CASES AND MATERIALS ON
PRIVATE INTERNATIONAL LAW

22.50

Cases and Materials on
Private International Law

J.H.C. Morris QC, DCL (OXON), LLD (CANTAB), FBA
Honorary Bencher of Gray's Inn; Honorary Fellow of Magdalen College, Oxford;
Emeritus Reader in the Conflict of Laws in the University of Oxford

P.M. North DCL (OXON)
Law Commissioner for England and Wales;
Fellow of Keble College, Oxford; Principal elect of Jesus College, Oxford

London
Butterworths
1984

England	Butterworth & Co (Publishers) Ltd, 88 Kingsway, LONDON WC2B 6AB
Australia	Butterworths Pty Ltd, SYDNEY, MELBOURNE, BRISBANE, ADELAIDE and PERTH
Canada	Butterworth & Co (Canada) Ltd, TORONTO Butterworth & Co (Western Canada) Ltd, VANCOUVER
New Zealand	Butterworths of New Zealand Ltd, WELLINGTON
Singapore	Butterworth & Co (Asia) Pte Ltd, SINGAPORE
South Africa	Butterworth Publishers (Pty) Ltd, DURBAN
USA	Mason Publishing Co, ST PAUL, Minnesota Butterworth Legal Publishers, SEATTLE, Washington; BOSTON, Massachusetts; and AUSTIN, Texas D & S Publishers, CLEARWATER, Florida

© Butterworth & Co (Publishers) Ltd 1984

British Library Cataloguing in Publication Data

Morris, J.H.C.
  Cases and materials on private international law.
  1. International law—Cases
  I. Title   II. North, P.M.
  341'.026   JX68

  ISBN Hardcover 0 406 25264 5
      Softcover 0 406 25265 3

Typeset and printed by The Whitefriars Press Ltd, Tonbridge

Preface

This book is intended primarily for those studying private international law (or the conflict of laws) at undergraduate or postgraduate level at universities and polytechnics in this country and for those studying the subject for professional examinations.

Editors of casebooks have to face a number of difficult choices. The first is that, because of limitations of space, certain topics have to be omitted. To assist us in making this choice, we sought information from what we hope was a representative group of law schools in this country, as to subjects which are usually included in, or excluded from, the syllabus. In the light of that helpful advice, for which we are most grateful, we decided, regretfully, to omit altogether any discussion of negotiable instruments, bankruptcy, winding up of companies and trusts—none of which were taught in any of the law schools we consulted. We have included a separate chapter (chapter 30) dealing with the theoretical and methodological developments in the subject in the USA. It was suggested to us that it would be of considerable use to have some of the relevant material collected together in a casebook. We have also included chapters dealing with financial relief in matrimonial proceedings (chapter 11) and with guardianship and custody proceedings (chapter 12), despite the fact that they contain, of necessity, a rather heavy diet of somewhat indigestible statutory material and despite the fact that they are topics not taught in some law schools. We take the view that these are both areas of very real practical importance, a view shared by our respondents including those from law schools where the topics are not currently taught.

Our choice of cases is intended to strike a balance between the older classic cases and the newer ones, with perhaps a bias towards the new. We have tried to select cases which, because of their interesting facts or trenchant judgments, are most likely both to inform and interest students and to make our book readable. We have included a sprinkling of cases from Scotland, Canada, Australia, South Africa and rather more from the United States, as well as cases decided by the European Court of Justice on the interpretation of the Brussels Convention of 1968. This is because under section 3 (1) of the Civil Jurisdiction and Judgments Act 1982 that Court has the last word in interpreting the Convention. At one time we considered including the opinions of the Advocate-General as well as the judgments of the Court, because they are often more interesting and more articulate. But ultimately we decided to omit them, because the Advocate-General is not part of the Court for the purposes of section 3 (1), and because the inclusion of his Opinions would have meant that nearly one-tenth of our book would have been occupied by cases from the European Court, which we thought excessive.

We realise that English statutes are not noted for their readability, but we have had to include a good many of them, because there is an increasing tendency in this subject for statutes to encroach more and more on the sphere of the common law.

We make no apology for the amount of law reform material that we have included, for this is not always easily accessible to students, and because each of us has long been interested in law reform.

We should emphasise that we are not trying to write a substitute for a textbook, since each of us is the author or editor of standard students' texts. This book is intended to supplement the use of a textbook. We have, however, included a number of explanatory Notes on recent material or material of some particular difficulty of which by far the most important is the Civil Jurisdiction and Judgments Act 1982. We have also included Questions (some of which we fully realise are insoluble) designed to make the student pause and reflect on what he has read.

A recurrent problem for authors of legal works is that of timing, and this book provides no exception. At the time of writing this Preface, neither the provisions of the Civil Jurisdiction and Judgments Act 1982 implementing the EEC Conventions of 1968 and 1978 on jurisdiction and the enforcement of judgments in civil and commercial matters, nor the related amendments to the Rules of the Supreme Court (especially Order 11) have been brought into force. This is because the Conventions cannot come into force for the United Kingdom until they have been ratified by all six original member states of the EEC. So ratification by the United Kingdom depends, in effect, on the speed with which the governments and legislatures elsewhere in the EEC act. Whilst we expect the legislation to be brought into effect in 1984, there is, at the moment, no certainty of this. Nevertheless we have assumed that the 1982 Act, and the relevant Rules of the Supreme Court, are fully in force. In chapter 24 we have included the Foreign Limitation Periods Act 1984. At the time of writing, this is still a Bill (based on an earlier draft Bill appended to a Law Commission Report), but it has passed the Report stage in the House of Lords, and we have assumed, not too rashly we hope, that it will complete its passage through Parliament in the form in which it appears in this book. We have been more cautious in chapter 11 where we include the draft Overseas Divorces (Financial Relief) Bill, though the substance of this provision has been included as Part III of the Matrimonial and Family Proceedings Bill which has completed its Committee stage in the House of Lords.

We express our grateful thanks to Mr Lawrence Collins for allowing us to make full use of the material he contributed to the Second Supplement to Dicey and Morris on the *Conflict of Laws* on the Civil Jurisdiction and Judgments Act 1982. Our publishers have provided us with every assistance on a variety of matters and for this we are most grateful. Finally, we should like to thank our wives for their active help and encouragement during this book's fairly short gestation period.

Orford and Oxford   J H C M
New Year's Day 1984   P M N

Acknowledgments

Grateful acknowledgment is made to all authors and publishers of extract material. In particular the following permissions are noted:

Page 388   Council of Europe Convention on Recognition and Enforcement of the Decisions concerning Custody of Children and on Restoration of Custody of Children (1980). Extracts reproduced by kind permission of the Council of Europe.

Page 393   Hague Convention on the Civil Aspects of International Child Abduction (1980). Extracts reproduced by kind permission of the Hague Conference on Private International Law.

Pages 698, 731   Leflar *American Conflicts Law* (3rd edn) pp 193–195, 198–200. Reproduced by kind permission of The Michie Company.

Page 700   P. Westen 'False Conflicts' 55 Calif L Rev 75–78, 122 (1967). Copyright © 1967, California Law Review, Inc. Reprinted by permission.

Page 708   Copyright © 1983 by the Directors for the Columbia Law Review Association, Inc. All rights reserved. This article, 'Comments on Babcock v Jackson', originally appeared at 63 Colum L Rev 1241–1243 (1963). Reprinted by permission.

Page 719   Cavers *The Choice of Law Process* (1965). Extract reproduced by kind permission of the University of Michigan Press. Copyright © The University of Michigan Press.

Pages 728, 733   Restatement of the Conflict of Laws, Second, para s 6, 145. Copyright © 1971 by the American Law Institute. Extracts reprinted with the permission of the American Law Institute.

Contents

ix

Table of Statutes

References in this Table to *Statutes* are to Halsbury's Statutes of England (Third Edition) showing the volume and page at which the annotated text of the Act will be found. Page references printed in bold type indicate where the Act is set out in part or in full.

xi

Table of International Conventions

Table of Rules of the Supreme Court

List of Cases

Page numbers printed in bold type indicate where a case is set out.

Introduction

Domicile and Habitual Residence

If a domicile of choice is abandoned, and a fresh domicile of choice is not acquired, the domicile of origin revives.

Udny v Udny (1869) LR 1 Sc & Div 441, 7 Macq 89 (House of Lords)

Appeal from the First Division of the Court of Session in Scotland.

Colonel Udny, of Udny in the county of Aberdeen, was born in 1779 at Leghorn (where his father was consul) with a Scottish domicile of origin. In 1797 he became an officer in the Guards. In 1802 he succeeded to the family estate. In 1812 he married, retired from the Army, and took a leasehold house in London, where he resided for thirty-two years, paying occasional visits to Aberdeenshire.

In 1844, having got into pecuniary difficulties, he broke up his establishment in London and moved to Boulogne, where he remained for nine years, occasionally, as before, visiting Scotland. In 1846 his wife died.

Some time after the death of his wife Colonel Udny formed at Boulogne a connexion with Miss Ann Allatt, which resulted in the birth of a son (the respondent) in Surrey in 1853. Colonel Udny married Miss Ann Allatt at Ormiston in Scotland in 1854, and the question was whether the respondent had become legitimate per subsequens matrimonium.

The Court of Session decided that Colonel Udny's domicile of origin was Scottish, that he had never altered or lost it, notwithstanding his long absences from Scotland; and that therefore the respondent, though illegitimate at his birth, was legitimated by the subsequent marriage of his parents. Hence this appeal.

Lord Westbury: The law of England, and of almost all civilised countries, ascribes to each individual at his birth two distinct legal states or conditions; one by virtue of which he becomes the subject of some particular country, binding him by the tie of natural allegiance, and which may be called his political status; another, by virtue of which he has ascribed to him the character of a citizen of some particular country, and as such is possessed of certain municipal rights, and subject to certain obligations, which latter character is the civil status or condition of the individual, and may be quite different from his political status. The political status may depend on different laws in different countries; whereas the civil status is governed universally by one single principle, namely, that of domicile, which is the criterion established by law for the purpose of determining civil status. For it is on this basis that the personal rights of the party, that is to say, the law which determines his majority or minority, his marriage, succession, testacy, or intestacy, must depend. International law depends on rules which, being

3

in great measure derived from the Roman law, are common to the jurisprudence of all civilised nations. It is a settled principle that no man shall be without a domicile, and to secure this result the law attributes to every individual as soon as he is born the domicile of his father, if the child be legitimate, and the domicile of the mother if illegitimate. This has been called the domicile of origin, and is involuntary. Other domiciles, including domicile by operation of law, as on marriage, are domiciles of choice. For as soon as an individual is sui juris it is competent to him to elect and assume another domicile, the continuance of which depends upon his will and act. When another domicile is put on, the domicile of origin is for that purpose relinquished, and remains in abeyance during the continuance of the domicile of choice; but as the domicile of origin is the creature of law, and independent of the will of the party, it would be inconsistent with the principles of which it is by law created and ascribed, to suppose that it is capable of being by the act of the party entirely obliterated and extinguished. It revives and exists whenever there is no other domicile, and it does not require to be regained or reconstituted animo et facto, in the manner which is necessary for the acquisition of a domicile of choice.

Domicile of choice is a conclusion or inference which the law derives from the fact of a man fixing voluntarily his sole or chief residence in a particular place, with an intention of continuing to reside there for an unlimited time. This is a description of the circumstances which create or constitute a domicile, and not a definition of the term. There must be a residence freely chosen, and not prescribed or dictated by any external necessity, such as the duties of office, the demand of creditors, or the relief from illness; and it must be residence fixed not for a limited period or particular purpose, but general and indefinite in its future contemplation. It is true that residence originally temporary, or intended for a limited period, may afterwards become general and unlimited, and in such a case so soon as the change of purpose, or animus manendi, can be inferred the fact of domicile is established.

The domicile of origin may be extinguished by act of law, as, for example, by sentence of death or exile for life, which puts an end to the status civilis of the criminal; but it cannot be destroyed by the will and act of the party.

Domicile of choice, as it is gained animo et facto, so it may be put an end to in the same manner. Expressions are found in some books, and in one or two cases, that the first or existing domicile remains until another is acquired. This is true if applied to the domicile of origin, but cannot be true if such general words were intended (which is not probable) to convey the conclusion that a domicile of choice, though unequivocally relinquished and abandoned, clings, in despite of his will and acts, to the party, until another domicile has animo et facto been acquired. The cases to which I have referred are, in my opinion, met and controlled by other decisions. A natural-born Englishman may, if he domiciles himself in Holland, acquire and have the status civilis of a Dutchman, which is of course ascribed to him in respect of his settled abode in the land, but if he breaks up his establishment, sells his house and funiture, discharges his servants, and quits Holland, declaring that he will never return to it again, and taking with him his wife and children, for the purpose of travelling in France or Italy in search of another place of residence, is it meant to be said that he carries his Dutch domicile, that is, his Dutch citizenship, at his back, and that it clings to him pertinaciously until he has finally set up his tabernacle in another country? Such a conclusion would be absurd; but there is no absurdity and, on the contrary, much reason, in holding that an acquired domicile may be effectually abandoned by unequivocal intention and act; and that when it is so determined the domicile of origin revives until a new domicile of choice be acquired. According to the dicta in the books and cases referred to, if the Englishman whose case we have been supposing lived for twenty years after he had finally quitted Holland, without acquiring a new domicile, and afterwards died intestate, his personal estate would be administered according to the law of Holland, and not according to that of his native country. This is an irrational consequence of the supposed rule. But when a proposition supposed to be authorised by one or more decisions involves absurd results, there is great reason for believing that no such rule was intended to be laid down.

In Mr Justice Story's *Conflict of Laws* (the last edition) it is stated that 'the moment the foreign domicile (that is the domicile of choice) is abandoned, the native domicile or domicile of origin is reacquired'. And such appears to be the just conclusion from several decided cases, as well as from the principles of the law of domicile.

In adverting to Mr Justice Story's work, I am obliged to dissent from a conclusion stated in the last edition of that useful book, and which is thus expressed, 'The result of the more recent English cases seems to be, that for a change of national domicile there must be a definite and effectual change of nationality'. In support of this proposition the editor refers to some words which appear to have fallen from a noble and learned lord in addressing this House in the case of *Moorhouse v Lord*[1] when in speaking of the acquisition of a French domicile, Lord Kingsdown says, 'A man must intend to become a Frenchman instead of an Englishman'. These words are likely to mislead, if they were intended to signify that for a change of domicile there must be a change of nationality, that is, of natural allegiance. That would be to confound the political and civil states of an individual, and to destroy the difference between patria and domicilium.

The application of these general rules to the circumstances of the present case is very simple. I concur with my noble and learned friend that the father of Colonel Udny, the consul at Leghorn, and afterwards at Venice, and again at Leghorn, did not by his residence there in that capacity lose his Scotch domicile. Colonel Udny was, therefore, a Scotchman by birth. But I am certainly inclined to think that when Colonel Udny married, and (to use the ordinary phrase) settled in life and took a long lease of a house in Grosvenor Street, and made that a place of abode of himself and his wife and children, becoming, in point of fact, subject to the municipal duties of a resident in that locality; and when he had remained there for a period, I think, of thirty-two years, there being no obstacle in point of fortune, occupation, or duty, to his going to reside in his native country; under these circumstances, I should come to the conclusion, if it were necessary to decide the point, that Colonel Udny deliberately chose and acquired an English domicile. But if he did so, he has certainly relinquished that English domicile in the most effectual way by selling or surrendering the lease of his house, selling his furniture, discharging his servants, and leaving London in a manner which removes all doubt of his ever intending to return there for the

1 (1863) 10 HLCas 272, 1 New Rep 555.

purpose of residence. If, therefore, he acquired an English domicile he abandoned it absolutely animo et facto. Its acquisition being a thing of choice, it was equally put an end to by choice. He lost it the moment he set foot on the steamer to go to Boulogne, and at the same time his domicile of origin revived. The rest is plain. The marriage and the consequences of that marriage must be determined by the law of Scotland, the country of his domicile.

Lords Hatherley, Chelmsford, and Colonsay delivered judgment to the same effect.

Appeal dismissed.

A domicile of origin is retained until a new domicile of choice is acquired. A domicile of origin cannot be lost by mere abandonment.

Bell v Kennedy (1868) LR 1 Sc & Div 307, 6 Macq 69 (House of Lords)

Appeal from the Second Division of the Court of Session in Scotland.

Mr Bell was born in Jamaica of Scottish parents domiciled in Jamaica. He was educated in Scotland but returned to Jamaica in 1823 soon after attaining his majority. In 1828 he married in Jamaica. In April 1837 he left Jamaica for good and went to Scotland, where he lived with his mother-in-law and looked around for an estate on which to settle down. Owing to the bad weather and to the high price of land he became dissatisfied with Scotland and undecided whether to settle there or in England or the south of France. On 28 September 1838, his wife died and the question was: Where was he domiciled on that date? The Second Division of the Court of Session held that he had become domiciled in Scotland.

Lord Westbury: What appears to me to be the erroneous conclusion at which the Court of Session arrived is in great part due to the circumstance, frequently lost sight of, that the domicile of origin adheres until a new domicile is acquired. In the argument, and in the judgments, we find constantly the phrase used that he had abandoned his native domicile. That domicile appears to have been regarded as if it had been lost by the abandonment of his residence in Jamaica. Now, residence and domicile are two perfectly distinct things. It is necessary in the administration of the law that the idea of domicile should exist, and that the fact of domicile should be ascertained, in order to determine which of two municipal laws may be invoked for the purpose of regulating the rights of parties. We know very well that succession and distribution depend upon the law of the domicile. Domicile, therefore, is an idea of law. It is the relation which the law creates between an individual and a particular locality or country. To every adult person the law ascribes a domicile and that domicile remains his fixed attribute until a new and different attribute usurps its place. Now this case was argued at the Bar on the footing, that as soon as Mr Bell left Jamaica he had a settled and fixed intention of taking up his residence in Scotland. And if, indeed, that had been ascertained as a fact, then you would have had the animus of the party clearly demonstrated, and the factum, which alone would remain to be proved, would in fact be proved, or, at least, would result immediately upon his arrival in Scotland.

The true inquiry, therefore, is—Had he this settled purpose, the moment he left Jamaica, or in course of the voyage, of taking up a fixed and settled abode in Scotland? Undoubtedly, part of the evidence is the external act of the party; but the only external act we have here is the going down with his wife to Edinburgh, the most natural thing in the world, to visit his wife's relations. We find him residing in Scotland from that time; but with what animus or intention his residence continued there we have yet to ascertain. For although residence may be some small prima facie proof of domicile, it is by no means to be inferred from the fact of residence that domicile results, even although you do not find that the party had any other residence in existence or in contemplation.

I take it that Mr Bell may be more properly described by words which occur in the Digest; that when he left Jamaica he might be described as 'quaerens, quo se conferat, atque ubi constituat domicilium'.[2] Where he was to fix his habitation was to him at that time a thing perfectly unresolved; and, as appears from the letters which your Lordships have heard, that irresolution, that want of settled fixity of purpose, certainly continued down to the time when he actually became the purchaser of Enterkine. But the punctum temporis to which our inquiries are to be directed as to Mr Bell's intention is of an earlier date than that. The question is, had he any settled fixed intention of being permanently resident in Scotland on 28 September 1838? I quite agree with an observation which was made in the Court of Session, that the letters are the best evidence in the case. To those letters your Lordships' attention has been directed, and whether you refer to the language of the wife's letters, or look exclusively at the language of the husband's letters written to his familiar friends or his relatives whom he had left in Jamaica, it is impossible to predicate of him that he was a man who had a fixed and settled purpose to make Scotland his future place of residence, to set up his tabernacle there, to make it his future home. And unless you are able to shew that with perfect clearness and satisfaction to yourselves, it follows that the domicile of origin continues. And therefore I think we can have no hesitation in answering the question where he was settled on 28 September. It must be answered in this way; he was resident in Scotland, but without the animus manendi, and therefore he still retained his domicile of origin.

Lords Cairns, Cranworth, Chelmsford and Colonsay delivered judgment to the same effect.

Appeal allowed.

Stronger evidence is required to prove the abandonment of a domicile of origin than the abandonment of a domicile of choice.

Winans v Attorney General [1904] AC 287, 73 LJKB 613 (House of Lords)

William Louis Winans was born in the United States in 1823. In 1859 he came to England and lived there in various places till his death in 1897. By

2 D 50, 1, 27.

his will he gave an annuity to a relative. If he died domiciled in England, legacy duty was payable; otherwise not. The Attorney General filed an information against the executors to recover the duty. Kennedy and Phillimore JJ held that the duty was payable. This decision was affirmed by the Court of Appeal (Collins MR, Stirling and Matthew LJJ). The executors appealed.

Lord Macnaghten: My Lords, there is, I think, hardly any branch of law which has been more frequently or more fully discussed in this House in comparatively modern times than the law of domicile. Difficulties have arisen, and difficulties must arise now and then, in coming to a conclusion upon the facts of a particular case. But those difficulties, as Lord Cottenham said, are 'much diminished by keeping steadily in view the principle which ought to guide the decision as to the application of the facts'.

Domicile of origin, or as it is sometimes called, perhaps less accurately, 'domicile of birth', differs from domicile of choice mainly in this—that its character is more enduring, its hold stronger, and less easily shaken off.

In *Munro v Munro*[3] Lord Cottenham observed that it was one of the principles adopted, not only by the law of England, but generally by the laws of other countries, 'that the domicile of origin must prevail until the party has not only acquired another, but has manifested and carried into execution an intention of abandoning his former domicile and acquiring another as his sole domicile . . . Residence alone', he adds, 'has no effect per se, though it may be most important as a ground from which to infer intention'. 'The law', said Lord Cairns LC in *Bell v Kennedy*,[4] 'is beyond all doubt clear with regard to the domicile of birth that the personal status indicated by that term clings and adheres to the subject of it until an actual change is made by which the personal status of another domicile is acquired'. The onus of proving that a domicile has been chosen in substitution for the domicile of origin lies upon those who assert that the domicile of origin has been lost.

'Residence and domicile', as Lord Westbury points out, 'are two perfectly distinct things . . . Although residence may be some small primâ facie proof of domicile, it is by no means to be inferred from the fact of residence that domicile results, even although you do not find the party had any other residence in existence or in contemplation'. Lord Chelmsford's opinion—*Udny v Udny*[5]—was that 'in a competition between a domicile of origin and an alleged subsequently acquired domicile there may be circumstances to shew that however long a residence may have continued, no intention of acquiring a domicile may have existed at any one moment during the whole of the continuance of such residence. The question in such a case is not whether there is evidence of an intention to retain the domicile of origin, but whether it is proved that there was an intention to acquire another domicile'.

Such an intention, I think, is not to be inferred from an attitude of indifference or a disinclination to move increasing with increasing years, least of all from the absence of any manifestation of intention one way or the other. It must be, to quote Lord Westbury again, a 'fixed and settled purpose'. 'And', says his Lordship, 'unless you are able to shew that with

3 (1840) 7 Cl & F 876.
4 (1868) LR 1 Sc & Div 307, 6 Macq 69 (p 6 above).
5 (1869) LR 1 Sc & Div 441, 7 Macq 89 (p 3 above).

perfect clearness and satisfaction to yourselves, it follows that a domicile of origin continues'. So heavy is the burden cast upon those who seek to shew that the domicile of origin has been superseded by a domicile of choice! And rightly, I think. A change of domicile is a serious matter—serious enough when the competition is between two domiciles both within the ambit of one and the same kingdom or country—more serious still when one of the two is altogether foreign. The change may involve far-reaching consequences in regard to succession and distribution and other things which depend on domicile.

To the same effect was the inquiry which Lord Cairns proposed for the consideration of the House in *Bell v Kennedy*. It was this: Whether the person whose domicile was in question had 'determined' to make, and had, in fact, made the alleged domicile of choice 'his home with the intention of establishing himself and his family there, and ending his days in that country'? In a later case, *Douglas v Douglas*,[6] which came before Wickens V-C, who was an excellent lawyer, and owing to the official position which he long held peculiarly conversant with cases of this sort, all the authorities were reviewed. The competition there was between a Scotch domicile of origin and an alleged English domicile of choice. The learned Vice-Chancellor thought the case 'a peculiar and difficult one'. He put the question in this way: 'What has to be here considered', he said, 'is whether the testator . . . ever actually declared a final and deliberate intention of settling in England, or whether his conduct and declarations lead to the belief that he would have declared such an intention if the necessity of making the election between the countries had arisen'.

My Lords, if the authorities I have cited are still law, the question which your Lordships have to consider must, I think, be this: Has it been proved 'with perfect clearness and satisfaction to yourselves' that Mr Winans had at the time of his death formed a 'fixed and settled purpose'—'a determination'—'a final and deliberate intention'—to abandon his American domicile and settle in England?

Considering the amount of Mr Winans' fortune, which was between two and three millions in marketable securities, and the length of his residence in this country, it is somewhat singular that the evidence offered on the question before your Lordships should be so meagre. There is not a single letter written by or to him, or a memorandum or note of any sort made by him, which bears directly on the point. There is nothing but long-continued residence in England on the one hand and some oral declarations and some words in some legal documents on the other. There is nothing else except such inference as may be drawn from a consideration of Mr Winans' character and disposition, the life he led here, and the objects which he seems to have had most at heart.

The principal events in Mr Winans' life may be stated briefly. He was born in the United States in 1823. He lived there till 1850, residing in Baltimore with his father, a railway contractor, and employed in his father's business. Mr Winans' eldest son, Walter, who was examined in this case, says that when he spoke of Baltimore he always called it 'home'. In 1850 Mr Winans went to Russia. He was employed by the Russian government, as his father had been, in equipping railways there on the American system.

6 (1871) LR 12 Eq 617, 41 LJCh 74.

During the Crimean War he rendered assistance to the Russian government in the construction and the equipment of gunboats to be used against the enemy—England and England's ally. In Russia he married a Guernsey lady, the daughter of a gentleman also employed by the Russian government. He had two sons by her. In 1859 his health broke down. There were symptoms of consumption, and he was warned by his doctor that another winter in Russia would probably be fatal. He was advised to winter in Brighton in England. Very reluctantly, under medical orders, he left St Petersburg and spent the winter in a hotel at Brighton, returning to Russia when the winter was over. In 1860 he took a furnished house in Brighton, No 2, Chichester Terrace, for a term of five years, determinable at the end of any year. He also took the next house, No 1, for a term of twenty-one years, determinable in the fifth, seventh, or fourteenth year. He connected the two houses structurally. He held both these houses at the time of his death—the furnished house, No 2, as tenant from year to year, and No 1, on a tenancy similar to that on which it was originally taken. From 1860 down to 1870 or 1871 he used to spend the winter at Brighton and about eight months of the year in Russia. In 1870 he gave up his house in St Petersburg, and took a lease of some shooting in Scotland, apparently for the sake of his sons, for he shot very little himself. From 1871 to 1883 he spent about two months in Russia, two or three months in Kissingen in Germany, and the rest of the year in Brighton, Scotland, or London. In 1883 he ceased to visit Russia, thenceforward dividing his time between Kissingen, Brighton, London, and Scotland. This mode of life continued until 1893. After that date he spent the whole of the year in England—in London, Brighton, and the country. He never bought an estate in England for himself or for either of his sons. As far as he was concerned 'he preferred living in furnished houses or hotels'—so his son says.

Mr Winans was a person of considerable ability and of singular tenacity of purpose, self-centred, and strangely uncommunicative. He was not interested in many things, and whatever he did he did, as his son says, thoroughly. He became completely absorbed in a scheme when he took it up. At the same time he lived a very retired—almost a secluded—life. He took no part in general or municipal politics. He rarely went into society. He had no intimate friends, if, indeed, he had any friends at all, in this country. There is no evidence that he was interested in any charity or charitable or philanthropic institution in England. Although he was on affectionate terms with his two sons, he never let them into his secrets. 'He always worked his business himself', his son says, 'and never brought us into the business affairs in any way'. And although at odd times he mentioned his property in America, he never allowed even his eldest son 'to understand much about it'.

Mr Winans had three objects in life. His first object was his health. He nursed and tended it with wonderful devotion. He took his temperature several times a day. He had regular times for taking his temperature, and regular times for taking his various waters and medicines.

Besides the care of his health, there were two other objects which engrossed his thoughts. The first was the construction of spindle-shaped vessels commonly called cigar ships. This form of vessel was, as Mr Winans asserted, an invention of the Winans family. Many patents were taken out for it both in England and in America. It was claimed that vessels of this type would be able to cross the Atlantic without pitching or rolling. In an application to Congress in the year 1892 Mr Winans represented himself as attached heart and soul to his country, and asked for protection for a long term of years in consideration of the great expenditure which he and his family had incurred in perfecting the invention, and the vast benefits that would result from it to the people of the United States. Mr Winans declared his confident expectation that a fleet of spindle-shaped vessels subsidised by Congress would restore to America the carrying trade which had fallen into the hands of England and other foreign nations, secure to America the command of the sea, and make it impossible for Great Britain to maintain war against the United States. Such a fleet as he described in his application could, he said, 'meet war vessels in open sea near the European side and destroy one vessel after another, so that none of them would be able to reach our shores'. In the development of his invention Mr Winans stated that he had incurred an expense nearly equal to four millions of dollars.

Mr Winans' confidence in this project remained unshaken to the end of his life, and he kept an office in Beaufort Gardens where a staff of engineers and draftsmen was engaged in working out the problem.

There was another scheme which Mr Winans hoped to develop and work in connection with his fleet of spindle-shaped vessels. In 1859 a property in Baltimore, about 200 acres in extent, called Ferry Bar, was purchased on behalf of the Winans family originally for the purpose of being used, as Mr Winans states in a letter of 31 January 1882, 'for the service of the sea-going steamers of the spindle-shaped form'. The scheme was that the water frontage should be used for wharves and docks, while a portion of the property should be laid out for the building of first-class houses as a sort of Belgravia. There Mr Winans intended to build a big house for himself and control the undertaking, which would make the property, he thought, when developed, worth one million sterling. Nothing practical came of this scheme, because the members of the family could not agree among themselves how the property was to be developed. So Mr Winans determined to wait until he could get the whole into his own hands. Then he would develop the property himself in his own way and according to his own ideas. He did not succeed in acquiring the entire interest until just before his death. At the date of his death, his son says, 'he was working night and day on it'. I find that in the conveyances of the last portion of the Ferry Bar property, which were prepared just before his death, and which are dated 16 June 1897, Mr Winans is described as 'of City of Baltimore, but now sojourning in the City of London, England'.

Of course, to us these schemes of Mr Winans appear wild, visionary and chimerical. But I have no doubt that to a man like Mr Winans, wholly wrapt up in himself, they were very real. They were the dream of his life. For forty years he kept them steadily in view. And one was anti-English and the other wholly American.

It was argued on behalf of the Crown that, although Mr Winans may have been prevented by the state of his health from returning to America when he left Russia, and although he could not have safely attempted the voyage in the latter years of his life, yet there was a time in which he might have ventured to cross the Atlantic in an ordinary liner. The obvious answer is that at that time, when divided counsels and family disagreements prevented the development of the Ferry Bar property, he had no object in going to Baltimore.

Then it was said that the length of time during which Mr Winans resided in this country leads to the inference that he must have become content to make this country his home. Length of time is of course a very important element in questions of domicile. An unconscious change may come over a man's mind. If the man goes about and mixes in society that is not an improbable result. But in the case of a person like Mr Winans, who kept himself to himself and had little or no intercourse with his fellow men, it seems to me that at the end of any space of time, however long, his mind would probably be in the state it was at the beginning. When he came to this country he was a sojourner and a stranger, and he was, I think, a sojourner and a stranger in it when he died.

On the whole I am unable to come to the conclusion that Mr Winans ever formed a fixed and settled purpose of abandoning his American domicile and settling finally in England. I think up to the very last he had an expectation or hope of returning to America and seeing his grand schemes inaugurated. To take the test proposed by Wickens V-C, 'if the question had arisen in a form requiring a deliberate or solemn determination', I have no doubt Mr Winans, who was, as his son says, 'entirely American in all his ideas and sympathies', would have answered it in favour of America.

I am therefore of opinion that the Crown has not discharged the onus cast upon it, and I think that the order appealed from ought to be reversed.

Lord Halsbury delivered judgment to the same effect.

Lord Lindley (dissenting): . . . He had one and only one home, and that was in this country; and long before he died I am satisfied that he had given up all serious idea of returning to his native country . . .
Appeal allowed.

Ramsay v Liverpool Royal Infirmary [1930] AC 588, 99 LJPC 134 (House of Lords)

Appeal against an interlocutor of the First Division of the Court of Session in Scotland affirming an interlocutor of the Lord Ordinary (Lord Mackay).

George Bowie, whose domicile of origin was Scottish, but who had lived the latter part of his life in Liverpool, died in Liverpool on 5 November 1927, leaving a holograph will dated 7 August 1927, which was valid by the law of Scotland but was not valid by the law of England.

This action was brought by the respondents, the residuary legatees under the will, against the appellant, the testator's sole next of kin, for a declaration that the testator's domicile at the date of his death was Scottish.

The Lord Ordinary held that the defender had failed to prove that the testator had changed his domicile and granted the declaration, and the First Division (the Lord President, Lord Blackburn (doubting but not formally dissenting), and Lord Morison) affirmed his decision.

Lord Thankerton: My Lords, the deceased George Bowie died in Liverpool, on 5 November 1927, aged 82 years and unmarried. Originally employed as a commercial traveller in Glasgow, he gave up that employment about 1882, and did no work for the rest of his life. About 1891 or 1892 he came to Liverpool, where a brother and sister were already settled, and resided in Liverpool for the remaining thirty-five or thirty-six years of his life. His domicile of origin was Scottish, and the question in the present appeal is whether he still retained that domicile at his death, or was then domiciled in England.

George Bowie left a holograph will, which was made by him in Liverpool on 7 August 1927. That will is valid according to Scottish law and invalid under English law. The appellant, as next of kin, maintains that George Bowie died domiciled in England and that the will is invalid. The respondents are the residuary legatees under the will, and maintain its validity on the ground that George Bowie retained his Scottish domicile.

Admittedly the appellant undertakes the burden of proving that George Bowie acquired an English domicile animo et facto; his long residence established the factum, but there remains the question of the animus. It seems clear on the authorities that mere length of residence by itself is insufficient evidence from which to infer the animus; but the quality of the residence may afford the necessary inference. For instance, the purchase of a house or estate coupled with long residence therein and non-retention of any home in the domicile of origin, might be sufficient to prove the intention to acquire a new domicile. But the long residence of George Bowie in Liverpool is remarkably colourless and suggests little more than inanition.

George Bowie went to Liverpool to live on the bounty of his brother Alexander, and, during his residence there, his means of existence were supplied by that brother and his sister Isabella. He received a legacy of £1,000 from the former and succeeded to the latter's whole estate on her death in 1920. He lived in lodgings until 1914, when he went to live with his sister Isabella, then the only other surviving member of the family, in a leased house, where he lived till his death. With the exception of family ties, he appears to have had few, if indeed any, ties either in Scotland or England.

Apart from residence, the evidence bearing on animus is vague and indecisive. It is not certain whether he knew that his will would be invalid in England, but he named his cousin, a Glasgow writer, as trustee, and he directed that his residuary bequests, of one-fourth each to three Glasgow infirmaries and one Liverpool infirmary, should be given anonymously as from a 'Glasgow Man'. He told people that he was proud to be a Glasgow man, and received a Glasgow weekly newspaper. With his sister Isabella's estate he became owner of a tenement property in Glasgow, which he desired to sell, but a bad market prevented its sale, and he retained it till his death. There is some evidence of his declining on one or two occasions to move to Glasgow and to visit Glasgow, but until 1912 he was dependent on his brother's bounty, and after 1912 it is probable that his disinclination was owing to the inertness of age and indifferent health. He was buried in Liverpool, but that was alongside of his brother Alexander and three sisters in ground for which Alexander had paid.

I am unable to find in this case sufficient evidence of a definite intention on the part of George Bowie to abandon his domicile of origin and to acquire a new domicile. The law on this subject is well fixed; the difficulty is found in its application to oft varying combinations of circumstances. The present case appears to me to be directly affected by the opinions (a) of Lord Westbury in *Bell v Kennedy*,[7] where he says: 'Although residence may be some small prima facie proof of domicile, it is by no means to be inferred from the

<hr />

7 (1868) LR 1 Sc & Div 307, 6 Macq 69; p 6 above.

fact of residence that domicile results, even although you do not find that the party had any other residence in existence or in contemplation'; (b) of Lord Chelmsford in *Udny v Udny*,[8] that 'in a competition between a domicile of origin and an alleged subsequently-acquired domicile there may be circumstances to shew that however long a residence may have continued no intention of acquiring a domicile may have existed at any one moment during the whole of the continuance of such residence. The question in such a case is not, whether there is evidence of an intention to retain the domicile of origin, but whether it is proved that there was an intention to acquire another domicile'; and (c) of Lord Macnaghten in *Winans v A-G*[9] where he states: 'Such an intention, I think, is not to be inferred from an attitude of indifference or a disinclination to move increasing with increasing years, least of all from the absence of any manifestation of intention one way or the other.' This last opinion appears to apply exactly to the circumstances of George Bowie's residence in Liverpool.

Accordingly, I am of opinion that the appellant has failed to prove the intention on the part of George Bowie to acquire an English domicile, and that the appeal fails.

Lords Buckmaster, Dunedin, and Macmillan delivered judgment to the same effect.

Appeal dismissed.

Re Fuld [1968] P 675, [1965] 3 All ER 776 (Probate Division)

Peter Fuld was born in Germany in 1921 with a German domicile of origin. His father was a wealthy man of Jewish origin with a flourishing business in Frankfurt, where Peter was brought up. His mother came from an old German family. In 1939, some years after the death of his father, he came to England as a student. After the outbreak of war in 1939 he was interned in England. In 1940 he was transferred as an internee to Canada. He was released from internment in 1942 and entered the University of Toronto as a law student, eventually graduating with first class honours. He acquired Canadian nationality in 1946 and soon afterwards returned to Europe. From 1946 until his death in 1962 his base was European, not American, though he often visited North America on business. From 1946 onwards he had a house in London (8 Blomfield Road). But he spent much time in Germany, built a house in Frankfurt (14 Annastrasse), registered himself with the police in Frankfurt as a resident of that city, and allowed his German wife Marina to divorce him in Munich. He did not live in the house in Frankfurt, where he installed his mother, because she was exceedingly possessive and jealous and they quarrelled incessantly. He was unsuccessful in persuading his father's associates to accept him as a colleague in the family business. In 1959 he entered the London Clinic for brain surgery owing to a tumour which was diagnosed as malignant. He made a temporary recovery from the tumour which however eventually killed him. During the last nine months of his life he made a will in England and a codicil in Germany. A second codicil was made in England and two more codicils in Germany. He made many

8 (1869) LR 1 Sc & Div 441 at 455; p 3 above.
9 [1904] AC 287 at 291; p 7 above.

statements referring to London as his home. He died in Frankfurt leaving an estate valued at £6m, of which about one-sixth was situated in England.

The executors under the will and first codicil (an English solicitor and accountant) propounded those instruments for probate in solemn form, but challenged the validity of the other three codicils. There were 14 defendants to the action, all beneficiaries under the will and codicils. After a trial lasting six months or 93 working days Scarman J pronounced in favour of the will and first codicil and against the other three codicils. His judgment is printed here only on the issue of domicile.

Scarman J   (having stated the facts and issues, continued):

Domicile—Law

Domicile is 'that legal relationship between a person . . . and a territory subject to a distinctive legal system which invokes the system as [his] personal law . . .': see *Henderson v Henderson*.[10] It is a combination of residence and intention. It takes two forms—domicile of origin and domicile of choice. A classic description of the concept is to be found in Lord Westbury's speech in *Udny v Udny*.[11] Two features of his description are of particular importance in the present case. First, that the domicile of origin prevails in the absence of a domicile of choice, ie, if a domicile of choice has never been acquired or, if once acquired, has been abandoned. Secondly, that a domicile of choice is acquired when a man fixes voluntarily his sole or chief residence in a particular place with an intention of continuing to reside there for an unlimited time.

It is necessary to consider both these features a little more fully and in the light of the more important authorities. But, before I do so, a word of warning. This branch of the law is adorned by a great number of cases, not all of which is it easy to harmonise. The difficulty arises not from a lack of clarity in judicial thought but from the nature of the subject. Domicile cases require for their decision a detailed analysis and assessment of facts arising within that most subjective of all fields of legal inquiry—a man's mind. Each case takes its tone from the individual propositus whose intentions are being analysed: anglophobia, mental inertia, extravagant habits, vacillation of will—to take four instances at random—have been factors of great weight in the judicial assessment and determination of four leading cases. Naturally enough in so subjective a field different judicial minds concerned with different factual situations have chosen different language to describe the law. For the law is not an abstraction: it lives only in its application, and its concepts derive colour and shape from the facts of the particular case in which they are studied, and to which they are applied. Thus the relationship of law and fact is a two-way one: each affects the other.

Subject to this warning, I now turn to the few cases which alone, in my opinion, I need consider. First in time, and still of great importance, is *Moorhouse v Lord*.[12] It was a case in which the propositus, a Dr Cochrane, was held not to have acquired a French domicile of choice but to have retained his Scots domicile of origin. The reasoning—particularly that of

10 [1967] P 77 at 79, [1965] 1 All ER 179 at 180.
11 (1869) LR 1 Sc & Div 441; p 3 above.
12 (1863) 10 HLCas 272 at 285.

Lord Kingsdown—has been criticised for an apparent confusion of the concepts of nationality and domicile. But, although the speeches have now to be considered in the light of *Douglas v Douglas*,[13] and *Udny v Udny*, the view expressed by Lord Chelmsford as to the nature of the intention required for the acquisition of domicile of choice is supported by later authority. In an earlier case, *Whicker v Hume*,[14] Lord Cranworth had described the necessary intention as that of making a place one's permanent home. Lord Chelmsford accepted this description and gave his view as to its meaning in these words:

> 'The present intention of making a place a person's permanent home can exist only where he has no other idea than to continue there, without looking forward to any event, certain or uncertain, which might induce him to change his residence.'

In *Douglas v Douglas*, Sir John Wickens V-C effectively annihilated the view that a man must intend to abandon one civil status and to acquire another before he can be said to acquire a domicile of choice. Thus the intention with which the law is concerned is an intention as to residence, and nothing else.

Bell v Kennedy[15] was a case in which the propositus, whose domicile of origin was Jamaican, was held at the time of death of his wife not to have acquired a domicile of choice in Scotland, though it was abundantly clear that later, when he bought a Scottish estate, he did acquire a domicile in Scotland. The decision turned simply on the finding that at the critical time he had not made up his mind whether to settle in England or Scotland. The case illustrates the strongly adhesive quality of the domicile of origin—for he had no intention of returning to Jamaica—and the necessity of affirmative proof of the requisite intention for the acquisition of a domicile of choice. Strictly considered, it is not binding authority as to the nature of the intention required.

In *Udny v Udny* Lord Westbury emphasised that the intention must be formed free of external constraining factors, eg, the demands of creditors—but expressed the opinion that 'permanent' in this context means no more than 'general and indefinite in its future contemplation'. The difference in emphasis between this dictum and that of Lord Chelmsford in *Moorhouse v Lord* is noticeable: but, if studied in the light of the general considerations to which I have alluded, of no great moment.

In *Winans v A-G*,[16] the case of the anglophobic American millionaire whose years of life in England were spent in the elaboration of eccentric schemes for making America master of the seas, the House of Lords underlined the adhesive strength of the domicile of origin. The same point was made again in *Ramsay v Liverpool Royal Infirmary*[17] upon which decision Dr Cheshire, in his *Private International Law*,[18] fairly comments that evidence was completely lacking of the slightest indication that the propositus, whose domicile of origin was Scottish, intended to live anywhere else than in England. Each of these decisions turns on the necessity of there being

13 (1871) LR 12 Eq 617, 41 LJCh 74.
14 (1858) 7 HLCas 124, 28 LJCh 396.
15 (1868) LR 1 Sc & Div 307, 6 Macq 69; p 6 above.
16 [1904] AC 287, 73 LJKB 613; p 7 above.
17 [1930] AC 588, 99 LJPC 134; p 12 above.
18 7th edn (1965) p 147.

satisfactory evidence of a positive intention to reside permanently in the new territory. Absence of such evidence, if there are other explanations for long residence in the territory, is fatal to the acquisition of a domicile of choice, and the domicile of origin persists.

In the light of these cases, the law, so far as relevant to my task, may be stated as follows: (1) The domicile of origin adheres—unless displaced by satisfactory evidence of the acquisition and continuance of a domicile of choice; (2) a domicile of choice is acquired only if it be affirmatively shown that the propositus is resident within a territory subject to a distinctive legal system with the intention, formed independently of external pressures, of residing there indefinitely. If a man intends to return to the land of his birth upon a clearly foreseen and reasonably anticipated contingency, eg, the end of his job, the intention required by law is lacking; but, if he has in mind only a vague possibility, such as making a fortune (a modern example might be winning a football pool), or some sentiment about dying in the land of his fathers, such a state of mind is consistent with the intention required by law. But no clear line can be drawn: the ultimate decision in each case is one of fact—of the weight to be attached to the various factors and future contingencies in the contemplation of the propositus, their importance to him, and the probability, in his assessment, of the contingencies he has in contemplation being transformed into actualities. (3) It follows that, though a man has left the territory of his domicile of origin with the intention of never returning, though he be resident in a new territory, yet if his mind be not made up or evidence be lacking or unsatisfactory as to what is his state of mind, his domicile of origin adheres. And, if he has acquired but abandoned a domicile of choice either because he no longer resides in the territory or because he no longer intends to reside there indefinitely, the domicile of origin revives until such time as by a combination of residence and intention he acquires a new domicile of choice.

There remains the question of standard of proof. It is beyond doubt that the burden of proving the abandonment of a domicile of origin and the acquisition of a domicile of choice is upon the party asserting the change. But it is not so clear what is the standard of proof: is it to be proved beyond reasonable doubt or upon a balance of probabilities, or does the standard vary according to whether one seeks to establish abandonment of a domicile of origin or merely a switch from one domicile of choice to another? Or is there some other standard?

In *Moorhouse v Lord*, Lord Chelmsford said that the necessary intention must be clearly and unequivocally proved. In *Winans v A-G*, Lord Macnaghten said that the character of a domicile of origin 'is more enduring, its hold stronger and less easily shaken off'. In *Ramsay v Liverpool Royal Infirmary*, the House of Lords seemed to have regarded the continuance of a domicile of origin as almost an irrebuttable presumption. Danger lies in wait for those who would deduce legal principle from descriptive language. The powerful phrases of the cases are, in my opinion, a warning against reaching too facile a conclusion upon a too superficial investigation or assessment of the facts of a particular case. They emphasise as much the nature and quality of the intention that has to be proved as the standard of proof required. What has to be proved is no mere inclination arising from a passing fancy or thrust upon a man by an external but temporary pressure, but an intention freely formed to reside in a certain territory indefinitely. All the elements of the intention must be shown to exist if the change is to be established: if any one element is not proved, the case for a change fails. The court must be satisfied as to the proof of the whole; but I see no reason to infer from these salutary warnings the necessity for formulating in a probate case a standard of proof in language appropriate to criminal proceedings.

The formula of proof beyond reasonable doubt is not frequently used in probate cases, and I do not propose to give it currency. It is enough that the authorities emphasise that the conscience of the court must be satisfied by the evidence. The weight to be attached to evidence, the inferences to be drawn, the facts justifying the exclusion of doubt and the expression of satisfaction, will vary according to the nature of the case. Two things are clear—first, that unless the judicial conscience is satisfied by evidence of change, the domicile of origin persists: and secondly, that the acquisition of a domicile of choice is a serious matter not to be lightly inferred from slight indications or casual words.

Domicile—Facts

(His Lordship reviewed the events in Peter Fuld's life and the evidence—often conflicting—of his intentions at various times and continued):

Nurse Cooney was the night nurse at the London Clinic. Her conversations with Peter Fuld were at a superficial level and casual in character. She got the impression—a very reasonable one—that he was a German living in England. She understood—I quote her words—that 'he lived between Germany and spent a lot of time in London'. If by that she meant he lived between Germany and London, she was a deal nearer the truth than many of the profound and learned minds which have addressed themselves to the problem of Peter Fuld's domicile.

Miss Oberlander is Marina's aunt, but she has lived in England since 1936. She saw something of Peter Fuld and Marina after their marriage. She remembers particularly their early days before they acquired the house at 8 Blomfield Road. In the course of conversations at that time Peter Fuld said he would nowhere like to live but in England, but never said for how long, and it was a very vague kind of conversation.

Such is our law that even conversations, casual, superficial, vague, such as these of which Nurse Cooney and Miss Oberlander speak, are relevant; but their weight is quite another matter.

I have drawn attention to some of the evidence; it is not my intention to catalogue all of it. Nevertheless, I have indicated in the foregoing the findings which I regard as decisive in determining whether Peter Fuld ever did acquire a domicile of choice in England. I now propose to state my conclusions on the point quite shortly.

I am satisfied that Peter Fuld resided in London from 1946 to November 1961. But London was not his sole residence. He also had a place of residence in Germany. For most of the time, however, and particularly in his later years, he regarded London as his chief place of residence. He did so because of his immediate circumstances, of which the most important was the presence of his mother in Frankfurt. I am not satisfied that he ever made up his mind to settle in England, or, to put it in the language of the authorities to which I have referred, that he ever formed the intention of continuing to reside in England for an unlimited time. It may be, as Mr Parker (counsel for the plaintiffs) has submitted, that he never made up his mind. I think it more likely that his innermost wish was at all times, and more particularly after he had married the German girl Marina, to return to Germany, to live in Annastrasse and to play an active part in the management of the family business. Immediate external circumstances, ie, the presence of his mother in Germany, the strain of their relationship, and the reluctance of those in control of the family business to let him into its management, alone thwarted him. But 14 Annastrasse was there, his mother was old, and his stake and rights in the businesss were so immense that the realisation of this intention was no mere pipe-dream but, in his mind and in all objective probability, something to be achieved sooner rather than later.

All this is consistent with his love for Canada and later for London. For him Canada would always remain the land of romance of his salad days. He would always feel its pull, especially as in December 1960, during periods of unhappiness. London was the haven of his later years, where he could choose his own friends, live his own life, pleasantly removed from the influence of the jealous and possessive mother, yet near enough to Frankfurt, which remained the key to his fortunes, the foundation upon which the structure of his life, wherever it was spent, was necessarily based.

Thus, though my judgment rests on the negative proposition that those who assert the acquisition of a domicile of choice have failed to prove the intention required by law, I must add that I think in fact Peter Fuld never did acquire such an intention. He may never have made up his mind as to his permanent home, but I believe that, deep down, he never abandoned an intention to return to live in Frankfurt. He was waiting his opportunity when disease, fatal in the event, struck him.

In my opinion, therefore, Peter Fuld was at all material times domiciled in Germany.

Domicile and Matrimonial Proceedings Act 1973

PART I

DOMICILE

1.—(1) Subject to subsection (2) below, the domicile of a married woman as at any time after the coming into force of this section[19] shall, instead of being the same as her husband's by virtue only of marriage, be ascertained by reference to the same factors as in the case of any other individual capable of having an independent domicile.

(2) Where immediately before this section came into force a woman was married and then had her husband's domicile by dependence, she is to be treated as retaining that domicile (as a domicile of choice, if it is not also her domicile of origin) unless and until it is changed by acquisition or revival of another domicile either on or after the coming into force of this section.

(3) This section extends to England and Wales, Scotland and Northern Ireland.

3.—(1) The time at which a person first becomes capable of having an independent domicile shall be when he attains the age of sixteen or marries

19 The Act came into force on 1 January 1974.

under that age; and in the case of a person who immediately before 1st
January 1974 was incapable of having an independent domicile, but had
then attained the age of sixteen or been married, it shall be that date.

(2) This section extends to England and Wales and Northern Ireland (but
not to Scotland).

4.—(1) Subsection (2) of this section shall have effect with respect to the
dependent domicile of a child as at any time after the coming into force of
this section when his father and mother are alive but living apart.

(2) The child's domicile as at that time shall be that of his mother if—
(a) he then has his home with her and has no home with his father; or
(b) he has at any time had her domicile by virtue of paragraph (a) above
      and has not since had a home with his father.

(3) As at any time after the coming into force of this section, the domicile
of a child whose mother is dead shall be that which she last had before she
died if at her death he had her domicile by virtue of subsection (2) above
and he has not since had a home with his father.

(4) Nothing in this section prejudices any existing rule of law as to the
cases in which a child's domicile is regarded as being, by dependence, that of
his mother.

(5) In this section, 'child' means a person incapable of having an
independent domicile; and in its application to a child who has been
adopted, references to his father and his mother shall be construed as
references to his adoptive father and mother.

(6) This section extends to England and Wales, Scotland and Northern
Ireland.

*A woman with a domicile of origin in one country who acquires a domicile of dependency
in another by marriage before 1974 and whose domicile of dependency is converted into a
domicile of choice on 1 January 1974 by section 1(2) of the Domicile and Matrimonial
Proceedings Act 1973 does not lose that domicile of choice until she abandons it.*

IRC v Duchess of Portland [1982] Ch 314, [1982] 1 All ER 784
(Chancery Division)

Case stated by the Commissioners for the Special Purposes of the Income
Tax Acts.

The taxpayer, now the Duchess of Portland, was born in Canada in 1911
with a domicile of origin in Quebec. She was and remained a Canadian
citizen. In 1948 she married the present Duke of Portland, who was
domiciled in England. She and her husband set up house in London. She
maintained close links with Quebec throughout her married life. When she
married she intended to stay in the United Kingdom so long as her husband
worked there. She intended to return to Quebec if he should predecease her
and hoped to persuade him to live in Quebec on his retirement. Throughout
her marriage she returned to Quebec for some ten or twelve weeks in the
summer in every year. Her husband would go with her but had to return to
London after some six weeks to resume his work. For the last twenty years
they stayed during these summer visits at a house in Metis Beach, Quebec,
which belonged originally to the taxpayer's family and later to the taxpayer.

In 1975 she and her husband agreed that when he retired they would leave London and take up full-time residence at the house in Metis Beach.

The Special commissioners upheld the taxpayer's contention that for the purposes of section 1(2) of the Domicile and Matrimonial Proceedings Act 1973 she had abandoned her domicile of choice in England when she went on her annual visit to Canada in 1974 and was not thereafter domiciled in England.

The Crown appealed.

Nourse J: (His Lordship stated the facts, read section 1 of the Domicile and Matrimonial Proceedings Act 1973,[20] and continued):

As will appear, the effect of those provisions is to treat women who were married before 1 January 1974 somewhat less favourably than those who marry on or after that date.

Immediately before 1 January 1974, the taxpayer had her husband's English domicile by dependency. She was therefore to be treated as retaining that domicile as a domicile of choice unless and until it was changed by acquisition or revival of another domicile. Before the commissioners the taxpayer put her case in three different ways, but on this appeal she has claimed only that her English domicile of dependency was changed by the revival of her Quebec domicile of origin when she went to Canada for her annual visit in July 1974.

I will now attempt some general observations on section 1 (2) of the Act of 1973. First, it is a deeming provision. Secondly, that which is deemed in a case where the domicile of dependency is not the same as the domicile of origin is the retention of the domicile of dependency as a domicile of choice. I think that that must mean that the effect of the subsection is to reimpose the domicile of dependency as a domicile of choice. The concept of an imposed domicile of choice is not one which it is very easy to grasp, but the force of the subsection requires me to do the best I can. It requires me to treat the taxpayer as if she had acquired an English domicile of choice, even though the facts found by the commissioners tell me that that would have been an impossibility in the real world. In my judgment it necessarily follows that the question whether, after 1 January 1974, the taxpayer abandoned her deemed English domicile of choice must be determined by reference to the test appropriate to the abandonment of a domicile of choice and not by reference to the more lenient test appropriate to the abandonment of one of dependency.

There can no longer be any doubt as to the test appropriate to the abandonment of a domicile of choice. The leading case on the subject is *Udny v Udny*.[1] The law is stated with accuracy and concision in rule 13 (1) in Dicey and Morris *The Conflict of Laws*,[2] which is in these terms:

'A person abandons a domicile of choice in a country by ceasing to reside there and by ceasing to intend to reside there permanently or indefinitely, and not otherwise.'

There are therefore two requirements which, with deference to certain arguments which have been advanced on behalf of the taxpayer, must be

20 P 19 above.
 1 (1869) LR 1 Sc & Div 441, 7 Macq 89; p 3 above.
 2 10th edn (1980) vol 1, p 128.

kept entirely separate. For the purposes of this case they are more conveniently stated in the reverse order. First, the domiciliary must cease to intend to reside permanently or indefinitely in the country in question. Secondly, he must actually cease to reside there. Adapting the first requirement to the provisions of section 1 (2), it is agreed in the present case that the taxpayer ceased to intend to reside permanently or indefinitely in England after, or more accurately on, 1 January 1974. That is the corollary of her enduring intention to return to Quebec, which is a present intention to reside there permanently or indefinitely in the future. The primary question therefore is whether the taxpayer actually ceased to reside here after 1 January 1974. Residence in a country for the purposes of the law of domicile is physical presence in that country as an inhabitant of it. If the necessary intention is also there, an existing domicile of choice can sometimes be abandoned and another domicile acquired or revived by a residence of short duration in a second country. But that state of affairs is inherently improbable in a case where the domiciliary divides his physical presence between two countries at a time. In that kind of case it is necessary to look at all the facts in order to decide which of the two countries is the one he inhabits.

Although section 1 (2) effects a change of domicile, it is important to bear in mind that the change is not necessarily dependent on a change either of intention or of residence. I have already touched on this point in relation to the taxpayer's intention in the present case. I can take the example of a woman with a foreign domicile of origin married to a domiciled Englishman who left her husband and returned to live in her country of origin with the intention of permanent or indefinite residence there before 1 January 1974. Consistently with the rule which would have applied if the husband had died before 1 January 1974 (see *Re Scullard*[3]), the wife's domicile of dependency would have changed by revival of her domicile of origin on 1 January 1974, without the need for any further act on her part. Accordingly, section 1 (2) of the Act of 1973 requires you first to look at the state of affairs prevailing on 1 January 1974, to see whether there has been any automatic change on that date. If there has not, you are required to look at events after that date in order to see whether any change has occurred subsequently.

I now return to the material facts of the present case. I start with the fact that the taxpayer has ever since 1948 returned to Quebec for some 10 to 12 weeks in each year to visit her parents, when they were alive, and other relatives, and generally to maintain her links with Canada. In 1956 she made an additional visit to look after her mother who was then ill. For the past 14 years or so she has owned, maintained at her own expense and kept ready for her occupation at all times the family house in Metis Beach at which she and her husband had stayed for the previous eight years. But since 1948 she has otherwise lived with her husband in England. There has been no significant change in the pattern of her life between 1948 and 1978, the latter being the last of the years of assessment with which the revenue claim in this case is concerned. On those facts it appears clear to me that since 1948 the taxpayer has been physically present in this country as an inhabitant of it. Her physical presence in Quebec has been for periods of limited duration and for the purpose of maintaining her links with the country to which it is

3 *Re Scullard, Smith v Brock* [1957] Ch 107, [1956] 3 All ER 898.

her intention ultimately to return. That is not enough to have made her an inhabitant of Quebec. In my judgment it is clear that she was resident in England on 1 January 1974, and that that residence was not displaced when she went to Canada in July 1974 or at any other time during the material period.

Sir John Foster, who appears for the taxpayer, pointed to the fact that if she and her husband had been married on or after 1 January 1974, the effect of section 1 (1) of the Act of 1973 on the facts of this case would have been to preserve the taxpayer's domicile of origin: see *IRC v Bullock*[4]. That point is accepted by the Crown. Sir John then submitted that because the manifest intention of Parliament was to abolish what Lord Denning MR described in *Gray v Formosa*[5] as 'the last barbarous relic of a wife's servitude', a less stringent test should be applied to the abandonment of this deemed domicile of choice than that which is appropriate to a true domicile of choice. That was an approach which appears to have found favour with the commissioners. But I regret that the language of section 1 (2) does not permit it. It seems clear that a woman living in England with her husband who was married before 1 January 1974, can only free herself from the shackles of dependency by choosing to leave her husband for permanent residence in another country. That is a very limited freedom and it is less than that available under section 1 (1) to those who marry on or after 1 January 1974. Be that as it may, Parliament did not, as it might have done, provide that a woman who was married before 1 January 1974, was to be treated as if she had never acquired her domicile of dependency. Section 1 (2) having taken the form which it has, by treating the married woman as retaining her domicile of dependency as a domicile of choice, I regret that I have no choice but to attach to it all the consequences which the law has long recognised the latter domicile to have. I should add, for the sake of clarity, that so construed section 1 (2) does not in my view lead to any result which is unjust, anomalous or absurd.

On that footing Sir John Foster made an alternative submission to the following effect. He said, as a general proposition in relation to the abandonment of a domicile of choice, that a person who has the necessary intention both to cease to reside permanently or indefinitely in the country of his former choice and so to reside in another country in the future can actually cease to reside there merely by visiting the other country for a short period, perhaps only for a day, albeit that he then returns to the first country and lives there for another 10 years. It seems to me that that submission cannot possibly be correct. The intention to reside in the second country is merely to do so in the future. Such an intention can neither transmute the visit to the second country into residence nor cause there to be a cessation of residence in the first. Sir John said that this is a point not covered by authority. My respectful answer to that is that, but for this case, I would have doubted that it was a point for which authority was needed.

My conclusion is that the taxpayer did not cease to reside in this country either in July 1974 or at any other material time and that means that she did not abandon the English domicile of choice which was imposed on her by section 1 (2) of the Act of 1973.

Appeal allowed

4 [1976] 3 All ER 353, [1976] 1 WLR 1178.
5 [1963] P 259, [1962] 3 All ER 419.

QUESTION

H, domiciled in Scotland, marries W, domiciled before her marriage in England. They live together in Scotland until 1983, when W returns to England, intending to remain there permanently. Later in the same year W gives birth to C, who is the child of H. What is C's domicile of origin?

For the purposes of an English rule of the conflict of laws, the question where a person is domiciled is determined according to English law.

Re Martin, Loustalan v Loustalan [1900] P 211, 69 LJP 75; p 586 below.

Re Annesley, Davidson v Annesley [1926] Ch 692, 95 LJCh 404; p 655 below.

New South Wales Domicile Act 1979

5. The rule of law whereby a married woman has at all times the domicile of her husband is abolished.

6. The rule of law whereby the domicile of origin revives upon the abandonment of a domicile of choice without the acquisition of a new domicile of choice is abolished and the domicile a person has at any time continues until he acquires a different domicile.

7.—(1) A person is capable of having an independent domicile if—
(a) he has attained the age of 18 years; or
(b) he is, or has at any time been, married,
and not otherwise.
　(2) Subsection (1) does not apply to a person who, under the rules of law relating to domicile, is incapable of acquiring a domicile by reason of mental incapacity.

8.—(1) In this section—
(a) 'child' means a person under the age of 18 years who is not, and has not at any time been, married; and
(b) references to the parents of a child include references to parents who are not married to each other.
　(2) Where, at any time, a child has his principal home with one of his parents but his parents are living separately and apart or the child does not have another living parent, the domicile of the child at that time is the domicile that that parent has at that time and thereafter the child has the domicile that that parent has from time to time or, if that parent has died, the domicile that that parent has at the time of death.
　(3) Where a child is adopted, his domicile—
(a) if, upon his adoption, he has two parents—is, at the time of the adoption and thereafter, the domicile he would have if he were a child born in wedlock to those parents; and

(b) if, upon his adoption, he has one parent only—is, at the time of the adoption, the domicile of that parent and thereafter is the domicile that that parent has from time to time or, if that parent has died, the domicile that that parent had at the time of death.

(4) A child ceases to have, by virtue of subsection (2), the domicile or last domicile of one of his parents if—

(a) he commences to have his principal home with his other parent; or

(b) his parents resume or commence living together.

(5) Where a child has a domicile by virtue of subsection (2) or (3) immediately before he ceases to be a child, he retains that domicile until he acquires a domicile of choice.

(6) Where the adoption of a child is rescinded, the domicile of the child shall thereafter be determined in accordance with any provisions with respect to that domicile that are included in the order rescinding the adoption and, so far as no such provision is applicable, as if the adoption had not taken place.

9. The intention that a person must have in order to acquire a domicile of choice in a country is the intention to make his home indefinitely in that country.

10. A person who is, in accordance with the rules of the common law as modified by this Act, domiciled in a union but is not, apart from this section, domiciled in any particular one of the countries that together form the union is domiciled in that one of those countries with which he has for the time being the closest connection.

11. The acquisition of a domicile of choice in place of a domicile of origin may be established by evidence that would be sufficient to establish the domicile of choice if the previous domicile had also been a domicile of choice.

NOTE

This is one of a number of Uniform Domicile Acts in force throughout Australia (and there is similar legislation in New Zealand). It will be seen that as well as making similar but not identical provision for the domicile of married women and children (ss 5, 7 and 8) as that made by ss 1, 3 and 4 of the Domicile and Matrimonial Proceedings Act 1973 (p 3 above), the Uniform Act abolishes the rule in *Udny v Udny* (p 19 above) as to the revival of a domicile of origin (s 6) and the rule in *Winans v A-G* (p 7 above) that stronger evidence is required to displace a domicile of origin than a domicile of choice (s 11). It also defines the intention required for the acquisition of a domicile of choice (s 9) and provides for the domicile of persons domiciled in a 'union', eg the Commonwealth of Australia, the United Kingdom, the United States or Canada, who are not domiciled in any of the countries that form the union (s 10).

In the United States, a domicile of choice continues until a new domicile is acquired: the domicile of origin does not revive.

Re Jones' Estate (1921) 182 NW 227 (Supreme Court of Iowa)

Evan Jones was born in Wales about 1850 with a Welsh domicile of origin. He was an industrious, thrifty, hardworking Welsh coal miner who by the end of his life had accumulated a considerable amount of property. In 1883 he put a Welsh girl in the family way. She instituted affiliation proceedings against him. To escape this prospect he emigrated to the United States and acquired a domicile of choice in Iowa. He married an American wife and became a naturalised American citizen. In 1915, after the death of his wife, he decided to return to Wales for good and live with his sister there. He realised all his property, purchased a draft for $2000 and, on the advice of his bank manager, deposited the rest (some $20,000) in the bank in Iowa. He sailed from New York on 1 May 1915 in the Lusitania, which on 7 May was torpedoed by a German submarine off the Old Head of Kinsale, southern Ireland. Like most of the passengers he was drowned. He died intestate. If he died domiciled in Wales, his brothers and sisters were entitled to his estate. If he died domiciled in Iowa it went to the illegitimate daughter from whom he had fled (before she was born) over thirty years before. The trial court held that the brothers and sisters were entitled. The daughter appealed.

Faville J (after stating the facts, and distinguishing between domicile of origin, domicile of choice, and domicile by operation of law, continued):   At the outset, it is obvious that under the circumstances of the instant case the domicile of the decedent at the time of his death must in any event be determined by the assumption of a fiction. All will agree that the decedent did not have a domicile on the Lusitania. In order to determine his domicile, then, one of two fictions must be assumed, either that he retained the Iowa domicile until one was acquired in Wales, or that he acquired a domicile in Wales the instant he abandoned the Iowa domicile and started for Wales, with the intent and purpose of residing there. Which one of these fictions shall we assume for the purpose of determining the disposition of his personal property? This question first came before the courts at an early day, long before our present easy and extensive methods of transportation, and at a time before the present ready movement from one country to another. At that time men left Europe for the Western Continent or elsewhere largely for purposes of adventure or in search of an opportunity for the promotion of commerce. It was at a time before the invention of the steamboat and before the era of the oceanic cable. Men left their native land knowing that they would be gone for long periods of time, and that means of communication with their home land were infrequent, difficult, and slow. The traditions of their native country were strong with these men. In the event of death, while absent, they desired that their property should descend in accordance with the laws of the land of their birth. Many such men were adventurers who had the purpose and intent to eventually return to the land of their nativity. There was a large degree of patriotic sentiment connected with the first announcement of the rules of law in the matter of the estates of such men. The idea found expression in the phrase, 'Once an Englishman, always an Englishman', and in the kindred declaration, 'A man must intend to become a Frenchman instead of an Englishman', *Moorhouse v Lord*.[6] This popular and patriotic idea was expressed in the familiar lines of Sir Walter Scott:

> 'Breathes there the man, with soul so dead,
>   Who never to himself hath said,

6 (1863) 10 HLCas 272, 1 New Rep 555.

"This is my own, my native land".
Whose heart hath ne'er within him burned,
As home his footsteps he hath turned,
    From wand'ring on a foreign strand?'

Many men, especially of English birth, became traders in the American colonies or in India. The Englishman of that day was a firm believer in the law of primogeniture and desired that his estate should descend according to the established law of his native land.

These reasons, which were, to an extent at least, historical and patriotic, found early expression in the decisions of the courts on the question of domicile. The general rule was declared to be that a domicile is retained until a new domicile has been actually acquired. At an early time, however, an exception was ingrafted upon this rule to the effect that, for the purposes of succession, a party abandoning a domicile of choice with the intent to return to his domicile of origin regains the latter the instant that the former domicile is abandoned.

It will be observed that this exception involves two elements: First, that the party is seeking to return from a domicile of choice to a domicile of origin[7] and, second, that the question arises in a case involving succession to an estate.[8] It is apparent that this exception to the general rule grew out of the conditions that we have before suggested and was a recognition of the desire on the part of the English trader in distant lands to have his estate administered according to the laws of the land of his birth.

In 1834, Mr Justice Story wrote the first edition of his great work on the Conflict of Laws. In it he stated (section 47):

'If a man has acquired a new domicile different from that of his birth, and he removes from it with an intention to resume his native domicile, the latter is reacquired even while he is on his way in itinere, for it reverts from the moment the other is given up'.

In section 48, he said:

'A national character acquired in a foreign country by residence changes when the party has left the country animo non revertendi, and is on his return to the country where he had his antecedent domicile. And especially if he be in itinere to his native country with that intent, his native domicile revives while he is yet in transitu, for the native domicile easily reverts. The moment the foreign domicile is abandoned the native domicile is reacquired'.

This pronouncement of Mr Justice Story has been frequently referred to by the courts, both English and American, in discussing this question, and has been the basis for decisions, particularly in the English courts. (The court elaborately reviewed the English and American authorities, especially *Udny v Udny*, and continued):

Perhaps no better case could be found than the instant case to illustrate the effect of the adoption of the exception to the general rule. The decedent

---

7 Sed quaere: The English rule is not so limited (*Ed*).
8 Sed quaere. In *Udny v Udny* (1869) LR 1 Sc & Div 441, 7 Macq 89 (p 3 above) the question arose in the context of legitimation by subsequent marriage, not in the context of succession (*Ed*).

in this case had not only acquired a domicile in the United States, but had become a citizen of this country. Under the general rule, if he had abandoned his domicile in Iowa with the intention of acquiring a domicile in Norway or in France, and had been on the ill-fated Lusitania, it would have been universally held that the domicile in Iowa was still retained.[9] No one will dispute that proposition. But, because, although a citizen of the United States, and residing here for many years, he was en route to Wales, the land of his birth, instead of to some other country, it is contended that he acquired a domicile in that country instantly upon abandoning his domicile in Iowa. If some native of Iowa had done exactly what the decedent did, had disposed of his property with the avowed and declared intention of abandoning his domicile in Iowa and of securing one in Wales, and had accompanied Jones on his trip, and had gone down on the same boat, his estate would have been administered according to the laws of the state of Iowa, because he had not yet acquired a new domicile anywhere else, while Jones' estate, under the theory of the English rule, would be administered according to the laws of Wales, because he happened to have been born in that country. If such a rule is to be applied as between different states of the Union, with our freedom of movement between the various states, it would lead to very startling results. The laws of the states differ greatly in regard to descent. There is no logical reason why the rule should not be applied between different states of the Union as readily as between different governments. Under such a doctrine, if applied between the various states of the Union, if a man had been born in the state of New York, and at an early age had removed to Iowa, and had lived in this commonwealth for many years, had voted here and had become familiar with our laws, and should finally decide to remove to New York to live, and should die in itinere, he would be regarded as domiciled in New York, If, however, under identical circumstances, he intended to remove to Massachusetts, he would be regarded as domiciled in Iowa.

What good reason is there why 'native allegiance' to the state of New York, where he was born, should be the determining factor which would prevail in such instance? One reason that is persuasive why such a rule should not be adopted is that a person who in these days abandons his domicile of origin and acquires a legal domicile in another jurisdiction, presumably, at least, is familiar with the laws of the jurisdiction of the latter domicile, and there is, to say the least, as strong a presumption that he desires his estate to be administered according to the laws of that jurisdiction as of the jurisdiction of the domicile of origin. While there may have been a good reason for the establishment of the English rule at the time and under the conditions under which it was announced, we do not believe that any good reason exists for the recognition of such a rule under the circumstances disclosed in this case. The general rule that a domicile once legally acquired is retained until a new domicile is secured, and that, in the acquisition of such new domicile, both the fact and the intention must concur, it seems to us is a rule of universal and general application and that there is neither good logic nor substantial reason for the application of an exception to that rule in the case where the party is in itinere toward the domicile of origin. In other words, going back to the original proposition, the fiction is assumed

9 Not in England (*Ed*).

generally that any domicile, either of choice or of origin, is retained until a new domicile has been legally acquired. We see no good reason for changing that rule in the one instance where the descent of property is involved and the party is in itinere to the domicile of origin. We believe that the general rule is the better rule, and that the exception laid down by Story and followed by the English courts should not be recognised either as between the states of the union or between this country and a foreign country, under the facts disclosed in this case.

It therefore follows that the domicile of the decedent was in the state of Iowa until a new domicile had been actually acquired in Wales. No such domicile having been acquired, at the time of his death, his personal estate must be administered according to the laws of Iowa. We think the general rule should be followed, even though the decedent was in itinere to his domicile of origin at the time of his death. We have examined the record and hold that the appellant was legally recognised as the child of the decedent, as required by our statute and the decisions of this court, and is his lawful heir.

It follows that the judgment of the trial court must be, and the same is, reversed.

Evans CJ and Stevens, Arthur, and De Graff JJ concur.

QUESTION

Was the result in this case more or less sensible than the result which would have been reached under the much-criticised revival doctrine of *Udny v Udny*?

Habitual residence means a regular physical presence which must endure for some time. It means something more than ordinary residence and something less than domicile.

Cruse v Chittum [1974] 2 All ER 940 (Family Division)

Husband's petition for a declaration that a foreign divorce was valid.

The husband and wife, both domiciled in England, married there in 1950. They lived together in England until 1961 when the wife left with a sergeant in the American forces. The husband lost touch with her until August 1964 when he received a letter from her from an address in Mississippi saying: 'I think it is only right to tell you that I have got a divorce so you are a free man now'. The husband took no steps in the matter until 1971 when he wished to marry. His solicitors discovered that the wife had been granted a divorce in Mississippi in July 1963. The decree recited that the wife was an actual bona fide resident of Harrison County, Mississippi, and had been for more than a year immediately preceding the filing of the complaint.

Section 3 of the Recognition of Divorces and Legal Separations Act 1971 provides that the validity of an overseas divorce shall be recognised if at the date of the institution of the proceedings in the country in which it was obtained (inter alia) either spouse was habitually resident in that country. Section 5 provides that any finding of fact made by the foreign court shall (if only one spouse took part in the proceedings) be sufficient proof of that fact unless the contrary is shown.

Lane J: The first question which arises in determining whether or not this court should recognise that decree is what is meant by the phrase 'habitually resident in that country'. Counsel for the petitioner submits that habitual residence requires an element of intention, an intention to reside in that country. He further submits that 'habitual' must indicate a quality of residence rather than a period of residence. He argues that as no period of residence is specified in the 1971 Act, this of itself points to the importance of the quality of residence in order to make it habitual. This submission derives support from the fact that in s 5 (2) of the Domicile and Matrimonial Proceedings Act 1973, the same phrase 'habitually resident' appears, but for the purposes of that subsection is required to be one year's duration. Counsel says further that one may point to characteristics of residency which will not make it habitual but other than habitual. For example the residence must not be temporary or of a secondary nature. He urges that the phrase in the decree of the American court that the residence was 'actual' and 'bona fide' really defines what is meant by 'habitual' in this context, and denotes a regular physical presence which must endure for some time. He further submits that ordinary residence is different from habitual residence in that the latter is something more than the former and is similar to the residence normally required as part of domicile, although in habitual residence there is no need for the element of animus which is necessary in domicile. I accept those submissions. (Her Ladyship referred to s 5 of the 1971 Act and continued):

I am satisfied that a valid decree of dissolution of the petitioner's marriage was pronounced in the Mississippi court on 17 July 1963, and that sufficient facts are apparent therefrom and from other evidence before me to show that the respondent at the time she instituted the proceedings in that court was habitually resident in the country where the decree was pronounced. I am fortified in my view by the fact that under s 5 (2) of the Domicile and Matrimonial Proceedings Act 1973 the court has jurisdiction to entertain proceedings for divorce if either party to the marriage has been habitually resident here throughout a period of one year ending with the date when divorce proceedings are begun. It would therefore be somewhat anomalous if habitual residence in a foreign country granting a decree were required to be of more than a year's duration in order that the decree should be recognised here.

These being my conclusions, I grant the declaration sought that the petitioner's marriage was validly dissolved and that the decree may be recognised here.

QUESTION

In the light of the increasing reliance on habitual residence as a connecting factor, what justification is there for retaining domicile in the law as a connecting factor?

CHAPTER 2

Proof of Foreign Law

Foreign law is a question of fact for the judge to be proved by expert evidence.

Lazard Brothers & Co v Midland Bank [1933] AC 289, 102 LJKB
191 (House of Lords)

Before the Bolshevik Revolution in Russia in October 1917, the Banque
Industrielle de Moscou (hereinafter called the Moscow Bank), a Russian
bank, kept current accounts with the Midland Bank Ltd and at the end of
1917 these accounts were in credit to an amount exceeding £300,000. At the
same time the Moscow Bank were indebted to Lazard Brothers & Co,
bankers in London, in a sum which, though large, was less than that owed
by the Midland Bank to the Moscow Bank. Both these debts were English
debts, payable in England and governed by English law.

On 27 October 1930 Lazard Brothers & Co obtained an order from
Branson J in Chambers for leave to issue a writ against the Moscow Bank
and to serve notice thereof at Moscow by sending it by registered post to the
Moscow Bank. In pursuance of this order Lazard Brothers & Co issued a
writ against the Moscow Bank claiming the sums owing to them, and sent
notice of it by registered post to Moscow. On 24 November 1930 judgment
in default of appearance was given for Lazard Brothers, who on 28
November 1930 received a letter from the Soviet Embassy returning the
notice of writ and stating that it could not be delivered because the Moscow
Bank had gone out of existence during the Revolution of October 1917.

On 12 December 1930 Lazard Brothers obtained a garnishee order nisi
against the Midland Bank attaching all debts owing from the Midland Bank,
the garnishees, to the Moscow Bank, the judgment debtors, to answer the
judgment of 24 November. On the same day a copy of this order was sent by
registered post to the Moscow Bank, but the envelope was returned marked
'Unknown'.

On 20 January 1931 a garnishee issue was directed between Lazard
Brothers as judgment creditors and the Midland Bank as garnishees, the
issue being whether the garnishees were indebted to the judgment debtors,
the Moscow Bank. Roche J made an order absolute that they were so
indebted. His judgment was reversed by the Court of Appeal on the ground
that the Moscow Bank had ceased to exist as a juristic person before 1930
and that therefore the writ and judgment, and consequently the garnishee
proceedings, were null and void.

The judgment creditors appealed.

Lord Wright: . . . The Moscow Bank was a corporation established by an
Act of the Tsar; but the governing authority in Russia, as recognised in the
English courts, is now and has been since October 1917 the Soviet state.

Soviet law is accordingly the governing law from the same date in virtue of the recognition de facto in 1921 and de jure in 1924 by this country of the Soviet state as the sovereign power in Russia. The effect of such recognition is retroactive and dates back to the original establishment of Soviet rule which was in the 1917 October Revolution, as was held by the Court of Appeal in *Luther v Sagor*.[1] The question, therefore, is whether by Soviet law the Moscow Bank was at the date of the issue of the writ in this action, that is on 27 October 1930, an existing juristic person. What the Russian Soviet law is in that respect is a question of fact, of which the English court cannot take judicial cognizance, even though the foreign law has already been proved before it in another case. The court must act upon the evidence before it in the actual case. The recent enactment, s 102 of the Supreme Court of Judicature (Consolidation) Act 1925,[2] which provides that this question of fact must be decided by the judge alone instead of by the jury, if there be a jury, expressly treats the question as depending on the evidence given with respect to the foreign law. No earlier decision of the court can relieve the judge of the duty of deciding the question on the actual evidence given in the particular case. On what evidence of the foreign law a court can act has often been discussed. The evidence it is clear must be that of qualified experts in the foreign law. If the law is contained in a code or written form, the question is not as to the language of the written law, but what the law is as shown by its exposition, interpretation and adjudication; so in effect it was laid down by Coleridge J in *Baron de Bode*;[3] in the *Sussex Peerage* case,[4] Lord Denman stated his opinion to the same effect as he had done in *Baron de Bode's*. He said that if there be a conflict of evidence of the experts, 'you (the judge) must decide as well as you can on the conflicting testimony, but you must take the evidence from the witnesses'. Hence the court is not entitled to construe a foreign code itself: it has not 'organs to know and to deal with the text of that law' (as was said by Lord Brougham in the *Sussex Peerage* case). The text of the foreign law if put in evidence by the experts may be considered, if at all, only as part of the evidence and as a help to decide between conflicting expert testimony. . . .

(His Lordship reviewed the evidence of Soviet law and came to the conclusion that the Moscow Bank had by Soviet law ceased to exist long before 1930, although in *Russian Commercial and Industrial Bank v Comptoir d'Escompte de Mulhouse*[5] the House of Lords had held that a Russian bank had not been dissolved by the same Soviet decrees as were in issue in this case.)

Lords Buckmaster, Blanesburgh, Warrington of Clyffe, and Russell of Killowen concurred.

Appeal dismissed.

Civil Evidence Act 1972

4.—(1) It is hereby declared that in civil proceedings a person who is suitably qualified to do so on account of his knowledge or experience is competent to

1 *A. M. Luther v James Sagor & Co* [1921] 3 KB 532, 90 LJKB 1202.
2 Now s 69(5) of the Supreme Court Act 1981 (*Ed*).
3 (1845) 8 QB 208 at 266.
4 (1844) 11 Cl & Fin 85 at 116.
5 [1925] AC 112, 93 LJKB 1098.

give expert evidence as to the law of any country or territory outside the United Kingdom, or of any part of the United Kingdom other than England and Wales, irrespective of whether he has acted or is entitled to act as a legal practitioner there.

(2) Where any question as to the law of any country or territory outside the United Kingdom, or of any part of the United Kingdom other than England and Wales, with respect to any matter has been determined (whether before or after the passing of this Act) in any such proceedings as are mentioned in subsection (4) below, then in any civil proceedings (not being proceedings before a court which can take judicial notice of the law of that country, territory or part with respect to that matter)—

(a) any finding made or decision given on that question in the first-mentioned proceedings shall, if reported or recorded in citable form, be admissible in evidence for the purpose of proving the law of that country, territory or part with respect to that matter; and

(b) if that finding or decision, as so reported or recorded, is adduced for that purpose, the law of that country, territory or part with respect to that matter shall be taken to be in accordance with that finding or decision unless the contrary is proved:

Provided that paragraph (b) above shall not apply in the case of a finding or decision which conflicts with another finding or decision on the same question adduced by virtue of this subsection in the same proceedings.

(3) Except with the leave of the court, a party to any civil proceedings shall not be permitted to adduce any such finding or decision as is mentioned in subsection (2) above by virtue of that subsection unless he has in accordance with rules of court given to every other party to the proceedings notice that he intends to do so.

(4) The proceedings referred to in subsection (2) above are the following, whether civil or criminal, namely—

(a) proceedings at first instance in any of the following courts, namely the High Court, the Crown Court, a court of quarter sessions, the Court of Chancery of the county palatine of Lancaster and the Court of Chancery of the county palatine of Durham;

(b) appeals rising out of any such proceedings as are mentioned in paragraph (a) above;

(c) proceedings before the Judicial Committee of the Privy Council on appeal (whether to Her Majesty in Council or to the Judicial Committee as such) from any decision of any court outside the United Kingdom.

(5) For the purposes of this section a finding or decision on any such question as is mentioned in subsection (2) above shall be taken to be reported or recorded in citable form if, but only if, it is reported or recorded in writing in a report, transcript or other document which, if that question had been a question as to the law of England and Wales, could be cited as an authority in legal proceedings in England and Wales.

CHAPTER 3

The Exclusion of Foreign Law

English courts will not enforce the penal laws of foreign countries. What is a foreign penal law is a matter to be decided by the English court.

Huntington v Attrill [1893] AC 150, 62 LJPC44 (Privy Council)

Appeal from the Ontario Court of Appeal.

In June 1880 the appellant became a creditor for money lent to the Rockaway Beach Improvement Co, which was incorporated and carried on business in the State of New York. A New York statute provided in section 21 that 'if any certificate or report made by the officers of any such corporation shall be false in any material representation, all the officers who shall have signed the same shall be jointly and severally liable for all the debts of the corporation contracted while they are officers thereof'. The respondent was in June 1880 a director, and in that capacity an officer of the company within the meaning of the statute. On the 30th of that month he and the other officers of the company signed and verified on oath a certificate stating that the whole capital stock had been paid up in cash.

In 1883 the appellant sued the respondent in the Supreme Court of New York for the unpaid balance of his loan to the company, alleging that the certificate contained representations which were material and false, and that the respondent had incurred personal liability for the debt as provided by section 21. In 1886 the court gave judgment for the appellant for the sum of $100,240.

Having failed to recover payment, the appellant brought an action on the New York judgment in the High Court of Ontario, where the respondent resided. The respondent pleaded that the New York judgment was for a penalty which could not be recovered in the courts of a foreign state. The trial judge dismissed the action with costs. The Ontario Court of Appeal was equally divided and dismissed the appeal.

The judgment of their Lordships (Lords Halsbury, Watson, Branwell, Hobhouse, Morris and Stand) was delivered by
Lord Watson: . . . Their Lordships cannot assent to the proposition that, in considering whether the present action was penal in such sense as to oust their jurisdiction, the courts of Ontario were bound to pay absolute deference to any interpretation which might have been put upon the Statute of 1875 in the State of New York. They had to construe and apply an international rule, which is a matter of law entirely within the cognizance of the foreign court whose jurisdiction is invoked. Judicial decisions in the state where the cause of action arose are not precedents which must be followed, although the reasoning upon which they are founded must always receive careful consideration, and may be conclusive. The court appealed to must

determine for itself, in the first place, the substance of the right sought to be enforced; and, in the second place, whether its enforcement would, either directly or indirectly, involve the execution of the penal law of another state. Were any other principle to guide its decision, a court might find itself in the position of giving effect in one case and denying effect in another, to suits of the same character, in consequence of the causes of action having arisen in different countries; or in the predicament of being constrained to give effect to laws which were, in its own judgment, strictly penal.

The general law upon this point has been correctly stated by Mr Justice Story in his 'Conflict of Laws', and by other text-writers; but their Lordships do not think it necessary to quote from these authorities in explanation of the reasons which have induced courts of justice to decline jurisdiction in suits somewhat loosely described as penal, when these have their origin in a foreign country. The rule has its foundation in the well-recognised principle that crimes, including in that term all breaches of public law punishable by pecuniary mulct or otherwise, at the instance of the state government, or of someone representing the public, are local in this sense, that they are only cognizable and punishable in the country where they were committed. Accordingly no proceeding, even in the shape of a civil suit, which has for its object the enforcement by the state, whether directly or indirectly, of punishment imposed for such breaches by the lex fori, ought to be admitted in the courts of any other country.

Their Lordships have already indicated that, in their opinion, the phrase 'penal actions', which is so frequently used to designate that class of actions which, by the law of nations, are exclusively assigned to their domestic forum, does not afford an accurate definition. In its ordinary acceptation, the word 'penal' may embrace penalties for infractions of general law which do not constitute offences against the state; it may for many legal purposes be applied with perfect propriety to penalties created by contract; and it therefore, when taken by itself, fails to mark that distinction between civil rights and criminal wrongs which is the very essence of the international rule. The phrase was used by Lord Loughborough and by Mr Justice Buller in a well-known case (*Folliott v Ogden*[1] and *Ogden v Folliott*[2]) and also by Chief Justice Marshall, who, in *The Antelope*[3] thus stated the rule with no less brevity than force: 'The courts of no country execute the penal laws of another'. Read in the light of the context, the language used by these eminent lawyers is quite intelligible, because they were dealing with the consequences of violations of public law and order, which were unmistakably of a criminal complexion. But the expressions 'penal' and 'penalty', when employed without any qualification, express or implied, are calculated to mislead, because they are capable of being construed so as to extend the rule to all proceedings for the recovery of penalties, whether exigible by the state in the interest of the community, or by private persons in their own interest.

The Supreme Court of the United States had occasion to consider the international rule in *Wisconsin v the Pelican Insurance Co.*[4] By the statute law of the State of Wisconsin, a pecuniary penalty was imposed upon corporations carrying on business under it who failed to comply with one of its

1 (1789) 1 Hy Bl 123 at 135.
2 (1790) 3 Term Rep 726 at 734.
3 (1825) 10 Wheat 123.
4 (1888) 127 US 265.

enactments. The penalty was recoverable by the commissioner of insurance, an official entrusted with the administration of the Act in the public interest, one half of it being payable into the State Treasury, and the other to the commissioner who was to defray the costs of prosecution. It was held that the penalty could not be enforced by the Federal Court, or the judiciary of any other state. In delivering the judgment of the bench, Mr Justice Gray, after referring to the textbooks, and the dictum by Chief Justice Marshall already cited, went on to say: 'The rule that the Courts of no country execute the penal laws of another applies not only to prosecutions and sentence for crimes and misdemeanours, *but to all suits in favour of the state* for the recovery of pecuniary penalties for any violation of statutes for the protection of its revenue or other municipal laws, and to all judgments for such penalties'.

Their Lordships do not hesitate to accept that exposition of the law, which, in their opinion, discloses the proper test for ascertaining whether an action is penal within the meaning of the rule. A proceeding, in order to come within the scope of the rule, must be in the nature of a suit in favour of the state whose law has been infringed. All the provisions of municipal statutes for the regulation of trade and trading companies are presumably enacted in the interest and for the benefit of the community at large; and persons who violate these provisions are, in a certain sense, offenders against the state law, as well as against individuals who may be injured by their misconduct. But foreign tribunals do not regard these violations of statute law as offences against the state, unless their vindication rests with the state itself, or with the community which it represents. Penalties may be attached to them, but that circumstance will not bring them within the rule, except in cases where these penalties are recoverable at the instance of the state, or of an official duly authorised to prosecute on its behalf, or of a member of the public in the character of a common informer. An action by the latter is regarded as an actio popularis pursued, not in his individual interest, but in the interest of the whole community.

The New York Statute of 1875 provides for the organisation and regulation of corporations formed for the purpose of carrying on all kinds of lawful business with the exception of certain branches therein specified. It confers rights and privileges upon persons who choose to form a trading association, and to become incorporated under its provisions, with full or with limited liability; and, in either case, it varies and limits the rights and remedies which, under the common law, would have been available to creditors of the association, as against its individual members. On the other hand, for the protection of those members of the public who may deal with the corporation, the Act imposes upon its directors and officers various stringent obligations, the plain object of which is to make known, from time to time, to all concerned, the true condition of its finances. Thus they are required (s 18) to publish an annual report stating the amount of capital, the proportion actually paid in, the amount and nature of existing assets and debts, the names of the shareholders and the dividends, if any, declared since last report; and (s 37) to certify the amount of capital stock paid in within thirty days after payment of the last instalment. In both cases the consequence of the report or certificate being false in any material representation, is that every director or officer who vouched its accuracy becomes, under s 21, liable personally for all the debts of the corporation contracted during his period of office.

The provisions of s 21 are in striking contrast to the enactments of s 34, which inflicts a penalty of $100 upon every director or officer of a corporation with limited liability, who authorises or permits the omission of the word 'limited' from its seal, official publications, or business documents. In that case, the penalty is recoverable 'in the name of the people of the State of New York by the district attorney of the county in which the principal office of such corporation is located, and the amounts recovered shall be paid over to the proper authorities for the support of the poor of such county'. It does not admit of doubt that an action by the district attorney would be a suit in favour of the state, and that neither the penalty, nor the decree of a New York court for its amount, could be enforced in a foreign country.

In one aspect of them, the provisions of s 21 are penal in the wider sense in which the term is used. They impose heavy liabilities upon directors, in respect of failure to observe statutory regulations for the protection of persons who have become or may become creditors of the corporation. But, in so far as they concern creditors, these provisions are in their nature protective and remedial. To use the language of Mr Justice Osler in the court below, they give 'a civil remedy only to creditors whose rights the conduct of the company's officers may have been calculated to injure, and which is not enforceable by the state or the public'. In the opinion of their Lordships, these enactments are simply conditions upon which the Legislature permits associations to trade with corporate privileges, and constitute an implied term of every contract between the corporation and its creditors. . . .

Appeal allowed.

Nor will English courts enforce foreign revenue laws.

Government of India v Taylor [1955] AC 491, [1955] 1 All ER 292 (House of Lords)

The Delhi Electric Supply and Traction Co Ltd was incorporated in the United Kingdom but carried on business in India. In 1947 it sold the whole of its undertaking to the appellant, the government of India, for the sum of 82, 11, 580 rupees. This sum was paid to the company in India and remitted to England a few days later. In 1949 the company went into voluntary liquidation in England and the respondent was appointed liquidator. The government of India claimed to prove in the liquidation for the sum of 16, 54, 945 rupees which consisted of Indian capital gains tax on the sale of the company's undertakings. The liquidator rejected this claim and Vaisey J and the Court of Appeal (Evershed MR, Jenkins and Morris LJJ) held that he was entitled to do so. The government of India appealed.

Viscount Simonds: My Lords, I admit that I was greatly surprised to hear it suggested that the courts of this country would and should entertain a suit by a foreign state to recover a tax. For at any time since I have had any acquaintance with the law I should have said as Rowlatt J said in *King of the Hellenes v Brostrom*:[5] 'It is perfectly elementary that a foreign government

5 (1923) 16 Ll LRep 190 at 193.

cannot come here—nor will the courts of other countries allow our government to go there—and sue a person found in that jurisdiction for taxes levied and which he is declared to be liable to in the country to which he belongs.' That was in 1923. In 1928 Tomlin J in *Re Visser*,[6] after referring to the case of *Sydney Municipal Council v Bull*,[7] in which the same proposition had been unequivocally stated by Grantham J, and saying that he was bound to follow it, added: 'My own opinion is that there is a well-recognised rule, which has been enforced for at least 200 years or thereabouts, under which these courts will not collect the taxes of foreign states for the benefit of the sovereigns of those foreign states; and this is one of those actions which these courts will not entertain.' My Lords, it is not seemly to weigh the pronouncements of living judges, but it is, I think, permissible to say that the opinions of few, if any, judges of the past command greater respect than those of Lord Tomlin and Rowlatt J, and what appeared to one of them to be a 'well-recognised rule' and to the other 'elementary' law cannot easily be displaced.

My Lords, the history and origin of the rule, if it be a rule, are not easy to ascertain and there is on the whole remarkably little authority upon the subject. I am inclined to agree with the Court of Appeal that the early cases of *A-G v Lutwydge*[8] and *Boucher v Lawson*,[9] to which some reference was made, do not give much help. It is otherwise when we advance a few years to the age of Lord Mansfield CJ. That great judge in a series of cases repeated the formula: 'For no country ever takes notice of the revenue laws of another'. See *Planché v Fletcher*,[10] *Holman v Johnson*,[11] and *Lever v Fletcher*.[12] It is true that Lord Mansfield was not directly concerned with the case of a foreign power suing in an English court to recover revenue, but with the validity of a contract made abroad where the seller was not implicated in smuggling operations which contravened the revenue laws of this country or with the rights of insurers where a ship which had cleared for Ostend went direct to Nantes thereby affecting the customs dues payable abroad. But in each case he could not have reached his conclusion but for the fact that he applied the rule that no country ever takes notice of the revenue laws of another. Where Lord Mansfield led, Lord Kenyon CJ followed, though he was not a judge who followed blindly. I agree with the learned Master of the Rolls that it is clear from such cases as *Clugas v Penaluna*,[13] *Bernard v Reed*,[14] and *Waymell v Reed*[15] that Lord Kenyon accepted without qualification the broad rule which Lord Mansfield had formulated. I pass over a number of cases where the question was as to the admissibility of documents made in a foreign country and not stamped according to the law of that country, pausing only to remind your Lordships that in *James v Catherwood*[16] Lord Tenterden (then Abbott CJ) said: 'This point is too plain for argument. It has been settled, or

6 [1928] Ch 877 at 884.
7 [1909] 1 KB 7; 78 LJKB 45.
8 (1729) Bunb 280.
9 (1735) Cunn 144.
10 (1779) 1 Doug KB 251 at 253.
11 (1775) 1 Cowp 341 at 343.
12 (1780, unreported).
13 (1791) 4 Term Rep 466.
14 (1794) 1 Esp 91.
15 (1794) 5 Term Rep 599.
16 (1823) 3 Dow & Ry KB 190.

at least considered as settled, ever since the time of Lord Hardwicke that in a British court we cannot take notice of the revenue laws of a foreign State.' The learned Chief Justice went on to apply the rule in a manner that may not have been justified, but that does not detract from the importance of his unqualified assertion of it.

Here, my Lords, is a formidable array of authority. It is possible that the words 'take notice of' might, if applied without discrimination, lead to too wide an application of the rule; for as Lord Tomlin pointed out in *Re Visser*, there may be cases in which our courts, although they do not enforce foreign revenue law, are bound to recognise some of the consequences of that law, and for this reason the terms of Lord Mansfield's proposition have been criticised. But in its narrower interpretation it has not been challenged except in the three cases mentioned earlier in this opinion and in them it was unequivocally affirmed.

Nor does the matter rest there. For Sir Andrew Clark, who argued the case for the appellant with equal vigour and candour, admitted that he knew of no case in which a foreign state had recovered taxes by suit in this country nor of any case in any foreign country in which the government of this country had done so. And in this connection it is worthy of note that, as my noble and learned friend, Lord Somervell of Harrow, has by his independent researches discovered and will presently tell your Lordships, this same rule is stated in at least one French textbook of high authority.[17]

The matter is carried one step further by the fact that the rule appears to have been recognised by Parliament. For I see no other reason for the exclusion from the advantages of the Foreign Judgments (Reciprocal Enforcement) Act 1933 of a judgment for 'a sum payable in respect of taxes or other charges of a like nature or in respect of a fine or other penalty' (s 1 (2) (b)), except that it was regarded as axiomatic that the courts of one country do not have regard to the revenue laws of another and therefore will not allow judgments for foreign taxes to be enforced.

It may well be asked, then, upon what grounds this appeal is founded. I think that counsel relied upon two main grounds, first that Lord Mansfield's proposition, which I have more than once quoted, extended to revenue law a doctrine properly applicable only to penal law and (I think it must be faced) that Lord Mansfield was wrong in so extending it and everyone who has since followed him was wrong: and secondly that, whatever may have been the rule in the past, there ought to be and is a trend towards a mitigation of the rule, particularly as between states which are united by the bonds of federal union or by such looser ties as bind the British Commonwealth of nations.

My Lords, these seem to me frail weapons with which to attack a strong fortress. The suggestion that Lord Mansfield's proposition was too wide was supported partly by the fact that in *Huntington v Attrill*[18] the proposition was somewhat more narrowly stated, as it was also in the case of *A-G for Canada v William Schulze & Co.*[19] In those cases the question was of enforcement of a penalty imposed by a foreign state and the observations of the court were directed to that question. This seems to me an inadequate reason for

17 Pillet *Traité de Droit International Privé* (1924) s 674.
18 [1893] AC 150, 62 LJPC 44; p 34 above.
19 1901 9 SLT 4.

challenging a wider statement in regard to a different subject-matter. Further, upon the assumption which must be made, that the decision in *Huntington v Attrill* was correct, it was conceded that it must cover not only a penalty strictly so-called but also any tax which could be regarded as penal or confiscatory. This seems to me to create a difficult task of discrimination, which is not made easier by the test suggested by counsel. 'If a tax', he said, 'is the sort of tax which is recognised in this country, it is not penal.' I am little disposed to introduce so nice a refinement into a rule which has hitherto been stated in terms that are easy to understand and to apply. . . .

The second branch of the argument for the appellant was directed to showing that in the United States of America there had been in certain states a disposition to relax the rigidity of the rule, and counsel was able to point to certain cases not cited to the Court of Appeal where the courts of one state had admitted and enforced claims for revenue by another state, notably in the States of Missouri and Kentucky. And reference was made also to the fact that in the 1948 supplement to the well-known 'Restatement' some doubt was cast upon the rule (Conflict of Laws, s 610). But it was conceded that this was not the trend in all states, the States of New York and of Delaware continuing to apply the old rule. My Lords, I do not think it necessary to occupy your time by an examination of the American cases. I am ever willing to get help from seeing how the law, which is our common heritage, has developed on the other side of the Atlantic, but a development which is not universal, and is in any case confined to relations between state and state within the Union, can have no weight in determining what the law is in this country.

Finally, it was urged that, whatever might be the position as between this country and a foreign country, it was not the same as between different members of the British Commonwealth, including those members which, though within the Commonwealth, do not acknowledge the sovereignty of the Queen. For such a distinction there is no authority and I can see no reason. If such a change is to be made, it is not for the courts to make it. It will be the task of governments and perhaps of Parliaments. I do not think that it will be an easy task.

(His Lordship proceeded to hold that s 302 of the Companies Act 1948 which provides that in a voluntary winding-up the liquidator is bound to discharge the liabilities of the company, did not assist the appellant, because the word 'liabilities' did not include an obligation to pay foreign taxes.)

Lords Morton and Reid concurred. Lords Keith of Avonholm and Somervell delivered judgments to the same effect.
Appeal dismissed.

NOTE

Although English courts will not *enforce* foreign penal or revenue laws, they frequently *take notice* of them. Thus in *Regazzoni v Sethia* [1958] AC 301, [1957] 3 All ER 286, the Indian government had, as a political protest against the treatment of Indians in South Africa, prohibited the shipment of jute from India to South Africa. By a contract the proper law of which was English, made between the plaintiff, who resided in Switzerland, and the defendants, merchants in India, the defendants agreed to sell a quantity of jute bags to the plaintiff, who (as the defendants knew) intended to reship them to South Africa. Both parties knew that this was illegal by Indian law. The defendants repudiated the contract. It was held that the plaintiff could not recover damages. Lord Simonds said (at 322 and 292, respectively): 'It does not follow from the fact that today the court will not enforce a revenue law at the suit of a foreign state that today it will enforce a contract which requires the doing of an act in a foreign country which violates the revenue law of that country. The two things are not complementary or co-extensive. This may be seen if for revenue law penal law is substituted. For an English court will not enforce a penal law at the suit of a foreign state, yet it would be surprising if it would enforce a contract which required the commission of a crime in that state'. Lord Keith of Avonholm said (at 328 and 296, respectively): 'I agree with the view entertained by some of your Lordships and by all the Lords Justices in the Court of Appeal that the proposition that "no country ever takes notice of the revenue laws of another" is too widely expressed'.

English courts will (perhaps) not enforce foreign public laws.

Attorney General of New Zealand v Ortiz [1982] 3 All ER 432, [1982] 3 WLR 570 (Court of Appeal)

Interlocutory appeal from Staughton J.

In 1972 a Maori tribesman found an ancient Maori carving in a swamp in New Zealand. He sold it to the third defendant, a dealer in primitive works of art, for NZ $6,000. The third defendant exported it from New Zealand in contravention of a New Zealand statute, section 12(2) of the Historic Articles Act 1962, which provided that historic articles exported from New Zealand without permission 'shall be forefeited to Her Majesty'. This was interpreted to mean 'shall be liable to be forfeited'. The third defendant sold the carving to the first defendant, Ortiz, who was a collector of Oceanic works of art, for US $65,000. At the time of the hearing it was said to be worth £300,000.

The Attorney General of New Zealand, suing on behalf of the Queen in right of the government of New Zealand, brought an action in England claiming delivery up of the carving and damages for its detention. The defence was that the New Zealand statute was a foreign penal, revenue or public law.

Staughton J on a preliminary question of law gave judgment for the plaintiff. The defendants appealed.

Lord Denning MR: . . .   This suit by a foreign state to enforce its laws is to be distinguished altogether from a suit between private firms or individuals which raises a question as to whether a contract has been broken by one or the other or whether a wrong has been done by one to the other. In such a suit our courts will often recognise the existence of the laws of a foreign state. We will recognise the foreign law so much that we will refuse to enforce a contract which is in breach of the laws of the foreign state: see the Prohibition case of *Foster v Driscoll*,[20] and the jute case of *Regazzoni v Sethia*.[1]

This present case is different. It is a suit by a foreign state brought in the

---

20 [1929] 1 KB 470, 98 LJKB 282.
 1 [1958] AC 301, [1957] 3 All ER 286.

English courts here to enforce its laws. No one has ever doubted that our courts will not entertain a suit brought by a foreign sovereign, directly or indirectly, to enforce the penal or revenue laws of that foreign state. We do not sit to collect taxes for another country or to inflict punishments for it. Now the question arises whether this rule extends to 'other public laws'. Dicey & Morris[2] say it does. I agree with them. The term 'other public laws' is very uncertain. But so are the terms 'penal' and 'revenue'. The meaning of 'penal' was discussed in *Huntington v Attrill*[3] and *Loucks v Standard Oil Co of New York*.[4] The meaning of 'revenue' was discussed in *Government of India v Taylor*.[5] But what are 'other public laws?' I think they are laws which are eiusdem generis with 'penal' or 'revenue' laws.

Then what is the genus? Or, in English, what is the general concept which embraces 'penal' and 'revenue' laws and others like them? It is to be found, I think, by going back to the classification of acts taken in international law. One class comprises those acts which are done by a sovereign 'jure imperii', that is, by virtue of his sovereign authority. The others are those which are done by him 'jure gestionis', that is, which obtain their validity by virtue of his performance of them. The application of this distinction to our present problem was well drawn by Dr FA Mann 28 years ago in an article 'Prerogative Rights of Foreign States and the Conflict of Laws'.[6]

Applied to our present problem the class of laws which will be enforced are those laws which are an exercise by the sovereign government of its sovereign authority over property within its territory or over its subjects wherever they may be. But other laws will not be enforced. By international law every sovereign state has no sovereignty beyond its own frontiers. The courts of other countries will not allow it to go beyond the bounds. They will not enforce any of its laws which purport to exercise sovereignty beyond the limits of its authority.

If this be right, we come to the question: what is meant by the 'exercise of sovereign authority?' It is a term which we will have to grapple with, sooner or later. It comes much into the cases on sovereign immunity and into the State Immunity Act 1978: see sections 3 (3) (c) and 14 (2) (a). It was much discussed recently in *I Congreso del Partido*[7] and by Hazel Fox 'State Immunity: The House of Lords' Decision in I Congreso de Partido' in the *Law Quarterly Review*.[8] It can provoke much difference of opinion as is shown by the differences amongst the Law Lords on the facts of that very case. But, difficult as it is, it must be tackled.

I suggest that the first thing in such a case as the present is to determine which is the relevant act. Then to decide whether it is of a sovereign character or a non-sovereign character. Finally, to ask whether it was exercised within the territory of the sovereign state—which is legitimate, or beyond it—which is illegitimate.

In solving the question, we can get guidance from the decided cases. I will

---

2 *Conflict of Laws* (10th edn, 1980) vol 1, p 90, rule 3.
3 [1893] AC 150, 62 LJPC 44; p 34 above.
4 (1918) 224 NY 99, 120 NE 198.
5 [1955] AC 491, [1955] 1 All ER 292; p 37 above.
6 (1954) 40 Tr Gro Soc 25, reprinted in his *Studies in International Law* (1973) pp 492–514.
7 [1983] 1 AC 244, [1981] 1 All ER 1092.
8 (1982) 98 LQR 94.

take therefore the cases decided in the English courts about tangible things which have been confiscated—or attempted to be confiscated—by a sovereign government.

Don Alonso v Cornero[9]

This case was decided in 1611. According to Dicey & Morris,[10] it is the only reported English case which approaches the problem. Sir Walter Raleigh had recently introduced tobacco into Europe. It was a growth industry. Senor Cornero, a Spanish subject, committed crimes in Spain and fled in a ship to England, carrying with him 3,000 lbs of tobacco. His very flight was in Spanish law a cause of forfeiture of his goods, as it was in English law at that time: see *Blackstone's Commentaries*.[11] So these goods were 'forfeited upon the high sea' to the King of Spain: see 2 Brownl 29. On arrival in England, Cornero unloaded the tobacco and sold it to Sir John Watts for £800.

The Spanish ambassador then on behalf of the King took proceedings in rem in the Court of Admiralty on the ground that the cargo was the property of the King of Spain. (This procedure in Admiralty for forfeiture is well recognised to this day: see section 1 (1) (s) of the Administration of Justice Act 1956[12] and *The Skylark*.[13] The Admiralty marshal served the warrant of arrest on the cargo in the hands of Sir John Watts. Sir John Watts then moved the Court of Common Pleas for a writ of prohibition to prevent the Spanish ambassador from proceeding any further with the arrest. The court granted his application. Prohibition was granted. The goods were released. Sir John Watts kept the tobacco and sold it—or smoked it. The King of Spain took nothing.

The report of the case in Hob 212 tells us that the judges were quite willing to allow the Spanish ambassador to bring proceedings on behalf of the King of Spain—'they would not let [ie prevent] the ambassador from prosecuting his master's subject'. As to the goods, the judges said, 'if any subject of a foreign prince bring goods into the kingdom, though they were confiscate before, the property of them shall not here be questioned but at the common law.' As I understand it, that means that the courts of this country would not enforce the forfeiture. Our courts would not enforce the title claimed by the Spanish King. Our courts of 'common law' would enforce a possessory title by trespass or trover, but this would not avail the King of Spain because he never had possession: see *Isaack v Clark*.[14]

The confiscation was an act done in the exercise of sovereign authority outside the territory of Spain—it was done on the high seas. So our court would not enforce it. So also when many centuries later the Spanish Constituent Cortes passed a decree confiscating all the private property of the ex-King, it was held that it would not be enforced against his property in England: see *Banco de Vizcaya v Don Alfonso de Borbon y Austria*.[15]

---

9 (1611) Hob 212, 2 Brownl 29.
10 *Conflict of Laws* (10th edn, 1980) vol 1, p 94, n 22.
11 17th edn (1830) vol 4, p 387.
12 Now s 21(1) (s) of the Supreme Court Act 1981 (*Ed*).
13 [1965] P 474, [1965] 3 All ER 380.
14 (1615) 2 Bulst 306.
15 [1935] 1 KB 140, 104 LJKB 46.

King of Italy v Marquis Cosimo de Medici Tornaquinci[16]

In Italy the Marquis of Medici had a most valuable collection of historical manuscripts covering a period of 700 years. They were known as the Medici archives. Some of them were official communications and belonged to the Italian state. The government had allowed the Marquis to hold them on behalf of the state. Others were family papers coming down in the Medici family. They belonged to the marquis himself. In 1909 the Italian government passed a law by which the state papers were to be kept in Italy. They belonged to the state. By the same law the Italian government prohibited the export of the family papers without a permit and there was a heavy export duty when a permit was granted. The state also had the right to purchase the family papers. The marquis brought these Medici archives to England and put them into the hands of Christie's for sale. Peterson J held that the state papers belonged to the State of Italy and granted an injunction to prevent their being disposed of. But he refused to grant any injunction, at the suit of the Italian government, in respect of the family papers. It was only at the interlocutory stage. Peterson J is reported as having said, at 624:

> 'Article 9 prohibited their exportation, but it was manifest that this only applied so long as they remained in Italy. The question arose whether there was any probability, at the trial of the action, that these documents, apart from the state papers, would be ordered to be returned to Italy. He did not think that the court would undertake such a burden.'

The prohibition of export of the family papers was an exercise of sovereign authority by the King of Italy. It would not be enforced in our courts.

Princess Paley Olga v Weisz[17]

Princess Paley Olga was the widow of Grand Duke Paul of Russia. She occupied the Paley Palace near St Petersburg, full of valuable furniture, pictures and objets d'art. In 1918 the revolutionaries took possession of it. The Princess fled to England. The Soviet government passed decrees declaring all of its contents to be the property of the Soviet Republic. They turned it into a state museum. In 1928 the Soviet government sold some of the articles to Mr Weisz for £40,000. He brought them to England. The Princess claimed that they belonged to her. She sued Mr Weisz to recover them. She failed. Scrutton LJ said, at 725:

> 'Our Government has recognised the present Russian Government as the de jure Government of Russia, and our courts are bound to give effect to the laws and acts of that Government *so far as they relate to property within* that jurisdiction when it was affected by those laws and acts.' (Emphasis added.)

The confiscation by the Soviet government was an exercise of sovereign authority within its own territory. It would therefore be enforced in England. If the Princess had removed the articles from the museum in St

16 (1918) 34 TLR 623.
17 [1929] 1 KB 718, 98 LJKB 465; p 557 below.

Petersburg and brought them to England, the English courts would have made her give them up to the Soviet government.

Brokaw v Seatrain (UK) Ltd[18]

Mr and Mrs Shaheen were United States citizens living in the United States. Their daughter married Mr Brokaw, an Englishman. The parents determined to send to their daughter their furniture and household effects so as to set up house in England. They were shipped on an American ship for delivery in England. While the vessel was on the high seas, the United States government served a notice of levy on the shipowners. They claimed possession of the goods on the ground that Mr and Mrs Shaheen owed them money for taxes and they were entitled by United States law to levy upon all the property of Mr and Mrs Shaheen. This court held that the United States government had no right to the goods. I said, at 482:

> 'If this notice of levy had been effective to reduce the goods into the possession of the United States government, it would, I think, have been enforced by these courts, because we would then be enforcing an actual possessory title. There would be no need for the United States government to have recourse to their revenue law. I would apply to this situation some words of the United States Supreme Court in *Compania Espanola de Navegacion Maritima SA v The Navemar*[19] in an analogous case: ". . . since the decree was in invitum, actual possession by some act of physical dominion or control on behalf of the Spanish Government, was needful."'

The notice of levy was an act done in the exercise of sovereign authority. It was not done in the territory of the United States but outside it. It would not be enforced by our courts. But if the United States government had actually reduced the goods into their possession in the United States, that act would have been done within its own territory. It would therefore have been enforced in our courts.

I have not gone into any of the cases on intangible things or on foreign exchange regulations, such as *Kahler v Midland Bank Ltd*[20] and *Re Lord Cable*;[1] but I would suggest that they might be solved by adopting the distinction between acts done in the exercise of a sovereign authority within its own territory, and those outside it.

Conclusion

Returning to our present case, I am of opinion that if any country should have legislation prohibiting the export of works of art, and providing for the automatic forfeiture of them to the state should they be exported, then that falls into the category of 'public laws' which will not be enforced by the courts of the country to which it is exported, or any other country, because it is an act done in the exercise of sovereign authority which will not be enforced outside its own territory.

18 [1971] 2 QB 476, [1971] 2 All ER 98.
19 (1938) 303 US 68 at 75.
20 [1950] AC 24, [1949] 2 All ER 621.
 1 [1976] 3 All ER 417, [1977] 1 WLR 7.

Ackner LJ: . . . It is common ground that if the question in this case was one of *recognising* the Historic Articles Act 1962, then it is a law which the English courts would recognise. Thus, if the carving had been seized and condemned in New Zealand, thereby being reduced into the possession of the New Zealand government, then that government would have been entitled to enforce its proprietary title in this country by reference to the Historic Articles Act 1962. . . .

The question whether a foreign law is penal must be decided by the English court. It must determine for itself, in the first place, the substance of the right sought to be enforced; and in the second place, whether its enforcement would, either directly or indirectly, involve the execution of the penal law of another state. The rule has its foundation in the well-recognised principle that crimes, including in that term all breaches of public law, punishable by pecuniary mulct, or otherwise, at the instance of the state government, or someone representing the public, are local in this sense, that they are only cognisable and punishable in the country where they were committed. Accordingly, no proceeding, even in the shape of a civil suit, which has for its object the enforcement by the state, whether directly or indirectly, of punishment imposed for such breaches by the lex fori, ought to be admitted in the courts of any other country: per Lord Watson in *Huntington v Attrill*.

It was readily accepted that forfeiture may, in certain circumstances, be a penalty. In *R v Nat Bell Liquors Ltd*[2] forfeiture of whisky to the Crown in the Province of Alberta was held to be a penalty; so also in *Banco de Vizcaya v Don Alfonso de Borbon y Austria* a decree expropriating all property of the defendant on the ground that he was guilty of high treason was held to be a penal law and unenforceable in this country. But, urges Mr Gray, the whole scheme of the Historic Articles Act 1962 is to preserve in New Zealand articles to which the Act applies. The provisions for forfeiture are but a deterrent by-product. The fact that it carries with it unpleasant consequences no more makes it penal than did the Massachusetts statute which was the foundation of the dispute in the case in the Court of Appeals of the State of New York, *Loucks v Standard Oil Co of New York*.

That statute provided for the recovery on behalf of the widow or children or next of kin of any person killed by negligence of damages 'in the sum of not less than $500, nor more than $10,000, to be assessed with reference to the degree of . . . culpability' of the wrongdoer. It thus provided for penal damages. To my mind, this decision, so far from assisting the Attorney-General, does the contrary. Cardozo J, giving the judgment of the court, followed *Huntington v Attrill* by repeating that a penal statute is one which awards a penalty to the state, or to a public officer on its behalf, or to a member suing in the interest of the whole community, to redress a public wrong. The purpose must be, not reparation to one aggrieved, but vindication of the public justice. Mrs Loucks was not a member of the public suing in the interests of the whole community. She was suing in her own interest. Nor was she suing to redress a public wrong—to vindicate the public justice. She was suing to vindicate a private right—reparation owed to one who was aggrieved.

2 [1922] 2 AC 128.

In the instant submission, the claim is made by the Attorney General on behalf of the state. It is not a claim by a private individual. Further, the cause of action does not concern a private right which demands reparation or compensation. It concerns a public right—the preservation of historic articles within New Zealand—which right the state seeks to vindicate. The vindication is not sought by the acquisition of the article in exchange for proper compensation. The vindication is sought through confiscation. It is of course accepted that the provision of section 5 (2) of the Historic Articles Act 1962, which provides for a fine not exceeding £200 for the same offence as gives rise to forfeiture, is a penal provision. However, in the majority of cases, forfeiture is a far more serious consequence. This case is a dramatic example. The current value of the carving is asserted by one of the parties to these proceedings to be in the region of £300,000.

It seems to me to be wholly unreal to suggest that when a foreign state seeks to enforce these forfeiture provisions in another country, it is not seeking to enforce a foreign penal statute. No doubt the general purpose of the Act of 1962 is to preserve in New Zealand its historic articles. However, this does not mean that a suit to enforce the forfeiture provisions contained in section 12 is not a suit by the state to vindicate the public justice. I therefore cannot agree with the judge that section 12 is not a penal provision. Accordingly, if I am wrong in the answer I have given to the first question raised in this action, I would still dismiss the Attorney General's claim on this point of public international law.

In these circumstances it is unnecessary for me to consider the question of whether there is a third category of foreign laws which our courts do not enforce, namely public law, and if so, what it comprises. Without reaching any firm conclusion, I am impressed by the reasoning of the judge that there is no such vague general residual category and, that if the test is one of public policy, there is no reason why English courts should not enforce section 12 of the Historic Articles Act 1962 of New Zealand.

I accordingly would also allow this appeal.

O'Connor LJ delivered a judgment agreeing with Ackner LJ.
Appeal allowed.

NOTE

This decision was affirmed by the House of Lords [1983] 2 All ER 93, [1983] 2 WLR 809, but only on the ground that the Court of Appeal were right in interpreting the New Zealand statute to mean 'shall be liable to be forfeited'. The House expressed no opinion on whether the New Zealand Act was a penal or public law. On the contrary, they said that this part of the judgments of the Court of Appeal was obiter. But we print them here because of their intrinsic interest and because they so nearly amount to a decision on the point.

It is not easy to see why the location of the property at the material time should be relevant in determining whether a foreign law is a 'penal or other public law'. The Master of the Rolls saw the difficulty but cleverly skated round it. The Lords Justices evidently did not. So one is entitled to ask them, if the New Zealand Act in this case was penal, why were not the Russian confiscatory decrees in *Princess Paley Olga v Weisz* [1929] 1 KB 718, 98 LJKB 465 (p 557 below) penal too?

English courts will exceptionally refuse to apply a foreign law or recognise a foreign judgment if that would be contrary to English public policy.

Jurisdiction of the English Courts

CHAPTER 4

Sovereign Immunity

State Immunity Act 1978

Proceedings in United Kingdom by or against other States

Immunity from jurisdiction

1.—(1) A State is immune from the jurisdiction of the courts of the United Kingdom except as provided in the following provisions of this Part of this Act.

(2) A court shall give effect to the immunity conferred by this section even though the State does not appear in the proceedings in question.

Exceptions from immunity

2.—(1) A State is not immune as respects proceedings in respect of which it has submitted to the jurisdiction of the courts of the United Kingdom.

(2) A State may submit after the dispute giving rise to the proceedings has arisen or by a prior written agreement; but a provision in any agreement that it is to be governed by the law of the United Kingdom is not to be regarded as a submission.

(3) A State is deemed to have submitted—

(a) if it has instituted the proceedings; or

(b) subject to subsections (4) and (5) below, if it has intervened or taken any step in the proceedings.

(4) Subsection (3) (b) above does not apply to intervention or any step taken for the purpose only of—

(a) claiming immunity; or

(b) asserting an interest in property in circumstances such that the State would have been entitled to immunity if the proceedings had been brought against it.

(5) Subsection (3) (b) above does not apply to any step taken by the State in ignorance of facts entitling it to immunity if those facts could not reasonably have been ascertained and immunity is claimed as soon as reasonably practicable.

(6) A submission in respect of any proceedings extends to any appeal but not to any counter-claim unless it arises out of the same legal relationship or facts as the claim.

(7) The head of a State's diplomatic mission in the United Kingdom, or the person for the time being performing his functions, shall be deemed to have authority to submit on behalf of the State in respect of any proceedings; and any person who has entered into a contract on behalf of and with the

authority of a State shall be deemed to have authority to submit on its behalf in respect of proceedings arising out of the contract.

3.—(1) A State is not immune as respects proceedings relating to—
(a) a commercial transaction entered into by the State; or
(b) an obligation of the State which by virtue of a contract (whether a commercial transaction or not) falls to be performed wholly or partly in the United Kingdom.

(2) This section does not apply if the parties to the dispute are States or have otherwise agreed in writing; and subsection (1) (b) above does not apply if the contract (not being a commercial transaction) was made in the territory of the State concerned and the obligation in question is governed by its administrative law.

(3) In this section 'commercial transaction' means—
(a) any contract for the supply of goods or services;
(b) any loan or other transaction for the provision of finance and any guarantee or indemnity in respect of any such transaction or of any other financial obligation; and
(c) any other transaction or activity (whether of a commercial, industrial, financial, professional or other similar character) into which a State enters or in which it engages otherwise than in the exercise of sovereign authority;
but neither paragraph of subsection (1) above applies to a contract of employment between a State and an individual.

4.—(1) A State is not immune as respects proceedings relating to a contract of employment between the State and an individual where the contract was made in the United Kingdom or the work is to be wholly or partly performed there.

(2) Subject to subsections (3) and (4) below, this section does not apply if—
(a) at the time when the proceedings are brought the individual is a national of the State concerned; or
(b) at the time when the contract was made the individual was neither a national of the United Kingdom nor habitually resident there; or
(c) the parties to the contract have otherwise agreed in writing.

(3) Where the work is for an office, agency or establishment maintained by the State in the United Kingdom for commercial purposes, subsection (2) (a) and (b) above do not exclude the application of this section unless the individual was, at the time when the contract was made, habitually resident in that State.

(4) Subsection (2) (c) above does not exclude the application of this section where the law of the United Kingdom requires the proceedings·to be brought before a court of the United Kingdom.

(5) In subsection (2) (b) above 'national of the United Kingdom' means
(a) a British citizen, a British Dependent Territories citizen or a British Overseas citizen; or
(b) a person who under the British Nationality Act 1981 is a British subject; or
(c) a British protected person (within the meaning of that Act).[1]

1 Sub-s (5) is printed as amended by the British Nationality Act 1981, Sch 7 (*Ed*).

(6) In this section 'proceedings relating to a contract of employment' includes proceedings between the parties to such a contract in respect of any statutory rights or duties to which they are entitled or subject as employer or employee.

5. A State is not immune as respects proceedings in respect of—
(a) death or personal injury; or
(b) damage to or loss of tangible property,
caused by an act or omission in the the United Kingdom.

6.—(1) A State is not immune as respects proceedings relating to—
(a) any interest of the State in, or its possession or use of, immovable property in the United Kingdom; or
(b) any obligation of the State arising out of its interest in, or its possession or use of, any such property.

(2) A State is not immune as respects proceedings relating to any interest of the State in movable or immovable property, being an interest arising by way of succession, gift or bona vacantia.

(3) The fact that a State has or claims an interest in any property shall not preclude any court from exercising in respect of it any jurisdiction relating to the estates of deceased persons or persons of unsound mind or to insolvency, the winding up of companies or the administration of trusts.

(4) A court may entertain proceedings against a person other than a State notwithstanding that the proceedings relate to property—
(a) which is in the possession or control of a State; or
(b) in which a State claims an interest,
if the State would not have been immune had the proceedings been brought against it or, in a case within paragraph (b) above, if the claim is neither admitted nor supported by prima facie evidence.

7. A State is not immune as respects proceedings relating to—
(a) any patent, trade-mark, design or plant breeders' rights belonging to the State and registered or protected in the United Kingdom or for which the State has applied in the United Kingdom;
(b) an alleged infringement by the State in the United Kingdom of any patent, trade-mark, design, plant breeders' rights or copyright; or
(c) the right to use a trade or business name in the United Kingdom.

8.—(1) A State is not immune as respects proceedings relating to its membership of a body corporate, an unincorporated body or a partnership which—
(a) has members other than States; and
(b) is incorporated or constituted under the law of the United Kingdom or is controlled from or has its principal place of business in the United Kingdom,
being proceedings arising between the State and the body or its other members or, as the case may be, between the State and the other partners.

(2) This section does not apply if provision to the contrary has been made by an agreement in writing between the parties to the dispute or by the constitution or other instrument establishing or regulating the body or partnership in question.

9.—(1) Where a State has agreed in writing to submit a dispute which has arisen, or may arise, to arbitration, the State is not immune as respects proceedings in the courts of the United Kingdom which relate to the arbitration.

(2) This section has effect subject to any contrary provision in the arbitration agreement and does not apply to any arbitration agreement between States.

10.—(1) This section applies to—
(a) Admiralty proceedings; and
(b) proceedings on any claim which could be made the subject of Admiralty proceedings.

(2) A State is not immune as respects—
(a) an action in rem against a ship belonging to that State; or
(b) an action in personam for enforcing a claim in connection with such a ship,

if, at the time when the cause of action arose, the ship was in use or intended for use for commercial purposes.

(3) Where an action in rem is brought against a ship belonging to a State for enforcing a claim in connection with another ship belonging to that State, subsection (2) (a) above does not apply as respects the first-mentioned ship unless, at the time when the cause of action relating to the other ship arose, both ships were in use or intended for use for commercial purposes.

(4) A State is not immune as respects—
(a) an action in rem against a cargo belonging to that State if both the cargo and the ship carrying it were, at the time when the cause of action arose, in use or intended for use for commercial purposes; or
(b) an action in personam for enforcing a claim in connection with such a cargo if the ship carrying it was then in use or intended for use as aforesaid.

(5) In the foregoing provisions references to a ship or cargo belonging to a State include references to a ship or cargo in its possession or control or in which it claims an interest; and, subject to subsection (4) above, subsection (2) above applies to property other than a ship as it applies to a ship.

(6) Sections 3 to 5 above do not apply to proceedings of the kind described in subsection (1) above if the State in question is a party to the Brussels Convention[2] and the claim relates to the operation of a ship owned or operated by that State, the carriage of cargo or passengers on any such ship or the carriage of cargo owned by that State on any other ship.

11. A State is not immune as respects proceedings relating to its liability for—
(a) value added tax, any duty of customs or excise or any agricultural levy; or
(b) rates in respect of premises occupied by it for commercial purposes.

Procedure

12.—(1) Any writ or other document required to be served for instituting proceedings against a State shall be served by being transmitted through the

---

2 The International Convention for the Unification of Certain Rules Concerning the Immunity of State-owned Ships signed in Brussels on 10 April 1926: s 17 (1). This convention was ratified by the United Kingdom in 1979 (*Ed*).

Foreign and Commonwealth Office to the Ministry of Foreign Affairs of the State and service shall be deemed to have been effected when the writ or document is received at the Ministry.

(2) Any time for entering an appearance (whether prescribed by rules of court or otherwise) shall begin to run two months after the date on which the writ or document is received as aforesaid.

(3) A State which appears in proceedings cannot thereafter object that subsection (1) above has not been complied with in the case of those proceedings.

(4) No judgment in default of appearance shall be given against a State except on proof that subsection (1) above has been complied with and that the time for entering an appearance as extended by subsection (2) above has expired.

(5) A copy of any judgment given against a State in default of appearance shall be transmitted through the Foreign and Commonwealth Office to the Ministry of Foreign Affairs of that State and any time for applying to have the judgment set aside (whether prescribed by rules of court or otherwise) shall begin to run two months after the date on which the copy of the judgment is received at the Ministry.

(6) Subsection (1) above does not prevent the service of a writ or other document in any manner to which the State has agreed and subsections (2) and (4) above do not apply where service is effected in any such manner.

(7) This section shall not be construed as applying to proceedings against a State by way of counter-claim or to an action in rem; and subsection (1) above shall not be construed as affecting any rules of court whereby leave is required for the service of process outside the jurisdiction.

Supplementary provisions

14.—(1) The immunities and privileges conferred by this Part of this Act apply to any foreign or commonwealth State other than the United Kingdom; and references to a State include references to—

(a) the sovereign or other head of that State in his public capacity;

(b) the government of that State; and

(c) any department of that government,

but not to any entity (hereafter referred to as a 'separate entity') which is distinct from the executive organs of the government of the State and capable of suing or being sued.

(2) A separate entity is immune from the jurisdiction of the courts of the United Kingdom if, and only if—

(a) the proceedings relate to anything done by it in the exercise of sovereign authority; and

(b) the circumstances are such that a State (or, in the case of proceedings to which section 10 above applies, a State which is not a party to the Brussels Convention) would have been so immune.

(5) Section 12 above applies to proceedings against the constituent territories of a federal State; and Her Majesty may by Order in Council provide for the other provisions of this Part of this Act to apply to any such constituent territory specified in the Order as they apply to a State.

(6) Where the provisions of this Part of this Act do not apply to a

constituent territory by virtue of any such Order subsections (2) and (3) above shall apply to it as if it were a separate entity.

15.—(1) If it appears to Her Majesty that the immunities and privileges conferred by this Part of this Act in relation to any State—

(a) exceed those accorded by the law of that State in relation to the United Kingdom; or

(b) are less than those required by any treaty, convention or other international agreement to which that State and the United Kingdom are parties,

Her Majesty may by Order in Council provide for restricting or, as the case may be, extending those immunities and privileges to such extent as appears to Her Majesty to be appropriate.

(2) Any statutory instrument containing an Order under this section shall be subject to annulment in pursuance of a resolution of either House of Parliament.

Part III

Miscellaneous and Supplementary

20.—(1) Subject to the provisions of this section and to any necessary modifications, the Diplomatic Privileges Act 1964 shall apply to—

(a) a sovereign or other head of State;

(b) members of his family forming part of his household; and

(c) his private servants,

as it applies to the head of a diplomatic mission, to members of his family forming part of his household and to his private servants.

21. A certificate by or on behalf of the Secretary of State shall be conclusive evidence on any question—

(a) whether any country is a State for the purposes of Part I of this Act, whether any territory is a constituent territory of a federal State for those purposes or as to the person or persons to be regarded for those purposes as the head or government of a State;

(b) whether a State is a party to the Brussels Convention mentioned in Part I of this Act;

(c) whether a State is a party to the European Convention on State Immunity, whether it has made a declaration under Article 24 of that Convention or as to the territories in respect of which the United Kingdom or any other State is a party;

(d) whether, and if so when, a document has been served or received as mentioned in section 12 (1) or (5) above.

CHAPTER 5

Jurisdiction in Actions in Personam

Section A. At common law

As a general rule,[1] English courts have jurisdiction in actions in personam if the defendant is present in England and served there with the writ.

Maharanee of Baroda v Wildenstein [1972] 2 QB 283, [1972] 2 All ER 689 (Court of Appeal)

Interlocutory appeal from Bridge J.

The plaintiff, who resided in France, was an Indian princess with social and sporting connections with England, Ireland and India. The defendant, who also resided in France, was an art dealer of international repute with business connections with England, Ireland, the USA and elsewhere. The defendant sold a picture to the plaintiff in France and represented that it was painted by the French artist Boucher. The plaintiff was later advised in England that the picture was not painted by Boucher. She issued a writ against the defendant claiming rescission of the contract and repayment of the price. Her reasons for preferring to sue in England and not in France were that in England she could get a speedier trial and could subpoena expert witnesses. The writ was served on the defendant at Ascot races during a temporary visit to England. He moved to set it aside. The master and judge set it aside. The plaintiff appealed.

Lord Denning MR: In this case the writ has been properly served on the defendant in this country. This makes the case very different from those in which the defendant is in a foreign country and the plaintiff has to seek leave to serve him out of the jurisdiction. It is also different from those cases in which the plaintiff has already started an action in another country, and the question is whether he should be allowed to start another action in this country on the same subject matter. In this case the plaintiff has validly invoked the jurisdiction of our courts in this, the one and only action she has brought.

---

1 The exceptions are when an international convention to which the United Kingdom is a party otherwise provides. The most important of these conventions is the Brussels Convention on jurisdiction and the enforcement of judgments in civil and commercial matters, implemented by the Civil Jurisdiction and Judgment Act 1982, p 79 below. This case would be differently decided now because of articles 2 and 3 of the Convention. But the principle of the case remains valid if the defendant is not resident in another EEC state or in another part of the United Kingdom (*Ed*).

The principle applicable to such a case was stated by Scott LJ in *St Pierre v South American Stores (Gath & Chaves) Ltd:*[2]

> 'The true rule about a stay under section 41 [of the Supreme Court of Judicature Act, 1925][3] so far as relevant to this case, may I think be stated thus: (1) A mere balance of convenience is not a sufficient ground for depriving a plaintiff of the advantages of prosecuting his action in an English court if it is otherwise properly brought. The right of access to the King's court must not be lightly refused. (2) In order to justify a stay two conditions must be satisfied, one positive and the other negative: (a) the defendant must satisfy the court that the continuance of the action would work an injustice because it would be oppressive or vexatious to him or would be an abuse of the process of the court in some other way; and (b) the stay must not cause an injustice to the plaintiff. On both the burden of proof is on the defendant.'

We have to apply that principle to this case when the plaintiff was only able to serve the defendant because he happened to be in this country on a short visit. There are only two cases in the books of this nature—*Egbert v Short*[4] and *Re Norton's Settlement.*[5] In each case the defendant was resident in India, but had returned to England on a short visit. Each case concerned an entirely Indian matter. In each case the action was not brought bona fide for the purpose of obtaining justice, but for the purpose of harassing and annoying the defendant. It would have been a great injustice to the defendant to compel him to fight it in England. So each action was stayed.

A similar case was put by Sir Gorell Barnes P in *Logan v Bank of Scotland (No 2):*[6]

> 'If, for instance, as was put in argument, a dispute of a complicated character had arisen between two foreigners in a foreign country, and one of them were made defendant in an action in this country by serving him with a writ while he happened to be here for a few days' visit, I apprehend that, although there would be jurisdiction in the court to entertain the suit, it would have little hesitation in treating the action as vexatious and staying it.'

The judge seems to have taken that instance given by Sir Gorell Barnes P and founded on it a presumption which he stated in these words: 'But a presumption arises that the proceedings are oppressive if the defendant is served when he appears to be here on a visit.' I cannot agree with that statement. There is no such presumption. If a defendant is properly served with a writ while he is in this country, albeit on a short visit, the plaintiff is prima facie entitled to continue the proceedings to the end. He has validly invoked the jurisdiction of the Queen's courts; and he is entitled to require those courts to proceed to adjudicate upon his claim. The courts should not strike it out unless it comes within one of the acknowledged grounds, such as that it is vexatious or oppressive, or otherwise an abuse of the process of the court: see RSC Ord 18, r 19. It does not become within those grounds simply

2 [1936] 1 KB 382 at 398.
3 See now s 49, Supreme Court Act 1981 (*Ed*).
4 [1907] 2 Ch 205, 76 LJ Ch 520.
5 [1908] 1 Ch 471, 77 LJ Ch 312.
6 [1906] 1 KB 141 at 152.

because the writ is served on the defendant while he is on a visit to this country. If his statement of claim discloses a reasonable cause of action, he is entitled to pursue it here, even though it did arise in a foreign country. It is not to be stayed unless it would plainly be unjust to the defendant to require him to come here to fight it, and that injustice is so great as to outweigh the right of the plaintiff to continue it here.

Mr Wilmers likened this case to a road accident in Rome, when two Italian citizens were in collision. Suppose that one of them was served with an English writ while on a short holiday in England. I would agree that such an action would be stayed. The issue would be solely Italian. But here the main issue is whether this painting was a genuine Boucher or not. That issue is one of fact which is crucial to the case in French law as well as in English law. It is not solely a French issue. The art world is so international in character today that this issue has itself something of an international character. The parties on either side are citizens of the world. The Maharanee has associations, not only with France, but also with India, England and Ireland. M. Wildenstein himself has, of course, close associations with France, but also with America, England and Ireland. He was for years the principal director of the English company of Daniel Wildenstein Ltd, and was so at the beginning of this action. He has now ceased to be a director, but he is still a shareholder. If anybody could be said to have an international reputation, it is he.

Furthermore, there might be difficulties, if not injustice, in requiring the Maharanee to go to France to seek redress. We are told that the courts of France appoint their own court experts and might hesitate about receiving the opinion of experts from England. It would be a matter for their discretion. In any case, the French courts might not themselves see the witnesses or hear them cross-examined, but might only read their reports. It is true that even in England there may be difficulties. It appears that both the experts for the Maharanee are not willing to give evidence and may have to be subpoenaed. But there would be no difficulty in M. Wildenstein's experts giving evidence here orally with all the advantages that that carries with it. So there is no injustice in that regard in having it tried in England.

Apart from the admission of evidence, there is the question of delay. We have been shown a speech which was made by the Premier President de la Cour de Cassation on 2 October 1970, in which he greatly regretted the delays in the civil procedure in France. He gave instances, such as a case started on 22 December 1953, which was finally decided on 5 March 1970: another started in 1950 decided in 1968: another of 1957 decided in 1969. It is said that this is due to the delaying tactics of lawyers. We are used to something of the kind here, but somehow we get over them in less time. So it does appear that the delay would be a good deal greater in France than in England. I have no doubt that this case could be brought for trial in England within a year.

Weighing one thing with another, it appears to me that the case can be tried quickly, fairly and properly here. It is not like the Indian cases when it took weeks to travel. Paris and London are only one hour apart. The convenience of witnesses would be studied in every way. At any rate, the burden is on M. Wildenstein to show that it would be an injustice to him to have the case tried here. I do not think he has discharged that burden. The judge was, I think, in error, in raising the presumption that he did. We can review his discretion. On so doing, I think the case should continue in England. I would allow the appeal, accordingly.

Edmund Davies and Stephenson LJJ delivered judgments to the same effect.
Appeal allowed.

Section B. Under the Rules of the Supreme Court and the Companies Act 1948

Rules of the Supreme Court, Order 81[7]

PARTNERS

Actions by and against firms within jurisdiction

1. Subject to the provisions of any enactment, any two or more persons claiming to be entitled, or alleged to be liable, as partners in respect of a cause of action and carrying on business within the jurisdiction may sue, or be sued, in the name of the firm (if any) of which they were partners at the time when the cause of action accrued.

Service of writ

3.—(1) Where by virtue of rule 1 partners are sued in the name of a firm, the writ may, except in the case mentioned in paragraph (3), be served—
(a) on any one or more of the partners, or
(b) at the principal place of business of the partnership within the jurisdiction, on any person having at the time of service the control or management of the partnership business there; or
(c) by sending a copy of the writ by ordinary first-class post (as defined in Order 10, rule 1 (2)) to the firm at the principal place of business of the partnership within the jurisdiction
and subject to paragraph (2) where service of the writ is effected in accordance with this paragraph, the writ shall be deemed to have been duly served on the firm, whether or not any member of the firm is out of the jurisdiction.

(2) Where a writ is served on a firm in accordance with sub-paragraph (1) (c)—
(a) the date of service shall, unless the contrary is shown, be deemed to be the seventh day (ignoring Order 3, rule 2 (5)) after the date on which the copy was sent to the firm; and
(b) any affidavit proving due service of the writ must contain a statement to the effect that—
(i) in the opinion of the deponent (or, if the deponent is plaintiff's solicitor or an employee of that solicitor, in the opinion of the plaintiff) the copy of the writ, if sent to the firm at the address in question, will have come to the knowledge of one of the persons mentioned in paragraph (1) (a) or (b) within 7 days thereafter, and

---

7 Amended by RSC (Amendment No 2) 1979 (SI 1979/402); RSC (Amendment No 2) 1982 (SI 1982/1111).

(ii) the copy of the writ has not been returned to the plaintiff through the post undelivered to the addressee.

(3) Where a partnership has, to the knowledge of the plaintiff, been dissolved before an action against the firm is begun, the writ by which the action is begun must be served on every person within the jurisdiction sought to be made liable in the action.

(4) Every person on whom a writ is served under paragraph (1) (a) or (b) must at the time of service be given a written notice stating whether he is served as a partner or as a person having the control or management of the partnership business or both as a partner and as such a person; and any person on whom a writ is so served but to whom no such notice is given shall be deemed to be served as a partner.

Companies Act 1948

407.—(1) Oversea companies which, after the commencement of this Act, establish a place of business within Great Britain shall, within one month of the establishment of the place of business, deliver to the registrar of companies for registration:

(c) [⁸ a list in the prescribed form of] the names and addresses of some one or more persons resident in Great Britain authorised to accept on behalf of the company service of process and any notices required to be served on the company.

412. Any process or notice required to be served on an oversea company shall be sufficiently served if addressed to any person whose name has been delivered to the registrar under the foregoing provisions of this Part of this Act and left at or sent by post to the address which has been so delivered:

Provided that—

(a) where any such company makes default in delivering to the registrar the name and address of a person resident in Great Britain who is authorised to accept on behalf of the company service of process or notices; or

(b) if at any time all the persons whose names and addresses have been so delivered are dead or have ceased so to reside, or refuse to accept service on behalf of the company, or for any reason cannot be served;

a document may be served on the company by leaving it at or sending it by post to any place of business established by the company in Great Britain.

437.—(2) Where a company registered in Scotland carries on business in England, the process of any court in England may be served on the company by leaving it at or sending it by post to the principal place of business of the company in England, addressed to the manager or other head officer in England of the company.

(3) Where process is served on a company under subsection (2) of this section the person issuing out the process shall send a copy thereof by post to the registered office of the company.

---

8 Words inserted by Companies Act 1976, Sch 1.

Rules of the Supreme Court, Order 10[9]

General provisions

1.—(1) A writ must be served personally on each defendant by the plaintiff or his agent.

(2) A writ for service on a defendant within the jurisdiction may, instead of being served personally on him, be served—

(a) by sending a copy of the writ by ordinary first-class post to the defendant at his usual or last known address, or

(b) if there is a letter box for that address, by inserting through the letter box a copy of the writ enclosed in a sealed envelope addressed to the defendant.

(4) Where a defendant's solicitor indorses on the writ a statement that he accepts service of the writ on behalf of that defendant, the writ shall be deemed to have been duly served on that defendant and to have been so served on the date on which the indorsement was made.

(5) Subject to Order 12, rule 7, where a writ is not duly served on a defendant but he acknowledges service of it, the writ shall be deemed, unless the contrary is shown, to have been duly served on him and to have been so served on the date on which he acknowledges service.

Service of writ on agent of oversea principal

2.—(1) Where the Court is satisfied on an ex parte application that—

(a) a contract has been entered into within the jurisdiction with or through an agent who is either an individual residing or carrying on business within the jurisdiction or a body corporate having a registered office or a place of business within the jurisdiction, and

(b) the principal for whom the agent was acting was at the time the contract was entered into and is at the time of the application neither such an individual nor such a body corporate, and

(c) at the time of the application either the agent's authority has not been determined or he is still in business relations with his principal,

the Court may authorise service of a writ beginning an action relating to the contract to be effected on the agent instead of the principal.

(2) An order under this Rule authorising service of a writ on a defendant's agent must limit a time within which the defendant must acknowledge service.

(3) Where an order is made under this Rule authorising service of a writ on a defendant's agent, a copy of the order and of the writ must be sent by post to the defendant at his address out of the jurisdiction.

Service of writ in pursuance of contract

3.—(1) Where—

(a) a contract contains a term to the effect that the High Court shall have jurisdiction to hear and determine any action in respect of a contract or,

---

9 Amended by RSC (Amendment No 2) 1983 (SI 1983/1181).

apart from any such term, the High Court has jurisdiction to hear and determine any such action, and

(b) the contract provides that, in the event of any action in respect of the contract being begun, the process by which it is begun may be served on the defendant, or on such other person on his behalf as may be specified in the contract, in such manner, or at such place (whether within or out of the jurisidiction), as may be so specified,

then, if an action in respect of the contract is begun in the High Court and the writ by which it is begun is served in accordance with the contract, the writ shall, subject to paragraph (2), be deemed to have been duly served on the defendant.

(2) A writ which is served out of the jurisdiction in accordance with a contract shall not be deemed to have been duly served on the defendant by virtue of paragraph (1) unless leave to serve the writ, or notice thereof, out of the jurisdiction has been granted under Order 11, rule 1 (1) or service of the writ is permitted without leave under Order 11, rule 1 (2).

(3) Where a contract contains an agreement conferring jurisdiction to which Article 17 of Schedule 1 or 4 to the Civil Jurisdiction and Judgments Act 1982[10] applies and the writ is served under Order 11, rule 1 (2) the writ shall be deemed to have been duly served on the defendant.

Rules of the Supreme Court, Order 11[11]

Principal cases in which service of writ out of jurisdiction is permissible

1.—(1) Provided that the writ does not contain any claim mentioned in Order 75, rule 2 (1) and is not a writ to which paragraph (2) of this rule applies, service of a writ out of the jurisdiction is permissible with the leave of the Court if in the action begun by the writ—

(a) relief is sought against a person domiciled within the jurisdiction;

(b) an injunction is sought ordering the defendant to do or refrain from doing anything within the jurisdiction (whether or not damages are also claimed in respect of a failure to do or the doing of that thing);

(c) the claim is brought against a person duly served within or out of the jurisdiction and a person out of the jurisdiction is a necessary or proper party thereto;

(d) the claim is brought to enforce, rescind, dissolve, annul or otherwise affect a contract, or to recover damages or obtain other relief in respect of the breach of a contract, being (in either case) a contract which—

    (i) was made within the jurisdiction, or

    (ii) was made by or through an agent trading or residing within the jurisdiction on behalf of a principal trading or residing out of the jurisdiction, or

    (iii) is by its terms, or by implication, governed by English law, or

    (iv) contains a term to the effect that the High Court shall have jurisdiction to hear and determine any action in respect of the contract;

---

10 See pp 90, 102 below.
11 As amended by RSC (Amendment No 2) 1983 (SI 1983/1181).

(e) the claim is brought in respect of a breach committed within the jurisdiction of a contract made within or out of the jurisdiction, and irrespective of the fact, if such be the case, that the breach was preceded or accompanied by a breach committed out of jurisdiction that rendered impossible the performance of so much of the contract as ought to have been performed within the jurisdiction;

(f) the claim is founded on a tort and the damage was sustained, or resulted from an act committed, within the jurisdiction;

(g) the whole subject-matter of the action is land situate within the jurisdiction (with or without rents or profits) or the perpetuation of testimony relating to land so situate;

(h) the claim is brought to construe, rectify, set aside or enforce an act, deed, will, contract, obligation or liability affecting land situate within the jurisdiction;

(i) the claim is made for a debt secured on immovable property or is made to assert, declare or determine proprietary or possessory rights, or rights of security, in or over movable property, or to obtain authority to dispose of movable property, situate within the jurisdiction;

(j) the claim is brought to execute the trusts of a written instrument being trusts that ought to be executed according to English law and of which the person to be served with the writ is a trustee, or for any relief or remedy which might be obtained in any such action;

(k) the claim is made for the administration of the estate of a person who died domiciled within the jurisdiction or for any relief or remedy which may be obtained in any such action;

(l) the claim is brought in a probate action within the meaning of Order 76;

(m) the claim is brought to enforce any judgment or arbitral award;

(n) the claim is brought against a defendant not domiciled in Scotland or Northern Ireland in respect of a claim by the Commissioners of Inland Revenue for or in relation to any of the duties or taxes which have been, or are for the time being, placed under their care and management.

(2) Service of a writ out of the jurisdiction is permissible without the leave of the Court provided that each claim made by the writ is either:

(a) a claim which by virtue of the Civil Jurisdiction and Judgments Act 1982[12] the Court has power to hear and determine, made in proceedings to which the following conditions apply—

(i) no proceedings between the parties concerning the same cause of action are pending in the Courts of any other part of the United Kingdom or of any other Convention territory, and

(ii) either—

the defendant is domiciled in any part of the United Kingdom or in any other Convention territory, or

the proceedings begun by the writ are proceedings to which Article 16 of Schedule 1 or Schedule 4 refers, or

the defendant is a party to an agreement conferring jurisdiction to which Article 17 of Schedule 1 or Schedule 4 to that Act applies,

or

(b) a claim which by virtue of any other enactment the High Court has

12 P 79 below.

power to hear and determine notwithstanding that the person against whom the claim is made is not within the jurisdiction of the Court or that the wrongful act, neglect or default giving rise to the claim did not take place within its jurisdiction.[13]

(4) For the purposes of this rule, and of rule 9 of this Order, domicile is to be determined in accordance with the provisions of sections 41 to 46 of the Civil Jurisdiction and Judgments Act 1982 and 'Convention territory' means the territory or territories of any Contracting State, as defined by section 1 (3) of that Act, to which the Conventions as defined in section 1 (1) of that Act apply.

Application for, and grant of, leave to serve writ out of jurisdiction

4.—(1) An application for the grant of leave under rule 1 (1) must be supported by an affidavit stating—
(a) the grounds on which the application is made,
(b) that in the deponent's belief the plaintiff has a good cause of action,
(c) in what place or country the defendant is, or probably may be found, and
(d) where the application is made under rule 1 (1) (c), the grounds for the deponent's belief that there is between the plaintiff and the person on whom a writ has been served a real issue which the plaintiff may reasonably ask the Court to try.

(2) No such leave shall be granted unless it shall be made sufficiently to appear to the Court that the case is a proper one for service out of the jurisdiction under this Order.

Leave to serve the writ out of the jurisdiction under Order 11 will not normally[14] *be granted if there is a foreign jurisdiction clause which is not void ab initio.*

Mackender v Feldia [1967] 2 QB 590, [1966] 3 All ER 847 (Court of Appeal)

Appeal from McNair J.

By a contract made in London in 1964 the plaintiffs, Lloyd's underwriters, issued a jewellers' block insurance policy covering the defendants, who were diamond merchants incorporated in Switzerland, Belgium and Italy, against loss or damage to their stock anywhere in the world. The policy provided that it was governed exclusively by Belgian law and that any disputes should be exclusively subject to Belgian jurisdiction. In January 1965 a loss of diamonds occurred in Naples. The defendants made a claim for £48,266. After investigation the plaintiffs rejected the claim, alleging that the defendants had made a practice of smuggling diamonds into Italy, that it was contrary to English policy to insure goods which were intended to be

13 This refers to international conventions implemented by Carriage by Air Act 1961, Carriage by Air (Supplementary Provisions) Act 1962, Carriage of Goods by Road Act 1965, Protection of Trading Interests Act 1980, and Civil Aviation Act 1982, s 24 and Sch 4.
14 Leave was exceptionally granted in *Evans Marshall & Co Ltd v Bertola SA* [1973] 1 All ER 992, [1973] 1 WLR 349, although there was a foreign jurisdiction clause (*Ed*).

smuggled into a friendly foreign country, and that the defendants had been guilty of non-disclosure of this practice. The defendants started proceedings in Belgium claiming payment of their loss. Wanting the dispute to be tried in England, the plaintiffs issued a writ asking that the policy be declared void for illegality and voidable for non-disclosure, and that it be rescinded or annulled. The plaintiffs obtained leave from McNair J to serve the writ on the defendants out of the jurisdiction on the ground that the contract had been made within the jurisdiction. The defendants appealed.

Lord Denning MR (after stating the facts): Where is the dispute to be tried? Lloyd's underwriters would like it tried in England. They have issued a writ in the English courts asking that the policy be declared void for illegality and voidable for non-disclosure, and that it be rescinded or annulled. They applied for leave to serve this writ out of the jurisdiction on the diamond merchants. Roskill J granted leave ex parte. McNair J, after hearing the diamond merchants, affirmed the decision. Now the diamond merchants appeal to this court. They point out that the policy contains the foreign jurisidiction clause and they ask that this dispute be decided in Belgium. The diamond merchants have themselves filed proceedings in the Belgian court claiming payment of this £48,266 on account of the loss. They appear to have obtained leave from the Belgian courts to serve proceedings on Lloyd's underwriters and those proceedings are being carried on in Belgium. The question we have to decide is whether the English proceedings should now be continued.

The rules of court are wide enough to cover the case for service out of the jurisdiction. RSC Ord 11, r 1 (f),[15] says that it is permissible if an action is brought to annul or otherwise affect a contract 'made within the jurisdiction'. This contract was undoubtedly made within the jurisdiction. The negotiations between the underwriters and the brokers were here in London, the slip signed here, and the policy issued out of and signed at Lloyd's policy signing office.

But although there is jurisdiction to give leave, it is a matter of discretion as to whether it should be granted. Mr Dunn for the diamond merchants says that, in view of the foreign jurisdiction clause, the court should not give leave. But Mr MacCrindle for the underwriters says that the foreign jurisdiction clause ought not to be given such importance in this case. He says that the foreign jurisdiction clause only applies where a contract has been truly created and formed. Here he says that owing to the non-disclosure, there was no true contract—no real consent by the underwriters—and that, on this basis, the contract itself falls down, including even the foreign jurisdiction clause.

I can well see that if the issue was whether there ever had been any contract at all, as, for instance, if there was a plea of non est factum, then the foreign jurisdiction clause might not apply at all. But here there was a contract, and when it was made, it contained the foreign jurisdiction clause. Even if there was non-disclosure, nevertheless non-disclosure does not automatically avoid the contract. It only makes it voidable. It gives the insurers a right to elect. They can either avoid the contract or affirm it. If they avoid it, it is avoided in this sense, that the insurers are no longer bound

---

15 See now RSC Ord 11, r 1 (1) (d), p 63 above (*Ed*).

by it. They can repudiate the contract and refuse to pay on it. But things already done are not undone. The contract is not avoided from the beginning but only from the moment of avoidance. In particular, the foreign jurisdiction clause is not abrogated. A dispute as to non-disclosure is 'a dispute arising under' the policy and remains within the clause: just as does a dispute as to whether one side or other was entitled to repudiate the contract: see *Heyman v Darwins Ltd.*[16]

It seems to me that Mr MacCrindle's argument (to the effect that non-disclosure strikes out the whole contract) is not well founded. The foreign jurisdiction clause is a positive agreement by the underwriters that the policy is governed exclusively by Belgian law. Any dispute under it is to be exclusively subject to Belgian jurisdiction. That clause still stands and is a strong ground why discretion should be exercised against leave to serve out of the jurisdiction.

As to illegality, I would only say this: the underwriters were clearly innocent. The diamond merchants may have had an unlawful intention to smuggle goods into a friendly foreign country. But their illegality would not affect the formation of the contract. It would only make it unenforceable. It would mean that they could not recover on the policy. This dispute again comes within the foreign jurisdiction clause.

It all comes to this: the English courts have discretion whether or not to give leave to serve this writ out of the jurisdiction. Seeing that the underwriters have agreed to a foreign jurisdiction clause which gives exclusive jurisdiction to the Belgian courts, I think we should allow these disputes to be decided in the courts of Belgium. We should not give leave to serve this writ out of the jurisdiction.

I would therefore allow the appeal.[17]

Diplock and Russell LJJ delivered judgments to the same effect.
Appeal allowed.

Two cases on when a contract is 'by its terms or by implication' governed by English law within the meaning of RSC Ord 11, r 1 (1) (d) (iii).

Coast Lines Ltd v Hudig & Veder Chartering NV [1972] 2 QB 34, [1972] 1 All ER 451[18] (Court of Appeal)

Appeal from Roskill J.

The plaintiffs, English shipowners, let a ship on a voyage charter to Dutch charterers. The charterparty was negotiated between the charterers and

---

16 [1942] AC 356, [1942] 1 All ER 337.
17 This case would now be decided the same way but by a different route. First, as will be explained later in this chapter (below, pp 95, 102), if the defendant is 'domiciled' in another EEC state or in another part of the United Kingdom, the rules in Order 11 do not apply. Secondly, if one of the parties is domiciled in another EEC state or another part of the United Kingdom, their chosen court has exclusive jurisdiction and discretion does not enter into the matter (*Ed*).
18 This case would now be differently decided because of articles 2 and 3 of the Brussels Convention (1968). But the principle of the case remains valid if the defendant is not resident in another EEC state or in another part of the United Kingdom (*Ed*).

brokers in Cardiff acting for the owners. It was drawn up and signed in Rotterdam for carriage of cargo from Rotterdam to Drogheda in the Republic of Ireland. It contained a clause exempting the owners from liability for loss of or damage to the cargo in the absence of personal fault on their part or that of their manager. The bill of lading was issued in Rotterdam. It made the shipowners liable to the cargo owners for want of due diligence. Since the charterers were responsible for the presentation of the bill of lading which imposed a greater liability on the shipowners than that provided by the charterparty, the charterers were by English law liable to indemnify the shipowners in respect of that greater liability.

During the voyage the ship ran into very bad weather conditions. When she arrived at Drogheda it was found that 65 tons of sea water had come aboard which badly damaged the cargo. The water got in by a broken bilge pipe. The ship was unseaworthy when she left Rotterdam, but not because of the personal fault of the shipowners or their manager. The cargo owners claimed damages from the shipowners who admitted liability to them and claimed to be indemnified by the charterers. But by article 517d of the Netherlands Commercial Code as it stood when the cargo was loaded, the shipowners were not entitled to any indemnity, irrespective of the proper law of the contract.

The shipowners obtained leave from Roskill J to serve notice of the writ on the charterers out of the jurisdiction on the ground that the charterparty by its terms or by implication was governed by English law. The charterers appealed.

Lord Denning MR (having stated the facts):   In view of this difference (sc between Netherlands and English law), we have to consider these points:

1. What is the proper law of the contract? If it is Netherlands law, then the Netherlands Commercial Code will apply. The shipowners will not be entitled to an indemnity. If it is English law, and the case is allowed to proceed in the English courts, then the English courts will apply English law, and will give the shipowners an indemnity. But, if the shipowners are forced to sue in the Netherlands courts, those courts will (despite the contract being governed by English law) apply the Netherlands Code to it, and will refuse an indemnity.

2. If the proper law is English law, ought these courts to allow service out of the jurisdiction so that the case can proceed in the English courts? Or should they refuse and force the shipowners to go to the Netherlands courts?

In order to determine the proper law of the contract, the courts at one time used to have a number of presumptions to help them. Now we have to ask ourselves: What is the system of law with which the transaction has the closest and most real connection? This is not dependent on the intentions of the parties. They never thought about it. They had no intentions upon it. We have to study every circumstance connected with the contract and come to a conclusion. This new test is all very well. It is often easy to apply. But, there are sometimes cases where it is quite indecisive. The circumstances do not point to one country only. They point equally to two countries, or even to three. What then is a legal adviser to do? What is an arbitrator or a judge to do? Is he to toss up a coin and see which way it comes down? Surely not. The law ought to give some help. It ought to provide a pointer to a solution, if only as a last resort. One such pointer is that, in a contract of charterparty, other things being equal, the law of the ship should govern: see *Lloyd v Guibert*[19] and *The Assunzione*.[20]

Apply the test here. One important circumstance is that the contract was made in Rotterdam by Dutch charterers for shipment at Rotterdam. That points to Netherlands law. Another important circumstance is that contract was for carriage in an English ship owned by English owners for carriage on the high seas. That points to English law. Put those two into the scales, one on one side, the other on the other. You find they are equal. Other circumstances point one way, then another. There is nothing to choose. So, as a last resort, you take the law of the flag, which is English law.

But then there is a further consideration. The contract contained an exemption clause which was valid under English law, but invalid under Netherlands law. That, I think, is important. In the maritime law of this country—and I believe of all other maritime countries—it is an accepted principle that a contract is, if possible, to be construed so as to make it valid rather than invalid. The latin maxim is well-known. A stipulation must be construed ut res magis valeat quam pereat. Applying it here, the exemption clause in the charterparty is valid by English law, but invalid by Netherlands law. That is a pointer to English law as the proper law of the contract. For this simple reason: it cannot be assumed that the Dutch charterers put their signatures to a contract which they did not intend to honour. This is supported by opinion of the Privy Council in *Peninsular and Oriental Steam Navigation Co v Shand*[1] and by the judgment of Lord Halsbury LC in *Re Missouri Steamship Co*.[2]

I would add another consideration also. The commercial judge (Roskill J) has held that the proper law is English law. We should be slow to differ from him on such a point. As Lord Wilberforce said recently: '. . . decision by the commercial judge should end the matter': see *Compagnie Tunisienne De Navigation SA v Compagnie D'Armement Maritime SA*.[3]

I am of opinion, therefore, that the proper law of this contract is English law, and not Netherlands law.

Once it is held that the charterparty is by implication governed by English law, the next question is whether leave should be given to serve the writ out of the jurisdiction? This is a very serious question. The charterers are a Netherlands company. They owe no allegiance here. They have no place of business here. They have, as yet, no assets here. It is a strong thing to force them to come to England to contest a case against them. So we must be exceedingly careful before doing so. That was pointed out long ago: *The Hagen*.[4] If the Netherlands courts were free to apply the proper law of the contract (ie English law), I would not be disposed to grant leave to serve out of the jurisdiction. But the Netherlands courts are not free. They are compelled by the Netherlands law to allow to apply a special law of the Netherlands, ie, article 517d, which is not the proper law of the contract and which is out of line with the maritime law of all other countries. The

---

19 (1865) LR 1 QB 115, 35 LJQB 74; p 433 below.
20 [1954] P 150 at 193–194, [1954] 1 All ER 278 at 300; p 439 below.
 1 (1865) 3 Moo PC NS 272 at 291–292; p 431 below.
 2 (1889) 42 Ch D 321 at 337.
 3 [1971] AC 572 at 600, [1970] 3 All ER 71 at 89; p 441 below.
 4 [1908] P 189, 77 LJP 124.

Netherlands courts are compelled to apply a law which is contrary to the general understanding of commercial men.

In these circumstances, I do not think we should send the English owners to the Netherlands courts. We should retain the case in these courts where we can and will apply English law, which is the proper law of the contract.

I know that the charterers can avoid our English law by refusing to submit to the jurisdiction of the English courts. In that case any judgment of the English courts will not be enforceable in the Netherlands under the arrangements for the reciprocal enforcement of judgment: see The Reciprocal Enforcement of Foreign Judgments (the Netherlands) Order 1969.[5] The English owners would then be forced to sue in the Netherlands, and the courts there would, no doubt, apply the Netherlands Commercial code. So, in a sense, the matter rests with the charterers. But, so far as these courts are concerned, I think that leave should be given to serve out of the jurisdiction.

I agree with the judgment of Roskill J, and I would dismiss the appeal.

Megaw LJ: What is the proper law of the contract? In this charterparty the parties did not express their actual intention as to the proper law. No inference can be drawn from any one or more of the express terms of the contract as to the *actual* common intention of the parties. Hence the question to be answered is: what is the system of law with which the transaction has its closest and most real connection? This test has its origin with Professor Westlake: see Cheshire's *Private International Law*.[6] It was first adopted by Lord Simonds in delivering the judgment of the Privy Council in *Bonython v Commonwealth of Australia*.[7] A decade later it was accepted explicitly for purposes of English private international law by the House of Lords in *Re United Railways of Havana and Regla Warehouses Ltd*:[8] see Lord Denning's speech at 1068, and that of Lord Morris of Borth-y-Gest at 1081. It has recently been reaffirmed in *Compagnie Tunisienne de Navigation SA v Compagnie d'Armement Maritime SA*, in which Lord Reid, at 583, Lord Morris of Borth-y-Gest at 587 and Lord Diplock at 603, accepted and applied the *Bonython* test of the closest and most real connection with the transaction.

I think it is not without significance to note that the connection which has to be sought is expressed to be connection between the *transaction*—that is, the transaction contemplated by the contract—and the system of law. That, I believe, indicates that, where the *actual* intention of the parties as to the proper law is not expressed in, and cannot be inferred from, the terms of the contract (so that it is impossible to apply the earlier part of the *Bonython* fomula: 'the system of law by reference to which the *contract was* made') more importance is to be attached to what is to be done under the contract—its substance— than to considerations of the form and formalities of the contract or considerations of what may, without disrespect, be described as lawyers' points as to inferences to be drawn from the terms of the contract.

With which system of law did this transaction—the business transaction of the provision of a ship which would carry goods from Rotterdam to Drogheda—have its closest and most real connection? The owners were

5 SI 1969/1063, Sch, art III (2) (a) and IV (1).
6 8th edn (1970) pp 199, 200, 202.
7 [1951] AC 201 at 219; p 437 below.
8 [1961] AC 1007, [1960] 2 All ER 332.

English; the charterers were Dutch. The charterparty, having been negotiated across the seas, was dated 'Rotterdam'. It was only in that somewhat technical sense that the contract was 'made' there. It was in the English language. In the light of the uncontradicted evidence, that is not a matter of great weight in this case in favour of the English legal system. The fact that the freight and demurrage were expressed in sterling deserves slightly greater weight, though, again, it is not a strong factor in the light of the evidence. The loading of the vessel was to take place in Rotterdam and bills of lading were to be issued there. To that extent performance of the obligations of the contract was connected with the Netherlands. So far as the bills of lading were concerned, it might well be that the fact that they were issued in Rotterdam in respect of goods loaded there would be a conclusive, or at least a powerful, indication that the proper law of the contracts to which they might give rise would be the law of the Netherlands. But different considerations apply to the two types of contract—charterparty contracts and bill of lading contracts, as is indeed evidenced by the Hague Rules, based on international convention, to which I shall have to refer further on the second issue.

Against this connection with the Netherlands system of law, arising out of the fact that an important part of the transaction was to be carried out in Netherlands territory, it is necessary to set the fact that the principal subject-matter of the charterparty, on a sensible business view of the transaction, was the ship. A voyage charterparty, while normally containing detailed provision for dealing with the goods to be carried, not only at the port or ports of loading but also during the voyage and at the port or ports of discharge, is primarily and in essence a contract for the provision of services of—the use of—a specified, named, ship. This may be contrasted with a bill of lading contract where it could sensibly be said that the principal subject-matter of the contract is the goods covered by the bill of lading. The ship here chartered was, to put it shortly, English. The flag was British, with English registration and English ownership. It would not be right to place too much stress on the rule of public international law (see Oppenheim's *International Law*,[9]) that 'vessels, and the things and persons thereon, remain during the time they are on the open sea under the jurisdiction of the state under whose flag they sail', and that they are in many respects to be treated as 'floating portions of the flag state'. But to my mind the fact that the subject-matter of the charterparty was an English ship and that the whole of the transaction contemplated by the contract concerned the activities of that English ship, in loading, carrying and discharging the cargo, produces the result that the transaction, viewed as a whole and weighing all the relevant factors, has a closer and more real connection with English law than with the law of the Netherlands.

It may be suggested that this is to bring back into English private international law a presumption—the presumption of the law of the flag—as prima facie determinant of the proper law. Presumptions, once fashionable during the earlier development of English private international law, are now, whether for good or for ill, out of fashion and rejected. That, indeed, is a necessary result of the adoption of the 'closest and most real connection' test. No single factor is to be treated as, prima facie, providing the answer. I

9 8th edn (1955) vol 1, pp 330, 597.

would go so far as to say that in a charterparty case the flag of the vessel is likely normally to be important. But it must be considered along with all the other relevant factors. Weighing it, as best I can, with and against the other relevant aspects of this transaction. I think that the result is as I have indicated. Therefore English law is the proper law of the charterparty contract.

Stephenson LJ delivered judgment to the same effect.
Appeal allowed.

Amin Rasheed Shipping Corporation v Kuwait Insurance Co
[1983] 2 All ER 884, [1983] 3 WLR 241 (House of Lords)

The plaintiffs, a Liberian corporation carrying on business in Dubai, owned a small cargo vessel which they insured against war and marine risks with the defendants, a Kuwaiti insurance company. The policy was in the English language and followed closely the wording of the Lloyd's SG policy scheduled to the Marine Insurance Act 1906, with additional war and strike clauses attached. The policy was expressed to be made in Kuwait in April 1979 and claims (if any) were expressed to be payable in Kuwait. The policy was however the second renewal of similar policies of which the first was issued in April 1977. The original policy was negotiated by brokers in London, premiums were paid to those brokers, and claims were settled through them. There was evidence that in 1979 there was no indigenous law of marine insurance in Kuwait, though there was a Commercial Code; and that a Kuwaiti court would probably apply English law since only thus could it give a sensible and precise meaning to the policy.

The vessel was detained in Saudi Arabia on suspicion of smuggling oil (which the plaintiffs strenuously denied) and the master and crew were imprisoned for several months. The plaintiffs gave notice of abandonment to the insurers and brought an action in England claiming as for a constructive total loss. Leave to serve the writ out of the jurisdiction under RSC Ord 11, r 1 (1) (f) (iii)[10] on the ground that the contract was governed by English law was granted ex parte by Robert Goff J. Bingham J set aside his order on the grounds (1) that the proper law was that of Kuwait and (2) that even if he had jurisdiction he would refuse leave as a matter of discretion. His reasons for (2) were that the issue whether the vessel had been engaged in smuggling oil was one of fact and could equally well be decided by a Kuwaiti judge; that the jurisdiction sought to be invoked was an exorbitant one; and that there was an alternative forum where justice could be done. His decision was affirmed by a majority of the Court of Appeal, Sir John Donaldson MR and May LJ holding that the proper law was that of Kuwait and Robert Goff LJ that it was English, but May LJ held that Bingham J was right on the discretion point while Sir John Donaldson MR took the view that the discretion should be exercised in favour of granting leave. Robert Goff LJ expressed no opinion on the discretion point.

The plaintiff appealed.

Lord Wilberforce: My Lords, the question in this appeal is whether service of a writ upon the respondents outside the jurisdiction of the English courts

---

10 Now r 1 (1) (d) (iii) (*Ed*).

should be set aside. The provision in the Rules of the Supreme Court which is relied upon as justifying such service is that contained in RSC Ord 11, r 1 (1) (f) (iii), which requires, in the case of an action being brought to enforce a contract, that the contract: 'is by its terms, or by implication, governed by English law'. The contract in question is a policy of marine insurance, dated 28 April 1979, between the appellants and the respondents, and the first question is, therefore, whether this contract comes within the quoted words. If it is held so to do, so that the court has jurisdiction to order service of the writ in Kuwait, a second question arises whether it should do so in the circumstances of the case.

It has been generally accepted, in my opinion rightly, that the formula used in paragraph (f) (iii) above is equivalent to a requirement that the proper law of the contract should be English law. This involves treating the words 'by implication' as covering both the situation where the parties' mutual intention can be inferred and the situation where, no such inference being possible, it is necessary to seek the system of law with which the contract has its closest and most real connection. Although these situations merge into each other, I regard this case as falling rather within the latter words since I can find no basis for inferring, as between the parties to this contract, an intention that the contract should be governed either by English law or by the law of Kuwait. (I should add here that, as was indicated during the hearing, we cannot, consistently with recent authority, have regard to conduct of the parties subsequent to the making of the contract— here the original policy of 1977.) The court's task must be to have regard objectively to the various factors pointing one way or the other and to estimate, as best it can, where the preponderance lies.

The search is for the 'proper law': the law which governs the contract and the parties' obligations under it; the law which determines (normally) its validity and legality, its construction and effect, and the conditions of its discharge. It is clear that, as regards this contract, there are only two choices, English law and the law of Kuwait. It is worth considering at the outset what these alternatives involve.

The Lloyd's SG form of policy, which the policy in this case is with insignificant departures, its obsolete and, in parts, unintelligible language, is one which has been used for centuries, almost without change. The Marine Insurance Act 1906, a codification Act, passed after 12 years of gestation, which schedules the Lloyd's SG policy as a permissible form of policy, also provides in the Schedule a number of definitions. These definitions may be regarded as a form of glossary based on established law, and the substantive provisions in the Act (binding by statutory force only if the proper law is English), as evidence of the established and customary law of marine insurance. I think that we can accept that if Kuwaiti law were regarded as the proper law, it would resort to the definitions and would have regard to commercial custom as (inter alia) manifested by the Act. The expert evidence, in my opinion, establishes so much in relation to the relevant law of Kuwait prior to 1980 when Kuwait introduced its own insurance legislation. Thus, whether English or Kuwaiti law is the proper law, the terms of the contract would be given the meaning ascribed to them by English statute, custom, and decisions.

There is nothing unusual in a situation where, under the proper law of a contract, resort is had to some other system of law for purposes of interpretation. In that case, that other system becomes a source of the law upon which the proper law may draw. Such is frequently the case where a given system of law has not yet developed rules and principles in relation to an activity which has become current, or where another system has from experience built up a coherent and tested structure—as, for example, in banking, insurance or admiralty law, or where countries exist with a common legal heritage such as the common law or the French legal system. In such a case, the proper law is not applying a 'conflicts' rule (there may, in fact, be no foreign element in the case) but merely importing a foreign product for domestic use.

There is evidence before us that in relation to insurance, and in particular to cases where Lloyd's SG policies are used, courts in Europe do this, and that the courts in Kuwait would act in a similar way, resorting, as to a source of their own domestic law, to English law directly or indirectly via Turkish law.

So returning to the choice before us, it is between the proper law being English law, or the proper law being Kuwaiti law, drawing in part at least on English interpretations. This analysis, if correct, thus early in the discussion calls in question the validity of one line of argument used to support the appellants' case (that the governing law is English law). That argument is simply (I am tempted to say simplistically) that since this contract is in English language and form and embodies many technical expressions which can only be explained by resort to English law, that shows that the proper law, the law governing the contract, must be English law. There are three reasons why this cannot be correct:

(1) As a matter of reasoning it inverts the process which has to be followed. Instead of arguing from the proper law to that which governs interpretation it does the reverse. The form of the contract may indeed be a factor to be considered in the search for the proper law—it is so here, and an important one, but one to be considered with other factors.

(2) It is inconsistent with authority including that of this House. In *Whitworth Street Estates Ltd v Miller*[11] the question for decision was whether the proper law was that of England or of Scotland. The contract was on an English RIBA form which had 'many connections with English law' (Lord Hodson, at 606). It had, in fact, been built up and amended from time to time as the result of English decisions. The decision, by a scarcely discernible majority, was that the proper law was English, but this decison was arrived at by a careful weighing of factors, including the nature and origin of the form. There can be little doubt that on either view, whichever the proper law was held to be, the contract would have fallen to be interpreted according to English law, but this circumstance alone was not regarded as decisive. Similarly, in *Compagnie Tunisienne de Navigation SA v Compagnie d'Armement Maritime SA*,[12] the use of an English form of charter was regarded as a factor to be considered, and the decision was that the proper law was French. Reliance was placed on some observations of Lord Wright in the Privy Council case of *Vita Food Products Inc v Unus Shipping Co Ltd*.[12a] But, as I understand him, Lord Wright was concerned only with the difference in terminology between that case and *The Torni*.[12b] I do not read his observations

11 [1970] AC 583, [1970] 1 All ER 796; p 206 below.
12 [1971] AC 572, [1970] 3 All ER 71; p 441 below.
12a [1939] AC 277 at 298, [1939] 1 All ER 513; p 443 below.
12b [1932] P 78, 101 LJP 44.

as equating the law governing construction with the proper law: if they were
so intended, I could not, with respect, agree with them.

(3) The simple proposition that because a form of contract has to be
interpreted in accordance with English rules, or even decisions, the proper
law must be English law would have very unfortunate consequences. It is
well known, and not disputed, that this Lloyd's SG policy is widely used, not
only in the British Commonwealth, or countries under British influence, but
elsewhere, including countries in Europe. It is regularly used in the Middle
East and in the Arabian Gulf. It is a strong thing to say that, in the absence
of an express choice of law clause, the proper law of all such policies is to be
regarded by an English court as English.

The wide use made of this form of policy calls, on the contrary, for a
careful examination in each case of the question what proper law is
appropriate, the English law form or derivation of the form being an
(important) factor. I do not believe, with respect, that this argument, which
both Bingham J and Robert Goff LJ regarded as important, can be disposed
of by describing it as contending for an internationalised, or floating,
contract, unattached to any system of law—to do so does not do it justice.
The argument is that the Lloyd's SG form of policy is taken into a great
number of legal systems, sometimes by statute, as in Australia, sometimes as
a matter of commercial practice, as in Belgium or Germany, or in the
Arabian Gulf, and that in such cases, though their legal systems may, and on
the evidence do, resort to English law in order to interpret its terms, the
contract may be regarded as an Australian, Belgian, German, etc contract.
What has to be done is to look carefully at all those factors normally
regarded as relevant when the proper law is being searched for, including of
course the nature of the policy itself, and to form a judgment as to the system
of law with which that policy in the circumstances has the closest and most
real connection.

In my opinion, therefore, the classic process of weighing the factors must
be followed, with all the difficulties inherent in the process. They are well
and clearly listed in the judgment of Sir John Donaldson MR. I agree with
him that the majority of the ingredients said to connect the policy with
English law are irrelevant or lacking in weight—these include payment of
premiums in sterling in London and the use of J. H. Minet & Co Ltd,
London brokers. The significant factors remain: (1) the use of this form of
policy expressed in the English language and requiring interpretation
according to English rules and practice; (2) the nationality of the parties, the
defendants being incorporated and carrying on business in Kuwait and the
plaintiffs being Liberian and resident in Dubai (ie neither in England nor in
Kuwait); (3) the use of English sterling as the money of account; (4) the issue
of the policy in Kuwait—this I regard as of little weight; (5) provision in
claims to be paid in Kuwait. This, too, is of minor consequence in view of
the practice, established at the time of contracting, of settling claims in
London. I think also, for myself, that it is not without importance that the
policy contains no choice of law clause. With a policy in a form so essentially
English, the absence of such a factor leaves the form and language, as a
pointer towards English law, without what one would consider as its natural
counterweight. I agree that omission of the Lombard Street or Royal
Exchange or London clause is insignificant, but I regard the incorporation of
the Institute Clauses, with express reference to English law provisions, as
important. With no great confidence, and reluctantly differing as to the

ultimate conclusion from Bingham J and Robert Goff LJ, whose reasoning in principle I approve and follow, I have reached the conclusion that English law is the proper law of this particular contract.

That makes it necessary to decide whether, even so, service of this writ outside the jurisdiction should be allowed to stand. RSC Ord 11, r 1 merely states that, given one of the stated conditions, such service is permissible, and it is still necessary for the plaintiff (in this case the appellant) to make it 'sufficiently to appear to the court that the case is a proper one for service out of the jurisdiction under this Order' (r 4 (2)). The rule does not state the considerations by which the court is to decide whether the case is a proper one, and I do not think that we can get much assistance from cases where it is sought to stay an action started in this country, or to enjoin the bringing of proceedings abroad. The situations are different. The intention must be to impose upon the plaintiff the burden of showing good reasons why service of a writ, calling for appearance before an English court, should, in the circumstances, be permitted upon a foreign defendant. In considering this question the court must take into account the nature of the dispute, the legal and practical issues involved, such questions as local knowledge, availability of witnesses and their evidence and expense. It is not appropriate, in my opinion, to embark upon a comparison of the procedures, or methods, or reputation or standing of the courts of one country as compared with those of another. In this case, Bingham J having first decided there was no jurisdiction to order service in Kuwait, then proceeded, after a review of the factors, to express the opinion that, if there was jurisdiction, he would not consider that it should be exercised. This in my opinion was a substantive decision on the point, viz an alternative ground of decision of the case before him, not a mere obiter dictum. It is, of course, appealable and was considered, without definitive result, by the Court of Appeal. Having weighed the factors involved and having the benefit of the analysis of them by my noble and learned friend, Lord Diplock, I have come to the conclusion that his decision on this point was right.

For this reason I would dismiss the appeal.

Lord Diplock gave judgment to the same effect. Lords Roskill, Brandon of Oakbrook and Brightman concurred.

Appeal dismissed.

A case on whether a contract is made in England within the meaning of Ord 11, r 1 (1) (d) (i).

Brinkibon Ltd v Stahag Stahl [1983] 2 AC 34, [1982] 1 All ER 293 (House of Lords)

On 26 April 1979 Brinkibon sent a telex from London to Stahag Stahl in Vienna offering to buy a quantity of mild steel bars on certain terms. On 3 May 1979 Stahag Stahl sent a telex from Vienna to Brinkibon in London offering to sell the steel on different terms. On 4 May 1979 Brinkibon sent a telex to Stahag Stahl accepting this counter-offer and instructed their bank in London to open a letter of credit in favour of Stahag Stahl with a Swiss firm in Switzerland. Later in May 1979 Stahag Stahl complained that Brinkibon had not opened a proper letter of credit and withdrew from the contract. Brinkibon issued a writ against Stahag Stahl and sought leave to serve it on them out of the jurisdiction under RSC Ord, 11 r 1 (1) (f) and (g)[13] on the grounds that the contract had been made and broken in England. Mocatta J granted leave on the first ground but not on the second. His decision was reversed by the Court of Appeal which refused leave on both grounds. Brinkibon appealed.

Lord Wilberforce: The question whether a contract was made within the jurisdiction will often admit of a simple answer: if both parties are in England at the time of making it, or if it is contained in a single document signed by both parties in England, there is no difficulty. But in the case of contracts involving negotiations, where one party is abroad, the answer may be difficult to find. Sophisticated analysis may be required to decide when the last counter-offer was made into a contract by acceptance, or at what point a clear consensus was reached and by virtue of what words spoken or of what conduct. In the case of successive telephone conversations it may indeed be most artificial to ask where the contract was made: if one asked the parties, they might say they did not know—or care. The place of making a contract is usually irrelevant as regards validity, or interpretation, or enforcement. Unfortunately it remains in Order 11 as a test for purposes of jurisdiction, and courts have to do their best with it.

In the present case it seems that if there was a contract (a question which can only be decided at the trial), it was preceded by and possibly formed by a number of telephone conversations and telexes between London and Vienna, and there are a number of possible combinations upon which reliance can be placed. At this stage we must take the alternatives which provide reasonable evidence of a contract in order to see if the test is satisfied. There are two: (i) A telex dated 3 May 1979, from the respondents in Vienna, said to amount to a counter-offer, followed by a telex from the appellants in London to the respondents in Vienna dated 4 May 1979, said to amount to an acceptance. (ii) The above telex dated 3 May 1979, from the respondents followed by action, by way of opening a letter of credit, said to have amounted to an acceptance by conduct.

The first of these alternatives neatly raises the question whether an acceptance by telex sent from London but received in Vienna causes a contract to be made in London, or in Vienna. If the acceptance had been sent by post, or by telegram, then, on existing authorities, it would have been complete when put into the hands of the post office—in London. If on the other hand it had been telephoned, it would have been complete when heard by the offerer—in Vienna. So in which category is a telex communication to be placed? Existing authority of the Court of Appeal decides in favour of the latter category, ie a telex is to be assimilated to other methods of instantaneous communication: see *Entores Ltd v Miles Far East Corpn.*[14] The appellants ask that this case, which has stood for 30 years, should now be reviewed.

Now such review as is necessary must be made against the background of

13 Now rule 1 (1) (d) and (e) (*Ed*).
14 [1955] 2 QB 327, [1955] 2 All ER 493.

the law as to the making of contracts. The general rule, it is hardly necessary to state, is that a contract is formed *when* acceptance of an offer is communicated by the offeree to the offeror. And if it is necessary to determine *where* a contract is formed (as to which I have already commented) it appears logical that this should be at the place where acceptance is communicated to the offeror. In the common case of contracts, whether oral or in writing inter praesentes, there is no difficulty; and again logic demands that even where there is not mutual presence at the same place and at the same time, if communication is instantaneous, for example by telephone or radio communication, the same result should follow.

Then there is the case—very common—of communication at a distance, to meet which the so-called 'postal rule' has developed. I need not trace its history: it has firmly been in the law at least since *Adams v Lindsell*[15]. The rationale for it, if left somewhat obscure by Lord Ellenborough CJ, has since been well explained. Mellish LJ in *Re Imperial Land Co of Marseilles (Harris' Case)*[16] ascribed it to the extraordinary and mischievous consequences which would follow if it were held that an offer might be revoked at any time until the letter accepting it had been actually received: and its foundation in convenience was restated by Thesiger LJ in *Household Fire and Carriage Accident Insurance Co Ltd v Grant*.[17] In these cases too it seems logical to say that the place, as well as the time, of acceptance should be *where* (as *when*) the acceptance is put into the charge of the post office.

In this situation, with a general rule covering instantaneous communication inter praesentes, or at a distance, with an exception applying to non-instantaneous communication at a distance, how should communications by telex be categorised? In *Entores Ltd v Miles Far East Corpn* the Court of Appeal classified them with instantaneous communications. Their ruling, which has passed into the textbooks, including Williston on *Contracts*,[18] appears not to have caused either adverse comment, or any difficulty to businessmen. I would accept it as a general rule. Where the condition of simultaneity is met, and where it appears to be within the mutual intention of the parties that contractual exchanges should take place in this way, I think it a sound rule, but not necessarily a universal rule.

Since 1955 the use of telex communication has been greatly expanded, and there are many variants on it. The senders and recipients may not be the principals to the contemplated contract. They may be servants or agents with limited authority. The message may not reach, or be intended to reach, the designated recipient immediately: messages may be sent out of office hours, or at night, with the intention, or upon the assumption, that they will be read at a later time. There may be some error or default at the recipient's end which prevents receipt at the time contemplated and believed in by the sender. The message may have been sent and/or received through machines operated by third persons. And many other variations may occur. No universal rule can cover all such cases: they must be resolved by reference to the intentions of the parties, by sound business practice and in some cases by a judgment where the risks should lie: see *Household Fire and Carriage Accident*

15 (1818) 1 B & Ald 681.
16 (1872) 7 Ch App 587 at 594.
17 (1879) 4 Ex D 216 at 223.
18 3rd edn (1957).

Insurance Co Ltd v Grant per Baggallay LJ and *Henthorn v Fraser*[19] per Lord Herschell.

The present case is, as *Entores Ltd v Miles Far East Corpn* itself, the simple case of instantaneous communication between principals, and, in accordance with the general rule, involves that the contract (if any) was made when and where the acceptance was received. This was on 3 May 1979, in Vienna.

(His Lordship held that the contract was not made in England when Brinkibon instructed their bank to open the letter of credit, and that it was not broken in England.)

Lords Fraser of Tullybelton and Brandon of Oakbrook delivered judgments to the same effect. Lords Russell of Killowen and Bridge of Harwich concurred.

Appeal dismissed.

Section C. Under the Civil Jurisdiction and Judgments Act 1982

Civil Jurisdiction and Judgments Act 1982

PART I

IMPLEMENTATION OF THE CONVENTIONS

1.—(1) In this Act—
'the 1968 Convention' means the Convention on jurisdiction and the enforcement of judgments in civil and commercial matters (including the Protocol annexed to that Convention), signed at Brussels on 27 September 1968;
'the 1971 Protocol' means the Protocol on the interpretation of the 1968 Convention by the European Court, signed at Luxembourg on 3 June 1971;
'the Accession Convention' means the Convention on the accession to the 1968 Convention and the 1971 Protocol of Denmark, the Republic of Ireland and the United Kingdom, signed at Luxembourg on 9 October 1978;
'the Conventions' means the 1968 Convention, the 1971 Protocol and the Accession Convention.
   (2) In this Act, unless the context otherwise requires—
(a) references to, or to any provision of, the 1968 Convention or the 1971 Protocol are references to that Convention, Protocol or provision as amended by the Accession Convention; and
(b) any reference to a numbered Article is a reference to the Article so numbered of the 1968 Convention, and any reference to a sub-division of a numbered Article shall be construed accordingly.
   (3) In this Act 'Contracting State' means—
(a) one of the original parties to the 1968 Convention (Belgium, the Federal Republic of Germany, France, Italy, Luxembourg and the Netherlands); or
(b) one of the parties acceding to that Convention under the Accession Convention (Denmark, the Republic of Ireland and the United Kingdom),

19 [1892] 2 Ch 27, 61 LJ Ch 373.

being a state in respect of which the Accession Convention has entered into force in accordance with Article 39 of that Convention.

2.—(1) The Conventions shall have the force of law in the United Kingdom, and judicial notice shall be taken of them.

(2) For convenience of reference there are set out in Schedules 1, 2 and 3 respectively the English texts of—

(a) the 1968 Convention as amended by Titles II and III of the Accession Convention;

(b) the 1971 Protocol as amended by Title IV of the Accession Convention; and

(c) Titles V and VI of the Accession Convention (transitional and final provisions),

being texts prepared from the authentic English texts referred to in Articles 37 and 41 of the Accession Convention.

3.—(1) Any question as to the meaning or effect of any provision of the Conventions shall, if not referred to the European Court in accordance with the 1971 Protocol, be determined in accordance with the principles laid down by and any relevant decision of the European Court.

(2) Judicial notice shall be taken of any decision of, or expression of opinion by, the European Court on any such question.

(3) Without prejudice to the generality of subsection (1), the following reports (which are reproduced in the Official Journal of the Communities), namely—

(a) the reports by Mr P. Jenard on the 1968 Convention and the 1971 Protocol; and

(b) the report by Professor Peter Schlosser on the Accession Convention,

may be considered in ascertaining the meaning or effect of any provision of the Conventions and shall be given such weight as is appropriate in the circumstances.

10.—(1) The provisions of this section have effect for the purpose of allocating within the United Kingdom jurisdiction in certain proceedings in respect of which the 1968 Convention confers jurisdiction on the courts of the United Kingdom generally and to which section 16 does not apply.

(2) Any proceedings which by virtue of Article 5 (6) (trusts) are brought in the United Kingdom shall be brought in the courts of the part of the United Kingdom in which the trust is domiciled.

(3) Any proceedings which by virtue of the first paragraph of Article 14 (consumer contracts) are brought in the United Kingdom by a consumer on the ground that he is himself domiciled there shall be brought in the courts of the part of the United Kingdom in which he is domiciled.

Part II

Jurisdiction, and Recognition and Enforcement of Judgments, within United Kingdom

16.—(1) The provisions set out in Schedule 4 (which contains a modified version of Title II of the 1968 Convention) shall have effect for determining, for each part of the United Kingdom, whether the courts of law of that part, or any particular court of law in that part, have or has jurisdiction in proceedings where—

(a) the subject-matter of the proceedings is within the scope of the 1968 Convention as determined by Article 1 (whether or not the Convention has effect in relation to the proceedings); and

(b) the defendant or defender is domiciled in the United Kingdom or the proceedings are of a kind mentioned in Article 16 (exclusive jurisdiction regardless of domicile).

(3) In determining any question as to the meaning or effect of any provision contained in Schedule 4—

(a) regard shall be had to any relevant principles laid down by the European Court in connection with Title II of the 1968 Convention and to any relevant decision of that court as to the meaning or effect of any provision of that Title; and

(b) without prejudice to the generality of paragraph (a), the reports mentioned in section 3 (3) may be considered and shall, so far as relevant, be given such weight as is appropriate in the circumstances.

(4) The provisions of this section and Schedule 4 shall have effect subject to the 1968 Convention and to the provisions of section 17.

PART IV

MISCELLANEOUS PROVISIONS

Provisions relating to jurisdiction

24.—(1) Any power of a court in England and Wales or Northern Ireland to grant interim relief pending trial or pending the determination of an appeal shall extend to a case where—

(a) the issue to be tried, or which is the subject of the appeal, relates to the jurisdiction of the court to entertain the proceedings; or

(b) the proceedings involve the reference of any matter to the European Court under the 1971 Protocol.

25.—(1) The High Court in England and Wales or Northern Ireland shall have power to grant interim relief where—

(a) proceedings have been or are to be commenced in a Contracting State other than the United Kingdom or in a part of the United Kingdom other than that in which the High Court in question exercises jurisdiction; and

(b) they are or will be proceedings whose subject-matter is within the scope of the 1968 Convention as determined by Article 1 (whether or not the Convention has effect in relation to the proceedings).

(2) On an application for any interim relief under subsection (1) the court may refuse to grant that relief if, in the opinion of the court, the fact that the court has no jurisdiction apart from this section in relation to the subject-matter of the proceedings in question makes it inexpedient for the court to grant it.

(3) Her Majesty may by Order in Council extend the power to grant interim relief conferred by subsection (1) so as to make it exercisable in relation to proceedings of any of the following descriptions, namely—

(a) proceedings commenced or to be commenced otherwise than in a Contracting State;

(b) proceedings whose subject-matter is not within the scope of the 1968 Convention as determined by Article 1;

(c) arbitration proceedings.

PART V

SUPPLEMENTARY AND GENERAL PROVISIONS

Domicile

41.—(1) Subject to Article 52 (which contains provisions for determining whether a party is domiciled in a Contracting State), the following provisions of this section determine, for the purposes of the 1968 Convention and this Act, whether an individual is domiciled in the United Kingdom or in a particular part of, or place in, the United Kingdom or in a state other than a Contracting State.

(2) An individual is domiciled in the United Kingdom if and only if—

(a) he is resident in the United Kingdom; and

(b) the nature and circumstances of his residence indicate that he has a substantial connection with the United Kingdom.

(3) Subject to subsection (5), an individual is domiciled in a particular part of the United Kingdom if and only if—

(a) he is resident in that part; and

(b) the nature and circumstances of his residence indicate that he has a substantial connection with that part.

(4) An individual is domiciled in a particular place in the United Kingdom if and only if he—

(a) is domiciled in the part of the United Kingdom in which that place is situated; and

(b) is resident in that place.

(5) An individual who is domiciled in the United Kingdom but in whose case the requirements of subsection (3) (b) are not satisfied in relation to any particular part of the United Kingdom shall be treated as domiciled in the part of the United Kingdom in which he is resident.

(6) In the case of an individual who—

(a) is resident in the United Kingdom, or in a particular part of the United Kingdom; and

(b) has been so resident for the last three months or more,

the requirements of subsection (2) (b) or, as the case may be, subsection (3) (b) shall be presumed to be fulfilled unless the contrary is proved.

(7) An individual is domiciled in a state other than a Contracting State if and only if—

(a) he is resident in that state; and

(b) the nature and circumstances of his residence indicate that he has a substantial connection with that state.

42.—(1) For the purposes of this Act the seat of a corporation or association (as determined by this section) shall be treated as its domicile.

(2) The following provisions of this section determine where a corporation or association has its seat—

(a) for the purpose of Article 53 (which for the purposes of the 1968 Convention equates the domicile of such a body with its seat); and

(b) for the purposes of this Act other than the provisions mentioned in section 43 (1) (b) and (c).

(3) A corporation or association has its seat in the United Kingdom if and only if—

(a) it was incorporated or formed under the law of a part of the United

Kingdom and has its registered office or some other official address in the United Kingdom; or

(b) its central management and control is exercised in the United Kingdom.

(4) A corporation or association has its seat in a particular part of the United Kingdom if and only if it has its seat in the United Kingdom and—

(a) it has its registered office or some other official address in that part; or

(b) its central management and control is exercised in that part; or

(c) it has a place of business in that part.

(5) A corporation or association has its seat in a particular place in the United Kingdom if and only if it has its seat in the part of the United Kingdom in which that place is situated and—

(a) it has its registered office or some other official address in that place; or

(b) its central management and control is exercised in that place; or

(c) it has a place of business in that place.

(6) Subject to subsection (7), a corporation or association has its seat in a state other than the United Kingdom if and only if—

(a) it was incorporated or formed under the law of that state and has its registered office or some other official address there; or

(b) its central management and control is exercised in that state.

(7) A corporation or association shall not be regarded as having its seat in a Contracting State other than the United Kingdom if it is shown that the courts of that state would not regard it as having its seat there.

(8) In this section—

'business' includes any activity carried on by a corporation or association, and 'place of business' shall be construed accordingly;

'official address', in relation to a corporation or association, means an address which it is required by law to register, notify or maintain for the purpose of receiving notices or other communications.

43.—(1) The following provisions of this section determine where a corporation or association has its seat for the purposes of—

(a) Article 16 (2) (which confers exclusive jurisdiction over proceedings relating to the formation or dissolution of such bodies, or to the decisions of their organs);

(b) Articles 5A and 16 (2) in Schedule 4; and

(c) Rules 2 (12) and 4 (1) (b) in Schedule 8.

(2) A corporation or association has its seat in the United Kingdom if and only if—

(a) it was incorporated or formed under the law of a part of the United Kingdom; or

(b) its central management and control is exercised in the United Kingdom.

(3) A corporation or association has its seat in a particular part of the United Kingdom if and only if it has its seat in the United Kingdom and—

(a) subject to subsection (5), it was incorporated or formed under the law of that part; or

(b) being incorporated or formed under the law of a state other than the United Kingdom, its central management and control is exercised in that part.

(5) A corporation or association incorporated or formed under—

(a) an enactment forming part of the law of more than one part of the United Kingdom; or

(b) an instrument having effect in the domestic law of more than one part
     of the United Kingdom,

shall, if it has a registered office, be taken to have its seat in the part of the
United Kingdom in which that office is situated, and not in any other part of
the United Kingdom.

   (6) Subject to subsection (7), a corporation or association has its seat in a
Contracting State other than the United Kingdom if and only if—
(a) it was incorporated or formed under the law of that state; or
(b) its central management and control is exercised in that state.

   (7) A corporation or association shall not be regarded as having its seat in
a Contracting State other than the United Kingdom if—
(a) it has its seat in the United Kingdom by virtue of subsection (2) (a); or
(b) it is shown that the courts of that other state would not regard it for the
     purposes of Article 16 (2) as having its seat there.

   (8) In this section 'official address' has the same meaning as in section 42.

44.—(1) This section applies to—
(a) proceedings within Section 3 of Title II of the 1968 Convention
     (insurance contracts), and
(b) proceedings within Section 4 of that Title (consumer contracts).

   (2) A person who, for the purposes of proceedings to which this section
applies arising out of the operations of a branch, agency or other
establishment in the United Kingdom, is deemed for the purposes of the
1968 Convention to be domiciled in the United Kingdom by virtue of—
(a) Article 8, second paragraph (insurers); or
(b) Article 13, second paragraph (suppliers of goods, services or credit to
     consumers),

shall, for the purposes of those proceedings, be treated for the purposes of this
Act as so domiciled and as domiciled in the part of the United Kingdom in
which the branch, agency or establishment in question is situated.

45.—(1) The following provisions of this section determine, for the purposes
of the 1968 Convention and this Act, where a trust is domiciled.

   (2) A trust is domiciled in the United Kingdom if and only if it is by
virtue of subsection (3) domiciled in a part of the United Kingdom.

   (3) A trust is domiciled in a part of the United Kingdom if and only if the
system of law of that part is the system of law with which the trust has its
closest and most real connection.

SCHEDULE 1

CONVENTION ON JURISDICTION AND THE ENFORCEMENT OF JUDGMENTS IN CIVIL
AND COMMERCIAL MATTERS

TITLE I

SCOPE

ARTICLE 1

   This Convention shall apply in civil and commercial matters whatever the
nature of the court or tribunal. It shall not extend, in particular, to revenue,
customs or administrative matters.

   The Convention shall not apply to:

(1) the status or legal capacity of natural persons, rights in property arising out of a matrimonial relationship, wills and succession;
(2) bankruptcy, proceedings relating to the winding-up of insolvent companies or other legal persons, judicial arrangements, compositions and analogous proceedings;
(3) social security;
(4) arbitration.

TITLE II

JURISDICTION

Section 1   General provisions

ARTICLE 2

Subject to the provisions of this Convention, persons domiciled in a Contracting State shall, whatever their nationality, be sued in the courts of that State.

Persons who are not nationals of the State in which they are domiciled shall be governed by the rules of jurisdiction applicable to nationals of that State.

ARTICLE 3

Persons domiciled in a Contracting State may be sued in the courts of another Contracting State only by virtue of the rules set out in Sections 2 to 6 of this Title.

In particular the following provisions shall not be applicable as against them:

—in Belgium:	Article 15 of the civil code (*Code civil—Burgerlijk Wetboek*) and Article 638 of the Judicial code (*Code judiciaire—Gerechtelijk Wetboek*);
—in Denmark:	Article 248 (2) of the law on civil procedure (*Lov om rettens pleje*) and Chapter 3, Article 3 of the Greenland law on civil procedure (*Lov for Grønland om rettens pleje*);
—in the Federal Republic of Germany:	Article 23 of the code of civil procedure (*Zivilprozessordnung*);
—in France:	Articles 14 and 15 of the civil code (*Code civil*);
—in Ireland:	the rules which enable jurisdiction to be founded on the document instituting the proceedings having been served on the defendant during his temporary presence in Ireland;
—in Italy:	Article 2 and Article 4, Nos 1 and 2 of the code of civil procedure (*Codice di procedura civile*);
—in Luxembourg:	Articles 14 and 15 of the civil code (*Code civil*);

—in the Netherlands: Article 126 (3) and Article 127 of the code of civil procedure (*Wetboek van Burgerlijke Rechtsvordering*);

—in the United Kingdom: the rules which enable jurisdiction to be founded on :

    (a) the document instituting the proceedings having been served on the defendant during his temporary presence in the United Kingdom; or

    (b) the presence within the United Kingdom of property belonging to the defendant; or

    (c) the seizure by the plaintiff of property situated in the United Kingdom.[20]

ARTICLE 4

If the defendant is not domiciled in a Contracting State, the jurisdiction of the courts of each Contracting State shall, subject to the provisions of Article 16, be determined by the law of that State.

As against such a defendant, any person domiciled in a Contracting State may, whatever his nationality, avail himself in that State of the rules of jurisdiction there in force, and in particular those specified in the second paragraph of Article 3, in the same way as the nationals of that State.

Section 2   Special jurisdiction

ARTICLE 5

A person domiciled in a Contracting State may, in another Contracting State, be sued:

(1) in matters relating to a contract, in the courts for the place of performance of the obligation in question;

(2) in matters relating to maintenance, in the courts for the place where the maintenance creditor is domiciled or habitually resident or, if the matter is ancillary to proceedings concerning the status of a person, in the court which, according to its own law, has jurisdiction to entertain those proceedings, unless that jurisdiction is based solely on the nationality of one of the parties;

(3) in matters relating to tort, delict or quasi-delict, in the courts for the place where the harmful event occurred;

(4) as regards a civil claim for damages or restitution which is based on an act giving rise to criminal proceedings, in the court seised of those proceedings, to the extent that that court has jurisdiction under its own law to entertain civil proceedings;

(5) as regards a dispute arising out of the operations of a branch, agency or other establishment, in the courts for the place in which the branch, agency or other establishment is situated;

(6) in his capacity as settlor, trustee or beneficiary of a trust created by the operation of a statute, or by a written instrument, or created orally and

---

20 Paras (b) and (c) relate to the jurisdiction of the Scottish, not the English, courts (*Ed*).

evidenced in writing, in the courts of the Contracting State in which the trust is domiciled;

(7) as regards a dispute concerning the payment of remuneration claimed in respect of the salvage of a cargo or freight, in the court under the authority of which the cargo or freight in question:
   (a) has been arrested to secure such payment, or
   (b) could have been so arrested, but bail or other security has been given;

   provided that this provision shall apply only if it is claimed that the defendant has an interest in the cargo or freight or had such an interest at the time of salvage.

ARTICLE 6

A person domiciled in a Contracting State may also be sued:
(1) where he is one of a number of defendants, in the courts for the place where any one of them is domiciled;
(2) as a third party in an action on a warranty or guarantee or in any other third party proceedings, in the court seised of the original proceedings, unless these were instituted solely with the object of removing him from the jurisdiction of the court which would be competent in his case;
(3) on a counterclaim arising from the same contract or facts on which the original claim was based, in the court in which the original claim is pending.

Section 3   Jurisdiction in matters relating to insurance

ARTICLE 7

In matters relating to insurance, jurisdiction shall be determined by this Section, without prejudice to the provisions of Articles 4 and 5 (5).

ARTICLE 8

An insurer domiciled in a Contracting State may be sued:
(1) in the courts of the State where he is domiciled, or
(2) in another Contracting State, in the courts for the place where the policy-holder is domiciled, or
(3) if he is a co-insurer, in the courts of a Contracting State in which proceedings are brought against the leading insurer.

   An insurer who is not domiciled in a Contracting State but has a branch, agency or other establishment in one of the Contracting States shall, in disputes arising out of the operations of the branch, agency or establishment, be deemed to be domiciled in that State.

ARTICLE 9

In respect of liability insurance or insurance of immovable property, the insurer may in addition be sued in the courts for the place where the harmful event occurred. The same applies if movable and immovable property are covered by the same insurance policy and both are adversely affected by the same contingency.

ARTICLE 10

In respect of liability insurance, the insurer may also, if the law of the court permits it, be joined in proceedings which the injured party has brought against the insured.

The provisions of Articles 7, 8 and 9 shall apply to actions brought by the injured party directly against the insurer, where such direct actions are permitted.

If the law governing such direct actions provides that the policy-holder or the insured may be joined as a party to the action, the same court shall have jurisdiction over them.

ARTICLE 11

Without prejudice to the provisions of the third paragraph of Article 10, an insurer may bring proceedings only in the courts of the Contracting State in which the defendant is domiciled, irrespective of whether he is the policy-holder, the insured or a beneficiary.

The provisions of this Section shall not affect the right to bring a counterclaim in the court in which, in accordance with this Section, the original claim is pending.

ARTICLE 12

The provisions of this Section may be departed from only by an agreement on jurisdiction:
(1) which is entered into after the dispute has arisen, or
(2) which allows the policy-holder, the insured or a beneficiary to bring proceedings in courts other than those indicated in this Section, or
(3) which is concluded between a policy-holder and an insurer, both of whom are at the time of conclusion of the contract domiciled or habitually resident in the same Contracting State, and which has the effect of conferring jurisdiction on the courts of that State even if the harmful event were to occur abroad, provided that such an agreement is not contrary to the law of that State, or
(4) which is concluded with a policy-holder who is not domiciled in a Contracting State, except in so far as the insurance is compulsory or relates to immovable property in a Contracting State, or
(5) which relates to a contract of insurance in so far as it covers one or more of the risks set out in Article 12A.

ARTICLE 12A

The following are the risks referred to in Article 12 (5):
(1) Any loss of or damage to
    (a) sea-going ships, installations situated offshore or on the high seas, or aircraft, arising from perils which relate to their use for commercial purposes,
    (b) goods in transit other than passengers' baggage where the transit consists of or includes carriage by such ships or aircraft;
(2) Any liability, other than for bodily injury to passengers or loss of or damage to their baggage,

  (a) arising out of the use or operation of ships, installations or aircraft as referred to in (1) (a) above in so far as the law of the Contracting State in which such aircraft are registered does not prohibit agreements on jurisdiction regarding insurance of such risks,

  (b) for loss or damage caused by goods in transit as described in (1) (b) above;

(3) Any financial loss connected with the use or operation of ships, installations or aircraft as referred to in (1) (a) above, in particular loss of freight or charter-hire;

(4) Any risk or interest connected with any of those referred to in (1) to (3) above.

Section 4 Jursidiction over consumer contracts

ARTICLE 13

In proceedings concerning a contract concluded by a person for a purpose which can be regarded as being outside his trade or profession, hereinafter called the 'consumer', jurisdiction shall be determined by this Section, without prejudice to the provisions of Articles 4 and 5 (5), if it is:

(1) a contract for the sale of goods on instalment credit terms, or

(2) a contract for a loan repayable by instalments, or for any other form of credit, made to finance the sale of goods, or

(3) any other contract for the supply of goods or a contract for the supply of services and

  (a) in the State of the consumer's domicile the conclusion of the contract was preceded by a specific invitation addressed to him or by advertising, and

  (b) the consumer took in that State the steps necessary for the conclusion of the contract.

Where a consumer enters into a contract with a party who is not domiciled in a Contracting State but has a branch, agency or other establishment in one of the Contracting States, that party shall, in disputes arising out of the operations of the branch, agency or establishment, be deemed to be domiciled in that State.

This Section shall not apply to contracts of transport.

ARTICLE 14

A consumer may bring proceedings against the other party to a contract either in the courts of the Contracting State in which that party is domiciled or in the courts of the Contracting State in which he is himself domiciled.

Proceedings may be brought against a consumer by the other party to the contract only in the courts of the Contracting State in which the consumer is domiciled.

These provisions shall not affect the right to bring a counterclaim in the court in which, in accordance with this Section, the original claim is pending.

ARTICLE 15

The provisions of this Section may be departed from only by an agreement:

(1) which is entered into after the dispute has arisen,
     or
(2) which allows the consumer to bring proceedings in courts other than
     those indicated in this Section,
     or
(3) which is entered into by the consumer and the other party to the
     contract, both of whom are at the time of conclusion of the contract
     domiciled or habitually resident in the same Contracting State, and
     which confers jurisdiction on the courts of that State, provided that such
     an agreement is not contrary to the law of that State.

Section 5   Exclusive jurisdiction

ARTICLE 16

The following courts shall have exclusive jurisdiction, regardless of domicile:
(1) in proceedings which have as their object rights *in rem* in, or tenancies
     of, immovable property, the courts of the Contracting State in which
     the property is situated;
(2) in proceedings which have as their object the validity of the
     constitution, the nullity or the dissolution of companies or other legal
     persons or associations of natural or legal persons, or the decisions of
     their organs, the courts of the Contracting State in which the company,
     legal person or association has its seat;
(3) in proceedings which have as their object the validity of entries in public
     registers, the courts of the Contracting State in which the register is
     kept;
(4) in proceedings concerned with the registration or validity of patents,
     trade marks, designs, or other similar rights required to be deposited or
     registered, the courts of the Contracting State in which the deposit or
     registration has been applied for, has taken place or is under the terms
     of an international convention deemed to have taken place;
(5) in proceedings concerned with the enforcement of judgments, the
     courts of the Contracting State in which the judgment has been or is to
     be enforced.

Section 6   Prorogation of jurisdiction

ARTICLE 17

If the parties, one or more of whom is domiciled in a Contracting State, have
agreed that a court or the courts of a Contracting State are to have
jurisdiction to settle any disputes which have arisen or which may arise in
connection with a particular legal relationship, that court or those courts
shall have exclusive jurisdiction. Such an agreement conferring jurisdiction
shall be either in writing or evidenced in writing or, in international trade or
commerce, in a form which accords with practices in that trade or commerce
of which the parties are or ought to have been aware. Where such an
agreement is concluded by parties, none of whom is domiciled in a
Contracting State, the courts of other Contracting States shall have no
jurisdiction over their disputes unless the court or courts chosen have
declined jurisdiction.

The court or courts of a Contracting State on which a trust instrument has conferred jurisdiction shall have exclusive jurisdiction in any proceedings brought against a settlor, trustee or beneficiary, if relations between these persons or their rights or obligations under the trust are involved.

Agreements or provisions of a trust instrument conferring jurisdiction shall have no legal force if they are contrary to the provisions of Articles 12 or 15, or if the courts whose jurisdiction they purport to exclude have exclusive jurisdiction by virtue of Article 16.

If an agreement conferring jurisdiction was concluded for the benefit of only one of the parties, that party shall retain the right to bring proceedings in any other court which has jurisdiction by virtue of this Convention.

ARTICLE 18

Apart from jurisdiction derived from other provisions of this Convention, a court of a Contracting State before whom a defendant enters an appearance shall have jurisdiction. This rule shall not apply where appearance was entered solely to contest the jurisdiction, or where another court has exclusive jurisdiction by virtue of Article 16.

Section 7   Examination as to jurisdiction and admissibility

ARTICLE 19

Where a court of a Contracting State is seised of a claim which is principally concerned with a matter over which the courts of another Contracting State have exclusive jurisdiction by virtue of Article 16, it shall declare of its own motion that it has no jurisdiction.

ARTICLE 20

Where a defendant domiciled in one Contracting State is sued in a court of another Contracting State and does not enter an appearance, the court shall declare of its own motion that it has no jurisdiction unless its jurisdiction is derived from the provisions of this Convention.

The court shall stay the proceedings so long as it is not shown that the defendant has been able to receive the document instituting the proceedings or an equivalent document in sufficient time to enable him to arrange for his defence, or that all necessary steps have been taken to this end.

The provisions of the foregoing paragraph shall be replaced by those of Article 15 of the Hague Convention of 15 November 1965 on the Service Abroad of Judicial and Extrajudicial Documents in Civil or Commercial Matters, if the document instituting the proceedings or notice thereof had to be transmitted abroad in accordance with that Convention.

Section 9   Provisional, including protective, measures

ARTICLE 24

Application may be made to the courts of a Contracting State for such provisional, including protective, measures as may be available under the law of that State, even if, under this Convention, the courts of another Contracting State have jurisdiction as to the substance of the matter.

Title V

General Provisions

Article 52

In order to determine whether a party is domiciled in the Contracting State whose courts are seised of the matter, the court shall apply its internal law.

If a party is not domiciled in the State whose courts are seised of the matter, then, in order to determine whether the party is domiciled in another Contracting State, the court shall apply the law of that State.

The domicile of a party shall, however, be determined in accordance with his national law if, by that law, his domicile depends on that of another person or on the seat of an authority.

Article 53

For the purposes of this Convention, the seat of a company or other legal person or association of natural or legal persons shall be treated as its domicile. However, in order to determine that seat, the court shall apply its rules of private international law.

In order to determine whether a trust is domiciled in the Contracting State whose courts are seised of the matter, the court shall apply its rules of private international law.

Title VII

Relationship to other Conventions

Article 59

This Convention shall not prevent a Contracting State from assuming, in a convention on the recognition and enforcement of judgments, an obligation towards a third State not to recognise judgments given in other Contracting States against defendants domiciled or habitually resident in the third State where, in cases provided for in Article 4, the judgment could only be founded on a ground of jurisdiction specified in the second paragraph of Article 3.

However, a Contracting State may not assume an obligation towards a third State not to recognise a judgment given in another Contracting State by a court basing its jurisdiction on the presence within that State of property belonging to the defendant, or the seizure by the plaintiff of property situated there:
(1) if the action is brought to assert or declare proprietary or possessory rights in that property, seeks to obtain authority to dispose of it, or arises from another issue relating to such property, or,
(2) if the property constitutes the security for a debt which is the subject-matter of the action.

Schedule 2

Text of 1971 Protocol, as Amended

Article 1

The Court of Justice of the European Communities shall have jurisdiction to give rulings on the interpretation of the Convention on Jurisdiction and the

Enforcement of Judgments in Civil and Commercial Matters and of the Protocol annexed to that Convention, signed at Brussels on 27 September 1968, and also on the interpretation of the present Protocol.

The Court of Justice of the European Communities shall also have jurisdiction to give rulings on the interpretation of the Convention on the Accession of the Kingdom of Denmark, Ireland and the United Kingdom of Great Britain and Northern Ireland to the Convention of 27 September 1968 and to this Protocol.

ARTICLE 2

The following courts may request the Court of Justice to give preliminary rulings on questions of interpretation:
(1) in the United Kingdom: the House of Lords and courts to which application has been made under the second paragraph of Article 37 or under Article 41 of the Convention;
(2) the courts of the Contracting States when they are sitting in an appellate capacity;
(3) in the cases provided for in Article 37 of the Convention, the courts referred to in that Article.

ARTICLE 3

(1) Where a question of interpretation of the Convention or of one of the other instruments referred to in Article 1 is raised in a case pending before one of the courts listed in Article 2 (1), that court shall, if it considers that a decision on the question is necessary to enable it to give judgment, request the Court of Justice to give a ruling thereon.

(2) Where such a question is raised before any court referred to in Article 2 (2) or (3), that court may, under the conditions laid down in paragraph (1), request the Court of Justice to give a ruling thereon.

ARTICLE 4

(1) The competent authority of a Contracting State may request the Court of Justice to give a ruling on a question of interpretation of the Convention or of one of the other instruments referred to in Article 1 if judgments given by courts of that State conflict with the interpretation given either by the Court of Justice or in a judgment of one of the courts of another Contracting State referred to in Article 2 (1) or (2). The provisions of this paragraph shall apply only to judgments which have become res judicata.

(2) The interpretation given by the Court of Justice in response to such a request shall not affect the judgments which gave rise to a request for interpretation.

(3) The Procurators-General of the Courts of Cassation of the Contracting States, or any other authority designated by a Contracting State, shall be entitled to request the Court of Justice for a ruling on interpretation in accordance with paragraph (1).

(4) The Registrar of the Court of Justice shall give notice of the request to the Contracting States, to the Commission and to the Council of the European Communities; they shall then be entitled within two months of the notification to submit statements of case or written observations to the Court.

NOTE

1. Introduction

In accordance with article 220 of the Treaty of Rome a Convention on jurisdiction and the enforcement of judgments in civil and commercial matters was signed by the six original member states of the EEC in September 1968 and came into force between them on 1 February 1973, together with a Protocol on Interpretation of 1971. Article 63 of the Convention declares that any state which becomes a member of the EEC must accept the Convention (with or without adjustments), and this was a term of the United Kingdom's accession to the EEC. Negotiations between the original six and the three new member states proceeded for six years in Brussels and resulted in an Accession Convention which was signed in October 1978. The accession of Greece was agreed in October 1982 with a minimum of amendments.

The United Kingdom, of course, took no part in drafting the original Convention, which reflects concepts and attitudes peculiar to the civil law. Many changes designed to make it more palatable for United Kingdom consumption were effected in the Accession Convention, but not so many as the United Kingdom would have wished.

Part I of the Civil Jurisdiction and Judgments Act 1982 gives effect in the law of the United Kingdom to the Brussels Convention of 1968 as amended by the Accession Convention of 1978 ('the Convention'). The Act sets out in Schedule 1 the English text of the Convention and its Protocol, and in Schedule 2 the English text of the 1971 Protocol on Interpretation, both of which are to have the force of law in the United Kingdom: s 2 (1). This Note is concerned with the jurisdictional provisions of the Convention. Its provisions on recognition and enforcement of judgments are noted in chapter 7, p 193 below.

2. Interpretation

Any question as to the meaning or effect of the Convention shall, if not referred to the European Court, be determined in accordance with the principles laid down by that court, of which judicial notice shall be taken: s 3 (1) and (2). The reports of Mr Jenard on the original Convention and of Professor Schlosser on that Convention as amended by the Accession Convention may be considered by United Kingdom courts in interpreting the Convention: s 3 (3). They are published in the *Official Journal of the European Communities*, 1979 No C59, at pp 1 and 71 respectively. The Jenard Report has had great influence on the interpretation of the Convention in national courts and in the European Court. The Schlosser Report will have a similar influence. It has great significance for the United Kingdom because many of the amendments sought by the United Kingdom during the accession negotiations were given effect to by 'understandings' recorded in the Report and not by formal amendments to the Convention.

The 1971 Protocol sets out the conditions under which references may be made to the European Court for a preliminary ruling on the interpretation of the Convention where a national court considers that a decision on the question is necessary to enable it to give judgment: Sch 2, arts 2 and 3. In England, a court sitting in an appellate capacity *may* make such a reference and the House of Lords *must* do so. The European Commission and the member states are entitled to make submissions to the court: Sch 2, art 4 (4); the United Kingdom (as well as other states and the Commission) has sometimes availed itself of this facility.

Courts of the six original contracting states have referred several cases on the Convention to the European Court, which has given judgment in some 30 cases. Since the European Court has the last word on the interpretation of the Convention, we print some of these cases in this chapter and in chapter 7. But, as the reader will see, the European Court is not a court which articulates its reasons very clearly. Nor of course is it bound by its own decisions.

An important question which has arisen several times is whether the Court should interpret the Convention according to an independent convention concept or according to national law, ie the law of the national court requesting the preliminary ruling. The Court has nearly always preferred the former alternative: see Case 29/76: *LTU v Eurocontrol* [1976] ECR 1541, [1977] 1 CMLR 88, which is the leading case. It is obvious that this is the only way in which the Convention can be made to mean the same thing in all contracting states. Only in one case has the Court preferred to interpret the Convention in accordance with national law: Case 12/76: *Tessili v Dunlop AG* [1976] ECR 1473, [1977] 1 CMLR 26, p 109 below.

3. Scope of the Convention

The scope of the Convention is very wide: it applies to almost the whole range of 'civil and commercial matters', with a few exceptions listed in article 1. With reference to 'rights in property arising out of a matrimonial relationship', see Case 143/78: *De Cavel v De Cavel (No 1)* [1979] ECR 1055, [1979] 2 CMLR 547, p 103 below. The exception for arbitration means that such matters as judicial control over arbitrators, the enforcement of arbitration awards and (in the view of the United Kingdom government) the validity and effect of arbitration agreements are not within the Convention: see Schlosser, para 61. If the main proceedings are outside the scope of the Convention, ancillary claims may fall within it, eg claims for maintenance in divorce proceedings: Case 120//79: *De Cavel v De Cavel (No 2)* [1980] ECR 731, [1980] 3 CMLR 1.

4. General scheme of the Convention

The primary basis of jurisdiction is the 'domicile' of the defendant within the contracting state. In addition there are other special bases of jurisdiction; and there are certain cases where specified courts have exclusive jurisdiction regardless of domicile. Provision is also made for submission to the jurisdiction by contract or appearance, and for certain other procedural matters, including lis alibi pendens and jurisdiction to order provisional or protective measures. As a general rule the domicile of the plaintiff is irrelevant: he need not even be domiciled in a contracting state. There are exceptions in articles 5 (2), 8 (1) (2) and 14 (1).

The jurisdictional rules of the Convention make two important departures of principle from English law as it was before the Act came into force. First, English courts cannot exercise jurisdiction over defendants domiciled in another contracting state merely by virtue of the temporary presence of the defendant in England at the time of service of the writ. Secondly, where a defendant is outside England at that time and the English court has jurisdiction under the Convention, service of the writ outside England is no longer a matter for the discretion of the court but a matter of right: see RSC Ord 11, rule 1 (2), p 64 above.

5. Domicile

(a) *Individuals.* The Convention made no attempt to define 'domicile' although it is the primary basis of jurisdiction. Article 52 (1) provides that in order to determine whether a party is domiciled in the contracting state whose courts are seised of the matter, the court shall apply its internal law. The traditional concept of domicile in English law would have been a quite unsuitable criterion for jurisdiction under the Convention, not only because it is sometimes so artificial and so difficult to ascertain, but also because it differs so much from the concept of domicile in the six original contracting states, where it means something much the same as habitual residence. Section 41 of the Act provides a new definition of domicile which applies only for the purposes of the Act and the Convention. The effect is broadly as follows: an individual is domiciled in the United Kingdom (or a part of it) if he is resident in and has a substantial connection with the United Kingdom (or that part); if he is resident in the United Kingdom but has no substantial connection with any part of the United Kingdom he is domiciled in that part in which he is resident. Substantial connection is presumed from residence for three months or more, unless the contrary is proved.

It is sometimes necessary to determine in what place an individual is domiciled, eg for the purposes of article 5 (2) (maintenance), 6 (1) (co-defendants) or 8 (2) (insurance). Section 41 (4) provides that an individual is domiciled in a particular place in the United Kingdom if he is domiciled in the part of the United Kingdom in which that place is situated and is resident in that place.

If the defendant is not domiciled in any part of the United Kingdom, the English court may have to decide whether he is domiciled in another contracting state in order to determine whether the Convention applies. The effect of article 52 (2) is that in such circumstances the English court is to apply the law of that other state. But if the party is not domiciled in that other state by its law, or is alleged to be domiciled in a non-contracting state, then his domicile will be determined by English law as the lex fori, which for this purpose is set out in section 41 (7) of the Act. This applies similar tests to those in the preceding subsections, except that there is no presumption from length of residence.

It would perhaps have been better to have defined domicile for the purposes of the Convention simply as habitual residence. That would have avoided the rather complicated definitions in section 41. It would also have avoided adding one more jurisdictional factor to those already used by English law, ie domicile in the traditional sense, ordinary residence and habitual residence. It seems no objection that the Convention sometimes contemplates that domicile differs from habitual residence, eg in articles 5 (2), 15 (3) and 59. Unfortunately the editors of this book found themselves in the minority when this question was discussed by the Lord Chancellor's Working Party on Foreign Judgments. You can imagine our chagrin, gentle reader, when some years later we read a case in the European Court in which throughout its judgment the court used the phrase 'habitual residence' as synonymous with domicile: Case 166/80: *Klomps v Michel* [1981] ECR 1593, [1982] 2 CMLR 773.

(b) *Corporations and associations.* Article 53 (1) provides that the 'seat' of a company or other legal person or association shall be treated as its domicile, and that in order to determine that seat the court shall apply its rules of private international law. Because the 'seat' of a corporation is a term unknown in the law of the United Kingdom, section 42 (3) and (4) of the Act provide for the determination of the seat of corporations and associations. It will be noticed that under section 42 (4) a company incorporated under the Companies Acts with its registered office in England will have its seat not only in England but also in Scotland if its central management and control is exercised there, and also in Northern Ireland if it has a place of business there. Section 42 (5) provides for those cases where it is necessary to determine the 'place' of the seat. Sections 42 (6) and (7) provide for the seat of a corporation or association which does not have its seat in the United Kingdom.

(c) *Trusts.* Article 52 (3) provides that in determining the domicile of a trust, the court shall apply its rules of private international law. Section 45 of the Act provides that a trust is domiciled in a part of the United Kingdom if the system of law of that part is the system of law with which the trust has its closest and most real connection. Of course it is artificial and novel to speak of the domicile of a trust at all. But continental lawyers seem to think that a trust is some kind of unincorporated association; and it seemed best to go along with them where it did no obvious harm.

6. General jurisdiction

Section 1 of Title II of the Convention (articles 2–4) sets out the general rule of jurisdiction. First, persons domiciled in a contracting state should be sued in that state, and may be sued in another contracting state only by virtue of the special rules in Sections 2–6: arts 2 (1), 3 (1). Secondly, the Convention blacklists certain 'exorbitant' bases of jurisdiction which may not be used against persons domiciled in a contracting state: art 3 (2). But as against a person not domiciled in a contracting state, the jurisdiction of courts of contracting states is, apart from the exclusive jurisdictional provisions of article 16, subject to national law: art 4. This means that as against, eg a New York resident, the rule of jurisdiction based on service of the writ on the defendant during his temporary presence in England and the rules in Order 11 will continue to apply.

7 Special jurisdiction

Section 2 (articles 5–6) sets out the special bases of jurisdiction under the Convention. These are additional to the primary basis of domicile. They only apply if the defendant is domiciled in a contracting state other than the one in which he is sued. For if he is domiciled in that state, jurisdiction will be derived from his domicile there under article 2, and there is no need for any special jurisdiction; while if he is not domiciled in any contracting state, the Convention does not apply and jurisdiction depends on national law, ie in England on service of the writ on the defendant during his temporary presence in England or on the rules in Order 11.

The effect on the jurisdiction of the English court of the more important of these special bases of jurisdiction is as follows.

(1) *Contract.* In matters relating to a contract, the English court has jurisdiction if England is the place of performance of the obligation in question: art 5 (1). This very important article has given rise to great difficulty in interpretation, partly because there were significant discrepancies between the different language versions, all of them equally authentic, but mainly because it is not drafted with sufficient precision. In Case 14/76: *De Bloos v Bouyer* [1976] ECR 1497, [1977] 1 CMLR 60, p 105 below, the European Court held, in the context of an exclusive sales and distribution agreement, that 'the obligation in question' meant the obligation which is the basis of the plaintiff's claim. But in Case 133/81: *Ivenel v Schwab* [1982] ECR 1891, p 106 below, the Court adopted a different approach in the context of a contract of employment. The Court, much influenced by the doctrine of 'characteristic performance' in the EEC Convention on the Law Applicable to Contractual Obligations (p 459 below), though it is not yet in force, held that the obligation in question was the one which was characteristic of the contract, namely, the obligation to work.

In Case 12/76: *Tessili v Dunlop AG* [1976] ECR 1473, [1977] 1 CMLR 26, p 109 below, the Court held that it was for the national court, applying its own conflict rules, to determine where the obligation is to be performed. But this case was the first case on the Convention to reach the European Court, and the Court preferred to interpret the Convention in accordance with national law and not in accordance with an independent Convention concept. Since then the current of authority has flowed strongly in the opposite direction, and it may be that the Court will one day depart from its ruling in *Tessili v Dunlop AG*.

If the parties agree on England as the place of performance, whether in writing or orally, that agreement will be effective to confer jurisdiction, at any rate if the agreement is not a sham: Case 56/79: *Zelger v Salinitri* [1980] ECR 89, [1980] 2 CMLR 635, p 110 below.

This head of jurisdiction applies even if the defendant disputes the existence of the contract: Case 38/81: *Effer SpA v Kantner* [1982] ECR 825, p 111 below.

(2) *Maintenance.* Article 5 (2) allows a maintenance creditor to sue in the courts of the place where he is domiciled or habitually resident. This is considered in chapter 11, p 342 below.

(3) *Tort.* In matters relating to a tort, the English court has jurisdiction if England is

the place where the harmful event occurred: art 5 (3). The place where the harmful event occurred is, at the option of the plaintiff, either the place where the wrongful act occurred or the place where the damage was suffered: Case 21/76: *Bier BV v Mines de Potasse d'Alsace* [1976] ECR 1735, p 113 below.

(4) *Civil claims in criminal proceedings.* Article 5 (4) gives the English court hearing a criminal charge against a defendant domiciled in another contracting state jurisdiction to order him to make restitution under the Criminal Justice Act 1972.

(5) *Branches and agencies.* The English court has jurisdiction as regards a dispute arising out of the operations of a branch, agency or other establishment if it is situated in England: art 5 (5). The tests for determining whether an entity is a branch or agency are whether it is subject to the direction and control of the parent body and has the appearance of permanence: Case 14/76: *De Bloos v Bouyer* [1976] ECR 1497, [1977] 1 CMLR 60; Case 139/80: *Blanckaert & Willems PVBA v Trost* [1981] ECR 819, [1982] 2 CMLR 1. The dispute must arise out of the operations of the branch, such as contracts into which it has entered: Case 33/78: *Somafer SA v Saar-Ferngas AG* [1978] ECR 2183, [1979] 1 CMLR 490. This head of jurisdiction was intended to apply to disputes between the branch and third parties, not to disputes between the branch and the parent body: *De Bloos v Bouyer,* above, at 1519.

(6) *Trusts.* The English court has jurisdiction in proceedings relating to a trust against a person domiciled in another contracting state in his capacity as settlor, trustee or beneficiary, if the trust is domiciled in England: art 5 (6). The trust must have been created by statute or by a written instrument; resulting or constructive trusts are not included. Nor are trusts arising under wills or intestacies, because wills and succession are outside the scope of the Convention: art 1 (1); Schlosser, para 52. Article 5 (6) applies to disputes relating to the internal relationships of the trust, such as disputes between beneficiaries or between trustees and beneficiaries, and not to disputes relating to its external relations, such as the enforcement by third parties of contracts made by trustees: Schlosser, para 120. As to the domicile of a trust, see p 96 above.

(7) *Co-defendants.* A person domiciled in another contracting state may be sued in England where he is one of a number of defendants, if one of the other defendants is domiciled in England: art 6 (1). This jurisdiction is analogous to the 'necessary and proper' party' provisions of RSC Ord 11, r 1 (1) (c) (p 63 above). But there is no room for discretion under article 6 (1), and it allows a plaintiff to sue a foreign defendant on the ground that England is the domicile of another, less important, defendant. There must however be a connection between the claims made against each of the defendants: Jenard, p 26.

(8) *Third parties.* The English court has jurisdiction over a person as a third party, in an action on a warranty or guarantee or in any other third party proceedings, if it has jurisdiction in the original proceedings, unless these were instituted solely with the object of removing the third party from the jurisdiction of the court which would be competent in his case: art 6 (2).

(9) *Counterclaims.* The English court has jurisdiction over a counterclaim arising from the same contract or facts on which the original claim was based if the original claim is pending in England: art 6 (3).

8. Jurisdiction in matters relating to insurance

The original Convention made special provision in articles 7–12 for jurisdiction in matters of insurance in order to protect the policy-holder, the supposedly weaker party. As Schlosser says (para 136), the accession of the United Kingdom introduced a totally new dimension to the insurance business as it had hitherto been practised within the EEC. This was because the London insurance market has such a large share of world-wide insurance business, particularly in the international insurance of large risks. In such business the policy-holder is likely to be a powerful multinational corporation which does not need the protection which the original Convention sought to give to an individual policy-holder insuring his house, his car or his life.

During the accession negotiations the United Kingdom sought to adapt the Convention to meet the new situation, and some changes were made. The result is the very complicated rules now contained in articles 7–12A (which have to be read with section 44 of the Act). These provisions are exclusive except that they are without prejudice to articles 4 and 5 (5). It will be seen that they are heavily weighted in favour of the policy-holder. He can sue the insurer in the courts for the place where he is domiciled as well as in the courts of the insurer's domicile: art 8. In liability insurance or the insurance of a house or its contents, he can also sue in the courts for the place where the harmful event occurred: art 9. But the policy-holder may be sued only in the courts of the contracting state in which he is domiciled: art 11. Moreover, article 12 (1)–(3) severely restricts the power of the parties (ie in practice the insurer) to contract out of these rules by means of a jurisdiction agreement in the contract of insurance. Articles 12 (4) and (5) and 12A (which were added by the Accession Convention) relax these restrictions if the policy-holder is not domiciled in a contracting state, or in the case of the large risks listed in article 12A.

9. Jurisdiction over consumer contracts

Section 4 (articles 13–15) of the Convention contains special provisions for jurisdiction over consumer contracts in order to protect the consumer, the economically weaker party. These provisions are exclusive except that they are without prejudice to articles 4 and 5 (5). 'Consumer' and 'consumer contracts' are defined in article 13 (1). The effect of articles 13 (2) and 14 and of section 44 of the Act is broadly that the consumer can only be sued in England if he is domiciled there; but the consumer can sue the other party if the defendant or the consumer is domiciled in England, or if the defendant has a branch or agency in England and the dispute arises out of the operations of the branch. Article 15 severely restricts the power of the parties (in practice the seller or lender) to contract out of these rules by means of a jurisdiction agreement in the contract.

10. Exclusive jurisdiction

Article 16 of the Convention provides for cases where courts in contracting states are to have exclusive jurisdiction, regardless of the parties' domicile. This exclusive jurisdiction applies even if the defendant is not domiciled in a contracting state: art 4. The five cases of exclusive jurisdiction listed in article 16 are as follows.

(1) *Immovable property.* The expression 'proceedings which have as their object rights in rem in or tenancies of' immovable property situated in England will not be easy for English courts to apply. Such proceedings are those involving title or possession, and not those for damage caused to an immovable; nor do they include actions on the purely contractual aspects of a property transaction: Schlosser, paras 163, 169–172. As to leases and tenancies, article 16 (1) includes actions for forfeiture or possession and disputes between lessors and lessees as to the existence or interpretation of a lease: Case 73/77: *Sanders v Van der Putte* [1977] ECR 2383, [1978] 1 CMLR 331; but probably not actions for rent: Jenard, p 35.

(2) *Corporations.* Article 16 (2) does not apply to proceedings for the winding-up of insolvent companies, which are outside the scope of the Convention: art 1 (2). But it does include proceedings for the winding-up or reconstruction of solvent companies: Schlosser, paras 57–58. Section 43 of the Act contains special provisions for the determination of the 'seat' of a corporation for the purposes of article 16 (2).

(3) *Public registers.* Article 16 (3) is not likely to be of practical significance in

England except in connection with proceedings relating to registered land, most of which would in any event come within article 16 (1).

(4) *Industrial property rights:* article 16 (4).

(5) *Judgments.* Article 16 (5) is not likely to be of great practical importance in England, but it may have the effect of preventing English courts from enjoining the enforcement of a judgment in the courts of another contracting state.

11. Jurisdiction agreements

Article 17 sets out the circumstances in which an agreement on jurisdiction will be effective. The agreement must either be in writing or, in international trade or commerce, in a form which accords with practices in that trade or commerce of which the parties are or ought to have been aware. The formula relating to international trade or commerce was added by the Accession Convention (at the instance of the United Kingdom) to overcome the very restrictive interpretation of the requirement of writing adopted by the European Court in Case 24/76: *Salotti v Rüwa* [1976] ECR 1831, [1977] 1 CMLR 345 and Case 25/76: *Segoura v Bonakdarian* [1976] ECR 1851, [1977] 1 CMLR 361. Article 17 applies even if the courts of more than one contracting state are contemplated by the contract: Case 23/78: *Meeth v Glacetal SARL* [1978] ECR 2133, [1979] 1 CMLR 520, p 115 below.

If one or more of the parties is domiciled in a contracting state and they have chosen the jurisdiction of a court in a contracting state, that court has exclusive jurisdiction. If neither of the parties is domiciled in a contracting state, the courts of other contracting states have no jurisdiction unless the court chosen has declined jurisdiction. The defendant may waive the clause, eg by submitting to the jurisdiction of another court: Case 150/80: *Elefanten Schuh GmbH v Jacqmain* [1981] ECR 1671, [1982] 3 CMLR 1, p 117 below.

National law may not invalidate jurisdiction agreements which comply with the formal requirements of article 17: *Elefanten Schuh v Jacqmain*, above.

Article 17 contains similar provisions relating to jurisdiction clauses in trust instruments.

12. Submission

Article 18 provides that, apart from jurisdiction derived from other provisions of the Convention, a court of a contracting state before whom a defendant enters an appearance shall have jurisdiction. This rule does not apply where appearance was entered solely to contest the jurisdiction, or where another court has exclusive jurisdiction under article 16. But it does apply where the parties have chosen another court under article 17: Case 150/80: *Elefanten Schuh GmbH v Jacqmain* [1981] ECR 1671, [1982] 3 CMLR 1, p 117 below. The rule that appearance solely to contest the jurisdiction does not amount to submission has to be flexibly applied so as to allow for different procedural rules in the contracting states. Otherwise, under some systems of law (not English law: see RSC Ord 12, r 8) the defendant might be barred from contesting the merits if his plea to the jurisdiction failed: *Elefanten Schuh v Jacqmain*, above.

13. Examination as to jurisdiction

Articles 19 and 20 require national courts to investigate of their own motion whether they have jurisdiction under the Convention if the case is principally concerned with a matter over which the courts of another contracting state have exclusive jurisdiction under article 16, or if the defendant is domiciled in another contracting state and does not enter an appearance. Moreover, the court must stay the proceedings if it is not shown that the defendant had been able to receive the document instituting the proceedings in sufficient time to enable him to arrange for his defence. These requirements that the court must act on its own motion are a novelty in English law with its adversary procedure. They have had to be implemented by detailed Rules of Court: see the amendments to Order 6, rule 7 and to Order 13, rule 7 made by RSC (Amendment No 2) 1983 (SI 1983/1181).

The Hague Convention of 1965 mentioned in article 20 (3) is in force between the United Kingdom and all other member states of the EEC except the Republic of Ireland. It is implemented in England by RSC Ord 11, r 5.

14. Lis alibi pendens and related actions

Articles 21–23 deal with these matters; they are printed in chapter 6, pp 140–141 below.

15. Provisional and protective measures

Article 24 provides that application may be made to the courts of a contracting state for such provisional, including protective, measures as may be available under the law of that state, even if, under the Convention, the courts of another contracting state have jurisdiction as to the substance of the matter. This article applies only to provisional measures in cases within the scope of the Convention: Case 25/81: *W v H* [1982] ECR 1189.

Typical of the protective measures contemplated by article 24 is the saisie conservatoire of French law, under which French courts have drastic powers to seize the defendant's property, put it under seal or freeze his bank account, even when the property or account is situated outside France. In that case of course the order of the French court, to be effective, would need to be enforced in the State where the property or account is situated. The courts of all the other original member states have similar powers. The efficacy of such protective measures frequently depends on the element of surprise, so that they are often made ex parte and without notice to the defendant. But then they cannot be enforced under the Convention in other contracting states, because article 27 (2) provides that a judgment shall not be recognised if it was given in default of appearance, if the defendant was not duly served with the document instituting the proceedings in sufficient time for him to arrange for his defence. See Case 125/79: *Denilauler v SNC Couchet Frères* [1981] ECR 1553, [1981] 1 CMLR 62, p 198 below, where article 27 (2) was applied to orders for protective measures. Article 24 meets this situation by enabling protective measures to be applied for in eg the courts of the state where the property is situated. It may be important in the interests of the plaintiff to achieve a surprise effect; but it is equally important in the interests of the defendant (and of third parties) that such measures should be rapidly brought to the notice of all concerned and that they should have the opportunity to take immediate countermeasures. See *Denilauler v SNC Couchet Frères*, pp 198–199 below.

From our point of view, perhaps the most important 'protective measures' known to English law are Anton Piller orders[20a] and Mareva injunctions,[1] both of which are of recent origin. An Anton Piller order is an order for the inspection of premises to discover important documents or valuable chattels to which the plaintiff may be entitled. Such an order has been made even where the premises in question were situated abroad.[2] The Mareva injunction was invented by the Court of Appeal in 1975 and subsequently developed and refined. It is an interlocutory injunction restraining a defendant from removing his assets out of the jurisdiction pending trial. But it was held by the House of Lords in *The Siskina*[3] that a Mareva injunction could not be granted where the defendant is not amenable to the jurisdiction of the court independently of the claim for an injunction.

20a After *Anton Piller KG v Manufacturing Processes Ltd* [1976] Ch 55, [1976] 1 All ER 779.
1 After *Mareva Compania Naviera SA v International Bulkcarriers SA* [1980] 1 All ER 213, [1975] 2 Lloyd's Rep 509.
2 *Cook Industries Inc v Galliher* [1979] Ch 439, [1978] 3 All ER 945.
3 [1979] AC 210, [1977] 3 All ER 803.

Strictly speaking there was no need to alter English law as laid down by the House of Lords in this case, for article 24 only applies to 'such protective measures as may be available under the law of' the state applied to. But it would have been contrary to the spirit of the Convention, and would have looked extremely odd, if courts in England and Northern Ireland were the only ones in the EEC which had no power to order protective measures unless they had jurisdiction in the main action. Accordingly section 25 (1) of the 1982 Act reverses the decision of the House of Lords in *The Siskina* and in effect restores that of the Court of Appeal (p 120 below) in cases where the main proceedings have been or are to be commenced in another contracting state or another part of the United Kingdom. Section 24 deals with cases where the jurisdiction of the court is doubtful, rather than non-existent.

16. Jurisdiction within the United Kingdom

Section 16 of the Act applies a modified form of the jurisdictional provisions of the Convention as between the different parts of the United Kingdom. This is set out in Schedule 4. It applies where (a) the subject-matter of the proceedings is within the scope of the Convention, and (b) the defendant is domiciled in the United Kingdom or the proceedings are of a kind mentioned in article 16 (ie exclusive jurisdiction): s 16 (1). In interpreting any provision in Schedule 4 the court is to have regard to any relevant principles laid down by the European Court on Title II of the Convention and to the Jenard and Schlosser reports: s 16 (3).

The principal differences between the rules set out in Schedule 4 and those of the Convention set out in Schedule 1, Title II, are as follows.
(1) The version of article 5 (3) in Schedule 4 makes it clear that the jurisdiction applies where the tort is merely threatened.
(2) There is a new article 5 (8), the effect of which is to give the English court jurisdiction in proceedings to enforce a debt secured on immovable property or to determine proprietary or possessory rights or rights of security in or over movable property, in each case where the property is situated in England.
(3) There is a new article 5A which confers jurisdiction, in proceedings which have as their object a decision of an organ of a company or association, on the courts of that part of the United Kingdom in which the company or association has its seat. The 'seat' will be determined in accordance with section 43.
(4) There is no provision for insurance contracts, which therefore come within the general rule of domicile or the special provisions of articles 5 (1) (contract) or 5 (5) (branch or agency).
(5) Article 13 (consumer contracts) is modified so as to exclude the references to advertising, and so as to make it clear that it does not apply to insurance.
(6) In article 16 (exclusive jurisdiction) there is no provision for patents or other industrial property rights. Otherwise, all patent litigation would have had to take place in England, because the Patent Office for the whole United Kingdom is situated in London.
(7) In article 17 (jurisdiction agreements) there is no requirement as to writing.
(8) The provisions concerning lis pendens and related actions are omitted.

The effect of Schedule 4, article 3 is that English courts can no longer exercise jurisdiction based on the service of the writ on the defendant during his temporary presence in England or on Order 11, if the defendant is domiciled in Scotland or Northern Ireland.

Section 10 of the Act deals with two miscellaneous allocations of jurisdiction in proceedings brought in the United Kingdom by virtue of article 5 (6) (trust domiciled in the United Kingdom) or of article 14 (1) (consumer domiciled in the United Kingdom).

For a comprehensive account of the Act and the Convention, see Collins *The Civil Jurisdiction and Judgments Act 1982* (1983).

The phrase 'rights in property arising out of a matrimonial relationship' in article 1 of the Convention includes not only property arrangements specifically envisaged by certain national systems but also any proprietary relationships resulting directly from the matrimonial relationship or its dissolution.

De Cavel v De Cavel (No. 1) Case 143/78: [1979] ECR 1055, [1979] 2 CMLR 547 (European Court of Justice)

Request by the Bundesgerichtshof (Supreme Federal Court of Germany) for a preliminary ruling.

Mr and Mrs De Cavel were resident in Frankfurt am Main, Germany. They had a flat there and also one in Cannes, France. The husband was a French citizen. The wife was of German origin. The husband instituted divorce proceedings against his wife before the Tribunal de Grande Instance of Paris. He alleged that his wife had removed from the flat in Cannes some valuable carpets which were his property, and had also removed a number of objects from the flat in Frankfurt. He applied to the Tribunal de Grande Instance for protective measures (saisie conservatoire). The Judge in Matrimonial Matters of the Tribunal ordered first the placing of seals on the furniture and effects in the flat in Frankfurt and on a safe deposit box hired in the wife's name at a bank in Frankfurt, and secondly the freezing of two accounts in the wife's name with banks in Frankfurt. That order was made ex parte in accordance with French law. The husband applied to the Landgericht (lower regional court) of Frankfurt for enforcement of the order under article 31 of the Convention. His application was rejected because he had not produced the documents required by article 47 (1) establishing that the French judgment had been served on the wife. He appealed to the Oberlandesgericht (higher regional court) of Frankfurt which also refused to enforce the order on the different ground that since the interim measures were made in the course of divorce proceedings they were measures relating to the status of natural persons and so fell outside the scope of the Convention under article 1. In the view of the Oberlandesgericht it made no difference that the object of the measures was to protect interests of a proprietary nature, since article 1 refers to 'rights in property arising out of a matrimonial relationship'. The husband appealed to the Bundesgerichtshof, which referred to the European Court the questions (1) whether the Convention applies to an ancillary order made in proceedings in which the substantive claim is outside the scope of the Convention, ie divorce proceedings; and if so (2) whether the measures ordered by the French judge in the present case related to 'the status of natural persons' or to 'rights in property arising out of a matrimonial relationship' within the meaning of article 1.

The Court delivered the following judgment:

The Commission and the appellant argue that the answer should be given that the proceedings referred to fall within the scope of the Convention, while the governments of the United Kingdom and of the Federal Republic of Germany and the respondent contend that the answer should be that the Convention is inapplicable.

It appears from the file on the case that the matters in dispute before the German courts concern, on the one hand, the connection between the measures ordered by the French judge of family matters and the divorce proceedings and, on the other, the question whether the Convention is applicable in view of the proprietary nature of the protective measures in question.

In the words of article 1, the Convention is to apply in 'civil and commercial matters'.

Nevertheless, because of the specific nature of certain matters, including 'the status or legal capacity of natural persons, rights in property arising out of a matrimonial relationship, wills and succession', disputes relating to such matters are excluded from its scope.

The enforced settlement on a provisional basis of proprietary legal relationships between spouses in the course of proceedings for divorce is closely linked to the grounds for the divorce and the personal situation of the spouses or any children of the marriage and is, for that reason, inseparable from questions relating to the status of persons raised by the dissolution of the matrimonial relationship and from the settlement of rights in property arising out of the matrimonial relationship.

Consequently, the term 'rights in property arising out of a matrimonial relationship' includes not only property arrangements specifically and exclusively envisaged by certain national legal systems` in the case of marriage but also any proprietary relationships resulting directly from the matrimonial relationship or the dissolution thereof.

Disputes relating to the assets of spouses in the course of proceedings for divorce may therefore, depending on the circumstances, concern or be closely connected with:

(1) questions relating to the status of persons; or
(2) proprietary legal relationships between spouses resulting directly from the matrimonial relationship or the dissolution thereof; or
(3) proprietary legal relations existing between them which have no connection with the marriage.

Whereas disputes of the latter category fall within the scope of the Convention, those relating to the first two categories must be excluded therefrom.

The foregoing considerations are applicable to measures relating to the property of spouses whether they are provisional or definitive in nature.

As provisional protective measures relating to property—such as the affixing of seals or the freezing of assests—can serve to safeguard a variety of rights, their inclusion in the scope of the Convention is determined not by their own nature but by the nature of rights which they serve to protect.

Furthermore, in relation to the matters covered by the Convention, no legal basis is to be found therein for drawing a distinction between provisional and definitive measures.

That conclusion is not affected by article 24 of the Convention whereby: 'Application may be made to the courts of a contracting state for such provisional, including protective, measures as may be available under the law of that State, even if, under this Convention, the courts of another contracting state have jurisdiction as to the substance of the matter'.

In fact that provision expressly envisages the case of provisional measures in a contracting state where 'under this Convention' the courts of another contracting state have jurisdiction as to the substance of the matter and it cannot, therefore, be relied on to bring within the scope of the Convention provisional or protective measures relating to matters which are excluded therefrom.

It may therefore be concluded that judicial decisions authorising provisional protective measures—such as the placing under seal or the freezing of the assets of the spouses—in the course of proceedings for divorce do not fall within the scope of the Convention as defined in article 1 thereof if those measures concern or are closely connected with either questions of the status of the persons involved in the divorce proceedings or propriety legal relations resulting directly from the matrimonial relationship or the dissolution thereof.[4]

The 'obligation in question' in article 5 (1) of the Convention generally means the obligation which is the basis of the plaintiff's claim.

De Bloos v Bouyer Case 14/76: [1976] ECR 1497, [1977] 1 CMLR 60 (European Court of Justice)

Request for a preliminary ruling by the Cour d'Appel of Mons, Belgium.

The French company Bouyer granted the Belgian company De Bloos the exclusive right to distribute their products in Belgium, Luxembourg and the Belgian Congo (now Zaire). De Bloos complained of a unilateral breach of the contract without notice by Bouyer and brought an action against Bouyer in the Tribunal de Commerce of Tournai, Belgium, seeking dissolution of the contract and damages. Bouyer objected that the court had no jurisdiction. The court upheld the objection. De Bloos appealed to the Cour d'Appel of Mons. That court formulated the following question for the European Court: In an action brought by the grantee of an exclusive sales concession against the grantor in which he claims that the latter has infringed the exclusive concession, may the term 'obligation' in article 5 (1) of the Convention be applied to the obligation in dispute or forming the basis of the legal proceedings?

The Court delivered the following judgment:

Under article 5 (1) of the Convention, a person domiciled in a contracting state may, in another contracting state, be sued 'in matters relating to a contract, in the courts for the place of performance of the obligation in question'.

As stated in its preamble, the Convention is intended to determine the international jurisdiction of the courts of the contracting states, to facilitate the recognition and to introduce an expeditious procedure for securing the enforcement of judgments.

These objectives imply the need to avoid, so far as possible, creating a situation in which a number of courts have jurisdiction in respect of one and the same contract.

---

4 This was an enforcement case and therefore properly belongs to chapter 7, but it is included here because it illustrates one of the matters excluded from the scope of the Convention by article 1.

  The European Court has subsequently held that provisional or protective measures cannot be enforced in another contracting state if they were made ex parte without the defendant being given an opportunity to be heard: Case 125/79: *Denilauler v Couchet Frères* [1980] ECR 1553, [1981] 1 CMLR 62, p 198 below.

Because of this, article 5 (1) of the Convention cannot be interpreted as referring to any obligation whatsoever arising under the contract in question.

On the contrary, the word 'obligation' in the article refers to the contractual obligation forming the basis of the legal proceedings.

It follows that for the purposes of determining the place of performance within the meaning of article 5, quoted above, the obligation to be taken into account is that which corresponds to the contractual right on which the plaintiff's action is based.

In a case where the plaintiff asserts the right to be paid damages or seeks a dissolution of the contract on the ground of the wrongful conduct of the other party, the obligation referred to in article 5 (1) is still that which arises under the contract and the non-performance of which is relied upon to support such claims.

For these reasons, the answer to the first question must be that, in disputes in which the grantee of an exclusive sales concession charges the grantor with having infringed the exclusive concession, the word 'obligation' contained in article 5 (1) of the Convention refers to the obligation forming the basis of the legal proceedings, namely the contractual obligation of the grantor which corresponds to the contractual right relied upon by the grantee in support of the application.

In disputes concerning the consequences of the infringement by the grantor of a contract conferring an exclusive concession, such as the payment of damages or the dissolution of the contract, the obligation to which reference must be made for the purposes of applying article 5 (1) of the Convention is that which the contract imposes on the grantor and the non-performance of which is relied upon by the grantee in support of the application for damages or for the dissolution of the contract.

In the case of actions for the payment of compensation by way of damages, it is for the national court to ascertain whether, under the law applicable to the contract, an independent contractual obligation or an obligation replacing the unperformed contractual obligation is involved.

But in the case of claims based on different obligations arising under a contract of employment, the obligation in question is that which is characteristic of the contract.

Ivenel v Schwab Case 133/81: [1982] ECR 1891 (European Court of Justice)

Request by the French Cour de Cassation for a preliminary ruling.

Mr Roger Ivenel of Strasbourg, France, was employed by Schwab, a German engineering firm of Oettingen, Germany, as a traveller and commercial representative in France. Mr Ivenel sued Schwab before the Conseil de Prud'hommes, Strasbourg for commission and other sums alleged to be due to him. Schwab contested the jurisdiction of the court on the ground that by both French and German law the sums claimed were payable at Oettingen and therefore the French court had no jurisdiction. There was also a dispute between the parties as to whether the contract between them was a contract of employment or a contract of representation (agency). The court dismissed the defendant's objection to the jurisdiction.

On appeal by Schwab to the Cour d'Appel of Colmar that court, following Case 14/76: *De Bloos v Bouyer SA*,[5] allowed the appeal. On further appeal by Ivenel to the Cour de Cassation, that court referred the question to the European Court.

The Court delivered the following judgment:

It must be observed that, as the Court of Justice has already stated, in particular in its judgment in Case 12/76: *Tessili v Dunlop*,[6] the 'place of performance' within the meaning of article 5 (1) of the Convention is to be determined in accordance with the law which governs the obligation in question according to the conflict rules of the court before which the matter is brought.

The question raised by the national court concerns the obligation to be taken into account for the purposes of that definition when the claim before the court is based on different obligations under a single contract for representation which has been classified by the courts concerned with the substance of the case as a contract of employment.

In its judgment in Case 14/76: *De Bloos v Bouyer SA* the Court has already stated that the obligation to be taken into account for the purposes of article 5(1) of the Convention in the case of a claim based on a contract granting an exclusive sales concession between two commercial undertakings is that which forms the basis of the legal proceedings. The problem raised by this case is whether the same criterion must be applied to cases of the kind described by the national court.

It is appropriate to examine that problem in the light of the objectives of the Convention and the general scheme of its provisions.

Adoption of the special rules of jurisdiction as contained in articles 5 and 6 of the Convention is justified inter alia by the fact that there must be a close connecting factor between the dispute and the court with jurisdiction to resolve it. The Jenard Report stresses that connection by stating inter alia that the court for the place of performance of the obligation will be useful in proceedings for the recovery of fees since the creditor will have a choice between the courts of the state where the defendant is ordinarily resident by virtue of the general provisions contained in article 2 of the Convention and the courts of another state within whose jurisdiction the services were provided, particularly where, according to the appropriate law, the obligation to pay must be performed where the services were provided.

The above-mentioned Report also refers to the reasons why those drafting the Convention did not consider it appropriate to insert into the Convention a provision giving exclusive jurisdiction in contracts of employment. According to the Report it is desirable as far as possible for disputes to be brought before the courts of the state whose law governs the contract whereas at the time the Convention was being drafted work was in progress to harmonise the application of the rules of employment law in the member states of the Community. The Report concludes that at present the existing provisions of the Convention, such as article 2 stipulating the forum for the place where the defendant is ordinarily resident and article 5 (1) the forum for the place of performance of the obligation, are likely to satisfy the relevant interests.

5 [1976] ECR 1497, [1977] 1 CMLR 60; p 105 above.
6 [1976] ECR 1473, [1977] 1 CMLR 26; p 109 below.

It should be noted that on 19 June 1980 a Convention on the law applicable to contractual obligations was opened for signature by the member states.[7] Article 6 thereof provides that a contract of employment is to be governed, in the absence of choice of the applicable law, by the law of the country in which the employee habitually carries out his work in performance of the contract unless it appears from the circumstances as a whole that the contract is more closely connected with another country.

The experts' report on the Convention on the law applicable to contractual obligations[8] explains in that respect that the adoption of a special conflict rule in relation to contracts of employment was intended to provide an appropriate arrangement for matters in which the interests of one of the contracting parties were not the same as those of the other and to secure thereby adequate protection for the party who from the socio-economic point of view was to be regarded as the weaker in the contractual relationship.

It follows from the foregoing account that in the matter of contracts article 5 (1) of the Convention is particularly concerned to attribute jurisdiction to the court of the country which has a close connection with the case; that in the case of a contract of employment the connection lies particularly in the law applicable to the contract; and that according to the trend in the conflict rules in regard to this matter that law is determined by the obligation which is characteristic of the contract in question and is normally the obligation to carry out work.

It emerges from an examination of the provisions of the Convention that in establishing special or even exclusive jurisdiction for insurance, instalment sales and tenancies of immovable property those provisions recognise that the rules on jurisdiction, too, are inspired by concern to afford proper protection to the party to the contract who is the weaker from the social point of view.

Those factors must be taken into account in answering the question which has been put to the Court.

In a case such as the one in point, where the national court has before it claims relating to obligations under a contract for representation, some of which concern remuneration due to the employee from an undertaking established in one state and others concern compensation based on the manner in which the work has been done in another state, it is necessary to interpret the provisions of the Convention in such a way that the national court is not compelled to find that it has jurisdiction to adjudicate upon certain claims but not on others.

Such a result would be even less compatible with the objectives and general structure of the Convention in the case of a contract of employment for which, as a general rule, the law applicable contains provisions protecting the worker and is normally that of the place where the work which is characteristic of the contract is carried out.

It follows from the foregoing considerations, taken as a whole, that the obligation to be taken into account for the purposes of the application of article 5 (1) of the Convention in the case of claims based on different obligations arising under a contract of employment as a representative binding a worker to an undertaking is the obligation which is characteristic of the contract.

7 OJ 1980 No L 266, p 1; p 459 below.
8 OJ 1980 No C 282, p 1.

The place of performance in article 5 (1) of the Convention may (semble) be determined by national law.

Tessili v Dunlop AG Case 12/76: [1976] ECR 1473, [1977] 1 CMLR 26 (European Court of Justice)

Request by the Oberlandesgericht (higher regional court), Frankfurt am Main for a preliminary ruling.

The German company Dunlop AG of Hanau bought a quantity of women's ski suits from the Italian company Tessili of Como. The suits were delivered but Dunlop AG complained that they were defective and not in conformity with the agreed specification. They brought an action against Tessili before the Landsgericht (lower regional court) at Hanau claiming rescission of the contract and damages. Tessili appeared in the proceedings but only to contest the jurisdiction of the court. The court held that it had jurisdiction. Tessili appealed to the Oberlandesgericht at Frankfurt. That court considered that the matter should be brought before the European Court.

The Court delivered the following judgment:

The interpretation of the Convention in general

Article 220 of the EEC Treaty provides that member states shall, so far as necessary, enter into negotiations with each other with a view to securing for the benefit of their nationals the establishment of rules intended to facilitate the achievement of the Common Market in the various spheres listed in that provision. The Convention was established to implement Article 220 and was intended according to the express terms of its preamble to implement the provisions of that article on the simplification of formalities governing the reciprocal recognition and enforcement of judgments of courts or tribunals and to strengthen in the Community the legal protection of persons therein established. In order to eliminate obstacles to legal relations and to settle disputes within the sphere of intra-Community relations in civil and commercial matters the Convention contains, inter alia, rules enabling the jurisdiction in these matters of courts of member states to be determined and facilitating the recognition and execution of courts' judgments. Accordingly the Convention must be interpreted having regard both to its principles and objectives and to its relationship with the Treaty.

The Convention frequently uses words and legal concepts drawn from civil, commercial and procedural law and capable of a different meaning from one member state to another. The question therefore arises whether these words and concepts must be regarded as having their own independent meaning and as being thus common to all the member states or as referring to substantive rules of the law applicable in each case under the rules of conflict of laws of the court before which the matter is first brought.

Neither of these two options rules out the other since the appropriate choice can only be made in respect of each of the provisions of the Convention to ensure that it is fully effective having regard to the objectives of article 220 of the Treaty. In any event it should be stressed that the interpretation of the said words and concepts for the purpose of the Convention does not prejudge the question of the substantive rule applicable to the particular case.

The question raised by the national court

Article 5 of the Convention provides: 'A person domiciled in a Contracting State may, in another Contracting State, be sued: (1) in matters relating to a contract, in the courts for the place of performance of the obligation in question'. This provision must be interpreted within the framework of the system of conferment of jurisdiction under Title II of the Convention. In accordance with article 2 the basis of this system is the general conferment of jurisdiction on the court of the defendant's domicile. Article 5 however provides for a number of cases of special jurisdiction at the option of the plaintiff.

This freedom of choice was introduced in view of the existence in certain well-defined cases of a particularly close relationship between a dispute and the court which may be most conveniently called upon to take cognisance of the matter. Thus in the case of an action relating to contractual obligations article 5 (1) allows a plaintiff to bring the matter before the court for the place 'of performance' of the obligation in question. It is for the court before which the matter is brought to establish under the Convention whether the place of performance is situate within its territorial jurisdiction. For this purpose it must determine in accordance with its own rules of conflict of laws what is the law applicable to the legal relationship in question and define in accordance with that law the place of performance of the contractual obligation in question.

Having regard to the differences obtaining between national laws of contract and to the absence at this stage of legal development of any unification in the substantive law applicable, it does not appear possible to give any more substantial guide to the interpretation of the reference made by article 5 (1) to the 'place of performance' of contractual obligations. This is all the more true since the determination of the place of performance of obligations depends on the contractual context to which these obligations belong.

In these circumstances the references in the Convention to the place of performance of contractual obligations cannot be understood otherwise than by reference to the substantive law applicable under the rules of conflict of laws of the court before which the matter is brought.

The parties may agree on the place of performance for the purposes of article 5 (1), whether orally or in writing.

Zelger v Salinitri Case 56/79: [1980] ECR 89, [1980] 2 CMLR 635 (European Court of Justice)

Request by the Bundesgerichtshof (Supreme Federal Court of Germany) for a preliminary ruling.

Zelger, a merchant in Munich, and Salinitri, a merchant in Mascali, Sicily, had had business dealings for many years. A dispute arose over repayment of a loan which Zelger had made to Salinitri. Zelger commenced proceedings before the Landsgericht (lower regional court) of Munich, claiming that the parties had made an express oral agreement that Munich was to be the place of performance for the repayment. That court dismissed the claim on the ground that it had no jurisdiction. Zelger's appeal to the

Oberlandesgericht (higher regional court) of Munich was also unsuccessful. That court held that a mere oral agreement on the place of performance did not suffice to found international jurisdiction. Zelger appealed to the Bundesgerichtshof, which formulated the following question for the European Court: Does an informal agreement which is effective under national—in this case German—law concerning the place of performance of the obligation suffice to found jurisdiction under article 5 (1) of the Convention, or must the agreement observe the form laid down in article 17?

The Court delivered the following judgment:

It is appropriate to point out that article 5 (1), which occurs in Section 2 of Title II of the Convention entitled 'special jurisdiction', creates a ground of jurisdiction which is an exception to the general rule of jurisdiction provided for in article 2 of the Convention; the provisions of article 5, which provide that in matters relating to a contract a defendant domiciled in a contracting state may be sued in the courts for the place of performance of the obligation in question, introduce a criterion for jurisdiction, the selection of which is at the option of the plaintiff and which is justified by the existence of a direct link between the dispute and the court called upon to take cognisance of it.

By contrast, article 17, which occurs in Section 6 of the Convention entitled 'Prorogation of jurisdiction' and which provides for the exclusive jurisdiction of the court designated by the parties in accordance with the prescribed form, puts aside both the rule of general jurisdiction—provided for in article 2—and the rules of special jurisdiction—provided for in article 5—and dispenses with any objective connection between the legal relationship in dispute and the court designated. It thus appears that the jurisdiction of the court for the place of performance (provided for in article 5 (1)) and that of the selected court (provided for in article 17) are two distinct concepts and only agreements selecting a court are subject to the requirements of form prescribed by article 17 of the Convention.

Consequently, if the parties to the contract are permitted by the law applicable to the contract, subject to any conditions imposed by that law, to specify the place of performance of an obligation without satisfying any special condition of form, an agreement on the place of performance of the obligation is sufficient to found jurisdiction in that place within the meaning of article 5 (1) of the Convention.

The answer to the question put by the Bundesgerichtshof must therefore be that if the place of performance of a contractual obligation has been specified by the parties in a clause which is valid according to the national law applicable to the contract, the court for that place has jurisdiction to take cognisance of disputes relating to that obligation under article 5 (1) of the Convention of Brussels of 27 September 1968, irrespective of whether the formal conditions provided for under article 17 have been observed.

The jurisdiction under article 5 (1) of the Convention can be exercised even when the defendant disputes the existence of the contract.

Effer SpA v Kantner Case 38/81: [1982] ECR 825 (European Court of Justice)

Request by the Bundesgerichtshof (Supreme Federal Court of Germany) for a preliminary ruling.

The Italian company Effer of Bologna was a manufacturer of cranes. These were distributed for Effer in Germany by the German company Hydraulikkran, now in liquidation. In order to ascertain whether the sale of Effer's cranes would infringe certain German patents, Mr Kantner, a patent agent carrying on business in Darmstadt, Germany, was employed to carry out investigations in Germany. He was commissioned by Hydraulikkran, but the parties were not agreed as to whether Hydraulikkran commissioned him in the name of Effer or in its own name. Kantner sued Effer for his fee in the Landgericht (lower regional court), Frankfurt. Effer contended that there was no contract between it and Kantner and therefore that there was no jurisdiction. The plaintiff succeeded at first instance and on appeal. On further appeal by Effer to the Bundesgerichtshof, that court formulated the following question for the European Court: May the plaintiff invoke the jurisdiction of the courts of the place of performance in accordance with article 5 (1) of the Convention even when the existence of the contract is in dispute between the parties?

The Court delivered the following judgment:

It is established that the wording of article 5 (1) of the Convention does not resolve this question unequivocally. Whilst the German version of that provision contains the words 'Vertrag oder Ansprüche aus einem Vertrage', the French and Italian versions contain the expressions 'en matière contractuelle' and 'in materia contrattuale' respectively. Under these circumstances, in view of the lack of uniformity between the different language versions of the provision in question, it is advisable, in order to arrive at the interpretation requested by the national court, to have regard both to the context of article 5 (1) and to the purpose of the Convention.

It is clear from the provisions of the Convention, and in particular from the preamble thereto, that its essential aim is to strengthen in the Community the legal protection of persons therein established. For that purpose, the Convention provides a collection of rules which are designed inter alia to avoid the occurrence, in civil and commercial matters, of concurrent litigation in two or more member states and which, in the interests of legal certainty and for the benefit of the parties, confer jurisdiction upon the national court territorially best qualified to determine a dispute.

It follows from the provisions of the Convention, and in particular from those in Section 7 of Title II, that, in the cases provided for in article 5 (1) of the Convention, the national court's jurisdiction to determine questions relating to a contract includes the power to consider the existence of the constituent parts of the contract itself, since that is indispensable in order to enable the national court in which proceedings are brought to examine whether it has jurisdiction under the Convention. If that were not the case, article 5 (1) of the Convention would be in danger of being deprived of its legal effect, since it would be accepted that, in order to defeat the rule contained in that provision it is sufficient for one of the parties to claim that the contract does not exist. On the contrary, respect for the aims and spirit of the Convention demands that that provision should be construed as meaning that the court called upon to decide a dispute arising out of a contract may examine, of its own motion even, the essential preconditions for its jurisdiction, having regard to conclusive and relevant evidence adduced by the party concerned, establishing the existence or the non-existence of the contract. This interpretation is, moreover, in accordance with that given in the judgment in Case 73/77: (*Sanders v Van der Putte*[9]) concerning the jurisdiction of the courts of the State where the immovable property is situated in matters relating to tenancies of immovable property (article 16 (1) of the Convention). In that case the Court held that such jurisdiction applies even if there is a dispute as to the 'existence' of a lease.

It is therefore necessary to reply to the question put by the Bundesgerichtshof that the plaintiff may invoke the jurisdiction of the courts of the place of performance in accordance with article 5 (1) of the Convention even when the existence of the contract on which the claim is based is in dispute between the parties.

'The place where the harmful act occurred' in article 5 (3) of the Convention means, at the option of the plaintiff, either the place where the wrongful act occurred or the place where the damage was suffered.

Handelskwekerij Bier v Mines de Potasse D'Alsace SA Case 21/76: [1978] QB 708, [1976] ECR 1735 (European Court of Justice)

Request by the Gerechtshof (appeal court) of The Hague for a preliminary ruling.

The plaintiff carried on business as a nursery gardener near Rotterdam. He used a water catchment area surrounding his property for watering and irrigating his seed beds. This water came principally from the Rhine. The salinity of the water caused damage to the seed beds. He brought an action before the Arrondissements-rechtsbank (court of first instance) of Rotterdam against a French company, Mines de Potasse d'Alsace, alleging that it discharged more than 10,000 tonnes of chlorides every day into the Rhine, with the result that the salt content of the river was considerably augmented. The defendant company, reserving its defence as to the substance of the matter, objected that the court had no jurisdiction because the defendant was not domiciled in the Netherlands. The court upheld this objection, and Bier appealed to the Gerichtshof of The Hague, relying on article 5 (3) of the Convention. That court formulated the following question for the European Court: Must the phrase 'the place where the harmful act occurred' in article 5 (3) of the Convention be interpreted as meaning 'the place where the damage occurred' or 'the place where the act causing the damage was done'?

The Court delivered the following judgment:

Article 5 of the Convention provides: 'A person domiciled in a contracting state may, in another contracting state, be sued:... (3) in matters relating to tort, delict or quasi-delict, in the courts for the place where the harmful event occurred'.

That provision must be interpreted in the context of the scheme of conferment of jurisdiction which forms the subject-matter of Title II of the Convention.

That scheme is based on a general rule, laid down by article 2, that the courts of the state in which the defendant is domiciled shall have jurisdiction.

9 [1977] ECR 2383, [1978] 1 CMLR 331.

However, article 5 makes provision in a number of cases for a special jurisdiction, which the plaintiff may opt to choose.

This freedom of choice was introduced having regard to the existence, in certain clearly defined situations, of a particularly close connecting factor between a dispute and the court which may be called upon to hear it, with a view to the efficacious conduct of the proceedings.

Thus in matters of tort, delict or quasi-delict article 5 (3) allows the plaintiff to bring his case before the courts for 'the place where the harmful event occurred'.

In the context of the Convention, the meaning of that expression is unclear when the place of the event which caused the damage is situated in a state other than the one in which the place where the damage occurred is situated, as is the case inter alia with atmospheric or water pollution beyond the frontiers of a state.

The form of words 'place where the harmful event occurred', used in all the language versions of the Convention, leaves open the question whether, in the situation described, it is necessary, in determining jurisdiction, to choose as the connecting factor the place of the event giving rise to the damage, or the place where the damage occurred, or to accept that the plaintiff has an option between the one and the other of those two connecting factors.

As regards this, it is well to point out that the place of the event giving rise to the damage no less than the place where the damage occurred can, depending on the case, constitute a significant connecting factor from the point of view of jurisdiction.

Liability in tort, delict or quasi-delict can only arise provided that a causal connection can be established between the damage and the event in which that damage originates.

Taking into account the close connection between the component parts of every sort of liability, it does not appear appropriate to opt for one of the two connecting factors mentioned to the exclusion of the other, since each of them can, depending on the circumstances, be particularly helpful from the point of view of the evidence and of the conduct of the proceedings.

To exclude one option appears all the more undesirable in that, by its comprehensive form of words, article 5 (3) of the Convention covers a wide diversity of kinds of liability.

Thus the meaning of the expression 'place where the harmful event occurred' in article 5 (3) must be established in such a way as to acknowledge that the plaintiff has an option to commence proceedings either at the place where the damage occurred or the place of the event giving rise to it.

This conclusion is supported by the consideration, first, that to decide in favour only of the place of the event giving rise to the damage would, in an appreciable number of cases, cause confusion between the heads of jurisdiction laid down by articles 2 and 5 (3) of the Convention, so that the latter provision would, to that extent, lose its effectiveness.

Secondly, a decision in favour only of the place where the damage occurred would, in cases where the place of the event giving rise to the damage does not coincide with the domicile of the person liable, have the effect of excluding a helpful connecting factor with the jurisdiction of a court particularly near to the cause of the damage.

Moreover, it appears from a comparison of the national legislative provisions and national case-law on the distribution of jurisdiction—both as regards internal relationships, as between courts for different areas, and in international relationships—that, albeit by differing legal techniques, a place is found for both of the two connecting factors here considered and that in several states they are accepted concurrently.

In these circumstances, the interpretation stated above has the advantage of avoiding any upheaval in the solutions worked out in the various national systems of law, since it looks to unification, in conformity with article 5 (3) of the Convention, by way of a systematisation of solutions which, as to their principle, have already been established in most of the states concerned.

Thus it should be answered that where the place of the happening of the event which may give rise to liability in tort, delict or quasi-delict and the place where that event results in damage are not identical, the expression 'place where the harmful event occurred', in article 5 (3) of the Convention, must be understood as being intended to cover both the place where the damage occurred and the place of the event giving rise to it.

The result is that the defendant may be sued, at the option of the plaintiff, either in the courts for the place where the damage occurred or in the courts for the place of the event which gives rise to and is at the origin of that damage.

Article 17 of the Convention allows the parties to a contract to submit their disputes to the courts of different contracting states, depending on which of them institutes the proceedings.

Meeth v Glacetal SARL Case 23/78: [1978] ECR 2133, [1979] 1 CMLR 520 (European Court of Justice)

Request by the Bundesgerichtshof (Federal Supreme Court of Germany) for a preliminary ruling.

By a contract in writing Glacetal, a French company, undertook to deliver to Meeth, a German undertaking manufacturing windows, certain quantities of glass. The contract provided that if Meeth sued Glacetal the French courts alone should have jurisdiction; if Glacetal sued Meeth the German courts alone should have jurisdiction. Meeth failed to pay for certain deliveries made by Glacetal. Glacetal then instituted proceedings against Meeth before the Landsgericht (lower regional court) of Trier to recover the sum due. That court ordered Meeth to pay Glacetal the sum due. Meeth appealed to the Oberlandesgericht (higher regional court) of Koblenz, claiming to reduce the amount due by reason of a set-off for damages for delayed delivery. The Oberlandesgericht held that the jurisdiction agreement precluded Meeth from claiming a set-off before any courts except those of France. Meeth appealed to the Bundesgerichtshof requesting a ruling that its claim for a set-off was admissible. That court formulated the following questions for the European Court: (1) Does the first paragraph of article 17 of the Convention permit an agreement under which the two parties to a contract, who are domiciled in different states, can be sued only in the courts of their respective states? (2) Does such a clause automatically rule out any set-off which one of the parties has against the other?

The Court delivered the following judgment:

The first question

According to the first paragraph of article 17 'if the parties... have agreed that a court or the courts of a contracting state are to have jurisdiction to settle any disputes which have arisen or which may arise in connection with a particular legal relationship, that court or those courts shall have exclusive jurisdiction'.

With regard to an agreement conferring reciprocal jurisdiction in the form in which it appears in the contract whose implementation forms the subject-matter of the dispute, the interpretation of that provision gives rise to difficulty because of the fact that article 17, as it is worded, refers to the choice by the parties to the contract of a single court or the courts of a single state.

That wording, which is based on the most widespread business practice, cannot, however, be interpreted as intended to exclude the right of the parties to agree on two or more courts for the purpose of settling any disputes which may arise.

This interpretation is justified on the ground that article 17 is based on a recognition of the independent will of the parties to a contract in deciding which courts are to have jurisdiction to settle disputes falling within the scope of the Convention, other than those which are expressly excluded pursuant to the second paragraph of article 17.

This applies particularly where the parties have by such an agreement reciprocally conferred jurisdiction on the courts specified in the general rule laid down by article 2 of the Convention.

Although such an agreement coincides with the scope of article 2 it is nevertheless effective in that it excludes, in relations between the parties, other optional attributions of jurisdiction, such as those detailed in articles 5 and 6 of the Convention.

The reply to the first question must accordingly be that the first paragraph of article 17 of the Convention cannot be interpreted as prohibiting an agreement under which the two parties to a contract for sale, who are domiciled in different states, can be sued only in the courts of their respective states.

The second question

According to the first paragraph of article 17, jurisdiction is conferred on a given court or courts in order to settle any disputes which have arisen or which may arise 'in connection with a particular legal relationship'.

The question of the extent to which a court before which a case is brought pursuant to a reciprocal jurisdiction clause, such as that appearing in the contract between the parties, has jurisdiction to decide on a set-off claimed by one of the parties on the basis of the disputed contractual obligation must be determined with regard both to the need to respect individuals' right of independence, upon which article 17, as has been noted above, is based, and the need to avoid superfluous procedure, which forms the basis of the Convention as a whole of which article 17 is part.

In the light of both of these objectives article 17 cannot be interpreted as preventing a court before which proceedings have been instituted pursuant to a clause conferring jurisdiction of the type described above from taking into account a claim for a set-off connected with the legal relationship in dispute if such court considers that course to be compatible with the letter and spirit of the clause conferring jurisdiction.

Accordingly the reply to the second question must be that where there is a clause conferring jurisdiction such as that described in the reply to the first question the first paragraph of article 17 of the Convention cannot be interpreted as prohibiting the court before which a dispute has been brought in pursuance of such a clause from taking into account a set-off connected with the legal relationship in dispute.

National law may not impose formal requirements for the validity of jurisdiction agreements additional to those imposed by article 17 of the Convention.

A court of a contracting state before which a defendant enters an appearance (other than an appearance solely to contest the jurisdiction) has jurisdiction under article 18, even if the parties validly chose another court under article 17.

Elefanten Schuh GmbH v Jacqmain Case 150/80: [1981] ECR 1671, [1982] 3 CMLR 1 (European Court of Justice)

Request by the Hof van Cassatie (Belgian Cour de Cassation) for a preliminary ruling.

The German undertaking Elefanten Schuh of Kleve, Germany, employed Mr Jacqmain of Antwerp, Belgium, as sole sales agent for the Belgian provinces of Antwerp, Brabant and Limburg. The contract was in the German language. It contained a clause providing that the court at Kleve should have exclusive jurisdiction over any dispute. Elefanten Schuh dismissed Mr Jacqmain without notice. He brought an action before the Arbeidsrechtbank (Labour tribunal) of Antwerp claiming damages for breach of contract. Elefanten Schuh appeared, pleaded to the merits and nine months later pleaded that the tribunal had no jurisdiction because of the jurisdiction clause. The tribunal, applying Belgian law, rejected the plea as to jurisdiction and ordered Elefanten Schuh to pay most of the damages claimed. On appeal the Arbeidshof (Labour appeal court) of Antwerp held, applying Belgian law, that the court below had jurisdiction; and also held, again applying Belgian law, that the contract was void because it was not written in Flemish. On appeal the Hof van Cassatie formulated the following questions for the European Court: (1) (a) Is article 18 of the Convention applicable if the parties have agreed to confer jurisdiction on another court within the meaning of article 17? (b) Is the rule on jurisdiction contained in article 18 applicable if the defendant has not only contested jurisdiction but has in addition made submissions on the action itself? (c) If it is, must jurisdiction be contested in limine litis? (3) Does it conflict with article 17 to rule that an agreement conferring jurisdiction is void if it is not drawn up in the language which is prescribed by national law?[10]

The Court delivered the following judgment:

Question 1

Articles 17 and 18 form Section 6 of Title II of the Convention which deals

10 Question 2 was concerned with a procedural matter relating to article 22.

with prorogation of jurisdiction; article 17 concerns jurisdiction by contract and article 18 jurisdiction implied from submission as a result of the defendant's appearance. The first part of the question seeks to determine the relationship between those two types of prorogation.

In the first sentence, article 18 of the convention lays down the rule that a court of a contracting state before whom a defendant enters an appearance is to have jurisdiction and in the second sentence it provides that that rule is not to apply where appearance was entered solely in order to contest the jurisdiction, or where another court has exclusive jurisdiction by virtue of article 16 of the Convention.

The case envisaged in article 17 is not therefore one of the exceptions which article 18 allows to the rule which it lays down. Moreover neither the general scheme nor the objectives of the Convention provide grounds for the view that the parties to an agreement conferring jurisdiction within the meaning of article 17 are prevented from voluntarily submitting their dispute to a court other than that stipulated in the agreement.

It follows that article 18 of the Convention applies even where the parties have by agreement designated a court which is to have jurisdiction within the meaning of article 17.

The second and third parts of the question envisage the case in which the defendant has appeared before a court within the meaning of article 18 but contests the jurisdiction of that court.

The Hof van Cassatie first asks if article 18 has application where the defendant makes submissions as to the jurisdiction of the court as well as on the substance of the action.

Although differences between the different language versions of article 18 of the Convention appear when it is sought to determine whether, in order to exclude the jurisdiction of the court seised, a defendant must confine himself to contesting that jurisdiction, or whether he may on the contrary still achieve the same purpose by contesting the jurisdiction of the court as well as the substance of the claim, the second interpretation is more in keeping with the objectives and spirit of the Convention. In fact under the law of civil procedure of certain contracting states a defendant who raises the issue of jurisdiction and no other might be barred from making his submissions as to the substance if the court rejects his plea that it has no jurisdiction. An interpretation of article 18 which enabled such a result to be arrived at would be contrary to the right of the defendant to defend himself in the original proceedings, which is one of the aims of the Convention.

However, the challenge to jurisdiction may have the result attributed to it by article 18 only if the plaintiff and the court seised of the matter are able to ascertain from the time of the defendant's first defence that it is intended to contest the jurisdiction of the court.

The Hof van Cassatie asks in this regard whether jurisdiction must be contested in limine litis. For the purposes of interpreting the Convention that concept is difficult to apply in view of the appreciable differences existing between the legislation of the contracting states with regard to bringing actions before courts of law, the appearance of defendants and the way in which the parties to an action must formulate their submissions. However, it follows from the aim of article 18 that if the challenge to jurisdiction is not preliminary to any defence as to the substance it may not in any event occur after the making of the submissions which under national procedural law are considered to be the first defence addressed to the court seised.

Therefore the answer to the second and third parts of Question 1 should be that article 18 of the Convention must be interpreted as meaning that the rule on jurisdiction which that provision lays down does not apply where the defendant not only contests the court's jurisdiction but also makes submissions on the substance of the action, provided that, if the challenge to jurisdiction is not preliminary to any defence as to the substance, it does not occur after the making of the submissions which under national procedural law are considered to be the first defence addressed to the court seised.

Question 3

It appears that the Hof van Cassatie is solely concerned with the validity of an agreement conferring jurisdiction which is rendered void by the national legislation of the court seised as having been written in a language other than that prescribed by that legislation.

Article 17 stipulates that the agreement conferring jurisdiction must take the form of an agreement in writing or an oral agreement evidenced in writing.

According to the Report on the Convention submitted to the governments of the contracting states at the same time as the draft Convention those formal requirements were inserted out of the concern not to impede commercial practice, yet at the same time to cancel out the effects of clauses in contracts which might go unread, such as clauses in printed forms for business correspondence or in invoices, if they were not agreed to by the party against whom they operate. For those reasons jurisdiction clauses should be taken into consideration only if they are the subject of a written agreement, and that implies the consent of all the parties. Furthermore, the draftsmen of article 17 were of the opinion that, in order to ensure legal certainty, the formal requirements applicable to agreements conferring jurisdiction should be expressly prescribed.

Article 17 is thus intended to lay down itself the formal requirements which agreements conferring jurisdiction must meet; the purpose is to ensure legal certainty and that the parties have given their consent.

Consequently contracting states are not free to lay down formal requirements other than those contained in the Convention.

When those rules are applied to provisions concerning the language to be used in an agreement conferring jurisdiction they imply that the legislation of a contracting state may not allow the validity of such an agreement to be called in question solely on the ground that the language used is not that prescribed by that legislation.

Moreover, any different interpretation would run counter to article 17 of the Convention the very purpose of which is to enable a court of a contracting state to be chosen by agreement where that court, if not so chosen, would not normally have jurisdiction. That choice must therefore be respected by the courts of all the contracting states.

Consequently, the answer to Question 3 must be that article 17 of the Convention must be interpreted as meaning that the legislation of a contracting state may not allow the validity of an agreement conferring jurisdiction to be called in question solely on the ground that the language used is not that prescribed by that legislation.

A case on article 24 of the Convention (provisional and protective measures).

Denilauler v Couchet Frères (p 198 below).

English courts have a discretionary power under section 25 of the Civil Jurisdiction and Judgments Act 1982 to grant interim relief in cases where proceedings have been or are to be commenced in another contracting state or in another part of the United Kingdom.

Siskina (Cargo Owners) v Distos SA [1979] AC 210, [1977] 3 All ER 803 (Court of Appeal)

Appeal from Kerr J.

Lord Denning MR: The *Siskina* is now sunk to the bottom of the Mediterranean Sea. In her lifetime she was a motor vessel owned by a 'one ship' Panamanian company; but she was managed by Greeks in Piraeus. Early in 1976 she was chartered by an Italian firm for a voyage from North Italy to the Red Sea. She arrived at the port of Carrara on the Gulf of Genoa and took on a cargo of general merchandise. Six thousand tons of it. We are much concerned with this cargo. It came from the industrial north of Italy and was destined for the rich land of Saudi Arabia. There were marble slabs and tiles for the wealthy homes. Refrigerators and gas cookers for the kitchens. And blankets in thousands for the cold nights. All to be carried to the port of Jeddah on the Red Sea. So the cargo was a very mixed bag. Many different parcels from many different sellers for many different consignees.

The buyers in Saudi Arabia had paid for all this cargo in advance. They had bought it from the sellers in North Italy on cif terms by means of irrevocable letters of credit. So they had not only paid the price of the goods themselves. They had in addition paid the freight for the voyage and also the insurance to cover it. All the documents were in order. The shipowners, or someone on their behalf, had given bills of lading to the shippers acknowledging the receipt of the goods on board. They had stamped them boldly in large letters 'Freight pre-paid'. These documents, including the bills of lading, had been handed by the Italian shippers to the bank and they had obtained cash against documents. The shippers duly endorsed the bills of lading to the consignees in Saudi Arabia: and sent them on to the buyers there. Then, in the ordinary course, when the ship arrived at Jeddah, the buyers would present the bills of lading to the ship and obtain the goods. If the goods had been delayed or damaged in transit, the consignees would have to resort to the Italian courts in Genoa: because there was a clause in the bills of lading giving exclusive jurisdiction to those courts.

The vessel, however, never got to Jeddah or anywhere near it. She went through the Mediterranean till she was near the entrance to the Suez Canal. There she stopped. The shipowning company, the defendants, said that the charterers—the Italian firm—had not paid them the freight due under the charterparty. That was, of course, very different from the freight under the bills of lading. The cargo-owners had already paid the bill of lading freight, and got the bills of lading marked 'Freight pre-paid'. But the charterers had not paid the charter freight to the shipowning company. It should have been paid to the shipowning company in Piraeus as soon as the bills of lading were signed. The charterers had not paid it; or, at any rate, not all of it. So the shipowning company said that they were not going to take the vessel through the Suez Canal—with all the dues and expense that that entailed—unless they were paid the full balance of the charter freight. So the *Siskina* waited outside the entrance to the canal. She waited there for over four weeks—from 6 March 1976 to 6 April 1976. The charterers paid two instalments amounting to a large sum and said it was all that was due. But the shipowning company said it was not enough. Not being enough, they ordered the master to turn back and go to Cyprus and unload the cargo there. This was not the first occasion of the kind. We are told that during the last year there have been about 20 cases in which vessels, due for discharge in the Middle East, have been diverted to Cyprus. They have there discharged their cargoes rather than carry them to their proper destinations. They pay scant regard to their obligations to the cargo-owners.

See what happened in this very case. The vessel went back to the port of Limassol in Cyprus. As soon as she got there the shipowning company issued a writ in rem against the cargo—although the cargo-owners were not in fault at all. The shipowning company applied to the Supreme Court of Cyprus for a warrant for the arrest of the cargo and for an order for it to be discharged and placed in warehouses. This writ and application were not served on the owners of the cargo. They knew nothing about it. It was only served on the cargo itself like the arrest of a ship. It was supported by an affidavit by a lawyer saying that he had got his information from the master. It said that the bills of lading had been marked 'Freight pre-paid' owing to the fraudulent misrepresentation of the charterers: and that the shipowning company were entitled to charter freight, of which a considerable sum was still outstanding; and that they were entitled to a lien on the cargo for the balance. So they sought to make the cargo-owners pay for the misdeeds of the charterers.

On 10 April 1976, the Supreme Court of Cyprus made the order asked. It issued a warrant for the arrest of the cargo. It appointed a company called Cyprian Seaways Agencies Ltd to discharge the cargo from the vessel to a safe place of storage, the cost to be a first charge on the cargo. Cyprian Seaways Ltd put up a bond of £10,000 as security. Soon afterwards the cargo was unloaded. The marble tiles and slabs were left in the open and suffered a lot of breakage and chipping. Machinery was left out and was damaged by rain. Other goods were taken to warehouse. The value of the cargo was, we are told, some $5,000,000.

Soon after the discharge, the vessel about 20 April 1976, left Limassol in ballast with no cargo. She has never been heard of since. All that we are told is that six weeks later, on 2 June 1976, she sank near Astipalaia Island and became a total loss. That island is one of the Dodecanese on the way from Cyprus to Greece. We know of no reason why she sank. All we know is that the shipowning company have made a claim on the London underwriters: and that the sum payable for the loss of the vessel will be more than $750,000.

The cargo-owners knew nothing of all this. They were merchants in Saudi Arabia, not well-versed in the intricacies of transport by sea. They made inquiries of the shippers, who inquired of the charterers. It was only on 31 May 1976, that their lawyers in Genoa first heard that the goods had been taken to Cyprus, unloaded there and arrested by the shipowning company alleging a lien for freight. They immediately instructed lawyers in Cyprus: but by that time the vessel had disappeared without trace. They also instructed lawyers in London.

In Cyprus in June and July 1976, the cargo-owners did all they could to get their goods released. The shipowning company refused to release them unless each cargo-owner paid them his 'proportion'—so-called—of the charter freight and demurrage expenses. The shipping company had no right whatever to claim any such sum; because each of the cargo-owners had paid for his goods and had paid the freight to Jeddah for his parcel; and none was liable for this sum. Yet they were so anxious to get their goods that some of them submitted. They paid the sums demanded, whereupon the shipowners asked the Cyprus court to release the goods to them: and the court did so. In this way the shipowners collected sums amounting to over $75,000. That was much more than the balance outstanding to the shipowners (even if they had carried the goods all the way to Jeddah). So the shipowning company made a good profit. The unfortunate cargo-owners, in order to get their goods to Jeddah, had, in addition, to pay the storage charges and the expenses of reloading the goods on other vessels and carrying them on to Jeddah—very substantial sums indeed.

The rest of the cargo-owners did not agree to pay their 'proportion'. They applied to the court in Cyprus for the release of the goods; and for higher security as a condition of their continued arrest; and for the shipowners to be answerable in damages in connection with the arrest of the cargo.

In England the cargo-owners were anxious about the insurance moneys which were payable in London to the shipowners for the loss of the *Siskina*. The shipowning company had no assets except these insurance moneys; and the cargo-owners (or their insurers) did not want these moneys paid over to the shipowners, because they would then be beyond reach. So the cargo-owners on 2 July 1976, drafted a writ in the Commercial Court against the shipowners. They asked for leave to issue it and to serve notice of it on the shipowners in Greece out of the jurisdiction. The writ was endorsed with

'claims for loss in respect of cargo lately carried on the defendant's vessel *Siskina* from Carrara in Italy and bound for Jeddah in Saudi Arabia under bills of lading dated ..., but wrongfully diverted to and detained at Limassol in Cyprus, as follows: (i) damages for breach of duty and/or contract, (ii) an injunction to restrain the defendants by themselves, their servants or agents or otherwise from disposing of their assets within the jurisdiction, and in particular the insurance proceeds in respect of the vessel *Siskina* or their claims thereto or removing the same out of the jurisdiction. ...'

On that self-same day, 2 July 1976, the cargo-owners went ex parte before Mocatta J. He gave the leave asked and granted an injunction in those very terms to restrain the shipowners from disposing of the insurance moneys. Subsequently, on 20 August 1976, the underwriters agreed to deposit the insurance moneys in a joint account at an English bank within the jurisdiction.

On hearing of this injunction, the Cyprus court took it into account in fixing further security. It did not order a big sum. It only ordered the shipowners to lodge additional security in the comparatively small sum of £20,000 as a condition of continuing the arrest of the cargo. The shipowners have given a bond for this £20,000.

So the position today is that goods of much value are still languishing on shore in Cyprus. I suppose about $3,000,000 worth. Some in the open exposed to the weather. Others in warehouses in unknown conditions. Storage charges are running up day by day. These will have to be paid before the goods are released: and the cargo-owners will have to pay the cost of carrying them to Jeddah: although they have paid it once already. The shipowners still claim to have a lien on them against the cargo-owners for their 'proportion' of the chartered freight.

The shipowners are a 'one ship' company, whose one ship the *Siskina* is sunk beneath the waves. They have no other ship. They have no business and have no intention of carrying on any business. They have no assets except the insurance moneys of $750,000 payable by London underwriters for the loss of the *Siskina*.

The cargo-owners have a claim against the shipowners for substantial damages for failing to carry the goods to Jeddah as promised by the bills of lading, all marked 'Freight Pre-paid': and for damages for wrongfully diverting the vessel to Limassol and wrongfully discharging the cargo there under an unwarranted claim of lien. The damages are put at some $250,000, and are no doubt increasing daily.

The cargo-owners want the insurance moneys of $750,000 retained in England—or a sufficent part of it—until their claim for damages is settled. Otherwise they are afraid—with good reason—that the $750,000 will be paid out to the shipowners and deposited in Switzerland, or in some foreign land; and the cargo-owners will have no chance of getting anything for all the damage they have suffered.

The jurisdiction of various courts

This does, however, give rise to important questions of jurisdiction. The contracts contained these provisions: The charterparty was between the shipowners and the Italian firm of charterers—Intermediterranea Genova. It was on the Gencon form. It provided for the master to sign clear bills of lading marked 'Freight Pre-paid': for the charter freight to be 'fully pre-paid on signing respective bills of lading'. There was an express clause: 'Arbitration in London. English law to Apply'. The cargo-owners have no claim under the charterparty. So they cannot use that clause so as to found jurisdiction to serve the shipowners out of the jurisdiction.

The bills of lading were all stamped 'Freight Pre-paid'. They contained a clause giving exclusive jurisdiction to the courts of Genoa. That clause shows that the cargo-owners would undoubtedly be able to pursue their claim by taking proceedings against the shipowners in the court of Genoa. A judgment by that court would be both recognised and enforced in England: see Dicey and Morris, *The Conflict of Laws*.[11] But a judgment there alone

11 9th edn (1973), r 180, pp 993–994.

would not be of much use because the shipowners have no assets there. Again the shipowners have arrested the cargo in rem in Cyprus. The cargo-owners can counterclaim there for damages. But a judgment in Cyprus alone would not be of much use because the shipowners have no assets there. Their one asset, the ship, has gone and sunk. They have only lodged security in £30,000, which would only go to a small part of the counter-claim—and may not be available for it. The only courts in which a judgment would be of any use is England, where the insurance moneys are.

If the ship had remained afloat, the cargo-owners would have been able to arrest the ship in rem if she put into a port in England or elsewhere—so as to enforce their claim for damages. As she is sunk, the cargo-owners wish to arrest the insurance moneys which are in London and take the place, so to speak, of the ship. This is the most hopeful line. And the cargo-owners have taken it.

The Mareva injunction

During the last two years the courts of this country have rediscovered a very useful procedure which used to be known as 'foreign attachment'. It is now called the *Mareva* injunction. It is a procedure by which the courts can come to the aid of a creditor when the debtor has absconded or is overseas, but has assets in this country. The courts are ready now to issue an injunction so as to prevent the debtor from disposing of those assets or removing them from this country—thus defeating the creditor of his claims. It is a procedure familiar to all the countries of the continent of Europe and to the United States of America, and to the province of Quebec. If you read the facts in *Mareva Compania Naviera SA v International Bulkcarriers SA*,[12] you will see how desirable and important it is that the courts should have jurisdiction to issue such an injunction. It was challenged before us recently in *Rasu Maritima SA v Perusahaan Pertambangon Minyak Dan Gas Bumi Negara*,[13] but the challenge failed. The procedure is now established beyond question. It has been used repeatedly in the Commercial Court to the satisfaction of all concerned. Up to the present, however, it has only been applied in cases where the defendant is abroad, but leave would be given to serve him out of the jurisdiction. Assuming it to be so confined, I turn to consider whether this is a case where leave to serve out would be given.

Leave to serve out of the jurisdiction

In many of the *Mareva* cases both creditor and debtor have been foreigners resident out of the jurisdiction of this court. The only connection with this country is that the money has been deposited in a bank or other safe hands in London. Yet the creditor has been granted an injunction to restrain their removal. He has, however, been able to point to some cause of action which will enable him to serve notice of the writ on the debtor out of the jurisdiction: such as, that the debt arose under a contract that was governed by English law: see RSC Ord 11, r 1 (1) (f) (iii).[14] In the present case, however, the cargo-owners, who are the plaintiffs, cannot bring their case

12 [1980] 1 All ER 213, [1975] 2 Lloyd's Rep 509.
13 [1978] QB 644, [1977] 3 All ER 324.
14 Now RSC Ord 11, r 1 (1) (d) (iii) (*Ed*).

within any of the heads of Ord 11, r 1 (1) except (i).[15] They cannot bring it within (f) (iii) because the bill of lading was governed by Italian law. They cannot bring it within (h)[16] because the tort was committed outside the jurisdiction. They can only bring it within rule 1 (1) (i), which says that service out of the jurisdiction is permissible:

> 'if in the action begun by the writ an injunction is sought ordering the defendant to do or refrain from doing anything within the jurisdiction (whether or not damages are also claimed in respect of a failure to do or the doing of that thing); . . .'

I must say that it seems to me that in our present case the injunction sought falls entirely within the words of that rule. An injunction is sought by the cargo-owners ordering that the shipowners be restrained: 'from disposing of their assets within the jurisdiction including and in particular the insurance proceeds in respect of the vessel *Siskina*'. It is true that damages are claimed against the shipowners 'for breach of duty and/or contract': but that is not necessary: for the rule applies whether damages are claimed, or not.

(His Lordship reviewed the cases on Ord 11, r 1 (1) (i) and continued):

Community law

Mr Lloyd (counsel for the defendants) also reminded us of the caution which the courts exercise in allowing service out of the jurisdiction under RSC Ord 11. That is for reasons of comity. But comity in this case is all in favour of granting an injunction seeing that it is a close parallel to 'saisie conservatoire' with which other countries are very familiar. I go further. Now that we are in the common market it is our duty to do our part in harmonising the laws of the countries of the nine (article 3 (h) of the EEC Treaty): see *Trendtex Trading Corpn v Central Bank of Nigeria*.[17]

It is our duty to apply the Treaty according to the spirit and not the letter: see *James Buchanan & Co Ltd v Babco Forwarding and Shipping (UK) Ltd*.[18] Now under article 220 it is the duty of the member states to seek to secure the 'reciprocal recognition' of the 'judgments of courts'. To do so in this case means that we should regard a determination by the Italian courts—one of the countries of the common market—with the same respect as a determination of the English courts: and that we should give our aid to the enforcement of it to the same extent as we would our own. In particular, we should take protective measures to see that the moneys here are not spirited away pending the decision of the Italian courts.

In this context it is instructive to study the way in which article 220 has been implemented by the original six countries of the common market in the 1968 Convention on Jurisdiction and the Enforcement of Judgments. This will in due course be extended to cover all the nine countries which are now members. When the creditor and debtor live in different countries of the common market, the Convention adopts the principle that the creditor must

---

15 Now RSC Ord 11, r 1 (1) (b) (*Ed*).
16 Now RSC Ord 11, r 1 (1) (f) (*Ed*).
17 [1977] QB 529 at 557–558, [1977] 1 All ER 881 at 892.
18 [1977] QB 208 at 213; [1977] 1 All ER 518 at 522. Lord Denning's judgment in this case did not meet with the approval of the House of Lords: [1978] AC 141, [1977] 3 All ER 1048: p 687 below (*Ed*).

seek out the debtor and sue him in the country in which the debtor lives: see article 2. The creditor cannot sue the debtor in his own (the creditor's) country so as to enforce the substance of the debt save in particular defined circumstances: see article 3. But meanwhile the creditor can apply to the courts of his own (the creditor's) country for protective measures to be taken against the assets of the debtor—when those assets are situate in the creditor's country—so as to prevent the debtor disposing of them before the creditor obtains his judgment in the substantive case: see article 24. So a German creditor, who has a debtor living in the Netherlands *must* sue him in the Netherlands for the substance of the debt, but meanwhile—even before starting proceedings in the Netherlands—he can take interim protective measures in Germany against any assets which the Netherlands debtor may have in Germany: see the decision of the Hamburg court summarised in the 'Synopsis of Case-Law' issued in the last few days by the European Court of Justice.[19] The typical protective measure is that known as saisie conservatoire under which the assets of the debtor can be frozen until judgment in order to prevent the debtor divesting himself of them.

When the debtor does not live in one of the countries of the common market, but outside it, then the creditor is at liberty to sue the debtor in whatever way the laws of his (the creditor's) country allow: and to take such protective measures as his (the creditor's) country permits against the assets of the debtor situate in the creditor's country: see article 4. So a German creditor who has a debtor in Panama or Greece can sue him in whatever way German law permits, and meanwhile he can take protective measures such as saisie conservatoire against the assets of such a debtor. Likewise, a creditor in England (who obtains leave to serve out of the jurisdiction on the foreign debtor) can take protective measures by way of a *Mareva* injunction.

In order to harmonise the laws of the common market countries, it is therefore appropriate that we should apply protective measures here so as to prevent these insurance moneys being disposed of before judgment.

Now suppose that the cargo-owners had a claim pending against the shipowning company in the English courts, it is clear that we would grant a *Mareva* injunction to restrain the removal of the assets. So also we should do the same when the claim is pending in the Italian courts. It is clear also that if these bills of lading were governed by English law, we should give leave to serve out and would grant a *Mareva* injunction. So also we should grant such an injunction when the bills are governed by Italian law—which no doubt is much the same as English law in this respect. In either case it is simple justice to the creditor that the assets should be preserved—and not removed—pending the determination of his claim, whether in the English courts or the Italian courts. So on this broad ground also—of the harmonisation of the laws of the European Economic Community—I would also grant the *Mareva* injunction and give leave to serve out.

Conclusion

I have, I hope, now dealt with all the submissions of Mr Lloyd. To my mind this case comes within the very words of RSC Ord 11, r 1 (1) (i), and within the principle of the *Mareva* case. I would, therefore, allow the appeal and grant an injunction to restrain the removal of the insurance moneys (or such

19 *Case No 37: Firma NRG & Co v Firma GSK BV* (1975).

part of them as would suffice to cover the claim of the cargo-owners) pending the determination of the dispute in the courts of Italy, or Cyprus, by arbitration, or any other lawful method: but I would put the cargo-owners on terms to proceed speedily in the courts of Genoa or Cyprus to determine their claim.

It was suggested that this course is not open to us because it would be legislation: and that we should leave the law to be amended by the Rules Committee. But see what this would mean: The shipowning company would be able to decamp with the insurance moneys and the cargo-owners would have to whistle for any redress. To wait for the Rules Committee would be to shut the stable door after the steed had been stolen. And who knows that there will ever again be another horse in the stable? Or another ship sunk and insurance moneys here? I ask, why should the judges wait for the Rules Committee? The judges have an inherent jurisdiction to lay down the practice and procedure of the courts: and we can invoke it now to restrain the removal of these insurance moneys. To the timorous souls I would say in the words of William Cowper:

'Ye fearful saints, fresh courage take,
The clouds ye so much dread
Are big with mercy, and shall break
In blessings on your head.'

Instead of 'saints', read 'judges'. Instead of 'mercy', read 'justice'. And you will find a good way to law reform.

I would allow the appeal.

Lawton LJ delivered judgment to the same effect.

Bridge LJ dissented.

Appeal allowed.

NOTE

This decision was reversed by the House of Lords on the ground that a *Mareva* injunction could not be granted where the defendant was not amenable to the jurisdiction of the court independently of the claim for an injunction. In the course of his speech Lord Diplock said: 'My Lords, there may be merits in Lord Denning MR's alternative proposals for extending the jurisdiction of the High Court over foreign defendants but they cannot, in my view, be supported by considerations of comity or by the common market treaties. They would require at least subordinate legislation by the Rules Committee under section 99 of the Supreme Court of Judicature (Consolidation) Act 1925, if not primary legislation by Parliament itself. It is not for the Court of Appeal or for your Lordships to exercise these legislative functions, however tempting this may be.' But the decision of the House of Lords was reversed by section 25 of the Civil Jurisdiction and Judgments Act 1982 (p 81 above). Hence the decision of the Court of Appeal is still good law if (a) proceedings had been or were to be commenced in Italy, or (b) the section had been extended to Cyprus by Order in Council under section 25 (3).

CHAPTER 6

Jurisdiction to Stay Actions

Section A: Lis Alibi Pendens

English courts have jurisdiction to stay an action in England or to restrain proceedings in foreign courts. In order to justify a stay, two conditions must be satisfied, one positive and the other negative: (a) the defendant must satisfy the court that there is another forum to whose jurisdiction he is amenable in which justice can be done between the parties at substantially less inconvenience and expense, and (b) the stay must not deprive the plaintiff of a legitimate personal or juridical advantage which would be available to him if he invoked the jurisdiction of the English court.

MacShannon v Rockware Glass Ltd [1978] AC 795, [1978] 1 All ER 625 (House of Lords)

Consolidated appeals from two decisions of the Court of Appeal (Stephenson and Waller LJJ; Lord Denning MR dissenting) and (under the 'leap-frog' procedure) from two decisions of Griffiths J.

Lord Diplock: My Lords, each of these four appeals is concerned with a claim for damages for personal injury or disability (deafness) sustained by the plaintiff in the course of his employment in a factory in Scotland, and alleged to be due to negligence on the part of his employer. In each case the employer was a company whose head office is in England. It is this alone that made it possible for a High Court writ to be served upon the employer in England. None of the four actions has any other connection with England and each of the employers could have been served at their places of business in Scotland with proceedings in the local Sheriff Court or the Court of Session.

All three members of the Court of Appeal acknowledged that Scotland was the natural and appropriate forum for the Fyfe and MacShannon actions. Stephenson LJ expressed it most emphatically in terms which I am ready to adopt, when he said: 'Anyone with nothing but common sense to guide him would say that they ought to be tried in Scotland'. Nevertheless he considered that the decision of this House in *The Atlantic Star*[1] compelled him to follow a course which was contrary to common sense, and so to allow the actions to proceed in England. It thus becomes necessary for this House to consider whether the ratio decidendi of the majority of this House in *The Atlantic Star* must indeed have this lamentable consequence.

In *The Atlantic Star* what divided the majority of the House (Lord Reid, Lord Wilberforce and Lord Kilbrandon) from the minority (Lord Morris of

---

1 [1974] AC 436, [1973] 2 All ER 175.

Borth-y-Gest and Lord Simon of Glaisdale) was not a difference as to the terms in which the relevant law had been laid down in the previous cases. The speeches of both Lord Wilberforce and Lord Morris of Borth-y-Gest contain very similar analyses of the authorities, of which the most important had been decided in the 1880s within a few years after the coming into force of the Supreme Court of Judicature Act 1873. Both the majority and the minority accepted that the existing law as it had been understood for some ninety years before *The Atlantic Star* was accurately stated in the oft-cited passage from the judgment of Scott LJ in *St. Pierre v South American Stores (Gath & Chaves) Ltd*:[2]

> 'The true rule about a stay under section 41 (of the Supreme Court of Judicature (Consolidation) Act 1925),[3] so far as relevant to this case, may I think be stated thus: (1) A mere balance of convenience is not a sufficient ground for depriving a plaintiff of the advantages of prosecuting his action in an English court if it is otherwise properly brought. The right of access to the King's court must not be lightly refused. (2) In order to justify a stay two conditions must be satisfied, one positive and the other negative: (a) the defendant must satisfy the court that the continuance of the action would work an injustice because it would be oppressive or vexatious to him or would be an abuse of the process of the court in some other way; and (b) the stay must not cause an injustice to the plaintiff. On both the burden of proof is on the defendant. These propositions are, I think, consistent with and supported by the following cases: *McHenry v Lewis*;[4] *Peruvian Guano Co v Bockwold*;[5] *Hyman v Helm*;[6] *Thornton v Thornton*;[7] and *Logan v Bank of Scotland (No 2)*.[8]'

The positive condition which must be satisfied to justify staying an action of which process has been lawfully served upon the defendant is here stated to be conduct which can be characterised as 'oppressive' or 'vexatious'. Both in ordinary parlance and as terms of art in relation to the procedure of the courts these terms connote an element of moral blameworthiness—a desire on the plaintiff's part to harass the defendant by putting him to unnecessary trouble or expense, rather than to improve the plaintiff's own prospects of success or enhance what he stands to gain from the litigation. As pointed out by Lord Morris of Borth-y-Gest, this was the meaning which had been uniformly attributed to the words 'oppressive' and 'vexatious' by judges in all cases subsequent to *St Pierre* in which Scott LJ's statement of the law had been applied.

In *The Atlantic Star*, this House was specifically invited to discard Scott LJ's statement as an authoritative exposition of the principles on which a stay of proceedings ought to be granted in English law and to substitute for it the Scottish legal doctrine of forum non conveniens. The House unanimously rejected this invitation. The minority were of opinion that this House should

2 [1936] 1 KB 382 at 398.
3 See now Supreme Court Act 1981, s 49 (*Ed*).
4 (1882) 22 Ch D 397, 52 LJCh 325.
5 (1883) 23 Ch D 225, 52 LJCh 714.
6 (1883) 24 Ch D 531, 49 LT 376.
7 (1886) 11 PD 176, 55 LJP 40.
8 [1906] 1 KB 141 at 150, 151.

leave unchanged the English law upon the topic as it had hitherto been expounded and applied, particularly in admiralty jurisdiction. The majority, however, were of opinion that the time was ripe for some further development of the common law which, as Lord Reid put it, would bring it more into line with the policy of Parliament and the movement of public opinion, and render it less reminiscent of 'the good old days, the passing of which many may regret, when the inhabitants of this island felt an innate superiority over those unfortunate enough to belong to other races'.

It would not be consonant with the traditional way in which judicial precedent has played its part in the development of the common law of England, to attempt to incorporate holus-bolus from some other system of law, even so close as that of Scotland, doctrines or legal concepts that have hitherto been unrecognised in English common law. The progress of the common law is gradual. It is undertaken step by step as what has been stated in a previous precedent to be the law is re-examined and modified so as to bring it into closer accord with the changed conditions in which it falls to be applied today. But this is not to say that the result of proceeding by the latter course of reasoning will necessarily be very different from that which would have been achieved by adopting into English law a concept from some other legal system. Destinations that are very close to one another may be reached by different routes. So there would be nothing surprising in the fact that in rejecting as the appropriate route the importation into English common law of the Scots doctrine of forum non conveniens in favour of the more traditional method of developing this branch of the common law from where the precedent in *St Pierre* had left it in 1936, the majority of the House had nevertheless reached a result which could invite the comment by Lord Simon of Glaisdale: 'That would be to admit by the back door a rule that your Lordships consider cannot be welcomed at the front'. Whether true or not, this, with respect, is not a valid criticism of the reasoning of the majority, particularly in a case in which the English Court of Admiralty, whose jurisdiction has been invoked in rem, was prima facie a natural and appropriate forum in which to bring the action and was recognised as such by international convention.

As a result of their re-examination of the statement of the law by Scott LJ in *St Pierre* the majority were of opinion that the modification that was called for could be best achieved by giving to the words 'oppressive' and 'vexatious' what was described by Lords Reid and Wilberforce as a more liberal interpretation. Put bluntly what this comes to is that if Scott LJ's judgment in *St Pierre* is still to be treated as the framework on which the statement of the law is built, the words 'oppressive' and 'vexatious' are no longer to be understood in their natural meaning, but in some strained and 'morally neutral meaning' (per Lord Kilbrandon). To continue to use these words to express the principle to be applied in determining whether an action brought in England should be stayed can, in my view, lead only to confusion—as I believe it has in the instant cases.

If these expressions are eliminated from Scott LJ's statement of the rule, the gist of the three speeches of Lord Reid, Lord Wilberforce and Lord Kilbrandon, in my opinion, enables the second part of it to be restated thus:

'(2) In order to justify a stay two conditions must be satisfied, one positive and the other negative: (a) the defendant must satisfy the court that there is another forum to whose jurisdiction he is amenable in which justice can be done between the parties at substantially less inconvenience or expense, and (b) the stay must not deprive the plaintiff of a legitimate personal or juridical advantage which would be available to him if he invoked the jurisdiction of the English court'

omitting the reference to burden of proof which follows these words. If the distinction between this restatement of the English law and the Scottish doctrine of forum non conveniens might on examination prove to be a fine one, I cannot think that it is any the worse for that.

My Lords, each of the instant actions arises out of an industrial accident or disability alleged to have been sustained by a plaintiff who lives in Scotland in the course of his employment in a factory in Scotland. All the witnesses to fact likewise live in Scotland and unless they have since retired earn their livings there. The plaintiff was treated for his injuries or disability by doctors practising in Scotland. Medical and other expert witnesses accustomed to giving evidence in industrial injury actions are available in Scotland. A mere recital of these features of the actions is sufficient to establish a prima facie case that each of them could be tried at the local sheriff court or the Court of Session at substantially less expense and inconvenience than in England. In considering inconvenience it would, in my view, be wrong to confine this to the convenience of the parties themselves. Witnesses, too, who are required to play a part essential to the administration of justice, are entitled to consideration, and so is disruption caused to others by the absence from their places of work of witnesses required to be present at the court of trial. This it is that prima facie makes the Scottish courts the only natural or appropriate forum for each of these actions and throws upon the plaintiffs the onus of showing what Lord Reid called 'some reasonable justification' for his choice of an English court or, as I have ventured to express it, of showing that if they brought their actions in a Scottish court they would be deprived of a legitimate personal or juridical advantage which would have been available to them in the High Court of England.

The advantage must be a real one. The plaintiff's own belief that there is an advantage or, what is more likely to determine where the action is to be brought, the belief of his legal advisers, however genuinely it may be held, is not enough. The advantage that is relied upon as a ground for diverting the action from its natural forum must be shown objectively and on the balance of probability to exist. So long as it was necessary to show 'oppressive' or 'vexatious' conduct by the plaintiff in the ordinary meaning of those words, the test remained subjective: an unsubstantiated but bona fide belief by the plaintiff or his legal advisers in an advantage to be obtained for him by suing in the English courts might be a sufficient answer to the defendant's application for a stay. Since *The Atlantic Star* this is no longer so.

My Lords, the decision whether or not to grant a stay involves the application of a judicial discretion to the facts of the particular case; but the judge in his consideration of the facts should not wear blinkers. In each of the actions the plaintiff and the defendant are the parties between whom justice is to be done; but in deciding how best it can be done it is a relevant fact that they are 'trade union cases'; had it been otherwise it is inconceivable that they should have been brought elsewhere than in

Scotland. The trade union of which the plaintiff is a member has taken up his case. It has referred him to its English solicitors who regularly conduct industrial injury cases on behalf of its members and to whom the union makes itself responsible for the plaintiff's own costs. It will indemnify the plaintiff against any liability he may incur to pay costs to the other party. The defendants for their part are insured against their liability to the plaintiffs and the conduct of their defence is in the hands of the insurance company's solicitors. It would be idle to suppose that the choice of forum in any of the individual cases has been made by the plaintiff himself rather than by the trade union's English solicitors. It is the solicitors who believe that it would be better for the plaintiff to sue in England instead of Scotland, and have stated the grounds for their belief in affidavits. I must summarise these grounds a little later, but that they are general in character and not personal to the individual plaintiff is confirmed by the fact that within the last three years, 44 similar cases of industrial injuries in Scotland have been started in the High Court in England in many of which the solicitors instructed on behalf of the plaintiffs are those who are instructed on behalf of three of the plaintiffs in the instant case.

My Lords, in the courts below the fact that many other actions for industrial injury actions sustained by Scotsmen in Scotland were being brought in England was treated as irrelevant. It was said, and rightly said, that the sole consideration which should influence the judge in exercising his discretion in each individual case was to do justice as between that plaintiff and that defendant. Nevertheless, the judge must be realistic. The decision whether or not to stay an action must be taken promptly. If the action is one for personal injuries which will be tried on oral evidence it is not possible at that early stage to enter into a nice calculation of what additional expense and inconvenience to all concerned will be involved if the action is allowed to proceed to trial in England instead of Scotland. So in the absence of any special features that are apparent even at that early stage, he can only act upon the assumption that it will turn out to be a run-of-the-mill industrial injuries action, of which he will himself have had considerable experience. Furthermore, if justice is to be seen to be done, the discretion, which will fall to be exercised by different judges in different cases, must manifest a reasonable consistency as between one case and another. In run-of-the-mill cases discretion, if exercised judicially, ought to be predictable so that lawyers may know broadly what advice to give to their clients. Lastly, there is an element of public policy involved; that the administration of justice within the United Kingdom should be conducted in such a way as to avoid any *unnecessary* diversion to the purposes of litigation, of time and efforts of witnesses and others which would otherwise be spent on activities that are more directly productive of national wealth or well-being. Many a mickle makes a muckle; and if it were to become the common practice to bring Scottish industrial injury cases in England, the total waste of time and effort would be substantial.

My Lords, your Lordships have had evidence in the Jardine and Paterson appeals as to the additional cost which would be incurred on travel and overnight accommodation alone if a run-of-the-mill industrial injury case from the industrial belt in Scotland were tried in London, Newcastle or Carlisle instead of in the local Sheriff Court or the Court of Session in Scotland. This evidence was not available to the Court of Appeal in the Fyfe and MacShannon appeals. Even upon these items of expenditure the difference is substantial, ranging from £200 to £450 according to the place of trial in England. This evidence throws up too the added inconvenience to witnesses and the additional time during which ordinary work will be disrupted by their having to attend a trial in an English court rather than a Scottish one. Prima facie this evidence, in my view, amply satisfies the requirement that the defendant must show that Scotland provides a forum in which justice can be done between the parties at substantially less expense and inconvenience than in the High Court in England.

So in each of these cases in my view it was for the plaintiff to show that to compel him to seek his remedy in a Scottish court would deprive him of a legitimate personal or juridical advantage which would be available to him if he were allowed to proceed with his action in the High Court in England.

In none of the cases was any personal advantage to the plaintiff relied on. All of them live in Scotland, their personal convenience both as respects the trial and preparation for it would be better served by litigation in a Scottish court. The advantages claimed for litigating industrial injury actions in England instead of Scotland were judicial and general in character. There were ten altogether set out in the affidavit of Mr Skidmore, a partner in the firm of solicitors for the plaintiff in the MacShannon case. Robert Goff J condensed them into four which he expressed thus:

'. . . first of all a suggestion that the level of damages in England may be higher; secondly, that the legal process in Scotland involves a greater length of time than the process in this country; thirdly, that Scottish proceedings are more expensive and, fourthly, that successful proceedings are not so likely to cover indemnities as to his costs as it would be in this country in the sense that he is unlikely to recover party and party costs'.

In Fyfe's case his solicitor relied primarily on the second and third of these reasons, which I should add, are largely based upon distrust by both deponents of the Scots system of pleading. These contentions as to the superiority of English over Scottish courts as the forum in which the victim of an industrial accident could obtain justice started a veritable war of affidavits. They were hotly denied by Scottish lawyers whose experience in their own jurisdiction was comparable to that of Mr Skidmore in his. Before Robert Goff J and the Court of Appeal Scots law and practice was a question of fact to be proved by expert evidence wherever the presumption that 'foreign' law is the same as English law is sought to be displaced. The judge did not attempt what he and Stephenson LJ described as 'the invidious and impossible task' of deciding which country's procedure was the quicker or the cheaper or whether English courts were likely to give higher damages or award more generous party and party costs. Neither did the Court of Appeal. They regarded themselves as absolved from undertaking such an investigation because the advice to bring his action in England given to the plaintiff by his solicitor and based upon the latter's bona fide belief that the plaintiff would fare better in the English High Court than in a Scots court, provided in itself a sufficient ground on which to refuse a stay. This was, in my view, an error of law which vitiates the exercise of his discretion by the judge and its confirmation by the Court of Appeal. It leaves the way open to your Lordships to decide how the discretion should have been exercised. Where prima facie England is not the natural or appropriate forum in which to bring the plaintiff's action and the plaintiff relies upon juridical, as distinct from personal, advantages in bringing his action here instead, it is for him to prove by expert evidence the respects in which the substantive or procedural law of the natural forum differs from the corresponding English law to the disadvantage of the plaintiff. This is so as respects the law of foreign states. In the High Court and Court of Appeal in England it is also true as respects Scots law.

The appellate jurisdiction of this House, however, in civil matters extends to Scotland as well as England. When an appeal comes before your Lordships, Scots law is not a question of fact to be proved by expert evidence, your Lordships are entitled and bound to take judicial notice of it.

My Lords, as respects the measure of damages in actions for personal injuries in Scotland there is no difference between English and Scots law; and Scots courts have since 1972 been enjoined by the Inner House of the Court of Session to take account of awards made by English courts in comparable cases: *Allan v Scott*.[9] So on this score the plaintiff's prospects are the same in both countries.

As respects the length and expense of process in Scotland said to result from the Scots system of pleading, reliance is placed upon some observations of my own in *Gibson v British Insulated Callenders' Construction Co Ltd*,[10] when I expressed disenchantment with the way in which the method of pleading had, in that particular case, operated, as I thought, to the disadvantage of the defendant and the corresponding advantage of the plaintiff in an industrial injury action. The circumstances in which the pleading point arose in that case were exceptional and my criticisms were repudiated in the speech of my noble and learned friend, Lord Kilbrandon. It is natural that lawyers from the two countries should prefer that system of pleading with which they are the more familiar. The English and Scottish system of pleading and procedure differ, but your Lordships would not be justified in holding as a generalisation that one offers more advantages to plaintiffs in industrial injury actions than does the other.

My Lords, there remain the questions of expense and the amount of costs recoverable from the losing party. So far as expense of travel and overnight accommodation is concerned, this has already been dealt with. The balance in favour of Scotland is substantial. There remain court fees and the costs of legal representation. Your Lordships have no reason to think that if Scots solicitors and counsel were engaged to prosecute proceedings in the Sheriff Court or the Court of Session the costs would be any greater than if English solicitors and counsel were engaged to prosecute proceedings in the High Court in England. The claim in the affidavits of the plaintiffs' solicitor that the lawyers' costs of proceeding in Scotland would be higher appears to contemplate that an English solicitor should be instructed on behalf of the plaintiff—as is the fact in each of the instant cases—and that the proceedings in Scotland should be undertaken by Scots solicitors on an agency basis. I can well understand that it may be convenient to a trade union with a membership covering England and Scotland to channel all claims by its members for damages for personal injuries through one firm of solicitors and

9 1972 SC 59, 1972 SLT 45.
10 1973 SC (HL) 15, 1973 SLT 2 at 7–9.

that if the headquarters of the trade union are in England and the majority of claims come from there, it may be convenient that that firm of solicitors should be English. But the fact that as part of the service which a trade union offers to its members, the plaintiff's action is underwritten by his trade union, does not, in my view, justify it in instructing an English solicitor on his behalf, if Scotland is the natural forum, and then relying, as a ground for not litigating in Scotland, on the increased cost of conducting proceedings in Scotland through Scottish solicitors on an agency basis instead of instructing the Scottish solicitor direct.

My Lords, I have treated the case of MacShannon and Fyfe as run-of-the-mill industrial injury cases—for that is what they are. The cases of Jardine and Paterson are claims for industrial deafness. If fought they will involve calling specialist medical witnesses and expert witnesses on acoustics and audiometry; but the evidence shows, not surprisingly, that such specialists and experts are available in Scotland as well as in England. I can see no ground on which a relevant distinction can be drawn between these two appeals and the MacShannon and Fyfe appeals. In none of them, in my view, has the plaintiff shown any legitimate personal or juridical advantage which would be available to him in an action in the English courts but of which he would be deprived if forced to litigate in Scotland.

I would allow all these appeals.

Lords Salmon, Fraser of Tullybelton, Russell of Killowen and Keith of Kinkel delivered judgments to the same effect.
Appeals allowed.

The fact that the plaintiff will probably recover higher damages in the foreign proceedings than he would in England is a legitimate personal or juridical advantage which may justify the court in refusing an injunction to restrain the foreign proceedings.

Castanho v Brown & Root (UK) Ltd [1981] AC 557, [1981] 1 All ER 143 (House of Lords)

The plaintiff, a Portuguese subject resident in Portugal, was severely injured by an accident in February 1977 while he was employed by the second defendants, a Panamanian company, on an American ship lying in Great Yarmouth. The first defendants, an English company, provided shore services for the ship. Both defendants were associates of a large Texas-based group of companies (Jackson Marine Corporation or JMC). While the defendant was in hospital in England a writ was issued on his behalf by English solicitors in September 1977 claiming damages for his injuries. In November 1977 the plaintiff was taken back to Portugal. During 1978 a firm of Texas attorneys persuaded the plaintiff to bring proceedings in Texas, where higher damages could be obtained, on the terms that if he was successful the attorneys would receive 40% of the sum recovered. In April 1979 proceedings on behalf of the plaintiff were started in a Texas state court and were subsequently transferred to a federal court in Texas. Meanwhile the defendants delivered a defence in the English proceedings admitting liability and claimed an injunction restraining the plaintiff from continuing proceedings in the United States. Parker J granted the injunction. The Court of Appeal by a majority (Brandon and Shaw LJJ: Lord Denning MR dissenting) discharged the injunction. The defendants appealed.

Lord Scarman (having stated the facts): The question in the appeal is, therefore, whether the plaintiff should be restrained by the English court from pursuing his claim for damages in the American courts. It is a question of great importance to the parties. In the American courts the plaintiff claims punitive as well as compensatory damages ($5m compensation, and 'at least' $10m punitive or exemplary). In England he has no claim for punitive damages: and the scale of compensatory damages is much less. It is conceded that, had he begun in Texas in the first place, the English courts would not grant an injunction to restrain him from continuing there. The defendants base their case upon the fact that he started in England, and upon the disadvantages, in the circumstances which have arisen, of their being sued in America. . . .

Injunction, being an equitable remedy, operates in personam. It has been used to order parties amenable to the court's jurisdiction 'to take, or to omit to take, any steps and proceedings in any other court of justice, whether in this country, or in a foreign country'; Leach V-C in *Bushby v Munday*.[11] The English court, as the Vice-Chancellor went on to say, 'does not pretend to any interference with the other court; it acts upon the defendant by punishment for his contempt in his disobedience to the order of the court'. The jurisdiction, which has been frequently exercised since 1821, was reviewed by the Court of Appeal in *Ellerman Lines Ltd v Read*.[12] Scrutton LJ in that case quoted with approval a passage from the judgment of Lord Brougham LC in *Lord Portarlington v Soulby*[13] where the Lord Chancellor affirmed that 'the injunction was not directed to the foreign court, but to the party within the jurisdiction here'. I would not, however, leave *Ellerman's* case without a reference to the warning of Eve J at 158: 'No doubt the jurisdiction is to be exercised with caution'.

The considerable case law to which your Lordships have been referred does not, in terms, express any limitation upon the sort of cases in which it may be appropriate to exercise the jurisdiction. Counsel for the plaintiff however, submitted that it is to be found to have been exercised only in two classes of case: (1) 'lis alibi pendens', where the object is to prevent harassment: he cited as examples *The Christiansborg*,[14] with especial reference to the judgment of Baggallay LJ at 152–153, *The Hagen*[15] and *The Janera*:[16] and (2) where there is a right justiciable in England, which the court seeks to protect.

In support of his second class, counsel cited a passage from the speech of my noble and learned friend, Lord Diplock, in *The Siskina*:[17]

'A right to obtain an interlocutory injunction is not a cause of action. . . . It is dependent upon there being a pre-existing cause of action against the defendant arising out of an invasion, actual or threatened by him, of

11 (1821) 5 Madd 297 at 307.
12 [1928] 2 KB 144, 97 LJKB 366.
13 (1834) 3 My & K 104 at 107.
14 (1885) 10 PD 141, 54 LJP 84.
15 [1908] P 189 at 202.
16 [1928] P 55, 97 LJP 58.
17 [1979] AC 210 at 256, [1977] 3 All ER 803 at 824.

a legal or equitable right of the plaintiff for the enforcement of which the defendant is amenable to the jurisdiction of the court.'

No doubt, in practice, most cases fall within one or other of these two classes. But the width and flexibility of equity are not to be undermined by categorisation. Caution in the exercise of the jurisdiction is certainly needed: but the way in which the judges have expressed themselves from 1821 onwards amply supports the view for which the defendants contend that the injunction can be granted against a party properly before the court, where it is appropriate to avoid injustice.

The plaintiff went home to Portugal after his accident (in fact, on 1 November, 1977), where he has ever since remained. He is neither a British subject nor resident in England. But he has sued in England, where he has agents, ie the solicitors acting for him: and his cause of action arose in England. Is this a sufficient connection with England to enable an English court to grant an injunction against him? The point was considered by Megaw J, as he then was, in *The Tropaioforos (No 2)*[18] where it was sought to discharge an injunction restraining a party from proceeding in a foreign court after the English proceedings had come to an end. Counsel for the applicant in that case submitted that an English court has no jurisdiction to restrain a foreigner who is not resident here (and who has no assets against which an order could be enforced) from instituting or continuing proceedings in a foreign court, unless this would constitute an abuse of the process of the English court. The point does not arise for decision, if your Lordships refuse to accept, as I do, that the English action in the present case had come to an end before the injunction was granted. But, if I may respectfully express an opinion, I would think that the approach of Megaw J in *The Tropaioforos* was correct in principle; namely, that it is a question of fact to be determined in the light of the particular circumstances of the case whether one who is suing abroad has sufficient connection with England to justify the granting of an injunction restraining him from proceeding with his foreign suit. In that case the existence of a contract was held to have provided the connection.

There remains the point that to grant an injunction in the circumstances of this case against the respondent would be useless, a mere brutum fulmen. The answer was given succinctly by the Court of Appeal in *Re Liddell's Settlement Trusts*[19] Romer LJ observing: 'It is not the habit of this court in considering whether or not it will make an order to contemplate the possibility that it will not be obeyed', and Slesser LJ, at 373 'We are not to assume that the lady will necessarily disobey the court. . . .'

I turn to consider what criteria should govern the exercise of the court's discretion to impose a stay or grant an injunction. It is unnecessary now to examine the earlier case law. The principle is the same whether the remedy sought is a stay of English proceedings or a restraint upon foreign proceedings. The modern statement of the law is to be found in the majority speeches in *The Atlantic Star*.[20] It had been thought that the criteria for staying (or restraining) proceedings were two-fold: (1) that to allow the proceedings to continue would be oppressive or vexatious, and (2) that to

18 [1962] 1 Lloyd's Rep 410.
19 [1936] Ch 365 at 374, [1936] 1 All ER 239.
20 [1974] AC 436, [1973] 2 All ER 175.

stay (or restrain) them would not cause injustice to the plaintiff: see Scott LJ in *St Pierre v South American Stores (Gath & Chaves) Ltd.*[1] In *The Atlantic Star* this House, while refusing to go as far as the Scottish doctrine of forum non conveniens, extended and reformulated the criteria, treating the epithets 'vexatious' and 'oppressive' as illustrating but not confining the jurisdiction. My noble and learned friend Lord Wilberforce put it in this way. The 'critical equation', he said at 468, was between 'any advantage to the plaintiff' and 'any disadvantage to the defendant'. Though this is essentially a matter for the court's discretion, it is possible, he said, to 'make explicit' some elements. He then went on, at 468–469:

'The cases say that the advantage must not be "fanciful"—that a "substantial advantage" is enough ... A bona fide advantage to a plaintiff is a solid weight in the scale, often a decisive weight, but not always so. Then the disadvantage to the defendant: to be taken into account at all this must be serious, more than mere disadvantage of multiple suits; ... I think too that there must be a relative element in assessing both advantage and disadvantage—*relative to the individual circumstances of the plaintiff and defendant.*' (Emphasis supplied.)

In *MacShannon v Rockware Glass Ltd*[2] my noble and learned friend, Lord Diplock, interpreted the majority speeches in *The Atlantic Star*, as an invitation to drop the use of the words 'vexatious' and 'oppressive' (an invitation which I gladly accept) and formulated his distillation of principle in words which are now very familiar:

'In order to justify a stay two conditions must be satisfied, one positive and the other negative: (a) the defendant must satisfy the court that there is another forum to whose jurisdiction he is amenable in which justice can be done between the parties at substantially less inconvenience or expense, and (b) the stay must not deprive the plaintiff of a legitimate personal or juridical advantage which would be available to him if he invoked the jurisdiction of the English court.'

Transposed into the context of the present case, this formulation means that to justify the grant of an injunction the defendants must show: (a) that the English court is a forum to whose jurisdiction they are amenable in which justice can be done at substantially less inconvenience and expense, *and* (b) the injunction must not deprive the plaintiff of a legitimate personal or juridical advantage which would be available to him if he invoked the American jurisdiction.

The formula is not, however, to be construed as a statute. No time should be spent in speculating as to what is meant by 'legitimate'. It, like the whole of the context, is but a guide to solving in the particular circumstances of the case the 'critical equation' between advantage to the plaintiff and disadvantage to the defendants.

No question arises on (a). I will assume that justice can be done in the English proceedings at substantially less expense to the defendants. The balance of convenience is, however, less heavily tipped against them, Texas being their headquarters. The judge directed himself correctly as to the

1 [1936] 1 KB 382 at 398.
2 [1978] AC 795 at 812, [1978] 1 All ER 625; p 128 above.

applicable law, founding himself on the *MacShannon* formulation and dealing with (b) at length. The challenge that is made to his decision is that, in exercising his discretion to grant the injunction, he wrongly analysed the relevant factors, giving weight to something which he ought not to have taken into account and failing to give weight to something which he ought to have taken into account. It is, indeed, submitted that the judge's exercise of his discretion was plainly wrong—a submission which Brandon LJ must have accepted, since he embarked on his own analysis of the factors relevant to discretion. The attack upon the judge's exercise of discretion stands or falls upon a consideration of the paragraph in his judgment beginning [1980] 1 WLR 833 at 845.

Having acknowledged that the prospect of higher damages in America can be a legitimate advantage for a plaintiff, he gives two reasons for considering the advantage to be of little weight in this case. First, he instances a situation in which two plaintiffs 'suffering identical personal injuries' sue in England but one sues also in Texas because his defendant has an office and assets there. The judge considers it would be unjust to allow the second plaintiff to recover more in Texas than the first can recover in England. But this example, upon which he heavily relies for his conclusion, is an irrelevancy. The criterion, as was emphasised in *The Atlantic Star*, is the critical equation between the advantage to the plaintiff and the disadvantage to the defendant; but not, as the judge assumes, a comparison between different plaintiffs in their separate claims against different defendants. The judge, though he pays lip service to the principle that he must do justice *between* the parties, relies in this instance upon a comparison not between them but with others. He ignores 'the relative element' of which my noble and learned friend spoke in *The Atlantic Star*.

Secondly, he treats as 'the question of real importance' whether the plaintiff is likely to obtain a lower award in England than he would in the country where he lives, ie Portugal. There being no evidence that an English award would be treated as unjustly low in Portugal, he considers the prospects of a higher recovery in Texas to be 'of little weight'. I reject the reasoning and its relevance. The fact that the plaintiff can sue in Texas defendants who have an office and substantial assets in Texas and that under the law there he has the legitimate personal and juridical advantage of the prospect of a much greater recovery than if he were to sue in England cannot be discarded as of little weight merely because an English award would not be regarded as unjustly low in Portugal. The discretion is not to be exercised upon such a comparison, even if there were (which there was not) any evidence to guide the judge's speculation as to the Portuguese possibilities. The balance is between the English and the American proceedings; the relative elements of plaintiff's advantage and defendant's disadvantage in each have to be weighed. The balance is not to be confused by uncertain legal, social and economic elements arising outside the two sets of litigation.

It is, therefore, open to this House to review the exercise of the judge's discretion. My Lords, upon this aspect of the case I find the judgment of Brandon LJ convincing. He found that to restrain the plaintiff from proceeding in Texas would deprive him of a legitimate personal or juridical advantage: I agree. If he had been advised early enough to sue the JMC group in Texas first, they could not have compelled him to sue in England. The only additional expense incurred by the defendants as a result of the plaintiff suing first in England has been that of legal costs, which are recoverable by the defendants. Texas is as natural and proper a forum for suing a group of Texan-based companies as England—even though England, as the scene of the accident, is also a natural and proper forum. The admission of liability obtained in the English action, which could in some cases be a significant factor, is not in this case: for as Brandon LJ said: 'it is clear beyond doubt that [the accident] was caused by negligence of the ship's chief engineer'. Finally, there is the possible injustice to the defendants that, if the Texan court should decline jurisdiction the plaintiff can start afresh here: but the court can safeguard the defendants either by putting the plaintiff upon terms or by staying whatever English action is in being. For the reasons which Brandon LJ gives I agree with his conclusion 'that the balance comes down clearly in the plaintiff's favour'.

My conclusion is, therefore, that the Court of Appeal was right to discharge the injunction.

Much time was spent below upon evidence and argument on the propriety of the conduct of the American attorneys of the plaintiff. They certainly approached him with the object, in which they were successful, of persuading him to sue in America; and they will receive for themselves the substantial benefit of a fee on a contingency basis—40% of the damages recovered, nothing if he fails. The agreement they reached with him was said to contain terms unethical by the standards of the American bar, though it is conceded a contingency fee basis is itself acceptable, and common practice.

I venture to suggest, my Lords, that these matters are for the American authorities, and not for your Lordships' House. They have no place in the 'critical equation' which is fundamental to the proper exercise of the discretion in this case.

Lords Wilberforce, Diplock, Keith of Kinkel and Bridge of Harwich concurred.

Appeal dismissed.

Civil Jurisdiction and Judgments Act 1982

49. Nothing in this Act shall prevent any court in the United Kingdom from staying, sisting, striking out or dismissing any proceedings before it, on the ground of forum non conveniens or otherwise, where to do so is not inconsistent with the 1968 Convention.

SCHEDULE 1

Section 8   Lis Pendens—Related actions

ARTICLE 21

Where proceedings involving the same cause of action and between the same parties are brought in the courts of different Contracting States, any court other than the court first seised shall of its own motion decline jurisdiction in favour of that court.

A court which would be required to decline jurisdiction may stay its proceedings if the jurisdiction of the other court is contested.

ARTICLE 22

Where related actions are brought in the courts of different Contracting States, any court other than the court first seised may, while the actions are pending at first instance, stay its proceedings.

A court other than the court first seised may also, on the application of one of the parties, decline jurisdiction if the law of that court permits the consolidation of related actions and the court first seised has jurisdiction over both actions.

For the purposes of this Article, actions are deemed to be related where they are so closely connected that it is expedient to hear and determine them together to avoid the risk of irreconcilable judgments resulting from separate proceedings.

ARTICLE 23

Where actions come within the exclusive jurisdiction of several courts, any court other than the court first seised shall decline jurisdiction in favour of that court.

Section B. Foreign Jurisdiction Clauses

If a contract provides that all disputes between the parties are to be referred to the exclusive jurisdiction of a foreign tribunal, prima facie the English court will stay proceedings instituted in England in breach of such agreement; but the court may in its discretion allow them to continue.

The Fehmarn [1958] 1 All ER 333, [1958] 1 WLR 159 (Court of Appeal)

Appeal by the defendants from a decision of Willmer J.

Russian shippers loaded a cargo of turpentine on a German ship at Ventspils, a Russian port in the Baltic. The bill of lading provided (inter alia) that the shipowners were bound to make the ship seaworthy before and at the beginning of the voyage; and that all disputes should be judged in the USSR. The ship sailed to London and the Russian shippers sold the turpentine to English buyers, who became holders of the bill of lading.

After the turpentine was unloaded in England the English importers complained to the German shipowners of short delivery and contamination. They alleged that there were some three tons short on delivery and that the shipowners had failed to make the ship seaworthy and fit for the reception of the turpentine. They said that the ship's tanks had carried linseed oil on previous voyages and that they had not been properly cleaned out before the turpentine was loaded, with the result that there was a skin of linseed oil on the inside on the tanks, which dissolved and so contaminated the turpentine.

The English importers brought an action against the German shipowners in the Admiralty Division of the High Court, claiming damages. The German owners moved to set aside the writ on the ground that the English courts had no jurisdiction or alternatively that the parties had agreed that all disputes should be adjudged in the courts of Russia and not in this country.

Lord Denning: As to the first point, it is not now suggested that the Court of Admiralty has not jurisdiction. By s 1 (1) (g) of the Administration of Justice Act 1956[3] (following previous statutes), it is plain that the Court of Admiralty in England has jurisdiction to deal with such a claim as this.

Then the next question is whether the action ought to be stayed because of the provision in the bill of lading that all disputes are to be judged by the Russian courts. I do not regard this provision as equal to an arbitration clause, but I do say that the English courts are in charge of their own proceedings: and one of the rules they apply is that a stipulation that all disputes should be judged by the tribunals of a particular country is not absolutely binding. It is a matter to which the courts of this country will pay much regard and to which they will normally give effect, but it is subject to the overriding principle that no one by his private stipulation can oust these courts of their jurisdiction in a matter that properly belongs to them.

I would ask myself therefore: Is this dispute a matter which properly belongs to the courts of this country? Here are English importers who, when they take delivery of the goods in England, find them contaminated. The goods are surveyed by surveyors on both sides, with the result that the English importers make a claim against the German shipowners. The vessel is a frequent visitor to this country. In order to be sure that their claim, if substantiated, is paid by the shipowners, the English importers are entitled by the procedure of our courts of Admiralty to arrest the ship whenever she comes here in order to have security for their claim. There seems to me to be no doubt that such a dispute is one that properly belongs for its determination to the courts of this country. But still the question remains: Ought these courts in their discretion to stay this action?

It has been said by Mr Roche that this contract is governed by Russian law and should be judged by the Russian courts, who know that law. And the dispute may involve evidence from witnesses in Russia about the condition of the goods on shipment. Then why, says Mr Roche, should it not be judged in Russia as the condition says?

I do not regard the choice of law in the contract as decisive. I prefer to look to see with what country is the dispute most closely concerned. Here the Russian element in the dispute seems to me to be comparatively small. The dispute is between the German owners of the ship and the English importers. It depends on evidence here as to the condition of the goods when they arrived here in London and on evidence of the ship, which is a frequent visitor to London. The correspondence leaves in my mind, just as it did in the judge's mind, the impression that the German owners did not object to the dispute being decided in this country but wished to avoid the giving of security.

I think the dispute is more closely connected with England than Russia, and I agree with the judge that sufficient reason has been shown why the proceedings should continue in these courts and should not be stayed. I would therefore dismiss the appeal.

Hodson and Morris LJJ delivered judgments to the same effect.
Appeal dismissed.

---

3 Now s 20(2)(g) of the Supreme Court Act 1981 (*Ed*).

The Eleftheria [1970] P 94, [1969] 2 All ER 64 (Admiralty Division)

Roumanian shippers loaded a cargo of plywood on a Greek ship at the Roumanian port of Galatz for carriage to London and Hull. The bill of lading provided that any dispute should be decided in the country where the carrier had his place of business and that the law of that country should apply. It also provided that in the event of strikes at the port of discharge the master might discharge the cargo at any safe or convenient port. The ship sailed to London and discharged part of her London cargo. Because of labour troubles in the London and Hull docks the ship then sailed to Rotterdam and discharged the rest of her London cargo and all her Hull cargo.

The plaintiffs, who were English indorsees of the bill of lading in respect of the Hull cargo, brought an action in rem against the ship claiming the cost of carriage from Rotterdam to Hull. The defendant shipowners, whose place of business was in Athens, asked for a stay.

Brandon J (after quoting the cases cited by counsel, continued): The principles established by the authorities can, I think, be summarised as follows: (1) Where plaintiffs sue in England in breach of an agreement to refer disputes to a foreign court, and the defendants apply for a stay, the English court, assuming the claim to be otherwise within its jurisdiction, is not bound to grant a stay but has a discretion whether to do so or not. (2) The discretion should be exercised by granting a stay unless strong cause for not doing so is shown. (3) The burden of proving such strong cause is on the plaintiffs. (4) In exercising its discretion the court should take into account all the circumstances of the particular case. (5) In particular, but without prejudice to (4), the following matters, where they arise, may properly be regarded:

(a) In what country the evidence on the issues of fact is situated, or more readily available, and the effect of that on the relative convenience and expense of trial as between the English and foreign courts.

(b) Whether the law of the foreign court applies and, if so, whether it differs from English law in any material respects.

(c) With what country either party is connected, and how closely.

(d) Whether the defendants genuinely desire trial in the foreign country, or are only seeking procedural advantages.

(e) Whether the plaintiffs would be prejudiced by having to sue in the foreign court because they would:
  (i) be deprived of security for their claim;
  (ii) be unable to enforce any judgment obtained;
  (iii) be faced with a time-bar not applicable in England; or
  (iv) for political, racial, religious or other reasons be unlikely to get a fair trial.

In the present case there has been no suggestion that there is any risk of the plaintiffs not getting a fair trial in Greece. I approach the matter therefore on the assumption that, so far as fairness of trial is concerned, there is no distinction between the Greek and English courts. There is further no question of the plaintiffs' claim being time-barred in Greece, while as regards security the defendants are content that, if a stay is granted, it should be on terms that the security obtained by the plaintiffs in the action, or other security equivalent to it, shall be available to answer any judgment which the plaintiffs may later get in Greece.

(His Lordship summarised the arguments of counsel on each side and continued): These being the arguments on either side I must now state my view of the matter. I shall do so under four heads. First, the prima facie case for a stay arising from the Greek jurisdiction clause; second, factors tending to rebut that prima facie case; third, factors tending to reinforce that prima facie case; fourth, conclusion.

First, as to the prima facie case for a stay arising from the Greek jurisdiction clause. I think that it is essential that the court should give full weight to the prima facie desirability of holding the plaintiffs to their agreement. In this connection I think that the court must be careful not just to pay lip service to the principle involved, and then fail to give effect to it because of a mere balance of convenience. I am strengthened in that view by the strong observations on the topic made by the Court of Appeal in two recent cases on RSC Ord 11, namely *Mackender v Feldia AG*[4] and *Unterweser Reederei GmbH v Zapata Offshore Co, The Chaparral*.[5] I recognise that the point for decision in those cases was not the same as that for decision in the present case. The point for decision in those cases was whether the plaintiffs should be allowed to bring their action by being given leave to serve out of the jurisdiction; the point for decision in the present case is whether the plaintiffs, who have begun an action here which they needed no leave to begin, should be prevented from going on with it. In *Mackender v Feldia AG*[4] the court had to bear in mind, as a basic starting point, the caution always used by it in giving leave for service out of the jurisdiction under RSC Ord 11 r 1. The reasons for such caution were explained by Diplock LJ at 599. In *Unterweser Reederei GmbH v Zapata Off-Shore Co, The Chaparral*,[5] the application was under RSC Ord 11, r 2, so that the same need for caution did not exist: see the reasons given by the same Lord Justice at 163. Allowing, however, for the fact that the point for decision was not the same, and that in the earlier of the two cases the special considerations affecting the giving of leave under RSC Ord 11, r 1, had to be taken into account, the governing factor in both decisions was the principle that a party should be bound by a jurisdiction clause to which he has agreed, unless there is strong reason to the contrary. This principle was stressed in the earlier case by Lord Denning MR at 598, and Diplock LJ at 604, and in the later case by Willmer LJ at 162 and 163 and Diplock LJ at 164, where he repeated what he had said in the earlier case. It is further to be observed that Willmer LJ in dealing with the principle involved, treated *The Fehmarn*,[6] one of the leading cases on the question of stay, as being directly relevant.

Second, as to the factors tending to rebut the prima facie case for a stay. I think that there is much force in the main point taken by counsel for the plaintiffs, that the bulk of the factual evidence is in England. While it may be that some of the facts with regard to labour disputes, etc., can be agreed or proved by documents, I accept the plaintiffs' case that they will probably wish to call a substantial number of witnesses on this topic, and that, if they have to take them to Greece, it will cause them substantial inconvenience and expense. The evidence of such witnesses would, moreover, have to be interpreted, with the difficulties and further expense involved in that process.

4 [1967] 2 QB 590, [1966] 3 All ER 847; p 65 above.
5 [1968] 2 Lloyd's Rep 158.
6 [1958] 1 All ER 333, [1958] 1 WLR 159; p 141 above.

Against all that it must be borne in mind that, if the dispute is tried in England, the reverse situation will arise as regards at least one, and perhaps two witnesses of fact for the defendants, certainly in relation to inconvenience and expense, and possibly, though not necessarily, also in relation to interpretation.

These considerations about evidence must, however, be viewed in perspective. Many commercial and Admiralty disputes are tried or arbitrated in England every year, in which most or all of the evidence comes from abroad. In these cases the parties are often content to have their disputes decided here, even though it causes inconvenience and expense with regard to bringing witnesses to England and examining them through interpreters. Bearing in mind these matters, I cannot regard the inconvenience and expense which the plaintiffs would suffer through having to take witnesses to Greece as being in any way overwhelming or insuperable.

Third, as to factors tending to reinforce the prima facie case for a stay. Of these I regard as carrying some weight the very real connection of the defendants with Greece and their willingness to protect the plaintiffs in relation to security for their claim. I further regard, of substantial importance the circumstance that Greek law governs, and is, in respects which may well be material, different from English law.

I recognise that an English court can, and often does, decide questions of foreign law on the basis of expert evidence from foreign lawyers. Nor do I regard such legal concepts as contractual good faith and morality as being so strange as to be beyond the capacity of an English court to grasp and apply. It seems to be clear, however, that in general, and other things being equal, it is more satisfactory for the law of a foreign country to be decided by the courts of that country. That would be my view, as a matter of common sense, apart from authority. But if authority be needed, it is to be found in *The Cap Blanco*[7] and in *Settlement Corpn v Hochschild*.[8] This last case was not cited to me in argument but appears to me to be helpful on the general point involved.

It is true that in *The Athenée*[9] and *The Fehmarn*, in both of which a stay was refused, the circumstance that the law of the foreign country governed does not appear to have been given much weight. But in those cases there was no evidence that the foreign law was different in any material respects from English law, whereas in the present case there is.

Apart from the general advantage which a foreign court has in determining and applying its own law, there is a significant difference in the position with regard to appeal. A question of foreign law decided by a court of the foreign country concerned is appealable as such to the appropriate appellate court of that country. But a question of foreign law decided by an English court on expert evidence is treated as a question of fact for the purposes of appeal, with the limitations in the scope of an appeal inherent in that categorisation. This consideration seems to me to afford an added reason for saying that, in general and other things being equal, it is more satisfactory for the law of a foreign country to be decided by the courts of

7 [1913] P 130 at 136.
8 [1966] Ch 10 at 18, [1965] 3 All ER 486 at 491.
9 (1922) 11 Ll LRep 6.

that country. Moreover, by more satisfactory I mean more satisfactory from the point of view of ensuring that justice is done.

Fourth, as to my conclusion. I have started by giving full weight to the prima facie case for a stay, and I have gone on to weigh on the one hand the factors tending to rebut that prima facie case, and on the other hand the factors tending to reinforce it. With regard to these, it appears to me that there are considerations of substantial weight on either side, which more or less balance each other, leaving the prima facie case for a stay largely, if not entirely, intact. On this basis I have reached the clear conclusion that the plaintiffs, on whom the burden lies, have not, on the whole of the matter, established good cause why they should not be held to their agreement. The question whether to grant a stay or not, and if so on what terms, is one for the discretion of the court. Having arrived at the clear conclusion which I have stated, I shall exercise my discretion by granting a stay, subject to appropriate terms as regards security.

Stay granted.

MacKender v Feldia (p 65 above)

Civil Jurisdiction and Judgments Act 1982

SCHEDULE 1

ARTICLE 17 (p 90 above).

PART III

Foreign Judgments and Arbitration

CHAPTER 7

Foreign Judgments in Personam

Section A. At common law

No action lies in England on a foreign judgment in personam unless the defendant either submitted to the jurisdiction or was present in the foreign country at the date of the issue of the writ.

Schibsby v Westenholz (1870) LR 6 QB 155 (Court of Queen's Bench)

The plaintiff was a Dane resident in France. The defendants were also Danes, resident in London and carrying on business there. A written contract between the plaintiff and defendants, which was in English and made in London, provided that the defendants should ship in Sweden a cargo of Swedish oats on board a French or Swedish vessel to Caen in France. The plaintiff complained of short delivery. He issued a writ against the defendants in France, which was served on the Procureur Impérial, who forwarded it to the French consul in London, who then served a copy of the citation on the defendants. The plaintiff obtained judgment in France in default of appearance. There was evidence from a French avocat that by French law a French subject might sue a foreigner, though not resident in France, and that for this purpose an alien, if resident in France, was considered as a French subject.

When sued on the French judgment in England the defendants pleaded (third plea) that they were not resident or domiciled in France, or in any way subject to the jurisdiction of the French court, nor did they appear; and that they were not summoned, nor had any notice or knowledge of the pending of the proceedings, or any opportunity of defending themselves therefrom.

The judgment of the court (Blackburn, Mellor, Lush and Hannen JJ) was delivered by

Blackburn J: The following admissions were made, namely: that the judgment was regular according to French law; that it was given in favour of the plaintiff, a foreigner domiciled in France, against the defendants, domiciled in England, and in no sense French subjects, and having no property in France.

I then ruled that I could not enter into the question whether the French judgment was according to the merits, no fraud being alleged or shown.

I expressed an opinion (which I have since changed) that, subject to the third plea, the plaintiff was entitled to the verdict, but reserved the point.

The jury found that the defendants had notice and knowledge of the summons and the pendency of the proceedings in time to have appeared and defended the action in the French court. I then directed the verdict for the plaintiff, but reserved leave to enter the verdict for the defendants on these facts and this finding.

A rule was accordingly obtained by Sir George Honyman, against which cause was shewn in the last term and in the sittings after it before my brothers Mellor, Lush, Hannen, and myself. During the interval between the obtaining of the rule and the shewing cause the case of *Godard v Gray*,[1] on which we have just given judgment, was argued before my brothers Mellor, Hannen, and myself, and we had consequently occasion to consider the whole subject of the law of England as to enforcing foreign judgments.

My brother Lush, who was not a party to the discussions in *Godard v Gray*, has, since the argument in the present case, perused the judgment prepared by the majority in *Godard v Gray* and approves of it; and, after hearing the argument in the present case, we are all of opinion that the rule should be made absolute.

It is unnecessary to repeat again what we have already said in *Godard v Gray*.

We think that, for the reasons there given, the true principle on which the judgments of foreign tribunals are enforced in England is that stated by Parke B, in *Russell v Smyth*,[2] and again repeated by him in *Williams v Jones*,[3] that the judgment of a court of competent jurisdiction over the defendant imposes a duty or obligation on the defendant to pay the sum for which judgment is given, which the courts in this country are bound to enforce; and consequently that anything which negatives that duty, or forms a legal excuse for not performing it, is a defence to the action.

We were much pressed on the argument with the fact that the British legislature has, by the Common Law Procedure Act 1852, ss 18 and 19,[4] conferred on our courts a power of summoning foreigners, under certain circumstances, to appear, and in case they do not, giving judgment against them by default. It was this consideration principally which induced me at the trial to entertain the opinion which I then expressed and have since changed. And we think that if the principle on which foreign judgments were enforced was that which is loosely called 'comity', we could hardly decline to enforce a foreign judgment given in France against a resident in Great Britain under circumstances hardly, if at all, distinguishable from those under which we, mutatis mutandis, might give judgment against a resident in France; but it is quite different if the principle be that which we have just laid down.

Should a foreigner be sued under the provisions of the statute referred to, and then come to the courts of this country and desire to be discharged, the only question which our courts could entertain would be whether the Acts of the British legislature, rightly construed, gave us jurisdiction over this foreigner, for we must obey them. But if, judgment being given against him in our courts, an action were brought upon it in the courts of the United States (where the law as to the enforcing foreign judgments is the same as

1 (1870) LR 6 QB 139, 40 LJQB 62; p 165 below.
2 (1842) 9 M & W 810 at 819.
3 (1845) 13 M & W 628 at 633.
4 Now RSC Ord 11, r 1 (1) p 63 above (*Ed*).

our own), a further question would be open, viz, not only whether the British legislature had given the English courts jurisdiction over the defendant, but whether he was under any obligation which the American courts could recognise to submit to the jurisdiction thus created. This is precisely the question which we have now to determine with regard to a jurisdiction assumed by the French jurisprudence over foreigners.

Again, it was argued before us that foreign judgments obtained by default, where the citation was (as in the present case) by an artificial mode prescribed by the laws of the country in which the judgment was given, were not enforceable in this country because such a mode of citation was contrary to natural justice, and if this were so, doubtless the finding of the jury in the present case would remove that objection. But though it appears by the report of *Buchanan v Rucker*[5] that Lord Ellenborough in the hurry of nisi prius at first used expressions to this effect, yet when the case came before him in banco in *Buchanan v Rucker*,[6] he entirely abandoned what (with all deference to so great an authority) we cannot regard as more than declamation, and rested his judgment on the ground that laws passed by our country[7] were not obligatory on foreigners not subject to their jurisdiction. 'Can', he said, 'the island of Tobago pass a law to bind the rights of the whole world?'

The question we have now to answer is, Can the empire of France pass a law to bind the whole world? We admit, with perfect candour, that in the supposed case of a judgment, obtained in this country against a foreigner under the provisions of the Common Law Procedure Act, being sued on in a court of the United States, the question for the court of the United States would be, Can the Island of Great Britain pass a law to bind the whole world? We think in each case the answer should be, No, but every country can pass laws to bind a great many persons; and therefore the further question has to be determined whether the defendant in the particular suit was such a person as to be bound by the judgment which it is sought to enforce.

Now on this we think some things are quite clear on principle. If the defendants had been at the time of the judgment subjects of the country whose judgment is sought to be enforced against them, we think that its laws would have bound them.[8] Again, if the defendants had been at the time when the suit was commenced resident in the country, so as to have the benefit of its laws protecting them, or, as it is sometimes expressed, owing temporary allegiance to that country, we think that its laws would have bound them.

If at the time when the obligation was contracted the defendants were within the foreign country, but left it before the suit was instituted, we should be inclined to think the laws of that country bound them;[9] though before finally deciding this we should like to hear the question argued. But every one of those suppositions is negatived in the present case.

Again, we think it clear, upon principle, that if a person selected, as

5 (1807) 1 Camp 63.
6 (1808) 9 East 192.
7 Sic in the report: evidently a misprint for 'one country' (*Ed*).
8 As to this see p 154 n 14 below.
9 It has since been held that the foreign court has no jurisdiction in such a case: *Sirdar Gurdyal Singh v Rajah of Faridkote* [1894] AC 670; *Emanuel v Symon* [1908] 1 KB 302, 77 LJKB 180; p 153 below (*Ed*).

plaintiff, the tribunal of a foreign country as the one in which he would sue, he could not afterwards say that the judgment of that tribunal was not binding upon him.

In the case of *General Steam Navigation Co v Guillou*,[10] on a demurrer to a plea, Parke B, in delivering the considered judgment of the Court of Exchequer, then consisting of Lord Abinger CB, Parke, Alderson, and Gurney BB, thus expresses himself:

> 'The substance of the plea is that the cause of action has been already adjudicated upon, in a competent court, against the plaintiffs, and that the decision is binding upon them, and that they ought not to be permitted again to litigate the same question. Such a plea ought to have had a proper commencement and conclusion. It becomes, therefore, unnecessary to give any opinion whether the pleas are bad in substance; but it is not to be understood that we feel much doubt on that question. They do not state that the plaintiffs were French subjects, or resident, or even present in France when the suit began, so as to be bound by reason of allegiance or temporary presence by the decision of a French court, and they did not select the tribunal and sue as plaintiffs, in any of which cases the determination might have possibly bound them. They were mere strangers, who put forward the negligence of the defendant as an answer, in an adverse suit in a foreign country, whose laws they were under no obligation to obey'.

It will be seen from this that those very learned judges, besides expressing an opinion conformable to ours, also expressed one to the effect that the plaintiffs in that suit did not put themselves under an obligation to obey the foreign judgment, merely by appearing to defend themselves against it. On the other hand, in *Simpson v Fogo*,[11] where the mortgagees of an English ship had come into the courts of Louisiana, to endeavour to prevent the sale of their ship seized under an execution against the mortgagors, and the courts of Louisiana decided against them, the Vice-Chancellor and the very learned counsel who argued in the case seem all to have taken it for granted that the decision of the Court in Louisiana would have bound the mortgagees, had it not been in contemptuous disregard of English law. The case of *General Steam Navigation Co v Guillou* was not referred to, and therefore cannot be considered as dissented from; but it seems clear that they did not agree in the latter part of the opinion there expressed.

We think it better to leave this question open, and to express no opinion as to the effect of the appearance of a defendant, where it is so far not voluntary that he only comes in to try to save some property in the hands of the foreign tribunal. But we must observe that the decision in *De Cosse Brissac v Rathbone*[12] is an authority that where the defendant voluntarily appears and takes the chance of a judgment in his favour he is bound.

In *Douglas v Forrest*,[13] the court, deciding in favour of the party suing on a Scotch judgment, say: 'We confine our judgment to a case where the party owed allegiance to the country in which the judgment was so given against

10 (1843) 11 M & W 877 at 894.
11 (1863) 1 Hem & M 195, 1 New Rep 442.
12 (1861) 6 H & N 301, 30 LJ Ex 238.
13 (1828) 4 Bing 686 at 703.

him, from being born in it, and by the laws of which country his property was, at the time those judgments were given, protected. The debts were contracted in the country in which the judgments were given, whilst the debtor resided in it'. Those circumstances are all negatived here. We should, however, point out that, whilst we think that there may be other grounds for holding a person bound by the judgment of the tribunal of a foreign country than those enumerated in *Douglas v Forrest*, we doubt very much whether the possession of property, locally situated in that country and protected by its laws, does afford such a ground. It should rather seem that, whilst every tribunal may very properly execute process against the property within its jurisdiction, the existence of such property, which may be very small, affords no sufficient ground for imposing on the foreign owner of that property a duty or obligation to fulfil the judgment. But it is unnecessary to decide this, as the defendants had in this case no property in France.

We think, and this is all that we need decide, that there existed nothing in the present case imposing on the defendants any duty to obey the judgment of a French tribunal.

Judgment for defendants.

The possession of property in a foreign country is not sufficient to give the courts of that country jurisdiction in personam over the owner thereof.

Emanuel v Symon [1908] 1 KB 302, 77 LJKB 180 (Court of Appeal)

Appeal from the judgment of Channell J.

In 1895 the defendant, who was then residing and carrying on business in Western Australia, entered into partnership with five other persons, whose interests were now represented by the plaintiffs, for the purpose of working and developing a gold mine situate in that colony and owned by the partnership. The defendant subsequently gave up his business in Western Australia, and in 1899 he left the colony permanently and came to live in England.

In November 1901 a writ was issued by the plaintiffs against the defendant in the Supreme Court of Western Australia, claiming a dissolution of partnership, a sale of the mine, accounts and inquiries, and other relief as in an ordinary partnership action. On 13 November 1901 that writ was served on the defendant in England, but he did not enter an appearance, or take any other step to defend the action. He was, however, kept informed from time to time of the proceedings in the action.

On 25 July 1902 the Supreme Court of Western Australia, in default of appearance by the defendant, pronounced a decree for the dissolution of the partnership as from that date, and ordered the mine to be sold and the usual accounts to be taken by the taxing officer. The sale was carried out and the accounts were taken, and the taxing officer issued his certificate shewing liabilities of the partnership amounting to a sum of £7,687 9s 9d. In May 1903 the final order of the court was pronounced, under which the plaintiffs paid the sum found to be due from the partnership. They subsequently issued the writ in this action to recover from the defendant the sum of £1,281 4s 11d as his share of the sum of £7,687 9s 9d paid by them as aforesaid.

The defendant denied that he was bound by the finding or order of the colonial court, on the ground that he was a British subject resident and domiciled in England; that neither at the commencement nor during the continuance of the action was he resident or domiciled in Western Australia, or subject to the jurisdiction of the courts of that colony; and that he had neither appeared to the process nor agreed to submit himself to the jurisdiction of those courts.

Channell J held that by entering into a partnership in Western Australia relating to real estate in that colony the defendant had impliedly agreed to submit to the jurisdiction of the colonial court as to disputes arising during the continuance and on the termination of the partnership, and was therefore bound by the findings of that court. He accordingly gave judgment for the plaintiffs.

The defendant appealed.

Buckley LJ: In actions in personam there are five cases in which the courts of this country will enforce a foreign judgment: (1) Where the defendant is a subject of the foreign country in which the judgment has been obtained;[14] (2) where he was resident in the foreign country when the action began; (3) where the defendant in the character of plaintiff has selected the forum in which he is afterwards sued;[15] (4) where he has voluntarily appeared; and (5) where he has contracted to submit himself to the forum in which the judgment was obtained. The question in the present case is whether there is yet another and a sixth case. In *Rousillon v Rousillon*,[16] Fry J, after enumerating the five cases above mentioned, added these words, 'and, possibly, if *Becquet v MacCarthy*[17] be right, where the defendant has real estate within the foreign jurisdiction, in respect of which the cause of action arose whilst he was within that jurisdiction'. The principle upon which this court proceeds in enforcing foreign judgments is stated by Blackburn J in *Schibsby v Westenholz*[18] in these words: (His Lordship read the passage on p 150, above, beginning 'We think that for the reasons there given' and ending 'as a defence to the action'). In other words, the courts of this country enforce foreign judgments because those judgments impose a duty or obligation which is recognised in this country and leads to judgment here also. Referring to *Becquet v MacCarthy*, Mr Dicey in his work on the Conflict of Laws has, at p 373, the following comment: 'But whether this case has reference to the possession of real property by the defendant as a ground of jurisdiction?' That comment is justified, and the doubt there expressed recognised, if indeed a negative answer to the question was not given in a substantive form, and without any doubt, by Lord Selborne in *Sirdar Gurdyal Singh v Rajah of Faridkote*.[19] *Becquet v MacCarthy* has been the subject of

14 This is supported by a long chain of dicta from 1828 to 1948, but was rejected in *Blöhn v Desser* [1962] 2 QB 116 at 123, [1961] 3 All ER 1 at 4; *Rossano v Manufacturers Life Insurance Co Ltd* [1963] 2 QB 352 at 382–3, [1962] 2 All ER 214 at 232; *Vogel v R & A Kohnstamm Ltd* [1973] QB 133, [1971] 2 All ER 1428; p 156 below; and *Rainford v Newall-Roberts* [1962] IR 95. (*Ed*).

15 Query 'as the one in which he would sue' (*Ed*).

16 (1880) 14 Ch D 351 at 371.

17 (1831) 2 B & Ad 951.

18 (1870) LR 6 QB 155, 40 LJQB 73; p 149 above.

19 [1894] AC 670.

adverse comment—first, in *Schibsby v Westenholz*,[20] where Blackburn J said: 'Whilst we think that there may be other grounds for holding a person bound by the judgment of the tribunal of a foreign country than those enumerated in *Douglas v Forrest*,[1] we doubt very much whether the possession of property, locally situated in that country and protected by its laws, does afford such a ground'; secondly, by Fry J in *Rousillon v Rousillon*, where that learned judge said, 'and possibly, if *Becquet v MacCarthy* be right, where the defendant has real estate within the foreign jurisdiction, in respect of which the cause of action arose whilst he was within that jurisdiction'; and, thirdly, by Lord Selborne in *Sirdar Gurdyal Singh v Rajah of Faridkote*, where he said: 'Of *Becquet v MacCarthy* it was said by great authority in *Don v Lippmann*[2] that it "had been supposed to go to the verge of the law"; and it was explained (as their Lordships think correctly) on the ground that "the defendant held a public office in the very colony in which he was originally sued". He still held that office at the time when he was sued; the cause of action arose out of, or was connected with it; and, though he was in fact temporarily absent, he might, as the holder of such an office, be regarded as constructively present in the place where his duties required his presence, and therefore amenable to the colonial jurisdiction. If the case could not be distinguished on that ground from that of any absent foreigner who, at some previous time, might have been in the employment of a colonial government, it would, in their Lordships' opinion, have been wrongly decided; and it is evident that Fry LJ in *Rousillon v Rousillon* took that view.' Lord Selborne then goes on to discuss the question whether it makes any difference that the defendant, at the time when the obligation was contracted, was resident in the foreign country, but left it before the suit was instituted; and, after observing that Blackburn J, delivering the opinion of the Court of Queen's Bench in *Schibsby v Westenholz*, inclined to the view that the laws of the foreign country would bind the defendant, though he declined to decide that point without further argument, Lord Selborne said: 'Their Lordships do not doubt that, if he'—ie, Blackburn J—'had heard argument upon the question, whether an obligation to accept the forum loci contractus, as having, by reason of the contract, a conventional jurisdiction against the parties in a suit founded upon that contract for all future time, wherever they might be domiciled or resident, was generally implied, he would have come (as their Lordships do) to the conclusion, that such obligation, unless expressed, could not be implied.' Having regard to these passages, *Becquet v MacCarthy*, if and in so far as it decides that a person, who merely possesses property or enters into a contract in a foreign country, binds himself to submit to the jurisdiction of the foreign country, can, I think, no longer be sustained; and the proposition on which Channell J based his judgment, namely, that inasmuch as the defendant had become a party to a contract of partnership in Western Australia he must be taken to have bound himself to submit to the jurisdiction of the courts of that colony, is not sound. This appeal must therefore be allowed.

Lord Alverstone CJ and Kennedy LJ delivered judgment to the same effect. *Appeal allowed.*

---

20 P 153 above.
1 (1828) 4 Bing 686 at 703.
2 (1837) 5 Cl & F 1.

A corporation is not resident in a foreign country for jurisdictional purposes merely because it has a representative there who has authority to elicit orders from customers but not to make contracts on its behalf.

Submission to the jurisdiction of a foreign court must be express: it cannot be implied.

Vogel v R and A Kohnstamm Ltd [1973] QB 133, [1971] 2 All ER 1428 (Queen's Bench Division)

The plaintiff was a leather merchant carrying on business in Tel Aviv, Israel. The defendants were an English company with a registered office in England and no office or place of business in Israel. They entered into an agreement with a Mr Kornbluth, a resident of Israel, whereby they gave him authority to elicit orders from customers but not to enter into contracts on their behalf. He was paid by commission. He introduced the plaintiff as a customer and two contracts were made for the supply of suede skins by the defendants to the plaintiff. The plaintiff, being dissatisfied with the quality of the skins, issued a writ against the defendants in Israel claiming damages for breach of contract, and obtained leave from the Israeli court to serve it on the defendants out of the jurisdiction. The defendants wrote to the President of the Israeli court saying they did not admit that the court had jurisdiction and stating that their letter was not to be taken as an appearance. Nevertheless the court assumed jurisdiction and in the absence of the defendants gave judgment against them for a sum of money. The plaintiff brought an action at common law to enforce that judgment in England.

Ashworth J: This claim is brought at common law and I am not concerned with the Foreign Judgments (Reciprocal Enforcement) Act 1933, nor with the Administration of Justice Act 1920. (His Lordship stated the facts and continued): Fortunately in some ways one can start with a measure of agreement between the parties as to the applicable principle. The most convenient place to find them is in a judgment given by Buckley LJ in *Emanuel v Symon*.[3] He said, at 309:

> 'In actions in personam there are five cases in which the courts of this country will enforce a foreign judgment: (1) Where the defendant is a subject of the foreign country in which the judgment has been obtained;'

I break off to say that that first class now seems to have been sufficiently questioned to be a doubtful authority.

> '(2) where he was resident in the foreign country when the action began;
> (3) where the defendant in the character of plaintiff has selected the forum in which he is afterwards sued; (4) where he has voluntarily appeared; and (5) where he has contracted to submit himself to the forum in which the judgment was obtained.'

For the plaintiff here Mr Waldman contends that this case falls within class (2), shortly described as residence; or class (5), where he has contracted to submit himself to that jurisdiction. And I agree with him in some measure, those two classes are apt to overlap. At any rate in this case the

---

3 [1908] 1 KB 302, 77 LJKB 180; p 154 above.

relevant considerations are common in large measure to both principles. Accordingly it is submitted on behalf of the plaintiff that the defendants were within the Israeli court's jurisdiction either because they were resident there or because they had by implication agreed to submit to the jurisdiction. I stress the words 'by implication', though I shall have to return to them, because Mr Waldman rightly concedes that in this particular case there can be no question of an express agreement to accept the Israeli court's jurisdiction.

I find it more convenient to consider the question whether the defendants can be said to have been at the material time resident in the State of Israel. As has been said in many cases, residence is a question of fact and when one is dealing with human beings one can normally approach the matter on the footing that residence involves physical residence by the person in question. I keep open the possibility that even in regard to such a person he may be constructively resident in another country although his physical presence is elsewhere. But in the case of a corporation there is broadly speaking no question of physical residence. A corporation or company, if resident in another country, is resident there by way of agents.

A number of cases have been cited, all of them having some bearing on the matter, and I must refer to a number of them. I am dealing only at the moment with the question of residence. In *Littauer Glove Corpn v FW Millington (1920) Ltd*,[4] the headnote reads:

'To constitute residence by a British company in a foreign state so as to render the company subject to the jurisdiction of the courts of that state, the company must to some extent carry on business in that state at a definite and reasonably permanent place.'

The main feature of that case is very different from any matter which arises in the present case because the person through whom the defendant corporation was said to have residence in the United States was not a person with any fixed or reasonably permanent place; whereas it is common ground that at all material times Mr Kornbluth had an office in Tel Aviv and could be described as having both a definite and reasonably permanent place. Accordingly in that case, the facts of which I need not recite, the so-called residence of the director of the defendant company was of much too fleeting a character and so lacking in permanence that the court had no difficulty in holding that the English company was not resident in the United States for the purpose of conferring jurisdiction upon those courts.

The matter was also considered by Mocatta J in *Sfeir & Co v National Insurance Co of New Zealand Ltd*.[5] In that case there was a body in Ghana which in some sense could be called an agent or agents of the defendant insurance company, who, as their name implies, were domiciled or resident in New Zealand. The entity in Ghana had a limited authority to act for the defendants. They were allowed to deal with minor claims and indeed settle them on the defendant's behalf. In cases where the loss did not exceed £5, and the entity was reasonably satisfied that the claim was presented in all good faith, they were authorised to dispense with a survey. All claims exceeding £1,000 and all unusual claims had to be submitted to the

4 (1928) 44 TLR 746.
5 [1964] 1 Lloyd's Rep 330.

defendants for approval. Having examined the facts in a lengthy judgment the judge came to the conclusion that this limited authority vested in the agent in Accra was not sufficient to render the defendants resident in Ghana and therefore subject to the jurisdiction of the Ghanaian courts.

Of course each case must depend on its own facts and I am only citing those to show that every effort has been made to find a case which could fairly be regarded as parallel to the present.

Dealing still only with residence I now have to examine in what sense can it be said that the defendants were resident in Israel. They had no office of their own there. All the material correspondence was conducted with them in England and their connection with the State of Israel was limited, in my view, to their dealings through Mr Kornbluth.

In examining how far the presence of a representative or agent will, so to speak, impinge on the absent company so as to render that absent company subject to the relevant jurisdiction, I find help to be obtained from cases in which the converse situation has been considered: namely, where the English courts have been invited to allow process to issue to foreign companies on the footing that such foreign companies are 'here'.

Much the most useful authority which has been cited to me is *Okura & Co Ltd v Forsbacka Jernverks Aktiebolag*.[6] It is worth reading the headnote:

'The defendants were a foreign corporation carrying on business in Sweden as manufacturers. They employed as their sole agents in the United Kingdom a firm in London who also acted as agents for other firms and carried on business as merchants on their own account. The agents had no general authority to enter into contracts on behalf of the defendants, but they obtained orders and submitted them to the defendants for their approval. On being notified by the defendants that they accepted the orders the agents signed contracts with the purchasers as agents for the defendants. The goods were shipped direct from the defendants in Sweden to the purchasers. The agents in some cases received payment in London from the purchasers and remitted the amount to the defendants less their agreed commission:— *Held*, that the defendants were not carrying on their business at the agents' office in London so as to be resident at a place within the jurisdiction, and that service of a writ on the agents at their office was, therefore, not a good service on the defendants.'

As Mr Boreham (counsel for the defendants) said, having read to me the headnote, if that was the view of the court in that case how much stronger in his favour is the present, because on the face of it there are details in the facts of that case which might have led the court to think that the corporation in question was indeed 'here', whereas such features are absent in the present case. There is force in that, but the matter for which I am citing the authority is the passage from Buckley LJ's judgment where he said, 718–719:

'In one sense, of course, the corporation cannot be "here." The question really is whether this corporation can be said to be "here" by a person who represents it in a sense relevant to the question which we have to decide. The point to be considered is, do the facts show that this

6 [1914] 1 KB 715, 83 LJKB 561.

corporation is carrying on its business in this country? In determining that question, three matters have to be considered. First, the acts relied on as showing that the corporation is carrying on business in this country must have continued for a sufficiently substantial period of time. That is the case here. Next, it is essential that these acts should have been done at some fixed place of business. If the acts relied on in this case amount to a carrying on of a business, there is no doubt that those acts were done at a fixed place of business. The third essential, and one which it is always more difficult to satisfy, is that the corporation must be "here" by a person who carries on business for the corporation in this country. It is not enough to show that the corporation has an agent here; he must be an agent who does the corporation's business for the corporation in this country.'

Then he goes on to refer to authorities, all of them relevant and all of them in a sense interesting as showing the line of distinction which the courts have drawn in the past between the situations which were, on the face of it, somewhat similar.

At the end of the day there is a test which the courts have used as part of the material on which to reach a conclusion, namely, is the person in question doing his business or doing the absent corporation's business? Conversely, are they doing business through him or by him?

I confess I find these aphorisms, if that is what they are, apt to lead one astray; one can find the choice phrase and then fit the facts to it and so on. But they are useful and I have asked myself anxiously in this case whether in any real sense of the word the defendants can be said to have been there in Israel; and all that emerges from this case is that there was a man called Kornbluth who sought customers for them, transmitted correspondence to them and received it from them, had no authority whatever to bind the defendants in any shape or form. I have come to the conclusion really without any hesitation that the defendants were not resident in Israel at any material time.

It is fair to Mr Waldman to say that he himself accepted that if he was limited to the question of residence as the basis of this action he might find himself in difficulty. But he has another approach, overlapping, but separate. What he says is that on these facts and on the decided cases the fair conclusion to draw is that the defendants by implication agreed to submit themselves to the jurisdiction of the Tel Aviv court.

Before I examine the authorities on that issue I would start with this comment; in considering whether a term should be implied, courts have laid down over and over again that the test is not whether it would be reasonable to imply a term and I follow that guidance. But I do venture to suggest that one test which a court can at least look at is the test whether it would be unreasonable to imply such a term. And I can think of no reason in this world why the defendants should have wished to submit themselves to the jurisdiction of the Israeli courts in respect of these skins which they were selling to customers in Israel. True they might have agreed to do so but I would have thought that one can at least start with the premise that it would be surprising if by implication they had committed themselves to that result.

The problem is lamentably bedevilled by the fact that not every decided case to which I have been referred sings the same tune. If this case had been

decided in 1909, after the decision in *Sirdar Gurdyal Singh v Rajah of Faridkote*[7]
and of *Emanuel v Symon*, I venture to think it would have taken a shorter time
than it has taken before me. But since that date there have been two
decisions, each of which is relied on and rightly relied on by Mr Waldman,
which have set the matter in balance.

Let me start with the firm ground of ancient authority. In 1894 there
came before the Privy Council *Sirdar Gurdyal Singh v Rajah of Faridkote*, and in
summary form the issue there was whether the defendant, as he originally
was, could be sued in the Faridkote court for the money which was said to be
due from him for misfeasance committed by him when he was treasurer in
Faridkote. By the time the action had been brought he had made his way to
the neighbouring state of Jhind. Action was brought in the Faridkote court,
successfully in the end, and it came before the Privy Council. In the course of
giving the judgment of their Lordships Lord Selborne dealt with this matter.
I believe all I need cite, despite the fact that much is relevant, is a passage at
the end of the judgment. Lord Selborne, referring to a doubt expressed by
Blackburn J in a previous case, said, at 686:

> 'their Lordships do not doubt that, if he had heard argument upon the
> question, whether an obligation to accept the forum loci contractus as
> having, by reason of the contract, a conventional jurisdiction against the
> parties in a suit founded upon that contract for all future time whether
> they might be domiciled or resident, was generally to be implied, he
> would have come (as their Lordships do) to the conclusion that such
> obligation, unless expressed, could not be implied.'

In that single sentence there is, as I see it, a firm declaration that this
contractual submission to the jurisdiction of another country's courts must, if
it is to be effective, be expressed and cannot be implied.

Fourteen years later *Emanuel v Symon* came before the Court of Appeal.
(His Lordship stated the facts and decision in that case and continued): The
headnote observes that *Sirdar's* case, which I have already cited, was followed.

It is in my view interesting to note that the unsuccessful plaintiffs, who
were the respondents in the Court of Appeal, were represented by Mr
Holman Gregory. In the course of his argument he raised the very
contention Mr Waldman has been raising before me in this form:

> 'When persons agree to become partners in a business or transaction
> which can only be carried on or effected in a foreign country, there is
> necessarily implied an agreement to submit to the jurisdiction of the
> foreign courts.'

That provoked Kennedy LJ to intervene. He said, as recorded, 'Such an
agreement, in order to be binding, must be express. It is not to be implied:'
and he cites *Sirdar*. Mr Boreham was good enough to read to me most of
Lord Alverstone's judgment and Mr Waldman read some of Buckley LJ's
judgment: but the real gem of the collection I think is to be found in the
judgment of Kennedy LJ. It is quite true that it does not go so far as his
intervention but it goes a long way. What he says is this:

> 'the decision of the Privy Council is clear that there is no implied
> obligation on a foreigner to the country of that forum to accept the

7 [1894] AC 670.

forum loci contractus, as having, by reason of the contract, acquired a conventional jurisdiction over him in a suit founded upon that contract for all future time, wherever the foreigner may be domiciled or resident at the time of the institution of the suit. Such an obligation may exist by express agreement, as in the case of *Copin v Adamson*,[8] and as in many cases of foreign contracts where the parties by articles of agreement bind themselves to accept the jurisdiction of foreign tribunals; but such an obligation, as is pointed out in the decision of the Privy Council, [*Sirdar*] is not to be implied from the mere fact of entering into a contract in a foreign country.'

Those two cases in my view establish the principle that an implied agreement to assent to the jurisdiction of a foreign tribunal is not something which courts of this country have entertained as a legal possibility. Recognising that such an agreement may be made expressly they have in terms decided that implication is not to be relied upon.

There the matter might have rested but for the fact that in 1961 there came before Diplock J the case of *Blohn v Desser*.[9] That was a case in which the plaintiff, an Austrian resident in Vienna, had obtained in the Commercial Court of Vienna a judgment against a partnership there. The defendant was a partner in the firm and her name was registered as such in the commercial register in Vienna. But she was only a sleeping partner receiving no income from the firm and at all material times was resident in England. The plaintiff brought an action against the defendant personally in England on, inter alia, the Austrian judgment. As counsel all agree it would have been quite possible for the judge to dispose of that claim on the short and simple ground on which he eventually did dismiss it, but in the course of giving judgment he entertained argument and gave his views upon a topic which was not necessary for his decision, and places those who come after in some difficulty when it is realised that what he there said runs completely counter to the passages which I have cited from *Sirdar* and from *Emanuel v Symon*. The curious thing is, if I might say so, that Diplock J then had cited to him *Emanuel v Symon* for the purpose of showing to him the five types of cases listed by Buckley LJ which I have already referred to. But then having set out those five cases the judge said, at 123:

'There may be some doubt as to whether today it would be held that the jurisdiction exists in the first category of cases, but the other four cases have never been questioned. It is also, I think, clear law that the contract referred to in the fifth case, to submit to the forum in which the judgment was obtained, may be express or implied.'

I suppose that eminent as counsel were who were engaged in that case none of them directed his Lordship's attention to the intervention of Kennedy LJ or the passage in his judgment which I have cited; if they had done so I can hardly believe that he would have said that the contrary was clear law. He went on to say:

'It seems to me that, where a person becomes a partner in a foreign firm with a place of business within the jurisdiction of a foreign court, and

8 (1874) LR 9 Ex 345, 43 LJ Ex 161.
9 [1962] 2 QB 116, [1961] 3 All ER 1.

appoints an agent resident in that jurisdiction to conduct business on behalf of the partnership at that place of business, and causes or permits, as in the present case, these matters to be notified to persons dealing with that firm by registration in a public register, he does impliedly agree with all persons to whom such a notification is made—that is to say, the public—to submit to the jurisdiction of the court of the country in which the business is carried on in respect of transactions conducted at that place of business by that agent.'

That passage has, as I am informed, and as I find in the current edition of Dicey and Morris, *Conflict of Laws*,[10] been the subject of critical comment. It would be impudent on my part to add criticism of my own: it is enough for me to say that faced with the choice between that passage and the earlier authorities I feel no hesitation in preferring the older authorities.

It is only fair to Mr Waldman to add that Mocatta J, in a case already mentioned, *Sfeir & Co v National Insurance Co of New Zealand Ltd* does seem in terms to have accepted that an agreement to submit to the jurisdiction of the foreign tribunal may be implied. Once again there were other reasons why his decision in favour of the defendants was certainly maintainable and correct and I leave it there. Leaving it there I can only say that there are clearly dicta to the contrary of what I am deciding, but at least I am fortified by having authority of high weight in favour of the view which I now take.

Of course, as Mr Waldman says, once I have reached that conclusion his claim goes. It must go because there is no express agreement here, none could be relied on, by which the defendants could be held to have agreed to submit themselves to the jurisdiction of the Israeli court.

Nonetheless because so much care has been taken in presenting this case I ought to add that if it were necessary for me to decide the point I should rule that there is no such implied agreement to be deduced in the present case. That is to say, assuming that such an agreement would give the plaintiff the relief he seeks, the facts are not enough to give rise to the implication. The facts relied on by Mr Waldman were (a) that the contract was made within the jurisdiction of the foreign tribunal; (b) by or through an agent residing there; (c) such agent was a person carrying on business residentially within that jurisdiction; and (d) the contract was to be performed within the jurisdiction. In my judgment while proposition (c) is established, namely that Mr Kornbluth was carrying on business residentially within that jurisdiction, none of the other material factors are established at all. I hold that Kornbluth was not an agent. I hold that the contract was not made within the foreign jurisdiction. And lastly I hold it was not to be performed there. On these grounds there must be judgment for the defendants.

A foreign judgment cannot be sued on in England unless it is final and conclusive.

Nouvion v Freeman (1889) 15 App Cas 1, 59 LJCh 337 (House of Lords)

Appeal from a decision of the Court of Appeal (Cotton, Lindley, and Lopes LJJ) reversing a judgment of North J.

10 8th edn (1967) p 980.

In 1878 the plaintiff obtained judgment against the defendant in Spain for a large sum of money. The judgment was a 'remate' judgment and the proceedings were summary or 'executive'. In such proceedings the defendant could plead such defences as payment or waiver, but could not set up any defence denying the validity of the contract. Either plaintiff or defendant, if unsuccessful in the 'executive' proceedings, might take separate and independent proceedings in the same Spanish court called 'ordinary' or 'plenary' proceedings, in which the 'remate' judgment could not be pleaded as res judicata or otherwise made use of. In such 'plenary' proceedings all defences and the whole merits of the matter might be gone into.

The plaintiff brought an action in England on the 'remate' Spanish judgment. The Court of Appeal held that the action failed. The plaintiff appealed.

Lord Herschell: . . . My Lords, there can be no doubt that in the courts of this country effect will be given to a foreign judgment. It is unnecessary to inquire upon what principle the courts proceed in giving effect to such a judgment, and in treating it as sufficient to establish the debt. Reliance was placed upon a dictum by Parke B and Alderson B in the case of *Williams v Jones*[11] where the law is thus stated: 'Where a court of competent jurisdiction has adjudicated a certain sum to be due from one person to another, a legal obligation arises to pay that sum, on which an action of debt to enforce the judgment may be maintained'. But it was conceded, and necessarily conceded, by the learned counsel for the appellant, that a judgment, to come within the terms of the law as properly laid down, must be a judgment which results from an adjudication of a court of competent jurisdiction, such judgment being final and conclusive. I shall of course have something to say upon the meaning which must be given to those words, but the general proposition in that form is not disputed by the learned counsel for the appellant. They contend that this judgment is final and conclusive, and no doubt in a certain sense that must be conceded. It puts an end to and absolutely concludes that particular action. About that there can be no manner of doubt—in that sense it is final and conclusive. But the same may be said of some interlocutory judgments upon which there can be no question that an action could not be maintained; they do settle and conclude the particular proceeding, the interlocutory proceeding, in which the judgment is pronounced. It is obvious, therefore, that the mere fact that the judgment puts an end to and finally settles the controversy which arose in the particular proceeding, is not of itself sufficient to make it a final and conclusive judgment upon which an action may be maintained in the courts of this country, when such judgment has been pronounced by a foreign court.

My Lords, I think that in order to establish that such a judgment has been pronounced it must be shewn that in the court by which it was pronounced it conclusively, finally, and for ever established the existence of the debt of which it is sought to be made conclusive evidence in this country, so as to make it res judicata between the parties. If it is not conclusive in the same court which pronounced it, so that notwithstanding such a judgment the existence of the debt may between the same parties be afterwards contested in that court, and upon proper proceedings being taken and such contest being adjudicated upon, it may be declared that there existed no obligation

11 (1845) 13 M & W 628 at 633.

to pay the debt at all, then I do not think that a judgment which is of that character can be regarded as finally and conclusively evidencing the debt, and so entitling the person who has obtained the judgment to claim a decree from our courts for the payment of that debt.

The principle upon which I think our enforcement of foreign judgments must proceed is this: that in a court of competent jurisdiction, where according to its established procedure the whole merits of the case were open, at all events, to the parties, however much they may have failed to take advantage of them, or may have waived any of their rights, a final adjudication has been given that a debt or obligation exists which cannot thereafter in that court be disputed, and can only be questioned in an appeal to a higher tribunal. In such a case it may well be said that giving credit to the courts of another country we are prepared to take the fact that such adjudication has been made as establishing the existence of the debt or obligation. But where, as in the present case, the adjudication is consistent with the non-existence of the debt or obligation which it is sought to enforce, and it may thereafter be declared by the tribunal which pronounced it that there is no obligation and no debt, it appears to me that the very foundation upon which the courts of this country would proceed in enforcing a foreign judgment altogether fails.

It has been suggested that a judgment obtained in an 'executive' action may be regarded as analogous to a judgment obtained in a common law action in the time prior to the Judicature Act, the execution of which might be restrained by a Court of Equity, so as to prevent the plaintiff who had succeeded in such an action from obtaining the fruits of his judgment. I do not think that such an analogy is a complete one; but even if it were more complete than I think it to be, it appears to me that it would afford very little assistance to your Lordships unless we could know what had been the course adopted with regard to such judgments in countries in whose system of law the same force and effect are given to foreign judgments as are given in the courts of this country. Upon that point we have had no information whatsoever.

Then, my Lords, it is said that such a judgment is analogous to a judgment which has been obtained upon which a suit may be instituted in the courts of this country, even although an appeal may be pending. It appears to me that there is a vital distinction between the two cases. Although an appeal may be pending, a court of competent jurisdiction has finally and conclusively determined the existence of a debt, and it has none the less done so because the right of appeal has been given whereby a superior court may overrule that decision. There exists at the time of the suit a judgment which must be assumed to be valid until interfered with by a higher tribunal, and which conclusively establishes the existence of the debt which is sought to be recovered in this country. That appears to me to be in altogether a different position from a 'remate' judgment, where the very court which pronounced the 'remate' judgment (not the Court of Appeal) may determine, if proper proceedings are taken, that the debt for which this 'remate' judgment is sought to be used as conclusive evidence has no existence at all.

My Lords, the plaintiff in such a suit, an executive suit, is not, by the decision which is now under appeal, deprived of his rights. He may still sue upon the original cause of action. Of course it may happen, as in this particular case, that such a suit is barred by lapse of time, but that is an accident. The right of the plaintiff to sue on his original cause of action is not at all interfered with by the judgment which has been pronounced; and in such an action, if it were brought, all questions upon which the rights of the parties depend, and by the solution of which the obligation to pay must ultimately be determined, would be open to consideration and could be dealt with by the courts, and finally and conclusively settled. I do not, therefore, see that there is any wrong or any hardship done by holding that a judgment which does not conclusively and for ever as between the parties establish the existence of a debt in that court cannot be looked upon as sufficient evidence of it in the courts of this country. . . .

For these reasons I move your Lordships that the judgment appealed from be affirmed, and the appeal dismissed with costs.

Lords Watson, Bramwell and Ashbourne delivered judgments to the same effect.

Appeal dismissed.

A foreign judgment cannot be impeached on its merits even if the foreign tribunal has proceeded on a mistaken view of English law.

Godard v Gray (1870) LR 6 QB 139, 40 LJQB 62 (Court of Queen's Bench)

Blackburn J: In this case the plaintiffs declare on a judgment of a French tribunal, averred to have jurisdiction in that behalf.

The question arises on a demurrer to the second plea, which sets out the whole proceedings in the French court. By these it appears that the plaintiffs, who are Frenchmen, sued the defendants, who are Englishmen, on a charterparty made at Sunderland, which charterparty contained the following clause: 'Penalty for non-performance of this agreement, estimated amount of freight'. The French court below, treating this clause as fixing the amount of liquidated damages, gave judgment against the defendants for the amount of freight on two voyages. On appeal, the superior court reduced the amount to the estimated freight of one voyage, giving as their reason that the charterparty itself 'fixait l'indemnité à laquelle chacune des parties aurait droit pour inexécution de la convention par la faute de l'autre; que moyennant paiement de cette indemnité chacune des parties avait le droit de rompre la convention', and the tribunal proceeds to observe that the amount thus decreed was after all more than sufficient to cover all the plaintiffs' loss.

All parties in France seem to have taken it for granted that the words in the charterparty were to be understood in their natural sense; but the English law is accurately expressed in *Abbott on Shipping*,[12] and had that passage been brought to the notice of the French tribunal, it would have known that in an English charterparty, as is there stated, 'Such a clause is not the absolute limit of damages on either side; the party may, if he thinks fit, ground his action upon the other clauses or covenants, and may, in such action, recover damages beyond the amount of the penalty, if in justice they shall be found to exceed it. On the other hand, if the party sue on such a

12 5th edn, p 170.

penal clause, he cannot, in effect, recover more than the damage actually sustained'. But it was not brought to the notice of the French tribunal that according to the interpretation put by the English law on such a contract, a penal clause of this sort was in fact idle and inoperative. If it had been, they would, probably, have interpreted the English contract made in England according to the English construction. No blame can be imputed to foreign lawyers for not conjecturing that the clause was merely a brutum fulmen. The fault, if any, was in the defendants, for not properly instructing their French counsel on this point.

Still the fact remains that we can see on the face of the proceedings that the foreign tribunal has made a mistake on the construction of an English contract, which is a question of English law; and that, in consequence of that mistake, judgment has been given for an amount probably greater than, or, at all events, different from that for which it would have been given if the tribunal had been correctly informed what construction the English contract bore according to English law.

The question raised by the plea is, whether this is a bar to the action brought in England to enforce that judgment, and we are all of opinion that it is not, and that the plaintiff is entitled to judgment.

The following are the reasons of my brother Mellor and myself. My brother Hannen, though agreeing in the result, qualifies his assent to these reasons to some extent, which he will state for himself.

It is not an admitted principle of the law of nations that a state is bound to enforce within its territories the judgment of a foreign tribunal. Several of the continental nations (including France) do not enforce the judgments of other countries, unless where there are reciprocal treaties to that effect. But in England and in those states which are governed by the common law, such judgments are enforced, not by virtue of any treaty, nor by virtue of any statute, but upon a principle very well stated by Parke B, in *Williams v Jones*:[13] 'Where a court of competent jurisdiction has adjudicated a certain sum to be due from one person to another, a legal obligation arises to pay that sum, on which an action of debt to enforce the judgment may be maintained. It is in this way that the judgments of foreign and colonial courts are supported and enforced.' And taking this as the principle, it seems to follow that anything which negatives the existence of that legal obligation, or excuses the defendant from the performance of it, must form a good defence to the action. It must be open, therefore, to the defendant to shew that the court which pronounced the judgment had not jurisdiction to pronounce it, either because they exceeded the jurisdiction given to them by the foreign law, or because he, the defendant, was not subject to that jurisdiction; and so far the foreign judgment must be examinable. Probably the defendant may shew that the judgment was obtained by the fraud of the plaintiff, for that would shew that the defendant was excused from the performance of an obligation thus obtained; and it may be that where the foreign court has knowingly and perversely disregarded the rights given to an English subject by English law, that forms a valid excuse for disregarding the obligation thus imposed on him; but we prefer to imitate the caution of the present Lord Chancellor, in *Castrique v Imrie*,[14] and to leave those

13 (1845) 13 M & W 628 at 633.
14 (1870) LR 4 HL 414 at 445.

questions to be decided when they arise, only observing that in the present case, as in that, 'the whole of the facts appear to have been inquired into by the French courts, judicially, honestly, and with the intention to arrive at the right conclusion, and having heard the facts as stated before them they came to a conclusion which justified them in France in deciding as they did decide'. . . .

The decisions of the Court of Queen's Bench in *Bank of Australasia v Nias*,[15] of the Court of Common Pleas in *Bank of Australasia v Harding*,[16] and of the Court of Exchequer in *De Cosse Brissac v Rathbone*,[17] seem to us to leave it no longer open to contend, unless in a court of error, that a foreign judgment can be impeached on the ground that it was erroneous on the merits; or to set up as a defence to an action on it, that the tribunal mistook either the facts or the law.

But there still remains a question which has never, so far as we know, been expressly decided in any court.

It is broadly laid down, by the very learned author of Smith's Leading Cases, in the original note to *Doe v Oliver*,[18] that 'it is clear that if the judgment appear on the face of the proceedings to be founded on a *mistaken notion* of the English law', it would not be conclusive. . . . We think that the defendant can no more set up as an excuse, relieving him from the duty of paying the amount awarded by the judgment of a foreign tribunal having jurisdiction over him and the cause, that the judgment proceeded on a mistake as to English law, than he could set up as an excuse that there had been a mistake as to the law of some third country incidentally involved, or as to any other question of fact.

It can make no difference that the mistake appears on the face of the proceedings. That, no doubt, greatly facilitates the proof of the mistake; but if the principle be to inquire whether the defendant is relieved from a prima facie duty to obey the judgment, he must be equally relieved, whether the mistake appears on the face of the proceedings or is to be proved by extraneous evidence. Nor can there be any difference between a mistake made by the foreign tribunal as to English law, and any other mistake. No doubt the English court can, without arrogance, say that where there is a difference of opinion as to English law, the opinion of the English tribunal is probably right; but how would it be if the question had arisen as to the law of some of the numerous portions of the British dominions where the law is not that of England? The French tribunal, if incidentally inquiring into the law of Mauritius, where French law prevails, would be more likely to be right than the English court; if inquiring into the law of Scotland it would seem that there was about an equal chance as to which took the right view. If it was sought to enforce the foreign judgment in Scotland, the chances as to which court was right would be altered. Yet it surely cannot be said that a judgment shewn to have proceeded on a mistaken view of Scotch law could be enforced in England and not in Scotland, and that one proceeding on a mistaken view of English law could be enforced in Scotland but not in England.

If, indeed, foreign judgments were enforced by our courts out of politeness

15 (1851) 16 QB 717, 20 LJQB 284.
16 (1850) 9 CB 661, 19 LJCP 345.
17 (1861) 6 H & N 301, 30 LJ Ex 238.
18 (1829) 2 Sm LC (2nd edn) p 448.

and courtesy to the tribunals of other countries, one could understand its being said that though our courts would not be so rude as to inquire whether the foreign court had made a mistake, or to allow the defendant to assert that it had, yet that if the foreign court itself admitted its blunder they would not then act; but it is quite contrary to every analogy to suppose that an English court of law exercises any discretion of this sort. We enforce a legal obligation, and we admit any defence which shews that there is no legal obligation or a legal excuse for not fulfilling it; but in no case that we know of is it ever said that a defence shall be admitted if it is easily proved, and rejected if it would give the court much trouble to investigate it. Yet on what other principle can we admit as a defence that there is a mistake of English law apparent on the face of the proceedings, and reject a defence that there is a mistake of Spanish or even Scotch law apparent in the proceedings, or that there was a mistake of English law not apparent on the proceedings, but which the defendant avers that he can shew did exist?

The whole law was much considered and discussed in *Castrique v Imrie*, where the French tribunal had made a mistake as to the English law, and under that mistake had decreed the sale of the defendant's ship. The decision of the House of Lords was, that the defendant's title derived under that sale was good, notwithstanding that mistake: Lord Colonsay pithily saying, 'It appears to me that we cannot enter into an inquiry as to whether the French courts proceeded correctly, either as to their own course of procedure or their own law, nor whether under the circumstances they took the proper means of satisfying themselves with respect to the view they took of the English law. Nor can we inquire whether they were right in their views of the English law. The question is, whether under the circumstances of the case, dealing with it fairly, the original tribunal did proceed against the ship, and did order the sale of the ship.'

The question in *Castrique v Imrie* was as to the effect on the property of a judgment ordering a ship, locally situate in France, to be sold, and therefore was not the same as the question in this case as to what effect is to be given to a judgment against the person. But at least the decision in *Castrique v Imrie* establishes this, that a mistake as to English law on the part of a foreign tribunal does not operate in all cases so as to prevent the courts of this country from giving effect to the judgment. . . .

For these reasons we have come to the conclusion that judgment should be given for the plaintiffs.

Hannen J, while expressing no final opinion on the question whether the French judgment might not be impeached on the ground that it appeared on its face to have proceeded on an incorrect view of English law, agreed in the result on the ground that the defendants should have taken steps to bring the English law to the notice of the French tribunal.

Judgment for the plaintiff.

A foreign judgment given by a court having jurisdiction is not void in England merely because the court mistook or misapplied its own procedure.

Pemberton v Hughes [1899] 1 Ch 781, 68 LJCh 281 (Court of Appeal)

This was an action by Mrs Pemberton who claimed to be the widow of Francis Pemberton asking for a declaration that under a deed poll executed by him in 1891 she was entitled to a jointure or rentcharge of £200 pa issuing out of certain lands in Cambridgeshire. The lands were settled by the will of a testator who died in 1850 on Francis Pemberton for life with remainders over, with power for every tenant for life in possession by deed to appoint a rentcharge to any woman whom he should marry or have married, to commence from the death of such tenant for life. Francis Pemberton died in 1892.

The defence was that the plaintiff was married to one Holmes Erwin in Florida in 1884, both parties being domiciled in Florida; that in 1888 Erwin obtained a divorce from a Florida court on the ground of the plaintiff's violent and ungovernable temper; that this divorce was invalid because the rules of the Florida court required that ten days should intervene between the day on which process was issued and the day on which it was returnable, whereas in the present case only nine clear days had intervened; that Erwin was still living when the plaintiff went through a ceremony of marriage with Francis Pemberton; and that therefore the plaintiff's marriage with Francis Pemberton was void and she was not within the power of jointuring conferred by the settlement.

Kekewich J held that the Florida divorce was void and dismissed the action with costs.

The plaintiff appealed.

Lindley MR (after stating the facts, and holding that the Florida court had jurisdiction because the plaintiff and Erwin were domiciled in Florida, and stating that he was not satisfied on the evidence that the alleged defect of procedure rendered the divorce void in Florida, continued): Assuming that the defendants are right, and that the decree of divorce is void by the law of Florida, it by no means follows that it ought to be so regarded in this country. It sounds paradoxical to say that a decree of a foreign court should be regarded here as more efficacious or with more respect than it is entitled to in the country in which it was pronounced. But this paradox disappears when the principles on which English courts act in regarding or disregarding foreign judgments are borne in mind. If a judgment is pronounced by a foreign court over persons within its jurisdiction and in a matter with which it is competent to deal, English courts never investigate the propriety of the proceedings in the foreign court, unless they offend against English views of substantial justice. Where no substantial justice, according to English notions, is offended, all that English courts look to is the finality of the judgment and the jurisdiction of the court, in this sense and to this extent— namely, its competence to entertain the sort of case which it did deal with, and its competence to require the defendant to appear before it. If the court had jurisdiction in this sense and to this extent, the courts of this country never inquire whether the jurisdiction has been properly or improperly exercised, provided always that no substantial injustice, according to English notions, has been committed.

There is no doubt that the courts of this country will not enforce the decisions of foreign courts which have no jurisdiction in the sense above explained—ie, over the subject-matter or over the persons brought before them: *Schibsby v Westenholz*;[19] *Rousillon v Rousillon*;[20] *Price v Dewhurst*;[1]

19 (1870) LR 6 QB 155, 40 LJQB 73; p 149 above.
20 (1880) 14 Ch D 351, 49 LJ Ch 338.
1 (1838) 4 My & Cr 76, 8 LJ Ch 57.

Buchanan v Rucker;[2] *Sirdar Gurdyal Singh v Rajah of Faridkote*.[3] But the jurisdiction which alone is important in these matters is the competence of the court in an international sense—ie, its territorial competence over the subject-matter and over the defendant. Its competence or jurisdiction in any other sense is not regarded as material by the courts of this country. This is pointed out by Mr Westlake[4] and by Foote,[5] and is illustrated by *Vanquelin v Bouard*.[6] That was an action on a judgment obtained in France on a bill of exchange. The court was competent to try such actions, and the defendant was within its jurisdiction. He let judgment go by default, and in the action in this country on the judgment he pleaded that by French law the French court had no jurisdiction, because the defendant was not a trader and was not resident in a particular town where the cause of action arose. In other words, the defendant pleaded that the French action was brought in the wrong court (see the 13th plea). The Court of Common pleas held the plea bad, and that the defence set up by it should have been raised in the French action. The French action in *Vanquelin v Bouard* was an action in personam, and the parties to the action in France were also the parties to the action brought in this country on the French judgment. The decision, therefore, does not exactly cover the present case, but it goes far to show that the defendants' contention in this case cannot be supported.

The defendants' contention entirely ignores the distinction between the jurisdiction of tribunals from an international and their jurisdiction from a purely municipal point of view. But that distinction rests on good sense, and is recognised by modern writers on private international law. . . .

It may be safely said that, in the opinion of writers on international law, and for international purposes, the jurisdiction or the competency of a court does not depend upon the exact observance of its own rules of procedure. The defendants' contention is based upon the assumption that an irregularity in procedure of a foreign court of competent jurisdiction in the sense above explained is a matter which the courts of this country are bound to recognise if such irregularity involves nullity of sentence. No authority can be found for any such proposition; and, although I am not aware of any English decision exactly to the contrary, there are many which are so inconsistent with it as to show that it cannot be accepted.

A judgment of a foreign court having jurisdiction over the parties and subject-matter—ie, having jurisdiction to summon the defendants before it and to decide such matters as it has decided—cannot be impeached in this country on its merits: *Castrique v Imrie*[7] (in rem); *Godard v Gray*[8] (in personam); *Messina v Petrococchino*[9] (in personam). It is quite inconsistent with those cases, and also with *Vanquelin v Bouard*, to hold that such a judgment can be impeached here for a mere error in procedure. And in *Castrique v Imrie* Lord Colonsay said that no inquiry on such a matter should be made.

2 (1808) 9 East 192.
3 [1894] AC 670.
4 *Private International Law* (3rd edn) s 328.
5 *Private International Jurisprudence* (2nd edn) p 547.
6 (1863) 15 CB NS 341, 3 New Rep 122.
7 (1870) LR 4HL 414, 39 LJCP 350.
8 (1870) LR 6 QB 139, 40 LJQB 62; p 165 above.
9 (1872) LR 4 PC 144, 8 Moo PCC NS 375.

A decree for divorce, altering as it does the status of the parties and affecting, as it may do, the legitimacy of their afterborn children, is much more like a judgment in rem than a judgment in personam: see *Niboyet v Niboyet*.[10] And where there are differences between the two, the decisions on foreign judgments in rem are better guides for the determination of this case than decisions on foreign judgments in personam. The leading cases on foreign judgments in rem are *Doglioni v Crispin*;[11] *Castrique v Imrie*; *Re Trufort*.[12] There is nothing, however, in the decisions in these cases to assist the defendants. On the contrary, the judgments delivered in them are, in my opinion, adverse to the defendants' contention. . . .

Rigby and Vaughan Williams LJJ delivered judgments to the same effect.
Appeal allowed.

A foreign judgment can be impeached on the ground of fraud, even if (a) the fraud alleged is such that it cannot be proved without retrying the questions adjudicated upon by the foreign court, or (b) the defendant could have taken the point in the foreign court, but did not.

Syal v Heyward [1948] 2 KB 443, [1948] 2 All ER 576 (Court of Appeal)

Interlocutory appeal from Jones J.

In February 1947 the plaintiff, an Indian moneylender, obtained judgment against the defendants, two English lieutenant-colonels, from a court at Saharanpur, India, on a plaint in which he alleged that the defendants had borrowed 20,000 rupees from him in October 1946, and had executed a promissory note for that amount. The defendants did not defend this action. In November 1947 this judgment was ordered to be registered in the High Court pursuant to the Foreign Judgments (Reciprocal Enforcement) Act 1933 (p 180 below). The defendants applied for an order that the registration of the judgment should be set aside under s 4 (1) (a) (iv) of the Act on the ground that the judgment had been obtained by fraud. They alleged that the amount which they had borrowed from the plaintiff was not 20,000 rupees but only 10,800 rupees, the difference being made up in part of commission and in part of interest; and that the plaintiff had deceived the Indian court by pretending that he had lent 20,000 rupees, whereas in fact he had lent only 10,800 rupees, thereby concealing from the court the possibility that the defendants might have a defence under the Indian Usurious Loans Act 1918.

The master dismissed the defendants' application on the ground that all the facts on which they relied were known to them at all material times and could have been raised by way of defence in the Indian proceedings. Jones J reversed this decision and directed an issue to be tried. The plaintiff appealed.

The judgment of the court (Scott, Cohen and Wrottesley LJJ) was read by Cohen LJ: Mr Foot [counsel for the plaintiff] submitted that: (1) The fraud contemplated by s 4 of the Foreign Judgments (Reciprocal

10 (1878) 4 PD 1, 48 LJP 1.
11 (1866) LR 1 HL 301, 35 LJP & M 129.
12 (1887) 36 Ch D 600, 57 LJ Ch 135.

Enforcement) Act 1933 is fraud on the court. Unless the court has been deceived, the section is not applicable. (2) An application under s 4 should be treated in the same way as, before the Act of 1933 came into force, an action to set aside a judgment would have been treated. (3) Precisely the same tests apply whether the judgment sought to be set aside is a foreign judgment or an English judgment. (4) Where a judgment is sought to be set aside on the ground of fraud, the fraud must have been discovered by the applicants since the date of the judgment. (5) It was plain that the facts relied on in the present case were all known to the defendants before the date of the Indian judgment.

[Counsel for the defendants] agreed with the first of these propositions and he did not, we think, dispute the second. The third is supported by the observations of Lindley LJ in *Vadala v Lawes*,[13] where he said: 'First of all, there is the rule which is perfectly well established and well known, that a party to an action can impeach the judgment in it for fraud. Whether it is the judgment of an English court or of a foreign court does not matter; using general language, that is a general proposition unconditional and undisputed.' It is unnecessary for us on this appeal to consider how far those observations go.

The fifth proposition is also plainly correct if Mr Foot means only that the defendants knew they were being sued for a sum in excess of 10,800 rupees and that in the plaint, verified by affidavit, the plaintiff was alleging that they had borrowed 20,000 rupees, but there is no evidence that they knew that the plaint so verified would be the only evidence before the court if in fact that was the position.

Be that as it may, Mr Foot's real difficulty is in his fourth proposition. For it he relied on *Boswell v Coaks (No 2)*,[14] a decision of the House of Lords applied in *Birch v Birch*.[15] These cases, no doubt, establish that in proceedings to set aside an English judgment, the defendants cannot ask for a retrial of the issue of fraud as between them and the plaintiff on facts known to them at the date of the earlier judgment; but in cases under s 4 of the Act of 1933, the question is not one of fraud on the plaintiff,[16] but of fraud on the court, and it seems to us to be clearly established by authority binding on us, that if the defendant shows a prima facie case that the court was deceived, he is entitled to have that issue tried even though in trying it the court may have to go into defences which could have been raised at the first trial. See *Abouloff v Oppenheimer*,[17] as explained in *Vadala v Lawes*, where Lindley LJ, immediately after the passage we have already cited, says: 'Another general proposition which, speaking in equally general language, is perfectly well settled, is, that when you bring an action on a foreign judgment, you cannot go into the merits which have been tried in the foreign courts. But you have to combine those two rules and apply them in the case where you cannot go into the alleged fraud without going into the merits. Which rule is to prevail? That point appears to me to have been one of very great difficulty before the case of *Abouloff v Oppenheimer*. At the time when that case was decided, namely, in 1882, there was a long line of authorities

13 (1890) 25 QBD 310 at 316.
14 (1894) 86 LT 365n, 6R 167.
15 [1902] P 130, 71 LJP 58.
16 Sic in the report: evidently a misprint for defendant (*Ed*).
17 (1882) 10 QBD 295, 52 LJQB 1.

including *Bank of Australasia v Nias*,[18] *Ochsenbein v Papelier*,[19] and *Cammell v Sewell*,[20] all recognising and enforcing the general proposition, that in an action on a foreign judgment you cannot retry the merits. But until *Abouloff's* case the difficulty of combining the two rules and saying what ought to be done where you could not enter into the question of fraud to prove it without reopening the merits, had never come forward for explicit decision. That point was raised directly in the case of *Abouloff v Oppenheimer*, and it was decided. I cannot fritter away that judgment, and I cannot read the judgments without seeing that they amount to this: that if the fraud upon the foreign court consists in the fact that the plaintiff has induced that court to come to a wrong conclusion, you can reopen the whole case even although you will have in this court to go into the very facts which were investigated and which were in issue in the foreign court. The technical objection that the issue is the same is technically answered by the technical reply that the issue is not the same, because in this court you have to consider whether the foreign court has been imposed upon. That, to my mind, is only meeting technical argument by a technical answer, and I do not attach much importance to it; but in that case the court faced the difficulty that you could not give effect to the defence without retrying the merits. The fraud practised on the court, or alleged to have been practised on the court, was the misleading of the court by evidence known by the plaintiff to be false. That was the whole fraud. The question of fact, whether what the plaintiff had said in the court below was or was not false, was the very question of fact that had been adjudicated on in the foreign court; and, notwithstanding that was so, when the court came to consider how the two rules, to which I have alluded, could be worked together, they said: "Well, if that foreign judgment was obtained fraudulently, and if it is necessary, in order to prove that fraud, to retry the merits, you are entitled to do so according to the law of this country". I cannot read that case in any other way.'

In the present case it is plain that the defendants are alleging a fraud on the court and it is, therefore, immaterial that to establish their allegation they will have to adduce evidence which was available to them before the date of the Indian judgment.

As a subsidiary point, Mr Foot contended that the defendants had failed to establish a prima facie case of fraud. We are unable to accede to this argument. It may well be that the plaintiff will rebut that prima facie case, but we think that the evidence filed by the defendants discloses sufficient evidence of a case to entitle them to an issue.

Appeal dismissed.

English courts will not enforce a foreign judgment for a fine or other penalty. But if a foreign criminal court imposes a fine on the defendant and also orders him to pay compensation to the injured party, the latter part of the judgment can be enforced in England.

Raulin v Fischer [1911] 2 KB 93, 80 LJKB 811 (King's Bench Division)

The defendant, a young American lady, while recklessly galloping her horse

18 (1851) 16 QB 717, 20 LJQB 284.
19 (1873) 8 Ch App 695, 42 LJ Ch 861.
20 (1860) 5 H & N 728, 29 LJ Ex 350; p 544 below.

in the Bois de Boulogne, Paris, ran into the plaintiff, a French officer, and seriously injured him. She was prosecuted before the Civil Court of First Instance of the Seine, sitting as a correctional court, under article 320 of the Penal Code. The plaintiff intervened in the proceedings as partie civile in accordance with French law and claimed damages. The defendant was convicted and ordered to pay a fine of 100 francs and (at a later sitting of the court) ordered to pay to the plaintiff 15,000 francs as damages and also costs. The plaintiff brought an action in England to enforce that judgment.

Hamilton J: On the judgment of the French court the plaintiff is in my opinion entitled to recover the English equivalent of the 15,000 francs that have been awarded him as damages. It was not disputed by the defendant's counsel that he would be so entitled but for the rule of private international law that a penal judgment of a court in one country cannot be enforced by action in another country. The point raised for the defendant was that the judgment sued on was in truth a penal judgment within that rule, and that though part of it might be more or less civil in its character there was no power in this court to dissect the judgment and enforce here that part which was enforceable by action though the judgment as a whole was not enforceable. Although the French courts might refuse to distinguish between the parts of a judgment which may be called principal and the parts which may be called accessory, the parts which are by way of punishment and the parts which are by way of civil remedy, it does not follow that the English courts in dealing with a French judgment should take the same course. The rule which governs such a question is that laid down by the Privy Council in *Huntington v Attrill*.[1] (His Lordship quoted from that case and continued): I have therefore to inquire first of all whether this judgment in so far as it concerns the present plaintiff is one for the satisfaction of a private wrong or for the punishment of an infraction of public law; and secondly whether, if it be as regards him only for the satisfaction of a private wrong, it is one which can be separated from the rest of the judgment, so that he may sue upon the judgment in spite of the fact that a considerable part of it relates to purely criminal proceedings. Certain French expert witnesses were called before me, and the effect of their evidence was this. In various respects the remedy in the form in which it was pursued differs from the form in which it might have been pursued. The result of M Raulin having pursued his remedy for compensation by intervention in the prosecution instead of bringing a separate civil action was that he came before a court especially assigned to criminal business. That court decided both in the prosecution and in the civil intervention, and to that extent the plaintiff obtained his judgment from a correctional tribunal. But in other respects it does not appear to me that his remedy differed in its character from the remedy which he might have pursued by a separate civil action. The prosecution abates with the death of the accused. The civil remedy does not. The liability to imprisonment in order to enforce payment of the damages is in law an incident both of the intervention in the action publique and of the separate civil action. The course of procedure differs because, instead of the whole conduct of the action on the intervener's side resting with the plaintiff as it would have done in civil proceedings, he has to adapt himself to the control of the proceedings by the

1 [1893] AC 150, 62 LJPC 44; p 34 above.

Procurator of the Republic. But the issues remain unchanged. The issue between the Procurator and the accused was whether she had broken the law against driving negligently contained in article 320 of the Penal Code. On that issue the contributory negligence of the plaintiff would have afforded no defence, but the contributory negligence of the plaintiff would have been material to the question of damages claimed by him as an intervening party, and that issue, if the facts justified it, would be raised just as much in the civil intervention in the action publique as it could in a separate action civile. It seems to me that there is no doubt that the public prosecution and private suit are two quite separate and distinct proceedings although they are for purposes of procedure combined in one. The judgment for the 15,000 francs is not in any respect a judgment in a proceeding 'in favour of the state whose law has been infringed'. It is a judgment in what is substantially a civil suit for the compensation of a person who has sustained a private wrong.

The other question is whether it is practicable to distinguish the portion of the adjudication which was not part of the criminal suit from that portion of it which was. In this connection certain decisions of French courts were cited to me, but not much assistance is to be gained from them, especially in view of the evidence that according to the jurisprudence of France the decisions of the courts are not binding even upon courts of inferior jurisdiction unless they are pronounced in the same cause or matter, and, consequently, though the decisions of the courts are constantly cited, they are cited by way of edification only and not as authority. In any case, according to the judgment of the Privy Council, this is not a matter in which I am bound by the view of the French courts. It is one in which I must determine for myself whether the enforcement of the plaintiff's rights would either directly or indirectly involve the execution of the penal law of another state. In my opinion it would not. Moreover here the decision awarding the final damages was not even pronounced at the same time as the decision inflicting the fine. It was given at a time when the only issue being contested was of a private and civil character, and one with which the state had nothing whatever to do. I think the decision must be for the plaintiff. I am fortified in this view by the passage which has been cited from Sir Francis Piggott's work on Foreign Judgments in which he deals with this very provision of the French law, that civil proceedings for a tort are allowed to be tacked on to criminal proceedings for the offence and damages may be awarded to the person injured, and suggests that the award of damages in such case is a civil judgment recognisable in England in the usual way.

Civil Jurisdiction and Judgments Act 1982

Part IV

Miscellaneous Provisions

32.—(1) Subject to the following provisions of this section a judgment given by a court of an overseas country in any proceedings shall not be recognised or enforced in the United Kingdom if—

(a) the bringing of those proceedings in that court was contrary to an agreement under which the dispute in question was to be settled otherwise than by proceedings in the courts of that country; and

(b) those proceedings were not brought in that court by, or with the agreement of, the person against whom the judgment was given; and

(c) that person did not counterclaim in the proceedings or otherwise submit to the jurisdiction of that court.

(2) Subsection (1) does not apply where the agreement referred to in paragraph (a) of that subsection was illegal, void or unenforceable or was incapable of being performed for reasons not attributable to the fault of the party bringing the proceedings in which the judgment was given.

(3) In determining whether a judgment given by a court of an overseas country should be recognised or enforced in the United Kingdom, a court in the United Kingdom shall not be bound by any decision of the overseas court relating to any of the matters mentioned in subsection (1) or (2).

(4) Nothing in subsection (1) shall affect the recognition or enforcement in the United Kingdom of—

(a) a judgment which is required to be recognised or enforced there under the 1968 Convention.

33.—(1) For the purposes of determining whether a judgment given by a court of an overseas country should be recognised or enforced in England and Wales or Northern Ireland, the person against whom the judgment was given shall not be regarded as having submitted to the jurisdiction of the court by reason only of the fact that he appeared (conditionally or otherwise) in the proceedings for all or any one or more of the following purposes, namely—

(a) to contest the jurisdiction of the court;

(b) to ask the court to dismiss or stay the proceedings on the ground that the dispute in question should be submitted to arbitration or to the determination of the courts of another country;

(c) to protect, or obtain the release of, property seized or threatened with seizure in the proceedings.

(2) Nothing in this section shall affect the recognition or enforcement in England and Wales or Northern Ireland of a judgment which is required to be recognised or enforced there under the 1968 Convention.

34. No proceedings may be brought by a person in England and Wales or Northern Ireland on a cause of action in respect of which a judgment has been given in his favour in proceedings between the same parties, or their privies, in a court in another part of the United Kingdom or in a court of an overseas country, unless that judgment is not enforceable or entitled to recognition in England and Wales or, as in the case may be, in Northern Ireland.

NOTE

As we have seen,[2] the Civil Jurisdiction and Judgments Act 1982 was passed primarily to implement the Brussels Convention of 1968 on jurisdiction and the enforcement of judgments in civil and commercial matters. But the opportunity was

2 P 94 above.

taken to remove some blemishes from the common law. Sections 32–34 fall into this category.

Section 32 generalises a provision of the Foreign Judgments (Reciprocal Enforcement) Act 1933 (s 4(3) (b), now repealed as redundant). That sub-section provided that the courts of a foreign country should not be deemed to have jurisdiction for the purposes of the Act if the bringing of the proceedings was contrary to an agreement under which the dispute in question was to be settled otherwise than by proceedings in the courts of that country (eg under a jurisdiction clause or an arbitration clause), unless the defendant submitted or agreed to submit to the jurisdiction. There was no authority for that proposition at common law. The gap has now been filled by section 32. The section does not apply if the foreign judgment is required to be recognised or enforced under the Brussels Convention: sub-s (4) (a). The reason for this is twofold. First, the fact that a judgment of a court in an EEC state was given in breach of a jurisdiction clause is not a ground under the Convention for refusing to enforce it in England: see article 27. Secondly, although the United Kingdom government hopes that the same does not apply to a judgment given in breach of an arbitration clause, this hope is based on the somewhat tenuous ground that the Convention does not apply to arbitration (article 1). That interpretation may at any moment be proved wrong by a decision of the European Court, which would be binding on English courts (s 3). If that happens, section 32 will not apply to any EEC judgment within the Convention, but will continue to apply at common law.

Section 33 reverses the decision of the Court of Appeal in *Henry v Geoprosco International Ltd.*[3] That was an action in England at common law to enforce an Alberta judgment for breach of a contract governed by English law and containing an arbitration clause. The defendant, which was not in any sense resident in Alberta nor carried on business there, sought to have the service of the writ set aside on the ground that Alberta was not the forum conveniens and also sought a stay of the proceedings because of the arbitration clause. When these applications failed the defendant took no further part in the proceedings and judgment was given against it. The judgment was held to be enforceable in England. The Court of Appeal held that there is a voluntary appearance where the defendant invites the court in its discretion not to exercise a jurisdiction which it has under its local law; or if the defendant's protest against the jurisdiction of the foreign court takes the form of what in England would be regarded as a conditional appearance. The court left open the question whether an appearance solely to protest against the jurisdiction of the foreign court would be a voluntary appearance. The decision has been heavily criticised by academic writers[4] and was extremely unpopular with the English business community. Few will regret its demise.

Sections 32 and 33 were applied in *Tracomin SA c Sudan Oil Seeds Co Ltd (No 1)*,[5] the first reported case on the Act.

Section 34 abolishes what used to be called the non-merger rule, under which a foreign judgment (unlike an English judgment) did not extinguish the plaintiff's cause of action, but left him free to bring an action in England on the original cause of action if it suited him to do so, as in some situations it did. Like the now exploded doctrine that a foreign judgment is merely evidence of a debt and therefore impeachable upon the merits, the non-merger rule was derived from the technical rule that a foreign court is not in the eyes of English law a court of record. Whereas one branch of that rule was finally exploded in *Godard v Gray* (1870) (p 165 above) the other remained an illogical anomaly, in conflict with the general policy of the law ut sit finis litium. No modern English case supported it, though Lord Herschell made a passing reference to it in *Nouvion v Freeman* (p 164 above), and three of their

3 [1976] QB 726, [1975] 2 All ER 702.
4 See eg *Cheshire and North* (10th edn) pp 638–641; *Morris* (2nd edn) pp 410–411.
5 [1983] 1 All ER 404, [1983] 1 WLR 662; affd [1983] 3 All ER 137, [1983] 1 WLR 1026.

Lordships accepted it (obiter) in *Carl Zeiss Stiftung v Rayner & Keeler (No 2)*.[6] However, in the same case Lord Wilberforce regarded it as 'illogical' and its continued existence as 'precarious'. Section 34 now gives it the coup de grace.

Section B. Under Statute

Administration of Justice Act 1920

PART II

RECIPROCAL ENFORCEMENT OF JUDGMENTS IN THE UNITED KINGDOM AND IN OTHER PARTS OF HIS MAJESTY'S DOMINIONS

9.—(1) Where a judgment has been obtained in a superior court in any part of His Majesty's dominions outside the United Kingdom to which this Part of this Act extends, the judgment creditor may apply to the High Court in England or [7Northern] Ireland or to the Court of Session in Scotland, at any time within twelve months after the date of the judgment, or such longer period as may be allowed by the court, to have the judgment registered in the court, and on any such application the court may, if in all the circumstances of the case they think it just and convenient that the judgment should be enforced in the United Kingdom, and subject to the provisions of this section, order the judgment to be registered accordingly.

(2) No judgment shall be ordered to be registered under this section if—

(a) the original court acted without jurisdiction; or

(b) the judgment debtor, being a person who was neither carrying on business nor ordinarily resident within the jurisdiction of the original court, did not voluntarily appear or otherwise submit or agree to submit to the jurisdiction of that court; or

(c) the judgment debtor, being the defendant in the proceedings, was not duly served with the process of the original court and did not appear, notwithstanding that he was ordinarily resident or was carrying on business within the jurisdiction of that court or agreed to submit to the jurisdiction of that court; or

(d) the judgment was obtained by fraud; or

(e) the judgment debtor satisfies the registering court either that an appeal is pending, or that he is entitled and intends to appeal, against the judgment; or

(f) the judgment was in respect of a cause of action which for reasons of public policy or for some other similar reason could not have been entertained by the registering court.

(3) Where a judgment is registered under this section—

(a) the judgment shall, as from the date of registration, be of the same force and effect, and proceedings may be taken thereon, as if it had been a judgment originally obtained or entered up on the date of registration in the registering court;

(b) the registering court shall have the same control and jurisdiction over

---

6 [1967] 1 AC 853, [1966] 2 All ER 536.
7 The restriction to Northern Ireland was made by SR & O 1921/1802 (*Ed*).

the judgment as it has over similar judgments given by itself, but in so far only as relates to execution under this section;

(c) the reasonable costs of and incidental to the registration of the judgment (including the costs of obtaining a certified copy thereof from the original court and of the application for registration) shall be recoverable in like manner as if they were sums payable under the judgment.

(5) In any action brought in any court in the United Kingdom on any judgment which might be ordered to be registered under this section, the plaintiff shall not be entitled to recover any costs of the action unless an application to register the judgment under this section has previously been refused or unless the court otherwise orders.

10. (*Provisions for issue of certified copies of UK judgments.*)

11. (*Power to make rules of court.*)

12.—(1) In this Part of this Act, unless the context otherwise requires—

The expression 'judgment' means any judgment or order given or made by a court in any civil proceedings, whether before or after the passing of this Act, whereby any sum of money is made payable, and includes an award in proceedings on an arbitration if the award has, in pursuance of the law in force in the place where it was made, become enforceable in the same manner as a judgment given by a court in that place:

The expression 'original court' in relation to any judgment means the court by which the judgment was given:

The expression 'registering court' in relation to any judgment means the court by which the judgment was registered:

The expression 'judgment creditor' means the person by whom the judgment was obtained, and includes the successors and assigns of that person:

The expression 'judgment debtor' means the person against whom the judgment was given, and includes any person against whom the judgment is enforceable in the place where it was given.

13. (*Extension to protectorates etc.*)

14.—(1) Where His Majesty is satisfied that reciprocal provisions have been made by the legislature of any part of His Majesty's dominions outside the United Kingdom for the enforcement within that part of His dominions of judgments obtained in the High Court in England, the Court of Session in Scotland, and the [High Court in Northern Ireland], His Majesty may by Order in Council declare that this Part of this Act shall extend to that part of His dominions, and on any such Order being made this Part of this Act shall extend accordingly.

(2) An Order in Council under this section may be varied or revoked by a subsequent Order.

(3)[8] Her Majesty may by Order in Council under this section consolidate any Orders in Council under this section which are in force when the consolidating Order is made.

8 This sub-s was added by s 35 (3) of the Civil Jurisdiction and Judgments Act 1982 (*Ed*).

Foreign Judgments (Reciprocal Enforcement) Act 1933[9]

Part I

Registration of Foreign Judgments

1.—(1) If, in the case of any foreign country, Her Majesty is satisfied that, in the event of the benefits conferred by this Part of this Act being extended to, or to any particular class of, judgments given in the courts of that country or in any particular class of those courts, substantial reciprocity of treatment will be assured as regards the enforcement in that country of similar judgments given in similar courts of the United Kingdom, she may by Order in Council direct—

(a) that this Part of this Act shall extend to that country;

(b) that such courts of that country as are specified in the Order shall be recognised courts of that country for the purposes of this Part of this Act; and

(c) that judgments of any such recognised court, or such judgments of any class so specified, shall, if within subsection (2) of this section, be judgments to which this Part of this Act applies.

(2) Subject to subsection (2A) of this section, a judgment of a recognised court is within this subsection if it satisfies the following conditions, namely—

(a) it is either final and conclusive as between the judgment debtor and the judgment creditor or requires the former to make an interim payment to the latter; and

(b) there is payable under it a sum of money, not being a sum payable in respect of taxes or other charges of a like nature or in respect of a fine or other penalty; and

(c) it is given after the coming into force of the Order in Council which made that court a recognised court.

(2A) The following judgments of a recognised court are not within subsection (2) of this section—

(a) a judgment given by that court on appeal from a court which is not a recognised court;

(b) a judgment or other instrument which is regarded for the purposes of its enforcement as a judgment of that court but which was given or made in another country;

(c) a judgment given by that court in proceedings founded on a judgment of a court in another country and having as their object the enforcement of that judgment.

(3) For the purposes of this section, a judgment shall be deemed to be final and conclusive notwithstanding that an appeal may be pending against it, or that it may still be subject to appeal, in the courts of the country of the original court.

(4) His Majesty may by a subsequent Order in Council vary or revoke any Order previously made under this section.

2.—(1) A person, being a judgment creditor under a judgment to which this Part of this Act applies, may apply to the High Court at any time within six

9 This Act is printed as amended by Schs 10 and 14 of the Civil Jurisdiction and Judgments Act 1982 (*Ed*).

years after the date of the judgment, or, where there have been proceedings by way of appeal against the judgment, after the date of the last judgment given in those proceedings, to have the judgment registered in the High Court, and on any such application the court shall, subject to proof of the prescribed matters and to the other provisions of this Act, order the judgment to be registered:

Provided that a judgment shall not be registered if at the date of the application—

(a) it has been wholly satisfied; or

(b) it could not be enforced by execution in the country of the original court.

(2) Subject to the provisions of this Act with respect to the setting aside of registration—

(a) a registered judgment shall, for the purposes of execution, be of the same force and effect; and

(b) proceedings may be taken on a registered judgment; and

(c) the sum for which a judgment is registered shall carry interest; and

(d) the registering court shall have the same control over the execution of a registered judgment;

as if the judgment had been a judgment originally given in the registering court and entered on the date of registration:

Provided that execution shall not issue on the judgment so long as, under this Part of this Act and the Rules of Court made thereunder, it is competent for any party to make an application to have the registration of the judgment set aside, or, where such an application is made, until after the application has been finally determined.

3. (*Power to make rules of court.*)

4.—(1) On an application in that behalf duly made by any party against whom a registered judgment may be enforced, the registration of the judgment—

(a) shall be set aside if the registering court is satisfied—

(i) that the judgment is not a judgment to which this Part of this Act applies or was registered in contravention of the foregoing provisions of this Act; or

(ii) that the courts of the country of the original court had no jurisdiction in the circumstances of the case; or

(iii) that the judgment debtor, being the defendant in the proceedings in the original court, did not (notwithstanding that process may have been duly served on him in accordance with the law of the country of the original court) receive notice of those proceedings in sufficient time to enable him to defend the proceedings and did not appear; or

(iv) that the judgment was obtained by fraud; or

(v) that the enforcement of the judgment would be contrary to public policy in the country of the registering court; or

(vi) that the rights under the judgment are not vested in the person by whom the application for registration was made;

(b) may be set aside if the registering court is satisfied that the matter in dispute in the proceedings in the original court had previously to the date of the judgment in the original court been the subject of a final and conclusive judgment by a court having jurisdiction in the matter.

(2) For the purposes of this section the courts of the country of the original court shall, subject to the provisions of subsection (3) of this section, be deemed to have had jurisdiction—

(a) in the case of a judgment given in an action in personam—
    (i) if the judgment debtor, being a defendant in the original court, submitted to the jurisdiction of that court by voluntarily appearing in the proceedings; or
    (ii) if the judgment debtor was plaintiff in, or counterclaimed in, the proceedings in the original court; or
    (iii) if the judgment debtor, being a defendant in the original court, had before the commencement of the proceedings agreed, in respect of the subject matter of the proceedings, to submit to the jurisdiction of that court or of the courts of the country of that court; or
    (iv) if the judgment debtor, being a defendant in the original court, was at the time when the proceedings were instituted resident in, or being a body corporate had its principal place of business in, the country of that court; or
    (v) if the judgment debtor, being a defendant in the original court, had an office or place of business in the country of that court and the proceedings in that court were in respect of a transaction effected through or at that office or place;

(b) in the case of a judgment given in an action of which the subject matter was immovable property or in an action in rem of which the subject matter was movable property, if the property in question was at the time of the proceedings in the original court situate in the country of that court;

(c) in the case of a judgment given in an action other than any such action as is mentioned in paragraph (a) or paragraph (b) of this subsection, if the jurisdiction of the original court is recognised by the law of the registering court.

(3) Notwithstanding anything in subsection (2) of this section, the courts of the country of the original court shall not be deemed to have had jurisdiction—

(a) if the subject matter of the proceedings was immovable property outside the country of the original court; or

(c) if the judgment debtor, being a defendant in the original proceedings, was a person who under the rules of public international law was entitled to immunity from the jurisdiction of the courts of the country of the original court and did not submit to the jurisdiction of that court.

5.—(1) If, on an application to set aside the registration of a judgment, the applicant satisfies the registering court either that an appeal is pending, or that he is entitled and intends to appeal, against the judgment, the court, if it thinks fit, may, on such terms as it may think just, either set aside the registration or adjourn the application to set aside the registration until after the expiration of such period as appears to the court to be reasonably sufficient to enable the applicant to take the necessary steps to have the appeal disposed of by the competent tribunal.

(2) Where the registration of a judgment is set aside under the last

foregoing subsection, or solely for the reason that the judgment was not at the date of the application for registration enforceable by execution in the country of the original court, the setting aside of the registration shall not prejudice a further application to register the judgment when the appeal has been disposed of or if and when the judgment becomes enforceable by execution in that country, as the case may be.

(3) Where the registration of a judgment is set aside solely for the reason that the judgment, notwithstanding that it had at the date of the application for registration been partly satisfied, was registered for the whole sum payable thereunder, the registering court shall, on the application of the judgment creditor, order judgment to be registered for the balance remaining payable at that date.

6. No proceedings for the recovery of a sum payable under a foreign judgment, being a judgment to which this Part of this Act applies, other than proceedings by way of registration of the judgment, shall be entertained by any court in the United Kingdom.

7.—(1) His Majesty may by Order in Council direct that this Part of this Act shall apply to His Majesty's dominions outside the United Kingdom and to judgments obtained in the courts of the said dominions as it applies to foreign countries and judgments obtained in the courts of foreign countries, and, in the event of His Majesty so directing, this Act shall have effect accordingly and Part II of the Administration of Justice Act 1920, shall cease to have effect except in relation to those parts of the said dominions to which it extends at the date of the Order.

(2) If at any time after His Majesty has directed as aforesaid an Order in Council is made under section one of this Act extending Part I of this Act to any part of His Majesty's dominions to which the said Part II extends as aforesaid, the said Part II shall cease to have effect in relation to that part of His Majesty's dominions.

Part II

Miscellaneous and General

8.—(1) Subject to the provisions of this section, a judgment to which Part I of this Act applies or would have applied if a sum of money had been payable thereunder, whether it can be registered or not, and whether, if it can be registered, it is registered or not, shall be recognised in any court in the United Kingdom as conclusive between the parties thereto in all proceedings founded on the same cause of action and may be relied on by way of defence or counterclaim in any such proceedings.

(2) This section shall not apply in the case of any judgment—
(a) where the judgment has been registered and the registration thereof has been set aside on some ground other than—
   (i) that a sum of money was not payable under the judgment; or
   (ii) that the judgment had been wholly or partly satisfied; or
   (iii) that at the date of the application the judgment could not be enforced by execution in the country of the original court; or
(b) where the judgment has not been registered, it is shown (whether it could have been registered or not) that if it had been registered the registration thereof would have been set aside on an application for that

purpose on some ground other than one of the grounds specified in paragraph (a) of this subsection.

(3) Nothing in this section shall be taken to prevent any court in the United Kingdom recognising any judgment as conclusive of any matter of law or fact decided therein if that judgment would have been so recognised before the passing of this Act.

9.—(1) If it appears to His Majesty that the treatment in respect of recognition and enforcement accorded by the courts of any foreign country to judgments given in the courts of the United Kingdom is substantially less favourable than that accorded by the courts of the United Kingdom to judgments of the courts of that country, His Majesty may by Order in Council apply this section to that country.

(2) Except in so far as His Majesty may by Order in Council under this section otherwise direct, no proceedings shall be entertained in any court in the United Kingdom for the recovery of any sum alleged to be payable under a judgment given in a court of a country to which this section applies.

(3) His Majesty may by a subsequent Order in Council vary or revoke any Order previously made under this section.

10. (*Provision for issue of certificates of UK judgments.*)

10A. The provisions of this Act, except sections 1 (5) and 6, shall apply, as they apply to a judgment, in relation to an award in proceedings on an arbitration which has, in pursuance of the law in force in the place where it was made, become enforceable in the same manner as a judgment given by a court in that place.

11.—(1) (*Definitions.*)

(2) For the purposes of this Act, the expression 'action in personam' shall not be deemed to include any matrimonial cause or any proceedings in connection with any of the following matters, that is to say, matrimonial matters, administration of the estates of deceased persons, bankruptcy, winding up of companies, lunacy, or guardianship of infants.

12. (*Application to Scotland.*)

13. (*Application to Northern Ireland.*)

Foreign Limitation Periods Act 1984

3. Where a court in any country outside England and Wales has determined any matter wholly or partly by reference to the law of that or any other country (including England and Wales) relating to limitation, then, for the purposes of the law relating to the effect to be given in England and Wales to that determination, that court shall, to the extent that it has so determined the matter, be deemed to have determined it on its merits.

NOTE

In *Harris v Quine*[10] the Court of Queen's Bench held that a Manx judgment dismissing an action for a debt on the ground that it was barred by the Manx statute

10 (1869) LR 4 QB 653, 10 B & S 644.

of limitation was not a conclusive judgment on the merits and therefore did not prevent the plaintiff from bringing a subsequent action in England within the English limitation period to recover the same debt. The court intimated that the result would have been different if the Manx law had extinguished the debt as well as barring the remedy. In *Black-Clawson International Ltd v Papierewerke Waldhof-Aschaffenburg AG*[11] the House of Lords held that the same result followed under section 8 (1) of the Foreign Judgments (Reciprocal Enforcement) Act 1933 (p 183 above). In *Harris v Quine* the debt was governed by Manx law, in the *Black-Clawson* case it was governed by English law, but this made no difference. These cases were a corollary of the English rule that foreign statutes of limitation were regarded as procedural if they merely barred the remedy without extinguishing the right. This rule, which went back to *Huber v Steiner* in 1835,[12] was often criticised. The Law Commission recommended the abolition of the rule,[13] and the opportunity was taken to recommend the abolition of the rule in *Harris v Quine* and the *Black-Clawson* case, which was considered unsatisfactory. Both recommendations have been implemented by the Foreign Limitation Periods Act 1984,[14] the latter recommendation by section 3 of the Act. It will be seen that it applies whether the foreign court applied its own statute of limitation or that of some other country, including England.

Civil Jurisdiction and Judgments Act 1982

PART I

IMPLEMENTATION OF THE CONVENTIONS

4.—(1) A judgment, other than a maintenance order, which is the subject of an application under Article 31 for its enforcement in any part of the United Kingdom shall, to the extent that its enforcement is authorised by the appropriate court, be registered in the prescribed manner in that court.

In this subsection 'the appropriate court' means the court to which the application is made in pursuance of Article 32 (that is to say, the High Court or the Court of Session).

(2) Where a judgment is registered under this section, the reasonable costs or expenses of and incidental to its registration shall be recoverable as if they were sums recoverable under the judgment.

(3) A judgment registered under this section shall, for the purposes of its enforcement, be of the same force and effect, the registering court shall have in relation to its enforcement the same powers, and proceedings for or with respect to its enforcement may be taken, as if the judgment had been originally given by the registering court and had (where relevant) been entered.

(4) Subsection (3) is subject to Article 39 (restriction on enforcement where appeal pending or time for appeal unexpired), to section 7 and to any provision made by rules of court as to the manner in which and conditions subject to which a judgment registered under this section may be enforced.

6.—(1) The single further appeal on a point of law referred to in Article 37,

11 [1975] AC 591, [1975] 1 All ER 810.
12 (1835) 2 Bing NC 202, 1 Hodg 206.
13 Law Com No 114 (1982).
14 For sections 1, 2 and 4 of the Act, see pp 627–628 below.

second paragraph and Article 41 in relation to the recognition or enforcement of a judgment other than a maintenance order lies—

(a) in England and Wales or Northern Ireland, to the Court of Appeal or to the House of Lords in accordance with Part II of the Administration of Justice Act 1969 (appeals direct from the High Court to the House of Lords);

(b) in Scotland, to the Inner House of the Court of Session.

(2) Paragraph (a) of subsection (1) has effect notwithstanding section 15 (2) of the Administration of Justice Act 1969 (exclusion of direct appeal to the House of Lords in cases where no appeal to that House lies from a decision of the Court of Appeal).

7.—(1) Subject to subsection (4), where in connection with an application for registration of a judgment under section 4 or 5 the applicant shows—

(a) that the judgment provides for the payment of a sum of money; and

(b) that in accordance with the law of the Contracting State in which the judgment was given interest on that sum is recoverable under the judgment from a particular date or time,

the rate of interest and the date or time from which it is so recoverable shall be registered with the judgment and, subject to any provision made under subsection (2), the debt resulting, apart from section 4 (2), from the registration of the judgment shall carry interest in accordance with the registered particulars.

Part II

Jurisdiction, and Recognition and Enforcement of Judgments, within the United Kingdom

18.—(1) In relation to any judgment to which this section applies—

(a) Schedule 6 shall have effect for the purpose of enabling any money provisions contained in the judgment to be enforced in a part of the United Kingdom other than the part in which the judgment was given; and

(b) Schedule 7 shall have effect for the purpose of enabling any non-money provisions so contained to be so enforced.

(2) In this section 'judgment' means any of the following (references to the giving of a judgment being construed accordingly)—

(a) any judgment or order (by whatever name called) given or made by a court of law in the United Kingdom;

(b) any judgment or order not within paragraph (a) which has been entered in England and Wales or Northern Ireland in the High Court or a county court;

(c) any document which in Scotland has been registered for execution in the Books of Council and Session or in the sheriff court books kept for any sheriffdom;

(d) any award or order made by a tribunal in any part of the United Kingdom which is enforceable in that part without an order of a court of law;

(e) an arbitration award which has become enforceable in the part of the United Kingdom in which it was given in the same manner as a judgment given by a court of law in that part;

and, subject to the following provisions of this section, this section applies to all such judgments.

(3) Subject to subsection (4), this section does not apply to—

(a) a judgment given in proceedings in a magistrates' court in England and Wales or Northern Ireland;

(b) a judgment given in proceedings other than civil proceedings;

(c) a judgment given in proceedings relating to—

(i) bankruptcy; or

(ii) the winding up of a corporation or association; or

(iii) the obtaining of title to administer the estate of a deceased person.

(8) A judgment to which this section applies, other than a judgment within paragraph (e) of subsection (2), shall not be enforced in another part of the United Kingdom except by way of registration under Schedule 6 or 7.

19.—(1) A judgment to which this section applies given in one part of the United Kingdom shall not be refused recognition in another part of the United Kingdom solely on the ground that, in relation to that judgment, the court which gave it was not a court of competent jurisdiction according to the rules of private international law in force in that other part.

(2) Subject to subsection (3), this section applies to any judgment to which section 18 applies.

(3) This section does not apply to—

(a) the documents mentioned in paragraph (c) of the definition of 'judgment' in section 18 (2);

(b) the awards and orders mentioned in paragraphs (d) and (e) of that definition.

31.—(1) A judgment given by a court of an overseas country against a state other than the United Kingdom or the state to which that court belongs shall be recognised and enforced in the United Kingdom if, and only if—

(a) it would be so recognised and enforced if it had not been given against a state; and

(b) that court would have had jurisdiction in the matter if it had applied rules corresponding to those applicable to such matters in the United Kingdom in accordance with sections 2 to 11 of the State Immunity Act 1978.[15]

(2) Reference in subsection (1) to a judgment given against a state include references to judgments of any of the following descriptions given in relation to a state—

(a) judgments against the government, or a department of the government, of the state but not (except as mentioned in paragraph (c)) judgments against an entity which is distinct from the executive organs of government;

(b) judgments against the sovereign or head of state in his public capacity;

(c) judgments against any such separate entity as is mentioned in paragraph (a) given in proceedings relating to anything done by it in the exercise of the sovereign authority of the state.

(4) Sections 12, 13 and 14 (3) and (4) of the State Immunity Act 1978 (service of process and procedural privileges) shall apply to proceedings for the recognition or enforcement in the United Kingdom of a judgment given

15 See pp 51–54 above.

by a court of an overseas country (whether or not that judgment is within subsection (1) of this section) as they apply to other proceedings.

(5) In this section 'state', in the case of a federal state, includes any of its constituent territories.

SCHEDULE I

TITLE III

RECOGNITION AND ENFORCEMENT

ARTICLE 25

For the purposes of this Convention, 'judgment' means any judgment given by a court or tribunal of a Contracting State, whatever the judgment may be called, including a decree, order, decision or writ of execution, as well as the determination of costs or expenses by an officer of the court.

Section 1   Recognition

ARTICLE 26

A judgment given in a Contracting State shall be recognised in the other Contracting States without any special procedure being required.

Any interested party who raises the recognition of a judgment as the principal issue in a dispute may, in accordance with the procedures provided for in Sections 2 and 3 of this Title, apply for a decision that the judgment be recognised.

If the outcome of proceedings in a court of a Contracting State depends on the determination of an incidental question of recognition that court shall have jurisdiction over that question.

ARTICLE 27

A judgment shall not be recognised:
(1) if such recognition is contrary to public policy in the State in which recognition is sought;
(2) where it was given in default of appearance, if the defendant was not duly served with the document which instituted the proceedings or with an equivalent document in sufficient time to enable him to arrange for his defence;
(3) if the judgment is irreconcilable with a judgment given in a dispute between the same parties in the State in which recognition is sought;
(4) if the court of the State in which the judgment was given, in order to arrive at its judgment, has decided a preliminary question concerning the status or legal capacity of natural persons, rights in property arising out of a matrimonial relationship, wills or succession in a way that conflicts with a rule of the private international law of the State in which the recognition is sought, unless the same result would have been reached by the application of the rules of private international law of that State;
(5) if the judgment is irreconcilable with an earlier judgment given in a non-Contracting State involving the same cause of action and between the same parties, provided that this latter judgment fulfils the conditions necessary for its recognition in the State addressed.

ARTICLE 28

Moreover, a judgment shall not be recognised if it conflicts with the provisions of Sections 3, 4 or 5 of Title II, or in a case provided for in Article 59.

In its examination of the grounds of jurisdiction referred to in the foregoing paragraph, the court or authority applied to shall be bound by the findings of fact on which the court of the State in which the judgment was given based its jurisdiction.

Subject to the provisions of the first paragraph, the jurisdiction of the court of the State in which the judgment was given may not be reviewed; the test of public policy referred to in Article 27 (1) may not be applied to the rules relating to jurisdiction.

ARTICLE 29

Under no circumstances may a foreign judgment be reviewed as to its substance.

ARTICLE 30

A court of a Contracting State in which recognition is sought of a judgment given in another Contracting State may stay the proceedings if an ordinary appeal against the judgment has been lodged.

A court of a Contracting State in which recognition is sought of a judgment given in Ireland or the United Kingdom may stay the proceedings if enforcement is suspended in the State in which the judgment was given by reason of an appeal.

Section 2   Enforcement

ARTICLE 31

A judgment given in a Contracting State and enforceable in that State shall be enforced in another Contracting State when, on the application of any interested party, the order for its enforcement has been issued there.

However, in the United Kingdom, such a judgment shall be enforced in England and Wales, in Scotland, or in Northern Ireland when, on the application of any interested party, it has been registered for enforcement in that part of the United Kingdom.

ARTICLE 32

The application shall be submitted:
— in the United Kingdom:
(1) in England and Wales, to the High Court of Justice, or in the case of a maintenance judgment to the Magistrates' Court on transmission by the Secretary of State;
(2) in Scotland, to the Court of Session, or in the case of a maintenance judgment to the Sheriff Court on transmission by the Secretary of State;
(3) in Northern Ireland, to the High Court of Justice, or in the case of a maintenance judgment to the Magistrates' Court on transmission by the Secretary of State.

The jurisdiction of local courts shall be determined by reference to the place of domicile of the party against whom enforcement is sought. If he is

not domiciled in the State in which enforcement is sought, it shall be
determined by reference to the place of enforcement.

ARTICLE 34

The court applied to shall give its decision without delay; the party against
whom enforcement is sought shall not at this stage of the proceedings be
entitled to make any submissions on the application.

The application may be refused only for one of the reasons specified in
Articles 27 and 28.

Under no circumstances may the foreign judgment be reviewed as to its
substance.

ARTICLE 36

If enforcement is authorised, the party against whom enforcement is sought
may appeal against the decision within one month of service thereof.

If that party is domiciled in a Contracting State other than that in which
the decision authorising enforcement was given, the time for appealing shall
be two months and shall run from the date of service, either on him in person
or at his residence. No extension of time may be granted on account of
distance.

ARTICLE 37

An appeal against the decision authorising enforcement shall be lodged in
accordance with the rules governing procedure in contentious matters:
— in the United Kingdom:
(1) in England and Wales, with the High Court of Justice, or in the case of
     a maintenance judgment with the Magistrates' Court;
(2) in Scotland, with the Court of Session, or in the case of a maintenance
     judgment with the Sheriff Court;
(3) in Northern Ireland, with the High Court of Justice, or in the case of a
     maintenance judgment with the Magistrates' Court.
The judgment given on the appeal may be contested only:
—in the United Kingdom, by a single further appeal on a point of law.

ARTICLE 39

During the time specified for an appeal pursuant to Article 36 and until any
such appeal has been determined, no measures of enforcement may be taken
other than protective measures taken against the property of the party
against whom enforcement is sought.

The decision authorising enforcement shall carry with it the power to
proceed to any such protective measures.

ARTICLE 40

If the application for enforcement is refused, the applicant may appeal:
—in the United Kingdom:
(1) in England and Wales, to the High Court of Justice, or in the case of a
     maintenance judgment to the Magistrates' Court;
(2) in Scotland, to the Court of Session, or in the case of a maintenance
     judgment to the Sheriff Court;

(3) in Northern Ireland, to the High Court of Justice, or in the case of a maintenance judgment to the Magistrates' Court.

The party against whom enforcement is sought shall be summoned to appear before the appellate court. If he fails to appear, the provisions of the second and third paragraphs of Article 20 shall apply even where he is not domiciled in any of the Contracting States.

ARTICLE 41

A judgment given on an appeal provided for in Article 40 may be contested only:
—in the United Kingdom, by a single further appeal on a point of law.

Section 3   Common provisions

ARTICLE 46

A party seeking recognition or applying for enforcement of a judgment shall produce:
(1) a copy of the judgment which satisfies the conditions necessary to establish its authenticity;
(2) in the case of a judgment given in default, the original or a certified true copy of the document which establishes that the party in default was served with the document instituting the proceedings or with an equivalent document.

ARTICLE 47

A party applying for enforcement shall also produce:
(1) documents which establish that, according to the law of the State in which it has been given, the judgment is enforceable and has been served;
(2) where appropriate, a document showing that the applicant is in receipt of legal aid in the State in which the judgment was given.

SCHEDULE 6

ENFORCEMENT OF UK JUDGMENTS (MONEY PROVISIONS)

Preliminary

1. In this Schedule—
'judgment' means any judgment to which section 18 applies and reference to the giving of a judgment shall be construed accordingly;
'money provision' means a provision for the payment of one or more sums of money;
'prescribed' means prescribed by rules of court.

Certificates in respect of judgments

2.—(1) Any interested party who wishes to secure the enforcement in another part of the United Kingdom of any money provisions contained in a judgment may apply for a certificate under this Schedule.

(2) The application shall be made in the prescribed manner to the proper officer of the original court.

Registration of certificates

5.—(1) Where a certificate has been issued under this Schedule in any part of the United Kingdom, any interested party may, within six months from the date of its issue, apply in the prescribed manner to the proper officer of the superior court in any other part of the United Kingdom for the certificate to be registered in that court.

(2) In this paragraph 'superior court' means, in relation to England and Wales or Northern Ireland, the High Court and, in relation to Scotland, the Court of Session.

(3) Where an application is duly made under this paragraph to the proper officer of a superior court, he shall register the certificate in that court in the prescribed manner.

General effect of registration

6.—(1) A certificate registered under this Schedule shall, for the purposes of its enforcement, be of the same force and effect, the registering court shall have in relation to its enforcement the same powers, and proceedings for or with respect to its enforcement may be taken, as if the certificate had been a judgment originally given in the registering court and had (where relevant) been entered.

Cases in which registration of a certificate must or may be set aside

10. Where a certificate has been registered under this Schedule, the registering court—
(a) shall set aside the registration if, on an application made by any interested party, it is satisfied that the registration was contrary to the provisions of this Schedule;
(b) may set aside the registration if, on an application so made, it is satisfied that the matter in dispute in the proceedings in which the judgment in question was given had previously been the subject of a judgment by another court or tribunal having jurisdiction in the matter.

SCHEDULE 7

ENFORCEMENT OF UK JUDGMENTS (NON-MONEY PROVISIONS)

Preliminary

1. In this Schedule—
'judgment' means any judgment to which section 18 applies and references to the giving of a judgment shall be construed accordingly;
'non-money provision' means a provision for any relief or remedy not requiring payment of a sum of money;
'prescribed' means prescribed by rules of court.

Certified copies of judgments

2.—(1) Any interested party who wishes to secure the enforcement in another part of the United Kingdom of any non-money provisions contained in a judgment may apply for a certified copy of the judgment.

(2) The application shall be made in the prescribed manner to the proper officer of the original court.

Registration of judgments

5.—(1) Where a certified copy of a judgment has been issued under this Schedule in any part of the United Kingdom, any interested party may apply in the prescribed manner to the superior court in any other part of the United Kingdom for the judgment to be registered in that court.

(2) In this paragraph 'superior court' means, in relation to England and Wales or Northern Ireland, the High Court and, in relation to Scotland, the Court of Session.

(3) An application under this paragraph for the registration of a judgment must be accompanied by—
(a) a certified copy of the judgment issued under this Schedule; and
(b) a certificate issued under paragraph 4 (1) (b) in respect of the judgment not more than six months before the date of the application.

(4) Subject to sub-paragraph (5), where an application under this paragraph is duly made to a superior court, the court shall order the whole of the judgment as set out in the certified copy to be registered in that court in the prescribed manner.

(5) A judgment shall not be registered under this Schedule by the superior court in any part of the United Kingdom if compliance with the non-money provisions contained in the judgment would involve a breach of the law of that part of the United Kingdom.

General effect of registration

6.—(1) The non-money provisions contained in a judgment registered under this Schedule shall, for the purposes of their enforcement, be of the same force and effect, the registering court shall have in relation to their enforcement the same powers, and proceedings for or with respect to their enforcement may be taken, as if the judgment containing them had been originally given in the registering court and had (where relevant) been entered.

Cases in which registered judgment must or may be set aside

9. Where a judgment has been registered under this Schedule, the registering court—
(a) shall set aside the registration if, on an application made by any interested party, it is satisfied that the registration was contrary to the provisions of this Schedule;
(b) may set aside the registration if, on an application so made, it is satisfied that the matter in dispute in the proceedings in which the judgment was given had previously been the subject of a judgment by another court or tribunal having jurisdiction in the matter.

NOTE

1. Introduction

An earlier Note in chapter 5 dealt with the jurisdictional provisions of the Brussels Convention as set out in Schedule 1 of the Civil Jurisdiction and Judgments Act

1982. This Note deals with its provisions on recognition and enforcement of judgments.

For reasons of clarity of exposition we have dealt in separate chapters with the jurisdictional provisions of the Convention and with its provisions on recognition and enforcement. But we cannot stress too strongly that the Convention is one and indivisible and should be read as a whole. Its provisions on recognition and enforcement are intended to mesh with its provisions on jurisdiction. The latter provide ample guarantees for the defendant: as a general rule he can only be sued in the courts of his domicile: arts 2 and 3; his right to defend himself is safeguarded: art 18; if he does not enter an appearance the court itself must protect him by declaring of its own motion that it has no jurisdiction, unless its jurisdiction is derived from the provisions of the Convention: art 20 (1); the court must stay the proceedings unless satisfied that the defendant had an opportunity to be heard: art 20 (2). The strictness of these provisions has its counterpart in the extreme liberality of the provisions on recognition and enforcement, which are designed to allow judgments given in one contracting state to run freely throughout the rest of the Community.

Of course the provisions on recognition and enforcement only apply to judgments within the scope of the Convention as defined in article 1. But subject to that, 'judgment' includes any judgment given by a court or tribunal of a contracting state, whatever it may be called: art 25.

The Convention makes two important departures of principle from the English rules for recognition and enforcement at common law and under the Foreign Judgments (Reciprocal Enforcement) Act 1933. First, the Convention is not limited to money judgments, but extends also to eg injunctions and orders for specific performance. Secondly, as a general rule (but subject to some limitations) the court in which enforcement is sought may not investigate the jurisdiction of the court which gave the judgment. The scheme of the Convention is that, in general, it is for the original court to determine that it has jurisdiction; once it has so determined, the court in which enforcement is sought cannot, in general, question its decision.

It is important to note that under the Convention the enforcement procedures apply to all judgments within its scope, whether or not they are against persons domiciled in a contracting state. Thus an English judgment against a New York resident where the jurisdiction of the English court was based on the temporary presence of the defendant in England is enforceable in France; and a French judgment against a New York resident where the jurisdiction of the French court was based on the French nationality of the plaintiff under article 14 of the French Civil Code is enforceable in England. But article 59 of the Convention allows a contracting state to assume in relation to a non-contracting state the obligation not to recognise judgments given in other contracting states against defendants domiciled or habitually resident in the third state where the basis of jurisdiction could only be one of the so-called 'exorbitant' bases of jurisdiction listed in article 3 (2). Negotiations for such a bilateral convention between the United Kingdom and the United States did not proceed to a conclusion. Negotiations are continuing between the United Kingdom and Canada and Australia.

2. Mode of enforcement

The enforcement of EEC judgments in the United Kingdom is by way of registration under section 4 of the Act and article 31 (2) of the Convention. It is implicit in the decision of the European Court in Case 42/76: *De Wolf v Cox* [1976] ECR 1759, [1977] 2 CMLR 43, p 196 below, that no other mode of enforcement is available, eg an action on the judgment at common law. Registration is to be in the High Court: s 4 (1) and article 32. The application for registration must be made ex parte in the first instance: art 34 (1). At this stage of the proceedings the defendant has no right to be heard, or even to be informed of the application for registration. This is intended to preserve the element of surprise and to prevent him from removing his assets out of the state where enforcement is sought. The applicant must produce the documents specified in articles 46 and 47. If enforcement is authorised, the defendant may then apply to the High Court to set aside the registration; thereafter he may appeal once only on a point of law: arts 36 and 37. If enforcement is refused, the plaintiff may reapply to the High Court (art 40) and there is a further right of appeal by either party, but once only on a point of law (art 41). The single appeal on a point of law under articles 37 and 41 is to the Court of Appeal or, under the 'leap-frog' procedure of the Administration of Justice Act 1969, to the House of Lords: s 6.

Provisional or protective orders are enforceable: Case 143/78: *De Cavel v De Cavel (No. 1)* [1979] ECR 1055, [1979] 2 CMLR 547, p 103 above; but not if they are granted ex parte without the defendant being given an opportunity to be heard: Case 125/79: *Denilauler v SNC Couchet Frères* [1980] ECR 1553, [1981] 1 CMLR 62, p 198 below.

The Convention does not deal with interest on money judgments, ie interest for the period after judgment. This is dealt with in section 7 of the Act.

3. Grounds on which recognition or enforcement may be refused

The grounds on which recognition may be refused are set out in articles 27 and 28. These apply equally to enforcement: art 34 (2). It will be noted that article 27 does not include the fact that the judgment was obtained by fraud. This is because in continental law this ground for refusal is included in the head of public policy. English courts have had no difficulty in deciding that a foreign decree of divorce obtained by fraud need not be recognised in England since recognition would be contrary to public policy.[16]

The court in which enforcement is sought is not entitled to review the merits of the judgment: arts 29, 34 (3). Nor can it question the jurisdiction of the court which gave the judgment, except where it conflicts with the provisions of articles 7–12A (insurance), 13–15 (consumer contracts) or 16 (exclusive jurisdiction): art 28. But even in these cases, the court in which enforcement is sought is bound by the findings of fact on which the original court based its jurisdiction. However, the court in which enforcement is sought is not bound by the findings of the original court as to whether the case is within the scope of the Convention: Case 29/76: *LTU v Eurocontrol* [1976] ECR 1541, [1977] 1CMLR 88. Nor is it bound by the findings of the original court as to whether the defendant was duly served with the writ in sufficient time to enable him to arrange for his defence as required by article 20: Case 228/81: *Pendy Plastic Products BV v Pluspunkt* [1982] ECR 2723, [1983] 1 CMLR 665.

4. The European Communities (Enforcement of Judgments) Order 1972

The judgments whose recognition and enforcement is governed by the Brussels Convention are those of national courts within the EEC. The enforcement of judgments and decisions given by the courts and institutions of the EEC itself is regulated by the European Communities (Enforcement of Judgments) Order 1972.[17] This renders enforceable in this country, for example, judgments (as opposed to preliminary rulings) of the European Court of Justice or decisions of the Commission of the EEC in competition matters. The judgments which are enforceable are not confined to money judgments. Enforcement is by registration in the High Court after the Secretary of State has appended an order for enforcement.

5. Reciprocal enforcement within the United Kingdom

The reciprocal enforcement of judgments within the United Kingdom now depends on section 18 and Schedules 6 and 7 of the Civil Jurisdiction and Judgments Act 1982, which replace the Judgments Extension Act 1868 and the Inferior Courts

16 *Kendall v Kendall* [1977] Fam 208, [1977] 3 All ER 471; p 307 below.
17 SI 1972/1590.

Judgments Extension Act 1882. The principal difference between the 1982 Act and those which it replaces is that the former applies equally to money and non-money judgments. Thus under the 1982 Act injunctions or orders for specific performance granted or made in one part of the United Kingdom are enforceable in other parts. Section 18 does not apply to judgments in proceedings other than civil proceedings, nor to maintenance orders or orders concerning the status or legal capacity of an individual, including judicial separation, guardianship and custody: s 18 (3), (5) and (6).

Enforcement is by way of registration in the court in which enforcement is sought of a certificate granted by the court which gave the judgment. Registration (even of certificates of judgments of inferior courts) is in superior courts only, ie the High Court in England or Northern Ireland, or the Court of Session in Scotland. Schedule 6 contains the procedure for enforcement of certificates of money judgments, and Schedule 7 for enforcement of certificates of non-money judgments. Schedule 6 para 10 and Schedule 7 para 9 indicate when registration must or may be set aside. It will be seen that it is not a ground for setting registration aside that the original court had no jurisdiction over the defendant, or that the judgment was obtained by fraud, or that the proceedings were opposed to natural justice, or that enforcement would be contrary to public policy.

The judgment may not be enforced except by registration under Schedules 6 or 7: s 18 (8).

Section 19 contains provisions for the recognition, as opposed to enforcement, of judgments to which section 18 applies.

A judgment of a court in one contracting state can only be enforced in another contracting state by means of the procedure laid down in articles 31 et seq of the Convention.

De Wolf v Cox Case 42/76: [1976] ECR 1759, [1977] 2 CMLR 43 (European Court of Justice)

Request by the Hoge Raad (Supreme Court of the Netherlands) for a preliminary ruling.

Mr De Wolf of Turnhout, Belgium, was owed a small sum by the Cox undertaking of Boxmeer, the Netherlands. He sued his debtor before the juge de paix of the First Canton of Turnhout and recovered judgment.[18] When Cox failed to comply with this judgment Mr De Wolf sued him before the Kantonrechter of Boxmeer. Instead of using the enforcement procedure laid down in the Convention, he based his claim on the original debt, and relied on the judgment of the Turnhout court as evidence of its existence. The Boxmeer court held that he was entitled to do so because the cost of proceedings under article 31 would be higher than under the Netherlands summary procedure for the recovery of small debts.

Mr De Wolf had previously attempted to use the same procedure in the Kantonrechter of Tilburg, the Netherlands, to recover another debt found to

18 The report does not indicate the ground on which the Belgian court at Turnhout took jurisdiction over a defendant presumably domiciled in the Netherlands. We have to assume either that the place of performance was at Turnhout within article 5 (1); or that the debt arose out of the operations of a branch which the defendant had at Turnhout within article 5 (5); or that there was a jurisdiction clause conferring jurisdiction on the court at Turnhout within article 17; or that the defendant entered an appearance before that court within article 18 (*Ed*).

be due from Cox by the same court at Turnhout. The Kantonrechter held that he could not rely on the Netherlands summary procedure.

Alerted by the court officer who represented Mr De Wolf's interests before the court at Tilburg, the Procurator-General of the Hoge Raad, acting as amicus curiae, brought an appeal against the judgment of the Boxmeer court. The Hoge Raad formulated the following question for the European Court: Does article 31 of the Convention, by itself or in conjunction with other provisions of the Convention, prevent a plaintiff who has obtained a judgment in his favour in a contracting state, being a judgment for which an order for enforcement within the meaning of article 31 may issue in another contracting state, from making an application to a court in that other state, in accordance with article 26, for a judgment against the other party in the same terms as the judgment delivered in the first state?

The Court delivered the following judgment:

The first paragraph of article 26 of the Convention provides: 'A judgment given in a contracting state shall be recognised in the other contracting states without any special procedure being required'.

Although articles 27 and 28 lay down certain exceptions to this duty of recognition, article 29 nevertheless provides that 'under no circumstances may a foreign judgment be reviewed as to its substance'.

When an application for a review as to substance is declared admissible, the court before which the application is heard is required to decide whether it is well founded, a situation which could lead that court to conflict with a previous foreign judgment and, therefore, to fail in its duty to recognise the latter.

To accept the admissibility of an application concerning the same subject-matter and brought between the same parties as an application upon which judgment has already been delivered by a court in another contracting state would therefore be incompatible with the meaning of the provisions quoted. It also results from article 21 of the Convention, which covers cases in which proceedings 'involving the same cause of action and between the same parties are brought in the courts of different contracting states' and requires that a court other than the first seised shall decline jurisdiction in favour of that court, that proceedings such as those brought before the Kantonrechter of Boxmeer are incompatible with the objectives of the Convention.

That provision is evidence of the concern to prevent the courts of two contracting states from giving judgment in the same case.

Finally, to accept the duplication of main actions such as has occurred in the present case might result in a creditor's possessing two orders for enforcement on the basis of the same debt.

The fact that there may be occasions on which, according to the national law applicable, the procedure set out in articles 31 et seq of the Convention may be found to be more expensive than bringing fresh proceedings on the substance of the case does not invalidate these considerations.

In this respect, it must be observed that the Convention, which, in the words of the preamble thereto, is intended 'to secure the simplification of formalities governing the reciprocal recognition and enforcement of judgments of courts or tribunals', ought to induce the contracting states to ensure that the costs of the procedure described in the Convention are fixed so as to accord with that concern for simplification.

The question raised by the Hoge Raad of the Netherlands should therefore be answered in the affirmative.

Orders for provisional or protective measures made in one contracting state are enforceable in another contracting state, but not if they are made ex parte without the defendant being given an opportunity to be heard.

Denilauler v SNC Couchet Frères Case 125/79: [1980] ECR 1553, [1981] 1 CMLR 62 (European Court of Justice)

Request by the Oberlandesgericht (higher regional court) of Frankfurt am Main for a preliminary ruling.

The French undertaking Couchet Frères transported goods for the German undertaking Denilauler. After failing to receive payment Couchet sued Denilauler before the Tribunal de Grande Instance, Montbrison, which ordered Denilauler to pay the sums due.[19] In the course of the proceedings the President of the court made an order authorising Couchet to freeze Denilauler's bank account in Frankfurt as security for payment of the sums claimed. That order was made ex parte and without notice to Denilauler. Couchet applied to the Landgericht (lower regional court) of Wiesbaden requesting that court to declare the protective measure enforceable and that an order be made enabling Couchet to attach the banking account. The Landgericht granted the application. Denilauler appealed to the Oberlandesgericht Frankfurt on the ground that the application to the French court for the protective measure had not been served on him. The Oberlandesgericht formulated the following questions for the European Court: (1) Do articles 27 (2) and 46 (2) of the Convention also apply to proceedings in which provisional protective measures are taken without the opposite party's being heard? (2) Is article 47 (1) of the Convention to be interpreted as meaning that the party applying for enforcement must also produce the documents which establish that the judgment has been served, even if that judgment concerns a provisional and purely protective measure?

The Court delivered the following judgment:

Questions 1 and 2 may be taken together.

The Commission, the Italian government and the plaintiff in the main action express the opinion in their observations that judgments for provisional or protective measures must be recognised as enforceable in the contracting state addressed without prior service on the party against which they are directed.

The specific object of this type of provisional or protective measure is thought to be to produce a surprise effect intended to safeguard the threatened rights of the party seeking them by preventing the party against whom they are directed from removing the assets in its possession, whether they be the subject-matter of the dispute or constitute the creditor's security. To stipulate that the recognition and the enforcement of such types of judgments must be subject to their prior service on the other party and from the stage of the proceedings in the contracting state of origin would, it is said, make them totally meaningless.

19 Once again the report does not indicate on what ground the French court took jurisdiction over a defendant presumably domiciled in Germany. See note on p 196 above (*Ed*).

The United Kingdom government, on the other hand, is of the opinion that the recognition and the enforcement of these judgments must be subject to the conditions set out in articles 27, 46 and 47 as regards service on the other party. It acknowledges that this requirement removes the surprise effect peculiar to such decisions and destroys all their practical value so that it virtually amounts to a refusal to recognise and enforce the decisions in question. However, it feels that the effect of this is not so serious as what it regards the intolerable risks which would have to be run by undertakings having assets in different contracting states as a result of a procedure which obliges the courts of the state addressed to authorise measures freezing assets located in that state without the owner of those assets having ever had the opportunity to put forward his version of the case either before the court of the state of origin or before the court of the state addressed when such assets may have been legitimately intended to meet other obligations. Only the court having jurisdiction in the state in which the assets are located is in a position to determine, in the full knowledge of the facts of the case, the necessity to authorise this type of provisional or protective measure. The United Kingdom government further contends that its point of view does not create a lacuna in the scheme of the Convention because article 24 enables any party to apply to the courts of a contracting state for such provisional or protective measures as may be available under the law of that state, even if the courts of another contracting state have jurisdiction as to the substance of the matter.

Article 27 of the Convention sets out the conditions to be fulfilled for the recognition in a contracting state of judgments given in another contracting state. Under article 27 (2) a judgment shall not be recognised 'if the defendant was not duly served with the document which instituted the proceedings in sufficient time to enable him to arrange for his defence'. Article 46 (2) stipulates that a party seeking recognition or applying for enforcement of a judgment given in default in another contracting state must produce amongst other documents the document which establishes that the party in default was served with the document instituting the proceedings or notice thereof.

These provisions were clearly not designed in order to be applied to judgments which, under the national law of a contracting state, are intended to be delivered in the absence of the party against whom they are directed and to be enforced without prior service on him. It is apparent from a comparison of the different language versions of the words in question and in particular from the terms used to describe the party who does not appear that these provisions are intended to refer to proceedings in which in principle both parties participate but in which the court is nevertheless empowered to give judgment if the defendant, although duly summoned, does not appear.

The same applies to article 47 (1) of the Convention under which the party seeking enforcement must produce documents which establish that, according to the law of the state in which it has been given, the judgment is enforceable and has been served. This provision which relates to judgments in cases in which both parties participate as well as to judgments in default delivered in the state of origin cannot by definition apply to judgments such as the type in dispute, which have a different character.

However, it cannot be inferred from the fact that articles 27 (2), 46 (2) and 47 (1) cannot apply to decisions of the type in question, save by distorting their substance and scope, that such decisions must nevertheless be recognised and enforced in the state addressed. It is necessary to consider whether judicial decisions of this type, having regard to the scheme and objects of the Convention, may be dealt with under the simplified procedure for recognition and enforcement provided by the Convention.

In favour of an affirmative answer, the Commission and the Italian government maintain that, according to article 25, the Convention covers all decisions given by the courts of the contracting states without distinguishing between those involving adversary proceedings and those given without the other party's being summoned to appear. As is apparent from article 24 the field of application of the Convention embraces protective and provisional measures which, under the law of the different contracting states and by reason of their very nature or their urgency are often adopted without the opposite party's having first been heard. The contracting states cannot have intended to restrict the field of application of the Conventions to such an extent without express mention being made to that effect. Finally, it may clearly be seen from article 34 of the Convention, which states that in the proceedings for an enforcement order 'the party against whom enforcement is sought shall not at this stage of the proceedings be entitled to make any submissions on the application', that the Convention itself recognises that proceedings in which only one party is heard are, where circumstances justify them, in keeping with the basic principle of the rights of the defence.

These arguments cannot prevail over the scheme of the Convention and the principles underlying it.

All the provisions of the Convention, both those contained in Title II on jurisdiction and those contained in Title III on recognition and enforcement, are intended to ensure that, within the scope of the objectives of the Convention, proceedings leading to the delivery of judicial decisions take place in such a way that the rights of the defence are observed. It is because of the guarantees given to the defendant in the original proceedings that the Convention, in Title III, is very liberal in regard to recognition and enforcement. In the light of these considerations it is clear that the Convention is fundamentally concerned with judicial decisions which, before the recognition and enforcement of them are sought in a state other than the state of origin, have been, or have been capable of being, the subject in that state of origin and under various procedures, of an inquiry in adversary proceedings. It cannot therefore be deduced from the general scheme of the Convention that a formal expression of intention was needed in order to exclude judgments of the type in question from recognition and enforcement.

Nor is the argument by analogy, based on article 34 of the Convention, of such a nature as to turn the scale. Although enforcement proceedings may be unilateral—but only provisionally so—this fact has to be brought into accord with the liberal character of the Convention as regards the procedure for enforcement, which is justified by the guarantee that in the state of origin both parties have either stated their case or had the opportunity to do so. Whilst another reason for the unilateral character of the enforcement procedure under article 34 is to produce the surprise effect which this procedure must have in order to prevent a defendant from having the opportunity to protect his assets against any enforcement measures, the surprise effect is attenuated since the unilateral proceedings are based on the assumption that both parties will have been heard in the state of origin.

An analysis of the function attributed under the general scheme of the Convention to article 24, which is specifically devoted to provisional and protective measures, leads, moreover, to the conclusion that, where these types of measures are concerned, special rules were contemplated. Whilst it is true that procedures of the type in question authorising provisional and protective measures may be found in the legal system of all the contracting states and may be regarded, where certain conditions are fulfilled, as not infringing the rights of the defence, it should however be emphasised that the granting of this type of measure requires particular care on the part of the court and detailed knowledge of the actual circumstances in which the measure is to take effect. Depending on each case and commercial practices in particular the court must be able to place a time-limit on its order or, as regards the nature of the assets or goods subject to the measures contemplated, require bank guarantees or nominate a sequestrator and generally make its authorisation subject to all conditions guaranteeing the provisional or protective character of the measure ordered.

The courts of the place or, at least, of the contracting state, where the assets subject to the measures sought are located, are those best able to assess the circumstances which may lead to the grant or refusal of the measures sought or to the laying down of procedures and conditions which the plaintiff must observe in order to guarantee the provisional and protective character of the measures ordered. The Convention has taken account of these requirements by providing in article 24 that application may be made to the courts of a contracting state for such provisional, including protective, measures as may be available under the law of that state, even if, under the Convention, the courts of another contracting state have jurisdiction as to the substance of the matter.

Article 24 does not preclude provisional or protective measures ordered in the state of origin pursuant to adversary proceedings—even though by default—from being the subject of recognition and an authorisation for enforcement on the conditions laid down in articles 25 to 49 of the Convention. On the other hand the conditions imposed by Title III of the Convention on the recognition and the enforcement of judicial decisions are not fulfilled in the case of provisional or protective measures which are ordered or authorised by a court without the party against whom they are directed having been summoned to appear and which are intended to be enforced without prior service on that party. It follows that this type of judicial decision is not covered by the simplified enforcement procedure provided for by Title III of the Convention. However, as the government of the United Kingdom has rightly observed, article 24 provides a procedure for litigants which to a large extent removes the drawbacks of this situation.

The reply to Questions 1 and 2 should therefore be that judicial decisions authorising provisional or protective measures, which are delivered without the party against which they are directed having been summoned to appear and which are intended to be enforced without prior service do not come within the system of recognition and enforcement provided for by Title III of the Convention.

State Immunity Act 1978

PART II

JUDGMENTS AGAINST UNITED KINGDOM IN CONVENTION STATES

18.—(1) This section applies to any judgment given against the United Kingdom by a court in another State party to the European Convention on State Immunity, being a judgment—

(a) given in proceedings in which the United Kingdom was not entitled to immunity by virtue of provisions corresponding to those of sections 2 to 11 above; and

(b) which is final, that is to say, which is not or is no longer subject to appeal or, if given in default of appearance, liable to be set aside.

(2) Subject to section 19 below, a judgment to which this section applies shall be recognised in any court in the United Kingdom as conclusive between the parties thereto in all proceedings founded on the same cause of action and may be relied on by way of defence or counterclaim in such proceedings.

(3) Subsection (2) above (but not section 19 below) shall have effect also in relation to any settlement entered into by the United Kingdom before a court in another State party to the Convention which under the law of that State is treated as equivalent to a judgment.

(4) In this section references to a court in a State party to the Convention include references to a court in any territory in respect of which it is a party.

19.—(1) A court need not give effect to section 18 above in the case of a judgment—

(a) if to do so would be manifestly contrary to public policy or if any party to the proceedings in which the judgment was given had no adequate opportunity to present his case; or

(b) if the judgment was given without provisions corresponding to those of section 12 above having been complied with and the United Kingdom has not entered an appearance or applied to have the judgment set aside.

(2) A court need not give effect to section 18 above in the case of a judgment—

(a) if proceedings between the same parties, based on the same facts and having the same purpose—

(i) are pending before a court in the United Kingdom and were the first to be instituted; or

(ii) are pending before a court in another State party to the Convention, were the first to be instituted and may result in a judgment to which that section will apply; or

(b) if the result of the judgment is inconsistent with the result of another judgment given in proceedings between the same parties and—

(i) the other judgment is by a court in the United Kingdom and either those proceedings were the first to be instituted or the judgment of that court was given before the first-mentioned judgment became final within the meaning of subsection (1) (b) of section 18 above; or

(ii) the other judgment is by a court in another State party to the Convention and that section has already become applicable to it.

(3) Where the judgment was given against the United Kingdom in proceedings in respect of which the United Kingdom was not entitled to immunity by virtue of a provision corresponding to section 6 (2) above, a court need not give effect to section 18 above in respect of the judgment if the court that gave the judgment—

(a) would not have had jurisdiction in the matter if it had applied rules of jurisdiction corresponding to those applicable to such matters in the United Kingdom; or

(b) applied a law other than that indicated by the United Kingdom rules of private international law and would have reached a different conclusion if it had applied the law so indicated.

(4) In subsection (2) above references to a court in the United Kingdom include references to a court in any dependent territory in respect of which the United Kingdom is a party to the Convention, and references to a court in another State party to the Convention include references to a court in any territory in respect of which it is a party.

Protection of Trading Interests Act 1980

5.—(1) A judgment to which this section applies shall not be registered under Part II of the Administration of Justice Act 1920 or Part I of the Foreign Judgments (Reciprocal Enforcement) Act 1933 and no court in the United Kingdom shall entertain proceedings at common law for the recovery of any sum payable under such a judgment.

(2) This section applies to any judgment given by a court of an overseas country, being—

(a) a judgment for multiple damages within the meaning of subsection (3) below;

(b) a judgment based on a provision or rule of law specified or described in an order under subsection (4) below and given after the coming into force of the order; or

(c) a judgment on a claim for contribution in respect of damages awarded by a judgment falling within paragraph (a) or (b) above.

(3) In subsection (2) (a) above a judgment for multiple damages means a judgment for an amount arrived at by doubling, trebling or otherwise multiplying a sum assessed as compensation for the loss or damage sustained by the person in whose favour the judgment is given.

(4) The Secretary of State may for the purposes of subsection (2) (b) above make an order in respect of any provision or rule of law which appears to him to be concerned with the prohibition or regulation of agreements, arrangements or practices designed to restrain, distort or restrict competition in the carrying on of business of any description or to be otherwise concerned with the promotion of such competition as aforesaid.

(5) The power of the Secretary of State to make orders under subsection (4) above shall be exercisable by statutory instrument subject to annulment in pursuance of a resolution of either House of Parliament.

(6) Subsection (2) (a) above applies to a judgment given before the date of the passing of this Act as well as to a judgment given on or after that date but this section does not affect any judgment which has been registered

before that date under the provisions mentioned in subsection (1) above or in respect of which such proceedings as are there mentioned have been finally determined before that date.

6.—(1) This section applies where a court of an overseas country has given a judgment for multiple damages within the meaning of section 5 (3) above against—

(a) a citizen of the United Kingdom and Colonies;[20] or

(b) a body corporate incorporated in the United Kingdom or in a territory outside the United Kingdom for whose international relations Her Majesty's Government in the United Kingdom are responsible; or

(c) a person carrying on business in the United Kingdom,

(in this section referred to as a 'qualifying defendant') and an amount on account of the damages has been paid by the qualifying defendant either to the party in whose favour the judgment was given or to another party who is entitled as against the qualifying defendant to contribution in respect of the damages.

(2) Subject to subsections (3) and (4) below, the qualifying defendant shall be entitled to recover from the party in whose favour the judgment was given so much of the amount referred to in subsection (1) above as exceeds the part attributable to compensation; and that part shall be taken to be such part of the amount as bears to the whole of it the same proportion as the sum assessed by the court that gave the judgment as compensation for the loss or damage sustained by that party bears to the whole of the damages awarded to that party.

(3) Subsection (2) above does not apply where the qualifying defendant is an individual who was ordinarily resident in the overseas country at the time when the proceedings in which the judgment was given were instituted or a body corporate which had its principal place of business there at that time.

(4) Subsection (2) above does not apply where the qualifying defendant carried on business in the overseas country and the proceedings in which the judgment was given were concerned with activities exclusively carried on in that country.

(5) A court in the United Kingdom may entertain proceedings on a claim under this section notwithstanding that the person against whom the proceedings are brought is not within the jurisdiction of the court.

(6) The reference in subsection (1) above to an amount paid by the qualifying defendant includes a reference to an amount obtained by execution against his property or against the property of a company which (directly or indirectly) is wholly owned by him; and references in that subsection and subsection (2) above to the party in whose favour the judgment was given or to a party entitled to contribution include references to any person in whom the rights of any such party have become vested by succession or assignment or otherwise.

(7) This section shall, with the necessary modifications, apply also in relation to any order which is made by a tribunal or authority of an overseas country and would, if that tribunal or authority were a court, be a judgment for multiple damages within the meaning of section 5 (3) above.

20 This now means a British citizen, a British Dependent Territories citizen or a British Overseas citizen: British Nationality Act 1981, s 51(3)(a)(ii).

(8) This section does not apply to any judgment given or order made before the passing of this Act.

NOTE

These sections are directed against the tendency of American courts to interpret United States anti-trust legislation in such a way as to give it extra-territorial effect, contrary to international law. This tendency has given rise to misgivings in the United Kingdom and other trading nations for many years: see *British Nylon Spinners Ltd v Imperial Chemical Industries Ltd*[1] and *Re Westinghouse Electric Corpn Uranium Contract Litigation MDL Docket No 235.*[2]

Section 5 gives the defendant a shield when a judgment for multiple damages has been given against him in the United States or elsewhere and it is sought to enforce that judgment in the United Kingdom. The section makes the whole judgment unenforceable, not merely that part of it which exceeds the loss or damage actually sustained by the judgment creditor.

Section 6 goes much further and gives the defendant a sword enabling him to recover in the United Kingdom so much of the damages which he has paid as exceeds the sum assessed by the foreign court as compensation for the loss or damage sustained. The section is confined to 'qualifying defendants' as defined in sub-ss (1), (3) and (4). The section contains the unusual provision that proceedings under it may be brought notwithstanding that the plaintiff in the foreign proceedings is not within the jurisdiction of the United Kingdom court: sub-s (5).

1 [1953] Ch 19, [1952] 2 All ER 780.
2 [1978] AC 547, [1978] 1 All ER 434.

CHAPTER 8

Arbitration

Whatever the proper law of the contract, the High Court may not exercise its powers of judicial control over an arbitration unless the arbitration is governed by English law. Prima facie the proper law of the arbitration will be the law of the country where it takes place.

Whitworth Street Estates Ltd v James Miller and Partners Ltd [1970] AC 583, [1970] 1 All ER 796 (House of Lords)

The respondents, an English company, owned a factory in Scotland. The appellants, a Scottish company, agreed to convert the factory into a bonded warehouse. The contract, which was made in Scotland, was in the standard form published by the Royal Institute of British Architects, a body composed of Scottish as well as English members. The architect was English and it was at his suggestion that the RIBA form was used. That form was 'redolent of English law'. It contained an arbitration clause providing for the appointment of an arbitrator by the President of the RIBA. There was no provision as to the place of arbitration or as to its procedure. Disputes arose, and the President appointed a Scottish architect as arbitrator and the arbitration proceedings took place in Scotland. Points of law arose, and the English company asked the arbitrator to state his award in the form of a special case. The arbitrator refused to do so. The English company then applied to the High Court for an order under section 21 (1) of the Arbitration Act 1950 (since repealed) compelling the arbitrator to state his award in the form of a special case. The master made the order. Eveleigh J allowed an appeal by the Scottish company and rescinded it. The Court of Appeal (Lord Denning MR, Davies and Widgery LJJ) reversed his decision, holding that the proper law of the contract was English. The Scottish company appealed.

Lord Wilberforce (after holding that the proper law of the contract was Scottish, continued): I turn to the second question: what law is to govern the arbitration procedure? If the proper law of the contract is Scottish there could be no argument in favour of the intrusion of English law into the arbitration. But if the proper law is English, an interesting question arises. One must ask first whether, in principle, it is possible for the law governing the arbitral procedure to differ from that governing the substance of the contract. No authority was cited to us which explicitly answers this question one way or the other, but I have no doubt as to the answer. It is a matter of experience that numerous arbitrations are conducted by English arbitrators in England on matters governed by contracts whose proper law is or may be that of another country, and I should be surprised if it had ever been held that such arbitrations were not governed by the English Arbitration Act in procedural matters, including the right to apply for a case to be stated. (I leave aside as a special case arbitrations conducted under the rules of the International Chamber of Commerce, though even these may be governed by the law of the place of arbitration.) The principle must surely be the same as that which applies to court proceedings brought in one country concerning a contract governed by the law of another, and that such proceedings as regards all matters which the law regards as procedural are governed by the lex fori has been accepted at least since Lord Brougham's judgment in *Don v Lippmann*.[1] In my opinion, the law is correctly stated by Professor Kahn-Freund and Dr Morris in *Dicey and Morris*,[2] where they say:

'It cannot however be doubted that the courts would give effect to the choice of a law other than the proper law of the contract. Thus, if parties agreed on an arbitration clause expressed to be governed by English law but providing for arbitration in Switzerland, it may be held that, whereas English law governs the validity, interpretation and effect of the arbitration clause as such (including the scope of the arbitrators' jurisdiction), the proceedings are governed by Swiss law. It is also submitted that where the parties have failed to choose the law governing the arbitration proceedings, those proceedings must be considered, at any rate prima facie, as being governed by the law of the country in which the arbitration is held, on the ground that it is the country most closely connected with the proceedings.'

The first part of this is well supported by *Hamlyn & Co v Talisker Distillery*[3] and also by *N. V. Kwik Hoo Tong Handel Maatschappij v James Finlay & Co Ltd*,[4] and both parts rest solidly on common sense.

What law, then, should be taken to apply to the procedure here? The arbitration clause itself is silent, and I would agree that in the normal case, where the contract itself is governed by English law, any arbitration would be held under English procedure. Moreover, the mere fact that the arbitrator was to sit either partly or exclusively in another part of the United Kingdom, or, for that matter, abroad, would not lead to a different result: the place might be chosen for many reasons of convenience or be purely accidental; a choice so made should not affect the parties' rights. But here there was much more than the fortuitous or convenient choice of a Scottish location. The selected arbitrator, an architect practising in Glasgow, near where the works were situated, immediately on his acceptance announced the appointment of a Scottish solicitor as clerk in the submission and invited both parties to state if they wished advice as to 'any points in our procedure'. The indication that the arbiter (as he should now be called) intended to conduct the proceedings in the Scottish manner, advised by a Scots lawyer, could not have been clearer, and neither party objected. It would not be right to place too much emphasis on the form of pleadings adopted: pleadings are, after all, only the manner in which parties state the facts on which they rely and arbitrations may use pleadings in any form with any degree of legal mystique, or no form at all. But, on a later occasion (24 May

1 (1837) 5 Cl & Fin 1.
2 *Conflict of Laws* (8th edn, 1967) p 1048.
3 [1894]AC 202, 71 LT 1, per Lord Herschell LC and Lord Watson.
4 [1927] AC 604, 96 LJKB 902.

1962), the arbiter through his clerk again explicitly took the position that he intended to act in accordance with Scottish arbitration procedure, again without objection, and he maintained this position when formally asked to state a case.

The respondents' argument was that the arbitration had from the beginning been firmly placed under the control of the Arbitration Act 1950. They pointed to the fact that in the application which the appellants made to the president of the Royal Institute of British Architects to nominate an arbitrator there was an explicit reference to the Act, and contended that this was both deliberate and decisive. In my opinion, it was neither: the reference, taken from the standard Royal Institute of British Architects' application form, was merely a means of describing the nature of the arbitration clause in the contract—as a submission to arbitration—so as to activate the nomination by the president, and had no bearing upon the procedure of the arbitration when instituted. This was the respondents' main (and unsuccessful) contention, but they also argued that, until their application for a case, the arbiter had been concerned merely with trivia and that there had been no real committal of the proceedings to any decisively Scottish form. I cannot agree with this. The right to ask for a case to be stated, which may, under the Arbitration Act 1950, be invoked at any stage in the arbitration, is essentially a matter of procedure—the respondents did not, indeed, dispute this. It is clear that the arbiter embarked upon a continuous and close-knit process, starting with definition of the issues both of fact and of pleas in law and continuing with the hearing of evidence, which was inconsistent with the exercise by a foreign (sc, English) court of the powers of direction and control contained in the English Act, whether the general procedural powers of section 12 or the special powers contained in section 21.

I find no basis on which the English courts are entitled to exercise authority over the arbiter: in my opinion, he was bound to conclude the proceedings in accordance with the law of Scotland. In my opinion, the order of Eveleigh J of 31 October 1968, rescinding the master's order was correct and should be restored and the appeal consequently allowed.

Lord Reid delivered judgment to the same effect. Lords Hodson, Guest and Dilhorne held that the proper law of the contract was English, but they agreed in the result.

Appeal allowed.
Judgment of Eveleigh J restored.

A foreign arbitration award may be final and thus enforceable in England under Part II of the Arbitration Act 1950 or (semble) at common law even though the law governing the arbitration proceedings requires a judgment or order of a court to make the award enforceable.

Union Nationale des Cooperatives Agricoles de Céréales v Robert Catterall & Co Ltd [1959] 2 QB 44, [1959] 1 All ER 721 (Court of Appeal)

A contract for the sale of wheat seed made between English sellers and French buyers contained a clause referring all disputes to the Arbitration

Chamber of Copenhagen. The French buyers obtained an award from the Copenhagen Arbitration Chamber ordering the English sellers to pay them £183,000. Under the rules of the committee, awards made by the committee were final. But there was evidence that by Danish law the award was not enforceable in Denmark until a judgment of a Danish court had been obtained. However, only objections of a formal nature could be taken in the proceedings to obtain a judgment, which were in no sense a rehearing. The French buyers applied to the High Court for an order under section 26 of the Arbitration Act 1950 giving leave to enforce the award. Hinchcliffe J made the order. The English sellers appealed.

Lord Evershed MR stated the facts, read sections 26, 36 (1), 37 and 39 of the Arbitration Act 1950 (pp 211–212 below), and continued: The contest, which I shall more elaborately state in a moment, turns, as I have said, upon the question: is this award final? I would, however, observe this, that the question seems to me to depend upon section 37 (1) (d). We are not here concerned with what use might be given to the word 'final' for other purposes, for example, in certain contexts and in certain places what might be said to be the effect of the convention in the second schedule. It must be borne in mind, as a background, that, if the conditions are satisfied, a foreign award is to be put in pari materia, so to speak, with an English award. The question, therefore, is: Has it become final, as we understand that phrase, in the country in which it was made? Of course, the question whether it is final in Denmark will depend no doubt upon Danish law, but the Danish law is directed to showing whether it is final as that word is understood in English. On the face of the matter, as I have narrated the facts, it would appear plain enough that, according to the bargain made between these two parties, this award is final. The two contracting parties have said that they would submit their differences to this arbitration chamber, which will settle 'en dernier ressort' the matter in dispute. They have by necessary implication submitted to the rules and regulations of the Danish tribunal, one of which, paragraph 14, states that if the presidency decide against an appeal, then the award is final. If the matter, therefore, rested alone on the documents and the bargain as I find it in the documents, it must be final, I would have said, within the section.

(His Lordship considered the evidence of Danish law and continued): At first sight, of course, it might appear that Mr Heyman is saying that, according to the law of the country in which this award was made, viz, Denmark, the award is not final as that word is used in section 37 (1) (d). But I confess I have come myself to the clear conclusion that that is not right. If it were so (as I think it must follow, and there is much force in this point which Mr Grieve made) it would mean that you could never in fact enforce an award, as such, in such cases as this; you would have to wait until you got the judgment of the court of the country where the award was made, and then you would not be enforcing the award but the judgment. I venture again to refer to the vital fact, as I think, that Part II, and the conditions to be complied with, is intending to put a foreign award in the same condition as an English award. But looking more closely at the evidence, it seems to me that what clearly has arisen here is a confusion—I am not using the word, and I certainly do not intend to, in a sense critical of the deponents—between finality as intended by the section and enforceability. Reverting to the textbook writer, I think that is made clear enough. He says that an award once final, of course must be valid, and speaks of an award not necessarily being final because it is valid. Those are somewhat philosophical considerations. He goes on, it will be observed, to speak of the possibility of taking objections, contemplating, as it seems to me, perhaps rather as subsection (3) of section 37 does, a challenge being made by the aggrieved party in the appropriate court of competent jurisdiction. But when he comes to his conclusion, introduced by the word 'therefore', it is clear that the textbook writer is concerned with enforcement: 'Therefore, any person will have to obtain legal confirmation . . . before seeking enforcement'.

Now the question of enforcement here is a matter of English law. Can it now be enforced by the terms of the Arbitration Act? It seems to me, with all respect to Mr Milmo's argument, that it is reasonably clear that it can. This award is, to my way of thinking, final according to the bargain made and according to the law of Denmark, so far as it is concerned with the problem with which we are presented. It is no doubt not enforceable directly in Denmark or anywhere else; but it is, I think, final within the contemplation of the section. I would add that there is here, so far as I know, no question of any formal challenge. I agree with Mr Milmo that when it speaks of formal defects, the language, according to the deponents (and particularly in that shown by Mr Heyman's own affidavit), is not limited to defects on the face of the award, mere matters of form; it will extend to compliance with the rules under which the award was given. But there is, so far as I know, no challenge on that basis; indeed, no precise challenge, so far as I know, at all.

The matter is, I think, not one which admits of useful elaboration, and I therefore say no more than this, that I have come to a clear conclusion in my own mind, in conformity with that of the judge, that for the purposes of section 37 (1) (d) this award must be treated as having become 'final' according to the relevant law of Denmark, and, that being so, the conditions in other respects being satisfied, section 36 (1) applies to it and it is enforceable in the same way as an English award.

I would, therefore, dismiss the appeal.

Pearce LJ delivered judgment to the same effect.
Appeal dismissed.

Arbitration Act 1950

Part I

GENERAL PROVISIONS AS TO ARBITRATION

4.—(1) If any party to an arbitration agreement, or any person claiming through or under him, commences any legal proceedings in any court against any other party to the agreement, or any person claiming through or under him, in respect of any matter agreed to be referred, any party to those legal proceedings may at any time after appearance, and before delivering any pleadings or taking any other steps in the proceedings, apply to that court to stay the proceedings, and that court or a judge thereof, if satisfied that there is no sufficient reason why the matter should not be referred in accordance with the agreement, and that the applicant was, at the time when the proceedings were commenced, and still remains, ready and willing to do all things necessary to the proper conduct of the arbitration, may make an order staying the proceedings.

26. An award on an arbitration agreement may, by leave of the High Court or a judge thereof, be enforced in the same manner as a judgment or order to the same effect, and where leave is so given, judgment may be entered in terms of the award.

Part II

Enforcement of certain Foreign Awards

35.—(1) This Part of this Act applies to any award made after the twenty-eighth day of July, nineteen hundred and twenty-four—

(a) in pursuance of an agreement for arbitration to which the protocol set out in the First Schedule to this Act applies; and

(b) between persons of whom one is subject to the jurisdiction of some one of such Powers as His Majesty, being satisfied that reciprocal provisions have been made, may by Order in Council declare to be parties to the convention set out in the Second Schedule to this Act, and of whom the other is subject to the jurisdiction of some other of the Powers aforesaid; and

(c) in one of such territories as His Majesty, being satisfied that reciprocal provisions have been made, may by Order in Council declare to be territories to which the said convention applies;

and an award to which this Part of this Act applies is in this Part of this Act referred to as 'a foreign award'.

(2) His Majesty may by a subsequent Order in Council vary or revoke any Order previously made under this section.

36.—(1) A foreign award shall, subject to the provisions of this Part of this Act, be enforceable in England either by action or in the same manner as the award of an arbitrator is enforceable by virtue of section twenty-six of this Act.

(2) Any foreign award which would be enforceable under this Part of this Act shall be treated as binding for all purposes on the persons as between whom it was made, and may accordingly be relied on by any of those persons by way of defence, set off or otherwise in any legal proceedings in England, and any references in this Part of this Act to enforcing a foreign award shall be construed as including references to relying on an award.

37.—(1) In order that a foreign award may be enforceable under this Part of this Act it must have—

(a) been made in pursuance of an agreement for arbitration which was valid under the law by which it was governed;

(b) been made by the tribunal provided for in the agreement or constituted in manner agreed upon by the parties;

(c) been made in conformity with the law governing the arbitration procedure;

(d) become final in the country in which it was made;

(e) been in respect of a matter which may lawfully be referred to arbitration under the law of England;

and the enforcement thereof must not be contrary to the public policy or the law of England.

(2) Subject to the provisions of this subsection, a foreign award shall not be enforceable under this Part of this Act if the court dealing with the case is satisfied that—

(a) the award has been annulled in the country in which it was made; or

(b) the party against whom it is sought to enforce the award was not given notice of the arbitration proceedings in sufficient time to enable him to present his case, or was under some legal incapacity and was not properly represented; or

(c) the award does not deal with all the questions referred or contains decisions on matters beyond the scope of the agreement for arbitration:

Provided that, if the award does not deal with all the questions referred, the court may, if it thinks fit, either postpone the enforcement of the award or order its enforcement subject to the giving of such security by the person seeking to enforce it as the court may think fit.

(3) If a party seeking to resist the enforcement of a foreign award proves that there is any ground other than the non-existence of the conditions specified in paragraphs (a), (b) and (c) of subsection (1) of this section, or the existence of the conditions specified in paragraphs (b) and (c) of subsection (2) of this section, entitling him to contest the validity of the award, the court may, if it thinks fit, either refuse to enforce the award or adjourn the hearing until after the expiration of such period as appears to the court to be reasonably sufficient to enable that party to take the necessary steps to have the award annulled by the competent tribunal.

38.—(1) The party seeking to enforce a foreign award must produce—

(a) the original award or a copy thereof duly authenticated in manner required by the law of the country in which it was made; and

(b) evidence proving that the award has become final; and

(c) such evidence as may be necessary to prove that the award is a foreign award and that the conditions mentioned in paragraphs (a), (b) and (c) of subsection (1) of the last foregoing section are satisfied.

(2) In any case where any document required to be produced under subsection (1) of this section is in a foreign language, it shall be the duty of the party seeking to enforce the award to produce a translation certified as correct by a diplomatic or consular agent of the country to which that party belongs, or certified as correct in such other manner as may be sufficient according to the law of England.

39. For the purposes of this Part of this Act, an award shall not be deemed final if any proceedings for the purpose of contesting the validity of the award are pending in the country in which it was made.

40. Nothing in this Part of this Act shall—

(a) prejudice any rights which any person would have had of enforcing in England any award or of availing himself in England of any award if neither this Part of this Act nor Part I of the Arbitration (Foreign Awards) Act 1930 had been enacted; or

(b) apply to any award made on an arbitration agreement governed by the law of England.

Arbitration Act 1975

Effect of arbitration agreement on court proceedings

1.—(1) If any party to an arbitration agreement to which this section applies, or any person claiming through or under him, commences any legal proceedings in any court against any other party to the agreement, or any person claiming through or under him, in respect of any matter agreed to be referred, any party to the proceedings may at any time after appearance, and before delivering any pleadings or taking any other steps in the proceedings, apply to the court to stay the proceedings; and the court, unless satisfied that the arbitration agreement is null and void, inoperative or incapable of being performed or that there is not in fact any dispute between the parties with regard to the matter agreed to be referred, shall make an order staying the proceedings.

(2) This section applies to any arbitration agreement which is not a domestic arbitration agreement; and neither section 4 (1) of the Arbitration Act 1950 nor section 4 of the Arbitration Act (Northern Ireland) 1937 shall apply to an arbitration agreement to which this section applies.

(4) In this section 'domestic arbitration agreement' means an arbitration agreement which does not provide, expressly or by implication, for arbitration in a State other than the United Kingdom and to which neither—

(a) an individual who is a national of, or habitually resident in, any State other than the United Kingdom; nor

(b) a body corporate which is incorporated in, or whose central management and control is exercised in, any State other than the United Kingdom;

is a party at the time the proceedings are commenced.

Enforcement of Convention awards

2. Sections 3 to 6 of this Act shall have effect with respect to the enforcement of Convention awards; and where a Convention award would, but for this section, be also a foreign award within the meaning of Part II of the Arbitration Act 1950, that Part shall not apply to it

3.—(1) A Convention award shall, subject to the following provisions of this Act, be enforceable—

(a) in England and Wales, either by action or in the same manner as the award of an arbitrator is enforceable by virtue of section 26 of the Arbitration Act 1950.

(2) Any Convention award which would be enforceable under this Act shall be treated as binding for all purposes on the persons as between whom it was made, and may accordingly be relied on by any of those persons by way of defence, set off or otherwise in any legal proceedings in the United Kingdom; and any reference in this Act to enforcing a Convention award shall be construed as including references to relying on such an award.

4. The party seeking to enforce a Convention award must produce—

(a) the duly authenticated original award or a duly certified copy of it; and

(b) the original arbitration agreement or a duly certified copy of it; and

(c) where the award or agreement is in a foreign language, a translation of it certified by an official or sworn translator or by a diplomatic or consular agent.

5.—(1) Enforcement of a Convention award shall not be refused except in the cases mentioned in this section.

(2) Enforcement of a Convention award may be refused if the person against whom it is invoked proves—

(a) that a party to the arbitration agreement was (under the law applicable to him) under some incapacity; or

(b) that the arbitration agreement was not valid under the law to which the parties subjected it or, failing any indication thereon, under the law of the country where the award was made; or

(c) that he was not given proper notice of the appointment of the arbitrator or of the arbitration proceedings or was otherwise unable to present his case; or

(d) (subject to subsection (4) of this section) that the award deals with a difference not contemplated by or not falling within the terms of the submission to arbitration or contains decisions on matters beyond the scope of the submission to arbitration; or

(e) that the composition of the arbitral authority or the arbitral procedure was not in accordance with the agreement of the parties or, failing such agreement, with the law of the country where the arbitration took place; or

(f) that the award has not yet become binding on the parties, or has been set aside or suspended by a competent authority of the country in which, or under the law of which, it was made.

(3) Enforcement of a Convention award may also be refused if the award is in respect of a matter which is not capable of settlement by arbitration, or if it would be contrary to public policy to enforce the award.

(4) A Convention award which contains decisions on matters not submitted to arbitration may be enforced to the extent that it contains decisions on matters submitted to arbitration which can be separated from those on matters not so submitted.

(5) Where an application for the setting aside or suspension of a Convention award has been made to such a competent authority as is mentioned in subsection (2) (f) of this section, the court before which enforcement of the award is sought may, if it thinks fit, adjourn the proceedings and may, on the application of the party seeking to enforce the award, order the other party to give security.

6. Nothing in this Act shall prejudice any right to enforce or rely on an award otherwise than under this Act or Part II of the Arbitration Act 1950.

General

7.—(1) In this Act—

'arbitration agreement' means an agreement in writing (including an agreement contained in an exchange of letters or telegrams) to submit to arbitration present or future differences capable of settlement by arbitration;

'Convention award' means an award made in pursuance of an arbitration agreement in the territory of a State, other than the United

Kingdom, which is a party to the New York Convention; and
'the New York Convention' means the Convention on the Recognition
and Enforcement of Foreign Arbitral Awards adopted by the United
Nations Conference on International Commercial Arbitrations on 10th
June 1958.

(2) If Her Majesty by Order in Council declares that any State specified
in the Order is a party to the New York Convention the Order shall, while
in force, be conclusive evidence that that State is a party to that Convention.

(3) An Order in Council under this section may be varied or revoked by a
subsequent Order in Council.

NOTE

Section 18 (2) (e) of the Civil Jurisdiction and Judgments Act 1982 (p 186 above)
defines a judgment for the purposes of that section so as to include an arbitration
award which has become enforceable as a judgment in the part of the United
Kingdom where it was given. The Act thus provides machinery for the reciprocal
enforcement of such awards within the United Kingdom. Such awards made in
Scotland or Northern Ireland can be enforced in England under Schedule 6 of the
Act if they order payment of a sum or sums of money or under Schedule 7 if they
order any relief or remedy not requiring payment of a sum of money (see pp 195–196
above). But registration under those Schedules is not the only way in which such
awards can be enforced, as it is with judgments: section 18 (8). They can also be
enforced in England at the option of the plaintiff under the summary procedure of
section 26 of the Arbitration Act 1950 (p 211 above) or presumably by action at
common law.

Section 19 of the 1982 Act (p 187 above), which provides for the recognition as
opposed to the enforcement of judgments within the United Kingdom, does not apply
to arbitration awards.

PART IV

Family Law

CHAPTER 9

Marriage

Section A: Formalities

The formalities of marriage are governed (in general) by the lex loci celebrationis.

Berthiaume v Dastous [1930] AC 79, 99 LJPC 66 (Privy Council)

Appeal from a judgment of the Court of King's Bench for Quebec affirming a judgment of the Superior Court, District of Montreal.

The judgment of their Lordships (Viscount Dunedin, Lord Warrington of Clyffe, Mr Justice Duff, and Sir Lancelot Sanderson) was delivered by

Viscount Dunedin: In 1913 the respondent, a French Canadian of the Roman Catholic faith, being then a girl seventeen years of age who had just graduated from a convent in a small town in Montreal, went on a trip to Europe with her father. She there met the appellant, a member of a Quebec family and also of the Roman Catholic faith, who had been living in Paris for several years. He proposed to her, and she accepted. The appellant asked the respondent to make the necessary arrangements, and she called on the curé of the parish where her fiancé had been residing and where she was then temporarily residing. The curé informed her that there were certain civil formalities to be gone through and that he would celebrate the marriage. She asked her fiancé to attend to the civil formalities, and he took her to the British consulate where certain papers were signed and a certificate issued which was given to her fiancé. After that the parties proceeded to the church, the certificate was handed to the curé, who then proceeded to celebrate the marriage according to the form of the Roman Catholic Church. The parties lived together as husband and wife until the year 1926, when on returning from an absence from home the respondent discovered that the appellant had been guilty of infidelity and had introduced a mistress into their home. The respondent then applied to the Court in Paris for a divorce. That Court before proceeding further demanded the exhibition of a civil certificate of marriage. This the respondent was unable to produce. She then discovered that the certificate which her fiancé had procured at the British consulate was only a notice of intended marriage, and that the officiating curé had carelessly omitted to notice that it was not a certificate of marriage. As a matter of fact he had exposed himself to severe penalty by celebrating the religious ceremony without the production of a certificate. As no certificate of marriage could be produced—none such ever having been in existence—the Court declined to proceed with the case for divorce. The respondent then raised another action in the French courts, craving a judgment 'pour faire statuer le mariage', and craving alternatively that if the marriage was declared void it should be held that she had contracted it in good faith and was entitled to a declaration of civil effects in her favour. The appellant appeared and denied the jurisdiction, he having still retained his Canadian domicile. This plea was sustained and the action dismissed. The respondent then raised the present action in the Superior Court of the Montreal district. The action sought a declaration of marriage, decree of separation, a dissolution of the communauté des biens—the marriage having been without a marriage contract, communauté des biens would ensue—and a judgment for alimony. Damages were also claimed, but that claim was departed from. Alternatively a declaration was sought that as the respondent had been in good faith, the marriage was a putative marriage and in terms of article 164 of the Civil Code produced civil effects. The case depended before Loranger J who held the marriage valid, pronounced a decree of separation, dissolved the community of goods and granted a decree against the appellant for an alimentary allowance of $1,500 a month. On appeal the Court of King's Bench by a majority upheld the judgment. Bernier J dissented, and held that the marriage was null and that a null marriage could not be a putative marriage. The present appeal is from that judgment.

Their Lordships are unable to agree with the judgment under appeal. If there is one question better settled than any other in international law, it is that as regards marriage—putting aside the question of capacity—locus regit actum. If a marriage is good by the laws of the country where it is effected, it is good all the world over, no matter whether the proceeding or ceremony which constituted marriage according to the law of the place would or would not constitute marriage in the country of the domicile of one or other of the spouses. If the so-called marriage is no marriage in the place where it is celebrated, there is no marriage anywhere, although the ceremony or proceeding if conducted in the place of the parties' domicile would be considered a good marriage. These propositions are too well fixed to need much quotation. They were laid down long ago in England in the well known case of *Dalrymple v Dalrymple*[1] and in *Scrimshire v Scrimshire*,[2] approved by Lord Stowell in *Ruding v Smith*.[3] . . .

Now in the face of the facts set forth in the narrative above given, and these facts were found by all the judges of the courts below and are amply borne out by the evidence, it is clear that under international law there was no marriage in this case. The law of France is peremptory. There must be a civil ceremony of marriage, and if‚ that has not taken place any religious ceremony is an idle performance so far as the law is concerned. . . .

(His Lordship proceeded to hold that as there was good faith on the part of the respondent, the marriage, though null, was capable of producing civil effects, including the right to alimony, under article 164 of the Quebec Civil Code, and that the case should be remitted to the court below to determine its amount.)

Appeal allowed.

1 (1811) 2 Hag Con 54.
2 (1752) 2 Hag Con 395.
3 (1821) 2 Hag Con 371, 1 State Tr NS 1054.

Retrospective legislation in the locus celebrationis validating a formally invalid marriage will be given effect to, even though the parties are domiciled in England at the date when it takes effect.

Starkowski v Attorney General [1954] AC 155, [1953] 2 All ER 1272 (House of Lords)

Henryka Juszczkiewicz and Richard Urbanski were born in Poland with a Polish domicile of origin. In 1944 they moved to Kitzbühel in Austria but remained domiciled in Poland. They were both Roman Catholics and anxious to be married in a church by a priest. Owing to the German occupation of Austria there were difficulties in their way and the priest at Kitzbühel at first refused to marry them, but when the Germans were driven out there was much confusion and he eventually agreed to do so on 19 May 1945, when they went through a ceremony of marriage according to the rites of their Church in the parish church at Kitzbühel. In June 1945 a daughter Barbara was born to them.

Henryka and Richard arrived in England in the autumn of 1946 and became domiciled here. In 1947 they separated. In March 1949 Henryka gave birth to a son Christopher of whom Michael Starkowski, a Pole domiciled in England, was the father. On 11 February 1950 Henryka went through a form of marriage with Michael at the register office in Croydon.

Christopher, suing by his mother as next friend, petitioned for a declaration under the Legitimacy Act 1926 and section 17 of the Matrimonial Causes Act 1950,[4] that his parents were lawfully married and that by that marriage he became legitimated.

By the German marriage law in force in Austria on 19 May 1945 a religious ceremony did not constitute a valid marriage since a civil ceremony was required. On 26 June 1945 the Austrian government promulgated an Order (No 31) enacting that religious marriages celebrated between 1 April 1945 and the date of the decree should be valid as soon as they were registered in the Family Book kept by the registry office. By some oversight the religious ceremony between Henryka and Richard was not registered until 18 July 1949. Before that date the law of Austria would not have regarded the parties as married, but after that date it would have regarded them as having been validly married on 19 May 1945.

Barnard J and the Court of Appeal held that Christopher was not legitimated because the marriage of his parents was void, his mother being at that date validly married to Richard. The petitioner appealed.

Lord Reid: The question to be determined is whether the law of England can give effect to the retrospective Austrian legislation, and the present case appears to me to be indistinguishable from a simple case where two English people domiciled here go through a ceremony of marriage in another country which is invalid in form and return to this country, and then retrospective legislation is enacted in that country which validates the marriage in that country as from the date of its celebration.

If the respondent is right, then it is possible for foreign legislation to alter

---

4 Now s 45 of the Matrimonial Causes Act 1973, p 412 below (*Ed*).

the status of English people who were neither domiciled, resident nor present in the foreign country when the legislation was passed nor at any time thereafter. It is certainly unusual that foreign legislation should have that effect whether it purports to be retrospective or not, but I do not think that it can be laid down as a universal rule that it can never have that effect and therefore it is necessary to consider more closely the circumstances of cases like the present case.

It has long been settled that the formal validity of a marriage must be determined by the law of the place where the marriage was celebrated. But if there has been retrospective legislation there, then a further question arises: are we to take the law of that place as it was when the marriage was celebrated, or are we to inquire what the law of that place now is with regard to the formal validity of that marriage? This question does not appear to have arisen for decision in England. There are many cases in which there have been statements of high authority of the general principle and of its application in various circumstances, but I do not think it helpful to analyse these statements of the law. I can find nothing to indicate that the present question was even in contemplation in any of these cases, and at best one could only make a speculative inference from words used as to what their author might have thought if he had had to consider the present question. Some other authorites were cited, but they do not appear to me to carry one very far. To my mind the best way of approaching this question is to consider the consequences of a decision in either sense. The circumstances are such that no decision can avoid creating some possible hard cases, but if a decision in one sense will on the whole lead to much more just and reasonable results, that appears to me to be a strong argument in its favour.

Cases calling for retrospective legislation have frequently occurred in England. The common case is that some fact has been discovered which shows that marriages celebrated in particular circumstances were invalid: sometimes many marriages extending over a long period were involved, but no one had suspected that these marriages were other than valid. It was then thought proper to pass legislation which had the effect of validating these marriages ab initio. If that had not been done there would have been great confusion and in many cases great injustice. It can be assumed that some of the marriages involved were between persons domiciled in other countries, and similar cases may well have occurred abroad.

Persons domiciled in England may have been married in another country by ceremonies apparently valid but later discovered to be invalid, and retrospective legislation may then have been passed in that country. If people have lived and acted and brought up families in the reasonable belief that they were married, it is highly desirable that the law should recognise some practical way of neutralising a belated and fortuitous discovery that their marriage was formally invalid. But if retrospective legislation in the country where the marriage was celebrated is to be of no avail to persons domiciled outside that country, it will seldom be possible for the country of their domicile to afford any remedy. If validating legislation is passed soon after the cause of the invalidity has been discovered, it is not easy to see how any practical difficulties or hardships can result from it.

But serious difficulties could arise if there were a long interval between the discovery of the invalidity and the remedial legislation. If the spouses are still living together when the invalidity is discovered, they can avoid most of the difficulties by remarrying. But if they have separated they would be in the position of knowing that they are for the moment unmarried but are liable at any time to become married against their wishes by retrospective legislation. It was argued that we should only recognise foreign retrospective legislation if the spouses in some way consented to its operation, but that argument is based on a misapprehension of what such retrospective legislation sets out to do. It has no concern with the state of affairs at the time when it is enacted: its purpose is to validate the original ceremony, and if there was then the necessary consent to marry, that is all that matters. Then it was argued that no valid consent was given in this case at the ceremony in 1945 because the wife Henryka knew that the ceremony was insufficient to constitute a legal marriage; but it is not proved that the husband Urbanski also knew that, and the wife cannot be heard to say that her consent freely given in church was not a consent to marry. I need not consider what the position would be if both parties knew at the time that the ceremony was insufficient in law.

It was suggested in argument that the law of England might recognise foreign retrospective legislation subject to certain qualifications or exceptions. For example, it was said that if one of the parties had entered into another marriage before the retrospective legislation took effect, then a different rule should apply; and it was suggested that if an English court of competent jurisdiction had decided that either party was unmarried, then subsequent retrospective foreign legislation should not affect that decision. It would not be proper to attempt to decide such questions in advance, but I shall assume for the purpose of the present argument that such exceptions would not be made and that a person who knew that his marriage abroad was invalid for want of form might be left in complete uncertainty if the circumstances were such as to make it at all reasonable to suppose that validating legislation might be passed. If that is so, there is at first sight compelling force in the appellant's argument that a person ought at any time to be able to find out with certainty whether he or she is married or not, and that the law of England ought not to recognise a principle which may result in a person being for the moment unmarried in law but knowing that he is liable to become married retrospectively. If there were any substantial likelihood of this happening I would be inclined to agree, but one must look at realities. I find it difficult to suppose that in any country there would be substantial delay in deciding whether to legislate retrospectively once the reason for the invalidity had come to light, and I cannot think that anyone who had discovered that his marriage was formally invalid would for long be in any real doubt whether there was to be remedial legislation. In the present case remedial leglislation was promptly enacted, and this could have been discovered and, indeed, may have been known to the parties: it was only by a mischance that the necessary executive action in Austria was delayed for four years.

Accordingly, in my opinion the balance of justice and convenience is clearly in favour of recognising the validity of such retrospective legislation (subject, it may be, to some exceptions), and the objections to doing so are not substantial and are not founded on any compelling principle. Once it is settled that the formal validity of a marriage is to be determined by reference to the law of the place of celebration, there is no compelling reason why the reference should not be to that law as it is when the question arises for decision. I therefore agree that this appeal should be dismissed.

Lords Morton of Henryton, Tucker, Asquith of Bishopstone and Cohen delivered judgments to the same effect.

Appeal dismissed.

QUESTION

What would have been the position if
(a) Henryka had married Michael before her marriage to Richard was registered in the Family Book?
(b) Henryka was, at the time of her (second) marriage to Michael, domiciled in a country which did not recognise the retrospective effect of the validation of the first marriage?

A requirement of parental consent imposed by foreign law, no matter how stringently expressed, is regarded as a formality in England.

Ogden v Ogden (p 240 below)

The validity of proxy marriages is a question of form, not a question of capacity to marry.

Apt v Apt [1948] P 83, [1947] 2 All ER 677 (Court of Appeal)

Appeal from Lord Merriman P.

On 15 January 1941, while the appellant was in this country, she being not only resident but domiciled here, a ceremony of marriage was celebrated at Buenos Aires between her and the respondent. She was represented by a person whom, by a power of attorney executed on 8 November 1940 in London, she had named as her representative to contract the marriage. The husband, as found by Lord Merriman P, was resident and domiciled in the Argentine at all material times. The wife gave evidence that she had at no material time any intention of revoking the power of attorney, that she was informed in due course of the performance of the ceremony, and that she was not merely ready and willing, but eager, to join her husband in Buenos Aires, but was prevented from doing so during the war. She further deposed that when, after the war, she renewed her efforts to join the husband, he took no steps to assist her and ignored her alternative suggestion of a meeting in the United States of America, and that it was this conduct on his part which decided her to present the petition in this matter.

A Dr Palacios was called to give evidence as to the relevant Argentine law, and the result of his evidence, so far as material, may be summarised as follows: (1) Argentine law recognises proxy marriages. Accordingly by that law the ceremony was valid and effectual, and the marriage would be recognised as a valid marriage by the law of the intended matrimonial domicile. (2) The intending spouse could revoke the power of attorney at any time before the ceremony, but if the power had been acted on before either the other spouse or the proxy had notice of the revocation the marriage would be valid. (3) If, however, the spouse giving the power of attorney had meanwhile lost the capacity to contract the marriage, for example, by an intervening marriage, or by becoming of unsound mind, although the marriage certificate would be prima facie evidence of the ceremony's having been performed, the court would declare the marriage null and void. The wife's petition for a decree of nullity having been dismissed, she now appealed.

The judgment of the court (Tucker, Bucknill, and Cohen LJJ) was delivered by

Cohen LJ: On this evidence counsel for the wife contended that, in the circumstances above stated, it would be contrary to public policy for the English courts to recognise the validity of the marriage, and that, accordingly, his client was entitled to the decree which she sought. The petition was undefended, but, having regard to the importance of the matter, the President invoked the assistance of the King's Proctor, and the case was fully argued. The President in a considered judgment dismissed the petition. After a careful review of all the authorities, English and American, to which his attention had been called, he summarised his conclusions as follows: 'My conclusions therefore are: that the contract of marriage in this case was celebrated in Buenos Aires; that the ceremony was performed strictly in accordance with the law of that country; that the celebration of marriage by proxy is a matter of the form of the ceremony or proceeding, and not an essential of the marriage; that there is nothing abhorrent to Christian ideas in the adoption of that form; and that, in the absence of legislation to the contrary, there is no doctrine of public policy which entitles me to hold that the ceremony, valid where it was performed, is not effective in this country to constitute a valid marriage. For these reasons, whatever may be the petitioner's remedies as a wife, I am obliged to hold that this petition must be dismissed.'

With these conclusions and with the reasons which the President gives for them we so fully agree that it is only because of the importance of the matter, and out of respect to the arguments addressed to us by counsel on both sides, that we state shortly our reasons for rejecting the arguments addressed to us for the wife. These arguments may be summarised as follows: (1) It is contrary to the public policy of England to recognise any marriage by proxy; (2) it is not however necessary to reach a conclusion on the first point, since in any event it is contrary to the public policy of England to recognise a marriage by proxy if (a) the party giving the proxy is domiciled in England or (b) the power of attorney conferring authority on the proxy is executed in England or (c) the power of attorney authorises a marriage by proxy in a country where the law will recognise, as does Argentine law, the validity of a marriage contracted thereunder, notwithstanding the revocation of the proxy, if the revocation has not been communicated to the other spouse or the proxy before the ceremony takes place; and (3) the granting of a power of attorney in England is governed as to essential validity by English law, and it is contrary to English law to recognise powers of attorney given for the purpose of celebrating a marriage.

The first argument is, in our opinion, ill-founded. Counsel was unable to suggest any statutory provision which was relevant to it. He referred us to s 22 of the Marriage Act 1823, which prohibits marriages otherwise than in a church or without banns or licence, but he admitted that this section only applies to marriages within the English jurisdiction: see s 33 of the Act. A proxy marriage, such as we are considering, is clearly a Christian marriage within the definition given by Lord Penzance in *Hyde v Hyde*:[5] 'the voluntary union for life of one man and one woman, to the exclusion of all others.' A proxy marriage was recognised as valid by the canon law: see Swinburne's *Treatise of Spousals or Matrimonial Contracts*[6] where, as the President points out, the conditions of such a marriage are described. It is recognised as valid in a number of Christian countries beside the Argentine. The preponderance of the American authorities to which the President refers indicates that such a marriage is recognised as valid in many states of the United States of America: see especially *Ex parte Suzanna*.[7] It was argued that *R v Millis*[8] precluded us from holding that such a marriage would be recognised in England, but that case concerned only marriages celebrated in England or Ireland; it did not expressly cover the point, and is in any event no authority for the general proposition that all proxy marriages, wherever celebrated, are void. See *Wolfenden v Wolfenden*[9] where the President pointed out the limited operation of *R v Millis*.

Counsel for the wife invited us, none the less, to hold that proxy marriages were contrary to public policy since they would facilitate clandestine marriages, make easy the bestowal of British nationality on foreigners and the carrying on of the white-slave traffic, and make it possible for two minors to get married in, for example, Mexico, although they were both domiciled in England. So far as the argument is based on clandestine marriages, we have to bear in mind that the English courts have not regarded all such marriages as contrary to public policy; for example, Gretna Green marriages were held to be valid until they were prohibited by statute. Moreover, we have to bear in mind the frequent injunctions of the highest tribunal as to the danger of allowing judicial tribunals to roam unchecked in the field occupied by that unruly horse, public policy: see, for example, per Lord Atkin in *Fender v Mildmay*.[10] In any event, a consideration of what is 'public policy' in a case where the matter is not governed by statute or by clearly established principle must necessarily involve balancing advantages against disadvantages. As against the considerations advanced by counsel must be weighed the following factors: (1) The unsatisfactory position that would arise in that, if Mr Foster is right, the parties would be married in the Argentine, the place of the intended matrimonial domicile, but not married in England; (2) the fact that, if Mr Foster is right, any children that might result from the marriage would be bastards in the eye of English law; and, above all, (3) we should in effect be holding that the law of the Argentine was contrary to essential justice and morality, a conclusion to which we should hestitate to come....

In all the circumstances, we are satisfied that we cannot properly extend public policy to invalidate all proxy marriages....

Finally, on this point we would repeat the citation from Lord Dunedin's speech in *Berthiaume v Dastous*[11] which was quoted by the President. (His

5 (1866) LR 1 P & D 130, 35 LJP & M 57.
6 (1686) pp 162, 163.
7 (1924) 295 F 713.
8 (1844) 10 Cl & Fin 534, 8 Jur 717.
9 [1946] P 61, [1945] 2 All ER 539; p 229 below.
10 [1938] AC 1 at 10, [1937] 3 All ER 402 at 406.
11 [1930] AC 79, 99 LJPC 66; p 220 above.

Lordship quoted the passage beginning 'If a marriage is good' and ending 'to need much quotation', and continued): In our opinion, the method of giving consent as distinct from the fact of consent is essentially a matter for the lex loci celebrationis, and does not raise a question of capacity, or, as Mr Foster preferred to call it, essential validity.

It will be convenient next to consider Mr Foster's third point, since it seems to us to founder on the same rock as his first. Counsel was constrained to admit that there was no question of incapacity in the donor of the power, or of any statutory invalidity, and that, if the power had related to a commercial transaction, its validity could not be challenged, since the act to be performed under it was valid by the law of the intended place of performance: see *Chatenay v Brazilian Submarine Telegraph Co Ltd*.[12]... Counsel argued, however, that this power relates to a contract of marriage, and that this is not a mere matter of contract of marriage, but affects status. This is, if anything, an understatement, since the main element in the marriage contract is its effect on status;... but, as the status sought to be created by the proxy marriage now in question is, as we have already pointed out, that of a Christian marriage such as English law recognises and approves, the argument does not really assist counsel and he is driven to argue that the power of attorney is bad because proxy marriages are against the public policy of England, an argument which we have already given our reasons for rejecting.

We return to the second point. In our opinion, this also fails. As regards sub-division (a) thereof, we are unable to see any reason in public policy which would require the English courts, if they recognise the validity of proxy marriages celebrated outside the United Kingdom, to deny to a person domiciled in this country the right of so celebrating a marriage, provided, of course, that he or she has in other respects capacity to marry and does not infringe any provision of English law. (b) is really another way of stating the third argument presented for the wife. We think it impossible to hold that, in the absence of some statutory prohibition, it is contrary to public policy to execute in England a power of attorney which the same person could validly execute in the Argentine, the power of attorney being intended to authorise an act in the Argentine which is lawful by the law of that country. As regards (c), we agree with the President that this point does not arise. If a case occurs where the proxy is revoked before the ceremony takes place but the other spouse and the proxy are unaware of the revocation, it may be that the courts of this country would hold that the purported marriage was void; but that would not be because of any general objection to proxy marriages, but because, on the facts of the particular case, the court was satisfied that the marriage was not a voluntary union.

Appeal dismissed.

Foreign Marriage Act 1892

1. All marriages between parties of whom one at least is a British subject[13] solemnised in the manner in this Act provided in any foreign country or

---

12 [1891] 1 QB 79, 60 LJQB 295.
13 This now means a Commonwealth citizen: see British Nationality Act 1981, s 51 (1). For the meaning of Commonwealth citizen, see s 37 (1) (*Ed*).

place by or before a marriage officer within the meaning of this Act shall be as valid in law as if the same had been solemnised in the United Kingdom with a due observance of all forms required by law.

8.—(1) After the expiration of fourteen days after the notice of an intended marriage has been entered under this Act, then, if no lawful impediment to the marriage is shown to the satisfaction of the marriage officer, and the marriage has not been forbidden in manner provided by this Act, the marriage may be solemnised under this Act.

(2) Every such marriage shall be solemnised at the official house of the marriage officer, with open doors, between the hours of [[14]eight in the forenoon and six in the afternoon] in the presence of two or more witnesses, and may be solemnised by another person in the presence of the marriage officer, according to the rites of the Church of England, or such other form and ceremony as the parties thereto see fit to adopt, or may, where the parties so desire, be solemnised by the marriage officer.

(3) Where such marriage is not solemnised according to the rites of the Church of England, then in some part of the ceremony, and in the presence of the marriage officer and witnesses, each of the parties shall declare,

'I solemnly declare, that I know not of any lawful impediment why I *A. B.* [*or C. D.*] may not be joined in matrimony to *C. D.* [*or A. B.*].'

And each of the parties shall say to the other,

'I call upon these persons here present to witness, that I *A. B.* [*or C. D.*] take thee, *C. D.* [*or A. B.*], to be my lawful wedded wife [*or husband*].'

13.—(1) After a marriage has been solemnised under this Act it shall not be necessary, in support of the marriage, to give any proof of the residence for the time required by or in pursuance of this Act of either of the parties previous to the marriage, or of the consent of any person whose consent thereto is required by law, nor shall any evidence to prove the contrary be given in any legal proceeding touching the validity of the marriage.

(2) Where a marriage purports to have been solemnised and registered under this Act in the official house of the British ambassador or consul, ...[15] it shall not be necessary in support of the marriage, to give any proof of the authority of the marriage officer by or before whom the marriage was solemnised and registered nor shall any evidence to prove his want of authority, whether by reason of his not being a duly authorised marriage officer or of any prohibitions or restrictions under the marriage regulations or otherwise, be given in any legal proceeding touching the validity of the marriage.

19. A marriage officer shall not be required to solemnise a marriage, or to allow a marriage to be solemnised in his presence, if in his opinion the solemnisation thereof would be inconsistent with international law or the comity of nations;

Provided that any person requiring his marriage to be solemnised shall, if the officer refuses to solemnise it or allow it to be solemnised in his presence, have the right to appeal to the Secretary of State given by this Act.

14 Words substituted by Marriage (Extension of Hours) Act 1934, s 1 (2).
15 Words repealed by Foreign Marriage Act 1947, s 4 (2)

23. Nothing in this Act shall confirm or impair or in anywise affect the validity in law of any marriage solemnised beyond the seas, otherwise than as herein provided, and this Act shall not extend to the marriage of any of the Royal family.

Foreign Marriage Order 1970[16]

3.—(1) Before a marriage is solemnised in a foreign country under the Foreign Marriage Acts 1892 to 1947, the marriage officer must be satisfied:
(a) that at least one of the parties is a British subject; and
(b) that the authorities of that country will not object to the solemnisation of the marriage; and
(c) that insufficient facilities exist for the marriage of the parties under the law of that country; and
(d) that the parties will be regarded as validly married by the law of the country to which each party belongs.

A valid common law marriage may be celebrated abroad if there is an insuperable difficulty in using the local form.

Wolfenden v Wolfenden [1946] P 61, [1945] 2 All ER 539 (Divorce Division)

Petition for nullity of marriage on the ground of lack of form.

The parties, both Canadian, went through a ceremony of marriage in October 1938 at a Church of Scotland Mission church in a remote part of China. It was performed by the minister of the mission, without banns or licence. He was not episcopally ordained nor authorised to perform a marriage under the Foreign Marriage Act 1892.

Lord Merriman P, having stated the facts, continued: The question is whether or not this ceremony, although the parties undoubtedly thought it was not fully effective, did effect a valid marriage. That it did not conform with the Foreign Marriage Act is made quite clear—indeed there is no dispute about it—by a Foreign Office Certificate dated 4 June 1945, under the hand of the late Prime Minister and under the seal of the Foreign Office duly put in before me. It was suggested that I might have to consider whether the marriage conformed to the law of the place where it was celebrated. I have no evidence at all of Chinese law and I am bound to say, having considered the matter, I do not think I could possibly hold that in the circumstances of this case that law was applicable. I do not propose to examine that proposition further. The real question on the supposition that the local law had nothing to do with it, and the marriage admittedly not being validated by the Foreign Marriage Act, is whether it is valid as a common law marriage, although it was not performed by an episcopally ordained priest.

In *R v Millis*,[17] it was decided that so far as England and Ireland are

---

16 SI 1970/1539.
17 (1844) 10 Cl & Fin 534, 8 Jur 717.

concerned it is the law that a common law marriage can only be validly celebrated before an episcopally ordained priest. It is not in the least to the purpose to point out that that result was arrived at in a somewhat curious way. It arose out of a trial for bigamy, inasmuch as the accused had gone through the form of a second marriage after an earlier ceremony performed according to the rites of the Presbyterian Church. He could not, of course, be convicted of bigamy unless the first ceremony was valid. The court in Ireland was equally divided two against two, but in order to raise the question one of the judges withdrew his opinion. The matter came up to the House of Lords and there again six Law Lords were equally divided, the result being that the appellant failed and it was held that the original marriage performed according to the rites of the Presbyterian Church was invalid. Nevertheless it must be taken that that is the law as regards England and Ireland.

The question in this case is whether, in order to effect a valid common law marriage in the District of Ichang, in the Province of Hupeh, in China, in the year 1938, it was or was not necessary that the ceremony should be performed by an episcopally ordained priest. If the decision in *R v Millis* had never been qualified it manifestly would compel me to decide in the same sense, but that is not the position. In 1847, Dr Lushington, in *Catterall v Catterall*[18] held that a marriage in New South Wales before a Presbyterian Minister, where there was in fact consent between the parties to become husband and wife, was a valid marriage notwithstanding the fact that the ceremony did not comply with the provisions of a local Act. In that Act, however, there were no words which constituted the ceremony a nullity failing compliance with the Act. Dr Lushington held that there was a valid marriage on which he could base a decree. He so held not merely notwithstanding the terms of the Australian Act (which as he had held earlier did not of itself nullify any ceremony not performed in accordance with the Act) but also notwithstanding the decision in *R v Millis*. He held, in effect, that that case did not apply with full force to a marriage performed in New South Wales.

I need not examine *Catterall v Catterall* any further, because the matter was dealt with in what I regard as conclusive fashion by Sir Erskine Perry C J, delivering the judgment of the full Court of the Supreme Court of Judicature of Bombay in *Maclean v Cristall*[19] in 1849. In that case the matter arose because the husband was suing an adulterer in an action for criminal conversation. The marriage had been celebrated at Surat by a 'Minister of the Gospel and Missionary' who was not in Holy Orders but belonged to a sect called Congregationalist or Independents, and it was admitted that no person in Holy Orders was present at the ceremony. If, therefore, *R v Millis* applied to a marriage in Surat it would be impossible for the action of criminal conversation to proceed. The matter was fully considered and the Chief Justice delivered a considered judgment in the course of which, after setting out the full effect of *R v Millis*, he discussed the question whether that judgment applied in India with all its full effect. In the course of so doing he said: 'But the next step of the reasoning, as to the extent to which the English law has been introduced into India, is the point on which the judgment in

18 (1847) 1 Rob Eccl 580, 11 Jur 914.
19 (1849) Perry's Oriental Cases 75.

the present case must depend. The rule on this subject is afforded by the doctrine of the common law with respect to colonies, which, though not strictly analogous, is more in point than any of the other rules in our law books. The rule in such case is, that although colonists take the law of England with them to their new home, they only take so much of it as is applicable to their situation and condition. In many cases no question will arise as to the inapplicability of several provisions of English law, which are clearly seen to be merely municipal; but whenever a question does spring up, it must be decided, like other disputed points of law in the Law Courts of the country. Blackstone lays down the rule very authoritatively on this subject: 'What shall be admitted and what rejected, at what times, and under what restrictions, must, in case of dispute, be decided in the first instance by their (the colonists') own provincial judicature, subject to the revision and control of the King and Council.'

Not only in respect of that last quotation but in respect of the earlier proposition that though 'colonists take the law of England with them to their new home, they only take so much of it as is applicable to their situation and condition', the learned Chief Justice was relying on the corresponding statement in Blackstone's Commentaries. He came to the same conclusion as Dr Lushington, that in effect it was surely inconsistent with the theory on which the incorporation of British law into a colony was based that this particular requirement of the common law marriage should apply in India. It is not suggested that either of these two authorities has ever been questioned—as far as I know they have stood for the best part of one hundred years—and the question is whether they do, or do not, govern this case.

It was suggested that there was a distinction, inasmuch as we are here dealing with a place to which the Foreign Marriage Act applies, and a place in which, at the time in question, British citizens had extra-territorial rights. It is common ground in this case that the Chinese Order in Council of 1925 applied to the Province of Hupeh. The Order recites that 'Whereas by treaty, grant, usage, sufferance, and other lawful means, His Majesty the King has jurisdiction within the Dominion of the Republic of China His Majesty by virtue of and in exercise of the powers in this behalf was pleased to pass an Order in Council' setting out a system of judicature in that province, to the details of which it is unnecessary to refer. It was suggested, therefore, that that raised a different situation; that in such a situation, at any rate, the principles available to the first entry of colonists into a new territory and the like could not apply, and if the theory is that this particular province (or any other place to which extra-territoriality applies) is British, then the whole law of England, without any exception, must apply also—in other words, that the decision in *R v Millis* would apply with full force and effect. I do not think that that can be so for two reasons. First of all, I do not see any distinction in principle between applying in a colony, as New South Wales was at the time of Dr Lushington's judgment, only so much of the English law as suited the situation (but applying it notwithstanding the fact that there was a local Act of Parliament) and applying only so much of the English law as is suited to the situation of a British subject in this Province of Hupeh, notwithstanding that by Order in Council having the effect of legislation the courts of law are set up there to administer British justice. Unless there is something in either case which excludes anything but that which is laid down in the legislation it seems to me that precisely the same principles apply in the one case as in the other.

In fact, there is nothing in the legislation which is inconsistent with that view, for I find in s 104 of the Chinese Order in Council this provision: 'Subject to the provisions of this Order the civil jurisdiction of every court acting under this Order shall, as far as circumstances admit, be exercised on the principles of and in conformity with English law for the time being in force.' That certainly cannot possibly be said to be exclusive. It seems to me that whether one puts it on this basis that one of the circumstances which must be taken into account is that the English law is being imported into a foreign country which in all material respects is indistinguishable from a colony, so far as access to priests of the Established Church and the like is concerned, or whether one puts it on the other basis, that when it is indicated that the jurisdiction of the court shall 'be exercised on the principles of and in conformity with the English law for the time being in force', the English law for the time being in force consists not only of the decision in *R v Millis* but of the decision in *R v Millis* as interpreted, as far as such a situation is concerned, by the decisions in *Catterall v Catterall* and *Maclean v Cristall*, one comes to the same result. In such a territory as this there is, so far as the requirements of English law are concerned in relation to a common law marriage, no obligation that the ceremony shall be performed in the presence of an episcopally ordained priest.

In my opinion, therefore, so far as the first point is concerned, it seems to me that the petition on the ground of nullity must fail, and that it is my duty to say that this marriage was a valid marriage.

QUESTION

What is the justification for applying English common law to determine the validity of a marriage in China, between two Canadians, celebrated by a Church of Scotland Minister?

Section B: Capacity to marry

Capacity to marry is governed (in general) by the lex domicilii of each party immediately before the marriage.

Brook v Brook (1861) 9 HLCas 193, 4 LT 93 (House of Lords)

Appeal from a decision of Stuart V-C.

William Charles Brook (hereinafter called the testator) married Charlotte Armitage in England in 1840. She died in 1847 and there were issue of that marriage one daughter and one son. In 1850 the testator married Emily Armitage, the sister of his deceased wife, in Holstein, Denmark. That marriage was valid by Danish law but void for consanguinity by English law. There were issue of that marriage one son and two daughters. The testator and Emily Armitage were British subjects domiciled in England and had merely gone over to Denmark on a temporary visit. In 1855 Emily

Armitage died of cholera and two days later the testator died of the same complaint, leaving all five children him surviving.

By his will the testator gave all the residue of his property to his five children by name.

In 1856 Charles Armitage Brook, the son of the second marriage, died an infant and intestate. A bill was filed by his sisters and half-sister against his half-brother and the Attorney General claiming that Charles Brook's share of the testator's real estate descended to his half-brother as heir at law and that his share of the testator's personal estate passed to his half-brother and the plaintiffs as next of kin. The Attorney General alleged that the marriage of the testator and Emily Armitage was not valid, that Charles Brook therefore was a bastard without collateral relatives and that his share of the testator's property passed to the Crown.

Stuart V-C having consulted Cresswell J held that the marriage was not valid and that the real and personal estate of Charles Brook had become vested in the Crown.

Lord Campbell LC: My Lords, the question which your Lordships are called upon to consider in the present appeal is, whether the marriage celebrated on 9 June 1850 in the duchy of Holstein, in the kingdom of Denmark, between William Leigh Brook, a widower, and Emily Armitage, the sister of his deceased wife, they being British subjects then domiciled in England, and contemplating England as their place of matrimonial residence, is to be considered valid in England, marriage between a widower and the sister of his deceased wife being permitted by the law of Denmark?

I am of opinion that this depends upon the question whether such a marriage would have been held illegal, and might have been set aside in a suit commenced in England in the lifetime of the parties before the passing of the Marriage Act 1835, commonly called Lord Lyndhurst's Act.

There can be no doubt that before Lord Lyndhurst's Act passed, a marriage between a widower and the sister of his deceased wife, if celebrated in England, was unlawful, and in the lifetime of the parties could have been annulled. Such a marriage was expressly prohibited by the legislature of this country, and was prohibited expressly on the ground that it was 'contrary to God's law'. Sitting here, judicially, we are not at liberty to consider whether such a marriage is or is not 'contrary to God's law', nor whether it is expedient or inexpedient.

Before the Reformation the degrees of relationship by consanguinity and affinity, within which marriage was forbidden, were almost indefinitely multiplied; but the prohibition might have been dispensed with by the Pope, or those who represented him. At the Reformation, the prohibited degrees were confined within the limits supposed to be expressly defined by Holy Scripture, and all dispensations were abolished. The prohibited degrees were those within which intercourse between the sexes was supposed to be forbidden as incestuous, and no distinction was made between relationship by blood or by affinity. The marriage of a man with a sister of his deceased wife is expressly within this category. *Hill v Good*[20] and *R v Chadwick*[1] are solemn decisions that such a marriage was illegal; and if celebrated in England such a marriage unquestionably would now be void.

20 (1674) Freem KB 167, Vaugh 302.
1 (1847) 11 QB 173 at 205.

Indeed, this is not denied on the part of the appellants. They rest their case entirely upon the fact that the marriage was celebrated in a foreign country, where the marriage of a man with the sister of his deceased wife is permitted.

There can be no doubt of the general rule, that 'a foreign marriage, valid according to the law of a country where it is celebrated, is good everywhere'. But while the forms of entering into the contract of marriage are to be regulated by the lex loci contractus, the law of the country in which it is celebrated, the essentials of the contract depend upon the lex domicilii, the law of the country in which the parties are domiciled at the time of marriage, and in which the matrimonial residence is contemplated. Although the forms of celebrating the foreign marriage may be different from those required by the law of the country of domicile, the marriage may be good everywhere. But if the contract of marriage is such, in essentials, as to be contrary to the law of the country of domicile, and it is declared void by that law, it is to be regarded as void in the country of domicile, though not contrary to the law of the country in which it was celebrated.

This qualification upon the rule that 'a marriage valid where celebrated is good everywhere', is to be found in the writings of many eminent jurists who have discussed the subject.

Mr Justice Story, in his valuable treatise on 'the Conflict of Laws', while he admits it to be the 'rule that a marriage valid where celebrated is good everywhere', says (s 113a) there are exceptions; those of marriages involving polygamy and incest, those positively prohibited by the public law of a country from motives of policy, and those celebrated in foreign countries by subjects entitling themselves, under special circumstances, to the benefit of the laws of their own country, he adds (s 114), 'in respect to the first exception, that of marriages involving polygamy and incest, Christianity is understood to prohibit polygamy and incest, and, therefore, no Christian country would recognise polygamy or incestuous marriages; but when we speak of incestuous marriages care must be taken to confine the doctrine to such cases as by the general consent of all Christendom are deemed incestuous'. The conclusion of this sentence was strongly relied upon by Sir FitzRoy Kelly, who alleged that many in England approve of marriage between a widower and the sister of his deceased wife; and that such marriages are permitted in Protestant states on the Continent of Europe and in most of the states in America.

Sitting here as a judge to declare and enforce the law of England as fixed by Kings, Lords, and Commons, the supreme power of this realm, I do not feel myself at liberty to form any private opinion of my own on the subject, or to inquire into what may be the opinion of the majority of my fellow citizens at home, or to try to find out the opinion of all Christendom. I can as judge only look to what was the solemnly pronounced opinion of the legislature when the laws were passed which I am called upon to interpret. What means am I to resort to for the purpose of ascertaining the opinions of foreign nations? Is my interpretation of these laws to vary with the variation of opinion in foreign countries? Change of opinion on any great question, at home or abroad, may be a good reason for the legislature changing the law, but can be no reason for judges to vary their interpretation of the law.

Indeed, as Story allows marriages positively prohibited by the public law of a country, from motives of policy, to form an exception to the general rule as to the validity of marriage, he could hardly mean his qualification to apply to a country like England, in which the limits of marriages to be considered incestuous are exactly defined by public law.

That the Parliament of England in framing the prohibited degrees within which marriages were forbidden, believed and intimated the opinion, that all such marriages were incestuous and contrary to God's word, I cannot doubt. All the degrees prohibited are brought into one category, and although marriages within those degrees may be more or less revolting, they are placed on the same footing, and before English tribunals, till the law is altered, they are to be treated alike....

It is quite obvious that no civilised state can allow its domiciled subjects or citizens, by making a temporary visit to a foreign country, to enter into a contract to be performed in the place of domicile, if the contract is forbidden by the law of the place of domicile as contrary to religion, or morality, or to any of its fundamental institutions.

A marriage between a man and the sister of his deceased wife, being Danish subjects domiciled in Denmark, may be good all over the world, and this might likewise be so, even if they were native born English subjects, who had abandoned their English domicile, and were domiciled in Denmark. But I am by no means prepared to say that the marriage now in question ought to be, or would be, held valid in the Danish courts, proof being given that the parties were British subjects domiciled in England at the time of the marriage, that England was to be their matrimonial residence, and that by the law of England such a marriage is prohibited as being contrary to the law of God. The doctrine being established that the incidents of the contract of marriage celebrated in a foreign country are to be determined according to the law of the country in which the parties are domiciled and mean to reside, the consequence seems to follow that by this law must its validity or invalidity be determined.

Sir FitzRoy Kelly argued that we could not hold this marriage to be invalid without being prepared to nullify the marriages of Danish subjects who contracted such a marriage in Denmark while domiciled in their native country, if they should come to reside in England. But on the principles which I have laid down, such marriages, if examined, would be held valid in all English courts, as they are according to the law of the country in which the parties were domiciled when the marriages were celebrated.

I will now examine the authorities relied upon by the counsel for the appellants. They bring forward nothing from the writings of jurists except the general rule, that contracts are to be construed according to the lex loci contractus, and the saying of Story with regard to a marriage being contrary to the precepts of the Christian religion, upon which I have already commented.

But there are various decisions which they bring forward as conclusive in their favour. They begin with *Compton v Bearcroft*[2] and the class of cases in which it was held that Gretna Green marriages were valid in England, notwithstanding Lord Hardwicke's Marriage Act 1753. In observing upon them, I do not lay any stress on the proviso in this Act that it should not extend to marriages in Scotland or beyond the seas; this being only an intimation of what might otherwise have been inferred, that its direct

2 (1769) Bull NP 113, 2 Hag Con 444, n.

operation should be confined to England, and that marriages in Scotland and beyond the seas should continue to be viewed according to the law of Scotland and countries beyond the seas, as if the Act had not been passed. But I do lay very great stress on the consideration that Lord Hardwicke's Act only regulated banns and licences, and the formalities by which the ceremony of marriage shall be celebrated. It does not touch the essentials of the contract or prohibit any marriage which was before lawful, or render any marriage lawful which was before prohibited. The formalities which it requires could only be observed in England, and the whole frame of it shows it was only territorial. The nullifying clauses about banns and licences can only apply to marriages celebrated in England. In this class of case the contested marriage could only be challenged for want of banns or licence in the prescribed form. These formalities being observed, the marriages would all have been unimpeachable. But the marriage we have to decide upon has been declared by the legislature to be 'contrary to God's law', and on that ground is absolutely prohibited.

The appellants' counsel next produced a new authority, the very learned and lucid judgment of Dr Radcliff, in *Steele v Braddell*.[3] The Irish statute, 9 Geo 2, c 11, enacts, 'that all marriages and matrimonial contracts, when either of the parties is under the age of twenty-one, had without the consent of the father or guardian, shall be absolutely null and void to all intents and purposes; and that it shall be lawful for the father or guardian to commence a suit in the proper Ecclesiastical Court in order to annul the marriage'. A young gentleman, a native of Ireland, and domiciled there, went while a minor into Scotland, and there married a Scottish young lady without the consent of his father or guardian. A suit was brought by his guardian in an Ecclesiastical Court in Ireland, in which Dr Radcliff presided, to annul the marriage on the ground that this statute created a personal incapacity in minors, subjects of Ireland, to contract marriage, in whatever country, without the consent of father or guardian. But the learned judge said, 'I cannot find that any Act of Parliament such as this has ever been extended to cases not properly within it, on the principle that parties endeavoured to evade it'. And after an elaborate view of the authorities upon the subject, he decided that both parties being of the age of consent, and the marriage being valid by the law of Scotland, it could not be impeached in the courts of the country in which the husband was domiciled, and he dismissed the suit. But this was a marriage between parties who, with the consent of parents and guardians, might have contracted a valid marriage according to the law of the country of the husband's domicile, and the mode of celebrating the marriage was to be according to the law of the country in which it was celebrated. But if the union between these parties had been prohibited by the law of Ireland as 'contrary to the word of God', undoubtedly the marriage would have been dissolved.

Another new case was brought forward, decided very recently by Sir Cresswell Cresswell, *Simonin v Mallac*.[4] This was a petition by Valerie Simonin for a declaration of nullity of marriage. The petitioner alleged that a pretended ceremony of marriage was had between the petitioner and Leon Mallac of Paris, in the parish church of St Martin's-in-the-Fields; that about

3 (1838) Milw Ecc Rep (Ir) 1.
4 (1860) 2 Sw & Tr 67, 29 LJPM & A 97.

two days afterwards the parties returned to Paris, but did not cohabit, and the marriage was never consummated; that the pretended marriage was in contradiction to and in evasion of the Code Napoléon; that the parties were natives of and domiciled in France, and that subsequently to their return to France the Civil Tribunal of the department of the Seine had declared the said pretended marriage to be null and void. Leon Mallac was served at Naples with a citation and a copy of the petition, but did not appear. Proof was given of the material allegations of the petition, and that the parties coming to London to avoid the French law, which required the consent of parents or guardians to their union, were married by licence in the parish church of St Martin's-in-the-Fields. Sir Cresswell Cresswell, after the case had been learnedly argued, discharged the petition. But was there anything here inconsistent with the opinion which the same learned judge delivered as assessor to Stuart V-C in *Brook v Brook*? Nothing whatever; for the objection to the validity of the marriage in England was merely that the forms prescribed by the Code Napoléon for the celebration of a marriage in France had not been observed. But there was no law of France, where the parties were domiciled, forbidding a conjugal union between them; and if the proper forms of celebration had been observed, this marriage by the law of France would have been unimpeachable. The case, therefore, comes into the same category as *Compton v Bearcroft* and *Steele v Braddell*. None of these cases can show the validity of a marriage which the law of the domicile of the parties condemns as incestuous, and which could not, by any forms or consents, have been rendered valid in the country in which the parties were domiciled. . . .

Lords Cranworth, St Leonards, and Wensleydale delivered judgments to the same effect.

Appeal dismissed.

Sottomayor v De Barros (No. 1) (1877) 3 PD 1, 47 LJP 23 (Court of Appeal)

Woman's petition for nullity of marriage.

The petitioner Ignacia Clara Maxima Pacheco Pereira Pamplona da Cunha Sottomayor was born in Portugal in 1851. The respondent Gonzalo Lobo Pereira Caldos De Barros, who was the petitioner's first cousin, was born in Portugal in 1850. In 1858 the petitioner, her father and mother, and her uncle De Barros and his family, including the respondent, his eldest son, came to England, and the two families occupied a house jointly in Dorset Square, London. The petitioner's father came to this country for the benefit of his health, and De Barros for the education of his children and to superintend the sale of wine. On 21 June 1866 the petitioner, at that time of the age of $14\frac{1}{2}$ years, and the respondent, of the age of 16 years, were married at a registry office in London. No religious ceremony accompanied or followed the marriage, and although the parties lived together in the same house until the year 1872, they never slept together, and the marriage was never consummated. The petitioner stated that she went through the form of marriage contrary to her own inclination, by the persuasion of her uncle and mother, on the representation that it would be the means of preserving her father's Portuguese property from the consequences of the bankruptcy of the wine business. The petitioner returned to Portugal in 1873 and the respondent in 1874. By the law of Portugal first cousins are incapable of contracting marriage by reason of consanguinity, and any such marriage is held to be incestuous and therefore null and void, unless solemnised under the authority of a papal dispensation.

The petitioner applied for a decree of nullity on the ground that she and the respondent were under a personal incapacity to contract marriage. The suit was undefended and Phillimore J ordered the papers to be sent to the Queen's Proctor, who filed an answer alleging (inter alia) that at the time of the marriage the petitioner and respondent were domiciled in England and not in Portugal; and that the petitioner and respondent intended at the time of the marriage to live together as man and wife in England, and did so live for six years, and that the validity of the marriage was to be determined by the law of England. By consent of the parties it was ordered that the question of law should be argued before the questions of fact.

Phillimore J dismissed the petition. The petitioner appealed.

The judgment of the court (James, Baggallay and Cotton LJJ) was delivered by

Cotton LJ (After stating the facts, and observing that the petitioner and respondent were domiciled in Portugal at all times, his Lordship continued): Under these circumstances the petitioner, in November 1874, presented her petition for the object above mentioned, and Sir R. Phillimore, before whom the case was heard, declined to declare the marriage invalid and dismissed the petition, but did so, as we understand, rather because he felt himself bound by the decision in the case of *Simonin v Mallac*[5] than because he considered that on principle the marriage ought to be held good. If the parties had been subjects of Her Majesty domiciled in England, the marriage would undoubtedly have been valid. But it is a well-recognised principle of law that the question of personal capacity to enter into any contract is to be decided by the law of domicile. It is, however, urged that this does not apply to the contract of marriage, and that a marriage valid according to the law of the country where it is solemnised is valid everywhere. This, in our opinion, is not a correct statement of the law. The law of a country where a marriage is solemnised must alone decide all questions relating to the validity of the ceremony by which the marriage is alleged to have been constituted; but, as in other contracts, so in that of marriage, personal capacity must depend on the law of the domicile; and if the laws of any country prohibit its subjects within certain degrees of consanguinity from contracting marriage, and stamp a marriage between persons within the prohibited degrees as incestuous, this, in our opinion, imposes on the subjects of that country a personal incapacity, which continues to affect them so long as they are domiciled in the country where this law prevails, and renders invalid a marriage between persons both at the time of their marriage subjects of and domiciled in the country which imposes this restriction, wherever such marriage may have been solemnised.

But it is said that the impediment imposed by the law of Portugal can be removed by a Papal dispensation, and, therefore, that it cannot be said there is a personal incapacity of the petitioner and respondent to contract marriage. The evidence is clear that by the law of Portugal the impediment

5 (1860) 2 Sw & Tr 67, 29 LJPM & A 97.

to the marriage between the parties is such that, in the absence of Papal dispensation, the marriage would be by the law of that country void as incestuous. The statutes of the English parliament contain a declaration that no Papal dispensation can sanction a marriage otherwise incestuous; but the law of Portugal does recognise the validity of such a dispensation, and it cannot in our opinion be held that such a dispensation is a matter of form affecting only the sufficiency of the ceremony by which the marriage is effected, or that the law of Portugal, which prohibits and declares incestuous, unless with such a dispensation, a marriage between the petitioner and respondent, does not impose on them a personal incapacity to contract marriage. It is proved that the courts of Portugal, where the petitioner and respondent are domiciled and resident, would hold the marriage void, as solemnised between parties incapable of marrying, and incestuous. How can the courts of this country hold the contrary, and, if appealed to, say the marriage is valid? It was pressed upon us in argument that a decision in favour of the petitioner would lead to many difficulties, if questions should arise as to the validity of a marriage between an English subject and a foreigner, in consequence of prohibitions imposed by the law of the domicile of the latter. Our opinion on this appeal is confined to the case where both the contracting parties are, at the time of their marriage, domiciled in a country the laws of which prohibit their marriage. All persons are legally bound to take notice of the laws of the country where they are domiciled. No country is bound to recognise the laws of a foreign state when they work injustice to its own subjects, and this principle would prevent the judgment in the present case being relied on as an authority for setting aside a marriage between a foreigner and an English subject domiciled in England, on the ground of any personal incapacity not recognised by the law of this country.

The counsel for the petitioner relied on the case of *Brook v Brook*[6] as a decision in his favour. If, in our opinion, that case had been a decision on the question arising on this petition, we should have thought it sufficient without more to refer to that case as decisive. The judgment in that case, however, only decided that the English courts must hold invalid a marriage between two English subjects domiciled in this country, who were prohibited from intermarrying by an English statute, even though the marriage was solemnised during a temporary sojourn in a foreign country. It is, therefore, not decisive of the present case; but the reasons given by the Lords who delivered their opinions in that case strongly support the principle on which this judgment is based.

It only remains to consider the case of *Simonin v Mallac*. The objection to the validity of the marriage in that case, which was solemnised in England, was the want of the consent of parents required by the law of France, but not under the circumstances by that of this country. In our opinion, this consent must be considered a part of the ceremony of marriage, and not a matter affecting the personal capacity of the parties to contract marriage; and the decision in *Simonin v Mallac* does not, we think, govern the present case. We are of opinion that the judgment appealed from must be reversed, and a decree made declaring the marriage null and void.

Appeal allowed.

6 (1861) 9 HL Cas 193, 4 LT 93; p 232 above.

NOTE

The case was remitted to the Divorce Division in order that the questions of fact raised by the Queen's Proctor's pleas should be determined. On it appearing that the husband's domicile at the date of the marriage was not Portuguese but English, Sir James Hannen P pronounced the marriage valid[7] in reliance on the dictum of the Court of Appeal in *Sottomayor v De Barros* (p 239 above) that 'our opinion on this appeal is confined to the case where both the contracting parties are, at the time of their marriage, domiciled in a country the laws of which prohibit their marriage'. This decision compelled Dicey to make an exception to his general rule on capacity to marry which he formulated as follows: 'The validity of a marriage celebrated in England between persons of whom the one has an English, and the other a foreign, domicile is not affected by any incapacity which, though existing under the law of such foreign domicile, does not exist under the law of England.' *Ogden v Ogden* (below) is an example of this exception. It does not apply to the prohibited degrees of affinity: see s 1 (3) of the Marriage (Enabling) Act 1960, below. But it may perhaps apply to consent of parties: see *Vervaeke v Smith*.[8]

Marriage (Enabling) Act 1960

1.—(1) No marriage hereafter contracted (whether in or out of Great Britain) between a man and a woman who is the sister, aunt or niece of a former wife of his (whether living or not), or was formerly the wife of his brother, uncle or nephew (whether living or not), shall by reason of that relationship be void or voidable under any enactment or rule of law applying in Great Britain as a marriage between persons within the prohibited degrees of affinity.

(2) In the foregoing subsection words of kinship apply equally to kin of the whole and of the half blood.

(3) This section does not validate a marriage, if either party to it is at the time of the marriage domiciled in a country outside Great Britain, and under the law of that country there cannot be a valid marriage between the parties.

The validity of a marriage celebrated in England between persons of whom the one has an English, and the other a foreign, domicile is not affected by any incapacity which, though existing under the law of such foreign domicile, does not exist under the law of England.

Ogden v Ogden [1908] P 46, 77 LJP 34 (Court of Appeal)

Appeal from a decision of Bargrave Deane J.

In September 1898 the appellant, an Englishwoman domiciled in England, married in England a man named Léon Philip, a Frenchman domiciled in France, then aged 19 years. The marriage took place without the knowledge either of his parents or of her parents.

After a short time Philip's father came to hear of the marriage. He took his son back to France (where he has ever since remained) and instituted proceedings in France to have the marriage annulled in accordance with the following provisions of the French Civil Code:

---

7 *Sottomayor v De Barros (No 2)* (1879) 5 PD 94, 49 LJP 1.
8 [1981] Fam 77, [1981] 1 All ER 55. The point was not mentioned in the House of Lords: see [1983] 1 AC 145, [1982] 2 All ER 144.

Article 148. The son who has not attained the full age of 25 years, the daughter who has not attained the full age of 21 years, cannot contract marriage without the consent of their father and mother.

Article 151. Where the children of a family have attained the majority fixed by article 148, they are required previously to contracting marriage to demand by a respectful and formal act the consent of their father and mother.

Article 152. From the majority fixed by article 148 until the age of 30 years completed for sons, and until the age of 25 years completed for daughters, the respectful act required by the preceding article, and on which consent to marriage shall not have been obtained, shall be twice more renewed from month to month; and one month after the third act it shall be lawful to proceed with the celebration of the marriage.

Article 170. A marriage contracted in a foreign country between natives of France and between a native of France and a foreigner shall be valid if celebrated according to the forms used in that country, provided that it has been preceded by the publications prescribed in article 63, under the title 'Of acts of the civil power', and that the Frenchman has not infringed the regulations contained in the preceding chapter.

Article 182. A marriage contracted without the consent of the father and mother in cases where such consent was necessary can be impeached only by those whose consent was necessary, or by such of the two married persons as stood in need of that consent.

In November 1901 a decree was pronounced by the Civil Tribunal of First Instance of the Seine annulling the marriage for lack of consent of parents in accordance with article 148. The appellant never went to France and did not appear personally in those proceedings.

After the decree Léon Philip married again in France, and in July 1903 the appellant instituted a suit in the High Court in England for a dissolution of her marriage on the ground of her husband's desertion and adultery. Her petition also asked for a declaration that her marriage was annulled. The petition was undefended, but was dismissed for want of jurisdiction, Léon Philip being domiciled in France.

In October 1904 the appellant went through a ceremony of marriage in England with the present petitioner, William Ogden. In July 1906 Ogden instituted the present suit against the appellant for a decree of nullity of marriage on the ground that at the time of the ceremony Léon Philip was still alive, and that the marriage of the appellant and Léon Philip had not been annulled or dissolved for any cause competent to the law of England.

The appellant by her answer denied that she was lawfully married to Léon Philip and pleaded that her marriage with him was annulled by the French decree.

Bargrave Deane J pronounced a decree nisi, declaring the marriage between the petitioner and the appellant null and void on the ground that the appellant had a husband living at the time of her marriage with the petitioner. From this decision the present appeal was brought.

The judgment of the court (Cozens-Hardy MR, Sir Gorell Barnes P, and Kennedy LJ) was delivered by

Sir Gorell Barnes P: ... Two points were made for the appellant by her counsel, Sir Edward Clarke; the first, that her marriage with Léon Philip was not valid, inasmuch as, although the marriage was celebrated according to the forms required by the law of England, it was invalid both in this country and in France because Léon Philip was, by the law of France, being the law of his country and his domicile, incapable of contracting the marriage; the second, that the effect of the French decree was to annul the marriage, both in France and in this country. If both or either of these points were established in favour of the appellant, the contention on her part which followed as a matter of course was that at the time of the ceremony of marriage between herself and Mr Ogden she was free to contract a marriage with him, and that, therefore, her marriage with him was valid, and his petition should be dismissed. . . .

(After discussing the provisions of the French Civil Code set out above, and observing that they rendered the marriage voidable, not void, his Lordship continued:) The simple question for determination in the present case upon the first point is whether or not a marriage taking place in England between an English person domiciled in England with a foreigner temporarily residing in this country, which it was not disputed would be held in England to be a valid marriage if celebrated between two inhabitants of this country, ought to be held invalid on the ground that the foreigner was by the statute law of his country subjected to the necessity of complying with certain formalities in order to be at liberty to enter into the marriage. It is desirable to state this limited proposition very clearly, because, with regard to questions which may be raised as to the validity of marriages in England between persons domiciled abroad, certain cases have been decided (to which reference will be made further on in this judgment) which do not necessarily involve the consideration of the particular point already indicated, or any decision thereupon; and it is desirable, therefore, to avoid the confusion which appears to have arisen sometimes between the consideration of the principles which have been laid down for determining the validity of a marriage where the ceremony alone was in question, and of those which have been considered, in determining whether it was lawful for the parties to intermarry at all.

Now, the argument for the appellant in the present case was that, although the marriage between her and Léon Philip was celebrated according to the forms required by the English law, it was invalid universally because Léon Philip was a minor in France, and under a disability by the law of France from contracting such marriage without the consent of his father, and without complying with the other formalities required by the law of France. In substance this contention amounted to this—that in regard to entering into a marriage in England with an inhabitant thereof, Léon Philip carried with him into this country an incapacity, which ought to be recognised by the law of England, to enter into matrimonial relationship with such inhabitant without complying with the provisions of the French code. It was urged that this principle had been recognised in this country, and cases were cited which it was said supported the contention. The cases cited, however, do not support it, and in truth the argument on behalf of the appellant appears to be based upon views which have been expressed by foreign jurists, but which have not been adopted in this country, where the English courts have not been very ready to admit a personal law of status and capacity dependent on domicile, and travelling with the person from country to country, although there has been, perhaps, less unwillingness in later years to give effect to the lex domicilii to some extent: see, for instance, *Re Goodman's Trusts*.[9]

It may be doubted whether there is much substantial difference of opinion between foreign and English jurists as to the general rule that between persons sui juris the validity of the marriage is to be decided by the law of the place where it is celebrated. There are certain exceptions, as, for instance, when the lex loci celebrationis violates the precepts of religion, or of public morals, as in the case of bigamy, or where the marriages are such as are generally recognised as incestuous. When, however, the competency of the parties to contract marriage is considered, there appears to be a diversity of opinion, not merely between foreign jurists and English jurists, but amongst the foreign jurists themselves, certain foreign jurists, but not all, maintaining that a person who is in his minority by the law of his native or acquired domicile is to be deemed everywhere in the same state or condition. This appears to be based upon the conception that the laws which have for their object the regulation of the capacity of persons are to be treated as personal laws and of absolute obligation everywhere when they have once attached upon the person by the law of his domicile. This conception would appear to result from the application of principles derived from sources of law different from those from which the English common law has been derived, and from considerations which have not had the same force in this country as abroad.

...We are concerned in this case only with the question of a disability imposed by foreign law upon one of the parties to the marriage in respect only of want of parental consent, and compliance with certain formalities required by such foreign law.

There appears to be no case in this country (certainly no case was cited to us in argument on this appeal) in which in such a case as last mentioned the view has been expressed that such a marriage would be held invalid in this country. We know of no principle recognised by English law which would justify the court in coming to the conclusion that such a marriage ought to be held invalid; for, although to a certain extent the lex domicilii is recognised in this country, for instance, in the familiar case where it is held that mobilia sequuntur personam, yet such recognition appears never to have been extended to the case of a matrimonial engagement entered into in this country between an inhabitant of another country and an inhabitant of this country. In such a case, where there are two different systems of law, one may well ask, which is to prevail? Why should it be recognised that a person who comes over to this country and validly enters into a marriage with one of its inhabitants according to English law should be held unable to do so here because of the regulations of a foreign system of jurisprudence which places upon him a personal incapacity to contract unless he complies with formalities required by the foreign law? It may be observed here that the 3rd section of article 1 of the French Civil Code ordains that the French laws relating to the conditions and privileges of persons are to govern Frenchmen although residing in a foreign country, so that it would seem from this provision that the French rule as to competency by reason of minority is not based upon domicile, but upon nationality, and therefore that even in the case of a Frenchman domiciled in England celebrating a marriage with a

9 (1881) 17 Ch D 266, 50 LJCh 425; p 412 below.

domiciled Englishwoman the French courts would be at liberty, if the question arose before them, to declare such a marriage null and void, on the ground that it was governed by the laws of France, although celebrated in this country; but it could hardly be contended in England, if both persons parties to a marriage were domiciled in this country, that our courts ought to hold such a marriage invalid because one of the parties by the laws of his or her nationality may not have adequate competency to enter into the contract. . . .

The case of *Brook v Brook*[10] was much relied upon by the appellant's counsel. That case, however, so far from supporting the contention of the appellant, is, when carefully considered, a decision adverse to her. (His Lordship stated the facts and the decision in *Brook v Brook,* and after observing that it had not met with approval in America, continued:) The reason why the case of *Brook v Brook* may be considered to be adverse to the appellant is that the distinction is there drawn between the question of the validity of a marriage absolutely prohibited by the law of the domicile of both parties and the case in which a marriage, valid by the law of the place of celebration, if it took place between two inhabitants of that place, is called in question because one of the persons is domiciled abroad, and has not complied with certain forms and obtained certain consents required by the law of the place of his or her domicile. The Lord Chancellor (Lord Campbell) said: (His Lordship quoted the passage on p 234 above, beginning 'There can be no doubt of the general rule' and ending 'the law of the country in which it was celebrated'.) Again, in commenting on the case of *Simonin v Mallac,*[11] next hereinafter referred to, Lord Campbell remarks: (His Lordship quoted the passage on p 237 above, beginning 'The objection to the validity of the marriage' and ending 'in which the parties were domiciled'.)

It was contended that *Simonin v Mallac* was wrongly decided, and therefore it is desirable to refer to it in some detail. (In that case a marriage celebrated in England between a man aged 29 and a woman aged 22, both of whom were domiciled in France, was held valid, although the parties had not obtained the consent of their parents as required by articles 151 and 152 of the French Civil Code, and although the marriage had been annulled in France on that ground. His Lordship stated the facts in *Simonin v Mallac* and continued:) The argument was very much the same as that which was addressed to this court, viz, that the law of the country of the domicile placed on the parties an incapacity to contract marriage without attending to the formalities prescribed, and that such incapacity travelled with them everywhere, and rendered them incapable of making a valid contract in any other country, especially where the intention was to evade the law of their own country. In the course of the judgment it was noted that according to the evidence the incapacity to contract was not absolute, but conditional only, and that the marriage, having been contracted between a man and woman of the respective ages of 29 and 22 without attending to the formalities prescribed by the Code Napoléon, articles 151, 152, 153, and 154, might receive a different consideration from one absolutely prohibited by article 148 by parties respectively under those ages. The court, however,

10 (1861) 9 HLCas 193, 4 LT 93; p 232 above.
11 (1860) 2 Sw & Tr 67, 29 LJPM & A 97.

dealt with the case on the broad ground that by the decree of the French court, as evidenced by the law of France,[12] the marriage was void, and the question considered was whether the marriage was to be judged of here by the law of France or by the law of England.... That case is in accordance with the general views to be found expressed in the English decisions, and has met with approval in this court and in the House of Lords, or at least it may be said that where mentioned in those tribunals it has not been dissented from.

The case principally relied on by the appellant was the case of *Sottomayor v De Barros*.[13] (His Lordship stated the facts in that case, read the passage beginning 'But it is a well-recognised principle of law' and ending 'wherever such marriage may have been solemnised', p 238 above, and continued:) Now this court hearing this appeal is bound by the decision of the Court of Appeal in the case of *Sottomayor v De Barros*. It is not necessary, even if we were at liberty to do so, to consider whether that case was rightly decided, but it is permissible to point out that the commencement of the paragraph above set out could scarcely be considered correct in stating that 'it is a well-recognised principle of law that the question of personal capacity to enter into any contract is to be decided by the law of domicile', for, if so, it would logically seem to follow that that part of the judgment which indicates that the opinion of the court was confined to cases where both the contracting parties were, at the time of their marriage, domiciled in a country, the laws of which prohibited their marriage, should not have expressed that limitation, and that the case of *Simonin v Mallac* should have been overruled, and yet that case, according to our reading of the judgment, is approved. The probability is that that sentence should be read with the context and be confined to the case present to the minds of the court in relation to marriages which could not be contracted at all by the laws of the country of domicile. Even then it may be questioned whether that sentence is correct, and whether the question of capacity is really raised at all in such a case; that is to say, where both the parties are capable of entering into a marriage but may not marry each other because such a marriage would be illegal in their own country. That is rather a question of illegality than of capacity, and it may, perhaps, not be unreasonable for one country to refuse to recognise a marriage contracted in it between two persons by the laws of whose domicile a marriage between them is illegal, and yet it may be quite proper and reasonable for a country, in which a marriage takes place between persons domiciled in another country, to recognise it as a valid marriage when it would be legal in such other country if contracted after compliance with all formalities required in such other country, and, further, to protect its citizens in all cases of marriages where one of the contracting parties is domiciled in the country first referred to—that is to say, where the marriage takes place—and the other is domiciled in a foreign country, and there is a conflict between the laws of the two countries as to the validity of the marriage. The passage in the judgment expressly confining the decision to the case then before the court is as follows: (his Lordship read the passage beginning 'It was pressed upon us in argument' and ending 'not recognised by the law of

12 Sic in the report: evidently a slip for 'by the law of France, as evidenced by the decree of the French court' (*Ed*).
13 (1877) 3 PD 1, 47 LJP 23; p 237 above.

this country' p 239 above and continued:) It was upon this passage that, when the case subsequently came before Lord Hannen, he was able to decide in favour of the marriage being valid notwithstanding the fact that one of the parties was domiciled in Portugal.

The concluding passage in the judgment of the Court of Appeal is as follows: (his Lordship read it). That may perhaps be considered only a dictum by the learned Lords Justices, but it is really a very strong statement that *Simonin v Mallac* is clearly distinguishable from the case before them, and we regard it as an approval of the decision in that case, and, if so, it is an authority adverse to the contention of the appellant on the present appeal.

...After very careful consideration of the present case we have come to the conclusion that the first point must be decided against the appellant, and that the marriage between her and Léon Philip must be declared valid in England.

(His Lordship proceeded (1) to hold that the French decree of nullity was not entitled to recognition in England: but as to this, see p 327 below; (2) to suggest that the appellant's suit for divorce ought not to have been dismissed for want of jurisdiction: but this suggestion has not been followed).

Appeal dismissed.

QUESTION

What would happen if, on similar facts, the French husband (or his father) petitioned for nullity in England and not in France? What arguments would you expect to be deployed on either side? Could you write a more convincing judgment than that of the Court of Appeal?

No marriage is valid if either party is domiciled in England and one party (not necessarily the party domiciled in England) is under the age of sixteen.

Pugh v Pugh [1951] P 482, [1951] 2 All ER 680 (Divorce Division)

The wife was born in Hungary with a Hungarian domicile of origin. In 1945 she left Hungary with her parents to escape from the Russian advance and went to Austria. There she met the husband, who was a serving British officer domiciled in England. They were married in Austria in October 1946 when the wife was fifteen years of age. They lived together in Austria and Germany at places where the husband was stationed. It was the husband's intention to return to England with his wife after his service abroad. The parties came to England in October 1950 but parted soon afterwards. The wife petitioned the High Court for a decree of nullity on the ground that at the time of the marriage she was under age.

By Hungarian law the marriage was voidable until the wife's seventeenth birthday when it became valid. By Austrian law the marriage was valid. By section 1 of the Age of Marriage Act 1929 (now section 2 of the Marriage Act 1949) 'a marriage between persons either of whom is under the age of sixteen shall be void'.

Pearce J: Mr Simon, for the wife, makes two submissions. The first is this:—The Age of Marriage Act 1929 applies to the husband as a British subject with an English domicile, wherever he may marry. Its effect is extra-territorial and is not merely confined to marriages in the United Kingdom. Therefore it makes this marriage void. His second submission is this:—The validity of such a marriage as this has to be tested as to its essentials by the law of the country of the husband's domicile, or alternatively (see *De Reneville v De Reneville*[14]), by the law of the country of the proposed matrimonial home. On either alternative that is English law, and by English law the Age of Marriage Act 1929 makes such a marriage void. If either of those submissions is correct the wife is entitled to a decree of nullity.

(His Lordship considered the scope of the statute, quoted from *Brook v Brook*[15] and *Mette v Mette*,[16] and continued): It is urged on me that the statute is ambiguous and also (rightly in my opinion) that if I am in doubt as to its meaning the marriage is to be deemed valid and the wife has failed to make out her case.

But is the statute ambiguous? The words are clear and general. It must be remembered that personal status and capacity to marry are considered to be the concern of the country of domicile. It is right and reasonable that the country of domicile should (as it did by Lord Lyndhurst's Act) from time to time vary and affect the personal status of its subjects and their capacity to marry as changing religious, moral, and social conditions may demand.

I see no reason to put upon the words any other limitation than the obvious one that they are not intended to apply to marriages abroad of persons who are not domiciled here and who are not the concern of or subject to the laws of Parliament.

In *Heydon's Case* in 1584[17] the Barons of the Exchequer resolved: 'that for the sure interpretation of all statutes in general (be they penal or beneficial, restrictive or enlarging of the common law), four things are to be discerned and considered: First, what was the common law before the making of the Act. Second, what was the mischief and defect for which the common law did not provide. Third, what remedy the Parliament hath resolved and appointed to cure the disease of the commonwealth. And fourth, the true reason of the remedy; and then the office of all the judges is always to make such construction as shall suppress the mischief, and advance the remedy, and to suppress subtle inventions and evasions for continuance of the mischief, and pro privato commodo, and to add force and life to the cure and remedy, according to the true intent of the makers of the Act, pro bono publico'.

It is helpful to consider this case in the light of those resolutions. The common law before the Age of Marriage Act 1929 was this: By canon law which continued after and in spite of the Reformation a boy of fourteen years could marry a girl of twelve. The 'mischief and defect for which the common law did not provide' was this: According to modern thought it is considered socially and morally wrong that persons of an age, at which we now believe them to be immature and provide for their education, should have the stresses, responsibilities and sexual freedom of marriage and the physical strain of childbirth. Child marriages are by common consent believed to be bad for the participants and bad for the institution of marriage. Acts making

14 [1948] P 100, [1948] 1 All ER 56.
15 (1861) 9 HLCap 193, 4 LT 93; p 232 above.
16 (1859) 1 Sw & Tr 416, 28 LJP & M 117.
17 (1584) 3 Co Rep 7a at 7b.

carnal knowledge of young girls an offence are an indication of modern views on this subject. The remedy that 'the Parliament has resolved' for this mischief and defect is to make marriages void where either of the parties is under sixteen years of age.

To curtail the general words of the Act so that a person can evade its provisions by merely going abroad and entering into a marriage where one of the parties is under sixteen in some country like Northern Ireland where canon law still prevails,[18] and then returning to live in this country after the marriage, seems to me to be encouraging rather than suppressing 'subtle inventions and evasions for the continuance of the mischief'.

Parliament must be deemed to have known the effect of *Brook v Brook*. In my view it was by the Age of Marriage Act 1929 deliberately legislating on a matter that is its own peculiar concern, namely, the personal status of its subjects and their capacity to contract marriage. This Act was intended, as was Lord Lyndhurst's Act, to affect that capacity in all persons domiciled in the United Kingdom wherever the marriage might be celebrated.

I come now to the second submission. So far as the form of marriage is concerned it is clearly established that the law of the place of the marriage is the effective law; but so far as concerns the essential validity of a marriage the position is different.

In *Conway v Beazley*,[19] as early as 1831, Dr Lushington held that 'The lex loci contractus as to marriage will not prevail when either of the contracting parties is under a legal incapacity by the law of the domicile; and therefore a second marriage, had in Scotland on a Scotch divorce a vinculo from an English marriage between parties domiciled in England at the times of such marriages and divorce, is null.'

I have already considered *Brook v Brook* and *Mette v Mette*, which show that the law of domicile is the law which regulates the essentials of the marriage and that Lord Lyndhurst's Act, as part of that law, in those cases avoided the marriages.

In *Sottomayor v De Barros*[20] it was held that, the parties being by the law of the country of their domicile under a personal disability to contract marriage, their marriage ought to be declared null and void. In delivering the judgment of the court, Cotton, LJ, said (His Lordship quoted the passage on p 238 above beginning 'But it is a well-recognised principle of law' and ending 'must depend on the law of domicile').

In *Re De Wilton*,[1] it was decided that the capacity of persons professing the Jewish religion who were also domiciled British subjects to contract marriage is regulated by the law of England. Therefore, where a marriage was solemnised abroad according to Jewish rites between a niece and her maternal uncle, both the contracting parties being at the time of the solemnisation domiciled British subjects and adherents of the Jewish faith, although the marriage was valid both by Jewish law and by the law of Wiesbaden where the marriage took place, it was held that the marriage was invalid.

18 See now the Age of Marriage Act (NI) 1951, which is in the same terms as the English Act (*Ed*).
19 (1831) 3 Hag Ecc 639.
20 (1877) 3 PD 1, 47 LJP 23; p 237 above.
 1 [1900] 2 Ch 481, 69 LJCh 717.

In *Re Paine*[2] a lady while domiciled in England married her deceased sister's husband, who was a German subject. The marriage took place in Germany and was in accordance with the laws of Germany, by which such a marriage was valid. Bennett J held that according to English law the marriage was invalid, because by English law the lady had not the capacity to contract it.

In view of those authorities it is clear that this marriage was not valid since by the law of the husband's domicile it was a marriage into which he could not lawfully enter.

On both submissions put forward by counsel for the wife she is entitled to succeed. There will be a decree of nullity on the wife's petition.

QUESTION

Was it really the object of the statute to protect British Army officers from the wiles of designing foreign teenagers? Contrast the more refined provisions of section 1 of the Marriage (Scotland) Act 1977, p 678 below.

The general rule on capacity to marry applies to cases of bigamy.

Shaw v Gould (p 401 below)

Padolecchia v Padolecchia [1968] P 314, [1967] 3 All ER 863 (Divorce Division)

Man's undefended petition for nullity of marriage on the ground of his own bigamy.

The petitioner, Ciro Padolecchia, an Italian national domiciled in Italy, married Maria Rosa in Italy in 1953. That marriage was indissoluble under Italian law. In 1957 the petitioner went to Venezuela and in December 1958 obtained a divorce by proxy from Maria Rosa in Mexico. He never set foot in Mexico, nor did Maria Rosa. That divorce was recognised in Venezuela but not in Italy. In 1963 the petitioner was transferred by his employers to Denmark. There he met the respondent Birte Leis, a Danish citizen domiciled in Denmark. On 1 February 1964 he and the respondent came to England for one day and were married at a London register office. They intended to settle in Denmark and live together there. There was intermittent cohabitation between them in Denmark for three or four months when the respondent left the matrimonial home and did not return.

In 1966 the petitioner presented his petition for nullity, alleging that at the time of the Mexican divorce he was domiciled in Venezuela and that he was now domiciled in Luxembourg, and that Maria Rosa was still alive on 1 February 1964. The respondent did not appear and was not represented.

Sir Jocelyn Simon P stated the facts, and held that he had jurisdiction to hear the case because the marriage was celebrated in England. This part of the judgment is omitted because under section 5 (3) of the Domicile and

2 [1940] Ch 46, 108 LJCh 427.

Matrimonial Proceedings Act 1973 (p 295 below) there is no longer
jurisdiction to annul a marriage on this ground. He continued: I turn then to
consider the validity of this marriage—in other words, choice of law in
contradistinction to jurisdiction. The marriage having taken place in
England, where monogamy is the rule, neither party could contract
matrimony with a person who was partner in a subsisting marriage. The
question which arises is, therefore, whether the petitioner's marriage to
Maria Rosa was still subsisting on 1 February 1964, or had been validly
dissolved by the Mexican decree of December 1958. That itself involves two
questions, which I may perhaps call 'a space problem' and 'a time problem'.
The space problem is: by what law does one ascertain whether the marriage
was still subsisting or had been validly dissolved? The time problem is: at
what time does one ascertain such law; in the context of the present case, is it
at the time of the Mexican decree in December 1958, or at the time of the
English marriage on 1 February 1964?

First, then, for the space problem. Each party must be capable of
marrying by the law of his or her respective antenuptial domicile: see *Dicey
and Morris*.[3] Moreover, since nobody who is still married can validly contract
a marriage in a monogamous country, nor can anybody validly contract
marriage in a monogamous country with a person who is already married, if
either party is already married by either's personal law, the marriage is
invalid (cf *Re Paine*;[4] *Pugh v Pugh*[5]).

I must therefore ascertain what the relevant domiciliary laws say about
this matter. It is conceded that Venezuelan law would recognise the
Mexican divorce as validly terminating the marriage. It is clear that Italian
law would not recognise the Mexican decree as having such effect.

(His Lordship considered an affidavit on Danish law from which it
appeared that Danish law would probably not recognise the Mexican
divorce. He said that the affidavit was technically defective because the
deponent did not state the source of his information, and that if the case
turned on Danish law it might be necessary to investigate the matter further.
He also considered an affidavit on Luxemburg law from which it appeared
that the recognition of the Mexican divorce was an open question in
Luxembourg law and could not be determined until a decree of the
Luxembourg court was applied for by an appropriate claimant. He
continued:)

But in my view none of these questions needs to be resolved in the present
case, for the following reasons. Although the petitioner affirms that he was
domiciled in Venezuela at the time of the Mexican divorce decree, and
domiciled in Luxembourg at the time of the English marriage and later, there
is no evidence that satisfies me that the petitioner ever abandoned his
domicile of origin in Italy. Indeed, apart from his own declarations (which
are admittedly made against his interest) there is every indication to the
contrary. I therefore hold that the petitioner retained his domicile of origin
in Italy at all material times; and there can be no doubt that his Italian
domiciliary personal law does not recognise and at no time recognised the
Mexican divorce decree as valid to terminate his marriage to Maria Rosa.

3 *Conflict of Laws* (8th edn, 1967) p 254, rule 31.
4 [1940] Ch 46, 108 LJCh 427.
5 [1951] P 482, [1951] 2 All ER 680; p 246 above.

Since I have found that the petitioner at all material times retained his Italian domicile of origin, the time problem does not fall for necessary decision. . . .

My conclusions therefore are as follows: (1) I have jurisdiction to make a decree of nullity in respect of the marriage of 1 February 1964, because it was celebrated in England. (2) The petitioner was at all material times domiciled in Italy. (3) By the Italian law of his immediate antenuptial domicile his marriage to Maria Rosa was still subsisting and had not been dissolved by the Mexican decree of December 1958. (4) The petitioner was on 1 February 1964, by his personal law incapable, by reason that he was partner of a still subsisting marriage, of entering into a fresh marriage in England. (5) Accordingly the ceremony of 1 February 1964 was incapable of constituting a valid marriage and was null and void. (6) I so decree.

QUESTION

Is it necessary, or desirable, for the same test to be applied to determine capacity to marry, irrespective of the alleged ground of incapacity? (Cf *Radwan v Radwan* p 280 at 283 below.)

R v Brentwood Superintendent Marriage Registrar, ex parte Arias [1968] 2 QB 956, [1968] 3 All ER 279 (Divisional Court)

Application for an order of mandamus.

Signor Galli, an Italian national domiciled in Switzerland, married a Swiss national in Switzerland. They were divorced in Switzerland and the wife remarried. Signor Galli and the applicant, a spinster of Spanish nationality and Swiss domicile, desired to marry in England. Notice of intended marriage was given to the registrar, but he refused to issue a certificate on the ground that in his view there was an impediment to the marriage. By Swiss law, capacity to marry is governed by the law of the nationality, and by Italian law Signor Galli had no capacity to remarry. The parties came to England temporarily to evade Swiss law; they both intended to return to Switzerland after their marriage. The marriage would not be recognised as valid in Switzerland or in most of the countries of western Europe. The applicant applied for an order of mandamus to compel the registrar to issue a certificate.

Sachs LJ: . . . Naturally one has considerable sympathy with those who, though already de facto living together, desire to obtain the benefit of clergy for that state of affairs, and that sympathy of course extends to the benefit of a registrar's marriage lines. But a court's decision cannot be given simply on grounds of sympathy. Especially is that the case when important questions of law involving status are involved, for any question relating to marriage ipso facto involves status, and status is particularly a matter for the law of the country in which the parties are domiciled. As is stated in one section of Dicey and Morris *Conflict of Laws*,[6] '. . . a person's capacity to marry is a matter of public concern to the country of his domicile.'

6 8th edn (1967) p 257.

That passage reflects what has been stated over many generations to be the law and policy of this country on that subject. It is only necessary to refer to a passage in the speech of Lord Campbell LC in *Brook v Brook* where he said:[7] (His Lordship read the passage on p 235 above, beginning 'It is quite obvious' and ending 'fundamental institutions').

The fact that the parties to a proposed marriage cannot marry according to the law of the country in which they are domiciled is, as a normal rule, a lawful impediment to their being married in this country. That follows from what in Dicey and Morris *Conflict of Laws,* is stated as rule 31: 'Capacity to marry is governed by the law of each party's antenuptial domicile.'

Mr de Pinna (counsel for the applicant) accordingly sought to get round that formidable obstacle by establishing that the case fell within an exception to the normal rule. He submitted that as Signor Galli's ex-wife was able to remarry whilst he was unable so to do, the law of Switzerland was such that the courts of this country should ignore it. The grounds for ignoring it were put forward as follows: that because of its discrimination between husband and wife or because it was penal or because it involved factors, religious or otherwise, which this country would disregard, the Swiss law was, to use the phraseology of Sir Jocelyn Simon P in *Cheni v Cheni*:[8] '... so offensive to the conscience of English courts that they should refuse to recognise and give effect to it.'

In aid of this submission numerous authorities were cited by Mr de Pinna but none of them concerned proposed marriages, and none even concerned a marriage where at the date of its celebration both parties were domiciled in the same foreign country and intended to remain domiciled there. On the contrary, those cases, which included *Chetti v Chetti*,[9] concerned marriages in which one party was domiciled at the relevant time in this country and thus related to what Dicey and Morris *Conflict of Laws*,[10] refers to as exception 3:

'The validity of a marriage celebrated in England between persons of whom the one has an English and the other a foreign domicile is not affected by an incapacity which, though existing under the law of such foreign domicile, does not exist under the law of England.'

Accordingly, it does not seem necessary to discuss those authorities, for they do not touch a case where both parties have the same foreign domicile and that is also their intended domicile after the marriage, if any, has been celebrated.

The Swiss law on the particular matter under consideration—under which a divorce has been decreed but the husband is yet not free to remarry—may well not seem attractive to those who sit in these courts, but it is one which Mr de Pinna has conceded would be recognised in all the countries contiguous to Switzerland: indeed that concession, as already indicated, applies to all the other countries of western Europe. Suffice it then to say that Mr de Pinna has not convinced me that this particular facet of Swiss law falls within any exception which he has urged upon this court. The mere fact that the law of another European country is different from that obtaining here

---

7 (1861) 9 HL Cas 193 at 212.
8 [1965] P 85 at 99, [1962] 3 All ER 873 at 883; p 259 at 264 below.
9 [1909] P 67, 78 LJP 23.
10 8th edn, p 269.

and is not attractive to those who sit in these courts is clearly not in the above circumstances sufficient to bring it within exceptions of that type.

I would, incidentally, refer in this behalf to a passage in the judgment of Pearce J in *Igra v Igra*,[11] when a parallel submission was made to him about recognition of decrees of divorce, and he said:

'It has long been accepted that the court of the domicile is the proper tribunal to dissolve a marriage. Its decision should, as far as reasonably possible, be acknowledged by other countries in the interests of comity. Different countries have different personal laws, different standards of justice and different practice. The interests of comity are not served if one country is too eager to criticise the standards of another country or too reluctant to recognise decrees that are valid by the law of the domicile.'

Mutatis mutandis, to my mind, that passage applies equally where questions of capacity to marry come under consideration.

One might perhaps add that those who live in legal glass houses, however well-constructed, should perhaps not be over-astute to throw stones at the laws of other countries. Our own divorce laws have facets which may well seem unusual to or even to lack attractions for those who apply a continental system of jurisprudence. For instance, as a result of section 40 (1) of the Matrimonial Causes Act 1965,[12] an Italian wife after residing for three years in this country can secure a decree of divorce against an Italian domiciled husband, yet the husband in question is not entitled in the proceedings here to cross-petiton for divorce against the wife even though the offence of which he complains is graver and earlier than that complained of by her....

Lord Parker CJ and Bridge J concurred.
Application refused.

Perrini v Perrini [1979] Fam 84, [1979] 2 All ER 323 (Family Division)

Woman's petition for nullity of marriage.

In September 1957 the husband, Ennio Giovanni Perrini, an Italian national domiciled and resident in Italy, was married at Bari in Italy to Irene Santonastaso, an American woman resident in New Jersey on holiday in Italy. The marriage was never consummated and Irene immediately returned to her mother's home in New Jersey. In October 1960 a New Jersey court annulled the marriage for non-consummation. Jurisdiction was founded on the bona fide residence of Irene within the state for at least six months prior to her application. The decree would not be recognised in Italy and by Italian law the husband was not free to remarry. In 1967 the husband, still domiciled in Italy, married in London an Englishwoman whom he had met while she was on holiday in Italy. At that time Irene was still alive. Later in 1967 the husband acquired a domicile of choice in England.

Sir George Baker P stated the facts, and continued: I now come to the question in the case which is: was the husband free to marry in England, or

---

11 [1951] P 404 at 412.
12 Now repealed (*Ed*).

was he still married by the Bari marriage, despite the New Jersey decree? The argument for the wife is founded on the rule that each party must be capable of marrying by the law of his or her respective antenuptial domicile: see *Pugh v Pugh*;[13] *Padolecchia v Padolecchia*[14] and Dicey & Morris *The Conflict of Laws*.[15]

In *Padolecchia v Padolecchia*, the fourth conclusion of Sir Jocelyn Simon P was: 'The petitioner was on 1 February 1964, [the date of his English marriage] by his personal law incapable, by reason that he was partner of a still subsisting marriage, of entering into a fresh marriage in England.' In that case the husband, who had at all material times retained his Italian domicile, had married an Italian woman in Italy. A Mexican court granted him a proxy divorce which was not recognised by Italian law as validly dissolving the Italian marriage. Substitute New Jersey decree for Mexican decree and the material facts are the same as in the present case.

(His Lordship referred to *Indyka v Indyka*,[16] a case on the recognition of foreign divorces, and continued): So there is an exception to the domicile rule in that a divorce decree based on residence of the appropriate quality is capable of recognition in England although it would not be recognised in Italy.

In *Law v Gustin*[17] Bagnall J applied *Indyka v Indyka* to a decree of nullity; I respectfully agree with his decision. It follows that a further category must be added to rule 50 in Dicey & Morris *The Conflict of Laws*,[18] which, as is pointed out at p 369, cannot be said to be exhaustive. As reliance has been placed on rule 50, it is pertinent to point out that it is: 'A foreign decree of nullity will be recognised in England... (3) If the nullity decree would be recognised by the courts of the country where, at the date of the commencement of the proceedings, the parties were domiciled.' That merely states one in an incomplete catalogue of circumstances in which a decree would be recognised. It does not purport to lay down that other decrees not based on such domicile cannot be recognised.

In my judgment the New Jersey decree can be recognised in England with the result, if it is so recognised, that both parties—Irene and the husband— were free to marry in England from the date of the New Jersey decree.

Should it be recognised? At the time of the New Jersey decree an English court had jurisdiction to entertain proceedings by a wife for divorce or nullity by section 18 (1) (b) of the Matrimonial Causes Act 1950:

'... if the wife is resident in England and has been ordinarily resident there for a period of three years immediately preceding the commencement of the proceedings, and the husband is not domiciled in any other part of the United Kingdom...'

This provision was re-enacted by section 40 of the Matrimonial Causes Act 1965 and section 46 of the Matrimonial Causes Act 1973 which was repealed by the Domicile and Matrimonial Proceedings Act 1973, Schedule 6, but restated in section 5 (3) of that Act as follows:

13 [1951] P 482, [1951] 2 All ER 680; p 246 above.
14 [1968] P 314, [1967] 3 All ER 863; p 249 above.
15 9th edn (1973) p 258, Rule 34.
16 [1969] 1 AC 33, [1967] 2 All ER 689.
17 [1976] Fam 155, [1976] 1 All ER 113.
18 9th edn, p 364.

'The court shall have jurisdiction to entertain proceedings for nullity of marriage if (and only if) either of the parties... (b) was habitually resident in England and Wales throughout the period of one year ending with that date' [when proceedings were begun].

Lord Pearce said in *Indyka*:[19] 'In my opinion the question whether a foreign decree should be recognised should be answered by the court in the light of its present policy, regardless within reason of when the decree was granted.'

True, the New Jersey jurisdiction was founded only on a requirement of bona fide residence of at least six months before the application, so even applying Lord Pearce's opinion the present 12 months' habitual residence required by English law might not be fulfilled, but on any view of the evidence before the New Jersey court there was bona fide residence within that jurisdiction for 'at least two years' and 'for the last three years' before the application. In *Robinson-Scott v Robinson-Scott*[20] Karminski J answered the question whether the courts in this country can recognise a foreign decree where in fact the wife was resident in the territory of the foreign court for three years immediately preceding the commencement of the proceedings there even though the jurisdiction of the foreign court was based on different grounds, thus:

> 'where, in fact, there has been three years' residence by a wife in the territory of the foreign court assuming jurisdiction in a suit for dissolution, the English court should accept that as a ground for exercising jurisdiction, because it would itself accept jurisdiction on proof of similar residence in England. It is not essential for recognition by this court that the foreign court should assume jurisdiction on the grounds laid down by section 18 of the Matrimonial Causes Act 1950. It is sufficient that facts exist which would enable the English courts to assume jurisdiction.'

This passage was approved as 'recognised in practice as a proper test' by Lord Reid in *Indyka*.[1]

I am unable to discover any reason why any different principle should apply to a decree of nullity and as the English statutory provisions cover both divorce and nullity there is every reason why the principle should apply. It follows that independently of anything said in *Indyka* the New Jersey decree ought to be recognised by this court and I recognise it. Once recognised it must be taken to have declared the pretended marriage a nullity, with each party free to marry. It does not deal only with the status of Irene—a sort of one-legged decree—but with the status of both. This is best illustrated, if that be necessary, by supposing Irene to have been an English woman living, for the requisite three years, with her parents in New Malden instead of New Jersey. A decree of nullity in the English court would leave each free to marry by a civil ceremony in England or Wales. Once the New Jersey decree is recognised here the fact that the respondent could not marry in Italy, the country of his domicile, on 8 April 1967, is, in my opinion, no bar to his marrying in England where by the New Jersey decree he was free to marry. No incapacity existed in England law.

19 At 91 and 717, respectively.
20 [1958] P 71 at 87–88, [1957] 3 All ER 473 at 478.
 1 At 57 and 695, respectively.

The result is then that on the issue I find that the London wedding was and is valid. I cannot pretend to be other than satisfied with this result because I think first the court should if possible uphold a marriage; second, it would be unfortunate if the respondent, on the facts of this case, were to be thought to have committed bigamy even by mistake; third, the result can demonstrate that in nullity also the courts can throw off the shackles of domicile, and, finally, it does not matter to the petitioner, to whom I have already given leave to file a further petition based on five years' separation should it be necessary. That petiton is to be undefended and I shall now hear it forthwith.

Declaration accordingly.

QUESTION

Can you reconcile this case with *R v Brentwood Superintendent Marriage Registrar*, p 251 above? If so, how? You will find the answer in [1979] Camb LJ 289, but try and work it out for yourself first.

Schwebel v Ungar (p 671 below)

Recognition of Divorces and Legal Separations Act 1971

7.[2] Where the validity of a divorce obtained in any country is entitled to recognition by virtue of sections 1 to 5 or section 6 (2) of this Act or by virtue of any rule or enactment preserved by section 6 (5) of this Act, neither spouse shall be precluded from re-marrying in the United Kingdom on the ground that the validity of the divorce would not be recognised in any other country.

NOTE

This section reverses the actual decision in *R v Brentwood Superintendent Marriage Registrar*, above. It applies to divorces obtained before as well as after the commencement of the Act: s 10 (4), p 305 below. Its limited scope should be noticed. It is confined to remarriages in the United Kingdom after a foreign (not English) decree of divorce (not nullity). The anomalous result may be that a foreign decree of divorce may have a greater effect in England than an English decree, because the validity of a remarriage in the United Kingdom after a foreign divorce is preserved by section 7, while that of a remarriage in the United Kingdom after an English divorce is not. See Cheshire & North, *Private International Law* (10th edn), pp 345–347; Morris, *Conflict of Laws* (2nd edn), pp 117–118.

However, in an unpublished Consultation Paper circulated to a selected audience in May 1983, the Law Commission and the Scottish Law Commission provisionally recommend that section 7 should be widened so as to provide that where a divorce or nullity decree is entitled to recognition in the United Kingdom, neither spouse should be regarded as incapable of remarrying, whether in the United Kingdom or elsewhere, on the ground that the divorce or annulment would not be recognised in any other country. They also recommend that a person whose marriage is dissolved or annulled in the United Kingdom should be regarded as free to remarry, whether

2 This section is printed as amended by the Domicile and Matrimonial Proceedings Act 1973 (*Ed*).

in the United Kingdom or elsewhere, notwithstanding that the law of his domicile would not recognise the divorce or annulment. A third recommendation is that a person whose foreign divorce or annulment is not recognised in the United Kingdom should not be regarded here as free to remarry, notwithstanding that the law of his domicile would recognise the divorce or annulment. This last recommendation would have the effect of reversing the controversial Canadian decision in *Schwebel v Ungar* [1965] SCR 148, 48 DLR (2d) 644, p 671 below.

An incapacity to marry imposed by a foreign lex loci celebrationis does not invalidate a marriage which is valid by the laws of the parties' antenuptial domicile.

Reed v Reed (1969) 69 WWR 327, 6 DLR (3d) 617 (Supreme Court of British Columbia)

Woman's petition for nullity of marriage on the ground of consanguinity.

Harvey J: The parties, then and now domiciled in British Columbia, went through a form of marriage in the State of Washington in 1948, and thereafter returned at once to British Columbia, where they continued to reside until their separation in 1968. They are first cousins and went to Washington to be married because of parental disapproval. As the plaintiff was a minor, aged 18, her parents' consent to her marriage was required by the laws of British Columbia but not by the laws of Washington. However, unknown to the parties, the laws of the State of Washington, unlike British Columbia, prohibited the marriage of first cousins by reason of consanguinity. An attorney at law from that state gave evidence that this prohibition has been in effect since statehood and that a 'marriage' entered into between persons of this degree of consanguinity is unlawful and void ab initio. The claim for a declaration of nullity of marriage is based on this situation and this alone. It is conceded (in fact proved) that the laws of Washington were observed with reference to the formalities of a marriage ceremony. The matter of parental consent is considered to be part of the ceremony of marriage and not a matter affecting the personal capacity of the parties to enter into a contract of marriage. Hence the absence of parental consent is governed not by the laws of British Columbia but by those of Washington: *Halsbury's Laws of England*;[3] *Solomon v Walters*.[4] Apart, therefore, from the matter of consanguinity there is no doubt that the parties are lawfully married. As to this the plaintiff contends that the laws of Washington apply so as to render the marriage void.

The plaintiff bases her case on *Berthiaume v Dastous*,[5] a judgment of the Privy Council in a Canadian appeal. (His Honour stated the facts in that case and quoted the passage beginning 'If there is one question better settled than another' and ending 'would be considered a good marriage' on p 220 above, and continued):

It is quite clear that this judgment deals only with the formal requirements of a marriage and not with the capacity of the parties to enter into a contract of marriage. Their Lordships were expressly 'putting aside the question of

3 3rd edn, vol 7, p 93.
4 (1956) 18 WWR 257, 3 DLR (2d) 78.
5 [1930] AC 79, 99 LJPC 66; p 219 above.

capacity'. This is a question having to do with the essentials and the intrinsic validity of the contract of marriage. The distinction was made clear in an earlier case in the House of Lords—*Brook v Brook*,[6] in which Lord Campbell LC said at 207: 'But while the forms of entering into the contract of marriage are to be regulated by the lex loci contractus, the law of the country in which it is celebrated, the essentials of the contract depend upon the lex domicilii, the law of the country in which the parties are domiciled at the time of the marriage, and in which the matrimonial residence is contemplated.'

It is urged, however, by the plaintiff that even as regards capacity the lex loci celebrationis cannot be disregarded when, under that law, the marriage is illegal. Support for this view may be found in the writings of learned authors but, as in the passage I have italicised from the following citation from Cheshire *Private International Law*,[7] it is conceded to lack judicial sanction:

'The contention, however, that the law of the matrimonial home is the proper law to govern the validity of a marriage, except with regard to formalities, does not mean that the law of the place where the marriage is actually solemnised is to be disregarded. That would be impossible. Obviously no system of law can allow its procedure to be used as an instrument for the contracting of unions which it considers void owing to youthfulness, incest, or any other reason. Every legal system requires that a marriage contracted under its protection shall conform not only to the local formalities but also to the local rules with regard to matrimonial capacity. *Therefore, if we were free to lay down the law without reference to authority,* we should prefer to say that a marriage which lacks essential validity either by the law of the place where it is solemnised, or by the law of the matrimonial home, is void everywhere. Conversely, that a marriage which is valid by the law of the matrimonial home is valid everywhere, provided that, if it is solemnised in some country other than that of the matrimonial home, it complies with the lex loci celebrationis with regard to both form and capacity.'

[Italics added.]

I have also been referred to Dicey and Morris on *The Conflict of Laws*,[8] in which this appears:

'A more difficult question is the validity of a marriage celebrated in a foreign country which the parties had capacity to contract by the law of their domicile, but not by the law of the place of celebration... in *Breen v Breen*,[9] Karminski J was prepared to hold that the parties' incapacity to marry by the lex loci celebrationis was fatal to the validity of their marriage, even though this would have meant denying the validity of a decree of divorce pronounced by the High Court.'

Having read with care the report of *Breen v Breen*, I can find no intimation that Karminski J was prepared to make the finding attributed to him. What he did find was that the laws of Eire did not prohibit the remarriage in Eire

6 (1861) 9 HLCas 193, 4 LT 93; p 232 above.
7 3rd edn, p 277. The passage cited does not appear in the 10th edn (*Ed*).
8 8th edn (1967) p 268.
9 [1964] P 144, [1961] 3 All ER 225.

of a man whose prior marriage had been dissolved by a court of the country of his domicile (England). His judgment in no way supports the proposition that incapacity to marry by the lex loci celebrationis but not by lex domicilii is fatal to the validity of a marriage. I have been referred to no authority which goes this far or which supports the views expressed by Cheshire, above, although it can fairly be said that difficulty does exist in reconciling the many cases I have examined.

As the parties to this action were domiciled in British Columbia at the time of their marriage and intended to and did remain so domiciled, and as they had capacity to marry under the laws of this Province notwithstanding that they were first cousins, their marriage in the State of Washington, conforming as it did with the formal requirements of that jurisdiction, is a valid marriage. The claim for a declaration of nullity of marriage is dismissed.

NOTE

In *Breen v Breen*, above, the parties were at all material times domiciled in England. They married in Dublin during the lifetime of the husband's first wife, from whom he had been divorced in England. The second wife petitioned for a decree of nullity on the ground that the divorce decree would not be recognised in the Republic of Ireland, and that therefore the husband lacked capacity to marry by Irish law. A clause in the Irish Constitution provided somewhat obscurely that a remarriage by either party in the lifetime of a former spouse after a decree of divorce was void. There were conflicting dicta in the Irish courts as to whether this extended to divorces granted in the country of the parties' domicile. Karminski J reviewed these dicta and preferred those which indicated that the Constitution did not extend to such divorces. He therefore pronounced the remarriage valid. But if he had preferred the other set of dicta, he would evidently have been prepared to hold that the remarriage was void, even if this meant declining to recognise a decree pronounced by the High Court in England. Therefore it is submitted that the passage from Dicey and Morris quoted in *Reed v Reed*, above, is quite correct.

QUESTION

Could the headnote to *Reed v Reed* have been correctly formulated without the word 'foreign'? In other words, if a marriage is celebrated in England, eg between uncle and niece or between parties one of whom is under 16, would incapacity by English law invalidate the marriage if it was valid by the law of the parties' domicile? See the dictum of Pearce J in *Pugh v Pugh*, p 247 above.

It is not contrary to public policy to recognise a marriage between uncle and niece if it was valid by the law of the parties' antenuptial domicile.

Cheni v Cheni [1965] P 85, [1962] 3 All ER 873 (Divorce Division)

Woman's petition for nullity of marriage on the ground of consanguinity.

The parties were Sephardic Jews domiciled in Egypt. They went through a ceremony of marriage in Jewish form in Cairo in 1924. The husband was the wife's maternal uncle. In 1926 a child was born. They lived in Egypt until 1957 when they left for England and acquired a domicile here. The wife then petitioned for nullity. By Egyptian law, the religious law of the parties determined the validity of their marriage. By Jewish law, a marriage between uncle and niece was valid. The marriage was potentially polygamous at its inception but became monogamous when the child was born.

Sir Jocelyn Simon P (having held that the marriage had become monogamous and therefore he had jurisdiction to adjudicate on the validity of the marriage, continued): On this part of the case Dr Gaon (Chief Rabbi of the Spanish and Portuguese Jewish community in Great Britain and religious leader of the Sephardic Jewish community here) told me that a marriage between uncle and niece is in accordance with general Jewish law. This was spelt out further by Professor James, Professor of the History of Religions at London University, and formerly a member of the Archbishops' Commission on Kindred and Affinity, 1937. In the Levitical Code marriage between aunt and nephew was prohibited, but not marriage between uncle and niece (see The Book of Leviticus, Ch 18, verses 12–14). The distinction reflected the Jewish emphasis on the family as a primary unit of society, the aunt-nephew relationship reversing the natural order of authority, whereas in the uncle-niece relationship there is no confusion of authority. In Christianity up to the schism between the Eastern and Western Catholic Churches marriage was prohibited up to the relationship of first cousins, so that the relationship of uncle and niece, which was closer, invalidated a marriage. After 1064 the Western Church maintained its prohibition of marriages between uncle and niece and first cousins, but the impediment was capable under special circumstances of dispensation by the Pope. The uncle-niece impediment would be dispensed with only to avoid some greater evil, generally of a political nature. This is still much the situation in the Roman Catholic Church: the Revised Codex of 1918 shows that close consanguinous relationship in marriage is discouraged, though dispensable up to the first degree collaterally, ie, the brother-sister relationship. The Reformation involved a general reaction against the papal system of dispensation. Luther dismissed the whole process and returned to the Levitical Code as the expression of God's will. The uncle-niece relationship is therefore permitted in many Lutheran churches, and the aunt-nephew relationship prohibited; though some Lutheran churches, such as those in this country and the United States, follow, as they are bound to, the law of the land. Calvin, on the other hand, did not accept the Levitical Code literally, but applied it by parity of reasoning. Uncle-niece and aunt-nephew stand in the same degree of blood relationship; the Levitical prohibition of aunt-nephew marriages was therefore applied to uncle-niece marriages. The Anglican communion in this respect followed the Calvinist line.

Mr Stirling (counsel for the petitioner) accepts that this marriage was valid by the law of the parties' domicile, which is the proper law by which capacity to marry is to be tested. But, he says, there is an exception to this general rule, in that the courts of this country will not recognise the validity of a marriage which, even though valid by its proper law, is incestuous by the general consent of all Christendom, or, as he prefers to put it, by the general consent of civilised nations or by English public policy. A marriage between uncle and niece is such a marriage. The foundation of Mr Stirling's argument is a passage from the famous book on Conflict of Laws, by Story J (8th edn, 1883) p 188. This reads: 'The most prominent . . . exceptions to the rule are marriages involving polygamy and incest . . . Christianity is understood to prohibit polygamy and incest, and therefore no Christian country would recognise polygamy or incestuous marriages. But when we speak of incestuous marriages, care must be taken to confine the doctrine to such cases as by the general consent of all Christendom are deemed incestuous.' But there are two preliminary points to be noted. First, it is now clear that English courts will recognise for most purposes the validity of polygamous marriages, notwithstanding that they are prohibited by Christianity. Secondly, Story himself quotes with approval (p 190) the observation of Kent Ch (2 Kent Com 83, 84) that it will be found difficult to carry the exception as to incest further in the collateral line than the first degree, save where the legislature has expressly provided such a prohibition. Mr Stirling nevertheless says that the present case falls within the exception. He argues that the words '*all* Christendom' are not to be taken literally, since otherwise the word 'general' is without force. As regards the Roman Catholic Church, uncle-niece marriages are considered incestuous, even though there may be in very exceptional circumstances a papal dispensation. They are so regarded by the Anglican communion and by Calvinist churches; and many Lutheran churches follow the law of the land in prohibiting them. Only a handful of Lutheran national churches will regard such marriages as other than incestuous. This means that in truth they are incestuous by the general, even though not the universal, consent of Christendom.

It does not appear that Story J's exception as to marriages incestuous by the general consent of Christendom has ever been applied to invalidate a marriage good by the law of its domicile.

In *Brook v Brook*[10] the House of Lords held to be void a marriage in Denmark between brother-in-law and sister-in-law, on the ground that such a marriage was prohibited as 'contrary to God's law' by a statute which was part of the law not only of the forum but of the parties' common domicile in England. Lord Cranworth quoted the passage from Story with approval, but explained that Story was speaking of a country whose marriage laws were silent as to polygamy and incest. He went on: 'It could never be held that the subjects of such a country were guilty of incest in contracting a marriage allowed and approved by a large proportion of Christendom.' Lord Wensleydale agreed with this explanation; as did also the Court of Appeal in *Sottomayor v De Barros*,[11] where it was said: 'It is hardly possible to suppose that the law of England, or of any Christian country, would consider as valid a marriage which the general consent of Christendom declared to be incestuous.' As appears from the evidence, several Christian countries do consider a marriage between uncle and niece as valid. In *Re De Wilton*,[12] uncle and niece, domiciled British subjects, went through a ceremony of marriage in Wiesbaden according to Jewish rites. The marriage was valid by the law of the place of celebration as well as by Jewish law. The case is at least of negative significance, since Story's exception was apparently not

10 (1861) 9 HLC 193, 4 LT 93; p 232 above.
11 (1877) 3 PD 1, 47 LJP 23; p 237 above.
12 [1900] 2 Ch 481, 69 LJCh 717.

considered relevant, as it was not referred to, the case turning on the English domicile of the parties and being governed by *Brook v Brook*. It is, moreover, of interest in showing the acceptance of such a marriage in a Lutheran country. In *Re Bozzelli's Settlement*,[13] the court was concerned with a marriage in Italy between two domiciled Italians who were brother and sister-in-law. The comments on Story in *Brook v Brook* were cited, but the marriage was held to be valid in England notwithstanding Lord Lyndhurst's Act. Swinfen Eady J said: 'I have a marriage which is not only valid according to the law of the particular domicile, but is also valid by the law of many other countries, and certainly cannot be regarded as incestuous by the general consent of Christendom.' *Peal v Peal*[14] was a suit for restitution of conjugal rights; the respondent filed a cross-petition for a decree of nullity on the ground that the petitioner was his aunt. The parties were British subjects of the Roman Catholic faith whose families had been resident in India for four generations. A special dispensation for the celebration of their marriage had been granted by their proper ecclesiastical authority. Lord Merrivale P assumed an Indian domicile of the parties, and the case turned on what law in that event governed their capacity to marry and whether that law permitted the removal of the impediment to their marriage. It was held that the relevant Indian statutes left the capacity to marry to be determined by the personal law; the parties in question being British subjects of European origin, this under the law of British India was English law. Marriage between persons in the relationship of the petitioner and the respondent was therefore precluded, and nothing in the local statutes permitted its dispensation, so that a decree of nullity was pronounced. Once again the case turned on the fact that the personal law of the parties imposed an incapacity. It does, however, indicate that the power of papal dispensation for the relationship in question is not in modern times confined in its exercise to persons or occasions of political importance. Indeed, it appears from Esmein *Mariage en Droit Canonique*,[15] that the Council of Trent had endeavoured to establish the principle that dispensation in the second degree should be accorded grudgingly, but without achieving any serious influence.

In the first edition of his book on Conflict of Laws, Professor Dicey followed Story in excepting from the general rule that capacity to marry is governed by the law of the domicile those marriages which are incestuous by the laws of all Christian countries. He omitted the exception from subsequent editions in deference to Westlake's observation,[16] that there was no necessity for it, 'because no country with which the communion of private international law exists has such marriages'. The editor of the current edition of *Dicey*[17] observes: 'It may be doubted, however, whether there is much realism in the notion of a charmed circle of "civilised" countries within which the "communion" of private international law exists, and outside which it does not. Accordingly it is believed that a marriage between (for example) a half-brother and half-sister, or between persons one of whom was a very young child, or a marriage entered into under duress, would for most

13 [1902] 1 Ch 751, 71 LJCh 505.
14 [1931] P 97, 100 LJP 69.
15 2nd edn (1935) Vol 2, p 391.
16 *Private International Law*, s 21.
17 7th edn (1957) p 253.

purposes be refused recognition in England on grounds of public policy, even if it was valid by the lex loci celebrationis and by the law of each party's antenuptial domicile.' *Halsbury's Laws of England*,[18] also states that 'The English courts refuse to recognise any marriage regarded as incestuous by the general consent of Christendom' and continues: '...the expression "Christendom" cannot be easily defined at the present day when in so many countries, whose inhabitants profess the Christian faith, legislative enactments have made marked departures from the canon law which was universal when the Church of Rome was the only Christian Church and practically the sole maker of matrimonial laws. In general the phrase nowadays would seem to embrace civilised nations, and not exclusively those which profess the doctrines of Christianity....' It is on the first of these authorities that Mr Stirling relies in invoking English public policy, on the second in substituting 'civilised nations' for the words 'all Christendom' in Story. In this connection he seeks, although no evidence was adduced on the point, to refer to Burge's *Colonial and Foreign Law*,[19] in order to show that in both Hindu and Mohammedan law marriage between uncle and niece is unlawful. The vast majority of the civilised world, therefore, he argues, rejects such marriages.

So far as public policy is concerned, Mr Stirling truly says that such marriages are void here by section 1 (1) of and Schedule I to the Marriage Act 1949. This is, however, expressly limited to marriages in England and affords me no guidance on how our law would regard foreign marriages good by their proper law. Mr Stirling also relies on *Burgess v Burgess*,[20] where the office of the judge was successfully promoted to separate an uncle and niece who were cohabiting without marriage as if husband and wife. Mr Argyle (counsel for the respondent) replies, I think with force, that current public policy on incestuous relationships is to be ascertained less by looking at an ecclesiastical criminal jurisdiction which is now obsolete than by examining the modern statutes proscribing incest. Neither by the Incest Act 1908, whereby incest was for the first time cognisable by our lay criminal law, nor by its re-enactment in the Sexual Offences Act 1956, ss 10 and 11, is it an offence for an uncle to have sexual intercourse with his niece. Even though the criminal law prohibits bigamy, public policy does not prevent our recognising and generally giving effect to polygamous marriages valid by their proper law; and it would be strange if public policy demanded our rejection of marriages constituted by a relationship of which our criminal law takes no notice. In any event, the law proceeds charily where grounds of public policy are invoked.

As I have said, there is no case in which Story's exception of marriages regarded as incestuous by the common consent of all Christendom has been applied, and I think that Westlake's criticism of it is valid. It does not, in my judgment, represent the law. Nor is there sufficient reason or any authority for rephrasing or glossing the passage in the alternative ways suggested. I believe the true rule to be that the courts of this country will exceptionally refuse to recognise and give effect to a capacity or incapacity to marry by the law of the domicile on the ground that to give it recognition and effect would

18 3rd edn (1954) Vol 7, p 90.
19 New edn (1910), Vol 3, pp 144–145.
20 (1804) 1 Hag Con 384.

be unconscionable in the circumstances in question. The rule is thus an example of a wider class which has received authoritative judicial acknowledgment in our private international law. 'No country is bound to recognise the laws of a foreign state when they work injustice to its own subjects', said Cotton LJ, giving the judgment of the Court of Appeal in *Sottomayor v De Barros*. Nor do I think that the principle is necessarily limited to protection of British subjects. As long ago as *Sommersett's* case[1] the Court of the King's Bench refused to recognise and give effect to a foreign status of slavery. In *Pemberton v Hughes*[2] the Court of Appeal laid down that a judgment by a foreign court of competent jurisdiction will be treated as conclusive, provided the proceedings do not offend against English notions of substantial justice; and this statement of the law was approved by the House of Lords in *Von Lorang v Administrator of Austrian Property*;[3] see especially per Viscount Haldane and per Viscount Dunedin. The proviso was applied in the recent case of *Gray v Formosa*,[4] where the Court of Appeal refused to accept a decree of nullity pronounced by the court of the husband's domicile on the ground that to do so would be contrary to our notions of justice. In *Re Langley's Settlement Trusts*[5] the Court of Appeal held that it had a discretion to refuse to give operation to the results of a status of incompetency imposed on a settlor by the Californian law of his domicile where to do so would be manifestly unjust and illogical. In *Russ v Russ*[6] the Court of Appeal distinguished *R v Superintendent Registrar of Marriages, Hammersmith; ex p Mir-Anwaruddin*[7] on the ground, inter alia, that the court was there exercising just such a discretionary power to disregard the law of the domicile.

But whatever test is adopted, the marriage in this case was in my judgment a valid one. I do not consider that a marriage which may be the subject of papal dispensation and will then be acknowledged as valid by all Roman Catholics, which without any such qualification is acceptable to all Lutherans, can reasonably be said to be contrary to the general consent of Christendom; and the passages I have quoted from Story himself and from those who have commented on him bear this out. If the general consent of civilised nations were to be the test, I do not think that the matter can be resolved by, so to speak, taking a card-vote of the United Nations and disregarding the views of the many civilised countries by whose laws these marriages are permissible. As Mr Argyle observed, Eygpt, where these people lived and where the marriage took place, is itself a civilised country. If domestic public policy were the test, it seems to me that the arguments on behalf of the husband, founded on such inferences as one can draw from the scope of the English criminal law, prevail. Moreover, they weigh with me when I come to apply what I believe to be the true test, namely, whether the marriage is so offensive to the conscience of the English court that it should refuse to recognise and give effect to the proper foreign law. In deciding that question the court will seek to exercise common sense, good manners and a reasonable tolerance. In my view it would be altogether too queasy a judicial

1 (1772) 20 State Tr 1.
2 [1899] 1 Ch 781, 68 LJCh 281; p 168 above.
3 [1927] AC 641, 96 LJPC 105; p 318 below.
4 [1963] P 259, [1962] 3 All ER 419.
5 [1962] Ch 541, [1961] 3 All ER 803.
6 [1964] P 315, [1962] 3 All ER 193.
7 [1917] 1 KB 634, 86 LJKB 210.

conscience which would recoil from a marriage acceptable to many peoples of deep religious convictions, lofty ethical standards and high civilisation. Nor do I think that I am bound to consider such marriages merely as a generality. On the contrary, I must have regard to this particular marriage, which, valid by the religious law of the parties' common faith and by the municipal law of their common domicile, has stood unquestioned for 35 years. I must bear in mind that I am asked to declare unmarried the parents of a child who is unquestionably legitimate in the eyes of the law: *Re Bischoffsheim.*[8] In my judgment, injustice would be perpetrated and conscience would be affronted if the English court were not to recognise and give effect to the law of the domicile in this case. I therefore reject so much of the prayer of the petition as asks that this marriage be declared null and void.

Section C. Consent of parties

No marriage is valid if by the law of either party's domicile he or she does not consent to marry the other.

Szechter v Szechter [1971] P 286, [1970] 3 All ER 905 (Divorce Division)

Sir Jocelyn Simon P: By her amended petition, originally dated 15 August 1969, Nina Maria Szechter (otherwise Nina Maria Karsov)—whom I shall call 'Nina'—petitioned for a declaration of nullity, alleging that a ceremony of marriage performed (according to the certificate of registration) at Warsaw, but in fact in the Mokotow prison in Warsaw, between herself and Szymon Szechter—whom I shall call 'the respondent'—was inoperative to give rise to the status of marriage by reason of the fact, as she alleges, that she went through the ceremony as a result of duress.

It would be affectation to pretend that any judge could listen to the evidence given in this case unmoved by the courage and generosity of the persons principally concerned or by the horror of the circumstances (though I appreciate that I have heard only one side and that few, it any, peoples can claim to have been entirely and at all times innocent of inhumanity or tyranny). But part of the comparative felicity which we have enjoyed in this country has been because we have lived under the rule of law. And not only does law, as Burke said, stand in dreadful enmity to arbitrary power; the rule of law, as Dicey pointed out, stands in contradistinction to (among other things) wide discretionary authority.

There is obviously a temptation for a court, faced with a situation of hardship brought about by heroism in the teeth of cruelty and oppression, to try if necessary to stretch the law a little here or a little there. The principles of the law are indeed essentially adaptable to varying circumstances; but the principles themselves are those which have been established by juristic authority or parliamentary enactment. The operation of the law is thus

8 [1948] Ch 79, [1947] 2 All ER 830; p 404 below.

reasonably certain and predictable; and it is no service to those who live under its rule to introduce uncertainty and capriciousness, even with the ostensibly laudable aim of meeting a hard case. If there is a substantial area of hardship which the existing law does not reach, the remedy nowadays lies in the hands of Parliament, which has at its service the advice of the executive as to all foreseeable repercussions of the decision (an advantage denied to courts of law); and if even the most sagaciously framed general rule is still liable to throw up, exceptionally, some cases of hardship, it is open to Parliament, should it be so advised, to establish a court of equity to deal with such cases on their merits. But it is not open to a court of law to deal out what is sometimes called 'palm-tree justice'.

The story which has been unfolded in this court is so extraordinary as to be liable to strain credence, were it not that Nina and the respondent, who were its main narrators, were in their different ways as impressive witnesses as I have ever had before me.

Nina was born in Poland on 10 June 1940. She was of Jewish parentage, though it was only in the course of interrogation by the Polish security police in 1967 that she came to know this. When she was very young she was despatched by the Germans with her mother to an extermination camp. On the way there her mother threw her out of the railway train into the snow, hoping thereby to save her life. Her mother was successful in this object, though Nina's health was permanently impaired by the shock and exposure, her back being injured and her fingers requiring amputation. Her mother subsequently met death in an extermination camp and her father committed suicide. Nina was rescued and brought up in Warsaw by a Mrs Karsov, whom she thought to be her real mother. Mrs Karsov was a Roman Catholic and brought Nina up in that faith.

Mrs Karsov had fought with the Polish resistance movement and had been wounded in the rising of 1944. Nevertheless, in 1949 she was arrested, and after an investigation lasting 27 months she was condemned to imprisonment for 10 years for allegedly collaborating with the Germans. It was only five years later that Mrs Karsov was exculpated and released, it being accepted that she had in truth been helping to save Jews. This cruel miscarriage of justice had a profound effect on Nina. Moreover, during the time of Mrs Karsov's imprisonment Nina continued to suffer from ill-health. She contracted tuberculosis and also a pathological condition of the thyroid gland. Every year she had to spend two months in hospital for treatment of her spinal complaint. But she triumphed over all these disabilities sufficiently to gain admittance to Warsaw University, where she studied from 1958 to 1963, graduating Master of Arts. Thereafter she worked as a journalist and as an historical researcher. She also began to take an interest in the political trials then going on in Poland, generally in secret. She managed to obtain permission to attend some of these. This was a perilous privilege, since the western press was keenly interested in what was going on. Her historical and political interests brought her into contact with the respondent, a distinguished Polish historian of Jewish origin, and his wife Lydia (by which name I shall hereafter refer to her). The respondent had been blinded while fighting against the Germans. Nina became the respondent's secretary and they collaborated in written work. By 1966 Nina was being treated like a daughter of the family by the respondent and Lydia and their children.

On 12 August 1966, the respondent, Lydia and Nina were all arrested by the security police. The respondent, who was a public figure, was released 48 hours later, though Nina did not know of this for many months. She herself was detained under interrogation, without trial, in the Mokotow Prison for 10 months, and then a further four months awaiting trial. For the first four months she was kept in a cell measuring 2½ by 2 metres, which she left only for 20 minutes' exercise daily and for interrogation. She shared this cell with two other women; one a common criminal, the other accused of economic malversation. For 10 months she had no visitors, no letters, no news of the outside world. She was allowed no writing materials, nor any book until after three months.

The food was exiguous and very poor. For breakfast she had unsweetened corn coffee, half a loaf of black bread and 10 grammes of margarine. At midday she had unpeeled beetroot soup and cold, badly peeled, rotten potatoes. In the evening she had only the unsweetened coffee. At no time did she eat meat, fruit or fresh vegetables.

Her health had at all times been frail; and while she was in prison it deteriorated rapidly. After a couple of weeks the prison doctor decided that Nina ought to go to the prison hospital. This was refused by the examining judges. Nina suffered from Basedow's syndrome, a condition of hyper-thyroid, requiring controlled hormone treatment, only safely to be carried out in hospital. Such uncontrolled treatment as she was given in prison affected her heart, resulting in severe tremulousness and loss of weight. She knew already that absence of, or uncontrolled, treatment would be exceedingly dangerous for her. The condition of her heart had previously caused anxiety. Her tuberculosis could become active again.

At first her interrogation took place every day and sometimes twice a day. It was conducted by the security police. A session generally lasted seven to eight hours, although there was sometimes a half-hour's break when the police got tired. During an interrogation Nina received no food, although she sometimes watched the police eating their own food.

She had been arrested in the summer months when she was wearing only a skirt and blouse. No warmer clothes were provided during the extreme cold of the Polish winter, though the respondent had sent some for her. The prison and cell were unheated. For her ablutions she was supplied with icy-cold water—a particular torment to Nina with her injured hands. Her only furniture consisted of a wooden bed and a pillow filled with hay. She was supplied with a single blanket only.

The main object of the interrogation was to get Nina to inculpate her 'accomplices' (particularly the respondent and students) in what her interrogators seemed to regard as activities inimical to the regime. The interrogations included threats; these took several forms.

First, the police insinuated that Nina was mentally deranged, and threatened that she would be sent to a mental hospital. This was a particularly terrifying threat, since Nina had knowledge which led her to believe that she would have little chance of release, the 'hospitals' in question being controlled by the security police.

Secondly, she was threatened by the police with a severe sentence of imprisonment. She knew that the sentence for the crime alleged against her—'anti-state activities'—was likely to be between three and 15 years.

Thirdly, she was threatened with rearrest after any such prison sentence. This, she believed, was far from unlikely; she had known of many political prisoners who had been rearrested after serving their full term of imprisonment.

Fourthly, she was told that she would never be able to lead a normal life again after the trial. With state control of the economy and professions she knew that she would never be able to get any job or employment other than that of a menial nature. She was also told that she would not be allowed to live in Warsaw; this would have further grave consequences on her prospects of employment owing to the housing shortage. It was also liable to lead to failure to supply the police with her address, with consequent liability to rearrest on this ground.

It was emphasised that she would have no money and therefore would not be able to support Mrs Karsov. To reinforce this threat she was told, fifthly, that Mrs Karsov—who was by now 76% disabled—would lose her pension.

Finally, she was told that she would never be allowed to leave the country.

To further the effect of these threats and her privations, it was now divulged to her for the first time, and in the most offensive manner, that she was Jewish by birth. This was meant still more to undermine her morale in view of the prevalent anti-semitic sentiments. (In fact the knowledge had no such effect since, as Nina told me, she had been brought up by Mrs Karsov to value her fellow-beings according only to their human qualities.) And, for all the threats and ill-treatment, Nina continued to deny to her persecutors the information they were seeking.

While all this was going on, the respondent was exercising his energies, and using such influence as he had, to get Nina freed and into hospital; he knew the disastrous effect a long term of imprisonment would have on her health. But he himself was subjected to the pressures of the security police. He was a figure of some standing and his presence in Poland was an embarrassment to the regime. He was told that if he helped the police he and his family would be allowed to go to Israel. However, he thought that his continued presence in Poland might have a restraining effect on the police's treatment of Nina and he did not take advantage of the overtures made to him.

But the knowledge that the police were far from unwilling to see him out of the country led the respondent and Lydia, after their failure to get Nina freed and into hospital, to make fresh plans, including the extraordinary one which has led to these proceedings.

Their first idea was to adopt Nina as their daughter; she would then be able to accompany them to Israel as a member of their family. But this proved to be impossible under Polish law owing to the fact that Nina was over the age of 18.

After being 10 months in prison, and her interrogation being completed, Nina was for the first time allowed to receive a lawyer, who had been briefed by the respondent. This was the first news Nina had of the Szechters since her arrest. The lawyer put to Nina the fresh plan that Lydia and the respondent had concocted as the only way to help Nina. This was that the respondent and Lydia should obtain a divorce and that the respondent should then go through a ceremony of marriage with Nina and take her to Israel as his wife, there to join up with, and the respondent to remarry, Lydia. In fact the respondent and Lydia had already anticipated Nina's knowledge of, and agreement with, this plan; secretly (so as not to excite the vigilance of the security police) they were divorced on 14 April 1967, and

Lydia left for Israel as a single woman, taking her younger son with her, her elder son being already there. In spite of her peril, Nina did not immediately give her consent to the plan; she did not know when she would be brought to trial or how long her sentence would be and therefore when it would be that the respondent and Lydia could be reunited. In the end, however, she came to see that it was the only solution for her. She believed that she would never survive a long, or even medium, prison sentence and that the desire of the authorities to see the respondent out of the country might lead to her earlier release if she were married to him. She also knew that the respondent would be in a better position to help her in prison if they were married; for example, he could probably visit her or send her parcels.

On 2 October 1967 Nina was finally brought to trial. On 26 October 1967 she was convicted and was sentenced to three years' imprisonment. As she was being led away after sentence, she noticed the respondent holding a conference in court with representatives of the western press. This act of courage on her behalf, unexampled to her knowledge, made a deep impression on Nina and probably ultimately clinched her consent to the Szechters' plans.

After Nina's conviction her conditions improved in some respects. She was allowed one 30-minute visit a month. On the other hand, her health continued to deteriorate in spite of treatment for her thyroid and spinal complaints, now, at last, in hospital (where conditions were, however, deplorable). She came to the conclusion that she would not be able to survive three years' imprisonment. After three applications the respondent had been given permission to marry Nina, despite the objections of the security police; and Nina herself now consented—attempts by the security police to dissuade her only increased her resolve.

On 2 February 1968 Nina and the respondent went through a ceremony of marriage in Mokotow Prison—it took five minutes only and they were at no point allowed to speak to each other during the ceremony. But I have been satisfied on expert evidence that qua formalities it constituted a valid marriage in Polish law, which is unquestionably the proper foreign law.

On 5 September 1968 Nina was released—in other words, after serving less than one year of her three-year sentence. Fantastic as it seemed, the Szechters' scheme had succeeded. Nina was in very bad health; but she and the respondent were under pressure to renounce their Polish citizenship and to leave for Israel, though they had to pay £300 each before they would be allowed to leave. They gladly complied with all the conditions demanded, and in early November 1968, Nina and the respondent went to Austria as stateless persons, where they were looked after by the International Rescue Committee. Amnesty International brought them to England at the end of 1968, the Home Office giving them leave to stay until December 1969 (later extended to December 1970).

In August 1969 Lydia came to England with her younger son. Having achieved their object in extricating Nina from prison and from Poland, the respondent and Lydia now wished to resume their married life together, and Nina, too, wished to be free of a marriage into which she had entered solely in the hope of thereby securing her release from prison. (Needless to say, the marriage had not been consummated.) So on 15 August 1969, Nina presented her petition for a declaration of nullity.

Nina is studying as a post graduate at the London School of Economics and Political Science for a Master of Science degree. Lydia is learning English with a view either to taking up a teaching post in this country or to using her qualification of civil engineer in employment here. The respondent is a visiting fellow at the London School of Economics and Political Science. All wish now to remain in this country if they are permitted to do so by the authorities.

The evidence of Nina and the respondent as to the socio-political background was borne out by a written statement made by a Mrs Stypulkowska, which was admitted under the provisions of the Civil Evidence Act 1968.

Since Nina and the respondent coincided in wishing the marriage to be declared a nullity, since the annulment of any marriage is a serious matter, and since some difficult questions of law might emerge, I requested the independent assistance of the Queen's Proctor. In the event, counsel instructed by the Queen's Proctor supported Nina's counsel in her submissions. Both counsel have placed the court in their debt.

There are two preliminary questions to be considered. The first is whether an English court has jurisdiction to make the decree which Nina seeks. (His Lordship reviewed the authorities, which are obsolete since the Domicile and Matrimonial Proceedings Act 1973, p 295 below, and continued):

I am therefore satisfied that I have jurisdiction to entertain this petition on the grounds of both common residence and common domicile in England.

The second preliminary question is what is the proper law to apply in order to determine whether an ostensible marriage is defective by reason of duress. There is little direct authority on this matter. But the effect of duress goes to reality of consent and I respectfully agree with the suggestion in rule 32 of Dicey and Morris *The Conflict of Laws*,[9] that no marriage is valid if by the law of either party's domicile one party does not consent to marry the other. This accords with the old distinction between, on the one hand, 'forms and ceremonies', the validity of which is referable to the lex loci contractus, and, on the other hand, 'essential validity', by which is meant (even though by, as the editors of *Rayden on Divorce*[10] remark, 'not a happy terminology') all requirements for a valid marriage other than those relating to forms and ceremonies, for the validity of which reference is made to the lex domicilii of the parties: *Rayden on Divorce*;[11] *De Reneville v De Reneville*[12] by Lord Greene MR. So far as capacity (also a matter of 'essential validity') is concerned, there can be no doubt that no marriage is valid if by the law of either party's domicile one of the parties is incapable of marrying the other: *Re Paine*;[13] *Pugh v Pugh*.[14]

Moreover, in *Way v Way*[15] Hodson J said:

'Questions of consent are to be dealt with by reference to the personal law of the parties rather than by reference to the law of the place where

9 8th edn (1967) p 271. The rule has now been changed and is the same as the headnote to this case (*Ed*).
10 10th edn (1967) p 121.
11 Pp 120, 121.
12 [1948] P 100 at 114, [1948] 1 All ER 56 at 61.
13 [1940] Ch 46, 108 LJCh 427.
14 [1951] P 482, [1951] 2 All ER 680; p 246 above.
15 [1950] P 71 at 78–79, [1949] 2 All ER 959 at 963.

the contract was made. This view is not covered by direct authority, but it is, I think, supported by the judgment of Lord Merriman P in *Apt v Apt*.[16] ...

When giving the judgment of the Court of Appeal dismissing the petitioner's appeal in this [*Apt's*] case, Cohen LJ said:[17] 'In our opinion the method of giving consent as distinct from the fact of consent is essentially a matter of lex loci celebrationis and does not raise the question of capacity.' Marriage is essentially a voluntary union and as Dr Idelson put it (and I cannot improve on the phrase) 'consent is an emanation of personality'. It is therefore, I think, justifiable and consistent with authority to apply the matrimonial law of each of the parties.'

When that case went to the Court of Appeal, under the name of *Kenward v Kenward*,[18] Sir Raymond Evershed MR at 133 assumed that what Hodson J had said about the relevant law to be applied was correct.

Both Nina and the respondent were domiciled in Poland at the time of the ceremony of marriage on 2 February 1968. It is therefore for Polish law to answer whether, on the facts as I have found them, the marriage was invalid by reason of duress. If I also look (as I propose to do) at what English law says on the matter, it is because the annulment of a marriage is a very serious step, and because the expert witness on Polish law had to go into hospital for an operation, so that he had to give his evidence by affidavit and was not available for oral examination. (His Lordship considered the evidence of Mr Jaxa, the expert witness on Polish law, and continued):

Mr Jaxa sums up his opinion as follows:

'I am of the firm opinion that if the agreement of the parties to enter into matrimony was given under constraint, that marriage is void in Polish law. I am well aware of the facts of the "marriage" which is the subject of this suit, and in my opinion, if such a case were to come before the Polish courts, it would be held to be void, and would have been void at the date of the marriage, that is, 2 February 1968.'

So far as English law is concerned, private reservations or motives are not in general matters cognisable to vitiate an ostensibly valid marriage.... [But] as the American writer Bishop states in his *Commentaries on the Law of Marriage and Divorce*:[19] 'Where a formal consent is brought about by force, menace, or duress—a yielding of the lips, not of the mind—it is of no legal effect. This rule, applicable to all contracts, finds no exception in marriage.'

In the nature of things the source of the fear and the agent of duress will generally be the other party to the marriage. But this is not necessarily so. Thus, in *H v H*[20] the source of fear was the political and social danger to the life, liberty and virtue of the petitioner in her native country of Hungary. In order to obtain a foreign passport she went through a ceremony of marriage

16 [1947] P 127 at 146, [1947] 1 All ER 620 at 630.
17 P 227 above.
18 [1951] P 124, [1950] 2 All ER 297.
19 6th edn (1881) vol 1, para 210, p 177.
20 [1954] P 258, [1953] 2 All ER 1229.

with a French citizen, and by agreement separated from him immediately thereafter. She was able thereby to escape to England, and in due course she presented here a petition for nullity on the ground of alleged duress. No allegation was made against the respondent or his agents. Karminski J heard argument not only on behalf of the petitioner but also by the Attorney General on behalf of the Queen's Proctor. In a reserved judgment he held that the petitioner's fears were reasonably entertained, and were of such a kind as to negative her consent to the marriage, which was accordingly void. (It appeared that there was no material difference between English and Hungarian law, both deriving from the canon law.)

Again in *Buckland v Buckland*[1] the petitioner, a Maltese employed by the British authorities in Malta as a dockyard policeman, in 1953 was charged under Maltese law with the corruption of a 15-year-old girl. Although stating he was innocent of the offence, he was advised by his solicitor that he would certainly be found guilty of the charge; that he would probably be sentenced to a long period of imprisonment and ordered to support for 15 or 16 years the child with which the girl concerned was believed to be pregnant; and that his only alternatives were either to marry the girl or to go to prison. The terrified petitioner preferred to marry the girl and went through a ceremony of marriage with her at a church in Malta. He left Malta a few days later and came to England, where he had lived ever since and acquired a domicile. He petitioned the English court for the annulment of the marriage on the ground that it was void for want of his consent. There was no evidence of Maltese law and Scarman J therefore apparently applied English law. He followed *H v H,* and an Irish case, *Griffith v Griffith*[2] (in which it was held that the fear must arise from some external circumstance for which the petitioner is not himself responsible) and held that the petitioner agreed to the marriage because of fears, reasonably entertained, which arose from external circumstances for which he was in no way responsible, and that accordingly the marriage ceremony was null and void.

I am content to follow those decisions. Indeed, the instant case seems to me to be stronger than either *H v H* or *Buckland v Buckland*.

It is, in my view, insufficient to invalidate an otherwise good marriage that a party has entered into it in order to escape from a disagreeable situation, such as penury or social degradation. In order for the impediment of duress to vitiate an otherwise valid marriage, it must, in my judgment, be proved that the will of one of the parties thereto has been overborne by genuine and reasonably held fear caused by threat of immediate danger (for which the party is not himself responsible) to life, limb or liberty, so that the constraint destroys the reality of consent to ordinary wedlock. I think that in the instant case that test is satisfied. In my view, English law returns the same answer to the juridical situation as the Polish law as deposed to by Mr Jaxa.

In those circumstances I made a decree nisi of nullity at the conclusion of the argument, reserving my reasons, which I have now delivered.[3]

Decree nisi of nullity.

1 [1968] P 296, [1967] 2 All ER 300.
2 [1944] IR 35.
3 Szymon Szechter established a publishing house in England, which he named 'Nina Karsov', see his obituary, *The Times,* 14 July 1983 (*Ed*).

Section D: Polygamous marriages

A potentially polygamous marriage may become monogamous by the happening of subsequent events, eg in some legal systems the birth of a child.

Cheni v Cheni [1965] P 85, [1962] 3 All ER 873 (Divorce Division)

The facts are stated on p 259 above.

Sir Jocelyn Simon P referred to the facts of the marriage and the evidence as to Egyptian law, and continued: I had the advantage of evidence from Dr Solomon Gaon, Chief Rabbi of the Spanish and Portuguese Jewish community of Great Britain and religious leader of the Sephardic Jewish community here. He is also head of the Sephardic Beth Din in this country, the Rabbinical Court of the Portuguese and Spanish Jews, and was acknowledged to speak with authority on matters of Jewish law. His evidence was as follows. The practice of polygamy among Jews has the sanction of the Bible and the Talmud. In the ninth century, however, Rabbi Gershon (or Gersonides) enjoined monogamy in marriage; and his tenets came to be accepted by the Askkenazim, that is, Jewish communities of Central Europe and Russia, and by many Sephardim, that is, Jewish communities of Mediterranean and Middle Eastern countries. But certain Jewish communities living in predominantly Moslem countries where polygamy was the rule did not accept the reforms of Rabbi Gershon. Chief Rabbi Gaon quoted from a book, Nahar Misrayim, which was written by an Egyptian Rabbi and considered a work of authority: 'Although we who live in Egypt have not accepted the ban of Gersonides, yet this is a place in which it is customary not to take two wives.' This may be partly due to the strict conditions which had to be satisfied before a second wife could be taken during the subsistence of the first marriage. It could not in any event be done without investigation and sanction by the Beth Din. The marriage had to subsist in childlessness for 10 years (or longer if so stipulated in the Katouba), and the period must not be interrupted by absence abroad or enforced separation or serious illness. The husband had to satisfy the court that the failure of progeny was solely the responsibility of the wife, and that it was irremediable in her. The wife would be given the choice of being divorced rather than sharing her husband with another wife, and she would be examined separately by the court to ensure that her choice was a free one. But if these conditions were satisfied and the first wife freely consented, the Beth Din could permit the husband to take a second wife. The first wife would retain her full rights in every respect—consortium, maintenance, conjugal rights. On the birth of a child within 10 years such a marriage became irrevocably and inevitably monogamous for all purposes.

In these circumstances, Mr Argyle (counsel for the husband) submitted that this court had no jurisdiction to pronounce on the marriage. The law is, indeed, clear that if a marriage is potentially polygamous, even though in fact no second wife is taken, the machinery of the English matrimonial law is inappropriate and unavailable.[4] *Hyde v Hyde and Woodmansee*[5] is the leading

4 But see now Matrimonial Causes Act 1973, s 47, p 294 below (*Ed*).
5 (1866) LR 1 P & D 130, 35 LJP & M 57.

authority, and the recent decision of the Court of Appeal in *Sowa v Sowa*[6] shows that, even though it is now accepted (contrary to what was for some time thought to have been the effect of *Hyde v Hyde and Woodmansee*) that for many purposes our courts will recognise the efficacy of a polygamous marriage which is valid by its proper law, the parties to such a marriage are not entitled to the remedies, the adjudication or the relief of our matrimonial law. Mr Stirling (counsel for the wife) replied that since the desire and intention of the parties was that this marriage should be monogamous, and since the conditions permitting a second wife were highly unlikely to be satisfied, the marriage should be regarded as monogamous from its inception. But to my mind it is unescapable that this marriage was in its inception potentially polygamous, however remote the possibility and the intention of the parties that it should be monogamous is irrelevant: see *Ohochuku v Ohochuku*,[7] per Wrangham J; *Muhammad v Suna*[8], per the Lord Ordinary, Lord Walker.

This poses the question of the relevant date for examining the marriage as to its polygamous potential—the inception of the marriage or the inception of the proceedings. If the inception of the marriage, the marriage in this case was potentially polygamous and the court has no jurisdiction over it. If the date of the proceedings, this marriage was by then monogamous and the court may proceed. But the question has significance beyond the circumstances of the present case. Two spouses may contract a valid polygamous union and subsequently join a monogamous sect, or go through a second ceremony in a place where monogamy is the law. Again, a marriage in its inception potentially polygamous though in fact monogamous may be rendered monogamous for all time by legislative action proscribing polygamy: this, according to the evidence, has in fact happened in the State of Israel in relation to the marriages of Sephardic Jews who are her nationals. Will the English court regard such marriages as monogamous or potentially polygamous for the purpose of exercising jurisdiction?

In favour of the inception of the marriage as the decisive date, Mr Argyle relied on three authorities. *Nachimson v Nachimson*[9] established that the inception of the marriage is the decisive date for ascertaining whether it is a union for life. It would be anomalous, said Mr Argyle, to take a different date for establishing whether it fulfils the analogous requirement for it to constitute marriage in the eyes of English law, namely, that it should be the union of one man with one woman: see *Mehta v Mehta*,[10] per Barnard J. But the two requirements are not in truth analogous: if the union were in its inception for a term less than life English law would not recognise it as a marriage at all, whatever name it might bear in its local law; whereas English law does for most purposes recognise a polygamous union as a marriage, even though not for the purpose of direct matrimonial relief. Moreover, the two rationes decidendi of *Nachimson v Nachimson* have no relevance at all to polygamous marriages. These were, first, that the defeasibility of a contract is not a test of its initial validity; and, secondly, that divorce is not an incident of the marriage contract to be governed by

6 [1961] P 70, [1961] 1 All ER 687.
7 [1960] 1 All ER 253, [1960] 1 WLR 183.
8 1956 SC 366 at 370.
9 [1930] P 217, 99 LJP 104.
10 [1945] 2 All ER 690 at 693–694.

the lex loci contractus, but an incident of status to be disposed of by the law of the domicile, whereas the polygamous or monogamous character of a marriage does fall for determination by the lex loci.

In *Mehta v Mehta* it was held that the English court has jurisdiction if the marriage is monogamous in its inception, notwithstanding that by a change of sect a second wife could validly be taken. If the inception of the marriage is the relevant date for determining that it is monogamous, it must also, it is argued, be the relevant date for determining whether it is potentially polygamous. But I do not think that this necessarily follows. If parties marry monogamously the law will readily and reasonably presume that they will not relapse into polygamy. After all, there are no marriages which are not potentially polygamous, in the sense that they may be rendered so by a change of domicile and religion on the part of the spouses. But, particularly in these days of widespread interpenetration of societies in different stages of development, it is not a reasonable presumption that spouses who marry polygamously will not by personal volition or act of state convert their marriages or have them converted into monogamous unions. An alternative way of putting the matter that commends itself to me is that of the editor of Dicey's *Conflict of Laws*[11] that the marriage has, so to speak, the benefit of the doubt as far as jurisdiction is concerned, so that it is sufficient that it is either monogamous in its inception, or has become so by the time of the proceedings. The marriage in *Mehta v Mehta* was apparently still monogamous at the time of the proceedings. I therefore do not think that the case is authority which compels me to hold that if a marriage is potentially polygamous in its inception the English matrimonial court will refuse its relief, even though by the time of proceedings the marriage is undoubtedly monogamous.

The *Sinha Peerage* case[12] established that the eldest son of a potentially polygamous Hindu marriage was entitled to succeed to a peerage conferred on his father, the parties having joined a monogamous sect before the claimant was born or the peerage created. Lord Maugham LC expressly stated that the decision had nothing to do with the jurisdiction of the divorce court. Mr Argyle argued that this showed that whereas it was sufficient for inheritance of a peerage that the marriage had assumed a monogamous character before the birth of the claimant or the creation of the peerage, in the case of matrimonial proceedings the marriage must be monogamous from its inception. But it is clear that Lord Maugham LC was not considering at all the point which arises in this case. If anything, the case is authority in favour of the wife, as showing that the law of this country will recognise and give effect to a change in the character of a marriage which was potentially polygamous in its inception.

There is further and more direct authority in favour of the wife's contention. Lord Merriman P in the Divisional Court in *Sowa v Sowa* implied that the marriage there, which was potentially polygamous in its inception, could have been converted into a monogamous marriage, and that the English matrimonial court would then have had jurisdiction. He said: 'There was evidence that this was a perfectly valid marriage in Ghana, and . . . that it could be converted into a perfectly valid marriage in England', and '. . . the

11 7th edn (1958) p 272.
12 [1946] 1 All ER 348n.

fact is that that change in the nature of the marriage has never been effected, from which it follows that it comes within the class of case dealt with in *Hyde v Hyde and Woodmansee*.' Again in *Ohochuku v Ohochuku* the court was concerned with a polygamous marriage, valid by the Nigerian law of the place of celebration and of the parties' domicile, which was followed by a second ceremony at a London register office. Wrangham J treated the latter as having converted the original and potentially polygamous marriage into a monogamous union, and pronounced a decree dissolving the marriage.

Moreover, the reasoning in *Hyde v Hyde and Woodmansee* and *Sowa v Sowa* is applicable only to a marriage that is still potentially polygamous at the time of the proceedings. It was that the structure and machinery of our matrimonial law is so inappropriate to resolving the problems thrown up by adjudication upon potentially polygamous marriages as to show that such terms as 'marriage', 'husband', 'wife' and 'married woman' must be used in the matrimonial statutes with a strictly monogamous connotation: see also *Baindail v Baindail*,[13] per Lord Greene MR. This reasoning has no relevance to a marriage of originally polygamous potentiality which has become strictly monogamous by the time of the proceedings. In *Sowa v Sowa* Holroyd Pearce LJ reluctantly denied the jurisdiction of the court to the parties on the ground that 'the only tie that binds them is a potentially polygamous marriage'. In the present case the only tie that binds the parties is a marriage from which all polygamous potential has been removed. Finally, on this part of the case, it is useful to bear in mind the observation of the Lord Ordinary, Lord Walker, in *Muhammed v Suna*: 'It is perhaps not altogether satisfactory that a man who enters into a polygamous union while domiciled abroad should, on acquiring a domicile in this country, be unable to sue in the court of his domicile for divorce (*Hyde's* case), and yet be regarded by the court of his domicile as not free to marry (*Baindail's* case)'. This, as well as the general undesirability of closing the doors of our courts to suitors, is an argument against any unnecessary extension of the rule in *Hyde v Hyde and Woodmansee*.

Therefore, on weight of authority, on principle and on ground of convenience I am of opinion that if the marriage is monogamous at the time of the proceedings, albeit potentially polygamous on its inception, the court has jurisdiction to adjudicate upon it.[14]

For the purposes of section 11 (d) of the Matrimonial Causes Act 1973, a marriage is not polygamous if neither party can under his or her personal law take another spouse during the subsistence of the marriage.

Hussain v Hussain [1983] Fam 26, [1982] 3 All ER 369 (Family Division)

Appeal from Manchester County Court.

The husband and wife were Muslims by religion. They were married in Pakistan in 1979 in accordance with the Muslim Family Laws Ordinance 1961. Under that form of marriage, by Pakistani law, a husband could

13 [1946] P 122, [1946] 1 All ER 342; p 286 below.
14 For the second part of the judgment, see p 259 above.

marry a second wife during the subsistence of the marriage, but a wife could not marry a second husband. At the time of the ceremony the husband was domiciled in England and the wife in Pakistan. The parties came to England and the wife petitioned for a decree of judicial separation. The husband contended that the marriage was void under section 11 (d) of the Matrimonial Causes Act 1973.

Ormrod LJ read the judgment of the court (Ormrod, Griffiths and Slade LJJ): The question in this appeal is purely one of construction of section 11 (d), and it turns on the meaning to be given to the phrase, 'a polygamous marriage' in the context in which it appears. Section 11, so far as material, is in the following terms:

> 'A marriage celebrated after 31 July 1971, shall be void on the following grounds only, that is to say—... (b) that at the time of the marriage either party was already lawfully married; ... (d) in the case of a polygamous marriage entered into outside England and Wales, that either party was at the time of the marriage domiciled in England and Wales. For the purposes of paragraph (d) of this subsection a marriage may be polygamous although at its inception neither party has any spouse additional to the other.'

Miss Bracewell, for the husband, contends that 'a polygamous marriage' refers to the character and incidents of marriage under the relevant régime. If the régime permits polygamy in any form, she submits that such marriage is void if either party to it is domiciled in England or Wales at the date on which it was entered into. Mr Jackson, for the wife, contends that it refers, not to marriages which may be categorised as polygamous in general terms, but to the particular marriage which is in question. He submits that a marriage which is not actually polygamous at its inception, and incapable of becoming actually polygamous, by reason of the personal laws of the parties at the time it was entered into, is not void under this paragraph. On the facts of this case the husband, by English law, is incapable of contracting a valid marriage when he is already lawfully married (section 11 (b)), and the wife, by Pakistani law, cannot marry another man so long as she is married to the husband, so this marriage can never become polygamous. Consequently, the marriage was not polygamous at its inception and cannot become polygamous at any time in the future. It is, therefore, not avoided by section 11 (d).

Miss Bracewell's submission is supported by the proposition which appears in leading text books that 'the nature of the ceremony, according to the lex loci celebrationis, and not the personal law of either party, determines whether a marriage is monogamous or polygamous': Dicey & Morris *The Conflict of Laws*,[15] *Halsbury's Laws of England*,[16] but see Cheshire and North's *Private International Law*.[17]

No authority is cited in support of this proposition,[18] but it is clearly

---

15 10th edn (1980) vol 1 pp 309–310.

16 4th edn, vol 8 (1974) para 474.

17 10th edn (1979) p 349. (But at pp 301–302 the editor comes to the same conclusion as Dicey & Morris and Halsbury: *Ed.*)

18 Sed quaere: 14 cases are cited for this proposition in Dicey & Morris, and 20 in Halsbury (*Ed*).

derived from cases concerned with polygamous marriages which were decided before the passing of the Matrimonial Proceedings (Polygamous Marriages) Act 1972, which radically altered the law relating to polygamous marriages. Prior to this Act, the law was governed by the decision in *Hyde v Hyde and Woodmansee*[19] that a 'marriage' which did not create a monogamous union between a man and a woman was not a marriage at all. Stated perhaps more precisely, the word 'marriage', where it appeared in the matrimonial legislation, did not, as a matter of construction, include any kind of ceremony which did not create a monogamous relationship of the kind adopted by Christianity. Consequently, in all the cases before 1972 it was the nature and incidents of the ceremony which were crucial, and these could only be ascertained by reference to the lex loci celebrationis.

Since the Matrimonial Proceedings (Polygamous Marriages) Act 1972[20] was passed, the position is quite different; section 1 of that Act provided that a court in England and Wales shall not be precluded from granting matrimonial relief by reason only that the marriage in question was entered into under a law which permits polygamy. It is no longer necessary, therefore, to characterise the nature and incidents of the status created by the lex loci celebrationis for jurisdiction purposes. The only question is whether the marriage under consideration is valid by English law, which is a question of capacity. The proposition in the textbooks, therefore, does not assist Miss Bracewell's argument.

Section 11 (d) of the Matrimonial Causes Act 1973 is not very happily phrased and does not fit in at all well with the rest of the section, and in the process of consolidation, it has become widely separated from its proper context. It was originally section 4 of the Matrimonial Proceedings (Polygamous Marriages) Act 1972, and was passed to deal with the new situation created by section 1 of that Act (now section 47 of the Act of 1973). Section 11 (d) must be read, therefore, with section 47.

When these two provisions are read together a significant difference can be seen between the language used in section 47 and in section 11 (d). Section 47 refers to 'a marriage entered into under a law which permits polygamy'. This is the exact equivalent in English law of the proposition in the textbooks; it clearly refers to the lex loci celebrationis and not the law of either party's domicile. But section 11 (d) refers simply to 'a polygamous marriage' and goes on to provide that a marriage may be polygamous although at its inception neither party has an additional spouse.

Miss Bracewell's argument has to overcome the difficulty that if her construction of section 11 (d) is right, the draftsman, originally, in the Matrimonial Proceedings (Polygamous Marriages) Act 1972 used two very different formulations to express the same idea in a short Act containing only two relevant sections (sections 1 and 4). Had the intention of Parliament been to prevent persons domiciled in England and Wales from entering into marriages under the Muslim Family Laws Ordinance, or under other similar laws which 'permit polygamy', it would have been easy to say so in so many words. On the other hand, once the position of *Hyde v Hyde and Woodmansee* had been abandoned, the question of the capacity of persons domiciled in England and Wales to enter into polygamous or potentially polygamous

19 (1866) LR 1 P & D 130, 35 LJP & M 57.
20 Now s 47 of the Matrimonial Causes Act 1973; p 294 below (*Ed*).

marriages had to be considered. Actually polygamous marriages were already covered by what is now section 11 (b) of the Act of 1973, but potentially polygamous marriages were not completely covered by the existing law. The spouse domiciled in England and Wales is, of course, incapable of marrying a second spouse, but if one of the spouses in the first marriage retains a domicile, the law of which permits polygamy, a situation could arise in which the spouse domiciled in this country becomes a party to a polygamous union. Mr Jackson submits that section 4 of the Matrimonial Proceedings (Polygamous Marriages) Act 1972 (now section 11 (d) of the Matrimonial Causes Act 1973) was passed to prevent this situation from arising. The effect would be that a marriage between a woman domiciled in England and Wales, and a man domiciled in Pakistan, would be a polygamous marriage because the husband has the capacity, by his personal law, to take a second wife, but not vice versa.

The language used by the draftsman is, at least, consistent with this construction. The insertion of the qualifying words at the end of section 11 (d) suggests that without them the phrase 'polygamous marriage' would, or might be, confined to a marriage which was actually polygamous at its inception, that is, one in which one of the spouses was already married to another spouse. The use of the word 'may' in the qualifying words suggests that the draftsman had some contingency in mind, the happening of which would make a marriage between two unmarried persons polygamous, within the meaning of the provision, that is, as it is called, a potentially polygamous marriage. A marriage can only be potentially polygamous if at least one of the spouses has the capacity to marry a second spouse.

On a broader view, it is difficult to conceive any reason why Parliament, in an increasingly pluralistic society, should have thought it necessary to prohibit persons, whose religious or cultural traditions accept polygamy, from marrying in their own manner abroad, simply because they are domiciled in England and Wales. On the other hand, it is obvious that Parliament, having decided to recognise polygamous marriages as marriages for the purposes of our matrimonial legislation, would think it right to preserve the principle of monogamy for persons domiciled here.

Finally, the consequences of accepting Miss Bracewell's submission in this case would be far reaching and very serious. It would mean that all marriages contracted abroad by people domiciled in this country, in accordance with the local law, would be void if that law permitted polygamy in any form. The repercussions on the Muslim community alone in this country would be widespread and profound.

For these reasons the narrower construction of section 11 (d) of the Matrimonial Causes Act 1973 is to be preferred. On the facts, the marriage in this case is monogamous and should be held to be a valid marriage. The husband's contention, therefore, fails and his appeal should be dismissed. The petition should be restored to the list as soon as possible for the pronouncement of the decree of judicial separation.

Appeal dismissed.

NOTE

From 1972 to 1982, government departments, practising lawyers and academic lawyers all believed that section 11 (d) of the Matrimonial Causes Act 1973 and its predecessor section 4 of the Matrimonial Proceedings (Polygamous Marriages) Act 1972 meant what they said; and that in this context as in others the nature of the ceremony according to the law of the place of celebration, and not the law of either party's domicile, would determine whether a marriage was monogamous or polygamous. This belief was shattered by the decision of the Court of Appeal in *Hussain v Hussain* (above), which was delivered on the very day on which the Law Commission's Working Paper No 83 on capacity to contract a polygamous marriage was due to go to the printer. The decision renders many marriages valid which were thought to be void, with consequent administrative problems relating to social security, taxation, nationality, succession, etc. It may also invalidate many marriages which were thought to be valid, eg if one of the parties had remarried without first obtaining a decree of nullity. If one of the parties had obtained such a decree, any subsequent remarriage would be valid, since a decree of nullity operates in rem. The decision is open to the grave objection that it lays down one rule for men and another for women. Thus a marriage celebrated in Muslim form in Pakistan between a Muslim man domiciled in England and a Muslim woman domiciled in Pakistan is valid; but a marriage celebrated in Muslim form in Pakistan between a woman domiciled in England and a Muslim man domiciled in Pakistan is void.

In their Working Paper No 83 the Law Commission provisionally recommend that section 11 (d) should be confined to actually polygamous marriages; and that the concept of potentially polygamous marriages should be abolished.

See Rhona Shuz (1983) 46 MLR 653.

Capacity to contract a polygamous marriage may (semble) be governed by the law of the intended matrimonial home.

Radwan v Radwan (No 2) [1973] Fam 35, [1972] 3 All ER 1026 (Family Division)

Wife's petition for divorce.

The husband, a Muslim domiciled in Egypt, and the wife, then domiciled in England, were married before the Egyptian Consul-General in Paris in 1951 in polygamous form. At that time the husband had a wife living in Egypt whom he divorced by talaq in 1952. The parties lived together in Egypt in accordance with their antenuptial intentions until 1956. Owing to the Suez affair they moved to England where the husband acquired a domicile of choice by 1959. They had eight children. The wife petitioned for divorce on the ground of cruelty. The husband cross-petitioned on the same ground.

Cumming-Bruce J (having held that there was insufficient evidence to rebut the presumption that the marriage was formally valid by French law, continued): Though much has been written, and many observations made in English cases, this is the first time an English court has had to decide whether the wife's capacity to enter into a polygamous marriage abroad is governed by the law of her domicile at the time of marriage, or by the law of the country of intended matrimonial residence, which often, as in this case, is the same as the law of the husband's domicile. I have, with proper humility, to grasp the nettle and decide whether to award the accolade of this court to Dr J. H. C. Morris, the editor of Dicey & Morris, *Conflict of Laws*[1] for his statement of rule 35 in his chapter on marriage, or to Professor Cheshire who

1 8th edn (1967) p 283.

has for many years advanced the contrary view. To pose the problem a little differently, in *De Reneville v De Reneville*[2] Lord Greene MR and Bucknill LJ, with both of whom Somervell LJ agreed, held that the law of the matrimonial domicile governs essential validity in relation to nullity on the ground of incapacity or wilful refusal to consummate.[3] And in *Kenward v Kenward*,[4] Denning LJ said obiter and without argument, that capacity to enter into polygamous marriage depends upon the law of the matrimonial domicile. Yet in a number of cases extending over the last 100 years judges of first instance have stated that the law of prenuptial domicile governs capacity to marry. Who is right? What is the law? Many are confident that the question is already settled, and that the rule of dual domicile is settled English law governing all questions of capacity save for the one exception given as exception no 3 to rule 31 in *Dicey & Morris*, based on *Sottomayor v De Barros (No 2)*[5] and exceptions founded on the penal or oppressive characteristics of foreign law. So the Law Commission in their *Report on Polygamous Marriage*[6] stated: 'Thus, if a person domiciled in England goes through a polygamous form of marriage abroad, that marriage will, under English law, be void, even if it was only potentially polygamous.' And at para 89, 'The marriage is also regarded as void if either party lacks capacity to marry under the law of the domicile of that party'; though there is a footnote to that proposition which gives *Brook v Brook*[7] as the authority and states: 'There is another line of authority which has been interpreted as implying that it is the law of the matrimonial domicile which is decisive.' It is to be observed that in *Ponticelli v Ponticelli*,[8] where counsel for the husband had argued in favour of choice of the law of matrimonial residence. Sachs LJ expressly left the point open as it was unnecessary to his decision. Against that background I examine the authorities.

(His Lordship referred at considerable length to *Brook v Brook, Warrender v Warrender*[9] and *De Reneville v De Reneville* and continued):

Mr Ewbank, for the Queen's Proctor, submitted that rule 35 of *Dicey* correctly states the law. Both parties must have capacity to enter into a polygamous marriage at date of contract. He relied upon five cases as establishing that from 1888 to 1968 successive judicial pronouncements have affirmed the dual domicile test of capacity.

In *Re Bethell*,[10] Stirling J refused to regard as valid the polygamous union of a domiciled Englishman with a woman of a semi-barbarous tribe in Bechuanaland. But the ground of the decision was that the union could not be regarded by English law as constituting any recognisable marriage, and does not appear to me to throw any light upon the law of capacity.

2 [1948] P 100, [1948] 1 All ER 56.
3 Sed quaere. They merely held that the law of the matrimonial domicile determined whether the marriage was void or voidable for the purpose of the jurisdiction of the English court (*Ed*).
4 [1951] P 124, [1950] 2 All ER 297. This was a virtually dissenting judgment holding that the doctrine of frustration applied to marriage (*Ed*).
5 (1879) 5 PD 94, 49 LJP 1.
6 Law Com No 42 (1971), para 18.
7 (1861) 9 HLCas 193 at 234; p 232 above.
8 [1958] P 204, [1958] 1 All ER 357; p 298 below.
9 (1835) 2 Cl & Fin 488, 9 Bli NS 89.
10 (1888) 38 Ch D 220, 57 LJCh 487.

The three most important modern cases appear to be *Re Paine*;[11] *Pugh v Pugh*[12] and *Padolecchia v Padolecchia*.[13]

In *Re Paine*,[11] Bennett J decided that by English law the domiciled Englishwoman had no capacity to marry her German domiciled deceased sister's husband. He said: 'In my view that point is settled by the decision of Sir Cresswell Cresswell in *Mette v Mette*.'[14] The same result would have been reached had the law of the matrimonial home been applied.

In *Pugh v Pugh*, Mr Simon argued that essential validity should be tested by the law of the husband's domicile, or alternatively by the law of the country of proposed matrimonial home, both of which were English law. Pearce J, at 493, referring to *Conway v Beazley*;[15] *Brook v Brook*; *Mette v Mette*; *Sottomayor v De Barros*;[16] *Re De Wilton*[17] and *Re Paine*, concluded, at 494: 'In view of those authorities it is clear that this marriage was not valid since by the law of the husband's domicile it was a marriage into which he could not lawfully enter.' The issue was lex loci contractus versus law of dual domicile or law of country of proposed matrimonial home, and it was immaterial from Mr Simon's position upon which ground he succeeded. But it is clear that without hearing argument upon the respective merits of Mr Simon's two arguments, Pearce J took the view that the dual domicile test was good law, and he quoted with approval the statement of the law by Cotton LJ in *Sottomayor v De Barros*. (His Lordship quoted the passage beginning 'The law of a country where a marriage is solemnised' and ending 'may have been solemnised' on p 238 above, and continued): But on the facts of this case too, the parties were not only both domiciled in Portugal, but Portugal was the country of matrimonial residence,[18] so that it can reasonably be said that there is nothing in the judgment of Pearce J inconsistent with the matrimonial residence test. The significant point is that Pearce J selected the dual domicile test as being the test which in English law governed capacity.

In passing I refer to *Sottomayor v De Barros (No 2)*. It appears an anomalous decision, and the ratio should not in my view contribute to the instant problem.

In *Padolecchia v Padolecchia* one problem for decision was by what law did one ascertain whether each party had capacity to marry. Sir Jocelyn Simon P unhesitatingly stated the answer in these terms, at 336: 'Each party must be capable of marrying by the law of his or her respective antenuptial domicile: see *Dicey & Morris* (8th edn) p 254, r 31.' In this case, the law of the husband's antenuptial domicile was Italy, and the law of intended matrimonial residence was Denmark. Sir Jocelyn Simon P unhesitatingly declared the test of dual domicile and approved *Dicey and Morris's* statement of the rule. Two criticisms may be made of the relevance of this ratio decidendi to the instant case. The first is that it was an undefended case, and Mr Louis Blom-Cooper never suggested the alternative test of matrimonial

---

11 [1940] Ch 46, 108 LJCh 427.
12 [1951] P 482, [1951] 2 All ER 680; p 246 above.
13 [1968] P 314, [1967] 3 All ER 863; p 249 above.
14 (1859) 1 Sw & Tr 416, 28 LJP & M 117.
15 (1831) 3 Hag Ecc 639.
16 (1877) 3 PD 1, 47 LJP 23; p 237 above.
17 [1900] 2 Ch 481, 69 LJCh 717.
18 Sed quaere. The parties lived together in England for six years after the marriage. They never lived together in Portugal (*Ed*).

residence: see *Padolecchia v Padolecchia* at 321. The second point is that the problem was whether the husband had lost his capacity for monogamous marriage because he had a wife already, so that the choice of law problem was concerned with the recognition of the Mexican divorce. It is arguable that it is an over-simplification of the common law to assume that the same test for purposes of choice of law applies to every kind of incapacity—non age, affinity, prohibition of monogamous contract by virtue of an existing spouse, and capacity for polygamy. Different public and social factors are relevant to each of these types of incapacity, and Mr Davies (counsel for the husband) submitted that I should beware of assuming that the adverse rationes decidendi in cases which have nothing to do with capacity for polygamy should influence my judgment, particularly as in all the later cases, except the undefended case of *Padolecchia v Padolecchia*, the same result would have been reached by the choice of law of matrimonial residence. But I do not blind myself to the fact that Sir Jocelyn Simon P was perfectly familiar with *De Reneville v De Reneville*, and that it is significant that with his great experience he stated the law of capacity in such unqualified terms.

Mr Ewbank, for the Queen's Proctor, has asked me to take into consideration two recent statutes, from which he submits an inference can be drawn that Parliament has in 1960 and in 1972 legislated on the assumption that the existing law applies the dual domicile test. By section 1 (3) of the Marriage (Enabling) Act 1960 it is enacted:

'This section does not validate a marriage, if either party to it is at the time of the marriage domiciled in a country outside Great Britain, and under the law of that country there cannot be a valid marriage between the parties.'

This subsection, it is submitted, is a statutory application of the dual domicile rule. I agree, and it is evidence that Parliament decided to show this respect for the laws of affinity of the country of a foreign intending spouse. This is not necessarily a safe guide to a belief in Parliament that the dual domicile test applies to capacity for polygamy where the British subject intends to live permanently with his spouse in a polygamous country. Then by section 4 of the Matrimonial Proceedings (Polygamous Marriages) Act 1972, it is provided:

'In section 1 of the Nullity of Marriage Act 1971[19] (which states as respects England and Wales the grounds on which a marriage taking place after commencement of that Act is void) after paragraph (c) there shall be added—(d) in the case of a polygamous marriage entered into outside England and Wales, that either party was at the time of the marriage domiciled in England and Wales. For the purposes of paragraph (d) of this section a marriage may be polygamous although at its inception neither party has any spouse additional to the other.'

To discover the operation and extent of this section, it is necessary to turn to the substantive Act, the Nullity of Marriage Act 1971.[20] There one finds that section 4 specifically restricts the operation of section 1 as follows:

19 Now s 11 of the Matrimonial Causes Act 1973 (*Ed*).
20 Now s 14 of the Matrimonial Causes Act 1973 (*Ed*).

'(1) Where, apart from this Act, any matter affecting the validity of a marriage would fall to be determined (in accordance with the rules of private international law) by reference to the law of the country outside England and Wales, nothing in section 1, 2 or 3 (1) of this Act, shall—

(a) preclude the determination of that matter as aforesaid; or

(b) require the application to the marriage of the grounds or bar there mentioned except so far as applicable in accordance with those rules.'

So that if by the common law capacity to enter into a polygamous marriage depends upon the law of intended matrimonial residence, being a foreign country such as Egypt, section 1, as amended by section 4 of the Matrimonial Proceedings (Polygamous Marriages) Act 1972, does not affect the marriage. This being so, unless Parliament was legislating on the understanding that the existing law upon capacity of marriage was dual domicile, the amendment in section 4 of the Act of 1972 appears only to have little if any content. Mr Davies submitted it would apply to the type of case where a person of English domicile makes a temporary stay abroad and there enters into a polygamous union. But on any view this case would not be a valid marriage on the matrimonial home test. If the matrimonial home test is correct, I find very great difficulty in giving much content to section 4 of the Act of 1972. It probably is the case that the draftsmen of section 4 of the Act of 1972 took the view that the dual domicile test represented the common law upon the capacity of a domiciled Englishman or Englishwoman to enter into polygamous marriage. It is clear that the Bill was presented to Parliament after reception of the *Law Commission Report*[1] on polygamous marriage, and that save for a footnote the Law Commission had reported that *Dicey and Morris'* rule 35 described the law. But I am concerned with the common law rights of the lady who in 1951 was Miss Mary Magson. Those rights are not to be cut down by any misapprehension about the common law entertained by the Law Commission, by the government, or by Parliament. I regard *Brook v Brook* and *Warrender v Warrender* as valuable guides as to the meaning of lex domicilii for the purposes of the instant case. I respect and agree with the decisions of the cases affirming the test of dual domicile in the cases to which I have referred, but I regard the rationes decidendi as an unsafe guide upon the problem which has been argued for the first time in this court. Profoundly as I respect the judgment of Sir Jocelyn Simon P in *Padolecchia v Padolecchia*, I am far from satisfied that he contemplated that his decision or his reasoning would be regarded as an authority upon capacity to enter into a polygamous union, the problems of which had not been brought in argument to his notice.

(His Lordship referred to *R v Brentwood Marriage Registrar, ex p Arias*[2] and continued):

And so the question that I have to decide is really this. It is clear that at the time of *Brook v Brook* and *Warrender v Warrender*, the factor of the intended matrimonial home played a part in the formulation of the concept of domicile. But that since then the factor of intended matrimonial home

1 Law Com No 42 (1971).
2 [1968] 2 QB 956, [1968] 3 All ER 279; p 251 above.

appears long to have been disregarded as relevant to choice of law in relation to capacity to marry, certainly in relation to polygamous marriage. Hence, Mr Ewbank rightly drew my attention to the confidence and the unqualified character of the dicta in the cases to which he referred, and the rationes decidendi, and reminded me there is no vestige in any of those cases of a continuing appreciation on the part of judges of the courts that matrimonial residence is relevant. But that may well be because the matter has never been argued until today, and I have to consider whether the assumption that has been made as a result of the expressions of view in the cases to which I have referred is solidly founded upon the common law foundations that are supposed to lie beneath them, and I have come to the conclusion that Mr Michael Davies is right in his submission that it is my duty to return to examine the foundations in *Brook v Brook* and *Warrender v Warrender* of the propositions that have since been founded upon them. And my conclusion is that Miss Magson had the capacity to enter into a polygamous union by virtue of her prenuptial decision to separate herself from the land of her domicile and to make her life with her husband in his country, where the Mohammedan law of polygamous marriage was the normal institution of marriage. I recognise that this decision may make it necessary for Parliament to consider a further amendment to the Nullity of Marriage Act 1971, if it is indeed the policy of Parliament to prevent such unions on the part of domiciled Englishmen and women, and to require a change of domicile before there is capacity to enter into them. But this court is only concerned with the common law rights of Miss Magson, as she was in 1951, and with the status, if any, that she acquired as a result of her decision to enter into a polygamous union with a domiciled Egyptian. My decision is that by that contract she became the wife of the respondent. Nothing in this judgment bears upon the capacity of minors, the law of affinity, or the effect of bigamy upon capacity to enter into a monogamous union. Having had the benefit of argument, I do not think that this branch of the law relating to capacity for marriage is quite as tidy as some very learned authors would have me believe, and I must face their displeasure with such fortitude as I can command.

NOTE

It seems safe to say that few cases on the English conflict of laws decided in the last 50 years have had a worse press than this one. Academic lawyers are almost unanimous in regarding it as wrongly decided: see *Cheshire & North*, pp 349–350, and *Morris*, p 128, and articles there cited. The chief grounds of criticism are (1) that the judge was wrong to prefer the dicta (for they were no more) in the early cases of *Warrender v Warrender* (1835) and *Brook v Brook* (1861) to the later decisions in *Pugh v Pugh* and *Padolecchia v Padolecchia*; (2) that his decision (as he conceded) made nonsense of section 4 (1) of the Nullity of Marriage Act 1971 (now section 14 (1) of the Matrimonial Causes Act 1973); and (3) that he was more solicitous for what he called the 'common law rights of Miss Mary Magson in 1951' than were her own counsel, who argued that the marriage was void, as did counsel for the Queen's Proctor. The case is printed here not because the present editors have changed their minds but in order to present the student with the opposing view, wrong though we believe it to be.

A polygamous marriage will be recognised as valid in England unless there is some strong reason to the contrary. Thus it constitutes a bar to a subsequent monogamous marriage by one of the parties.

Baindail v Baindail [1946] P 122, [1946] 1 All ER 342 (Court of Appeal)

In 1928 the respondent, a Hindu domiciled in India, married an Indian woman in India according to Hindu rites. This marriage was a polygamous marriage by the customs and laws of the Hindu race and was valid in India. In 1939, while his Indian wife was still living, the respondent went through a ceremony of marriage with the petitioner, an Englishwoman domiciled in England, at a registry office in London. In 1944 the petitioner, having discovered an invitation to the respondent's former Hindu marriage, presented a petition for nullity on the ground of bigamy. Barnard J granted a decree. The respondent appealed.

Lord Greene MR: The point raised by the appeal is a very short one. It was said that for the purposes of a claim to a decree of nullity the existence of the Hindu marriage must be disregarded by the courts of this country with the consequence that on 5 May 1939, the respondent was an unmarried man and was therefore not debarred by any existing union from marrying the petitioner. In support of that proposition a number of observations in decided cases have been cited. But it is to be observed that in no one of those cases was the question to which the court was addressing its observations in any way similar to the present question; it is not, in my opinion, legitimate to take those observations from their context and apply them to what is essentially a different question. I do not propose to go through all the cases cited to us but I will take what I think has been properly described as the high-water mark, the well-known decision of Lord Penzance in *Hyde v Hyde*.[3] The headnote starts with this general proposition: 'Marriage as understood in Christendom is the voluntary union for life of one man and one woman, to the exclusion of all others.' But that, of course, does not enable any general answer to be given to the question: 'What is to be understood by "marriage" for the purpose of the various branches of English law in which the question of marriage is relevant?' For the purpose of enforcing the rights of marriage, or for the purpose of dissolving a marriage, it has always been accepted as the case, following Lord Penzance's decision, that the courts of this country exercising jurisdiction in matrimonial affairs do not and cannot give effect to, or dissolve, marriages which are not monogamous marriages.[4] The word 'marriage' in the Matrimonial Causes Act, has to be construed for the purpose of ascertaining what the jurisdiction of the English courts is in these matters. The reasons are that the powers conferred on the courts for enforcing or dissolving a marriage tie are not adapted to any form of union between a man and a woman save a monogamous union. If a man by the law of his domicile is entitled to have four wives and then becomes domiciled in this country and wishes to be divorced here, nice questions would necessarily arise as to whether in consorting with the other wives he had

3 (1866) LR 1 P & M 130, 35 LJP & M 57.
4 See now Matrimonial Causes Act 1973, s 47; p 294 below (*Ed*).

been guilty of adultery and various questions of that kind. At any rate, rightly or wrongly, the courts have refused to regard a polygamous marriage as one which entitles the parties to come for matrimonial relief to the courts of this country.... Lord Penzance quite clearly saw how undesirable it would be to attempt to lay down any comprehensive rule as to the manner in which a polygamous marriage ought to be regarded by the courts of this country for purposes different from that with which he was immediately concerned. I do not feel myself bound by anything said in *Hyde v Hyde* or any of the other cases on which reliance was placed in this connection to hold that, for the purposes of the present petition, the court is bound, or ought, to disregard the existence of the Hindu marriage.

The problem, as it seems to me, requires to be approached de novo and from quite a different angle; that was the view which the learned judge took and, if I may respectfully say so, I entirely agree with the decision to which he came. The question as it presents itself to my mind is simply this: On 5 May 1939, when the respondent took the petitioner to the registry office, was he, or was he not, a married man so as to be incapable of entering into another legitimate union? The proposition I think would not be disputed that in general the status of a person depends on his personal law, which is the law of his domicile. By the law of the respondent's domicile at the time of his Hindu marriage he unquestionably acquired the status of a married man according to Hindu law; he was married for all the purposes of Hindu law, and he had imposed upon him the rights and obligations which that status confers under that law. That status he never lost. Nothing that happened afterwards, save the dissolution of the marriage, if it be possible according to Hindu law, could deprive him of the status of a married man which he acquired under Hindu law at the time of his Hindu marriage; he was therefore a married man on 5 May 1939, according to Hindu law. Did that circumstance prevent him from entering into a valid marriage in this country? It is said that it did not because, whatever Hindu law may say and whatever his position may be in India, this country will not recognise the validity of the Hindu marriage. We are not considering in this case the question of construction of any words such as 'marriage', 'husband', 'wife', and so forth in the Divorce Acts. We are considering whether, according to what would have been the old ecclesiastical law, the existence of the Hindu marriage formed a bar. For the purpose of that consideration, what was his status on 5 May 1939? Unquestionably, as I have said, it was that of a married man. Will that status be recognised in this country? English law certainly does not refuse all recognition of that status. For many purposes, quite obviously, the status would have to be recognised. If a Hindu domiciled in India died intestate in England leaving personal property in this country, the succession to the personal property would be governed by the law of his domicile; and in applying the law of his domicile effect would have to be given to the rights of any children of the Hindu marriage and of his Hindu widow, and for that purpose the courts of this country would be bound to recognise the validity of a Hindu marriage so far as it bears on the title to personal property left by an intestate here; one can think of other cases.

Lord Maugham LC, who delivered the leading opinion of the Committee of Privileges in *Lord Sinha's* case[5] said this: 'On the other hand it cannot, I

5 (1939) 171 Lords' Journals 350; [1946] 1 All ER 348, n.

think, be doubted now, notwithstanding some earlier dicta by eminent judges, that a Hindu marriage between persons domiciled in India is recognised by our courts, that issue are regarded as legitimate and that such issue can succeed to property, with the possible exception to which I refer later'; that was the well-known exception of real estate. We have not been referred to the cases, if any, to which the learned Lord Chancellor was referring, and, in fact, I do not know of any English cases; there are cases no doubt in the Privy Council, but whether there are any purely English cases I do not know. But I do get assistance from that paragraph, quite apart from the question of authorities, as showing the way in which these problems were striking a great master of the law, and one particularly familiar with problems of private international law. If he was not asserting that the law had been settled by decisions of the English courts, he was at least expressing his own opinion and to that I would pay the greatest respect. But quite apart from that, it seemes to me that the matter rests in this way: the courts of this country do for some purposes give effect to the law of the domicile as affixing or imposing a particular status on a given person. It would be wrong to say that for all purposes the law of the domicile is necessarily conclusive as to capacity arising from status. There are some things which the courts of this country will not allow a person in this country to do whatever status with its consequential capacity or incapacity the law of his domicile may give him. The case of slavery, of course, is an obvious case. The status of slavery would not be recognised here, and a variety of other things involved in status will not be recognised here. In the case of infants where different countries have different laws, it certainly is the view of high authority here that capacity to enter in England into an ordinary commercial contract is determined not by the law of the domicile but by the lex loci. I refer to the illustrations in order to show that there cannot be any hard and fast rule relating to the application of the law of the domicile as determining status and capacity for the purpose of transactions in this country.

The practical question in this case appears to be: Will the courts of this country, in deciding upon the validity of this English marriage, give effect to the status possessed by the respondent? That question we have to decide with due regard to common sense and some attention to reasonable policy. We are not fettered by any concluded decision on the matter. The learned judge set out in a striking manner some of the consequences which would flow from disregarding the Hindu marriage for present purposes. I think it is certainly a matter to bear in mind that the prospect of an English court saying that it will not regard the status of marriage conferred by a Hindu ceremony would be a curious one when very little more than a mile away the Privy Council might be sitting and coming to a precisely opposite conclusion as to the validity of such a marriage on an Indian appeal. I do not think we can disregard that circumstance. We have to apply the law in a state of affairs in which this question of the validity of Hindu marriages is necessarily of very great practical importance in the everyday running of our Commonwealth and Empire.

If the marriage with the petitioner was a valid marriage it would have this consequence: that she is entitled to the consortium of her husband to the exclusion of any other woman, that he is entitled to the consortium of his wife, and that she is bound according to our notions of law to live with him provided he gives her a suitable home. If he decided to go back to India it would be her duty as a wife to follow him to the home that he would provide. Assume that this takes place. Directly they land in India by the law of India he is a man married to the Indian lady, and assuming as I think we are bound to assume that Hindu law would be the same in this respect as English law, that Hindu lady is his lawful wife in India and as such would be entitled to his consortium, he would be entitled to insist that she should live with him and she would be entitled to insist that he should provide a home for her. The position therefore would be that this English lady would find herself compelled in India either to leave her husband or to share him with his Indian wife. What the position would be with regard to divorce in India I do not know, but if he had an Indian domicile she apparently could not divorce him in England.[6] Whether or not she could divorce him in India because in India he was associating with a woman who under Indian law was his lawful wife I do not know and I do not stop to inquire. Is it right that the courts of this country should give effect to a ceremony of marriage, the result of which would be to put the petitioner into such a position? It seems to me that effect must be given to common sense and decency and that on a question which is not covered by authority considerations of that kind must carry very great weight. On principle it seems to me that the courts are for this purpose bound to recognise the Indian marriage as a valid marriage and an effective bar to any subsequent marriage in this country.

Those are the short grounds on which I think this appeal should be decided. If we have not thought it necessary to reserve judgment in order to study more fully the cases which have been cited it is not that we have failed to appreciate them, but because at any rate so far as I am concerned I do not find it necessary to examine them very closely. The opinion which I have formed relates and relates solely to the facts of the present case which are connected with the validity of the English marriage in the circumstances of this case. I must not be taken as suggesting that for every purpose and in every context an Indian marriage such as this would be regarded as a valid marriage in this country. Mr Pritt in his reply drew an alarming picture of the effect of our decision on the law of bigamy if we were to decide against him. I think it right therefore to say that so far as I am concerned nothing that I have said must be taken as having the slightest bearing on the law of bigamy. On the question of whether a person is 'married' within the meaning of the statute (which is a criminal statute) when he has entered into a Hindu marriage in India I am not going to express any opinion whatever. It seems to me a different question in which other considerations may well come into play. I hope sincerely that nobody will endeavour to spell out of what I have said anything to cover such a question.

Morton and Bucknill LJJ concurred.
Appeal dismissed.

And the summary remedy provided by section 17 of the Married Women's Property Act 1882 applies to the parties to a valid polygamous marriage.

Chaudhry v Chaudhry [1976] Fam 148, [1976] 1 All ER 805 (Family Division)

6 See now Domicile and Matrimonial Proceedings Act 1973, s 5 (2) (*Ed*).

In 1959 the parties were married under Islamic law in Pakistan, where they were domiciled. The marriage was potentially polygamous. In 1963 they came to England without acquiring a domicile here. In July 1972 the husband divorced the wife by talaq in the Pakistani Embassy in London. This divorce became final in October 1972. At that date the talaq would have been recognised by the English courts as validly dissolving the marriage, because it was pronounced before section 16 of the Domicile and Matrimonial Proceedings Act 1973 (p 307 below) came into force on 1 January 1974. Under section 39 of the Matrimonial Proceedings and Property Act 1970 the wife had three years from the date of dissolution of the marriage in which to issue a summons under section 17 of the Married Women's Property Act 1882. That section provides that in any question between husband and wife as to the title to or possession of property, either party may apply to a judge by summons and the judge may make such order with respect to the property in dispute as he thinks fit. In February 1974, well within the time limit, the wife issued a summons asking for a declaration that she was entitled to an interest in the former matrimonial home in London. The registrar transferred the application to the High Court for the determination of a preliminary question of law.

Dunn J (having stated the facts):   Counsel for the husband submits that at common law, as it was stated in the leading case of *Hyde v Hyde and Woodmansee*,[7] the parties would not have been recognised as husband and wife, and that the words 'husband and wife' in section 17 of the Act of 1882 did not apply to the parties to polygamous marriages. He submitted that the indications to the contrary in the textbooks and in the *Report on Polygamous Marriages*[8] at paragraphs 123 and 124 were incorrect. He also submitted that there was nothing in section 1 of the Matrimonial Proceedings (Polygamous Marriages) Act 1972, now replaced by section 47 of the Matrimonial Causes Act 1973,[9] sufficient to alter the common law, and he reminded me of the canon of construction that there is a presumption against changes in the common law, and that if Parliament had intended that the wives of polygamous marriages should have the right to apply under section 17 of the Act of 1882, then it would have said so. Counsel for the husband went so far as to submit that all that the Matrimonial Proceedings (Polygamous Marriages) Act 1972 had done was to enable the court to grant decrees of divorce, nullity, and judicial separation, and make orders for wilful neglect to maintain and alterations of maintenance agreements, and that it was significant that there was nothing in section 1 which referred to property; and he submitted that if Parliament had intended that the rights of parties to polygamous marriages in property should be altered, then it could easily have said so.

I cannot accept that particular submission. Section 47 (2) (d) of the Matrimonial Causes Act 1973 gives the court power, notwithstanding that the marriage was a polygamous one, to make 'an order under any provision of this Act which confers a power exercisable in connection with, or in connection with proceedings for, any such decree or order as is mentioned in paragraphs (a) to (c) above;...' In my judgment, that

7 (1866) LR 1 P & D 130, 30 LJP & M 57.
8 Law Com No 42 (1971).
9 P 294 below.

provision gives the court power not only to grant relief under Part I of the Act of 1973 but also to make orders for financial relief under Part II, and orders for the protection and custody of children under Part III, notwithstanding that the marriage was a polygamous marriage.

But the matter does not rest there, because counsel's submission is that, whatever changes in the law have been made or not made by the Act of 1972, there is no express or implied reference in that Act to section 17 of the Married Women's Property Act 1882 and that the common law position with regard to section 17 still is that the English court would not recognise a polygamous marriage when deciding property rights between the parties.

He referred me to a number of cases, *Ali v Ali*;[10] *Imam Din v National Assistance Board*;[11] *Baindail v Baindail*[12] and *Sowa v Sowa*[13] and he submitted finally that all that the Act of 1972 had done was to change the law in regard to the granting of matrimonial relief, but that so far as section 17 of the Act of 1882 was concerned, the English courts would not regard these two people as husband and wife.

Counsel for the wife suggested that, as the law has developed, at common law a polygamous marriage would be recognised for the purpose of an application under section 17 of the Married Women's Property Act 1882 just as it has been recognised when considering what is meant by a husband and wife in other legislation, noticeably the Supplementary Benefit Act 1966, and he submitted that for the purpose of this application the wife was entitled as a wife.

Counsel for the wife further submitted that from 29 June 1972, when the Matrimonial Proceedings (Polygamous Marriages) Act 1972 received the royal assent, this wife could have come to this court and obtained as full and complete matrimonial relief as if she had been party to a monogamous marriage. He said that the only reason why she did not do so was because at that time she had not received advice and she allowed the talaq to go through, and that it would be quite anomalous if a wife was able to make applications in relation to financial provision and transfer of property under the Matrimonial Causes Act 1973 and not be able to make an application under the Married Women's Property Act 1882, which he pointed out is only a procedural matter, the substantive law so far as real property is concerned, at any rate, being the law of England.

Counsel also submitted that, quite apart from the provisions of the Matrimonial Proceedings (Polygamous Marriages) Act 1972, the parties had been married according to the law of their domicile and that consequently the English courts would give them the status of husband and wife according to that law, and that when one came to construe the words 'husband and wife' in section 17 of the Act of 1882, one should look at the status of the husband and wife according to the law of their domicile, and by that law these parties were undoubtedly husband and wife, notwithstanding that the marriage was potentially polygamous.

I accept that submission of counsel for the wife. It is, I think, important to

---

10 [1968] P 564, [1966] 1 All ER 664.
11 [1967] 2 QB 213, [1967] 1 All ER 750.
12 [1946] P 122, [1946] 1 All ER 342; p 286 above.
13 [1961] P 70, [1961] 1 All ER 687.

remember what was decided in *Hyde v Hyde and Woodmansee* and what was not decided. Lord Penzance said, at 138:

> 'This court does not profess to decide upon the rights of succession or legitimacy which it might be proper to accord to the issue of the polygamous unions, nor upon the rights or obligations in relation to third persons which people living under the sanction of such unions may have created for themselves. All that is intended to be here decided is that as between each other they are not entitled to the remedies, the adjudication, or the relief of the matrimonial law of England.'

It is that authoritative statement of the law which was finally changed by the Matrimonial Proceedings (Polygamous Marriages) Act 1972 as a result of the *Report on Polygamous Marriages*. But before that change was made there were a number of cases, which have been cited to me, referring to different statutes in which the words 'husband and wife' fell to be construed in which the courts held that the parties were husband and wife for the purpose of the statute, notwithstanding that the marriage was a polygamous one.

In *Baindail v Baindail* Lord Greene MR said, at 127: (His Lordship quoted the passage beginning 'what was his status on 5 May 1939?' and ending 'one can think of other cases' on p 287, above, and continued):

In my judgment, the parties having been married according to the law of their domicile, the English court would regard them as husband and wife for the purpose of deciding any application by either of them under section 17 of the Married Women's Property Act 1882. Any other conclusion would, in my judgment, be most impractical and an affront to common sense, because one would have the highly inconvenient situation that parties to a polygamous marriage could apply for transfers and settlement of property under the Matrimonial Causes Act 1973 but could not apply for their rights to be determined or for sale under section 17 of the Married Women's Property Act 1882.

For those reasons, my view of the preliminary issue is that the wife in this case is entitled to proceed under the section.

NOTE

An appeal from this decision was dismissed: [1976] 1 WLR 221. It may be added that modern statutes dealing with property rights between husband and wife (at least if they emanate from the Law Commission) often make express provision that the statute applies to polygamous marriages. Thus, section 10 (2) of the Matrimonial Homes Act 1983 provides that 'this Act applies as between husband and wife notwithstanding that the marriage in question was entered into under a law which permits polygamy'.

Social Security and Family Allowances (Polygamous Marriages) Regulations 1975[14]

2.—(1) Subject to the following provisions of these regulations, a polygamous marriage shall, for the purpose of the Social Security Act and the Family

14 SI 1975/561.

Allowances Act and any enactment construed as one with those Acts, be treated as having the same consequences as a monogamous marriage for any day, but only for any day, throughout which the polygamous marriage is in fact monogamous.

(2) In this and the next following regulation—

(a) a polygamous marriage is referred to as being in fact monogamous when neither party to it has any spouse additional to the other; and

(b) the day on which a polygamous marriage is contracted, or on which it terminates for any reason, shall be treated as a day throughout which that marriage was in fact monogamous if at all times on that day after it was contracted, or as the case may be, before it terminated, it was in fact monogamous.

CHAPTER 10

Matrimonial Causes

Section A. Jurisdiction of the English courts

Matrimonial Causes Act 1973

47.—(1) A court in England and Wales shall not be precluded from granting matrimonial relief or making a declaration concerning the validity of a marriage by reason only that the marriage in question was entered into under a law which permits polygamy.

(2) In this section 'matrimonial relief' means—

(a) any decree under Part I of this Act;

(b) a financial provision order under section 27 above;

(c) an order under section 35 above altering a maintenance agreement;

(d) an order under any provision of this Act which confers a power exercisable in connection with, or in connection with proceedings for, any such decree or order as is mentioned in paragraphs (a) to (c) above;

(e) an order under Part I of the Domestic Proceedings and Magistrates' Courts Act 1978.

(3) In this section 'a declaration concerning the validity of a marriage' means—

(a) a declaration that a marriage is valid or invalid; and

(b) any other declaration involving a determination as to the validity of a marriage;

being a declaration in a decree granted under section 45 above or a declaration made in the exercise by the High Court of its jurisdiction to grant declaratory relief in any proceedings notwithstanding that a declaration is the only substantive relief sought in those proceedings.

(4) This section has effect whether or not either party to the marriage in question has for the time being any spouse additional to the other party; and provision may be made by rules of court—

(a) for requiring notice of proceedings brought by virtue of this section to be served on any such other spouse; and

(b) for conferring on any such other spouse the right to be heard in any such proceedings,

in such cases as may be prescribed by the rules.

QUESTION

H, domiciled in Pakistan, and W¹, domiciled in England, marry in a register office in London. Later H marries W², a Pakistan domiciliary, in a mosque in Pakistan. Will W¹'s petition to the English courts for divorce succeed:

i) on the basis of H's adultery with W[2] (under s 1 (2) (a) of the Matrimonial Causes Act 1973) or

ii) On the basis of H's unreasonable behaviour (under s 1 (2) (b) of the 1973 Act)? As to (i), *Dicey and Morris*, pp 330–331, suggests the petition will fail; *Cheshire and North*, pp 354–355, thinks it might succeed.

Domicile and Matrimonial Proceedings Act 1973

PART II

JURISDICTION IN MATRIMONIAL PROCEEDINGS (ENGLAND AND WALES)

5.—(1) Subsections (2) to (5) below shall have effect, subject to section 6 (3) and (4) of this Act, with respect to the jurisdiction of the court to entertain—

(a) proceedings for divorce, judicial separation or nullity of marriage; and

(b) proceedings for death to be presumed and a marriage to be dissolved in pursuance of section 19 of the Matrimonial Causes Act 1973;

and in this Part of this Act 'the court' means the High Court and a divorce county court within the meaning of the Matrimonial Causes Act 1967.

(2) The court shall have jurisdiction to entertain proceedings for divorce or judicial separation if (and only if) either of the parties to the marriage—

(a) is domiciled in England and Wales on the date when the proceedings are begun; or

(b) was habitually resident in England and Wales throughout the period of one year ending with that date.

(3) The court shall have jurisdiction to entertain proceedings for nullity of marriage if (and only if) either of the parties to the marriage—

(a) is domiciled in England and Wales on the date when the proceedings are begun; or

(b) was habitually resident in England and Wales throughout the period of one year ending with that date; or

(c) died before that date and either—

(i) was at death domiciled in England and Wales, or

(ii) had been habitually resident in England and Wales throughout the period of one year ending with the date of death.

(4) The court shall have jurisdiction to entertain proceedings for death to be presumed and a marriage to be dissolved if (and only if) the petitioner—

(a) is domiciled in England and Wales on the date when the proceedings are begun; or

(b) was habitually resident in England and Wales throughout the period of one year ending with that date.

(5) The court shall, at any time when proceedings are pending in respect of which it has jurisdiction by virtue of subsection (2) or (3) above (or of this subsection), also have jurisdiction to entertain other proceedings, in respect of the same marriage, for divorce, judicial separation or nullity of marriage, notwithstanding that jurisdiction would not be exercisable under subsection (2) or (3).

(6) Schedule 1 to this Act shall have effect as to the cases in which matrimonial proceedings in England and Wales are to be, or may be, stayed by the court where there are concurrent proceedings elsewhere in respect of

the same marriage, and as to the other matters dealt with in that Schedule; but nothing in the Schedule—

(a) requires or authorises a stay of proceedings which are pending when this section comes into force; or

(b) prejudices any power to stay proceedings which is exercisable by the court apart from the Schedule.

SCHEDULE 1

STAYING OF MATRIMONIAL PROCEEDINGS (ENGLAND AND WALES)

Interpretation

1. The following five paragraphs have effect for the interpretation of this Schedule.

2. 'Matrimonial proceedings' means any proceedings so far as they are one or more of the five following kinds, namely, proceedings for—

divorce,

judicial separation,

nullity of marriage,

a declaration as to the validity of a marriage of the petitioner, and

a declaration as to the subsistence of such a marriage.

3.—(1) 'Another jurisdiction' means any country outside England and Wales.

(2) 'Related jurisdiction' means any of the following countries, namely, Scotland, Northern Ireland, Jersey, Guernsey and the Isle of Man (the reference to Guernsey being treated as including Alderney and Sark).

4.—(1) References to the trial or first trial in any proceedings do not include references to the separate trial of an issue as to jurisdiction only.

(2) For purposes of this Schedule, proceedings in the court are continuing if they are pending and not stayed.

5. Any reference in this Schedule to proceedings in another jurisdiction is to proceedings in a court of that jurisdiction, and to any other proceedings in that jurisdiction, which are of a description prescribed for the purposes of this paragraph; and provision may be made by rules of court as to when proceedings of any description in another jurisdiction are continuing for the purposes of this Schedule.

6. 'Prescribed' means prescribed by rules of court.

Duty to furnish particulars of concurrent proceedings in another jurisdiction

7. While matrimonial proceedings are pending in the court in respect of a marriage and the trial or first trial in those proceedings has not begun, it shall be the duty of any person who is a petitioner in the proceedings, or is a respondent and has in his answer included a prayer for relief, to furnish, in such manner and to such persons and on such occasions as may be prescribed, such particulars as may be prescribed of any proceedings which—

(a) he knows to be continuing in another jurisdiction; and

(b) are in respect of that marriage or capable of affecting its validity or subsistence.

Obligatory stays

8.—(1) Where before the beginning of the trial or first trial in any proceedings for divorce which are continuing in the court it appears to the court on the application of a party to the marriage—

(a) that in respect of the same marriage proceedings for divorce or nullity of marriage are continuing in a related jurisdiction; and

(b) that the parties to the marriage have resided together after its celebration; and

(c) that the place where they resided together when the proceedings in the court were begun or, if they did not then reside together, where they last resided together before those proceedings were begun, is in that jurisdiction; and

(d) that either of the said parties was habitually resident in that jurisdiction throughout the year ending with the date on which they last resided together before the date on which the proceedings in the court were begun,

it shall be the duty of the court, subject to paragraph 10 (2) below, to order that the proceedings in the court be stayed.

(2) References in sub-paragraph (1) above to the proceedings in the court are, in the case of proceedings which are not only proceedings for divorce, to the proceedings so far as they are proceedings for divorce.

Discretionary stays

9.—(1) Where before the beginning of the trial or first trial in any matrimonial proceedings which are continuing in the court it appears to the court—

(a) that any proceedings in respect of the marriage in question, or capable of affecting its validity or subsistence, are continuing in another jurisdiction; and

(b) that the balance of fairness (including convenience) as between the parties to the marriage is such that it is appropriate for the proceedings in that jurisdiction to be disposed of before further steps are taken in the proceedings in the court or in those proceedings so far as they consist of a particular kind of matrimonial proceedings,

the court may then, if it thinks fit, order that the proceedings in the court be stayed or, as the case may be, that those proceedings be stayed so far as they consist of proceedings of that kind.

(2) In considering the balance of fairness and convenience for the purposes of sub-paragraph (1) (b) above, the court shall have regard to all factors appearing to be relevant, including the convenience of witnesses and any delay or expense which may result from the proceedings being stayed, or not being stayed.

(3) In the case of any proceedings so far as they are proceedings for divorce, the court shall not exercise the power conferred on it by sub-paragraph (1) above while an application under paragraph 8 above in respect of the proceedings is pending.

(4) If, at any time after the beginning of the trial or first trial in any matrimonial proceedings which are pending in the court, the court declares by order that it is satisfied that a person has failed to perform the duty imposed on him in respect of the proceedings by paragraph 7 above, sub-

paragraph (1) above shall have effect in relation to those proceedings and, to the other proceedings by reference to which the declaration is made, as if the words 'before the beginning of the trial or first trial' were omitted; but no action shall lie in respect of the failure of a person to perform such a duty.

Supplementary

10.—(1) Where an order staying any proceedings is in force in pursuance of paragraph 8 or 9 above, the court may, if it thinks fit, on the application of a party to the proceedings, discharge the order if it appears to the court that the other proceedings by reference to which the order was made are stayed or concluded, or that a party to those other proceedings has delayed unreasonably in prosecuting them.

(2) If the court discharges an order staying any proceedings and made in pursuance of paragraph 8 above, the court shall not again stay those proceedings in pursuance of that paragraph.

Section B. Choice of Law

Choice of law issues relating to formalities of marriage, capacity to marry or consent of parties which arise in the context of a nullity petition are decided on the same principles as are applicable generally to marriage.

Apt v Apt (p 224 above)

Pugh v Pugh (p 246 above)

Szechter v Szechter (p 265 above)

The question what law determines whether a marriage should be annulled for wilful refusal to consummate is (to put it mildly) not satisfactorily settled.

Ponticelli v Ponticelli [1958] P 204, [1958] 1 All ER 357 (Divorce Division)

An Italian national, domiciled and resident in England, married by proxy in Italy a girl domiciled and resident in Italy. The marriage was arranged for them by their relations. The ceremony took place in Italy in July 1955 in the absence of the husband. The wife arrived at Paddington station in October 1955. She considered that she had been forced into marriage by her relatives and soon afterwards returned to Italy. Proxy marriages are valid by Italian law. The husband petitioned for nullity on the ground of the wife's wilful refusal to consummate.

Sachs J (after stating the facts, and holding that the proxy marriage was valid,[1] continued): The next issue is, what law is applicable to the plea of nullity by reason of wilful refusal to consummate the marriage? The importance of that issue in the present case derives from the fact that such a refusal, if established, (a) is a ground on which a decree of nullity may be granted, according to the law of this country, under section 8 (1) of the Matrimonial Causes Act 1950;[2] (b) is not a ground for such a decree of nullity before a civil court in Italy; and (c) is not a ground for such a decree before a consistory court there, unless the intention to refuse to consummate the marriage existed at the moment of the ceremony itself.

I pause to note that on the evidence before me it is not clear whether in Italy it would be a civil or a consistory court which has jurisdiction over this particular marriage—but most probably it would be the latter.

As regards the authorities on the question of which law applies, I first refer to *Robert v Robert*.[3] In that case Barnard J said: 'I have come to the conclusion that I ought to apply the lex loci celebrationis, for the following reasons. Wilful refusal to consummate a marriage, in order to be justified on principle as a ground for annulment and not dissolution, must be considered as a defect in marriage, an error in the quality of the respondent'; considered that wilful refusal did not relate to the personal capacity of the respondent spouse and decided that the lex domicilii could not be applied.

In *Rayden on Divorce*,[4] the law is stated as follows: 'Wilful refusal to consummate a marriage has been held in one case to be a defect in the marriage, so as to make the lex loci contractus applicable, rather than as something affecting capacity to contract.'

In *Way v Way*,[5] however, Hodson J took a contrary view. That was the case which concerned the validity of four marriages by British members of military missions and other organisations concerned with the prosecution of the war when they were on duty in Russia during the period 1941 to 1945. In all four cases the main point put forward by the petitioners was that the marriages were void for want of form according to the law of the USSR, a plea rejected by Hodson J. Brigadier Way, however, succeeded at trial on his alternative plea of wilful refusal to consummate and Hodson J said: 'In the case of Way, however, on the facts stated, accepting as I do his evidence, the respondent has wilfully refused to consummate the marriage and the marriage is accordingly voidable by English law, which is the law of the matrimonial domicile. The petitioner is accordingly entitled to a decree.'

It is true that there seems to have been little or no argument in that case as to whether it was lex loci or lex domicilii which was applicable, and there is no trace of the judgment of Barnard J having been cited. It is also true that on appeal by another of the above four petitioners, the Court of Appeal held that the marriages were void for want of form (*Kenward v Kenward*),[6] and thus the point as to wilful refusal to consummate should perhaps strictly

1 Following *Apt v Apt* [1948] P 83, [1947] 2 All ER 677; p 224 above.
2 Now s 12 (b) of the Matrimonial Causes Act 1973 (*Ed*).
3 [1947] P 164, [1947] 2 All ER 22.
4 7th edn (1958) p 93.
5 [1950] P 71, [1949] 2 All ER 959.
6 [1951] P 124, [1950] 2 All ER 297.

not have been decided in the *Way* case. None the less, the judgment of
Hodson J retains considerable persuasive effect and, moreover, it is
reinforced by the fact that later when he wrote the introduction to Mr
Jackson's work on the Formation and Annulment of Marriage (1951 edition)
he stated: 'Wilful refusal being a post-nuptial fact, it is difficult to see how,
for example, the lex loci celebrationis could have any application thereto.'

Next I should refer to the judgments of the Court of Appeal in *De Reneville
v De Reneville*.[7] That well-known case concerned the jurisdiction of the court
where the marriage had taken place in Paris—the petitioner being an
Englishwoman, who, previous to the marriage, was domiciled in England,
the husband being a French national who was domiciled in Paris both at the
date of the marriage and at the date of the petition, and France being the
place of the matrimonial home. The wife there alleged incapacity on the part
of the husband or, alternatively, wilful refusal to consummate the marriage.
Lord Greene MR, whose judgment was supported in toto by Somervell LJ,
stated that the wife's allegations went to the essential validity of the marriage
and then proceeded to say: 'In my opinion, the question whether the
marriage is void or merely voidable is for French law to answer. My reasons
are as follows: The validity of a marriage so far as regards the observance of
formalities is a matter for the lex loci celebrationis. But this is not a case of
forms. It is a case of essential validity. By what law is that to be decided? In
my opinion by the law of France, either because that is the law of the
husband's domicile at the date of the marriage or (preferably, in my view)
because at that date it was the law of the matrimonial domicile in reference
to which the parties may have been supposed to enter into the bonds of
marriage.' And the following passage is to be found in the judgment of
Bucknill LJ: 'The wife consented to marry her husband in France and
intended to live with him there and also impliedly intended to take her
husband's French domicile on the assumption that the marriage was valid.
Under these circumstances it seems to me that the question as to the validity
of the marriage should be decided by French law.' The phrasing of those
judgments and the reference to the place where the marriage took place
may, of course, be argued to leave open the question, which did not arise in
De Reneville v De Reneville, as to which law should prevail if there was a
conflict between the lex loci and lex domicilii—they simply tend against lex
fori.

Turning from authority to general principles, the position is that matters
touching the validity of a marriage have, at any rate since *Sottomayor
v De Barros*,[8] been generally regarded as divided into two broad categories.
The first related to matters of form and ceremony, to be determined by lex
loci. The second related to matters 'affecting the personal capacity of the
parties' at the moment of marriage. Indeed, earlier, Lord Campbell, in his
much quoted speech in *Brook v Brook*[9] said: 'But while the forms of entering
into the contract of marriage are to be regulated by the lex loci contractus,
the law of the country in which it is celebrated, the essentials of the contract
depend upon the lex domicilii, the law of the country in which the parties

---

7 [1948] P 100, [1948] 1 All ER 56.
8 (1877) 3 PD 1, 47 LJP 23; p 237 above.
9 (1861) 9 HLCas 193, 4 LT 93; p 232 at 234 above.

are domiciled at the time of the marriage, and in which the matrimonial residence is contemplated.'

Wilful refusal to consummate a marriage, clearly, cannot be said to fall within the categories of matters of form and ceremony. To my mind the true question is whether it should be treated as falling within the category of matters affecting the personal capacity of the spouse, in which case lex domicilii (which normally coincides with the law pertaining to the country of the husband's domicile at the time of marriage) applies, or whether it should be treated as something akin to matters for which the true remedy is divorce, in which case lex fori (eg, the law pertaining to the domicile of the husband at the date of presentation of the petition, or the law pertaining to the residence of a wife who may bring herself within the provisions of section 18 (1) of the Matrimonial Causes Act 1950),[10] applies.

It is first to be noted that no direct decision has been cited to me on the question of whether sexual incapacity should be regarded as a matter of 'personal capacity' within the meaning of the words used by Cotton LJ in *Sottomayor v De Barros* when delivering the judgment of the court. Mr Ormrod (counsel for the wife) submitted that it should be so regarded, but that any claim for a decree of nullity where a marriage was voidable, as opposed to void, should be decided according to lex fori. Dicey on *Conflict of Laws*,[11] treats the point as being open and submits the choice lies between lex domicilii or lex fori. It is there suggested, on the one hand: 'it would be logically and historically correct to hold that, even if the court has jurisdiction in the case of a voidable marriage, it can only pronounce a decree if the ground upon which it is sought is recognised by the law of the husband's domicile at the date of the marriage.' The opposing view is then put as follows: 'In answer it may be urged, however, that, as the practice of "looking behind the form and regarding the substance of the matter" has been approved by the Court of Appeal when the question is one of jurisdiction in the case of a voidable marriage, it must be adopted when the question is one of choice of law. The substance of the matter is that someone is claiming to terminate an existing status, and his right to do so should be referred to the law of his domicile at the date the claim is made.'

It is next to be observed that upon the authority of the judgment of Denning LJ in *Ramsay-Fairfax v Ramsay-Fairfax*,[12] I feel bound to take the view that there is no distinction in regard to the present issue to be drawn because the proceedings are for wilful refusal to consummate the marriage, rather than for sexual incapacity. The words of the judgment, albeit in a jurisdiction case, were: 'No one can call a marriage a real marriage when it has not been consummated; and this is the same, no matter whether the want of consummation is due to incapacity or to wilful refusal. Let the theologians dispute as they will, so far as the lawyers are concerned, Parliament has made it quite plain that wilful refusal and incapacity stand together as grounds of nullity and not for dissolution.' Mr Dobry (counsel for the husband) put the opposite and logical view in a persuasive manner, but I am unable to accede to his argument, supported though it may be by other judicial dicta. I would add that the reasoning in *De Reneville v De Reneville*

10 Now repealed; see Domicile and Matrimonial Proceedings Act 1973, s 5, p 295 above *(Ed)*.
11 6th edn (1949) p 267.
12 [1956] P 115, [1955] 3 All ER 695.

also implicitly rules out any attempt to distinguish between the two in relation to the point now under consideration.

In the light of the matters mentioned above, I find myself unable to agree with Barnard J that lex loci is the proper law applicable to the husband's plea. The choice, in my view, is between lex domicilii and lex fori. As between those, lex domicilii is favoured by Hodson J, by the fact that it was chosen as being the proper alternative by Barnard J in *Robert v Robert* if he was wrong as to lex loci, and by the fact that the judgments in *De Reneville v De Reneville* clearly tend against the applicability of lex fori. For myself, I would, in support of applying the lex domicilii, urge that it would be unfortunate indeed if a marriage were to be held valid or invalid according to which country's courts adjudicated on the issue: and the danger of differences of that type arising is now all the more to be feared by reason of the provisions of section 18 (1) of the Matrimonial Causes Act 1950. It is surely a matter of some importance that the initial validity of a marriage should, in relation to all matters except form and ceremony (to which a uniform general rule already applies), be consistently decided according to the law of one country alone—a point of view which seems to be supported by the judgment of Bucknill LJ in *De Reneville v De Reneville*—and that consistency cannot be attained if the test is lex fori.

Being of the opinion that the relevant proper law is either lex domicilii or lex fori, it is not, however, in the present case essential to come to a final conclusion as between the two. The husband having been domiciled in England, both at the date of the marriage and when he presented his petition, it is the law of this country that applies in each case. Further, if, and in so far as there may be, according to Mr Dobry's submission, a third alternative as to the law to be applied in the present case, viz, the law of the intended matrimonial domicile (should that be distinguishable from lex domicilii), again, no difference would be involved, for both spouses originally intended to live and settle here after the marriage. (His Lordship reviewed the evidence and granted a decree nisi.)

QUESTION

H and W marry in Germany where they are both domiciled. Later W becomes domiciled and habitually resident in England and petitions for annulment of her marriage on the ground of her mistake as to the attributes of H. This is not a ground for annulment under English law, though it is under German law (see *Mitford v Mitford* [1923] P 130, 92 LJP 90). What law will the English court apply?

Matrimonial Causes Act 1973

14.—(1) Where, apart from this Act, any matter affecting the validity of a marriage would fall to be determined (in accordance with the rules of private international law) by reference to the law of a country outside England and Wales, nothing in section 11, 12 or 13 (1) above[13] shall—

13 Section 11 states the grounds on which a marriage is void in English law. Section 12 states the grounds on which a marriage is voidable. Section 13 (1) states one of the bars to relief in cases where the marriage is voidable (*Ed*).

(a) preclude the determination of that matter as aforesaid; or
(b) require the application to the marriage of the grounds or bar there mentioned except so far as applicable in accordance with those rules.

QUESTION

Why is it the case that, although s 14 permits the English courts to apply foreign law to determine the validity of a marriage, a divorce petition in England is always governed by English law, even when the parties are both domiciled abroad?

Section C. Recognition of Foreign Divorces

Recognition of Divorces and Legal Separations Act 1971[14]

Decrees of divorce and judicial separation granted in British Isles

1. Subject to section 8 of this Act, the validity of a decree of divorce or judicial separation granted after the commencement of this section shall, if it was granted under the law of any part of the British Isles, be recognised throughout the United Kingdom.

Overseas divorces and legal separations

2. Sections 3 to 5 of this Act shall have effect, subject to section 8 of this Act, as respects the recognition in the United Kingdom of the validity of overseas divorces and legal separations, that is to say, divorces and legal separations which—
(a) have been obtained by means of judicial or other proceedings in any country outside the British Isles; and
(b) are effective under the law of that country.

3.—(1) The validity of an overseas divorce or legal separation shall be recognised if, at the date of the institution of the proceedings in the country in which it was obtained—
(a) either spouse was habitually resident in that country; or
(b) either spouse was a national of that country.
   (2) In relation to a country the law of which uses the concept of domicile as a ground of jurisdiction in matters of divorce or legal separation, subsection (1) (a) of this section shall have effect as if the reference to habitual residence included a reference to domicile within the meaning of that law.
   (3) In relation to a country comprising territories in which different systems of law are in force in matters of divorce or legal separation, the foregoing provisions of this section (except those relating to nationality) shall have effect as if each territory were a separate country.

4.—(1) Where there have been cross-proceedings, the validity of an overseas divorce or legal separation obtained either in the original proceedings or in the cross-proceedings shall be recognised if the requirements of paragraph

14 This Act is printed as amended by the Domicile and Matrimonial Proceedings Act 1973 (*Ed*).

(a) or (b) of section 3 (1) of this Act are satisfied in relation to the date of the institution either of the original proceedings or of the cross-proceedings.

(2) Where a legal separation the validity of which is entitled to recognition by virtue of the provisions of section 3 of this Act or of subsection (1) of this section is converted, in the country in which it was obtained, into a divorce, the validity of the divorce shall be recognised whether or not it would itself be entitled to recognition by virtue of those provisions.

5.—(1) For the purpose of deciding whether an overseas divorce or legal separation is entitled to recognition by virtue of the foregoing provisions of this Act, any finding of fact made (whether expressly or by implication) in the proceedings by means of which the divorce or legal separation was obtained and on the basis of which jurisdiction was assumed in those proceedings shall—

(a) if both spouses took part in the proceedings, be conclusive evidence of the fact found; and

(b) in any other case, be sufficient proof of that fact unless the contrary is shown.

(2) In this section 'finding of fact' includes a finding that either spouse was habitually resident or domiciled in, or a national of, the country in which the divorce or legal separation was obtained; and for the purposes of subsection (1) (a) of this section, a spouse who has appeared in judicial proceedings shall be treated as having taken part in them.

General provisions

6.—(1) In this section 'the common law rules' means the rules of law relating to the recognition of divorces or legal separations obtained in the country of the spouses' domicile or obtained elsewhere and recognised as valid in that country.

(2) In any circumstances in which the validity of a divorce or legal separation obtained in a country outside the British Isles would be recognised by virtue only of the common law rules if either—

(a) the spouses had at the material time both been domiciled in that country; or

(b) the divorce or separation were recognised as valid under the law of the spouses' domicile,

its validity shall also be recognised if subsection (3) below is satisfied in relation to it.

(3) This subsection is satisfied in relation to a divorce or legal separation obtained in a country outside the British Isles if either—

(a) one of the spouses was at the material time domiciled in that country and the divorce or separation was recognised as valid under the law of the domicile of the other spouse; or

(b) neither of the spouses having been domiciled in that country at the material time, the divorce or separation was recognised as valid under the law of the domicile of each of the spouses respectively.

(4) For any purpose of subsection (2) or (3) above 'the material time', in relation to a divorce or legal separation, means the time of the institution of proceedings in the country in which it was obtained.

(5) Sections 2 to 5 of this Act are without prejudice to the recognition of the validity of divorces and legal separations obtained outside the British

Isles by virtue of the common law rules (as extended by this section), or of any enactment other than this Act; but, subject to this section, no divorce or legal separation so obtained shall be recognised as valid in the United Kingdom except as provided by those sections.

8.—(1) The validity of—

(a) a decree of divorce or judicial separation granted under the law of any part of the British Isles; or

(b) a divorce or legal separation obtained outside the British Isles,

shall not be recognised in any part of the United Kingdom if it was granted or obtained at a time when, according to the law of that part of the United Kingdom (including its rules of private international law and the provisions of this Act), there was no subsisting marriage between the parties.

(2) Subject to subsection (1) of this section, recognition by virtue of sections 2 to 5 or section 6 (2) of this Act or of any rule preserved by section 6 (5) thereof of the validity of a divorce or legal separation obtained outside the British Isles may be refused if, and only if—

(a) it was obtained by one spouse—

    (i) without such steps having been taken for giving notice of the proceedings to the other spouse as, having regard to the nature of the proceedings and all the circumstances, should reasonably have been taken; or

    (ii) without the other spouse having been given (for any reason other than lack of notice) such opportunity to take part in the proceedings as, having regard to the matters aforesaid, he should reasonably have been given; or

(b) its recognition would manifestly be contrary to public policy.

(3) Nothing in this Act shall be construed as requiring the recognition of any findings of fault made in any proceedings for divorce or separation or of any maintenance, custody or other ancillary order made in any such proceedings.

10.—(1) This Act may be cited as the Recognition of Divorces and Legal Separations Act 1971.

(2) In this Act 'the British Isles' means the United Kingdom, the Channel Islands and the Isle of Man.

(3) In this Act 'country' includes a colony or other dependent territory of the United Kingdom but for the purposes of this Act a person shall be treated as a national of such a territory only if it has a law of citizenship or nationality separate from that of the United Kingdom and he is a citizen or national of that territory under that law.

(4) The provisions of this Act relating to overseas divorces and legal separations and other divorces and legal separations obtained outside the British Isles apply to a divorce or legal separation obtained before the date of the commencement of those provisions as well as to one obtained on or after that date and, in the case of a divorce or legal separation obtained before that date—

(a) require, or, as the case may be, preclude, the recognition of its validity in relation to any time before that date as well as in relation to any subsequent time; but

(b) do not affect any property rights to which any person became entitled before that date or apply where the question of the validity of the divorce or legal separation has been decided by any competent court in the British Isles before that date.

QUESTIONS

1. What is the significance of the distinction drawn in section 10 (4) of this Act between 'overseas divorces' and 'other divorces obtained outside the British Isles'?
2. What is the meaning of 'effective under the law of that country' in section 2 (b)? Does it mean that the divorce must be effective in eg the American state where it was obtained, or in the United States as a whole? At first sight the former may seem the more convenient interpretation, because the latter would require the English court to be satisfied that the American divorce would be entitled to full faith and credit in the other states. Yet this is precisely what may have to be done under the rule in *Armitage v A-G*,[15] preserved by section 6 (3) of the Act, if one or both parties are domiciled in one American state but divorced in another. On the other hand, the former interpretation would mean that an American divorce would have to be recognised in England even if it would not be recognised in any other American state: which seems absurd. Consider *Cruse v Chittum*,[16] where the Mississippi divorce was recognised in England although there was no evidence that it would be recognised in other states. Yet *Cheshire & North*, pp 374–375, and *Morris*, pp 147–148, insists that 'country' in section 2 (b) means eg the United States and not the individual state. Which is right?
3. H, who is at all material times a French national habitually resident in France, marries W, who is at all material times a British citizen habitually resident in England. H obtains a divorce from W in France. Will this divorce be recognised in England?
4. H, domiciled at all material times (in the English sense) in France, marries W, domiciled at all material times (in the English sense) in England. H obtains a divorce from W in France. Will this divorce be recognised in England?
5. H and W are domiciled at all material times (in the English sense) in England. In 1965 W goes to New York and obtains a divorce there after three years' ordinary residence there. In 1970 the Court of Session in Edinburgh declines to recognise this divorce. But it would have been recognised in England under the rule in *Travers v Holley*,[17] now abolished by section 6 (5) of the Act. In 1984 the validity of the divorce arises in English proceedings. Will the English court follow the decision of the Scottish court (in which case the marriage will 'limp' as between England (and Scotland) and New York)? Or will it apply the rule in *Travers v Holley* and recognise the divorce (in which case the marriage will 'limp' as between England and Scotland)? See section 10 (4) (b).

NOTE

In an unpublished Consultation Paper circulated to a selected audience in May 1983, the Law Commission and the Scottish Law Commission identify some defects in this Act which they provisionally recommend should be abolished. First they recommend that the confusing and unnecessary distinction between 'overseas divorces' and 'other divorces obtained outside the British Isles should be abolished, and that sections 4 and 5 of the Act should apply to all divorces obtained outside the British Isles.

15 [1906] P 135, 75 LJP 42.
16 [1974] 2 All ER 940; p 29 above.
17 [1953] P 246, [1953] 2 All ER 794.

Secondly they recommend that section 6 should be amended so that if the divorce was obtained or recognised in the domicile of only one party it should be recognised in the United Kingdom even if it would not be recognised in the domicile of the other party. Thirdly they recommend that section 8 (1) should be redrafted so as to provide that recognition of a foreign divorce should be refused if it is inconsistent with a previous decision of another court in the British Isles. The object of this last recommendation is to pave the way for a redrafted section 8 (1) to be extended to foreign nulity decrees (p 335 below), to which in its present form it is obviously inappropriate.

Domicile and Matrimonial Proceedings Act 1973

16.—(1) No proceeding in the United Kingdom, the Channel Islands or the Isle of Man shall be regarded as validly dissolving a marriage unless instituted in the courts of law of one of those countries.

(2) Notwithstanding anything in section 6 of the Recognition of Divorces and Legal Separations Act 1971 (as substituted by section 2 of this Act), a divorce which—

(a) has been obtained elsewhere than in the United Kingdom, the Channel Islands and the Isle of Man; and

(b) has been so obtained by means of a proceeding other than a proceeding instituted in a court of law; and

(c) is not required by any of the provisions of sections 2 to 5 of that Act to be recognised as valid,

shall not be regarded as validly dissolving a marriage if both parties to the marriage have throughout the period of one year immediately preceding the institution of the proceeding been habitually resident in the United Kingdom.

(3) This section does not affect the validity of any divorce obtained before its coming into force and recognised as valid under rules of law formerly applicable.

A case on the meaning of 'contrary to public policy' in section 8 (2) (b) of the Recognition of Divorces and Legal Separations Act 1971.

Kendall v Kendall [1977] Fam 208, [1977] 3 All ER 471 (Family Division)

The husband, who was domiciled in England, married the wife, a Cypriot, in Cyprus in 1964. The matrimonial home was in Newbury, England. In 1972 the husband was posted by his employers to Bolivia. The wife joined him there in March 1973. In June 1974 the wife returned to England with the children. Before she left Bolivia she was induced by the husband to sign some papers in Spanish (a language which she did not understand) asking for a divorce which she did not want. The husband told her that her signature was necessary to enable the children to leave the country. In

August 1975 a Bolivian court pronounced a decree of divorce on the wife's petition. The decree stated several things which were not true: that there were no children; that the wife worked; and that neither party owned any property. Soon afterwards the husband returned to England. The wife petitioned under RSC Order 15, rule 16, for a declaration that the Bolivian divorce was invalid.

Hollings J: This declaration is sought pursuant to the provisions of the Recognition of Divorces and Legal Separations Act 1971, an Act which came into being as a result of an international convention, the Hague Convention on Recognition of Divorces and Legal Separations of 1970, and it provides for the recognition of foreign decrees of divorce, given certain conditions set out in that Act, and also provides for non-recognition in certain exceptional circumstances. (His Lordship read section 3 (1) (a) and continued): I do not need to refer to the alternative. I am satisfied, and Mr Lines on behalf of the wife concedes, that at the time of the Bolivian decree of 25 August 1975, the husband was habitually resident in Bolivia. So, pursuant to that section, unless there is an exception under a later section, I am bound to recognise the validity of that decree. The exceptions are set out in section 8 (2). (His Lordship read section 8 (2) (a) and continued): One notices that there is a discretion allowed.

Mr Lines acknowledges the difficulty, if not the impossibility, of relying upon that exception, because in this case the decree on its face states that it has been obtained by her; so the provision as to notice by the other spouse is not apt or relevant, she being the person who, on the face of the decree, brought the proceedings, ex hypothesi does not need notice of the proceedings. That exception plainly refers to a person seeking a declaration of non-validity who was the respondent in the relevant divorce proceedings. Mr Lines, therefore, relies on the next exception in sub-paragraph (b) which is to the effect that a decree may be refused, and only refused if, 'its recognition would manifestly be contrary to public policy'. Mr Lines acknowledges that this is no doubt an Act which starts de novo, as it were, and founded, as I have said, upon an international convention, and he acknowledges that reference to earlier authorities in relation to recognition of foreign decrees at common law may not be, and indeed probably is not, of assistance or relevance; but he did refer me to the authorities, the effect of which is set out in *Rayden on Divorce*,[18] where it is stated, for example:

'Even if the foreign court had jurisdiction to grant a decree, the common law position is that such decree would not be afforded recognition if it offends English views of substantial justice. This residual discretion to refuse recognition to a foreign decree was applied particularly in cases on foreign nullity decrees but also in divorce cases.'

I refrain from quoting further from that paragraph, but it does give other examples of occasions when the court has decided that substantial justice dictates a decree that a foreign decree should not be recognised notwithstanding other factors rendering it recognisable. Mr Lines also referred me to the judgment of Cairns J in *Middleton v Middleton*,[19] where

18 12th edn (1974) vol 1, p 95.
19 [1967] P 62 at 69, [1966] 1 All ER 168 at 172.

Cairns J set out the propositions of English law which he had to consider.
Proposition 2 states:

> 'If a decree of divorce has been obtained in a foreign court by false
> evidence about the matrimonial offence relied on, it will not on that
> ground be treated by the English court as invalid provided it has not
> been set aside in the foreign court.'

The authority there referred to is *Bater v Bater*.[20]

I accept that that was indeed the position at common law and, if
considerations of common law applied here, therefore the mere fact that false
evidence had been placed before the Bolivian court would not be a ground of
non-recognition or a declaration of non-validity. Mr Lines, however, does
submit that the next two propositions are of relevance. Proposition 3 states:
'If a decree has been obtained in a foreign court contrary to natural justice,
the English court must treat it as invalid.' *MacAlpine v MacAlpine*.[1] In both
that authority and *Bater v Bater* the facts are so dissimilar as to render
reference to them unnecessary as a comparison with the facts of this case.
Then proposition 4: 'The English court has a discretion to refuse to recognise
a foreign decree which offends against English ideas of substantial justice.'
The authority there is *Gray v Formosa*[2] and *Lepre v Lepre*.[3]

Mr Lines submits that this is an approach one can still make when
considering whether to withhold recognition on the ground of public policy.
I have looked at what the editor of Dicey & Morris, *The Conflict of Laws*,[4] has
to say about this. He says, in relation to recognition manifestly contrary to
public policy, at 326:

> 'There does not appear to be a reported case in which a foreign divorce
> has been refused recognition on this ground. The word 'manifestly' is
> therefore probably redundant. It appears in section 8 (2) of the Act
> because it appears in article 10 of the Convention . . .'

That is the Convention to which I have already referred.

> ' . . . where it was inserted to discourage the excessive reliance by the
> courts of some countries on alleged grounds of public policy. On the
> other hand, English judges have claimed a 'residual discretion' to refuse
> recognition to divorces which offended their sense of justice . . .'

And some of the authorities to which I have already made reference are
there referred to.

> ' . . . and have occasionally exercised it: *Middleton v Middleton*. This
> discretion appears to have been abolished by the Act, and such divorces
> could now be refused recognition only on the ground of public policy.
> The difference may be purely verbal.'

I have stated enough already to indicate my view that the proceedings in the
Bolivian court were, on the evidence before me, obtained by deception.

20 [1906] P 209, 75 LJP 60.
 1 [1958] P 35, [1957] 3 All ER 134.
 2 [1963] P 259, [1962] 3 All ER 419.
 3 [1965] P 52, [1963] 2 All ER 49; p 325 below.
 4 9th edn (1973).

Manifestly, as I have said, the Bolivian court was deceived, certainly deceived, it would appear, by lawyers, possibly—I will say no more—with the collusion and the connivance or at the instigation of the husband. In those circumstances, is it not, I ask myself, manifestly contrary to public policy that a decree obtained in such circumstances should be given any force or effect or should be accorded any recognition? I bear in mind, however, that one must pay regard to the principles of comity and observe or accept decisions, so far as one otherwise can without injustice, of foreign courts. I am sure that, if the Bolivian court was apprised of the circumstances that I find existing, it would without hesitation take steps effectually to invalidate the decree.

In those circumstances I have no hesitation in saying that in the extraordinary circumstances of this case the exception under section 8 (2) (b) of the Act of 1971 applies, that is, that the recognition of that decree in those circumstances would manifestly be contrary to public policy, and I so declare.

Declaration accordingly.

In Canada and the United States a spouse who obtains an invalid foreign divorce, or who remarries on the strength of one, or who acquiesces in the other spouse obtaining one, may sometimes be precluded or 'estopped' from denying its validity.

Downton v Royal Trust Co (1972) 34 DLR (3d) 403 (Supreme Court of Canada)

Dr and Mrs Downton were domiciled at all material times in Newfoundland. They separated in 1960. In May 1960 a separation agreement provided that the husband would pay his wife the monthly sum of $350. In 1965 the husband went to Nevada and lived there for six weeks in order to obtain a divorce. His Nevada lawyer wrote to the wife asking her to sign a power of attorney to authorise an appearance on her behalf. The power of attorney specified that the terms of the separation agreement would be incorporated in the divorce decree. The wife signed and returned the power of attorney. The divorce was granted, and the husband remarried and returned to Newfoundland. The husband died in 1969 having by his will left the bulk of his estate to his second wife. The first wife applied to the Newfoundland court for an order for financial provision under the Newfoundland Family Provision Act on the ground that she was the deceased's lawful widow. It was not disputed that the Nevada divorce was without effect in Newfoundland.

Furlong CJ made an order in the widow's favour for $20,000. The Newfoundland Court of Appeal reversed his decision on the ground that the widow, having accepted the jurisdiction of the Nevada court and having her rights under the separation agreement incorporated in the decree, was precluded from denying the validity of the decree. The widow appealed.

Laskin J (having stated the facts, and having reviewed the conflicting Canadian case law, continued): My canvass of typical cases which have reached Canadian courts indicates that the only claim to consistency that they exhibit is the application of a preclusion doctrine against a spouse who, having obtained a decree of divorce or nullity from a foreign court incompetent to give it, seeks thereafter to assert that incompetence in order to gain a pecuniary advantage against his or her spouse or the estate of the spouse. The doctrine has an ethical basis: a refusal to permit a person to insist, to his or her pecuniary advantage, on a relationship which that person has previously deliberately sought to terminate. The ethical basis is lost, however, where there has been both invocation and submission to the foreign jurisdiction by the respective spouses; and if there is to be a modification or rejection of the preclusion doctrine in respect of one or both of the spouses, other considerations must be brought into account; there may be, for example, an alleviating explanation for the submission to the jurisdiction of an incompetent foreign court. So too, where third parties are involved in a case where a spouse who has obtained an invalid foreign divorce or decree of nullity seeks to rely on its invalidity.

Any ethical factors underlying the preclusion doctrine are submerged in overriding considerations when an invalid foreign decree is pressed in a strictly matrimonial cause in which divorce or nullity is sought. Marital status per se cannot be altered or perpetuated by a preclusion doctrine, and hence a spouse should not be denied the right to seek a divorce before a competent court merely because that spouse earlier invoked the jurisdiction of an incompetent foreign court.

This result appears to me to be consonant with a public policy which today more than before recognises that parties whose marriage has failed should be allowed to dissolve it. I see no inconsistency between this position and the application of a preclusion doctrine against a spouse who has ignored the jurisdictional requirements for a valid dissolution and who would none the less insist to his or her own pecuniary advantage that the law be applied strictly in his or her favour in disregard of an attempted dissolution which is invalid.

The American Law Institute, Restatement of the Law, Second, Conflict of Laws, (1971), has recognised the difficulty of formulating precise rules by adopting in this area of the law a broad and flexible approach which commends itself to me. Section 74 reads as follows:

> A person may be precluded from attacking the validity of a foreign divorce decree if, under the circumstances, it would be inequitable for him to do so.

In the succeeding comment on the scope of this rule, there are the following passages:

> The rule is not limited to situations of what might be termed 'true estoppel' where one party induces another to rely to his damage upon certain representations as to the facts of the case. The rule may be applied whenever, under all the circumstances, it would be inequitable to permit a particular person to challenge the validity of a divorce decree. Such inequity may exist when action has been taken in reliance on the divorce or expectations are based on it or when the attack on the divorce is inconsistent with the earlier conduct of the attacking party.
>
> The rule's scope of application varies from state to state and, even within the confines of a single state, is often clouded with uncertainty. In general, it may be said that a person who obtains a divorce and then

remarries will not be permitted to attack the validity of the divorce in order to free himself from his obligations to his second spouse or in order to claim an inheritance from the estate of the first spouse. On the other hand, if both parties to a divorce attack its validity in a subsequent action, neither should be estopped from making such an attack since neither is placing reliance upon the validity of the divorce. An example is where after a husband has obtained an ex parte divorce, the wife brings an action against him for separation and support, and the husband in turn seeks to counterclaim for divorce. He should be permitted to do so. The wife is attacking the validity of the divorce in her action for separation, and there is no reason under the circumstances why the husband should not be allowed to do the same.

A spouse who has accepted benefits under the divorce will usually be held estopped to attack it. So an invalid ex parte divorce obtained by a husband will be held immune from attack by a wife who has remarried. Usually, such a divorce will also be held immune from attack by a wife who has accepted alimony under the original decree or who has waited an unreasonably long time before attacking the divorce, particularly if the husband has remarried in the meantime.

The cases are divided on the question whether third persons may be estopped from attacking a divorce decree. Such an estoppel has at times been imposed upon one who persuades a woman to seek a divorce in order that he may marry her, particularly if he finances the divorce and provides a lawyer. Likewise, a person may be estopped from attacking a divorce if his claim is derived from a person who would have been estopped.

In the present case, I am satisfied that the lawful wife submitted to the foreign court as she did to protect her existing benefits which were given as a result of her separation from her husband in Newfoundland. Her submission was, accordingly, a special one and could have no effect against her in Newfoundland in enforcing the separation terms, since she would not have to rely there upon the foreign decree in order to enforce them. This is not a case where the appellant's maintenance benefits rested on the foreign divorce decree alone and where she had taken those benefits until the deceased's death, and then sought to assert that she was the lawful wife in order to gain additional benefits. . . .

The present case stands, therefore, as one where the wife's formal submission to the foreign court was not followed by any act or conduct in reliance upon it nor was there any acceptance by her of benefits under it. I am unable to agree, therefore, that the appellant is precluded from denying the validity of the foreign divorce decree in Newfoundland and from insisting on her status as the lawful widow of the deceased.

Appeal allowed. Order of Furlong CJ restored.

NOTE

There is very little English authority on this question, and what there is is uniformly hostile to the adoption of a doctrine of preclusion or estoppel. It is true however that the English courts have not yet been confronted with such starkly unmeritorious claims as the American and Canadian courts have sometimes been.

Extra-judicial divorces obtained by talaq in Pakistan in accordance with the Muslim Family Laws Ordinance 1961 are obtained by 'judicial or other proceedings' within the meaning of section 2 of the Recognition of Divorces and Legal Separations Act 1971.

Quazi v Quazi [1980] AC 744, [1979] 3 All ER 897 (House of Lords)

The parties were Pakistan nationals born in India. They married there in 1963. In 1968, when they were both domiciled in Thailand, the marriage was dissolved by khula (a consensual form of Muslim divorce). The husband came to England and in 1973 bought a small house in Wimbledon for £3000 with money borrowed from a friend. On 30 July 1974, during a temporary visit to Pakistan, the husband pronounced a talaq (a form of Muslim divorce obtainable at the will of the husband alone). This talaq would take effect under Pakistani law 90 days thereafter, ie on 28 November 1974. On 23 December 1974, the wife instituted divorce proceedings against the husband in England, claiming (inter alia) a share in the house in Wimbledon. On 18 June 1975 the husband petitioned for a declaration that the marriage had been dissolved, and the wife's petition was stayed pending the result of that of the husband. Wood J after a trial lasting 14 days held that both the khula and the talaq could be recognised in England. The Court of Appeal (Orr, Ormrod and Browne LJJ) after a hearing lasting seven days reversed this decision. The husband appealed.

Lord Diplock: My Lords, to dispose of this appeal it is sufficient if the appellant succeeds in showing that either of the foreign divorces that he relies on in the alternative as having dissolved his marriage to the respondent, is entitled to recognition by the English courts. The validity of a divorce by talaq obtained by a Pakistani national in accordance with Pakistani law raises a question as to the true construction of the Recognition Act and its application to talaqs obtained in Pakistan. This is of general importance in view of the number of Pakistani nationals who are settled in the United Kingdom either accompanied or unaccompanied by their wives. On the other hand, the validity of a divorce by khula entered into in Thailand by Pakistani nationals who are domiciled there, is not a question that is very likely to require consideration by an English court in any subsequent case. It depends on the domestic law of Thailand, the Thai rules of conflict of laws, the application by the Thai courts of the doctrine of renvoi, and under that doctrine, the applicability of Muslim Family Laws Ordinance 1961 of Pakistan to consensual divorces. These are questions of fact to be decided by an English court upon expert evidence of the foreign law concerned. In the instant case the expert evidence on these matters was inadequate, conflicting and confusing and any decision of the Court of Appeal or of this House that was based upon that evidence would be valueless as a precedent in any subsequent case between other parties even in the unlikely event that the circumstances were similar.

It was for this reason that it was decided to hear argument in this House restricted in the first instance to the question of the validity of the divorce by talaq under the Recognition Act. At the conclusion of this argument your Lordships were all of the opinion, which I also share, that even if the marriage were still subsisting on 30 July 1973, it was effectively dissolved on 28 November 1974 by a divorce by talaq that is entitled to recognition under sections 2 and 3 of the Recognition Act. So in order to avoid unnecessary prolongation of a costly hearing in a case which has been throughout conducted entirely upon legal aid, this House has limited its consideration to the only question that is of general importance, the validity of the Pakistani talaq, and has decided the appeal upon that point alone.

The preamble to the Recognition Act makes it plain that its principal, though not its only, purpose was to enable the United Kingdom to give effect in its domestic law to the Hague Convention on the Recognition of Divorces and Legal Separations of 1970 ('the Recognition Convention').[5] The mischief that the Convention was designed to cure was that of 'limping marriages', that is, marriages that were recognised in some jurisdictions as having been validly dissolved, but in other jurisdictions as still subsisting. The cause of these discrepancies in the recognition of foreign divorces by the courts of different states was that some states under their rules of conflict of laws treated the nationality of the parties as the sole ground of jurisdiction in matters of divorce, others treated as the only ground of jurisdiction 'domicile' in the strict sense in which that concept plays a part in English common law, and yet others 'domicile' in the looser sense, in which that term is used in civil law as meaning habitual residence. The solution adopted by the Recognition Convention was to require all contracting states to recognise as valid grounds of jurisdiction in matters of divorce and legal separation all three concepts, nationality, domicile and habitual residence. Article 17, however, left them at liberty to apply rules of law *more* favourable to the recognition of foreign divorces than those called for by the Convention.

The sections of the Recognition Act that are relevant to the recognition of the divorce by talaq in the instant case are sections 2 and 3. (His Lordship read them.)

It is not disputed that both spouses in the instant case have at all relevant times been nationals of Pakistan; nor is it disputed that if the procedural requirements of the Muslim Family Laws Ordinance 1961 of Pakistan were complied with the divorce would be effective under the law of that country—though there is a dispute of fact (to which I will have to revert later) as to whether one of those requirements was satisfied. This leaves as the only question of law arising under the Recognition Act: was the divorce by talaq 'obtained by means of judicial or other proceedings' which took place in Pakistan, within the meaning of that phrase as used in section 2?

One must therefore first look to see what it was that was done in Pakistan which resulted in the divorce by talaq being effective there. The concept of divorce by talaq under the classic religious law of Islam is one with which English courts have become familiar. It is effected by the husband solemnly pronouncing the word 'talaq' either once or thrice in the presence of witnesses. Neither the presence of the wife nor even any notice to her is required by the classic religious law of Islam. The absence of any requirement of notice or publicity in this classic or 'bare' form of talaq, has led certain Muslim states, of which Pakistan is one, to pass legislation requiring additional formalities to be complied with in order to make a bare talaq effective to dissolve the marriage. The relevant law in Pakistan is to be found in sections 1 and 7 of the Muslim Family Laws Ordinance 1961, and is in the following terms:

5 Cmnd 6248.

'1 (2). [The Ordinance] extends to the whole of Pakistan, and applies to all Muslim citizens of Pakistan, wherever they may be.... 7. Talaq—(1) Any man who wishes to divorce his wife shall, as soon as may be after the pronouncement of talaq in any form whatsoever, give the chairman notice in writing of his having done so, and shall supply a copy thereof to the wife. (2) Whoever contravenes the provisions of subsection (1) shall be punishable with simple imprisonment for a term which may extend to one year or with fine which may extend to 5,000 rupees or with both. (3) Save as provided in sub-section (5), a talaq unless revoked earlier, expressly or otherwise, shall not be effective until the expiration of 90 days from the day on which notice under subsection (1) is delivered to the chairman. (4) Within 30 days of the receipt of notice under subsection (1), the chairman shall constitute an arbitration council for the purpose of bringing about a reconciliation between the parties, and the arbitration council shall take all steps necessary to bring about such reconciliation. (5) If the wife be pregnant at the time talaq is pronounced talaq shall not be effective until the period mentioned in subsection (3) or the pregnancy, whichever be later, ends. (6) Nothing shall debar a wife whose marriage has been terminated by talaq effective under this section from remarrying the same husband, without an intervening marriage with a third person, unless such termination is for the third time so effective.'

The 'chairman' referred to in this section is the chairman of the union council, an administrative, not a judicial body, although the chairman in the instant case happened to be a judge. Rules made under the Ordinance (West Pakistan Rules under the Muslim Family Laws Ordinance 1961) (as amended) provide, inter alia, which union council shall have jurisdiction in the case of notice of talaq, and lay down the procedure to be followed by the arbitration council constituted under section 7 (4). The relevant rules are:

'3. The union council which shall have jurisdiction in the matter for purposes of clause (d) of section 2 shall be as follows, namely:—... (b) in the case of notice of talaq under subsection (1) or section 7, it shall be the union council of the union or town where the wife in relation to whom talaq has been pronounced was residing at the time of the pronouncement of talaq: Provided that if at the time of pronouncement of talaq such wife was not residing in any part of West Pakistan, the union council that shall have jurisdiction shall be—(i) in case such wife was at any time residing with the person pronouncing the talaq in any part of West Pakistan, the union council of the union or town where such wife so last resided with such person; and (ii) in any other case, the union council of the union or town where the person pronouncing the talaq is permanently residing in West Pakistan; ... 6. (1) Within seven days of receiving an application under subsection (2) of section 6 or under subsection (1) of section 9, or a notice under subsection (1) of section 7, the chairman shall, by order in writing, call upon each of the parties to nominate his or her representative, and each such party shall, within seven days of receiving the order, nominate in writing a representative and deliver the nomination to the chairman or send it to him by registered post: provided that where a party on whom the order is to be served is residing outside Pakistan, the order may be served on

such party through the consular officer of Pakistan in or for the country
where such party is residing.'

It appears to be the practice, though it is not required by the rules, for the
chairman of the union council at the request of either of the spouses after the
90 days have expired without the talaq having been revoked, to issue a
document recording that the procedure laid down in the Ordinance and
Rules has been followed and that the talaq dissolving the marriage is
confirmed.

Although the Ordinance is primarily procedural the evidence shows that it
does involve at least two substantive changes in the classic religious law of
Islam. Whereas under the classic religious law the talaq once pronounced
takes effect immediately and is irrevocable, under the Ordinance (a) it
cannot take effect until at least 90 days after it has been pronounced or even
longer if notice is not delivered promptly to the chairman of the union
council; and (b) until it does take effect it can be revoked. If notice is not
given to the chairman at all it would appear that the talaq never does take
effect.

There is nothing to compel either spouse to take part in conciliation
proceedings before the arbitration council. If, as happened in the instant
case, the husband chooses not to do so, then, subject to his having given the
required notice of talaq to the chairman of the union council and supplied a
copy to his wife, divorce by talaq is still obtainable at the husband's will
alone, and no authority in Pakistan, whether judicial or administrative, has
any power to prevent its taking effect automatically the moment that the 90
day period expires.

It was the absence of such power that led the Court of Appeal to hold that
the procedure for which the Ordinance and Rules provide does not make a
divorce by talaq obtained in Pakistan a divorce that has 'been obtained by
means of judicial or other proceedings' within the meaning of section 2 of the
Recognition Act.

It was not the appellant's case that the divorce by talaq was obtained in
Pakistan by proceedings that were 'judicial'; it is the reference in the section
to 'other proceedings' on which he relied. The argument for the respondent
is that these words, which on the face of them would include any proceedings
that were *not* judicial, are to be read as limited to proceedings that are quasi-
judicial, by application of the ejusdem generis rule. This involves reading
'other' as if it meant 'similar' and, as it seems to me, is based upon a
misunderstanding of that well-known rule of construction that is regrettably
common. As the latin words of the label attached to it suggest, the rule
applies to cut down the generality of the expression 'other' only where it is
preceded by a list of two or more expressions having more specific meanings
and sharing some common characteristics from which it is possible to
recognise them as being species belonging to a single genus and to identify
what the essential characteristics of that genus are. The presumption then is
that the draftsman's mind was directed only to that genus and that he did
not, by his addition of the word 'other' to the list, intend to stray beyond its
boundaries, but merely to bring within the ambit of the enacting words those
species which complete the genus but have been omitted from the preceding
list either inadvertently or in the interests of brevity. Where, however, as in
section 2 of the Recognition Act, the word 'other' as descriptive of

proceedings is preceded by one expression only that has a more specific meaning, viz, 'judicial' there is no room for the application of any ejusdem generis rule; for unless the draftsman has indicated at very least two different species to which the enacting words apply there is no material on which to base an inference that there was some particular genus of proceedings to which alone his mind was directed when he used the word 'other' which on the face of it would embrace all proceedings that were *not* judicial, irrespective of how much or little they resemble judicial proceedings.

The fact that the ejusdem generis rule is not applicable does not, however, necessarily mean that where the expression 'other' appears in a statute preceded by only one expression of greater specificity its generality may not be cut down if to give it its wide prima facie meaning would lead to results that would be contrary to the manifest policy of the Act looked at as a whole, or would conflict with the evident purpose for which is was enacted.

In the instant case, however, this does not help the respondent wife; it helps the appellant husband. The purpose for which the Recognition Act was passed is declared by the preamble to be with a view to the ratification by the United Kingdom of the Recognition Convention and for other purposes. Where Parliament passes an Act amending the domestic law of the United Kingdom in order to enable this country to ratify an international treaty and thereby assume towards other states that are parties to the treaty an obligation in international law to observe its terms, it is a legitimate aid to the construction of any provisions of the Act that are ambiguous or vague to have recourse to the terms of the treaty in order to see what was the obligation in international law that Parliament intended that this country should be enabled to assume. The ambiguity or obscurity is to be resolved in favour of that meaning that is consistent with the provisions of the treaty: *Salomon v Customs and Excise Comrs*[6] and *Post Office v Estuary Radio Ltd.*[7]

Article 1 of the Recognition Convention provides that it shall apply to the

'recognition in one contracting state of divorces and legal separations obtained in another contracting state which follow judicial or other proceedings officially recognised in that state and which are legally effective there.'

It is rightly conceded on behalf of the respondent that the divorce by talaq which was obtained in Pakistan followed upon acts which though not judicial do fall within the description 'other proceedings officially recognised' in that country. The pronouncement of the talaq was required by law to be notified to a public authority, the chairman of the union council; he in turn was required by law to constitute an arbitration council for the purposes of conciliation and to invite each spouse to nominate a representative. These are 'proceedings'; none the less so because in the event neither spouse elects to take advantage of the opportunity for conciliation which the arbitration council presents. They are proceedings that are not merely officially recognised but are also enforced by penal sanctions under the Muslim Family Laws Ordinance 1961. Without such proceedings the divorce by talaq never becomes effective. The proceedings come first, the divorce follows them 90 days after they have been commenced.

6 [1967] 2 QB 116, [1966] 3 All ER 871.
7 [1968] 2 QB 740, [1967] 3 All ER 663.

My Lords, the presumption is that the draftsman of the Recognition Act, by his use of the phrase 'obtained by means of judicial or other proceedings in any country outside the British Isles', intended to provide for the recognition of all divorces to which the recognition Convention applies, for to fail to do so would be a breach of that Convention by this country. The ordinary meaning of the phrase he used is amply wide enough to cover at least them. It may even have been intended to cover more, since article 17 permits contracting states to be more favourable to the recognition of foreign divorces than is needed to comply with the provisions of the Convention. This, however, is not a matter that arises for decision in the present appeal. It suffices for this House to hold that the phrase must have been intended to embrace divorces by talaq obtained in Pakistan under the provisions of the Muslim Family Laws Ordinance 1961.

It remains to notice a subsidiary argument advanced for the respondent; that the notice of pronouncement of the talaq was given to the Chairman of a union council on whom jurisdiction was not conferred under rule. This depended upon whether the respondent wife was 'residing' in Karachi when the talaq was pronounced on 30 July 1973. She was physically present in London on that date, but the judge was entitled on the evidence to find, as he did, that this was but a temporary absence from Karachi which continued to be her place of residence.

For these reasons I would allow the appeal. Since it has not been necessary to consider the validity of the alleged divorce by khula, the declarations 2 and 3 made by Wood J relating to it and to the divorce by talaq respectively are inappropriate and his order should be varied by replacing them by a single declaration 'that the said marriage [the Indian marriage] had been dissolved on or before 28 November 1974.'

Lords Dilhorne, Salmon, Fraser of Tullybelton and Scarman delivered judgments to the same effect. Lord Scarman also held that the khula could also be recognised.

Appeal allowed.

QUESTION

Should it be possible to object to the recognition of a foreign talaq divorce on the ground that the wife had had no notice of it (under s 8 (2) (a) of the Recognition of Divorces and Legal Separations Act 1971, above) even though the wife could not, by notice, prevent the pronunciation of the talaq?

Section D. Recognition of Foreign Nullity Decrees

A foreign decree of nullity of marriage pronounced by the courts of the country in which the parties were domiciled will be recognised in England.

Von Lorang v Administrator of Austrian Property [1927] AC 641, 96 LJPC 105 (House of Lords)

Appeal from an interlocutor of the First Division of the Court of Session in Scotland recalling an interlocutor of the Lord Ordinary in an action of multiplepoinding.

In June 1897 the appellant, formerly Miss Salvesen, a British subject domiciled in Scotland, went through a form of marriage in Paris with Herr von Lorang, an Austrian subject. The parties thereafter settled in Wiesbaden, in Germany, where they lived together as man and wife, except during the period of the war, when Herr von Lorang served with the Austrian army and the appellant lived in Switzerland, until 1923. In that year the respondent claimed the movable property of the appellant in Scotland, which was then in the hands of her agents and bankers, under the Treaty of Peace (Austrian) Order 1920, and an Amending Order of 1921, on the ground that she became an Austrian national by her marriage. The holders of the movable property brought an action of multiplepoinding to have it determined who was entitled to the property and to obtain their discharge. The property was claimed by the respondent and by the appellant, who averred that she had recently discovered that her marriage in Paris was null and void because certain formalities required by the law of France had not been observed, and intimated that she intended to bring a suit of nullity of marriage in the civil Court of Wiesbaden, the court of the domicile of Herr von Lorang and herself, and the action of multiplepoinding was sisted for this purpose. The nullity suit was brought (the respondent not intervening), and the Court of Wiesbaden in 1924 declared the marriage null and void on the ground that it was formally invalid by French law. Herr von Lorang appeared and was represented by an advocate, but took no active part in the proceedings. Thereupon the respondent raised several objections to the validity of the decree of the German court, and in particular averred that the decree was obtained by collusion, and that it proceeded upon a mistaken view of the law of France; but the jurisdiction of the German court was admitted. The question for determination was whether the decree of the German court should be held binding on the Scottish courts for the purpose of excluding the respondent's averments from inquiry.

The Lord Ordinary (Lord Morison) repelled the respondent's claim for a proof, and preferred the appellant to the property.

The First Division, by a majority (the Lord President, Lord Blackburn and Lord Ashmore; Lord Sands dissenting), recalled the interlocutor of the Lord Ordinary and remitted the case to him to allow the parties a proof of their respective averments.

Lord Haldane (having stated the facts, and having found that the appellant and Herr von Lorang were domiciled at Wiesbaden in 1923, continued): My Lords, I do not think that there are any materials before us on which exception can be taken to the judgment in Germany as having been obtained by what amounts in law to collusion. I will assume that both the husband and his wife had as their main motive to obtain that judgment in order, if possible, to avoid the application of the Austrian administrator's title to claim, but I think that, on the grounds assigned by the Lord Ordinary and Lord Sands, if they had the legal right to do this the motive for which they exercised it could make no difference in a case in which fraud practised on the German tribunal is not now alleged, and no collusion in any attempt to deceive that tribunal is established. The real question is simply whether the court of the domicile was competent to dispose conclusively and finally of the question before it. If so it does not matter in law whether it had an exclusive jurisdiction. Had the question been one of divorce for adultery there could today have been no controversy as to the binding effect of the German decree. The status of married persons as dependent on divorce is a matter for which the court of their domicile is the appropriate court, and its decision is treated by our courts as not only being valid but as conclusive. The case before us is, however, not one of dissolving an existing marriage but of deciding that no valid marriage ever took place. The marriage was declared by the court of the domicile to have been void by reason of non-compliance with the formalities required by the law of France, where it was celebrated. If this was a judgment determining the status of the supposed husband and wife it may well be that it should be regarded as having been binding on third parties as having been a judgment in rem. For what does status mean in this connection? Something more than a mere contractual relation between the parties to the contract of marriage. Status may result from such a contractual relationship, but only when the contract has passed into something which private international law recognises as having been superadded to it by the authority of the state, something which the juris-prudence of that state under its law imposes when within its boundaries the ceremony has taken place. This juridical result is more than any mere outcome of the agreement inter se to marry of the parties. It is due to a result which concerns the public generally, and which the state where the ceremony took place superadds; something which may or may not be capable of being got rid of subsequently by proceedings before a competent public authority, but which meantime carries with it rights and obligations as regards the general community until so got rid of. There is nothing unusual in this doctrine.

I cannot see how, for instance, a husband could plead as a good answer to a claim for necessaries supplied to his wife that the marriage which had been publicly celebrated was one which he was entitled if he took proceedings to have declared void for either impotency or for want of compliance with formalities which the public authority which had celebrated the marriage had assumed to have been complied with. For the marriage gives the husband and wife a new legal position from which flow both rights and obligations with regard to the rest of the public. The status so acquired may vary according to the laws of different communities. The disability of monastic celibacy, for example, or that of a minor, or that of consanguinity, may be binding by the law of one country so as to invalidate the married status, while not binding by that of another. When, therefore, it is necessary to determine what married status implies and how far rights or acts are affected by it, it is necessary to determine the law by which they are fixed. It may be going too far to assert that these are all recognised in this country as referable only to the law of the domicile. But at least it is now established, since the decisions in *Le Mesurier v Le Mesurier*;[8] *Lord Advocate v Jaffrey*;[9] and *A-G for Alberta v Cook*,[10] that for a decree of dissolution of a marriage the court of the domicile is the true court of jurisdiction. That jurisdiction ought on principle to be regarded as exclusive. But for the purpose of the present case it is not necessary to refer to the point, for if the German court was competent to pronounce the judgment it did in the case before us the

8 [1895] AC 517, 64 LJPC 97.
9 [1921] 1 AC 146, 89 LJPC 209.
10 [1926] AC 444, 95 LJPC 102.

judgment, being that of the court of the domicile, was conclusive in our courts here, so far as competency is concerned, unless there is something in the decree of dissolution for nullity which distinguishes such a proceeding from one for divorce for adultery. In *Niboyet v Niboyet*,[11] in which the judgment of the majority of the court is no longer law, Brett LJ, in the dissenting judgment which he delivered, observed that the court of the domicile was the only court that was entitled to alter the status of married people; but he went on to indicate that the principle, while it applies so as to include suits for judicial separation and for restitution of conjugal rights, did not apply to suits for a declaration of nullity. He gives no reasons for saying this. Whether there cannot be jurisdiction which is not that of the domicile in restricted instances to entertain a suit for nullity is a question we have not before us for determination. For, as I have pointed out, the only relevant issue is whether the German court was competent as against all other courts conclusively to declare the marriage in the present case void. I am unable as matter of principle to see how its competence as the court of the domicile can be successfully challenged, and if it was competent the decree brought the claim, even of the respondent who was not a party before it, to an end. For the decree did undoubtedly alter the status of the husband and wife. They ceased retrospectively to have been married people in the community of their country. For the purpose of the question raised that status must be taken to have been a res and the judgment was therefore one in rem.

My Lords, if the status in question was a res within the meaning of the principle, the duty of our courts is clear. In *Castrique v Imrie*[12] this House, adopting the language of Blackburn J, who was one of the judges who advised it, laid down that the inquiry is, first, whether the subject-matter was so situated as to be within the lawful control of the state under the authority of which the court sits; and, secondly, whether the sovereign authority of that state has conferred on the court jurisdiction to decide on the disposition of the thing, and the court has acted within its jurisdiction. . . .

There does not appear to be any reason why a judgment of nullity, even on such restricted grounds as the Lord President mentions, should not be regarded as disposing of the status of married persons. It does not do so the less because third parties may have it open to them to litigate elsewhere questions of validity in certain restricted instances before such questions have been disposed of in the court of the domicile. Such status is not dependent only on the contract of the parties to the marriage. Before Lord Lyndhurst's Act, for example, a man and woman in England standing in an affinity within the prohibited degrees might marry, and the marriage, though voidable, could only be got rid of by the sentence of an Ecclesiastical Court pronounced within the lifetime of the parties. But the status though voidable was not the less a status, a res with which the court could deal. That shows that though voidable and not void, it was that as to which the sentence of the appropriate court was essential for its dissolution.

My Lords, for these reasons I am unable to agree with the view of the Lord President that the foreign judgment in the case before us did not as soon as given establish conclusively against the respondent and every one else

11 (1878) 4 PD 1, 48 LJP 1.
12 (1870) LR 4 HL 414 at 429.

that the appellant, at the relevant date in the multiplepoinding proceedings, was not an Austrian national qua wife of an Austrian subject. If so, the claim of the administrator in the multiplepoinding became inept on 28 March 1924, the date of the decree of the Wiesbaden Court, which was made final on 4 May in that year. The interlocutor of the Lord Ordinary repelling the claim for the administrator was not pronounced until 21 April 1925, and ought accordingly to receive effect.

There were cited numerous authorities for the contention of the respondent in the Court of Session. These I have examined, but they do not appear to me to modify the conclusion at which I have arrived as to the principle which must be applied. In considering them it should be borne in mind that some of the dicta in the older cases have been affected by the English Divorce Act of 1857, which for the first time enabled divorce a vinculo to be granted by a court of general law in England. Before that year it was the prevalent view that a marriage duly celebrated in England could not be got rid of (except by Act of Parliament) validly so far as England was concerned, even by a foreign decree, at least when the domicile at the time of the marriage was English. In the report of *Warrender v Warrender*,[13] *Lolley's* case[14] which had been decided by eminent English judges, is explained, and it is yet more precisely explained by Lord Westbury in *Shaw v Gould*[15] and by Lord Selborne in *Harvey v Farnie*.[16] *Lolley's* case appears in reality to have turned on domicile as much as on the indissoluble character of an 'English marriage'. After 1857 the indissoluble character of an English marriage disappeared, and the effect of this disappearance is noticeable in the later decisions. In the judgment in *Le Mesurier v Le Mesurier* the modern doctrine of domicile as the true test prevails unrestrainedly. . . .

In considering the application of other authorities cited to us it is essential to bear in mind the limited scope of the only question before us. It is simply whether, when the court of the domicile of both the parties has pronounced their marriage to be invalid on the ground of nullity for want of formalities, a court here where they are not domiciled can review that decision. The reasons given by Lindley MR in *Pemberton v Hughes*[17] are, in my opinion, conclusive against any attempt to reopen any such case on the footing of supposed irregularity of procedure. Our courts, as he says, never inquire whether a competent foreign court has exercised its jurisdiction improperly, provided that no substantial injustice according to our notions has been committed. In the present case the question was not divorce by way of dissolution for any offence but because of nullity for want of essentials required for the contract. It is said that this makes a difference, inasmuch as the marriage if a nullity could not change the domicile of the supposed wife. That is possibly true, on the grounds assigned by the then President of the Divorce Court, Sir Gorell Barnes, in his elaborate judgment in *Ogden v Ogden*.[18] But it does not affect the litigation before us, in which the decree of nullity in the court of the husband's domicile was pronounced with retrospective effect before the claim of the Administrator of Austrian

---

13　(1835) 2 Cl & Fin 488, 9 Bli NS 89.
14　(1812) 2 Cl & Fin 567n, Russ & Ry 237.
15　(1868) LR 3 HL 55 at 58.
16　(1882) 8 App Cas 43 at 54.
17　[1899] 1 Ch 781, 68 LJCh 281; p 168 above.
18　[1908] P 46, 77 LJP 34; p 240 above.

Property could be established. None of the cases cited to us seem to me to affect this simple point.

My Lords, for the reason that the judgment of the Wiesbaden Court was both competent and binding upon us, I think that we ought to recall the interlocutor of the First Division and to restore that of the Lord Ordinary. The appellant should have her costs in the Inner House and here. I move accordingly.

Viscount Dunedin: My Lords, although I had made up my mind as to what, according to my opinion, the judgment of the House ought to be in this case, yet before I had penned a single sentence of the opinion which I should deliver, I had the advantage of reading the opinions of the noble Viscount on the Woolsack and of Lord Phillimore. Agreeing as I do with these opinions and also with every word of what I may without offence term the exceedingly able judgment of Lord Sands, if this were an ordinary case I should simply announce my concurrence. But the case is so important to the law that I need not apologise for adding some remarks of my own; only, as it would be useless to retrace the ground so thoroughly explored in the opinions mentioned, these remarks will be necessarily discursive, but I hope may serve some purpose.

First I would like to say that I thoroughly endorse the view of Lord Phillimore that the outlook of the English courts was necessarily different before and after 1857. I would like to add that I think there is another date of great moment, namely, the date of the decision of *Warrender v Warrender* in this House, namely, 1835. Now I venture to say this: that before that judgment, without my considering whether it really was the law or not, any English lawyer would have said that the law of England is, that an English marriage is indissoluble by any court; it is something that cannot be broken, indissoluble in essence, and looking to *Lolley's* case, who could say he was wrong? I think satisfactory proof of this may be found in the argument of Sir John Campbell A-G, afterwards Lord Chancellor, in the *Warrender* case, wherein he says: 'It may be considered as absolutely certain that the bar of England could not have furnished a single counsel who would have set his name to the opinion, that judicial indissolubility was not a legal quality of every English marriage.' But when *Warrender's* case was decided, that, as an abstract proposition, could no longer hold, though I doubt whether the majority of English lawyers appreciated it. They did not in those days pay much attention to Scotch cases. Besides, as a decision it did not necessarily say *Lolley's* case was wrong, because Lolley was an Englishman and only went to Scotland for the purpose of obtaining a divorce, while Warrender was a Scotchman. In other words, if the law of *Le Mesurier* had then been fully known, Lolley's divorce in Scotland was no divorce at all. No one can read Lord Brougham's judgment without coming to the conclusion that he thought *Lolley's* case was wrong in what it laid down, and when Lord Lyndhurst twitted him with having gone out of his way to approve *Lolley's* case in *M'Carthy v De Caix*,[19] when he was Chancellor, Lord Brougham retorted that he was then only sitting in Chancery, and was bound by *Lolley's* case, but now he was in the House of Lords and was not. My Lords, I do not think it necessary to consider whether I should follow the iconoclastic

19 (1831) 2 Russ & M 614, 2 Cl & Fin 568, n.

tendencies of my fellow-countryman. All I want to point out is that I think all early English decisions, certainly up to 1835, and I think up to 1857, must be read in the light of the general opinion of the indissolubility of an English marriage.

The other point on which I want to say a few words is the question of what is a judgment in rem. All are agreed that a judgment of divorce is a judgment in rem, but the whole argument of the majority of the judges in the Court of Session turns on the distinction between divorce and nullity. The first remark to be made is that neither marriage nor the status of marriage is, in the strict sense of the word, a 'res', as that word is used when we speak of a judgment in rem. A res is a tangible thing within the jurisdiction of the court, such as a ship or other chattel. A metaphysical idea, which is what the status of marriage is, is not strictly a res, but it, to borrow a phrase, savours of a res, and has all along been treated as such. Now the learned judges make this distinction. They say that in an action of divorce you have to do with a res, to wit, the status of marriage, but that in an action of nullity there is no status of marriage to be dealt with, and therefore no res. Now it seems to me that celibacy is just as much a status as marriage. I notice that in the Oxford dictionary the word 'status' is defined (inter alia) as 'The legal standing or position of a person . . . condition in respect, eg, of liberty or servitude, marriage or celibacy, infancy or majority'. The judgment in a nullity case decrees either a status of marriage or a status of celibacy.

The learned judges rest strongly on what was said on the subject in *Ogden v Ogden*, but, first, I am not bound by *Ogden v Ogden*, and so far as the dicta contradict what I have just said, I do not agree with them. And, further, a close perusal of the judgment in *Ogden v Ogden* will show that it is very much wrapped up with the question of jurisdiction, and if the first marriage was null, there was no jurisdiction in the French court against the so-called wife defending.[20] But here the jurisdiction is undoubted. On this point I would cite the words of Sir James Hannen in the case of *Turner v Thompson*:[1] 'A woman when she marries a man, not only by construction of law, but absolutely as a matter of fact, does acquire the domicile of her husband, if she lives with him in the country of his domicile. There is no ground here for contending that she did not take up that domicile. She had the intention of taking up her permanent abode with him, and of making his country her permanent home.' These words exactly fit this case. I am therefore of opinion that a decree of nullity savours of a res just as much as a decree of divorce. I accept the conditions laid down by Lord Lindley when he was Master of the Rolls in *Pemberton v Hughes*. In order for a foreign decree to be immune from disturbance by an English court—and in my opinion Scottish may with perfect justice be substituted for English—it must be pronounced between persons subject to the foreign jurisdiction, and deal with a matter with which the court is competent to deal, and it must not offend against English ideas of substantial justice.

Although, as I said before, these remarks are discursive, and I do not wish to retrace traversed ground, yet I would put in the form of short propositions

---

20 However, the first marriage in *Ogden v Ogden* was voidable, not void, and therefore the woman acquired the domicile of the man by operation of law: *De Reneville v De Reneville* [1948] P 100, [1948] 1 All ER 56 (*Ed*).

1 (1888) 13 PD 37 at 41.

the points I hold proved, the proof of several of them being worked out, not by me, but by the opinions of my noble and learned friends.

1. The German court had jurisdiction over the parties, they being domiciled in Germany equally whether there was marriage or no marriage.

2. This was a genuine action, and there was no collusion or fraud used to deceive the German court.

3. The validity of the marriage depended on French law, that being the law of the locus celebrationis.

4. The German court took proper steps to inform itself of the French law, and gave judgment according to the law proved before it.

5. That judgment is a judgment which is equivalent to a judgment in rem, and is therefore binding on the Scotch court without further inquiry.

It follows that I agree with the motion made from the Woolsack.

Lords Phillimore, Blanesburgh, and Warrington delivered judgments to the same effect.

Appeal allowed.

So will a decree pronounced by the courts of the country in which only one party is domiciled.

Lepre v Lepre [1965] P 52, [1963] 2 All ER 49 (Divorce Division)

The wife was born and lived most of her life in England. The husband was born and brought up in Malta and was a Roman Catholic. In April 1955 they went through a ceremony of marriage at the Portsmouth register office. That marriage was valid according to English law. The parties went to Malta in May 1955, but the wife returned to England with the child of the marriage in 1956, and in April 1957 obtained from the Portsmouth justices an order for maintenance for herself and the child. In order to enforce the order against the husband she started proceedings to secure its registration in Malta, but her application was adjourned by the Maltese court when the husband alleged the invalidity of the civil marriage ceremony by Maltese law. In December 1957 the husband issued a writ in the Civil Court of Malta praying for a decree of nullity on the ground that his marriage did not comply with canon law. In March 1960 the Maltese court pronounced a decree of nullity, holding that the husband was at all times domiciled in Malta and that by the law of his Maltese domicile he had an incapacity to contract a marriage otherwise than in accordance with canon law and that the marriage celebrated in the register office failed to comply with canon law because no Roman Catholic priest was present.

In December 1960 the wife filed a petition in the High Court seeking a declaration that the Maltese decree of nullity was invalid and of no effect in England and further praying that the marriage should be dissolved on the grounds of the husband's cruelty and desertion. The husband did not defend the petition and took no part in the proceedings.

Sir Jocelyn Simon P: I have to consider initially whether the decree of the Maltese court of 28 March 1960, should be recognised in England as annulling the marriage. That itself raises two questions: first, should such a

decree in principle be recognised in the absence of fraud or of offence against
our notions of justice; secondly, does the decree in this case in fact offend
against our notions of justice?

On the first question differing views of great weight have been expressed.
On the one side stand Willmer J in *Chapelle v Chapelle*[2] and Lord Denning
MR and Donovan LJ in *Gray v Formosa*:[3] they would not recognise the
decree as effective to annul the marriage. On the other side are Pearson LJ
in *Gray v Formosa*, Herbstein J in *De Bono v De Bono*,[4] Reed J in *Vassallo
v Vassallo*[5] and the distinguished academic figures who have commented on
Chapelle v Chapelle: they hold that the decree ought to be recognised. Those
who take the first view argue in this way: the Maltese court can make a
binding and conclusive decree annulling the marriage if both parties were
domiciled in Malta at the commencement of the suit there (*Von Lorang
v Administrator of Austrian Property*);[6] the Maltese decree, however, declared
the marriage void; the wife, therefore, never acquired the husband's Maltese
domicile by operation of the law, but retained her English domicile
throughout; it follows that the decree of the Maltese court was not a decree
of the court of common domicile and was not binding and conclusive. Those
who take the contrary view, that we should recognise the decree, retort that
such a refusal to recognise the Maltese decree as effectively annulling the
marriage involves that the parties remain married in the eye of English law;
and the wife had thus, at the commencement of the Maltese proceedings, a
domicile in law dependent on her husband's, which was then admittedly
Maltese; both parties were therefore domiciled within the jurisdiction of the
Maltese court, which in consequence had jurisdiction over their marriage.
The views expressed by the Court of Appeal in *Gray v Formosa* were obiter on
this part of the case. I must therefore proceed to my own judgment guided
but not governed by what has been said elsewhere.

The apparent dilemma is, in my view, to be resolved by, first, carefully
isolating the legal system to which reference should be made in order to
ascertain whether the Maltese court had a conclusive jurisdiction, and,
secondly, bearing constantly in mind the crucial time for invoking such legal
system. That time is unquestionably the commencement of the Maltese
proceedings. The husband being then domiciled in Malta, where was the
wife domiciled? (His Lordship proceeded to hold that since the marriage was
valid, or at most merely voidable, the wife was domiciled in Malta. But since
this part of his judgment is rendered obsolete by section 1 of the Domicile
and Matrimonial Proceedings Act 1973,[7] it is omitted here.)

But even if this marriage were void ipso jure, so that the husband alone
was domiciled in Malta at the start of the proceedings there, in my judgment
we should still accord recognition to the Maltese decree. In the case of a
marriage void ipso jure, such as a marriage alleged to be fundamentally
defective as to formalities, the English court assumes jurisdiction in nullity if
the petitioner alone is domiciled in England: *De Reneville v De Reneville*,[8] *Apt*

2 [1950] P 134, [1950] 1 All ER 236.
3 [1963] P 259, [1962] 3 All ER 419.
4 1948 (2) SA 802.
5 [1952] SASR 129.
6 [1927] AC 641, 96 LJPC 105; p 317 above.
7 p 19 above.
8 [1948] P 100, [1948] 1 All ER 56.

v Apt,[9] *Kenward v Kenward,*[10] to cite only authorities in the Court of Appeal. Moreover, in such circumstances we purport to operate on the status not only of the petitioner who is domiciled within the jurisdiction but also of the respondent who is not; it is for this reason that we insist that he or she should be made a party to the proceedings, so as to be bound by our decree. If we ourselves claim a ground of jurisdiction we must concede a similar ground of jurisdiction to foreign courts: *Travers v Holley,*[11] *Corbett v Corbett.*[12] Therefore, even if the wife were, contrary to my view, domiciled in England at the start of the Maltese proceedings by reason of the nullity of the marriage, we should nonetheless concede recognition to the Maltese decree, because we would regard ourselves as competent to pronounce a decree of nullity of a marriage void ipso jure were the husband domiciled in England and the wife in Malta. In so far as *Ogden v Ogden*[13] appears to be to the contrary, it is in my judgment in conflict with the reasoning of the later authorities in the Court of Appeal to which I have referred and must be taken to be confined to its particular facts—if, indeed, it can today stand at all in the light of the House of Lords decisions in *Von Lorang v Administrator of Austrian Property* and *Ross Smith v Ross Smith.*[14]

Furthermore, such assumption and concession of a binding jurisdiction in nullity based on the domicile of one party only seems to me to accord with principle. A judgment declaratory of the status of some subject-matter legally situated within the national and international jurisdiction of the court pronouncing the judgment constitutes a judgment in rem which is universally conclusive. The husband was legally situated within the jurisdiction of the Maltese court because he was domiciled in Malta. That court was, therefore, competent to declare his status by a decree of nullity; such a decree constitutes a judgment in rem, and should be regarded universally as conclusive as to his status, that is to say, that he is unmarried. [Counsel for the wife] conceded that for the purpose of criminal proceedings in this country we would be bound so to regard him; but not, he said, for the purpose of matrimonial proceedings, because the wife (on the present hypothesis) was not domiciled in Malta, so that her status was not within the competence of the Maltese court. The wife therefore, it is claimed, remains married to the husband, even though he is not married to her: the concept is no more difficult of acceptance than a finding that a respondent has committed adultery with a co-respondent, but not he with her. Such schizoid situations reflect little credit on the law, though the latter one is reasonably based on differential admissibility of evidence. But I cannot conceive how our courts could accept as conclusive the decree of a competent court of the husband's domicile that he is unmarried and, at the same time, purport to dissolve a marriage to which he is the other party. Moreover, there is high persuasive authority to suggest that this contention for the wife is not correct: see *Williams v North Carolina,*[15] a decision of the Supreme Court of the

9 [1948] P 83, [1947] 2 All ER 677; p 224 above.
10 [1951] P 124, [1950] 2 All ER 297 (see now s 5 (3) of the Domicile and Matrimonial Proceedings Act 1973; p 295 above (*Ed*)).
11 [1953] P 246, [1953] 2 All ER 794.
12 [1957] 1 All ER 621, [1957] 1 WLR 486.
13 [1908] P 46, 77 LJP 34; p 240 above.
14 [1963] AC 280, [1962] 1 All ER 344.
15 (1942) 317 US 287.

United States, where comparable recognition problems arise after divorce owing to their rule that a wife retains during marriage a domicile independent of her husband's. Incidentally, further authority from the same eminent source indicates that recognition of the nullity decree of the court of the husband's domicile only might not necessarily exclude our courts from enforcing in favour of the wife in appropriate circumstances financial obligations arising out of the marriage—for example, under a prior maintenance order made in this country: see *Estin v Estin*.[16]

Therefore, in my judgment, we should accept the Maltese decree as binding and conclusive—primarily as a decree of the court of the common domicile at the commencement of the proceedings there, though alternatively as a decree of the husband's domicile alone at that time—provided always that it is not vitiated by fraud or contrary to natural justice.

That brings me to the second main issue in this part of the case. I confess that I approach it with some misgiving. We are concerned here with the decree of a superior court of a Commonwealth country. Its procedure was manifestly solicitous of the forensic interests of the wife. The code of law applied was an ancient and honoured one. Moreover, limping marriages are themselves inherently liable to cause hardship and injustice: suppose, for example, the wife had remarried and had offspring in reliance on the Maltese decree—or, for that matter, the husband. The refusal to recognise an otherwise binding foreign judgment or rule of law on the ground that it is manifestly unjust is nowadays put as a matter of discretion. But as Lord Mansfield said in *R v Wilkes*:[17] 'discretion when applied to a court of justice means sound discretion guided by law. It must be governed by rule, not by humour: it must not be arbitrary, vague, and fanciful; but legal and regular.' In short, there must be a reasonable consistency in its exercise. In *Corbett v Corbett* Barnard J recognised a foreign decree of nullity based on two grounds, one apparently identical with that which constituted the defect in the present case, the other—that a Jewess was incapable of marrying out of her faith—not easily distinguishable in principle: see also *Igra v Igra*.[18] But in *Gray v Formosa* the Court of Appeal, though not expressly adverting to *Corbett v Corbett*, was unanimous that a decree pronounced by a Maltese court on a ground indentical with that in the present case and in largely similar circumstances offended so grossly against our notions of justice that it should not be recognised. It is true that the present case differs in certain details from *Gray v Formosa*. The husband here was not proved to have acquired an English domicile at the time of the marriage, and I am not satisfied that the child would be adversely affected by recognition of the decree. But to differentiate this case and *Corbett v Corbett* from *Gray v Formosa* on these grounds would be, in my opinion, to introduce idle distinctions into the law and throw it into confusion. Not least in matters relating to marriage is it incumbent on the law to speak with a clear, consistent and unequivocal voice. In truth, I do not believe that it was a mere cumulation of detail which impelled the Court of Appeal to their conclusion. I think the crux of their decision was that it was an intolerable injustice that a system of law

16 (1947) 334 US 541.
17 (1770) 4 Burr 2539.
18 [1951] P 404, [1951] 2 TLR 670.

should seek to impose extra-territorially, as a condition of the validity of a marriage, that it should take place according to the tenets of a particular faith. . . . Just as in *Chetti v Chetti*[19] Sir Gorell Barnes P refused to give effect to an incapacity to marry outside his caste or religion imposed extra-territorially on the husband by the law of his domicile, so, I think, the Court of Appeal discerned in *Gray v Formosa* an attempt by Maltese law to impose an analogous incapacity based on creed: they would refuse to recognise the incapacity, so they refused to recognise the domiciliary decree founded upon it.

If that is so, the present case cannot be distinguished; and I am bound to hold that the Maltese decree of nullity, although on general jurisdictional grounds conclusive, should not be accorded recognition because it must be taken to offend intolerably against the concept of justice which prevails in our courts. It follows that the marriage is valid and subsisting.

(His Lordship then pronounced a decree nisi of divorce on the grounds of the husband's cruelty and desertion.)

Order accordingly.

So will a decree pronounced by the courts of the country with which the petitioner had a real and substantial connection.

Perrini v Perrini (p 253 above)

A foreign decree of nullity will not be recognised in England if recognition would be contrary to English public policy or if the decree is inconsistent with a prior English judgment between the parties which is final and conclusive

Vervaeke v Smith 1 [1983] AC 145, [1982] 2 All ER 144 (House of Lords)

The appellant, Marie Therese Rachelle Vervaeke, who was of Belgian nationality and domicile, went through a ceremony of marriage at Paddington register office in 1954 with William George Smith, a British subject domiciled in England. William George Smith was down and out, drinking and out of work. He was induced to go through the ceremony by a bribe of £50 and a ticket to South Africa.

The appellant's object in going through the ceremony was to enable her to apply for British nationality and a British passport (in which she was successful) so that she could ply her trade as a prostitute in London without being deported as an undesirable alien. She and Smith never had any intention of living together as man and wife, and they parted at the doors of the register office.

The appellant worked as a prostitute between 1954 and 1963 in various brothels in London run by the Messina organisation. During this period she accumulated over 100 convictions for soliciting.

In March 1970 the appellant was married in Italy to Eugenio Messina,

19 [1909] P 67 at 72.

one of the principals in the organisation which had been managing her activities as a prostitute. Eugenio Messina died on the day of the wedding, at a celebration party.

The appellant then took steps to have her marriage with Smith annulled so that she could claim a share in Eugenio's estate in England. She obtained a decree nisi of nullity alleging that she had not consented to the marriage as she did not know that the ceremony at Paddington register office was a marriage at all. It so happened that in the county court that day was a barrister, waiting for another case, who had been advising the Messina family on other matters. He reported the decision to them and both they and the Queen's Proctor intervened in proceedings before Ormrod J[20] to prevent the decree nisi being made absolute. The Queen's Proctor had discovered that Smith had been married before, in Shanghai in 1937, to a Russian woman who divorced him in Nevada in 1946. At this stage, the appellant then added the further petition for nullity on the ground that the Nevada divorce was invalid in England. Ormrod J dismissed this second petition on the ground that the divorce was recognised as valid in England. He set aside the decree nisi on the first petition, holding that the appellant knew at the time of her marriage to Smith that she was taking part in a marriage ceremony, and that it was immaterial to the validity of the marriage that the parties did not intend to live together as man and wife. An appeal from this decision was dismissed with costs with the appellant's consent in March 1972.

Meanwhile in December 1971 the appellant applied to the Kortrijk District Court in Belgium for a declaration of nullity of her marriage to Smith. Her application was made on two grounds, (a) that she was mistaken as to the nature of the ceremony, and (b) that the marriage was entered into for an ulterior purpose and not with any intention of cohabiting. The first ground was rejected by the Belgian court as res judicata. On the second ground the appellant succeeded and obtained a decree of nullity. That decision was affirmed by the Court of Appeal in Ghent in April 1973. The court said: 'As the parties delusively indulged in a marriage ceremony without in fact really consenting to the marriage, they behaved against public policy'.

In September 1973 the appellant petitioned the High Court under RSC Order 15, rule 16, for a declaration that the Belgian decree of nullity should be recognised in England. In 1979 Waterhouse J dismissed the petition on the ground that the statutory procedure under section 45 of the Matrimonial Causes Act 1973[1] was available and provided better safeguards for third parties; but he granted the appellant leave to petition under that section for a declaration that her marriage in Italy to Eugenio Messina was a valid marriage. William George Smith was a nominal respondent but took no part in the proceedings, and died before the appeal to the House of Lords was heard. The real respondents were two brothers of Eugenio Messina and the Attorney-General.

Waterhouse J dismissed the petition and his decision was affirmed by the Court of Appeal (Sir John Arnold P, Cumming-Bruce and Eveleigh LJJ).

Lord Simon of Glaisdale: In the end the case comes down to considering

---

20 *Messina v Smith* [1971] P 322, [1971] 2 All ER 1046.
 1 p 400 below.

the effect of the Belgian judgment in our private international law. It is true that the section 45 proceedings are concerned with the Italian marriage; but the validity of that marriage depends on the capacity of the appellant to contract it; this in turn depends on whether she was subsequently bound in matrimony by the English marriage; and the appellant relies on the Belgian judgment as effectively declaring to English law that she was not.

My noble and learned friend on the Woolsack (Lord Hailsham of Marylebone LC) bases his judgment partly on res judicata arising from the Ormrod judgment; but he invokes also wider considerations of public policy which lead to a refusal to recognise the efficacy of the Belgian judgment. My noble and learned friend Lord Diplock, while agreeing with the Lord Chancellor, puts the main weight of his argument on res judicata.

The application of the doctrine of res judicata may itself seem to be no more than an application of English public policy. But this is apt to be misleading in a case such as the instant. It is true that the doctrine of res judicata has two bases—first, that it is a hardship on an individual that he should be twice vexed with the same matter and, secondly, public policy, (interest reipublicae ut sit finis litium). Nevertheless, the doctrine of res judicata consists of legal rules; and public policy, in the sense in which it arises in this appeal, denotes considerations of wider social interests which call for modification of a normal legal rule (in this case the conflict rule which normally leads to accord of recognition to the judgment of a foreign court of competent jurisdiction). That the distinction between the two aspects of the appeal—res judicata and public policy—is a real one can be seen by consideration that, even if there had been no English proceedings culminating in the Ormrod judgment, your Lordships might still be concerned with whether English public policy calls for refusal of recognition of the Belgian judgment and for affirmation of the validity of the English marriage.

Notwithstanding any predilection for a narrow rather than a wide ground of decision, I agree with my noble and learned friends on the issue of public policy as well as of res judicata.

Res judicata

The appellant relied on two matters in seeking from the Belgian court a decree of nullity in respect of the English marriage: (1) that she had been mistaken as to the nature of the formalities at the Paddington Register Office; (2) that, in accordance with the facts as found by Ormrod J, it was no marriage at all. As to (1) the Belgian court held that the Ormrod judgment constituted rem judicatam against the appellant; but not (2).

In coming to this decision the Belgian court was understandably unaware of the peculiar duty of a judge in English matrimonial proceedings. He does not exercise the role of a merely passive arbiter over adversary proceedings. Having a claim for nullity before him, based on an allegation of absence of consent, and having ascertained the true facts, Ormrod J, as a matrimonial judge, was bound to act as he did—namely, consider whether the marriage was in the true circumstances null and void as alleged. That this is what he did appears from the following passage in the Ormrod judgment:

'In one sense it was an unreal marriage in that it was never intended that the normal relationship of husband and wife should be established between Mr. Smith and herself. But this cannot affect *the question which I have to determine, namely, whether the marriage was, in law, a valid marriage.* Where a man and a woman consent to marry one another in a formal ceremony, conducted in accordance with the formalities required by law, knowing that it is a marriage ceremony, it is immaterial that they do not intend to live together as man and wife.' (My italics.)

Having addressed himself to this question, Ormrod J found the marriage to be valid, and dismissed the petition. I doubt whether he heard argument on the point: it is clear beyond argument. If he had found that the true facts rendered the marriage void he would (possibly ordering the petition to be amended appropriately) have pronounced a decree of nullity. The validity of the marriage on the true facts thereby passed, in English law, into rem judicatam. It was established as a fact, and could not be relitigated.

Two conflict rules are relevant to the decision of the Belgian court that the alleged invalidity of the English marriage by reason of its ulterior purpose and the common intention not to cohabit was not res judicata by Ormrod J. First, English courts never examine the judgment of a foreign court to see whether it has correctly applied its own or any relevant rule of foreign (even English) law: *Godard v Gray*;[2] *Castrique v Imrie*.[3] But, secondly, rules of adjectival (in contradistinction to substantive) law, including rules of evidence, fall for decision according to the lex fori (in the instant case, English law). Whether an estoppel per rem judicatam is substantive or adjective is not entirely clear (see eg, Dicey & Morris, *The Conflict of Laws*)[4] My own view is that the estoppel per rem judicatam in question here is on principle a rule of adjectival, evidentiary, law and that the balance of authority also favours this view. But I do not pause to undertake the considerable argument involved, in view of the fact that in my judgment the appeal also fails on the issue of public policy.

There is abundant authority that cause of action estoppel applies to foreign judgments, and on principle the same must be true of issue estoppel: see Cheshire & North, *Private International Law*.[5] Section 4 (1) (b) of the Foreign Judgments (Reciprocal Enforcement) Act 1933, though dealing not with recognition but with setting aside a registered foreign judgment on the ground of res judicata, lends some weight to the authorities to which Cheshire & North refers.

Assuming, as I do, that English law applies, I agree with my noble and learned friend on the Woolsack that the much quoted judgment of Wigram V-C in *Henderson v Henderson*[6] would if necessary be applicable to the instant case:

'The plea of res judicata applies, except in special cases, not only to points upon which the court was actually required by the parties to form an opinion and pronounce a judgment, but to every point which properly belonged to the subject of litigation, and which the parties,

---

2 (1870) LR 6 QB 139, 40 LJQB 62; p 165 above.
3 (1870) LR 4 HL 414.
4 10th edn (1980) vol 2, p 1190.
5 10th edn (1979) pp 651–655, 658.
6 (1843) 3 Hare 100 at 115.

exercising reasonable diligence, might have brought forward at the time.'

It seems to me that parties seeking to impugn a marriage should be expected to bring forward at the outset whatever they allege might invalidate it and not proceed from one alleged defect to another and from forum to forum.

Public policy

It is clear from the citations made by my noble and learned friend on the Woolsack from the Belgian proceedings that the Belgian judgment was the result of application of Belgian public policy to the same facts as were finally ascertained by Ormrod J. That the English rule, which leads to a contrary result, is also based on public policy appears most clearly from *Brodie v Brodie*;[7] though that case is only the culmination of a long line of authority. In *Brodie v Brodie* a wife, petitioning for restitution of conjugal rights, had been expecting to be delivered of a child of whom the respondent was the father. She pressed him to marry her, and he agreed to do so if, and only if, she would sign an agreement to separate after marriage. This she did; and a ceremony took place forthwith at a register office. It was held that the agreement not to cohabit was void as against public policy; and a decree of restitution of conjugal rights was pronounced. Such a decree is a judgment affirming the validity of the marriage in question.

English and Belgian law, both based clearly on respective public policy, being thus contradictory as to the validity and consequences of a marriage such as that instantly in issue, the question arises whether English law is bound to surrender its own concept of the public policy involved and defer to that of Belgian law as expressed in the Belgian judgment.

If your Lordships should hold that English public policy justifies refusal to accord binding recognition to the Belgian judgment, your Lordships are in the light of *Brodie v Brodie*, acting within the principle stated by Lord Thankerton in *Fender v St John-Mildmay*:[8]

'the proper function of the courts in questions of public policy . . . is to expound, and not to expand, such policy. That does not mean that they are precluded from applying an existing principle of public policy to a new set of circumstances where such circumstances are clearly within the scope of the policy.'

Non-recognition of the Belgian judgment will, of course, involve a 'limping marriage'. This is a situation which our law will generally seek to avoid; and under an ideal system of conflict of laws it would not arise. But it is bound to happen in a juristically imperfect world where there is not universal agreement on such concepts as characterisation and the appropriate connecting factor. Its main evil, that a marriage valid in one country might be invalidated in another with which a party has some real and substantial connection, does not seem to arise here. Although in her petition in the section 45 proceedings the appellant claimed to be a British subject, it appears both in that petition and in the earlier one in the recognition

7 [1917] P 271, 86 LJP 140.
8 [1938] AC 1 at 23, [1937] 3 All ER 402 at 414.

proceedings that she is permanently resident in Belgium; she may, moreover, have double nationality—the Belgian court made no reference to English as her personal law.

There is abundant authority that an English court will decline to recognise or apply what would otherwise be the appropriate foreign rule of law when to do so would be against English public policy; although the court will be even slower to invoke public policy in the field of conflict of laws than when a purely municipal legal issue is involved. There is little authority for refusing, on the ground of public policy, to recognise an otherwise conclusive foreign judgment—no doubt because the conclusiveness of a judgment of a foreign court of competent jurisdiction is itself buttressed by the rule of public policy interest reipublicae ut sit finis litium, the 'commonwealth' in conflict of laws extending to the whole international community. Nevertheless, there is some judicial authority that the English court will in an appropriate case refuse on the ground of public policy to accord recognition to the judgment of a foreign court of competent jurisdiction (*Re Macartney*;[9] see also *Gray v Formosa*[10] as explained in *Lepre v Lepre*);[11] and the leading textbooks acknowledge this exception to the general recognition rules (see, eg, Dicey & Morris, *The Conflict of Laws*,[12] repeating a rule similarly expressed in earlier editions). Although an English court will exercise such a jurisdiction with extreme reserve, in my judgment the instant is a case where it should be invoked, for the following reasons:

(1) Quite apart from its having been legally adopted and its being consonant with our general law of contract (see *Dalrymple v Dalrymple*,[13] per Sir William Scott), the English policy towards the sort of marriage in question here seems as soundly based, morally, socially and in reason, as the Belgian; and there appears to be no inherent reason why, giving every weight to the international spirit of the conflict of laws, we should surrender our own policy to that of any foreign society. The type of 'sham' marriage in question is not necessarily entered into for a nefarious purpose. Auden married the daughter of the great German novelist, Thomas Mann, in order to facilitate her escape from persecution in Nazi Germany: see also *Szechter v Szechter*.[14]

(2) Although an English court will take cognisance of English public policy irrespective of plea, it hardly lies in the mouth of the appellant to invoke in her favour the maxim interest reipublicae ut sit finis litium. She started proceedings in England, entered an appeal to the English Court of Appeal, switched to the Belgian forum, and then returned to England in the recognition proceedings. And here she is as appellant in your Lordships' House.

(3) English proceedings (in which English public policy became relevant on the ascertainment of the true facts) were started by the appellant before ever she invoked the jurisdiction of the Belgian court to apply their own contradictory rule of public policy; and the Ormrod judgment expressing

9 [1921] 1 Ch 522, 90 LJCh 314.
10 [1963] P 259, [1962] 3 All ER 419.
11 [1965] P 52, [1963] 2 All ER 49; pp 328–329 above.
12 10th edn (1980) rule 188.
13 (1811) 2 Hag Con 54 at 105–106.
14 [1971] P 286, [1970] 3 All ER 905; p 265 above.

English public policy towards this marriage was, therefore, prior to the Belgian judgment expressing their contrary public policy . . .

I would dismiss the appeal.

Lords Hailsham of Marylebone LC and Diplock delivered judgments to the same effect. Lords Keith of Kinkel and Brandon of Oakbrook concurred.

Appeal dismissed.

NOTE

Unlike the English rules for the recognition of divorces, the English rules for the recognition of nullity decrees still depend upon the common law. They draw no distinction between decrees obtained within and without the British Isles; and they are marked by a great deal of uncertainty. In particular the 'real and substantial connection' test borrowed from *Indyka v Indyka*[15] (a case on divorce recognition) and applied to nullity decrees in *Law v Gustin*[16] and *Perrini v Perrini*[17] is not specific enough to provide a basis for recognition without the necessity for constant recourse to the courts. During the brief reign of *Indyka* before it was abolished for divorce by section 6 (5) of the Recognition of Divorces and Legal Separations Act 1971 large numbers of people simply did not know whether or not they were married, and if so, to whom. The only reason why it has not produced a similar situation of chaos in relation to the recognition of foreign nullity decrees is that these are so much less numerous than foreign divorces.

In the unpublished Consultation Paper previously mentioned, the Law Commission and the Scottish Law Commission provisionally recommend that the rules for the recognition of foreign nullity decrees should be reduced to statutory form and assimilated as nearly as possible to the amended statutory rules for the recognition of foreign divorces. That is to say, a decree of nullity granted under the law of any part of the British Isles should be entitled to automatic recognition throughout the United Kingdom, subject only to the res judicata rule in the redrafted section 8 (1) (p 307 above); and annulments obtained outside the British Isles should be recognised in the United Kingdom on the same grounds and to the same extent as divorces are recognised under section 3 of the Act and the redrafted section 6.

15 [1969] 1 AC 33, [1967] 2 All ER 689.
16 [1976] Fam 155, [1976] 1 All ER 113.
17 [1979] Fam 84, [1979] 2 All ER 323; p 253 above.

CHAPTER 11

Financial Relief

Section A. Jurisdiction of the English courts

(1) *Financial relief ancillary to divorce etc*

The High Court or a divorce county court has jurisdiction to make any of the ancillary orders for financial relief mentioned in sections 21–24A of the Matrimonial Causes Act 1973 whenever it has jurisdiction in the main suit for divorce, nullity of marriage or judicial separation, provided its order would not be wholly ineffectual.

This jurisdiction is unaffected by the Civil Jurisdiction and Judgments Act 1982: see Schedules 1 and 4, article 5 (2) (p 342 below).

Cammell v Cammell [1965] P 467, [1964] 3 All ER 255 (Divorce Division)

The husband and wife were married in England in 1954. There was one child of the marriage, born in 1959. After the birth of the child the husband left the wife and went to live permanently in France. He transferred the matrimonial home in Hampstead to the wife, subject to a mortgage, and at the time of the suit had no asset of any value in England. In June 1962 the wife filed a petition for divorce in England on the ground of desertion, alleging that the husband was domiciled in England immediately before the desertion, or that she was ordinarily resident in England for a period of three years immediately preceding the presentation of the petition. The husband by his answer denied that he had ever been lawfully married to the wife, alleged that he was domiciled in France, and that in July 1963 he began proceedings for annulment in France. There was evidence that by French law maintenance of a wife or child can only be awarded if there has been a valid marriage, and that the French courts would not acknowledge that the English courts had jurisdiction either to dissolve the marriage or to make a maintenance order against the husband.

The Registrar made a maintenance order against the husband ordering him to pay £2 10s per week for the benefit of the child. The husband appealed.

Scarman J (having stated the facts, continued): Mr Davidson for the husband submits that the court has no jurisdiction to make an order: if this be wrong, he submits that the court has a discretion to decline jurisdiction and in the circumstances of this case should decline. Each of these alternative ways of putting his case rests upon the same basis, namely, the contention that any order now made by the English court for the maintenance of the child would be wholly ineffectual.

The husband's first proposition is one of law, namely, that the jurisdiction of the court depends upon the effectiveness of the order sought. Reliance for this proposition is placed upon *Tallack v Tallack and Broekema*,[1] a decision of Lord Merrivale whereby he refused to order the settlement of a guilty wife's property. The wife (or more accurately, the ex-wife) at the time of the application was resident and domiciled in Holland; the property sought to be settled was situate in Holland; and there was evidence to show that the Dutch courts would not recognise or enforce an order of the English court, if made. Mr Davidson has also relied upon the recent decision of Sir Jocelyn Simon P in *Wyler v Lyons*.[2]

Such jurisdiction as the court has to make an order for the maintenance of the child at this stage of the suit is to be found in section 26 of the Matrimonial Causes Act 1950.[3] That section confers on the court jurisdiction to make an order 'in any proceedings for divorce or nullity of marriage or judicial separation . . . from time to time, either before or by or after the final decree.' No limitation upon the court's jurisdiction such as that for which Mr Davidson contends is to be found in the express terms of the statute: but, as Lord Merrivale remarked in *Tallack v Tallack and Broekema*: 'Questions of difficulty arise which are not provided for in terms in the statutes': more especially does this happen, I would respectfully add, when the question of difficulty is a point as to the conflict of laws. Accordingly, Mr Davidson argues that the statute must be construed as subject to the general principle as to the jurisdiction for which he contends and he accepts that the effect of his contention, if it be correct, is that, notwithstanding the general language of the statute, there are certain proceedings in which the court lacks jurisdiction to make an order for the maintenance of a child the marriage of whose parents is the subject of those proceedings. But, in my view, the court in construing the statute should have regard not only to the general principle which Mr Davidson invokes from the sphere of conflict of laws but also to the policy of the law that where in any proceeding before any court the custody or upbringing of an infant is in question, the court, in deciding that question shall regard the welfare of the infant as the first and paramount consideration: Section 1 of the Guardianship of Infants Act 1925.[4] Such being the policy of the law in relation to children, I would be loth to read into section 26 of the Matrimonial Causes Act 1950 a limitation upon the jurisdiction of the court which Parliament has not by express words introduced into the section.

Does *Tallack v Tallack and Broekema*, which I accept as a decision I ought to follow, compel the court to construe the jurisdiction conferred by the section as subject to the limitation for which Mr Davidson contends? I think not. In my opinion the true relevance of that decision is not as to the interpretation of section 26 of the Matrimonial Causes Act 1950, but as a guide to the exercise of the discretion conferred by the section upon the court. With respect, I think the law is accurately stated in Dicey's *Conflict of Laws*,[5] in the

1 [1927] P 211, 96 LJP 117.
2 [1963] P 274, [1963] 1 All ER 821.
3 Now s 23 of the Matrimonial Causes Act 1973 (*Ed*).
4 Now s 1 of the Guardianship of Minors Act 1971, p 370 below (*Ed*).
5 7th edn (1958), p 293.

paragraph entitled 'Ancillary relief in matrimonial causes' 'It is conceived that, in all cases in which it has jurisdiction in the main suit, the court has (where otherwise appropriate) jurisdiction to entertain applications for ancillary relief by way of alimony pending suit, permanent alimony, permanent maintenance, periodical payments, a settlement of the wife's property, variation of settlements and custody, education and maintenance of children. The court will, however, decline to exercise jurisdiction in cases where any order that it might make would be wholly ineffective.' In other words the jurisdiction exists, but ordinarily will not be exercised if there is no chance of the court's order being effectual. This view of the law certainly accords with the practice of the court in matters of custody: for the court does not hesitate in a proper case to make a custody order in respect of a child who is out of the jurisdicition or to grant an injunction against a parent who is out of the jurisdiction in respect of a child also out of the jurisdiction: see for illustrations of the court's practice *Philips v Philips*;[6] *Harben v Harben*;[7] *Fabbri v Fabbri*.[8]

The question, therefore, becomes one of discretion. Ought the court in this case to decline jurisdiction? Clearly the court may decline to make an order if it thinks its order will be wholly ineffectual or will constitute an infringement of the authority of a foreign court. Mr Davidson submits that it would be highly undesirable in this case to make an order. Neither the person nor the property of the husband is within the jurisdiction: the courts of his domicile, it is said, would themselves make no order in present circumstances, and would neither recognise nor enforce an English order, if made. If all this be so, a very serious situation could arise: for the logic of the argument is that neither the courts of the country in which the husband is to be found nor those of the country in which the wife and child reside can or ought to make an order. The argument over-reaches itself: if in truth the courts of France are powerless, it would seem to be highly desirable that the courts of England should not decline jurisdiction. And I am by no means persuaded that the court's order, if made, would be totally ineffectual. I accept Mr Ross-Munro's submission that there is a very real probability, in view of the terms of the answer, that the husband will come to England for the hearing of the suit. If he does, the court's order can be enforced in personam. In *Tallack's* case an order, if made, would, because it was directed to property situate abroad, have been wholly ineffectual: but it would also have worn the appearance of an infringement of the authority of the Dutch courts who had exclusive jurisdiction over the subject-matter of the proposed order. I am not impressed with the comparable argument put forward in this case that an order requiring a father resident in France to make weekly payments for the maintenance of his child who lives in England would infringe French sovereignty. In *Hunter v Hunter and Waddington*[9] this court felt itself able to make an order settling a guilty wife's English property because it could be enforced within the jurisdiction and without infringement of the authority of the courts of her domicile. In the present case I think, as I have already said, that there is a very reasonable chance of an order, if made,

6 (1944) 60 TLR 395.
7 [1957] 1 All ER 379, [1957] 1 WLR 261.
8 [1962] 1 All ER 35, [1962] 1 WLR 13.
9 [1962] P 1, [1961] 2 All ER 121.

becoming enforceable by process in personam within the jurisdiction—process which would in no way infringe the authority of the French courts.

I, therefore, see no reason why the court should in its discretion decline jurisdiction. Further, it would seem to be in the interests of the child to make an order. Although the wife has the benefit of the matrimonial home which the husband transferred to her and derives some sort of income from her profession as an actress, her circumstances are such that the husband ought to contribute to the maintenance, if not wholly to maintain, his own child. And even if for the time being the order has no more than moral force, it is as well that his obligation to provide for his child should be both publicly recognised by the courts of the country where the child has his home and immediately enforceable in the event of his coming to that country. . . .

Appeal dismissed.

Domicile and Matrimonial Proceedings Act 1973

Schedule 1

Staying of Matrimonial Proceedings

11.—(1) The provisions of sub-paragraphs (2) and (3) below shall apply (subject to sub-paragraph (4)) where proceedings for divorce, judicial separation or nullity of marriage are stayed by reference to proceedings in a related jurisdiction[10] for divorce, judicial separation or nullity of marriage; and in this paragraph—

'custody' includes access to the child in question;

'education' includes training;

'lump sum order' means such an order as is mentioned in paragraph (f) of section 23 (1) of the Matrimonial Causes Act 1973 (lump sum payment for children), being an order made under section 23 (1) or (2) (a);

'the other proceedings', in relation to any stayed proceedings, means the proceedings in another jurisdiction by reference to which the stay was imposed;

'relevant order' means—

(a) an order under section 22 of the Matrimonial Causes Act 1973 (maintenance for spouse pending suit),

(b) such an order as is mentioned in paragraph (d) or (e) of section 23 (1) of that Act (periodical payments for children) being an order made under section 23 (1) or (2) (a),

(c) an order under section 42 (1) (a) of that Act (orders for the custody and education of children), and

(d) except for the purposes of sub-paragraph (3) below, any order restraining a person from removing a child out of England and Wales or out of the custody, care or control of another person; and

'stayed' means stayed in pursuance of this Schedule.[11]

---

10 'Related jurisdiction' is defined in para 3 (2) (p 296 above) as meaning Scotland, Northern Ireland, Jersey, Guernsey (including Alderney and Sark) and the Isle of Man (*Ed*).
11 See pp 296–298 above.

(2) Where any proceedings are stayed, then, without prejudice to the effect of the stay apart from this paragraph—

(a) the court shall not have power to make a relevant order or a lump sum order in connection with the stayed proceedings except in pursuance of paragraph (c) below; and

(b) subject to paragraph (c) below, any relevant order made in connection with the stayed proceedings shall, unless the stay is previously removed or the order previously discharged, cease to have effect on the expiration of the period of three months beginning with the date on which the stay was imposed; but

(c) if the court considers that, for the purpose of dealing with circumstances needing to be dealt with urgently, it is necessary during or after that period to make a relevant order or a lump sum order in connection with the stayed proceedings or to extend or further extend the duration of a relevant order made in connection with the stayed proceedings, the court may do so and the order shall not cease to have effect by virtue of paragraph (b) above.

(3) Where any proceedings are stayed and at the time when the stay is imposed an order is in force, or at a subsequent time an order comes into force, which was made in connection with the other proceedings and provides for any of the four following matters, namely, periodical payments for a spouse of the marriage in question, periodical payments for a child, the custody of a child and the education of a child then, on the imposition of the stay in a case where the order is in force when the stay is imposed and on the coming into force of the order in any other case—

(a) any relevant order made in connection with the stayed proceedings shall cease to have effect in so far as it makes for a spouse or child any provision for any of those matters as respects which the same or different provision for that spouse or child is made by the other order;

(b) the court shall not have power in connection with the stayed proceedings to make a relevant order containing for a spouse or child provision for any of those matters as respects which any provision for that spouse or child is made by the other order; and

(c) if the other order contains provision for periodical payments for a child, the court shall not have power in connection with the stayed proceedings to make a lump sum order for that child.

(4) If any proceedings are stayed so far as they consist of matrimonial proceedings of a particular kind but are not stayed so far as they consist of matrimonial proceedings of a different kind, sub-paragraphs (2) and (3) above shall not apply to the proceedings but, without prejudice to the effect of the stay apart from this paragraph, the court shall not have power to make a relevant order or a lump sum order in connection with the proceedings so far as they are stayed; and in this sub-paragraph references to matrimonial proceedings do not include proceedings for a declaration.

(5) Nothing in this paragraph affects any power of the court—

(a) to vary or discharge a relevant order so far as the order is for the time being in force; or

(b) to enforce a relevant order as respects any period when it is or was in force; or

(c) to make a relevant order or a lump sum order in connection with proceedings which were but are no longer stayed.

(2) *Failure to provide maintenance*

Matrimonial Causes Act 1973

27.[12]—(1) Either party to a marriage may apply to the court for an order under this section on the ground that the other party to the marriage (in this section referred to as the respondent)—

(a) has failed to provide reasonable maintenance for the applicant, or

(b) has failed to provide, or to make a proper contribution towards, reasonable maintenance for any child of the family.

(2) The court shall not entertain an application under this section unless—

(a) the applicant or the respondent is domiciled in England and Wales on the date of the application; or

(b) the applicant has been habitually resident there throughout the period of one year ending with that date; or

(c) the respondent is resident there on that date.

(3) *Financial provision in magistrates' courts*

Domestic Proceedings and Magistrates' Courts Act 1978

30.—(1) A magistrates' court shall, subject to section 11 of the Administration of Justice Act 1964 and any determination of the committee of magistrates thereunder, have jurisdiction to hear an application for an order under this Part of this Act if at the date of the making of the application either the applicant or the respondent ordinarily resides within the commission area for which the court is appointed.

(3) In relation to an application for an order under this Part of this Act (other than an application in relation to which jurisdiction is exercisable by virtue of section 24 of this Act) the jurisdiction conferred by subsection (1) above—

(a) shall be exercisable notwithstanding that the respondent resides in Scotland or Northern Ireland if the applicant resides in England and Wales and the parties last ordinarily resided together as man and wife in England and Wales, and

(b) is hereby declared to be exercisable where the applicant resides in Scotland or Northern Ireland if the respondent resides in England and Wales.

(5) It is hereby declared that any jurisdiction conferred on a magistrates' court by this Part of this Act is exercisable notwithstanding that any party to the proceedings is not domiciled in England.

NOTE

In *Forsyth v Forsyth*[13] and *Macrae v Macrae*[14] it was held that a magistrates' court had no jurisdiction to order one party to a marriage to make payments to the other party

12 Sub-ss (1) and (2) of this section are printed as amended by s 6 (1) of the Domicile and Matrimonial Proceedings Act 1973 and s 63 (1) of the Domestic Proceedings and Magistrates' Courts Act 1978 (*Ed*).

13 [1948] P 125, [1947] 2 All ER 623.

14 [1949] P 397, [1949] 2 All ER 34.

unless the respondent was resident (or perhaps merely present) in England at the date of the application, even if he submitted to the jurisdiction of the court. This was because the principle of submission has no application to courts of inferior jurisdiction which derive their jurisdiction from statute. This is still the law if the respondent is resident (or present) outside the United Kingdom and is not domiciled (in the sense of the Civil Jurisdiction and Judgments Act 1982) in another part of the United Kingdom or in another EEC state. If he is resident (or present) in Scotland or Northern Ireland, the actual decisions in *Forsyth v Forsyth* and *Macrae v Macrae* were altered by section 1 (1) of the Maintenance Orders Act 1950, now section 30 (3) (a) of the Domestic Proceedings and Magistrates' Courts Act 1978. 'Last ordinarily resided together as husband and wife' seems to mean little more than, in plain English, 'copulated'.[15]

If the respondent is domiciled (in the sense of the Civil Jurisdiction and Judgments Act 1982) in another EEC state or in another part of the United Kingdom, the jurisdiction of the English magistrates' courts is further extended by articles 5 (2) and 18 of Schedules 1 and 4 of that Act: see below.

(4) *Under the Brussels Convention 1968*

Civil Jurisdiction and Judgments Act 1982

Schedule 1

ARTICLE 5 (2)[16]

A person domiciled in a Contracting State may, in another Contracting State, be sued:

(2) in matters relating to maintenance, in the courts for the place where the maintenance creditor is domiciled or habitually resident, or, if the matter is ancillary to proceedings concerning the status of a person, in the court which, according to its own law, has jurisdiction to entertain those proceedings, unless that jurisdiction is based solely on the nationality of one of the parties.

NOTE

The Brussels Convention on jurisdiction and the enforcement of judgments in civil and commercial matters applies to judgments for maintenance, whether they order periodical payments or payment of a lump sum. Hence, English courts have no jurisdiction to make a maintenance order if the defendant is domiciled (in the sense of the Civil Jurisdiction and Judgments Act 1982) in another EEC state or in Scotland or Northern Ireland: Sch 1, art 3; Sch 4, art 3, unless the maintenance creditor is domiciled (in that sense) or habitually resident in England: Sch 1, art 5 (2); Sch 4, art 5 (2), or unless the defendant enters an appearance within the meaning of article 18. The only exception to this proposition is that they have jurisdiction to make ancillary maintenance orders in proceedings for divorce, nullity of marriage or judicial separation whenever they have jurisdiction in the main suit. Such orders are 'ancillary to proceedings concerning the status of a person' within the meaning of article 5 (2). The exception at the end of article 5 (2) has no relevance for English

15 *Lowry v Lowry* [1952] P 252, [1952] 2 All ER 61.
16 See also arts 3 (p 85 above) and 18 (p 91 above). Sch 4, arts 3, 5 (2) and 18 (dealing with cases where the defendant is domiciled in Scotland or Northern Ireland) are to the same effect.

courts, because they do not exercise jurisdiction in divorce, nullity of marriage or judicial separation on the basis of nationality: see Domicile and Matrimonial Proceedings Act 1973, s 5, p 295 above.

'Maintenance' in article 5 (2) means maintenance imposed by law and not maintenance payable under an agreement between the parties. Such agreements will therefore come within article 5 (1) (contract) and not within article 5 (2): Schlosser, *Official Journal of the European Communities*, 1979 No C59, para 92.

Section B. Enforcement of Foreign Orders

Recognition of Divorces and Legal Separations Act 1971

8.—(3) Nothing in this Act shall be construed as requiring the recognition of any findings of fault made in any proceedings for divorce or separation or of any maintenance, custody or other ancillary order made in any such proceedings.

At common law a foreign maintenance order will not be enforced in England if the foreign court can vary the amounts payable, because then the order is not final and conclusive. But if the foreign court has no power to vary the amount of past instalments, then the arrears can be recovered in England.

Beatty v Beatty [1924] 1 KB 807, 93 LJKB 750 (Court of Appeal)

Appeal from Horridge J.

The parties were divorced in 1911 by a decree of the Supreme Court of New York. In 1912 the former wife obtained an order from that court for the payment of twenty dollars a week. The order directed that she should have liberty to apply for a modification of the order in the event of a change of circumstances.

The former wife sued her former husband in England in 1915 for £819 alleged to be arrears due under the New York order. The defendant pleaded that the order was obtained by fraud. In 1921 an order was made for the issue of a commission for the examination of the plaintiff's witnesses in New York. An American lawyer deposed that the New York order was a final judgment and enforceable as such. When the case came to trial before Horridge J the defence of fraud was abandoned but for some reason the evidence of the American lawyer was not referred to. In the absence of that evidence Horridge J assumed that the New York rule was the same as the English rule, namely, that an action would not lie to recover arrears of alimony.

The plaintiff appealed.

Scrutton LJ: On an appeal being brought to this court we were informed that a decision of the Supreme Court of the United States in a case of *Sistare v Sistare*[17] was in conflict with the learned judge's view, and we thereupon adjourned the hearing in order that evidence as to the law of New York in

17 (1910) 218 US 1.

this respect might be given in the ordinary way. Again, for some reason which I do not understand the legal advisers of the parties returned to this court without the necessary evidence, and proposed to discuss the effect of the decision in *Sistare v Sistare*. But the question as to what is the law of a foreign State on a particular matter is treated in our courts as a question, not of law, but of fact. We are not entitled to look at an American report, and say on the authority of that report that the American law is so and so. It must be proved by the evidence of experts in that law. Under those circumstances the question arose, What was this court to do? The regular course would have been to send the case down for retrial in order that evidence of the facts might be given, but we were not desirous of putting the parties to further expense, and we asked them to agree to this court deciding the matter as arbitrators on the materials before it, and in that way we are now deciding it. Whether the effect of that will be that our decision will be of no authority as a reported case is a matter on which I express no opinion.

Is then this judgment of the court of New York a final judgment which this court will enforce on an action being brought for the purpose? The principle which we have to apply was thus stated by Lord Herschell in *Nouvion v Freeman*:[18] 'I think that in order to establish that such a judgment has been pronounced'—that is a final judgment which this court can enforce—'it must be shewn that in the court by which it was pronounced it conclusively, finally, and for ever established the existence of the debt of which it is sought to be made conclusive evidence in this country, so as to make it res judicata between the parties.' That statement of the principle, however, although very widely expressed, must not be understood as meaning that the fact that a judgment may be reversed on appeal, and that an appeal is even pending at the time, makes the judgment the less final, if it is final in the particular court in which it was pronounced. What then is the evidence as to the effect of this judgment in the State of New York where it was pronounced? In England, as I have said, an order for the payment of alimony is not a final judgment within the rule, for it is always open to the court to vary its order even in respect of instalments already accrued due, and if that had been the position in New York this order could not now be sued upon. But the evidence of the New York lawyer and the decision in *Sistare v Sistare* show that in the State of New York, when an order for alimony has been made and instalments have accrued due, the court has no power to vary that order as regards the instalments so in arrear, however much the position of the parties may have changed, and the order in respect of those arrears is a final judgment.

It was, however, suggested that there are certain recent decisions which go to show that this action is not maintainable. In *Re Macartney*,[19] where the action was for arrears due under an affiliation order made by the Court of Appeal in Malta, Astbury J held that the judgment was not final and conclusive. He did so on the evidence of an expert in Maltese law that the maintenance awarded by the judgment might be varied from time to time or terminated, according to the circumstances of the child. But as it did not appear whether he was referring only to future maintenance, or also to instalments already due, I must take it that that case was decided on the

18 (1889) 15 App Cas 1, 59 LJCh 337; p 163 above.
19 [1921] 1 Ch 522, 90 LJCh 314.

principle applicable to an English order for alimony—namely, that a power to vary the order prevents it from being final even as regards arrears. The same observation applies to the judgment of Sankey J in *Harrop v Harrop*,[20] where no evidence was given that the court of the State of Perak had no power to alter its order as to accrued instalments. And *M'Donnell v M'Donnell*[1] proceeded on the same grounds, that there was no evidence as to the law of the State of Montana, and the court expressly said that in the absence of evidence as to the foreign law they took the order of the foreign court to be analogous to our orders for alimony, and to be liable to variation whether instalments had accrued or not. None of those cases therefore are in conflict with the view we are here taking. For these reasons I agree that the appeal should be allowed.

Bankes and Sargant LJJ delivered judgments to the same effect.
Appeal allowed.

Civil Jurisdiction and Judgments Act 1982

5.—(1) The function of transmitting to the appropriate court an application under Article 31 for the recognition or enforcement in the United Kingdom of a maintenance order shall be discharged—
(a)   as respects England and Wales and Scotland, by the Secretary of State;
(b)   as respects Northern Ireland, by the Lord Chancellor.
   In this subsection 'the appropriate court' means the magistrates' court or sheriff court having jurisdiction in the matter in accordance with the second paragraph of Article 32.
   (2) Such an application shall be determined in the first instance by the prescribed officer of that court.
   (3) Where on such an application the enforcement of the order is authorised to any extent, the order shall to that extent be registered in the prescribed manner in that court.
   (4) A maintenance order registered under this section shall, for the purposes of its enforcement, be of the same force and effect, the registering court shall have in relation to its enforcement the same powers, and proceedings for or with respect to its enforcement may be taken, as if the order had been originally made by the registering court.
   (5) Subsection (4) is subject to Article 39 (restriction on enforcement where appeal pending or time for appeal unexpired), to section 7 and to any provision made by rules of court as to the manner in which and conditions subject to which an order registered under this section may be enforced.

6.—(3) The single further appeal on a point of law referred to in Article 37, second paragraph and Article 41 in relation to the recognition or enforcement of a maintenance order lies—
(a)   in England and Wales, to the High Court by way of case stated in accordance with section 111 of the Magistrates' Courts Act 1980.

8.—(1) Sums payable in the United Kingdom under a maintenance order by virtue of its registration under section 5, including any arrears so payable, shall be paid in the currency of the United Kingdom.

20 [1920] 3 KB 386, 90 LJKB 101.
 1 [1921] 2 IR 148.

(2) Where the order is expressed in any other currency, the amounts shall be converted on the basis of the exchange rate prevailing on the date of registration of the order.

(3) For the purposes of this section, a written certificate purporting to be signed by an officer of any bank in the United Kingdom and stating the exchange rate prevailing on a specified date shall be evidence, and in Scotland sufficient evidence, of the facts stated.

SCHEDULE 1

Section 2 Enforcement

ARTICLE 31

A judgment given in a Contracting State and enforceable in that State shall be enforced in another Contracting State when, on the application of any interested party, the order for its enforcement has been issued there.

However, in the United Kingdom, such a judgment shall be enforced in England and Wales, in Scotland, or in Northern Ireland when, on the application of any interested party, it has been registered for enforcement in that part of the United Kingdom.

ARTICLE 32

The application shall be submitted:
—in the United Kingdom:
   (1) in England and Wales, to the High Court of Justice, or in the case of a maintenance judgment to the Magistrates' Court on transmission by the Secretary of State.

NOTE

Maintenance judgments given in another EEC state, in order to be enforced in England, are sent, not to the High Court like other judgments, but to the Secretary of State (ie the Home Office) so that he can transmit them to the appropriate magistrates' court for registration: Civil Jurisdiction and Judgments Act 1982, Sch 1, arts 31 (2) and 32, s 5. The application for registration must be made ex parte in the first instance: art 34 (1). (For the reasons for this, see pp 194–195 above.) The application will be determined in the first instance by the prescribed officer, almost certainly the clerk to the justices. If enforcement is authorised, the defendant may then appeal to the magistrates' court to set aside the registration; thereafter he may appeal once only on a point of law: arts 36 and 37. If enforcement is refused, the applicant may appeal to the magistrates' court (art 40) and there is a further right of appeal by either party, but once only on a point of law (art 41). The single appeal on a point of law under articles 37 and 41 is to the High Court by way of case stated: s 6 (3) (a).

The grounds on which recognition may be refused are set out in article 27 (p 188 ground of refusal which is of special relevance to maintenance orders. Its effect is that if eg a French divorce court orders a man to pay maintenance to a woman on the footing that she is his wife, but by English rules of private international law she is not his wife, the order cannot be enforced in England.

Conversion of foreign currencies into sterling is governed by section 8 of the Act. See the Note to chapter 16, p 526 below.

Maintenance orders made in Scotland and Northern Ireland are enforced in England under Part II of the Maintenance Orders Act 1950 (p 347 below): 1982 Act, s 18 (5) (a).

Section C. Reciprocal Enforcement

Maintenance Orders Act 1950

PART II

ENFORCEMENT

16.—(1) Any order to which this section applies (in this Part of this Act referred to as a maintenance order) made by a court in any part of the United Kingdom may, if registered in accordance with the provisions of this Part of this Act in a court in another part of the United Kingdom, be enforced in accordance with those provisions in that other part of the United Kingdom.

17.—(1) An application for the registration of a maintenance order under this Part of this Act shall be made in the prescribed manner to the appropriate authority, that is to say—

(a) where the maintenance order was made by a court of summary jurisdiction in England, a justice or justices acting for the same place as the court which made the order;

(b) where the maintenance order was made by a court of summary jurisdiction in Northern Ireland, a resident magistrate acting for the same petty sessions district as the court which made the order;

(c) in every other case, the prescribed officer of the court which made the order.

(2) If upon application made as aforesaid by or on behalf of the person entitled to payments under a maintenance order it appears that the person liable to make those payments resides in another part of the United Kingdom, and that it is convenient that the order should be enforceable there, the appropriate authority shall cause a certified copy of the order to be sent to the prescribed officer of a court in that part of the United Kingdom in accordance with the provisions of the next following subsection.

(3) The Court to whose officer the certified copy of a maintenance order is sent under this section shall be—

(a) where the maintenance order was made by a superior court, the Supreme Court of Judicature in England, the Court of Session or the Supreme Court of Judicature of Northern Ireland, as the case may be;

(b) in any other case, a court of summary jurisdiction acting for the place in England or Northern Ireland in which the defendant appears to be, or, as the case may be, the sheriff court in Scotland within the jurisdiction of which he appears to be.

(4) Where the prescribed officer of any court receives a certified copy of a maintenance order sent to him under this section, he shall cause the order to be registered in that court in the prescribed manner, and shall give notice of the registration in the prescribed manner to the prescribed officer of the court which made the order.

18.—(1) Subject to the provisions of this section, a maintenance order registered under this Part of this Act in a court in any part of the United Kingdom may be enforced in that part of the United Kingdom in all respects as if it had been made by that court and as if that court had had jurisdiction to make it; and proceedings for or with respect to the enforcement of any such order may be taken accordingly.

21.—(1) The registration of a maintenance order in a superior court under this Part of this Act shall not confer on that court any power to vary or discharge the order, or affect any jurisdiction of the court in which the order was made to vary or discharge the order.

22.—(1) Where a maintenance order is for the time being registered under this Part of this Act in a court of summary jurisdiction or sheriff court, that court may, upon application made in the prescribed manner by or on behalf of the person liable to make [²periodical] payments under the order or the person entitled to those payments, by order make such variation as the court thinks fit in the rate of the payments under the maintenance order; but no such variation shall impose on the person liable to make payments under the maintenance order a liability to make payments in excess of the maximum rate (if any) authorised by the law for the time being in force in the part of the United Kingdom in which the maintenance order was made.

(4) Except as provided by subsection (1) of this section, no variation shall be made in the rate of the payments under a maintenance order which is for the time being registered under this Part of this Act in a court of summary jurisdiction or sheriff court, but without prejudice to any power of the court which made the order to discharge it or vary it otherwise than in respect of the rate of the payments thereunder.

Maintenance Orders (Facilities for Enforcement) Act 1920

1.—(1) Where a maintenance order has, whether before or after the passing of this Act, been made against any person by any court in any part of His Majesty's dominions outside the United Kingdom to which this Act extends, and a certified copy of the order has been transmitted by the governor of that part of His Majesty's dominions to the Secretary of State, the Secretary of State shall send a copy of the order to the prescribed officer of a court in England or Ireland for registration; and on receipt thereof the order shall be registered in the prescribed manner, and shall, from the date of such registration, be of the same force and effect, and, subject to the provisions of this Act, all proceedings may be taken on such order as if it had been an order originally obtained in the court in which it is so registered, and that court shall have power to enforce the order accordingly.

(2) The court in which an order is to be so registered as aforesaid shall, if the court by which the order was made was a court of superior jurisdiction, be the [³Family Division] of the High Court, or in Ireland the King's Bench Division (Matrimonial) of the High Court of Justice in Ireland, and, if the court was not a court of superior jurisdiction, be a court of summary jurisdiction.

2. Where a court in England or Ireland has, whether before or after the commencement of this Act, made a maintenance order against any person, and it is proved to that court that the person against whom the order was

2 Word inserted by Domestic Proceedings and Magistrates' Courts Act 1978, Sch 2, para 14.
3 Words substituted by Administration of Justice Act 1970, Sch 2, para 2.

made is resident in some part of His Majesty's dominions outside the United Kingdom to which this Act extends, the court shall send to the Secretary of State for transmission to the governor of that part of His Majesty's dominions a certified copy of the order.

3.—(1) Where an application is made to a court of summary jurisdiction in England or Ireland for a maintenance order against any person, and it is proved that that person is resident in a part of His Majesty's dominions outside the United Kingdom to which this Act extends, the court may, in the absence of that person, if after hearing the evidence it is satisfied of the justice of the application, make any such order as it might have made if a summons had been duly served on that person and he had failed to appear at the hearing, but in such case the order shall be provisional only, and shall have no effect unless and until confirmed by a competent court in such part of His Majesty's dominions as aforesaid.

(2) The evidence of any witness who is examined on any such application shall be put into writing, and such deposition shall be read over to and signed by him.

(3) Where such an order is made, the court shall send to the Secretary of State for transmission to the governor of the part of His Majesty's dominions in which the person against whom the order is made is alleged to reside the depositions so taken and a certified copy of the order, together with a statement of the grounds on which the making of the order might have been opposed if the person against whom the order is made had been duly served with a summons and had appeared at the hearing, and such information as the court possesses for facilitating the identification of that person, and ascertaining his whereabouts.

(4) Where any such provisional order has come before a court in a part of His Majesty's dominions outside the United Kingdom to which this Act extends for confirmation, and the order has by that court been remitted to the court of summary jurisdiction which made the order for the purpose of taking further evidence, that court or any other court of summary jurisdiction sitting and acting for the same place shall, after giving the prescribed notice, proceed to take the evidence in like manner and subject to the like conditions as the evidence in support of the original application.

If upon the hearing of such evidence it appears to the court that the order ought not to have been made, the court may rescind the order, but in any other case the depositions shall be sent to the Secretary of State and dealt with in like manner as the original depositions.

(5) The confirmation of an order made under this section shall not affect any power of a court of summary jurisdiction to vary or rescind that order: Provided that on the making of a varying or rescinding order the court shall send a certified copy thereof to the Secretary of State for transmission to the governor of the part of His Majesty's dominions in which the original order was confirmed, and that in the case of an order varying the original order the order shall not have any effect unless and until confirmed in like manner as the original order.

(6) The applicant shall have the same right of appeal, if any, against a refusal to make a provisional order as he would have had against a refusal to make the order had a summons been duly served on the person against whom the order is sought to be made.

4.—(1) Where a maintenance order has been made by a court in a part of His Majesty's dominions outside the United Kingdom to which this Act extends, and the order is provisional only and has no effect unless and until confirmed by a court of summary jurisdiction in England or Ireland, and a certified copy of the order, together with the depositions of witnesses and a statement of the grounds on which the order might have been opposed has been transmitted to the Secretary of State, and it appears to the Secretary of State that the person against whom the order was made is resident in England or Ireland, the Secretary of State may send the said documents to the prescribed officer of a court of summary jurisdiction, with a requisition that a summons be issued calling upon the person to show cause why that order should not be confirmed, and upon receipt of such documents and requisition the court shall issue such a summons and cause it to be served upon such person.

(2) A summons so issued may be served in England or Ireland in the same manner as if it had been originally issued or subsequently endorsed by a court of summary jurisdiction having jurisdiction in the place where the person happens to be.

(3) At the hearing it shall be open to the person on whom the summons was served to raise any defence which he might have raised in the original proceedings had he been a party thereto, but no other defence, and the certificate from the court which made the provisional order stating the grounds on which the making of the order might have been opposed if the person against whom the order was made had been a party to the proceedings shall be conclusive evidence that those grounds are grounds on which objection may be taken.

(4) If at the hearing the person served with the summons does not appear or, on appearing, fails to satisfy the court that the order ought not to be confirmed, the court may confirm the order either without modification or with such modifications as to the court after hearing the evidence may seem just.

(5) If the person against whom the summons was issued appears at the hearing and satisfies the court that for the purpose of any defence it is necessary to remit the case to the court which made the provisional order for the taking of any further evidence, the court may so remit the case and adjourn the proceedings for the purpose.

(6) Where a provisional order has been confirmed under this section, it may be varied or rescinded in like manner as if it had originally been made by the confirming court, and where on an application for rescission or variation the court is satisfied that it is necessary to remit the case to the court which made the order for the purpose of taking any further evidence, the court may so remit the case and adjourn the proceedings for the purpose.

(7) Where an order has been so confirmed, the person bound thereby shall have the same right of appeal, if any, against the confirmation of the order as he would have had against the making of the order had the order been an order made by the court confirming the order.

10. For the purposes of this Act, the expression 'maintenance order' means an order other than an order of affiliation for the periodical payment of sums of money towards the maintenance of the wife or other dependants of the person against whom the order is made, and the expression 'dependants'

means such persons as that person is, according to the law in force in the part of His Majesty's dominions in which the maintenance order was made, liable to maintain; the expression 'certified copy' in relation to an order of a court means a copy of the order certified by the proper officer of the court to be a true copy, and the expression 'prescribed' means prescribed by rules of court.

Maintenance Orders (Reciprocal Enforcement) Act 1972[4]

PART I

RECIPROCAL ENFORCEMENT OF MAINTENANCE ORDERS MADE IN UNITED KINGDOM OR RECIPROCATING COUNTRY

1.—(1) Her Majesty, if satisfied that, in the event of the benefits conferred by this Part of this Act being applied to, or to particular classes of, maintenance orders made by the courts of any country or territory outside the United Kingdom, similar benefits will in that country or territory be applied to, or to those classes of, maintenance orders made by the courts of the United Kingdom, may by Order in Council designate that country or territory as a reciprocating country for the purposes of this Part of this Act; and, subject to subsection (2) below, in this Part of this Act 'reciprocating country' means a country or territory that is for the time being so designated.[5]

(2) A country or territory may be designated under subsection (1) above as a reciprocating country either as regards maintenance orders generally, or as regards maintenance orders other than those of any specified class, or as regards maintenance orders of one or more specified classes only; and a country or territory which is for the time being so designated otherwise than as regards maintenance orders generally shall for the purposes of this Part of this Act be taken to be a reciprocating country only as regards maintenance orders of the class to which the designation extends.

2.—(1) Subject to subsection (2) below, where the payer under a maintenance order made, whether before or after the commencement of this Part of this Act, by a court in the United Kingdom is residing or has assets in a reciprocating country, the payee under the order may apply for the order to be sent to that country for enforcement.

(2) Subsection (1) above shall not have effect in relation to a provisional order or to an order made by virtue of a provision of Part II of this Act.

(3) Every application under this section shall be made in the prescribed manner to the prescribed officer of the court which made the maintenance order to which the application relates.

(4) If, on an application duly made under this section to the prescribed officer of a court in the United Kingdom, that officer is satisfied that the payer under the maintenance order to which the application relates is

---

4 The following extracts from this Act are printed as amended by ss 54, 55, 56, 58 and Sch 2, para 34 of the Domestic Proceeding and Magistrates' Courts Act 1978, by Sch 2, para 18 of the Justices of the Peace Act 1979, and by Sch 11 of the Civil Jurisdiction and Judgments Act 1982 (*Ed*).

5 For reciprocating countries, see SI 1974/566, SI 1975/2187, SI 1979/115 and SI 1983/1125.

residing or has assets in a reciprocating country, the following documents, that is to say—

(a) a certified copy of the maintenance order;

(b) a certificate signed by that officer certifying that the order is enforceable in the United Kingdom;

(c) a certificate of arrears so signed;

(d) a statement giving such information as the officer possesses as to the whereabouts of the payer and the nature and location of his assets in that country;

(e) a statement giving such information as the officer possesses for facilitating the identification of the payer; and

(f) where available, a photograph of the payer;

shall be sent by that officer to the Secretary of State with a view to their being transmitted by the Secretary of State to the responsible authority in the reciprocating country if he is satisfied that the statement relating to the whereabouts of the payer and the nature and location of his assets in that country gives sufficient information to justify that being done.

(5) Nothing in this section shall be taken as affecting any jurisdiction of a court in the United Kingdom with respect to a maintenance order to which this section applies, and any such order may be enforced, varied or revoked accordingly.

3.—(1) Where a complaint is made to a magistrates' court against a person residing in a reciprocating country and the complaint is one on which the court would have jurisdiction by virtue of any enactment to make a maintenance order if—

(a) that person were residing in England and Wales; and

(b) a summons to appear before the court to answer to the complaint had been duly served on him,

the court shall have jurisdiction to hear the complaint and may, subject to subsection (2) below, make a maintenance order on the complaint.

(2) A maintenance order made by virtue of this section shall be a provisional order.

(3) If the court hearing a complaint to which subsection (1) above applies is satisfied—

(a) that there are grounds on which a maintenance order containing a provision requiring the making of payments for the maintenance of a child may be made on that complaint, but

(b) that it has no jurisdiction to make that order unless it also makes an order providing for the legal custody of that child,

then, for the purpose of enabling the court to make the maintenance order, the complainant shall be deemed to be the person to whom the legal custody of that child has been committed by an order of the court which is for the time being in force.

(4) No enactment empowering a magistrates' court to refuse to make an order on a complaint on the ground that the matter in question is one which would be more conveniently dealt with by the High Court shall apply in relation to a complaint to which subsection (1) above applies.

(5) Where a court makes a maintenance order which is by virtue of this section a provisional order, the following documents, that is to say—

(a) a certified copy of the maintenance order;

(b) a document, authenticated in the prescribed manner, setting out or summarising the evidence given in the proceedings;

(c) a certificate signed by the prescribed officer of the court certifying that the grounds stated in the certificate are the grounds on which the making of the order might have been opposed by the payer under the order;

(d) a statement giving such information as was available to the court as to the whereabouts of the payer;

(e) a statement giving such information as the officer possesses for facilitating the identification of the payer; and

(f) where available, a photograph of the payer;

shall be sent by that officer to the Secretary of State with a view to their being transmitted by the Secretary of State to the responsible authority in the reciprocating country in which the payer is residing if he is satisfied that the statement relating to the whereabouts of the payer gives sufficient information to justify that being done.

(6) A maintenance order made by virtue of this section which has been confirmed by a competent court in a reciprocating country shall be treated for all purposes as if the magistrates' court which made the order had made it in the form in which it was confirmed and as if the order had never been a provisional order, and subject to section 5 of this Act, any such order may be enforced, varied or revoked accordingly.

5. (*Variation of maintenance orders made in the UK.*)

6.—(1) This section applies to a maintenance order made, whether before or after the commencement of this Part of this Act, by a court in a reciprocating country, including such an order made by such a court which has been confirmed by a court in another reciprocating country but excluding a provisional order which has not been confirmed.

(2) Where a certified copy of an order to which this section applies is received by the Secretary of State from the responsible authority in a reciprocating country, and it appears to the Secretary of State that the payer under the order is residing or has assets in the United Kingdom, he shall send the copy of the order to the prescribed officer of the appropriate court.

(3) Where the prescribed officer of the appropriate court receives from the Secretary of State a certified copy of an order to which this section applies, he shall, subject to subsection (4) below, register the order in the prescribed manner in that court.

(4) Before registering an order under this section an officer of a court shall take such steps as he thinks fit for the purpose of ascertaining whether the payer under the order is residing or has assets within the jurisdiction of the court, and if after taking those steps he is satisfied that the payer is not residing and has no assets within the jurisdiction of the court he shall return the certified copy of the order to the Secretary of State with a statement giving such information as he possesses as to the whereabouts of the payer and the nature and location of his assets.

7.—(1) This section applies to a maintenance order made, whether before or after the commencement of this Part of this Act, by a court in a reciprocating country being a provisional order.

(2) Where a certified copy of an order to which this section applies together with—

(a) a document, duly authenticated, setting out or summarising the evidence given in the proceedings in which the order was made; and

(b) a statement of the grounds on which the making of the order might have been opposed by the payer under the order,

is received by the Secretary of State from the responsible authority in a reciprocating country, and it appears to the Secretary of State that the payer under the order is residing in the United Kingdom, he shall send the copy of the order and documents which accompanied it to the prescribed officer of the appropriate court, and that court shall—

(i) if the payer under the order establishes any such defence as he might have raised in the proceedings in which the order was made, refuse to confirm the order; and

(ii) in any other case, confirm the order either without alteration or with such alterations as it thinks reasonable.

(3) In any proceedings for the confirmation under this section of a provisional order, the statement received from the court which made the order of the grounds on which the making of the order might have been opposed by the payer under the order shall be conclusive evidence that the payer might have raised a defence on any of those grounds in the proceedings in which the order was made.

(4) For the purpose of determining whether a provisional order should be confirmed under this section the court shall proceed as if an application for a maintenance order against the payer under the provisional order had been made to it.

(5) The prescribed officer of a court having power under this section to confirm a provisional order shall, if the court confirms the order, register the order in the prescribed manner in that court, and shall, if the court refuses to confirm the order, return the certified copy of the order and the documents which accompanied it to the Secretary of State.

(6) If a summons to appear in the proceedings for the confirmation of the provisional order cannot be duly served on the payer under that order the officer by whom the certified copy of the order was received shall return that copy and the documents which accompanied it to the Secretary of State with a statement giving such information as he possesses as to the whereabouts of the payer.

8.—(1) Subject to subsection (2) below, a registered order may be enforced in the United Kingdom as if it had been made by the registering court and as if that court had had jurisdiction to make it; and proceedings for or with respect to the enforcement of any such order may be taken accordingly.

(2) Subsection (1) above does not apply to an order which is for the time being registered in the High Court under Part I of the Maintenance Orders Act 1958 or to an order which is for the time being registered in the High Court of Justice in Northern Ireland under Part II of the Maintenance and Affiliation Orders Act (Northern Ireland) 1966.

9. (*Variation of maintenance orders registered in the UK.*)

21.—(1) In this Part of this Act—

'the appropriate court' in relation to a person residing or having assets in England and Wales or in Northern Ireland means a magistrates' court;

'court' includes any tribunal or person having power to make, confirm, enforce, vary or revoke a maintenance order;

'maintenance order' means an order (however described) of any of the following descriptions, that is to say—

(a) an order (including an affiliation order or order consequent upon an affiliation order) which provides for the payment of a lump sum or the making of periodical payments towards the maintenance of any person, being a person whom the person liable to make payments under the order is, according to the law applied in the place where the order was made, liable to maintain;

'payee', in relation to a maintenance order, means the person entitled to the payments for which the order provides;

'payer', in relation to a maintenance order, means the person liable to make payments under the order;

'provisional order' means (according to the context)—

(a) an order made by a court in the United Kingdom which is provisional only and has no effect unless and until confirmed, with or without alteration, by a competent court in a reciprocating country; or

(b) an order made by a court in a reciprocating country which is provisional only and has no effect unless and until confirmed, with or without alteration, by a court in the United Kingdom having power under this Part of this Act to confirm it.

(2) For the purposes of this Part of this Act an order shall be taken to be a maintenance order so far (but only so far) as it relates to the payment of a lump sum or the making of periodical payments as mentioned in paragraph (a) of the definition of 'maintenance order' in subsection (1) above.

(3) Any reference in this Part of this Act to the payment of money for the maintenance of a child shall be construed as including a reference to the payment of money for the child's education.

Part II

Reciprocal Enforcement of Claims for the Recovery of Maintenance

26.—(1) Where a person in the United Kingdom ('the applicant') claims to be entitled to recover in a convention country[6] maintenance from another person, and that other person is for the time being subject to the jurisdiction of that country, the applicant may apply to the Secretary of State, in accordance with the provisions of this section, to have his claim for the recovery of maintenance from that other person transmitted to that country.

(2) Where the applicant seeks to vary any provision made in a convention country for the payment by any other person of maintenance to the applicant, and that other person is for the time being subject to the jurisdiction of that country, the applicant may apply to the Secretary of State, in accordance with the provisions of this section, to have his application for the variation of that provision transmitted to that country.

(3) An application to the Secretary of State under subsection (1) or (2) above shall be made through the appropriate officer, and that officer shall assist the applicant in completing an application which will comply with the requirements of the law applied by the convention country and shall send

6 The convention referred to is the United Nations Convention for the Recovery Abroad of Maintenance (1956). For convention countries, see SI 1975/423, as amended by SI 1978/279 and SI 1982/1530 (*Ed*).

the application to the Secretary of State, together with such other documents, if any, as are required by that law.

(4) On receiving an application from the appropriate officer the Secretary of State shall transmit it, together with any accompanying documents, to the appropriate authority in the convention country, unless he is satisfied that the application is not made in good faith or that it does not comply with the requirements of the law applied by that country.

(5) The Secretary of State may request the appropriate officer to obtain from the court of which he is an officer such information relating to the application as may be specified in the request, and it shall be the duty of the court to furnish the Secretary of State with the information he requires.

(6) Where the applicant is residing in England and Wales the appropriate officer for the purposes of this section is the clerk of a magistrates' court acting for the petty sessions area in which the applicant is residing.

27.—(1) Where the Secretary of State receives from the appropriate authority in a convention country an application by a person in that country for the recovery of maintenance from another person who is for the time being residing in England and Wales, he shall send the application, together with any accompanying documents, to the clerk of a magistrates' court acting for the petty sessions area in which that other person is residing; and the application shall be treated for the purposes of any enactment as if it were a complaint and references in this section and in sections 28, 28A, 29, 29A and 30 of this Act to the complaint, the complainant and the defendant shall be construed accordingly.

(2) Where the complaint is for an affiliation order, a magistrates' court appointed for the commission area (within the meaning of the Justices of the Peace Act 1979), in which the defendant is residing shall have jurisdiction to hear the complaint.

(4) If a summons to appear before a magistrates' court having jurisdiction to hear the complaint cannot be duly served on the defendant, the clerk of the court shall, subject to subsection (5) below, return the complaint and the accompanying documents to the Secretary of State with a statement giving such information as he possesses as to the whereabouts of the defendant, and unless the Secretary of State is satisfied that the defendant is not residing in the United Kingdom he shall deal with the complaint in accordance with subsection (1) above or section 31 of this Act, as the circumstances of the case require.

(5) If the clerk of a magistrates' court to whom the complaint is sent in pursuance of a provision of this section is satisfied that the defendant is residing within the jurisdiction of another magistrates' court in that part of the United Kingdom in which the first-mentioned court is he shall send the complaint and accompanying documents to the clerk of that other court and shall inform the Secretary of State that he has done so.

(6) The clerk of a court to whom the complaint is sent under subsection (5) above shall proceed as if it had been sent to him under subsection (1) above.

(7) When hearing the complaint a magistrates' court shall proceed as if the complainant were before the court.

(8) If a magistrates' court makes an order on the complaint, the clerk of the court shall register the order in the prescribed manner in that court.

28A.—(1) Where on an application under section 27 (1) of this Act for the recovery of maintenance from a person who is residing in England and Wales—

(a) that person is a former spouse of the applicant in a convention country who is seeking to recover maintenance, and

(b) the marriage between the applicant and the former spouse has been dissolved by a divorce granted in a convention country which is recognised as valid by the law of England and Wales, and

(c) an order for the payment of maintenance for the benefit of the applicant or a child of the family has, by reason of the divorce proceedings in the convention country, been made by the court which granted the divorce or by any other court in that country,

the application shall, notwithstanding that the marriage has been dissolved, be treated as a complaint for an order under section 2 of the Domestic Proceedings and Magistrates' Courts Act 1978, and the provisions of this section shall have effect.

(2) On hearing a complaint by virtue of this section the magistrates' court may, if satisfied that the defendant has failed to comply with the provisions of any such order as is mentioned in subsection (1) (c) above, make any order which it has power to make under section 2 or section 19 (1) (i) of the Domestic Proceedings and Magistrates' Courts Act 1978 except that—

(a) an order for the making of periodical payments for the benefit of the applicant or any child of the family shall not be made unless the order made in the convention country provides for the making of periodical payments for the benefit of the applicant or, as the case may be, that child, and

(b) an order for the payment of a lump sum for the benefit of the applicant or any child of the family shall not be made unless the order made in the convention country provides for the payment of a lump sum to the applicant or, as the case may be, to that child.

(4) A divorce obtained in a convention country shall be presumed for the purposes of this section to be one the validity of which is recognised by the law of England and Wales, unless the contrary is proved by the defendant.

(5) The reference in subsection (1) (b) above to the dissolution of a marriage by divorce shall be construed as including a reference to the annulment of the marriage and any reference in this section to a divorce or to divorce proceedings shall be construed accordingly.

(6) In this section the expression 'child of the family' has the same meaning as in section 88 of the Domestic Proceedings and Magistrates' Courts Act 1978.

PART III

MISCELLANEOUS AND SUPPLEMENTAL

40. Where Her Majesty is satisfied—

(a) that arrangements have been or will be made in a country or territory outside the United Kingdom to ensure that maintenance orders made by courts in the United Kingdom can be enforced in that country or territory or that applications by persons in the United Kingdom for the recovery of maintenance from persons in that country or territory can be entertained by courts in that country or territory; and

(b) that in the interest of reciprocity it is desirable to ensure that maintenance orders made by courts in that country or territory can be enforced in the United Kingdom or, as the case may be, that applications by persons in that country or territory for the recovery of maintenance from persons in the United Kingdom can be entertained by courts in the United Kingdom,

Her Majesty may by Order in Council make provision for applying the provisions of this Act, with such exceptions, adaptations and modifications as may be specified in the Order, to such orders or applications as are referred to in paragraphs (a) and (b) above and to maintenance and other orders made in connection with such applications by courts in the United Kingdom or in that country or territory.[7]

QUESTION

W, who is domiciled in England and resident in Oxford, has been deserted by her husband, H. Advise W as to how she can best obtain a maintenance order against H in Oxford magistrates' court, assuming that H is domiciled and resident (a) in another part of the United Kingdom, (b) in another EEC state, (c) in a reciprocating country designated by Order in Council under section 1 of the Maintenance Orders (Reciprocal Enforcement) Act 1972, or (d) in a convention country to which Part II of that Act applies.

Section D. Effect of Foreign Order in England

A valid foreign divorce does not necessarily terminate the husband's financial obligations to his former wife under an English maintenance order.

Wood v Wood [1957] P 254, [1957] 2 All ER 14 (Court of Appeal)

A husband and wife were married in 1945, both parties being domiciled in England. On 7 February 1950 the wife obtained a maintenance order against the husband in a magistrates' court on the ground of his desertion. The husband was ordered to pay to the chief clerk of the court a weekly sum of £3 for the wife and 15s for each of the two children of the marriage. In January 1953 the husband, who was a showman exercising his profession through a troupe of performing chimpanzees, took the animals to the United States, and in May found his way to Las Vegas, Nevada. He decided to make his home in that state, partly because the climate suited his chimpanzees, and partly because the rate of income-tax compared favourably with that in his native land. He invited the wife to join him there, but she refused to go as he was accompanied by another woman who was pregnant by him at the time.

On 29 September 1954 the court in Las Vegas granted the husband a divorce on the ground that he and his wife had not lived together for three years. The qualification for obtaining such a decree was residence in Las

---

7 Versions of Part I of the Act (with considerable modifications) have been applied to the Republic of Ireland (SI 1974/2140) and to Hague Convention countries (SI 1979/1317 as amended by SIs 1981/837, 1545, 1674 and SIs 1983/885 and 1523). A version of Part II has been applied to most states of the USA (SI 1979/1314 as amended by SI 1981/606) (*Ed*).

Vegas for six weeks. The wife knew nothing of the decree as service of the proceedings was by advertisement in a Las Vegas newspaper. Thereafter the husband married the other woman and ceased to make the payments ordered in 1950.

In 1956 he came to England to exhibit the chimpanzees at the Palladium in London, and on 18 May 1956 he appeared at the North London Magistrates' court on a warrant for arrears of maintenance, then amounting to £260. The husband applied to have the order discharged under section 7 of the Summary Jurisdiction (Married Women) Act 1895,[8] on the ground that he was now divorced. That section (as amended) provided as follows: 'A court of summary jurisdiction . . . may, on the application of the married woman or of her husband, and upon cause being shown upon fresh evidence to the satisfaction of the court at any time, alter, vary or discharge any . . . order. . . .' The wife applied for an order increasing the sums payable by the husband on the ground that his circumstances had improved, the troupe of chimpanzees, exhilarated no doubt by the climate of Nevada, having increased his disposable income to six or eight times what it had been in 1950.

The magistrate found that the husband was domiciled in Nevada at the time of the divorce; that the wife knew nothing of the proceedings until after the decree; and that the wife had committed no matrimonial offence, since she was justified in refusing to accompany her husband to the United States as junior partner to a troupe formed by his family of chimpanzees and his pregnant mistress. Relying on *Bragg v Bragg*,[9] where it was held that magistrates had a discretion to continue a maintenance order made in favour of a wife notwithstanding an English decree of divorce subsequently obtained by her, he dismissed the husband's application and increased the sums payable to the maximum permitted amounts, namely, £5 a week for the wife and 30s a week for each child.

The Divisional Court (Lord Merriman P and Collingwood J) reversed this decision and discharged the order on the grounds that comity required the English courts to recognise the Nevada decree, and that there was no reported case in which a maintenance order made in favour of a wife had been held to survive a divorce decree (English or foreign) subsequently obtained by the husband.

The wife appealed to the Court of Appeal.

Hodson LJ: The following questions arise on this appeal: (1) Does an order for maintenance payable by a husband to a married woman under the provisions of the Summary Jurisdiction Acts survive a divorce? (2) Does the answer to the first question depend on whether the divorce is pronounced in favour of the wife? (3) Does it depend on whether the decree of divorce is pronounced by an English or by a foreign court? (4) If the order survived the divorce, must the court discharge the order on being informed of the divorce? (5) If there is no compulsion to discharge the order, is there a discretion to discharge and vary the order and how is that discretion to be exercised?

There is much to be said for the view that the effect of the dissolution of

8 Now s 20 of the Domestic Proceedings and Magistrates' Courts Act 1978 (*Ed*).
9 [1925] P 20, 94 LJP 11.

the marriage is to destroy automatically the obligations that arise therefrom. As Douglas J graphically put it in the American case of *Estin v Estin*,[10] 'the tail must go with the hide'. This result is logical, but the question turns on the construction of an English Act of Parliament, namely, the Summary Jurisdiction (Married Women) Act 1895, s 7. (His Lordship read the section, so far as material, and continued:) On the construction of this section it can be fairly argued that since the title of the Act is the Summary Jurisdiction (Married Women) Act and the words 'married woman' and 'husband' are used throughout to describe the persons who may apply for orders and the persons against whom orders may be made, so such orders must expire with the marriage.

Section 7 contains the power in the court to vary or discharge an order and it is argued that 'married woman' and 'husband' must bear the same meaning in this section as in the rest of the Act and cannot include divorced women and divorced husbands. Moreover, the power to discharge an order is normally exercised when, for example, the desertion upon which the order was founded has come to an end and the right to receive separate maintenance is therefore at an end. When the husband and wife are divorced the order can never be discharged on this ground, since their right to consortium having gone the possibility of desertion no longer exists. Hence it is said that the statute has no application to divorced persons and any order made thereunder must die with the marriage when a decree of divorce takes effect.

In *Bragg v Bragg*, however, decided by the Divisional Court, an opposite conclusion was reached. It was held that the decree does not ipso facto discharge a maintenance order obtained under the Act of 1895 nor does such dissolution compel the court to discharge such an order. Every such case, it was held, comes within the discretion given to the court by section 7 of the Act to vary or discharge the order on evidence of fresh facts. Horridge J pointed out that there were no words in the Act to show that the order itself is to be limited to the period of the marriage. Sir Henry Duke P thought that there were grounds of common sense why an order which dealt with maintenance and not with general obligations of married life should continue to subsist. *Bragg v Bragg* was decided in 1924 and has been followed consistently since; and Parliament when amending the Act of 1895 in 1925 and again in 1951 has not taken the opportunity of limiting the scope of the Act as interpreted by the Divisional Court.

If *Bragg*'s case was correctly decided the answer to the first question is in the affirmative. In my opinion it was, and there is nothing contrary to common sense or the plain language of the statute in this construction even though it produces the result of what is called in the United States, 'divisible divorce', that is to say, it does not follow that because a marriage is dissolved the prior financial obligations of a husband to a wife must necessarily fall with it.

In *Estin v Estin*, the Supreme Court of the United States held that a New York support decree survived a subsequent Nevada divorce. The decision of the Supreme Court turned mainly on article IV, section 1, of the Constitution, the 'full faith and credit' clause, but it appears from the decision that the New York court had maintained that its order was not

10 (1948) 334 US 541 at 544.

destroyed by the Nevada decree. See also *Vanderbilt v Vanderbilt*,[11] a decision of the New York Court of Appeals which maintains the same principle; although carrying it to a length outside the scope of the English Summary Jurisdiction Act or the Matrimonial Causes Act which in the first case does not provide for an application for the first time after divorce and in the second does not provide for such an application after a decree which is not an English decree. See section 19 of the Matrimonial Causes Act 1950.[12] These cases are of persuasive authority.

As to the second question, the Divisional Court seems to have thought that the *Bragg* principle should not be applied when the wife is the unsuccessful party to the divorce except in a limited class of case, of which this is not one. See also the observations of Lord Merriman P in *Wood v Wood*,[13] who, however, was careful to make clear that he was not saying that in no circumstances can justices exercise their discretion to keep an order alive in favour of an unsuccessful wife.

The court will, if it has a discretion under section 7 of the Act, be entitled to receive evidence as to the facts. In this case we know that on the facts proved the husband deserted the wife prior to the divorce. The order of the court of summary jurisdiction was made on that ground and, as the Divisional Court stated, there appears to be no reason to suppose that the desertion had been terminated at the time of the foreign decree, the only suggestion to that effect being that when the husband went to America the wife declined to go with him, her explanation of this refusal having been found to be that she was unwilling to make a third with the husband and his pregnant mistress.

The validity of the Nevada divorce is not in question and the grounds upon which relief was claimed (immaterial to the question of jurisdiction) were that the parties had not lived together for three years. No matrimonial offence was there alleged and there are no facts to justify the conclusion that because the wife was not the petitioner or actor in the divorce proceedings she should, therefore, be in a worse position than if she had been a successful supplicant for relief. . . .

On the facts it seems difficult to envisage a set of circumstances more favourable to the wife and I cannot regard the fact that she was respondent to the proceedings and divorced on the prayer of her husband as a matter to be put in the scales against her. Indeed, the Nevada proceedings exemplify a tendency to be found in the modern exercise of divorce jurisdiction to permit proceedings to be taken not on the ground of an injury inflicted on the petitioner or claimant by the opposite spouse but on the ground that it is thought desirable or expedient that there should be a divorce. The ground of three years' separation involved no imputation of guilt.

The case of a wife who, as in this case, has no knowledge of proceedings taken at the instance of her husband which have the effect of bringing her marriage to an end is, I should have thought, a stronger one than that of the petitioner in such a case as *Kirk v Kirk*.[14] In that case a wife who had

11 (1956) 1 NY (2d) 242; affirmed by the Supreme Court of the United States (1957) 354 US 416 (*Ed*).
12 Now s 23 of the Matrimonial Causes Act 1973 (*Ed*).
13 [1949] WN 59, 93 Sol Jo 200.
14 [1947] 2 All ER 118, 177 LT 151.

obtained a maintenance order under the Summary Jurisdiction Act in England subsequently sued her husband for divorce in Scotland. It was held in effect by the Divisional Court that she must take the consequences and rely on such remedies as the Scottish courts could give her and she was not permitted to enforce the summary jurisdiction order. In the present case the wife, on the other hand, has been quite helpless in the divorce proceedings from beginning to end and had had no part in them.

As to the third question, once the question of the validity of the foreign decree is determined, the position is, in my opinion, exactly the same as if the decree had been an English one: compare *Mezger v Mezger*[15] and *Kirk v Kirk*. In the former case the exercise of discretion by a court of summary jurisdiction was reversed since neither of the reasons given, to one of which I return later, showed a judicial exercise of discretion, and further because the wife's allegations of failure to maintain had been disproved in the foreign proceedings to which she was an active party. In *Kirk v Kirk*, where there had been a Scottish divorce following upon an English order for maintenance, the court expressly refrained from deciding against the wife merely because the foreign decree ipso facto destroyed her right to maintenance.

It was suggested in argument that the form of the Nevada decree which ends with the words 'the said parties are hereby released from all the obligations thereof and restored to the status of single persons' is destructive of the wife's claim and brings the case into line with *Mezger*'s case, in which the maintenance obligation had been litigated between the parties. I do not accept this contention since here there was no evidence that the Nevada court ever entertained, much less adjudicated upon, a claim for maintenance, and there is no reason on this account why any discretion there may be to keep the order alive should not be exercised in favour of the wife.

As to the fourth question, it was contended that even accepting the construction put upon the Act of 1895 in *Bragg*'s case to the effect that the order survived the divorce, the court must upon proof of a valid decree discharge the order. This argument was based on the reasoning of Hill J in *Pastre v Pastre*,[16] the headnote of which reads as follows: 'The basis of a wife's right to receive permanent alimony from her husband is that the marriage is subsisting and that she is still a wife. If after a decree for judicial separation and an order for the payment of alimony the marriage is put an end to by the decree of a court of competent jurisdiction the status of the woman as wife and her consequential right to alimony have ceased to exist. The order for alimony, however, which in its common form is limited till further order, remains effective till an application is made for its discharge.'

Hill J said that the order was expressed to be until further order, and that until further order it was effective. He added: 'I am now asked to make a further order—namely, to discharge the order for payment in the future. In my opinion I have no alternative but to do so. I cannot order a man who has ceased to be a husband to pay alimony to a woman who has ceased to be a wife. The whole basis of an order for permanent alimony is gone'. He

15 [1937] P 19, [1936] 3 All ER 130.
16 [1930] P 80, 99 LJP 20. In this case Hodson LJ had been counsel for the unsuccessful wife (*Ed*).

distinguished *Bragg v Bragg* as depending upon the terms of the Summary Jurisdiction (Married Women) Act, which he described as an Act of a very special nature giving magistrates powers which the divorce courts did not possess in some respects.

The jurisdiction to order alimony depends on statute, the then relevant provision being section 190 (4) of the Supreme Court of Judicature (Consolidation) Act 1925,[17] which reads as follows: 'Where any decree for restitution of conjugal rights or judicial separation is made on the application of the wife, the court may make such order for alimony as the court thinks fit.' If the order for alimony survives the decree, as Hill J thought, there is nothing in the statute to show that it must be discharged on divorce any more than there is a provision to that effect in the Summary Jurisdiction (Separation and Maintenance) Act 1925.

It may be that different considerations apply to alimony, but I am not persuaded by the reasoning of Hill J that the decision in *Bragg*'s case that a maintenance order could be permitted to remain in force after a divorce was wrong. It is to be noted that the decision in *Pastre*'s case could in any event be supported on the ground that the wife was an active participant in the French divorce proceedings.

As to the fifth question, if there is no compulsion to discharge the order, it is, I think, clear on the language of section 7 of the Act of 1895 that there is a discretion in the justices to alter, vary or discharge the order upon cause being shown to the satisfaction of the court at any time. This discretion was exercised by the stipendiary magistrate by refusing the husband's application to discharge the order and by varying the amount payable to the wife in an upward direction. It is not suggested that the amount payable under the proposed variation is in itself excessive.

In considering the question of discretion I have been indebted to an article by Dr Morris in the *British Year Book of International Law* (1952), pp 286 et seq, who has considered the American doctrine of divisible divorce. It is necessary on this matter to distinguish between the decree dissolving the marriage and any ancillary relief which may be claimed. The grounds for divorce are irrelevant so far as the status of the spouses is concerned and the fact that the wife received no notice of the proceedings does not affect this conclusion, as was rightly held in my opinion in *Boettcher v Boettcher*[18] and *Igra v Igra*.[19] Dr Morris points out that if effective notice were necessary, the decree of divorce being analogous to a judgment in rem, great uncertainty in family relationships would result in cases where parties have remarried in reliance on a foreign decree, for if want of notice were a ground for contesting a foreign decree the defect could not be waived by the party who received no notice. The same considerations do not apply to orders for support or maintenance.

If the wife litigates the maintenance at the same time as the foreign divorce and fails, it is not to be expected that she will be permitted to relitigate the same question in the English courts. Such a case was *Mezger v Mezger*, which in my opinion was rightly decided upon that ground.

---

17 See now s 23 of the Matrimonial Causes Act 1973. The term 'alimony' is no longer used in English law (*Ed*).

18 [1949] WN 83, 93 Sol Jo 237.

19 [1951] P 404, [1951] 2 TLR 670.

The New York Court of Appeals has held in *Lynn v Lynn*[20] that the principle of *Estin v Estin* does not apply in a case where the wife participates in the Nevada divorce. When, however, the wife, as here, takes no part in the Nevada proceedings of which she was unaware, there is no obstacle of the particular kind which confronted the wife in *Mezger*'s case to the exercise of the discretion in her favour.

The court is, in my view, entitled to look at the grounds of the foreign divorce before deciding whether it is just to continue the existing maintenance order in her favour. I would, therefore, take a different view from the Divisional Court in *Mezger*'s case in so far as it criticised the justices for exercising their discretion by relying in part on the fact that the foreign divorce was pronounced on a ground not sufficient by English law.

The Divisional Court ended its judgment in the present case: 'In our opinion, it is most important to avoid any suggestion that effect is not being given to the foreign decree because of the grounds on which it is based, or on the ground that the substituted service was ineffectual, or that it is being assumed, without any evidence of the foreign law, that the husband's adultery or his desertion would be fatal according to the foreign law to his obtaining a decree on the ground of a three years' separation.' These considerations apply forcefully to the recognition of the foreign decree as affecting the status but do not conclude the matter, in my view, as regards rights in personam such as property rights of the wife which, as I have endeavoured to show, are subject to different considerations.

Accordingly, taking into account the wife's conduct throughout, the Nevada decree pronounced against her without effective notice and the ground of the decree, I am of opinion that the exercise of discretion under review is not open to criticism and I would allow the appeal.

Lord Evershed MR and Ormrod LJ delivered judgments to the same effect.
Appeal allowed.

But English courts have no jurisdiction to order financial relief for the first time after a valid foreign divorce.

Torok v Torok [1973] 3 All ER 101, [1973] 1 WLR 1066 (Family Division)

The husband and wife were Hungarian by origin. They came to England at the time of the Hungarian rising in 1956. They married in Scotland in 1957 and had two children, Kathleen and Andrew. They lived together mainly in England until 1967, when the husband went to Canada, leaving the wife and children in England. Neither of the parties had been back to Hungary since they left in 1956. In 1964 they became naturalised British subjects.

The wife received out of the blue a summons from a Hungarian court dated 28 November 1972, notifying her that proceedings for divorce would take place in Budapest on 18 December 1972. She consulted a Dr Baracs, a Hungarian lawyer living in England, who instructed a lawyer in Budapest to apply for an adjournment. In due course the wife entered an appearance

20 (1951) 302 NY 193, 97 NE (2d) 748.

indicating that she did not object to a divorce and asking for maintenance for herself and that the matrimonial home in England (which was in joint names) should be dealt with. The court did not deal with these matters but pronounced a partial decree, subject to a delay of 15 days from the date of service of that judgment on the advocate for the wife. He gave notice of appeal but the appeal had not yet been heard at the time of the hearing of the wife's petition for divorce in England, nor had the marriage then been dissolved by the Hungarian court. Dr Baracs gave evidence that though the Hungarian court had jurisdiction to award maintenance to wives, it very rarely exercised that power, and had no jurisdiction to deal with immovable property outside Hungary.

Ormrod J: This case raises a very difficult problem, and I think has revealed a dangerous gap in the existing legislation, for reasons which I will try to demonstrate. (His Lordship stated the facts and continued): While this court has jurisdiction under the Guardianship of Minors Act 1971 to deal with the children, of course, unless this court pronounces a decree itself the various powers which the court has under the Matrimonial Proceedings and Property Act 1970[1] cannot be exercised because all those powers depend upon there having been a decree absolute of this court; and there can be no doubt that the decree which is referred to throughout the Act of 1970 is a decree absolute—or nisi as the case may be, but in most cases decree absolute—of this court. And so if this marriage is dissolved by the Hungarian court, there will be no court which has jurisdiction to deal with the house where the wife and the children are living, and there will be no court which has any effective jurisdiction to order maintenance for the wife (if that is appropriate on the figures) because as I have already said the Hungarian court's order is valueless in Canada, and probably an order of this court in Canada would be a much more valuable thing.

The problem in this case arises, I think, entirely out of the recent Recognition of Divorces and Legal Separations Act 1971,[2] because under the law as it was before that Act was passed there would clearly, I think, have been in the view of this court no jurisdiction in the Hungarian court; because certainly the husband could not set up a domicile in the Hungarian court— he has clearly abandoned his domicile, having become a naturalised British subject in 1964 together with his wife. That would, I should have thought, in the circumstances of this case have effectively cut off any connection with the Hungarian court which could have been regarded before the Act of 1971 was passed as an adequate basis for jurisdiction. But section 3 (1) of the Act provides:

'The validity of an overseas divorce or legal separation shall be recognised if, at the date of the institution of the proceedings in the country in which it was obtained—(a) either spouse was habitually resident in that country; or (b) either spouse was a national of that country.'

In this case jurisdiction was taken by the Hungarian court on the basis that the petitioning husband there was a national of Hungary. That might have given rise to an interesting question in view of his naturalisation in this

1 Now ss 21–24 of the Matrimonial Causes Act 1973 (Ed).
2 P 303 above.

country had that issue as to whether or not he was an Hungarian national had to be decided by the law of England. But by section 5 (1) of the Act of 1971 it is expressly provided:

> 'For the purpose of deciding whether an overseas divorce or legal separation is entitled to recognition by virtue of the foregoing provisions of this Act, any finding of fact made (whether expressly or by implication) in the proceedings by means of which the divorce or legal separation was obtained and on the basis of which jurisdiction was assumed in those proceedings shall—(a) if both spouses took part in the proceedings, be conclusive evidence of the fact found; . . .'

Clearly in this case both parties did take part in the proceedings. But even if that had not been so, section 5 (2) puts the matter beyond any doubt because that subsection enacts:

> 'In this section "finding of fact" includes a finding that either spouse was habitually resident or domiciled in, or a national of, the country in which the divorce or legal separation was obtained; and for the purposes of subsection (1) (a) of this section, a spouse who has appeared in judicial proceedings shall be treated as having taken part in them.'

So the finding of fact depends, therefore, on the Hungarian law in relation to whether or not the husband, at the time when the proceedings were instituted, was a national of that country. I am told by Dr Baracs that in Hungary the fact that a person has become a naturalised citizen of another country does not ipso facto terminate his Hungarian nationality or citizenship as the case may be; and that in such a situation the Hungarian courts consider such a person to have dual nationality.

So there is no doubt that under the Act of 1971 this court is bound, or would be bound, to recognise any decree of the Hungarian court made in this case on these facts, which would have the effect, if that decree were made before a decree in this court, of shutting out this court's jurisdiction to deal with the property belonging to the spouses in this country—which of course is to produce a ridiculous situation, where two people have been living in England since 1956, married in England, with children who have been brought up in England and who have English Christian names, whose matrimonial home—and whose only matrimonial home—was in this country, and whose future is obviously here or in Canada or some other place, but certainly not Hungary. And this, I think, must be an unforeseen situation, unforeseen that is at the time when the Act of 1971 was drafted; because the effect of the Act is to oust the jurisdiction of this court to deal with a family living in this country and with a property—a matrimonial home or a house in joint names—in this country. Now, that is a situation which plainly should be avoided at all cost.

My view is, for reasons I have already stated, that not only have I jurisdiction to grant a decree nisi in this case, I should be obliged to—there could be no ground on which I could withhold it. The more difficult question, and equally the most vital question, is whether it would be proper in the circumstances of this case—in spite of the recent Presidential direction[3]—to expedite the decree absolute.

3 *Practice Note (Divorce: Decree Absolute)* [1972] 3 All ER 461, [1972] 1 WLR 1261.

Fortunately, Miss Booth (counsel for the wife) was able to assure me that the husband had been notified (true, by cable) of the intention to ask for the decree absolute to be expedited as much as possible. Now this is a pure matter of discretion so far as this court is concerned and, as I understand it, it is a discretion which has to be exercised with the primary object (like all discretions) of doing justice between the parties. The first question I have to ask myself is, if I expedite the decree absolute in this case can I, by any process that I can imagine, cause an injustice to the husband, who is not here to protest and not here to put his case, if any, before the court?

First of all, it is clear that he could not possibly have a section 6 situation as against the wife.[4] Secondly, I can conceive of no hardship or no injustice to him by expediting the divorce because he wants the marriage dissolved, unless it is that in some way by doing so he will lose an advantage in the Hungarian court. It may well be that he hasn't even got as far as thinking that the Hungarian court decree offers him some advantage; but the only conceivable thing that he could lose by my making the decree absolute is an opportunity, as it were, to deny his wife a right of access to this court in relation to her own maintenance and in relation to the house which she lives in and which is in joint names, and that cannot in itself conceivably be, as I think, a denial of justice because all that is being sought is an opportunity for this court to deal justly with those two items.

If one looks at it from the other side, if the decree is not expedited will the wife suffer any injustice? I agree with Miss Booth that the answer is that she may suffer a very severe injustice by being disabled from using or taking advantage of the legislation in this country which is passed for the protection of spouses, particularly women as a rule, in relation to her own maintenance and in relation to property rights in the house in question. So that I think the overwhelming balance of advantage lies in favour of my expediting the decree.

I have had some natural hesitation in doing it because it looks as though this court and the Hungarian court might be engaged in a competition for jurisdiction, which is never a very dignified situation for courts to be in, and one in which the normal rules as to comity are designed to avoid. And certainly, no judge of this court is at all happy if he is led, as it were, to trespass on the jurisdiction of a foreign court. But I think here that I am not doing anything, and I certainly do not intend to do anything, which could possibly be regarded as lack of respect for the Hungarian court. What I am doing is adopting a procedural technique which is necessary to give this court a jurisdiction over matters I have mentioned, which for reasons which I have already given the Hungarian court has no jurisdiction over. So that over anything that really matters in this case there is, in fact, no conflict of jurisdiction. Therefore I feel justified in taking the wholly exceptional steps which I propose to take, namely, to pronounce a decree nisi today and to direct that the decree absolute be made forthwith.

4 This refers to s 6 of the Divorce Reform Act 1969 (now s 10 (2)–(4) of the Matrimonial Causes Act 1973) which provides that the court shall not make absolute a decree of divorce based on 2 or 5 years' separation unless it is satisfied (a) that the petitioner should not be required to make any financial provision for the respondent, or (b) that the financial provision made by the petitioner for the respondent is reasonable and fair or the best that can be made in the circumstances (*Ed*).

Quazi v Quazi (p 313 above).

Draft Overseas Divorces (Financial Relief) Bill[5]

1.—(1) Where—
(a) a marriage has been dissolved or annulled, or the parties to a marriage have been legally separated, by means of judicial or other proceedings in an overseas country, and
(b) the divorce, annulment or legal separation is entitled to be recognised as valid in England and Wales,
either party to the marriage may apply to the High Court in the manner prescribed by rules of court for an order for financial relief under this Act.

(2) A party to a marriage which has been dissolved or annulled in an overseas country shall not be entitled to make an application under subsection (1) above in relation to that marriage if he or she has remarried.

2.—(1) No application for an order for financial relief shall be made under this Act unless the leave of the High Court has been obtained in accordance with rules of court; and the court shall not grant leave to make such an application unless it considers that there is substantial ground for the making under this Act of an application for financial relief.

(2) The High Court may grant leave under subsection (1) above notwithstanding that an order has been made by a court in a country outside England and Wales requiring the other party to the marriage to make any payment or transfer any property to the applicant or a child of the family.

(3) The High Court may grant leave under subsection (1) above subject to such conditions as it thinks fit.

4. Subject to section 14 of this Act, the High Court shall have jurisdiction to entertain an application for an order for financial relief under this Act if (and only if)—
(a) either of the parties to the marriage was domiciled in England and Wales on the date of the application for leave under section 2 of this Act or was so domiciled on the date on which the divorce, annulment or legal separation obtained in the overseas country took effect in that country; or
(b) either of the parties to the marriage was habitually resident in England and Wales throughout the period of one year ending with the date of the application for leave or was so resident throughout the period of one year ending with the date on which the divorce, annulment or legal separation obtained in the overseas country took effect in that country; or
(c) either or both of the parties to the marriage had at the date of the application for leave a beneficial interest in possession in a dwelling-house situated in England and Wales which was at some time during the marriage a matrimonial home of the parties to the marriage.

---

5 This draft Bill was annexed to the Law Commission's Report on Financial Relief after Foreign Divorce, Law Com No 117 (1982). The Matrimonial and Family Proceedings Bill, introduced into Parliament in November 1983 contains provisions (Part III) to similar effect to those in the Law Commission's draft Bill.

5.—(1) Before making an order for financial relief on an application under this Act the High Court shall consider whether in all the circumstances of the case it would be appropriate for such an order to be made by a court in England and Wales, and if the court is not satisfied that it would be appropriate, the court shall dismiss the application.

(2) The following matters shall be included among the circumstances which the court is required to consider under subsection (1) above, that is to say—

(a) the connection which the parties to the marriage have with England and Wales;

(b) the connection which those parties have with the country in which the marriage was dissolved or annulled or in which they were legally separated;

(c) the connection which those parties have with any other country outside England and Wales;

(d) any financial benefit which the applicant or a child of the family has received, or is likely to receive, in consequence of the divorce, annulment or legal separation, by virtue of any agreement or the operation of the law of a country outside England and Wales;

(e) in a case where an order has been made by a court in a country outside England and Wales requiring the other party to the marriage to make any payment or transfer any property for the benefit of the applicant or a child of the family, the financial relief given by the order and the extent to which the order has been complied with or is likely to be complied with;

(f) any right which the applicant has, or has had, to apply for financial relief from the other party to the marriage under the law of any country outside England and Wales and if the applicant has omitted to exercise that right the reason for that omission;

(g) the availability in England and Wales of any property in respect of which an order under this Act in favour of the applicant could be made;

(h) the extent to which any order made under this Act is likely to be enforceable;

(i) the length of time which has elapsed since the date of the divorce, annulment or legal separation.

14. Where the subject-matter of an application under this Act and the other circumstances of the case are such that the jurisdiction of a court in England and Wales to entertain the application is determined by the Civil Jurisdiction and Judgments Act 1982, then, notwithstanding anything in section 4 or 12 (1) of this Act, a court in England and Wales shall have jurisdiction to entertain that application if (and only if) it has jurisdiction by virtue of that Act.

19.—(2) For the removal of doubt it is hereby declared that the reference in section 1 (2) of this Act to remarriage includes a reference to a marriage which is by law void or voidable.

CHAPTER 12

Guardianship and Custody of Minors

Guardianship of Minors Act 1971

1. Where in any proceedings before any court (whether or not a court as defined in section 15 of this Act)—
(a) the custody or upbringing of a minor; or
(b) the administration of any property belonging to or held on trust for a minor, or the application of the income thereof,
is in question, the court, in deciding that question, shall regard the welfare of the minor as the first and paramount consideration, and shall not take into consideration whether from any other point of view the claim of the father, . . .[1] in respect of such custody, upbringing, administration or application is superior to that of the mother, or the claim of the mother is superior to that of the father.

The High Court has jurisdiction to appoint a guardian for a minor or to make a custody order in respect of him if he is a British citizen or owes local allegiance to the Crown by virtue of his ordinary residence or presence in England

Re P (GE) (an infant) [1965] Ch 568, [1964] 3 All ER 977 (Court of Appeal)

Appeal from Plowman J.
 The infant was born in Egypt of Jewish parents in 1956. His parents brought him to England in 1957 because of the Suez crisis. The parents were both stateless persons. In January 1962 they set up a matrimonial home in Brighton. In August 1962 the mother left the matrimonial home and went to live with her own mother in Hendon. By arrangement the infant lived with his mother in Hendon and went to school there during the week, and spent weekends with his father in Brighton. On 9 November 1962 the father collected the infant as usual but did not return him to the mother on 11 November. Instead, he flew with him to Israel where they remained ever since. On 4 January 1963 the mother issued an originating summons in the High Court asking that the infant be made a ward of court and for custody of him. She obtained leave to serve the summons on the father in Israel. The father issued a summons asking that the mother's originating summons should be set aside for lack of jurisdiction. Plowman J set it aside, holding that he had no jurisdiction to make the infant a ward of court unless the

---

1 Words repealed by Guardianship Act 1973, Sch 3 (*Ed*).

infant was a British subject or was present in England at the date of the commencement of the proceedings. The mother appealed.

Lord Denning MR (after stating the facts):   I say nothing about the merits of the case—nothing as to whether it is best for the son to be with his father in Jerusalem or to be brought back to his mother here. We are concerned only with the question whether the court here has jurisdiction to hear the mother's case. And this is a matter which must be determined as at the time when the mother issued her summons on 4 January 1963. The father has recently issued a summons in the courts of Israel. Those courts would, I should think, clearly have jurisdiction as the boy is there. But the question is whether the courts here also have jurisdiction over the custody of the child.

Let me say at once that if the mother had instituted proceedings here for divorce, the Divorce Court would clearly have jurisdiction over the child. If the mother had any ground for saying that the father had committed a matrimonial offence, she could bring a petition for divorce, and the Divorce Court here would have jurisdiction over the marriage. If the father retained his English domicile, she could rely on the English domicile as a ground of jurisdiction in the English court; or, if the father had taken up his domicile in Israel, she could rely on the ground that she was herself resident here and had been 'ordinarily resident' here for three years before the proceedings: see section (18) (1) (b) of the Matrimonial Causes Act 1950.[1] Once the divorce proceedings were properly brought here, the Divorce Court would have jurisdiction to make provision for the custody, maintenance and education of the child, even though the child was far away in Israel: see section 26 (1) of the Act of 1950[2] and *Harben v Harben*.[3]

No divorce proceedings have, however, been taken. The mother has simply applied in the Chancery Division to make the child a ward of court under section 9 of the Law Reform (Miscellaneous Provisions) Act 1949,[4] and for custody under the Guardianship of Infants Acts, 1886 and 1925.[5] And the question is whether the Court of Chancery has jurisdiction. Those Acts give no guidance as to the geographical jurisdiction of the court, and we have to determine it on principle by reference to the inherent jurisdiction.

It is quite plain that if the child had been a *British subject* the Court of Chancery would have had jurisdiction to make an order as to its custody, maintenance or education, even though the child itself was out of the country and in a foreign land. The court here always retains a jurisdiction over a British subject wherever he may be, though it will only exercise it abroad where the circumstances clearly warrant it: see *Hope v Hope*;[6] *Re Willoughby*;[7] *R v Sandbach Justices, ex p Smith*.[8] So also if the child was *physically present* here, the Court of Chancery would have jurisdiction over it (just as the Queen's Bench would on habeas corpus), even though the child was not living here and only passing through on a journey. That happened recently when a child in transit was stopped in England from being taken to

1 See now Domicile and Matrimonial Proceedings Act 1973, s 5 (2), p 295 above (*Ed.*)
2 Now s 42 of the Matrimonial Causes Act 1973 (p 374 below) (*Ed*).
3 [1957] 1 All ER 379, [1957] 1 WLR 261.
4 Now s 41 of the Supreme Court Act 1981 (*Ed*).
5 Now the Guardianship of Minors Act 1971 (*Ed*).
6 (1854) 4 DeGM & G 328, 23 LJCh 682.
7 (1885) 30 ChD 324, 54 LJCh 1122.
8 [1951] 1 KB 62, [1950] 2 All ER 781.

Russia and was sent back to America. See such cases as *Johnstone v Beattie*[9] and *Re D (an infant)*.[10]

Mr Godfrey (counsel for the father) submitted to us that the jurisdiction of the court was limited to those two cases—a child who is a British subject and a child who is physically present here—and could not be extended further. No case could be found, he said, to warrant any extension. That is the sort of argument we have heard many times, and as often as not we have rejected it. When we come upon a situation which has not arisen before, we must say what we believe the law to be upon the matter. We are not to be deterred by the absence of authority in the books. Our forefathers always held that the law was locked in the breasts of the judges, ready to be unlocked whenever the need arose.

Mr Lazarus (counsel for the mother) invited us to hold that the Court of Chancery has jurisdiction over any child who is *domiciled* here. He asked us to follow the Scottish law, supported by the latest edition of Dicey's *Conflict of Laws*.[11] It appears that the Scottish courts hold that they have jurisdiction over any child under 16 who is *domiciled* in Scotland even though the child is not resident in Scotland nor physically present there. The custody of a child, say the Scotsmen, is a matter of status, and is governed by the law of the *domicile*. An order for custody, made by the court of the *domicile*, is, they say, a judgment in rem and should be recognised everywhere. Inasmuch as the child takes the *domicile* of its father, this means that, in Scottish eyes, the pre-eminent jurisdiction rests in the courts of the domicile of the father of the child: see *Ponder v Ponder*.[12]

I do not think that we should follow the Scottish courts in this matter. The tests of *domicile* are far too unsatisfactory. In order to find out a person's domicile, you have to apply a lot of archaic rules. They ought to have been done away with long ago. But they still survive. Particularly the rule that a wife takes the domicile of her husband. And the rule that a child takes the domicile of its father. If you were to ask what was the domicile of the child in this case, you would have a pretty problem. The child would take the domicile of the father. But what was the father's domicile? His domicile of origin was Palestine. His domicile of choice was England. But in November 1962, he left England for Israel, taking the child with him. What was the father's domicile then? It all depends on his intention. Goodness knows how you are to find that out. His intention may at first have been to go to Israel for a short time. Later, when he found work there, he may have intended to make his home there permanently. When did his domicile change? Are you to take his word for it? If so, he could always defeat the jurisdiction of the court by saying that, from the very outset, he intended never to return to England, and abandoned his English domicile.

As an alternative to *domicile*, Mr Lazarus invited us to apply the test of *ordinary residence*, and supported it by references to some cases where the word 'residence' was used and also to a case in the State of New York: *Descollonges v Descollonges*.[13] I think this is the right test. The fount of the jurisdiction of the Court of Chancery is the Crown which, as parens patriae, takes under its

9   (1843) 10 Cl & Fin 42, 1 LTOS 250.
10 [1943] Ch 305, [1943] 2 All ER 411.
11 7th edn (1958), p 390.
12 1932 SC 233.
13 (1959) 183 NYS 2d 943, 190 NYS 2d 314.

protection every infant child who is ordinarily resident within the realm, whether he is a British subject or an alien. As Lord Campbell said in *Johnstone v Beattie*, 'I do not doubt the jurisdiction of the Court of Chancery on this subject, whether the infant be domiciled in England or not. The Lord Chancellor, representing the Crown as parens patriae, has a clear right to interpose the authority of the court for the protection of the person and property of *all infants resident* in England'.

The Crown protects every child who has his home here and will protect him in respect of his home. It will not permit anyone to kidnap the child and spirit it out of the realm. Not even its father or mother can be allowed to do so without the consent of the other. The kidnapper cannot escape the jurisdiction of the court by such a stratagem. If, as in this case, it is the father who flies away with the child, the mother is not bound to follow him to a foreign clime. She can bring her proceedings against him in England. I know that it will be difficult for her to enforce any order the court may make. But it is not impossible. The father may have assets here. Or he may return here for a visit. And if she has eventually to apply to the courts of the foreign country, they will surely respect an order made by the courts of the ordinary residence—just as we should—for the simple reason that it is his home and, as such, is entitled to special consideration.

I hold therefore that the Court of Chancery has jurisdiction to make an order for the custody, education and maintenance of an alien child who is ordinarily resident in this country, even though the child is for the time being absent from this country or taken out of it. But then we are faced with the question, what is the ordinary residence of a child of tender years who cannot decide for himself where to live, let us say under the age of 16? So long as the father and mother are *living together in the matrimonial home*, the child's ordinary residence is the home—and it is still his ordinary residence, even while he is away at boarding school. It is his base, from whence he goes out and to which he returns. When father and mother are at variance and living *separate and apart* and by arrangement the child resides *in the house of one of them*—then that home is his ordinary residence, even though the other parent has access and the child goes to see him from time to time. I do not see that a child's ordinary residence, so found, can be changed by kidnapping him and taking him from his home, even if one of his parents is the kidnapper. Quite generally, I do not think a child's ordinary residence can be changed by one parent without the consent of the other. It will not be changed until the parent who is left at home, childless, acquiesces in the change, or delays so long in bringing proceedings that he or she must be taken to acquiesce. Six months' delay would, I should have thought, go far to show acquiescence. Even three months might in some circumstances. But not less. . . .

Applied to this case, it is plain that the child's ordinary residence was at Hendon. That was his home, so arranged by both mother and father. The father broke the arrangement and took him off to Israel. That did not mean that his ordinary residence ceased to be in England. The father could not change the home without the mother's consent. His ordinary residence was still in England when the mother took out the summons two months later. That means that the English court has jurisdiction over him. I do not say that the court would exercise that jurisdiction in the special circumstances of the case. I do not suggest that it would order the child to be brought back to

England. The father says that in these two years he has settled down well in Jerusalem. The court will consider what is best for the child. Suffice it for us to hold that the court has jurisdiction. I would allow the appeal accordingly.

Pearson and Russell LJJ delivered judgments to the same effect. In the course of his judgment, Russell LJ said: 'The whole trend of English authority on the parental jurisdiction of the Crown over infants bases that jurisdiction on protection as a corollary of allegiance in some shape or form. Domicile is an artificial concept which may well involve no possible connection with allegiance'.

Appeal allowed

Matrimonial Causes Act 1973

42.—(1) The court may make such order as it thinks fit for the custody and education of any child of the family who is under the age of eighteen—
(a) in any proceedings for divorce, nullity of marriage or judicial separation, before or on granting a decree or at any time thereafter (whether, in the case of a decree of divorce or nullity of marriage, before or after the decree is made absolute);
(b) where any such proceedings are dismissed after the beginning of the trial, either forthwith or within a reasonable period after the dismissal;
and in any case in which the court has power by virtue of this subsection to make an order in respect of a child it may instead, if it thinks fit, direct that proper proceedings be taken for making the child a ward of court.

(2) Where the court makes an order under section 27 above,[14] the court shall also have power to make such order as it thinks fit with respect to the custody of any child of the family who is for the time being under the age of eighteen; but the power conferred by this subsection and any order made in exercise of that power shall have effect only as respects any period when an order is in force under that section and the child is under that age.

Guardianship of Minors Act 1971

15.[15]—(1) Subject to the provisions of this section, 'the court' for the purposes of this Act means—
(b) the county court of the district in which the respondent (or any of the respondents) or the applicant or the minor to whom the application relates resides; or
(c) a magistrates' court having jurisdiction in the place in which any of the said persons resides.

(3) A county court or magistrates' court shall not have jurisdiction under this Act in any case where the respondent or any of the respondents resides in Scotland or Northern Ireland—
(a) except in so far as such jurisdiction may be exercisable by virtue of the following provisions of this section; or

14 P 341. above.
15 These subss. are printed as amended by the Guardianship Act 1973, Sch 2, Pt I, para 3 (*Ed*).

(b) unless a summons or other originating process can be served and is served on the respondent or, as the case may be, on the respondents in England or Wales.

(4) An order under this Act giving the custody of a minor to a person resident in England or Wales, whether with or without an order requiring payments to be made towards the minor's maintenance, may be made, if one parent resides in Scotland or Northern Ireland and the other parent and the minor in England or Wales, by a magistrates' court having jurisdiction in the place in which the other parent resides.

(5) It is hereby declared that a magistrate's court has jurisdiction—

(a) in proceedings under this Act by a person residing in Scotland or Northern Ireland against a person residing in England or Wales for an order relating to the custody of a minor (including . . . an order requiring payments to be made towards the minor's maintenance);

(b) in proceedings by or against a person residing in Scotland or Northern Ireland for the revocation, revival or variation of any such order.

(6) Where proceedings for an order under subsection (1) of section 9 of this Act[16] relating to the custody of a minor are brought in a magistrates' court by a person residing in Scotland or Northern Ireland, the court shall have jurisdiction to make any order in respect of the minor under that section on the application of the respondent in the proceedings.

Domestic Proceedings and Magistrates' Courts Act 1978, section 30[17] (p 341 above)

The welfare of the minor is the paramount consideration to which all others must yield, including the order of a foreign court of competent jurisdiction.

McKee v McKee [1951] AC 352, [1951] 1 All ER 942 (Privy Council)

Appeal from the Supreme Court of Canada.

The infant was born in California of American parents in July 1940. The parents separated in December 1940 and in September 1941 agreed in writing that neither of them should remove the infant out of the United States without the written permission of the other. In December 1942, in divorce proceedings before the Supreme Court of California, custody of the child was awarded to the father. In August 1945 the previous custody order was modified to provide that full custody of the infant be awarded to the mother with reasonable access for the father. On Christmas Eve 1946 the father, on hearing that his final appeal against that order had failed, took the child from Michigan to Ontario without the knowledge or consent of the mother. She instituted habeas corpus proceedings in the Supreme Court of Ontario seeking to have the infant delivered to her. In October 1947 Wells J after a trial lasting eleven days ordered that custody of the infant be awarded

---

16 This section empowers the court to make a custody order in favour of the father or mother of a minor (*Ed*).

17 See the Note relating to the magistrates' court jurisdiction, p 341 above.

to the father. This judgment was affirmed by the Ontario Court of Appeal (Hogg and Aylesworth JJA, Robertson CJ dissenting) but reversed by the Supreme Court of Canada (Kerwin, Estey, Locke and Cartwright JJ, Taschereau, Kellock and Fauteux JJ dissenting). The father appealed to the Privy Council.

The judgment of their Lordships (Lords Merriman, Simonds, Morton of Henryton, Radcliffe and Tucker) was delivered by

Lord Simonds (after stating the facts):   It is possible that a case might arise in which it appeared to a court, before which the question of custody of an infant came, that it was in the best interests of that infant that it should not look beyond the circumstances in which its jurisdiction was invoked and for that reason give effect to the foreign judgment without further inquiry. But it is the negation of the proposition, from which every judgment in this case has proceeded, namely, that the infant's welfare is the paramount consideration, to say that where the trial judge has in his discretion thought fit not to take the drastic course above indicated, but to examine all the circumstances and form an independent judgment, his decision ought for that reason to be overruled. Once it is conceded that the court of Ontario had jurisdiction to entertain the question of custody and that it need not blindly follow an order made by a foreign court, the consequence cannot be escaped that it must form an independent judgment on the question, though in doing so it will give proper weight to the foreign judgment. What is the proper weight will depend on the circumstances of each case. It may be that, if the matter comes before the court of Ontario within a very short time of the foreign judgment and there is no new circumstance to be considered, the weight may be so great that such an order as the Supreme Court made in this case could be justified. But if so, it would be not because the court of Ontario, having assumed jurisdiction, then abdicated it, but because in the exercise of its jurisdiction it determined what was for the benefit of the infant.

It cannot be ignored that such consequences might follow as are suggested by Cartwright J. The disappointed parent might meet stratagem by stratagem and, taking the child into the Province of Manitoba, invoke the protection of its courts, whose duty it would then be to determine the question of custody. That is a consideration which, with others, must be weighed by the trial judge. It is not, perhaps, a consideration which in the present case should have weighed heavily.

It has been said that the weight or persuasive effect of a foreign judgment must depend on the circumstances of each case. In the present case there was ample reason for the trial judge, in the first place, forming the opinion that he should not take the drastic course of following it without independent inquiry and, in the second place, coming to a different conclusion as to what was for the infant's benefit. For not only was the child two years older at an age when two years make a material difference, but the facts, which, as appeared on the face of the Californian order, had influenced that court had substantially changed. No longer was the choice between California and 'a place not accessible, snowbound in winter': no longer was the child under the care and supervision for most of the time of aged employees hired by the father, nor was he many miles from adequate transportation and adequate school facilities. This conspicuous change of circumstances demanded an independent inquiry, and their Lordships see no reason for thinking that the judge, whose full and exhaustive inquiry they have already recognised, came to a wrong conclusion.

In the course of the proceedings a large number of authorities have been discussed. It is necessary only to refer to them shortly. For their Lordships concur in the review of them which is to be found in the judgment of Kellock J in the Supreme Court of Canada. It is the law of Ontario (as it is the law of England) that the welfare and happiness of the infant is the paramount consideration in questions of custody: see Re Laurin,[18] following Ward v Laverty.[19] So, also, it is the law of Scotland (see M'Lean v M'Lean)[20] and of most, if not all, of the states of the United States of America. To this paramount consideration all others yield. The order of a foreign court of competent jurisdiction is no exception. Such an order has not the force of a foreign judgment: comity demands, not its enforcement, but its grave consideration. This distinction, which has long been recognised in the courts of England and Scotland (see Johnstone v Beattie[1] and Stuart v Marquis of Bute),[2] and in the courts of Ontario (see, eg, Re Ethel Davis[3] and Re Gay),[4] rests on the peculiar character of the jurisdiction and on the fact that an order providing for the custody of an infant cannot in its nature be final.

Counsel relied (as had the Supreme Court of Canada) on the observations of Page Wood V-C in Nugent v Vetzera[5] and of James V-C in Di Savini v Lousada.[6] It is true that in both these cases particular emphasis was laid on the respect to be paid by an English court to a foreign judgment relating to custody. But in the former case Page Wood V-C was careful to observe that he guarded himself against anything like an abdication of the jurisdiction of his court to appoint guardians. This can only mean that, if he thought that the welfare of the infants required the appointment of guardians by an English court, he would appoint them notwithstanding the foreign order. There is in fact no via media between the abdication of jurisdiction, which he rejected, and the consideration of the case on its merits, in which the respect payable to a foreign order must always be in the foreground. In the latter case James V-C used language which appears to amount to blind surrender to a foreign order. 'I think', he said, 'that I am bound without exercising any judgment of my own to recognise their authority'. 'Their' authority appears to mean the authority of the Italian guardians who had been appointed by an Italian court, though this is not quite clear. If the Vice-Chancellor intended by this observation to apply a general proposition, their Lordships cannot accept it as an accurate statement of the law. It is, however, probable that he no more than Page Wood V-C intended an abdication of jurisdiction. In their Lordships' opinion the nature and limits of the jurisdiction of a court alike in England and Ontario in relation to the custody of an infant are correctly stated by Morton J in Re B's Settlement.[7]

18 (1927) 60 OLR 409, [1927] 3 DLR 136.
19 [1925] AC 101, 94 LJPC 17.
20 1947 SC 79, 1947 SLT 36.
 1 (1843) 10 Cl & Fin 42, 1 LTOS 250.
 2 (1861) 9 HLCas 440, 4 LT 382.
 3 (1894) 25 OR 579.
 4 (1926) 59 OLR 40, [1926] 3 DLR 349.
 5 (1866) LR 2 Eq 704, 35 LJCh 777.
 6 (1870) 18 WR 425.
 7 [1940] Ch 54, 109 LJCh 20.

But they would add that too much stress should not be laid on the provisions of the Guardianship of Infants Act 1925. Section 1 of that Act[8] introduced no new principle of law, but merely enacted the rule which had long been acted on in the Chancery Division of the High Court of Justice: see *Re Thain*.[9] It is true, as pointed out in the judgment of Cartwright J, that the judgment in *Re B's Settlement* has been criticised by some writers whose opinions are entitled to consideration, but it has not, so far as their Lordships are aware, been the subject of adverse judicial comment. In their opinion it is not only consistent with authority but, as they have already observed, proceeds inevitably from the nature of the jurisdiction and of the subject matter in regard to which it is exercised.

Appeal allowed.

Re E (D) (an infant) [1967] Ch 761, [1967] 2 All ER 881 (Court of Appeal)

Appeal from Cross J.

Diana was born in New Mexico in September 1959 of American parents resident in that state. In June 1960 the mother obtained a divorce from the father on the ground of incompatibility. The divorce was granted by Judge Reidy, sitting at Albuquerque, New Mexico. He awarded the custody of Diana to the mother. But in March 1962 Judge Reidy transferred the custody to the father on the ground that the mother was not a fit and proper person to have the custody of a small child.

In August 1962 the father, presumably having a premonition of impending death, executed an unusual document in which he said that he did not regard either the mother or her parents as suitable persons to have the custody of Diana, and expressed the wish that his sister (the present plaintiff), who was married and living in England, should take over the custody in the event of his premature death. In August 1965 he brought Diana to England on a holiday trip in the course of which they stayed with the present plaintiff. He extracted a promise from her that in the event of his death she would look after Diana. Meanwhile the mother had remarried and gone to live with her present husband in Portland, Oregon, which is about 3000 miles[10] from Albuquerque.

In December 1965 the father was killed in a motor accident. Diana was with him in the car, and although not seriously injured she was emotionally upset and taken to hospital in Durango, Colorado, just over the border from New Mexico. The father's father, Dr E, telephoned to the plaintiff, who was on holiday in Europe, and arranged for her to fly at once to New York to take over the custody of Diana. He himself travelled from his home in New Jersey to Durango with his attorney and they succeeded in spiriting Diana away from the hospital and flew with her direct to New York so as to be ready for the plaintiff when she arrived from Europe.

Meanwhile the mother heard what had happened. She flew south from Portland, Oregon, and obtained an order from Judge Reidy on 3 January 1966, directed to Dr E and his attorney, requiring them to deliver Diana to her maternal grandmother. But before the order could be served, the

8 Now s 1 of the Guardianship of Minors Act 1971, p 370 above (*Ed*).
9 [1926] Ch 676, 95 LJCh 292.
10 Sic in the report. The distance is in fact about 1200 miles (*Ed*).

plaintiff and Diana flew to England via Montreal, arriving on 7 January. On 10 January Judge Reidy made a further order awarding temporary custody of Diana to the mother, though of course without a full investigation.

The mother, who was not a wealthy woman, was unable for some months to follow Diana across the Atlantic. She saved and borrowed money until she could afford the fare. She came to England early in May 1966 and met the plaintiff and Diana. Fearing that the mother might try to rekidnap Diana, the plaintiff made her a ward of court and asked for directions for her care and control. Cross J held that Diana should continue to be brought up in England in the care and control of the plaintiff. The mother appealed.

Willmer LJ (having stated the facts): On those facts I think that the judge was faced with a peculiarly difficult problem. On the one hand he quite rightly felt that it was his duty to condemn in the most forthright terms the conduct of Dr E, and to a lesser extent that of the plaintiff, in smuggling the child out of the United States in defiance of an order made by the court of the domicile of which the child was already a ward. On the other hand, he also had to consider as the first and paramount consideration the welfare of the child. I do not think that is was at all an easy matter, in the very unusual circumstances of this case, to maintain a correct balance between these conflicting considerations.

At the outset of his judgment, after expressing his concern at what he described as the growing tendency, which has recently been apparent, of kidnapping children in this way and removing them from the jurisdiction of a foreign court, the judge proceeded as follows:

'The courts in all countries ought, as I see it, to be careful not to do anything to encourage this tendency. The substitution of self help for due process of law in this field can only harm the interests of wards generally, and a judge should, as I see it, pay regard to the orders of the proper foreign court, unless he is satisfied beyond reasonable doubt that to do so would inflict serious harm on the child.'

First of all, I would like to say, by way of comment on that passage, that I wholly agree with, and would wish to support, everything that the judge said about the duty of all courts not to countenance behaviour of the kind there referred to. The other comment that I would make upon it is that it seems to me that in that passage the judge was giving himself exactly the same direction as he had previously given himself in the earlier case of *Re H (infants)*.[11] That was a case which undoubtedly did have a number of features in common with the present case. But it was different in one very essential respect, namely, that in that case both the father and mother were alive, and both of them had settled homes in the State of New York. In that case it was the mother who had smuggled the children out of the State of New York and brought them to this country in defiance of an order of the New York Court. The judge there came to the conclusion that the children would come to no harm if he ordered their immediate return to their father's home in New York, and he accordingly made an order that they should be so returned so that the New York court could decide as to their future. There was an appeal to this court from the decision of the judge in that case, but we in this court upheld his decision.

11 [1966] 1 All ER 886, [1966] 1 WLR 381.

This case, as I have said, is radically different in that very essential respect, for here the only home that the child Diana has ever known in the United States was effectively destroyed by her father's death. In the present case, therefore, the effect of transferring care and control of Diana to her own natural mother would necessarily be to uproot her from the new home in this country in which she has now happily settled down, to take her away from her aunt, who has more or less established a relationship of mother to the child, and to transfer her to surroundings which would be wholly strange to her, namely, in Portland, Oregon. It might be different if the child was to go back to Albuquerque where, I suppose, she might find herself among her own friends and some of her own people; but, of course, in Portland, Oregon, she would be a complete stranger.

In those circumstances, the judge, having asked himself substantially the same question as he had asked himself in the previous case of *Re H* (*infants*), arrived in this case at the opposite answer. What he said, having referred to the conduct of Dr E in taking the child away from the hospital, was this:

> 'But however much one may disapprove of his action—and I am very far indeed from condoning it—one cannot shut one's eyes to the results which have flowed from it. Having heard Mrs Z' (that is, the plaintiff) 'in the witness-box, I have no doubt whatever that she now stands in the relation of mother to the child and to take the child away from her would be utterly disastrous for the child.'

To be fair to the mother, I do not read this as meaning that the judge took an adverse view of her. On the contrary, he rather went out of his way to pay tribute to the mother for the way in which she had behaved; he described her as 'a woman of charm and intelligence'. But it is also fair to say that he did bear in mind the strictures which had been made about her moral behaviour in the past. What the judge was concerned with in using the word 'disastrous', I think, was the danger of taking the child away from the plaintiff, having regard to the relationship which had been built up between them. To take the child away from the plaintiff would involve removing her from the only home which she now knows, and setting her adrift in wholly strange surroundings.

In view of the judge's finding that it would be disastrous for the child to take her away, it is indeed difficult to see what order he could properly have made other than the one that he did. We invited counsel for the mother to direct our attention to any evidence which there might be tending to rebut this finding of the judge. But in answer to that invitation, the only reply which Mr Comyn was able to give was that the judge ought never to have got into the position of asking himself that question at all. What was submitted was that the proper course would have been to adjourn the case, though maintaining the wardship in being for the time being, without forming (and certainly without expressing) any view as to the merits of the case, or as to the effect on the child, so as to give time and opportunity for the whole matter to be thrashed out and decided by Judge Reidy in the court at Albuquerque. That point had been argued also before Cross J, and he dealt with it in this way:

> 'Mr Comyn suggested that a possible solution would be for me to leave the ward here for the time being, while asking the New Mexico court to

decide on her future and impliedly undertaking to abide by its decision. That to my mind would be to abdicate my responsibility. In cases of this sort either the child must go back, or this court must decide on its future. As *Re H (infants)* shows, unless there are compelling reasons to the contrary, the child ought to be sent back; but here in my judgment there are such reasons.'

Let me say that in my judgment the judge dealt with this submission in the proper way. I am abundantly satisfied that he was right, and indeed was only carrying out the duty entrusted to him, in himself considering what would be the effect on Diana of such order as he might be disposed to make. As I have said, he gave himself the same direction that he gave himself in the earlier case, and I think that in doing so he asked himself the right question.

Once he had decided, as he did, that it would be 'disastrous' to take Diana away from the plaintiff and from the only home that she now knows, I think that he was not only entitled but bound to say so in no uncertain terms, and to give effect to his view, as he did, by directing that the plaintiff should have the care and control of the child.

I cannot refrain from expressing my sympathy with the mother, who has fought valiantly to recover care and control of her own daughter. I have no doubt that in the course of doing so she has subjected herself to a good deal of expense and hardship in her efforts. I feel sympathy all the more because I fully recognise the obvious difficulties, on geographical grounds, in making any satisfactory provision for the mother having regular access. But in view of the judge's finding as to the effect of removing Diana from the care and control of the plaintiff, I do not think that any other decision was open to him. In those circumstances in my judgment the appeal must be dismissed.

Danckwerts LJ delivered judgment to the same effect. Winn LJ concurred.
Appeal dismissed.

Re L (Minors) [1974] 1 All ER 913, [1974] 1 WLR 250 (Court of Appeal)

Appeal from Cumming-Bruce J.

The father was a German national domiciled and resident in Germany. The mother was English by origin. The matrimonial home was near Munich. There were two children of the marriage, a girl aged ten and a boy aged eight. In July 1972 the mother brought the children to England, ostensibly for a holiday, but with the settled intention to establish herself and the children permanently in England if she could. She was careful to conceal her address in England from the father. When the mother and children failed to return to Germany in time for the autumn school term, the father came to England to find them. Consequently in October 1972 the mother issued an originating summons making the children wards of court and sought an order giving her care and control. The father first discovered where his wife and children were when he was served with the summons. He proposed that the children should live with his spinster sister in Munich so that he could see a good deal of them. At the time of the hearing the mother was aged 48, the father 55 and his sister 64.

Cumming-Bruce J after a full investigation, and having seen the parents and the sister in the witness-box, considered that the children would be better off if they were brought up by their mother rather than by their aunt. But as this was a kidnapping case he ordered that the children should be sent back to Germany in the custody of their father. The mother appealed.

Buckley LJ (after stating the facts, and reviewing the authorities, ie *McKee v McKee*,[12] *Re H (infants)*,[13] *Re E (D) (an infant)*,[14] *Re T (infants)*,[15] *Re TA (infants)*[16] and *J v C*,[17] continued): Beyond doubt *J v C* establishes, if authority were needed, that where in a wardship case the court considers the facts and fully investigates the merits of a dispute, the welfare of the child concerned is not the only consideration but is the first and paramount consideration to be taken into account, whether the dispute be between a parent and a parent, or between parents and a stranger in blood or between one such stranger and another. As to the meaning of 'first and paramount consideration' it is, I think, useful to bear in mind what was said by Lord MacDermott in *J v C*, at 710–711:

> 'Reading these words in their ordinary significance, and relating them to the various classes of proceedings which the section has already mentioned, it seems to me that they must mean more than that the child's welfare is to be treated as the top item in a list of items relevant to the matter in question. I think they connote a process whereby, when all the relevant facts, relationships, claims and wishes of parents, risks, choices and other circumstances are taken into account and weighed, the course to be followed will be that which is most in the interests of the child's welfare as that term has now to be understood. That is the first consideration because it is of first importance and the paramount consideration because it rules upon or determines the course to be followed.'

Every matter having relevance to the welfare of the child should be taken into account and placed in the balance. Other matters, which may not directly relate to the child's welfare but are relevant to the situation, may be proper to be taken into account and given such weight as the court may think fit, subject always to the welfare of the child being treated as paramount. The interests, wishes and conduct of parents and of other members of the child's family and, indeed, of other persons, may fall under either of these heads.

Race, nationality or religion may very probably and quite properly affect parental wishes about how and where a child should be brought up. These are factors which may well have an important bearing on the child's growth to maturity and his welfare. In *J v C* Lord Guest observed that nationality is one of the factors which the judge should take into consideration. It must form one element in the balancing operation to be performed to determine

12 [1951] AC 352, [1951] 1 All ER 942, p 375 above.
13 [1966] 1 All ER 886, [1966] 1 WLR 381.
14 [1967] Ch 761, [1967] 2 All ER 881, p 378 above.
15 [1968] Ch 704, [1968] 3 All ER 411.
16 (1972) 116 Sol Jo 78.
17 [1970] AC 668, [1969] 1 All ER 788.

where the child's welfare lies. It is, however, no more than one of the balancing factors.

Where, as in the present case and in *J v C*, no order has been made by a foreign court relating to the custody or upbringing of the child, no question of comity arises. Even if an order has been made by a foreign court, an English court is nonetheless bound in duty to protect the child's welfare without being bound to enforce the foreign order or to follow it: see *J v C*, per Lord Guest, at 701; Lord MacDermott, at 714 and Lord Upjohn, at 720.

How, then, do the kidnapping cases fit these principles? Where the court has embarked upon a full-scale investigation of the facts, the applicable principles, in my view, do not differ from those which apply to any other wardship case. The action of one party in kidnapping the child is doubtless one of the circumstances to be taken into account and may be a circumstance of great weight; the weight to be attributed to it must depend upon the circumstances of the particular case. The court may conclude that notwithstanding the conduct of the 'kidnapper' the child should remain in his or her care: see *McKee v McKee*; *Re E (D) (an infant)* and *Re TA* (where the order was merely interim); or it may conclude that the child should be returned to his or her native country or the jurisdiction from which he or she has been removed: *Re T (infants)*. Where a court makes a summary order for the return of a child to a foreign country without investigating the merits, the same principles, in my judgment, apply, but the decision must be justified on somewhat different grounds.

To take a child from his native land, to remove him to another country where, maybe, his native tongue is not spoken, to divorce him from the social customs and contacts to which he has been accustomed, to interrupt his education in his native land and subject him to a foreign system of education, are all acts (offered here as examples and of course not as a complete catalogue of possible relevant factors) which are likely to be psychologically disturbing to the child, particularly at a time when his family life is also disrupted. If such a case is promptly brought to the attention of a court in this country, the judge may feel that it is in the best interests of the infant that these disturbing factors should be eliminated from his life as speedily as possible. A full investigation of the merits of the case in an English court may be incompatible with achieving this. The judge may well be persuaded that it would be better for the child that those merits should be investigated in a court in his native country than that he should spend in this country the period which must necessarily elapse before all the evidence can be assembled for adjudication here. Anyone who has had experience of the exercise of this delicate jurisdiction knows what complications can result from a child developing roots in new soil, and what conflicts this can occasion in the child's own life. Such roots can grow rapidly. An order that the child should be returned forthwith to the country from which he has been removed in the expectation that any dispute about his custody will be satisfactorily resolved in the courts of that country may well be regarded as being in the best interests of the child. In my judgment, the decision of this court in *Re H (infants)* was based upon considerations of this kind.

As citations which I have already made disclose, judges have more than once reprobated the acts of 'kidnappers' in cases of this kind. I do not in any way dissent from those strictures, but it would, in my judgment, be wrong to suppose that in making orders in relation to children in this jurisdiction the court is in any way concerned with penalising any adult for his conduct. That conduct may well be a consideration to be taken into account, but, whether the court makes a summary order or an order after investigating the merits, the cardinal rule applies that the welfare of the infant must always be the paramount consideration.

I can now return to a discussion of the grounds on which the judge finally disposed of the present case. After discussing the kidnapping cases on the lines which I have indicated, the judge stated his final conclusion thus:

> 'The concept of the welfare of the children in this context is not limited to questions as to which parent can produce the nicest surroundings, or even the best education. It goes much further than that. The correct approach is this: these are German children. They have always been brought up in Germany. They are German nationals. They ought to be able to look forward to a future in their own country. Are the proposals of the father or the mother likely to promote their welfare, having regard to those long-term objects? And it is perfectly plain that those considerations point overwhelmingly to their immediate return to their own country, to a resumption of their education in the appropriate schools in Germany, which was unfortunately interrupted by the decision of their mother. The factor which manifestly is the strongest factor pointing towards care and control by the mother is that she has always brought them up, that [the girl] is a child of an age where she ought to have a mother's care, and [the boy] is a little boy of an age who is likely to have very close emotional links with his mother which should not be rudely disrupted without risk of damage to his emotional life and his character. I am very alive to those factors. I regard it as highly desirable that the children should continue to be brought up by their mother. I think their father regards that as highly desirable, too. But I have no doubt on the facts of this case that the solution must be that the children must be restored to their own country, that their future destiny should be decided, if there is a dispute between the parents, by the courts in Germany where some proceedings are already pending; and that if the mother wishes to assert her right to care and control of the children, she should institute proceedings to that end in the court of the domicile, which is Germany.'

This passage, in my judgment, makes it plain that the judge weighed all the relevant factors in deciding where the true interests of the children lay. This was not a case in which the judge made a summary order. He considered and gave weight to all the relevant circumstances. He reached his decision on a full evaluation of the merits. In doing so he rightly took into account, amongst other things, the conduct of the mother in removing the children from Germany and its likely effect upon the children themselves, but he did not, I think, give undue weight to these factors. His conclusion was, in my opinion, one which he was fully entitled to reach on the material before him; and it is, moreover, one with which I agree.

I would accordingly dismiss this appeal.

Davies and Lawton LJJ concurred.
Appeal dismissed.

Re C (Minors) [1978] Fam 105, [1978] 2 All ER 230 (Court of Appeal)

Appeal from Judge McLellan, sitting as a deputy judge of the High Court.

The father, an Englishman, emigrated to the United States in 1966 at the age of 19 and in the following year he married the mother, who was an American. They came to England and set up home in Southampton where their three children were born in 1967, 1969 and 1971. The marriage was not happy and in 1973 the mother returned to California, taking the children with her with the consent of the father. The marriage was dissolved in 1975 and custody awarded to the mother by consent. Both parties remarried. The father married a girl of 17 who was a Jehovah's Witness and be became a convert to that faith. In February 1977 the mother died suddenly of a heart attack. The father, on hearing of her death, flew to California with his mother to bring the children back. Soon after he arrived the children's step-father and their maternal aunt and grandmother applied to the Superior Court of California for an order for custody of the children. The court made an interim order in their favour and, while a welfare officer's report was being prepared, made an order for the father to have access, including staying access over a weekend. During that weekend, in breach of the court's order, the father kidnapped the children, put them on a plane and brought them back to England. His subsequent explanation of this behaviour was that the Californian proceedings were taking longer to come to trial than he had expected, and he was running out of money. The judge disbelieved him but the Court of Appeal did not.

The step-father followed and issued a wardship summons in the High Court asking for an order for the peremptory return of the children to California. Judge McLellan formed a very unfavourable view of the father and a largely favourable view of the step-father. But he refused to make an order on the ground that the step-father smoked cannabis on social occasions, and so to return the children to him would expose them to serious moral danger.

The step-father appealed. The Court of Appeal had before it (as the judge did not) the Californian welfare officer's report and the report of an English welfare officer, Mr Chapman.

Ormrod LJ: This is a case which can properly be called an extremely tragic one for all concerned. It has caused the court a great deal of anxiety and worry. (His Lordship stated the facts, considered the Californian welfare officer's report in which she said that it would not be detrimental for the children to be with their natural father; that the law of California gave preference to a natural parent; and recommended to the Californian court that the step-father's petition for custody be denied. His Lordship also referred to a recent Californian case, Re BG,[18] in which the development of the law in California was traced, and which stated that, in order to award custody to a non-parent, the court must find that it would be detrimental to the child to award custody to a natural parent and that the best interests of the child would be served by awarding custody to a non-parent. His Lordship continued): That is the present state of the law in California. Perhaps one might properly comment that the evolution of the law in California seems to be following very much the same lines as the law in

18 (1974) 11 Cal 3d 725.

England has already followed from the time before the first of the Guardianship of Infants Acts in 1886, when a claim by a father was almost irresistible by the mother or anybody else unless he was shown to be a person who had totally unfitted himself to act as a parent, through a period after the Guardianship of Infants Acts 1886 and 1925 were passed, when the claim of a natural parent—particularly an unimpeachable natural parent—took precedence over the claims of any non-parent, to the present state of the law set out in *J v C*[19] by the House of Lords, which makes it clear that in England now the law requires the court, as I have already said, to make its decision based on the best interests of the children without gloss or qualification. The Californian court seems to be very much in the state that this court was in before *J v C* was finally decided by the House of Lords.

The importance of this consideration is that if this court decides that the proper order is to send these children back to California for their future to be decided by the Californian court, judging by the welfare officer's report and doing the best we can in a necessarily amateur way, it seems highly likely that the American court will conclude that the step-father is unable to demonstrate that it would be 'detrimental' to the interests of these children to be placed in the custody of their father, in which case the Californian court would have to make an order for custody in the father's favour, which would mean that the children would be returned, or have to be returned, to this country once more. It cannot possibly be in the best interests of children to expose them to a real risk—call it balance of probabilities or whatever, but I would prefer to speak of it as a real risk—of being taken back to California by the step-father, only to be sent back again here to be placed in the care of their natural father. It is only for that reason that, in my judgment, this court should assume jurisdiction, and it is for that reason that I agree that the order which the judge made was a right order, although I cannot agree with the grounds on which he made it. It is only in such a way that this court could justify this interference (as it were) with the court in California, and the justification for it is that this court is coming to a decision which, so far as it can judge, the Californian court would be likely to reach itself.

Mr Wood (counsel for the step-father) has tried to argue the case on the footing that he was appearing in the Californian court, trying to show that there was sufficient evidence here to establish 'detriment'. This is, of course, a difficult theoretical exercise, particularly before a court which does not know at all clearly how the word 'detriment' is interpreted in California. It has already got to be something more than 'not in the best interests of the children'.

The position as we find it in fact now is this, as I see it: the children had become and got completely used to their life in California, their friends and their relatives were there, and Mr Wood is perfectly justified in saying that they had put down their roots in California. They clearly had. They were, all the evidence shows, happy there, and their memories of England must have been comparatively faint. It is also right to say that the death of their mother has been the most terrible blow to each of them, and each of them no doubt is trying to deal with that blow in the child's own particular way. Mr Wood argues that what they need above all things is continuity.

19 [1970] AC 668, [1969] 1 All ER 788.

Certainly one can understand that. However, the great difficulty in the continuity argument is that they have been deprived by death of the one element in their particular environment the continuity of which is essential to them; and, without their mother, continuity (except in the most general sense) is very difficult to maintain, particularly for this step-father who has not at the present moment any female assistance in bringing them up with him, although he hopes to get such assistance. The thing that stands out a mile to my mind is that, so far as California is concerned, there is no visible mother-substitute for these children at the time when they very badly need one. The aunt and the grandmother have made it clear that they cannot, for various reasons, take on any close day-to-day role in looking after these children, and so some woman would have to be found. On the other hand, the father has a wife, a new wife, though, it is true, a very young woman to take on so great a responsibility, but he has got a wife and a home which is a two-parent home of an established kind. So he has a very powerful attraction in that respect. I think it is also wrong of us wholly to overlook the fact that he is the children's natural father. I do not mean to say that the scales should be weighted particularly heavily. If other indications point to the step-father, I would not hesitate for my part to make an order in favour of the step-father; but the fact is that his reaction over these children is a perfectly normal and natural reaction for a father whose children have suddenly been partially orphaned by the death of their mother. From Mr Chapman's report it is striking how the eldest child has taken to her step-mother. His impression (it is true of a fleeting visit) is that this child is really quite content. She appears to be quite pleased with her English school, and she actually expressed the view—in contrast to what she had said before—that she did not want to go back to California. She referred to the whole thing as a 'bore' and no doubt, poor child, she must feel at sea because she has lived since her mother died in an atmosphere of almost constant conflict. The second child is clearly very much disturbed and is adjusting with much greater difficulty; but the third child seems happy enough, so far as anyone can tell.

On that state of the evidence, it seems to me, with respect to Mr Wood's argument, very difficult to imagine how the court in California could find that it would be 'detrimental' to these children to be entrusted to the care and custody of their father.

The case is complicated by one matter which is always a difficulty, and that is, as I have mentioned earlier, that the father and step-mother are Jehovah's Witnesses. Mr Wood is quite right in saying that if the children remain with the father, they will be brought up as Jehovah's Witnesses. They are not by any means alone in this world as children being brought up as Jehovah's Witnesses. It is unfortunate that this particular persuasion does seem prone to lead to controversies in the courts from time to time, so that we are all very familiar with cases involving this particular persuasion. But the court must approach it as it approaches any other religious persuasion and do the best it can. There are certain aspects of the way of life of Jehovah's Witnesses which do seem to people who are not members of the persuasion somewhat awkward, difficult and not very good for children. There is a tendency to isolate them from other people at school to some extent. There is the unfortunate feature that Christmas and birthdays are not celebrated in the way that most people do, and a number of other matters.

But these are all matters of relatively light weight when the court is considering the welfare of the children in the sort of circumstances in which we are in this court today. My conclusion would be that it would be quite wrong to say, or for any court to say, that because the parents were Jehovah's Witnesses, this represented a 'detriment', however that word is construed in the American court.

The evidence, therefore, as it is before us—and I stress 'as it is before us' because we are relying on the welfare officer's report—is heavily in favour of leaving the children where they are, with their father. It is perfectly true that of course the fact that he took them unilaterally from California has produced a situation in which the children have actually been living with him for a short period which they would not otherwise have done. This, of course, is unfortunate from the point of view of the step-father. I mean forensically unfortunate, because it enables the court and the children to look at two situations in terms of reality, as opposed to looking at one situation in terms of reality and the other in terms of hypothesis. Children are often able, I think, to judge between two real situations of which they have experience very much better than they can judge between one which they have experienced and one which is put to them in the form of hypothesis. Mr Chapman's report indicates to me that the children, having regard to the appalling difficulties that they have had in the last couple of months, have really settled down remarkably well. I would regard it as plain that the best interests of the children are now that they remain where they are. I can well understand the attraction of the step-father, who might be able to give them a much freer, easier, outgoing sort of life; but he has, as I think, immense problems to tackle himself. I would hesitate for a long time to put upon him the burden of taking care of these three children, none of whom are related to him at all.

So, for all those reasons, I would dismiss the appeal from the judge's judgment.

Stamp LJ and Sir David Cairns concurred.

Appeal dismissed.
Judge's order varied by directing that wardship be continued until children respectively attain age 18 or until further order.
Care and control to father until children attain age of 18 or until further order.
Reasonable access to step-father.

Council of Europe Convention on Recognition and Enforcement of Decisions Concerning Custody of Children and on Restoration of Custody of Children (1980)

Article 1

For the purposes of this Convention:
(a) *child* means a person of any nationality, so long as he is under 16 years of age and has not the right to decide on his own place of residence under the law of his habitual residence, the law of his nationality or the internal law of the State addressed;
(b) *authority* means a judicial or administrative authority;
(c) *decision relating to custody* means a decision of an authority in so far as it

relates to the care of the person of the child, including the right to decide on the place of his residence, or to the right of access to him;

(d) *improper removal* means the removal of a child across an international frontier in breach of a decision relating to his custody which has been given in a Contracting State and which is enforceable in such a State; improper removal also includes:

(i) the failure to return a child across an international frontier at the end of a period of the exercise of the right of access to this child or at the end of any other temporary stay in a territory other than that where the custody is exercised;

(ii) a removal which is subsequently declared unlawful within the meaning of Article 12.

PART I

CENTRAL AUTHORITIES

Article 2

1. Each Contracting State shall appoint a central authority to carry out the functions provided for by this Convention.

2. Federal States and States with more than one legal system shall be free to appoint more than one central authority and shall determine the extent of their competence.

3. The Secretary General of the Council of Europe shall be notified of any appointment under this Article.

Article 3

1. The central authorities of the Contracting States shall co-operate with each other and promote co-operation between the competent authorities in their respective countries. They shall act with all necessary despatch.

2. With a view to facilitating the operation of this Convention, the central authorities of the Contracting States:

(a) shall secure the transmission of requests for information coming from competent authorities and relating to legal or factual matters concerning pending proceedings;

(b) shall provide each other on request with information about their law relating to the custody of children and any changes in that law;

(c) shall keep each other informed of any difficulties likely to arise in applying the Convention and, as far as possible, eliminate obstacles to its application.

Article 4

1. Any person who has obtained in a Contracting State a decision relating to the custody of a child and who wishes to have that decision recognised or enforced in another Contracting State may submit an application for this purpose to the central authority in any Contracting State.

2. The application shall be accompanied by the documents mentioned in Article 13.

3. The central authority receiving the application, if it is not the central authority in the State addressed, shall send the documents directly and without delay to that central authority.

4. The central authority receiving the application may refuse to intervene where it is manifestly clear that the conditions laid down by this Convention are not satisfied.

5. The central authority receiving the application shall keep the applicant informed without delay on the progress of his application.

Article 5

1. The central authority in the State addressed shall take or cause to be taken without delay all steps which it considers to be appropriate, if necessary by instituting proceedings before its competent authorities, in order:
(a) to discover the whereabouts of the child;
(b) to avoid, in particular by any necessary provisional measures, prejudice to the interests of the child or of the applicant;
(c) to secure the recognition or enforcement of the decision;
(d) to secure the delivery of the child to the applicant where enforcement is granted;
(e) to inform the requesting authority of the measures taken and their results.

2. Where the central authority in the State addressed has reason to believe that the child is in the territory of another Contracting State it shall send the documents directly and without delay to the central authority of that State.

3. With the exception of the cost of repatriation, each Contracting State undertakes not to claim any payment from an applicant in respect of any measures taken under paragraph 1 of this Article by the central authority of that State on the applicant's behalf, including the costs of proceedings and, where applicable, the costs incurred by the assistance of a lawyer.

4. If recognition or enforcement is refused, and if the central authority of the State addressed considers that it should comply with a request by the applicant to bring in that State proceedings concerning the substance of the case, that authority shall use its best endeavours to secure the representation of the applicant in the proceedings under conditions no less favourable than those available to a person who is resident in and a national of that State and for this purpose it may, in particular, institute proceedings before its competent authorities.

PART II

RECOGNITION AND ENFORCEMENT OF DECISIONS AND RESTORATION OF CUSTODY OF CHILDREN

Article 7

A decision relating to custody given in a Contracting State shall be recognised and, where it is enforceable in the State of origin, made enforceable in every other Contracting State.

Article 8

1. In the case of an improper removal, the central authority of the State addressed shall cause steps to be taken forthwith to restore the custody of the child where:

(a) at the time of the institution of the proceedings in the State where the decision was given or at the time of the improper removal, if earlier, the child and his parents had as their sole nationality the nationality of that State and the child had his habitual residence in the territory of that State, and

(b) a request for the restoration was made to a central authority within a period of six months from the date of the improper removal.

2. If, in accordance with the law of the State addressed, the requirements of paragraph 1 of this Article cannot be complied with without recourse to a judicial authority, none of the grounds of refusal specified in this Convention shall apply to the judicial proceedings.

3. Where there is an agreement officially confirmed by a competent authority between the person having the custody of the child and another person to allow the other person a right of access, and the child, having been taken abroad, has not been restored at the end of the agreed period to the person having the custody, custody of the child shall be restored in accordance with paragraphs 1(b) and 2 of this Article. The same shall apply in the case of a decision of the competent authority granting such a right to a person who has not the custody of the child.

Article 9

1. In cases of improper removal, other than those dealt with in Article 8, in which an application has been made to a central authority within a period of six months from the date of the removal, recognition and enforcement may be refused only if:

(a) in the case of a decision given in the absence of the defendant or his legal representative, the defendant was not duly served with the document which instituted the proceedings or an equivalent document in sufficient time to enable him to arrange his defence; but such a failure to effect service cannot constitute a ground for refusing recognition or enforcement where service was not effected because the defendant had concealed his whereabouts from the person who instituted the proceedings in the State of origin;

(b) in the case of a decision given in the absence of the defendant or his legal representative, the competence of the authority giving the decision was not founded:

  (i) on the habitual residence of the defendant, or

  (ii) on the last common habitual residence of the child's parents, at least one parent being still habitually resident there, or

  (iii) on the habitual residence of the child;

(c) the decision is incompatible with a decision relating to custody which became enforceable in the State addressed before the removal of the child, unless the child has had his habitual residence in the territory of the requesting State for one year before his removal.

2. Where no application has been made to a central authority, the provisions of paragraph 1 of this Article shall apply equally, if recognition and enforcement are requested within six months from the date of the improper removal.

3. In no circumstances may the foreign decision be reviewed as to its substance.

Article 10

1. In cases other than those covered by Articles 8 and 9, recognition and enforcement may be refused not only on the grounds provided for in Article 9 but also on any of the following grounds:
(a) if it is found that the effects of the decision are manifestly incompatible with the fundamental principles of the law relating to the family and children in the State addressed;
(b) if it is found that by reason of a change in the circumstances including the passage of time but not including a mere change in the residence of the child after an improper removal, the effects of the original decision are manifestly no longer in accordance with the welfare of the child;
(c) if at the time when the proceedings were instituted in the State of origin:
   (i) the child was a national of the State addressed or was habitually resident there and no such connection existed with the State of origin;
   (ii) the child was a national both of the State of origin and of the State addressed and was habitually resident in the State addressed;
(d) if the decision is incompatible with a decision given in the State addressed or enforceable in that State after being given in a third State, pursuant to proceedings begun before the submission of the request for recognition or enforcement, and if the refusal is in accordance with the welfare of the child.

2. In the same cases, proceedings for recognition or enforcement may be adjourned on any of the following grounds:
(a) if an ordinary form of review of the original decision has been commenced;
(b) if proceedings relating to the custody of the child, commenced before the proceedings in the State of origin were instituted, are pending in the State addressed;
(c) if another decision concerning the custody of the child is the subject of proceedings for enforcement or of any other proceedings concerning the recognition of the decision.

Article 11

1. Decisions on rights of access and provisions of decisions relating to custody which deal with the right of access shall be recognised and enforced subject to the same conditions as other decisions relating to custody.

2. However, the competent authority of the State addressed may fix the conditions for the implementation and exercise of the right of access taking into account, in particular, undertakings given by the parties on this matter.

3. Where no decision on the right of access has been taken or where

recognition or enforcement of the decision relating to custody is refused, the central authority of the State addressed may apply to its competent authorities for a decision on the right of access, if the person claiming a right of access so requests.

Article 12

Where, at the time of the removal of a child across an international frontier, there is no enforceable decision given in a Contracting State relating to his custody, the provisions of this Convention shall apply to any subsequent decision, relating to the custody of that child and declaring the removal to be unlawful, given in a Contracting State at the request of any interested person.

PART VI

FINAL CLAUSES

Article 26

1. In relation to a State which has in matters of custody two or more systems of law of territorial application:
(a) reference to the law of a person's habitual residence or to the law of a person's nationality shall be construed as referring to the system of law determined by the rules in force in that State or, if there are no such rules, to the system of law with which the person concerned is most closely connected;
(b) reference to the State of origin or to the State addressed shall be construed as referring, as the case may be, to the territorial unit where the decision was given or to the territorial unit where recognition or enforcement of the decision or restoration of custody is requested.

2. Paragraph 1(a) of this Article also applies mutatis mutandis to States which have in matters of custody two or more systems of law of personal application.

Hague Convention on the Civil Aspects of International Child Abduction (1980)

CHAPTER I—SCOPE OF THE CONVENTION

Article 1

The objects of the present Convention are—
(a) to secure the prompt return of children wrongfully removed to or retained in any Contracting State; and
(b) to ensure that rights of custody and of access under the law of one Contracting State are effectively respected in the other Contracting States.

Article 2

Contracting States shall take all appropriate measures to secure within their territories the implementation of the objects of the Convention. For this purpose they shall use the most expeditious procedures available.

Article 3

The removal or the retention of a child is to be considered wrongful where—
(a) it is in breach of rights of custody attributed to a person, an institution or any other body, either jointly or alone, under the law of the State in which the child was habitually resident immediately before the removal or retention; and
(b) at the time of removal or retention those rights were actually exercised, either jointly or alone, or would have been so exercised but for the removal or retention.

The rights of custody mentioned in sub-paragraph (a) above, may arise in particular by operation of law or by reason of a judicial or administrative decision, or by reason of an agreement having legal effect under the law of that State.

Article 4

The Convention shall apply to any child who was habitually resident in a Contracting State immediately before any breach of custody or access rights. The Convention shall cease to apply when the child attains the age of 16 years.

Article 5

For the purposes of this Convention—
(a) 'rights of custody' shall include rights relating to the care of the person of the child and, in particular, the right to determine the child's place of residence;
(b) 'rights of access' shall include the right to take a child for a limited period of time to a place other than the child's habitual residence.

CHAPTER II—CENTRAL AUTHORITIES

Article 6

A Contracting State shall designate a Central Authority to discharge the duties which are imposed by the Convention upon such authorities.

Federal States, States with more than one system of law or States having autonomous territorial organisations shall be free to appoint more than one Central Authority and to specify the territorial extent of their powers. Where a State has appointed more than one Central Authority, it shall designate the Central Authority to which applications may be addressed for transmission to the appropriate Central Authority within that State.

Article 7

Central Authorities shall co-operate with each other and promote co-operation amongst the competent authorities in their respective States to secure the prompt return of children and to achieve the other objects of this Convention.

In particular, either directly or through any intermediary, they shall take all appropriate measures—
(a) to discover the whereabouts of a child who has been wrongfully removed or retained;

(b) to prevent further harm to the child or prejudice to interested parties by taking or causing to be taken provisional measures;

(c) to secure the voluntary return of the child or to bring about an amicable resolution of the issues;

(d) to exchange, where desirable, information relating to the social background of the child;

(e) to provide information of a general character as to the law of their State in connection with the application of the Convention;

(f) to initiate or facilitate the institution of judicial or administrative proceedings with a view to obtaining the return of the child and, in a proper case, to make arrangements for organising or securing the effective exercise of rights of access;

(g) where the circumstances so require, to provide or facilitate the provision of legal aid and advice, including the participation of legal counsel and advisers;

(h) to provide such administrative arrangements as may be necessary and appropriate to secure the safe return of the child;

(i) to keep each other informed with respect to the operation of this Convention and, as far as possible, to eliminate any obstacles to its application.

CHAPTER III—RETURN OF CHILDREN

Article 8

Any person, institution or other body claiming that a child has been removed or retained in breach of custody rights may apply either to the Central Authority of the child's habitual residence or to the Central Authority of any other Contracting State for assistance in securing the return of the child.

The application shall contain—

(a) information concerning the identity of the applicant, of the child and of the person alleged to have removed or retained the child;

(b) where available, the date of birth of the child;

(c) the grounds on which the applicant's claim for return of the child is based;

(d) all available information relating to the whereabouts of the child and the identity of the person with whom the child is presumed to be.

The application may be accompanied or supplemented by—

(e) an authenticated copy of any relevant decision or agreement;

(f) a certificate or an affidavit emanating from a Central Authority, or other competent authority of the State of the child's habitual residence, or from a qualified person, concerning the relevant law of that State;

(g) any other relevant document.

Article 9

If the Central Authority which receives an application referred to in Article 8 has reason to believe that the child is in another Contracting State, it shall directly and without delay transmit the application to the Central Authority of that Contracting State and inform the requesting Central Authority, or the applicant, as the case may be.

Article 10

The Central Authority of the State where the child is shall take or cause to be taken all appropriate measures in order to obtain the voluntary return of the child.

Article 11

The judicial or administrative authorities of Contracting States shall act expeditiously in proceedings for the return of children.

If the judicial or administrative authority concerned has not reached a decision within six weeks from the date of commencement of the proceedings, the applicant or the Central Authority of the requested State, on its own initiative or if asked by the Central Authority of the requesting State, shall have the right to request a statement of the reasons for the delay. If a reply is received by the Central Authority of the requested State, that Authority shall transmit the reply to the Central Authority of the requesting State, or to the applicant, as the case may be.

Article 12

Where a child has been wrongfully removed or retained in terms of Article 3 and, at the date of the commencement of the proceedings before the judicial or administrative authority of the Contracting State where the child is, a period of less than one year has elapsed from the date of the wrongful removal or retention, the authority concerned shall order the return of the child forthwith.

The judicial or administrative authority, even where the proceedings have been commenced after the expiration of the period of one year referred to in the preceding paragraph, shall also order the return of the child, unless it is demonstrated that the child is now settled in its new environment.

Where the judicial or administrative authority in the requested State has reason to believe that the child has been taken to another State, it may stay the proceedings or dismiss the application for the return of the child.

Article 13

Notwithstanding the provisions of the preceding Article, the judicial or administrative authority of the requested State is not bound to order the return of the child if the person, institution or other body which opposes its return establishes that—

(a) the person, institution or other body having the care of the person of the child was not actually exercising the custody rights at the time of removal or retention, or had consented to or subsequently acquiesced in the removal or retention; or

(b) there is a grave risk that his or her return would expose the child to physical or psychological harm or otherwise place the child in an intolerable situation.

The judicial or administrative authority may also refuse to order the return of the child if it finds that the child objects to being returned and has attained an age and degree of maturity at which it is appropriate to take account of its views.

In considering the circumstances referred to in this Article, the judicial and administrative authorities shall take into account the information relating to the social background of the child provided by the Central Authority or other competent authority of the child's habitual residence.

Article 14

In ascertaining whether there has been a wrongful removal or retention within the meaning of Article 3, the judicial or administrative authorities of the requested State may take notice directly of the law of, and of judicial or administrative decisions, formally recognised or not in the State of the habitual residence of the child, without recourse to the specific procedures for the proof of that law or for the recognition of foreign decisions which would otherwise be applicable.

Article 15

The judicial or administrative authorities of a Contracting State may, prior to the making of an order for the return of the child, request that the applicant obtain from the authorities of the State of the habitual residence of the child a decision or other determination that the removal or retention was wrongful within the meaning of Article 3 of the Convention, where such a decision or determination may be obtained in that State. The Central Authorities of the Contracting States shall so far as practicable assist applicants to obtain such a decision or determination.

Article 16

After receiving notice of a wrongful removal or retention of a child in the sense of Article 3, the judicial or administrative authorities of the Contracting State to which the child has been removed or in which it has been retained shall not decide on the merits of rights of custody until it has been determined that the child is not to be returned under this Convention or unless an application under this Convention is not lodged within a reasonable time following receipt of the notice.

Article 17

The sole fact that a decision relating to custody has been given in or is entitled to recognition in the requested State shall not be a ground for refusing to return a child under this Convention, but the judicial or administrative authorities of the requested State may take account of the reasons for that decision in applying this Convention.

Article 18

The provisions of this Chapter do not limit the power of a judicial or administrative authority to order the return of the child at any time.

Article 19

A decision under this Convention concerning the return of the child shall not be taken to be a determination on the merits of any custody issue.

Article 20

The return of the child under the provisions of Article 12 may be refused if this would not be permitted by the fundamental principles of the requested State relating to the protection of human rights and fundamental freedoms.

CHAPTER V—GENERAL PROVISIONS

Article 31

In relation to a State which in matters of custody of children has two or more systems of law applicable in different territorial units—

(a) any reference to habitual residence in that State shall be construed as referring to habitual residence in a territorial unit of that State;

(b) any reference to the law of the State of habitual residence shall be construed as referring to the law of the territorial unit in that State where the child habitually resides.

NOTE

These two conventions are both concerned with the enforcement in one country of rights to the custody of a child existing in another country. However, they differ as to their scope and effect. They are also at different stages of acceptability to the government. The Council of Europe Convention was signed in 1980 by the United Kingdom (along with 14 other states, of which France, Luxembourg, Portugal and Switzerland have since ratified) but has not yet been ratified, whilst active consideration is now being given to whether the Hague Convention is acceptable in this country and should, therefore, be signed and ultimately ratified. The Hague Convention has, so far, been signed by 7 member states, and has been ratified by Canada, France, Switzerland and Portugal.

The Council of Europe Convention[20] deals with the recognition and enforcement in one contracting state of a custody order in relation to a child under the age of 16 obtained in another contracting state. Each state has to establish a central authority to handle applications for the recognition and enforcement of custody orders. If someone wants an order enforced in another country, an application is made to any central authority, not necessarily that of the country where the child is believed to be, and the application is then passed to the central authority in that country. It is then the duty of the central authority to whom the application is eventually passed without delay to discover the whereabouts of the child, to secure the enforcement of the foreign custody order and then to secure the delivery of the child to the applicant (art 5). The Council of Europe Convention rules on recognition and enforcement of foreign custody orders fall into two kinds—namely where the child has, or has not, been improperly removed (ie, removed across an international frontier in breach of an enforceable custody order given in a contracting state: art 1 (d)). If the removal is improper, then the contracting state to which application is made for the enforcement of the order must cause steps to be taken *forthwith* for the return of the child provided that the child and its parents were all nationals of, and the child was habitually resident in, the state whose order is sought to be enforced and provided that the application is made within six months of the improper removal (art 8 (1)). No grounds for refusing enforcement are provided in such a case. In other cases of improper removal, there is a limited number of grounds on which enforcement may be refused (art 9). If the removal is not improper but enforcement of the order is sought in a state other than that which granted it, then enforcement may be refused

20 See Jones, (1980) 30 ICLQ 467.

not only on the grounds listed in article 9 but also on a wider range of grounds listed in article 10. In fact the United Kingdom has exercised the power of reservation under article 17 to apply the welfare of the child principle and the other grounds listed in article 10 (1) as grounds for denying enforcement in cases of improper removal falling under both articles 8 and 9.

In summary, the Council of Europe Convention is limited to the recognition of custody *orders*, but it applies (with differing effects) whether or not the removal from one country to another was improper and there is no general time limit on enforcement of foreign orders. The convention is limited, in the first instance, to those states which are members of the Council of Europe, ie European states, with a fairly generous geographical interpretation of Europe. The power to extend the convention to non-member states of the Council of Europe is somewhat limited.

The Hague Convention[1] is both more limited and wider in scope than the Council of Europe Convention. It is more limited in that it applies only to cases of the wrongful removal of a child under the age of 16 habitually resident in a contracting state, but removal is wrongful (under article 3) not only if it is in breach of a custody order but also, and this is the wider aspect of the convention, if though there was no foreign order, the removal was in breach of custody rights in the country of the child's habitual residence. The machinery of the Hague Convention is similar to that of the Council of Europe Convention in that applications for the return of the child are to be made through central authorities established in each contracting state. There is a clear desire expressed in the Hague Convention that the return of the child should be speedy. For example, under article 12, if the child has been in the state to which application for his return is made for less than a year, the child must be returned *forthwith*. As in the Council of Europe Convention, there are a number of grounds on which return of the child may be refused (arts 13, 20) but they are more narrowly cast than those in the Council of Europe Convention, even in relation to improper removal under that convention. One of the issues for consideration in determining the acceptability of the Hague Convention will be whether the right balance has been struck between the desirability of ensuring the prompt return of a child who has been wrongfully removed and of ensuring that such a return would not cause greater harm or injustice. It is the narrowness of the grounds for refusal of enforcement on which attention is likely to be concentrated, especially bearing in mind the United Kingdom's decision to apply the welfare of the child principle to cases of improper removal under the Council of Europe Convention.

The Hague Convention has a broader potential geographical scope in that the 30 member states of the Hague Conference on Private International Law are drawn from all over the world, and are not just limited to Europe. It is also possible for any other state to accede to the convention but only in relation to those contracting states which accept the accession (art 38). It will have been seen that the focus of the two conventions is different. The Council of Europe Convention is concerned with the recognition of all foreign custody orders, whether or not improper removal is involved; the Hague Convention is concerned with the restoration of children who have been wrongfully removed, whether or not in breach of a foreign custody order. Some countries, such as the United Kingdom, are members of both the Council of Europe and of the Hague Conference and this raises the question whether both conventions should be implemented in this country. Although there is a danger of confusion, complexity and uncertainty in a proliferation of international instruments governing one area of law, as is illustrated by the rules relating to the recognition of foreign maintenance orders (pp 345–358 above),[2] the need for a wide degree of mutual international recognition of custody orders is a powerful argument for the United Kingdom accepting and implementing both these child custody conventions.

1 Anton, (1980) 30 ICLQ 536.
2 North, (1981) 6 Dalhousie LJ 417 at 438–441.

CHAPTER 13

Legitimacy, Legitimation, and Adoption

Section A. Legitimacy

Matrimonial Causes Act 1973

45.—(1) Any person who is a British subject,[1] or whose right to be deemed a British subject depends wholly or in part on his legitimacy or on the validity of any marriage, may, if he is domiciled in England and Wales or in Northern Ireland or claims any real or personal estate situate in England and Wales, apply by petition to the High Court for a decree declaring that he is the legitimate child of his parents, or that the marriage of his father and mother or of his grandfather and grandmother was a valid marriage or that his own marriage was a valid marriage.

(5) Applications to the High Court under the preceding provisions of this section may be included in the same petition, and on any application under the preceding provisions of this section the High Court or, as the case may be, the county court shall make such decree as it thinks just, and the decree shall be binding on Her Majesty and all other persons whatsoever, so however that the decree shall not prejudice any person—

(a) if it is subsequently proved to have been obtained by fraud or collusion; or

(b) unless that person has been given notice of the application in the manner prescribed by rules of court or made a party to the proceedings or claims through a person so given notice or made a party.

(6) A copy of every application under this section and of any affidavit accompanying it shall be delivered to the Attorney-General at least one month before the application is made, and the Attorney-General shall be a respondent on the hearing of the application and on any subsequent proceedings relating thereto.

(7) Where any application is made under this section, such persons as the court hearing the application thinks fit shall, subject to rules of court, be given notice of the application in the manner prescribed by rules of court, and any such persons may be permitted to become parties to the proceedings and to oppose the application.

---

1 This now means a Commonwealth citizen: see British Nationality Act 1981, s 51 (1) (b). For the meaning of Commonwealth citizen, see s 37 (1) (*Ed*).

A child not born or conceived in lawful wedlock (that is, a marriage valid by English conflict of laws rules) is in general illegitimate in England.

Brook v Brook [1861] 9 HLCas 193, 4 LT 93; p 232 above.

Shaw v Gould (1868) LR 3 HL 55, 37 LJCh 433 (House of Lords)

Appeal from a decision of Kindersley V-C.

John Wilson by his will dated 27 February 1832 bequeathed his personal estate upon certain trusts for the benefit of the child, children, or issue of his great-niece Elizabeth Hickson and devised his real estate to the first and other sons of the body of his said great-niece lawfully begotten. The testator died in 1835 domiciled in England.

On 10 June 1828 Elizabeth Hickson, being then about 16 years of age and domiciled in England, was induced by the fraud of a person named Buxton, also domiciled in England, to contract a marriage with him. The marriage was never consummated, and for his fraudful act Buxton was indicted, and convicted, and sentenced to three years' imprisonment. No formal dissolution of this fraudulently procured marriage ever took place in England.

In November 1844 Buxton was induced for a pecuniary consideration to go to Scotland so that Elizabeth Hickson, or Buxton, could divorce him. A suit was begun in the Court of Session in November 1845, and that court pronounced a decree of divorce in March 1846 on the ground of Buxton's adultery. Buxton thereupon returned to England.

In June 1846 Elizabeth Hickson went through a ceremony of marriage in Scotland with John Shaw, who was domiciled in Scotland. There were three children of that marriage, the present appellants. John Shaw died in 1852 (a few months after the death of Buxton). Mrs Shaw died in 1863.

In 1865 the appellants petitioned for maintenance out of the trust funds, which had been paid into court under the Trustee Relief Act 1859. The respondents, claiming to be interested in these funds in case the appellants should be declared not entitled to them, presented a cross-petition alleging that the appellants were not the children lawfully begotten of Elizabeth Hickson, because she still continued the wife of Buxton, the divorce from him having been obtained by collusion, and being in itself invalid for the purpose of dissolving an English marriage.

Kindersley V-C made an order refusing the petition of the appellants, and directing that the funds in court should be applied for the benefit of the respondents. That was the order appealed against.

Lord Cranworth: My Lords, the question to be decided in this case is one of a class which not unfrequently gives rise to great difficulties—the question, namely, how far the status of legitimacy or illegitimacy attaching on a subject of this country may or ought to be modified by the laws of another country. There is no dispute as to the facts material for the decision of this case:—[His Lordship stated them.]

If the law of Scotland on the subject of marriage and divorce was the same as that of England, the case would not have admitted of doubt. As Elizabeth Hickson was married to Thomas Buxton in 1828, and as she gave birth to three children during his lifetime, those children must, by the law of

England, supposing that law alone to be in question, either be his children or be bastards. The former conclusion is that which in bygone days would possibly have been adopted, so reluctant were the courts to receive any evidence of non-access by the husband while he was intra quatuor maria. Adopting, however, the more reasonable views on this subject by which the courts of this country are now guided, we may safely act on the hypothesis adopted by all parties in the argument of the case, that the children of Elizabeth are either her lawful children by John Shaw, or are illegitimate. That they are illegitimate, if we are to look only to the laws of England, is certain; for ex hypothesi they are not the children of Buxton, who was the husband of Elizabeth when they were born. This, therefore, brings us to consider whether, in order to help us in deciding this question, we are warranted in looking at any other law than that of England—whether we may to any extent be guided by the law of Scotland.

If the parties in this case had been Scotch, and not English, and if all which occurred had occurred not in England but in Scotland, there would, I presume, have been no question on the subject. If Thomas Buxton, being a domiciled Scotchman, had married in Edinburgh, Elizabeth Hickson, being a domiciled Scotchwoman, and afterwards, while their Scotch domicile continued, she had obtained a decree of divorce in the Court of Session, and then had married John Shaw, the issue of that marriage would certainly have been legitimate. The argument of the appellants is, that the consequence must be the same, though the parties were at the time of the first marriage domiciled in England, and were married there. The question, it is contended, is whether, when the second marriage was contracted, the parties to it had the capacity to contract marriage; in other words, whether the effect of the divorce was to enable them to enter into a valid contract of marriage, which, but for the divorce, they certainly could not have entered into. The whole, therefore, turns on the validity of the divorce. Now, the law of Scotland seems clear that a residence in Scotland for forty days makes that country the domicilium fori of any person so residing in the country, in which, for the purposes of litigation, he is to be treated as being domiciled. And it is assumed that this is true whatever be the nature of the litigation; that it holds equally in cases the decision in which may involve the personal status of those who may claim through the litigant parties; as also where it is a mere dispute between the litigant parties themselves. Taking this, however, to be the undoubted law of Scotland, the question is, whether that principle is one which this country is bound to recognise. I think it is not.

The facts of this case do not raise the question as to what would have been the status of these children if Buxton and Elizabeth Hickson, though married at Manchester, had always been Scotch persons, and had always lived in Scotland; or even what it would have been if, before the proceedings for the divorce, Buxton had actually bona fide quitted England permanently, and established himself in Scotland, so as to have acquired a Scotch domicile for all intents and purposes. It may be that in these circumstances the courts of this country would recognise the status of these children, so as to entitle them, after the death of their mother, to the fund given to her children; which, no doubt, must be construed as meaning her legitimate children. But on that point I express no opinion. The decision in *Doe v Vardill*,[2] though the

---

2 *Birtwhistle v Vardill* (1840) 7 Cl & Fin 895, 6 Bing NC 385.

case did not turn on any question depending on the validity of a divorce, yet rests on principles hardly, to my mind, distinguishable from it; and it may certainly be assumed that these children could not, in any circumstances, claim real estate in England by descent. But the opinions of the judges in that case, and of the noble Lords who spoke in the House, left untouched the question of legitimacy, except so far as it was connected with succession to real estate. I think they inclined to the opinion that for purposes other than succession to real estate, for purposes unaffected by the Statute of Merton, the law of the domicile would decide the question of status. No such decision was come to, for no question arose except in relation to heirship to real estate. But the opinions given in the case seem to me to shew a strong bias towards the doctrine that the question of status must, for all purposes unaffected by the feudal law, as adopted and acted on in this country, be decided by the law of the domicile. Even, however, if that had been expressly so decided, it would not affect this case. The domicile to produce that result must be a bona fide domicile for all purposes, not, that which alone existed in this case, a mere residence of forty days, so as to give jurisdiction to the Scotch courts.

The important differences on the subject of marriage and divorce which exist in the different parts of the United Kingdom often give rise to perplexing difficulties, and exhibit a state of our law little creditable to us. But these difficulties make it more than usually incumbent on those who have to administer the law to take care that wherever a clear line has been drawn by judicial decision the course which it has marked out should be rigidly followed. Now, whatever be the difficulties in such cases as the present, I think the doctrine that no divorce in Scotland resting merely on a forum domicilii had, at all events before the passing of our English Divorce Act in 1857, any effect in England on the validity of an English marriage, is established on the highest authority.

It is impossible to have a stronger authority for this than the case of *Lolley*,[3] for it was decided there by the twelve judges that by the second marriage he was guilty of bigamy, though on general principles every leaning in a criminal case would be in favour of the party accused.

That case was followed by Dr Lushington in *Conway v Beazley*.[4] There, as in the present case, the second marriage was had in Scotland, not, as in *Lolley's* case, in England; and it was attempted on that ground to distinguish the two cases. But Dr Lushington held that the principle was the same wherever the second marriage was solemnised, for that as neither of the parties to the first marriage had been, at any time, bona fide domiciled in Scotland the principle of *Lolley's* case must prevail.

The same question arose in this House in *Dolphin v Robins*.[5] The case was very fully considered, and the conclusion at which your Lordships arrived unanimously was, that the Scotch courts have no power to dissolve an English marriage where the parties are not really domiciled in Scotland, but have only gone there for such a time as, according to the doctrine of the Scotch courts, gives them jurisdiction in the matter.

These cases clearly decide the one now before the House, for if the first

3 *R v Lolley* (1812) 2 Cl & Fin 567, n, Russ & Ry 237.
4 (1831) 3 Hag Ecc 639.
5 (1859) 7 HLCas 390, 29 LJP & M11.

marriage here was not dissolved there could not have been a second marriage. Till the first was dissolved there was no capacity to contract a second. If after the second marriage Buxton and Elizabeth had again cohabited, and there had been an issue, that issue would certainly have been legitimate by the law of England, and it cannot be argued that the issue of both unions could share together.

The view which I take of this case relieves me from the necessity of considering whether the resort to Scotland for the purpose of the divorce, and the arrangements made among the parties for bringing about that object, were or were not of such a character as to taint the whole of the proceedings with fraud; I am not at all satisfied that they were, but I am glad to be relieved from the necessity of deciding on such a ground.

There is only one further observation which I desire to make; it is this: In saying that the Scotch courts have no power to dissolve an English marriage where the parties have only gone to Scotland for the purpose of obtaining there a domicilium fori, I do not mean to express any opinion as to what might be the effect of a divorce so obtained considered merely as a Scotch question. In the anomalous state of our laws relating to marriage and divorce, it may be that such a proceeding may be valid to the north of the Tweed, but invalid to the south. And I am painfully sensible of the inconveniences which may result from such a state of the law. But it must be for the legislature to set it right. The authorities seem to me to shew clearly that whatever may be the just decision of the Scotch courts in such a case as the present, on this subject of divorce according to Scotch law, it is one in which this country cannot admit any right in them to interfere with the inviolability of an English marriage, or with any of its incidents. To do so would be to allow a prejudice to English law to be created by the decisions of what, for this purpose, we must call a foreign law, thus going beyond what any country is called on to do.

On these short grounds I am of opinion that there was no foundation for this appeal, and I move your Lordships that it may be dismissed.

Lord Chelmsford: Whether the appellants answer the description respectively of 'sons lawfully begotten' and of 'children', depends upon whether their parents were lawfully married; and this again depends upon the effect of a divorce in Scotland dissolving the marriage of their mother with Thomas Buxton in England. (His Lordship proceeded to hold that the divorce was invalid in England, and therefore that the appellants were illegitimate and could not take under the will.)

Lords Westbury and Colonsay delivered judgments to the same effect.
Appeal dismissed.

But a child may be legitimate in England if it is legitimate by the law of the domicile of each of its parents at the date of its birth.

Re Bischoffsheim [1948] Ch 79, [1947] 2 All ER 830 (Chancery Division)

Henri Louis Bischoffsheim by his will, dated 26 August 1903, devised and bequeathed his residuary real and personal estate to his trustees on the usual trusts for sale, conversion, and investment. He directed his trustees to hold a share of his residuary estate (subject to certain prior interests) upon trust for his granddaughter Nesta Pamela Fitzgerald for life, with remainder to such of her child or children as being male should attain the age of twenty-one years or being female should attain that age or marry.

The testator died on 11 March 1908. On 30 April 1908 his granddaughter, Nesta Pamela Fitzgerald, married Lord Richard Wellesley. There were two children of that marriage, namely, the first and second defendants. On 29 October 1914 Lord Richard Wellesley was killed in action. On 12 March 1917 Nesta Pamela Wellesley married in New York, Lord George Wellesley, the brother of her first husband. There was one child of this marriage, namely, the third defendant, Richard Wellesley. Nesta Pamela Wellesley died on 21 February 1946.

The domicile of origin of Nesta Pamela Wellesley and of Lord George Wellesley was English. Accordingly, in 1917, a marriage between them in this country would have been void under the Marriage Act 1835. It was their intention, however, prior to their marriage to acquire a domicile of choice in the State of New York, where their marriage would have been valid. It was questioneed whether in fact they had succeeded in establishing such a domicile of choice at the date of the marriage but it was not disputed that they had established a domicile of choice in the State of New York in 1920, at the date when the third defendant, Richard Wellesley, was born.

This summons was taken out by the trustees of the testator's will for the determination of the question whether the defendant Richard Wellesley was entitled to share as a child of Nesta Pamela Wellesley in the share of the testator's residuary estate settled by his will on her for life, with remainder to her children.

Romer J: The domicile of origin both of Lord George Wellesley and his wife was English, and by the law of England a marriage between them would have been void under the Marriage Act 1835. Such a marriage was, on the other hand, unimpeachable by the law of New York, and the evidence plainly discloses that it was the definite aim both of Lord George and his bride to relinquish their domicile of origin and acquire an American domicile of choice before the marriage was celebrated. Whether or not they succeeded in doing so was one of the subjects discussed before me. Whatever be the truth of that matter, however, it was fairly and rightly conceded by Mr Gray, on behalf of the first two defendants, that Lord George and his wife had unquestionably acquired a domicile of choice in New York by the time that their son was born there in June 1920. From this fact sprang a different way of founding Mr Richard Wellesley's claim to share in the testator's estate, and I propose to consider this aspect of the matter first.

The argument on his behalf was briefly as follows: Admitting that only a legitimate child could take under the gift to Nesta Pamela Fitzgerald's children, legitimacy is a question of status. That status is conferred or withheld, as the case may be, by the law of the domicile of origin, which is the law of the domicile of the parents at the time when the person whose legitimacy is in question was born. The status, once conferred, remains with the person concerned throughout his or her life and will be recognised and given effect to by our courts, save only in cases where that person claims to succeed to real estate in England. It is established by the evidence that

Richard Wellesley received at birth the status of legitimacy by the law of New York and accordingly, it was contended, his claim, as a child of his parents, to a fund of English personalty will be recognised by the courts of this country.

There can be no doubt as to the general criterion of a person's legitimacy. 'In most cases', said Lord Brougham in *Fenton v Livingstone*,[6] 'the legitimacy of a party is to be determined by the law of his birthplace and of his parents' domicile.' Richard Wellesley undoubtedly received at birth the status of legitimacy from the law of his domicile of origin, and such status is, in general, accorded international recognition. It is said, however, on behalf of the first and second defendants, that our courts will not accord universal recognition to a status of legitimacy conferred by a foreign domicile of origin. The acceptance by our law of the status so conferred is, it is contended, subject to exceptions: and the particular exception relied on in the present case is this: that an English court will not recognise as legitimate the child of a marriage which is incestuous, or which is otherwise contrary to religion or sound morality, notwithstanding that the child is legitimate according to the law of his domicile at birth. In such cases, it is said, our courts are not content to act merely on the fact that the status of legitimacy was bestowed by the law of the birthplace; they will, on the contrary, fasten their attention on the marriage of the parents and, finding that incestuous, treat the issue as bastards here, however full the measure of legitimacy that may be conferred upon them in the foreign land of their birth.

So far, at all events, as a court of first instance is concerned, I am of opinion that on the authorities, and especially having regard to the majority judgments in *Re Goodman's Trusts*,[7] the contentions which were advanced on behalf of Richard Wellesley, and which I have already summarised, must prevail.

(His Lordship discussed the cases of *Re Goodman's Trusts* and *Re Andros*[8] and continued:) It is quite clear that in *Re Goodman's Trusts* both Cotton and James LJJ recognised only one exception to the general rule that the question of legitimacy or illegitimacy is to be decided exclusively by the law of the domicile of origin; and that exception relates to claims to succession to real estate (a term which would, of course, include titles of honour and dignity) in England. That, also, was the only exception referred to by Kay J in *Re Andros*. I was referred to no authority which, in my judgment, compels me to entertain the further exception which was contended for in the present case. In *Fenton v Livingstone* the House of Lords held that a person born of an English marriage between a man and his deceased wife's sister was not legitimate in Scotland as to the succession of real estate. Lord Brougham said 'Now it must be granted that the general rule is to determine the validity of a marriage by the law of the country where the parties were domiciled, and in most cases the legitimacy of a party is to be determined by the law of his birthplace and of his parents' domicile. But to this application of the lex loci contractus there are exceptions, from the nature of the case in which the question arises'. It is true that Lord Brougham there uses the word 'exceptions' in the plural. He proceeds, however: 'Thus, in deciding upon the

6 (1859) 3 Macq 497 at 532.
7 (1881) 17 Ch D 266, 50 LJCh 425; p 412 below.
8 (1883) 24 Ch D 637, 52 LJCh 793.

title to real estate, the lex loci rei sitae must always prevail', and then discusses the principles on which that exception is founded. The noble Lord did not, however, in the course of his speech, refer to any other exception to the general rule apart from claims to real estate. The other speeches in *Fenton v Livingstone* were consonant with the views expressed by Cotton and James LJJ in *Re Goodman's Trusts*, except that Lord Chelmsford did not wish to commit himself without further consideration. 'It seems to have been assumed', he said, 'throughout the argument before your Lordships, that if the claim in this case had been to movable property, the respondent would have succeeded; but I am not disposed, without further consideration, to concede that if the marriage is regarded in Scotland as an incestuous marriage, and it had become necessary, in order to make out the title to be next of kin, to prove such a marriage, that result would have followed. It is, however, unnecessary to consider that question, as we are dealing with a different description of property'. At what conclusion Lord Chelmsford would have arrived on this question had he given it further consideration, I cannot, of course, say. But in *Re Goodman's Trusts* the matter was amply considered by the Court of Appeal, to whom *Fenton v Livingstone* was cited. The case of *Brook v Brook*[9] does not really bear on the point which I am now considering. The question before the House was (as stated by Lord Wensleydale) whether a marriage celebrated in 1850 in Denmark between a widower and the sister of his deceased wife, both being then, and subsequently, British subjects domiciled in England, and contemplating England as their future matrimonial residence, was valid in England, such a marriage being permitted by the law of Denmark. The right of the children of that marriage to succeed to property (apparently consisting of, or at least including, real estate in England (per Lord St Leonards)), was in issue, but obviously their case could not be, nor was it, founded upon a status of legitimacy conferred upon them by a foreign domicile of origin, for their domicile at birth was English. Their right to succeed to property here, in the capacity of children of their parents, accordingly depended, and depended solely, on their being able to establish the validity of their parents' Danish marriage, and in this attempt they failed.

I should next, I think, refer to the much debated case of *Shaw v Gould*.[10] (After stating the facts in that case his Lordship continued:) The case came before Kindersley V-C, and he dismissed the children's claim. He held that at the time of the Scottish divorce (which was some eleven years prior to the passing of the Divorce Act 1857), the marriage between Buxton and Elizabeth Hickson was not only indissoluble by an English court but was indissoluble by any court at all; and that accordingly the Scottish decree was wholly inoperative to bring that marriage to an end. He also considered and rejected an alternative argument advanced on their behalf that they were entitled at all events to be treated under the law of Scotland as legitimate children of a putative marriage. When the case came before the House of Lords on appeal, the main point which was argued and debated was as to the validity of the Scottish proceedings and decree. 'The whole', said Lord Cranworth,[11] 'turns on the validity of the divorce'. He held that it was

9 (1861) 9 HLCas 193, 4 LT 93; p 232 above.
10 (1868) LR 3 HL 55, 37 LJCh 433; p 401 above.
11 P 402 above.

invalid on the ground that Buxton was a domiciled Englishman at the time of the divorce, and that accordingly the Court of Session had no jurisdiction to grant it. Lord Chelmsford also addressed himself primarily (for he also considered the 'putative marriage' point, which is irrelevant for present purposes) to inquiring into the validity of the proceedings in Scotland.[12] 'Whether', he said, 'the appellants answer the descriptions respectively of "sons lawfully begotten", and of "children", depends upon whether their parents were lawfully married; and this again depends upon the effect of a divorce in Scotland dissolving the marriage of their mother with Thomas Buxton in England.' . . . Lord Colonsay, with some reluctance, accepted the view that the validity of the divorce was a relevant subject for inquiry, notwithstanding that the legitimacy of the appellants might be recognised in the land of their birth. The other noble Lords, however, expressed no views of their own on this aspect of the matter. They approached the case, as also had Kindersley V-C, on the footing that the legitimacy of the appellants depended on the validity of their parents' marriage, which, in its turn, depended on the validity of the Scottish divorce. If the validity of the divorce was regarded as a legitimate subject for inquiry, and if it was invalid, as the Lords held it to be, it necessarily followed as a result of those considerations, when taken by themselves, that the appellants' domicile of origin was English, as their mother's domicile remained that of her lawful husband, Buxton. Accordingly, on the sequence of reasoning which was adopted by the House in their approach to the case as a whole, a claim founded on international acceptance of a status conferred by what was certainly the domicile of origin, if the validity of the divorce was disregarded as irrelevant, namely: by the law of Scotland, could not succeed or, indeed, arise; it was, so to speak, stillborn. It is not altogether surprising that, having regard to the very peculiar circumstances of the case, and to the fact that the important Divorce Act of 1857 had so recently been passed, the attention of the Lords (except, perhaps, Lord Colonsay) was attracted primarily to a consideration of the proceedings in Scotland. These proceedings were clearly relevant to the question whether John Shaw and Elizabeth were lawfully married, but this was not the question before the House; the point in issue was not as to the status of the parents but as to the status of the children, and that, as it seems to me, gave rise to different considerations. The relevance of the Scottish proceedings and of the decree which resulted therefrom appears to me to have been a matter rather of assumption by the House than one of direct decision. It is, however, to be noted that the claims under consideration were not confined to personal estate in England, for there was a claim to English real estate as well; and this may have had some effect on the line which was adopted both in the argument and in their Lordships' opinions.[13]

In view of the very special circumstances affecting *Shaw v Gould*, I do not

---

12 P 404 above.
13 Sed quaere. The rule in *Birtwhistle v Vardill* (1840) 7 Cl & Fin 895, 6 Bing NC 385, relates only to the case of descent of land upon an intestacy, and does not affect the case of a devise in a will to children': per Stirling J in *Re Grey's Trusts* [1892] 3 Ch 88 at 93. It was distinguished in *Re Goodman's Trusts* (p 412 below), emasculated by s 45 (1) of the Administration of Estates Act 1925 (which abolished descent to the heir in the case of fee simple estates), and finally abolished (in the case of deaths after 1 January 1976) by s 10 (4) of the Legitimacy Act 1976 (p 421 below) (*Ed*).

regard it as necessarily opposed to the majority view in *Re Goodman's Trusts*, nor did Cotton LJ so regard it. I accordingly propose to follow the view which prevailed in *Re Goodman's Trusts*, namely, that where succession to personal property depends on the legitimacy of the claimant, the status of legitimacy conferred on him by his domicile of origin (ie the domicile of his parents at his birth) will be recognised by our courts; and that, if that legitimacy be established, the validity of his parents' marriage should not be entertained as a relevant subject for investigation. It is true that in *Shaw v Gould* (as in the present case) the status in question was that of original legitimacy, whereas *Re Goodman's Trusts* and *Re Andros* were cases of legitimation (ie, original bastardy converted into legitimacy through the subsequent marriage of the parents) but, in my judgment, there is no real distinction between the two classes of case. If in fact the status of legitimacy is conferred by the law of the domicile of origin the time of, as also the reason for, its conferment are surely immaterial.

The conclusion which I have formed and expressed on the legitimacy at birth of Richard Wellesley relieves me of the necessity of inquiring into the domicile of his parents at the time of their marriage in New York. The question is one which is not altogether easy of solution, and I will express no concluded opinion on it.

I will declare, in answer to question 1 of the summons, that upon the true construction of the will of the testator, and in the events which have happened, the defendant Richard Wellesley is entitled to share as a child of Nesta Pamela Wellesley in the share of the residuary estate of the testator settled by his will on his granddaughter, Nesta Pamela Wellesley, for her life with remainder to her children.

QUESTIONS

1. Was Romer J justified in asserting that, according to the majority judgments in *Re Goodman's Trusts* (p 412 below), the question of legitimacy, whether original or acquired, is governed by the law of the child's domicile of origin? Suppose that before 1 January 1926 (when the Legitimacy Act 1926 came into operation) (a) a domiciled Englishman had an illegitimate child by a domiciled Dutch woman whom he subsequently married, or (b) a domiciled Dutchman had an illegitimate child by a domiciled English woman whom he subsequently married: (i) what would be the child's domicile of origin? (ii) would the child be legitimated by the subsequent marriage?

2. Was Romer J correct in assuming that a child's domicile of origin is the same as that of his parents at the date of his birth? What was the domicile of origin of the children in *Shaw v Gould* (p 401 above)?

3. Can the decision in *Re Bischoffsheim* be reconciled with *Shaw v Gould*? If so, how? Would the decision in *Shaw v Gould* have been different if Buxton had acquired a domicile in Scotland after the divorce but before the children were born?

4. Suppose that H, domiciled in Portugal, marries in England W, who is domiciled in England. They have a child C. The marriage is valid by English domestic law, but void by Portuguese law because H and W are first cousins. By Portuguese law C is illegitimate. What is his status in England?

Legitimacy Act 1976

1.—(1) The child of a void marriage, whenever born, shall, subject to subsection (2) below and Schedule 1 to this Act, be treated as the legitimate child of his parents if at the time of the act of intercourse resulting in the birth (or at the time of the celebration of the marriage if later) both or either of the parties reasonably believed that the marriage was valid.

(2) This section only applies where the father of the child was domiciled in England and Wales at the time of the birth or, if he died before the birth, was so domiciled immediately before his death.

10.—(1) 'void marriage' means a marriage, not being voidable only, in respect of which the High Court has or had jurisdiction to grant a decree of nullity, or would have or would have had such jurisdiction if the parties were domiciled in England and Wales.

SCHEDULE 1

3. Section 1 does not—
(a) affect any rights under the intestacy of a person who died before 29 October 1959, or
(b) affect the operation or construction of any disposition coming into operation before 29 October 1959 except so far as may be necessary to avoid the severance from a dignity or title of honour of property limited (expressly or not) to devolve (as nearly as the law permits) along with the dignity or title of honour.

4.—(1) Section 1 of this Act, so far as it affects the succession to a dignity or title of honour, or the devolution of property limited as aforesaid, only applies to children born after 28 October 1959.

(2) Apart from section 1, nothing in this Act shall affect the succession to any dignity or title of honour or render any person capable of succeeding to or transmitting a right to succeed to any such dignity or title.

(3) Apart from section 1, nothing in this Act shall affect the devolution of any property limited (expressly or not) to devolve (as nearly as the law permits) along with any dignity or title of honour.

This sub-paragraph applies only if and so far as a contrary intention is not expressed in the instrument, and shall have effect subject to the instrument.

5. It is hereby declared that nothing in this Act affects the Succession to the Throne.

Family Law Reform Act 1969

PART II

PROPERTY RIGHTS OF ILLEGITIMATE CHILDREN

14.—(1) Where either parent of an illegitimate child dies intestate as respects all or any of his or her real or personal property, the illegitimate child or, if he is dead, his issue, shall be entitled to take any interest therein to which he or such issue would have been entitled if he had been born legitimate.

(2) Where an illegitimate child dies intestate in respect of all or any of his real or personal property, each of his parents, if surviving, shall be entitled to take any interest therein to which that parent would have been entitled if the child had been born legitimate.

(3) In accordance with the foregoing provisions of this section, Part IV of the Administration of Estates Act 1925 (which deals with the distribution of the estate of an intestate) shall have effect as if—

(a) any reference to the issue of the intestate included a reference to any illegitimate child of his and to the issue of any such child;

(b) any reference to the child or children of the intestate included a reference to any illegitimate child or children of his; and

(c) in relation to an intestate who is an illegitimate child, any reference to the parent, parents, father or mother of the intestate were a reference to his natural parent, parents, father or mother.

(4) For the purposes of subsection (2) of this section and of the provisions amended by subsection (3)(c) thereof, an illegitimate child shall be presumed not to have been survived by his father unless the contrary is shown.

(5) This section does not apply to or affect the right of any person to take any entailed interest in real or personal property.

(8) In this section 'illegitimate child' does not include an illegitimate child who is—

(a) a legitimated person within the meaning of the said Act of 1926[14] or a person recognised by virtue of that Act or at common law as having been legitimated; or

(b) an adopted person under an adoption order made in any part of the United Kingdom, the Isle of Man or the Channel Islands or under an overseas adoption as defined in section 4(3) of the Adoption Act 1968.

(9) This section does not affect any rights under the intestacy of a person dying before the coming into force of this section.

15.—(1) In any disposition made after the coming into force of this section—

(a) any reference (whether express or implied) to the child or children of any person shall, unless the contrary intention appears, be construed as, or as including, a reference to any illegitimate child of that person; and

(b) any reference (whether express or implied) to a person or persons related in some other manner to any person shall, unless the contrary intention appears, be construed as, or as including, a reference to anyone who would be so related if he, or some other person through whom the relationship is deduced, had been born legitimate.

(2) The foregoing subsection applies only where the reference in question is to a person who is to benefit or to be capable of benefiting under the disposition or, for the purpose of designating such a person, to someone else to or through whom that person is related; but that subsection does not affect the construction of the word 'heir' or 'heirs' or of any expression which is used to create an entailed interest in real or personal property.

(7) There is hereby abolished, as respects dispositions made after the coming into force of this section, any rule of law that a disposition in favour of illegitimate children not in being when the disposition takes effect is void as contrary to public policy.

(8) In this section 'disposition' means a disposition, including an oral disposition, of real or personal property whether inter vivos or by will or codicil; and, notwithstanding any rule of law, a disposition made by will or

14 ie the Legitimacy Act 1926, now the Legitimacy Act 1976, p 420 below (*Ed*).

codicil executed before the date on which this section comes into force shall
not be treated for the purposes of this section as made on or after that date
by reason only that the will or codicil is confirmed by a codicil executed on
or after that date.

Section B: Legitimation

Matrimonial Causes Act 1973

45.—(2) Any person claiming that he or his parent or any remoter ancestor
became or has become a legitimated person may apply by petition to the
High Court, or may apply to a county court in the manner prescribed by
county court rules, for a decree declaring that he or his parent or remoter
ancestor, as the case may be, became or has become a legitimated person.

In this subsection 'legitimated person' means a person legitimated by the
Legitimacy Act 1926, and includes a person recognised under section 8 of
that Act[15] as legitimated.

(5) (6) (7) (see p 400 above).

*Legitimation by subsequent marriage is not recognised at common law unless the father is
domiciled both at the date of the child's birth and at the date of the subsequent marriage
in a country where the marriage legitimates the child.*

Re Goodman's Trusts [1881] 17 Ch D 266, 50 LJCh 425 (Court of Appeal)

This was an appeal by Hannah Pieret from a decision of Jessel MR
disallowing her claim as one of the next of kin of Rachel Goodman.

Rachel Goodman died unmarried in 1878, domiciled in England, and a
legacy given by her will having lapsed to her next of kin, was paid into
Court under the Trustee Relief Act, and the question for decision was who
were her next of kin at the time of her death.

It appeared that her sole next of kin were the children of her two deceased
brothers. One of these brothers, Leyon Goodman, had three illegitimate
children in England by Charlotte Smith, and in 1820 went to Holland with
the intention of permanently residing there. While in Amsterdam he had
another illegitimate child by Charlotte Smith, Hannah Pieret, the present
appellant. In 1822, while still in Amsterdam, he married Charlotte Smith,
and thereby the previously born children became legitimate according to the
law of Holland. They afterwards had another child, Anne Denis, who
claimed to be the only legitimate child according to the English law. The
Master of the Rolls decided that Hannah Pieret was illegitimate according to
English law, and she appealed from this decision.

James LJ: According to my view, the question as to what is the English law
as to an English child is entirely irrelevant. There is, of course, no doubt as
to what the English law as to an English child is. We have in this country

15 Now s 3 of the Legitimacy Act 1976, p 420 below (*Ed*).

from all time refused to recognise legitimation of issue by the subsequent marriage of the parents, and possibly our peculiarity in this respect may deserve all that was said in its favour by Professor, afterwards Mr Justice, Blackstone, the somewhat indiscriminate eulogist of every peculiarity and anomaly in our system of laws. But the question is, What is the rule which the English law adopts and applies to a non-English child? This is a question of international comity and international law. According to that law as recognised, and that comity as practised, in all other civilised communities, the status of a person, his legitimacy or illegitimacy, is to be determined everywhere by the law of the country of his origin—the law under which he was born. It appears to me that it would require a great force of argument derived from legal principles, or great weight of authority clear and distinct, to justify us in holding that our country stands in this respect aloof in barbarous insularity from the rest of the civilised world. On principle, it appears to me that every consideration goes strongly to shew, at least, that we ought not so to stand. The family relation is at the foundation of all society, and it would appear almost an axiom that the family relation, once duly constituted by the law of any civilised country, should be respected and acknowledged by every other member of the great community of nations. England has been for centuries a country of hospitality and commerce. It has opened its shores to thousands of political refugees and religious exiles, fleeing from their enemies and persecutors. It has opened its ports to merchants of the whole world, and has by wise laws induced and encouraged them to settle in our marts. But would it not be shocking if such a man, seeking a home in this country, with his family of legitimated children, should find that the English hospitality was as bad as the worst form of the persecution from which he had escaped, by destroying his family ties, by declaring that the relation of father and child no longer existed, that his rights and duties and powers as a father had ceased, that the child of his parental affection and fond pride, whom he had taught to love, honour, and obey him, for whom he had toiled and saved, was to be thenceforth, in contemplation of the law of his new country, a fatherless bastard? Take the case of a foreigner resident abroad, with such a child. If that child were abducted from his guardianship and brought to this country, can any one doubt that the courts of this country would recognise his parental right and guardianship, and order the child to be delivered to any person authorised by him? But suppose, instead of sending, he were to come himself to this country in person, would it be possible to hold that he would lose his right to the guardianship of the child in this country because of the historical or mythical legend that the English barons and earls many centuries ago cried out in Latin, Nolumus leges Angliae mutare? Can it be possible that a Dutch father, stepping on board a steamer at Rotterdam with his dear and lawful child, should on his arrival at the port of London find that the child had become a stranger in blood and in law, and a bastard, filius nullius?[16]

It may be suggested that that would not apply to a mere transient visit or a temporary commorancy, during which the foreign character of the visitor

16 After this famous purple patch, 'it is almost with a sense of anticlimax that one discovers that the only question on which the court was asked to pronounce was whether a girl who had been legitimated by the subsequent marriage of her parents in Holland could succeed to certain property as 'next of kin' on the intestacy of her English aunt' (Welsh, 63 LQR 65 at 77) (*Ed*).

and his family would be recognised, with all its incidents and consequences, but that it would only apply to a man electing to have a permanent English domicile. But what could, in that view, be more shocking than that a man, having such a family residing with him perhaps for years, in this country as his lawful family, recognised as such by every court in the kingdom, being minded at last to make this country his permanent domicile, should thereby bastardise his children; and that he could relegitimate them by another change of domicile from London to Edinburgh? And why should we on principle think it right to lay down a rule leading to such results? I protest that I can see no principle, no reason, no ground for this, except an insular vanity, inducing us to think that our law is so good and right, and every other system of law is naught, that we should reject every recognition of it as an unclean thing.

But it is not merely on principle, but on authority, to my mind conclusive, that this question ought to be determined in favour of the appellant. I will not go through the roll of authorities which the Lord Justice Cotton has cited. But I content myself with the one case of *Doe v Vardill*.[17] In that case we have the careful and elaborate judgment of the judges summoned to advise the House of Lords. And in that judgment, or advice, there are two distinct propositions clearly and distinctly enunciated. The first was that the claimant was for all purposes and to all intents legitimate. The second was that such legitimacy did not necessarily, and did not in fact in that case, include heirship to English land. The first proposition was accepted by the law lords without any doubt or question; the second was questioned. After further reference to the judges and further hearing, the case was at last determined in accordance with the second proposition. But the first proposition has never been really questioned. No doubt it may be said that the only decision was against the heirship in that case. But the weight of such an authority, particularly of advice tendered by the assembled judges to the House of Lords, is not affected by that consideration. It is the ratio decidendi, the rules, maxims, and principles of law which are to be found there, by which we are to guide ourselves. In fact, as is well known, the House has frequently put hypothetical states of fact, and abstract questions of law, for the advice and opinion of the judges, of which I recollect one notable instance in the *D'Este* case.[18] What the assembled judges said in *Doe v Vardill*, and what the Lords held, was, that the case of heirship to English land was a peculiar exception to the rights incident to that character and status of legitimacy, which was admitted by both judges and Lords to be the true character and status of the claimant. It was only an additional instance of the many anomalies which at that time affected the descent of land. Legitimate relationship in the first degree was of no avail if the claimant were an alien, or if he were of the half-blood, or in the direct ascending line, which, pace Professor Blackstone, were precious absurdities in the English law of real property. But in this particular case, the exception is, at all events, plausible. The English heirship, the descent of English land, required not only that the man should be legitimate, but as it were porphyro-genitus, born legitimate within the narrowest pale of English legitimacy. Heirship is an incident of land, depending on local law, the law of the country, the

17 *Birtwhistle v Vardill* (1840) 7 Cl & Fin 895, 6 Bing NC 385.
18 *Sussex Peerage Case* (1844) 11 Cl & Fin 85, 6 State Tr NS 79.

county, the manor, and even of the particular property itself, the forma doni.
Kinship is an incident of the person, and universal. It appears to me that a
statement of the law so given, and so accepted nearly fifty years ago, which
has been adopted without question by jurists as a correct statement of
English adhesion to the universal law and comity of nations, is not to be
questioned at this time by any tribunal short of the House of Lords, and I
should humbly think not by them. There is only one authority to the
contrary, the case of *Boyes v Bedale*,[19] on which I will say a few words. The
decision there was on the ground that, in an Englishman's will, the children
of a nephew must mean children who would be lawful children if they were
English children. That seems to me a violent presumption. It was an
accident in that case that the testator was an Englishman. But supposing it
had been the will of a Frenchman, dying domiciled in England, and made in
favour of his French relations and their children, or of his own children,
there being children legitimate and legitimated, what would have been said
of such a presumption and such a construction? In that case, by way of
obiter dictum, the learned Judge goes on to say that the same construction
would be applied to kindred under the Statute of Distributions. This point
was never argued and never considered, I believe, by counsel, and must, I
think, have been hastily uttered by the Vice-Chancellor at the close of an
oral judgment. It must be borne in mind that the Statute of Distributions is
not a statute for Englishmen only, but for all persons, whether English or
not, dying intestate and domiciled in England, and not for any Englishman
dying domiciled abroad. And it was to provide for what was thought an
equitable distribution of the assets, as to which a man had, through
inadvertence, not expressed his testamentary intentions. And, as the law
applies universally to persons of all countries, races, and religions
whatsoever, the proper law to be applied in determining kindred is the
universal law, the international law, adopted by the comity of states. The
child of a man would be his child so ascertained and so determined, and, in
the next degree, the lawful child of his brother or sister would be his nephew
or niece.

The real importance of the case of *Dalrymple v Dalrymple*[20] has not been
sufficiently appreciated. There must have been hundreds of cases in which a
Scotchman or a foreigner with legitimated children, or other kindred, elected
to domicile himself for business, or health, or pleasure, in London or
elsewhere in England. Can it be doubted that the English Court of Probate,
of whose conception of the law the case of *Dalrymple v Dalrymple* is an
authoritative exponent, would, without question, have admitted the right of
some child or next of kin to take out administration? And if such right had
ever been questioned, would not the fact of such a question, viz, whether a
man by changing his domicile had bastardised his child, have created a
sensation which would have vibrated throughout the civilised world,
wherever there was a writer on international law and comity? The fact that
no such case is to be found shews the universal consensus of all persons
conversant with the Court of Probate's administration (the appropriate
court in that behalf) that no such question in fact existed.

That consensus goes back not only to the year in which the judgment in

19 (1863) 1 Hem & M 798, 3 New Rep 290.
20 (1811) 2 Hag Con 54.

Dalrymple v Dalrymple was pronounced, 1811, but to the furthest limit to which the knowledge and experience of the learned judge who pronounced it extended. Moreover, if such a question had ever been raised in the distribution of assets by the Court of Chancery, the Chief Baron Alexander must, in his long experience in that court, have been aware of it, and would not have omitted to refer to it in the advice which, on behalf of the judges, he tendered to the House of Lords.

Cotton LJ delivered judgment to the same effect. Lush LJ dissented.
Appeal allowed.

The same rule applies at common law to other modes of legitimation, eg by parental recognition.

Re Luck's Settlement Trusts [1940] Ch 864, [1940] 3 All ER 307
(Court of Appeal)

Appeal from Farwell J.

Under the marriage settlement and will of a testator domiciled at all material times in England, investments were held by trustees upon trust for Frederick Charles Luck for life and after his death for his children in equal shares, provided in the case of the marriage settlement that they were born within twenty-one years after the decease of the survivor of the testator and his wife. The settlement was made in 1867, the testator's wife died in 1892 and the testator died in 1896.

In 1893 Frederick Charles Luck, whose domicile of origin was English, married his first wife and had two children by her. In 1905 he left them and went to the United States of America. From 1905 till 1918 one Martha Croft lived with him as his wife and in 1906 she bore him a son in California, David Luck.

In 1922 Frederick Luck's first marriage was dissolved by a Californian court and he married Alma Hyam. There was no issue of this marriage. In 1925 he made a declaration in writing publicly acknowledging David Luck as his child. The effect of this was that by s 230 of the Californian Civil Code, David Luck became the legitimate son of his father as from the date of his birth.

David Luck having claimed to be entitled to share in the trust funds settled by the marriage settlement and will, the trustees thereof took out a summons to determine whether he was so entitled.

Farwell J found that Frederick Luck acquired a domicile of choice in California some time after 1906 (the date of David's birth) and before 1925 (the date of the declaration of recognition). The Court of Appeal agreed with this finding. There was no evidence as to the domicile of Martha Croft, but the Court of Appeal assumed that her domicile of origin was English and that she had acquired a domicile of choice in California some time between 1906 and 1925.

Farwell J held that David Luck was legitimate and was entitled to share in the trust funds, although his father was not domiciled in California when David Luck was born. The two children of Frederick Charles Luck by his first marriage appealed.

Luxmoore LJ read the judgment of himself and Lord Greene MR prepared by Lord Greene: ...Apart from the principles of private international law which form part of the law of England, that law did not recognise legitimation of a child born illegitimate until the passing of the Legitimacy Act 1926. In this respect the law of England differed from the civil and the canon law and from the law of Scotland and that of many continental countries all of which recognised one particular form—and so far as we know one form only—of legitimation, namely, legitimation by subsequent marriage of the parents. Under the law of France (and possibly in other countries) it appears that in addition to the marriage of the parents a formal recognition of the child by both of them was required: see *Re Wright's Trusts*.[1] But in the eye of English law in the narrower sense legitimation was impossible, except, of course, by Act of Parliament. A child born illegitimate remained illegitimate until his death with all the consequences which that status implied. These consequences affected not merely the child itself, but its mother and its natural father whose rights and duties towards the child were governed accordingly. This rigid rule of English municipal law has been qualified to meet the case of legitimation by subsequent marriage of the parents in cases where the law of the father's domicile at the time of the birth of the child and the law of the father's domicile at the time of the subsequent marriage recognises such legitimation. In these cases the English courts recognise the legitimation as effective: but where the father's domicile at either of the two times stated did not recognise such legitimation the marriage was regarded as inoperative to effect legitimation notwithstanding that the law of the father's domicile at the other of the two times recognised legitimation by subsequent marriage: see *Re Wright's Trusts*; *Udny v Udny*,[2] *Re Grove*.[3] The special case of heirship to land in England need not be considered.

An alteration of the law has been effected by s 8 of the Legitimacy Act 1926,[4] which enables legitimation to take place where the law of the father's domicile (not being English) at the date of the marriage recognises the marriage as effective to legitimate the child. In such cases legitimation takes place as from the date of the commencement of the Act or the date of the marriage, notwithstanding that the law of the country where the father was domiciled at the date of the birth did not recognise legitimation by subsequent marriage. It is to be noticed that legitimation under the section is not retrospective and in none of the cases which were decided before the Act did any question of retrospective legitimation arise.

It so happens that the only form of legitimation which has hitherto come up for consideration by the English courts has been legitimation per subsequens matrimonium. This was the method of legitimation commonly found in systems of law other than our own and it was in relation to this method that the rules adopted by the English courts came to be formulated.

So far as we are aware this is the first case which has arisen in the English courts where a different method of legitimation, namely, by adoption, has had to be considered. The next point which arises is whether the

1 (1856) 2 K & J 595 at 613.
2 (1869) LR 1 Sc & Div 441; p 3 above.
3 (1888) 40 Ch D 216, 58 LJCh 57.
4 Now s 3 of the Legitimacy Act 1976, p 420 below (*Ed*).

requirements with regard to the domicile of the father which exist in the case
of legitimation per subsequens matrimonium must be complied with in such
a case, or whether, as Farwell J held, the matter falls to be decided by
reference only to the law of the country in which the child was domiciled at
the date when the legitimation is said to have taken place.

It is useful at the outset to consider certain consequences which flow from
the view adopted by Farwell J. The law of California provides for
legitimation per subsequens matrimonium as well as for legitimation by
adoption by the natural father. Accordingly, if Frederick Charles Luck had
on 27 July 1922, married Martha Anne Croft instead of Alma Hyam and
had not in addition adopted David Luck, the English courts would not
(apart from the operation of s 8 of the Legitimacy Act 1926) have regarded
David Luck as legitimate, since Frederick Charles Luck was domiciled in
England at the date of the birth. If, however, in addition to marrying
Martha Anne Croft, Frederick Charles Luck had adopted David Luck with
her consent, the English courts would have recognised the legitimation. This
result would, to say the least of it, be anomalous. A result even more
anomalous would follow in a case where a man had two illegitimate children
by two different women. If he subsequently married one of them but did not
trouble to adopt her child and then adopted with her consent the child of the
other woman, the former child would (apart always from the Legitimacy Act
1926) be regarded in this country as illegitimate, the latter as legitimated.
These considerations in our view afford some reason for adopting, upon
grounds of convenience, a uniform principle applicable to both cases. But
this by itself is not sufficient and it becomes necessary to examine the
authorities in which the rules applicable to cases of legitimation per
subsequens matrimonium have been laid down.

(His Lordship referred to *Munro v Munro*;[5] *Re Wright's Trusts*; *Udny v Udny*;
Re Goodman's Trusts;[6] and *Re Grove*, and continued:) In our judgment the
principles laid down in the authorities which we have cited are not limited to
the one case of legitimation per subsequens matrimonium. It is natural that
references to that form of legitimation should have found a place in the
statements of the law since that was the particular form that was relevant in
those cases. But the language used is, we think, of wider import. In
particular, Lord Hatherley in *Re Wright's Trusts* lays down the principle in
quite general terms which clearly cover the present case. He regards the law
of the father's domicile as 'fastening on' the child at its birth and as
determining the nature of their relationship. If by the law of that domicile
the relationship is immutably that of putative father and illegitimate child,
nothing thereafter can change it. If, on the other hand, by the law of that
domicile such relationship is not immutable but is capable of becoming that
of father and legitimate child, that capacity when duly fulfilled is to be
recognised by the courts of this country.

There appear to us to be sound reasons in principle why this should be the
law. Legitimacy is not a unilateral matter affecting the child alone. If an
illegitimate child is legitimated it is not only the status of the child which is
affected: the status of the putative father is also changed since he becomes
what he was not before, namely, the father of a legitimate child with all the

5 (1840) 7 Cl & Fin 842.
6 (1881) 17 Ch D 266, 50 LJCh 425; p 412 above.

consequential rights and duties which flow from that relationship. Moreover, the position of the child is changed as regards the father's relatives: for it acquires the capacity to succeed to their property as next of kin, while they similarly acquire a like right to succeed to his property. If the question of the effect of the adoption of David Luck upon his legitimacy is to be determined by the law of his domicile at the time, it would apparently follow that if he had been legitimated by a privilegium enacted by the legislature of California he would have been regarded as legitimate by the English courts, even if his father had been domiciled in England at the time. In other words, the English courts would recognise the jurisdiction of a foreign legislature to impose upon a domiciled Englishman the status of paternity which he did not acquire at the date of the child's birth and the potentiality of acquiring which he did not at the time possess. We cannot accept a view which would lead to that result.

When the question of legitimation per subsequens matrimonium first came up for examination in *Re Wright's Trusts* the law might have been laid down differently and it might have been held that the domicile of the father or of the child at the date of the marriage was the sole matter to be considered. Lord Hatherley's decision in that case was, we think, largely influenced by the Scotch law as laid down by the House of Lords in *Munro v Munro*. It was natural that the English law on this matter should be founded upon the same principles as Scotch law which required the potentiality of legitimation to exist at the date of the birth. The result is that the English authorities have been based upon the principle that before subsequent legitimation can take place the status of illegitimacy as acquired at birth under the law of the domicile of the putative father must have as an integral part of itself the potentiality of subsequent legitimation. If it has not this potentiality, it is incapable of change since the capacity to be changed exists and exists only by virtue of the potentiality. It is in our opinion only within these narrow limits that the English law recognises an exception to the principle that bastardy is indelible, a principle which it always steadfastly maintained in opposition to the civil and the canon law save in so far as it was forced to recognise an exception in cases of persons not domiciled in England.

It was suggested that a logical distinction between the present case and the case of legitimation per subsequens matrimonium might be found in the circumstance that the act of adoption by the father was done deliberately for the purpose of legitimising the child, whereas marriage is contracted for its own sake and the consequential legitimation is, so to speak, only a collateral result. There appears to us to be no substance in this distinction. Moreover, as we have already pointed out, it appears from *Re Wright's Trusts* that by French law an act of recognition was required in addition to the marriage and it was not suggested that this circumstance in any way affected the principles to be applied.

Scott LJ dissented.

Appeal allowed.

QUESTION

Farwell J and Scott LJ thought that David Luck could be recognised in England as having been legitimated, because in their view it was only necessary to refer to the law of California, where his father was domiciled at the date of the acknowledgment, and not to the law of England, where his father was domiciled at the date of David's birth. This is of course a reasonable view and arguably a better one than that of the majority. But do you think that Farwell J and Scott LJ were correct in thinking that David could succeed as a child of his father not only under the will but also under the marriage settlement? If so, what about the rule against perpetuities? Was David a legitimate child of his father in 1917 when the perpetuity period ended?

Legitimacy Act 1976

2. Subject to the following provisions of this Act, where the parents of an illegitimate person marry one another, the marriage shall, if the father of the illegitimate person is at the date of marriage domiciled in England and Wales, render that person, if living, legitimate from the date of the marriage.

3. Subject to the following provisions of this Act, where the parents of an illegitimate person marry one another and the father of the illegitimate person is not at the time of the marriage domiciled in England and Wales but is domiciled in a country by the law of which the illegitimate person became legitimated by virtue of such subsequent marriage, that person, if living, shall in England and Wales be recognised as having been so legitimated from the date of the marriage notwithstanding that, at the time of his birth, his father was domiciled in a country the law of which did not permit legitimation by subsequent marriage.

5.—(1) Subject to any contrary indication, the rules of construction contained in this section apply to any instrument other than an existing instrument, so far as the instrument contains a disposition of property.

(2) For the purposes of this section, provisions of the law of intestate succession applicable to the estate of a deceased person shall be treated as if contained in an instrument executed by him (while of full capacity) immediately before his death.

(3) A legitimated person, and any other person, shall be entitled to take any interest as if the legitimated person had been born legitimate.

(6) If an illegitimate person or a person adopted by one of his natural parents dies, or has died before the commencement of this Act, and—
(a) after his death his parents marry or have married; and
(b) the deceased would, if living at the time of the marriage, have become a legitimated person,
this section shall apply for the construction of the instrument so far as it relates to the taking of interests by, or in succession to, his spouse, children and remoter issue as if he had been legitimated by virtue of the marriage.

10.—(1) In this Act, except where the context otherwise requires,—
'disposition' includes the conferring of a power of appointment and any other disposition of an interest in or right over property;
'existing', in relation to an instrument, means one made before 1 January 1976;
'legitimated person' means a person legitimated or recognised as legitimated—
(a) under section 2 or 3 above; or
(b) under section 1 or 8 of the Legitimacy Act 1926; or
(c) except in section 8, by a legitimation (whether or not by virtue of the

subsequent marriage of his parents) recognised by the law of England and Wales and effected under the law of any other country; and cognate expressions shall be construed accordingly.

(2) For the purposes of this Act 'legitimated person' includes, where the context admits, a person legitimated, or recognised as legitimated, before the passing of the Children Act 1975.

(3) For the purpose of this Act, except where the context otherwise requires,—

(a) the death of the testator is the date at which a will or codicil is to be regarded as made;

(b) an oral disposition of property shall be deemed to be contained in an instrument made when the disposition was made.

(4) It is hereby declared that references in this Act to dispositions of property include references to a disposition by the creation of an entailed interest.

SCHEDULE 1

SAVINGS

1.—(1) Notwithstanding the repeal by this Act of sections 1 and 8 of the Legitimacy Act 1926 persons legitimated or recognised as legitimated under that Act shall continue to be legitimated or recognised as legitimated by virtue of section 1 or, as the case may be, section 8 of that Act.

(2) In any enactment whether passed before or after this Act references to persons legitimated or recognised as legitimated under section 1 or section 8 of the Legitimacy Act 1926 or under section 2 or section 3 of this Act shall be construed as including references to persons legitimated or recognised as legitimated under section 2 or section 3 of this Act or under section 1 or section 8 of the said Act of 1926 respectively.

2.—(1) The enactments repealed by Part II of Schedule 4 to the Children Act 1975 (which are superseded by section 5 of this Act) shall, notwithstanding those repeals, continue to have effect as respects existing instruments.

In this sub-paragraph 'instrument' has the same meaning as in section 5 of this Act.

(2) Subject to paragraph (3)(b) below, nothing in this Act or in the Legitimacy Act 1926 (in so far as the effect of that Act is preserved by subparagraph (1) above) shall affect the operation or construction of any disposition coming into operation before 1 January 1927 or affect any rights under the intestacy of a person dying before that date.

Section C. Adoption

Children Act 1975

10.—(1) Subject to sections 37(1) and 53(1), an adoption order may be made on the application of a married couple where each has attained the age of 21 but an adoption order shall not otherwise be made on the application of more than one person.

(2) An adoption order shall not be made on the application of a married couple unless—

(a) at least one of them is domiciled in a part of the United Kingdom, or in the Channel Islands or the Isle of Man, or

(b) the application is for a Convention adoption order and section 24 is complied with.

11.—(1) Subject to sections 37(1) and 53(1), an adoption order may be made on the application of one person where he has attained the age of 21 and—

(a) is not married, or

(b) is married and the court is satisfied that—

    (i) his spouse cannot be found, or

    (ii) the spouses have separated and are living apart, and the separation is likely to be permanent, or

    (iii) his spouse is by reason of ill health, whether physical or mental, incapable of making an application for an adoption order.

(2) An adoption order shall not be made on the application of one person unless—

(a) he is domiciled in a part of the United Kingdom, or in the Channel Islands or the Isle of Man, or

(b) the application is for a Convention adoption order and section 24 is complied with.

100.—(1) In this Act 'authorised court', as respects an application for an order relating to a child, shall be construed as follows.

(2) If the child is in England or Wales when the application is made, the following are authorised courts—

(a) the High Court;

(b) the county court within whose district the child is and, in the case of an application under section 14, any county court within whose district a parent or guardian of the child is;

(c) any other county court prescribed by rules made under section 102 of the County Courts Act 1959;

(d) a magistrates' court within whose area the child is and, in the case of an application under section 14, a magistrates' court within whose area a parent or guardian of the child is.

(3) If the child is in Scotland when the application is made, the following are authorised courts—

(a) the Court of Session;

(b) the sheriff court of the sheriffdom within which the child is.

(4) If, in the case of an application for an adoption order or an order under section 14, the child is not in Great Britain when the application is made, the following are authorised courts—

(a) the High Court;

(b) the Court of Session.

SCHEDULE 1

STATUS CONFERRED BY ADOPTION OR LEGITIMATION IN ENGLAND AND WALES

PART I

INTERPRETATION

1.—(1) This Part applies for the construction of this Schedule, except where the context otherwise requires.

(2) 'Adoption' means adoption—

(a) by an adoption order as defined in section 107,

(b) by an adoption order made under the 1958 Act or the Adoption Act 1950 or any enactment repealed by the Adoption Act 1950,

(c) by an order made in Northern Ireland, the Isle of Man or in any of the Channel Islands,

(d) which is an overseas adoption as defined by section 4(3) of the Adoption Act 1968, or

(e) which is an adoption recognised by the law of England and Wales, and effected under the law of any other country,

and cognate expressions shall be construed accordingly.

(4) [⁷This definition of adoption includes], where the context admits, [⁷an adoption effected] before the passing of this Act, and the date of an adoption effected by an order is the date of the making of the order.

(5) 'Existing', in relation to any enactment or other instrument, means one passed or made before 1 January 1976 (and whether or not before the passing of this Act).

(6) The death of the testator is the date at which a will or codicil is to be regarded as made.

Dispositions of property

2.—(1) In this Schedule—

'disposition' includes the conferring of a power of appointment and any other disposition of an interest in or right over property;

'power of appointment' includes any discretionary power to transfer a beneficial interest in property without the furnishing of valuable consideration.

(2) This Schedule applies to an oral disposition of property as if contained in an instrument made when the disposition was made.

PART II

ADOPTION ORDERS

Status conferred by adoption

3.—(1) An adopted child shall be treated in law—

(a) where the adopters are a married couple, as if he had been born as a child of the marriage (whether or not he was in fact born after the marriage was solemnised);

(b) in any other case, as if he had been born to the adopter in wedlock (but not as a child of any actual marriage of the adopter).

(2) An adopted child shall be treated in law as if he were not the child of any person other than the adopters or adopter.

(3) It is hereby declared that this paragraph prevents an adopted child from being illegitimate.

(4) This paragraph has effect—

(a) in the case of an adoption before 1 January 1976, from that date, and

(b) in the case of any other adoption, from the date of the adoption.

(5) Subject to the provisions of this Part, this paragraph applies for the

---

7 Words substituted by Legitimacy Act 1976, Sch 1, para 7.

construction of enactments or instruments passed or made before the adoption or later, and so applies subject to any contrary indication.

(6) Subject to the provisions of this Part, the paragraph has effect as respects things done, or events occurring, after the adoption, or after 31 December 1975, whichever is the later.

Vocabulary

4. A relationship existing by virtue of paragraph 3 may be referred to as an adoptive relationship, and—
(a) a male adopter may be referred to as the adoptive father;
(b) a female adopter may be referred to as the adoptive mother;
(c) any other relative of any degree under an adoptive relationship may be referred to as an adoptive relative of that degree,
but this paragraph does not prevent the term 'parent', or any other term not qualified by the word 'adoptive', being treated as including an adoptive relative.

Peerages, etc

10. An adoption does not affect the descent of any peerage or dignity or title of honour.

Entails

17. It is hereby declared that references in this Schedule to dispositions of property include references to a disposition by the creation of an entailed interest.

Adoption Act 1968

4.—(3) In this Act 'overseas adoption' means an adoption of such a description as the Secretary of State may by order specify, being a description of adoptions of infants appearing to him to be effected under the law of any country outside Great Britain; and an order under this subsection may contain provision as to the manner in which evidence of an overseas adoption may be given.

6.—(3) The court may, upon an application under this subsection—
(a) order that an overseas adoption or a determination shall cease to be valid in Great Britain on the ground that the adoption or determination is contrary to public policy or that the authority which purported to authorise the adoption or make the determination was not competent to entertain the case.
(4) Any court in Great Britain may, in any proceedings in that court, decide that an overseas adoption or a determination shall, for the purposes of those proceedings, be treated as invalid in Great Britain on either of the grounds mentioned in subsection (3) of this section.
(5) Except as provided by this section, the validity of an overseas adoption or a determination shall not be impugned in proceedings in any court in Great Britain.

An adoption made in any foreign country outside the United Kingdom, the Channel Islands, or the Isle of Man will be recognised as valid in England at common law if at the time of the adoption the adopter was domiciled in such foreign country.

Re Valentine's Settlement [1965] Ch 831, [1965] 2 All ER 226 (Court of Appeal)

Alastair Valentine was at all material times domiciled and resident in Southern Rhodesia. He was married and had one child, Simon, who was born in 1936. By orders of the Children's Court in Johannesburg, South Africa, Alastair and his wife adopted a girl Carole in 1939 and a boy Timothy in 1944. It was assumed that both Carole and Timothy were resident and domiciled in South Africa at the times of the respective adoption orders.

In 1946, by a settlement the proper law of which was English, Alastair's mother settled funds on trust for Alastair for life and then for his children at 21.

Alastair died in 1962 and the trustees of the settlement issued a summons to determine whether the settled funds devolved on Simon alone, or equally between Simon, Carole, and Timothy.

There was evidence that by South African law an adopted child was deemed to be the legitimate child of the adoptive parents, except that he did not become entitled to any property as a child of the adoptive parent under any instrument executed prior to the date of the adoption, nor could he inherit any property ab intestato from any relative of his adoptive parent. There was evidence that by the law of Southern Rhodesia an adoption order could not be made in favour of any applicant who was not domiciled and resident in the colony or in respect of any minor who was not so resident; and that the courts of Southern Rhodesia would not recognise as valid an adoption order granted by the courts of a country in which the adopter was not resident and domiciled.

Pennycuick J held that the settled funds were held on trust for Simon alone. Timothy appealed.

Lord Denning MR: In order to determine the case, we have to answer two questions. The first is whether the English courts will recognise the adoption orders so as to give the adopted children the status of children. If the answer is 'No', that will decide the case adversely to Carole and Timothy: for they will not be regarded as the children of Alastair in the eyes of English law at all: and Simon will take the whole because he is the only child recognised by English law. If the answer is 'Yes', so that the adopted children have the status of children, nevertheless the second question arises. It is whether the English courts will confer on these adopted children the rights and benefits given to 'children' by this settlement: for, whilst recognising their status, English law may not give them all the self-same rights and benefits as the natural-born child.

On both these points we have to consider the law as to adoption of South Africa, England and Southern Rhodesia. I will summarise the material provisions. [His Lordship did so, pointing out that by South African law Carole and Timothy would be regarded as entitled to succeed to the property under the settlement, but that by English and Southern Rhodesian domestic law they would not.]

Such being the various laws, I turn now to consider the first question, which is this: Do the courts of this country recognise the adoption orders made by the courts of South Africa so as to give these children the status of children?

I start with the proposition stated by James LJ in *Re Goodman's Trusts*:[8] 'The family relation is at the foundation of all society, and it would appear almost an axiom that the family relation, once duly constituted by the law of any civilised country, should be respected and acknowledged by every other member of the great community of nations.' That was a legitimation case, but the like principle applies to adoption.

But when is the status of adoption duly constituted? Clearly it is so when it is constituted in another country in similar circumstances as we claim for ourselves. Our courts should recognise a jurisdiction which mutatis mutandis they claim for themselves: see *Travers v Holley*.[9] We claim jurisdiction to make an adoption order when the adopting parents are domiciled in this country and the child is resident here. So also, out of the comity of nations, we should recognise an adoption order made by another country when the adopting parents are domiciled there and the child is resident there.[10]

Apart from international comity, we reach the same result on principle. When a court of any country makes an adoption order for an infant child, it does two things: (1) it destroys the legal relationship theretofore existing between the child and its natural parents, be it legitimate or illegitimate; (2) it creates the legal relationship of parent and child between the child and its adopting parents, making it their legitimate child. It creates a new status in both, namely, the status of parent and child. Now it has long been settled that questions affecting status are determined by the law of the domicile. This new status of parent and child, in order to be recognised everywhere, must be validly created by the law of the domicile of the adopting parent. You do not look to the domicile of the child: for that has no separate domicile of its own. It takes its parents' domicile. You look to the parents' domicile only. If you find that a legitimate relationship of parent and child has been validly created by the law of the parents' domicile at the time the relationship is created, then the status so created should be universally recognised throughout the civilised world, provided always that there is nothing contrary to public policy in so recognising it. That general principle finds expression in the judgment of Scott LJ in *Re Luck's Settlement Trusts*.[11] I think it is correct, notwithstanding that the majority in that case created a dubious exception to it. But it is an essential feature of this principle that the parents should be domiciled in the country at the time: for no provision of the law of a foreign country will be regarded in the English courts as effective to create the status of a parent in a person not domiciled in that country at the time: see *Re Grove*[12] (legitimation by subsequent marriage); *Re*

8 (1881) 17 Ch D 266 at 297; p 412 above.
9 [1953] P 246 at 257, [1953] 2 All ER 794 at 800.
10 Under ss 10 and 11 of the Children Act 1975 (p 421 above) there is no longer a requirement that the child must be resident in England in order to give the English courts jurisdiction to make an adoption order. Hence there should no longer be a requirement that the child must be resident in the foreign country in order that foreign adoptions may be recognised in England (*Ed*).
11 [1940] Ch 864; p 416 above.
12 (1888) 40 Ch D 216, 58 LJCh 57.

Wilson[13] (adoption). I ought to say, however, that in order for adoption to be recognised everywhere, it seems to me that, in addition to the adopting parents being domiciled in the country where the order is made, the child should be ordinarily resident there: for it is the courts of ordinary residence which have the pre-eminent jurisdiction over the child: see *Re P (GE) (an infant)*.[14] The child is under their protection and it would seem only right that those courts should be the courts to decide whether the child should be adopted or not.

In my opinion, therefore, the courts of this country will only recognise an adoption in another country if the adopting parents are domiciled there and the child is ordinarily resident there.

Now coming to this particular case, I fear that we in these courts cannot recognise these adoption orders as conferring the status of children on Carole and Timothy: for the simple reason that the adopting parents were not domiciled nor ordinarily resident in South Africa. So on the very first point Carole and Timothy fail.

I may, however, be wrong about this: because I recognise the force of the opinion which Salmon LJ will express, namely, that the courts of this country should recognise an adoption in another country if it is effected by an order of the courts of that country, provided always that their courts apply the same safeguards as we do. If this be right, then we should recognise the adoption orders in South Africa as conferring the status of children on Carole and Timothy: for their courts have the same safeguards as we. There then arises the second question: What is the effect of this recognition? Does it give the adopted children the self-same rights and benefits as natural-born children, especially in regard to succession to property? Or only the same rights and benefits as adopted children? (His Lordship proceeded to hold that Carole and Timothy could not take under the settlement, because it was executed before 1 January 1950. This part of his judgment is omitted here because it was rendered obsolescent by para 3 of Schedule 1 of the Children Act 1975, p 423 above).

In my judgment the decision of Pennycuick J was right and this appeal should be dismissed.

Danckwerts LJ delivered judgment to the same effect, except that he was 'not sure' that the child need be ordinarily resident in the country where he was adopted.

Salmon LJ (dissenting): . . .There is clearly much to be said for the argument that, as adoption affects the status not only of the child but also of the father, our courts should not recognise the power of the South African court to make an adoption order altering Alastair's status since he was not domiciled within its jurisdiction. Our courts will not ordinarily recognise a decree of divorce unless the husband was domiciled in the country where the decree was granted: *Le Mesurier v Le Mesurier*.[15] According to our law the wife takes the husband's domicile.[16] There could, therefore, be no nexus

---

13 [1954] Ch 733, [1954] 1 All ER 997.
14 [1965] Ch 568, [1964] 3 All ER 977; p 370 above.
15 [1895] AC 517, 64 LJPC 97. But see now Recognition of Divorces and Legal Separations Act 1971, ss 2 and 3, p 303 above (*Ed*).
16 But see now s 1 of the Domicile and Matrimonial Proceedings Act 1973, p 19 above (*Ed*).

between the foreign court and either of the parties to the divorce. The personal law of each would be alien to that of the court. Besides there are sound sociological reasons why such a divorce should not be recognised. In some countries the laws of divorce are far laxer than our own. If an Englishman could go abroad and obtain a divorce on almost any pretext and that divorce were to be recognised in England, the divorce rate might rise considerably. Such a weakening of the marriage tie is contrary to the interest of society. In the case of adoption, however, the position is very different when, as here, the foreign court certainly had jurisdiction over two of the parties concerned—the children and their natural parents. The evidence does not show whether or not the children were born legitimate. If they were legitimate, they, of course, took their father's domicile, and if illegitimate, their mother's. There is nothing in the evidence to suggest that the natural parent of either of them was domiciled or ordinarily resident anywhere other than in South Africa. Whilst it is, of course, a principle of English law that it will not recognise the right of a foreign court to impose a change of status upon anyone not domiciled within its jurisdiction, it is equally a principle of English law generally to recognise the right of a foreign court to make an order changing the status of anyone over whom it has jurisdiction. What happens, as here, when these two principles conflict? When the adopted child and its natural parents are domiciled within the jurisdiction of the foreign court and the adoptive father is not domiciled within its jurisdiction? There is no escape from the necessity of choosing between the two principles, for no compromise is possible. We could not regard the orders of the South African court as effective to sever the ties between the children and their natural parents and make them the children of Alastair and yet ineffective to make Alastair their father. The problem that confronts us has never yet arisen in this country. It has been suggested that according to the theory of our law no foreign adoption should be recognised unless, at the time it was made, both adopted child and adoptive parent were domiciled within the jurisdiction of the foreign country and that this appeal should be decided accordingly. Our law, however, develops in accordance with the changing needs of man. These have always been ascertained by experience rather than by the rigid application of abstract theory. Experience has shown that there are sound sociological reasons for recognising an adoption in circumstances such as these. Adoption—provided that there are proper safeguards—is greatly for the benefit of the adopted child and of the adoptive parents, and also, I think, of civilised society, since this is founded on the family relationship. It seems to me that we should be slow to refuse recognition to an adoption order made by a foreign court which applies the same safeguards as we do and which undoubtedly had jurisdiction over the adopted child and its natural parents.

The laws of adoption in South Africa are very nearly the same as our own. The principles underlying them are the same. The whole emphasis is upon the welfare of the child and elaborate precautions are laid down for assuring that the adoption order shall not be made unless it is for the benefit of the child; the consent of the natural parents is required. It is difficult to see why in these circumstances, unless compelled to do so, our courts should refuse to recognise these adoption orders made lawfully in South Africa which conferred nothing but benefits on all the parties concerned. . . .

Appeal dismissed.

PART V

Law of Obligations

Contracts

Section A: Doctrine of the proper law

The essential validity of a contract is governed by its proper law, ie the system of law by which the parties intended the contract to be governed, or, where their intention is neither expressed nor to be inferred from the circumstances, the system of law with which the transaction has its closest and most real connection.

Peninsular and Oriental Steam Navigation Company v Shand
(1865) 3 Moo PCC NS 272, 6 New Rep 387 (Privy Council)

Appeal from the Supreme Court of Mauritius.

The plaintiff, the Chief Justice of the court below, took a ticket in England for his passage from Southampton to Alexandria and from Suez to Mauritius on board the defendants' steamships, for which he paid one entire sum of £315. One of the conditions of carriage was that the defendants did not hold themselves liable for damage to or loss of passengers' baggage.

The voyage from Southampton to Alexandria was on board the *Ceylon* and from Suez to Mauritius on board the *Norna*. At Suez the *Norna* lay a little distance out at sea in consequence of the shallowness of the water; the passengers were conveyed to her in a small steamboat, the baggage in another vessel. It was on board this small vessel that the plaintiff's baggage (consisting of cloaks, an overcoat and plaids) was last seen. It was missed by the plaintiff when on board the *Norna*, and on arrival at Mauritius it was not forthcoming.

The Supreme Court of Mauritius held that the contract was governed by French law (which prevailed generally at Mauritius) and that by that law the defendants were liable in spite of the exemption clause.

The defendants appealed.

The judgment of their Lordships (Knight Bruce and Turner LJJ and Coleridge J) was delivered by

Turner LJ (after stating the facts his Lordship continued): The general rule is, that the law of the country where a contract is made governs as to the nature, the obligation, and the interpretation of it. The parties to a contract are either the subjects of the Power there ruling or as temporary residents owe it a temporary allegiance: in either case equally they must be understood to submit to the law there prevailing, and to agree to its actions upon their contract. It is, of course, immaterial that such agreement is not expressed in terms; it is equally an agreement in fact, presumed de jure, and a foreign court interpreting or enforcing it on any contrary rule defeats the intention of the parties, as well as neglects to observe the recognised comity of nations. Their Lordships are speaking of the general rule; there are, no doubt, exceptions and limitations on its applicability, but the present case is not affected by these, and seems perfectly clear as to the actual intention of the contracting parties.

This is a contract made between British subjects in England, substantially for safe carriage from Southampton to Mauritius. The performance is to commence in an English vessel, in an English port; to be continued in vessels which for this purpose carry their country with them; to be fully completed in Mauritius; but liable to breach, partial or entire, in several other countries in which the vessels might be in the course of the voyage. Into this contract, which the appellants frame and issue, they have introduced for their own protection a stipulation, professing in its terms to limit the liability which, according to the English law, the contract would otherwise have cast upon them. When they tendered this contract to the respondent, and required his signature to it, what must it be presumed that he understood to be their intention as to this stipulation? What would any reasonable man have understood that they intended? Was it to secure to themselves some real protection against responsibility for accidental losses of luggage and for damage to it; or to stipulate for something to which, however clearly expressed, the law would allow no validity? This question leaves untouched, it will be observed, the extent of the contemplated protection; it asks, in effect, was it intended that the stipulation in case of an alleged breach of contract should be construed by the rules of the English law, which would give some effect to it? or by those of the French or any other law, according to which it would have none, but be treated as a merely fruitless attempt to evade a responsibility inseparably fixed upon the appellants as carriers? The question appears to their Lordships to admit of one answer only; but if they take the respondent so to have understood the intention of the appellants, they must take him to have adopted the same intention; it would be to impute want of good faith on his part to suppose that with that knowledge he yet intended to enter into a contract wholly different on so important an article; he could not have done this if the intention had been expressed, and there is no difference as to effect between that which is expressed in terms and that which is implied and clearly understood.

The actual intention of the parties, therefore, must be taken clearly to have been to treat this as an English contract, to be interpreted according to the rules of English law; and as there is no rule of general law or policy setting up a contrary presumption, their Lordships will hold that the court below was wrong in not governing itself according to those rules.

It is a satisfaction to their Lordships to find that in the year 1864 the Cour de Cassation in France pronounced a judgment to the same effect in a case under precisely the same circumstances, which arose between the appellants and a French officer who was returning with his baggage from Hong Kong in one of their ships, the *Alma*, and who lost his baggage in the wreck of that vessel in the Red Sea. The same question arose as here on the effect to be given to the stipulation in the ticket; two inferior courts, those of Marseilles and Aix, decided it in favour of the plaintiff on the provisions of the French law; the Supreme Court reversed these decisions, and held that the contract having been made at Hong Kong, an English possession, and with an

English Company, was to receive its interpretation and effect according to English law.

(His Lordship proceeded to hold that by English law the clause in the contract exempted the appellants from liability.)

Appeal allowed.

Lloyd v Guibert (1865) LR 1 QB 115, 6 B & S 100 (Exchequer Chamber)

Willes J: The facts disclosed by the record are as follows: The plaintiff below, a British subject, at St Thomas, a Danish West India Island, chartered the ship *Olivier*, belonging to the defendants, who are Frenchmen, for a voyage from St Marc, in Hayti, to Havre, London, or Liverpool, at the charterer's option. The plaintiff must have known that the ship was French. The charter-party was entered into by the master in pursuance of his general authority as master, and not under any special authority from the owner. The plaintiff shipped a cargo at St Marc for Liverpool, with which the vessel sailed. On her voyage, she sustained damage from a storm, which compelled her to put into Fayal, a Portuguese port, for repair. There the master properly borrowed money upon bottomry of the ship, freight, and cargo, and repaired the ship, which proceeded with the cargo, and arrived in safety at Liverpool. The bondholder proceeded in the Court of Admiralty against the ship, freight, and cargo. The ship and freight were insufficient to satisfy the bond; the deficiency and costs fell upon the plaintiff as owner of the cargo, and in respect thereof he seeks to be indemnified by the defendants as shipowners.

The defendants abandoned the ship and freight; and it must be taken as fact (because it is alleged and not denied) that, by the law of France, they abandoned in time, and in such manner and under such circumstances as are required by the French law, and that according to such law, abandonment, by which we understand a giving up of the ship and freight to the shippers, absolved them from liability. This law, if applicable, is one which furnishes an absolute bar to the plaintiff's claim by way of satisfaction or discharge, and affected the validity of the claim, and not merely the mode of proceeding to enforce it.

By the English law, a shipowner, under such circumstances, is liable personally, and not merely to the value of the ship and freight. And it is alleged, and not denied, that the Danish Portuguese and Haytian laws agree in this respect with our own. The law of Hayti was not however relied upon in argument.

Upon these facts, it was insisted for the plaintiff that the decision ought to proceed upon either what was called the 'general maritime law', as regulating all maritime transactions between persons of different nationalities at sea; the Danish law, as that of the place where the contract was made (lex loci contractus); the Portuguese law, because the bottomry bond, which in one sense caused the question to arise, was given in a Portuguese port, and the rule that the place governs the act (locus regit actum) was supposed, therefore, to furnish a solution; or the English law, as being that of the place of the final act of performance by the delivery of the cargo (quasi lex loci solutionis), in either of which alternatives the liability of the defendants was established. And it was argued, that, the charter-party having been entered into bona fide in the ordinary course of business by the master, within the scope of his ostensible authority to contract for the employment of the vessel, which the owner, by appointing a master and sending him abroad in command, allows him to assume, the right of the charterer could no more be narrowed by a provision of foreign law unknown to him than by secret instructions from the owners, which would clearly be inoperative—a proposition which needs no authority in our law.

For the defendants, it was answered, that by the French law they are absolved; and that that law, as being that of the ship, governs the case, either because of the character of the transaction itself, showing that the plaintiff impliedly submitted his goods to the operation of the law of the ship, or because the master, who entered into the contract (although his doing so was within the scope of the authority which he was allowed by the owners to assume), was disabled by the French law from binding his owners, otherwise than with the exception expressed or implied of exemption from liability by abandonment, and that of such disability, or lack of authority, his flag was sufficient notice.

Upon this latter ground, the Court of Queen's Bench gave judgment for the defendants, not expressing any opinion upon the former; whereupon the plaintiff brought error, and the case was well argued at the sittings after Trinity Term last, before Erle CJ, Pollock CB, Martin B, Keating J, Pigott B, and myself, when we took time to consider.

In determining a question between contracting parties, recourse must first be had to the language of the contract itself, and (force, fraud, and mistake apart) the true construction of the language of the contract (lex contractus) is the touchstone of legal right. It often happens, however, that disputes arise, not as to the terms of the contract, but as to their application to unforeseen questions, which arise incidentally or accidentally in the course of performance, and which the contract does not answer in terms, yet which are within the sphere of the relation established thereby, and cannot be decided as between strangers.

In such cases it is necessary to consider by what general law the parties intended that the transaction should be governed, or rather to what general law it is just to presume that they have submitted themselves in the matter. . . .

In the diversity or conflict of laws, which ought to prevail, is a question that has called forth an amazing amount of ingenuity, and many differences of opinion. It is, however, generally agreed that the law of the place where the contract is made, is prima facie that which the parties intended, or ought to be presumed to have adopted as the footing upon which they dealt, and that such law ought therefore to prevail in the absence of circumstances indicating a different intention, as for instance, that the contract is to be entirely performed elsewhere, or that the subject-matter is immovable property situate in another country, and so forth; which latter, though sometimes treated as distinct rules, appear more properly to be classed as exceptions to the more general one, by reason of the circumstances indicating an intention to be bound by a law different from that of the place where the contract is made; which intention is inferred from the subject-matter and from the surrounding circumstances, so far as they are relevant to construe and determine the character of the contract.

The present question does not appear to have ever been decided in this country, and in America it has received opposite decisions, equally entitled to respect. We must therefore deal with it as a new question, and endeavour to be guided in its solution by a steady application of the general principle already stated, viz, that the rights of the parties to a contract are to be judged of by that law by which they intended, or rather by which they may justly be presumed to have bound themselves.

We must apply this test successively to the various laws which have been suggested as applicable; and first to the alleged general maritime law.

(His Lordship held that there was no general rule in maritime law upon the subject, and continued:) In one other point of view the general maritime law, as administered in England, or (to avoid periphrasis) the law of England, viz as the law of the contemplated place of final performance, or port of discharge, remains to be considered. It is manifest, however, that what was to be done at Liverpool (besides that, it might at the charterer's option have been done at Havre) was but a small portion of the entire service to be rendered, and that the character of the contract cannot be determined thereby. . . . It is unnecessary, however, to discuss this point further, because we have been anticipated and the question set at rest, in an instructive judgment of the Judicial Committee, delivered by the Lord Justice Turner, since the argument of the present case, in that of *Peninsular and Oriental Co v Shand*.[1]

Next, as to the law of Portugal: the only semblance of authority for resorting to that law, as being the law of the place where the bottomry bond was given, is *Cammell v Sewell*;[2] and we consider that the judgment in that case, if applicable at all, as to which we say nothing, could only affect the validity of the bottomry, and not the duties imposed upon the shipowner towards the merchant by the fact of the bottomry, which duties must be traced to the contract of affreightment and the bailment founded thereupon.

The law of Hayti was not mentioned nor relied upon in argument; and there remain only to be considered the laws of Denmark and of France, between which we must choose.

In favour of the law of Denmark, there is the cardinal fact that the contract was made within Danish territory; and, further, that the first act done towards performance was weighing anchor in a Danish port.

For the law of France, on the other hand, many practical considerations may be suggested; and, first, the subject-matter of the contract, the employment of a sea-going vessel for a service, the greater and more onerous part of which was to be rendered upon the high seas, where, for all purposes of jurisdiction, criminal or civil, with respect to all persons, things, and transactions, on board, she was, as it were, a floating island, over which France had as absolute, and for all purposes of peace as exclusive, a sovereignty as over her dominions by land, and which, even whilst in a foreign port, was never completely removed from French jurisdiction.

Further, it must be remembered that, although bills of lading are ordinarily given at the port of loading, charter-parties are often made elsewhere; and it seems strange and unlikely to have been within the contemplation of the parties that their rights or liabilities in respect of the identical voyage should vary, first, according as the vessel was taken up at

1 (1865) 3 Moo PCC NS 272, 6 New Rep 387; p 431 above.
2 (1860) 5 H & N 728, 29 LJEx 350; p 544 below.

the port of loading or not; and secondly, if she were taken up elsewhere, according to the law of the place where the charter-party was made, or even ratified. If a Frenchman had chartered the *Olivier* upon the same terms as the plaintiffs did, it would seem strange if he could appeal to Danish law against his own countryman because of the charter-party being made or ratified in a Danish port, though for a service to be rendered elsewhere, by a transient visitor, for the most part within French jurisdiction.

Moreover, there are many ports which have few or no seagoing vessels of their own, and no fixed maritime jurisprudence, and which yet supply valuable cargoes to the ships of other countries. Take Alexandria, for instance, with her mixed population and her maritime commerce almost in the hands of strangers. Is every vessel that leaves Alexandria with grain under a charter-party or bill of lading made there, and every passenger vessel leaving Alexandria or Suez, be she English, Austrian, or French, subject to Egyptian law? As to not a few half-savage places in Africa and Asia, with neither seagoing ships nor maritime laws, a similar question— what is the law in such cases, or is there none except that of the court within whose jurisdiction the litigation first arises?

Again, it may be asked, does a ship which visits many ports in one voyage, whilst she undoubtedly retains the criminal law of her own country, put on a new sort of civil liability, at each new country she visits, in respect of cargo there taken on board? An English steamer, for instance, starts from Southampton for Gibraltar, calling at Vigo, Lisbon, and Cadiz. A Portuguese going in her from Southampton to Vigo would naturally expect to sail subject in all respects to English law, that being the law of the place and the ship. But if the locality of the contract is to govern throughout, an Englishman going from Vigo to Lisbon on the same voyage would be under English law as to crimes and all obligations not connected with the contract of carriage, but under Spanish law as to the contract of carriage; and a Spaniard going from Lisbon to Cadiz, during the same voyage would enjoy Portuguese law as to his carriage, and be subject to English law in other respects.

The cases which we have thus put are not extreme nor exceptional; on the contrary, they are such as would ordinarily give rise to the question, which law is to prevail. The inconvenience and even absurdities which would follow from adopting the law of the place of contract in preference to that of the vessel, are strong to prove that the latter ought to be resorted to.

No inconvenience comparable to that which would attend an opposite decision has been suggested. The ignorance of French law on the part of the charterer is no more than many Englishmen contracting in England with respect to English matters might plead as to their own law, in case of an unforeseen accident.

Nor can we allow any weight to the argument, that this is an impolitic law, as tending to interfere with commerce, especially in making merchants cautious how they engage foreign vessels. That is a matter for the consideration of foreigners themselves, and nothing short of a violation of natural justice, or of our own laws, could justify us in holding a foreign law void because of being impolitic. No doubt the French law was intended to encourage shipping, by limiting the liability of shipowners, and in this respect it goes somewhat further than our own; but whether wisely or not is matter within the competence and for the consideration of the French legislature, and upon which, sitting here, we ought to pronounce no opinion.

Exceptional cases, should they arise, must be dealt with upon their own merits. In laying down a rule of law, regard ought rather to be had to the majority of cases upon which doubt and litigation are more likely to arise; and the general rule, that where the contract of affreightment does not provide otherwise, there, as between the parties to such contract, in respect of sea damage and its incidents, the law of the ship should govern, seems to be not only in accordance with the probable intention of the parties, but also most consistent and intelligible, and therefore most convenient to those engaged in commerce.

For these reasons we have arrived at the same conclusion as the Court of Queen's Bench; and without examining the grounds upon which the court proceeded, we are of opinion that the judgment was right, and ought to be affirmed.

Judgment affirmed.

R v International Trustee (p 506, below)

Mount Albert Borough Council v Australasian Temperance and General Mutual Life Assurance Society Ltd [1938] AC 224, [1937] 4 All ER 206 (Privy Council)

Appeal from the New Zealand Court of Appeal.

In 1926 the appellants, a New Zealand borough council, and a local body within the New Zealand Local Bodies' Loans Act 1926, borrowed money for public works from the respondents, a company incorporated in Victoria, Australia, and carrying on business in Australia and New Zealand. As security for the loan the appellants issued in New Zealand debentures totalling £130,000 repayable in Melbourne, Victoria, and bearing interest payable in Melbourne half-yearly. The debentures were issued under the Local Bodies' Loans Act 1913, of New Zealand, and the loan and interest were secured on a special rate of 3d in the £ on the rateable value of all rateable property in the borough of Mount Albert, ie they were charged on land in the borough.

The respondents claimed that the interest due on 1 March 1935 was £3,696 17s 6d. The appellants, however, paid £3,250, alleging that as the interest was payable at Melbourne, the payment was governed by the Financial Emergency Act 1931 of Victoria, which provided for a reduction in the rate of interest on mortgages and other securities.

In the action the respondents claimed £446 17s 6d as being the balance of interest alleged to be due to them. The New Zealand Court of Appeal gave judgment for the respondents (plaintiffs). The Mount Albert Borough Council now appealed.

The judgment of their Lordships (Lords Atkin, Macmillan, Wright, and Maugham) was delivered by

Lord Wright: . . . The debentures and the interest coupons in so far as they give a security on real property, namely, a portion of the local rate in New Zealand, are beyond question governed by the New Zealand law. The security can be enforced only in the Courts of New Zealand and in the manner provided by the Loans Act. It is not disputed that these rights are governed by New Zealand law. But in their Lordships' judgment it is equally true that the personal obligation to pay is a New Zealand contract, governed by New Zealand law. It seems impossible to sever this personal covenant from the mortgage provisions which secure it. Indeed, the whole tenor of the transaction is only consistent with its being governed by New Zealand law. The loan was agreed in New Zealand, the money under the loan was paid by the respondents to the appellants there. The appellants were a statutory body in New Zealand which in borrowing were acting under the statutory powers contained in the Loans Act as set out above. The respondents carried on business in New Zealand as well as in Australia. It is true that the place of repayment of the loan, and of payment of interest from time to time, was to be Melbourne, in Australia. But even that was fixed in accordance with s 32 of the Loans Act 1913, which required payment of the debt to be at the place within or out of New Zealand named in the debenture, so that the obligation to pay has statutory sanction. Mr O'Shea, in his able and exhaustive argument, has contended that the payment is governed by Victorian law because Victoria is the place of performance, and that Victorian law for this purpose includes s 19, sub-s 1, of the Financial Emergency Act. He further contends that s 19, sub-s 1, applies to the debt because it is a specialty debt and the coupon, which is the document of title, must necessarily be presented at the place of payment in Melbourne when payment is due and demanded, and thus at the relevant moment the lex situs applies so as to introduce the statutory reduction of interest. Their Lordships are not prepared to accept either contention. While they think that the lex situs applies to the security in New Zealand, they do not think that the lex situs of the actual coupon can be applied to the instrument, whether or not the personal obligation to pay is properly regarded as a specialty debt. Nor can they accept the view that the obligation to pay is here governed by the place where it is stipulated that payment is to be made, in the sense that the amount of the debt, as expressed in the instrument creating it, can lawfully be varied by the Victorian Financial Emergency Act so as to bind a foreign jurisdiction, or indeed at all. So to hold would be, in their Lordships' judgment, to confuse two distinct conceptions, that is, to confuse the obligation with the performance of the obligation. It is well established in the law of England and of New Zealand, which in this respect follows it, that the proper law of a contract has to be first ascertained where a question of conflict of laws arises.

The proper law of the contract means that law which the English or other court is to apply in determining the obligations under the contract. English law in deciding these matters has refused to treat as conclusive, rigid or arbitrary criteria such as lex loci contractus or lex loci solutionis, and has treated the matter as depending on the intention of the parties to be ascertained in each case on a consideration of the terms of the contract, the situation of the parties, and generally on all the surrounding facts. It may be that the parties have in terms in their agreement expressed what law they intend to govern, and in that case prima facie their intention will be effectuated by the court. But in most cases they do not do so. The parties may not have thought of the matter at all. Then the court has to impute an intention, or to determine for the parties what is the proper law which, as just and reasonable persons, they ought or would have intended if they had thought about the question when they made the contract. No doubt there are certain prima facie rules to which a court in deciding on any particular contract may turn for assistance, but they are not conclusive. In this branch of law the particular rules can only be stated as prima facie presumptions. It is not necessary to cite authorities for these general principles. Sometimes their application involves difficulty; but not in this case. It has been already pointed out that there are, in their Lordships' opinion, such circumstances as lead to the inference that in the present case the proper law of the contract is the law of New Zealand, and accordingly that law should prima facie govern the rights and obligations to be enforced under the contract by a court before which the matter comes, a fortiori a New Zealand court. It is true that, when stating this general rule, there are qualifications to be borne in mind, as for instance, that the law of the place of performance will prima facie govern the incidents or mode of performance, that is, performance as contrasted with obligation. Thus in the present case it is not contested that the word 'pound' in the debenture and coupon is to be construed with reference to the place of payment, and as referring to the 'pound' in Victorian currency.[3] Again, different considerations may arise in particular cases, as, for instance, where the stipulated performance is illegal by the law of the place of performance. But there is no question of illegality here, since the Victorian statute is not prohibitory. . . .

Appeal dismissed.

Bonython v Commonwealth of Australia (p 457 below)

The Assunzione [1954] P 150, [1954] 1 All ER 278 (Court of Appeal)

In pursuance of a charterparty signed in Paris after negotiations between brokers resident in France on behalf of French shippers, and brokers resident in Italy on behalf of Italian shipowners, the Italian steamship *Assunzione*, commanded by an Italian master, loaded a cargo of wheat at Dunkirk for delivery at Venice. During the voyage the cargo was damaged and the charterers sued the shipowners for short delivery and damage to the cargo. The charterparty was in the English language and used the printed form of Uniform General Charter of the Documentary Council of the Baltic and White Sea Conference ('Gencon'). It contained additional clauses in the French language. It provided that freight and demurrage should be paid in Italian lire in Naples. Bills of lading in the French language were signed by the master at Dunkirk and indorsed by the Italian consignees. The wheat was shipped under an exchange agreement made between the French and Italian governments, but the shipowners did not know this.

Willmer J on a preliminary point of law held that Italian and not French law should be applied to the contract of affreightment. The charterers appealed.

Singleton LJ (having stated the facts): We have had a considerable number of authorities cited to us upon the question of what law should be applied. The parties did not state their desire, or their intention, upon the

3 Such matters have since been held to be part of the substance of the obligation and so governed by the proper law of the contract: *Bonython v Commonwealth of Australia* [1951] AC 201, 66 TLR (pt 2) 969; p 457 below (*Ed*).

subject. It has been said that when that happens one must endeavour to find what the intention of the parties was on the matter. That does not appear to me to be very helpful, for in most cases neither party has given it a thought, and neither has formed any intention upon it; still less can it be said that they have any common intention. I am not sure how far it is necessary to consider all the authorities which have been cited to us, and which go back to the year 1865, but I must refer to some of them. Sir Robert Aske, on behalf of the plaintiffs, relies on what he described as the general rule; that is, that the law to be applied should be the law of the country in which the contract was made.

(His Lordship referred to *P & O Steam Navigation Co Ltd v Shand*,[4] *Lloyd v Guibert*,[5] *Chartered Mercantile Bank of India v Netherlands India Steam Navigation Co Ltd*,[6] *Re Missouri SS Co*,[7] *The Industrie*,[8] *Mount Albert Borough Council v Australasian Temperance and General Mutual Life Assurance Society Ltd*[9] and *R v International Trustee for the Protection of Bondholders AG*[10] and continued): Upon the authorities Sir Robert Aske submitted that it was not possible to spell out of the cases any rule other than that of the place where the contract was made. Mr Mocatta (counsel for the defendants) claimed that no stronger inference could be drawn from the place where the contract was made than from the flag of the country under which the ship sailed; indeed, he submitted that one ought, in the circumstances of this case, to have regard first to the flag which the ship wore, and he relied on the decision in *Lloyd v Guibert*. His main contention was that this was not a case of an inference to be drawn one way or the other; it was a case, he submitted, in which the facts should be weighed, and that if they were weighed, those pointing towards the application of the Italian law weighed down any which could be found pointing the other way.

Without doubt there are features in this case which appear to point one way, and others which appear to point in another direction. When there are a number of circumstances which have to be considered in deciding which system of law applies, a presumption or inference arising from one alone becomes of less importance. In such a case an inference which might be properly drawn may cancel another inference which would be drawn if it stood by itself. When such a position arises all the relevant circumstances must be borne in mind, and the tribunal must find, if it can, how a just and reasonable person would have regarded the problem. No good purpose is served by saying that the French charterers would never have agreed to the application of Italian law, or by saying that the Italian shipowners would never have agreed to the application of French law, for that would have meant that there would have been no contract; and there is a contract.

I can summarise the facts relied upon fairly shortly. The charterers, who were also shippers under the bills of lading, were a French organisation; the contract was entered into by a charterparty which was made in France, after discussions to which I have referred, and the bills of lading were issued in

4 (1865) 3 Moo PCC NS 272, 6 New Rep 387; p 431 above.
5 (1865) LR 1 QB 115, 6 B & S 100; p 433 above.
6 (1883) 10 QBD 521, 52 LJQB 220.
7 (1889) 42 ChD 321, 58 LJCh 721.
8 [1894] P 58, 63 LJP 84.
9 [1938] AC 224, [1937] 4 All ER 206; p 437 above.
10 [1937] AC 500, [1937] 2 All ER 164; p 506 below.

France. The language of the charterparty is English, but no one contends that English law is to be applied. Some support is given to the argument of counsel for the plaintiffs by the bills of lading which are in French, and which contain the particular terms which I have mentioned. Sir Robert relies, too, upon the exchange agreement; upon the fact that in making arrangements for the carriage of the wheat from Dunkirk to an Italian port the charterers were acting in pursuance of what had been agreed between two government departments. I do not see, in the circumstances of this case, that great help is given by that fact, if it be a fact. . . .

With regard to the circumstances which support the defendants' contention that Italian law should be applied, I mention these: The ship was an Italian ship owned by two Italians in partnership, and a ship wearing the Italian flag; the owners were Italians; the master was an Italian; the contract was for carriage from a French port to an Italian port; the cargo was to be delivered at an Italian port. It is right to say that loading was at a French port and discharging at an Italian port, and one may appear to cancel the other, but there are further considerations; the charterparty provided that freight and demurrage should be paid in Italian currency. . . . Although I believe it to be impossible to state any rule of general application, I feel that matters of very considerable importance are the form of, and place of, payment. In this case payment has to be made in Italian lire, and in Italy. In the circumstances of this case I regard it as a very important feature, coupled as it is with the facts that the ship was an Italian ship and that the destination was an Italian port. . . .

One must look at all the circumstances and seek to find what just and reasonable persons ought to have intended if they had thought about the matter at the time when they made the contract. If they had thought that they were likely to have a dispute, I hope it may be said that just and reasonable persons would like the dispute determined in the most convenient way and in accordance with business efficacy.

Applying the rule which I have stated, and weighing all the facts to which attention was directed, I am satisfied that the scale comes down in favour of the application of Italian law, and that the decision of Willmer J was right. In my opinion, the appeal should be dismissed.

Birkett and Hodson LJJ delivered judgments to the same effect.
Appeal dismissed.

Coast Lines Ltd v Hudig & Veder Chartering NV (p 67 above)

Amin Rasheed Shipping Corpn v Kuwait Insurance Co (p 72 above)

A clause in a contract providing for arbitration in London usually but not necessarily means that English law is the proper law of the contract.

Compagnie Tunisienne de Navigation SA v Compagnie d'Armement Maritime SA [1971] AC 572, [1970] 3 All ER 71 (House of Lords)

French shipowners agreed with a Tunisian company to carry a large quantity of oil over a period of nine months from one Tunisian port to another. The contract was made in Paris on an English printed form. Freight was payable in French francs in Paris. French law was assumed to prevail in Tunisia and no question arose as between French and Tunisian law. A clause in the contract provided for the settlement of disputes by arbitration in London. There was no other connection between the contract and English law.

Disputes arose and were referred to arbitration in London. The arbitrators made an interim award holding that French law was the proper law of the contract. This award was upheld by Megaw J but reversed by the Court of Appeal (Lord Denning MR, Salmon and Karminski LJJ), which held that English law was the proper law because of the arbitration clause. The French shipowners appealed.

Lord Reid: . . . In the absence of any positive indication of intention in the contract the law will determine the proper law by deciding with what country or system of law the contract has the closest connection. Here three countries are involved. The contract was negotiated and signed in France and the freight was payable in Paris in French francs. The contract was to be performed in Tunisia. The only connection with England was that any dispute was to be settled by arbitration in London. The contract is in the English language and in English form, but it was not argued, in my view rightly, that any great importance should be given to this.

Until this case reached this House it appears to have been assumed that France and Tunisia could be treated as one country or as having the same system of law. It is stated in the interim award that: 'The civil law of Tunisia (which until 1956 was a French colony) is based on the Code Napoléon' and that 'neither side contended for any other system of law' than French or English law. On that basis when one comes to weigh the various factors which tell in favour of French or of English law being regarded as the proper law, the fact that Tunisia was to be the place of performance of the contract would be put in the scale for French law. Then it is clear that the balance comes down heavily in favour of French law. On the one hand, there are the place where the contract was negotiated and signed, the place of performance, the place where and the currency in which the freight was to be paid, and the place where the parties resided and carried on business: on the other hand, there is only the place where disputes were to be settled by arbitration. But I wish to reserve my opinion as to how far in a case of this kind it is proper to disregard the fact that two countries are separate and independent countries, each with its own system of law, on the ground that those countries are or have recently been closely associated, or that their systems of law are very similar but both very different from English law.

The respondents do not deny that, if we are free to apply the general rule that the proper law is the law of the place with which the contract is most closely associated, then the proper law would be French law. Their case is that that general rule does not apply where there is an arbitration clause requiring disputes to be settled by arbitration in England. They admit that such a clause does not prevent the parties from agreeing that some other law shall be the proper law, but they maintain that if such an agreement cannot be deduced from the terms of the contract, then the arbitration clause is decisive as to the proper law and requires an English court to hold that the proper law is the law of England.

Of course the fact that the parties have agreed that arbitration shall take place in England is an important factor and in many cases it may be the decisive factor. But it would, in my view, be highly anomalous if our law required the mere fact that arbitration is to take place in England to be decisive as to the proper law of the contract. For the reasons given by others of your Lordships I agree that this is not the law of England.

I would therefore allow this appeal.

Lords Morris of Borth-y-Gest, Dilhorne, Wilberforce and Diplock delivered judgments to the same effect.

Appeal allowed.

The parties are at liberty to select the proper law of their contract, provided the choice is bona fide and legal and provided there is no reason for avoiding the choice on the ground of public policy.

Vita Food Products Inc v Unus Shipping Co Ltd [1939] AC 277, [1939] 1 All ER 513 (Privy Council)

Appeal from the Supreme Court of Nova Scotia.

The appellant was a body corporate incorporated under the laws of the State of New York; the respondent was a body corporate incorporated under the laws of the Province of Nova Scotia. The respondent owned a motor vessel called *The Hurry On* which was registered at Halifax, Nova Scotia. In January 1935 the respondent agreed to carry a cargo of herrings from Middle Arm, Newfoundland, for delivery to the appellant in New York, and accordingly bills of lading were signed in Newfoundland by the agents of the parties.

The Newfoundland Carriage of Goods by Sea Act 1932 provided in s 1 that 'subject to the provisions of this Act' the Rules set out in the Schedule thereto should 'have effect in relation to and in connection with the carriage of goods by sea in ships carrying goods from any port in this Dominion to any other port whether in or outside this Dominion'. Section 3 provided that 'Every bill of lading or similar document of title issued in this Dominion which contains or is evidence of any contract to which the Rules apply shall contain an express statement that it is to have effect subject to the provisions of the said Rules as expressed in this Act.' Sections 4, 5, and 6 contained certain provisions to which the Rules were subject.

The Rules scheduled to the Act were identical with those scheduled to the United Kingdom Carriage of Goods by Sea Act 1924. They are commonly called the Hague Rules and were settled by an International Conference on Maritime Law held at Brussels in 1922 and 1923. Article III, rule 8, provided that any clause, covenant, or agreement lessening the carrier's liability under the Rules should be null and void and of no effect. Article IV, rule 2, provided that 'neither the carrier nor the ship shall be responsible for loss or damage arising or resulting from (a) act, neglect, or default of the master, mariners, pilot or the servants of the carrier in the navigation or in the management of the ship; ... (c) perils, dangers and accidents of the sea or other navigable waters'.

Owing to the inadvertence of the parties in using obsolete forms the bills of lading did not contain the statement required by section 3 of the Newfoundland Act. The bills of lading conferred on the carrier a number of immunities, some of which were wider and some narrower than those contained in the Rules. Clause 7 of the bills provided that the carrier should not be liable for any loss or injury arising from any act or omission, negligence, default or error in judgment of the pilots, masters, mariners, engineers, stevedores, workmen or other men in the service of the carrier. They also contained a statement that 'this contract shall be governed by English law', and a provision that the United States Harter Act 1893 should apply to shipments from the United States and that save as so provided the bills of lading were subject to the terms and provisions of, and exemptions from liability contained in, the Canadian Water Carriage of Goods Act 1910 (which, however, only applied to shipments of goods from any port in Canada).

The Hurry On sailed from Middle Arm on 16 January 1935, bound for New York with the herrings on board. Two days later she ran into bad weather and ice off the coast of Nova Scotia. The captain decided to make for a port of refuge, but in an attempt to do so ran ashore on the coast of Nova Scotia in a gale of wind owing (as was ultimately admitted) to his negligence. The herrings were unloaded, reconditioned, and forwarded by another ship to New York, where the appellant took delivery of them in a damaged condition and paid freight.

The appellant brought an action against the respondent in Nova Scotia claiming damages for the failure of the respondent to deliver the cargo in New York in like condition as received on board. The appellant claimed that the respondent operated *The Hurry On* as a common carrier and that as such it was an insurer of the safety of the cargo. The respondent pleaded that the bills of lading or, alternatively, the Rules exempted it from liability, even if the damage was caused by the captain's negligence; and that the contract was governed by the law of Newfoundland. The appellant admitted that the contract was governed by the law of Newfoundland, but alleged in reply that the bills of lading were illegal, null and void under Newfoundland law in that, contrary to section 3 of the Act of 1932, they did not contain an express statement that they were to have effect subject to the Rules; and that therefore the respondent could not take advantage of any of the exemptions from liability provided by the Rules or by the bills of lading.

Chisholm CJ and the Supreme Court of Nova Scotia rejected the appellant's contention, and the Supreme Court also held that, if the bills of lading were illegal, the parties were in pari delicto and the action must fail. The appellant appealed.

The judgment of their Lordships (Lords Atkin, Russell of Killowen, Macmillan, Wright, and Porter) was delivered by

Lord Wright: ... The first question to determine is the true construction of ss 1 and 3 of the Act. Section 1 provides for the application of the rules to every bill of lading for the carriage of goods by sea in ships from any port in Newfoundland to any other port, whether in or outside that Dominion. The appellant contended that since s 1 only provided that the rules should have effect 'subject to the provisions of this Act,' the rules could not apply to a bill of lading unless the terms of s 3 were complied with. Their Lordships do not so construe the section. In their opinion the words 'subject to the provisions of this Act' merely mean in this connection that the rules are to apply but subject to the modifications contained in ss 2, 4, 5 and 6 sub-s 3 of the Act. To read these words as meaning that the rules are only to have effect if the requirements of s 3 are complied with, would be to put an unnecessarily wide interpretation upon them instead of the narrower meaning, which is more natural and obvious. In their Lordships' judgment s 1 is the dominant section. Section 3 merely requires the bill of lading to contain an express statement of the effect of s 1. This view of the relative effect of the sections raises the question whether the mandatory provision of s 3, which cannot change the effect of s 1, is under Newfoundland law directory or imperative, and, if imperative, whether a failure to comply with it renders the contract void, either in Newfoundland, or in courts outside that Dominion.

It will be convenient at this point to determine what is the proper law of the contract. In their Lordships' opinion the express words of the bill of lading must receive effect, with the result that the contract is governed by English law. It is now well settled that by English law (and the law of Nova Scotia is the same) the proper law of the contract 'is the law which the parties intended to apply'. That intention is objectively ascertained, and, if not expressed, will be presumed from the terms of the contract and the relevant surrounding circumstances. But as Lord Atkin, dealing with cases where the intention of the parties is expressed, said in *R v International Trustee for, the Bondholders AG*[11] (a case which contains the latest enunciation of this principle), 'Their intention will be ascertained by the intention expressed in the contract if any, which will be conclusive'. It is objected that this is too broadly stated and that some qualifications are necessary. It is true that in questions relating to the conflict of laws rules cannot generally be stated in absolute terms but rather as prima facie presumptions. But where the English rule that intention is the test applies, and where there is an express statement by the parties of their intention to select the law of the contract, it is difficult to see what qualifications are possible, provided the intention expressed is bona fide and legal, and provided there is no reason for avoiding the choice on the ground of public policy. In the present case, however, it might be said that the choice of English law is not valid for two reasons. It might be said that the transaction, which is one relating to the carriage on a Nova Scotian ship of goods from Newfoundland to New York between residents in these countries, contains nothing to connect it in any way with English law, and therefore that choice could not be seriously taken. Their Lordships reject this argument both on grounds of principle and on the facts. Connection with English law is not as a matter of principle essential. The provision in a contract (eg, of sale) for English arbitration imports English law as the law governing the transaction, and those familiar with international business are aware how frequent such a provision is even where the parties are not English and the transactions are carried on completely outside England. Moreover in the present case *The Hurry On*, though on a Canadian register, is subject to the Imperial statute, the Merchant Shipping Act 1894, under which the vessel is registered, and the underwriters are

11 [1937] AC 500 at 529, [1937] 2 All ER 164 at 166; p 506 below.

likely to be English. In any case parties may reasonably desire that the familiar principles of English commercial law should apply. The other ground urged is that the choice of English law is inconsistent with the provisions of the bill of lading, that in respect of certain goods the Harter Act or the Canadian Water Carriage of Goods Act of 1910 (now repealed, but in force at the date of the bill of lading) was to apply. It has been explained that the incorporation of these Acts may have only contractual effect, but in any case, though the proper law of the contract is English, English law may incorporate the provisions of the law of another country or other countries as part of the terms of the contract, and apart from such incorporation other laws may have to be regarded in giving effect to the contract. The proper law of the contract does indeed fix the interpretation and construction of its express terms and supply the relevant background of statutory or implied terms. But that part of the English law which is commonly called the conflict of laws requires, where proper, the application of foreign law; eg, English law will not enforce a performance contrary to the law of the place of performance in circumstances like those existing in *Ralli Bros v Compania Naviera Sota y Aznar*,[12] and the law of the place of performance, though it will not be effective to affect the construction of the contract in regard to its substance (which must be ascertained according to the rule of the proper law, as was held in *Jacobs v Crédit Lyonnais*[13]) will still regulate what were called in that case the incidents and mode of performance in that place. English law will in these and sometimes in other respects import a foreign law, but the contract is still governed by its proper law. The reference to the United States and the Canadian Acts does not on any view supersede English law which is to govern the contract, nor does Newfoundland law, though Newfoundland was the place where the contract was made, apply to oust English law from being the law of the contract, and as such from being the law which defines its nature, obligation and interpretation, though Newfoundland law might apply to the incidents of performance to be done in Newfoundland. There is, in their Lordships' opinion, no ground for refusing to give effect to the express selection of English law as the proper law in the bills of lading. Hence English rules relating to the conflict of laws[14] must be applied to determine how the bills of lading are affected by the failure to comply with s 3 of the Act.

If however, by reason of this failure to obey the Act the bills of lading were illegal in Newfoundland, it would not follow as a necessary consequence that a Nova Scotian court, applying the proper law of the contract, would in its own forum treat them as illegal, though the position of a court in Newfoundland might be different, if it held them illegal by Newfoundland law. A court in Newfoundland would be bound to apply the law enacted by its own Legislature, if it applied, and thus might treat the bills as illegal, just as the Supreme Court in the United States treated as void an exemption of negligence in a bill of lading issued in the United States, though in relation to the carriage of goods to England in an English ship; *Liverpool and Great Western Steam Co v Phenix Insurance Co*.[15] Such a clause, it was held, was

12 [1920] 2 KB 287, 89 LJKB 999; p 451 below.
13 (1884) 12 QBD 589, 53 LJQB 156; p 453 below.
14 As to this, see p 665 below.
15 (1889) 129 US 397.

against public policy and void by the law of the United States, which was not only the law of the forum but was also held to be the proper law of the contract. This decision may be contrasted with *Re Missouri SS Co*[16] where in similar circumstances the Court of Appeal, holding the proper law of the bill of lading to be English, held that English law did not apply the American rule of public policy, though the shipment took place in America and the bill of lading was issued there, and that the clause, being valid in English law, must receive effect.

With these considerations in mind it is necessary first to consider if the bills of lading are illegal by Newfoundland law. If they are not, the question of illegality cannot arise in the courts of another jurisdiction, eg, those of Nova Scotia. Illegality is a concept of so many varying and diverse applications, that in each case it is necessary to scrutinise the particular circumstances with precision in order to determine if there is illegality and if so what is its effect. ... Each case has to be considered on its merits. Nor must it be forgotten that the rule by which contracts not expressly forbidden by statute or declared to be void are in proper cases nullified for disobedience to a statute is a rule of public policy only, and public policy understood in a wider sense may at times be better served by refusing to nullify a bargain save on serious and sufficient grounds.

Are there such grounds for holding that the Newfoundland law does in Newfoundland nullify bills of lading such as those in question? In their Lordships opinion there are not. ... It would be a grave matter if business men when dealing with a bill of lading had in a case like the present to inquire into the foreign law ruling at the port of shipment. The omission of what is called the clause paramount does not make the bills of lading illegal documents, in whole or in part, either within Newfoundland or outside it. Section 3 is in their Lordships' judgment directory. It is not obligatory, nor does failure to comply with its terms nullify the contract contained in the bill of lading. This, in their Lordships' judgment, is the true construction of the statute, having regard to its scope and its purpose and to the inconvenience which would follow from any other conclusion. If that is so, the bills of lading are binding according to their terms and consequently the respondent is entitled to succeed in its defence.

But on the basis that the bills of lading were illegal in Newfoundland in that their issue without the clause paramount was prohibited by the law of that country it was argued that no court in any country would enforce their terms and exemptions, and the carriage would therefore be upon the terms implied where goods are taken for carriage by a common carrier, ie, subject only to the exception of the Act of God and the King's Enemies. No further terms, it was said, could be implied nor could any reliance be put upon the provisions of the Hague Rules, since they had not been incorporated in the bills of lading by the insertion of the clause paramount. The appellant contended that, unless the clause was inserted, no contract between carrier and shipper which included the provisions of the Hague Rules was entered into. Nor could the Act be said to have incorporated them even in Newfoundland itself, since s 1 only provided that the rules should have effect 'subject to the provisions of this Act', a phrase which the appellant maintained meant (inter alia) that the rules were not incorporated unless the

16 (1889) 42 ChD 321, 58 LJCh 721.

provisions of s 3 were complied with. For reasons already explained their
Lordships do not so construe the section.

But whatever view a Newfoundland court might take, whether they would
hold that the contracts contained in the bills of lading must be taken to have
incorporated the Hague Rules or whether they would hold them to have
been illegal, the result would be the same in the present case, where the
action was brought not in a Newfoundland but in a Nova Scotian court. It
may be that, if suit were brought on these bills of lading in a Newfoundland
court, and the court held they were illegal, the court would refuse to give
effect to them, on the basis that a court is bound to obey the laws of its own
legislature or its own common law, as indeed the United States Supreme
Court did in *Liverpool and Great Western Steam Co v Phenix Insurance Co*. But it
does not follow that any other court could properly act in the same way. If it
has before it a contract good by its own law or by the proper law of the
contract, it will in proper cases give effect to the contract and ignore the
foreign law. This was done in the *Missouri* case, both by Chitty J and by the
Court of Appeal. Lord Halsbury, having stated that the contrary view would
mean that no country would enforce a contract made in another country
unless their laws were the same, said 'that there may be stipulations which
one country may enforce and which another country may not enforce, and
that to determine whether they are enforceable or not you must have regard
to the law of the contract, by which I mean the law which the contract itself
imports to be the law governing the contract'. Having held that the law of
the contract was English, he went on to hold that the exception of
negligence, even if of no validity in the place where made, must receive effect
in English law, although the exception of negligence was invalid in the
United States as being against the public policy of that country, and
although to do an act contrary to public policy is one type of illegal action.
The same attitude is illustrated in *Dobell v SS Rossmore Co*,[17] where the
Harter Act, which declares certain stipulations to be unlawful and imposes
penalties on shipowners inserting them in bills of lading, was not considered
as affecting the English contract as a part of the contract where its provisions
were infringed, save so far as it was expressly incorporated. Foreign law was
also disregarded in *Trinidad Shipping Co v G R Alston & Co*,[18] where the
contract was an English contract and payment of certain rebates on freight
were rendered illegal by the law of the United States, where the freight was
payable. From the rule which he states Lord Halsbury in the *Missouri* case
puts aside 'questions in which the positive law of the country [sc the foreign
country] forbids contracts to be made. Where a contract is void on the
ground of immorality, or is contrary to such positive law as would prohibit
the making of such a contract at all, then the contract would be void all over
the world, and no civilised country would be called on to enforce it'. In this
passage Lord Halsbury would seem to be referring to matters of foreign law
of such a character that it would be against the comity of nations for an
English court to give effect to the transaction, just as an English court may
refuse in proper cases to enforce performance of an English contract in a
foreign country where the performance has been expressly prohibited by the
public law of that country. The exact scope of Lord Halsbury's proviso has

17 [1895] 2 QB 408, 64 LJQB 777.
18 [1920] AC 888, 89 LJPC 185.

not been defined. There may also be questions in some cases as to the effect of non-performance of conditions which by the foreign law of the place where a contract was entered into are essential to its formation, though even in that case the validity of the contract may depend on its proper law. But whatever the precise ambit of that saving expression, it is clear that it does not apply to such a statutory enactment as s 3, even if disobedience to it were regarded as rendering the bill of lading in some sense illegal. . . .

(His Lordship proceeded to express disapproval of *The Torni*,[19] and refused to distinguish it either on the ground that the bills of lading in that case provided that they were to be 'construed in accordance with' (not 'governed by') English law; or on the ground that s 4 of the Palestine Carriage of Goods by Sea Ordinance, which was otherwise identical with s 3 of the Newfoundland Act of 1932, contained the additional words 'and shall be deemed to have effect subject thereto, notwithstanding the omission of such express statement'.)

Appeal dismissed.

The Hollandia (p 682 below)

Unfair Contract Terms Act 1977

6.—(1) Liability for breach of the obligations arising from—

(a) section 12 of the Sale of Goods Act 1893 (seller's implied undertakings as to title, etc);

(b) section 8 of the Supply of Goods (Implied Terms) Act 1973 (the corresponding thing in relation to hire-purchase),

cannot be excluded or restricted by reference to any contract term.

(2) As against a person dealing as consumer,[20] liability for breach of the obligations arising from—

(a) section 13, 14 or 15 of the 1893 Act (seller's implied undertakings as to conformity of goods with description or sample, or as to their quality or fitness for a particular purpose);

(b) section 9, 10 or 11 of the 1973 Act (the corresponding things in relation to hire-purchase),

cannot be excluded or restricted by reference to any contract term.

(3) As against a person dealing otherwise than as consumer, the liability specified in subsection (2) above can be excluded or restricted by reference to a contract term, but only in so far as the term satisfies the requirement of reasonableness.

27.[1]—(1) Where the proper law of a contract is the law of any part of the United Kingdom only by choice of the parties (and apart from that choice would be the law of some country outside the United Kingdom) sections 2 to 7 and 16 to 21 of this Act do not operate as part of the proper law.

(2) This Act has effect notwithstanding any contract term which applies or purports to apply the law of some country outside the United Kingdom, where (either or both)—

19 [1932] P 78, 101 LJP 44.
20 'Dealt as consumer' is widely defined by s 12 (*Ed*).
1 See further on this section pp 677–678 below.

(a) the term appears to the court, or arbitrator or arbiter to have been imposed wholly or mainly for the purpose of enabling the party imposing it to evade the operation of this Act; or

(b) in the making of the contract one of the parties dealt as consumer, and he was then habitually resident in the United Kingdom, and the essential steps necessary for the making of the contract were taken there, whether by him or by others on his behalf.

QUESTION

Imagine a contract between two private individuals for the sale of a car. All the circumstances of the case are English, but for an express term that the contract is to be governed by French law. The buyer claims that the car is defective. Is French or English law to be applied to this issue? Would the answer be different if the contract was one of hire rather than sale? Would the answers be different if the EEC Convention on the Law Applicable to Contractual Obligations (p 459 below) was in force in this country?

Section B. Capacity

Capacity to contract is governed by the proper law of the contract.

Charron v Montreal Trust Co (1958) 15 DLR (2d) 240, [1958] OR 597 (Ontario Court of Appeal)

Peter Charron was domiciled in Quebec. In 1906 he came to Ontario and joined the Royal Canadian Mounted Police. In 1908 he married the plaintiff in Ontario and lived with her there until they separated in 1920. They entered into a separation agreement in Ontario form in 1920. Peter Charron then resigned from the Mounted Police and returned to Quebec, where he died in 1953 having by his will appointed the defendant his executor. The plaintiff sued to recover arrears of payments due under the separation agreement. One of the defences was that by Quebec law spouses have no capacity to enter into a separation agreement. McRuer CJ gave judgment for the plaintiff. The defendant appealed.

The judgment of the court (Aylesworth, Gibson, and Morden JJA) was delivered by

Morden JA (having stated the facts): I will assume for the purpose of this appeal that the husband and therefore his wife, the plaintiff, lacked the capacity by the law of their domicile to make this agreement.

Apart from marriage and marriage settlements in which situations capacity is regulated, broadly speaking, by the lex domicilii, there is no clear decision whether capacity to contract is to be tested by the lex loci contractus or the lex domicilii. Examples could be given in particular instances of the unfairness and unreality of applying one law or the other. To vary the facts of the instant case, let us assume the spouses had been both domiciled and resident in Quebec and had come to Ontario for a short visit during which the agreement under consideration was made; upon such assumption, in my opinion, it would be against common sense to decide the parties' capacity by Ontario law. In the present case, the marriage had taken place in Ontario and for many years thereafter and until the date of this agreement the parties had cohabited in Ontario. It would be unrealistic in the circumstances here to apply Quebec law in deciding the parties' capacity. The solution to this problem, in my opinion, is that adopted by the learned writers on private international law and to decide that a party's capacity to enter into a contract is to be governed by the proper law of the particular contract, that is, the law of the country with which the contract is most substantially connected.[2] In this case there is no doubt that the proper law of the agreement was the law of Ontario, and by that law neither party to the agreement lacked the necessary capacity. Therefore, I agree with the learned Chief Justice's statement that 'the contract is a good enforceable contract under the laws of Ontario'.

Appeal dismissed.

QUESTIONS

1. A, aged 20, is domiciled and resident in Ruritania. During a temporary visit to England he buys goods (not necessaries) on credit from a shop in London. Could he refuse to pay for them on the ground that by Ruritanian law, minority ends at 21?
2. B, aged 20, is domiciled and resident in England. During a temporary visit to Ruritania he buys goods (not necessaries) from a shop in Strelsau. Could he refuse to pay for them on the ground that by Ruritanian law, minority ends at 21?

Section C. Illegality

An English court will not enforce a contract which is valid by its proper law but the performance of which is illegal by the law of the place of performance: at any rate if (a) the proper law is English, or (b) the place of performance is in England.

Ralli Brothers v Compania Naviera Sota y Aznar [1920] 2 KB 287, 89 LJKB 999 (Court of Appeal)

In July 1918 an English firm chartered a Spanish steamship from the owners, a Spanish firm, to carry a cargo of jute from Calcutta to Barcelona at a freight of £50 per ton, one half to be paid to the owners in London on the vessel sailing from Calcutta, and the other half to be paid at Barcelona, after the arrival of the ship. The charter-party was made in London in the English language and form and the Court of Appeal held (what had not been disputed) that English law was its proper law. The steamship arrived at Barcelona in December 1918. Meanwhile in September 1918 there came into force in Spain a decree having the force of law which fixed the maximum freight on jute imported into Spain at 875 pesetas per ton, and imposed penalties upon persons infringing it. The freight reserved by the charter-party was largely in excess of 875 pesetas per ton. The receivers of the cargo

---

2 Cheshire *Private International Law* (5th edn) pp 221–4; Dicey's *Conflict of Laws* (7th edn) pp 769–74; Falconbridge *Conflict of Laws* (2nd edn) pp 383–5.

at Barcelona tendered the balance of the freight at this rate but refused to pay the balance at the rate reserved by the charter party. The Spanish shipowners then claimed to recover the balance of the freight from the charterers in England, notwithstanding that it exceeded the freight limited by Spanish law. The matter came before Bailhache J in the form of a special case stated by a commercial umpire. The learned judge decided in favour of the charterers. The shipowners appealed.

Scrutton LJ (after stating the facts, continued): I accept the contention of the shipowners that the charterers remain liable for the freight, in spite of the provision that half of it is to be paid by the receivers. But I think they remain liable to pay it in Spanish currency at the Spanish port of discharge to a Spanish company resident in Spain. To pay freight in Spain to a Spaniard for goods to be discharged in Spain at a rate in excess of the maximum freight fixed by Spanish law for the carriage of such goods is illegal by the law of Spain. What then is the effect on the contract of illegality by the law of the place where it is to be performed, such law not being British law?

In my opinion the law is correctly stated by Professor Dicey in *Conflict of Laws*[3] where he says: 'A contract . . . is, in general, invalid in so far as . . . the performance of it is unlawful by the law of the country where the contract is to be performed'—and I reserve liberty to consider whether it is any longer an exception to this proposition that this country will not consider the fact that the contract is obnoxious only to the revenue laws of the foreign country where it is to be performed as an obstacle to enforcing it in the English courts. The early authorities on this point require reconsideration in view of the obligations of international comity as now understood.

The argument addressed to us was that illegality by foreign law was only impossibility in fact, which the parties might have provided against by their contract, and for which they must be liable, if they had not expressly relieved themselves from liability. This is the old doctrine of *Paradine v Jane*:[4] 'When the party by his own contract creates a duty or charge upon himself, he is bound to make it good, if he may, notwithstanding any accident by inevitable necessity, because he might have provided against it by his contract.' It was emphasized by Lord Ellenborough in *Atkinson v Ritchie*,[5] where he said: 'No exception (of a private nature at least) which is not contained in the contract itself, can be engrafted upon it by implication, as an excuse for its non-performance.' And Lord Bowen as late as 1884 in the case of *Jacobs v Crédit Lyonnais*,[6] cited Lord Ellenborough's approval of *Paradine v Jane* with approval. But the numerous cases, of which *Metropolitan Water Board v Dick, Kerr & Co*[7] is a recent example, most of which are cited in McCardie J's exhaustive judgment in *Blackburn Bobbin Co v Allen & Sons*,[8] have made a serious breach in the ancient proposition. It is now quite common for exceptions, or exemptions from liability, to be grafted by implication on contracts, if the parties by necessary implication must have treated the continued existence of a specified state of things as essential

3 2nd edn (1908) p 553.
4 (1647) Aleyn 26 at 27.
5 (1809) 10 East 530 at 553.
6 (1884) 12 QBD 589, 53 LJQB 156; p 453 below.
7 [1918] AC 119, 87 LJKB 370.
8 [1918] 1 KB 540 at 546.

to liability on the express terms of the contract. If I am asked whether the true intent of the parties is that one has undertaken to do an act though it is illegal by the law of the place in which the act is to be done, and though that law is the law of his own country; or whether their true intent was that the doing of that act is subject to the implied condition that it shall be legal for him to do the act in the place where it has to be done, I have no hesitation in choosing the second alternative. 'I will do it provided I can legally do so' seems to me infinitely preferable to and more likely than 'I will do it, though it is illegal'.

. . . Where a contract requires an act to be done in a foreign country, it is, in the absence of very special circumstances, an implied term of the continuing validity of such a provision that the act to be done in the foreign country shall not be illegal by the law of that country. This country should not in my opinion assist or sanction the breach of the laws of other independent states.

Lord Sterndale MR and Warrington LJ delivered judgments to the same effect.

Appeal dismissed.

But an English court will enforce a contract which is valid by its proper law but illegal by the law of the place of contracting.

Vita Food Products Inc v Unus Shipping Co (p 443 above)

Section D. Discharge

The proper law of the contract, and not the law of the place of performance as such, determines what are excuses for non-performance.

Jacobs v Credit Lyonnais (1884) 12 QBD 589, 53 LJQB 156 (Court of Appeal)

Appeal from a Divisional Court (Denman and Manisty JJ).

The judgment of the Court of Appeal (Brett MR and Bowen LJ) was read by

Bowen LJ: The plaintiffs in this case are esparto merchants carrying on business in the city of London, and the defendants are a banking firm also carrying on business in the City.

By a contract made in London on the 6 October 1880, the defendants agreed to sell to the plaintiffs 20,000 tons of Algerian esparto, to be shipped from Algeria during the year 1881 by monthly deliveries on board ships or steamers to be provided by the plaintiffs, payment to be made by cash on arrival of the ship or steamer at her port of destination. The defendants delivered a portion of the esparto under the contract, but failed to deliver the remainder; and this action was brought by the plaintiffs for its non-delivery. The defendants in their statement of defence admitted the non-delivery complained of, but alleged that the insurrection in Algeria and the military operations connected with it had rendered the performance of the contract impossible; and that by the French Civil Code, which prevails throughout Algeria, 'force majeure' is an excuse for non-performance. The plaintiffs demurred to this defence on the ground that the contracts were governed by English law and not by the law of Algeria. . . . The Queen's Bench Division having given judgment upon [the demurrers] for the plaintiffs, the case now came before us upon appeal.

The first matter we have to determine is, whether this contract is to be construed according to English law or according to French. To decide this point we must turn to the contract itself, for it is open in all cases for parties to make such agreement as they please as to incorporating the provisions of any foreign law with their contracts. What is to be the law by which a contract, or any part of it, is to be governed or applied, must be always a matter of construction of the contract itself as read by the light of the subject-matter and of the surrounding circumstances. Certain presumptions or rules in this respect have been laid down by juridical writers of different countries and accepted by the courts, based upon common sense, upon business convenience, and upon the comity of nations; but these are only presumptions or prima facie rules that are capable of being displaced, wherever the clear intention of the parties can be gathered from the document itself and from the nature of the transaction. The broad rule is that the law of a country where a contract is made presumably governs the nature, the obligation and the interpretation of it, unless the contrary appears to be the express intention of the parties. 'The general rule', says Lord Mansfield, 'established ex comitate et jure gentium is that the place where the contract is made, and not where the action is brought, is to be considered in expounding and enforcing the contract. But this rule admits of an exception where the parties at the time of making the contract had a view to a different kingdom': *Robinson v Bland*[9] (see *P & O Steam Navigation Co v Shand*).[10] This principle was explained by the Exchequer Chamber in the case of *Lloyd v Guibert*[11] as follows. (His Lordship read the passage beginning 'It is, however, generally agreed' and ending 'the character of the contract', p 434 above and continued:) It is obvious, however, that the subject-matter of each contract must be looked at as well as the residence of the contracting parties or the place where the contract is made. The place of performance is necessarily in many cases the place where the obligations of the contract will have to be enforced, and hence, as well as for other reasons, has been introduced another canon of construction, to the effect that the law of the place of fulfilment of a contract determines its obligations. But this maxim, as well as the former, must of course give way to any inference that can legitimately be drawn from the character of the contract and the nature of the transaction. In most cases no doubt where a contract has to be wholly performed abroad, the reasonable presumption may be that it is intended to be a foreign contract determined by foreign law; but this prima facie view is in its turn capable of being rebutted by the expressed or implied intention of the parties as deduced from other circumstances. Again, it may be that the

9 (1760) 2 Burr 1077, 1 Wm Bl 256.
10 (1865) 3 Moo PCC NS 272, 6 New Rep 387; p 431 above.
11 (1865) LR 1 QB 115, 6 B & S 100; p 433 above.

contract is partly to be performed in one place and partly in another. In such a case the only certain guide is to be found in applying sound ideas of business, convenience, and sense to the language of the contract itself, with a view to discovering from it the true intention of the parties. Even in respect of any performance that is to take place abroad, the parties may still have desired that their liabilities and obligations shall be governed by English law; or it may be that they have intended to incorporate the foreign law to regulate the method and manner of performance abroad, without altering any of the incidents which attach to the contract according to English law. Stereotyped rules laid down by juridical writers cannot, therefore, be accepted as infallible canons of interpretation in these days, when commercial transactions have altered in character and increased in complexity: and there can be no hard-and-fast rule by which to construe the multiform commercial agreements with which in modern times we have to deal. In the present case the contract was made in London between merchants carrying on their business in the city of London, and payment was to be made in London. Presumably, therefore, we should infer that this was an English contract and intended to be governed by English law; but it still remains to be considered whether anything in the contract itself or the nature of its stipulations displaces this prima facie view either wholly or in part. Now it cannot be contended that the parties have in express terms provided that any portion of this contract is to be construed or applied otherwise than according to English law; but it was suggested by the appellants that such an intention ought to be inferred from certain provisions as to the collection of the esparto in Algeria and as to its shipment thence. The esparto was to be shipped by the Compagnie Franco-Algerienne, or their agents, from Arzew, or any other port with safe anchorage, by sailing ships or steamers during the year 1881. The quality of the esparto was to be finally approved by the plaintiff's representatives at the works of the Compagnie Franco-Algerienne, at Ain-el-Hadjar, in Algeria, before being baled, and no claim respecting quality was to be allowed after the delivery of the bales at Arzew. The necessary ships or steamers were to be supplied by the plaintiffs, otherwise the esparto was to be warehoused by the Compagnie Franco-Algerienne at the plaintiffs' peril and risk. Insurance was to be effected by the defendants for the invoice amount at selling price, and 2% over in the United Kingdom on the usual conditions. Payment to be made by cash on arrival of the ship or steamer at port of destination. Finally, the contract contained an arbitration clause, with a provision that it should be made a rule of the High Court of Judicature on the application of either of the contracting parties.

There is absolutely nothing in any part of this contract, as it appears to us, which can amount to an indication that it is in any way or in any part of it to be treated as anything except an English contract, unless it be the mere fact that the esparto is to be collected in Algeria, approved at the works of a French company in Algeria before shipment, and to be delivered on board ships of the plaintiffs at an Algerian port, after which it is to be at plaintiffs' risk. To hold that on this ground only the ordinary presumption is to be displaced, and that the parties must have meant some law other than the English to govern the construction of any portion of the contract as regards the liabilities of the contracting parties, would be to introduce a serious element of uncertainty into mercantile contracts. The mere fact that a contract of this description,—made in England between English resident houses, and under which payment is to be made in England upon delivery of goods from up country in an Algerian port,—is partly to be performed in Algeria, does not put an end to the inference that the contract remains an English contract between English merchants, to be construed according to English law, and with all the incidents which English law attaches to the non-performance of such contracts.

Now one of the incidents which the English law attaches to a contract is that (except in certain excepted cases as that of common carriers and bailees, of which this is not one) a person who expressly contracts absolutely to do a thing not naturally impossible, is not excused for non-performance because of being prevented by vis major.

'The rule laid down in the case of *Paradine v Jane*[12] has often', says Lord Ellenborough, 'been recognised in courts of law as a sound one; that when a party by his own contract creates a duty or charge upon himself, he is bound to make it good, if he may, notwithstanding any accident by inevitable necessity; because he might have provided against it by his contract': *Atkinson v Ritchie*.[13] If inevitable necessity occurring in this country would not excuse non-performance, why should non-performance be excused on account of the inevitable necessity arising abroad? So to hold would be to alter the liability which English law attaches to contracts, and would, in the absence of an expressed or implied intention to that effect, be contrary to authority as well as principle. The Solicitor-General, in his argument, admitted that he was driven to contend that the law of the place of fulfilment not merely governed the mode of performance of this particular contract, but governed also the obligations in respect of performance, and the liabilities in respect of non-performance of it. It seems to us, however, that the true principles of construction to be applied do not admit of this interpretation of this contract. To what extent foreign law is to be incorporated in any contract must be, as we have said, a question of construction of the contract itself read by the light of the surrounding circumstances. If a contract made in England by English subjects or residents, and upon which payment is to be made in England, has to be performed in part abroad, it might be not unreasonable to assume that the mode in which any part of it has to be performed abroad was intended to be in accordance with the law of the foreign country, and to construe the contract as incorporating silently to that extent all provisions of a foreign law which would regulate the method of performance, and which were not inconsistent with the English contract. But it cannot be gathered from such a contract as the present that the parties desired to go further and to discharge the defendants from performance whenever circumstances arose which would, according to foreign law, excuse them. The contract has absolutely provided that delivery of the esparto shall be duly made, not that the bargain as to such delivery need only be observed when the foreign law would insist upon such observance. The contract being an English contract, only such portions of the French Civil Code can be applied to its provisions as to performance in Algeria as are not inconsistent with the express language of the contract as interpreted according to English law. If the parties had wished, in addition to this, to incorporate a provision of French

12 (1647) Aleyn 27, Sty 47.
13 (1809) 10 East 530.

law which in the event of vis major would operate to excuse the contracting parties for non-performance, and thus to vary the natural construction of the instrument according to English law, they should have done so in express terms. Read by English law the contract is not susceptible of such an interpretation, and there is nothing to show that in this respect the parties desired the contract to be governed by the French.

For these reasons we are of opinion that the judgment of the court below was right and must be affirmed with costs.

Judgment affirmed.

The proper law of the contract, and not the law of the place of performance as such, determines the substance of the obligation.

Mount Albert Borough Council v Australasian Temperance and General Mutual Life Assurance Society Ltd (p 437 above)

Bonython v Commonwealth of Australia [1951] AC 201 (Privy Council)

Appeal from the High Court of Australia.

In 1895 the government of Queensland issued debentures of varying amounts to secure a loan of £2,000,000 of which £1,250,000 was raised in England and the balance in Australia. The debentures entitled the holders to repayment in 'pounds sterling' in 1945 (together with interest in the meantime) either in Brisbane, Sydney, Melbourne, or London at the holder's option. In 1931 the Australian pound was devalued in relation to the English pound by 25%. In 1932 the public debt of Queensland was taken over by the Commonwealth of Australia which issued consolidated inscribed stock maturing in 1945 in lieu of the debentures to the holders thereof.

The plaintiffs, who were holders of some of the inscribed stock, exercised their option for repayment in London and claimed to be entitled to be paid in London the face value of their stock in English currency or, alternatively, to be paid in Australia the equivalent in Australian currency of such value in English currency. The High Court of Australia by a majority rejected their claim. The plaintiffs appealed.

The judgment of their Lordships (Viscount Simon, Lords Simonds, Morton of Henryton, MacDermott, and Reid) was delivered by

Lord Simonds: ... The conclusion to which, as a matter of construction, their Lordships come, that the substantial obligation under the debenture is the same whatever the place of payment, clears the way to a solution of the whole problem. It has been urged that, if London is chosen as the place of payment, then English law as the lex loci solutionis governs the contract and determines the measure of the obligation. But this contention cannot be accepted. The mode of performance of the obligation may, and probably will, be determined by English law; the substance of the obligation must be determined by the proper law of the contract, ie the system of law by reference to which the contract was made or that with which the transaction has its closest and most real connection. In the consideration of the latter question, what is the proper law of the contract, and therefore what is the substance of the obligation created by it, it is a factor, and sometimes a decisive one, that a particular place is chosen for performance. . . .

In the present case it is clear that, if it had been provided that payment would be made in London only, that would have been an important factor in determining the substance of the obligation, though other factors could not be ignored. But payment in London was only one of four alternative modes of performance, and the fact that London might be chosen as the place of payment becomes a factor of little or no weight. If the substance of the obligation is in every case the same, how can it affect the rights of one debenture-holder who elects to be paid in Melbourne that another has elected to be paid in London?

The question, then, is what is the proper law of the contract, or, to relate the general question to the particular problem, within the framework of what monetary or financial system should the instrument be construed. On the assumption that express reference is made to none, the question becomes a matter of implication to be derived from all the circumstances of the transaction. Applying this test to the present case, their Lordships find in the circumstances overwhelming evidence that it was to the law of Queensland that the parties looked for the determination of their rights. The debentures were issued on the authority of a Queensland Act which empowered the Governor-in-Council to raise by way of loan not more than £2,000,000 for the public service of the colony. By the same Act the loan was secured on the public revenues of the colony, and was made repayable on 1 January 1945. These circumstances must be of great, if not decisive, weight in determining what is the proper law of the contract: see *R v International Trustee for the Protection of Bondholders AG*[14] and compare *Mount Albert Borough Council v Australasian etc Life Assurance Society Ltd.*[15] It is not inconceivable that the legislature of a self-governing colony should authorise the raising of a loan in terms of a currency other than its own, but where it uses terms which are apt to describe its own lawful money, it must require the strongest evidence to the contrary to suppose that it intended some other money. Here there are no countervailing features except (a) that the lender was given a choice of payment in London, and (b) that the larger part of the authorised loan of £2,000,000 was in fact raised in London. The weight of the first factor has already been discussed: the second is more difficult to assess. As has been pointed out by Dixon J, no details of this transaction have been given and the history and fate of the debentures issued in London were not revealed. The safer course is to examine the contract as between the present appellants or their predecessors in title and the government of Queensland and to disregard what must be a matter of mere speculation, whether the fact that similar debentures had been, or were to be, issued in London was a circumstance from which an intention could fairly or reasonably be implied that the debentures issued to them in Queensland were to be repaid in anything but the lawful money of Queensland. . . .

The government of a self-governing country, using the terms appropriate to its own monetary system, must be presumed to refer to that system whether or not those terms are apt to refer to another system also. It may be

---

14 [1937] AC 500, [1937] 2 All ER 164; p 506 below
15 [1938] AC 224, [1937] 4 All ER 206; p 437 above.

possible to displace that presumption,[16] but, unless it is displaced, it prevails, and, if it prevails, then it follows that the obligation to pay will be satisfied by payment of whatever currency is by the law of Queensland valid tender for the discharge of the nominal amount of the debt. It becomes an irrelevant consideration whether the parties ever thought that the money of account of Queensland and England might at a future date, though still bearing the same name, become disparate in value or whether in fact that divergence took place. The law of Queensland governs the contract and that law determines the meaning of the word 'pound'. . . .

The Lordships will humbly advise His Majesty that this appeal should be dismissed.

Appeal dismissed.

Re Helbert Wagg & Co Ltd's Claim (p 559 below)

Section E. EEC Contracts Convention

The EEC Convention on the Law Applicable to Contractual Obligations

TITLE I
SCOPE OF THE CONVENTION

ARTICLE 1

Scope of the Convention

1. The rules of this Convention shall apply to contractual obligations in any situation involving a choice between the laws of different countries.

2. They shall not apply to:
(a) questions involving the status or legal capacity of natural persons, without prejudice to Article 11;
(b) contractual obligations relating to:
   —wills and succession,
   —rights in property arising out of a matrimonial relationship,
   —rights and duties arising out of a family relationship, parentage, marriage or affinity including maintenance obligations in respect of children who are not legitimate;
(c) obligations arising under bills of exchange, cheques and promissory notes and other negotiable instruments to the extent that the obligations under such other negotiable instruments arise out of their negotiable character;
(d) arbitration agreements and agreements on the choice of court;
(e) questions governed by the law of companies and other bodies corporate or unincorporate such as the creation, by registration or otherwise, legal capacity, internal organisation or winding up of companies and other

---

16 This presumption was displaced in *National Mutual Life Association of Australasia Ltd v A-G for New Zealand* [1956] AC 369, [1956] 1 All ER 721 *(Ed)*.

bodies corporate or unincorporate and the personal liability of officers and members as such for the obligations of the company or body;

(f)   the question whether an agent is able to bind a principal, or an organ to bind a company or body corporate or unincorporate, to a third party;

(g)   the constitution of trusts and the relationship between settlors, trustees and beneficiaries;

(h)   evidence and procedure, without prejudice to Article 14.

3. The rules of this Convention do not apply to contracts of insurance which cover risks situated in the territories of the Member States of the European Economic Community. In order to determine whether a risk is situated in these territories the court shall apply its internal law.

4. The preceding paragraph does not apply to contracts of re-insurance.

ARTICLE 2

Application of law of non-contracting States

Any law specified by this Convention shall be applied whether or not it is the law of a Contracting State.

TITLE II
UNIFORM RULES

ARTICLE 3

Freedom of choice

1. A contract shall be governed by the law chosen by the parties. The choice must be expressed or demonstrated with reasonable certainty by the terms of the contract or the circumstances of the case. By their choice the parties can select the law applicable to the whole or a part only of the contract.

2. The parties may at any time agree to subject the contract to a law other than that which previously governed it, whether as a result of an earlier choice under this Article or of other provisions of this Convention. Any variation by the parties of the law to be applied made after the conclusion of the contract shall not prejudice its formal validity under Article 9 or adversely affect the rights of third parties.

3. The fact that the parties have chosen a foreign law, whether or not accompanied by the choice of a foreign tribunal, shall not, where all the other elements relevant to the situation at the time of the choice are connected with one country only, prejudice the application of rules of the law of that country which cannot be derogated from by contract, hereinafter called 'mandatory rules'.

4. The existence and validity of the consent of the parties as to the choice of the applicable law shall be determined in accordance with the provisions of Articles 8, 9 and 11.

ARTICLE 4

Applicable law in the absence of choice

1. To the extent that the law applicable to the contract has not been chosen in accordance with Article 3, the contract shall be governed by the law of the

country with which it is most closely connected. Nevertheless, a severable part of the contract which has a closer connection with another country may by way of exception be governed by the law of that other country.

2. Subject to the provisions of paragraph 5 of this Article, it shall be presumed that the contract is most closely connected with the country where the party who is to effect the performance which is characteristic of the contract has, at the time of conclusion of the contract, his habitual residence, or, in the case of a body corporate or unincorporate, its central administration. However, if the contract is entered into in the course of that party's trade or profession, that country shall be the country in which the principal place of business is situated or, where under the terms of the contract the performance is to be effected through a place of business other than the principal place of business, the country in which that other place of business is situated.

3. Notwithstanding the provisions of paragraph 2 of this Article, to the extent that the subject matter of the contract is a right in immovable property or a right to use immovable property it shall be presumed that the contract is most closely connected with the country where the immovable property is situated.

4. A contract for the carriage of goods shall not be subject to the presumption in paragraph 2. In such a contract if the country in which, at the time the contract is concluded, the carrier has his principal place of business is also the country in which the place of loading or the place of discharge or the principal place of business of the consignor is situated, it shall be presumed that the contract is most closely connected with that country. In applying this paragraph single voyage charter-parties and other contracts the main purpose of which is the carriage of goods shall be treated as contracts for the carriage of goods.

5. Paragraph 5 shall not apply if the characteristic performance cannot be determined, and the presumptions in paragraphs 2, 3 and 4 shall be disregarded if it appears from the circumstances as a whole that the contract is more closely connected with another country.

ARTICLE 5

Certain consumer contracts

1. This Article applies to a contract the object of which is the supply of goods or services to a person ('the consumer') for a purpose which can be regarded as being outside his trade or profession, or a contract for the provision of credit for that object.

2. Notwithstanding the provisions of Article 3, a choice of law made by the parties shall not have the result of depriving the consumer of the protection afforded to him by the mandatory rules of the law of the country in which he has his habitual residence:

—if in that country the conclusion of the contract was preceded by a specific invitation addressed to him or by advertising, and he had taken in that country all the steps necessary on his part for the conclusion of the contract, or

—if the other party or his agent received the consumer's order in that country, or

—if the contract is for the sale of goods and the consumer travelled from that country to another country and there gave his order, provided that the consumer's journey was arranged by the seller for the purpose of inducing the consumer to buy.

3. Notwithstanding the provisions of Article 4, a contract to which this Article applies shall, in the absence of choice in accordance with Article 3, be governed by the law of the country in which the consumer has his habitual residence if it is entered into in the circumstances described in paragraph 2 of this Article.

4. This Article shall not apply to:
(a) a contract of carriage;
(b) a contract for the supply of services where the services are to be supplied to the consumer exclusively in a country other than that in which he has his habitual residence.

5. Notwithstanding the provisions of paragraph 4, this Article shall apply to a contract which, for an inclusive price, provides for a combination of travel and accommodation.

Article 6

Individual employment contracts

1. Notwithstanding the provisions of Article 3, in a contract of employment a choice of law made by the parties shall not have the result of depriving the employee of the protection afforded to him by the mandatory rules of the law which would be applicable under paragraph 2 in the absence of choice.

2. Notwithstanding the provisions of Article 4, a contract of employment shall, in the absence of choice in accordance with Article 3, be governed:
(a) by the law of the country in which the employee habitually carries out his work in performance of the contract, even if he is temporarily employed in another country; or
(b) if the employee does not habitually carry out his work in any one country, by the law of the country in which the place of business through which he was engaged is situated;
unless it appears from the circumstances as a whole that the contract is more closely connected with another country, in which case the contract shall be governed by the law of that country.

Article 7

Mandatory rules

1. When applying under this Convention the law of a country, effect may be given to the mandatory rules of the law of another country with which the situation has a close connection, if and in so far as, under the law of the latter country, those rules must be applied whatever the law applicable to the contract. In considering whether to give effect to these mandatory rules,

regard shall be had to their nature and purpose and to the consequences of their application or non-application.[17]

2. Nothing in this Convention shall restrict the application of the rules of the law of the forum in a situation where they are mandatory irrespective of the law otherwise applicable to the contract.

ARTICLE 8

Material validity

1. The existence and validity of a contract, or of any term of a contract, shall be determined by the law which would govern it under this Convention if the contract or term were valid.

2. Nevertheless a party may rely upon the law of the country in which he has his habitual residence to establish that he did not consent if it appears from the circumstances that it would not be reasonable to determine the effect of his conduct in accordance with the law specified in the preceding paragraph.

ARTICLE 9

Formal validity

1. A contract concluded between persons who are in the same country is formally valid if it satisfies the formal requirements of the law which governs it under this Convention or of the law of the country where it is concluded.

2. A contract concluded between persons who are in different countries is formally valid if it satisfies the formal requirements of the law which governs it under this Convention or of the law of one of those countries.

3. Where a contract is concluded by an agent, the country in which the agent acts is the relevant country for the purposes of paragraphs 1 and 2.

4. An act intended to have legal effect relating to an existing or contemplated contract is formally valid if it satisfies the formal requirements of the law which under this Convention governs or would govern the contract or of the law of the country where the act was done.

5. The provisions of the preceding paragraphs shall not apply to a contract to which Article 5 applies, concluded in the circumstances described in paragraph 2 of Article 5. The formal validity of such a contract is governed by the law of the country in which the consumer has his habitual residence.

6. Notwithstanding paragraphs 1 to 4 of this Article, a contract the subject matter of which is a right in immovable property or a right to use immovable property shall be subject to the mandatory requirements of form of the law of the country where the property is situated if by that law those requirements are imposed irrespective of the country where the contract is concluded and irrespective of the law governing the contract.

---

17 The United Kingdom government, on signing the Convention, exercised the power of reservation conferred by article 22 not to apply article 7 (1), on the ground that it would lead to legal and commercial uncertainty (*Ed*).

ARTICLE 10

Scope of the applicable law

1. The law applicable to a contract by virtue of Articles 3 to 6 and 12 of this Convention shall govern in particular:
(a) interpretation;
(b) performance;
(c) within the limits of the powers conferred on the court by its procedural law, the consequences of breach, including the assessment of damages in so far as it is governed by rules of law;
(d) the various ways of extinguishing obligations, and prescription and limitation of actions;
(e) the consequences of nullity of the contract.[18]

2. In relation to the manner of performance and the steps to be taken in the event of defective performance regard shall be had to the law of the country in which performance takes place.

ARTICLE 11

Incapacity

In a contract concluded between persons who are in the same country, a natural person who would have capacity under the law of that country may invoke his incapacity resulting from another law only if the other party to the contract was aware of this incapacity at the time of the conclusion of the contract or was not aware thereof as a result of negligence.

ARTICLE 15

Exclusion of renvoi

The application of the law of any country specified by this Convention means the application of the rules of law in force in that country other than its rules of private international law.

ARTICLE 16

'Ordre public'

The application of a rule of the law of any country specified by this Convention may be refused only if such application is manifestly incompatible with the public policy ('ordre public') of the forum.

ARTICLE 17

No retrospective effect

This Convention shall apply in a Contracting State to contracts made after the date on which this Convention has entered into force with respect to that State.

---

18 The United Kingdom government, on signing the Convention, exercised the power of reservation conferred by article 22 not to apply article 10 (1) (e), on the ground that in English law the right eg to recover money paid in pursuance of a void contract is regarded as quasi-contractual, not contractual (*Ed*).

ARTICLE 19

States with more than one legal system

1. Where a State comprises several territorial units each of which has its own rules of law in respect of contractual obligations, each territorial unit shall be considered as a country for the purposes of identifying the law applicable under this Convention.

2. A State within which different territorial units have their own rules of law in respect of contractual obligations shall not be bound to apply this Convention to conflicts solely between the laws of such units.

NOTE

This Convention was concluded in 1980 between the then nine member states of the EEC.[19] It has since been signed by all of them, but not yet by Greece, though the Joint Declaration appended to the Convention expresses the view that 'any state which becomes a member of the European Communities should accede to this Convention'.[20] No state has ratified the Convention and it will not come into force until seven states have ratified it; though there is nothing to prevent a member state adopting the substantive rules of the Convention as part of its own law prior to the Convention coming into force. It would also be possible for a state to apply the choice of law rules in the Convention, as part of its internal law, to those matters excluded by article 1 from the scope of the Convention.

The Convention is world-wide in effect. In this it differs from the Judgments Convention (p 84 above) which, in general, only applies if the defendant is domiciled in the EEC. As and when the Contractual Obligations Convention is implemented in this country, it will apply to all cases coming before our courts which raise a choice of law issue, whether or not the case has any factual connection with a member state of the EEC

The current English choice of law rules in contract apply in general terms to all types of contract. The Convention differs in two main respects. Some matters are excluded from the scope of the Convention, of which the most significant are arbitration agreements and choice of court clauses (art 1 (2) (d)) and insurance contracts relating to risks within the EEC (art 1 (3)). On the other hand, some types of contract, namely consumer and employment contracts (arts 5 and 6), whilst included within the Convention have special choice of law rules applied to them. It might also be added that, in applying the general Convention choice of law rules under article 4, particular contracts (those concerning immovable property and carriage of goods) have special rebuttable presumptions applied to them.

The general choice of law rules in the Convention are not dissimilar from the English common law rules. The parties are free to choose the governing law (art 3), though two matters which are not finally settled in English law are made clear in article 3 (2) and (3), namely that the parties may vary the applicable law after the conclusion of the contract and that the parties may choose a law factually unconnected with the contract. The validity of the choice of the governing law is to

---

19 For a detailed analysis of the Convention and its impact both within and outside the EEC, see North *Contract Conflicts* (1982).

20 Unlike the Convention on jurisdiction and the enforcement of judgments in civil and commercial matters (pp 84, 188 above), the Contractual Obligations Convention is not one which falls within article 220 of the Treaty of Rome and to which new member states are required to accede. Furthermore, no decision has yet been taken as to whether the European Court of Justice should have jurisdiction over the interpretation of the Convention.

be determined by the putative proper law in the sense of the law chosen (arts 3 (4), 8).

In the absence of choice, the contract is to be governed by the law of the country with which it is most closely connected (art 4 (1)). In substance, this accords closely with the present rules of English law but the Convention then goes on to provide a number of presumptions for determining the proper law. In addition to those mentioned above, article 4 (2) states that a contract is presumed to be most closely connected with the country where the person who is to effect the performance which is characteristic of the contract has his habitual residence. The concept of 'characteristic performance',[1] which is borrowed from Swiss law, is not defined in the Convention, though it is exemplified in the Explanatory Report[2] which accompanies the Convention. It is there suggested that the payment of money is not the characteristic performance of a contract for the supply of goods or services, rather is it the performance of the obligation for which payment is due, ie, the provision of the goods or services. This means that there is a presumption in favour of the seller's law. At the end of the day, however, this is only a presumption which may be displaced (art 4 (5)) if the contract is more closely connected with another country. The end result is much the same as that achieved by present English law, but by a more complex route.

The Convention rules on formal validity (art 9) follow the general pattern of English law, namely a rule of double reference. A contract is formally valid if it satisfies the formal requirements of either the proper law or of the law of the place where it was concluded; though the Convention has detailed provisions to try to solve the conundrum, posed, for example, by different countries' postal rules, that the place of contracting may depend on the validity of the contract, which is the very matter in issue. Capacity to contract is not covered by the Convention, with the exception of the limited provisions of article 11. There is nothing, however, to prevent this country from applying the general rule of the Convention to other capacity issues.

The Convention refers in a number of places to mandatory rules (eg, arts 3, 5, 6 and 7) which are defined in article 3 (3) as rules which cannot be derogated from by contract. In most instances the relevance of such rules is that they may continue to have effect notwithstanding the parties' choice of a different governing law. However, under article 7 their effect is different. Article 7 (2) embodies the general rule that the forum may apply its mandatory rules whatever may be the proper law. This preserves the effect of section 27 (2) of the Unfair Contract Terms Act 1977 (p 449 above). However, article 7 (1) goes much further and permits the court to consider the mandatory rules of some third country, neither the forum nor that of the proper law. It was fear of the commercial and legal uncertainty created by such a rule that led the United Kingdom to exercise its power not to apply article 7 (1).

The end result of implementation of this Convention will be that our contract choice of law rules will be placed on a firm statutory basis in harmony with the rules in other EEC countries, whose judgments in contract, as in other, cases we have to recognise under the Civil Jurisdiction and Judgments Act 1982 (pp 185–193 above). However, there will be no substantial change in our choice of law rules and it will be rare for a court to reach a result on the Convention rules different from that which it would reach today.

1 See on this d'Oliviera, (1977) 25 Am Jo Comp Law 303.
2 By Professors Giuliano and Lagarde, OJ 1980, C 282/4.

CHAPTER 15

Torts

As a general rule, an act done in a foreign country is a tort and actionable as such in England, only if it is both (a) actionable as a tort according to English law, and (b) civilly actionable according to the law of the foreign country where it was done.

Phillips v Eyre (1870) LR 6 QB 1, 10 B & S 1004 (Exchequer Chamber)

Error from the judgment of the Court of Queen's Bench in favour of the defendant.

The judgment of the Court (Kelly CB, Martin, Channell, Pigott, and Cleasby BB, Willes and Brett JJ) was delivered by

Willes J: This is an action complaining of false imprisonment and other injuries to the plaintiff by the defendant in the island of Jamaica. The plea states in effect that the defendant was governor of the island; that a rebellion broke out there which the governor and others acting under his authority had arrested by force of arms; that an Act was afterwards duly passed by the legislature of the island, and received the royal assent, by which it was enacted by the governor, legislative council, and assembly of the island, amongst other things that the defendant and all officers and other persons who had acted under his authority, was thereby indemnified in respect of all acts, matters, and things done in order to put an end to the rebellion, and all such acts were 'thereby made and declared lawful, and were confirmed'. The plea further states that the grievances complained of in this action were measures used in the suppression of the rebellion, and were reasonably and in good faith considered by the defendant to be proper for the purpose of putting an end to, and bonâ fide done in order to put an end to, the rebellion, and so were included in the indemnity. To this plea the plaintiff demurred, and also replied that the defendant as governor was, by the law of Jamaica, a necessary party to the making of the Act. The defendant demurred to that replication, and issues in law were raised upon the validity of the plea and replication, upon which issues the Court of Queen's Bench gave judgment for the defendant, whereupon the plaintiff has assigned error.

It was agreed at the bar that, for the purpose of this argument, the decision ought to turn upon the colonial Act, and numerous objections were urged against its validity and effect....

(After considering the nature and effect of an Act of Indemnity, and disposing of objections (1) that the Crown had no power to create a legislative assembly in a settled colony; (2) that the Act in question was contrary to English statute law and was therefore void; (3) that the defendant was as governor a necessary party to the passing of the Act and so could take no benefit thereunder; (4) that the Act was retrospective in character and therefore contrary to natural justice, his Lordship continued:)

The last objection to the plea of the colonial Act was of a more technical character; that assuming the colonial Act to be valid in Jamaica and a defence there, it could not have the extra-territorial effect of taking away the right of action in an English court. This objection is founded upon a misconception of the true character of a civil or legal obligation and the corresponding right of action. The obligation is the principal to which a right of action in whatever court is only an accessory, and such accessory, according to the maxim of law, follows the principal, and must stand or fall therewith. 'Quae accessorium locum obtinent extinguuntur cum principales res peremptae sunt.' A right of action, whether it arise from contract governed by the law of the place or wrong, is equally the creature of the law of the place and subordinate thereto. The terms of the contract or the character of the subject-matter may shew that the parties intended their bargain to be governed by some other law; but, primâ facie, it falls under the law of the place where it was made. And in like manner the civil liability arising out of a wrong derives its birth from the law of the place, and its character is determined by that law. Therefore, an act committed abroad, if valid and unquestionable by the law of the place, cannot, so far as civil liability is concerned, be drawn in question elsewhere unless by force of some distinct exceptional legislation, superadding a liability other than and besides that incident to the act itself. In this respect no sound distinction can be suggested between the civil liability in respect of a contract governed by the law of the place and a wrong.

Our courts are said to be more open to admit actions founded upon foreign transactions than those of any other European country; but there are restrictions in respect of locality which exclude some foreign causes of action altogether, namely, those which would be local if they arose in England, such as trespass to land: *Doulson v Matthews*,[1] and even with respect to those not falling within that description our courts do not undertake universal jurisdiction. As a general rule, in order to found a suit in England for a wrong alleged to have been committed abroad, two conditions must be fulfilled. First, the wrong must be such a character that it would have been actionable if committed in England; therefore, in *The Halley*,[2] the Judicial Committee pronounced against a suit in the Admiralty founded upon a liability by the law of Belgium for collision caused by the act of a pilot whom the shipowner was compelled by that law to employ, and for whom, therefore, as not being his agent, he was not responsible by English law. Secondly, the act must not have been justifiable by the law of the place where it was done. Therefore in *Blad's Case*,[3] and *Blad v Bamfield*,[4] Lord Nottingham held that a seizure in Iceland, authorised by the Danish government and valid by the law of the place, could not be questioned by civil action in England, although the plaintiff, an Englishman, insisted that the seizure was in violation of a treaty between this country and Denmark— a matter proper for remonstrance, not litigation. And in *Dobree v Napier*,[5] Admiral Napier having, when in the service of the Queen of Portugal, captured in Portuguese water an English ship breaking blockade, was held

1 (1792) 4 Term Rep 503.
2 (1868) LR 2 PC 193, 5 Moo PCCNS 262.
3 (1673) 3 Swanst 603.
4 (1674) 3 Swanst 604.
5 (1836) 2 Bing NC 781, 3 State TR NS 621.

by the Court of Common Pleas to be justified, by the law of Portugal and of nations, though his serving under a foreign Prince was contrary to English law, and subjected him to penalties under the Foreign Enlistment Act. And in *R v Lesley*,[6] an imprisonment in Chile on board a British ship lawful there, was held by Erle C J, and the Court for Crown Cases Reserved, to be no ground for an indictment here, there being no independent law of this country making the act wrongful or criminal. As to foreign laws affecting the liability of parties in respect of bygone transactions, the law is clear that, if the foreign law touches only the remedy or procedure for enforcing the obligation, as in the case of an ordinary statute of limitations, such law is no bar to an action in this country; but if the foreign law extinguishes the right it is a bar in this country equally as if the extinguishment had been by a release of the party, or an act of our own legislature. This distinction is well illustrated on the one hand by *Huber v Steiner*,[7] where the French law of five years' prescription was held by the Court of Common Pleas to be no answer in this country to an action upon a French promissory note, because that law dealt only with procedure, and the time and manner of suit (tempus et modum actionis instituendae), and did not affect to destroy the obligation of the contract (valorem contractus); and on the other hand by *Potter v Brown*,[8] where the drawer of a bill at Baltimore upon England was held discharged from his liability for the non-acceptance of the bill here by a certificate in bankruptcy, under the law of the United States of America, the Court of Queen's Bench adopting the general rule laid down by Lord Mansfield in *Ballantine v Golding*,[9] and ever since recognised, that 'what is a discharge of a debt in the country where it is contracted is a discharge of it everywhere'. So that where an obligation by contract to pay a debt or damages is discharged and avoided by the law of the place where it was made, the accessory right of action in every court open to the creditor unquestionably falls to the ground. And by strict parity of reasoning, where an obligation, ex delicto, to pay damages is discharged and avoided by the law of the country where it was made, the accessory right of action is in like manner discharged and avoided. Cases may possibly arise in which distinct and independent rights or liabilities or defences are created by positive and specific laws of this country in respect of foreign transactions: but there is no such law (unless it be the Governor's Act already discussed and disposed of) applicable to the present case.

It may be proper to remark, before quitting this part of the subject, that the colonial Act could not be overruled upon either of these two latter grounds of objection without laying down that no foreign legislation could avail to take away civil liability here in respect of acts done abroad; so that, for instance, if a foreign country after a rebellion or civil war were to pass a general Act of oblivion and indemnity, burying in one grave all legal memory alike of the hostilities, and even the private retaliations which are the sure results of anarchy and violence, it would, if the argument for the plaintiff prevailed, be competent for a municipal court of any other country to condemn and disregard, as naturally unjust or technically ineffectual, the

6 (1860) Bell CC 220, 29 LJMC 97.
7 (1835) 2 Bing NC 202, 1 Hodg 206.
8 (1804) 5 East 124, 1 Smith KB 351.
9 (1784) 1 Cooke's Bankrupt Laws, 8 Ed 487.

law of a sovereign state, disposing, upon the same constitutional principles as have actuated our own legislature, of matters arising within its territory—a course which to adopt would be an unprecedented and mischievous violation of the comity of nations.

The judgment of the Court of Queen's Bench for the defendant was right, and is affirmed.

Judgment affirmed.

QUESTION

What is the justification for allowing a defendant to rely on defences available to him both under the lex loci delicti and under English law?
(See *M'Elroy v M'Allister*, p 666 below.)

But a particular issue between the parties may be governed by the law of the country which, with respect to that issue, has the most significant relationship with the occurrence and the parties.

Boys v Chaplin [1971] AC 356, [1969] 2 All ER 1085 (House of Lords)

The plaintiff and defendant were both normally resident in England but temporarily stationed in Malta in the British armed forces. While both were off duty, the plaintiff, while riding as a passenger on a motor scooter, was seriously injured in a collision in Malta with a motor car negligently driven by the defendant. By the law of Malta, the plaintiff could only recover special damages for his expenses and proved loss of earnings, which in the circumstances amounted to no more that £53. By English law, he could also recover general damages for pain and suffering.

Milmo J following *Machado v Fontes*[10] held that it was immaterial that no general damages could be recovered under the lex loci delicti; and awarded the plaintiff a total of £2303. The Court of Appeal by a majority affirmed his judgment, but for differing reasons. Lord Denning MR applied English law as the proper law of the tort since both parties were English. Lord Upjohn applied English law on the grounds (a) that in his opinion *Machado v Fontes* was rightly decided, and (b) that all questions relating to the remedy were a matter for the lex fori. Diplock LJ dissented and would have applied Maltese law as the lex loci delicti. Both Lord Denning and Diplock LJ agreed that *Machado v Fontes* was wrongly decided and should be overruled.

The defendant appealed.

Lord Hodson (after stating the facts): No difficulty arises in settling the place of the wrong which occurred entirely in Malta. As to the choice of law the generally accepted rule in this country is set out in Dicey and Morris, *Conflict of Laws*,[11] as follows:

> 'Rule 158.—An act done in a foreign country is a tort and actionable as such, in England, only if it is both

10 [1897] 2 QB 231, 66 LJQB 542.
11 8th edn (1967) p 919. The Rule has since been changed (*Ed*).

(1) actionable as a tort, according to English law, or in other words, is an act which, if done in England, would be a tort; and

(2) not justifiable, according to the law of the foreign country where it was done.'

Clause (1) of this rule was clearly stated in *The Halley*,[12] an Admiralty case in which a suit was brought against a British ship and her owners on account of a collision in Belgian waters. The defence was that the ship was under the control of a compulsory pilot so that both vessel and owners were relieved of responsibility. The plaintiffs replied that under Belgian law the owners were liable notwithstanding that the ship was being navigated at the time by a compulsory pilot. At first instance the plaintiff succeeded on the ground that the governing law was that of the place where the collision occurred. This decision was reversed by the Judicial Committee of the Privy Council which, in a judgment delivered by Selwyn LJ, declared the law as follows, at 204:

'...it is, in their Lordships' opinion, alike contrary to principle and to authority to hold, that an English court of justice will enforce a foreign municipal law, and will give a remedy in the shape of damages in respect of an act which, according to its own principles, imposes no liability on the person from whom the damages are claimed.'

It is to be noticed that there is no direct reference to public policy as such in this judgment.

Clause (2) of the rule has occasioned difficulty owing to the use of the words 'not justifiable'. 'Justification' according to the lex loci delicti is to be found in the opinion of Lord Nottingham in *Blad's* case.[13] A century later in the leading case of *Mostyn v Fabrigas*,[14] Lord Mansfield said: 'whatever is a justification in the place where the thing is done, ought to be a justification where the cause is tried.'

Dicey's rule is collected from the judgment delivered by Willes J in *Phillips v Eyre*[15] in the Exchequer Chamber. The action complained of false imprisonment and other injuries to the plaintiff inflicted in Jamaica by the defendant who was governor of the island. The defendant relied upon an act of indemnity passed by the legislature of Jamaica as in effect a subsequent justification of his actions. (His Lordship quoted the passages beginning 'A right of action' and ending 'determined by that law' on p 468 above, and the passage beginning 'As a general rule' and ending 'where it was done' on p 468 above).

The appellant's argument gains support from the passage I have read in which it is declared that the civil liability arising out of a wrong derives its birth from the law of the place and its character is determined by that law. Willes J was not, however, concerned with choice of law but only whether the courts of this country should entertain the action.

The judgment does not declare, as Lord Upjohn pointed out in the Court of Appeal, that the tortious act must be determined by the lex loci delicti. That would be to adopt what is called 'the obligation' theory formerly accepted in the United States of America and sponsored by Holmes J, of the

12 (1868) LR 2 PC 193, 5 Moo PCCNS 262.
13 (1673) 3 Swan 603.
14 (1774) 1 Cowp 161 at 175.
15 (1870) LR 6 QB 1, 10 B & S 1004; p 467 above.

Supreme Court of the United States. In *Slater v Mexican National Railroad Co*[16] he said:

> 'The theory of the foreign suit is that although the act complained of was subject to no law having force in the forum, it gave rise to an obligation ... and may be enforced wherever the person may be found.... But as the only source of this obligation is the law of the place of the act, it follows that the law determines not merely the existence of the obligation,... but equally determines its extent.'

Again in *Western Union v Brown*[17] Holmes J said:

> '...when a person recovers in one jurisdiction for a tort committed in another he does so on the ground of an obligation incurred at the place of the tort that accompanies the person of the defendant elsewhere, and that is not only the ground but the measure of the maximum recovery.'

As Diplock LJ pointed out, the courts have of recent years in a number of states of the United States departed from the lex loci in favour of another law which has been described as 'the proper law of the tort' (see *Babcock v Jackson*[18]).

In opposition to the obligation theory another distinguished American judge, Judge Learned Hand, said in *Guinness v Miller*:[19]

> 'When a court takes cognisance of a tort committed elsewhere, it is indeed sometimes said that it enforces the obligation arising under the law where the tort arises.... However, no court can enforce any law but that of its own sovereign, and, when a suitor comes to a jurisdiction foreign to the place of the tort, he can only invoke an obligation recognised by that sovereign. A foreign sovereign under civilised law imposes an obligation of its own as nearly homologous as possible to that arising in the place where the tort occurs.'

In the next year the same judge, in the case of *The James M'Gee*[20] said:

> 'In the very nature of things, courts can enforce no obligations which are created elsewhere; when dealing with such obligations, they merely recognise them as the original of the copies which they themselves enforce.'

I come to the much criticised decision of *Machado v Fontes*, a decision of the Court of Appeal upon an interlocutory matter. This case was doubted by the Privy Council in *Canadian Pacific Rly Co v Parent*.[1] It has been followed in Canada, rejected by the High Court of Australia in *Koop v Bebb*[2] and not accepted in Scotland. The case concerned two men, one of whom sued the other in England for a libel in the Portuguese language published in Brazil on the footing that the libel was actionable in England although it appeared

---

16 (1904) 194 US 120 at 126.
17 (1914) 234 US 542 at 547.
18 (1963) 12 NY 2d 473, 191 NE 2d 279, [1963] 2 Lloyd's Rep 286; p 501 below.
19 (1923) 291 F 769 at 770.
20 (1924) 300 F 93 at 96.
 1 [1917] AC 195, 86 LJPC 123; p 496 below.
 2 (1951) 84 CLR 629, [1952] ALR 37.

that in Brazil it was not actionable civilly but only punishable as a crime. Lopes LJ equated 'not justifiable' in Willes J's judgment with 'wrongful' and 'justifiable' with 'innocent'. Rigby LJ drew attention to the change from 'actionable' in the first branch of the rule to 'justifiable' in the second. He equated 'justifiable' with 'authorised or innocent or excusable'.

As Professor Cheshire pointed out in his *Private International Law*:[3]

> 'It seems reasonably clear that the word "justifiable" was used by Willes J to emphasise the established and obvious rule that what is a good defence in the locus delicti must be equally good in a foreign forum. His mind was addressed solely to "the civil liability arising out of the wrong", and there is nothing in his remarks to show that he contemplated the possibility of a successful action in England in respect of an act that is civilly, though not criminally, innocent in the locus delicti.'

Governor Eyre's acts were justified by statute passed after they were committed and did not by virtue of the statute merit the appellation of innocence. In that case and in the earlier cases in which they appear in like context the words 'not justifiable' must, I think, refer only to civil liability. That this may be the true view of the law is supported by the opinion of the High Court of Australia given in *Koop v Bebb*, referred to above. If the decision in *Machado v Fontes* could be supported on the ground that actionability is not essential the respondent must succeed but, in my opinion, that decision is wrong and should be overruled.

To put *Machado v Fontes* on one side is not, however, to dispose of this case. There is no doubt that an actionable wrong by Maltese law was committed in Malta when the respondent sustained his injuries and that subject to the difference in the laws of the two countries a wrong is actionable here. Prima facie the conditions set forth in the judgment of the Court of Exchequer Chamber in *Phillips v Eyre* are fulfilled, but it is proper to remember that the conditions were introduced by the words 'as a general rule' which I do not read as equivalent to 'as an invariable rule'. One gets some assistance from a case earlier than *Phillips v Eyre* where Willes J was also a member of the court. This is *Scott v Seymour*.[4] Lord Seymour had assaulted Mr Scott in Naples and Mr Scott sued Lord Seymour in England for damages. This action was, it is said, not available in Naples where only criminal proceedings lay. The case was decided on a special ground, but Wightman J in the course of his judgment said:

> ... whatever might be the case as between two Neapolitan subjects, or between a Neapolitan and an Englishman, I find no authority for holding that, even if the Neapolitan law gives no remedy for an assault and battery, however violent and unprovoked, by recovery of damages, that therefore a British subject is deprived of his right to damages given by the English law against another British subject.'

Willes J said: 'I am far from saying that I differ from any part of the judgment of my brother Wightman.'

This is an indication that at this point of time Willes J was content to

3 7th edn (1965) p 248.
4 (1862) 1 H & C 219, 32 LJEx 61.

adopt a flexible attitude to the position which he subsequently incorporated in the passage beginning with the words 'As a general rule'.

The American cases have shown that in recent years, particularly in instances arising from accidents occurring in motor car journeys or in aeroplanes on trans-continental trips where the place of the accident is likely to be fortuitious, an attempt has been made to arrive at a solution described as 'the proper law of the tort'. This has led to uncertain results and has not been fully developed in the United States. The analogy of the proper law of the contract is not useful since the parties to a contract usually have the opportunity of choosing the law to which they seek to submit. Choice of law rules here bring certainty, predictability and uniformity of result. These features are absent in tort. No doubt if the proper law of the tort were to be adopted as the solution of those cases which arise from transitory torts, it is not easy to improve on the test chosen by the Master of the Rolls from the American *Restatement*, namely, the place with which the parties had the most significant connection.

The respondent did not seek to argue that the American theory of the proper law of the tort should be adopted but he submitted, and I think submitted rightly, that the words 'As a general rule' should be interpreted so as to leave some latitude in cases where it would be against public policy to admit or to exclude claims. I am conscious that to resort to public policy is to mount an 'unruly horse'. It appears to me, however to be in the interests of public policy to discourage 'forum shopping' expeditions by the inhabitants of other countries. As Lord Cooper said in *M'Elroy v M'Allister:*[5]

'Pursuers should not be encouraged to improve their position vis-à-vis of their opponents by invoking some secondary forum in order to exact compensation for a type of loss which the primary forum would not regard as meriting reparation.'

It is necessary to permit some flexibility in applying the language of Willes J in *Phillips v Eyre*, which is to be applied as 'a general rule' and not invariably. I reach this conclusion not without reluctance since rules of law should be defined and adhered to as closely as possible lest they lose themselves in a field of judicial discretion where no secure foothold is to be found by litigants or their advisers. The search for justice in the individual case must often clash with fixed legal principles especially perhaps when choice of law is concerned.

So far as the instant case is concerned, there is no ground of public policy for rejecting the respondent's claim. The parties appear to have been British nationals resident in this country but temporarily in Malta on service at the time of the occurrence.

The substantial ground for rejecting the claim is that when *Machado v Fontes* is out of the way and 'innocence' by the local law no longer leaves the way clear for the application of the lex fori, one must look and see exactly what is the wrongful act sued upon which is actionable in the foreign country and also here.

The nature of a plaintiff's remedy is a matter of procedure to be determined by the lex fori. This includes the quantification of damages, but the question arises whether or not the English remedy sought and obtained

5 1949 SC 110 at 125.

by the judgment here fits in with the right as fixed by the foreign, that is the Maltese, law. It is argued that to award damages on the English principle is to make the right sought to be enforced a different right from that given by the lex loci delicti and that questions such as whether loss of earning capacity or pain and suffering are admissible heads of damage are questions of substantive law distinct from mere quantification which is purely a procedural matter.

The distinction between substance and procedure was clearly stated by Tindal CJ in *Huber v Steiner*[6] and by Lord Brougham in *Don v Lippmann*.[7] The latter said:

'The law on this point is well settled in this country, where this distinction is properly taken, that whatever relates to the remedy to be enforced, must be determined by the lex fori, the law of the country to the tribunals of which the appeal is made.'

If it were clear that there existed in Malta in this case civil liability for the wrong done there would be no obstacle in the respondent's way, for in principle a person should in such circumstances be permitted to claim in this country for the wrong committed in Malta. This is to state the general rule as generally accepted which takes no account of circumstances peculiar to the parties or the occurrence. The existence of the relevant civil liability is, however, not clear in this case. I was at first attracted by the submission that some liability under Maltese law being established, the remedy under Maltese law of compensation for actual loss of earnings and the remedy of damages in respect of the injury itself for pain and suffering could be merged. If this were done both heads of damage could be treated as if they related solely to the remedy and not to the substantive law involved, thus avoiding the difficulty presented by the distinction between substantive law and procedure. I am now, however, persuaded that questions such as whether loss of earning capacity or pain and suffering are admissible heads of damage must be questions of substantive law. The law relating to damages is partly procedural and partly substantive, the actual quantification under the relevant heads being procedural only. This view is supported by authority. The Supreme Court of Canada in *Livesley v Horst*[8] held that the question what kind of loss actually resulting from a breach of contract is actionable is a question of [substantive] law.

Here I think the question of right to damages for pain and suffering is a substantive right and the respondent would fail if that which I have described as the general rule of principle were applied. That would be a just result if both parties were Maltese residents or even if the defendant were a Maltese resident.

In a case such as the present the result is, if not plainly unjust, at least not to be regarded as satisfactory. The parties had no connection with Malta except by reason of their service which was of a temporary nature and the interest of justice in such a case where civil liability exists in the foreign country though not exactly corresponding to the civil liability in this country requires some qualification of the general rule. The observations of

6 (1835) 2 Bing NC 202, 1 Hodg 206; p 206.
7 (1837) 5 Cl & Fin 1 at 13.
8 [1925] 1 DLR 159, [1924] SCR 605.

Wightman J in *Scott v Seymour* lend support to this view, as the Master of the Rolls pointed out.

Likewise there is no apparent justification for one Maltese subject suing another in this country for damages in respect of pain and suffering where the wrong took place in Malta. That would be a bare-faced example of 'forum shopping'.

In personal injury cases it is not necessarily true that by entering a country you submit yourself to the special laws of that country.

I would for myself, therefore, adopt the *American Law Institute Restatement (Second) Conflict of Laws* (Proposed official draft 1 May 1968) set out in the speech which has been prepared by my noble and learned friend Lord Wilberforce. If controlling effect is given to the law of the jurisdiction which because of its relationship with the occurrence and the parties had the greater concern with the specific issue raised in the litigation, the ends of justice are likely to be achieved although, as the American authorities show, there is a difficult task presented for decision of the courts, and uncertainty has led to dissenting judgments in the appellate courts.

I would accordingly, in agreement with the Master of the Rolls, treat the law of England as applicable since even though the occurrence took place in Malta this was overshadowed by the identity and circumstances of the parties, British subjects temporarily serving in Malta.

It is to be expected that a court will favour its own policies over those of other states and be inclined to give its own rules a wider application than it will give to those of other states (see Willis L. M. Reese (of Columbia University) *Conflict of Laws Restatement (Second)*). This tendency is convenient. To insist on the choice of the law of the place where the wrong was committed has an attraction and leads to certainty but in modern conditions of speedy and frequent travel between countries the place of the wrong may be and often is determined by accidental circumstances, as in this case where the parties were but temporarily carrying out their service in Malta. Furthermore, difficulty and inconvenience is involved in many cases in ascertaining the details of the relevant foreign law.

On the facts of this case, giving the rule, as I understand it, which is propounded in *Phillips v Eyre* a flexible interpretation, I would dismiss the appeal.

Lord Guest: Before I deal with the main question, I should say that I would not, in any event, be in favour of applying 'the proper law of the tort' whatever that law might be. The principle of 'the proper law of the tort' has only been recently introduced into certain states of the United States of America due to the differing state laws in that country. It has never been part of the law of England. It produces uncertainty and for the reasons given by both Lord Upjohn and Diplock LJ I would not be in favour of its introduction here.

I propose to decide this case upon a very narrow ground. The difficulties arising from the decision of *Phillips v Eyre* have already been referred to by my noble and learned friends. I prefer to leave these questions to those of your Lordships who are more familiar with this aspect of English law. I am content to accept the position that to justify an action in England for a tort committed abroad the conduct must be actionable by English law and by the laws of the country in which the conduct occurred, the lex loci delicti.

Both these conditions are satisfied in this case as the negligent driving of the appellant was actionable both by the law of England and by the law of Malta. This line of reasoning would be in accord with the principles of the Scottish decision of *Naftalin v London Midland and Scottish Rly Co*[9] and *M'Elroy v M'Allister*. And nothing which I have to say hereafter is intended to throw any doubt on these cases which I think were rightly decided.

Assuming that the conduct was actionable in Malta, what law is to be applied to the ascertainment of the damages? Is it to be the substantive law, the law of Malta, or is it to be the procedural law which is the lex fori? In *Don v Lippmann* Lord Brougham said that whatever relates to the remedy to be enforced must be determined by the lex fori. There would appear to be a distinction between questions affecting heads of damages which are for the lex loci delicti and quantification of damages which is for the lex fori. This is well illustrated in Dicey and Morris, *Conflict of Laws*[10] where the kind of damage is a matter of substantive law and the method of compensating the plaintiff for his loss which is for the lex fori. Cheshire on *Private International Law*[11] is to the same effect. . . .

Although differing from some of the reasoning in the majority of the Court of Appeal, I would dismiss the appeal.

Lord Donovan: My Lords, I need not repeat the facts, I am content with the rule enunciated by Willes J in *Phillips v Eyre* and would leave it alone. In particular I would not substitute 'actionable' for 'not justifiable'. I think the latter expression was deliberately chosen; and it makes for justice. For example, if the present respondent had suffered only pain and suffering in Malta, it would have allowed him to bring an action for damages here which he could not have brought in Malta. And I think this would have been right.

If 'actionable' be substituted for 'not justifiable' a reason has to be found for allowing such damages in the present case. The one which has found favour with some of your Lordships is, I think, that while 'double actionability' ought to be the rule, yet departures may be made from it in individual cases where this appears to be justified by the circumstances. This introduces a new element of uncertainty into the law which I would prefer to exclude.

So far as *Machado v Fontes* is concerned we do not need to alter the rule laid down by Willes J. It is enough to say that the case in question, while within the rule, was an abuse of it; and that considerations of public policy would justify a court here in rejecting any such future case of blatant 'forum shopping'. I may say I am assuming that the parties were Brazilian though the report does not say so.

I do not think we should adopt any such doctrine as 'the proper law of the tort' with all its uncertainties. There is no need here for such a doctrine—at least while we remain a United Kingdom. Nor would I take the first step towards it in the name of flexibility. I would dismiss the present appeal on the ground that an English court was competent to entertain the action under the rule in *Phillips v Eyre* and that once it had done so it was right that it should award its own remedies. In short I entirely agree with the judgment of my noble and learned friend, Lord Upjohn, in the court below.

9 1933 SC 259.
10 8th edn, pp 944, 1092.
11 7th edn, p 602.

Lord Wilberforce: In the forefront of the appeal it is necessary to consider what is the basis of an action brought in England in respect of a foreign tort: to what extent (if any) the lex delicti enters into it. If it does, further questions arise, whether the awarding of damages generally is within the exclusive authority of the lex fori, whether any distinction is to be made between the quantification of damages and the definition of the heads of recoverable damages, and if so whether, as to the latter, the lex delicti should be held to govern. I state these questions provisionally in classical form and language and in terms which suggest that they can be answered through the formulation of definite rules of law. But I shall have to consider whether, after formulation of any general rules as is possible, it is necessary to admit some flexibility in their operation, in order to decide such a case as the present.

The existing English law. Apart from any revision which this House may be entitled, and think opportune, to make, I have no doubt that this is as stated in Dicey and Morris, *Conflict of Laws*, Rule 158, adopting with minor verbal adaptations the 'general rule' laid down by the Court of Exchequer Chamber in *Phillips v Eyre*. This is as follows: (His Lordship read it).

I am aware that different interpretations have been placed by writers of authority upon the central passage in the judgment of Willes J in which the general rule is contained. Like many judgments given at a time when the relevant part of the law was in course of formation, it is not without its ambiguities, or, as a century of experience perhaps permits us to say, its contradictions. And if it were now necessary to advance the law by reinterpretation, it would be quite legitimate to extract new meanings from words and sentences used. Two of the judgments in the Court of Appeal have done just this, reaching in the process opposite conclusions. I do not embark on this adventure for two reasons: first, because of the variety of interpretation offered us by learned writers no one of which can claim overwhelming support; secondly, and more importantly, because, on the critical points, I do not think there is any doubt what the rule as stated has come to be accepted to mean in those courts which apply the common law. And it is with this judicially accepted meaning and its applications that we are now concerned.

(a) The first part of the rule—'actionable as a tort according to English law'. I accept what I believe to be the orthodox judicial view that the first part of the rule is laying down, not a test of jurisdiction, but what we now call a rule of choice of law: is saying, in effect, that actions on foreign torts are brought in English courts in accordance with English law. I would be satisfied to rest this conclusion on the words of the rule itself 'if done [committed] in England' which seem clear enough to exclude the 'jurisdiction' theory but, since the point is important, I give some citations to support it. (His Lordship referred to *The Halley, Koop v Bebb, Anderson v Eric Anderson Radio and TV Pty Ltd,*[12] *Canadian National SS Co v Watson*[13] and *Story v Stratford Mill Building Co*[14]).

I am of opinion, therefore, that, as regards the first part of this rule, actionability as a tort under and in accordance with English law is required.

12 (1965) 114 CLR 20, [1966] ALR 423.
13 [1939] SCR 11, [1939] 1 DLR 273.
14 (1913) 30 OLR 271, 18 DLR 309.

(b) The second part of the rule—'not justifiable according to the lex loci delicti'. There can hardly be any doubt that when this formulation was made in *Phillips v Eyre*, it was intended to cover the justification by act of indemnity which had occurred in Jamaica—the word 'justification' is derived from or at least found in *Mostyn v Fabrigas* in a similar context. It might have been better for English law if the rule had continued to be so understood. But *Machado v Fontes* gave the authority of the then Court of Appeal to the proposition that 'not justifiable' included not only 'actionable' but 'liable to criminal penalty', or, putting it another way, that 'justifiable' means 'innocent'. Until the decision of the Court of Appeal in the present case this was undoubtedly still the law. And it was accepted as such with varying degrees of reluctance in courts in Australia and Canada (see *Koop v Bebb; Varawa v Howard Smith & Co Ltd (No 2)*;[15] *McLean v Pettigrew*).[16] In the Court of Appeal two members thought it should be overruled.

It results from the foregoing that the current English law is correctly stated by *Dicey and Morris*, it being understood (a) that the substantive law to be applied is the lex fori, (b) that, as a condition, non-justifiability under the lex delicti is required.

Is this a satisfactory rule? We need not hesitate to ask the question. Although *Phillips v Eyre* is just a century old, and has some more ancient roots, the reported cases in which it has been considered or even applied are not numerous. The rule was stated as well settled by Lord Macnaghten in *Carr v Fracis Times & Co*,[17] but the issue in that case turned upon the second part of the rule and the first did not arise for discussion. As Kitto J said in *Anderson v Eric Anderson Radio and TV Pty Ltd*, the first part of the rule was open to review, and I deal first with that.

It may be admitted that it bears a parochial appearance: that it rests on no secure doctrinal principle: that outside the world of the English-speaking common law it is hardly to be found. But can any better general rule be devised, or is the existing rule, with perhaps some adjustment, the best suited to our system?

There have, in the past, been powerful advocates for the lex delicti: if a simple universal test is needed, it is perhaps the most logical, the one with most doctrinal appeal. A tort takes place in France: if action is not brought before the courts in France, let other courts decide as the French courts would. This has obvious attraction. But there are two disadvantages. To adopt the lex delicti as the substantive law would require proof of a foreign law, an objection which should not be exaggerated since in practice it could be met by suitable pleadings and with the aid of a presumption that foreign law coincides with that of the forum. But the intrusion of this foreign element would complicate the task of the adviser, who would at least have to consider, to a greater extent than the present rule compels him to, the possible relevance of a foreign law to his client's case. The second disadvantage arises from the character of the majority of foreign torts. These are mainly in respect of personal injuries sustained by persons travelling away from the place of their residence. In many cases, the place where the wrong occurred is fortuitous: with the speed of travel increasingly so. To fix

15 [1910] VLR 509.
16 [1945] SCR 62, [1945] 2 DLR 65.
17 [1902] AC 176 at 182.

the liability of two or more persons according to a locality with which they may have no more connection than a temporary, accidental and perhaps unintended presence, may lead to an unjust result. Moreover, the more emphasis there is laid upon the locus delicti, the more oppressive may become the question (and research has shown how perplexing this can be) what the locus, in a particular case, is. It is difficulties of this character as well as injustices produced by a rigid and logical adherence to the lex delicti (see for a striking example *Slater v Mexican National Railroad Co*) which have driven the courts in the United States of America to abandon the lex delicti as a universal solvent, and to qualify it by means of a principle of 'contacts' or 'interests'. But if this kind of qualification is to be admissible, it may equally well be added to our existing rule. Before considering whether this should be done, I examine the second part of the *Phillips v Eyre* proposition.

In my opinion, in agreement with your Lordships and the Court of Appeal, *Machado v Fontes* ought to be overruled. The balance of judicial opinion is decidedly against it. It was powerfully attacked in the Court of Session by Lord Justice-Clerk Thompson (*M'Elroy v M'Allister*).

In *Koop v Bebb* it was discussed by the High Court of Australia. After referring to a reasoned criticism of it by Cussen J in the Supreme Court of Victoria (*Varawa v Howard Smith & Co Ltd (No 2)*) the judgment of Dixon, Williams, Fullagar and Kitto JJ contains this passage:

> 'It seems clear that the last word has not been said on the subject, and it may be the true view that an act done in another country should be held to be an actionable wrong in Victoria if, first, it was of such a character that it would have been actionable if it had been committed in Victoria, and, secondly, it was such as to give rise to a civil liability by the law of the place where it was done.'

In Canada the decision has been followed and found useful in certain cases where courts in one province have sought to escape from the consequences of an Ontario statute (and analogous USA legislation) depriving passengers (guests) of remedies against their drivers (hosts). The Privy Council, on Canadian appeals, has left it open.

For reasons I shall explain, I do not think that any principle established by this case is needed in order to resolve the difficulties of guest-host relationships—indeed, it only does so with a certain strain (see *McLean v Pettigrew* where the 'criminality' of the act in Ontario was relied on though in fact the defendant had been acquitted). On principle the decision for or against it must rest on a balance between the illogicality referred to by Lord Thompson, together with the inducement the case offers to 'forum shopping', on the one hand, against, on the other, a debatable advantage in allowing a national of the forum to sue there for torts committed by another such national abroad, if these are not actionable but criminal under the lex loci. This balance I find is decidedly against the authority of the decision.

But I do not think it is sufficient to rest here. For we should still be left with the test of 'non-justifiability' according to the lex delicti. I have no objection to the concept of 'non-justifiability' as the basis for the decision in *Phillips v Eyre*: to say that Governor Eyre could not be sued in England after his actions in Jamaica had been justified by an Act of Indemnity was sound enough. But I do not think that we need any longer confine ourselves within this phrase. Assuming that, as the basic rule, we continue to require actionability by the lex fori, subject to some condition as to what the lex delicti requires, we should, in my opinion, allow a greater and more intelligible force to the lex delicti than is included in the concept of unjustifiability as normally understood.

The broad principle should surely be that a person should not be permitted to claim in England in respect of a matter for which civil liability does not exist, or is excluded, under the law of the place where the wrong was committed. This non-existence or exclusion may be for a variety of reasons and it would be unwise to attempt a generalisation relevant to the variety of possible wrongs. But in relation to claims for personal injuries one may say that provisions of the lex delicti, denying, or limiting, or qualifying recovery of damages because of some relationship of the defendant to the plaintiff, or in respect of some interest of the plaintiff (such as loss of consortium) or some head of damage (such as pain and suffering) should be given effect to. I can see no case for allowing one resident of Ontario to sue another in the English court for damages sustained in Ontario as a passenger in the other's car, or one Maltese resident to sue another in the English courts for damages in respect of pain and suffering caused by an accident in Malta. I would, therefore, restate the basic rule of English law with regard to foreign torts as requiring actionability as a tort according to English law, subject to the condition that civil liability in respect of the relevant claim exists as between the actual parties under the law of the foreign country where the act was done.

It remains for me to consider (and this is the crux of the present case) whether some qualification to this rule is required in certain individual cases. There are two conflicting pressures: the first in favour of certainty and simplicity in the law, the second in favour of flexibility in the interest of individual justice. Developments in the United States of America have reflected this conflict: I now consider them.

The contact or interests principle. The process which has evolved is to segregate the relevant issue, which may be one only of those arising, and to consider in relation to that issue as it arises in the actual suit between the actual parties what rule of law, ie, the rule of which state or jurisdiction, ought to be applied. This method has mainly though not exclusively been used in relation to personal injury cases, whether air or motor car accidents and, as to the latter, mainly in relation to statutes excluding or limiting the liability of drivers of vehicles. Like other doctrines, including that of the 'proper law of the tort', it may represent a development from English seed. Professor Westlake's *Private International Law*[18] contains this:

> 'The truth is that by entering a country or acting in it you submit yourself to its special laws *only so far as science selects them as the rule of decision in each case.* Or more truly still, you give to its special laws the opportunity of working on you to that extent. The operation of the law depends on the conditions, and where the conditions exist the law operates as well on its born subjects as on those who have brought themselves under it.'

The germ of the doctrine may lie here but has only developed in recent United States cases towards passengers or generally. Those I have found of

18 7th edn (1925) p 281.

most interest are *Kilberg v Northeast Airlines Inc*,[19] *Babcock v Jackson* (law of the place which had most dominant contacts with matter in dispute); *Griffith v United Air Lines*[20] (the strict lex loci delicti rule should be abandoned in favour of a more flexible rule which permits analysis of the policies or interests underlying the particular issue before the court); *Dym v Gordon*;[1] *Miller v Miller*.[2] Interesting and suggestive as are the judgments in these cases, I forbear from detailed citation since they are, at the present stage, approximative to the definition of a rule.

A reference to *Babcock v Jackson* may sufficiently illustrate. There the plaintiff was a passenger in a car owned and driven by the defendant, both parties being resident in New York. The accident occurred in Ontario, Canada, during a weekend trip: the Highway Traffic Act 1960 of Ontario excluded any liability of driver to passenger,[3] but the law of New York (lex fori) did not. The plaintiff was allowed to recover. The basic law, as accepted in New York, as elsewhere in the United States of America, was the lex delicti, which, for the reasons I have given, ought not to become the basic law in England, but the judgment of the court established a principle equally applicable whatever the basic law might be.

> 'Justice, fairness and "the best practical result" . . . may best be achieved by giving controlling effect to the law of the jurisdiction which, because of its relationship or contact with the occurrence or the parties, has the greatest concern with the specific issue raised in the litigation.'

The general tendency is stated in the *American Law Institute Restatement (Second) Conflict of Laws* (proposed official draft, 1 May 1968). This states as the general principle that rights and liabilities of the parties with respect to an issue in tort are determined by the local law of the state, which, as to that issue, has the most significant relationship to the occurrence and the parties, and that separate rules apply to different kinds of torts. The importance of the respective contacts is to be evaluated according to their relevant importance with respect to the particular issue, the nature of the tort, and the purposes of the tort rules involved (see s 6, 145). In an action for a personal injury the local law of the state where the injury occurred (the basic rule in the United States of America) determines the rights and liabilities of the parties, unless *with respect to the particular issue* (emphasis supplied) some other state has a more significant relationship with the occurrence and the parties, in which event the local law of the other state will be applied.

This formulation has what is very necessary under a system of judge-made law, the benefit of hard testing in concrete applications. The criticism is easy to make that, more even than the doctrine of the proper law of the contract (cf *The Assunzione*[4]) where the search is often one of great perplexity, the task of tracing the relevant contacts, and of weighing them, qualitatively,

---

19 (1961) 9 NY 2d 34, 172 NE 2d 526; [1961] 2 Lloyd's Rep 406.
20 (1964) 416 Pa 1, 203 A 2d 796.
 1 (1965) 16 NY 2d 120, 209 NE 2d 792. In this case the facts were similar to those in *Babcock v Jackson* but the decision was different. It was not followed in *Macey v Rozbicki* (1966) 18 NY 2d 289, 221 NE 2d 380 and overruled in *Tooker v Lopez* (1969) 24 NY 2d 569, 249 NE 2d 394 *(Ed)*.
 2 (1968) 22 NY 2d 12, 237 NE 2d 877.
 3 This Act was repealed by the Highway Traffic Act Amendment Act 1977 *(Ed)*.
 4 [1954] P 150, [1954] 1 All ER 278; p 439 above.

against each other, complicates the task of the courts and leads to uncertainty and dissent: see particularly the powerful dissents in *Griffith* of Bell CJ, and in *Miller* of Breitel J.

There is force in this and for this reason I am not willing to go so far as the more extreme version of the respondent's argument would have us do and to adopt, in place of the existing rule, one based solely on 'contacts' or 'centre of gravity' which has not been adopted even in the more favourable climate of the United States. There must remain great virtue in a general well-understood rule covering the majority of normal cases provided that it can be made flexible enough to take account of the varying interests and considerations of policy which may arise when one or more foreign elements are present.

Given the general rule, as stated above, as one which will normally apply to foreign torts, I think that the necessary flexibility can be obtained from that principle which represents at least a common denominator of the United States decisions, namely, through segregation of the relevant issue and consideration whether, in relation to that issue, the relevant foreign rule ought, as a matter of policy or as Westlake said of science, to be applied. For this purpose it is necessary to identify the policy of the rule, to inquire to what situations, with what contacts, it was intended to apply; whether not to apply it, in the circumstances of the instant case, would serve any interest which the rule was devised to meet. This technique appears well adapted to meet cases where the lex delicti either limits or excludes damages for personal injury: it appears even necessary and inevitable. No purely mechanical rule can properly do justice to the great variety of cases where persons come together in a foreign jurisdiction for different purposes with different pre-existing relationships, from the background of different legal systems. It will not be invoked in every case or even, probably, in many cases. The general rule must apply unless clear and satisfying grounds are shown why it should be departed from and what solution, derived from what other rule, should be preferred. If one lesson emerges from the United States decisions it is that case to case decisions do not add up to a system of justice. Even within these limits this procedure may in some instances require a more searching analysis than is needed under the general rule. But unless this is done, or at least possible, we must come back to a system which is purely and simply mechanical.

I find in this approach the solution to the present case. The tort here was committed in Malta; it is actionable in this country. But the law of Malta denies recovery of damages for pain and suffering. Prima facie English law should do the same: if the parties were both Maltese residents it ought surely to do so; if the defendant were a Maltese resident the same result might follow. But in a case such as the present, where neither party is a Maltese resident or citizen, further inquiry is needed rather than an automatic application of the rule. The issue, whether this head of damage should be allowed, requires to be segregated from the rest of the case, negligence or otherwise, related to the parties involved and their circumstances, and tested in relation to the policy of the local rule and of its application to these parties so circumstanced.

So segregated, the issue is whether one British subject, resident in the United Kingdom, should be prevented from recovering, in accordance with English law, against another British subject, similarly situated, damages for pain and suffering which he cannot recover under the rule of the lex delicti. This issue must be stated, and examined, regardless of whether the injured person has or has not also a recoverable claim under a different heading (eg, for expenses actually incurred) under that law. This Maltese law cannot simply be rejected on grounds of public policy, or some general conception of justice. For it is one thing to say or presume that domestic rule is a just rule, but quite another, in a case where a foreign element is involved, to reject a foreign rule on any such general ground. The foreign rule must be evaluated in its application.

The rule limiting damages is the creation of the law of Malta, a place where both plaintiff and defendant were temporarily stationed. Nothing suggests that the Maltese state has any interest in applying this rule to persons resident outside it, or in denying the application of the English rule to these parties. No argument has been suggested why an English court, if free to do so, should renounce its own rule. That rule ought, in my opinion, to apply.

It may be that this appeal can be decided, quasi-mechanically, by the accepted distinction between substance and procedure, between solatium as a jus actionis and solatium as an ingredient in general damages. I have no wish to deprecate the use of these familiar tools. In skilful hands they can be powerful and effective, though I must add that in some applications, particularly in Scottish cases, they have led to results which give me no satisfaction. But I suspect that in the ultimate and difficult choice which has to be made between regarding damages for pain and suffering as a separate cause of action and so governed by the lex delicti, or treating them as merely part of general damages to calculate which is the prerogative of the lex fori, two alternatives which are surely closely balanced in this case, a not insubstantial makeweight, perhaps unconscious in its use, is to be found in a policy preference for the adopted solution (cf *Kilberg v Northeast Airlines Inc*: 'It is open to us . . . particularly in view of our own strong public policy as to death action damages, to treat the measure of damages . . . as being a procedural or remedial question controlled by our own state policies': per Desmond CJ). I note indeed that a purely legal analysis in the Court of Appeal led Lord Upjohn to one answer, Diplock LJ to another. So I prefer to be explicit about it. There certainly seems to be some artifice in regarding a man's right to recover damages for pain and suffering as a matter of procedure. To do so, at any rate, goes well beyond the principle which I entirely accept, that matters of assessment or quantification, including no doubt the manner in which provision is made for future or prospective losses, are for the lex fori to determine.

Yet, unless the claim can be classified as procedure, there seems no basis on the traditional approach for denying the application of the Maltese law. I find the basis for doing so only in the reasons I have stated. For those reasons I would dismiss the appeal.

Lord Pearson . . . : If the difference between the English law and the Maltese law could be regarded only as a difference of procedural (or adjectival or non-substantive) law, there would be an easy solution of the problem in this appeal. On that basis the nature and extent of the remedy would be matters of procedural law regulated by the lex fori, which is English, and the proper remedy for the plaintiff in this case according to

English law would be that he should recover damages for all the relevant consequences of the accident, including pain and suffering as well as pecuniary expense and loss, and the amount of such damages would be £2,303, the sum awarded by the learned judge.

But I am not convinced that the difference between the English law and the Maltese law can reasonably be regarded as only a difference of procedural law. There is a radical difference in the cause of action, the right of action, the jus actionis. A claim to be reimbursed or indemnified or compensated for actual economic loss is substantially different in character from a claim for damages for all the relevant consequences of the accident to the plaintiff, including pain and suffering. If an accident caused no economic loss, but only pain and suffering, there would be a cause of action according to English law, but not according to Maltese law. Surely that must be a matter of substantive law. Then if the validity of a claim for damages for pain and suffering is a matter of substantive law when that is the only claim, is it not a matter of substantive law equally when such a claim happens to be associated with a claim in respect of actual economic loss? I do not think there is any exact and authoritative definition of the boundary between substantive law and procedural (or adjectival or non-substantive) law, and the boundary remains to be settled by further decisions in particular cases. In the present case I think it would be artificial and incorrect to treat the difference between the English law and the Maltese law, which materially affects the determination of the rights and liabilities of the parties, as a matter only of procedural law.

Taking that view, I have to go on to consider the question whether the substantive law to be applied is English or Maltese or both. A choice of law is involved and, as it has to be made by the English court in which the action is brought, it must be governed by the principles of English law for making such a choice.

What, then, is the substantive law applicable in this case? Is it the law of England, or the law of Malta, or some combination of both? It is necessary to consider the authorities. The leading authority is a passage in the judgment of the Court of Exchequer Chamber, delivered by Willes J in *Phillips v Eyre*. But earlier authorities are of some assistance as leading up to it. (His Lordship cited *Mostyn v Fabrigas, Scott v Seymour* and *The Halley*. He quoted the passage in *Phillips v Eyre* beginning 'The last objection' and ending 'incident to the act itself' on p 468 above, and the passage beginning 'As a general rule' and ending 'place where it was done' on p 468 above).

I find some difficulty in reconciling the earlier passage with the later passage, but I think that when taken together they show that the applicable law, the substantive law determining liability or non-liability, is a combination of the lex fori and the lex loci delicti (which was conveniently called by Willes J 'the law of the place'). The act must take its character of wrongfulness from the law of the place: it must not be justifiable under the law of the place: if it is 'valid and unquestionable by the law of the place, it cannot, so far as civil liability is concerned, be drawn in question elsewhere'. But Willes J does not say that the wrongful act has to be actionable, or to give a cause of action for damages according to the law of the place. The actionability is by the lex fori: 'the wrong must be of such a character that it would have been actionable if committed in England'. The second condition has to be read in the light of what has gone before. The act referred to is one which is wrongful according to the law of the place in which it is committed. But there is no requirement that it must be actionable by the law of that place as well as by the law of England: double actionability is not required. The requirement is that the act must not be justifiable by the law of the place. The reason for that must be that a person could not fairly be held liable in damages for doing something which in the place where it was done was either originally lawful or made lawful by retrospective legislation. Willes J's statement of the conditions which have to be fulfilled (which may be called 'the Willes formula') shows that in such a case the substantive law of England plays the dominant role, determining the cause of action, whereas the law of the place in which the act was committed plays a subordinate role, in that it may provide a justification for the act and so defeat the cause of action but it does not in itself determine the cause of action.

Machado v Fontes raised directly, in an interlocutory appeal heard by two Lords Justices, the question whether the act committed abroad, if it was to found an action in England, had to be actionable by the law of the place in which the act was committed or merely wrongful by that law. There was a plea to the effect that the alleged libel published in Brazil was not actionable by the law of Brazil. The plea did not say that the publication was not wrongful by the law of Brazil: thus criminal liability was not excluded. The court, Lopes LJ and Rigby LJ, applying the Willes formula and relying also on the judgments in *The Mary Moxham*,[5] held that the plea was insufficient, because it did not allege that the publication of the libel was an innocent act in Brazil. That was a decision that the act committed abroad, if it was to found an action in England, had to be merely wrongful, not necessarily actionable, by the law of the foreign country. In my opinion, this decision involved a correct interpretation of the Willes formula. The cause of action for the libel was determined by English law, but the defendant would have a defence if he could show that the act complained of was 'justifiable' by the law of the place in which it was committed. It would not be 'justifiable' by that law, if it was a crime by that law. A criminal act would be even less justifiable than a tortious act. There may be an objection to the decision on a different ground, namely, that it may have been permitting a person whose natural forum was a Brazilian court to gain advantages by by-passing his natural forum and suing in the English court. That is a matter which I will consider at a later stage.

The English authorities show that the Willes formula has been accepted; that the first of his conditions gives the predominant role to the English substantive law; and that the second of his conditions does not require actionability by the law of the place where the act was committed, but only that the act should not be justifiable, ie, not excused or innocent by that law. That is the orthodox and established rule, and it has been maintained for a great many years. On the other hand, it has met with some unfavourable criticism both in this country and in Australia, and it is open to your Lordships to set aside or amend the rule by overruling *Machado v Fontes* and not following *The Halley*. But I do not think there could be any good ground for doing so unless either the rule was wrong from the beginning or it has become out of date by reason of changes in legal, social or economic conditions.

5 (1876) 1 PD 107, 46 LJP 17.

I am not persuaded that the rule was wrong from the beginning. It has certain advantages and certain disadvantages. The main advantages are, first, that it has a high degree of certainty and, secondly, that it enables an English court to give judgment according to its own ideas of justice. In *The Halley* it would then have seemed unjust to the English court to hold the defendants liable for the fault of a pilot whom they were compelled by the local law to engage and put in charge of their ship. In the present case it would have seemed unjust to an English court to award to the plaintiff only £53 as damages for serious injuries.

If the rule is to be set aside or amended, what should be put in its place or how should it be amended? There may be many suggestions, but I think the principal ones are:

(a) That the substantive law of the place where the act is committed should be given the predominant role so as to determine the cause of action, and the substantive law of the forum, the English court, should apply only to the extent of the court refusing to enforce the cause of action if it is repugnant to some rule of English public policy;

(b) That damages should be recoverable for a wrongful act committed out of England only if it is actionable both by the law of England and by the law of the country in which the act was committed;

(c) That a flexible rule, which has been referred to as 'the proper law of the tort', should be substituted. . . .

(a) The traditional American rule giving preference to the lex loci delicti has been shown by the opinions and experience of the American courts to have become out of date. With the modern ease and frequency of travel across frontiers (not only by air and not only in the United States) the place of the accident may be quite fortuitous and the law of that place may have no substantial connection with the parties or the issues in the action. It would be strange if the English courts now adopted a rule which the courts of many states of the United States have felt compelled to discard by reason of its unsuitability to modern conditions.

(b) It has been suggested—and there is some support for this suggestion in the Scottish and the Australian cases—that damages should be recoverable for a wrongful act committed out of England only if it is actionable both by the law of England and by the law of the place in which the act was committed. That involves a duplication of causes of action and is likely to place an unfair burden on the plaintiff in some cases. He has the worst of both laws. Also it would in some cases prevent the English court from giving judgment in accordance with its own ideas of justice. Suppose that in the present case there was no pecuniary expense or loss at all. By the law of Malta the plaintiff would have no cause of action in a Maltese court and therefore under the suggested rule his action in the English court would have to be dismissed in spite of his serious injuries and pain and suffering. If I am right in thinking that the question whether damages for pain and suffering are recoverable is a question of substantive law, the suggested rule would bar the plaintiff's claim for such damages even if it was associated with a claim for pecuniary loss.

(c) The new American flexible rule or flexible approach, with its full degree of flexibility, seems—at present at any rate, when the doctrine is of recent origin and further development may be expected—to be lacking in certainty and likely to create or prolong litigation. Nevertheless, it may help the English courts to deal with the danger of 'forum-shopping' which is inherent in the English rule.

The English rule, giving a predominant role to the lex fori in accordance with the Willes formula as interpreted in *Machado v Fontes*, is well established. It has advantages of certainty and ease of application. It enables the English courts to give judgment according to their own ideas of justice. I see no sufficient reason for discarding or modifying this established rule for the normal case in which the action is appropriately brought in the English courts. There is, however, the danger of 'forum-shopping', of which the case of *Machado v Fontes* may be an illustration. A plaintiff, who would naturally and appropriately be suing the defendant in the courts of some other country, may seek to take advantage of the English rule by suing in the English courts because their law is more favourable to him. In such a case it may be desirable as a matter of public policy for the English courts, for the purpose of discouraging 'forum-shopping', to apply the law of the natural forum. That is a possible, and I would think desirable, qualification of the established rule: it would prevent a repetition of what may have happened in *Machado v Fontes*. But it is not a necessary part of the decision in the present case, in which it cannot be said that it was inappropriate for the plaintiff to bring his action in the English courts.

In my opinion, it was right for the learned judge at the trial to apply the English substantive law, being the lex fori, in accordance with the established rule, and, as the majority of the Court of Appeal have affirmed his decision, I would dismiss the appeal.

Finally, I wish to add this. There ought to be a general rule so as to limit the flexibility and consequent uncertainty of the choice of the substantive law to be applied. But whatever rule may be adopted as the general rule some exception will be required in the interests of justice. If the general rule is that the substantive law is the law of the forum, an exception will be required in order to discourage 'forum-shopping'. On the other hand, if the general rule is that the alleged wrongful act must be actionable by the law of the place where it was committed or that it must be actionable both by that law and by the law of the forum, an exception will be required to enable the plaintiff in a case such as the present case to succeed in his claim for adequate damages.

Appeal dismissed.

QUESTIONS

1. What was the ratio decidendi of this case? (One is reminded of the celebrated remark of Lord Melbourne to his Cabinet: 'Gentlemen, it doesn't matter what we say, but for God's sake let's all say the same thing').

2. Two Italians, A and B, are on a motoring holiday in Malta when their car collides with one driven by C, an English tourist. The accident is caused by the combined negligence of B and C. A sues them both in England. Would you apply English, Italian or Maltese law to determine whether damages may be recovered for pain and suffering?

3. Two Maltese are on a motoring holiday in England. One injures the other by negligently driving the car and a claim for damages is brought in England. Would you apply English or Maltese law to determine whether damages may be recovered for pain and suffering?

Corcoran v Corcoran [1974] VR 164 (Supreme Court of Victoria)

The plaintiff, who was the wife of the defendant, was injured when she was travelling as a passenger in a motor car negligently driven by the defendant which was involved in an accident in New South Wales. The plaintiff and defendant were both resident and domiciled in Victoria and the car was registered there. By the law of New South Wales the plaintiff could not sue the defendant because the car was not registered in New South Wales. By the law of Victoria she could, because a Victorian statute had abolished the common law immunity of spouses in actions in tort for personal injuries.

Adams J: For the defendant Mr Winneke contended that the authorities clearly established that in an action of tort for personal injuries, such as the present, where the tortious act was committed in another state, not only must the act be one which is actionable according to the lex fori—the law of Victoria in this case—but also according to the lex delicti, here the law of New South Wales, where the tortious act was committed.

   The leading authority, of course, is *Phillips v Eyre*[6] where Willes J said: (His Honour quoted the passage on p 468 above, beginning 'As a general rule' and ending 'by the law of the place where it was done'). In the case of *Koop v Bebb*,[7] the High Court has held, in a manner binding on me and the other courts of this country, that the principles of *Phillips v Eyre* are binding and should be applied. Mr Winneke conceded that the first of the requirements or conditions in *Phillips v Eyre* had been complied with. By Act No 7768 of the State of Victoria the rule of the interspousal immunity from actions in tort for personal injuries which was originally a common law doctrine, and later embodied in statute, was abrogated, and, accordingly, this action between the wife and the husband for damages for personal injuries arising out of a tort is clearly one which would be actionable in Victoria, assuming that the act was committed here. The difficulty arises with the second of the requirements or conditions prescribed by *Phillips v Eyre* as a condition for maintaining an action on a foreign tort, that is the requirement that the tortious act should be one which was, to use the words of that case, 'not justifiable' according to the lex delicti.

   Mr Winneke contended that this second of the requirements or conditions, which I will refer to as the second limb in *Phillips v Eyre*, would be satisfied only if it could be shown that this cause of action relied upon by the plaintiff would have been actionable in New South Wales had the action been brought in the courts of that jurisdiction. In other words, his submission was that properly interpreted the propositions enunciated in *Phillips v Eyre* required double actionability between the same parties, actionability according to the lex fori in which the case was brought, and actionability according to the lex delicti where the tortious act was committed. Although the words 'not justifiable' as used in the rules enumerated in *Phillips v Eyre* do not, on their face, compel any such restricted interpretation, Mr Winneke's contention was that the body of authority in favour of his construction, as the preferred one, was much too strong for me at this age and place to disregard.

   Although no doubt the matter will continue to be hotly debated among

6 (1870) LR 6 QB 1 10 B & S 1004; p 467 above.
7 (1951) 84 CLR 629, [1952] ALR 37.

academic writers, concerned at times more with what the law should be, and may even still be considered open to review by the highest courts, the House of Lords decision in *Boys v Chaplin*[8] discourages any such hope. It was conceded by all parties that the present application should be decided by me on the basis that the answer is to be found upon the proper interpretation of the rules formulated by Willes J in *Phillips v Eyre*—the rules which indicate what should properly be taken into consideration in determining the actionability in one court of a claim for damages based on a tort committed within the territorial jurisdiction of another court.

For the plaintiff, Mr O'Bryan's main submission was that *Phillips v Eyre* properly understood and applied did not provide a defence in the circumstances of this case. One contention was that the second limb of *Phillips v Eyre* as well as the first was satisfied in the circumstances of this case. The validity of this submission depended, of course, on the meaning to be assigned to the words 'not justifiable' in the requirement that the tortious act must be one which was not justifiable in the country where it was committed.

In view of, and in deference to, the criticisms which the decision in *Machado v Fontes*[9] has excited over the years for its interpretation of the expression 'not justifiable' as meaning no more than 'not innocent', whether regarded civilly or criminally, Mr O'Bryan submitted that if the act was of a kind which might give rise to a civil cause of action under the lex delicti, it was to be regarded as 'not justifiable' within the meaning of the second limb in *Phillips v Eyre*. Thus in the present case he urged that although the wife could not have sued her husband in New South Wales in respect of the negligent driving of the motor car in New South Wales causing her personal injuries, as the husband's employer, if he had one, could have been liable to her on the basis of the vicarious liability for the wrongdoing or tort of a servant that was enough: see *Broom v Morgan*.[10] That decision is some authority for the proposition that notwithstanding the immunity of a husband from suit by his wife for damages for tort, his conduct, as it would have attracted liability albeit only in an action by the wife against the employer is of a tortious character sufficient to characterise it as 'not justifiable'.

Furthermore, Mr O'Bryan contended that this negligent driving by the husband, had it been a cause of injury to some other car, or perhaps to some passenger in the husband's car other than the wife, would have provided the foundation for civil liability against the husband in New South Wales. The very same act of the negligent driving, although not entitling the wife herself to sue in New South Wales because of the statutory bar, could not, so it was argued, be other than an act 'not justifiable' in New South Wales whatever reasonable restrictions are put on the width of the language thus used in *Phillips v Eyre*. How can it be said that an act by the husband having such consequences was an act which was 'justifiable' in New South Wales merely because the wife herself could not maintain an action in respect of it? As a further argument that the tortious act in this case was 'not justifiable' in New South Wales Mr O'Bryan relied on the decision of our Full Court in

8 [1971] AC 356, [1969] 2 All ER 1085; p 470 above.
9 [1897] 2 QB 231, 66 LJQB 542.
10 [1953] 1 QB 597, [1953] 1 All ER 849.

McKinnon v McKinnon,[11] which established that, notwithstanding the then bar under Victorian law in general preventing a wife from suing her husband in tort, where she suffered, in addition to personal injuries through some tortious act of her husband, damage to her separate estate or property—she could maintain, in Victoria, an action in tort against her husband although limited to the damage which was occasioned to her personal property. That was so by reason of the construction put on the local legislation which permitted actions of tort by a wife against her husband for the protection of her personal property, and only barred actions in tort otherwise, that is to say, in the main in so far as the damages extended to personal injuries.

In this case, notice of special damage has been filed, and as appears from that document there is included in the damages claimed by the wife which are in the main for personal injuries, damage to property, ie a frock damaged by blood, and stockings damaged by blood which together came to $11, and broken dentures the value of which is claimed to be $120. And so the argument is put that here the husband is liable at the suit of the wife in New South Wales which has similar legislation to this, to the extent at least of the damage to her personal property.

Although under the law of New South Wales, the husband is immune from any claim in respect of personal injuries to his wife in this case, how can it be said that the act of negligence which attracts civil liability of husband to wife although only to a limited extent is otherwise than an act 'not justifiable' according to the lex loci delicti.

I may say I have felt a great deal of force in Mr O'Bryan's submission as to the ambit of the expression 'not justifiable' in the rule in *Phillips v Eyre*. Unaided by authority I would have thought the negligent conduct of the husband leading, or capable of leading, to such consequences in New South Wales would answer the description of conduct 'not justifiable' according to the law of New South Wales consistently with the claim against her husband by this plaintiff being barred by the local legislation.

It seems to me that the justification for reading the requirement in *Phillips v Eyre* that the act should not be justifiable according to the lex delicti, as requiring that the act should give rise in the lex delicti to a cause of action of damages there and nothing less, has a theoretical justification only if in the choice of laws the lex delicti should be regarded as dominant, and the 'obligation' doctrine adopted. The doctrine that under the principles of private international law in the case of foreign torts the courts of this country are in effect enforcing an obligation arising and having its source under a foreign law, rather than an obligation arising under our own law, is one which has in the past commanded interest and influence in the courts of the United States, and I think at an earlier stage may have done so in the English courts; but one thing is clear, at least for me, that is that any notion that in enforcing a claim based on a foreign tort we are, by courtesy or for some other reason, giving effect to an accrued obligation arising in a foreign country is a doctrine which is not now acceptable. It was clearly repudiated in *Koop v Bebb*, by the High Court and is just as clearly repudiated by the House of Lords in the case of *Boys v Chaplin*. It is not part of the common law, this doctrine based on obligation, whatever future it might possibly

11 [1955] VLR 81, [1955] ALR 392.

have in the United States. That, as I say, seems to be the main theoretical justification for relying on the rule of double actionability which involves as being essential that there be a fully actionable cause of action arising in the country where the tort was committed, although our own law imposes an additional check on enforcing it in this country, by requiring that the act should have been an actionable tort in this country, if the act had been committed here.

With the rejection of the 'obligation' doctrine, it is difficult to see why, on principle, actionability in every respect in the foreign country should be insisted upon when the actionability according to the lex fori is of course insisted upon under the first limb in *Phillips v Eyre*.

A practical benefit, however, which flows undoubtedly from the rule of double actionability—actionability both under the lex fori and under the lex delicti—is the protection that that affords against the evils and injustices of forum shopping. If civil actionability under the lex delicti is insisted upon as a condition of bringing the action in another country, then clearly a plaintiff can gain no benefit from selecting his own forum because whatever forum he selects can only give effect to an action which is maintainable in the country in which the tortious act was done.

Although I am not persuaded that in strict theory I am bound by authority in this matter, I have concluded, I may say with some reluctance, that the weight of authority favours construing the second limb of *Phillips v Eyre* as in itself requiring that the act complained of as an actionable tort in the forum should be one which would give rise to an actionable tort by the lex loci. Not only has this conclusion the support of the High Court in *Koop v Bebb*, although not essential to that decision, but I consider that it also commands substantial support from the Lords in the case of *Boys v Chaplin*. I have thought it proper in the existing uncertain state of authority, for me to accept, as it appeals to me, what was said by Lord Wilberforce in *Boys v Chaplin*: (His Honour quoted the passage on pp 480–481 above, beginning 'Assuming that, as the basic rule' and ending 'reflected this conflict').

I agree it is very difficult to extract a ratio from the many opinions expressed by the House of Lords in *Boys v Chaplin*, but what Lord Wilberforce here says coupled with what Lord Hodson says in his speech, warrants me in concluding, I consider, that prima facie, without importing any notion of flexibility to the rule, the rule in *Phillips v Eyre* requires actionability both by the lex fori and by the lex delicti as a condition of maintaining an action in our courts on a foreign tort. But while accepting that as the broad principle to be applied prima facie, I think it rational to accept the qualification that in a particular case where there are special circumstances warranting it in the interests of justice the rule should be modified or departed from. I know this introduction of flexibility into the rule was not accepted in a recent case in New South Wales in the Full Court, *Kolsky v Mayne Nickless Ltd*.[12] With all due respect to that decision, I must say that I am not persuaded that I should follow it; in part because I think it attributes a proposition that flexibility is foreign to the rule in *Phillips v Eyre* and to certain observations of the High Court in the two cases that I have already referred to—*Koop v Bebb* and *Anderson v Eric Anderson Radio and TV*

---

12 [1970] 3 NSWR 511, 72 SR NSW 437.

Pty Ltd.[13] For myself I find nothing in either of these cases—in neither of which the point arose for decision and both of which were decided before the House of Lords made its observations in *Boys v Chaplin*—which is in any way inconsistent with the adoption of the views expressed by Lord Hodson and Lord Wilberforce in *Boys v Chaplin,* to the effect that the rules in *Phillips v Eyre* are not to be regarded as rigid inflexible rules. Indeed as clearly pointed out in *Boys v Chaplin* the rules in *Phillips v Eyre* are stated as rules to be applied 'in general' and not as inflexible rules.

I feel persuaded by the force of what Lord Wilberforce has said in the passage cited above and I propose in this last portion of this judgment to indicate why, in my opinion, this is clearly a case where the rules in *Phillips v Eyre* are flexible enough to admit of an action in the circumstances of this case although if rigidly applied they would defeat the wife's action.

Shortly, the reasons are that I consider that having due regard to the requirements of certainty and individual justice where, as in the present case, there is a conflict in one respect between the laws of New South Wales and the laws of Victoria, there are strong reasons why that conflict should be resolved in favour of the law of Victoria. I say the conflict here is in one respect only. Were it not for the immunity which a husband has in New South Wales from action by his wife in a suit in tort for personal injuries, (except in the use of a New South Wales registered motor vehicle) there would be no doubt whatever that the conduct of the husband would have been actionable in New South Wales in an action for tort.

It is only in that respect that the law of New South Wales differs from the law of Victoria; under the law of Victoria, interspousal immunity in actions of tort has been swept away and the wife is entitled to bring the action she has.

Why should, in this case, the rule applicable in New South Wales apply in preference to that of Victoria? The only connection, as I indicated before, between the facts or the ingredients of this action with New South Wales is that the accident giving rise to the wife's injuries happened to occur in New South Wales. But when it is realised that the parties, the husband and the wife, are both residents of Victoria, both domiciled in Victoria, were only fortuitously in New South Wales at the time of the accident, have no other connection whatsoever with New South Wales, and also that they were travelling in a car which is registered in Victoria, there would seem to me to be overwhelming reasons for treating this as a case where the Victorian law should be preferred to the New South Wales law on the issue, and the only issue where the laws conflict—the capacity of the wife to sue the husband. Not only has the cause of action a much closer contact with Victoria than with New South Wales but the interests of Victoria are more clearly involved than any interests of New South Wales. The interests of New South Wales in maintaining interspousal immunity primarily concern husbands and wives who are connected with New South Wales. There would seem to be no obvious connection between any such policy of immunity in the New South Wales legislation, and husbands and wives who are unconnected with New South Wales, being residents of Victoria.

Furthermore, if one is looking for some question of policy on which to decide whether the rule in *Phillips v Eyre* should be relaxed in this case, one

13 (1965) 114 CLR 20, [1966] ALR 423.

finds, I think, without much difficulty a policy evident in the New South Wales legislation which would favour the allowing of this action in Victoria between the Victorian husband and wife driving a Victorian car. From the New South Wales legislation, it is clear that the legislature there has thought it proper to relax the old doctrine of interspousal immunity when the result of it would be injustice to a wife without any benefit to the husband. One can readily enough understand a general policy of discouraging litigation between husband and wife in tort because of the wider interests involved if these actions were allowed without restraint.

The policy of the New South Wales legislation is to allow these actions, where by the requirements of its legislation the husband's car is subject to a policy of compulsory third-party insurance in New South Wales and, accordingly, there will in substance be no question of personal litigation between husband and wife. In such a case there is no reason founded on public policy for denying to a spouse a right to sue the other spouse for damages sustained by wrongful conduct. The same policy which lies behind the New South Wales legislation, which in terms is locally confined to a case where the motor vehicle concerned is registered in New South Wales is effectuated in Victoria, although in general terms, by its legislation which, inter alia, operates to remove any bar to one spouse suing the other for damages in tort where the motor vehicle is registered in Victoria with the like consequences of a compulsory third-party insurance. The circumstance that by allowing the present action in Victoria by wife against husband the policy manifested by the New South Wales Act would also operate in Victoria provides, in my opinion, an additional reason in justification of the relaxation of the second limb of the rule in *Phillips v Eyre*. To allow Victorian law to govern the matter so far from contravening the policy of the New South Wales legislation promotes it.

I might just add this: another thing which has persuaded me to this flexible application of *Phillips v Eyre*, is that I see no danger, by allowing this, of encouraging 'forum shopping'. It is to be recalled that this proceeding is arising in the natural forum of the parties, not any forum chosen at random with a view of benefiting the plaintiff. Other consequences may well arise were such an action as the present to come before what might be called a fortuitous forum. Here we have the natural forum, Victoria, where both the parties reside and where the car itself is registered, the link with New South Wales being entirely fortuitous, New South Wales is not a natural forum. And therefore by allowing this action to proceed in Victoria as maintainable according to Victorian law, I am doing nothing to encourage 'forum shopping'. Had the case been brought in some state which had no connection with the parties at all, and in that state the law allowed the action to be brought, whereas in the natural forum the law did not, one might well conclude that the rule in *Phillips v Eyre* should apply with all its rigour, namely, that it should require to be shown that the action brought was one which was maintainable and actionable according to the lex delicti.

While I may have not done full justice to the many submissions which have been raised before me, I have said sufficient to indicate why I must answer the question raised by the order as follows: 'As to the objection in point of law and the point of law raised by the defence, namely whether in the circumstances admitted in the pleadings and the statement of facts agreed between the parties, the plaintiff is entitled to maintain, and whether

the Supreme Court of Victoria has jurisdiction to entertain the action herein',
I answer, 'Yes'.

*If an exemption clause in a contract is pleaded as a defence to an action in tort, the
validity and scope of the exemption clause are governed by the proper law of the contract,
but whether the clause is available as a defence is governed by the lex delicti.*

Canadian Pacific Rly v Parent [1917] AC 195, 86 LJPC 123 (Privy Council)

Appeal from the Supreme Court of Canada.

Joseph Chalifour was a stockman employed by the Gordon Ironside and
Fares Co. Ltd. to bring cattle by the defendants' railway from Winnipeg in
Manitoba to Montreal in Quebec. The railway company had its head office
in Montreal. Chalifour, who was domiciled in Quebec, understood little
English and could not read or write, though he could sign his name. He
signed a pass issued by the defendants which exempted them from all
liability in respect of the death or injury of a person travelling at less than
full fare in charge of stock, whether such death or injury was caused by the
negligence of the defendants or their servants or otherwise. While on the
journey from Winnipeg to Montreal, Chalifour was killed in a collision in
Ontario which was due to negligence on the part of the defendants'
servants.

The widow and son of Chalifour brought an action in Quebec against the
defendants claiming damages under article 1056 of the Civil Code of
Quebec. The Chief Justice of Quebec held that the plaintiffs were entitled to
damages. His judgment was affirmed by the Court of King's Bench and (for
differing reasons) by a majority of the Supreme Court of Canada. The
railway company appealed to the Privy Council.

The judgment of their Lordships (Viscount Haldane, Lords Dunedin,
Parker, Parmoor and Wrenbury) was delivered by:

Viscount Haldane (having stated the facts):   By art 1056 of the Civil Code
of Quebec it is provided that 'in all cases where the person injured by the
commission of an offence or a quasi-offence dies in consequence, without
having obtained indemnity or satisfaction, his consort and his ascendant and
descendant relations have a right, but only within a year after his death, to
recover from the person who committed the offence or quasi-offence, or his
representatives, all damages occasioned by such death'. It is settled by the
decisions of this Board in *Robinson v Canadian Pacific Rly Co*[14] and *Miller v
Grand Trunk Rly Co*[15] that this article of the Code confers an independent and
personal right, and not one conferred, as in the English statute known as
Lord Campbell's Act, merely on the representatives as such of the deceased.
In Manitoba and Ontario it is otherwise. The analogous right there arises
only under statutes which are for this purpose substantially in the same terms
as Lord Campbell's Act. There was some doubt expressed in the courts of
Quebec in the present case as to whether the law of Manitoba, assuming it to

14 [1892] AC 481, 61 LJPC 79.
15 [1906] AC 187.

be relevant, was duly proved. If such proof was material in the Quebec court, their Lordships are of opinion that, when the case reached the Supreme Court of Canada, this doubt could not properly be entertained. For the Supreme Court is the common forum of the provinces of Canada, and is bound to take judicial notice of their laws. It is clear that if the law of either Manitoba or Ontario governs the case the respondents were precluded from claiming.

In these provinces the rule of the English common law prevails that in a civil court the death of a human being cannot be complained of as an injury. The application of this rule is modified by statute in a fashion analogous to what obtains in England under Lord Campbell's Act; but the modification contained in the statutes in these provinces has, like that contained in Lord Campbell's Act, no application unless the wrongful act done would, had not death ensued, have entitled the person injured to maintain an action and recover damages. If Chalifour validly contracted himself out of this right, his representatives could not therefore have sued if the law of either of these provinces governs.

The crucial questions which arise are whether Chalifour, by signing the pass under the circumstances in which he was accepted as a passenger in charge of the cattle at less than the full fare, bound himself to renounce what would otherwise have been his rights, and, if so, whether the respondents were precluded from claiming under the article in the Quebec Code. If that article applied, it is not in controversy that the widow and son were proper plaintiffs in this action. (His Lordship held that the exemption clause in the contract of carriage was valid under Canadian railway legislation; and that the defendants did enough to enable Chalifour to know what he was about when he signed the pass).

It follows that, as the statute law of Ontario, the province where the accident occurred which caused Chalifour's death, did not confer on any one claiming on his account a statutory right to sue, there was, so far as Ontario is concerned, no other right. For in Ontario the principle of the English common law applies, which precludes death from being complained of as an injury. If so, on the general principles which are applied in Canada and this country under the title of private international law, a common law action for damages for tort could not be successfully maintained against the appellants in Quebec. It is not necessary to consider whether all the language used by the English Court of Appeal in the judgments in *Machado v Fontes*[16] was sufficiently precise. The conclusion there reached was that it is not necessary, if the act was wrongful in the country where the action was brought, that it should be susceptible of civil proceedings in the other country, provided it is not an innocent act there. This question does not arise in the present case, where the action was brought, not against the servants of the appellants, who may or may not have been guilty of criminal negligence, but against the appellants themselves. It is clear that the appellants cannot be said to have committed in a corporate capacity any criminal act. The most that can be suggested is that, on the maxim respondeat superior, they might have been civilly responsible for the acts of their servants.

The other point that remains is whether art 1056 of the Quebec Code which has already been quoted conferred a statutory right to sue in the

16 [1897] 2 QB 231, 66 LJQB 542.

events which happened. Their Lordships answer this question in the negative. The offence or quasi-offence took place not in Quebec but in Ontario. The presumption to be made is that in enacting art 1056 the Quebec legislature meant, as an Act of the Imperial Parliament would be construed as meaning, to confine the special remedy conferred to cases of offences or quasi-offences committed within its own jurisdiction. There is, in their Lordships' opinion, nothing in the context of the chapter of the Code in which the article occurs which displaces this presumption in its construction. The rule of interpretation is a natural one where law, as in the case of both Quebec and England, owes its origin largely to territorial custom. No doubt the Quebec legislature could impose many obligations in respect of acts done outside the province on persons domiciled within its jurisdiction, as the railway company may have been by reason of having its head office at Montreal. But in the case of art 1056 there does not appear to exist any sufficient reason for holding that it has intended to do so, and by so doing to place claims for torts committed outside Quebec on a footing differing from that on which the general rule of private international law already referred to would place them.

Appeal allowed.

Sayers v International Drilling Co NV [1971] 3 All ER 163, [1971] 1 WLR 1176 (Court of Appeal)

Appeal from Bean J.

An American oil company, the Offshore Company of Houston, Texas, had subsidiaries in many parts of the world. One of them was an English company, the International Drilling Co Ltd, which had its head office in London and oil rigs in the North Sea. Another subsidiary was a Dutch company, the International Drilling Co NV, which had its head office at The Hague and drilling rigs in various parts of the world.

The plaintiff, an Englishman, was employed by the English company. In 1967 he agreed to go to Nigeria as an employee of the Dutch company. His contract of employment was made in England and was written in Americanised English. It provided for payment in sterling. It contained a provision stating that in case of accident the company had a 'Disability Compensation Program'. Clause 8 provided that the employee should in case of accident or disability accept the benefits to which he might be entitled under the Compensation Program as his exclusive remedy in lieu of any other claims whether at common law or under the statutes of the United Kingdom or any other nation.

Soon after arriving in Nigeria the plaintiff was injured in an accident on the drilling rig caused, as he alleged, by the negligence of his fellow employees. He brought an action in England against the Dutch company.

By section 1 (3) of the Law Reform (Personal Injuries) Act 1948, 'any provision contained in a contract of service or apprenticeship shall be void in so far as it would have the effect of excluding or limiting any liability of the employer in respect of personal injuries caused to the person employed or apprenticed by the negligence of persons in common employment with him'. By article 1638x of the Netherlands Civil Code, 'any condition whereby these obligations of the employer are excluded or restricted is void'. But that article only applied to domestic Dutch contracts, not to international contracts like the one signed by the plaintiff.

The master ordered a preliminary issue to be tried, namely whether the Dutch company could rely on the exemption clause as a defence to the action.

Lord Denning MR: The issue raises an important question of private international law. On the one hand, the claim by the plaintiff is a claim founded on tort. In considering that claim, we must apply the proper law of tort, that is, the law of the country with which the parties and the acts done have the most significant connection. That is how I put it in *Boys v Chaplin*.[17] I think it is confirmed by what Lord Wilberforce said in the House of Lords,[18] though he put it with more scholarship and precision than I could hope to do.

On the other hand, the defence by the defendants is a defence based on contract. In considering that defence we must apply the proper law of the contract, that is, the system of law with which the contract has its closest and most real connection: see *Compagnie Tunisienne de Navigation SA v Compagnie d'Armement Maritime SA*.[19]

But it is obvious that we cannot apply two systems of law, one for the claim in tort, and the other for the defence in contract. We must apply one system of law by which to decide both claim and defence. To decide it I would ask this question: What is the proper law by which to determine the issues in this case? And I would answer it by saying: it is the system of law with which the issues have the closest connection.

So far as the claim in tort is concerned, the accident took place in the territorial waters of *Nigeria*. But it took place on an oil drilling rig owned and controlled by a *Dutch* company and manned by employees of that company. The Nigerians had nothing to do with the rig. So Nigeria is out. The injured man was *English*, but his fellow employees (who were negligent) may have been English or American or of some other nationality. The only common bond between them was that they were employed by the Dutch company. So Dutch is in. If I were asked to decide the proper law of the *tort* (apart from contract) I should have said it was *Dutch* law.

So far as the defence in contract is concerned, the contract with Mr Sayers was negotiated and *made* in England. It was for the services of Mr Sayers, an *Englishman*, asking him to go overseas for a spell of work. It was in the *English* language. His salary was to be paid in the *English* currency, sterling. He was insured under the *English* national insurance scheme. He was to come back on leave to his home in *England*. True it is that the employers were Dutch (who employed personnel of all nationalities), but the contract was administered in London. The records were kept in London, Texas and Holland. If I were asked to decide the proper law of the contract (apart from the tort) I should be inclined to say that it was English.

But seeing that the action is founded on tort and the proper law of the tort is Dutch, I would say that, as between the two systems, English or Dutch, the issue of liability should be determined by Dutch law. In any case, there is

17 [1968] 2 QB 1 at 20, [1968] 1 All ER 283 at 286.
18 [1971] AC 356 at 391–392, [1969] 2 All ER 1085 at 1104; p 470 at 483 above.
19 [1971] AC 572, [1970] 3 All ER 71; p 441 above.

a provision in clause 8 of the contract which turns the scale against English law. (His Lordship read it.)

Seeing that English law is in terms excluded, I think that the issue of liability has its closest connection with Dutch law: and should be determined by Dutch law. According to that law this exemption clause is valid and effective to bar Mr Sayers' claim in tort. His claim must be limited to the benefits in the Dutch company's Compensation Program.

I agree with the judge that the matter is governed by Dutch law and is not to be determined by the English law. I would dismiss the appeal accordingly.

Salmon LJ: I agree that this appeal should be dismissed.

(His Lordship stated the facts and continued): It follows that the only point on this appeal is: was the judge right in coming to the conclusion that the proper law of the contract of employment is Dutch law? I confess that I do not find this at all an easy point. Sometimes commercial contracts expressly lay down what law shall govern them. It is not at all unusual to find merchants all over the world agreeing that the law of the contract shall be English law and that any dispute which shall arise between the parties shall be settled by arbitration in London or perhaps in the commercial court of this country. I have seen many such contracts, though the subject-matter of the contract has otherwise nothing whatsoever to do with the British system of law. Clauses such as those are introduced into contracts because of the confidence which merchants abroad repose in the administration of justice in this country. Well, there is no such clause in this contract; nor, of course, is there a clause which specifies any other system of law as applying to the contract. We are left to try and discern by inference from the contract itself which is the system of law by which the parties intended that it should be governed. Sometimes it is said that the test—and it is a very useful test— is: what system of law has the closest and most real connection with the contract? My difficulty in this case is that I can find very little clue in the contract as to what the parties intended, and very little indication that the contract has a very real or close connection with any particular system of law. I agree, however, with Lord Denning MR, that on the whole the conclusion at which the judge arrived ought not to be disturbed.

One thing about which everyone was agreed was that whatever system of law ought to be applied to this contract, it should not be the Nigerian system of law. The work under the contract was being carried out in the territorial waters of Nigeria. The contract itself, however, stated that although the work was expected to be done in Nigeria, the company had the right to change the venue of the work; in other words, under this contract the plaintiff could have been ordered to work in any part of the world other than the United Kingdom. So Nigerian law is out, and that leaves us with a choice of English or Dutch law. There are, as Lord Denning MR has said, a number of factors supporting the view that perhaps English law was intended to be the law governing the contract. The contract was made with an Englishman in England; it is in the English language and payment under it is to be made in sterling. I do not, however, think that in this case those factors have very much significance. Looking at the contract itself, one finds that it is entered into on a printed form of contract drawn up by the Dutch company for the purpose of engaging European personnel. The printed form leaves a blank for the country of origin of the servant to be engaged under the contract. He may be of any European nationality. It is apparent, I think, that although this contract is in the English language and refers to payment in sterling, it is using a language and a currency of convenience for the purpose of dealing with a multiplicity of nationals. Moreover, as Mr Kidwell points out without any disrespect, this contract, having regard to its phraseology and spelling, could be described as being in the American rather than in the English language, and therefore the fact that it is written in what may be English has even less significance than it would ordinarily have, and it never has very much. Anyone reading the contract would see that it had been drafted by an American and everyone concerned in this case knew that the parent of the defendant company was a United States company; but no one could have supposed that the law applicable to the contract was intended to be American law. The ordinary intelligent prospective servant reading through this contract would, I think, recognise—as indeed Mr Sayers did—that the form of contract could well be used for engaging an Italian, a Spaniard, a Greek and an Englishman or any other European. It could not be supposed that if, for example, an Italian were to be engaged in Italy under this form of contract he would expect the contract to be governed by English or even Italian law any more than would the Dutch company. The plaintiff entering into this form of contract in England must, I think, have recognised that when he went out to Nigeria or to whatever other part of the world he might be sent, he could well find himself working on a rig with an Italian, a Greek and a Spaniard. He could not have believed that his contractual rights would be governed by a different law from that of his fellow employees, still less that there would be five different laws governing the contractual rights of, say, five different employees. If it were so, it would be awkward for the employers, awkward for their employees, and difficult to give the contracts ordinary business efficacy. Therefore, in spite of the fact that the contract is in the English language, payment in sterling, and the nationality of the plaintiff is English, I cannot accept the argument that this contract is governed by English law.

It has been argued that the first part of clause 8 of the contract should be read as meaning that English law is not to apply. This is not a very happily drafted clause. Indeed, the latter part of it might be read as meaning that it merely excludes the plaintiff's English common law rights in respect of his employer's negligence. Now if that is the correct view of the clause, English law would apply to the contract, for otherwise there would be no reason for excluding the plaintiff's rights under English law.

I have, however, come to the conclusion, not without some doubt, that the correct view of clause 8 is that on balance it indicates that English law does not govern this contract. I should mention in passing that the employment under the contract does not begin until the plaintiff leaves the shores of this country, and the one place in the world in which the work cannot be carried out is within this country or its territorial waters.

If English and Nigerian law are to be excluded, this leaves only Dutch law as the law which governs the contract. I think that since the Dutch employers were engaging people of various nationalities in different parts of the world to work abroad together it certainly gives the greatest business efficacy to such contracts to presume that the parties must have intended to adhere to the law of Holland, or, put in a different way, that that system of law has the closest and most real connection with the contract.

Another pointer which I think indicates Dutch law is that under that system of law it is permissible, in this type of contract, to exclude the employer's ordinary liability in negligence and to substitute for it the rights under what is called the Compensation Program. This is a pointer (although its importance must not be exaggerated) which suggests that the parties may well have intended the contract to be governed by a system of law under which it would be valid rather than invalid, namely, Dutch law rather than English law.

On the whole, therefore, although not without doubt, I have come to the conclusion that the proper law of this contract is Dutch law and that accordingly this appeal should be dismissed.

Stamp LJ delivered a judgment to the same effect as Salmon LJ.

Appeal dismissed.

NOTE

This decision has been heavily criticised by academic writers: see eg *Cheshire & North*, pp 282–284; *Morris*, p 262; Collins, (1972) 21 1CLQ 914. It should be contrasted with the decision of the Court of Session on the same statute: *Brodin v A/R Seljan* 1973 SC 213; p 679 below.

Unfair Contract Terms Act 1977

2.—(1) A person cannot by reference to any contract term or to a notice given to persons generally or to particular persons exclude or restrict his liability for death or personal injury resulting from negligence.

(2) In the case of other loss or damage, a person cannot so exclude or restrict his liability for negligence except in so far as the term or notice satisfies the requirement of reasonableness.

(3) Where a contract term or notice purports to exclude or restrict liability for negligence a person's agreement to or awareness of it is not of itself to be taken as indicating his voluntary acceptance of any risk.

27.—(2) (p 449 above).

In most of the United States the rights and liabilities of the parties with respect to an issue in tort are determined by the law of the country which, with respect to that issue, has the most significant relationship to the occurrence and the parties.

Babcock v Jackson (1963) 12 NY 2d 473, 191 NE 2d 279 (New York Court of Appeals)

Fuld J: On Friday 16 September 1960 Miss Georgia Babcock and her friends, Mr and Mrs William Jackson, all residents of Rochester, NY, left that city in Mr Jackson's automobile, Miss Babcock as guest, for a week-end trip to Canada. Some hours later, as Mr Jackson was driving in the Province of Ontario, he apparently lost control of the car; it went off the highway into an adjacent stone wall, and Miss Babcock was seriously injured. Upon her return to this state, she brought the present action against William Jackson, alleging negligence on his part in operating his automobile.

At the time of the accident, there was in force in Ontario a statute providing that 'the owner or driver of a motor vehicle, other than a vehicle operated in the business of carrying passengers for compensation, is not liable for any loss or damage resulting from bodily injury to, or the death of, any person being carried in . . . the motor vehicle'.[20] Even though no such bar is recognised under this state's substantive law of torts, the defendant moved to dismiss the complaint on the ground that the law of the place where the accident occurred governs and that Ontario's guest statute bars recovery. The court at Special Term, agreeing with the defendant, granted the motion and the Appellate Division, over a strong dissent by Halpern J, affirmed the judgment of dismissal without opinion.

The question presented is simply drawn. Shall the law of the place of the tort[1] *invariably* govern the availability of relief for the tort or shall the applicable choice of law rule also reflect a consideration of other factors which are relevant to the purposes served by the enforcement or denial of the remedy?

The traditional choice of law rule, embodied in the original Restatement of Conflict of Laws and until recently unquestioningly followed in this court, has been that the substantive rights and liabilities arising out of a tortious occurrence are determinable by the law of the place of the tort. It had its conceptual foundation in the vested rights doctrine, namely, that a right to recover for a foreign tort owes its creation to the law of the jurisdiction where the injury occurred and depends for its existence and extent solely on such law. Although espoused by such great figures as Holmes J[2] and Professor Beale,[3] the vested rights doctrine has long since been discredited because it fails to take account of underlying policy considerations in evaluating the significance to be ascribed to the circumstance that an act had a foreign situs in determining the rights and liabilities which arise out of that act. 'The vice of the vested rights theory', it has been aptly stated, 'is that it affects to decide concrete cases upon generalities which do not state the practical considerations involved.'[4] More particularly, as applied to torts, the theory ignores the interest which jurisdictions other than that where the tort occurred may have in the resolution of particular issues. It is for this very reason that, despite the advantages of certainty, ease of application and predictability which it affords, there has in recent years been increasing criticism of the traditional rule by commentators[5] and a judicial trend towards its abandonment or modification. . . .

The 'center of gravity' or 'grouping of contacts' doctrine adopted by this court in conflicts cases involving contracts impresses us as likewise affording the appropriate approach for accommodating the competing interests in tort

20 RSO 1960 c 172 s 105 (2). This section was repealed by the Highway Traffic Amendment Act 1977, s 16 (1). All the remaining footnotes to this case form part of Fuld J's opinion. Many footnotes have had to be omitted (*Ed*).

1 In this case, as in nearly all such cases, the conduct causing injury and the injury itself occurred in the same jurisdiction. The phrase 'place of the tort', as distinguished from 'place of wrong' and 'place of injury', is used herein to designate the place where both the wrong and the injury took place.

2 See *Slater v Mexican National Railroad Co* (1904) 194 US 120.

3 *Conflict of Laws* Vol II, pp 1286–92.

4 Yntema, 37 Yale LJ 468 at 482–3.

5 See Dicey *Conflict of Laws* (7th edn) pp 937 et seq; Leflar *The Law of Conflict of Laws* pp 217 et seq; Stumberg *Principles of Conflict of Laws* (2nd edn) pp 201 et seq; Morris 'The Proper Law of a Tort', 64 Harv L Rev 881; Ehrenzweig, 69 Yale LJ 595; Currie, 10 Stan L Rev 205.

cases with multi-state contacts. Justice, fairness and 'the best practical result' may best be achieved by giving controlling effect to the law of the jurisdiction which, because of its relationship or contact with the occurrence or the parties, has the greatest concern with the specific issue raised in the litigation. The merit of such a rule is that 'it gives to the place having the most interest in the problem paramount control over the legal issues arising out of a particular factual context' and thereby allows the forum to apply 'the policy of the jurisdiction most intimately concerned with the outcome of the particular litigation'.[6]. . .

Comparison of the relative 'contacts' and 'interests' of New York and Ontario in this litigation, vis-à-vis the issue here presented, makes it clear that the concern of New York is unquestionably the greater and more direct and that the interest of Ontario is at best minimal. The present action involves injuries sustained by a New York guest as the result of the negligence of a New York host in the operation of an automobile, garaged, licensed and undoubtedly insured in New York, in the course of a week-end journey which began and was to end there. In sharp contrast, Ontario's sole relationship with the occurrence is the purely adventitious circumstance that the accident occurred there.

New York's policy of requiring a tortfeasor to compensate his guest for injuries caused by his negligence cannot be doubted—as attested by the fact that the legislature of this state has repeatedly refused to enact a statute denying or limiting recovery in such cases; and our courts have neither reason nor warrant for departing from that policy simply because the accident, solely affecting New York residents and arising out of the operation of a New York based automobile, happened beyond its borders. Per contra, Ontario has no conceivable interest in denying a remedy to a New York guest against his New York host for injuries suffered in Ontario by reason of conduct which was tortious under Ontario law. The object of Ontario's guest statute, it has been said, is 'to prevent the fraudulent assertion of claims by passengers, in collusion with the drivers, against insurance companies',[7] and quite obviously the fraudulent claims intended to be prevented by the statute are those asserted against Ontario defendants and their insurance carriers, not New York defendants and their insurance carriers. Whether New York defendants are imposed upon or their insurers defrauded by a New York plaintiff is scarcely a valid legislative concern of Ontario simply because the accident occurred there, any more so than if the accident had happened in some other jurisdiction.

It is hardly necessary to say that Ontario's interest is quite different from what it would have been had the issue related to the manner in which the defendant had been driving his car at the time of the accident. Where the defendant's exercise of due care in the operation of his automobile is in issue, the jurisdiction in which the allegedly wrongful conduct occurred will usually have a predominant, if not exclusive, concern. In such a case, it is appropriate to look to the law of the place of the tort so as to give effect to that jurisdiction's interest in regulating conduct within its borders, and it would be almost unthinkable to seek the applicable rule in the law of some other place.

6 *Auten v Auten* (1954) 308 NY 155, 124 NE 2d 99 at 102.
7 Survey of Canadian Legislation, 1 U of Toronto LJ 358 at 366.

The issue here, however, is not whether the defendant offended against a rule of the road prescribed by Ontario for motorists generally or whether he violated some standard of conduct imposed by that jurisdiction, but rather whether the plaintiff, because she was a guest in the defendant's automobile, is barred from recovering damages for a wrong concededly committed. As to that issue, it is New York, the place where the parties resided, where their guest-host relationship arose and where the trip began and was to end, rather than Ontario, the place of the fortuitous occurrence of the accident, which has the dominant contacts and the superior claim for application of its law. Although the rightness or wrongness of defendant's conduct may depend upon the law of the particular jurisdiction through which the automobile passes, the rights and liabilities of the parties which stem from their guest-host relationship should remain constant and not vary and shift as the automobile proceeds from place to place. Indeed, such a result, we note, accords with 'the interests of the host in procuring liability insurance adequate under the applicable law, and the interests of his insurer in reasonable calculation of the premium'.

Although the traditional rule has in the past been applied by this court in giving controlling effect to the guest statute of the foreign jurisdiction in which the accident occurred, it is not amiss to point out that the question here posed was neither raised nor considered in those cases and that the question has never been presented in so stark a manner as in the case before us with a statute so unique as Ontario's.[8] Be that as it may, however, reconsideration of the inflexible traditional rule persuades us, as already indicated, that, in failing to take into account essential policy considerations and objectives, its application may lead to unjust and anomalous results. This being so, the rule, formulated as it was by the courts, should be discarded.

In conclusion, then, there is no reason why all issues arising out of a tort claim must be resolved by reference to the law of the same jurisdiction. Where the issue involves standards of conduct, it is more than likely that it is the law of the place of the tort which will be controlling but the disposition of other issues must turn, as does the issue of the standard of conduct itself, on the law of the jurisdiction which has the strongest interest in the resolution of the particular issue presented.

The judgment appealed from should be reversed, with costs, and the motion to dismiss the complaint denied.

Desmond CJ and Dye, Burke and Foster JJ concurred with Fuld J.
Van Hoorhis and Scileppi JJ dissented.
Appeal allowed.

---

8 We note that the Supreme Court of Canada has upheld the refusal of the Quebec courts to apply the Ontario guest statute to an accident affecting Quebec residents which occurred in Ontario. (See *McLean v Pettigrew* [1945] SCR 62, [1945] 2 DLR 65.) This decision was dictated by the court's resort to the English choice of law rule, whereby the foreign tort is deemed actionable if actionable by the law of the forum and not justifiable by the law of the place of the tort. (See *Phillips v Eyre* (1870) LR 6 QB 1, 10 B & S 1004) However that may be, it would seem incongruous for this court to apply Ontario's unique statute in circumstances under which its own sister provinces would not.

QUESTIONS

1. What would have happened on converse facts, eg a defendant resident in Ontario gives a lift in Ontario to a plaintiff also resident in Ontario and injures him in New York? It might have been expected that the Ontario guest statute would be applied. But the intermediate appellate court in New York has, on three occasions, applied the law of New York and allowed recovery: *Kell v Henderson* (1966) 270 NYS 2d 552; *Rye v Colter* (1972) 333 NYS 2d 96; *Bray v Cox*, ibid, 783; contra, *Arbuthnot v Allbright* (1970) 316 NYS 2d 391. To the same effect is the decision of the Supreme Court of Wisconsin in *Conklin v Horner* (1968) 157 NW 2d 579 and of the Supreme Court of Minnesota in *Milkovich v Saari* (1973) 213 NW 2d 408.

2. Suppose that New York had retained the common law rule whereby contributory negligence bars the plaintiff's claim, but Ontario had introduced an apportionment statute like the English Law Reform (Contributory Negligence) Act 1945, and that Miss Babcock's negligence had contributed to the accident. Is there any reason why a court should decline to apply the Ontario guest statute and yet apply the Ontario apportionment statute? This is called *depeçage* (cutting up the carcase) by the French and 'picking and choosing' by the Americans.

CHAPTER 16

Foreign Currency Obligations

The validity, interpretation and effect of a gold clause in a contract are determined by the proper law of the contract.

R v International Trustee for the Protection of Bondholders AG [1937] AC 500, [1937] 2 All ER 164 (House of Lords)

Petition of right.

On 1 February 1917, before the United States entered the First World War, the British government obtained a loan of $250,000,000 on the New York money market. It was the only allied government whose credit was not exhausted by $2\frac{1}{2}$ years of war; and New York was the only place where a loan of such magnitude could be floated. The loan was in the form of short-term secured Notes convertible into bonds repayable in 1937. The Notes and the bonds were repayable at holder's option either in New York in gold coin of the United States of America of the standard of weight and fineness existing on 1 February 1917, or in the City of London in sterling money at the fixed rate of 4.86\frac{1}{2}$ to the pound, together with interest thereon at the rate of $5\frac{1}{2}\%$ payable twice a year.

In June 1933 the United States Congress passed a Joint Resolution (having the force of law) declaring that all gold coin and gold value clauses attached to dollar obligations were against public policy and that all dollar obligations incurred before or after the passing of the Resolution could be discharged upon payment, dollar for dollar, in any coin or currency which at the time of payment was legal tender for public or private debts.

The International Trustee for the Protection of Bondholders, being a holder of some of the bonds, petitioned the Crown for a declaration of its rights. The question was whether the bondholders were entitled to be paid in New York the present value of the amount of gold represented by the nominal value of the bonds, or were only entitled to be paid in New York in depreciated paper dollars.

Branson J held that the proper law of the contract was English law but that the gold clause was a gold coin clause which had become impossible of performance. The Court of Appeal held that it was a gold value clause and unaffected by the Joint Resolution of Congress because the proper law of the contract was English law. The Crown appealed.

Lord Atkin: Various questions have been raised in this case; but that which comes first under consideration is what is the proper law of the contract: for if that be answered in one way no further issues remain. I will therefore proceed to discuss that matter. The legal principles which are to guide an

English court on the question of the proper law of a contract are now well settled. It is the law which the parties intended to apply. Their intention will be ascertained by the intention expressed in the contract if any, which will be conclusive. If no intention be expressed the intention will be presumed by the court from the terms of the contract and the relevant surrounding circumstances. In coming to its conclusion the court will be guided by rules which indicate that particular facts or conditions lead to a prima facie inference, in some cases an almost conclusive inference, as to the intention of the parties to apply a particular law: eg, the country where the contract is made, the country where the contract is to be performed, if the contract relates to immovables the country where they are situate, the country under whose flag the ship sails in which goods are contracted to be carried. But all these rules but serve to give prima facie indications of intention: they are all capable of being overcome by counter indications, however difficult it may be in some cases to find such. The principle of law so stated applies equally to contracts to which a sovereign state is a party as to other contracts. In the present case both Branson J and the Court of Appeal appear to have considered themselves bound by authority to hold that where a sovereign state is party to a contract the only proper inference to be drawn is that it did not intend that any system of law should be applied to its contract other than its own: and that this conclusion is either necessitated or reinforced by the consideration that only in its own court if at all can it be sued. For this proposition two cases are cited. The first is *Smith v Weguelin*.[1] That was the case of a Peruvian loan negotiated in this country. So far as I can see Lord Romilly in dealing with the topic is doing no more than negativing a contention that where a government negotiates a loan in a foreign country the law of that country is necessarily the law of the contract. He points to the case where a foreign loan in this country is negotiated at the same time in the same terms in different foreign countries as conclusive to negative the inference that English law is intended, and he proceeds: 'So, if the English government were to negotiate a loan in Paris or in New York, the English law must be applied to construe and regulate the contract.' I cannot think that Lord Romilly was intending to lay down a rule applicable in all circumstances, as, for instance, if the contract expressly made the foreign law applicable. His remarks are in fact obiter, but in any event do not I think purport to lay down a rule of universal application. The other case is *Goodwin v Robarts*,[2] in a passage in the speech of Lord Selborne approving the remarks of Lord Romilly in *Smith v Weguelin* with which Lord Selborne was specially acquainted, having been counsel for the successful party. In *Goodwin v Robarts* what Lord Selborne said had little to do with the ground of the decision. The question in that case was whether the scrip of a Russian loan was negotiable. It had been agreed in the Divisional Court that if English law applied common law principles prevented the extension of negotiability to any choses in action not made so by statute. The Court of Exchequer held that the scrip was governed by Russian law and that the question did not arise. In the Exchequer Chamber Cockburn LCJ in that remarkable judgment which is one of the charters of the liberty of the common law pronounced that the proper law was immaterial, for by English law

1 (1869) LR 8 Eq 198 at 213.
2 (1876) 1 App Cas 476 at 495.

commercial custom could attach the qualities of negotiability to forms of
contract hitherto not negotiable. The House of Lords took the same view. It
would appear therefore that these cases afford little authority for the
proposition. In principle it must be illfounded. It cannot be disputed that a
government may expressly agree to be bound by a foreign law. It seems to
me equally indisputable that without any expressed intention the inference
that a government so intended may be necessarily inferred from the
circumstances: as where a government enters into a contract in a foreign
country for the purchase of land situate in that country in the terms
appropriate only to the law of that country: or enters into a contract of
affreightment with the owners of a foreign ship on the terms expressed in a
foreign bill of lading, or employs in a foreign country foreign labour in
circumstances to which foreign labour laws would apply. It appears
therefore that in every case whether a government be a party or not the
general principle which determines the proper law of the contract is the
same: it depends upon the intention of the parties either expressed in the
contract or to be inferred from the terms of the contract and the surrounding
circumstances, and in the latter case the inference may be drawn that the
parties intended a foreign law to apply. The circumstance that a government
is a party is entitled to great weight in drawing the appropriate inference,
but it is not conclusive and is only one factor in the problem.

We can therefore approach the question what is the proper law of this
contract untrammelled by any rule binding us to hold that it is English law.
(His Lordship read the lengthy documents in which the loan was recorded
and continued):

Now beginning with the Notes, what is the true inference as to the
intention of the parties as to the proper law of the contract contained in
them? They were issued in America, they were expressed in terms of
American currency, they were to be paid on one option in America on a
value estimated by reference to American coins. But there is the further fact
that they were secured by a pledge agreement also made in America,
performed in America by the deposit with an American company of
securities on terms which appear irresistibly to give rights governed by
American law as to maintaining margins of value, redemption, enforcement
by sale. They contemplate a judicial sale which in my opinion can only
mean a sale by orders of an American court; and they finally stipulate that
the company with which the securities are pledged shall be protected if it
acts in accordance with the opinion of counsel selected by it, which must, I
think, in this context mean American counsel advising on American law. I
do not overlook that there is an option to be paid in England, that there is a
clause stating that payment is to be made without deduction of British taxes,
and in particular the weighty circumstance that the borrowers are the British
government. But it is to be noted that the obligation to pay in England is
secured only by the American pledge agreement and that the provision as to
British taxes is a provision which might well be inserted ex majori cautela in
any contract under which a government has to make payment. But taking
all the circumstances into consideration I think that the irresistible inference
is that the proper law of the contract is American law, meaning thereby in
this contract the law of the State of New York. I come to this conclusion
without attempting to answer the question put in argument, What would

have been the result of the issue in America in 1917 if there had been expressed in the pledge agreement or in the Notes the term that the contract was to be governed by English law?

Now if the Notes were governed by American law how is it possible to avoid the conclusion that the bonds into which at the will of the holders they were convertible before maturity were intended to be governed by the same law? In substance the bonds are long term renewals, and I find it impossible to assume that the parties who on the hypothesis start with an American contract either in fact intended or in some way or another signified to each other the intention no longer to be bound by American law but for the future to substitute English law. In terms there is no substantial difference other than time between the obligation expressed in the Notes and in the bonds. There is the very material fact that the bonds are not secured by the pledge agreement, but I cannot regard this as countervailing the strong improbability that the holder of an American Note surrendered it in exchange for an English bond, the debtor and other terms remaining for this purpose the same. There are indeed expressions in the bond which bear an American complexion: but in themselves they are far from conclusive: and one must base the inference on the transaction viewed as a whole. It is, I think, unfortunate that the attention of the courts below does not seem to have been directed to the importance of the Notes and the pledge agreement as bearing on the question in issue. I think their decision might have been different. I need only add that the question before us has to be determined as of the time that the bonds were exchanged for the Notes. The fact that they were negotiable and possibly negotiated in other countries does not affect the question. Having reached this conclusion in favour of American law as the proper law of the contract I need add but a few words. It is admitted that the effect of the Joint Resolution of Congress, dated 5 June 1933, had the statutory effect in New York State as well as in all the other states of the United States of requiring a bond expressed in the present form to be discharged upon payment dollar for dollar of the nominal amount. As this is so the suppliants who only found their petition of right upon their claim to be paid in America a larger sum than the nominal amount of the bond must fail: and it becomes unnecessary to consider the other points which came under discussion in the courts below. I think it desirable to add, however, that as at present advised I agree with the construction placed upon the bond by the Court of Appeal applying English law,[3] and that it would appear from recent decisions of the Supreme Court that the same conclusion would be reached by applying American law. It is not, however, necessary finally to decide this. For the above reasons I proposed the motion allowing the appeal and restoring the judgment of Branson J which the House has already adopted.

Lords Russell of Killowen, Maugham and Roche delivered judgments to the same effect. Lord Macmillan concurred.

Appeal allowed

---

3 Ie that it was a gold value clause. In England this is usually known as the *Feist* construction, after *Feist v Société Intercommunale Belge d'Electricité* [1934] AC 161, 103 LJCh 41 (*Ed*).

Where there is doubt as to the currency in which a debt is expressed, the money of account will be ascertained by construing the contract in accordance with its proper law. This does not mean that the money of account is that of the country of the proper law; it means that the proper law furnishes the canons of construction for ascertaining the money of account.

Bonython v Commonwealth of Australia (p 437 above).

English courts can give judgment for a sum expressed in foreign currency.

Miliangos v George Frank (Textiles) Ltd [1976] AC 443, [1975] 3 All ER 801 (House of Lords)

In May 1971 the plaintiff, a Swiss national, agreed to sell a quantity of polyester yarn to the defendants, an English company. The price was expressed in Swiss francs. The proper law of the contract was Swiss and the money of account and of payment were Swiss francs. The yarn was delivered in November 1971 but not paid for. The writ was issued in April 1972. The defendants raised a number of defences but on 22 November 1974, just before the action was due to come on for trial, they wrote to say they would submit to judgment.

On 26 November 1974 the Court of Appeal (Lord Denning MR, Lawton LJ and Foster J) decided a case involving a claim in German currency, *Schorsch Meier GmbH v Hennin.*[4] Although they were faced with a unanimous decision of the House of Lords in *Re United Rlys of Havana and Regla Warehouses Ltd*[5] that judgment can only be given in sterling and that the foreign currency must be converted into sterling as at the date when the debt became due, the Court of Appeal held by a majority (Lawton LJ dissenting) that an English court could give a money judgment in a foreign currency. The court further held, unanimously, that where the creditor resided in an EEC country an English court was obliged by article 106 of the Treaty of Rome to give a judgment in the currency of the creditor, if that was the currency of the contract.

In the present case the plaintiff applied on 2 December 1974 to amend his statement of claim so as to claim the amount due to him in Swiss francs. Since sterling had fallen between 1971 and 1974 this would mean that he could recover in sterling terms £60,000 instead of £42,000.

Bristow J allowed the amendment. He found himself faced on the one hand with the decision of the House of Lords in the *Havana Railways* case, which clearly precluded him from giving judgment in Swiss francs or from awarding the sterling equivalent of the sum due converted at any other date than November 1971, and on the other hand with the recent decision of the Court of Appeal in *Schorsch Meier* which had declined to apply the *Havana Railways* decision. In these circumstances he decided that he ought to follow the *Havana Railways* case and that the decision in *Schorsch Meier* was given per

4 [1975] QB 416, [1975] 1 All ER 152.
5 [1961] AC 1007, [1960] 2 All ER 332.

incuriam. The Court of Appeal (Lord Denning MR, Stephenson and Geoffrey Lane LJJ) allowed the plaintiff's appeal. The defendants appealed to the House of Lords.

Lord Wilberforce: My Lords, although the 'breach date rule' has a long history, possibly, but, I think, not clearly, extending back to the Year Books, consideration of it at the present time as regards foreign money debts must start from the *Havana Railways* case. For that was a case of a money debt as to which it was sought to persuade this House that a different rule should be applied from that which was admitted to be relevant to claims for damages for tort or for breach of contract. The claim there was for a debt (or debts) in US dollars, due under a contract the proper law of which was held to be the law of Pennsylvania. The debtor (the United Havana Railways Co) was English: the creditor was American. The proceedings were by way of proof in the liquidation of the debtor, not by action by writ, but it was not suggested that this made any difference, and I say at once that I do not think that any distinction can be drawn on this ground. On the arguments presented which were at least strenuous, and after examination of the cases extending over a long period, the House unanimously decided that the provable sum in US dollars had to be converted into sterling at the rates of exchange prevailing when the relevant sums fell due and were not paid. They rejected the counter-suggestion that conversion should be made at the date of judgment. They did not take up or accept suggestions which had been made in some earlier cases that a separate rule applied to foreign money claims.

My Lords, even if I were inclined to question some of the arguments used in the speeches, I should find it inappropriate and unnecessary to say that, in the circumstances of the time and on the arguments and authorities presented, the decision was wrong or is open to distinction or explanation.

What we can do, and what is our responsibility, is to consider whether this decision, clear and comparatively recent, should be regarded as a binding precedent in today's circumstances. For that purpose it is permissible to examine the speeches in order to understand the considerations upon which the opinions there reached were based, for the ultimate purpose of seeing whether there have emerged fresh considerations which might have appealed to those who gave those opinions and so may appeal to their successors.

The leading opinion was given by Viscount Simonds. The kernel of this opinion is in the critical paragraph where Viscount Simonds says:

'The question, summarily stated, is what sum in sterling is recoverable by a plaintiff suing in the courts of this country, for a sum of money payable in foreign currency in a foreign country under an instrument of which the proper law is a foreign law. Admittedly, the claim must be for a sterling sum and the judgment must be in sterling. It is established by authority binding on this House that a claim for damages for breach of contract or for tort in terms of a foreign currency must be converted into sterling at the rate prevailing at the date of breach or tortious act: see, for example, *SS Celia v SS Volturno*.[6] But, it was said, doubts had been expressed whether the same rule applied where the claim arose from a failure to pay a debt expressed in terms of foreign currency, and

6 [1921] 2 AC 544, 90 LJP 385.

it was urged that on principle the plaintiff should recover sterling at the rate prevailing at the date of judgment or, alternatively, at the date of the writ or other initiating step of the proceedings. To this it was answered that without undue refinement the two cases, damages and foreign debt (as I will call a debt in foreign currency) could not be distinguished, that an action to recover a foreign debt was upon a sound analysis nothing else than an action for recovery of damages for breach of a contract to deliver foreign currency, that there was ample authority, ancient and modern, for this proposition, and that in any case convenience demanded that the same rule should obtain.'

There are three essential steps here: the first, which was accepted or assumed without argument, is that the claim must be in sterling and that judgment must be in sterling: the second, that an action to recover a foreign debt is an action in damages: the third, that authority and convenience requires that the same rules should obtain for all actions in damages whether for failure to pay a foreign debt or founded on tort or breach of contract. It is obvious that of these the first is fundamental and that the others in some degree follow from it.

(His Lordship quoted from the speeches of Lords Reid and Radcliffe and continued): Lord Denning opens with an emphatic statement: 'And if there is one thing clear in our law, it is that the claim must be made in sterling and the judgment given in sterling. We do not give judgments in dollars any more than the United States courts give judgments in sterling.' It is clear, and I think significant, that his Lordship, in the light of developments, has departed from these views in recent decisions.

My Lords, I have quoted extensively from these opinions, not only because they embody the standing authority on the question now at issue, but also in order to make clear what, I think, appears from all of them to be the basic presupposition. This is that procedurally an action cannot be brought here for recovery or payment of a sum expressed in foreign currency, and that, in effect, it can only be brought for a sum expressed in sterling, recoverable by way of damages. I now have to ask, what is the position at the present time? Have any fresh considerations of any substance emerged which should induce your Lordships to follow a different rule? I will endeavour to state those which appear to me to be significant.

1. The courts have evolved a procedure under which orders can be made for payment of foreign currency debts in the foreign currency. The Court of Appeal has given its approval to the form:

'It is adjudged . . . that the defendant do pay to the plaintiff [the sum in foreign currency] or the sterling equivalent at the time of payment.'

(See *Schorsch Meier GmbH v Hennin* per Lord Denning MR). I can find no reason in principle why such orders cannot be made. The courts have generally power to order delivery in specie whenever, in their opinion, damages are an inadequate remedy. In cases such as the present, indeed, one of the arguments against making orders for payment of foreign currency in specie has been that damages are an adequate remedy (see particularly *Lloyd Royal Belge SA v Louis Dreyfus & Co*[7] per Romer J). But if, in the

7 (1927) 27 Ll LRep 288 at 294.

circumstances of today, damages are not an adequate remedy, as they clearly may not be if the breach date rule is applied in times of floating currencies, this argument, in any case nothing more than an appeal to discretion, loses its force. The jurisdiction is clear, on general principle: how the courts' discretion is to be exercised depends on the circumstances. I return to this later. Further, I can find nothing in the Rules of the Supreme Court which prevents such orders being made: indeed, though I do not attach the same importance to the change as did the learned Master of the Rolls, the present form of the rules[8] is somewhat more favourable to the making of orders in this form than was the version in force in 1961. Lord Denning MR adhered to this position in the present case after further argument upon the rules, by which time any serious inconveniences or practical difficulties would have come to light. I shall return to this subject later with particular reference to the question of the date of conversion. At the present stage what is relevant is that orders in this form are jurisdictionally legitimate and procedurally workable.

2. The situation as regards currency stability has substantially changed even since 1961. Instead of the main world currencies being fixed and fairly stable in value, subject to the risk of periodic re- or devaluations, many of them are now 'floating', ie, they have no fixed exchange value even from day to day. This is true of sterling. This means that, instead of a situation in which changes of relative value occurred between the 'breach date' and the date of judgment or payment being the exception, so that a rule which did not provide for this case could be generally fair, this situation is now the rule. So the search for a formula to deal with it becomes urgent in the interest of justice. This leads to the next point.

3. The state of facts referred to under 2 has become recognised in those commercial circles which are closely concerned with international contracts. The reaction to them appears in the field of arbitration. In 1969 two of the most experienced arbitrators in the City of London made an award expressed in terms of US dollars and the validity of this came to be tested in the courts: *Jugoslavenska Oceanska Plovidba v Castle Investment Co Inc.*[9] In reserved judgments the Court of Appeal (Lord Denning MR, Cairns and Roskill LJJ), disagreeing with observations made in that court in *The Teh Hu*[10] held that the award was valid. What is more, and relevant in the present context, they held that it could be enforced under section 26 of the Arbitration Act 1950 which enables an award to be enforced 'in the same manner as a judgment or order to the same effect'. They pointed out that this was also the case as regards foreign awards which under section 36 (1) of the same Act 'shall be enforceable' in the same manner as an award 'is enforceable under section 26'. Roskill LJ, who has great experience in these matters, said that awards of this kind made in the City have been entirely satisfactory and honoured all over the world. He also referred to inquiries made by Kerr J, at first instance, of the Central Office of the High Court which showed that there is no difficulty in practice in enforcing foreign currency awards: the foreign currency is simply converted into sterling at the rate prevailing at the date of the award.

8 RSC Ord 42, r 1, Ord 45 and Forms 45 et seq; Appendix A.
9 [1974] QB 292, [1973] 3 All ER 498.
10 [1970] P 106 at 129, [1969] 3 All ER 1200 at 1206–1207.

I regard this development as of great importance for two reasons. First, it goes a long way towards removing the practical objections as regards enforcement which weighed so heavily in the *Havana Railways* case. If an award in a foreign currency case can be readily enforced, after conversion into a sterling sum, and since an award is enforceable as a judgment, it should follow that a judgment in a foreign currency can be similarly enforced, after conversion into a sterling sum. Secondly, it would be an intolerable situation if a different rule were to prevail as regards arbitrations upon debts expressed in foreign currency on the one hand and actions upon similar debts on the other. Counsel for the appellants was therefore obliged to argue that if he was to succeed the decision in the *Jugoslavenska* case must either be overruled, or narrowly confined. I can find no limits within which it can be confined which would not still enclose the present case, so, if the appeal were to be allowed, the case would have to be overruled. But if I am faced with the alternative of forcing commercial circles to fall in with a legal doctrine which has nothing but precedent to commend it or altering the doctrine so as to conform with what commercial experience has worked out, I know where my choice lies. The law should be responsive as well as, at times, enunciatory, and good doctrine can seldom be divorced from sound practice.

4. Further recognition of the need for, and practicality of, making orders in terms of foreign currencies was given in *The Halcyon the Great*,[11] where an order was made in Admiralty for the sale of a ship for US dollars, and for the lodgment of the price in a separate dollar account. The judgment of Brandon J contains a clear acceptance (contrary to the appellant's arguments here) of the proposition that US dollar currency may be regarded as 'money' within the meaning of English procedural rules and that the courts can easily adapt their procedure so as to give effect to foreign money claims in specie. The case indeed prompts the reflection that a similar procedure might have been regarded as acceptable in the *Havana Railways* case, the factual situation (ie, a debt in foreign currency secured upon a sum expressed in foreign currency) being in many respects similar.

5. I should mention at this stage the argument based upon article 106 of the EEC Treaty of Rome. I can understand the temptation, in the search for an argument why the *Havana Railways* case should not now be followed, to fasten upon the important development which the treaty represents. Although Switzerland is not an EEC member, the argument unanimously accepted by the Court of Appeal in *Schorsch Meier* was invoked by the respondent in this appeal and correspondingly attacked by the appellants. It cannot therefore be passed over in silence, all the less since there is a risk that it may be quoted as a precedent. There are two reasons for dealing with it here with restraint. First, there is no direct appeal against the decision in *Schorsch Meier*: secondly, the issue of the applicability and interpretation of article 106, if it were to be considered by this House, would necessitate a reference to the European Court under article 177 of the treaty. But nevertheless I feel bound to say that I entertain the strongest reservations concerning the use made by the Court of Appeal of article 106 in the present context, and I cannot believe that, if the court had heard argument on the other side (corresponding to that of the present appellants), very weighty

11 [1975] 1 All ER 882, [1975] 1 WLR 515.

arguments would not have been brought forward concerning such questions as the direct applicability of this article, its bearing on any question of the currency in which claims may be made in the courts of member states or its relevance at all to the ascertainment of the date of conversion of such claims, which arguments seem to have been unappreciated. Any other court in which such issues may arise would be well advised to refer them to the European Court for clarification. In this appeal, in my opinion, no argument based directly or indirectly upon article 106 of the treaty should be considered as available to the respondent.

My Lords, before attempting the task of deciding where, in the end, this House should stand as regards the *Havana Railways* rule there are some other general observations I think should be made.

First, I do not for myself think it doubtful that, in a case such as the present, justice demands that the creditor should not suffer from fluctuations in the value of sterling. His contract has nothing to do with sterling: he has bargained for his own currency and only his own currency. The substance of the debtor's obligations depends upon the proper law of the contract (here Swiss law): and though English law (lex fori) prevails as regards procedural matters, it must surely be wrong in principle to allow procedure to affect, detrimentally, the substance of the creditor's rights. Courts are bound by their own procedural law and must obey it, if imperative, though to do so may seem unjust. But if means exist for giving effect to the substance of a foreign obligation, conformably with the rules of private international law, procedure should not unnecessarily stand in the way.

There is, unfortunately, as Lord Radcliffe pointed out in the *Havana Railways* case, a good deal of confusion in English cases as to what the creditor's rights are. Appeal has been made to the principle of nominalism, so as to say that the creditor must take the pound sterling as he finds it. Lord Denning said so in the *Havana Railways* case and I can safely and firmly disagree with him in that because he has himself, since then, come to hold another view. The creditor has no concern with pounds sterling: for him what matters is that a Swiss franc for good or ill should remain a Swiss franc. This is substantially the reasoning of Holmes J in the important judgment of the US Supreme Court in *Deutsche Bank Filiale Nürnberg v Humphrey*.[12] Another argument is that the 'breach date' makes for certainty whereas to choose a later date makes the claim depend on currency fluctuations. But this is only a partial truth. The only certainty achieved is certainty in the sterling amount—but that is not in point since sterling does not enter into the bargain. The relevant certainty which the rule ought to achieve is that which gives the creditor neither more nor less than he bargained for. He bargained for 415,522.45 Swiss francs; whatever this means in (unstipulated) foreign currencies, whichever way the exchange into those currencies may go, he should get 415,522.45 Swiss francs or as nearly as can be brought about. That such a solution, if practicable, is just, and adherence to the 'breach date' in such a case unjust in the circumstances of today, adds greatly to the strength of the argument for revising the rule or, putting it more technically, it adds strength to the case for awarding delivery in specie rather than giving damages.

Secondly, and I must deal with this point more briefly than historically it

12 (1926) 272 US 517.

deserves, objections based on authority against making an order in specie for the payment or delivery of foreign money, are not, on examination, found to rest on any solid principle or indeed on more than the court's discretion. Your Lordships were referred to a number of early cases dealing with claims expressed, or which the courts thought should or could have been expressed, in terms of foreign money, but though the examination of them proved interesting (and I would like to express indebtedness to learned counsel for the respondent) I do not think they showed more than that English law up to the 17th century, as one would expect in the state of monetary theory and practice, took an empirical position, allowing claims to be made and enforced in various forms and showing a good deal of flexibility, or blurring, in the forms of action, debt, detinet, debt in the detinet, debt and detinet, being among the forms admitted. (His Lordship referred to a number of 16th and 17th century cases and to *Manners v Pearson*[13] and continued):

These considerations and the circumstances I have set forth, when related to the arguments which moved their Lordships in the *Havana Railways* case, lead me to the conclusion that, if these circumstances had been shown to exist in 1961, some at least of their Lordships, assuming always that the interests of justice in the particular case so required, would have been led, as one of them very notably has been led, to take a different view.

This brings me to the declaration made by this House in 1966. Under it, the House affirmed its power to depart from a previous decision when it appears right to do so, recognising that too rigid adherence to precedent might lead to injustice in a particular case and unduly restrict the proper development of the law. My Lords, on the assumption that to depart from the *Havana Railways* case would not involve undue practical difficulties, that a new and more satisfactory rule is capable of being stated, I am of opinion that the present case falls within the terms of the declaration. To change the rules would, for the reasons already explained, avoid injustice in the present case. To change it would enable the law to keep in step with commercial needs and with the majority of other countries facing similar problems. The latter proposition is well vouched by Dr F. A. Mann's work, *The Legal Aspect of Money*.[14]

I return then to the two preconditions.

1. Can a better rule be stated? I would make it clear that, for myself, I would confine my approval at the present time of a change in the breach-date rule to claims such as those with which we are here concerned, ie, to foreign money obligations, sc obligations of a money character to pay foreign currency arising under a contract whose proper law is that of a foreign country and where the money of account and payment is that of that country, or possibly of some other country but not of the United Kingdom.

I do not think that we are called upon, or would be entitled in this case, to review the whole field of the law regarding foreign currency obligations: that is not the method by which changes in the law by judicial decision are made. In my opinion it should be open for future discussion whether the rule applying to money obligations, which can be a simple rule, should apply as regards claims for damages for breach of contract or for tort. It is only because it has been thought that the same rule need apply to all these

13 [1898] 1 Ch 581, 67 LJCh 304.
14 3rd edn (1971) Ch 10.

situations that we have been forced into straitjacket solutions based on concepts, or on forms of action ('archaic legalistic nonsense' in the words of Lawton LJ in *Schorsch Meier*). But the principles on which damages are awarded for tort or breach of contract are both very intricate and not the same in each case, involve questions of remoteness (cf the speech of Lord Parmoor in *SS Celia (Owners) v SS Volturno (Owners), The Volturno*) and have no direct relevance to claims for specific things, in which I include specific foreign currency. To take one familiar point. Whereas in the case of the inevitable contract to supply a foreign cow, the intending purchaser has to be treated as going into the market to buy one as at the date of breach, this doctrine cannot be applied to a foreign money obligation, for the intending creditor has nothing to buy his own currency with—except his own currency. I therefore see no need to overrule or criticise or endorse such cases as *The Volturno* or *Di Ferdinando v Simon, Smits & Co Ltd*.[15]

As regards foreign money obligations (defined above), it is first necessary to establish the form of the claim to be made. In my opinion acceptance of the argument already made requires that the claim must be specifically for the foreign currency—as in this case for a sum stated in Swiss francs. To this may be added the alternative 'or the sterling equivalent at the date of...' (see below). As regards the conversion date to be inserted in the claim or in the judgment of the court, the choice, as pointed out in the *Havana Railways* case, is between (i) the date of action brought, (ii) the date of judgment, (iii) the date of payment. Each has its advantages, and it is to be noticed that the Court of Appeal in *Schorsch Meier* and in the present case chose the date of payment meaning, as I understand it, the date when the court authorises enforcement of the judgment in terms of sterling. The date of payment is taken in the convention annexed to the Carriage of Goods by Road Act 1965 (article 27 (2)). This date gets nearest to securing to the creditor exactly what he bargained for. The date of action brought, though favoured by Lord Reid and Lord Radcliffe in the *Havana Railways* case, seems to me to place the creditor too severely at the mercy of the debtor's obstructive defences (cf this case) or the law's delay. It may have been based on an understanding of the judgment of Holmes J in the *Deutsche Bank* case now seen to be probably mistaken (see Mann, *The Legal Aspect of Money*,[16] and cases cited). The date of judgment is shown to be a workable date in practice by its inclusion in the Carriage by Air Act 1961 which gave effect to the Hague Convention of 1965 varying, on this very point, the Warsaw Convention of 1929, but, in some cases, particularly where there is an appeal, may again impose on the creditor a considerable currency risk. So I would favour the payment date, in the sense I have mentioned. In the case of a company in liquidation, the corresponding date for conversion would be the date when the creditor's claim in terms of sterling is admitted by the liquidator.[17] In the case of arbitration, there may be a minor discrepancy, if the practice which is apparently adopted (see the *Jugoslavenska* case) remains as it is, but I can see no reason why, if desired, that practice should not be adjusted so as to enable

15 [1920] 3 KB 409, 89 LJKB 1039.
16 3rd edn (1971) p 355.
17 The date has subsequently been held to be the date of the winding up order or (in the case of a creditors' voluntary liquidation) the date of the winding up resolution, so that all creditors can be treated alike: *Re Dynamics Corpn of America* [1976] 2 All ER 669, [1976] 1 WLR 757; *Re Lines Bros Ltd* [1983] Ch 1, [1982] 2 All ER 183 (*Ed*).

conversion to be made as at the date when leave to enforce in sterling is given.

2. A rule in the form suggested above would not, in my opinion, give rise to any serious procedural difficulty. Suggestions were made at the Bar that as regards such matters as set off, counterclaim, payment into court, it would be difficult or impossible to apply. I would say as to these matters that I see no reason why this should be so: it would be inappropriate to discuss them here in detail and unnecessary since the Court of Appeal has assessed the procedural implications and has not been impressed with any difficulty. I have no doubt that practitioners, with the assistance of the Supreme Court, can work out suitable solutions. . . .

My Lords, in conclusion I would say that, difficult as this whole matter undoubtedly is, if once a clear conclusion is reached as to what the law ought now to be, declaration of it by this House is appropriate. The law on this topic is judge-made: it has been built up over the years from case to case. It is entirely within this House's duty, in the course of administering justice, to give the law a new direction in a particular case where, on principle and in reason, it appears right to do so. I cannot accept the suggestion that because a rule is long established only legislation can change it—that may be so when the rule is so deeply entrenched that it has infected the whole legal system, or the choice of a new rule involves more far-reaching research than courts can carry out. A recent example of the House changing a very old established rule is *West Midland Baptist (Trust) Association (Inc) v Birmingham Corp.*[18] Lord Reid thought that it was proper to re-examine a judge-made rule of law based on an assumption of fact (as to the stability of money) when the rule was formulated but which was no longer true and which in many cases caused serious injustice. So in that case the House selected a new date and did not think it necessary or right to wait for legislation and I would not think it necessary or right here. Indeed, from some experience in the matter, I am led to doubt whether legislative reform, at least prompt and comprehensive reform, in this field of foreign currency obligation, is practicable. Questions as to the recovery of debts or of damages depend so much upon individual mixtures of facts and merits as to make them more suitable for progressive solutions in the courts. I think that we have an opportunity to reach such a solution here. I would accordingly depart from the *Havana Railways* case and dismiss this appeal.

Lords Cross of Chelsea, Edmund Davies and Fraser of Tullybelton delivered judgments to the same effect. Lord Simon of Glaisdale dissented.

Appeal dismissed.

The same rule applies in actions for damages for tort. The damages will normally be awarded in the currency which the plaintiff uses in the course of his business and not the currency in which the loss immediately arose.

The Despina R [1979] AC 685, [1979] 1 All ER 421 (House of Lords)

Two Greek ships, *The Eleftherotria* and *The Despina R*, collided off Shanghai. *The Eleftherotria* sustained damage owing to the negligence of the master and

18 [1970] AC 874, [1969] 3 All ER 172.

crew of *The Despina R*. The owners of the two ships agreed that the owners of *The Despina R* would pay 85% of the loss and damage caused to the owners of *The Eleftherotria* by the collision.

After the collision *The Eleftherotria* proceeded to Shanghai for temporary repairs and then to Yokohama and later to Los Angeles for permanent repairs. Expenses and loss for detention were incurred in Chinese yuan, Japanese yen and United States dollars. The ship was managed for the owners by agents with their principal place of business in New York. The bank account used for all payments in respect of the ship was a United States dollar account.

Brandon J held that the owners' expenses must be expressed in the currency in which each item of loss was incurred. The Court of Appeal (Stephenson, Orr and Cumming-Bruce LJJ) varied his judgment and held that they must be expressed in United States dollars. The owners of the *The Despina R* appealed to the House of Lords.

Lord Wilberforce (after stating the facts, and pointing out that the choice of currency lay between United States dollars, the currency in which each item of loss was incurred and sterling converted at the time of the wrongful act, continued): I consider first *The Volturno*.[19] Although, as in this case, there had been expenses for repairs incurred in foreign currency these were not in issue on the appeal. That was only concerned with a claim for damages in respect of detention which was assessed in Italian lire. It was thought to be clear at that time that an English court could only give judgment for a sum in sterling, and it is this which formed the basis of the decision arrived at, namely, that conversion must be made at the date of the breach and not at the date of judgment. This most clearly appears in the speech of Lord Sumner. He states, at 558, the argument in favour of conversion at the date of judgment—the creditor in that event would get the exact sum to which he was entitled. This would inevitably, he says, introduce a speculative element into all transactions—waiting to convert the currency until the date of judgment only adds the uncertainty of exchange to the uncertainty of the law's delays. There is no answer to this, he continues, except that the claimant's right is exclusively a right to lire and would result in a judgment for lire, if only an English court was, so to speak, competent to express itself in Italian. Earlier he had described the agreed numbers of lire as only part of the foreign language in which the court is informed of the damage sustained, which, like the rest of the foreign evidence, must be translated into English as at the date when the damage accrues.

The whole of this process of argument flows from the accepted inability of the court to receive a claim in lire and to give judgment in lire. The same point underlies just as clearly the opinion of Lord Parmoor, at 560:

'The necessity for transferring into English money damages ascertained in a foreign currency arises in the fact that the courts of this country have no jurisdiction to order payment of money except in English currency.'

The contrary view—based firmly on the principle of restitutio in integrum—is clearly stated by Lord Carson at 566–567.

19 [1921] 2 AC 544, 90 LJP 385.

My Lords, I do not think that there can now be any doubt that, given the ability of an English court (and of arbitrators sitting in this country) to give judgment or to make an award in a foreign currency, to give a judgment in the currency in which the loss was sustained produces a juster result than one which fixes the plaintiff with a sum in sterling taken at the date of the breach or of the loss. I need not expand upon this because the point has been clearly made both in *Miliangos v George Frank (Textiles) Ltd,*[20] and in cases which have followed it, as well as in commentators who, prior to *Miliangos,* advocated abandonment of the breach-date-sterling rule. To fix such a plaintiff with sterling commits him to the risk of changes in the value of a currency with which he has no connection: to award him a sum in the currency of the expenditure or loss, or that in which he bears the expenditure or loss, gives him exactly what he has lost and commits him only to the risk of changes in the value of that currency, or those currencies, which are either his currency or those which he has chosen to use.

I shall consider the objections against the use of that currency or those currencies, but first it is necessary to decide between the expenditure currency and the plaintiff's currency—a matter which gave the judges below some difficulty. Brandon J would have preferred adoption of the plaintiff's currency but he considered himself prevented from doing so by *The Canadian Transport,*[1] a collision case decided by a strong Court of Appeal. There the loss was originally suffered in Argentinian pesos but a claim was made which involved converting pesos into sterling, sterling into francs at one rate and francs into sterling at another rate, thus producing an exchange profit for the cargo owners. The decision of the Court of Appeal, against the cargo owners, was based in part on their rejection of the treble exchange manoeuvre and in part on their acceptance of the necessity of giving judgment in sterling. They could not have given judgment in either sterling[2] or francs. In my opinion— and I agree with the Court of Appeal in the present case on this—this case, like *The Volturno* does not preclude a decision in favour of the plaintiff's currency or the currency of the loss (there it would have been francs or pesos) once the possibility of giving judgment in a foreign currency exists.

I return to consider the alternatives.

My Lords, in my opinion, this question can be solved by applying the normal principles, which govern the assessment of damages in cases of tort. These are the principles of restitutio in integrum and that of the reasonable foreseeability of the damage sustained. It appears to me that a plaintiff, who normally conducts his business through a particular currency, and who, when other currencies are immediately involved, uses his own currency to obtain those currencies, can reasonably say that the loss he sustains is to be measured not by the immediate currencies in which the loss first emerges but by the amount of his own currency, which in the normal course of operation, he uses to obtain those currencies. This is the currency in which his loss is felt, and is the currency which it is reasonably foreseeable he will have to spend.

There are some objections to this, but I think they can be answered. First, it is said that to use the method of finding the loss in the plaintiff's currency

20 [1976] AC 443, [1975] 3 All ER 801; p 510 above.
 1 (1932) 43 Ll LRep 409.
 2 Sic in the report: presumably pesos was meant (*Ed*).

would involve the court or arbitrators in complicated inquiries. I am not convinced of this. The plaintiff has to prove his loss: if he wishes to present his claim in his own currency, the burden is on him to show to the satisfaction of the tribunal that his operations are conducted in that currency and that in fact it was his currency that was used, in a normal manner, to meet the expenditure for which he claims or that his loss can only be appropriately measured in that currency (this would apply in the case of a total loss of a vessel which cannot be dealt with by the 'expenditure' method). The same answer can be given to the objection that some companies, particularly large multi-national companies, maintain accounts and operate in several currencies. Here again it is for the plaintiff to satisfy the court or arbitrators that the use of the particular currency was in the course of normal operations of that company and was reasonably foreseeable. Then it is said that this method produces inequality between plaintiffs. Two claimants who suffer a similar loss may come out with different sums according to the currency in which they trade. But if the losses of both plaintiffs are suffered at the same time, the amounts awarded to each of them should be equivalent even if awarded in different currencies: if at different times, this might justify difference in treatment. If it happened that the currencies of the two plaintiffs relatively changed in value before the date of judgment that would be a risk which each plaintiff would have to accept. Each would still receive, for himself, compensation for *his* loss.

Finally it is said (and this argument would apply equally if the expenditure currency were taken) that uncertainty will take the place of certainty under the present rule. Undoubtedly the present (sterling-breach-date) rule produces certainty—but it is often simpler to produce an unjust rule than a just one. The question is whether, in order to produce a just, or juster, rule, too high a price has to be paid in terms of certainty.

I do not think so. I do not see any reason why legal advisers, or insurers, should not be able, from their knowledge of the circumstances, to assess the extent of probable liability. The most difficult step is to assess the quantum of each head of damage. Once this is done, it should not be difficult, on the basis of information which the plaintiff must provide, to agree or disagree with his claim for the relevant currency. I wish to make it clear that I would not approve of a hard and fast rule that in all cases where a plaintiff suffers a loss or damage in a foreign currency the right currency to take for the purpose of his claim is 'the plaintiff's currency'. I should refer to the definition I have used of this expression and emphasise that it does not suggest the use of a personal currency attached, like nationality, to a plaintiff, but a currency which he is able to show is that in which he normally conducts trading operations. Use of this currency for assessment of damage may and probably will be appropriate in cases of international commerce. But even in that field, and still more outside it, cases may arise in which a plaintiff will not be able to show that in the normal course of events he would use, and be expected to use, the currency, or one of several currencies, in which he normally conducts his operations (the burden being on him to show this) and consequently the conclusion will be that the loss is felt in the currency in which it immediately arose. To say that this produces a measure of uncertainty may be true, but this is an uncertainty which arises in the nature of things from the variety of human experience. To resolve it is part of the normal process of adjudication. To attempt to confine this within a rigid formula would be likely to produce injustices which the courts and arbitrators would have to put themselves to much trouble to avoid.

Apart from these general considerations there are certain special problems which may arise in Admiralty cases to which attention was rightly drawn by Brandon J. I do not think it necessary, or wise, to comment on them in detail for I am satisfied that they do not in themselves create insuperable, or great, difficulties in the way of adopting the plaintiff's currency, where to do so is appropriate. Brandon J expressed upon them provisional views which must clearly command respect and which demonstrate that the problems are soluble. I think it best to leave such cases to be decided as they arise in the light of full argument. Lastly there are some difficulties foreseen by the Court of Appeal. I appreciate these but I think that the answer to them lies in the necessity for a plaintiff—claiming a judgment in the plaintiff's currency—to prove his case—that his loss was naturally and foreseeably borne in that currency. There should be no automatic and invariable rule to this effect: if, in the circumstances, he fails to satisfy the court or arbitrators, they may give judgment or award in whatever other currency represents his loss.

In my opinion the Court of Appeal reached a right conclusion on this case and I would dismiss the appeal.

Lord Russell of Killowen delivered judgment to the same effect. Lords Diplock, Salmon and Keith of Kinkel concurred.

Appeal dismissed.

The same rule applies to claims for damages for breach of contract. The currency will normally be that which most fully expresses the plaintiff's loss.

Services Europe Atlantique Sud of Paris v Rederiaktiebolag Svea [1979] AC 685, [1979] 1 All ER 421 (House of Lords)

Swedish shipowners chartered a ship to a French company for a round voyage from the Mediterranean to the east coast of South America. The contract contained a clause providing for arbitration in London. Its proper law was English law. Freight was expressed to be payable in United States dollars.

The French company shipped a cargo of onions at Valencia, Spain, for carriage to Santos, Brazil. Owing to a failure of the ship's refrigeration the onions arrived in a damaged condition and the French company was obliged to compensate the receivers of cargo. To discharge this liability they bought Brazilian cruzeiros with French francs, the currency in which they kept their accounts. The cruzeiro then declined in value by 50%.

The arbitrators awarded the French company a sum in French francs. Goff J set aside the arbitrators' award and held that damages should have been awarded in Brazilian cruzeiros. This judgment was in turn reversed by the Court of Appeal (Lord Denning MR, Ormrod and Geoffrey Lane LJJ) which restored the award of the arbitrators. The Swedish shipowners appealed to the House of Lords.

Lord Wilberforce: My Lords, the effect of the decision of this House in

Miliangos v George Frank (Textiles) Ltd[3] is that, in contractual as in other cases a judgment (in which for convenience I include an award) can be given in a currency other than sterling. Whether it should be and, in a case where there is more than one eligible currency, in which currency, must depend on general principles of the law of contract and on rules of conflict of laws. The former require application, as nearly as possible, of the principle of restitutio in integrum, regard being had to what was in the reasonable contemplation of the parties. The latter involve ascertainment of the proper law of the contract, and application of that law. If the proper law is English, the first step must be to see whether, expressly or by implication, the contract provides an answer to the currency question. This may lead to selection of the 'currency of the contract'. If from the terms of the contract it appears that the parties have accepted a currency as the currency of account and payment in respect of all transactions arising under the contract, then it would be proper to give a judgment for damages in that currency—this is, I think, the case which Lord Denning MR had in mind when he said in *Jugoslavenska Oceanska Plovidba v Castle Investment Co Inc*:[4] '[arbitrators] should make their award in that currency because it is the proper currency of the contract. By that I mean that it is the currency with which the payments under the contract have the closest and most real connection.'

But there may be cases in which, although obligations under the contract are to be met in a specified currency, or currencies, the right conclusion may be that there is no intention shown that damages for breach of the contract should be given in that currency or currencies. I do not think that Lord Denning MR was intending to exclude such cases. Indeed in the present case he said, in words which I would adopt 'the plaintiff should be compensated for the expense or loss in the currency which most truly expresses his loss'. In the present case the fact that US dollars have been named as the currency in which payments in respect of hire and other contractual payments are to be made, provides no necessary or indeed plausible reason why damages for breach of the contract should be paid in that currency. The terms of other contracts may lead to a similar conclusion.

If then the contract fails to provide a decisive interpretation, the damage should be calculated in the currency in which the loss was felt by the plaintiff or 'which most truly expresses his loss'. This is not limited to that in which it first and immediately arose. In ascertaining which this currency is, the court must ask what is the currency, payment in which will as nearly as possible compensate the plaintiff in accordance with the principle of restitution, and whether the parties must be taken reasonably to have had this in contemplation. It would be impossible to devise a simple rule, other than the general principles I have mentioned, to cover cases on the sale of goods, on contracts of employment, on international carriage by sea or air: in any of these types of contract the terms of the individual agreement will be important.

My Lords, it is obvious that this analysis, involving as it does a reversion to the ordinary law governing damages for breach of contract, necessitates a departure from older cases decided upon the 'breach-date-sterling' rule. I should comment upon some of the latter.

3 [1976] AC 443, [1975] 3 All ER 801; p 510 above.
4 [1974] QB 292, [1973] 3 All ER 498.

Di Ferdinando v Simon, Smits & Co Ltd[5] was clearly decided on the sterling-breach-date principle so that the foundations of it have been impaired. It is possible, as suggested by Lord Denning MR, that the same result could have been reached if judgment had been given so as truly to express the plaintiff's loss, but the case itself can no longer be regarded as authoritative. The decision of Eveleigh J in *Jean Kraut A-G v Albany Fabrics Ltd*[6] is in line with the principles I have endeavoured to state. The learned judge in effect applied to a claim in damages the same rule as the *Miliangos* case applied to debt, thus applying, in reverse, the principles which led Viscount Simonds in *Re United Railways of Havana and Regla Warehouses Ltd*[7] to apply the same rule to debt as he held to apply to damages. *Federal Commerce and Navigation Co Ltd v Tradax Export SA*[8] I would regard as a decision on the 'currency of the contract' and correct on that basis. *The Canadian Transport,*[9] I have already mentioned when dealing with the appeal in the *Despina R*. I regard the decision as depending on the sterling-breach-date rule which was thought to prevent a choice between the currency of expenditure and the currency of the plaintiff. Finally I would regard rule 172 of Dicey & Morris, *Conflict of Laws,*[10] based as it is upon existing authorities, as requiring revision, or reinterpretation, so as, at least, to reflect the principle that, subject to the terms of the contract, damages should be recoverable in the currency which most truly expresses the plaintiff's loss.

The present case is concerned with a charterparty for carriage by sea, the parties to which are Swedish and French. It was in the contemplation of the parties that delivery of the goods carried might be made in any of a number of countries with a currency different from that of either of the parties. Loss might be suffered, through non-delivery or incomplete delivery, or delivery of damaged or unsuitable goods, in any of those countries, and if any such loss were to fall upon the charterer, he in turn might have a claim against the shipowners. Although the proper law of the contract was accepted to be English by virtue of a London arbitration clause, neither of the parties to the contract, nor the contract itself, nor the claim which arose against the charterers, nor that by the charterers against the owners, had any connection with sterling, so that prima facie this would be a case for giving judgment in a foreign currency. This is not disputed in the present appeal, and the only question is which is the appropriate currency in which to measure the loss.

Prima facie, there is much to be said in favour of measuring the loss in cruzeiros: the argument for this was powerfully stated by Robert Goff J. The initial liability of the charterers was measured in that currency by the difference between the value of sound goods arrived at the port of discharge and the damaged value at that port. To require or admit a further conversion can be said to introduce an unnecessary complication brought about by an act of the charterers' choice. I am unable in the end to accept this argument. The essential question is what was the loss suffered by the respondents. I do not find this to be identical with that suffered by the cargo receivers: the charterers' claim against the owners is not one for indemnity in respect of

5 [1920] 3 KB 409, 89 LJKB 1039.
6 [1977] QB 182, [1977] 1 All ER 116.
7 [1961] AC 1007, [1960] 2 All ER 332.
8 [1977] QB 324, [1977] 2 All ER 41.
9 (1932) 43 Ll LRep 409; p 520 above.
10 The rule (now Rule 176 (4)) has since been altered (*Ed*).

expenditure sustained but is one for damages for breach of contract. Robert Goff J makes this plain in his judgment: '. . . the charterers' claim [as formulated] was a claim for damages on the basis that [they] incurred a personal liability to the receivers under the bills of lading which they were compelled to discharge . . .' I think it must follow from this that their loss, which they claim as damages, was the discharge of the receivers' claim, together with the legal and other expenses they incurred. They discharged all these by providing francs—until they provided the francs to meet the receivers' claim they suffered no loss. Then secondly was this loss the kind of loss which, under the contract, they were entitled to recover against the owners? The answer to this is provided by the arbitrators' finding that it was reasonable to contemplate that the charterers, being a French corporation and having their place of business in Paris, would have to use French francs to purchase other currencies to settle cargo claims arising under the bills of lading. So in my opinion the charterers' recoverable loss was, according to normal principle, the sum of French francs which they paid.

My Lords, there may be many variants of situations, *The Canadian Transport* is one, in which a loss arises immediately in the form of expenditure or indebtedness in one currency, but is ultimately felt in another, which other may be the normal trading currency of the plaintiff. In my opinion a decision in what currency the loss was borne or felt can be expressed as equivalent to finding which currency sum appropriately or justly reflects the recoverable loss. This is essentially a matter for arbitrators to determine. A rule that arbitrators may make their award in the currency best suited to achieve an appropriate and just result should be a flexible rule in which account must be taken of the circumstances in which the loss arose, in which the loss was converted into a money sum, and in which it was felt by the plaintiff. In some cases the 'immediate loss' currency may be appropriate, in others the currency in which it was borne by the plaintiff. There will be still others in which the appropriate currency is the currency of the contract. Awards of arbitrators based upon their appreciation of the circumstances in which the foreign currency came to be provided should not be set aside for, as such, they involve no error of law.

The arbitrators' decision in the present case was both within the permissible area of decision, and further was in my opinion right.

I agree with the Court of Appeal that the award ought not to have been set aside and with the judgments in that court. I would dismiss the appeal.

Lord Russell of Killowen delivered judgment to the same effect. Lords Diplock, Salmon and Keith of Kinkel concurred.
    Appeal dismissed.

NOTE

Although the English courts can now give judgment for a debt or damages expressed in foreign currency, for procedural reasons the amount of the judgment must be converted into sterling before execution can be levied. In the *Miliangos* case[11] the House of Lords held that the date for conversion was the date of payment, ie the date when the court authorises enforcement of the judgment in terms of sterling. As Lord

11 [1976] AC 443, [1975] 3 All ER 801; p 510 above.

Wilberforce said 'this date gets nearest to securing the creditor exactly what he bargained for'. And as he also pointed out, the same date is chosen by the Geneva Convention on the Carriage of Goods by Road.[12]

Sometimes a different date is prescribed by statute. This happens in two classes of case: (1) statutes implementing international conventions; (2) statutes enabling foreign judgments for periodical payments (eg maintenance orders) to be enforced in the United Kingdom.

(1) Under the Carriage by Air Act 1961,[13] implementing the Hague-Warsaw Convention, the date for conversion is the date of the judgment. Under the Merchant Shipping Act 1979[14] (not yet in force), which will implement the Athens Convention on the Carriage of Passengers by Sea, the date is the date of the judgment or the date agreed upon by the parties.

(2) It would clearly be impracticable for the sums due under a foreign maintenance order (which may be payable weekly) to vary from week to week in accordance with fluctuations in the value of the pound or of the relevant foreign currency. Therefore a different date is chosen by the Maintenance Orders (Reciprocal Enforcement) Act 1972.[15] This is the date on which the order became a registered order or (if earlier) the date on which it was confirmed by a court in the United Kingdom. If the order has been varied, the relevant date is the date on which the last order varying the order is registered or (if earlier) the date on which it was confirmed by a court in the United Kingdom. Under the Civil Jurisdiction and Judgments Act 1982, there is no question of a provisional order made in another EEC State being confirmed in the United Kingdom, and no court in the United Kingdom has power to vary the amounts payable under a maintenance order made in another EEC State. So the date for conversion is the date of registration of the order.[16]

---

12 Carriage of Goods by Road Act 1965, Sch, art 27 (2).
13 Sch 1, art 22 (5).
14 Sch 3, Part I, art 9 (2).
15 S 16.
16 S 8; pp 346–347 above.

PART VI

Law of Property

CHAPTER 17

Immovables

Section A: Distinction between Movables and Immovables

The primary division of property according to the English conflict of laws is into movables and immovables, not into realty and personalty.
 Leaseholds in England are interests in immovables.

Freke v Carbery (1873) LR 16 Eq 461, 21 WR 835 (Court of Chancery)

The testator was a domiciled Irishman who died in 1845. He was entitled to stocks and funds in England and to a leasehold house in Belgrave Square, London. By his will he gave his personal property to trustees on trusts for accumulation extending beyond any of the periods allowed by the Accumulations Act 1800, which did not apply to Ireland. The validity of the trusts for accumulation was not disputed so far as these related to the testator's stocks and funds; but the question was raised whether these trusts were valid as to the proceeds of sale of the house in Belgrave Square.

Lord Selborne LC: The only remaining question which has been argued is as to the leashold estate. Now I confess that is a point upon which I need no authority. The territory and soil of England, by the law of nature and of nations, which is recognised also as part of the law of England, is governed by all statutes which are in force in England. The leasehold property in Belgrave Square is part of the territory and soil of England, and the fact that the testator had a chattel interest in it, and not a freehold interest, makes it in no way whatever less so. An Act of Parliament, limiting the period for which accumulations are permitted, has as much force in Belgrave Square, as it has in any other part of England; and, for that purpose, it appears to me to be totally immaterial what is the quantity of interest dealt with by the will. All the general doctrines and maxims which are to be found in any of the books of authority really go the same way. The passage which Mr Fry quoted from *Story*, in which the words of Lord Loughborough[1] were cited with approbation, is simply a translation into the phraseology of the English law of the maxim of the general law, mobilia sequuntur personam, and is certainly not meant to apply arbitrarily in a new sense, because Lord Loughborough used the word 'personal' instead of 'movable'. The doctrine depends upon a principle which is expressed in the Latin words; and that is the only principle of the whole of our law as to domicile when applicable to the succession of what we call personal estate. It is so, not by any special law

1 In *Sill v Worswick* (1791) 1 Hy Bl 665 at 690.

of England, but by the deference which, for the sake of international comity, the law of England pays to the law of the civilised world generally. Domicile is allowed in this country to have the same influence as in other countries in determining the succession of movable estate; but the maxim of the law of the civilised world is mobilia sequuntur personam, and is founded on the nature of things. When 'mobilia' are in places other than that of the person to whom they belong their accidental situs is disregarded, and they are held to go with the person. But land, whether held for a chattel interest or held for a freehold interest, is in nature, as a matter of fact, immovable and not movable. The doctrine is inapplicable to it. . . .

I hold, therefore, that as to the proceeds of the house in Belgrave Square, they must necessarily follow the law applicable to the house itself, and are in no degree brought under a different law by the direction in the will; and that as to the house and the proceeds of the house the Thellusson Act does apply.

The lex situs determines whether an interest in a thing is an interest in a movable or in an immovable.

Mortgages on freehold land are interests in immovables.

Re Hoyles [1911] 1 Ch 179, 80 LJCh 274 (Court of Appeal)

A testator who died in February 1888, domiciled in England, gave one-third of his real and personal property after the death of his wife to charity. His property included $16,340 invested on legal mortgages of freehold land in the city of Toronto, in the province of Ontario, Canada. A summons was taken out to determine whether the charitable gift was void to any and what extent under the Mortmain Act 1736, which was in force at the date of the testator's death. It was proved that the Mortmain Act 1736 was in force in Ontario and that by the law of that province mortgages were impure personalty, and that bequests thereof to charity by persons domiciled in Ontario were void.

Swinfen Eady J held that the bequest of mortgages to charity was void.

Farwell LJ: I am of opinion that Swinfen Eady J's judgment is quite right.

At the date of the death of the testator the laws of England and of Ontario were the same, and the Statute of Mortmain of George II applied in Ontario as it then did in England. If a testator domiciled in England had devised to a charity a mortgage of real estate in England, it would have been void under the statute, and if a testator domiciled in Ontario had devised to a charity a mortgage of real estate in Ontario, that devise also would have been void under the statute. But it is argued that if a testator domiciled in England devises to a charity a mortgage on land in Ontario, or a testator domiciled in Ontario devises to a charity a mortgage on land in England, the statute has no application in either case. It is sought to establish this amazing proposition by an argument founded on the division of property in certain cases into movable and immovable. But this division is no part of the law either of England or of Ontario; in both England and Ontario the division is into real and personal property. The division into movable and immovable is only called into operation here when the English courts have to determine rights between domiciled Englishmen and persons domiciled in countries which do not adopt our division into real and personal property. In such cases, out of international comity and in order to arrive at a common basis on which to determine questions between the inhabitants of two countries living under different systems of jurisprudence, our courts recognise and act on a division otherwise unknown to our law into movable and immovable. But when there is no such difficulty there is no ground for attempting any such division. In this case the law is the same in both countries; the mortgaged property savours of the realty in both countries; the Statute of Mortmain applies in both countries; and any argument founded on what would be the case if the law of Ontario required us to consider movables and immovables is merely hypothetical and has no application to the present case. There is no necessity for ascertaining which law is applicable because the law in both countries is the same.

But even if this were not so, and the case were that put by Mr Sargant of a domiciled Frenchman, I should come to the same conclusion. International law is a matter of international comity. No country can be expected to allow questions affecting its own land, or the extent and nature of the interests in its own land which should be regarded as immovable, to be determined otherwise than by its own courts in accordance with its own interests.

... It is true that a mortgage is as between mortgagor and mortgagee regarded as personal estate for many purposes; but the fact that it is so for certain purposes in questions between our fellow subjects here has no bearing on the question whether such a mortgage should be regarded as movable or not in questions of international law. The mortgage undoubtedly affects the law directly; the mortgagee can enter and take possession at any time after his estate has become absolute at law; he can by foreclosure acquire the full title to the land in fee, and the legislature has forbidden any devises of land for any estate or interest whatsoever in any way charged or incumbered by any person or persons whatsoever in trust or for the benefit of any charitable use whatsoever and has made them void: Mortmain Act 1736, ss 1 and 2. And the reason is stated in the preamble: 'Whereas gifts or alienations of lands, tenements or hereditaments, in mortmain, are prohibited or restrained by Magna Charta, and divers other wholesome laws, as prejudicial to and against the common utility; nevertheless this public mischief has of late greatly increased by many large and improvident alienations or dispositions made by languishing or dying persons, or by other persons, to uses called charitable uses, to take place after their deaths, to the disherison of their lawful heirs.' It is for this court to determine whether mortgages on land are movables or immovables, and in order to come to a conclusion we are bound to consider the result of our decision on the general welfare of this country as shown by our laws, and if a decision in one way will involve results which our law considers prejudicial to the public interest, or immoral, or the like, it is our duty to decide the other way. Mr Sargant invites us to leave the Mortmain Act out of sight and decide as a preliminary abstract question whether mortgages on land are movable or immovable. But we should fail in our duty if we did not consider that Act and the effect of our decision upon devises within it. We must have regard to the fact that such gifts have been regarded as prejudicial to and against the public utility and a public mischief, and we must accordingly come to such conclusion as will avoid these evils.

Cozens-Hardy MR delivered judgment to the same effect.
Fletcher Moulton LJ doubted but did not dissent.
Appeal dismissed.

QUESTION

Do you prefer Farwell LJ's statement (above) that:

> 'The division into movable or immovable is only called into operation when the English courts have to determine rights between domiciled Englishmen and persons domiciled in countries which do not adopt our division into real and personal property'

or the approach of Robertson (*Characterisation in the Conflict of Laws* (1940) p 201) who asks:

> 'Is England to have one system of conflict of laws for the rest of the world and a different system for the common law countries?'

An interest in the proceeds of sale of English freeholds which are subject to a trust for sale but not yet sold is an interest in an immovable.

Re Berchtold [1923] 1 Ch 192, 92 LJCh 185 (Chancery Division)

Originating Summons.

On 2 April 1906 Count Richard Berchtold died, being a person of Hungarian nationality and domicile. He left a will in English form dealing with his estate in England. By that will he devised all his freehold estate in Birmingham to English trustees upon trust for sale and conversion with power to postpone such sale and conversion for so long as they should think fit. The proceeds of sale and the investments for the time being representing the same and the rents and profits of such part of the estate as should for the time being remain unsold were directed to be held in trust for his son Count Nicholas subject to the payment of an annual sum to the testator's wife during her life. Count Richard left him surviving his wife (who died in 1913), his only son Count Nicholas, and an only daughter, the defendant Countess Szokolyi.

Count Nicholas died intestate on 9 July 1911. He was of Hungarian nationality and domicile. He left him surviving his widow the plaintiff and one child only, Count Antoine, who was killed in action on 23 October 1915, under the age of 21 years. He was of Hungarian nationality and domicile. He died intestate leaving his mother, the plaintiff, his sole next of kin. The estate of Count Nicholas in this country consisted of his beneficial interest in the Birmingham freeholds under the will of Count Richard. No part of the Birmingham freeholds had been sold before the date of the summons.

The summons asked 'Whether the persons or person beneficially entitled to the proceeds of sale of the said real estate (if sold) and to the rents and profits thereof (until sale) are the persons or person who would be entitled according to English law or the persons or person who would be entitled according to the law of Hungary'.

Russell J: It is conceded that when a conflict of laws arises on the death of an intestate, the devolution of his immovables is governed by the lex situs; the devolution of his movables is governed by the lex domicilii. It is further conceded that whether particular property is a movable or an immovable is decided according to the lex situs.

The questions which arise in the present case, arise in regard to (1) the interest owned by Count Nicholas at his death in respect of the Birmingham freeholds which were subject to a trust for sale, and the other provisions contained in Count Richard's will; and (2) the interest owned by Count Antoine at his death in respect of the same freeholds. If these respective interests are immovable property according to the lex situs (ie, the law of England) the law applicable to their devolution will be the law of England, and being, according to English law, personal estate, they will devolve upon the persons entitled by English law to the intestate's personal estate. The result of this solution would be that the plaintiff would take one-third on the intestacy of Count Nicholas as his widow, and the remaining two-thirds on the intestacy of Count Antoine as his mother and sole next of kin. On the other hand, if these respective interests are movable property according to the lex situs, the law applicable to their devolution will be the lex domicilii or law of Hungary. The result of this solution would be that, subject to a usufruct in favour of the plaintiff as the widow of Count Nicholas (as to the extent of which usufruct there is a question) the whole devolves upon and belongs to the Countess Szokolyi as the only sister of Count Nicholas, Count Antoine having died intestate and without leaving him surviving any issue, or any brother and sister, or any issue of a deceased brother or sister, or a father, or any brother of his deceased father. It will thus be seen that the primary question for decision can thus be framed. Were the interests taken by Count Nicholas and Count Antoine under or by virtue of the will of Count Richard, so far as regards the Birmingham freeholds thereby devised upon trust for sale, immovable property or movable property according to English law? The distinction between real estate and personal estate under English law has nothing to do with the question. The alternatives and the only alternatives for consideration are immovable property or movable property. It is said that there is no decision of the English courts directly upon the point. There is a decision on the exact point in the Irish courts, which though entitled to the highest respect, is not binding on me. I will first consider the matter apart from that decision.

Different classes of property have come under the consideration of the courts of this country and have been held to be immovables. Leaseholds are immovables: *Freke v Lord Carbery*[2] and *Duncan v Lawson*.[3] A testatrix's share of a rent-charge issuing out of lands during the lives of herself and two others and the life of the longest liver was held to be an estate pur autre vie applicable by law as personal estate and chargeable with duty as personal estate under the Legacy Duty Act 1796; and was held not to be exempt from duty by reason of the foreign domicile of the testatrix because the property was as much land as if land to the annual value of the rent-charge had been given, and was accordingly immovable property: *Chatfield v Berchtoldt*.[4]

2 (1873) LR 16 Eq 461, 21 WR 835; p 529 above.
3 (1889) 41 Ch D 394, 58 LJCh 502.
4 (1872) 7 Ch App 192, 41 LJCh 255.

Scotch heritable bonds are immovables: *Re Fitzgerald*.[5] A mortgage debt secured by land is immovable property: *Re Hoyles*.[6] Numerous authorities were cited for the purpose of showing that an interest in the proceeds of sale of real estate subject to a trust for sale was under different statutes treated as an interest in land. I will refer to a few. (After referring to *Briggs v Chamberlain*,[7] *Brook v Badley*,[8] *Bowyer v Woodman*[9] and *Re Thomas*,[10] his Lordship continued:) These authorities are only decisions that the property in question in each case fell within the wording of the relevant statute, but they certainly show that an interest in property such as I have to consider in the present case is aptly described as being 'an interest in land', or 'a sum of money payable out of land'.

Let me now consider what rights existed in Count Nicholas during his lifetime and at his death in regard to the Birmingham freeholds by virtue of the dispositions contained in the will of Count Richard. Subject to his mother's £500 a year, he was absolutely entitled to the proceeds of sale if and when the sale took place. No sale in fact took place; the property continued to be land, immovable property. Subject to his mother's interest, Count Nicholas was entitled down to his death to the rents and profits of that immovable. . . . Further, subject to the interest of the mother of Count Nicholas, the land was his in equity. As to Count Antoine, his position was the same as regards so much of the benefit taken by Count Nicholas under Count Richard's will as passed to Count Antoine upon the intestacy of Count Nicholas, except that at the time of Count Antoine's death, the £500 a year had ceased to be payable owing to the previous death of Count Nicholas' mother. The rights and interests of Count Nicholas and Count Antoine, under or by virtue of the will of Count Richard in relation to the Birmingham freeholds and the proceeds of sale thereof being such as I have described, are those rights and interests more properly to be classified as immovable property, or as movable property? In my opinion, they should be classified as immovable property equally with the freehold land out of which the money is eventually to be paid. That is the conclusion to which I have come independently of the Irish decision to which I will now refer. (His Lordship referred to *Murray v Champernowne*,[11] and continued:) That decision seems to me to cover the exact point and is in my opinion right. . . .

On behalf of the Countess Szokolyi it was argued that according to English law land directed to be sold and turned into money must be considered to be money; and that on the principle that equity considers done what should be done, the Birmingham freeholds are, in the eye of the law, money. This argument, to be effective, must add the words 'for all purposes'. That the Birmingham freeholds are to be treated as money for some purposes, no one doubts. Thus the interest of the taker is personal estate. But this equitable doctrine of conversion only arises and comes into play where the question for consideration arises as between real estate and personal estate. It has no relation to the question whether property is movable or

5 [1904] 1 Ch 573, 73 LJCh 436.
6 [1911] 1 Ch 179, 80 LJCh 274; p 530 above.
7 (1853) 11 Hare 69, 1 Eq Rep 404.
8 (1868) 3 Ch App 672, 37 LJCh 884.
9 (1867) LR 3 Eq 313.
10 (1886) 34 Ch D 166, 56 LJCh 9.
11 [1901] 2 IR 232.

immovable. The doctrine of conversion is that real estate is treated as personal estate, or personal estate is treated as real estate; not that immovables are turned into movables, or movables into immovables. As Farwell LJ pointed out in *Re Hoyles*, the fact that a mortgage is regarded as personal estate for certain purposes in questions between our fellow subjects here has no bearing on the question whether such a mortgage should be regarded as a movable or not in questions of international law. . . .

I answer the second question in the summons by declaring that the persons or person beneficially entitled to the proceeds of sale of the Birmingham freeholds and to the rents and profits thereof until sale are the persons or person who would be entitled thereto according to the law of England.

Section B: Jurisdiction

English courts have no jurisdiction to adjudicate upon the right of property in or the right of possession to foreign immovables, unless the case falls within one of the two exceptions mentioned below.

British South Africa Company v Companhia de Moçambique
[1893] AC 602, 63 LJQB 70 (House of Lords)

By their statement of claim the plaintiffs, a Portuguese company, alleged that they were in possession of large tracts of land and mines and mining rights in South Africa; and that the defendant company by its agents wrongfully broke and entered and took possession of the said lands, mines, and mining rights, and ejected the plaintiff company, its servants, agents, and tenants therefrom. The plaintiffs claimed (1) a declaration that the plaintiff company were lawfully in possession and occupation of the lands, mines, and mining rights; (2) an injunction restraining the defendant company from continuing to occupy or from asserting any title to the said lands, mines, and mining rights; (3) £250,000 damages for trespass.

The defence alleged that the lands in question were in South Africa, out of the jurisdiction of the High Court, and that the statement of claim disclosed no cause of action.

By an order of Collins J in chambers the questions of law raised by the pleadings were set down for hearing before a Divisional Court.

The Divisional Court (Lawrance and Wright JJ) made an order that judgment be entered for the defendants dismissing the action for want of jurisdiction.

In the Court of Appeal the plaintiffs formally abandoned their claim for a declaration of title and an injunction, and that court by a majority (Fry and Lopes LJJ; Lord Esher MR dissenting) declared that the High Court had jurisdiction to entertain the claim for damages for trespass.

The defendants appealed to the House of Lords.

Lord Herschell: My Lords, the principal question raised by this appeal is whether the Supreme Court of Judicature has jurisdiction to try an action to recover damages for a trespass to lands situate in a foreign country.

It is not in controversy that prior to the Judicature Acts no such jurisdiction could have been exercised; but it is asserted on behalf of the respondents that the only barrier to its exercise was the technical one, that the venue in such a case must be local, and that the rules made under the Judicature Acts which have abolished local venues have removed the sole impediment which prevented the courts entertaining and adjudicating on cases of this description.

The nature of the controversy between the parties renders it necessary to consider the origin of the distinction between local and transitory actions, and the development of the law which determined the venue or place of trial of issues of fact.

It was necessary originally to state truly the venue—that is, the place in which it arose—of every fact in issue, whether those on which the plaintiff relied, or any matter stated by way of defence; and if the places were different, each issue would be tried by a jury summoned from the place in which the facts in dispute were stated to have arisen. After the statute 17 Car 2, c 8, which provided that 'after verdict judgment should not be stayed or reversed for that there was no right venue, so as the cause were tried by a jury of the proper county or place where the action was laid', the practice arose, which ultimately became regular and uniform, of trying all the issues by a jury of the venue laid in the action, even though some of the facts were laid elsewhere. When juries ceased to be drawn from the particular town, parish, or hamlet where the fact took place, that is, from amongst those who were supposed to be cognisant of the circumstances, and came to be drawn from the body of the county generally, and to be bound to determine the issues judicially after hearing witnesses, the law began to discriminate between cases in which the truth of the venue was material and those in which it was not so. This gave rise to the distinction between transitory and local actions, that is, between those in which the facts relied on as the foundation of the plaintiff's case have no necessary connection with a particular locality and those in which there is such a connection. In the latter class of actions the plaintiff was bound to lay the venue truly; in the former he might lay it in any county he pleased. It was, however, still necessary to lay every local fact with its true venue on peril of a variance if it should be brought in issue. Where a local matter occurred out of the realm, a difficulty arose, inasmuch as it was supposed that the issue could not be tried, as no jury could be summoned from the place, and it was by the general rule essential that a jury should be summoned from the venue laid to the fact in issue. It was, however, early decided that, notwithstanding the general rule, such matters might be tried by a jury from the venue in the action, and thus the difficulty was removed and the form was introduced of adding after the statement of the foreign place the words, 'To wit at Westminster in the county of Middlesex', or whatever else might happen to be the venue in the action. . . .

It is, I think, important to observe that the distinction between local and transitory actions depended on the nature of the matters involved and not on the place at which the trial had to take place. It was not called a local action because the venue was local, or a transitory action because the venue might be laid in any county, but the venue was local or transitory according as the action was local or transitory. It will be seen that this distinction is material when the Judicature Rule upon which so much turns comes to be examined.

My Lords, I cannot but lay great stress upon the fact that whilst lawyers made an exception from the ordinary rule in the case of a local[12] matter occurring outside the realm for which there was no proper place of trial in this country, and invented a fiction which enabled the courts to exercise jurisdiction, they did not make an exception where the cause of action was a local matter arising abroad, and did not extend the fiction to such cases. The rule that in local actions the venue must be local did not, where the cause of action arose in this country, touch the jurisdiction in the courts, but only determined the particular manner in which the jurisdiction should be exercised; but where the matter complained of was local and arose outside the realm, the refusal to adjudicate upon it was in fact a refusal to exercise jurisdiction, and I cannot think that the courts would have failed to find a remedy if they had regarded the matter as one within their jurisdiction, and which it was proper for them to adjudicate upon.

The earliest authority of importance is *Skinner v East India Company*.[13] The House of Lords in that case referred it to the judges to report whether relief could be obtained in respect of the matters mentioned in the petition, either at law or in equity, and if so in what manner. The judges answered, 'that the matters touching the taking away of the petitioner's ship and goods and assaulting of his person, notwithstanding the same were done beyond the seas, might be determined upon by His Majesty's ordinary Courts at Westminster. And as to the dispossessing him of his house and island, that he was not relievable in any ordinary Court of Law'.

Notwithstanding the opinion thus expressed, Lord Mansfield entertained and acted on the view that where damages only were sought in respect of a trespass committed abroad, an action might be maintained in this country, although it was one which would here be a local action (see *Mostyn v Fabrigas*[14])....

The view acted on by Lord Mansfield in the two cases referred to has not been followed. It came before the Court of Queen's Bench for consideration in *Doulson v Matthews*,[15] which was an action of trespass for entering the plaintiff's house in Canada and expelling him therefrom. The decisions of Lord Mansfield were relied on by the plaintiff, but the action was held not to lie. Buller J in delivering judgment said: 'It is now too late for us to inquire whether it were wise or politic to make a distinction between transitory and local actions: it is sufficient for the courts that the law has settled the distinction, and that an action quare clausum fregit is local. We may try actions here which are in their nature transitory, though arising out of a transaction abroad; but not such as are in their nature local.'

In saying that we may not try actions here arising out of transactions abroad which are in their nature local, I do not think that the learned judge was referring to the mere technical difficulty of there being no venue in this country in which these transactions could be laid, but to the fact that our courts did not exercise jurisdiction in matters arising abroad 'which were in their nature local'. The case of *Doulson v Matthews* has ever since been regarded as law, and I do not think it has been considered as founded merely

12 Sic in the report; evidently 'transitory' was meant (*Ed*).
13 (1665) 6 St Tr 710 at 719.
14 (1774) 1 Cowp 161 at 180.
15 (1792) 4 Term Rep 503.

on the technical difficulty that in this country a local venue was requisite in a local action. . . .

The question what jurisdiction can be exercised by the courts of any country according to its municipal law cannot, I think, be conclusively determined by a reference to principles of international law. No nation can execute its judgments, whether against persons or movables or real property, in the country of another. On the other hand, if the courts of a country were to claim, as against a person resident there, jurisdiction to adjudicate upon the title to land in a foreign country, and to enforce its adjudication in personam, it is by no means certain that any rule of international law would be violated. But in considering what jurisdiction our courts possess, and have claimed to exercise in relation to matters arising out of the country, the principles which have found general acceptance amongst civilised nations as defining the limits of jurisdiction are of great weight.

It was admitted in the present case, on behalf of the respondents, that the court could not make a declaration of title, or grant an injunction to restrain trespasses, the respondents having in relation to these matters abandoned their appeal in the court below. But it is said that the court may inquire into the title, and, if the plaintiffs and not the defendants are found to have the better title, may award damages for the trespass committed. My Lords, I find it difficult to see why this distinction should be drawn. It is said, because the courts have no power to enforce their judgment by any dealing with the land itself, where it is outside their territorial jurisdiction. But if they can determine the title to it and compel the payment of damages founded upon such determination, why should not they equally proceed in personam against a person who, in spite of that determination, insists on disturbing one who has been found by the court to be the owner of the property?

It is argued that if an action of trespass cannot be maintained in this country where the land is situate abroad a wrongdoer by coming to this country might leave the person wronged without any remedy. It might be a sufficient answer to this argument to say that this is a state of things which has undoubtedly existed for centuries without any evidence of serious mischief or any intervention of the legislature; for even if the Judicature Rules have the effect contended for, I do not think it can be denied that this was a result neither foreseen nor intended. But there appear to me, I confess, to be solid reasons why the courts of this country should, in common with those of most other nations, have refused to adjudicate upon claims of title to foreign land in proceedings founded on an alleged invasion of the proprietary rights attached to it, and to award damages founded on that adjudication.

The inconveniences which might arise from such a course are obvious, and it is by no means clear to my mind that if the courts were to exercise jurisdiction in such cases the ends of justice would in the long run, and looking at the matter broadly, be promoted. Supposing a foreigner to sue in this country for trespass to his lands situate abroad, and for taking possession of and expelling him from them, what is to be the measure of damages? There being no legal process here by which he could obtain possession of the lands, the plaintiff might, I suppose, in certain circumstances, obtain damages equal in amount to their value. But what would there be to prevent his leaving this country after obtaining these damages and repossessing himself of the lands? What remedy would the defendant have in such a case where the lands are in an unsettled country, with no laws or regular system of government, but where, to use a familiar expression, the only right is might? Such an occurrence is not an impossible or even an improbable hypothesis. It is quite true that in the exercise of the undoubted jurisdiction of the courts it may become necessary incidentally to investigate and determine the title to foreign lands; but it does not seem to me to follow that because such a question may incidentally arise and fall to be adjudicated upon, the courts possess, or that it is expedient that they should exercise, jurisdiction to try an action founded on a disputed claim of title to foreign lands.

Reliance was placed on the decisions of courts of equity, as showing that our courts were ready, when no technical difficulty of venue stood in the way, to adjudicate on the title to lands situate abroad. If the refusal of the common law courts to exercise jurisdiction in cases of the nature now under consideration had been regarded as the result of a mere technical difficulty, I cannot help thinking that the courts of equity, which were, in early days, at all events, keen to supplement the deficiencies of the common law, when the requirements of justice were impeded by technical difficulties, would have found some means of affording a remedy. Lord Mansfield, in his judgment in *Mostyn v Fabrigas*, refers to a case of an injury in the East Indies similar to that with which he had to deal in the case of Captain Gambier, in which Lord Hardwicke in a Court of Equity had directed satisfaction to be made in damages. But in this exercise of jurisdiction he has not been followed by any judge of the Court of Chancery.

Whilst courts of equity have never claimed to act directly upon land situate abroad, they have purported to act upon the conscience of persons living here. (His Lordship referred to *Lord Cranstown v Johnston*,[16] and continued:) My Lords, the decisions of the courts of equity do not, to my mind, afford any substantial support to the view that the ground upon which the courts of common law abstained from exercising jurisdiction in relation to trespasses to real property abroad was only the technical difficulty of venue. . . .

The terms of rule 1 of Order 36, which are relied on by the plaintiffs, are as follows: 'There shall be no local venue for the trial of any action except where otherwise provided by statute.' The language used appears to me important. The rule does not purport to touch the distinction between local and transitory actions—between matters which have no necessary local connection, and those which are local in their nature. It deals only with the place of trial, and enables actions, whatever their nature, to be tried in any county. But it is, in my opinion, a mere rule of procedure, and applies only to those cases in which the courts at that time exercised jurisdiction. It has been more than once held that the rules under the Judicature Acts are rules of procedure only, and were not intended to affect, and did not affect, the rights of parties. . . .

According to the contention of the respondents in this case the rule under consideration had the effect of conferring upon them a right of action in this country which they would not otherwise have possessed. As I have already pointed out, a person whose lands, situate in this country, were trespassed

16 (1796) 3 Ves 170.

upon always had a right of action in respect of the trespass. The rules relating to venue did no more than regulate the manner in which the right was to be enforced. But in respect of a trespass to land situate abroad there was no right of action, for an alleged right which the courts would neither recognise nor enforce did not constitute any right at all in point of law.

My Lords, I have come to the conclusion that the grounds upon which the courts have hitherto refused to exercise jurisdiction in actions of trespass to lands situate abroad were substantial and not technical, and that the rule of procedure under the Judicature Acts has not conferred a jurisdiction which did not exist before. If this conclusion be well founded, I do not think that the allegation contained in paragraph 16 of the statement of claim, 'that the defendant company did and committed the acts above mentioned and complained of with intent to injure and destroy the trade of the plaintiff company, and to deprive it of its aforesaid lands, territories, mines, minerals and mining rights and property', disclosed a cause of action cognisable by our courts any more than the paragraph complaining of trespass. . . .

Lord Halsbury delivered judgment to the same effect.
Lords Macnaghten and Morris concurred.
Appeal allowed: judgment of Divisional Court restored.

Civil Jurisdiction and Judgments Act 1982

30.—(1) The jurisdiction of any court in England and Wales or Northern Ireland to entertain proceedings for trespass to, or any other tort affecting, immovable property shall extend to cases in which the property in question is situated outside that part of the United Kingdom unless the proceedings are principally concerned with a question of the title to, or the right to possession of, that property.

(2) Subsection (1) has effect subject to the 1968 Convention and to the provisions set out in Schedule 4.

NOTE

This section reverses the much-criticised decision of the House of Lords in *Hesperides Hotels Ltd v Aegean Turkish Holidays Ltd*,[17] where it was held that the *Moçambique* rule precluded actions for damages for trespass to foreign land.

Sub-s (2) is a reminder to the courts that they cannot exercise the jurisdiction conferred by sub-s (1) if the defendant is domiciled in another EEC state or in Scotland or Northern Ireland (Sch 1, art 3; Sch 4, art 3), unless jurisdiction can be derived from some other part of the Brussels Convention. It probably does not mean that the jurisdiction cannot be exercised merely because the land is situated in some other EEC state or in Scotland or Northern Ireland. Article 16 (1), which gives exclusive jurisidiction to the courts of the situs in proceedings 'which have as their object rights in rem in or tenancies of immovable property', does not apply to actions for damages.[18]

17 [1979] AC 508, [1978] 2 All ER 1168.
18 Schlosser Report, OJ 1979 No C/71, para 163.

Civil Jurisdiction and Judgments Act 1982

SCHEDULE 1

Section 5 Exclusive jurisdiction

ARTICLE 16

The following courts shall have exclusive jurisdiction, regardless of domicile:
(1) in proceedings which have as their object rights in rem in, or tenancies of, immovable property, the courts of the Contracting State in which the property is situated.

Exception 1: English courts have jurisdiction to adjudicate upon rights in foreign immovables, if the defendant is affected by some personal obligation arising out of contract or implied contract, fiduciary relationship or fraud, or other conduct which in the view of a court of equity would be unconscionable.

Deschamps v Miller [1908] 1 Ch 856, 77 LJCh 416 (Chancery Division)

On 6 October 1831 a contract of marriage in French form was made in France in consideration of the then contemplated marriage of Jean Deschamps and Marie Taris, who were both then domiciled and residing in France. The agreement provided that the marriage should be governed by the régime dotal with community of acquired property under the French law. The plaintiff, Thomas Deschamps, the son of the marriage, alleged that by the law of France his mother, Marie Taris, became entitled, by virtue of the contract and marriage, to one-half of the after-acquired property of Jean Deschamps (with some unimportant exceptions), and also to a life interest, on his death, in the other half of the property.

About the year 1836 Jean Deschamps went to India, and there, in 1839, in the lifetime of his wife, Marie Deschamps, he went through a form of marriage in Madras with Cecilia Taylor.

By an indenture dated 14 February 1865, Jean Deschamps, in consideration of his natural love and affection for his so-called 'wife Cecilia Deschamps' and of a share in her father's estate which he had received, conveyed and assigned his business premises at Madras to a trustee, upon trust for Jean Deschamps for his life without impeachment of waste, and after his death upon trust to sell the same, and to hold the net proceeds of sale on trusts for the benefit of Cecilia Taylor and her children, if any, by Jean Deschamps, and in default of children for certain relations of Cecilia Taylor.

By deeds executed by him in 1866 and 1869 Jean Deschamps conveyed other real estate at Madras to be held upon the trusts of the settlement of 1865.

According to the plaintiff, all these properties were after-acquired property of Jean Deschamps settled without the knowledge of Marie Deschamps, and in breach of trust, and with intent to defraud her and deprive her of her rights in the property subject to the marriage contract of 1831; there was no good or valuable consideration for the settlement; by French law the husband could dispose of after-acquired property during the coverture, but only for 'good consideration', which meant full consideration in money or money's worth.

Jean Deschamps died on 14 December 1885, and his wife died intestate in France on 14 March 1890, and the plaintiff claimed that by the law of France he was entitled to all her rights under the marriage contract of 1831.

The defendants took the preliminary objection that the court had no jurisdiction.

Parker J: . . . It is said that the action relates to the title and possession of real estate out of the jurisdiction of the court, and therefore that it ought not to be entertained by the court, even though all parties to the action are resident within the jurisdiction. . . .

The question is whether under these circumstances the court ought to entertain jurisdiction. In my opinion the general rule is that the court will not adjudicate on questions relating to the title to or the right to the possession of immovable property out of the jurisdiction. There are, no doubt, exceptions to the rule, but, without attempting to give an exhaustive statement of those exceptions, I think it will be found that they all depend on the existence between the parties to the suit of some personal obligation arising out of contract or implied contract, fiduciary relationship or fraud, or other conduct which, in the view of a court of equity in this country, would be unconscionable, and do not depend for their existence on the law of the locus of the immovable property. Thus, in cases of trusts, specific performance of contracts, foreclosure, or redemption of mortgages, or in the case of land obtained by the defendant by fraud, or other such unconscionable conduct as I have referred to, the court may very well asssume jurisdiction. But where there is no contract, no fiduciary relationship, and no fraud or other unconscionable conduct giving rise to a personal obligation between the parties, and the whole question is whether or not according to the law of the locus the claim of title set up by one party, whether a legal or equitable claim in the sense of those words as used in English law, would be preferred to the claim of another party, I do not think the court ought to entertain jurisdiction to decide the matter.

In the present case there is, in my opinion, no such personal obligation as above mentioned, and I do not think I could assume jurisdiction in this case without acting contrary to the decision in *Norris v Chambres*.[19] In that case there was a contract for sale of immovables abroad, and a deposit was paid. The vendor refused to complete, and the purchaser claimed a lien for the deposit on the property agreed to be sold; but he claimed that lien, not as against the vendor with whom he had contracted, but against a third party who had purchased subsequently with notice of the prior contract and of the claim to the lien for the deposit. There was no personal obligation based on contract, fiduciary relationship, fraud, or other unconscionable conduct between the parties, and the right, if there was a right, to succeed in the action depended, therefore, solely on whether the law of the locus of the immovable property would recognise any lien as arising out of the contract for sale coupled with the payment of a deposit, and, if so, what was the position, with regard to such lien, of a purchaser with notice. The court refused to entertain the action. In a similar way here, the question depends

19 (1861) 29 Beav 246; affd 3 DeG F & J 583, 4 LT 345.

on whether the Indian law will recognise the French contract as having
created an interest in the wife, and, if so, what is the position with regard to
such interest of the defendants, who in their pleadings claim to have
purchased for value without notice. There is no obligation on the part of the
defendants to the plaintiff based on any contract, fiduciary relationship,
fraud, or other unconscionable conduct. Such obligation, if any, as exists
depends, in my opinion, on the Indian law relating to immovables, and on
that alone. It was suggested that the defendants have since action, or shortly
before action, sold some of the property in dispute, and that this at any rate
gives the court jurisdiction. I do not think, however, that I could so decide
without acting contrary to the decision of Kay J in *Re Hawthorne*.[20] In my
opinion, therefore, the preliminary objection which I have been discussing
succeeds.

*Exception 2: Where an English court has jurisdiction to administer the estate of a
deceased person or a trust arising under his will or intestacy and the property includes
movables or immovables situated in England and immovables situated abroad, the court
has jurisdiction to determine questions of title to the foreign immovables for the purposes
of the administration.*

Re Hoyles (p 530 above)

Re Ross (p 657 below)

Section C: Choice of Law

*In general, the lex situs determines all questions as to the essential validity of conveyances
and wills of immovables and who are entitled thereto on intestacy.*

Freke v Carbery (p 529 above)

Re Ralston (p 573 below)

Re Hoyles (p 530 above)

Re Berchtold (p 532 above)

Re Ross (p 657 below)

20 (1883) 23 Ch D 743, 52 LJCh 750.

CHAPTER 18

Transfer of Tangible Movables

If movable property is disposed of in a manner binding according to the law of the country where it is, that disposition is binding everywhere.

Cammell v Sewell (1860) 5 H & N 728 (Exchequer Chamber)

Error from the Court of Exchequer.

The plaintiffs were underwriters in Hull; the defendants merchants in London. The action was brought to recover part of a cargo of deals shipped on board the Prussian ship *Augusta Bertha* at Onega, in Russia, by the Onega Wood Company, for Messrs Simpson & Whaplate of Hull, and by them insured with the plaintiffs.

On 17 September 1852 *The Augusta Bertha*, having put into Haroe Roads in consequence of the shifting of her deck cargo, drove from her anchorage on the rocks at Smaage, about three miles from Molde in Norway. On the 19th the captain began discharging the cargo, which was ultimately stacked on two small islands. The cargo was not materially damaged. Witnesses, however, stated that as it stood it was exposed to injury from the weather and sea water: that possibly some of it might be washed away in storms; and that it would require to be watched. The wreck lay out of the track of shipping. There was no harbour; the anchorage at Smaage was bad, and ships could not have been readily obtained for the purpose of forwarding the cargo to its destination. There was a conflict of testimony as to whether or not a prudent owner, if uninsured, would have sold the cargo on the spot.

On 23 September the captain notified the consignees of the wreck. The consignees gave notice of abandonment to the plaintiffs who paid as for a total loss.

The captain instructed surveyors to survey the vessel and cargo, and on 27 September they reported that a sale of the cargo by public auction was best for all parties. On 15 October the sale was held, Mr Jervell, the representative of the plaintiffs, protesting against the sale. The cargo was bought by Mr Clausen, the British Vice-Consul.

Mr Jervell then instituted a suit before the superior diocesan Court of Trondhjem to set aside the sale, making the captain and his agent and Mr Clausen defendants: but on 25 November 1853[1] the court confirmed the sale.

The cargo remained in Norway throughout the winter, and in the spring it was shipped to London by a vessel called *The Mindet* under a bill of lading indorsed by Clausen to the defendants, who had made advances on the cargo. *The Mindet* arrived in the Thames in April 1853, when the plaintiffs immediately caused a notice to be served on the defendants requiring them

---

1 Sic in the report. It is thought that this is a misprint for 1852 (*Ed*).

to deliver up the deals. The cargo was afterwards sold by auction, and the net proceeds received by the defendants on 9 December 1853 were £1,470 4s 2d. The plaintiffs claimed this sum. By Norwegian law the sale conferred a good title on Clausen.

The Court of Exchequer (Pollock CB, Martin B, and Channell B) gave judgment for the defendants on the ground that the Norwegian judgment was in the nature of a judgment in rem and as such conclusively determined the title to the deals. The plaintiffs appealed.

Crompton J: In this case the majority of the court (Cockburn CJ, Wightman, Williams, Crompton, and Keating JJ) are of opinion that the judgment of the Court of Exchequer should be affirmed. At the same time we are by no means prepared to agree with the Court of Exchequer in thinking the judgment of the Diocesan Court in Norway conclusive as a judgment in rem, nor are we satisfied that the defendants in the present action were estopped by the judgment of that court or what was relied on as a judicial proceeding at the auction. It is not, however, necessary for us to express any decided opinion on these questions, as we think that the case should be determined on the real merits as to the passing of the property.

If we are to recognise the Norwegian law, and if according to that law the property passed by the sale in Norway to Clausen as an innocent purchaser, we do not think that the subsequent bringing the property to England can alter the position of the parties. The difficulty which we have felt in the case principally arises from the mode in which the evidence is laid before us in the mass of papers and depositions contained in the appendix.

We do not see evidence in the case sufficient to enable us to treat the transaction as fraudulent on the part of Clausen, although there are circumstances which would have made it better for him not to have become the purchaser. Treating him, therefore, as an innocent purchaser, it appears to us that the questions are—did the property by the law of Norway vest in him as an innocent purchaser? and are we to recognise that law? That question of what is the foreign law is one of fact, and here again there is great difficulty in finding out from the mass of documents what is the exact state of the law. The conclusion which we draw from the evidence is, that by the law of Norway the captain, under circumstances such as existed in this case, could not, as between himself and his owners, or the owners of the cargo, justify the sale, but that he remained liable and responsible to them for a sale not justified under the circumstances; whilst, on the other hand, an innocent purchaser would have a good title to the property bought by him from the agent of the owners.

It does not appear to us that there is anything so barbarous or monstrous in this state of the law as that we can say that it should not be recognised by us. Our own law as to market overt is analogous; and though it is said that much mischief would be done by upholding sales of this nature, not justified by the necessities of the case, it may well be that the mischief would be greater if the vendee were only to have a title in cases where the master was strictly justified in selling as between himself and the owners. If that were so, purchasers, who seldom can know the facts of the case, would not be inclined to give the value, and on proper and lawful sales by the master the property would be in great danger of being sacrificed.

There appears nothing barbarous in saying that the agent of the owners, who is the person to sell, if the circumstances justify the sale, and who must, in point of fact, be the party to exercise his judgment as to whether there should be a sale or not, should have the power of giving a good title to the innocent purchaser, and that the latter should not be bound to look to the title of the seller. It appears in the present case that the one purchaser bought the whole cargo; but suppose the farmers and persons in the neighbourhood at such a sale buy several portions of the goods, it would seem extremely inconvenient if they were liable to actions at the suit of the owners, on the ground that there was no necessity for the sale. Could such a purchaser coming to England be sued in our courts for a conversion, and can it alter the case if he re-sell, and the property comes to this country?

Many cases were mentioned in the course of the argument, and more might be collected, in which it might seem hard that the goods of foreigners should be dealt with according to the laws of our own or of other countries. Amongst others our law as to the seizure of a foreigner's goods for rent due from a tenant, or as to the title gained in them, if stolen, by a sale in market overt, might appear harsh. But we cannot think that the goods of foreigners would be protected against such laws, or that if the property once passed by virtue of them it would again be changed by being taken by the new owner into the foreigner's own country. We think that the law on this subject was correctly stated by the Lord Chief Baron in the course of the argument in the court below, where he says 'if personal property is disposed of in a manner binding according to the law of the country where it is, that disposition is binding everywhere'. And we do not think that it makes any difference that the goods were wrecked, and not intended to be sent to the country where they were sold. We do not think that the goods which were wrecked here would on that account be the less liable to our laws as to market overt, or as to the landlord's right of distress, because the owner did not foresee that they would come to England. . . .

In the present case, which is not like the case of *Freeman v East India Co*,[2] the case of an English subject purchasing in an English colony property which he was taken to know that the vendor had no authority to sell, we do not think that we can assume on the evidence that the purchase was made with the knowledge that the sellers had no authority, or under such circumstances as to bring the case within any exception to the foreign law, which seems to treat the master as having sufficient authority to sell, so as to protect the innocent purchaser where there is no representative of the real owner. It should be remarked also, that Lord Stowell, in the passage, cited in the case of *Freeman v East India Co*, from his judgment in the case of *The Gratitudine*,[3] states that if the master acts unwisely in his decision as to selling still the foreign purchaser will be safe under his acts. The doctrine of Lord Stowell agrees much more with the principles on which our judgment proceeds than with those reported to have been approved of in the case of *The Eliza Cornish*,[4] as, on the evidence before us, we cannot treat Clausen otherwise than as an innocent purchaser, and as the law of Norway appears to us, on the evidence, to give a title to an innocent purchaser, we think that the property vested in him, and in the defendants as sub-purchasers from

2 (1822) 5 B & Ald 617, 1 Dow & Ry KB 234.
3 (1801) 3 Ch Rob 240.
4 (1853) 1 Ecc & Ad 36, 22 LTOS 36.

him, and that, having once so vested, it did not become divested by its being subsequently brought to this country, and, therefore, that the judgment of the Court of Exchequer should be affirmed.

Byles J dissented on the grounds (1) that the law of Norway allowing indiscriminate sales of cargo by the masters of all ships wrecked on the Norwegian coast was so inconvenient and dangerous that effect could not be given to it in England; (2) that he could not concur in the universality of the proposition that a disposition of movable property, effectual by the law of the country where that property might at the time be locally situated, was necessarily binding without exception in any country to which it might afterwards come.

Judgment affirmed.

NOTE

This case was followed in *Winkworth v Christie, Manson & Woods Ltd*,[5] where works of art were stolen from the plaintiff's house in England, taken to Italy without his knowledge or consent, and sold there to the second defendant, an Italian, who sent them to the first defendants in England to be auctioned. By Italian law the second defendant had a good title. Slade J held that Italian law applied and that the plaintiff could not recover.

A title to goods acquired in accordance with the lex situs will be recognised as valid in England if the goods are removed from the country where they were situated when such title was acquired, until such title is displaced by a new title acquired in accordance with the law of the country to which they are removed.

Century Credit Corp v Richard [1962] OR 815, 34 DLR (2d) 291 (Ontario Court of Appeal)

Moses sold a car to Foldes under a conditional sales contract which reserved the title in Moses until the price was fully paid. At the time of the sale the car was situated and both parties resided in Montreal in the Province of Quebec. On the same day Moses assigned the contract for value to the plaintiff respondent.

Subsequently Foldes, without the knowledge of the respondent, brought the car into Ontario where it was sold in a damaged condition to Hamilton Car Refinishers and resold to the defendant appellant, who bought it without notice of the respondent's title.

The respondent sued the appellant claiming possession of the car and damages for its wrongful detention. Under the law of Quebec, the conditional sales contract was sufficient to reserve the title in the unpaid vendor until payment in full of the purchase price without the necessity for any registration of the contract. If the sale had taken place in Ontario, the vendor's reservation of title would have been invalid as against purchasers from Foldes unless the contract had been registered in Ontario.

The trial judge gave judgment for the plaintiff. The defendant appealed.

5 [1980] Ch 496, [1980] 1 All ER 1121.

The judgment of the court (Laidlaw, MacKay, and Kelly JJA) was
delivered by

Kelly JA: The point at issue in this appeal can be stated as follows: Does a
sale in Ontario to a purchaser in Ontario by a person who has agreed in
Quebec to buy a vehicle from a resident of Quebec under a contract by
which the title and ownership are reserved to the seller and who has
obtained possession of the vehicle with the consent of the seller to him,
transfer title to the purchaser in Ontario notwithstanding that the original
seller's right to the title and ownership would have been enforceable in
Ontario against the original buyer who signed the conditional sales
contract?

In considering the respective rights of the parties the respondent as
assignee of Moses, the original seller, stands in no higher position than its
assignor, and for the purpose of this judgment I will refer to the rights of the
respondent as those of an unpaid seller.

At the outset consideration must be given to the conflicts of law problem
presented by the facts. The applicable principles are stated in Dicey's *Conflict
of Laws*, 7th edn, in Rules 86 and 88. Rule 87 is inapplicable due to the
particular facts of this case.

Rule 86.—(1) A transfer of a tangible movable which is valid and effective
by the proper law of the transfer and by the law of the place where the
movable is at the time of the transfer (lex situs) is valid and effective in
England.

(2) A transfer of a tangible movable which is invalid and ineffective by the
proper law of the transfer and by the lex situs of the movable at the time of
the transfer is invalid or ineffective in England.

Rule 88.—A title to goods acquired or reserved in accordance with Rules
86 or 87 will be recognised as valid in England if the goods are removed out
of the country where they were situated at the time when such title was
acquired, until such title is displaced by a new title acquired in accordance
with the law of the country to which they are removed.

Applying these rules to the present facts the absence of registration in
Ontario is not a circumstance invalidating the contract in Ontario and the
title reserved by the respondent will remain valid in Ontario unless and until
it is superseded by a valid title acquired in accordance with the laws of
Ontario.

If the laws of Ontario were to seek to invalidate the respondent's title by
refusing to recognise that the transaction which took place in Quebec had
the effect of continuing the title in the respondent, this attempt of Ontario
law to invalidate a transaction taking place in Quebec would be bad because
the validity of a Quebec transaction must be decided according to the laws of
Quebec, the lex situs: to the extent that s 12 of the Conditional Sales Act of
Ontario seeks to make subject to that Act a contract made out of Ontario
with respect to goods not then in Ontario but subsequently brought into
Ontario, it is an attempt to legislate with respect to such a transaction, the
effects of which are to be decided according to the law of Quebec and for this
reason offends against the above-quoted Rule 86. However, if the laws of
Ontario provide that a later transaction which takes place wholly within
Ontario has the effect of overriding prior titles, then since Ontario does not
seek to give its laws any extraterritorial effect the laws of Ontario prevail and

the title created under the laws of Ontario displaces the title reserved in the Quebec transaction.

The sale by Foldes to Hamilton Car Refinishers took place in Ontario and its effect must be decided according to Ontario law. The applicable statutory provisions appear to be s 25 (2) of the Sale of Goods Act and s 2 (1) of the Factors Act:

25 (2). Where a person having bought or agreed to buy goods obtains, with the consent of the seller, possession of the goods or the documents of title to the goods, the delivery or transfer by that person, or by a mercantile agent acting for him, of the goods or documents of title, under a sale, pledge or other disposition thereof to a person receiving the same in good faith and without notice of any lien or other right of the original seller in respect of the goods, has the same effect as if the person making the delivery or transfer were a mercantile agent in possession of the goods or documents of title with the consent of the owner.

2 (1). Where a mercantile agent is, with the consent of the owner, in possession of goods or of the documents of title to goods, a sale, pledge or other disposition of the goods made by him when acting in the ordinary course of business of a mercantile agent, is, subject to this Act, as valid as if he were expressly authorised by the owner of the goods to make the disposition, if the person taking under it acts in good faith and has not at the time thereof notice that the person making is has not authority to make it.

The sale by Foldes in Ontario to a purchaser who received the vehicle in good faith and without notice of any lien or other right of the original seller, by reason of s 25 of the Sale of Goods Act, has the same effect as if Foldes in making the delivery and transfer were a mercantile agent in possession of the goods with the consent of the owner. Applying s 2 (1) of the Factors Act, this sale by Foldes is as valid as if it were expressly authorised by the owner and the title acquired by the purchaser by virtue of this sale is absolute. As I have said before the respondent can stand in no higher position than the original seller in Quebec and therefore respondent's title is displaced by the valid sale in Ontario. . . .

Appeal allowed.

CHAPTER 19

Assignment of Intangible Movables

The validity or invalidity of an assignment of a chose in action on the ground of lack of form or lack of capacity is governed by the proper law of the assignment.

Republica de Guatemala v Nunez [1927] 1 KB 669, 96 LJKB 441
(Court of Appeal)

Appeal from a judgment of Greer J.

In 1906 Manuel Estrada Cabrera, the then president of the republic of Guatemala, deposited with Messrs Lazard Bros, bankers of London, a sum of money which with interest amounted by the end of the year 1920 to £21,533. In April 1920 Cabrera was deposed and imprisoned by his political opponents. Subsequently the money so deposited with Lazard Bros was claimed on behalf of the republic of Guatemala. Lazard Bros refused to pay it over, as they had received notice that it was also claimed by one Nunez, an illegitimate son of Cabrera. In October 1921 an action was commenced on behalf of the republic of Guatemala against Lazard Bros to recover the money, whereupon the defendants took out an interpleader summons. They were ordered to pay the money into court, and were dismissed from the action, Nunez being substituted in their place as defendant.

The action then proceeded as between the republic of Guatemala as plaintiffs and Nunez as defendant. The plaintiffs alleged that the money was the money of the republic misappropriated by Cabrera and that Cabrera had transferred it to the republic as public funds by letters dated 12 July and 11 October 1921.

The defendant Nunez claimed the money as the assignee of his father Cabrera. In support of his claim a letter was produced on behalf of the defendant Nunez, dated 24 July 1919, signed by Cabrera, and addressed to Messrs Lazard Bros in New York, in which Cabrera requested them to transfer the balance of his account with their London house to Nunez. This letter Greer J held to be a genuine document signed before July 1921, and intended to operate as an assignment of the funds in question by Cabrera to his son Nunez. On 20 July 1921 the defendant Nunez and his solicitor gave oral notice of this assignment to Messrs Lazard Bros of New York, and on 22 July wrote to Messrs Lazard Bros, London, giving them written notice of the assignment, which notice was received in London on 4 August and acknowledged on that date.

Evidence was given that by Guatemalan law an assignment of money exceeding $100 in amount if without consideration was void, unless made by a written contract before a notary, duly stamped, and unless the assignee signed before the notary to signify his acceptance. These formalities had not been complied with in the present case. Further, by Guatemalan law a minor could not accept a voluntary assignment; it had to be made to and accepted by a tutor or legal representative appointed by a judge to act on his behalf. At the time of the assignment in question Nunez was a minor, and no legal representative had been appointed to act for him.

Greer J held that, the assignment having been executed in Guatemala, its validity must be determined by the law of that country, and by that law it was bad. He therefore dismissed the defendant's claim. He dismissed the plaintiff's claim also on the ground that the two documents on which they relied had been extorted by duress from Cabrera while he was in prison and that apart from those two documents there was no evidence that the money had been wrongfully appropriated by Cabrera.

The defendant appealed. The plaintiffs also appealed, and their appeal was dismissed, but it is not reported.

Scrutton LJ: This appeal raises a question of some difficulty. Freed from the picturesque facts, which do not assist the court to determine the dry question of law, the problem which emerges is this. (His Lordship stated the facts and continued:) It will be seen, therefore, that if Guatemalan law, being both the law of the domicile of both parties and the lex loci actus, is to be applied, the document was a nullity. If English law, as the law of the situs of the debt assigned, or the lex loci solutionis of the contract to pay, is to be followed, the document was effective. It is to be assumed, however, that in any case it is English law which the English courts enforce; the question is whether English law directs them to ascertain the validity of the assignment by the law of Guatemala, or by the law of England applicable to such documents.

On the question of the law applicable to an assignment of personal property invalid by the law of the country where the transaction takes place, or by the lex domicilii of the parties to the transaction, but valid by the law of the country where the property is, or is deemed to be, situate, the English authorities are scanty and unsatisfactory. Channel J in *Dulaney v Merry & Sons*[1] 'had not found any clear case of a transfer, good according to the law of the domicile of the owner, and made there, but held bad for not conforming to the law of the country where the goods are situate'. Mr Dicey has not found any clear case in reference to individual assignments by gift or sale as to the validity of an assignment good by the lex domicilii of the owner, but bad in the country where the goods are situate. Conversely, I have not been able to find, nor could counsel refer me to, any clear statement of the principles governing the question whether a transaction in personal property, as distinct from land, invalid by the law of the country where the transaction takes place, may be valid by the law of the place where the property is situate. Mr Foote[2] points out that in most of the judgments where general statements are made the transaction took place in the country where the property was, and a conflict between the lex loci actus and the lex loci rei sitae was not dealt with.

There seem to me, however, in this case to be two clear matters which help to a conclusion. First, in cases of personal property, the capacity of the

1 [1901] 1 KB 536.
2 *Private International Law* (5th edn) p 293.

parties to a transaction has always been determined either by the lex domicilii or the law of the place of the transaction; and where, as here, the two laws are the same it is not necessary to decide between them. In *Lee v Abdy*[3] an assignment was made in Cape Colony by a man there domiciled to his wife of a policy issued by an English company, and it was assumed for the purposes of the case that such an assignment was invalid by the law of the Colony, husband and wife not being capable of entering into such a transaction. A Divisional Court, composed of Day and Wills JJ held that, on that assumption, the assignment, though valid by the law of England, could not be enforced against the company in England. Neither judge draws a distinction between the lex domicilii or the lex loci actus. The Court of Appeal, in *Sottomayor v De Barros*,[4] a case of marriage, laid down in general terms: 'It is a well-recognised principle of law that the question of personal capacity to enter into any contract is to be decided by the law of domicile'; and Lord Halsbury says, in *Cooper v Cooper*,[5] that 'incapacity to contract by reason of minority . . . is regulated by the law of domicile'. Lord Macnaghten, in the same case, is more doubtful, treating the question as not finally settled, but with a preponderance of opinion in favour of the lex domicilii. 'But', he says, 'when the contract is made in the place where the person whose capacity is in question is domiciled there can be no room for dispute. It is difficult to suppose that Mrs Cooper (the infant) could confer capacity on herself by contemplating a different country as the place where the contract was to be fulfilled.' Lord Watson declines to decide the point, as the two laws are the same. The opinion of the Court of Appeal, in *Sottomayor v De Barros*, in favour of the lex domicilii, was criticised by the same court in *Ogden v Ogden*[6] and by Sir James Hannen in the later *Sottomayor* case.[7] But most of the authorities seem to agree that capacity to contract depends either on the lex domicilii or the lex loci actus, and here they are the same: see also per Lord Eldon in *Male v Roberts*[8] as to infancy. It seems to me, therefore, that Nunez, being a minor incapable by the law of his domicile or the law of the place where the transaction takes place, of receiving a valid donation, so that a gift to him, without the intervention of a next friend judicially appointed to receive it, would be void and a nullity in Guatemala, cannot claim that he has received a good title to the deposit by such an invalid donation.

This view would support the judgment of Greer J, but is not the express ground on which he puts his decision, which is, I think, that a contract void in the place where it is made, by reason of the omission of formalities required by the law of that place, is void elsewhere; the case of void contracts being distinguished from that of contracts merely inadmissible in evidence by reason of the absence of formalities, such as the requirements of stamp laws, not invalidating the contract itself. This seems to me a second point on which the authorities are fairly clear—namely, that where a transaction is invalid or a nullity by the law of the place where the transaction takes place

---

3 (1886) 17 QBD 309, 55 LT 297.
4 (1877) 3 PD 1, 47 LJP 23; p 237 above.
5 (1888) 13 App Cas 88 at 99.
6 [1908] P 46, 77 LJP 34; p 240 at 245 above.
7 (1879) 5 PD 94, 49 LJP 1.
8 (1800) 3 Esp 163.

owing to the omission of formalities or stamp, it will not be recognised in England. In *Bristow v Sequeville*,[9] Rolfe B agrees 'that if for want of a stamp a contract made in a foreign country is void, it cannot be enforced here', distinguishing it from a case where the contract is not void but only not admissible in evidence.... The negotiable instrument cases of *Alcock v Smith*[10] and *Embiricos v Anglo-Austrian Bank*[11] appear to proceed on the same principle. In each case a bill of exchange, accepted and payable in England and therefore representing an English debt, was dealt with in another country; in *Alcock's* case by execution in Norway; in *Embiricos'* case by purchase for valuable consideration in Vienna after theft and forgery of indorsement. In each case the foreign transaction would not have legal effect in England, but in each case it was held that, being valid by the lex loci actus, the English law would give effect to it. I cannot think that the suggested difference between the piece of paper and the chose in action represented by it is satisfactory. I refer to the judgments of Romer J and of Kay LJ in the former case. In the present case the private unstamped donation made in Guatemala from one Guatemalan subject to another was a nullity by the law of Guatemala. I think it was therefore a nullity by the law of England.

Reliance was, however, placed on the opinion of Mr Dicey as stated in rule 153[12] of his work on the *Conflict of Laws*, to which great weight is, of course, added by the opinion of Cozens-Hardy J in *Re Maudslay, Sons and Field*[13] that it is right. It is to be observed, however, firstly, that in this case the question was whether the English courts would give effect to seizure in France of a French debt as against English debenture-holders administering an English company's affairs; that is to say, the lex loci actus and, if debts have a situs, the lex loci rei sitae were the same; and the learned judge's opinion was therefore not necessary for the decision. Secondly, while Cozens-Hardy J thinks the opinion of Mr Dicey right, he also thinks the authorities cited by the author for that opinion do not support it; and Greer J, after consideration, has come to the same conclusion....

We were also referred to *Kelly v Selwyn*,[14] where, in the administration in England of the English estate of an English testator, priority was given to an English assignment, later in date but prior in notice, over an earlier New York assignment for which the law of New York did not require notice. Priorities have been said to be questions for the lex fori (*The Colorado*[15]), and I think this is the ground of the decision. It seems to me, therefore, that the authorities cited by Mr Dicey do not support the proposition that a transaction as to an English debt, void by the law of the country where it takes place and by the law of the domicile of the parties to it, will be treated as valid in the country where the debt is deemed to be situated. In my opinion, both the capacity of the parties to enter into such a transaction and the validity and effect of such a transaction in form and results must be

---

9 (1850) 5 Exch 275 at 279.
10 [1892] 1 Ch 238, 61 LJCh 161.
11 [1905] 1 KB 677, 74 LJKB 326.
12 See now rule 82 in the 10th edn.
13 [1900] 1 Ch 602, 69 LJCh 347.
14 [1905] 2 Ch 117, 74 LJCh 567; p 554 below.
15 [1923] P 102, 92 LJP 100.

determined by one or other of those laws; and in this case they are the same.

For these reasons, I think the judgment of Greer J dismissing the claim of Nunez should be affirmed on the grounds (1) that Nunez, as an infant, was not, by the law of Guatemala, capable of himself receiving a valid donation; and (2) that the transaction, apart from infancy, was void as not carried out in the way required by the law of Guatemala.

The result is that both claims on the fund in court fail. The court has notice that the trustee in bankruptcy of Cabrera claims the fund, and the fund must remain in court till that and any other claim made to the court is disposed of.

Bankes LJ agreed that the assignment to Nunez was invalid, on the ground that Cabrera and Nunez were domiciled in Guatemala.

Lawrence LJ held (1) that the validity of the assignment as regards form was governed by the lex situs (English law); (2) that the validity of the assignment as regards capacity was governed by the law of Guatemala.

Appeal dismissed.

Where there are two or more competing assignments of a chose in action, each valid by its own proper law, questions of priority are determined by the proper law of the original contract.

Kelly v Selwyn [1905] 2 Ch 117, 74 LJCh 567 (Chancery Division)

Under the will of his father A. H. Solomon, who died in March 1888, Arthur Hammond Selwyn was entitled to a protected life interest in the legacy of £20,000, and was also contingently entitled in reversion to certain other legacies bequeathed to various members of the testator's family. The will contained a trust for sale, under which, at the time of the events hereinafter mentioned, all the real estate had been converted, and the whole estate was invested in English trust securities.

By an indenture of 8 June 1891, A. H. Selwyn, being then domiciled in the State of New York, assigned to his wife, an American lady, all his share and interest of what nature or kind soever which he then had or might thereafter have in the estate of his late father A. H. Solomon under or by virtue of his said will or otherwise (except his life interest in the £20,000 legacy), whether in possession, reversion, remainder, or expectancy, for her sole and separate use absolutely. According to the law of the State of New York, notice to the trustees of the will was not necessary to complete an assignment of a chose in action or reversionary interest in personalty, and no notice of the deed of 8 June 1891 was sent to the English trustees.

By an indenture of 10 August 1894, A. H. Selwyn, being then in England, assigned all his share and interest in the estate of his late father, whether under his said will or otherwise, or whether in remainder, reversion, or expectancy (except his life interest in the £20,000 legacy), to the plaintiff Thomas Kelly by way of mortgage to secure £400 and interest. Notice of this assignment was forthwith given by the plaintiff to the trustees of A. H. Solomon's will.

In September 1903 notice of the assignment of 8 June 1891 was given to the trustees of the will on behalf of Mrs Selwyn.

A reversionary interest in A. H. Solomon's estate having recently fallen in, a portion of which would have been payable to A. H. Selwyn or persons claiming under him, the plaintiff commenced the present action against the trustees of the will and Mrs Selwyn, claiming a declaration that he was entitled by virtue of his security of 10 August 1894 to a first charge on A. H. Selwyn's interest in his father's estate in priority to any right or claim of Mrs Selwyn under the assignment in her favour of 8 June 1891.

Warrington J: The important question in this case has resolved itself into one of law upon which there does not seem to be any direct authority, though the case, I think, comes within certain well-known principles. [Having stated the facts, his Lordship continued:]

Under these circumstances the question I have to determine is which of these two assignments is to have priority. But for one circumstance, which I will mention directly, there can be no doubt, in the case of an English trust fund created by an English testator with trustees in England, that by the law of England, if that is the proper law to apply to this case, the mortgagee who first gave to the trustees notice of his security would take priority over the secret assignment (as I may call it) in favour of the wife, who did not give notice of it till later. But it is said on behalf of the wife (and this is the circumstance I referred to just now) that owing to the accident of the assignment in favour of the wife having been executed in the State of New York, where the English doctrines of notice are not recognised or are not in force, the law which I ought to regard myself as administering is not the law of England, but the law of New York, at any rate as far as that assignment is concerned.

A number of cases have been cited to me, none of which are actually in point; in fact, I do not think they were at all in point on the actual question which I have to determine. The first case, Re Queensland Mercantile and Agency Co,[16] merely decided that where there is a chose in action owing from persons residing in a particular country (in that case in Scotland), an assignment in that case by process of law of those choses in action, valid according to the law of Scotland, would be valid elsewhere. I do not think that case decided anything more. If it is of any value in assisting me in the present case (I do not think it is) it is rather in favour of the defendant Mrs Selwyn than in favour of the plaintiff; but I do not think that is the point which I have to decide. The assignment in New York is valid, but what I have to determine in administering an English trust fund, constituted by an English testator who may be taken to have made his will with the English law in his mind, is, in what order am I to treat the several claimants who come here with charges on the trust fund? The doctrine of notice, as I understand it, is that till notice is given, the assignee of a share in a trust fund is not completely constituted a cestui que trust, and that the order in which the fund is to be administered is the order in which the several claimants claiming to be assignees completely constituted themselves cestuis que trust. That is the point which I have to determine.

Another case that was cited and a good deal relied on is Lee v Abdy,[17] which seems to me like Re Queensland Mercantile and Agency Co, and merely

16 [1891] 1 Ch 536, 60 LJCh 579, [1892] 1 Ch 219, 61 LJCh 145.
17 (1886) 17 QBD 309, 55 LT 297.

decided this: that if a question arises whether an assignment of a chose in action is valid according to the law where it is executed, that question will be determined by the law of the place where it is executed. The question in *Lee v Abdy* was whether an assignment made by a husband to his wife, which according to the law of Cape Colony was for that reason void, was to be treated as a good assignment of an English policy of assurance.

I have listened to the citations from Foote, Dicey, and Westlake, but I do not think there is anything in those passages that actually guides me in what I have to decide in this case. The ground on which I decide it is that, the fund here being an English trust fund and this being the court which the testator may have contemplated as the court which would have administered that trust fund, the order in which the parties are to be held entitled to the trust fund must be regulated by the law of the court which is administering that fund. On that footing it seems to me that the assignment to the plaintiff of August 1894 is entitled to priority over the assignment to Mrs Selwyn of June 1891 by reason of the notice given by the plaintiff to the trustees of the will, and I must make a declaration to that effect.

QUESTION

What is the ratio of this case? Was English law applied as the lex fori, the lex situs of the debt, the proper law of the debt, or as the proper law of the second assignment?

EEC Convention on the Law Applicable to Contractual Obligations

ARTICLE 12

Voluntary assignment

1. The mutual obligations of assignor and assignee under a voluntary assignment of a right against another person ('the debtor') shall be governed by the law which under this Convention applies to the contract between the assignor and assignee.

2. The law governing the right to which the assignment relates shall determine its assignability, the relationship between the assignee and the debtor, the conditions under which the assignment can be invoked against the debtor and any question whether the debtor's obligations have been discharged.

CHAPTER 20

Governmental Seizure of Property

English courts will recognise a foreign decree affecting property situated within the territory of the foreign country at the time of the decree, even if the property is later brought to England.

Princess Paley Olga v Weisz [1929] 1 KB 718, 98 LJKB 465 (Court of Appeal)

Appeal from MacKinnon J.

The plaintiff, Princess Paley Olga, was a Russian who was married to the Grand Duke Paul of Russia without the consent of the Tsar. The marriage was therefore morganatic and she did not become a member of the Romanoff family. In 1917 the Princess owned valuable pictures which she kept in her palace at Tsarskoe Selo, near St Petersburg, now Leningrad. In 1918 a mob of revolutionaries, whose act was subsequently adopted by the Soviet government, took forcible possession of the palace and its contents while the Princess was in residence there. In 1919 she escaped to England without a passport. Meanwhile the palace was maintained by the Soviet government as a state museum. In 1921 a Soviet decree confiscated the property of all Russian citizens who fled from Russia. In 1923 another Soviet decree confiscated all works of art in state museums. The Soviet government was recognised by the British government as the de facto government of Russia as from the end of 1917, and as the de jure government in 1924. In 1928 the Soviet government sold some of the pictures to the defendants who brought them to England, where they were claimed by the plaintiff as her property.

MacKinnon J dismissed her claim.

Scrutton LJ (having stated the facts, and stated that the defendants alleged that by Russian law the goods claimed were the property of the Russian government): They did so for two reasons which the judge below has held to be valid. The first is by the Decree of 18 March 1923 (No 245), of the All-Russian Central Executive Committee and of the Council of People's Commissaries, s 5 of which is relevant: 'Works of art, antiques, and articles of historical interest being in museums and depositories, as forming part of the Museum Fund and being safeguarded by state means, are recognised to be state property.' I am quite satisfied on the evidence that from 1918 to the date of sale in Russia, the goods in question in this action were in a state museum in Russia, safeguarded at the expense of the state, having been in 1918 taken by force from the possession of Princess Paley by persons whose acts were adopted by the Russian government. I agree with and adopt the finding of MacKinnon J when he said: 'I am driven to the conclusion that it is shown that this Paley Palace was a museum which was being safeguarded by state means from funds provided by the Commissariat of Education, and that these articles, which had been put into an inventory, did form part of the Museum Fund.' Being the property of the Russian state, the Russian government has sold them; and I can find nothing in the Russian Decrees enabling their former owner to complain in these or any courts of the sale by the Russian government.

The second title in the Russian government alleged by the defendants is under s 1 of Decree No 111 of the Council of People's Commissaries, signed by Lenin as chairman of that body. That section reads: There is declared 'the property of the Russian Soviet Federal Socialist Republic all the moveable property of citizens fled outside the confines of the Republic, or hiding themselves up to the present time, and of whatever consisting, and wherever situated'. It is clear on the evidence, and is admitted by the Princess, that she escaped from Russia without a passport; and I am satisfied that this is 'fleeing from Russia' within the meaning of the Decree, and that thereby her property in Russia became automatically confiscated and the property of the Russian state without any necessity of further legal proceedings. On the ground of this Decree also I agree with MacKinnon J that the plaintiff fails.

There is, however, a third defence which he rejected, which I think should also succeed. Counsel for the defendants put in the front of his argument below and before us that if the seizure of this property began without legal justification, or only by revolutionary right, it was ultimately adopted by a government, which was recognised by the British government as the lawful government of the territory in which the property was, and that this was an act of state into the validity of which this court would not inquire.

Incidentally, he referred to the Decrees of May 1922 and sub-s or Note 1 to the Civil Code of 1923, by which, when by a change of policy the Russian government recognised to some extent private, as opposed to state, property, they yet prevented the original owner from asserting his original right against those who had by force or revolutionary right dispossessed him. The sub-section reads as follows: 'Note 1. Former owners whose property was expropriated in virtue of the revolutionary right or generally passed into the possession of the labouring classes or toilers before 22 May 1922 have no right to claim the return of such property.' The learned judge dealt with this rather summarily. He said it was a bad point, and not seriously relied on. As it was based on three decisions of the Supreme Court of the United States, followed by this court in *Luther v Sagor & Co*,[1] I regret that the learned judge did not indicate more precisely why it was a bad point. I think it was a good one. It may be that the learned judge was so satisfied that the Russian government had lawfully acquired the property that he thought it waste of time to consider what would happen if they claimed not by law but by title of force. The United States, situate in the neighbourhood of South and Central American Republics, where the life of any government is precarious and its death rarely by natural causes, frequently found in its territory property seized by a revolutionary force which ultimately succeeded in establishing itself in power and there sold the goods it had seized to persons

1 [1921] 3 KB 532, 90 LJKB 1202.

who exported them to the United States, where they were claimed by their original owners. In *Oetjen v Central Leather Co*[2] these facts occurred with reference to a seizure in Mexico of property of a Mexican citizen which when sold came into the United States, and in *Ricaud v American Metal Co*[3] they occurred again with respect to the property of a citizen of the United States. In each case the Supreme Court acted on the principle stated thus in *Oetjen's* case: 'It is also the result of the interpretation by this court of the principles of international law that when a government which originates in revolution or revolt is recognised by the political department of our government as the de jure government of the country in which it is established, such recognition is retroactive in effect and validates all the actions and conduct of the government so recognised from the commencement of its existence .... To these principles we must add that: "Every sovereign state is bound to respect the independence of every other sovereign state, and the courts of one country will not sit in judgment on the acts of another done within its own territory. Redress of grievances by reason of such acts must be obtained through the means open to be availed of by sovereign powers as between themselves." ' Two further authorities of the Supreme Court of the United States are cited in support of that proposition. This court acted on the principles laid down in the above cases in *Luther v Sagor*. For this reason also in my opinion the claim of the plaintiff fails.

I do not go more minutely into the Decrees and evidence in this case, as, except in the matter I have mentioned, I substantially agree with the careful judgment of MacKinnon J. Our government has recognised the present Russian government as the de jure government of Russia, and our courts are bound to give effect to the laws and acts of that government so far as they relate to property within that jurisdiction when it was affected by those laws and acts. The appeal must be dismissed with costs, with an order that the sum paid into court as security for costs be applied, after taxation, in satisfaction of the defendants' taxed costs.

Sankey and Russell LJJ delivered judgments to the same effect.
Appeal dismissed.

It is immaterial that the property belongs to persons who are not nationals of the foreign state and that no compensation is payable, unless the decree is penal (ie discriminatory).

Re Helbert Wagg & Co Ltd's Claim [1956] Ch 323, [1956] 1 All ER 129 (Chancery Division)

By a loan agreement made in 1924 between a German company ('the company') and Helbert Wagg & Co Ltd ('the claimant'), the claimant agreed to lend the company £350,000 at $7\frac{1}{2}\%$ interest. The loan was redeemable in 1945. The proper law of the contract was German. In June 1933 a German moratorium law provided that a Konversionskasse for foreign debts should be created, that debts payable in foreign currencies must be

2 246 US 297.
3 246 US 304.

converted into Reichsmarks and paid into the Konversionkasse, and that the debtor's liability should thereby be discharged. The company duly paid Reichsmarks into the Konversionkasse at the appropriate rate of exchange, and continued to do so after the outbreak of war in 1939. By 1945 the company had paid the full equivalent in Reichsmarks of the whole loan outstanding and interest thereon. On 3 September 1939 there was outstanding under the loan agreement £174,142 in respect of capital, and the claimant claimed, under the Distribution of German Enemy Property Act 1949, to rank as creditor in respect of that amount and interest thereon. The Administrator of German Property rejected the claim. The claimant appealed to the High Court.

Upjohn J: The first question that I must determine is whether the applicability of the Moratorium Law is to be tested by reference to the local situation of the debt or by the proper law of the contract. I am concerned with the effect of a law passed in 1933 upon a series of debts which, though accrued, only became payable on or after 3 September 1939. In my judgment, the question whether a liability to pay a debt payable on a future date has become modified or annulled by legislation must depend upon the question whether such legislation affects the contractual obligation, for the matter still rests in contract. Indeed, it does not seem appropriate to speak of a debt having a local situation until it is payable and can be recovered by suit, for its situs primarily depends upon the residence of the debtor when it is recoverable . . . . The power of legislation to affect a contract by modifying or annulling some term thereof is a question of discharge of the contract which, in general, is governed by the proper law (see *Kahler v Midland Bank Ltd*[4]).

(After holding that the proper law of the contract was German, his Lordship continued:) For the reasons I have already given, I do not think that the situs of the debt is the relevant consideration, but as the matter has been very fully argued before me. . .I think I ought to express my views thereon. (After holding that the situs of the debt was in Germany, his Lordship continued:) I start with the elementary proposition that it is part of the law of England, and of most nations, that in general every civilised state must be recognised as having power to legislate in respect of movables situate within that state and in respect of contracts governed by the law of that state, and that such legislation must be recognised by other states as valid and effectual to alter title to such movables and to sustain, modify or dissolve such contracts. The substantial question I have to determine is what limit is to be imposed upon that proposition when the effect of such legislation comes to be debated in the courts of other states. I may note in passing that the modern tendency is to deny extraterritorial validity to legislation, for example, upon movables situate outside the state at the time of the legislation: *Bank voor Handel en Scheepvart NV v Slatford*.[5]

To this general principle of recognition in foreign courts of territorial validity of legislation there are undoubted limitations or exceptions as the following examples show: (1) No state will enforce the fiscal laws, however proper, of another state, nor penal statutes, using that phrase in the strict

---

4 [1950] AC 24, [1949] 2 All ER 621.
5 [1953] 1 QB 248, [1951] 2 All ER 779; p 562 below.

sense of meaning statutes imposing penalties recoverable by the state for infringement of some law. 'The penal laws of foreign countries are strictly local and affect nothing more than they can reach and seize by virtue of their authority', per Lord Loughborough in *Folliott v Ogden*.[6] (2) English law will not recognise the validity of foreign legislation intended to discriminate against nationals of this country in time of war by legislation which purports to confiscate wholly or in part movable property situated in the foreign state. As long ago as 1817 such confiscation was described by Lord Ellenborough CJ in *Wolff v Oxholm*[7] as 'not conformable to the usage of nations' . . . . (3) English courts will not recognise the validity of foreign legislation aimed at confiscating the property of particular individuals or classes of individuals: *Banco de Vizcaya v Don Alfonso de Borbon y Austria*[8] which treated the Spanish laws purporting to expropriate the ex-King of Spain's property as examples of penal legislation; and see *Anglo-Iranian Oil Co v Jaffrate (The Rose Mary)*[9] where Campbell J, sitting in the Supreme Court of Aden, held certain laws of the State of Persia which he found to be passed to nationalise the plaintiff company only without compensation were confiscatory and ineffectual to pass title . . . .

I do not challenge the correctness of the decision in the *Rose Mary* case upon the facts of that case, but Campbell J came to the conclusion that the authorities both of this and other countries justified the formulation of a more general principle, namely: (1) all legislation that expropriates without compensation is contrary to international law; and (2) that such law is incorporated in the domestic law of Aden and accordingly such legislation will not be recognised as valid in the courts of Aden. Unless the law of England takes a different view of international law from the law of Aden, the judge's conclusions can only be correct if his interpretation of *Luther v Sagor*[10] and *Princess Paley Olga v Weisz*[11] is correct. Those cases, both in the Court of Appeal, were concerned with the effect of Russian legislation introduced shortly after the Russian Revolution of 1917 which in fact expropriated certain types of private property situate in Russia without any compensation. They established the principle that this court will not inquire into the legality of acts done by a foreign government in respect of property situate in its own territory. Campbell J considered that principle to be valid only where the property confiscated belongs (as in both those cases) to subjects of the confiscating state. However, all three judgments in *Luther v Sagor* laid down the principle in perfectly general terms and it was in no way limited, at any rate in express terms, to a recognition of the validity of such legislation in relation only to nationals of the confiscating state . . . .

In equally general terms were the judgments of two members of the court in *Princess Paley Olga v Weisz*. It seems clear that Scrutton LJ drew no distinction between the operation of legislation upon the property of a national of the confiscating state and a foreigner who had movables in that state . . . . It is true that Russell LJ, in that case, said: 'This court will not inquire into the legality of acts done by a foreign government against its own

6 (1789) 1 Hy Bl 123 at 135.
7 (1817) 6 M & S 92.
8 [1935] 1 KB 140, 104 LJKB 46.
9 [1953] 1 WLR 246.
10 [1921] 3 KB 532, 90 LJKB 1202.
11 [1929] 1 KB 718, 98 LJKB 465; p 557 above.

subjects in respect of property situate in its own territory', but it was sufficient for the decision of the case before him, and he dealt with the point very briefly.

Maugham J in *Re Russian Bank for Foreign Trade*,[12] also stated the principle in the same limited way but his remarks were obiter.

On the other hand, in *Perry v Equitable Life Assurance Society of the United States of America*,[13] the plaintiff, a British subject residing in Russia, took out a policy of life assurance with the defendants, the proper law of the contract being Russian. It was held that certain confiscatory decrees of the Russian government were effective to annul the contract, though it is true that no point was taken that such decrees could be valid only against Russian nationals. This case was quoted without disapproval by Lord Radcliffe in *Kahler v Midland Bank*.[14]

In *Re Banque des Marchands de Moscou (Koupetschesky), Royal Exchange Assurance v The Liquidator*[15] (which does not appear to have been cited to Campbell J), Vaisey J expressed the view that the general principle was not limited to nationals of the confiscating state. I respectfully agree with him, for it seems to me that on this question nationality must be irrelevant. If the principle be true in respect of a state in relation to its own nationals, it must surely be conceded in relation to those persons who, though not subjects of the state, nevertheless bring their movables within its jurisdiction for business or private reasons or for the like reasons enter into contracts governed by the law of the state, and in general enjoy the same benefits and protection and are subject to the same disadvantages and disabilities as subjects of the state.

With all respect to Campbell J I think that *Luther v Sagor* and *Princess Paley Olga v Weisz* laid down principles of general application not limited to nationals of the confiscating state.

In my judgment the true limits of the principle that the courts of this country will afford recognition to legislation of foreign states in so far as it affects title to movables in that state at the time of the legislation or contracts governed by the law of that state rest in considerations of international law, or in the scarcely less difficult considerations of public policy as understood by these courts. Ultimately I believe the latter is the governing consideration. But, whatever be the true view, the authorities I have reviewed do show that these courts have not on either ground recognised any principle that confiscation without adequate compensation is per se a ground for refusing recognition to foreign legislation. That view is further supported by the authorities on exchange control legislation which I must now consider . . . .

Appeal dismissed.

But English courts will not recognise a foreign decree purporting to affect property situated outside the territory of the foreign state.

Bank voor Handel en Scheepvart N V v Slatford [1953] 1 QB 248, [1951] 2 All ER 779 (Queen's Bench Division)

12 [1933] Ch 745, 102 LJ Ch 309.
13 (1929) 45 TLR 468.
14 [1950] AC 24 at 56, [1949] 2 All ER 621 at 641–642.
15 [1952] 1 All ER 1269, [1952] 1 TLR 739.

Before the war of 1939–45 the plaintiff, a Dutch bank, in the ordinary course of business deposited gold bars to the value of two million pounds with the City Safe Deposit in London. In May 1940 the Netherlands were invaded and became enemy territory. The plaintiff bank retained its commercial domicile in the Netherlands, and thus at once acquired enemy character on that ground. The Royal Netherlands government thereafter, with the approval of the British government, exercised their sovereign powers from London. On 24 May 1940 they issued a decree (called the A. 1 decree), with the object of preventing property belonging to persons resident in occupied Holland from being used in a manner incompatible with the interests of the Netherlands. This decree purported to transfer such property (including the gold bars) to the state for so long as might be necessary. On 3 July 1940 the Board of Trade, under the Trading with the Enemy Act 1939, made a vesting order transferring the gold to the custodian. On 24 July the custodian sold the gold and retained the proceeds as enemy property. On 19 May 1950 the Netherlands government made an order returning the property in the gold to the bank. The bank claimed against the custodian in conversion the present value of the gold bars, on the ground that the order of July 1940 was invalid since the property in the gold was then in the Netherlands Government by virtue of the A. 1 decree.

Devlin J: The custodian submits that the English courts will not enforce it [the A. 1 decree] since they will treat it as having no extraterritorial effect. The plaintiff's submission is that the general rule is to the contrary, and that the legislation of a foreign state affecting the title of its nationals to movables in England will be applied by the English courts unless, first, the legislation is contrary to public policy—as, for instance, confiscatory or penal legislation—or, secondly, its application would infringe English legislation. Alternatively, the plaintiffs submit that, if it be the general rule that foreign legislation is not enforceable, then the decree falls within an exceptional category.

I think it is convenient to begin by considering what is the general principle of our law with regard to foreign legislation affecting property within our territory. There is little doubt that it is the lex situs which as a general rule governs the transfer of movables when effected contractually. The maxim mobilia sequuntur personam is the exception rather than the rule, and is probably to be confined to certain special classes of general assignments such as marriage settlements and devolutions on death and bankruptcy. Upon this basis the A. 1 decree, not being a part of English law, would not transfer the property in this case. But decrees of this character have received in the authorities rather different treatment. Although there is not, as far as I am aware, any authority which distinguishes general legislation, such as part of a civil code, from ad hoc decrees, the effectiveness of such decrees does not appear on the authorities to be determined exclusively by the application of the lex situs. Apart from two recent cases on which the plaintiffs greatly rely, there has been no case in which such a decree has been enforced in this country, but the grounds for refusing effect to them have been variously put. Sometimes it is said that the decree is confiscatory. In the textbooks it is said sometimes that as a matter of public international law no state ought to seek to exercise sovereignty over property outside its own territory, and therefore the principle of comity is against enforcement; and sometimes it is said that the principle of effectiveness is against enforcement, since no state can expect to make its laws effective in the territory of another State. Dicey[16] states: 'A state's authority, in the eyes of other states and the courts that represent them, is, speaking very generally, coincident with, and limited by, its power. It is territorial. It may legislate for, and give judgments affecting, things and persons within its territory. It has no authority to legislate for, or adjudicate upon, things or persons not within its territory.'

The Solicitor-General has argued on principle that no foreign legislation, whether confiscatory or not, can be allowed to affect property in this country. It is beyond dispute that confiscatory legislation will not be allowed to do so, and the Solicitor-General contends that the distinction between confiscatory and non-confiscatory is not a satisfactory one. In *A/S Tallinna Laevauhisus v Estonian State SS Line*,[17] legislation which provided for compensation amounting to 25% of the value was held to be confiscatory. Presumably any decree which did not provide for full compensation would be held to be confiscatory. Now that decrees involving state acquisition and requisition are comparatively common, it may not be easy to ascertain whether full compensation is provided for or not. The Compensation (Defence) Act 1939 places certain limits on the amount of compensation: for example, no account is to be taken of any appreciation in value due to the war. While that is doubtless a healthy rule for British nationals, it might well result in a neutral getting less than the full value of his goods. If a decree, such as the A. 1 decree, contemplates that the property taken is to be preserved for the benefit of its owners and to be returned to them at the conclusion of the war, but contains no legal obligation to that effect, is the hope and expectation that the subject will get his property returned to him sufficient to save it from being confiscatory?

There are other considerations of principle which can be advanced in support of the defendants' argument. First, in the construction of our own statutory legislation we accept the principle that, unless the contrary is made clear, an Act of Parliament is not intended to have extraterritorial effect. Secondly, the principle as submitted by the defendants is in harmony with the principle which favours the lex situs generally. Thirdly, if extraterritorial effect is given to foreign property legislation, it can only be at the expense of English law affecting the same subject-matter . . . .

There are three comparatively recent authorities in point. In *Lorentzen v Lydden & Co Ltd*,[18] Atkinson J decided that a decree of the Royal Norwegian government acquiring, in return for compensation, property of its subjects in England was effective to transfer such property to the Norwegian government. In *O/Y Wasa SS Co Ltd v Newspaper Pulp and Wood Export Ltd*,[19] Morris J followed this decision and applied it to the decree A. 1 which I have to consider in this case. In both these cases the property concerned was a claim for damages for breach of a charterparty. The latter case involved a great number of points, and I am told by counsel concerned in this case that the principle in *Lorentzen v Lydden & Co Ltd* was not much debated. The main authority on which the plaintiffs rely is therefore

16 *Conflict of Laws* (6th edn, 1949) p 13.
17 (1946) 80 Ll L Rep 99.
18 [1942] 2 KB 202, 111 LJKB 327.
19 (1949) 82 Ll L Rep 936.

Lorentzen v Lydden & Co Ltd. I think that that case is directly in point; I am unable to distinguish it upon the ground suggested—namely, that the point that the decree was in conflict with the Trading with the Enemy legislation was not expressly taken in argument. The defendants rely mainly on *Government of the Republic of Spain v National Bank of Scotland (The El Condado)*,[20] a decision of the Inner House of the Court of Session and therefore of high persuasive authority. The court was considering a claim by the Spanish consul to the possession of a Spanish ship which he had sought to requisition while she was at Glasgow in accordance with powers granted by a Spanish decree. It does not appear from those parts of the decree set out in the report whether it provided for compensation or not, but it is clear that it was not treated by the court as confiscatory. The Scottish court refused to enforce the decree. The plaintiffs are unable to distinguish this case from *Lorentzen v Lydden & Co Ltd* or from the present case except by saying that different considerations of public policy are involved.

In *Lorentzen v Lydden & Co Ltd* Atkinson J surveyed the earlier authorities in order to arrive at his conclusion that there was no general rule preventing him from enforcing the Norwegian decree. I do not find it entirely clear whether he held that all foreign property legislation was enforceable unless contrary to public policy, or that the general rule excluded all such legislation, subject to certain exceptional categories, within one of which the Norwegian decree fell. I shall examine the cases to see if any general rule can be extracted from them.

(After considering *Lecouturier v Rey*,[1] *Sedgwick Collins & Co v Rossia Insurance Co of Petrograd.*,[2] *The Jupiter (No 3)*,[3] and *Re Russian Bank for Foreign Trade*,[4] his Lordship continued:) While it is true that in all these cases there was confiscatory legislation, I think it would be surprising if, with so many masters of the law all intending to restrict the statement of the principle to confiscatory legislation, no one of them had used in his statement of the principle some words of limitation. This consideration disposes me to think that the view of these dicta taken by the Court of Session in *The El Condado* is the right one. The Lord Justice Clerk, having stated that the principle clearly applies to confiscatory or penal laws, inquires whether it equally applies to legislation which is not confiscatory or penal in the full sense. He treats *The Jupiter (No. 3)* as being an authority in point, and concludes that the decree cannot apply to movable property outwith the territory and jurisdiction of the foreign sovereign state. Lord Mackay says that he finds in the cases 'a most emphatic train of eminent English judges in favour of the view that such "decrees" of a foreign country as purport to have extraterritorial effect, and to attach property in a subject situated, and at a time when it is situated, in this country or its territorial waters, will not be recognised by our laws and courts'. Lord Wark reviews all the English authorities and concludes by adopting the passage in *Dicey* which I have cited.

My recollection of the argument in *Lorentzen v Lydden & Co Ltd* is that Atkinson J was referred to *The El Condado*; but he does not distinguish it in

20 1939 SC 413, 1939 SLT 317.
 1 [1910] AC 262 at 265, 273.
 2 [1926] 1 KB 1 at 15.
 3 [1927] P 122 at 145.
 4 [1933] Ch 745 at 767.

his judgment. I recognise the force of the point that, if the principle were as wide as the custodian says it is, there would be no need for any case to have been decided on the basis that the legislation was confiscatory. But the dicta in the English cases seem to me to be sufficient to support the conclusion in *The El Condado*; and for the reasons that I have given I think that the rule there laid down is a sound one. If Atkinson J is to be taken as deciding that the general rule was otherwise, I respectfully prefer the decision in *The El Condado*.

The question next arises whether the A. 1 decree belongs to a special category which should form an exception to this general rule. The real ground stated by Atkinson J in *Lorentzen v Lydden & Co Ltd* for regarding the Norwegian decree as exceptional is that, England and Norway being engaged together in a desperate war for their existence, public policy required that effect should be given to the decree. This reasoning at once gives rise to three comments. The first is that it amounts to the formulation of a new head of public policy, and that is not a matter to be lightly undertaken. The second is that it is using public policy, not in accordance with precedent, as a restriction upon acts which are thought to be harmful to the community, but in a novel way as a positive force to give to an act validity which it would otherwise lack. The third is that it would appear to cast on the court the duty of considering to some extent the political merits of the decree itself.

The plaintiffs in their argument before me accept that it is not possible for the courts to judge of the expediency of any particular decree; and I think that they admit also that it would be beyond the wit of man to devise a principle which would admit the politically desirable decrees and exclude the undesirable. They therefore put their submission on this point in a form which seeks a middle way between these two extremities. They submit that the exceptional category consists of decrees of an allied Power in respect of the property of its nationals made in this country with the approval, or at least with the acquiescence, of His Majesty's Government with a view to keeping property out of the hands of a common enemy.... No doubt one could formulate a broad rule of policy that allied governments should be assisted in time of war. But the extent to which a particular decree serves that end seems to me to be entirely a matter for political decision by the government of the day, which would have to consider whether all its provisions or some or none of them fitted in with their war policy. A power at war is not bound to regard everything that its allies do as politically desirable....

In my judgment it would be unwise, in the light of these considerations and of the authorities, to propound as a new rule of public policy the principle for which the plaintiffs contend. I need hardly say that it is only after much thought that I have rejected the guidance given by the decision of Atkinson J in *Lorentzen v Lydden & Co Ltd*; and I have done so only because upon reflection I think that it cannot be made to conform with the authorities which regulate the use of public policy. In this respect I may say that I have had from the Solicitor-General the benefit of a much fuller and more able presentation of the relevant considerations than Atkinson J had in the unsuccessful argument before him.[5]

5 This argument was presented by Mr Devlin as he then was (*Ed*).

I have been dealing with public policy as a force which has to be invoked by the plaintiffs in order to succeed. Many of these considerations would also apply on the first part of the argument. If foreign legislation is as a general rule to be admitted, it would have to be excluded when politically harmful; and the difficulty of formulating any satisfactory principle of exclusion is in my view a formidable argument against the validity of the rule.

In my judgment the claim against the custodian fails.

Action dismissed.

A-G of New Zealand v Ortiz (p 41 above)

CHAPTER 21

Administration of Estates

Non-contentious Probate Rules 1954

29.[1] Where the deceased died domiciled outside England, a registrar may order that a grant do issue—
(a) to the person entrusted with the administration of the estate by the court having jurisdiction at the place where the deceased died domiciled,
(b) to the person entitled to administer the estate by the law of the place where the deceased died domiciled,
(c) if there is no such person as is mentioned in paragraph (a) or (b) of this rule or if in the opinion of the registrar the circumstances so require, to such person as the registrar may direct,
(d) if a grant is required to be made to, or if the registrar in his discretion considers that a grant should be made to, not less than two administrators, to such person as the registrar may direct jointly with any such person as is mentioned in paragraph (a) or (b) of this rule or with any other person:
Provided that without any such order as aforesaid—
(a) probate of any will which is admissible to proof may be granted—
   (i) if the will is in the English or Welsh language, to the executor named therein;
   (ii) if the will describes the duties of a named person in terms sufficient to constitute him executor according to the tenor of the will, to that person;
(b) where the whole of the estate in England consists of immovable property, a grant limited thereto may be made in accordance with the law which would have been applicable if the deceased had died domiciled in England.

Supreme Court Act 1981

114.—(1) Probate or administration shall not be granted by the High Court to more than four persons in respect of the same part of the estate of a deceased person.

(2) Where under a will or intestacy any beneficiary is a minor or a life interest arises, any grant of administration by the High Court shall be made either to a trust corporation (with or without an individual) or to not less than two individuals, unless it appears to the court to be expedient in all the circumstances to appoint an individual as sole administrator.

---

1 This rule is printed as amended by the Non-contentious Probate (Amendment) Rules 1967 and 1982 (*Ed*).

Administration of Estates Act 1971

1.—(1) Where a person dies domiciled in Scotland—

(a) a confirmation granted in respect of all or part of his estate and noting his Scottish domicile, and

(b) a certificate of confirmation noting his Scottish domicile and relating to one or more items of his estate,

shall, without being resealed, be treated for the purposes of the law of England and Wales as a grant of representation (in accordance with subsection (2) below) to the executors named in the confirmation or certificate in respect of the property of the deceased of which according to the terms of the confirmation they are executors or, as the case may be, in respect of the item or items of property specified in the certificate of confirmation.

(2) Where by virtue of subsection (1) above a confirmation or certificate of confirmation is treated for the purposes of the law of England and Wales as a grant of representation to the executors named therein then, subject to subsections (3) and (5) below, the grant shall be treated—

(a) as a grant of probate where it appears from the confirmation or certificate that the executors so named are executors nominate; and

(b) in any other case, as a grant of letters of administration.

(4) Subject to subsection (5) below, where a person dies domiciled in Northern Ireland a grant of probate of his will or letters of administration in respect of his estate (or any part of it) made by the High Court in Northern Ireland and noting his domicile there shall, without being resealed, be treated for the purposes of the law of England and Wales as if it had been originally made by the High Court in England and Wales.

Colonial Probates Act 1892

1. Her Majesty the Queen may, on being satisfied that the legislature of any British possession has made adequate provision for the recognition in that possession of probates and letters of administration granted by the courts of the United Kingdom, direct by Order in Council that this Act shall, subject to any exceptions and modifications specified in the Order, apply to that possession, and thereupon, while the Order is in force, this Act shall apply accordingly.

2.—(1) Where a court of probate in a British possession to which this Act applies has granted probate or letters of administration in respect of the estate of a deceased person. . .the probate or letters so granted may, on being produced to, and a copy thereof deposited with, a court of probate in the United Kingdom, be sealed with the seal of that court, and, thereupon, shall be of the like force and effect, and have the same operation in the United Kingdom, as if granted by that court.

In the administration of the English estate of a deceased person who died domiciled abroad, foreign creditors are entitled to dividends pari passu with English creditors.

Re Klœbe (1884) 28 Ch D 175, 54 LJ Ch 297 (Chancery Division)

This was an action for the administration of the estate in England of Charles Jules Alexander Klœbe, a domiciled Greek, who died at Syra on 15 February 1882, intestate and insolvent. The deceased carried on business in England in partnership under the style of Charles Klœbe & Co, and was possessed of property in England. It did not appear whether there were any foreign assets. The Chief Clerk had certified that the assets consisted of a sum of £1,710. 19s 2d, the balance of the administrator's account in court, and a sum of £1,837. 11s 9d. Consols also in court. That there was one separate debt of £50. 7s due to a foreign creditor, and that the partnership debts amounted to £3,432. 4s 7d due to English creditors, and £8,456. 18s 3d due to foreign creditors. The action now came on on further consideration.

Pearson J: At the end of the argument I stated I had no doubt what my decision should be, but in consequence of my being told that there were decisions of learned judges to whom I am bound to pay, and do pay, the greatest respect, who had supported a contrary contention, I thought it better to look at those judgments to see if they really supported that contention, and I am glad to find that they do not. It appeared to me, if that contention had anything in it, it must have been the practice of the court to inquire in actions for the administration of deceased persons domiciled abroad as to the nationality of creditors, and I can find no case in which the court in distributing assets has made an inquiry as to the nationality of different creditors, or ordered that English creditors should be paid in priority to others. There is not a fragment of authority for such a practice. I think Mr Westlake in a passage cited lays down the law perfectly correctly. In section 102 of the last edition of his work on *Private International Law*, he says: 'Every administrator, principal or ancillary, must apply the assets reduced into possession under his grant in paying all the debts of the deceased, whether contracted in the jurisdiction from which the grant issued or out of it, and whether owing to creditors domiciled or resident in that jurisdiction or out of it, in that order of priority which according to the nature of the debts or of the assets is prescribed by the laws of the jurisdiction from which the grant issued.' All that is there said, and no doubt correctly, is that although mobilia sequuntur personam, in the collection, the lex fori must be observed; so also is it to be observed in the administration of those assets when collected. Therefore, if a man dies domiciled in England, possessing assets in France, the French assets must be collected in France, and distributed according to the law of France. If the French creditors are entitled according to that law to be paid in priority, that rule must be observed, because it is the lex fori, and for no other reason. But if it should happen that a man died domiciled in France, leaving assets in England, those assets can only be collected under an English grant of administration, and being so collected must be distributed according to the law of England. No doubt in a case in which French assets were distributed so as to give French creditors, as such, priority, in distributing the English assets the court would be astute to equalise the payments, and take care that no French creditors should come in and receive anything till the English creditors had been paid a proportionate amount. But subject to that, which is for the purpose of doing what is equal and just to all the creditors, I know of no law under which the English creditors are to be preferred to foreigners. On the other hand the rule is they are all to be treated equally, subject to what priorities the law may give them, from whatever part of the world they come, and in the case cited by Mr Cookson of *De La Vega v Vianna*[2] Lord Tenterden says: 'A person suing in this country must take the law as he finds it; he cannot, by virtue of any regulation in his own country, enjoy greater advantages than other suitors here, and he ought not therefore to be deprived of any superior advantage which the law of this country may confer. He is to have the same rights which all the subjects of this kingdom are entitled to.' And that has been the rule in this country, as far as I know, from the earliest time . . . .

The law of England has always been that you must enforce claims in this country according to the practice and rules of our courts, and according to them a creditor, whether from the furthest north or the furthest south, is entitled to be paid equally with other creditors in the same class. I must refuse to alter that which has always been the law of this country, and which I must say, for the sake of honesty, I hope will always be the law of this country.

If in the administration of the English estate of a deceased person who died domiciled abroad there remain surplus assets in the hands of the administrator after all debts recoverable by English law have been duly paid, the surplus assets must be beneficially distributed in accordance with the law of the deceased's domicile, and not paid to the domiciliary administrator for the benefit of creditors whose claims are statute-barred by English law, but not by the law of the domicile.

Re Lorillard [1922] 2 Ch 638, 92 LJ Ch 148 (Court of Appeal)

Appeal from a decision of Eve J.

Lord Sterndale MR: This is an unusual question arising in certain administration proceedings in this country and in the United States of America. It seems to me to be entirely a matter of discretion, and I do not see my way to differ from the decision of Eve J. The testator, who was domiciled in America, died in this country. Administration proceedings are going on both in America and in England. In England there are no debts. There are debts in America which according to English law are statute barred, but not so according to the law of New York. If claims in respect of these debts had been made here they would rightly have been rejected. The English administrator asked for the directions of the court as to what course he ought to pursue. For the beneficiaries in England it was contended that the American creditors were completely barred, the debts being over twenty years old. For the creditors in New York it was contended that as the testator was at the time of his death domiciled there the American administration was the principal proceeding to which the English administration was merely ancillary, and that accordingly the applicant as administrator in New York was entitled to receive the surplus assets in England remaining after the satisfaction of the testator's debts in order that they might be applied in paying the debts of bona fide creditors in any part of the world and for this purpose they ought to be transferred to America. The authorities do not

2 (1830) 1 B & Ad 284, 8 LJOS KB 388.

throw much light upon the question as to the duty of the English administrator. It would seem to be his duty to see that the debts are paid— ie, debts which are due according to English law. Eve J has made an order giving the American creditors a period of two months within which to bring in their claims in this country, and intimating that if they did not do so the surplus assets would be distributed among the beneficiaries. The American creditors, however, did not present their claims, presumably knowing that if they did so they would be rejected. It is argued that it is still the duty of the English administrator to transfer the moneys in his hands to the American administrator. I cannot see any principle under which it is necessary for the English court in such circumstances to order the administrator here to hand over the surplus assets to the American administrator. No authority has been cited in favour of such a course, and I cannot say that Eve J has wrongly exercised his discretion in the matter. The appeal must therefore be dismissed.

Warrington and Younger LJJ delivered judgments to the same effect.

Appeal dismissed.

CHAPTER 22

Succession

Section A. Intestate Succession

Intestate succession to movables is governed by the law of the deceased's domicile at the date of his death. Intestate succession to immovables is governed by the lex situs.

Re Ralston [1906] VLR 689, 12 ALR 365 (Supreme Court of Victoria)

James Ralston died in 1905 intestate. He was domiciled in Tasmania at the date of his death. He left a surviving widow but no issue. He left real estate in Victoria worth £750 and personal estate there worth £8,612. By the Victorian Intestate Estates Act 1896 the widow was entitled to a charge against the estate for £1000, in addition to her other rights in the estate. This Act was modelled on the English Intestates Estates Act 1890, except that the amount of the charge (now called a statutory legacy) was £1000 and not £500. There was no similar Act in force in Tasmania.

The Victorian administrator of the estate took out an originating summons for the determination of the question (inter alia) of what part of the Victorian estate should be paid or transferred to the widow.

Weigall for the administrator.

Davis for the widow.

Winstall for the next of kin. The distribution of personal estate is governed by the law of the domicile—that is, in this case, by the law of Tasmania.

[Cussen J: I accept that as a general proposition, but the question in this case is whether it was not the intention of the Victorian Legislature that the widow should get this charge wherever the property was situated, and wherever the deceased was domiciled.]

Cussen J (after stating the facts, and disposing of two preliminary matters): Coming now to the construction of the Intestate Estates Act 1896, there are, I think, three possible views which may be taken:

(a) That it applies to the Victorian estate, whether movable or immovable, of every intestate leaving a widow, but no issue, whether such intestate was, at the time of his death, domiciled in Victoria or not.

(b) That it applies to the movable and immovable Victorian estate of such an intestate if domiciled in Victoria, but only to the immovables of an intestate not domiciled in Victoria.

(c) That it applies to the movable and immovable Victorian estate of such an intestate if domiciled in Victoria, but does not apply at all to the Victorian estate, whether movable or immovable, of such an intestate not domiciled in Victoria.

To arrive at the correct construction of the Act is, I think, a matter of much difficulty, but I have come to the conclusion that the intermediate view numbered (b) above is the right one. (His Honour reviewed the Victorian Act in its setting as part of Victorian legislation on intestate succession and subjected it to close scrutiny in order to arrive at its correct construction in the light of its background, policy and purpose. He continued):

If the ordinary rules as to succession and distribution are to govern, nothing is better settled than that while the local law governs as to both movables and immovables, with respect to immovables it applies its own rules, and with respect to movables it adopts and applies the rules on the subject which are law in the country of the domicile. These rules have been acted on with almost, if not quite, unbroken uniformity, and as Lord Selborne expresses it with regard to movables in *Ewing v Orr Ewing*[1] 'For the purpose of determining succession to movable estate, recourse must be had, not always or necessarily to the Court of the domicile, but always and necessarily to the law of the domicile.' Our courts, in other words, in distributing the distributable residue, act exactly as they think the courts in the country of the domicile would act if such courts were applying the law there at the time of the death: Dicey, *Conflict of Laws*.[2] These rules are so invariably and universally recognised that it is a rule of construction to be applied to all Acts of Parliament that they are not to be taken to be affected unless the contrary is expressed clearly and with certainty. With respect to immovables, the rule is so well settled that no authority need be cited. Now, I think it can hardly be successfully contended that the contrary is clearly expressed in the Act of 1896, and this is, in a large degree, the reason impelling me to decide as I do. The decisions as to movables show that they are based on the theory that they are, for purposes of succession, to be deemed to be situated in the country of the domicile: *Re Ewin*;[3] *A-G v Napier*:[4] *Freke v Lord Carbery*[5]—and in many cases of ancillary administration they or their proceeds are, in fact, sent to such country prior to distribution. It follows that in the case of an intestate not domiciled in Victoria, if the above rule applies, the intestate, for purposes of succession, is taken to have no movables in Victoria, and that the rule to this extent intercepts the operation of the statute. The main difficulty I have felt is whether the right conclusion is not exactly the other way—namely, whether the statute does not sufficiently clearly intercept the operation of the rule. But the authorities are very strong, and the court will not presume that the legislature intended to bring about a breach of international or interstate comity. I therefore think that the words property and estate used in the title and body of the Act respectively may in the case of an intestate domiciled in Victoria include both movable and immovable property (including possibly movables or their proceeds forwarded here by the ancillary administrator), but in the case of an intestate domiciled elsewhere the meaning of the words should be confined to immovables.

I am glad to find that in deciding as I have done I am following the

1 (1882) 9 App Cas 34, 53 LJCh 435.
2 1st edn (1896) p 678.
3 (1830) 1 Cr & J 151.
4 (1851) 6 Exch 217, 20 LJ Ex 173.
5 (1873) LR 16 Eq 461, p 529 above.

decision of Porter MR in *Re Rea*[6] because, as I understand, in that case the learned judge held that the Act did apply to the immovables of an intestate who was not domiciled in Victoria, and he adds, at 465: 'It would, of course, be a different question if the Australian (Victorian) assets had been movables, and therefore subject to the law of the country of the domicile.' His view resulted in the widow getting priority, both in respect of the Victorian estate and the Irish estate, since there was a similar Act there, and this result may, of course, follow in many cases. This, perhaps, was a result not contemplated by the Legislature. So far as it goes, it would rather tend to show that the Act should be confined to intestates who died domiciled in Victoria.

For the reasons I have given, I answer the questions asked as follows: 1. The defendant Amelia Ralston, as the widow of the said intestate, and having regard to the fact that he was domiciled in Tasmania, is entitled against and in priority to the said next of kin to the net value of the real estate in Victoria, so long as such net value does not exceed 1000*l*, but is not entitled, as against the said next of kin, to any further or other special charge, payment, or other preference.

QUESTIONS

1. In *Re Rea*, above, a man died intestate domiciled in Ireland. He left real and personal estate in Ireland and real estate in Victoria, which was sold and the proceeds remitted to Ireland soon after his death. He left a widow but no issue. Sir Andrew Porter MR held that the widow was entitled to two statutory legacies, one of £500 under the English Act (which extended to Ireland) payable rateably out of the real and personal estate in Ireland, and one of £1000 under the Victorian Act payable out of the proceeds of sale of the Victorian land. Do you approve of this decision? See Morris (1969) 85 LQR 339 at 348–352.

2. The statutory legacy payable to the surviving spouse, if the intestate leaves no issue, is now £85,000 in England[7] and Northern Ireland.[8] Suppose that a man dies intestate domiciled in Northern Ireland leaving a widow and no issue, and leaving movables in Northern Ireland worth £85,000 and land in England worth the same amount. Would the widow be entitled to two statutory legacies under the English and Northern Irish legislation, thereby leaving nothing for the next of kin (perhaps the mother of the intestate)? If not, can you suggest how this result could be arrived at? See Morris (1969) 85 LQR 339–340, 367–369.

3. Would it be more desirable for all intestate succession to be governed by the same rule, the law of the domicile, irrespective of the nature of the property as movable or immovable? Why is pre-eminence accorded to the lex situs in the case of succession to immovable property?

If the deceased died intestate and without next of kin and domiciled abroad, the State of his domicile is entitled to his movables in England as against the Crown's right to bona vacantia if the foreign State claims as ultimus heres, but not if it claims under a jus regale.

Re Maldonado [1954] P 223, [1953] 2 All ER 1579 (Court of Appeal)

6 [1902] 1 IR 451.
7 Administration of Estates Act 1925, s 46 (1) (i), para (3), as amended by Intestates' Estates Act 1952, s 1, Family Provision Act 1966, s 1(1) (b), and SI 1981/255.
8 Administration of Estates Act (NI) 1955, s 7, as amended by Family Provision Act (NI) 1969, s 1(c) and SR&O 1981/124.

Appeal from Barnard J.

Eloisa Hernandez Maldonado died at Santander, Spain, on 11 October 1924, a widow and intestate, with no ascendant, descendant, or collateral relative entitled to succeed to her estate under Spanish law. The deceased was a Spanish subject and at the time of her death was domiciled in Spain. Her English estate consisted of securities in the custody of Hambros Bank Ltd, London, which at the time of her death were valued at £13,515, but which now amounted to over £26,000.

The State of Spain brought proceedings in the Probate, Divorce, and Admiralty Division claiming that letters of administration to the estate of the intestate in England should issue to the duly constituted attorney of the Spanish state as the sole and universal heir to her estate by Spanish law. The defendant, the Treasury Solicitor, claimed that the deceased's estate in England passed to the Crown as bona vacantia.

Article 956 of the Spanish Civil Code provides that when a person dies intestate leaving no issue, parents or grandparents, surviving spouse or collaterals within the sixth degree, the state inherits as being the ultimus heres, the assets being devoted to charitable institutions as therein mentioned.

There was a conflict of evidence among the Spanish lawyers, the witnesses for the plaintiff asserting that under article 956 the Spanish state took the property of a deceased intestate as heir, and the witnesses for the defendant asserting that it took the property by virtue of a jus regale. Barnard J preferred the witnesses for the plaintiff on this point; he said: 'I am satisfied on the evidence before me that the State of Spain is a true heir just as any individual heir according to Spanish law.' That finding was not challenged in the Court of Appeal.

Barnard J decided in favour of the Spanish state. The Treasury Solicitor appealed.

Jenkins LJ: The general rule to be applied in a case such as this is summed up in the maxim mobilia sequuntur personam, and is thus stated in Dicey's *Conflict of Laws* (6th edn) p 814: 'Rule 177. The distribution of the distributable residue of the movables of the deceased is (in general) governed by the law of the deceased's domicile (lex domicilii) at the time of his death.' Thus, in the present case the personalty in question should, prima facie, devolve in accordance with Spanish law, and therefore go to the State of Spain for application in accordance with the provisions of article 956.

There is, however, an admitted exception to the general rule to the effect that if, according to the law of the foreign state in which the deceased is domiciled, there is no one entitled to succeed to the movable property of the deceased owing, for example, to the bastardy of the deceased, or to the failure of kin near enough in degree to qualify for succession under the law of the domicile, and, by the law of the foreign state, the state itself is, in such circumstances, entitled to appropriate the property of the deceased as ownerless property by virtue of of some jus regale corresponding to our law of bona vacantia, English law will not recognise the claim of the foreign state as part of the law of succession of the domicile, but will treat it merely as being the assertion by the foreign state of a prerogative right which has no extra-territorial validity and one which must yield to the corresponding prerogative right of the Crown. That appears from *Dicey* at p 818 in the passage to which Evershed MR has already referred: 'Where a person dies, eg, intestate and a bastard, and under the law of the country where he is domiciled there is no succession to his movables, but they are bona vacantia, and leaves movables situate in a country, eg England, in which he is not domiciled, the title to such movables is governed by the lex situs, ie, under English law the movables being situate in England, the Crown is entitled thereto. In such a case the foreign Treasury claims not by way of succession but because there is no succession.'

The law of the relevant foreign state, however, may be such as to constitute the state itself the successor to the deceased in the absence of any individual with a prior right of succession under that law, and the question then arises whether the claim of the foreign state should be recognised under the general rule as being the claim of a person entitled to succeed according to the law of the domicile, or whether it should be treated as falling within the exception, on the ground that the claim of the foreign state, as self-constituted successor, does not differ in substance, or in principle, from a claim by a foreign state by virtue of its paramount right to ownerless property within its dominions as bona vacantia or the equivalent.

Accordingly, two questions were debated below: first, whether under the Spanish Civil Code the state takes as a true heir or successor in the eye of Spanish law, or takes by virtue of a jus regale; and secondly, if it takes in the former capacity, whether English law will recognise the State of Spain as a true heir or successor for the purpose of the maxim mobilia sequuntur personam. Barnard J, having heard evidence on both sides in regard to the Spanish law, answered the first question in the former sense, and the second question in the affirmative, holding in effect that the answer to the second followed from the answer to the first. Barnard J's decision on the first question has not been challenged by the Crown in this court. The sole issue before us, therefore, is whether the State of Spain, being admittedly according to its own law the true heir of, or successor to, the intestate, should be recognised as such by English law in its application of the general rule that is expressed in the maxim mobilia sequuntur personam.

This question has not been the subject of any direct decision, but the distinction between a sovereign state claiming 'jure regali' and claiming as true heir or successor was recognised in Re Barnett's Trusts,[9] and Re Musurus.[10] Inasmuch as the foreign law in each of those cases was held to give the foreign state concerned a jus regale, as distinct from a true right of succession, there was no actual decision on the present question; but the distinction was recognised. Indeed, as it was pointed out, both those cases would have been susceptible of a short and simple answer if the view then taken of the law had been that in no circumstances could a foreign state claim the assets of a deceased intestate situated in this country, whether the claim was founded on jus regale or on a true right of succession.

The question has also been discussed in various textbooks on this branch of the law. In Dicey, at p 818, the passage cited above continues: 'It does not follow that the decision would be the same if the law of the domicile was such that the foreign Treasury claimed as ultimus heres. That would be a true case of succession and would, it is submitted, be governed by the law of the

9 [1902] 1 Ch 847, 71 LJCh 408.
10 [1936] 2 All ER 1666, 80 Sol Jo 637.

domicile.' There are also the passages in the works on Private International Law by Wolff (2nd ed, p 579), Bar (2nd edn, p 843) and Cheshire (4th edn, p 59), to which Evershed MR has referred. I treat those passages as incorporated in this judgment. The conclusion of Barnard J, therefore, has the support of no inconsiderable weight of learned opinion, and although, for my part, I find it difficult to embrace with enthusiasm either side of this highly technical question, his conclusion also commends itself to me on the ground of consistency.

In cases such as the present, English law professes to apply the law of the domicile to the devolution of the intestate's movables situated in this country. If the law of the domicile is that of a foreign state under whose law of intestacy the state itself is the successor, why should English law not give effect to that provision as part of the law of succession which it professes to apply?

The reasons why it is claimed that English law does not do so are expressed in a variety of ways. First, the distinction between succession by a sovereign state and the appropriation of bona vacantia by a foreign state is said to be a mere matter of words. This argument is not without persuasive force, but I do not think that the question can truly be said to be one of distinction without difference. The foreign state can only succeed under its own law of succession where the succession is governed by that law. On the other hand, where the case is not one of succession, but of appropriation of ownerless property, the right applies to any ownerless property which may be reached by the law of the foreign state concerned, irrespective of the law by which its devolution is governed, provided only that by the relevant law it is in fact ownerless.

Second, it is said that the foreign state, being omnipotent so far as its own law of succession is concerned, can constitute itself successor in circumstances in which it could equally well rely on a claim based on jus regale. But in accepting the foreign state's law of succession, English law recognises the foreign state as being the arbiter of what the succession is to be. The foreign state could, for instance, enact that older relatives should be preferred to younger, or that male relatives should be preferred to female, or vice versa, or even that fair-haired relatives should be preferred to dark-haired; and to such distinctions, unreasonable as they might seem, English law would, as I understand the matter, have no objection. Why, then, should English law stop short of recognising the foreign state itself as the successor where, according to its own law, it is indeed such? The answer that English law recognises it to be the function of the relevant foreign law to regulate succession as between individual subjects or citizens, but declines to recognise rights conferred by the foreign state on itself in exercise of that function, does not commend itself to me. It involves distinctions at least as arbitrary and artificial as those discerned by the Crown in the distinction between jus regale and true inheritance by the state. For example, it was, I think, conceded in argument that if the Spanish law of succession provided that in circumstances such as those of the present case the estate of the intestate was to go to some person, or body, or corporation, other than the state itself for application to charitable purposes such as those stated in article 956 of the Civil Code, there would be no reason why the English courts, in applying the general rule to the inheritance, should not recognise and allow effect to be given to that provision. Why, then, should not the same result ensue where, as here, the estate goes by Spanish law to the Spanish state itself for application to those same charitable purposes?

Third, it is said that private international law is concerned only with the rights of individuals and not with the competing rights of sovereign states. That may well be so. But it is clear that English law recognises the legitimate proprietary rights of foreign sovereign states, and I see no reason why a right of succession to an intestate's estate should not be held to answer that description.

Fourth, it is said that English law should not recognise as 'heir' or 'successor' any person not bound by some personal nexus with the deceased. I cannot follow this submission. The heir or successor is surely the person, whether related to the deceased or not, who under the relevant law is entitled to inherit or to succeed.

Fifth, it is said that there is no reciprocity, because Spanish law would not give effect to a claim by the Crown in respect of bona vacantia. But non constat that Spanish law would not recognise a right to succession belonging to the Crown if any such right existed, and it could easily be made to exist by Act of Parliament if that were thought expedient.

There might be a case where a so-called right of succession claimed by a foreign state could be shown to be in truth no more than a claim to bona vacantia. If so, it would, no doubt, be right to apply the recognised exception to the general rule; but this has not been shown to be such a case. On the contrary, it has been found (and the Crown has accepted the finding) that the State of Spain is, in the eye of Spanish law, the true heir; and I would add that, to my mind, notwithstanding what the President said in *Re Musurus*, the conclusion that this is a case of genuine succession is reinforced by the circumstance that the State of Spain is by article 956 of the Spanish Civil Code enjoined to apply the property of the intestate to the charitable purposes therein mentioned.

Accordingly, for the reasons given by Evershed MR and such additional reasons as I have been able to offer, I agree that this appeal fails and should be dismissed.

Sir Raymond Evershed MR and Morris LJ delivered judgments to the same effect.

Appeal dismissed.

Section B. Wills

Wills Act 1963

1. A will shall be treated as properly executed if its execution conformed to the internal law in force in the territory where it was executed, or in the territory where, at the time of its execution or of the testator's death, he was domiciled or had his habitual residence, or in a state of which, at either of those times, he was a national.

2.—(1) Without prejudice to the preceding section, the following shall be treated as properly executed—
(a) a will executed on board a vessel or aircraft of any description, if the execution of the will conformed to the internal law in force in the

territory with which, having regard to its registration (if any) and other relevant circumstances, the vessel or aircraft may be taken to have been most closely connected;

(b) a will so far as it disposes of immovable property, if its execution conformed to the internal law in force in the territory where the property was situated;

(c) a will so far as it revokes a will which under this Act would be treated as properly executed or revokes a provision which under this Act would be treated as comprised in a properly executed will, if the execution of the later will conformed to any law by reference to which the revoked will or provision would be so treated;

(d) a will so far as it exercises a power of appointment, if the execution of the will conformed to the law governing the essential validity of the power.

(2) A will so far as it exercises a power of appointment shall not be treated as improperly executed by reason only that its execution was not in accordance with any formal requirements contained in the instrument creating the power.

3. Where (whether in pursuance of this Act or not) a law in force outside the United Kingdom falls to be applied in relation to a will, any requirement of that law whereby special formalities are to be observed by testators answering a particular description, or witnesses to the execution of a will are to possess certain qualifications, shall be treated, notwithstanding any rule of that law to the contrary, as a formal requirement only.

4. The construction of a will shall not be altered by reason of any change in the testator's domicile after the execution of the will.

5. (*Repealed*).

6.—(1) In this Act—

'internal law' in relation to any territory or state means the law which would apply in a case where no question of the law in force in any other territory or state arose;

'state' means a territory or group of territories having its own law of nationality;

'will' includes any testamentary instrument or act, and 'testator' shall be construed accordingly.

(2) Where under this Act the internal law in force in any territory or state is to be applied in the case of a will, but there are in force in that territory or state two or more systems of internal law relating to the formal validity of wills, the system to be applied shall be ascertained as follows—

(a) if there is in force throughout the territory or state a rule indicating which of those systems can properly be applied in the case in question, that rule shall be followed; or

(b) if there is no such rule, the system shall be that with which the testator was most closely connected at the relevant time, and for this purpose the relevant time is the time of the testator's death where the matter is to be determined by reference to circumstances prevailing at his death, and the time of execution of the will in any other case.

(3) In determining for the purposes of this Act whether or not the execution of a will conformed to a particular law, regard shall be had to the

formal requirements of that law at the time of execution, but this shall not prevent account being taken of an alteration of law affecting wills executed at that time if the alteration enables the will to be treated as properly executed.

NOTE

Section 27 of the Administration of Justice Act 1982 provides that the Annex to the Convention on International Wills concluded at Washington on 26 October 1973 shall have the force of law in the United Kingdom. The Annex is set out in Schedule 2 to the Act. It provides in article 1 that a will shall be valid as regards form, irrespective of the place where it was made, of the location of the assets and of the nationality, domicile or residence of the testator, if it complies with articles 2 to 5. The will must be in writing and signed or acknowledged by the testator in the presence of two witnesses and of an 'authorised person' (a solicitor or notary public: section 28) who must then attest the will in the presence of the testator. The authorised person must attach to the will a certificate in the form prescribed by article 10 authenticating the will and its due execution. The will may (but need not) be deposited for safe custody in the Principal Registry of the Family Division. That Registry will keep a list of the states which have ratified the Washington Convention and will keep district probate registries informed.

In general, the material or essential validity of a gift of movables in a will is governed by the law of the testator's domicile at the date of his death.

Re Annesley [1926] Ch 692, 95 LJCh 404 (p 655 below)

Re Ross [1930] 1 Ch 377, 99 LJCh 67 (p 657 below)

Re Cohn [1945] Ch 5, 114 LJCh 97 (p 668 below)

The material or essential validity of a gift of immovables in a will is governed by the lex situs.

Freke v Carbery (1873) LR 16 Eq 461, 21 WR 835 (p 529 above)

Re Ross [1930] 1 Ch 377, 99 LJCh 67 (p 657 below)

The question whether a beneficiary under a will is put to his election is governed by the law of the testator's domicile at the date of his death.

Re Ogilvie [1918] 1 Ch 492, 87 LJCh 363 (Chancery Division)

Administration action.

Margaret Ogilvie died on 2 April 1908, a widow, domiciled in England, possessed of real and personal estate in England and Scotland, and, as absolute owner in equity, of a tramway undertaking at Asuncion, in Paraguay, the property of which consisted of (inter alia) land. She had eight children, of whom four sons (Glencairn, Fergus, Gordon, Campbell) and one daughter were living at her death; of the three who had died in her lifetime, two left issue who were living and sui juris, and one had died an infant and bachelor. By her will and codicils she gave benefits to her surviving daughter, to her sons Glencairn, Fergus, and Campbell, and to certain of her grandchildren, including the children of her two deceased children who had died leaving issue. She made no provision for her son Gordon. She did not dispose of the residue of the personal estate in England and Scotland. She gave to her sons Glencairn and Fergus and her grandson Gerald all her Paraguayan property upon trust for sale and to apply the proceeds for such charitable purposes as they should think fit. The tramway undertaking had been sold and the purchase-money paid into court. The case now came before the court on a summons to proceed with an inquiry which had been directed on further consideration, and for the purpose of enabling the court to ascertain the effect of Paraguayan law on the disposition of the Paraguayan property all parties agreed to be bound by an opinion of a Paraguayan jurist, which, shortly, was as follows: (1) By the law of Paraguay the testamentary dispositions of Mrs Ogilvie, in so far as the property situate in that republic is concerned, whether movable or immovable, real or personal, are governed by the law of Paraguay . . . . (3) They are not valid by the law of Paraguay, inasmuch as they infringe upon the legal portions, under that law, of the obligatory heirs, and the bequest in favour of charity must, accordingly, be reduced until these portions are provided for. (4) These portions are not to be affected in amount by reason of the obligatory heirs or some of them having, by the will, been given benefits out of property of the testatrix situate in other countries. The transmission of property locally situate is, by the law of Paraguay, considered as completely independent of any disposition of property situate outside the republic. (5) The legal portion of the lawful descendants is four-fifths of all the properties existing at the death: the children inherit per capita; the grandchildren, children of deceased children, inherit per stirpes. (6) One-fifth only of the Paraguayan property has by the will, according to the law of Paraguay, been effectually given for charitable purposes.

Younger J: It seems clear, in the first place, that the testatrix's son Gordon, as one of the Paraguayan obligatory heirs ·for whom no other provision is made by the will, is left free by the law of this country to take what the law of Paraguay gives him. Accordingly, one-seventh of four-fifths of the undisposed-of proceeds of the undertaking falls to him. The real question is whether those of the obligatory heirs who take other benefits under the will can be allowed at the same time to gain by the partial invalidity in Paraguay of Mrs Ogilvie's disposition of the tramway undertaking, or whether they must be put to their election either to treat the whole will as valid or, in case they find it to their interest in any instance to take advantage of its invalidity in Paraguay, to submit to make compensation, out of the other benefits given them by the will, to the charities ultimately disappointed by their refusal to allow the provision made for charity to have full effect.

In the main the authorities on this subject are clear. The testatrix here very plainly intended to deal by her will with her Paraguayan property as well as with her English movable and immovable estate. She purported to dispose of her Paraguayan property by express words of gift. There is, therefore, no room here for the difficulty which, although ultimately solved in the same sense, arose in the case of *Orrell v Orrell*.[11] Again, in these cases of election the court has always shown a special tenderness to the heir-at-law of English real estate as contrasted with the customary heir or the person compendiously described—pace Joyce J in *Re de Virte*[12]—as the 'foreign heir'. The principle is well established that, where a testator who dies domiciled in England makes a will which purports to dispose of, but is, in fact, inoperative to pass English real estate, his heir-at-law, as contrasted with the customary heir or the foreign heir in the corresponding case, is not put to his election between that realty and other benefits given him by the will—*Hearle v Greenbanks*[13]—unless there be contained in the will itself some such express condition, as, for instance, was found in *Boughton v Boughton*,[14] that if any who receive benefit by the will shall dispute any part of it they shall forfeit all claim under it.

This distinction between the English heir-at-law and any other heir is not very satisfactory, but, although frequently severely criticised, it was too well established, even in the time of Sir William Grant, to remain open to effective discussion. In *Brodie v Barry*,[15] Sir William Grant deal with the point. He says: 'If it were now necessary to discuss the principles, upon which the doctrine of election depends, it might be difficult to reconcile to those principles, or to each other, some of the decisions, which have taken place on this subject . . . . This is, or is not, a case of election according as the English will is, or is not, to be read against the Scotch heir. Where land and personal property are situated in different countries, governed by different laws, and a question arises upon the combined effect of those laws, it is often very difficult to determine, what portion of each law is to enter the decision of the question. It is not easy to say, how much is to be considered as depending on the law of real property; which must be taken from the country where the land lies; and how much upon the law of personal property; which must be taken from the country of the domicile; and to blend both together; so as to form a rule, applicable to the mixed question, which neither law separately furnishes sufficient materials to decide.' Then, after a discussion as to whether the law of England or the law of Scotland ought to determine the question in the case before him, and finding it unnecessary in that case to decide it, the result being the same under both, he proceeds: 'As to the law of England'—and this is the point—'a will of land in Scotland must be held analogous to that of copyhold estate in England; and the will is equally to be read against the heir.' And it is now, I think, clearly established that this is by the law of England always so if the realty in question is situate not in England, but, say, in Paraguay or in any other foreign country, and it is by the law of Paraguay or that country, and not by the law of England, that the devise of it fails to have effect. In such a case the Paraguayan or other foreign heir, to whom, say, a pecuniary legacy is given by the will, put to his election here in England, whether the will does or

11 (1871) 6 Ch App 302, 40 LJCh 539.
12 [1915] 1 Ch 920 at 926.
13 (1749) 3 Atk 695, 1 Ves Sen 298.
14 (1750) 2 Ves Sen 12.
15 (1813) 2 Ves & B 127 at 129, 133.

does not contain any such express condition as that found in *Boughton v Boughton*.

Further, it has since Sir William Grant's time become, I think, well settled, in accordance with what was plainly his own view, that the question whether in any particular case, like *Brodie v Barry* or like the present, a case of election is or is not raised depends upon the domicile of the testator at death—for it is the law of that domicile which governs it. The reasons for this are given by Lord Brougham in his judgment in *Dundas v Dundas*.[16] In that case a testator domiciled in Scotland had, by a will inoperative under the Statute of Frauds, purported to devise his English real estate to a stranger and had, by his same will, given benefits to his English heir-at-law. The Court of Session held that the heir-at-law was put to his election. The House of Lords affirmed that decision. And although the House of Lords in dealing with a Scotch appeal applies to it the principles of Scotch law applicable, *Orrell v Orrell*, to cite no other case, shows that in this respect the principles of the law of England are the same.

The result at first sight may seem strange. It would appear remarkable that the question whether the English heir of a Scottish testator resident in England at his death is or is not put to his election under his will may, in fact, turn upon the question whether the testator had or had not then lost his domicile of origin—a question which many testators in that situation might themselves find it difficult to answer. But the point is one of substance, and I am inclined to think that it discloses the clue by which the difficulty in the present case may be solved. If by the law of the domicile the gift of the tramway be, irrespective of its locality, to any extent invalid, there is no case of election; if it is only by the law of lex rei sitae that the gift is inoperative, then the foreign heirs are put to their election.

And the foreign heirs, in argument, ultimately accepted that position. But they said that by the law of England a foreign heir would not be put to his election in a case like the present, where the invalidity of the gift by the law of Paraguay was not due to any such formal matter as, for instance, a defect in signature or attestation, but was due to its being contrary to a cardinal principle of public policy adopted in Paraguay, the country where the property is situated. Cases like *Orrell v Orrell*, *Brodie v Barry*, and *Dundas v Dundas*, where the foreign heir was put to his election, were all of them, they pointed out, cases in which the devise of the foreign realty might have been effectively made if it had been made in due form; here, on the other hand, the devise of the tramway undertaking to charity could not to the extent of four-fifths of the property be by the law of Paraguay, made valid by any means whatever. To such a case, so it was said, this court must apply the principles of *Re Oliver's Settlement*,[17] and *Re Beales' Settlement*,[18] approved by the Court of Appeal in *Re Nash*,[19] and refuse to assist indirectly, by an application of the doctrine of election, a breach or evasion of positive rules of foreign law, just as in these cases it refused to, shall I say, encourage, by applying the doctrine, a breach of the rule against perpetuities. The argument is plausible, but, in my opinion, it is not sound. It is not open to

---

16 (1830) 2 Dow & Cl 349.
17 [1905] 1 Ch 191, 74 LJCh 62.
18 [1905] 1 Ch 256, 74 LJCh 67.
19 [1910] 1 Ch 1, 79 LJCh 1.

me to consider the correctness of the principle as applied to the rule against perpetuities upon which *Re Oliver's Settlement* and the cases following it proceed. That principle has been accepted by the Court of Appeal and is binding upon me. Some day it may come under the notice of the House of Lords, and then the powerful reasoning of Mr Theobald in the preface to the 7th edition of his *Law of Wills* and the views of the learned editors of *Jarman on Wills* (6th edn) p 851, may meet with more consideration than they have hitherto received, and even *Re Bradshaw*[20] may, as a decision, at the last come to its own, and the question may be asked whether any advantage is gained by driving testators, if they would attain the same end, to resort in that matter to the use of an express condition, the necessity for which, in cases then already established, was so deplored by Sir William Grant in *Brodie v Barry*. Accepting, however, as I must, the principle to the full, it does not, I think, apply here.

This court does not, in these cases of election, against a foreign heir, presume to sit in judgment upon the wisdom or the reverse according to its own notions of the municipal law of any foreign country. If it finds that an English testator has by his will manifested an intention to dispose of foreign heritage away from the foreign heir, and has, in fact, so far as words are concerned effectually so disposed of it, this court merely says that it is against conscience that that foreign heir, given a legacy by the same will, and to that extent an object of mere bounty on the part of the testator, shall take and keep, under the protection of the foreign law, the land by the will destined for another, without making to that other out of his English legacy, so far as it will go, compensation for his disappointment, thus effectuating the testator's whole intentions. That object, as I take it, is, in the eye of this court, always the paramount object of attainment. But in so attaining it the court violates no foreign law; it leaves that law, as it must, untouched. If the heir can obtain under the protection of the foreign law property which the testator destined for others, he will, so far as this court is concerned, be at perfect liberty to take it and keep it; it is the legacy subject to its own jurisdiction that the court alone will touch and administer and, if necessary, impound for the purpose of effectuating the testator's intention, and so doing justice as it sees it. And, in my opinion, the court will always take this course upon the conditions presupposed, unless the heir's legacy would, if applied in compensating the disappointed devisees of the foreign land, be applied in a way or for purposes for which the testator himself could not, by English law, validly by his will have directed that legacy to be so applied. It is with the English law only that the court at this stage is concerned. If, in the result, no principle of that law is violated, the hand of the court will not be stayed. The foreign heir will be put to his election; and compensation, partial or complete, will, if necessary, be provided for the disappointed devisee. From this point of view the question what precise principle or provision of the foreign law, as such, has been left unobserved by the testator becomes quite immaterial in this court, and I cannot doubt that it is for this reason that no such distinction as that suggested in argument here has, so far as I can find, ever before been taken.

In my opinion these Paraguayan heirs are in this case put to their election.

---

20 [1902] 1 Ch 436, 71 LJCh 230.

The question whether a will of movables is revoked by the subsequent marriage of the testator is governed by the law of his domicile at the date of the marriage.

Re Martin [1900] P 211, 69 LJP 75 (Court of Appeal)

In 1870 the testatrix, an unmarried Frenchwoman then in England in the domestic service of an English family, made a holograph will in one of the forms recognised as valid by French law which was not attested as required by the Wills Act 1837. By that will she gave the residue of her property to the plaintiff, her sister.

In 1874 the testatrix left domestic service, established a laundry business in London, and married a French refugee named Louis Guillard, known in London as Martin, who was then 51 years old.

Prior to 1868 Guillard, then a Professor of French in France, fled to Belgium to escape prosecution for an offence alleged to have been committed by him in connection with his professorship. In his absence he was convicted and sentenced by a French court to ten years' imprisonment, and in 1868 or 1869, after the date of his conviction, he came over from Belgium to England.

After the marriage the husband joined his wife in carrying on the laundry business. In 1890, the period of prescription of 20 years under French criminal law having expired, he separated from his wife and returned to France, where he remained and where he was still living at the date of the action.

In 1895 the testatrix, who had continued to carry on the laundry in London, died in a fire which occurred at the business premises.

Her next of kin were her sister, the plaintiff, and her brother, the defendant. As it was believed that she had died intestate, the brother took out letters of administration in England to her estate, the husband renouncing. Subsequently the sister propounded the will of 1870, claiming a grant of administration with the will annexed, and asking that the letters of administration granted to the brother should be revoked. There was evidence that by French law marriage does not revoke a will.

All the judges held that at the date of the testatrix's death the domicile of the husband, and therefore of the testatrix, was French; but there was a difference of opinion as to the domicile of the husband at the date of the marriage, Sir F. H. Jeune P and Lindley MR holding that it was French, and Rigby and Vaughan Williams LJJ that it was English.

Sir F. H. Jeune P held that the husband and wife, though domiciled in France, intended to marry in accordance with English matrimonial law, but that s 18 of the Wills Act 1837 (by which a will is revoked by the subsequent marriage of the testator), is part of the testamentary law of England and not part of the matrimonial law. He therefore held that the will was not revoked. The defendant appealed.

Lindley MR: The will which is in question in this case was made in this country by a Frenchwoman before her marriage, and was not attested as required by English law. By English law, by which I mean English law irrespective of all foreign law, the will is therefore clearly invalid. But foreign law must be taken into account. Those principles of private international law which are recognised in this country are part of the law of England; and on those principles the validity of the will, so far as it affects movable property, depends on the law of the domicile of the testatrix when she died. The domicile of the testatrix must be determined by the English Court of Probate according to those legal principles applicable to domicile which are recognised in this country and are part of its law. Until the question of the domicile of the testatrix at the time of her death is determined, the Court of Probate cannot tell what law of what country has to be applied. The testatrix was a Frenchwoman, but it would be contrary to sound principle to determine her domicile at her death by the evidence of French legal experts. The preliminary question, by what law is the will to be governed, must depend in an English court on the view that court takes of the domicile of the testatrix when she died. If authority for these statements is wanted, it will be found in *Bremer v Freeman*,[1] *Doglioni v Crispin*,[2] and *Re Trufort*.[3] In each of the last two cases a foreign court had determined the domicile and the English court had also to determine it, and did determine it to be the same as that determined by the foreign court. But, as I understand those cases, the English court satisfied itself as to the domicile in the English sense of the term, and did not simply adopt the foreign decisions. The course universally followed when domicile has to be decided by the courts of this country proceeds upon the principles to which I have alluded.

But, further, the validity of a will of movables made by a person domiciled in a foreign country at the time of such person's death not only may, but must, depend on the view its courts take of the validity of the will when made and on its subsequent revocation if that question arises. These questions may or may not turn on the domicile of the testator as understood in this country. For example, in this case it is agreed on all hands that by the law of France the will in question, being a holograph will made by a French subject, was valid when made, whatever her domicile may have been when she made it. It is also agreed on all hands that by French law marriage does not revoke the prior wills of the spouses. But the testatrix married a Frenchman in this country after she made her will, and the question whether her will was thereby revoked as to her movables is the real question on which this case turns.

By whatever court this question is to be decided, the English law of marriage, which in such a case involves and, indeed, turns on English views of domicile, must be considered. If this view be ignored, the effect of the marriage will be inadequately and, indeed, erroneously ascertained. If the domicile of the testatrix is to be treated as English, when she became a married woman her will was revoked by her marriage, for such is the law of England whatever the intentions of the parties may be: 1 *Jarman on Wills*, c 7; but if her domicile was French, her will would not be revoked by English law, and still less by French law. Both laws are alike in regarding her domicile as that of her husband as soon as she married him. The effect of her marriage must, therefore, depend on the English view of his domicile. It would be useless, and, indeed, entirely misleading, to ask a French expert what effect the French law would give to an English marriage, without explaining the English law to him, and no explanation of that law would be

---

1 (1857) 10 Moo PCC 306 at 359 et seq.
2 (1866) LR 1 HL 301, 35 LJP&M 129.
3 (1887) 36 Ch D 600, 57 LJCh 135.

adequate or correct if it excluded the English view of the domicile of the parties.

Having thus stated the principles which, in my opinion, ought to be applied to the case, I proceed to consider the facts and the evidence of the experts called at the trial.

(His Lordship referred to the facts and continued:) Upon the question of domicile (in the English sense) my own conclusions are that the domicile of the testatrix was French when she made her will; French up to the time she married; French by her marriage; and French when she died. Her domicile was French by and after marriage because, in my opinion, her husband's domicile was French.

The domicile of the testatrix being French when she made her will and when she died, it became necessary to ascertain the effect of her will on her movable property according to French law. The husband being, in my opinion, domiciled in France when she married, it became necessary to ascertain the effect of such marriage by French law upon her will; and if, in order to ascertain this, it became necessary for the French experts to be told what the English law was, they should have been told that it depended on the view which an English court would take of the domicile, in the English sense, of the husband; and if I am right in my view of his domicile, the experts should have been told that by English law the marriage in this case did not revoke the wife's will. It was not necessary or, indeed, proper on this occasion to pursue the inquiry further and to see what matrimonial régime the parties intended to adopt. It is not necessary to cite authorities to show that it is now settled that, according to international law as understood and administered in England, the effect of marriage on the movable property of spouses depends (in the absence of any contract) on the domicile of the husband in the English sense. This being clear the will was not revoked; and if not revoked it was clearly valid as regards the wife's movable property. Section 18 of the Wills Act does not apply to the wills of foreigners who die domiciled abroad, and the effect of the marriage was not to vest the wife's property in the husband. French law did not so vest it, neither did international law as understood and administered in this country. The English law applicable to English people, and according to which a woman's personal property formerly vested in her husband on marriage, and according to which her will was revoked by marriage even before the Wills Act, could not, on principle, apply to French spouses married in England, but (according to English views) domiciled in France when they married.

In my opinion the will has been properly admitted to probate; but it will not apply to leasehold property, for that is not regarded as movable property, to which the lex domicilii is applicable . . . .

Vaughan Williams LJ: I agree in the conclusion of Sir F. Jeune that the husband and wife intended to keep up an establishment in England, and that they intended to marry under English law, and to adopt it as their matrimonial law; but I base this conclusion on the fact, which Sir F. Jeune does not accept, that at the date of the marriage the husband had an English domicile, for I find no other evidence of an agreement embodying that intention, unless it be as an inference from the actual domicile at the date of the marriage . . . .

(His Lordship referred to the facts and continued:) This, in my judgment, is sufficient to show that his actual domicile at the time of the marriage was, according both to English and French law, English.

I gather, however, from the judgment of Sir F. Jeune that his view is that England became the matrimonial domicile by the agreement of the husband and wife at the time of the marriage; but I do not quite understand where he finds such an agreement unless it is to be inferred from a change of the husband's domicile. There is no express agreement, and I know of no English decision in which such an agreement has been inferred inconsistently with the fact of domicile. Husband and wife cannot by mere tacit agreement choose a matrimonial domicile.

Mr Westlake, in *Private International Law* (3rd edn) p 68, says:

'By the matrimonial domicile is to be understood that of the husband at the date of the marriage, with a possible exception in favour of any other which may have been acquired immediately after the marriage, in pursuance of an agreement to that effect made before it.'

If this exception can be supported, for which there is no English authority, no doubt there is evidence from which one may infer that the actual English domicile after marriage was in pursuance of an ante-nuptial agreement.

I doubt, however, if domicile can be directly affected by the marriage contract. Such an agreement as to the intended matrimonial place of residence may no doubt be evidence, and cogent evidence, of adoption of a new domicile as from a date anterior to the marriage; or it may be evidence of an agreement as to the law which shall govern the movable property of the parties marrying; but I can find no case in which an inferred agreement, as distinguished from an express agreement, has been allowed to outweigh the prima facie inference that the law of the country of the husband's domicile is to govern the movable property of the married couple.

If my conclusion is right, and if one ought to come to the conclusion—from the evidence of the husband's conduct in making his home in England for an indefinite time and going into such a business as by French law put an end to his French domicile and gave him an English domicile—that he adopted an English domicile at the time of his marriage, then at that time his wife's movables became his property; and I think that, his wife's property in the movables having thereby ceased, it follows, quite independently of the 18th section of the Wills Act, that this loss of the power of disposition put an end to her will while it was still ambulatory, and rendered it of no effect, and that nothing but republication could revive it.

If, however, the French domicile of the husband continued at and after the marriage and down to the wife's death, then it would follow that the French law, by which alone this will can be supported (for it is not in the form required by the English Wills Act), must govern the testamentary validity of this will, and also the rights of property of the husband and wife, unless there can be found some binding marriage contract determining the relative rights of the property of the husband and wife.

Sir F. Jeune has found, as I understand, that there is such an agreement or contract. Assuming that there is, I differ from his conclusion in law on this assumption, for I think that the rule of the English law which makes a woman's will null and void on her marriage is part of the matrimonial law, and not of the testamentary law, and that probate of this will ought not to be granted; but as I am not sure that we ought to infer that there was at the time of the marriage an agreement that the English law should govern the matrimonial property, I prefer to ground my judgment on the change of the husband's domicile at the time of marriage; and I think that, if he did change it from a French to an English domicile, then his subsequent reversion to a French domicile will not prevent English law continuing to govern the matrimonial property.

In my opinion, the effect of the husband's domicile on the matrimonial property is based on the presumption that you must read the law of the husband's domicile into the marriage contract as a term of it, unless there is an express agreement to the contrary.

I think, therefore, that the decision of the court below ought to be reversed, and the grant of letters of administration with the will annexed revoked.

Rigby LJ delivered a judgment concurring with the conclusions of Vaughan Williams LJ.

Appeal allowed.

The same rule applies to a will of immovables.

Re Micallef's Estate [1977] 2 NSWLR 929 (Supreme Court of New South Wales)

Joseph Micallef, who was at all material times domiciled and resident in Malta, owned land in New South Wales. In 1970 he made a will disposing of all his property including the land in New South Wales. The will was well executed according to Maltese law and the law of New South Wales. In 1972 he married a Maltese lady in Malta. In 1973 he died. By Maltese law, marriage did not revoke a will. By the law of New South Wales, it did. A beneficiary under the will applied for a grant of letters of administration with the will annexed.

Holland J (after stating the facts): The question is whether in these circumstances, according to New South Wales law, the mere fact that the Maltese owned real estate in New South Wales caused his marriage in Malta to a Maltese lady, both otherwise bound by Maltese law, to revoke his Maltese will in so far as it applied to New South Wales real estate.

Now it is unquestionable under New South Wales law that the Maltese marriage could have no such effect upon any movable property of whatever value in New South Wales, because it is firmly established for New South Wales law that the question whether marriage revokes an existing will disposing of movables is governed by the law of the testator's domicile when he married, in this case by Maltese law. Maltese law gave the marriage no invalidating effect to the Maltese will in respect of any class of property owned by the testator, wherever it was. Why then should New South Wales law? There are only two possible reasons that could be suggested: (1) a policy of New South Wales law with respect to disposition of land in New South Wales; or (2) a policy of New South Wales law concerning marriage.

It cannot be the first, because, but for the marriage, New South Wales law would have given effect to the Maltese will. If there is any policy contrary to the Maltese law which bound the parties to this marriage, it must in New South Wales law be found in the marriage. But this is a marriage between Maltese in Malta, governed by Maltese law. What interest could New South Wales law conceivably have in imposing on the parties to that marriage, by reason of the marriage, a ruling affecting the disposition of property belonging to one of the parties to the marriage different from that to which they were subjected by Maltese law? On the basis of marriage I can think of none whatever. It is understandable that, in relation to the marriage of persons subject at the time of the marriage to the law of New South Wales with respect to the consequences of their marriage upon their property rights, the New South Wales legislature has simply adopted and continued as part of New South Wales law the rule in England as enacted by s 18 of the Wills Act 1837. But it is quite another thing to say that the law of England was, and the law of New South Wales must accordingly be, that the rule was intended to apply in relation to foreigners marrying in their own country and subject at the time of their marriage to the law of their own country as to the consequences of marriage upon their property rights. In my opinion, common sense and the convenience of the parties would indicate that Maltese law should govern the matter, and I can see no reason in policy why New South Wales law should be held to apply in the circumstances of the present case. Certainly the provisions of the statute in question give no indication of an intention on the part of the legislature that the section was to be applied to foreigners who married abroad.

It is necessary then to turn to such authority in English law as bears directly upon the present problem. In *Re Earl Caithness*,[4] Chitty J, according to the report of his judgment, held that s 18 of the Wills Act 1837 applied to revoke the will of a domiciled Scotchman disposing of leasehold land situated in England, but he did not give any reason why the section should apply, except to say that there was, in English law, a general rule that succession to English land and all questions relating to the disposition of it by will or otherwise were governed by the law of England, including all statutes in force in England. Chitty J gave no attention to the question whether he was dealing with a matter of matrimonial law or a matter of testamentary law in applying this rule to a foreigner.

In *Re Martin*[5] the President, Sir Francis Jeune, said that s 18 was testamentary not matrimonial law in England. On appeal from his decision, however, the Master of the Rolls, Lord Lindley, said: '. . ., the English law of marriage, when considered with reference to its effect on property, involves, and in a case like this cannot be severed from, English views of domicile.'

The Master of the Rolls rejected the view that s 18 was part of English testamentary law, and held that, as by English law the effect of the marriage depended upon the domicile of the parties when the marriage took place, s 18 did not apply to the wills of foreigners domiciled out of England. It is not altogether clear from the judgment of Lord Lindley whether he intended to make a distinction between movables and immovables in expressing his views about the application of the section. The case was complicated by the fact that the testatrix had left a holograph will which would have been valid according to the laws of England to deal with her movables, if she had been

4 (1891) 7 TLR 354.
5 [1900] P 211 at 223, p 586 above.

domiciled in France. As Lord Lindley took the view that she had been domiciled in France, contrary to the view taken by the majority on the appeal, it was sufficient for him to say that the will was valid and admissible to probate in respect of movables which she owned. It could not have been valid in respect of immovables, because, in relation to wills dealing with real estate situated in England, it would have been necessary for the will, to be valid, to have been executed in accordance with the requirements of English law. But that was another subject matter. In so far as he characterised the nature of the rule contained in s 18 of the Wills Act 1837 Lord Lindley clearly held that the subject matter of that rule was matrimonial law. Vaughan Williams LJ who formed part of the majority on the appeal, in referring to a rule of English law which made a woman's will void on her marriage, held that the rule was part of matrimonial, and not testamentary, law and that its application depended upon the husband having at the time of the marriage an English domicile.

In my opinion, the views expressed in *Re Martin* by Lord Lindley and Vaughan Williams LJ have reopened the question whether s 18 of the Wills Act 1837 applies in the case of foreigners marrying abroad to immovables in England, in so far as it might be thought that the decision of Chitty J in *Re Earl Caithness* had determined that question. I think that the question must be regarded as reopened, because it clearly was the view of the majority of the Court of Appeal in *Re Martin* that, for the purpose of English rules of private international law, s 18 was directed to the consequences of marriage upon the property disposing rights of the parties to the marriage; in other words, it had to be regarded as part of English matrimonial law. I am independently of the same opinion, and would respectfully call in support the opinions of Lord Lindley MR and Vaughan Williams LJ. If that opinion be correct, I can see no logical or other reason for making any distinction between movable and immovable property in applying the foreign law relating to the marriage and its consequences to a will of one of the parties to the marriage. If marriage is the reason for the rule in England and English law recognises the foreign law of the marriage as governing the parties to the marriage, the nature or location of the property dealt with by the will is immaterial. I am, therefore, not prepared to follow the decision in *Re Caithness* in the present case, as Chitty J does not appear from the report to have taken what, in my view, was the real nature of the question into account in arriving at his decision.

For the reasons I have given, and on the footing that the question remains open, I have come to the conclusion that it ought not be held as a matter of New South Wales law that a marriage of foreigners domiciled abroad has the effect of revoking their wills, in so far as they deal with immovables in New South Wales, because of the provisions of s 15 of the Wills, Probate and Administration Act 1898.

The same conclusion was reached in *Davies v Davies*;[6] cf *Re Howard*.[7]

The subject has been the matter of comment by the text-writers, and the majority of the views of the learned authors would favour the conclusion which I have reached.

---

6 (1915) 8 WWR 803, 24 DLR 737.
7 [1924] 1 DLR 1062, 54 OLR 109.

Section C. Powers of Appointment

A will made in exercise of a power of appointment will be treated as properly executed if its execution conformed to (a) any system of law applicable under section 1 of the Wills Act 1963, or (b) the law governing the essential validity of the power.

Re Price [1900] 1 Ch 442, 69 LJCh 225 (Chancery Division)

Dame Elizabeth Price, by her will dated 28 March 1876, bequeathed a sum of £2,000 to trustees upon trust for investment and payment of the income to 'Maria the wife of Monsieur Adolphe Gay' during her life. The will then proceeded: 'And from and after her decease to pay and transfer the last-mentioned sum of £2,000 in such manner as she the said Maria Gay shall by her last will appoint, and, in default of such appointment, then to such person or persons as would at the time of her decease be the next of kin of the said Maria Gay in case she had died intestate and without being married.'

Lady Price died on 18 March 1878.

At the date of the will Maria Gay was the wife of Adolphe Gay, a French subject domiciled in France. Monsieur Gay died on 12 October 1882; and in October 1886 Madame Gay married Monsieur Auguste Dié Forfillier, also a French subject domiciled in France.

On 2 June 1887 Madame Forfillier made a holograph will in the French language, of which the following is a translation:

> 'I the undersigned declare that I bequeath to my dear husband Auguste Dié Forfillier, everything which I possess at the present moment, and which I hereafter may possess . . . . And I declare that this will annuls all the others, as I have informed Mr Archibald Willett, solicitor, Bromley, Kent, and that it shall thus be considered in England the same as in France, and I repeat that I leave everything which I possess at the present moment and which I may come to possess afterwards to my dear husband.'

The will was unattested.

On 16 February 1898 Madame Forfillier died, and on 30 October 1898 letters of administration with the will annexed were granted by the Probate Division to the defendant Edward Latter as the attorney of Monsieur Forfillier. At the date of her death Madame Forfillier had no interest in any property in England except the property subject to the power of appointment.

This summons was taken out by the trustees of the will of Lady Price to have it determined who was entitled to the fund of £2,000.

Madame Forfillier was at the time of her death a French subject by virtue of the Naturalisation Act 1870, s 10, sub-s 1. She was also domiciled in France. The law of France was stated in the evidence to be that the will of Madame Forfillier was a complete testamentary disposition of the whole of the property which the testatrix might have at her death or which she might by law dispose of; that the mode of disposition by appointment was not practised in France; and that if a French court had to consider the effect of the will in this respect it would inquire into and apply the English law bearing on this point; and would also take cognizance of and give effect to the fact that the testatrix had no interest in any property in England except that which was subject to the power of appointment.

Stirling J: Under the will of Lady Price the fund is to be paid and transferred in such manner as Madame Forfillier 'shall by her last will appoint'. The first question arises as to the word 'will' which there occurs— whether it means any instrument recognised by the law of England as a will or a will executed in accordance with the law of England. I shall first consider the three authorities which have been cited to me as bearing on this subject. The first is the case of *D'Huart v Harkness*.[8] There, under the will of an English lady, a sum of Consols was held upon trust for her daughter for her separate use for life, and after her decease upon trust for such persons as her said daughter 'by her last will and testament in writing duly executed' should direct or appoint. The daughter was an Englishwoman by birth, but she married a domiciled Frenchman and resided in France till her death; she made a will, which was not attested, whereby she bequeathed the sum of Consols to her husband. This will was valid by the law of France and had been admitted to probate in this country. It was held by Lord Romilly that the will was a valid execution of the power. It will be observed that, as regards the facts, that case is as near to the present case as one case can be to another. The material portion of the judgment is this:

'A sum of money is given simply, to such person as the Baroness shall by her last will duly executed appoint. What does that mean? It means a will so executed as to be good according to the English law. Here it is admitted to probate, and that is conclusive that it is good according to the English law. The English law admits two classes of wills to probate, first, those which follow the forms required by the Wills Act 1837, s 9, and secondly, those executed by a person domiciled in a foreign country, according to the law of that country, which latter are perfectly valid in this country. Accordingly, where a person domiciled in France executes a will in the mode required by the law of that country, it is admitted to proof in England, though the English formalities have not been observed. When a person simply directs that a sum of money shall be held subject to a power of appointment by will, he does not mean any one particular form of will recognised by the law of this country, but any will which is entitled to probate here. A power to appoint by will, simply, may be executed by any will which according to the law of this country is valid, though it does not follow the forms of the statute.'

(His Lordship referred to *Re Kirwan's Trusts*[9] and *Hummel v Hummel*[10] and continued:) I am of opinion that I ought to follow *D'Huart v Harkness* and not *Re Kirwan's Trusts*. But I go further. I think that on principle *D'Huart v Harkness* was well decided. The general rule on the subject is, as stated by Mr Dicey[11], that 'Any will of movables which is valid according to the law of the testator's domicile at the time of his death is valid' in England. It follows that the provisions of an English statute prescribing formalities with

---

8 (1865) 34 Beav. 324, 5 New Rep 440.
9 (1883) 25 Ch D 373, 52 LJCh 952.
10 [1898] 1 Ch 642, 67 LJCh 363.
11 *Conflict of Laws* (1st edn, 1896) p 684.

reference to wills do not apply to the wills of persons not domiciled in England.

In *Bremer v Freeman*[12] it appears to have been contended that the provisions of s 20 of the Wills Act as to the revocation of wills applied to the wills of persons domiciled abroad. Lord Wensleydale in delivering the judgment of the court said that for reasons referred to by him it was unnecessary to consider the point, but added:

> 'Their Lordships, however, do not wish to intimate any doubt that the law of the domicile at the time of the death is the governing law (see Story *Conflict of Laws* para 473), nor any that the Wills Act 1837 applies only to wills of those persons who continue to have an English domicile, and are consequently regulated by the English law.'

Section 9 of the Wills Act prescribes that 'no will shall be valid unless it shall be in writing and executed in manner hereinafter mentioned'. Notwithstanding this language, it is the practice of the Probate Division, on the principle just stated, to admit to probate or otherwise recognise as valid the wills of persons domiciled abroad, although not executed as prescribed by the Act. The present case affords an instance of this being done. I fail to see why the provisions of s. 10 of the Wills Act should apply to the will of Madame Forfillier any more than those of s. 9.

There is, however, a series of cases referred to in the argument which seems to establish that a will purporting to be made in execution of a power is valid if it satisfies the requirements of the instrument creating the power, although it would be invalid according to the law of the domicile of the testator at the time of his death: see *In the Goods of Alexander;*[13] *In the Goods of Hallyburton;*[14] *In the Goods of Huber.*[15] These cases, however, do not lay down that a power to appoint by will (without special formalities) conferred on a person domiciled abroad cannot be executed by a will valid by the law of the domicile of the donee of the power at the time of his death, and consequently do not appear to me to affect the decision of the present case . . . .

In my opinion, therefore, it was competent for Madame Forfillier to exercise the power conferred on her by Lady Price's will by such a will as has been recognised by the Probate Division. It remains to be considered whether she has done so. This question is one of construction.

In general, a will is to be construed according to the law of the domicile of the testator: 'but this is a mere canon of interpretation, which should not be adhered to when there is any reason, from the nature of the will, or otherwise, to suppose that the testator wrote it with reference to the law of some other country': Dicey *Conflict of Laws* p 695. Considering first the law of France, according to which prima facie the will is to be construed, the evidence shews that the will of Madame Forfillier is a complete disposition of all the property which she could dispose of; but it also appears that the mode of disposition by appointment is not practised in France, and that if a French court had to consider the effect of the will in this respect it would apply the English law. It is contended with regard to the law of England that the

12 (1857) 10 Moo PCC 306, 29 LT OS 251.
13 (1860) 29 LJ PM & A 93, 2 LT 56.
14 (1866) LR 1P & M 90, 35 LJP&M 122.
15 [1896] P 209, 65 LJP 119.

provisions of the Wills Act, including s 27, are inapplicable, and that consequently the law of England applicable is the law as it existed before that Act, and that, there being no reference in the will either to the power or to the property, it is not a good execution of the power. If I am to apply the law as it existed before the Wills Act, questions of difficulty might arise; but it appears to me that I can decide this case upon another ground. The testatrix says, 'I declare that this will annuls all the others ... and that it shall thus be considered in England the same as in France.' I think that that amounts to a declaration by the testatrix that she meant the will to operate as her last will in England as well as in France. I think it is indicated upon the face of the will that she wrote it with reference to the law of England as well as the law of France. Therefore I think that I am entitled to apply the rules of construction which would by English law be applied to a will expressed in the same terms and of the same date as that annexed to the letters of administration, including the rule of construction introduced by s 27 of the Wills Act.

No question arises between Monsieur Forfillier and the daughter of his wife by her first marriage, who by the law of France might have a claim if this fund had been part of Madame Forfillier's property; for she appears and supports the claim of Monsieur Forfillier.

In my opinion, therefore, the husband, Monsieur Forfillier, is entitled to the fund.

Wills Act 1963, s 2 (1) (d), (2) (p 580 above).

A general bequest in the will of a testator domiciled abroad exercises a general power of appointment conferred by an English instrument unless a contrary intention appears in the will.

A testator has capacity to exercise by will a power of appointment over movables conferred by an English instrument if he has testamentary capacity by the law of his domicile at the time of making his will.

Re Lewal's Settlement Trusts [1918] 2 Ch 391, 87 LJCh 588 (Chancery Division)

By an antenuptial settlement made in 1907 upon the marriage of Gertrude Loyd, an infant aged 19, to the defendant Maxime Lewal, an officer in the French Army, certain property belonging to the intended wife was settled after her death, and in the event (which happened) of there being no child of the marriage, upon trust for such person or persons as the wife should by deed or will (executed in such manner as to be valid by the law of her domicile) appoint, with a gift over in default of appointment. The settlement contained a statement that it should be construed, and that the rights of all parties claiming thereunder should in all respects be regulated, according to English law. The settlement was duly sanctioned by the court under the Infant Settlements Act 1855. The marriage was solemnised on 15 April 1907. The husband was at all material times a French citizen domiciled in France.

Immediately after the marriage the wife, then 19 years of age, signed at Versailles an unattested French holograph will as follows: J'institue mon mari pour mon légataire universel.' The wife died in June 1917 in the lifetime of the husband. Letters of administration with the French will annexed were granted in England to the wife's mother as attorney for the husband.

The trustees of the settlement took out a summons to determine whether and to what extent the will exercised the general power of appointment given to the wife by the settlement.

The evidence showed that the will was in point of form a valid will according to French law, and that as the wife at the time of making the will was over 16 but under 21 years of age, she was, under French law, competent to dispose by will of one-half of the property which she could have disposed of if she had been 21 years of age.

Peterson J: . . . It was contended, in the first place, that as she was, when she made her will, under 21 years of age, she could not thereby exercise the power of appointment at all, and reliance was placed on the provision that the rights of all parties claiming under the settlement were to be regulated by the law of England in the same way as if both husband and wife had throughout been domiciled in England. It could not be disputed that a holograph French will might operate as an exercise of the power, as it was expressly within the terms of the settlement, and if it had not been expressly provided for it would, on the authorities, be a will which was recognised in England as valid and therefore a will capable of exercising the power. But it was urged that the provisions in the settlement only related to the form of this will and did not affect the question of testamentary capacity, and that this question must be determined by English law, as the rights under the settlement were to be regulated by English law as if the husband and wife had been domiciled in England. This argument, in my opinion, is unsound. The settlement expressly enables the power of appointment to be exercised by Madame Lewal by a will executed in such manner as to be valid according to the law of her actual domicile as well as by a will executed in such manner as to be valid as such according to the law of England. It obviously contemplated that she should be able to exercise the power by a French will which might not comply with the requirements as to wills of the English law. Nor do I think that this provision related merely to the form of the will and to the presence or absence of attesting witnesses. What the settlement contemplated was a will which should be valid according to French law or a will which would be valid according to English law. This will is a good will according to French law notwithstanding the fact that Madame Lewal was under 21 years of age when she made it. This objection therefore, in my opinion, fails.

The next objection was that the will did not, in fact, exercise the power. It does not refer to the settlement or to the property comprised in the settlement, and it was said that s 27 of the Wills Act cannot be invoked for the purpose of interpreting a French will. This contention has given rise to a considerable difference in judicial opinion. In *Re D'Este's Settlement Trusts*,[16] Buckley J held that a will by a domiciled Frenchwoman, which appointed her husband her universal legatee and bequeathed to him all her personal estate, did not operate as an exercise of a general power of appointment, and

16 [1903] 1 Ch 898, 72 LJCh 305.

that reference could not be made to s 27 of the Wills Act for the purpose of interpreting the will, as the section was intended as a statutory rule for the interpretation of English wills and could not be applied to the interpretation of foreign wills, which must be construed according to the law of the domicile. This decision was followed by Kekewich J in *Re Scholefield*.[17] These two cases were, however, subjected to a very destructive criticism by Neville J in *Re Simpson*,[18] where it was held that an unattested holograph will of a British subject domiciled in France, by which she disposed of all the property and rights comprised in her estate, effectually exercised a general power of appointment which she had over the trust funds under the English settlement, the learned judge expressly dissenting from the decisions in the two earlier cases. In *Re Wilkinson's Settlement*,[19] Sargant J (although the point seems to have been unnecessary for the decision of that case) agreed with the opinion of Neville J and added some further reasons for disagreeing with the view of Buckley J and Kekewich J. In these circumstances I am at liberty to express my own opinion. The judgment of Buckley J is summarised in the following passage from his judgment: 'Then it is said that I must take this French document and read it, not as a will in the sense in which I have explained, but as if the directions contained in it were introduced into the instrument which contained the power. That is quite right: but how must I read it? I have, referentially, to introduce into the instrument which contains the power a foreign document. I have to see whether the power was exercised, and therefore to find out the meaning of what is expressed by the donee of the power. Now how am I to ascertain the meaning of the donee of the power? I must ascertain it according to the law of the place applicable to the document executed by the donee and to the domicile of that person, and that law is to be taken as the law governing its construction. If I do that, I have to read the French will and say what its meaning is according to the principle of French construction, excluding, therefore, s 27, which is a rule for English construction.' With all respect to the learned judge, it appears to me that his conclusion does not necessarily follow from his premises. If the French will was to be interpreted according to the principles of French construction it did not follow that s 27 of the Wills Act was to be excluded. As pointed out by Neville J, the French court does not know anything of powers of appointment and would require to be informed what a general power of appointment was and in what manner it might be exercised, and the answer to this question must involve the effect of s 27. A further argument indicated, I think, by Sargant J in *Re Wilkinson's Settlement*, against the view of Buckley J may be put in this way. Prior to the Wills Act the exercise of a general power of appointment by will had to refer either to the power or to the property subject to the power. After that Act the power could be exercised by a will which disposed of the personal estate of the appointor. This, in effect, amounted to a provision that every general power of appointment by will should be read as a power to appoint by a will which referred to the power, or to the property subject to the power, or disposed of the personal estate of the appointor in general words. The result then would in the present case be that the power authorised the appointment by a valid

17 [1905] 2 Ch 408, 74 LJCh 610.
18 [1916] 1 Ch 502, 85 LJCh 329.
19 [1917] 1 Ch 620, 86 LJCh 511.

French will which disposed of the appointor's estate in general terms and the will of Madame Lewal would be an exercise of the power. I agree with the opinions of Neville J and Sargant J, and therefore hold that the general power of appointment was exercised by the will of Madame Lewal.

I may add that in the present case there seems to be an additional reason why a French court, on being asked to determine whether the will operated as an exercise of the power of appointment, would be bound to ascertain what the English law on the subject was. In order to determine the question it would be necessary to refer to the settlement which contained the power in order to see what was authorised by the power, and it would then be found that the settlement contained a provision that the rights of all parties claiming under it should be regulated in the same way as if the husband and the wife were and continued to be domiciled in England—a clear reference to English law.

The question, however, remains whether the will of Madame Lewal effectively appoints the whole of the fund subject to the power. On the evidence Madame Lewal, when she made her will, had only a limited testamentary capacity. She could only dispose of one-half of the property which she could have disposed of if she had been 21. It appears to me that I am not concerned with the fact that one-quarter of her property went to her mother under art 14 of the Civil Code. Her mother cannot claim a share of the settled funds unless they have been appointed to her or she takes under the settlement in default of appointment.

The result, in my opinion, is that, as Madame Lewal's testamentary capacity was limited in the way which I have mentioned, her will only operated on one-half of the funds which were subject to the power, and that the other half goes as in default of appointment.

The material or essential validity of an exercise by will of a power of appointment over movables depends in the case of a special power on the law governing the instrument of creation, and in the case of a general power on the law governing the instrument of appointment (at any rate if the donee intended to take the appointed property out of the instrument creating the power for all purposes).

Re Pryce [1911] 2 Ch 286, 80 LJCh 525 (Court of Appeal)

Thomas Pryce died in 1904 domiciled in England and having by his will given a share of residue on certain trusts for his daughter Jane Pryce and her children if any, but if no child should attain a vested interest, then for such persons as Jane should by will appoint, and in default of appointment for the persons who would have been entitled if she had died intestate and a spinster.

In January 1908 Jane Pryce married G. H. O. Geertsema, a Dutch subject domiciled in the Netherlands. There was no issue of the marriage, and she died in October 1909, having by her will, which was dated in September 1909 and made in the Dutch language and form, appointed her husband as her 'sole heir of the whole of the estate of which the law in force at the time of her death should allow her to dispose of in his favour'.

According to Dutch law the exercise of the power had the effect of making the appointed property the assets of the testatrix for all purposes: but the testatrix's mother was entitled to one-eighth of her property and her husband to seven-eighths only.

The executor of Thomas Pryce took out an originating summons for the determination of the question who was entitled to the property subject to the power. Parker J held that the husband was entitled to the whole of such property. The testatrix's mother appealed.

Cozens-Hardy MR: .... It has not been, and it cannot be, seriously denied that the power has been fully exercised in this sense, that the persons entitled in default of appointment are completely cut out. The real question is whether the testatrix had such complete disposing power as the law of England gives, or only such as the law of Holland gives. Parker J has held that the husband is beneficially entitled to the whole fund. . . .

In the present case I think the lady has exercised the power in such a manner as to make the property her assets for all purposes. If so it seems to me to follow that her power of disposition over this property is neither greater nor less than over that which was strictly her own property. That power of disposition must depend upon the law of Holland, by which she could not beneficially dispose of more than seven-eighths.

Parker J based his judgment on three cases which it is necessary for me to consider. The first is *Re Bald*,[20] a decision of Byrne J. It is very shortly reported and no authority is cited. A general power of appointment given by a Scottish instrument was executed by an English will. Under English law the appointed fund would be assets for payment of the appointor's debts, but under Scotch law it would not. Byrne J held apparently that the appointment was specific and not such as to make the fund the appointor's own assets for all purposes, and accordingly he held that the fund went to the appointees, and was not assets of the appointor for the benefit of his creditors. The second case is *Pouey v Hordern*,[1] a decision of Farwell J. There the power was special and not general. The learned judge held, and, if I may respectfully say so, with perfect accuracy, that the will exercising the power was not a disposition of her own property, but was only a nomination of the persons whose names were to be inserted in the English settlement creating the power. But there are some observations which led me, in *Re Mégret*,[2] to suppose, as Parker J supposed, that Farwell J's view was that the same principle applied to a general as to a special power. If this statement is taken without any qualification, I think it is too wide. But on further consideration I am satisfied that the observations of Farwell J were addressed only to a case where the appointment under the general power is direct to the object of the appointor's bounty, and not in such a manner as to make the fund part of her own estate to be dealt with in one mass. The third case is *Re Mégret*, the facts of which are distinguishable from the facts in the present case. The appointment there was specific, in this sense, that it did not operate to make the fund a part of her own property for all purposes. My decision was, I think, correct on that view.

The proposition deduced from those cases in *Dicey on Domicil*,[3] (2nd edn)

20 (1897) 66 LJCh 524, 76 LT 462.
 1 [1900] 1 Ch 492, 69 LJCh 231.
 2 [1901] 1 Ch 547, 70 LJCh 451.
 3 Sic: Dicey's *Conflict of Laws* was really meant.

p 705, seems to me to be too widely stated. It should exclude cases in which the power has been so exercised as to throw the appointed fund into the appointor's own estate and to deal with the whole as one mass.

The present case seems to me to fall within the excepted class. The appointed fund is thrown into one mass with the appointor's own property. In this respect the English law is the same as the law of Holland.

With great respect to Parker J I am unable to concur in his view, and I think this appeal must be allowed.

I prefer to base my judgment on the above reasons rather than upon the peculiar terms of the gift to the husband.

Buckley LJ: . . . It is not necessary to consider whether *Re Mégret* was rightly decided or not. The present case is distinguishable inasmuch as the property the subject of the power was in *Re Mégret* the only property dealt with, while in the present case all the property of which the testatrix had power to dispose is dealt with in one mass. . . . .

Kennedy LJ concurred.
  Appeal allowed.

The law governing the instrument of creation determines whether a power of appointment is general or special.

Re Bauer's Trust (1964) 14 NY 2d 272, 200 NE 2d 207 (New York Court of Appeals)

In 1917 Dagmar Bauer, then domiciled in New York, executed in New York City an irrevocable trust indenture which stipulated that the income of the trust fund should be paid to her for life and the principal distributed after her death and that of her husband to such person or persons as she should by will appoint and in default of appointment to the settlor's next of kin pursuant to the statutes of the State of New York. The settlor's husband predeceased her and she died in 1956 domiciled in England having by her will and a codicil thereto appointed the trust funds to Midland Bank Executor and Trustee Co Ltd on trust for two nieces for life with remainder to Dr Barnardo's Homes.

By New York law the power was special and the appointment was invalid under the New York statutory rule against perpetuities (since repealed) because the power of alienation was suspended for longer than two lives in being at the creation of the power. By English law the power was general and the appointment was valid.

Desmond CJ: (1) The law to be applied here is the law of New York which was the donor's domicile and where there was executed the trust agreement containing the power of appointment. This rule applies where the same person is donor and donee.

(2) The trust was irrevocable and created a remainder interest but no reversionary interest in Mrs Bauer. She retained no more than a testamentary power of appointment and hers was, therefore, one of the 'measuring lives'.

(3) The original trust plus the codicil trust thus involved three lives in

being, resulting in unenforcibility under the applicable former New York law and thus the attempt in the will and codicil to exercise the power of appointment was ineffective.

(4) Since the residuary clause specifically excludes 'property otherwise disposed of by this . . . will or any codicil', it cannot be construed to refer to the appointive property as to which the will contained an invalid dispositive clause.

(5) Since, therefore, there has been no valid testamentary disposition of the trust principal it must, as directed by the indenture itself, be distributed to the settlor's next of kin pursuant to the statutes of New York.

Fuld J (dissenting): We deal here with a testatrix (Dagmar Dauer) who died in England, where she had long been domiciled, after there executing a will in which she exercised a general power of appointment, of which she was donor as well as donee, pursuant to a trust indenture executed in New York almost 40 years earlier. The court's decision to apply New York law to test the validity of Mrs Bauer's exercise in England (in 1954) of the power of appointment which she had reserved to herself (in 1917) strikes me as an unfortunate example of adherence to mechanical and arbitrary formulae. The same considerations which prompted a departure from the inflexible and traditional choice-of-law rules in other cases (see, eg, *Auten v Auten*,[4] *Babcock v Jackson*)[5], it seems to me, should move the court to re-examine the wisdom and justice of continuing to apply similarly inflexible rules, without regard to significant underlying factors, in disposing of cases such as the present one.

The traditional rule which identifies the instrument exercising the power with the instrument creating it, for the purpose of testing the validity of the exercise of the power, assumes that ownership of the appointive property remains at all times in the donor of the power and that the donee of the power serves merely as a conduit or agency through which the donor's intention with respect to the appointive property is realised. Such an assumption is, perhaps, justified where the power created is 'special' and confines the donee's exercise of the power within the limits prescribed by the instrument creating the power. However, the assumption is certainly not justified when the power created is 'general' or 'beneficial', whether exercisable by deed or will or by will alone, and no restrictions of any other kind are imposed on its exercise by the donee. In the latter case—and in the one before us upon the death of Mrs Bauer's husband—it is evident that the donee is vested with the equivalence of ownership as to the appointive property. (See, eg, *Cheshire Private International Law*, (6th edn, 1961) p 578). And this is particularly true where the donor and donee of the general power are the same person. This being so, it runs counter to reason to assume that the donor in such a case becomes his own agent to preserve an attachment to the place where the original trust agreement was executed, even though he has abandoned that place as his residence and acquired a new domicile in another jurisdiction, to the laws of which he voluntarily subjected himself.

In exercising the general power of appointment in England 37 years after she had conferred such power upon herself, Mrs Bauer was justified in

4 (1954) 308 NY 155, 124 NE 2d 99.
5 (1963) 12 NY 2d 473, 191 NE 2d 279 (p. 501 above).

treating the appointive property as her own, and it is reasonable to suppose that, in disposing of such property under a will executed in England by an English solicitor, designating an English institutional executor and trustee to administer the trust and conferring benefits, at least in part, upon an English charity, Mrs Bauer (through her English solicitor) had exercised the power in the light of English, rather than New York, law. The inference is inescapable that she intended the disposition of the appointive property to be governed by the same law which would govern the disposition of her personal estate, namely, the law of her last domicile. Since no discernible New York policy or interest dictates the application of its law to invalidate the disposition by the English testatrix valid under her personal law—and, indeed, now valid under present New York law—such intention should be given effect.

I do not, of course, mean to suggest that New York law would not govern the validity and effect of the provisions of the *trust indenture*. That instrument was executed in 1917 against the background of New York law, which Mrs Bauer at that time undoubtedly intended would control. (See *Hutchinson v Ross*;[6] *Shannon v Irving Trust Co*[7].) However, I reject as insupportable any suggestion that the law governing the trust conclusively governs the exercise of the power of appointment in every case, even to the extent of overriding the manifest intent of the donor-donee to have the law of his last domicile apply so as to effect a valid exercise of the general power.

In sum, then, I would disavow the rule requiring the inexorable application of the law governing the instrument creating the power and I would apply the law of the jurisdiction intended by the donor-donee to control—in the case before us, England which, quite obviously, has the principal, if not the sole, interest and concern with ' "the outcome of . . . [this] litigation" '. (*Auten v Auten*).

Van Voorhis, Burke and Scileppi JJ concurred with Desmond CJ. Dye and Bergan JJ concurred with Fuld J.

---

6 (1933) 262 NY 381, 187 NE 65.
7 (1937) 275 NY 95, 9 NE 2d 792.

CHAPTER 23

Effect of Marriage on Movables

In the absence of a marriage contract the rights of husband and wife to each other's movables, whether possessed at the time of the marriage or acquired afterwards, are governed by the law of the matrimonial domicile.

The matrimonial domicile means (in the absence of special circumstances) the husband's domicile at the time of the marriage.

Re Egerton's Will Trusts [1956] Ch 593, [1956] 2 All ER 817 (Chancery Division)

In May 1932 the testator, who was then domiciled in England, married a Frenchwoman domiciled in France. In 1934 they settled in France and acquired a domicile there in accordance with their antenuptial intention. In 1951 the testator died having by his will made provision for his wife which she regarded as unsatisfactory. She claimed to be entitled to share in his estate in accordance with the French doctrine of community of property.

Roxburgh J: ....Mr Wilberforce [counsel for the widow] has propounded an argument which might almost be said to set the professors by the ears. To start on a safe foundation, I will first read rule 171 in Dicey's *Conflict of Laws* (6th edn) p 795, which says: 'Where there is no marriage contract or settlement, and where no subsequent change of domicile on the part of the parties to the marriage has taken place, the rights of the husband and wife to each other's movables, whether possessed at the time of the marriage or acquired afterwards, are governed by the law of the matrimonial domicile, without reference to the law of the country where the marriage is celebrated or where the wife is domiciled before marriage.' That is indisputable law. So that, prima facie, the law applicable to the present case, on the finding of fact which I have just made, is English law. I have deliberately used the phrase 'prima facie'. I can disregard the words of the rule 'where no subsequent change of domicile on the part of the parties to the marriage has taken place'. In truth there was a subsequent change in the domicile in the present case. But I need not pursue that question further because, for reasons connected with French law, which I need not elaborate but which Mr Wilberforce found quite compelling, he did not base any argument on the subsequent change of domicile.

What Mr Wilberforce did was to explore the problem which has been the subject of debate between Dr Morris, the author of the note that I am going to read, and Dr Cheshire. The particular note refers to a somewhat different position, namely, where there is a marriage contract, but for the present purpose that is not important because it is really a discussion of the phrase 'matrimonial domicile'. The passage in the text of *Dicey* (at p 541) is as follows: 'The marriage contract, or settlement, will be construed with reference to the proper law of the contract, ie, in the absence of reason to the contrary, by the law of the husband's actual domicile at the time of the marriage. The husband's actual domicile at the time of the marriage is hereinafter termed the "matrimonial domicile".' I have read that passage in order to explain the note, because it is the note and not the passage which really raises the issue. Dr Morris says this: 'Whether in this Exception and in the rest of this Digest the term "matrimonial domicile" ought to be extended, so as to mean the intended domicile of the husband, when, as occasionally happens, he, though domiciled in one country, intends, to the knowledge of both parties to the marriage, to become immediately domiciled in another country (eg, France)',—and I stress at once the word 'immediately'—'is a question on which there is no decisive English authority. On the theory, however, of a tacit or express contract between the parties about to marry, that their mutual property rights shall be determined by the law of their matrimonial domicile, the extension of that term so as to include the country in which they intend to become, and do become, domiciled immediately after the marriage'—and I again stress that word—'seems to some authorities reasonable. For instance, if H, domiciled in England, marries in England W, domiciled in South Africa, and H and W sail to South Africa immediately after the ceremony'—and again I stress the word 'immediately'—'intending to make it their permanent home, it would seem reasonable at first sight to hold that South Africa, and not England, was their matrimonial domicile. The difficulty is, however, that there is no conclusive English authority in favour of this view, and there are practical difficulties in its application. What if H and W do not sail to South Africa until a month—or a year—after the ceremony? Where is the line to be drawn? Are the rights of the spouses to be in suspense until they actually acquire a new domicile in pursuance of their pre-matrimonial intention? It is submitted that the safer rule to adopt is that the matrimonial domicile means the husband's domicile at the time of the marriage. In a clear case where the parties change their domicile very shortly after the marriage'—and I do again stress the words 'in a clear case'—'in pursuance of a pre-matrimonial intention to that effect, the change of domicile might well be a "reason to the contrary" within the meaning of the Exception. This way of looking at the matter has the advantage of avoiding the use of a term of ambiguous meaning which suggests either that a change of domicile can be effected by mere intention, or that "matrimonial domicile" means something different from "domicile" simpliciter.'

Different, however, is the approach of Dr Cheshire in *Private International Law*. The passage is too long for me to read in extenso, and I am only going to read extracts. It begins with these words (4th edn p 491): 'Although there is no clear-cut and decisive authority, the prevalent view is that the determining domicile is that which the husband possesses *at the time of the marriage*. On the whole it is an unobjectionable view, for in the vast majority of cases the parties retain the husband's domicile immediately after the marriage. Nevertheless, a rule better calculated to function more justly and more conveniently in every case is one which selects the country of the intended matrimonial home. This is equivalent in the normal case to the domicile at the time of the marriage, but its merit is that it meets the not unusual case where the parties intend to settle immediately after marriage in another country.' After leaving something out, I read again (at p 492): 'It is respectfully submitted, however, that the just and reasonable view to take'— on the facts, which he had just mentioned—'is that the law of the country in which the parties intended to settle immediately, in which in fact they did settle, and in which so far as they could foresee they would remain for the rest of their married lives, should be allowed to govern their mutual proprietary rights. The reasonable inference from the circumstances is that they intended to submit themselves in toto to the matrimonial régime, proprietary as well as personal, obtaining in their future home.' Then he says (on p 493): 'The view that the matter should be governed by the law of the intended matrimonial home lacks neither doctrinal analogy nor juristic support.' Then he says later: 'It is undeniable, of course, that the practical application of the doctrine of the intended matrimonial home may in some cases encounter considerable difficulties. . . .How quickly must the intention to settle in the specified country be implemented? What if there is unforeseen delay or some accident which frustrates the design? Will effect be given to the alleged intention if it remains a secret locked in the breasts of the parties? These difficulties are no more insuperable than those which often attend the ascertainment of intention in a disputed case of domicile. Everything hinges on intention, but the dominion of the lex domicilii of the husband at the time of the marriage is not displaced unless the intention to acquire a new home is established by irrefragable evidence. In fact, the suggested rule goes no further than this: There is a strong presumption that the lex domicilii of the husband at the time of the marriage governs the mutual proprietary rights of the spouses. This presumption is rebutted if it is proved that they intended before the marriage to establish their home in some country other than the husband's domicile and that they have in fact carried this intention out. The presumption may be rebutted, though not lightly, if the question falls to be considered before the intention has been carried out.' If that suggested rule is in fact a rule of English law, then I think there is no doubt that Mr Wilberforce's client would succeed in the present case, because the [widow] has deposed to the following statement in an affidavit, she has not been cross-examined on it, and it is a statement which I accept. She says this: 'Neither before nor at the time of my marriage to the testator, nor at any time afterwards, was there any discussion or express agreement between us as to community or separation of property. It was however agreed between us before marriage that as soon as possible we would settle in France and establish our permanent and only home there. We carried this intention into effect, and neither of us ever had a permanent home outside France after the date of our marriage.'

I have, therefore, to approach this controversy between Dr Morris and Dr Cheshire with that caution and respect which they both deserve. I think a good starting point is a passage in the judgment of Vaughan Williams LJ in the Court of Appeal in *Re Martin*,[1] where he says this: 'In my opinion, the effect of the husband's domicile on the matrimonial property is based on the presumption that you must read the law of the husband's domicile into the marriage contract as a term of it, unless there is an express agreement to the contrary.' I must respectfully differ from those last words 'unless there is an

---

1 [1900] P 211, 69 LJP 75; p 590 above.

express agreement to the contrary', because I see no reason why, if the facts warrant it, an agreement which is sometimes erroneously called 'a tacit agreement' might not be as effective as an express agreement. . . .For my part, I see no reason why an appropriate agreement excluding the presumption could not be inferred from the conduct of the parties if the circumstances of the case justify such an inference, and it is, I think, something of that kind which Dicey must have contemplated when he used the somewhat wide phrase 'in the absence of reason to the contrary'.

There is one point which I must consider which I do not remember meeting before, and on which no authority has been cited to me, and which is very material in this case. Mr Wilberforce has submitted that in deciding whether or not an agreement is to be inferred from conduct, the only conduct which can be considered is conduct earlier than or contemporaneous with the date on which the alleged contract was made. I see no reason for such a limitation, which I should have thought would have put the court into blinkers and preclude it from doing palpable justice in some cases. I will give an example, though perhaps a fanciful one. Supposing that it might be relevant to determine whether there was to be inferred from the conduct of two parties an intention to make a voyage to South Africa, and supposing that the evidence before the date of the journey was that they had consulted tourist offices, obtained particulars of fares, possibly even booked some accommodation, had written to friends and said that they were coming, and supposing that it was quite uncertain at that date whether there was any reason to go to South Africa other that what was to be inferred. Then when the departure comes, they go to New Zealand. It would be ridiculous to exclude from the circumstances from which the inference has to be drawn the circumstance that in the end, at any rate, they went to New Zealand. That is perhaps an extreme case. But I certainly take the view that if it is a question of inferring something from conduct, the court must look at the conduct as a whole and not stop its investigation at any particular date. That approach, as I think, gets rid of all the difficulties.

I would, first of all, like to consider—though it is obiter in this case—the case where the parties agreed before the marriage to change their domicile immediately. I can well conceive that in certain circumstances that mere fact might be enough to lead the court to infer that the parties intended their proprietary rights to be regulated by the law of the new domicile from the moment of their marriage. Take, for example, the case of two comparatively poor persons, one, the woman, having a few National Savings Certificates, and the man being a weekly wage earner. They both decide to emigrate to Australia. I can well believe that the court might think that that was enough in those circumstances to lead to the inference that they intended their proprietary rights (which at that stage were nugatory, but which might thereafter become of great value) to be regulated from the beginning of their married life by the law of Australia. I can well believe that the court might in those circumstances draw some such inference. However, take the case of an elderly widower who was a director of half a dozen companies in England and held shares and debentures and exchequer bonds and various things in England. He marries a young wife, and being ill and in need of a warm climate, agrees to leave immediately to take up his home in South Africa. I cannot imagine that any court would ever draw the inference from the mere fact that they had decided immediately to leave for South Africa to make it their permanent home, and did so, that he intended that all his proprietary rights should, as from the date of their marriage, be governed by the law of South Africa. I have only given those illustrations to show that what inference the court might or might not draw from the circumstances of an immediate change of domicile would depend on all the circumstances of the case. There does not seem to me to be any particular difficulty. Indeed, I think that I am, roughly speaking, adopting the solution which Dr Morris has suggested, though in place of the somewhat vague phrase 'reason to the contrary' I should prefer to put it that an inference was to be drawn from all the circumstances of the case that the law of the new domicile was intended to apply as from the date of the marriage.

But I am not really concerned with that case, because the evidence of the [widow] is 'We would settle in France as soon as possible'. That very phrase, in my view, connotes that circumstances might not make it possible to settle there immediately, and indeed there were circumstances which did stand in the way of an immediate departure. There were certain circumstances connected with the testator's release from the army, and there may have been—though there is no evidence of that—financial and business reasons. The evidence is singularly meagre in this case. I think that the difficulties of inferring anything of that sort are very much greater because, if it is once conceded that the parties contemplated that a period of time is to elapse before they change their domicile, it is most improbable that they intend the new law, or rather, the law of the new domicile, to apply before they actually change their domicile. If, therefore, any inference of this nature is to be drawn, a dichotomy of property rights appears to result, so that they would have some property subject to the law of the matrimonial domicile, that is to say, the husband's domicile at the time of the marriage, and some property subject to the law of the state in which they had a newly acquired domicile. Such an agreement could be made—I see no juristic difficulty— but it seems to me an improbable arrangement and, therefore, strong evidence would be required to justify any such inference merely from conduct and without any express agreement, written or oral.

In the present case there is no evidence of any intention to substitute the new law, that is to say, the law of the changed domicile, for the law of England. All the matters on which Mr Wilberforce relies are equivocal and could not possibly be said to be evidence which would justify any such inference. I have deliberately said that, because, even if I am wrong in thinking that I am entitled to have regard to the declarations in the three documents to which I have referred, I should still hold that there was not enough evidence to justify the inference which Mr Wilberforce asks me to make. But if, as I think, I am entitled to look at those documents, then there is strong evidence that no agreement between these parties is to be inferred from their conduct that the law of France was to apply as soon as they took up their residence in France. I myself should have thought that if any kind of change of that sort was in contemplation the testator would, at some stage, have been bound to have discussed it with [his wife], and her evidence is that he never did. In my opinion, in the circumstances of this case, it would be quite fantastic to infer from what is merely the change of domicile that it was arranged at the time of the marriage, tacitly or by conduct, that French law should apply to their property rights as soon as they settled in France, and I decline to draw any such inference.

If that be the right basis in law, that is, of course, the end of the matter. If, however, Professor Cheshire's view is to be adopted, then I think that Mr Wilberforce would succeed, but I can find no foundation in the authorities for Professor Cheshire's view. In my judgment, it is reasonably plain that there is a presumption that the law of the husband's domicile applies to a marriage, and that the presumption can be rebutted. It can certainly be rebutted by express contract, and, in my judgment, it could also be rebutted by what is loosely called a tacit contract, if the circumstances warrant the inference of such a tacit contract. Therefore, in substance, I adhere to the view expressed by Dr Morris. The widow is not entitled to have the estate administered under the régime of community of property in accordance with French law.

Declaration accordingly.

Frankel's Estate v The Master 1950 (1) SA 220 (Appellate Division of the Supreme Court of South Africa)

A husband and wife were married in 1933 in Czechoslovakia, the husband being then domiciled in Germany (which was his domicile of origin) and the wife, immediately before the marriage, in Czechoslovakia. At the time of the marriage they intended and had determined and agreed to leave Germany and to establish their permanent home in Johannesburg where the husband had been promised employment. They arrived in Johannesburg about four months later, the husband entering upon the promised employment and both of them having the intention of settling there permanently. In 1937 the husband was appointed a director of a Durban company controlled by his employers, and in consequence he and his wife moved to Durban with the intention of settling there permanently. In 1938 the husband was naturalised as a British subject. The husband and wife lived in Durban until 1948 when the husband died. There was no antenuptial contract. The law of Germany in 1933 was that a marriage without antenuptial contract was a marriage out of community.

The widow applied for a declaration that the parties were married in community of property according to the laws of the Union of South Africa. The substantial respondent was the Commissioner for Inland Revenue. The Natal Provincial Division dismissed the application. The widow appealed.

Schreiner JA: The question in this appeal is whether, where a man and woman at the time of their marriage intend to settle in a country other than that of the man's domicile, that country's law, and not the law of the man's domicile, governs the proprietary rights of the spouses. It is not in dispute that where no question of intention to settle in some other country is involved the law of the man's domicile at the time of the marriage governs those rights, unless before the marriage the parties have expressly agreed otherwise; but it is contended for the appellants that where there is such an intention to settle in another country this intention has in law the same effect as if the parties had expressly agreed that their proprietary rights should be governed by the law of the country of proposed settlement.

The appellants support their case by reference to several lines of authority. Some writers advance as a reason for the adoption of the rule that the law of the man's domicile governs the proprietary rights of the spouses the fact that they will generally be going to live in that domicile; and this reason is claimed by the appellants to be the true general principle, of which the predominance of the law of the man's domicile is only the most important application. The practice of seeking a wider, underlying, principle behind a recognised specific rule is a valuable means of improving the form of the law, by making it more logical and harmonious, but the practice may, if pursued incautiously, have unsatisfactory effects on the law's substance. If some reason for a rule of law has appealed to the fertile brain of an early writer and has been accepted, possibly without re-examination, by later writers, it may take the place of the rule itself, although it was not in fact the reason or the only or most important reason for the adoption of the rule into the customary or statutory law. If the result is a better, fairer, clearer rule it may be of no importance that the modification rested on a weak foundation. But unless the result is good it is difficult to see why the rule should be changed because a writer or writers conceived a plausible but possibly erroneous reason for its introduction. The certainty of a generally accepted rule should not, without good cause, be weakened by doubts as to the reasons that may have led to its establishment. In the present case, whatever may have been written on the subject, I am not convinced that the domicile of the man was chosen, by whoever chose it, because that was where the parties were most likely to have their home after the marriage. It may be so but it may not. At least equally plausible seems to me to be the proposition that the law treated the husband as generally the dominant partner and when the need for fixing a law to govern the proprietary rights of the spouses was in question it was his law, that is under our system the law of his domicile, that was made to govern. At all events the possibility that the inaugurators of the generally accepted rule that the man's domicile provides the law of the marriage had in mind the fact that the parties would probably be living there seems to furnish no sufficient reason for doubting the full applicability of the rule.

The appellants rely upon another line of authorities who make the statement, sometimes with a confusing introduction of the place of celebration of the marriage as a factor, that the law of the woman's domicile will govern the proprietary rights of the spouses if the man intends to settle at that domicile after the marriage. But these statements are fairly explainable on the basis that the man may change his domicile when he comes to get married at the woman's home with the intention of going on living there.

The appellants, however, do have in their favour certain opinions expressed by jurists of importance in favour of the view for which they contend. So far as Pothier and Story are concerned there is no doubt that they did support the proposition that where at the time of the marriage the parties intend to make a particular country their home their proprietary rights should be governed by the law of that country and not by the law of the man's domicile at the date of the marriage. And some modern textbook writers have adopted the same view. But the considerations against this view seem to me to be preponderant. In the first place it may be remarked that Story's reasoning does not appear to have found favour in the United States of America.[2] Then, if one looks at the matter from the logical point of view, there seems to be a decided jump in inferring from a decision to settle in a particular country a tacit agreement that the law of that country is to govern the spouses' proprietary rights. It would depend on what assumption regarding the very question in issue is to be attributed to the parties. If they

2 See notes in 43 Harv L Rev 1286 and 44 Harv L Rev 523, citing Conflict of Laws Restatement, s 18.

assume that the law of the man's domicile will govern, the fact that they intend to settle in another country becomes irrelevant. The analogy of ordinary contracts, which are generally governed in regard to their performance by the law of the place of performance, seems to be a false one, for in regard to such contracts the law of the domicile of the parties to the contract is irrelevant. Where parties in marrying make no express contract as to the law that is to govern their proprietary rights the natural inference is that they intend those rights to be governed by whatever law is applicable, according to the law of the place where the issue arises. There seems to be no greater justification for attributing to them an assumption that their proprietary rights will be governed by the law of their proposed place of settlement, no matter what the law of the man's domicile is, than for attributing to them an assumption that the law of the man's domicile will apply, no matter where they make their home.

When one turns to considerations of convenience the appellants' contention is seriously weakened. In a matter of this sort it is of the greatest importance that there should, as far as possible, be certainty not only as to what the law is but as to its application. Now it is clear that, if the mere intention of the spouses regarding their future home is to decide what law is to govern their proprietary rights, a world of uncertainty is introduced into the problem. How firm or definite must their intention be? Must their resolve be fixed to remain in the new country permanently, whatever the conditions may prove to be? How soon must it be their intention to move thither? Answers of some kind to these and similar questions might no doubt be given if the facts could be established or if use were made of the burden of proof, but the result could only be to leave it in serious doubt what law would govern the rights of any married couple who at the time of their marriage considered migrating to another country. They themselves could not be certain of their position, especially if one spouse had somewhat different views from the other as to the advisability or urgency of moving to the new country. So far as other persons, like creditors, are concerned, they would be entirely unable to ascertain or prove the law governing the rights of the spouses. No doubt questions of considerable difficulty can arise as to where any particular person is domiciled but, by comparison, such questions, answerable as they are by external facts such as circumstances of birth and conduct, would appear to be simple.

These considerations lead me to the conclusion that the appeal must be dismissed with costs.

Watermeyer CJ, Centlivres JA, Greenberg JA, and Van den Heever JA delivered judgments to the same effect.
Appeal dismissed.

Where there is a marriage contract or settlement, it governs the rights of husband and wife over all movables comprised within its terms which are then possessed or afterwards during the coverture acquired, even if there is a change of domicile, and even if the contract is implied by law.

De Nicols v Curlier [1900] AC 21, 69 LJCh 109 (House of Lords)

In 1854 Nicolas Daniel Thevenon, a Frenchman, married a Frenchwoman in Paris. In accordance with French law and custom the municipal officer who performed the ceremony formally called upon the parties to declare whether they had executed any contract of marriage, to which they both replied in the negative, when their answers were duly recorded on the usual 'Minute'; and it appeared from the evidence in the present case that no contract of marriage was executed.

At the date of the marriage the husband was a man of no means whatever, being a working coachmaker in Paris at wages. The wife was an assistant in a linen business, and had a little property of her own amounting altogether to about £120. In October 1863 they came over to England, and with a sum of about £400, which represented their sole property, set up in London a small restaurant, called the 'Café Royal', in Glasshouse Street, Regent Street. Ultimately under their joint management this restaurant expanded into a large establishment of the same name in Regent Street. Shortly after their arrival in England the husband changed his name to 'Daniel Nicolas de Nicols', and in 1865 took out letters of naturalisation as a British subject under that name. He and his wife remained in England until his death, she actively assisting him in the management of the café. Out of that business, and from an interest in a valuable building site in London, the husband amassed a large fortune. On 28 February 1897 he died, having made a will dated 22 March 1895, in the English form, in which, after appointing three persons his executors and trustees and bequeathing various legacies, he devised and bequeathed to them his residuary real and personal estate in trust for sale, and to hold the proceeds upon trust for his wife for life, and after her death upon trust for his daughter (the only child of the marriage), her husband and children. The testator was at his death possessed of property of the total value of about £600,000, comprising considerable freehold and leasehold properties, besides investments in numerous stocks and shares. It was said that he also had £100,000 worth of wine in France. There was only one child of his marriage, a daughter, who was married and had several children, of whom one, a daughter, was now the wife of the Marquis de Bruille.

This was an originating summons taken out by Madame de Nicols, the testator's widow, against the executors and trustees of his will, his daughter and her children, to ascertain (amongst other things) what were the rights and interests of the plaintiff in the real and personal estate of her late husband, the testator, by reason of their having married without any marriage contract or settlement, the parties being at the time domiciled in France. Subsequently the question for decision was formulated in chambers as follows: 'Did the change of domicile alter the legal position of the parties to the marriage in reference to property?' The summons was then adjourned into court for argument on this question, and now came on for hearing. Upon the summons being opened it was arranged that the argument should, for the present, be confined to the effect of the change of domicile on the testator's 'movable goods' only.

Kekewich J decided in favour of the widow. His decision was reversed by the Court of Appeal. The widow appealed.

Lord Macnaghten: The question for your Lordships' consideration is whether Mr and Mrs De Nicols continued subject to the system of community of goods after they became domiciled in England. On the one hand it is contended that the change of domicile from French to English destroyed the community altogether, and, therefore, that the testator's will operated upon the whole of the property vested in him which, but for that change, would have been common. On the other hand it is said that the community continued notwithstanding the change of domicile, and that Mr De Nicols remained bound by the article of the Code Civil, which provides that a testamentary donation by the husband cannot exceed his share of the community.

If the case were not embarrassed by the judgment of this House in *Lashley v Hog*,[3] which was discussed so fully at the bar, it would not, I think, present much difficulty.

Putting aside *Lashley v Hog* for the moment, the only question would seem to be what was the effect according to French law of the marriage of Mr and Mrs De Nicols without a marriage contract? Upon that point there cannot, I think, be any room for doubt. It is proved by the evidence of M. Lax, the expert in French law called on behalf of the appellant, that, according to the law of France, a husband and wife intermarrying without having entered into an antenuptial contract in writing are placed and stand by the sole fact of the marriage precisely in the same position in all respects as if previously to their marriage they had in due form executed a written contract, and thereby adopted as special and express covenants all and every one of the provisions contained in arts 1401 to 1496 in Title V of the Code Civil, headed 'Of Marriage Contracts and the respective rights of spouses'. . . .

The expert who was called on behalf of the executors does not attempt to contravene this conclusion of law. He endeavours to minimise its effect by treating it as a self-evident proposition—as in fact being nothing more than what the Code declares. He adds, however, that in his opinion the effect of a change of domicile or nationality upon the community system was never considered by the framers of the Code. That may be so. But if there is a valid compact between spouses as to their property, whether it be constituted by the law of the land or by convention between the parties, it is difficult to see how that compact can be nullified or blotted out merely by a change of domicile. Why should the obligations of the marriage law, under which the parties contracted matrimony, equivalent according to the law of the country where the marriage was celebrated to an express contract, lose their force and effect when the parties become domiciled in another country? As M. Lax points out, change of domicile and naturalisation in a foreign country are not among the events specified in the Code as having the effect of dissolving or determining the community. Let us suppose a case the converse of the present one. Suppose an Englishman and an Englishwoman, having married in England without a settlement, go to France and become domiciled there. Suppose that at the time of the acquisition of the French domicile the husband has £10,000 of his own. Why should his ownership of that sum be impaired or qualified because he settles in France? There is nothing to be found in French law, nothing in the Code Civil, to effect this alteration in his rights. Community of goods in France is constituted by a marriage in France according to French law, not by married people coming to France and settling there. And the community must commence from the day of the marriage. It cannot commence from any other time. It appears to me, therefore, that the proposition for which the executors contend cannot

3 (1804) 4 Paton 581.

be supported on principle. That, I think, was the view of the Court of Appeal. But they considered that the judgment of Lord Eldon in *Lashley v Hog* compelled them to decide in favour of the executors. Mr and Mrs Roger Hog, an Englishman by domicile and an Englishwoman, intermarried in England without a settlement. Mr Hog made a fortune in England, settled in Scotland and became domiciled there. After this change of domicile the wife died in the lifetime of the husband. Some years later the husband died a domiciled Scotsman. There was a good deal of litigation as to the administration of Mr Hog's estate, and there were appeals to this House. In one of these appeals, among other things, this House determined that Mrs Lashley, who was one of the children of the marriage, had 'a claim in right of her mother the wife of the said Mr Roger Hog, who at the time of her death had his domicile in Scotland, to a share of the movable estate of her father at the time of her mother's death'.

No doubt if the law had not been altered by the Intestate Movable Succession (Scotland) Act 1855, s 6, that decision would be binding upon this House in a similar case. But when you are asked to apply the decision to a case where the circumstances are different, it seems to me that the proper course is to ascertain, if you can, the principle of the decision, and then to see if that principle is applicable to the circumstances of the case under consideration. This is the case of a French marriage with a settlement prescribed and constituted by the law of the land and followed by naturalisation in a foreign country. *Lashley v Hog* was the case of an English marriage without a settlement and a change of residence to another part of the United Kingdom.

Now, what was the principle on which Lord Eldon proceeded? After a long discussion Lord Eldon comes to the point by asking this question: 'Why should it be thought an unreasonable thing that where there is no express contract the implied contract should be taken that the wife is to look to the law of the country where the husband dies for the right she is to enjoy, in case the husband thinks proper to die intestate?' Then his Lordship goes on to say:

> 'This has been the principle, which it seems to me has been adopted, as far as we can collect what has been the principle adopted, in cases in those parts of the island with which we are best acquainted, and not being aware that there has been any decision which will countervail this; thinking that it squares infinitely better with those principles upon which your Lordships have already decided in this case, it does appear to me attending to the different sentiments to be found in the text-writers upon the subject that it is more consonant to our own laws, and more consonant to the general principle, to say that the implied contract is that the rights of the wife shall shift with the change of residence of the wife, that change of residence being accomplished by the will of the husband whom by the marriage contract in this instance she is bound to obey.'

I may observe in passing that in that passage Lord Eldon was referring to the difference of practice in the administration of intestates' effects then prevailing in the different provinces of York and Canterbury, and also to a previous decision in the case of *Lashley v Hog* on the question of legitim. It is not, I think, very easy to see how the principle which Lord Eldon selects as the ground of his decision could in the case of an English marriage and the subsequent acquisition of a Scotch domicile be legitimately extended so as to deprive the husband of his own property, and transfer it in his lifetime to the next of kin of his wife. It seems to me that the result can only be reached by one or other of two alternatives. Either it must be held that the implied contract on the part of the husband is that in case of a change of domicile the wife shall enjoy all the rights of a woman married in the country where the new domicile is established, and that he will surrender in her favour so much of his rights as may be inconsistent therewith; or else it must be assumed that marriage in Scotland is not required to create communion of goods, but that communion of goods is incidental to the status of married persons in Scotland; or, as Lord Eldon puts it, 'the law of Scotland "recognises" communion of goods "in the married state"'.

Now, if that assumption be necessary in order to support Lord Eldon's conclusion in *Lashley v Hog*, it is obvious that there is so wide a divergence between the law of Scotland, or what is assumed to be the law of Scotland, and the law of France as to make the decision inapplicable to the present case. If, on the other hand, Lord Eldon's conclusion is a legitimate extension or development of the principle on which his argument is founded, it seems to me that there is no room for the application of the principle in the circumstances of the present case. The principle, as Lord Eldon explains, is founded on the notion that upon an English marriage without an express settlement there is an implied contract that the expectations of the wife are to depend upon the domicile of the husband. Lord Eldon admits, and it was conceded at the bar, that, if there had been a written contract dealing with the whole property of the spouses present and future, the principle of *Lashley v Hog* could not apply. Now the effect of what took place on the occasion of the French marriage, so far as it amounted to a compact in respect of property, must, I think, be determined by French law; and it has been proved by the evidence in this case that what did take place was to all intents and purposes, according to the law of France, equivalent to a written contract.

It appears to me, therefore, that the case is not governed by the decision in *Lashley v Hog*, and I think the appeal ought to be allowed.

Lords Halsbury, Morris, Shand, and Brampton delivered judgment to the same effect.

Appeal allowed.

The essential validity of a marriage settlement or contract is governed by its proper law. The proper law is presumed to be (but is not necessarily) the law of the matrimonial domicile.

Duke of Marlborough v A-G [1945] Ch 78, [1945] 1 All ER 165 (Court of Appeal)

Appeal from Vaisey J.

This originating summons taken out by the tenth Duke of Marlborough raised the question whether, on the true construction of a settlement, dated 6 November 1895, and executed in New York on the occasion of the marriage between the ninth duke and Miss Consuelo Vanderbilt (now Madame Balsan) and in the events which happened, estate duty became payable on or in respect of the funds therein comprised by reason of the death of the ninth duke on 30 June 1934. Miss Vanderbilt was the daughter of Mr W. K. Vanderbilt, a citizen of the United States domiciled in New York. At the time of her marriage she was a minor. The settlement comprised a fund of two and a half million dollars in the stock of an American railway, and no English property at all. There was also a covenant by Mr Vanderbilt to settle an annual sum of $100,000 for the wife's separate use without power of anticipation during the joint lives of himself and the wife, and a covenant for the payment by his executors on his death of a further $2,500,000. There was a covenant for the settlement of the wife's after-acquired property 'with a minimum of £10,000'. The trustees were Mr Vanderbilt and the Hon Ivor Churchill Guest (afterwards Lord Wimborne). The investment clause provided a wide range of British and American securities in which the trustees might invest. In fact, the funds had always been invested in American securities, and the administration of the trust had taken place in America, but it was the intention of the parties that Miss Vanderbilt should marry a domiciled Englishman and that the matrimonial domicile of the parties should be English. The settlement contained a covenant that the husband and wife would as soon as possible take all necessary steps to procure the approval of the Chancery Division of the English High Court of Justice under the Infant Settlements Act 1855. Provision was made for the case of the court refusing to approve, and for the possibility of the wife repudiating the settlement. On 27 January 1896 Chitty J in chambers sanctioned the settlement. On the death of the duke the question arose whether for the purpose of succession duty (and therefore of estate duty) the settlement was to be treated as an American or an English settlement. Vaisey J held that it was an English settlement, and that both succession duty and estate duty became payable thereon on the death of the ninth duke. The tenth duke appealed.

The judgment of the court (Lord Greene MR, Finlay and Morton LJJ) was delivered by

Lord Greene MR: . . .Counsel for the duke and for the Crown were in agreement in submitting that in the case of a marriage settlement the question whether succession duty is payable under s 2 of the Succession Duty Act 1853 is to be answered by reference to the law governing the settlement—in other words, the proper law of the settlement. They agreed that duty attaches if, and only if, the proper law of the settlement is English (or Scottish as the case may be). . . .

It may well be the case that the proper law of a settlement can be changed by subsequent events, but we do not see how this can happen without the concurrence of the beneficiaries agreeing to a change in the proper law and thereby, in effect, making a new settlement. It cannot, we think, be effected by a change in trusteeship. . . .In determining what is the proper law of the settlement the nature and situation of the property settled is, no doubt, a matter to be taken into consideration, but the relevant date for this purpose can only be the date of the settlement itself since we do not see how a change, for example, from foreign investments to English investments can turn what was originally a foreign settlement into an English settlement. As in the case of trustees, so in the case of investments a change may be quite fortuitous and cannot affect the question what law governs the settlement. . . .We do not ourselves think that in the case of a marriage settlement what we may call the notional character or location of settled property (which, as we have said, is a relevant consideration) is to be ascertained by reference to the rule 'mobilia sequuntur personam'. That character and location is, we think, a relevant consideration for what it is in fact, not for what (for some purposes) it notionally is by virtue of a conventional rule of law. In the case of a wife who acquires the domicile of her husband on marriage it does not appear to us to be right to attribute to personal property which she settles a character and location by reference to her antenuptial domicile which ex hypothesi is going to be changed immediately after the marriage takes place. Moreover, in the case of both spouses, the matrimonial domicile is the one which must be taken to be in their contemplation when they execute the settlement. For these reasons, although, as we have said, the character and location of the settled property are relevant matters to be taken into consideration in deciding what is the proper law of the settlement they are not, in our opinion, to be ascertained by reference to anything but the true facts relating to the property. . . .

We have come to the conclusion that in the case of a marriage settlement succession duty is exigible only where the proper law of the settlement is English (or Scottish) law. The question, therefore, in the present case is whether that law is the law of England or the law of the State of New York. On what principle is it to be answered? On the same principle, as it seems to us, as a similar question arising in the case of any other personal contract. For this we cannot do better than quote the words of Lord Watson in *Hamlyn & Co v Talisker Distillery*.[4] 'When two parties living under different systems of law enter into a personal contract, which of these systems must be applied to its construction depends upon their mutual intention, either as expressed in their contract, or as derivable by fair implication from its terms. In the absence of any other clear expression of their intention it is necessary and legitimate to take into account the circumstances attendant upon the making of the contract and the course of performing its stipulations contemplated by the parties.' At the outset of the inquiry in the present case lies a question as to the admissibility of certain direct evidence as to the actual intention of the parties, particularly the intention of Mr W. K. Vanderbilt himself. We cannot see on what principle evidence of this character is admissible and counsel for the duke was unable to refer to any case in which it was admitted for the purpose of determining the proper law of a contract. The language of Lord Watson appears to us quite clearly to imply that such evidence is inadmissible. The question what law the parties to a contract contemplate as governing its meaning and operation is, we venture to think, a question of construction the answer to which depends, as Lord Watson says, on 'their mutual intention, either as expressed in their contract or as derivable by fair implication from its terms'. For this purpose, all such evidence of the circumstances as is generally admissible for the purpose of construing a written contract is admissible to ascertain its proper law. Direct evidence of intention is, in our opinion, clearly inadmissible for that purpose.

When we turn to the settlement in this case and such circumstances as are

4 [1894] AC 202 at 212.

admissible, we find the following matters to be considered. Miss Vanderbilt, the settlor of the railway stock, was at the date of the settlement domiciled in the State of New York but the matrimonial domicile of the parties was clearly to be English. The securities which she settled were American securities, but the terms of the settlement permitted their sale and the re-investment of the proceeds in English securities. Mr W. K. Vanderbilt himself was domiciled in the State of New York. Of the two trustees, one was Mr W. K. Vanderbilt, the other was Mr Ivor Guest, a domiciled Englishman resident in England, so that, presumably, both the courts of the State of New York and the English court would have been competent to enforce the trusts of the settlement. The settlement was executed in New York in triplicate, one part being handed to the English trustee, who brought it to England. For some reason he did not have it stamped, but this can have no bearing on the question what is the proper law of the settlement. The settlement itself was drafted in English form. Taking into account these considerations alone and attaching particular weight to the fact of the matrimonial domicile being English, we should have had little hesitation in deciding that the proper law of the settlement was English, but there are certain provisions in the settlement which appear to us to place this beyond all possible doubt. The first is the reference to 'the statutory power of appointing a new trustee', a phrase which would be quite meaningless if the law of the State of New York were contemplated. The next provision is the special indemnity given to the trustees 'in addition to the indemnity given by law to trustees'. The law referred to can only be the law of England since the evidence shows that the law of the State of New York, although it recognises the validity of a contractual indemnity to trustees, does not of itself provide for any indemnity. The last provision is that for the making of an application to the English courts under the Infant Settlements Act with a view to making Miss Vanderbilt's settlement binding on her by English law. It is true that this only affects her own part of the settlement. It points, however, quite clearly to English law as being the proper law of the settlement so far as her part in it was concerned, and we can see no reason for thinking that Mr W. K. Vanderbilt's part of the settlement was intended to be governed by a different law to that which was to govern the settlement of her property by his daughter. . . .

Appeal dismissed.

Re Bankes [1902] 2 Ch 333, 71 LJCh 708 (Chancery Division)

In 1877 Kate Gruinard Anderton, a widow, domiciled in England, became engaged to be married to Angelo Favaroni, an officer in the Italian army. At that time she was possessed of £4,000, and, in order to meet the requirements of the Italian government with reference to the marriage of officers, she deposited £1,000 with the military authorities in that country. On 28 March 1878 she and Favaroni executed in Italy a marriage settlement in English common form, whereby it was agreed that the trustee should hold the remaining sum of £3,000 in trust after the marriage, to permit it to remain in its then state of investment or call in and invest it, and pay the income during the joint lives of herself and Favaroni to her for her separate use without power of anticipation; and after the death of either of them to the survivor, and then for the children of the marriage; and subject thereto, if Mrs Favaroni survived her husband, upon trust after his death for her, her executors, administrators, and assigns; but if he survived her, then after his death as she should by will or codicil appoint; and in default of appointment, in trust for such person or persons as under the statutes for the distribution of the effects of intestates would have become entitled thereto at the decease of Mrs Favaroni had she died possessed thereof intestate and without having been married.

The settlement contained a covenant by Mrs Favaroni to settle her after-acquired property.

The marriage took place on 28 July 1878 at Florence, and Mr and Mrs Favaroni lived in Italy continuously after that time, and were domiciled there. There were no children of the marriage. By a decree dated the 8th and registered on 28 March 1898, of the Civil and Criminal Court of Florence, the court approved of the official report, declared by the President of the Court, of the legal voluntary separation which had taken place between Mr and Mrs Favaroni, subject to certain conditions, and ordered the execution of the report. Since the date of the decree Mr and Mrs Favaroni had lived apart from one another.

On the death of her mother in 1899 Mrs Favaroni became entitled to certain legacies bequeathed by the wills of her father and mother. Questions arose whether these legacies were caught by the agreement to settle after-acquired property contained in the settlement, or could be paid and transferred to Mrs Favaroni on her separate receipt.

The trustee of the settlement commenced an action to determine these questions, and claimed a declaration that the £1,000 legacy was subject to the covenant, and ought to be paid to him; and that the property bequeathed by Mr Bankes was also subject to the clause. There was evidence that according to Italian law the settlement was void because it was not executed before a notary, and because it altered the order of succession under that law; that after marriage the husband and wife remained entitled to their respective fortunes as before; that this position could not be affected by a settlement unless it was attested by a notary; that the separation had no effect upon the individual rights of property; and that the marriage continued after the separation.

Buckley J: The question I now have to determine is whether to this settlement, which was executed on 28 March 1878, the English law or the Italian law is to be applied.

The relevant facts are these: the document is in the English form; it contains this covenant to settle after-acquired property, which would be wholly inoperative if Italian law were applicable to the case. Beyond that the instrument as a whole would, according to the Italian law, have been perfectly invalid, for the evidence is that, inasmuch as it openly violates the legal order of succession established by Italian law, it can have no effect at all in Italy. The further fact is that the wife's domicile was English, and this document provides that the settled fund, which was an English mortgage, if realised and reinvested, should be reinvested in English investments. This is therefore an instrument dealing with the property of a lady who was English, dealing with property which was English, providing that in case that particular property changed its form the new form which it assumed should be English, the whole contained in a document which is in the common

English form, with the further fact that unless the English law is to be applied the whole thing was invalid, and might have been put behind the fire the moment it was executed, because in Italian law it had no effect at all. It seems to me that upon those facts I ought to arrive at the conclusion that the parties intended to contract according to the English law. The general proposition, as stated in Dicey's *Conflict of Laws,* at p 653, is this: 'A marriage contract or settlement will, in the absence of reason to the contrary, be construed with reference to the law of the matrimonial domicile.' The matrimonial domicile here was Italian, no doubt, so that prima facie this ought to be construed with reference to the law of the matrimonial domicile. But is there reason to the contrary? It seems to me, on the facts I have mentioned, there is reason to the contrary. I therefore think the English law, and not the Italian law, ought to be applied.

Then this is further argued—that although according to the English law the lady covenanted that she would at a future time so dispose of her after-acquired property as that it would come within the settlement, yet when she married an Italian she acquired an Italian domicile, and according to the Italian law such a covenant is invalid, and that therefore, upon the doctrine of *Viditz v O'Hagan,*[5] she could not when the covenant fell to be performed be called upon to perform it. It seems to me that is not so. In *Viditz v O'Hagan* the point was that the settlement was executed by an infant who could not bind herself, and the question was whether, by acts done after attaining majority, and after a foreign domicile had been acquired, there had been such an affirmation of the settlement as that it became binding; in other words, the settlement when executed was nothing, and, unless the English law as to affirmation and confirmation applied, it never became binding. Now, here, if I am right, the settlement at the outset was binding because it was executed by a person competent to bind herself. Then, if I am entitled to treat the English law as being applicable to it, she could according to our law bind herself in respect of her after-acquired property, and although it took the form of a covenant and not of an assignment, that would make no difference. On that ground it seems to me the covenant was effectual. I therefore hold that this matter is throughout to be governed by English law.

Capacity to make a marriage settlement contract is governed by its proper law.

Viditz v O'Hagan [1900] 2 Ch 87, 69 LJCh 507 (Court of Appeal)

Appeal against the decision of Cozens-Hardy J.

In November 1864 the Honourable Frances Netterville, then aged 18, the only child of Viscount Netterville, an Irish peer, was married at Berne in Switzerland to Mr Viditz, an Austrian. By marriage articles under seal in English form dated 24 November 1864, and executed before the marriage at the British Legation at Berne, and made between Mr Viditz of the first part, the Honourable Frances Netterville of the second part, trustees of the third part, and Viscount Netterville of the fourth part, it was declared and agreed that all personal property to which the wife was then entitled or to which she might become entitled during the joint lives of the husband and the wife

5 [1900] 2 Ch 87, 69 LJCh 507, below.

should be vested in the trustees upon the usual trusts for the benefit of the wife for life, and after her death upon trusts for the issue of the marriage, with an ultimate trust for Viscount Netterville absolutely.

The husband was domiciled in Austria before and after the marriage and it was contemplated that the parties should live in Austria, as in fact they did. Mrs Viditz attained 21 on 5 November 1867. Subsequently she became entitled to various sums of money and executed various documents appointing new trustees of the settlement of 1864 and, under a power in the settlement, appointing one fourth of the trust funds to one of her daughters.

In 1893 she and her husband executed in Austria and in accordance with Austrian law a notarial act by which they purported to revoke the deed of 1864 and to vest in Mrs Viditz the unrestricted administration of all her property.

In 1896 Mr and Mrs Viditz and their four children commenced this action against the trustees of the settlement claiming a declaration that by virtue of the notarial act of November 1893 the deed of 1864 was revoked and was void by Austrian law.

Expert evidence was given to the effect that by Austrian law the marriage articles of 1864 were void, not having been executed as notarial acts; that children do not acquire vested interests under the marriage contracts of their parents, but only an expectancy; that a husband and wife have a right to revoke their marriage contract, notwithstanding the birth of issue and acts of ratification, and that this right of revocation cannot be waived and is not lost by lapse of time.

Cozens-Hardy J held that the marriage articles were valid and were governed by English law, and that the wife, not having repudiated them within a reasonable time after she had attained 21, was absolutely bound by them.

The plaintiffs appealed.

Lindley MR: Two questions arise. The first is, whether, upon the true construction of the marriage articles of November 1864 (assuming that they are binding on the wife), the sum of £5,000, which is payable to her under the compromise of the probate action, is or is not comprised in the articles. (Having held that it was not, his Lordship continued:) This brings me to the second point, which is a much more difficult one, namely, whether the settlement has or has not become binding on the wife. She was an Irish lady, and was under twenty-one when she executed the marriage articles. They were executed in contemplation of her marriage with an Austrian gentleman, and it was contemplated that after their marriage they should (as they in fact did) live in Austria; in other words, that the wife should become domiciled in Austria, which was the domicile of the husband.

Now, according to English law, this settlement by her was a voidable contract in the sense explained by the House of Lords in *Edwards v Carter*.[6] After the marriage she lived with her husband in Austria, and in 1867 she became of age. By the Austrian law she was unable to ratify or confirm this contract; she could always repudiate it, but could never ratify it, ie, deprive herself of the right to repudiate it. This was the case in *Cooper v Cooper*,[7] but it

---

6 [1893] AC 360, 63 LJCh 100.
7 (1888) 13 App Cas 88, 59 LT1.

was not so in *Edwards v Carter*. We have to consider what is the consequence of that. In the course of her married life she executed some documents which, if they are to be governed by English law, clearly amounted to a ratification of the settlement. By the Austrian law these documents were invalid in so far as they purported to be irrevocable ratifications.

The position is a simple one. This lady never had, either before or after her marriage, power to make an irrevocable settlement. Can we in those circumstances hold that the settlement has become irrevocable? That is the paradox put to us. Cozens-Hardy J has taken this view of it. He says, first, that, upon the authority of *Van Grutten v Digby*,[8] this was an English settlement to be governed by an English law, and that by the English law as expounded by the House of Lords in *Edwards v Carter* (which affirmed a decision of this court) a covenant in a marriage settlement by an infant or a settlement made on his marriage by an infant is voidable, and it is binding on him unless it is repudiated within a reasonable time after he attains 21. It is said that this lady always had at all events power to repudiate the settlement—she could do that by Austrian law—and that, inasmuch as she did not repudiate it within a reasonable time after she attained twenty-one, the contract has become irrevocable. Is that reasoning sound? I think it is not, and for this reason. In the first place, as regards *Van Grutten v Digby*, the point which we have now to consider did not arise for determination. There was no question there about incapacity to contract. There was a settlement made by persons of mature age and binding upon them when it was made. Romilly MR was clearly right in saying that that contract must be governed by the law of England, regardless of any change of the domicile of the parties afterwards. But in the present case the difficulty arises from the incapacity to contract, and that difficulty, as it seems to me, is not touched and still less governed by *Van Grutten v Digby*.

Now, what is the effect of the English law as expounded by the House of Lords in *Edwards v Carter*? What is the theory of it? The theory is, I apprehend, this—that there are some contracts of infants which by English law are absolutely void. There are a few (not a great many) contracts which in the view of English law cannot possibly be for the benefit of the infant—take a bond with penalties as an illustration—and they are void. An infant cannot so contract. The great bulk of infants' contracts are only voidable. What does that mean? It means that when the infant comes of age he can elect either to affirm or to disaffirm the contract. If he does nothing within a reasonable time after he attains 21, the presumption is that he has affirmed the contract. The contract is binding and has been binding on him ever since he attained 21, unless he proves the contrary by repudiating it within a reasonable time. But I think it would be an entire mistake to apply that part of English law which relates to repudiation within a reasonable time if you shut out the other part which relates to the ability to ratify.

Now, by the alteration of the wife's domicile in this case her ability to ratify her contract was lost. Ought we then to apply what I may call the mutilated English doctrine relating to infants, and to say that this contract has become irrevocable because it was not repudiated within a reasonable time? It seems to me that this would be contrary to good sense, and it would land us in the paradox which I have already mentioned, namely, that the

---

8 (1862) 31 Beav 561, 1 New Rep 79.

contract had become irrevocable, although the lady never had, either before or after she was married, the capacity to enter into an irrevocable contract.

As to the authorities, the nearest case to the present which has been cited, and the nearest which I know, is *Cooper v Cooper*, in which a very similar difficulty had to be met by the House of Lords, but the question of reasonable time did not receive attention. In that case a lady did succeed in repudiating a marriage settlement made when she was an infant after the lapse of much more than a reasonable time, if you shut out of consideration the change of her domicile between the execution of the settlement and the repudiation. The question of reasonable time was not discussed there, but so far as it goes the case is in favour of the present appellants.

In my opinion, the effect of the change of domicile was that the English doctrine of reasonable time became inapplicable by reason of the impossibility after that change of the wife's effectually ratifying her contract. An alternative view of the case (perhaps it is only the same view in another shape) is that the effect of the change of domicile was to enlarge the reasonable time for repudiation. This may not perhaps be quite so satisfactory a way of putting it; but I confess I do not see how it can be said that a reasonable time for repudiation had expired when there was no possibility of her doing anything else but repudiate. However, I think the former is the truer view, and any other view would be difficult to reconcile with *Cooper v Cooper*.

I may refer to the observations of Lord Watson in that case. He said: 'Being of opinion that the capacity of the appellant to bind herself by the marriage contract must be determined by the law of England, I agree with your Lordships that the discharge which she seeks to set aside cannot stand in the way of her claiming her legal rights as a Scotch widow. The rule seems to be clear that an infant cannot, during minority, effectually subject herself to any contractual obligation which cannot be shewn to have been for her benefit. She may ratify the contract, after attaining majority, and so become liable to implement it, but, in the circumstances of the present case, any such ratification of the contract would, according to the law of Scotland, have been revocable by her as a donation inter virum et uxorem.' That, so far as it goes, although it does not quite touch the point, appears to me an authority in favour of the conclusion at which I have arrived.

I think, therefore, that the appeal must be allowed, and a declaration made in accordance with the plaintiff's claim.

Rigby and Collins LJJ concurred.
Appeal allowed.

PART VII

Law of Procedure

CHAPTER 24

Substance and Procedure

Foreign Limitation Periods Act 1984

1.—(1) Subject to the following provisions of this Act, where in any action or proceedings in a court in England and Wales the law of any other country falls (in accordance with rules of private international law applicable by any such court) to be taken into account in the determination of any matter—

(a) the law of that other country relating to limitation shall apply in respect of that matter for the purposes of the action or proceedings; and

(b) except where that matter falls within subsection (2) below, the law of England and Wales relating to limitation shall not so apply.

(2) A matter falls within this subsection if it is a matter in the determination of which both the law of England and Wales and the law of some other country fall to be taken into account.

(3) The law of England and Wales shall determine for the purposes of any law applicable by virtue of subsection (1) (a) above whether, and the time at which, proceedings have been commenced in respect of any matter; and, accordingly, section 35 of the Limitation Act 1980 (new claims in pending proceedings) shall apply in relation to time limits applicable by virtue of subsection (1)(a) above as it applies in relation to time limits under that Act.

(4) A court in England and Wales, in exercising in pursuance of subsection (1) (a) above any discretion conferred by the law of any other country, shall so far as practicable exercise that discretion in the manner in which it is exercised in comparable cases by the courts of that other country.

(5) In this section 'law', in relation to any country, shall not include rules of private international law applicable by the courts of that country or, in the case of England and Wales, this Act.

2.—(1) In any case in which the application of section 1 above would to any extent conflict (whether under subsection (2) below or otherwise) with public policy, that section shall not apply to the extent that its application would so conflict.

(2) The application of section 1 above in relation to any action or proceedings shall conflict with public policy to the extent that its application would cause undue hardship to a person who is, or might be made, a party to the action or proceedings.

(3) Where, under a law applicable by virtue of section 1 (1) (a) above for the purposes of any action or proceedings, a limitation period is or may be extended or interrupted in respect of the absence of a party to the action or proceedings from any specified jurisdiction or country, so much of that law as provides for the extension or interruption shall be disregarded for those purposes.

3. (*Foreign judgments on limitation points*; p 184 above.)

4.—(1) Subject to subsection (3) below, references in this Act to the law of any country (including England and Wales) relating to limitation shall, in relation to any matter, be construed as references to so much of the relevant law of that country as (in any manner) makes provision with respect to a period of limitation applicable to the bringing of proceedings in respect of that matter in the courts of that country and shall include—

(a)   references to so much of that law as relates to, and to the effect of, the application, extension, reduction or interruption of that period; and

(b)   a reference, where under that law there is no period of limitation which is so applicable, to the rule that such proceedings may be brought within an indefinite period.

(2) In subsection (1) above 'relevant law', in relation to any country, means the procedural and substantive law applicable, apart from any rules of private international law, by the courts of that country.

(3) References in this Act to the law of England and Wales relating to limitation shall not include the rules by virtue of which a court may, in the exercise of any discretion, refuse equitable relief on the grounds of acquiescence or otherwise; but, in applying those rules to a case in relation to which the law of any country outside England and Wales is applicable by virtue of section 1 (1) (a) above (not being a law that provides for a limitation period that has expired), a court in England and Wales shall have regard, in particular, to the provisions of the law that is so applicable.

NOTE

The rule of English private international law used to be that foreign statutes of limitation were procedural and therefore inapplicable in an English court, if they merely barred the plaintiff's remedy without extinguishing his right. This was so even if under the foreign law the relevant statute of limitation was substantive, or if (as in continental European law) the distinction between right and remedy was unknown. The rule went back to *Huber v Steiner*,[1] and was often criticised. The main grounds of criticism were as follows:

(1)   The distinction between right and remedy is an unreal one, for 'a right for which the legal remedy is barred is not much of a right'.[2]

(2)   The rule might bar a claim which was still alive in the jurisdiction in which it arose, eg if the English period of limitation was shorter than the foreign one.

(3)   Conversely, the rule might work hardship on a debtor in the opposite situation if, in reliance on the foreign law, he had destroyed his receipts.

(4)   The rule might encourage forum shopping.

(5)   It would be no more difficult for an English court to apply a foreign statute of limitation than any other rule of foreign law. Not to do so in a situation where the foreign statute of limitation, unlike most other foreign rules of procedure, would determine the outcome of the litigation seemed perverse.

In 1982, the Law Commission recommended[3] that the rule be abandoned and replaced by a rule whereby the English court should in general apply the foreign statute of limitation and not the English statute. This recommendation is implemented by section 1 (1) of the Foreign Limitation Periods Act 1984.[4] The qualification in section 1 (2) was necessary because of the double-barrelled nature of the English conflict rule for tort liability, whereby the foreign tort must normally be

1   (1835) 2 Bing NC 202, 1 Hodg 206.
2   Leflar *American Conflicts Law* (3rd edn, 1977) p 253.
3   Law Com No 114 (1982).
4   The Act is in very similar terms to the draft Bill appended to the Law Commission's Report.

actionable as a tort in English law and also civilly actionable by the lex loci delicti.[5] Section 1 (3) provides that, for practical reasons, English law and not the foreign law shall determine when time ceases to run. In English law this is the date of the institution, not the service, of the proceedings. Section 1 (4) provides that in the application of a foreign statute of limitation, any discretion vested in the foreign court by its law (eg to extend the time) shall be exercisable by the English court so far as practicable in the same manner as it would be exercised by the foreign court. This is an unusual provision, for English courts do not normally exercise a discretion vested in a foreign court: see eg *Phrantzes v Argenti*.[6] Section 1 (5) makes it clear that, in referring to 'law', the section means rules of law relating to limitation and does not include choice of law rules or other private international law rules.

Section 2 (1) provides an exception in those rare cases where the application of section 1 would be contrary to English public policy, eg if the foreign law provided a much shorter or much longer period than does English law. Section 2 (3) provides that a foreign rule providing for the suspension or interruption of a foreign period of limitation by reason of the absence of either party from the foreign country shall not be applied in England. Rules of this kind give rise to difficulties and are increasingly regarded with disfavour. English law at one time provided that time should stop running when either the plaintiff or the defendant was 'beyond the seas'. The rule was repealed in the case of plaintiffs in 1856[7] and in the case of defendants in 1939.[8]

Section 4 (1) and (2) implement the recommendation that, except, where otherwise provided (eg in section 2 (3)) the court shall have regard to foreign rules as to the application, extension, reduction or interruption of the period.

Section 4 (3) preserves the English rule whereby equitable relief may, apart from any statute of limitation, be refused if the plaintiff has been guilty of laches or acquiescence. But it goes on to provide that in applying that rule, the court shall have regard to the fact that a foreign period of limitation has not expired or that there is no foreign period of limitation.

The fourth section of the Statute of Frauds relates to procedure and not to substance.

Leroux v Brown (1852) 12 CB 801, 22 LJCP 1 (Court of Common Pleas)

Assumpsit. The declaration stated, that, on 1 December 1849, at Calais, in France, to wit, at Westminster, in the county of Middlesex, in consideration that the plaintiff, at the request of the defendant, then agreed with the defendant to enter into the service of the defendant as clerk and agent, and to serve the defendant in that capacity for one year certain, at certain wages, to wit, £100 a year, to be paid by the defendant to the plaintiff by equal quarterly payments during his continuance in such service, the defendant then promised the plaintiff to receive him into his said service, and to retain and employ him in his said service, at the wages aforesaid: Averment that the plaintiff was ready and willing to enter into the service of the defendant as aforesaid: Breach, that the defendant did not, nor would, at the time he was so requested as aforesaid, or at any other time, receive the plaintiff into his service as aforesaid, or retain or employ him, at such wages as aforesaid, or in any other way.

5 *Phillips v Eyre* (1870) LR 6 QB 1, 10 B & S 1004, p 467 above; *Boys v Chaplin* [1971] AC 356, [1969] 2 All ER 1085 p 470 above.
6 [1960] 2 QB 19, [1960] 1 All ER 778; p 633 below.
7 Mercantile Law Amendment Act 1856, s 10.
8 Limitation Act 1939, s 34 and Sch.

Pleas,—first, non assumpsit.

The cause was tried before Talfourd J. It appeared that an oral agreement had been entered into at Calais, between the plaintiff and the defendant, under which the latter, who resided in England, contracted to employ the former, who was a British subject resident at Calais, at a salary of £100 per annum, to collect poultry and eggs in that neighbourhood, for transmission to the defendant here,—the employment to commence at a future day, and to continue for one year certain.

Evidence was given on the part of the plaintiff to show, that, by the law of France, such an agreement is capable of being enforced, although not in writing.

For the defendant, it was insisted, that, notwithstanding the contract was made in France, when it was sought to enforce it in this country, it must be dealt with according to our law; and, being a contract not to be performed within a year, the Statute of Frauds 1677, s 4, required it to be in writing.

Under the direction of the learned judge, a verdict was entered for the plaintiff on the first issue,—leave being reserved to the defendant to move to enter a nonsuit or a verdict for him on that issue, if the court should be of opinion that the contract could not be enforced here.

Jervis CJ: I am of opinion that the rule to enter a nonsuit must be made absolute. There is no dispute as to the principles which ought to govern our decision. My brother Allen admits, that, if the 4th section of the Statute of Frauds applies, not to the validity of the contract, but only to the procedure, the plaintiff cannot maintain this action, because there is no agreement, nor any memorandum or note thereof, in writing. On the other hand, it is not denied by Mr Honyman,—who has argued this case in a manner for which the court is much indebted to him,—that, if the 4th section applies to the contract itself, or, as Boullenois expresses it, to the solemnities of the contract, inasmuch as our law cannot regulate foreign contracts, a contract like this may be enforced here. I am of opinion that the 4th section applies not to the solemnities of the contract, but to the procedure; and therefore that the contract in question cannot be sued upon here. The contract may be capable of being enforced in the country where it was made: but not in England. Looking at the words of the 4th section of the statute of frauds, and contrasting them with those of the 1st, 3rd, and 17th sections, this conclusion seems to me to be inevitable. The words of s 4 are, 'no action shall be brought upon any agreement which is not to be performed within the space of one year from the making thereof, unless the agreement upon which such action shall be brought, or some memorandum or note thereof, shall be in writing, and signed by the party to be charged therewith, or some other person thereto by him lawfully authorised'. The statute, in this part of it, does not say, that, unless those requisites are complied with, the contract shall be void, but merely that no action shall be brought upon it, and, as was put with great force by Mr Honyman, the alternative, 'unless the agreement, or some memorandum or note thereof, shall be in writing',—words which are satisfied if there be any written evidence of a previous agreement,— shows that the statute contemplated that the agreement may be good, though not capable of being enforced, if not evidenced by writing. This therefore may be a very good agreement, though, for want of a compliance with the requisites of the statute, not enforceable in an English court of justice. This view seems to be supported by the authorities; because, unless we are to infer that the courts thought the agreement itself good, though not made in strict compliance with the statute, they could not consistently have held, as was held in the cases referred to by Sir Edward Sugden, that a writing subsequent to the contract, and addressed to a third person, was sufficient evidence of an agreement, within the statute. It seems, therefore, that both authority and practice are consistent with the words of the 4th section. . . . I therefore think we are correct in holding that the contract in this case is incapable of being enforced by an action in this country, because the 4th section of the Statute of Frauds relates only to the procedure, and not to the right and validity of the contract itself. As to what is said by Boullenois in the passage last cited by my brother Allen, it is to be observed that the learned author is there speaking of what pertains ad vinculum obligationis et solemnitatem, and not with reference to the mode of procedure. Upon these grounds, I am of opinion that this action cannot be maintained, and that the rule to enter a nonsuit must be made absolute.

Maule and Talfourd JJ delivered judgments to the same effect.
  Rule absolute.

In California the court will not apply its statute of frauds to a contract governed by the law of another state unless California has an 'interest' in having its statute applied.

Bernkrant v Fowler (1961) 360 P 2d 906 (Supreme Court of California)

John Granrud orally agreed to make a will in favour of the plaintiff by forgiving him a debt. The plaintiff was domiciled and resident in Nevada; the contract was made there and the debt was secured by a mortgage on land in Nevada. Granrud died two years later domiciled in California but without having made the promised provision for the plaintiff. The trial court held that the action was barred by both the Nevada and the California statute of frauds. The California statute of frauds provided that 'an agreement not to be performed during the lifetime of the promisor, or to devise or bequeath any property or make any provision by will, is invalid unless the same or a note or memorandum thereof is in writing and subscribed by the party to be charged or his agent'. The plaintiff appealed.

Traynor J (having stated the facts, and decided that the agreement was not caught by the Nevada statute of frauds, continued): We are therefore confronted with a contract that is valid under the law of Nevada but invalid under the California statute of frauds if that statute is applicable. We have no doubt that California's interest in protecting estates being probated here from false claims based on alleged oral contracts to make wills is constitutionally sufficient to justify the legislature's making our statute of frauds applicable to all such contracts sought to be enforced against such estates. The legislature, however, is ordinarily concerned with enacting laws to govern purely local transactions, and it has not spelled out the extent to which the statute of frauds is to apply to a contract having substantial contacts with another state. Accordingly, we must determine its scope in the light of applicable principles of the law of conflict of laws. In the present case plaintiffs were residents of Nevada, the contract was made in Nevada, and plaintiffs performed it there. If Granrud was a resident of Nevada at the time the contract was made, the California statute of frauds, in the absence of a plain legislative direction to the contrary, could not reasonably be interpreted as applying to the contract even though Granrud subsequently moved to California and died here. The basic policy of upholding the expectations of the parties by enforcing contracts valid under the only law apparently applicable would preclude an interpretation of our statute of frauds that would make it apply to and thus invalidate the contract because Granrud moved to California and died here. Just as parties to local transactions cannot be expected to take cognizance of the law of other jurisdictions, they cannot be expected to anticipate a change in the local statute of frauds. Protection of rights growing out of valid contracts precludes interpreting the general language of the statute of frauds to destroy such rights whether the possible applicability of the statute arises from the movement of one or more of the parties across state lines or subsequent enactment of the statute.

In the present case, however, there is no finding as to where Granrud was domiciled at the time the contract was made. Since he had a bank account in California at that time and died a resident here less than two years later it may be that he was domiciled here when the contract was made. Even if he was, the result should be the same. The contract was made in Nevada and performed by plaintiffs there, and it involved the refinancing of obligations arising from the sale of Nevada land and secured by interests therein. Nevada has a substantial interest in the contract and in protecting the rights of its residents who are parties thereto, and its policy is that the contract is valid and enforceable. California's policy is also to enforce lawful contracts. That policy, however, must be subordinated in the case of any contract that does not meet the requirements of an applicable statute of frauds. In determining whether the contract herein is subject to the California statute of frauds, we must consider both the policy to protect the reasonable expectations of the parties and the policy of the statute of frauds. It is true that if Granrud was domiciled here at the time the contract was made, plaintiffs may have been alerted to the possibility that the California statute of frauds might apply. Since California, however, would have no interest in applying its own statute of frauds unless Granrud remained here until his death, plaintiffs were not bound to know that California's statute might ultimately be invoked against them. Unless they could rely on their own law, they would have to look to the laws of all of the jurisdictions to which Granrud might move regardless of where he was domiciled when the contract was made. We conclude, therefore, that the contract herein does not fall within our statute of frauds. Since there is thus no conflict between the law of California and the law of Nevada, we can give effect to the common policy of both states to enforce lawful contracts and sustain Nevada's interest in protecting its residents and their reasonable expectations growing out of a transaction substantially related to that state without subordinating any legitimate interest of this state.

The judgment is reversed.[9]

Gibson CJ and Schauer, McComb, Peters, White and Dooling JJ concur.

9 It will be noticed that the court decided the case without once mentioning the distinction between substance and procedure (Ed).

The English presumption of survivorship is substantive, not procedural.

Re Cohn (p 668 below)

English courts will enforce foreign rights which are unknown to English law, but will not do so if English law has no suitable machinery for enforcement.

Phrantzes v Argenti [1960] 2 QB 19, [1960] 1 All ER 778 (Queen's Bench Division)

A daughter, a Greek national who had recently married in England, claimed a declaration that under Greek law she was entitled to be provided with a dowry by her father, also a Greek national. By Greek law a father was obliged to provide a dowry for his daughter on her marriage. The amount of the dowry depended on his fortune, the number of his children, and his social position and that of his son-in-law. There was no obligation to provide the dowry if the daughter had committed such a 'fault' as would justify disinheritance. The dowry was constituted by a contract entered into with the husband in notarial form. It might consist of present or future property, which had to be specified, and could be land or movables. Should the father fail to provide a dowry the daughter, and the daughter alone, had a cause of action in the Greek courts to obtain an order condemning him to conclude a dowry contract with the husband in notarial form. If the father was abroad he could be condemned to enter into the contract before a Greek consul or a foreign notary public. In such proceedings the Greek court would decide what in all the circumstances was the appropriate amount of the dowry and might specify the assets to be handed over.

The father and daughter were both resident in England. The father denied that he was domiciled in Greece and objected that the statement of claim disclosed no cause of action. Master Lawrence ordered the trial of a preliminary issue, namely, whether on the assumption that the defendant was domiciled in Greece at all material times the plaintiff was entitled to the relief claimed.

Lord Parker CJ: In the first place, it is said on behalf of the defendant that even if what is sought to be enforced here is a proprietary right, which is denied, it will not be enforced unless it comes within one or other of the definite rules enumerated by Dicey, eg, in regard to infants, marriage, succession or bankruptcy. To go outside those rules would lay the way open to the enforcement of a number of rights which it is said these courts have never enforced. For example, the English courts will not enforce the duty under a foreign system of law of a parent to maintain his child or vice versa, cf Dicey's *Conflict of Laws*.[10] Again, in *Re Macartney*,[11] the court was asked to enforce the judgment of a Maltese court condemning the testator's estate to provide maintenance for his illegitimate daughter. Astbury J, while refusing to enforce the judgment on the ground that the recognition of an illegitimate

10 7th edn (1958) p 403.
11 [1921] 1 Ch 522, 90 LJCh 314.

child's right under Maltese law to be permanently maintained was contrary to public policy, went on to hold that the action could not be entertained on the ground that the judgment obtained was of such a character that it would not have supported an action in England. In advancing this second ground the judge followed the New York case of *De Brimont v Penniman*.[12] In that case a French citizen had married in France the daughter of two United States citizens. The wife died, leaving a child. Under French law the father-in-law and mother-in-law were bound to provide an allowance to the father for the support of the child. The father obtained the judgment of a French court against them while they were in France, requiring them to provide an annual allowance. On their return to the United States of America the father sued them in the American courts to recover arrears. Woodruff J refused to entertain the action. He held that the French law and the decree made under it were local in their nature and operation, were designed to guard against pauperism and were not of universal acceptance like judgments founded upon contract or other recognised rights.

Some criticism has been made of the decision in *Re Macartney*, cf Wolff's *Private International Law*,[13] in so far as the second ground of the decision is concerned. Be that as it may, I think that the present case is quite different from *Re Macartney* and *De Brimont v Penniman*. There is no question here of the foreign law being a law against pauperism. It is, moreover, intended to have extraterritorial effect since the Greek courts will, as I have said, condemn a father resident abroad to enter into a contract before the Greek consul or a foreign notary public.

Indeed, if this were the only point in the case I would hold that this was a right which could be enforced here. As Cardozo J said in *Loucks v Standard Oil Co of New York*:[14]

> 'If aid is to be withheld here, it must be because the cause of action in its nature offends our sense of justice or menaces the public welfare. . . . Our own scheme of legislation may be different. We may even have no legislation on the subject. That is not enough to show that public policy forbids us to enforce the foreign right. A right of action is property. If a foreign statute gives the right, the mere fact that we do not give a like right is no reason for refusing to help the plaintiff in getting what belongs to him. We are not so provincial as to say that every solution of a problem is wrong because we deal with it otherwise at home. . . . The courts are not free to refuse to enforce a foreign right at the pleasure of the judges, to suit the individual notion of expediency or fairness. They do not close their doors unless help would violate some fundamental principle of justice, some prevalent conception of good morals, some deep-rooted tradition of the common weal.'

The next point taken on behalf of the defence is that the right under Greek law is not a proprietary right at all. It is, so it is said, only a right in personam; a right to get the court to condemn the father to enter into a dowry contract. This, as it seems to me, must be the correct position. True it is connected with succession, being on account of the daughter's inheritance,

---

12 (1873) 10 Blatchford's Circuit Court Reports 436.
13 2nd edn (1950) pp 266–267.
14 (1918) 224 NY 99, 120 NE 198.

but the action is an action in personam. However, in my judgment, it matters not what label is given to the right. It is, I think, a right which could be enforced here if, for instance, it was a right to payment of a fixed sum of money or a definite proportion of the father's fortune simpliciter.

It is, however, at this point that the plaintiff's difficulties occur. The right is not the right to the payment of a sum of money. It is the right to an order condemning the father to instruct a notary public to draw up a dowry contract in accordance with the directions of the court, and to enter into that contract with the son-in-law who may not even be a party to the proceedings. Before the order can be made the court must inquire into the extent of the father's fortune and that of his daughter. The court must further consider the respective social position of the father and son-in-law, that is their positions in the Greek or other community where each is living, and decide what is the appropriate amount of dowry. It must decide, if the point is raised, whether the daughter has committed a fault within article 1497. It will often have to decide in all the circumstances what the dowry is to consist of, how much of it shall be land, how much movables, whether any part of it is to consist of the usufruct from property and, if so, for how long it is to be granted, whether the use of a house free of rent is to be provided, and, in addition, what are to be the terms as to ownership of the dowry whether movable or land (article 1412). Specimen contracts were put in evidence. All these inquiries and decisions are essentially matters for the domestic courts, and matters largely for the discretion of those courts and not our courts. It is true that in *Kornatzki v Oppenheimer*[15] Farwell J held that he was able to evaluate the sum which a German court in all the circumstances of the case would award as payable in discharge of a pre-war debt based on a provision of the German Civil Code, which provided that the debtor was bound to effect the performance of his obligations according to the requirements of good faith, ordinary usage being taken into consideration. He came to the conclusion in that case that the evaluation was really a question of fact which could be determined by the court in England, and that it was not a matter of discretion at all. He, however, clearly took the view that if discretion had entered into the matter it would have been a matter for the German courts alone, and that he would not have had any jurisdiction in the matter. Here it seems to me that the considerations which I have enumerated above, taken as a whole, must involve a very large measure of discretion, and that it would be quite wrong for our courts to claim jurisdiction in the matter.

The matter does not end there since, in my judgment, the lex fori, English law, does not provide a cause of action and relief appropriate to the enforcement of the foreign right, namely, a right to obtain an order condemning someone to enter into a contract in a particular form with a person not even a party to the proceedings. It is true, of course, that a plaintiff seeking to enforce a foreign right here can demand only those remedies recognised by English law, and that the claim will not be defeated merely because those remedies are greater or less than those in the courts of the foreign country: cf Dicey's *Conflict of Laws*,[16] and *Baschet v London*

15 [1937] 4 All ER 133.
16 7th edn (1958) p 1089.

Illustrated Standard Co.[17] But the remedies available must harmonise with the right according to its nature and extent as fixed by the foreign law: cf Cheshire *Private International Law.*[18] Put another way, if the machinery by way of remedies here is so different from that in Greece as to make the right sought to be enforced a different right, that right would not, in my judgment, be enforced in this country. This matter has been considered in the United States of America. Thus the Restatement of the Law of Conflict of Laws (1934), para 608, states:

'If no form of action is provided by the law of a state for the enforcement of a particular foreign right, no action to enforce that right can be maintained in the state. *Comment: a.* The form of action is a matter of procedure. A court will not invent a new form of action, unknown to the law of the forum, in order to give a remedy on a foreign cause of action.'

In the present case, even if the court granted a declaration and embarked on the necessary inquiry as to the extent of the dowry, it could do no more than order payment of the amount found to be appropriate and payment thereof to the plaintiff. That, however, would be to enforce a right which the plaintiff does not possess under Greek law. True, the courts here have power to order a deed to be entered into by a husband to secure payment of maintenance or to order a settlement of a wife's property, but that is a jurisdiction given by statute: cf sections 23 and 24 of the Matrimonial Causes Act 1950.[19] I know of no power in the court, inherent or otherwise, which would enable the court to give relief which was consistent with the plaintiff's right under Greek law.

For these reasons I have come to the conclusion that the answer to the question raised in the preliminary issue is 'No'. Since it is admitted that the claim fails if, contrary to the assumption in the issue, the defendant is not domiciled in Greece, it follows that the claim must be dismissed.

Remoteness of damage is a question of substance, governed by the proper law of the contract. The measure of damages is a question of procedure, governed by the lex fori.

D'Almeida Araujo Lda v Sir Frederick Becker & Co Ltd [1953] 2 QB 329, [1953] 2 All ER 288 (Queen's Bench Division)

On 20 March 1947 the plaintiffs, a firm of merchants carrying on business in Lisbon, agreed to sell to the defendants, an English company carrying on business as merchants in the City of London, 500 tons of palm oil at 14.20 escudos a kilogramme fob Angora, Portuguese West Africa, payment to be by open credit to be opened by 24 March. The proper law of the contract was Portuguese.

On the same date the plaintiffs had contracted with one Mourao for the purchase of 500 tons of palm oil which was designed to implement the plaintiffs' contract with the defendants. This contract provided that payment

17 [1900] 1 Ch 73, 69 LJCh 35. In this case the English court granted an injunction although only damages would have been awarded by the lex causae (*Ed*).
18 5th edn (1957) pp 667–668.
19 Now ss 23 and 24 of the Matrimonial Causes Act 1973 (*Ed*).

was to be by open credit to be opened by 24 March. The contract also provided that in the event of breach by either party the party in default should pay to the other as indemnity for the damages an amount corresponding to 5% of the total value of the contract. Mourao had entered into a similar contract with one Guimeraes for the purchase of the oil.

The defendants had agreed to resell the palm oil, payment for which was to be made by credit in their favour in Lisbon, but the sub-purchasers failed to open the credit, with the result that the defendants were unable to open the credit in favour of the plaintiffs. The plaintiffs were ready to complete the sale, if the defendants opened the credit, at least up to 12 April. On 14 April the plaintiffs advertised the palm oil for sale in a Lisbon newspaper against immediate opening credit, but were unable to sell it.

On 18 April Guimeraes cabled that if the credit was not opened on that day his contract would be cancelled.

The defendants having failed to open the credit in the plaintiffs' favour, the plaintiffs were unable to open the credit in favour of Mourao, and accordingly under their contract with him were bound to pay him the indemnity, which amounted to £3,500, and they did so pay him.

The plaintiffs claimed damages for the defendants' breach of contract under two heads, (1) £1,000 for the loss of profit which they would have made on the resale; and (2) £3,500 which they had had to pay Mourao for breach of their contract with him.

Pilcher J (having held that there was a contract and that the defendants had broken it and that the only remaining point was what damages, if any, the plaintiffs were entitled to recover, continued:) While it was common ground between the parties that the substantive contract between them was governed by Portuguese law, the plaintiffs contended that the damages which they were entitled to recover in the particular circumstances of the case were also to be determined in accordance with the principles of Portuguese law. The defendants, on the contrary, submitted that even in a case where the substantive contract was governed by foreign law, procedural or remedial questions, which included the question of damages, ought to be determined according to the lex fori, in this case, the law of England. Subject to the question of the obligation of an innocent party to mitigate the damages, to which I will refer in a moment, the question of the proper law to be applied in regard to the damages in this case has importance, because the plaintiffs are seeking to recover from the defendants the £3,500 as one head of damage—that being, of course, the sum which they had to pay to Mourao for failing to carry out their contract with him.

The loss sustained by the plaintiffs in paying that sum was clearly not a loss which was foreseeable by the defendants at the time when they negotiated this contract with the plaintiffs, and it is clear that under English law this sum of £3,500 would be irrecoverable by the plaintiffs from the defendants. It was argued by Mr Mocatta, on behalf of the plaintiffs, that they would, under Portuguese law, have been entitled to include this sum in their damages if damages were assessed on the principles of Portuguese law. While I feel no certainty that the plaintiffs' right to recover damages in this case will turn out in the end to be any different whether the principles of English or Portuguese law are applied, it is none the less desirable that I should state my view on the point.

I was referred to a number of textbooks on the particular point whether in a foreign contract which has to be determined by the lex loci contractus the issue of damages is, in the words of some of the textbook writers, 'a procedural or remedial matter' such as falls to be determined in accordance with the lex fori, or whether, on the other hand, it is part of the substantive contract between the parties and so to be determined in accordance with the lex loci contractus. I propose to read certain passages from the textbooks, because there is very little authority on this particular topic in English law. In Dicey's *Conflict of Laws* (6th edn) pp 649–50, this passage occurs:

> 'A further difficulty is created by the problem of how to distinguish between the effect of the contract and the remedies which are available for its enforcement. Whether a contract gives rise to a claim for performance or to a claim for damages, whether, in the event of a breach of contract, the other party has a right to rescind it, whether interest is payable on a debt—all these are matters which, on a proper analysis, should be regarded as affecting the rights and obligations to which the contract gives rise. While it is clear that, in the view of the English courts, the liability to pay contractual interest and the rate of such interest are determined by the proper law, it appears to be a generally accepted view that the measure of damages is, in an English court, governed by English law, whatever be the proper law of the contract. This principle is apt to deprive a party of rights he would have enjoyed under the proper law or to confer upon him an uncovenanted benefit merely owing to the fact that he happened to be able to invoke the jurisdiction of an English court. Its rigour could be mitigated if, following Cheshire's suggestion, the courts could separate from the question of the measure of damages that known as "remoteness of damage" and hold that it was one of the effects of a contract to determine what events may and must be taken into account in assessing the damages for which a party is liable.'

On p 862, under the head 'Procedure, Rule 193', the following passage occurs: 'While there is little authority, it appears that English courts, contrary to the prevailing American practice, tend to hold that damages are a matter of procedure in an action based on a foreign tort. In contract, there is no direct English authority, but it is submitted that questions of remoteness of damage should be determined by the proper law of the contract, and should not be treated as a matter of procedure', and a reference is then given to a case decided in the Supreme Court of Canada, *Livesley v Horst*,[20] to which I will refer. 'The rate of interest to be allowed (if any) for breach of a foreign contract must depend on its proper law.' Those are the relevant passages in *Dicey*.

There are also certain passages in Cheshire's *Private International Law* (4th edn) to which I must refer. After considering the principles on which damages are recoverable in this country in actions founded respectively in contract and tort, the author states at pp 659–60:

> 'The truth would appear to be that judicial pronouncements and the statements in textbooks are unintelligible unless two entirely different questions are segregated. In brief, remoteness of liability or remoteness

20 [1925] 1 DLR 159, [1924] SCR 605.

of damage must be distinguished from measure of damages. The rules relating to remoteness indicate what kind of loss actually resulting from the commission of a tort or from breach of contract is actionable; the rules for the measure of damages show the method by which compensation for an actionable loss is calculated. Damage may be, but damages can never be, too remote. In tort the rule of remoteness established by the *Polemis* case[1] is that a tortfeasor is responsible for all the direct consequences of his wrongful act, even though they could not reasonably have been anticipated. The analogous rule in contracts, however, is different. The breach of a contract, like the commission of a tort, causes material loss, and it is that loss to which the rule in *Hadley v Baxendale*[2] applies. In other words, it is impossible to claim monetary compensation in respect even of an admitted loss unless it arose naturally and in the ordinary course of things from breach of contract. But the rule that regulates the measure of damages is the same for contracts as it is for torts. It requires restitutio in integrum. In torts compensation must be paid for the whole of the direct loss; in contracts, as *Robinson v Harman*[3] insists, compensation must be paid for the whole of the natural or foreseeable loss.

Alive to the distinction between remoteness of liability and measure of damages we can now attempt to state the relevant principles of private international law.

There can be no doubt, at least on principle, that remoteness of liability must be governed by the proper law of the obligation that rests upon the defendant. Not only the existence, but also the extent, of an obligation, whether it springs from a breach of contract or the commission of a wrong, must be determined by the system of law from which it derives its source. The proper law admittedly determines the nature and content of the right created by a contract, and it is clear that the kind of loss for which damages are recoverable upon breach forms part of that contract. Both the nature and the content of a contractual right depend in part upon the question whether certain consequential loss that may ensue if the contract is unperformed will be too remote in the eye of the law. If the proper law determines what constitutes a breach, it is also entitled to determine the consequences of a breach.'

That passage from Professor Cheshire's book seems to me to be very closely reasoned and to offer considerable help in deciding this problem, which is not an easy one. The conclusion at which he arrives would seem to be that questions of remoteness of damage should be governed by the proper law of the contract, whereas the quantification of damage, which according to the proper law is not too remote, should be governed by the lex fori.

I must also refer to *Livesley v Horst*, the headnote of which reads: 'The right to damages for breach of a contract made in a foreign country and to be executed there is governed by the lex loci contractus and not by the lex fori.' (After quoting from that case at considerable length, his Lordship continued:)

1 *Re Polemis & Furness, Withy & Co Ltd* [1921] 3 KB 560, 90 LJKB 1353. See now *The Wagon Mound* [1961] AC 388, [1961] 1 All ER 404 (*Ed*).
2 (1854) 9 Exch 341, 23 LJEx 179.
3 (1848) 1 Exch 850, 18 LJEx 202.

The question which I have to determine here really depends, if I accept and adopt, as I do, the analysis given by Professor Cheshire, on whether the £3,500 which the plaintiffs have had to pay to Mourao is a head of damage which is recoverable or not on principles of remoteness of damage, or whether it is to be regarded as a mere established quantification of a part of the loss the plaintiffs have in fact sustained. While the decision in the Canadian case is not binding on me, and while the facts of that case can be distinguished from those of the present case, it is none the less a decision which I must, and do, treat with respect. I confess that in the absence of any direct authority I was attracted by the reasoning in the passage I have quoted from Professor Cheshire's work.

Fortified by the decision of the Supreme Court of Canada, I conclude that the question whether the plaintiffs are entitled to claim from the defendants the £3,500 which they have paid to Mourao, depends on whether such damage is or is not too remote. In my view, the question here is one of remoteness, and therefore falls to be determined in accordance with Portuguese law. Whether the plaintiffs are entitled to recover this sum under Portuguese law is, however, quite another matter.

(His Lordship proceeded to review the evidence of Portuguese law. He concluded that under that law, unlike English law, it was possible to recover unforeseeable damages, but that, as in English law, the plaintiff was under a duty to mitigate his damage. Assuming that the £3,500 could have been recovered under Portuguese law apart from this duty, his Lordship held that the plaintiffs could reasonably have mitigated their damage by reselling the palm oil on the Lisbon Produce Exchange at a price which would have been at least as high as, and almost certainly higher than, the contract price. He therefore awarded nominal damages of 40s only.)

Judgment for the plaintiffs for nominal damages.

The same rule applies in tort.

Boys v Chaplin (p 470 above)

A rule of foreign law to the effect that the defendant's liability is conditional on other persons being sued first is procedural and will be ignored in English proceedings.

Re Doetsch [1896] 2 Ch 836, 65 LJCh 855

Administration action.

Sundheim & Doetsch, a Spanish firm, was indebted to Matheson & Co, a firm carrying on business in the City of London. Doetsch, one of the partners in the Spanish firm, died. His will was proved in England by two of the executors therein named. Matheson & Co brought an action against them for the recovery of their debt. The executors pleaded that by Spanish law the executors of a deceased partner were not liable for the debts of the firm until the property of the firm was exhausted.

Romer J: It is admitted that the plaintiffs are creditors of the firm of Sundheim & Doetsch. As such creditors they ask for the usual administration of the estate of Mr Doetsch, who is dead—that is to say, they ask to have the separate assets of Mr Doetsch applied in payment of the joint debts after first satisfying the separate creditors. Objection is taken to that relief on the ground that the firm is a Spanish firm, and that by Spanish law the estate of one partner who dies cannot be reached by joint creditors of the firm until the estate of the firm has been proceeded against or is exhausted, or there is a proved insufficiency of the joint estate.

The objection fails, and for this reason. In the first place, it is clear that according to English law, as a matter of procedure and to avoid circuity of action, a creditor of a partnership of which one member is dead is entitled as a creditor to share in the administration of the estate of that deceased partner after the separate debts are paid, without first proving that the surviving partner is insolvent and without being obliged first to have recourse to the joint assets. Now, from the admissions before me—and there is no other evidence—it appears to me that the Spanish law only differs from the English law in a matter of procedure. The Spanish courts require that a joint creditor shall before he seeks to reach the estate of a deceased partner first proceed against and exhaust or prove the insolvency of the joint estate. In my opinion, that is a matter of procedure. It is clear that the Spanish firm was not a corporation. On the contrary, the admissions shew that the deceased partner's estate can be reached after proper procedure has been taken to exhaust or prove the insolvency of the joint estate; and certainly it cannot, I think, be successfully contended that the plaintiffs are to be considered as having contracted in any way not to take such proceedings as are before me. Now, that being so, there is nothing to prevent the plaintiffs from asking for the relief which they claim. The procedure of the Spanish courts does not bind the courts here; nor does the Spanish law at all affect the right of a creditor here to avail himself of the benefits given by the English courts in administering estates here. For that *Bullock v Caird*[4] is a sufficient authority. Speaking generally, English assets have to be distributed according to the English law—according to priorities recognised by courts in this country—according to the rules of procedure and course of distribution adopted here. That general proposition was pointed out, amongst other places, in *Thurburn v Steward*[5] by Lord Cairns, who says: 'The proper order and priority of distribution of assets is always a matter for the lex fori, and the country where the distribution takes place always claims to itself the right to regulate the course of distribution.'

For these reasons it appears to me that the objection fails. I need only add, that in my opinion the contract between the parties on which the plaintiffs' rights turn is to be governed by the lex loci contractûs—that is to say, by the English law.

The priority of competing claims against a ship in Admiralty is a question of procedure. A mortgagee of a ship has priority over a foreign necessaries man even if the foreign law gives the necessaries man a maritime lien.

The Halcyon Isle [1981] AC 221, [1980] 3 All ER 197 (Privy Council)

Appeal from the Court of Appeal of Singapore.

The *Halcyon Isle* was a British ship on which the appellants, an English bank, had a registered English mortgage. The respondents were American

4 (1875) LR 10 QB 276, 44 LJQB 124.
5 (1871) LR 3 PC 478, 7 Moo PCC NS 333.

ship-repairers who did repairs and supplied materials to the ship while it was in the port of New York. The ship was later arrested at Singapore since the ship-repairers and the mortgagees had issued writs in rem against it. The ship was sold by order of the court. The ship-repairers obtained a judgment for $237,011 and the mortgagees a judgment for $14,413,000. The proceeds of sale amounted to only $1,380,000. Under the domestic law of Singapore, which was the same as English law, mortgagees had priority over necessaries men, who did not have a maritime lien. Under United States law necessaries men had a maritime lien against the ship which would give them priority over prior or subsequent mortgagees.

The trial judge ruled in favour of the mortgagees. His judgment was reversed by the Court of Appeal, which followed the decision of the Supreme Court of Canada in *The Ioannis Daskalelis*.[6] The mortgagees appealed to the Privy Council.

The judgment of the majority of their Lordships (Lords Diplock, Elwyn Jones and Lane) was delivered by

Lord Diplock: Although the admiralty jurisdiction of the High Court of Singapore is statutory the order of priorities in the distribution of the proceeds of sale of a ship in an action in rem or in a limitation action is not. It is a matter of practice and procedure of that court in the exercise of its admiralty jurisdiction; and in matters of practice and procedure as well as the substantive law which it administers there is no relevant difference between the law of Singapore and the law of England. Since nearly all the cases to be cited will be English cases, their Lordship will be brevity use the expression 'English law' as embracing also the law of Singapore administered by the High Court of Singapore in the exercise of its admiralty jurisdiction.

At first sight, the answer to the question posed by this appeal seems simple. The priorities as between claimants to a limited fund which is being distributed by a court of law are matters of procedure which under English rules of conflict of laws are governed by the lex fori; so English law is the only relevant law by which the priorities as between the mortgagees and the necessaries men are to be determined; and in English law mortgagees take priority over necessaries men.

In the case of a ship, however, the classification of claims against her former owners for the purpose of determining priorities to participate in the proceeds of her sale may raise a further problem of conflict of laws, since claims may have arisen as a result of events that occurred not only on the high seas but also within the territorial jurisdictions of a number of different foreign states. So the lex causae of one claim may differ from the lex causae of another, even though the events which gave rise to the claim in each of those foreign states are similar in all respects, except their geographical location; the leges causarum of various claims, of which under English conflict rules the 'proper law' is that of different states, may assign different legal consequences to similar events. So the court distributing the limited fund may be faced, as in the instant case, with the problem of classifying the foreign claims arising under differing foreign systems of law in order to assign each of them to the appropriate class in the order of priorities under the lex fori of the distributing court.

6 *Todd Shipyards Corpn v Altema Compania Maritima SA, The Ioannis Daskalelis* (1972) 32 DLR (3d) 571.

The choice would appear to lie between (1) on the one hand classifying by reference to the events on which each claim was founded and giving to it the priority to which it would be entitled under the lex fori if those events had occurred within the territorial jurisdiction of the distributing court; or (2) on the other hand applying a complicated kind of partial renvoi by (i) first ascertaining in respect of each foreign claim the legal consequences, *other than those relating to priorities in the distribution of a limited fund*, that would be attributed under its own lex causae to the events on which the claim is founded; and (ii) then giving to the foreign claim the priority accorded under the lex fori to claims arising from events, however dissimilar, which would have given rise to the same or analogous legal consequences if they had occurred within the territorial jurisdiction of the distributing court. To omit the dissection of the lex causae of the claim that the second choice prescribes and to say instead that if under the lex causae the relevant events would give rise to a maritime lien, the English court must give to those claims all the legal consequences of a maritime lien under English law, would, in their Lordships' view, be too simplistic an approach to the questions of conflicts of law that are involved.

Even apart from the merit of simplicity, the choice in favour of the first alternative, classification by reference to events, appears to their Lordships to be preferable in principle. In distributing a limited fund that is insufficient to pay in full all creditors of a debtor whose claims against him have already been quantified and proved, the court is not any longer concerned with enforcing against the debtor himself the individual creditors' original rights against him. It is primarily concerned in doing evenhanded justice between competing creditors whose respective claims to be a creditor may have arisen under a whole variety of different and, it may be, conflicting systems of national law. It may be plausibly suggested that the moral and rational justification of the general conflicts of law rule, applied by English courts to claims arising out of foreign contracts, that the contract should be given the same legal consequences as would be accorded to it under its 'proper law', is that the legitimate expectations of the parties to the contract as to their rights against one another, which will result from entering into and carrying out the contract, ought not to be defeated by any change of the forum in which such rights have to be enforced. Rights of priority over other creditors of the defaulting party to such a contract, in a judicial distribution of a fund which is insufficient to satisfy all the creditors in full, are not, however, rights of the parties to the contract against one another. They are rights as between one party to the contract against strangers to the contract, the other creditors, who have done nothing to arouse any legitimate expectations in that party as to the priority to which he will be entitled in the distribution of such a fund. Every such creditor whose claim is based on contract or quasi-contract must have known that in so far as the legal consequences of his claim under its own lex causae included rights to priority over other classes of creditors in the distribution of a limited fund resulting from an action in rem against a ship, that particular part of the lex causae would be compelled to yield to the lex fori of any foreign court in which the action in rem might be brought.

Counsel for the necessaries men in the instant case, who are experienced litigants in courts of admiralty, has not suggested that they were not perfectly well aware of this when they allowed the *Halcyon Isle* to vacate the berth that she was occupying in their busy repair yard in Brooklyn and thereby relinquished their possessory lien for the unpaid work that they had done upon the ship. They would likewise know that if the *Halcyon Isle* were to enter a port in any of the major trading countries of the world while their bill *remained unpaid* they could have her arrested in an action in rem and in this way obtain the security of the ship itself for their claim; subject, however, to being postponed to any other claimants who might be entitled to priority under the lex fori of the country in which the action was brought. They, or their lawyers, would know, too, that the priorities as between various kinds of maritime claims accorded by the lex fori were subject to considerable variation as between one country and another.

In the case of claimants to a limited fund consisting of the proceeds of sale of a ship in an action in rem brought in a court which, like the High Court of Singapore, applies English admiralty law and practice, the problem of classifying foreign maritime claims for the purposes of determining priorities is complicated by the legal concept of 'maritime lien' to which some classes of maritime claims against a shipowner give rise in English law while other classes do not. This concept derived as it is from the civil law and not the common law may fairly be described as sui generis.

The classic description of a maritime lien in English law is to be found in *The Bold Buccleugh*,[7] a case decided by the Privy Council at a time when the English Court of Admiralty regarded itself as applying not so much English law as the 'general law of the sea of the whole of Europe'. Sir John Jervis described (at p 284) the concept as having its origin in the civil law. He adopted as correct Lord Tenterden's definition of 'maritime lien' in *Abbott on Shipping*, as meaning '. . . a claim or privilege upon a thing to be carried into effect by legal process;' and Sir John Jervis added: 'This claim or privilege travels with the thing, into whosesoever possession it may come. It is inchoate from the moment the claim or privilege attaches, and when carried into effect by legal process, by a proceeding in rem, relates back to the period when it first attached.' The expression 'privilege' in this description of a maritime lien is a reference to the concept of 'privilège' in the civil law from which the French Code Civil is derived. There, privilège is used in the sense of the right of a creditor of a particular class to be paid out of a particular fund or the proceeds of sale of a particular thing in priority to other classes of creditors of the owner or former owner of the fund or thing. In the French Code Civil it is distinguished from the concept of 'hypothèque', which was the subject of detailed analysis by the English Court of Appeal in *The Colorado*.[8]

Sir John Jervis, speaking in 1851, said that a maritime lien existed in every case in which the Court of Admiralty had jurisdiction to entertain an action in rem against a ship. Jurisdiction in rem and maritime lien went hand in hand. This had been true when the jurisdiction of the Court of Admiralty was at its lowest ebb in the early years of the 19th century as a result of harassment by the courts of common law. It has remained true in the law of the United States of America where today all maritime claims enforceable in rem are treated as giving rise to maritime liens; but it was no longer true in English law, even by 1851, after the jurisdiction of the Court of Admiralty

---

7 (1851) 7 Moo PCC 267, 19 LTOS 235.
8 [1923] P 102, 92 LJP 100.

had been extended by the Admiralty Court Act 1840 and the Merchant Shipping Act 1844. Subsequent extensions of jurisdiction in rem in respect of maritime claims were made by the Admiralty Court Act 1861 and by later Merchant Shipping Acts until its modern jurisdiction was laid down in the Administration of Justice Act 1956,[9] which is in the same terms as the High Court (Admiralty Jurisdiction) Act, of Singapore.

During the period that the English Court of Admiralty regarded itself as applying the 'general law of the sea' four classes of claims only were treated as giving rise to maritime liens on ships, viz: (1) salvage; (2) collision damage; (3) seamen's wages; and (4) bottomry. Bottomry is now obsolete, but historically it provided a normal means of providing security for the price of goods and services supplied to a ship by necessaries men outside its home port. Two additional classes of claims were added to this list by statute in the 19th century. These were (5) master's wages, and (6) master's disbursements. The ranking for the purpose of priority in the distribution of a limited fund that has been accorded by the English Court of Admiralty to claims within the various classes that were treated as giving rise to maritime liens was complicated. It still is. It can be found conveniently set out in *British Shipping Laws*[10] that deals with admiralty practice. For present purposes it is sufficient to observe that the priorities, whether between class and class or within one class, bear no relation to the general rule applicable to other charges upon property as security for a debt: qui prior est tempori potior est jure. This rule is based upon the principle that when the owner of a thing grants a charge on it as security for the payment of a sum of money, he transfers to the grantee part of his own proprietary rights in the thing and so deprives himself of the ability to transfer to a subsequent grantee anything more than such proprietary rights as remain to him.

This principle, based as it is upon the concept of a transfer of proprietary rights, cannot explain the priorities accorded to maritime liens. Indeed a later maritime lien for one class of claim may rank in priority to an earlier maritime lien for another class of claim, and even within a single class a later maritime lien may rank in priority to an earlier one.

Thus when Gorell Barnes J in *The Ripon City*[11] said of a maritime lien: 'It is a right acquired by one over a thing belonging to another—a jus in re aliena. It is, so to speak, a subtraction from the absolute property of the owner in the thing', the second sentence is inaccurate if it is to be regarded as suggesting that the owner of a ship, once it has become the subject of a maritime lien, can no longer create a charge on the *whole* property in the ship which will rank in priority to the existing lien. This he can do—as for instance by entering into a salvage contract or by signing on a crew.

In English admiralty law and practice claims of all those six classes that have hitherto been treated as giving rise to a maritime lien take priority over claims under mortgages in the distribution of a limited fund by the court, and mortgages themselves rank in priority to all classes of claims that have not been treated as giving rise to a maritime lien.

In view of the reference hereafter to be made to *The Colorado* it is also relevant to note that for the purpose of priority of ranking inter se mortgages

9 Now s 20 of the Supreme Court Act 1981 (*Ed*).
10 Vol 1 (1st edn, 1964) paras 1574 et seq.
11 [1897] P 226 at 242.

fall into two classes: (1) British registered mortgages (which can only be upon British ships) and (2) other mortgages, British or foreign (which can be upon either British or foreign ships). British registered mortgages rank in priority to all other mortgages and rank inter se in order of date of registration. All other mortgages regardless of whether they are British or foreign rank inter se in order of date of creation.

The pattern of priorities, which has been applied by the English Admiralty Court in the distribution of the fund representing the proceeds of sale of a ship in an action in rem, thus affords no logical basis for concluding that, if a new class of claim additional to the six that have hitherto been recognised were treated under its own lex causae as having given rise to a maritime lien, this should have any effect on its ranking for the purpose of priority under the lex fori in the distribution of the fund by the court and, in particular, no logical basis for concluding that this should entitle it to priority over mortgages.

There is, however, an additional legal characteristic of a maritime lien in English law which distinguishes it from maritime claims to which no maritime lien attaches and which is not confined to rights to a particular rank of priority in the distribution by a court of justice of a limited fund among the various classes of creditors of a single debtor. A maritime lien continues to be enforceable by an action in rem against the ship in connection with which the claim that gave rise to the lien arose, notwithstanding any subsequent sale of the ship to a third party and notwithstanding that the purchaser had no notice of the lien and no personal liability on the claim from which the lien arose. This characteristic points in the direction of a maritime lien partaking of the nature of a proprietary right in the ship.

It is true that in the instant case this complication does not in fact arise; there had been no change of ownership since the claim of the necessaries men arose. Nevertheless it would be wrong to overlook this special characteristic of a maritime lien (for which the French expression is droit de suite) in any consideration of how a claim, which under its own lex causae would be treated as having the same legal consequences as those of a maritime lien in English law, is to be classified under English rules of conflict of laws for the purpose of distribution of a fund under Singapore law as the lex fori; for a maritime lien does something more than merely affect priorities.

As explained in the passage from *The Bold Buccleugh* that has already been cited, any charge that a maritime lien creates on a ship is initially inchoate only; unlike a mortgage it creates no immediate right of property; it is, and will continue to be, devoid of any legal consequences unless and until it is 'carried into effect by legal process, by a proceeding in rem'. Any proprietary right to which it may give rise is thus dependent upon the lienee being recognised as entitled to proceed in rem against the ship in the court in which he is seeking to enforce his maritime lien. Under the domestic law of a number of civil law countries even the inchoate charge to which some classes of maritime claims give rise is evanescent. Unless enforced by legal process within a limited time, for instance, within one year or before the commencement of the next voyage, it never comes to life. In English law, while there is no specific time limit to a maritime lien the right to enforce it may be lost by laches.

If and when a maritime lien is carried into effect by legal process,

however, the charge dates back to the time that the claim on which it is
founded arose. It is only this retrospective consequence of his having been
able to enforce the legal process in a court of law that enables a claimant,
whose entitlement to a maritime lien is still inchoate and has not yet come
into effect, to pursue his claim to the lien, as it were proleptically, in a
proceeding in rem against the ship at a time when it no longer belongs to the
shipowner who was personally liable to satisfy the claim in respect of which
the lien arose.

This characteristic of a maritime lien is one that is unique in English law.
It has the result that the recognition of any new class of claim arising under
foreign law as giving rise to a maritime lien in English law because it does so
under its own lex causae, may affect not only priorities as between classes of
creditors of a particular debtor in the distribution of the proceeds of sale of a
particular ship in an action in rem, but such recognition may also extend the
classes of persons who are entitled to bring such an action against a
particular ship, ie by including among them some who, although they have
no claim against the current owner of the ship, have claims against his
predecessor in ownership. But any question as to who is entitled to bring a
particular kind of proceeding in an English court, like questions of priorities
in distribution of a fund, is a question of jurisdiction. It too under English
rules of conflict of laws falls to be decided by English law as the lex fori.

Their Lordships therefore conclude that, in principle, the question as to
the right to proceed in rem against a ship as well as priorities in the
distribution between competing claimants of the proceeds of her sale in an
action in rem in the High Court of Singapore falls to be determined by the
lex fori, as if the events that gave rise to the claim had occurred in
Singapore.

Although in the English cases involving claims to maritime liens, which
extend over a period of a century and a half, there is no apparent
recognition in the judgments that any hidden problems of conflict of laws
might be involved, the English Courts of Admiralty have consistently
applied English rules as to what classes of events give rise to maritime liens
wherever those events may have occurred. Not one single case has been
drawn to their Lordships' attention in which it has been treated as relevant
that a transaction or event did or did not give rise to a maritime lien under
the law of the country where the transaction or event took place; even
though the judges of the Court of Admiralty were fully aware that under the
law of many European countries claims falling outside the six classes
recognised by English law were treated by those countries as giving rise to
maritime liens. Claims for the supply of necessaries provided the most
widespread example of foreign recognition of the maritime lien; but, under
French law in particular, a wide variety of other maritime claims were
treated as giving rise to privilèges, ie maritime liens.

(His Lordship examined the authorities, in particular *The Colorado* in
which the Court of Appeal held that the holder of a French hypothèque over
a French ship took priority over a Cardiff necessaries man; and *The Ioannis
Daskalelis*, in which the Supreme Court of Canada held that American
necessaries men took priority over a mortgagee of a Greek ship. He observed
that the Supreme Court misunderstood the judgments in *The Colorado*).

In their Lordships' view the English authorities upon close examination
support the principle that, in the application of English rules of conflict of

laws, maritime claims are classified as giving rise to maritime liens which are enforceable in actions in rem in English courts where *and only where* the events on which the claim is founded would have given rise to a maritime lien in English law, if those events had occurred within the territorial jurisdiction of the English court.

(His Lordship considered the High Court (Admiralty Jurisdiction) Act of Singapore, which, like its English counterpart the Administration of Justice Act 1956, was probably passed to enable Singapore to ratify the Brussels Convention of 1952 on the Arrest of Seagoing Ships (though Singapore had not ratified it). He examined that Convention and pointed out that United Kingdom policy had been to reduce to a minimum the number of maritime liens so as to prevent secret charges arising and gaining priority over mortgagees and subsequent purchasers, while United States policy of granting maritime liens for practically all classes of maritime claims was quite different).

Their Lordships are accordingly of opinion that in principle, in accordance with long-established English authorities and consistently with international comity as evidenced by the wide acceptance of the International Convention relating to the Arrest of Seagoing Ships 1952, the question whether or not in the instant case the necessaries men are entitled to priority over the mortgagees in the proceeds of sale of *The Halcyon Isle* depends upon whether or not if the repairs to the ship had been done in Singapore the repairers would have been entitled under the law of Singapore to a maritime lien on *The Halcyon Isle* for the price of them. The answer to that question is that they are not. The mortgagees are entitled to priority.

Lords Salmon and Scarman delivered the following dissenting judgment: In *The Tolten*[12] Scott LJ described the maritime lien as 'one of the first principles of the law of the sea, and very far-reaching in its effects'. But, if the mortgagees are right, a maritime lien is in the modern law no more than a procedural remedy. So far from being far-reaching, its validity and effect will be subject to the domestic law of the forum in which it is sought to be enforced. If this be the law, we have travelled a great distance from the concept of a universal law of the sea. We have returned to the legal climate which in England prior to 1840 nourished the common law courts by excluding the Admiralty jurisdiction from 'the body of the country', ie, the internal waters, ports and dockyards of the country. In the climate of a dominating domestic law the concepts and principles of the law of the sea wilt and die.

First, certain matters which are not in dispute. Under United States law a ship-repairer has a maritime lien against the ship. According to the uncontradicted evidence of a New York 'attorney at law and proctor in admiralty' the rendition by the ship-repairer of services and repairs to the ship 'gives rise to a valid maritime lien . . . which confers upon [him] rights of the same nature and quality as are conferred upon the holder of a maritime lien under English law'. It is equally not in dispute that under the law of Singapore, as of England:

(1) 'whatever relates to the remedy to be enforced, must be determined by the lex fori': Lord Brougham, *Don v Lippmann*;[13]

12 [1946] P 135 at 144, [1946] 2 All ER 372 at 376.
13 (1837) 5 Cl & Fin 1 at 13.

(2)   the priority of creditors claiming against a fund in court (including the proceeds of the judicial sale of a ship) is governed by the lex fori;

(3)   the claim of a mortgagee has priority over the claim of a ship-repairer for repairs executed in Singapore;

(4)   ship-repairers do not have a maritime lien on a ship for repairs executed in Singapore;

(5)   a claimant who has a maritime lien recognised by the law has priority over a mortgagee.

These propositions are to be found stated in the Court of Appeal's judgment as being not in dispute. They narrow the issue to the question: does the law of Singapore recognise a foreign maritime lien as a substantive right of property vested in a claimant who can show that he enjoys it under the law of the place where he performed his services? The law, admittedly, gives effect to a validly established foreign mortgage, recognising that the mortgage is an essential element of the claim. Is a validly established foreign maritime lien to be treated in the same way, as part of the claim? Or is it a remedy made available by the lex fori?

The law of Singapore follows English law in restricting maritime liens arising under its domestic law to only a few cases; in modern conditions, they are for all practical purposes limited to salvage, wages (or salaries) of the crew, master's disbursements and liabilities incurred on behalf of the ship, and damage done by the ship: *The Ripon City*. Whether it be put in terms of the law of the sea or of the rules of private international law, the question has to be asked and answered in this appeal: does English and Singapore law recognise a foreign maritime lien, where none would exist, had the claim arisen in England or Singapore? Whatever the answer, the result is unsatisfactory. If in the affirmative, maritime states may be tempted to pass 'chauvinistic' laws conferring liens on a plurality of claims so that the claimants may obtain abroad a preference denied to domestic claimants; if in the negative, claimants who have given the ship credit in reliance upon their lien may find themselves sorely deceived. If the law of the sea were a truly universal code, those dangers would disappear. Unfortunately the maritime nations, though they have tried, have failed to secure uniformity in their rules regarding maritime liens: see the fate of the two Conventions of 1926 and 1967 (*British Shipping Laws*)[14] each entitled (optimistically) an International Convention for the Unification of Certain Rules of Law relating to Maritime Liens and Mortgages. Though it signed each of them, the United Kingdom has not ratified either of them; Singapore (fully independent since 1965) has signed neither of them. In such confusion policy is an uncertain guide to the law. Principle offers a better prospect for the future.

Against this background the submissions of the parties have to be considered. The basic submission of the mortgagees is that in determining priorities the lex fori looks to the nature of the claim, and has no regard to the existence, or absence, of a maritime lien. The nature of the claim determines the priority of the judgment debt founded upon it. The claim of the ship-repairer is that of a necessaries man and, by the lex fori, ranks after the claim of a mortgagee. The reference in the books to the ranking of maritime liens before mortgage debts means no more than that the claims

14 Vol 8 (2nd edn, 1973) pp 1392, 1397.

which under the domestic law have the benefit of a maritime lien—notably salvage, wages and for damage done by the ship—enjoy their priority not because they have the 'privilege' of a maritime lien but because of the nature of the claims themselves.

The ship-repairers submit that a maritime lien is a substantive property right given by the law as a security for the claim and attaching to the claim as soon as the cause of action arises, though it does not take effect until legal proceedings are brought against the ship. They submit that it is as absurd, in characterising a claim to which the law attaches the security of a maritime lien, to ignore the existence of the lien as it would be to characterise a mortgagee's claim as merely one for the repayment of money lent. In each the security is part of the nature of the claim. They further submit that both principle and the weight of authority (which it is conceded is not all one way) support the view, for which they contend,—that English law has regard to the maritime lien in determining the nature of the claim. If, therefore, the court finds that the claim has under its lex loci a valid maritime lien, the lex fori will give the claim the priority over a mortgagee which it accords to a claim having the benefit of an English lien. . . .

In England, the lex fori decides the priority of the rights which exist against a ship, eg the rights conferred by a maritime lien taking precedence over the rights of a mortgagee. The question is—does English law, in circumstances such as these, recognise the maritime lien created by the law of the United States of America, ie the lex loci contractus where no such lien exists by its own internal law? In our view the balance of authorities, the comity of nations, private international law and natural justice all answer this question in the affirmative. If this be correct then English law (the lex fori) gives the maritime lien created by the lex loci contractus precedence over the mortgagees' mortgage. If it were otherwise, injustice would prevail. The ship-repairers would be deprived of their maritime lien, valid as it appeared to be throughout the world, and without which they would obviously never have allowed the ship to sail away without paying a dollar for the important repairs upon which the ship-repairers had spent a great deal of time and money and from which the mortgagees obtained substantial advantages.

It is suggested in the majority judgment that the ship-repairers were well aware that the lex loci contractus, conferring upon them their maritime lien, was likely to be disregarded by overseas lex fori in its determination of priorities. We entirely disagree. The importance which the ship-repairers attached to their maritime lien is clearly shown by the ship repair contract which included the term: 'Nothing herein shall be deemed to constitute a waiver of our maritime lien.' Moreover, in many countries the lex loci gives priority to maritime liens over mortgages. In our opinion, the ship-repairers clearly relied upon the fact that overseas the lex loci and the maritime lien which it created would both be respected, and the lien would be given the priority which it rightly received from the Court of Appeal in Singapore according to the law of Singapore and of England. Finally, on this aspect of the matter, it must be remembered that the nations have failed to introduce a uniform code governing maritime liens. The two international conventions relating to maritime liens, upon which the majority places great weight, cannot affect, in our view, the result of this appeal. Neither of them has been signed by Singapore; and neither of them ratified by the United Kingdom.

It is submitted, however, by the mortgagees that the weight of authority supports their case. We do not agree: we think that the contrary is true. (Their Lordships examined the authorities, in particular *The Colorado* and continued):

In our opinion the English Court of Appeal in *The Colorado* adopted the approach which is correct in principle. A maritime lien is a right of property given by way of security for a maritime claim. If the Admiralty court has, as in the present case, jurisdiction to entertain the claim, it will not disregard the lien. A maritime lien validly conferred by the lex loci is as much part of the claim as is a mortgage similarly valid by the lex loci. Each is a limited right of property securing the claim. The lien travels with the claim, as does the mortgage: and the claim travels with the ship. It would be a denial of history and principle, in the present chaos of the law of the sea governing the recognition and priority of maritime liens and mortgages, to refuse the aid of private international law.

For these reasons, we think that the Court of Appeal reached the correct conclusion and would dismiss the appeal.

Appeal allowed.

NOTE

In *The Colorado*[15] there was a contest for priorities between two claimants against a French ship, namely, A, the holders of a French hypothèque or mortgage on the ship, and B, Welsh necessaries men who had repaired the ship at Cardiff. By English law necessaries men are postponed to mortgagees of a ship. The Court of Appeal examined the nature of a French hypothèque in French law and came to the conclusion that A had priority, even though by French law B had priority. Until 1981 it was generally assumed that the Court of Appeal in that case regarded a French hypothèque as conferring rights equivalent to a maritime lien. Scrutton LJ said so in terms, and so did Bankes and Atkin LJJ. But in *The Halcyon Isle* (above) the majority of the Privy Council said that Scrutton LJ can only have been speaking loosely and could hardly have been suggesting that a hypothèque would take priority over a prior English mortgage. The minority did not agree with this interpretation of Scrutton LJ's judgment in *The Colorado*. They said that the case was a neat application of two principles of law: (1) The court looks to the lex loci to determine the nature of the claim. (2) Having established its nature, the court applies the principles of its own law, the lex fori. The minority said that the effect of the decision was succinctly summarised in Cheshire's *Private International Law*:[16] 'French law determined the substance of A's right, English law determined whether a right of that nature ranked before or after the opposing claim'.

15 [1923] P 102, 92 LJP 100.
16 9th edn (1974) p 697.

PART VIII

General Considerations

CHAPTER 25

Renvoi

When a rule of the English conflict of laws refers to the 'law' of a foreign country, the reference sometimes means the 'whole' law of the foreign country, including its rules of the conflict of laws, in which case the English court will decide the case as nearly as possible as it would be decided by a court in the foreign country.

Re Annesley [1926] Ch 692, 95 LJCh 404 (Chancery Division)

The testatrix, a British subject who had lived in France since 1866, died in 1924. By clause 2 of her will (made in the English language and form) she gave pecuniary legacies to friends and servants. By clause 4 she gave the residue of her property on trust for sale and out of the proceeds to pay an annuity and a trust legacy. By clause 5 she gave the ultimate residue to one of her two daughters absolutely. By clause 8 she declared that it was not her intention to abandon her English domicile of origin and that she had made no application under Article 13 of the French Civil Code (since repealed) for permission to establish her domicile in France. As the testatrix left two children surviving her, by French domestic law she could only dispose of one-third of her movable property. The testatrix by her will purported to dispose of the whole of her movable property.

Russell J (after deciding that on the facts the testatrix was domiciled in France at the date of her death, notwithstanding the declaration in her will and her failure to comply with article 13, continued): I accordingly decide that the domicile of the testatrix at the time of her death was French. French law accordingly applies, but the question remains: what French law? According to French municipal law,[1] the law applicable in the case of a foreigner not legally domiciled in France is the law of that person's nationality, in this case British. But the law of that nationality refers the question back to French law, the law of the domicile; and the question arises, will the French law accept this reference back, or renvoi, and apply French municipal law?

Upon this question arises acute conflict of expert opinion. Two experts took the view that the renvoi would not be accepted, but that a French court would distribute the movables of the testatrix in accordance with English municipal law. One expert equally strongly took the view that a French court would accept the renvoi and distribute in accordance with French municipal law. I must come to a conclusion as best I can upon this question of fact upon the evidence after considering and weighing the reasons given

1 Evidently a slip for 'French private international law' (*Ed*)

by each side in support of their respective views. It is a case rather of views expressed by the experts as to what the French law ought to be, than what it is. Although there is in France no system of case law such as we understand it here—the decisions of higher courts not being binding upon inferior tribunals—yet I think I must pay some attention to the fact that this question of renvoi has at different times come for consideration before the Cour de Cassation, the highest court in France, and each time with the same result—namely, the acceptance of the renvoi and the application of the French municipal law. It is true that the Cour de Cassation is quite free to take the opposite view on a future occasion, but it has never done so. I refer to the cases which were discussed and expounded before me—namely, the *Forgo* case in 1882, and the *Soulié* case in 1910. In the former case, a decision of the Cour de Cassation, the renvoi was accepted, and French municipal law was applied to the disposition of the estate of a Bavarian national domiciled de facto in France (but not domiciled there according to French law), because according to Bavarian law the law of the domicile or usual residence was applicable. The *Forgo* case gave rise to grave differences of opinion among French jurists and was followed by many conflicting decisions in lower courts, some favouring the 'Théorie du Renvoi', others against it. The matter again came under the consideration of the branch of the Cour de Cassation entitled Chambre de Requêtes, one of whose functions is to decide whether or not an appeal to the Cour de Cassation should be allowed to proceed. That was the *Soulié* case, in which the court below had held that French municipal law governed the succession to the movable property of an American subject who had died in France with a de facto domicile in that country. The Chamber declined to allow an appeal to the Cour de Cassation to proceed. This decision, coming as it did after the grave differences of opinion which resulted from the *Forgo* case, strikes me as of great importance. As is pointed out in a note to the report in Clunet, it shows that the Supreme Court persists with energy in its former view, notwithstanding the views of text-writers to the contrary.

In these circumstances, and after careful consideration of the evidence of the experts called before me, I have come to the conclusion that I ought to accept the view that according to French law the French courts, in administering the movable property of a deceased foreigner who, according to the law of this country, is domiciled in France, and whose property must, according to that law, be applied in accordance with the law of the country in which he was domiciled, will apply French municipal law, and that even though the deceased had not complied with article 13 of the Code.

The result is that as regards her English personal estate and her French movable property the testatrix in this case had power only to dispose of one-third thereof by her will.

Speaking for myself, I should like to reach the same conclusion by a much more direct route along which no question of renvoi need be encountered at all. When the law of England requires that the personal estate of a British subject who dies domiciled, according to the requirements of English law, in a foreign country shall be administered in accordance with the law of that country, why should this not mean in accordance with the law which that country would apply, not to the propositus, but to its own nationals legally domiciled there? In other words, when we say that French law applies to the administration of the personal estate of an Englishman who dies domiciled in

France, we mean that French municipal law which France applies in the case of Frenchmen. This appears to me a simple and rational solution which avoids altogether that endless oscillation which otherwise would result from the law of the country of nationality invoking the law of the country of domicile, while the law of the country of domicile in turn invokes the law of the country of nationality, and I am glad to find that this simple solution has in fact been adopted by the Surrogate's Court of New York: *Re Tallmadge*.[2]

Certain other subsidiary questions arise. In consequence of the restrictions on the power of the testatrix to dispose of her property, the legacies bequeathed by the will cannot be paid in full. The will, in my opinion, is so worded that the pecuniary legacies given by clause 2 of the will must be paid in full before any of the sums mentioned in clause 4 of the will are set apart or paid. These last mentioned sums must if necessary abate rateably.

Re Ross [1930] 1 Ch 377, 99 LJCh 67 (Chancery Division)

Janet Anne Ross, a British subject domiciled in Italy, died in 1927 leaving movable property in England and Italy and immovable property in Italy. She left two wills, one in English and the other in Italian. By her English will she gave the residue of her property in England to her niece, the defendant Caroline Waterfield, absolutely. By her Italian will she appointed her grand-nephew Aymand Waterfield heir of her movable and immovable property in Italy, subject to a usufruct in favour of his mother Caroline Waterfield during her life. Neither will left anything to the plaintiff, who was the testatrix's only son. The plaintiff claimed a declaration that he was entitled, notwithstanding the testamentary dispositions of his mother, to one moiety of her movable and immovable property in Italy and one moiety of her movable property in England as his legitima portio under Italian law.

Article 8 of the Italian Code provided that succession, whether under an intestacy or under a will, was regulated by the national law of the deceased, whatever the nature of the property. Article 9 provided that the substance and effect of testamentary dispositions were deemed to be governed by the national law of the testator.

Luxmore J: ... I will deal first with the movable property. Both the plaintiff's and defendants' counsel agree that by English law, the succession to movable property wherever situate is governed by the law of the domicile, in this case the law of Italy. In Italy, as in most of the European countries, the law refuses to recognise domicile as governing succession and other personal rights, and accepts the law of the nationality as the governing law. ... The parties are agreed that 'the law of the domicile' governs the succession to the movable property. The dispute which arises between them and which I have to determine, is what is meant by 'the law of the domicile'. Does the phrase, so far as the English law is concerned, mean only that part of the domiciliary law which is applicable to nationals of the country of domicile (sometimes called 'the municipal law', or 'the internal law'); or does it mean the whole law of the country of domicile, including the rules of private international law, administered by its tribunals? If the former contention is correct, then the English court, in deciding a case like the

2 (1919) 181 NY Supp 336.

present, is not concerned to inquire what the courts of the country of domicile would in fact decide in the particular case, but what the courts of the domicile would decide if the propositus, instead of being domiciled in the foreign country, was also a national of that country. Whereas if the latter view is the correct one, the English court is solely concerned to inquire what the courts of the country of domicile would in fact decide in the particular case. In my opinion the latter is the correct view, as laid down by the English decisions, and there is no decision that has been quoted to me in argument or that I have been able to discover which supports the former view, though there is a dictum in the most recent case dealing with the question, which expresses approval of that view. I refer to the dictum of Russell J in *Re Annesley*.[3]

The argument against the view that the law of the country of domicile means the whole of the law of that country, including its rules of private international law, is based on a claim that if this be the meaning of the expression 'the law of the domicile', then logically the meaning of the expression 'the law of the nationality' must also mean the whole of that law, including its rules of private international law; and it is said that if this be the true rule, the English court, in effect, has to say—I am putting the argument in the concrete form applicable to the case before me—the Italian law provides that the law of the nationality (the English law) is to be the governing law on the basis that the domicile of origin is English; but as the English law considers the law of the domicile to be the governing law, there is a further reference back from it to the Italian law as the domiciliary law, the logical result being an endless oscillation backwards and forwards from one law to the other, the English court sending the case back according to the English doctrine of domicile to the Italian court, and the Italian court sending it back again to the English court according to the Italian doctrine of nationality, and so on ad infinitum; the result being the establishment of what has been called by some of the text-writers a 'circulus inextricabilis'. The circle can only be cut if and when one or other of the opposing systems of law—to use once more a phrase adopted by the text-writers—'accepts the renvoi'.

Is this argument well founded? Indeed, does it arise at all? It does not in fact arise if the true view of the English court is that, by the phrase 'the law of the country of domicile' is meant that law which the courts of the country of domicile apply to the decision of the case to which the rule refers. If this is the correct view, the English courts in deciding the case 'accept the renvoi'. Let me illustrate what I mean by a reference to the question before me. It is admitted on both sides that the English court must adhere to the rule that, Janet Anne Ross having died domiciled in Italy, the distribution of her movable property must be governed by the law of Italy. On the proposition with which I am dealing this means the law which the Italian courts would hold to be applicable to the case of Janet Anne Ross, she being a British subject with an English domicile of origin. If because of her nationality the Italian courts hold that her movable property ought to be distributed in accordance with English internal law as applicable to English nationals domiciled in England–then the English courts will distribute this property in exactly the same way as if Janet Anne Ross was in fact at her death

3 [1926] Ch 692, 95 LJCh 404; pp 656–657 above.

domiciled in England. If, on the other hand, the Italian courts should hold
that her movable property should be distributed in accordance with the
internal law of Italy applicable to Italian nationals, then the English courts
will distribute Janet Anne Ross's movable property in accordance with
Italian internal law. In other words, the English court will endeavour to
ascertain what the Italian courts would in fact decide with regard to that
part of Janet Anne Ross's movable property as might come under the actual
control of the Italian courts.

My attention has been called in the course of the argument of this case to
a number of authorities, and I have also considered a number of other
decisions. In my view the general trend of the authorities establishes that the
English courts have generally, if not invariably, meant by 'the law of the
country of domicile', the whole law of that country as administered by the
courts of that country, and with the exception of the dictum already referred
to, there is no case to the contrary.

(His Lordship reviewed the authorities and continued:) In my opinion the
present case must be decided in accordance with the law of Italy, as that law
would be expounded in the Italian courts. If the Italian court had in fact
dealt with the matter there would be no necessity to inquire into the law,
and it would be my duty simply to follow the decision. Since there is no
decision by the Italian court, I am bound to ascertain how the Italian court
would decide the case from the evidence of those competent to instruct me. I
am glad to say that the Italian lawyers who have been called on both sides
are unanimous in this conclusion, that if the case fell to be decided in the
Italian courts, it would be held that the testamentary dispositions of Mrs
Janet Anne Ross were valid, and provide for the total disposition of her
property in Italy; and that in no circumstances would the Italian court
recognise any right on the part of the plaintiff to any part of her property as
legitima portio, as it would have done had Mrs Janet Anne Ross been an
Italian national.

. . . This disposes of the case so far as the movables in Italy are concerned.
The position as to the immovable property in Italy seems to me to stand on a
different basis. It is true that the law of Italy provides, by articles 8 and 9 of
the Code, that the succession to movable and immovable property is
governed by the law of the nationality of the deceased owner, yet the English
law has never suggested that the law of the domicile has anything to do with
the succession to immovables. On the contrary, it has always recognised that
the lex situs governs the succession to immovables, and the lex situs must
necessarily be the law of the country where the property is situate, as it
would be expounded by the courts of that country; and domicile cannot
under any circumstances have any bearing on the case. But to some extent
the theory of the renvoi may apply, for the law of England refers the
question of succession to immovables to the lex situs (in this case the law of
Italy), and the lex situs (the Italian law) refers the case to the law of the
nationality, and this might mean the law of the nationality including the
rule relating to the lex situs, and once again the circulus inextricabilis would
be constituted. But in my view the lex situs must, for the reasons I have
already stated with regard to the meaning to be placed on the phrase, 'law of
the domicile', be construed in the way the courts of the country where the
immovables are situate would themselves determine. On this basis the expert
evidence is clear that the Italian courts would decide the succession to the

immovable property in the same manner as the English court would determine it if the immovable property in question belonged to an Englishman and was situate in England.

. . . In the result the plaintiff has failed to substantiate either of his claims in this action, and I therefore dismiss it with costs.

Re Askew [1930] 2 Ch 259, 99 LJCh 466 (Chancery Division)

By an English marriage settlement made in 1893 on the marriage of John Bertram Askew, a British subject then domiciled in England, it was provided that if John Bertram Askew should marry again he might by deed or will revoke in part the trusts of the husband's trust fund and might appoint that part upon such trusts for the benefit of any child of such subsequent marriage as he might think proper.

John Bertram Askew separated from his wife, and acquired a domicile of choice in Germany prior to 1911. In June 1911 a German court made a decree dissolving his marriage. In 1912 he married Anna Askew in Berlin. In January 1911, before the divorce, a daughter named Margarete Askew had been born to Anna Askew in Switzerland and she was acknowledged to be the daughter of John Bertram Askew.

By deed poll dated in 1913 John Bertram Askew purported to revoke part of the trusts of the husband's trust fund under the settlement of 1893 and to appoint that part to Margarete Askew absolutely.

The trustees of the settlement took out a summons for the determination of the question whether the power of appointment had been validly exercised in favour of Margarete Askew by the deed poll of 1913.

An affidavit by a German lawyer, accepted by all parties as correct, stated as follows: 'A general principle of German law is that the law of the country of which the father at the time of the marriage is a national governs the question of legitimation per subsequens matrimonium. I am informed and believe that John Bertram Askew was an Englishman. Therefore English law would be applied by the German court in deciding the question. (I am informed that the English law refers the question back to the law of the domicile, in the present case German law.) The German court would in these circumstances first have to decide whether to apply the municipal law of England only, or also the principles of international private law as interpreted by the English courts. The rule followed by the German court is that both the municipal law and the rules of international law, as interpreted by the English court, are to be applied. The German court therefore accepts the renvoi. There is no general statutory rule of German law as to which municipal law in the case of renvoi as in the present case is to be ultimately applied. The question has, however, been decided by numerous decisions of the Reichsgericht, the court of the highest instance in Germany. These decisions are to the effect that in a case where the German law provides that the law of the nationality is to govern a question and the law of nationality refers to the law of domicile and the domicile is German, the German court is to apply German municipal law.

'I am therefore of opinion that the German court would hold that according to German law Margarete Askew was legitimated by the marriage of her parents notwithstanding the fact that her father at the time of her birth was still married to a woman other than her mother and that by reason of the legitimation the child Margarete Askew has become issue of the marriage between John Bertram Askew and Anna Askew née Wengels.'

Maugham J: There is no doubt that, if German local law were applicable, the subsequent marriage of the parents of the defendant Margarete Askew would effect her legitimation, and that although she was born before the divorce, which was not made absolute until 27 July 1911. The trustees are naturally desirous of the protection of the court in relation to the question whether the power of appointment in question was validly exercised by the deed poll, and for this purpose it is necessary to determine whether the defendant Margarete Askew, though born out of wedlock during the continuance of a previous marriage, is, having regard to her father's domicile, legitimate. It is admitted that the Legitimacy Act 1926 would not have had that effect, having regard to the fact that John Bertram Askew was married to his first wife when the defendant Margarete Askew was born.[4]

The question of legitimation of a child by the subsequent marriage of its parents in a foreign country (apart from the provisions of the Legitimacy Act 1926, s 1, sub-s 2, and s 8) appears at first sight to be well settled. Dicey (Rule 137, Case I, in his *Conflict of Laws*) states the result of the decisions thus: 'If both the law of the father's domicile at the time of the birth of the child and the law of the father's domicile at the date of the subsequent marriage allow of legitimatio per subsequens matrimonium, the child becomes or may become legitimate on the marriage of the parents.' The authorities cited are *Udny v Udny*;[5] *Re Wright's Trusts*;[6] *Re Grove*,[7] and they bear out the proposition. Now, John Bertram Askew was admittedly domiciled in Germany both at the date of the birth and at the time of the subsequent marriage. But what is the meaning of the phrase 'the law of the father's domicile'? Does it refer to the municipal law or local law of Germany, or does it refer to the whole of the laws applicable in Germany, including the views entertained in Germany as to the rules of private international law? There is no doubt that Dicey means the latter (see his Interpretation of Terms, Definition II); but in my opinion it is very doubtful whether the courts who have dealt with the matter did not mean the former. The so-called doctrine of renvoi, which has been so much discussed by jurists of recent years, had not been formulated in earlier days; and those who look at the statement of the foreign law in the earlier cases (see, for example, *Re Wright's Trusts* and *Re Grove*) will find that the foreign law as stated was the local or municipal law, and that no evidence was adduced as to the rules of private international law applied in the foreign country. It would seem that rules of private international law, not being founded on custom or statute, but being based upon considerations of justice and what is called 'comity', ought to be the same in all countries, though it is now well known (contrary to the belief entertained by Lord Westbury: see *Udny v Udny*) that they are

---

4 This is a reference to s 1 (2) of the Legitimacy Act 1926, which was repealed by s 1 of the Legitimacy Act 1959. Another reason, not noticed in the judgment, why the Act was not available was that since Margarete was legitimated after the power of appointment was created, she was not an object of the power: see *Re Hoff* [1942] Ch 298, [1942] 1 All ER 547 (*Ed*).
5 (1869) LR 1 Sc & Div 441; p 3 above.
6 (1856) 2 K & J 595, 25 LJCh 621.
7 (1888) 40 Ch D 216, 58 LJCh 57.

not. I am convinced that 60 or 70 years ago it never would have occurred to lawyers who were proving, say, the law of Italy (or France) in relation to the succession to an Englishwoman dying domiciled in Italy (or France) to depose (first) that the Italian (or the French) law gave a son a legitima portio; (secondly) that foreigners domiciled in Italy (or France) were deemed to retain their personal law; (thirdly) that he was informed that according to English law an English testator had a free power of disposition; and (finally) that, accordingly, by an application of Italian (or French) rules of private international law, the son had not (or had) a right to a legitima portio. It is on evidence of this kind that English courts have now to decide cases relating to the succession to movables belonging to British subjects who die domiciled abroad, and other cognate matters. It may be added that there is generally an acute conflict of expert opinion as to the foreign law, which has to be proved afresh in each case. Foreign jurists and foreign courts take from time to time varying views on the subject of renvoi. The result is not always satisfactory. It may, then, be useful to consider the question from the point of view of principle before dealing with the four modern authorities which must, I think, guide me in the matter.

I will take the case of John Doe, a British subject, who goes to a foreign country, the Commonwealth of Utopia, and there acquires a permanent home without any intention of returning to his native land. He does not care to become a naturalised Utopian, and he does not trouble to fulfil the legal formalities which Utopia requires before legally admitting him to a Utopian domicile. Now the State of Utopia is one which (I assume) has adopted what is called the principle of nationality for foreigners, including those who have permanently settled in the realm, and it accordingly applies their national law in all questions relating to their status, capacity, and the succession to their surplus assets and the like. The first question that arises is whether in these circumstances John Doe in an English court can be said to have acquired a Utopian domicile. Clearly this depends upon the true meaning to be attached to the word 'domicile'. Until the decision of the House of Lords to be referred to later, this was at least doubtful; but it is now, I think, finally settled that in an English court John Doe must be taken to have been domiciled in Utopia, because domicile is a pure question of fact and does not in any true sense connote a legal relation. In English courts, English law must be applied; and by that law all these matters must be decided, at any rate prima facie, by the lex domicilii, that is, in the case under consideration, by the law of Utopia, and not the less that the courts of Utopia attach no importance in such a case to the lex domicilii. Now the second question arises—when the English courts refer the matter to the law of Utopia as the lex domicilii, do they mean the whole of that law, or do they mean the local or municipal law which in Utopia would apply to Utopian subjects? In order fully to appreciate this matter, it is necessary to answer the question, how comes it that an English court applies to John Doe the system of law of Utopia to which he does not owe allegiance? The answer must be that, in the view of an English court, John Doe, by acquiring a permanent home in Utopia, has attracted to himself the system of personal law which Utopia would apply to him, and it may be added that this would be in accordance with his presumed intention. Moreover, questions of private international law, in the absence of statute, depend largely on the historical views and the opinions of jurists which have been adopted in our courts; and it is the fact that, for some hundreds of years before the nineteenth century, continental and British jurists alike were practically united in the view that there existed in the world a number of civil societies based on domicile in the sense that the status and capacity of the members of those societies were governed by the lex domicilii, whatever their nationalities might be. In France, Italy, Germany and elsewhere a different principle—namely, that of nationality—has gradually been introduced and now prevails; but in the British Empire, including as it does within its area so many distinct systems of law, the old doctrine is retained, and domicile is still the criterion in our courts of the personal law. If the law of Utopia had taken the same view as the English courts and applied to John Doe the Utopian local law, there would of course be no difficulty whatever. But since the jurists of Utopia have adopted the principle of nationality as governing the question of his personal law, the result is that, when the English court makes an inquiry as to the Utopian law, the first answer may be that Utopia prima facie applies to John Doe the law of England. It is, I think, a misunderstanding of the problem to suggest that this leads to a deadlock. Like others before me, I have spoken of the lex domicilii as applying to John Doe; but it should not be forgotten that the English court is not applying Utopian law *as such*, and the phrase is really a short way of referring to rights acquired under the lex domicilii. The inquiry which the court makes is, of course, as to Utopian law as a fact, and one to be proved in evidence like any other. The inquiry might accurately be expanded thus: What rights have been acquired in Utopia by the parties to the English suit by reason of the de facto domicile of John Doe in Utopia? For the English court will enforce those rights, though, I repeat, it does not, properly speaking, enforce Utopian laws. It is evident that, so stated, the question involves this. Have the parties acquired rights in Utopia by reason of the personal law of John Doe being English local law or Utopian local law? There is this alternative and no other. It is apparent that there is no room here for a deadlock, and that the circulus inextricabilis is no better than a (perhaps amusing) quibble.

The English judges and the foreign judges do not bow to each other like the officers at Fontenoy. The English court has to decide a matter within its jurisdiction according to English law in the wide sense, and if the matter depends on foreign domicile it is only necessary to prove certain facts as to rights under the foreign law. It is therefore, I think, clear that, when we inquire whether John Doe has acquired rights in Utopia by Utopian law, we must mean by the whole of the laws of Utopia including any views of private international law which may be deemed to give him rights (or subject him to restrictions), though an Englishman settled in that land. A final question may sometimes remain—namely, whether the lex domicilii is one which the English courts can recognise. If it is (as it nearly always is), we have only to ascertain what the lex domicilii in the wider sense is. I will add that I am not aware of any satisfactory definition of the term renvoi; but it will be noted that, if I am right, an English court can never have anything to do with it, except so far as foreign experts may expound the doctrine as being part of the lex domicilii. . . .

(His Lordship discussed the cases of *Re Johnson*,[8] *Casdagli v Casdagli*,[9] *Re*

8 [1903] 1 Ch 821, 72 LJCh 682.
9 [1919] AC 145, 88 LJP 49.

Annesley,[10] and *Re Ross*[11] and the evidence of German law and continued:) For the reasons given above I hold that in an English court the lex domicilii in the wide sense must prima facie apply, and, this being a law which the English courts will recognise, the conclusion is that the defendant Margarete is a legitimate child of John Bertram Askew in our courts and that the power of appointment was effectively exercised in her favour.

I think it proper to add that in my opinion it is unsatisfactory to find that, upon the evidence adduced in the two cases of *Re Annesley* and *Re Ross*, the courts were bound to hold that, although both in France and in Italy the national law of the de cujus is held to prevail, yet, owing to a divergence on the theoretical question of renvoi, the property and capacity of an Englishman domiciled in Italy is held to be a matter of (local) English law, whilst the property and capacity of an Englishman domiciled in France is held to be a matter of (local) French law. Nor is there any certainty that a contrary result will not be reached upon the evidence adduced in the next two cases which arise as to persons dying in France and Italy respectively. Those who have any acquaintance with the extensive literature that has appeared on the Continent on the subject of renvoi and the great diversity of view that exists would not be surprised to find that the legal decisions in France and Italy, where legal decisions are not binding as authorities to be followed, had changed in their effect. An Englishman domiciled de facto in France can have no certainty that his personal law is the municipal law of France, nor can he be sure if he crosses the frontier and becomes domiciled de facto in Italy that the municipal law of England will become his personal law. It may be added that views which seem strange to an English lawyer are entertained on these matters in some Eastern countries and also in some of the states in South America; and in those countries the result of acquiring a domicile must be very doubtful. I cannot refrain from expressing the opinion that it is desirable that the position of British subjects who acquire domiciles in countries which do not agree with our views as to the effect of a foreign domicile should be made clear by a very short statute. There is much to be said for the 'simple and rational solution' suggested by Russell J in *Re Annesley*; but whether the municipal law of the foreign country or the municipal law of England is to be held applicable in British courts in these cases, it is clearly desirable that the matter should be certain and should not be held ultimately to depend on the doubtful and conflicting evidence of foreign experts.

QUESTIONS

1. What happens if the foreign law has the same rules as to renvoi as English law, as may be quite likely if the foreign law is that of another common law jurisdiction?
2. What law will an English court apply if our choice of law rules refer the issue to the law of the domicile and that law refers the issue to the law of the nationality and the person in question is a British citizen? (see *Re O'Keefe* [1940] Ch 124, [1940] 1 All ER 216)
3. What is the justification, in a case of renvoi, for the English court abandoning its choice of law rules in favour of those of the foreign law?

10 [1926] Ch 692, 95 LJCh 404; p 655 above.
11 [1930] 1 Ch 377, 99 LJCh 67; p 657 above.

Renvoi has no place in the law of contract.

Re United Railways of Havana and Regla Warehouses Ltd
[1960] Ch 52, [1959] 1 All ER 214 (Court of Appeal)

An English company owned a railway undertaking in Cuba. It raised loan capital in the United States through the 'Philadelphia Plan', ie the sale of its rolling stock to a Pennsylvania bank and its lease back by the bank to the company in consideration of rentals payable partly in Pennsylvania and partly in New York. The Court of Appeal held that the law of Pennsylvania and not that of Cuba was the proper law of the contract.

Jenkins LJ: While accepting the respondents' contention that the proper law of the trust agreement and of the lease was not the law of Cuba we are not prepared, as at present advised, to accept their alternative suggestion that had the proper law been Cuban the relevant law to apply would nevertheless, on the evidence of Dr Gorrin and by virtue of the renvoi doctrine, have been that of Pennsylvania. This view does seem to have been accepted by the judge and receives some support from the judgment of the Privy Council, delivered by Lord Wright, in *Vita Food Products Inc v Unus Shipping Co.*[12] This passage from the judgment of the Judicial Committee has, however, by no means escaped criticism (see, for example, *Dicey*;[13] and an article in vol 56 of the *Law Quarterly Review* (1940), pp 333 to 335, by Mr Morris and Dr Cheshire). Had it been necessary to decide the point on the present appeal (which it is not), we should have been disposed to hold that the principle of renvoi finds no place in the field of contract; and accordingly that if the parties to the lease here in question ought to be treated as having accepted Cuban law as the proper law of the contract, such law was the domestic law of Cuba and not the rules of the conflict of laws administered by the Cuban courts.[14]

Amin Rasheed Shipping Co v Kuwait Insurance Co [1983] 2 All
ER 884; [1983] 3 WLR 241 (House of Lords)

The facts are stated above, p 72.

Lord Diplock: One final comment upon what under English conflict rules is meant by the 'proper law' of a contract may be appropriate. It is the substantive law of the country which the parties have chosen as that by which their mutual legally enforceable rights are to be ascertained, but excluding any renvoi, whether of remission or transmission, that the courts of that country might themselves apply if the matter were litigated before them. For example, if a contract made in England were expressed to be governed by French law, the English court would apply French substantive law to it notwithstanding that a French court applying its own conflict rules might accept a renvoi to English law as the lex loci contractus if the matter were

---

12 [1939] AC 277 at 292, [1939] 1 All ER 513 at 522; p 446 above.
13 *Conflict of Laws*, 7th edn, 1958, pp 73, 721.
14 The decision of the Court of Appeal on the proper law of the contract was affirmed by the House of Lords [1961] AC 1007, [1960] 2 All ER 332, though varied in other respects (*Ed*).

litigated before it. Conversely, assuming that under English conflict rules English law is the proper law of the contract the fact that the courts of a country which under English conflict rules would be regarded as having jurisdiction over a dispute arising under the contract (in casu Kuwait) would under its own conflict rules have recourse to English law as determinitive of the rights and obligations of the parties, would not make the proper law of the contract any the less English law because it was the law that a Kuwaiti court also would apply.

EEC Convention on the Law Applicable to Contractual Obligations

ARTICLE 15

Exclusion of renvoi

The application of the law of any country specified by this Convention means the application of the rules of law in force in that country other than its rules of private international law.

It may well be that renvoi has no place in the law of tort, but there is no English authority for this proposition.

M'Elroy v M'Allister 1949 SC 110 (Court of Session)

The pursuer's husband was killed in a motor accident at Shap in Cumbria. He was a passenger in a lorry owned by his employers and negligently driven by their servant the defender. All parties concerned were natives of and resident in Glasgow. If the accident had happened in Scotland, the pursuer would have been entitled to substantial damages for solatium. If the action had been brought in England, she would have been entitled to substantial damages under the Fatal Accidents Act and also for loss of the deceased's expectation of life under the Law Reform (Miscellaneous Provisions) Act 1934.[15] But it was held by a special court of seven judges that she could only recover £40 in respect of funeral expenses, that being the only point at which Scots and English law coincided. The claim for solatium failed because it was a substantive and independent right of action and not a mere item in a claim for damages, and was not recognised by English law, the lex loci delicti. The claim under the Fatal Accidents Act failed because the action was begun more than 12 months after the accident, contrary to section 3 of the Act of 1846, which the court regarded as substantive and not procedural. The claim under the Law Reform (Miscellaneous Provisions) Act 1934 failed because in Scots law all rights of action for personal injuries due to negligence die with the injured person, and therefore the wrong was not actionable by the lex fori. Lord Keith (later Lord Keith of Avonholm) dissented on both the last two points.

Lord Russell: . . . In the consideration of the question raised by those

---

15 This head of liability under English law was abolished by s 1 of the Administration of Justice Act 1982 (*Ed*).

opposing arguments as thus briefly summarised, it is desirable to note that in referring to the lex loci delicti to ascertain by what rules the rights and liabilities of the parties to this action are there regulated this court refers to the internal domestic law of that locus and not to its private international law. The reference is thus to the English rules regulating a purely domestic case similar to the case presently under consideration. If so, it appears to me that decisions pronounced by English courts affirming and applying their principles of private international law—to the effect that foreign statutes of limitation affecting rights enjoyed in that foreign country, if merely such as to specify a period of time after which such rights cannot be enforced by action there, affect procedure only, and that accordingly such matter of procedure falls to be regulated by the lex fori—are not binding on a Scottish court.

Pfau v Trent Aluminium Co (p 704 at 707–708 below)

CHAPTER 26

Characterisation

The court does not necessarily characterise rules of foreign law in the same way as their nearest equivalents in English law.

Re Cohn [1945] Ch 5, 114 LJCh 97 (Chancery Division)

A mother and daughter, Mrs Cohn and Mrs Oppenheimer, were German nationals domiciled in Germany but resident in England. They were killed in an air raid in London as a result of the same explosion, and it could not be proved which of them survived the other. Mrs Oppenheimer was entitled to movable property under Mrs Cohn's will if she survived Mrs Cohn.

Uthwatt J: ... There is a difference between the law of England and the law of Germany regarding the presumption which is to be made about the order of the deaths in the circumstances stated. The law of England, by s 184 of the Law of Property Act 1925, prescribes that, where two or more persons have died in circumstances rendering it uncertain which of them survived the other or others, 'such deaths shall (subject to any order of the court), for all purposes affecting the title to the property, be presumed to have occurred in order of seniority, and accordingly the younger shall be deemed to have survived the elder'. The Civil Code of Germany makes different provision. In the first book of the German Civil Code, headed 'General Principles', the first chapter of the first part deals with 'Natural Persons'. Article 20 contained in that chapter provides that, if several persons perish in a common danger, it is presumed that they have died simultaneously. On 4 July 1939, this was replaced by the following article: 'If it cannot be proved that of several deceased persons or persons declared dead one has survived the other, it is presumed that they have died simultaneously.' It may be observed in passing that the date of the widening of the scope of article 20 affected by the amendment is of interest to the general historian. Under German law Mrs Oppenheimer can benefit under the will of Mrs Cohn only if she (Mrs Oppenheimer) was the survivor of the two.

It was argued by Mr Danckwerts, on behalf of those interested in Mrs Oppenheimer's estate, that the first question which the court was called on to ascertain was whether or not Mrs Oppenheimer survived Mrs Cohn; that, in ascertaining that fact, the method of proof was determined by the lex fori (the law of England)—a general proposition which cannot be disputed; and that, when once it was shown that it was uncertain which of them survived the other, s 184 of the Law of Property Act 1925 came into operation as part of the lex fori compelling the court to draw the inference or proceed on the footing that Mrs Oppenheimer survived Mrs Cohn. It was, according to his argument, only after reaching that point, that one turned to the law of the domicile.

In my opinion, this argument is not well founded. The law of the domicile, namely the law of Germany, is alone relevant in determining the effect of the testamentary dispositions of movables made by Mrs Cohn, the basis on which the movables are to be administered, and the facts which it is necessary to ascertain to administer that estate. If, for instance, under the law of Germany, it was not necessary for the efficacy of the disposition in her favour that Mrs Oppenheimer should survive Mrs Cohn, but was only necessary that she should survive either Mr or Mrs Cohn, no inquiry as to survivorship such as is here being made would have been necessary. The question of survivorship is, in fact, opened up by the provisions of German law as to inheritance and is formally not: 'Did or did not Mrs Oppenheimer survive Mrs Cohn?' but 'Is the administration of Mrs Cohn's estate to proceed on the footing that Mrs Oppenheimer survived Mrs Cohn or on the footing that she did not?' The purpose to which the inquiry as to survivorship is directed must be kept in mind. The mode of proving any fact bearing on survivorship is determined by the lex fori. The effect of any fact so proved is for the purpose in hand determined by the law of the domicile. The fact proved in this case is that it is impossible to say whether or not Mrs Oppenheimer survived Mrs Cohn. Proof stops there. Section 184 of the Law of Property Act 1925 does not come into the picture at all. It is not part of the law of evidence of the lex fori, for the section is not directed to helping in the ascertainment of any fact but contains a rule of substantive law directing a certain presumption to be made in all cases affecting the title to property. As a rule of substantive law the section is relevant where title is governed by the law of England. It has no application where title is determined by the law of any other country.

I turn now to consider the law of Germany in relation to the facts proved, unhampered by s 184 of the Law of Property Act 1925. In my view, the provision contained in the article of 4 July 1939 is part of the general substantive law of Germany and not part of its law of evidence. Its terms and the place in which the repealed article dealing with the same general subject-matter was to be found make that clear. That rule of law has to be applied, inter alia, as part of the Law of Inheritances, contained in the German Civil Code. Predicating of Mrs Oppenheimer that she is presumed to have died simultaneously with Mrs Cohn, it is clear that Mrs Oppenheimer was not a person living at the time when the succession to Mrs Cohn's estate opened, and that, accordingly, having regard to arts 1922 and 1923 of the German Civil Code, the defendants, Mrs Freudenthal and Siegfried Cohn, take Mrs Cohn's movable estate.

QUESTION

Hansel and Gretel, a brother and sister aged 25 and 27 respectively, are domiciled in Ruritania. While on holiday in England, they are killed in a motor accident in circumstances rendering it uncertain which of them survived the other. Hansel died intestate and a bachelor leaving movables in England. His sole next of kin are Gretel and another sister Elisabeth, who survives him. Gretel left a will in which she gave all her property to her friend Rudolf. By Ruritanian law, the male is deemed to die first; and this is a rule of procedure, not of substance. By English law, the elder is deemed to die first; and this is a rule of substance, not of procedure. Who is entitled to Hansel's movables?

Apt v Apt (p 224 above)

Ogden v Ogden (p 240 above)

Freke v Carbery (p 529 above)

Re Berchtold (p 532 above)

Re Maldonado (p 575 above)

Wills Act 1963, s 3 (p 580 above)

Re Martin (p 586 above)

Foreign Limitation Periods Act 1984 (p 627 above)

Leroux v Brown (p 629 above)

CHAPTER 27

The Incidental Question

The court may apply a foreign rule of the conflict of laws to determine some question which incidentally arises in the course of deciding the main question.

Schwebel v Ungar [1964] 1 OR 430, 42 DLR (2d) 622 (Ontario Court of Appeal)

The defendant was born in Hungary. In 1945 she married Joseph Waktor in Hungary according to the rites of the Jewish faith. Joseph Waktor was domiciled at that time in Hungary. Shortly after the marriage they both decided to leave Hungary and go to Israel. They were in several refugee camps in Europe and finally in one in Italy in the course of their efforts to get to Israel. While in the camp in Italy, and while still domiciled in Hungary, they were divorced by a gett (an extra-judicial Jewish divorce). A few weeks later, in December 1948, they both arrived in Israel. This divorce was not recognised as a valid divorce by the law of either Hungary or Italy but it was recognised as such by the law of Israel.

The defendant then lived in Israel for seven and a half years with her parents. She then came to New York and Toronto to visit relatives, and while in Toronto she met and married the plaintiff in April 1957.

The plaintiff petitioned for a decree of nullity on the ground that Joseph Waktor was still alive at the date of the plaintiff's marriage to defendant which was therefore bigamous. McRuer CJ granted a decree, holding that Joseph Waktor and the defendant had never lost their Hungarian domicile of origin. The defendant appealed.

The judgment of the court (MacKay, Kelly, and McLennan JJA) was delivered by

Mackay JA (after stating the facts, and holding that Waktor and the defendant acquired a domicile of choice in Israel before the defendant's second marriage): One of the requirements for a valid marriage in Ontario is that the parties entering into the marriage have the status of single persons and the question here is whether the personal status of the defendant was that of a married or single person at the time she entered into the marriage contract with the plaintiff in 1957.

If we determine the question by asking, (1) What was her domicile at that date? and (2) What was her personal status under the law of her country of domicile? the answer clearly is that she was domiciled in Israel; her status was that of a single person and therefore her marriage in 1957 was a valid marriage.

On the other hand, if we say her status in Israel is one based on the recognition by the law of Israel of a divorce obtained in another country where she was not domiciled and that divorce was one not recognised as valid by the law of her country of domicile at the time it was obtained, should we say: 'The status you claim of being a single person is valid only in Israel and cannot be recognised in Ontario.' In other words, should our enquiry as to personal status extend beyond the simple enquiry as to what was her status under the law of her country of domicile at the date of her marriage in 1957 in Ontario? Do we accept that law as establishing her status in Ontario?

(After quoting from *Le Mesurier v Le Mesurier*,[1] *Armitage v A-G*,[2] *Mountbatten v Mountbatten*,[3] *Har-Shefi v Har-Shefi (No 2)*,[4] and Dicey's *Conflict of Laws*,[5] the learned judge continued): The decision in the present case turns on the marital status of the defendant at the time of her marriage to the plaintiff. To determine that status, I think our enquiry must be directed not to the effect to be given under Ontario law to the divorce proceedings in Italy as at the time of the divorce, but to the effect to be given to those proceedings by the law of the country in which she was domiciled at the time of her marriage to the plaintiff in 1957, namely, Israel, a domicile that she retained until her marriage to the plaintiff was actually performed, or, to put it another way, the enquiry is as to her status under the law of her domicile and not to the means by which she acquired that status. To hold otherwise would be to determine the personal status of a person not domiciled in Ontario by the law of Ontario instead of by the law of that person's country of domicile. This would be contrary to a basic principle of private international law and would result in the social evil referred to by Lord Watson in the *Le Mesurier* case of a person being regarded as married in one jurisdiction and unmarried in another. If Waktor or the defendant, after arriving in Israel, had attempted to obtain a divorce, any such application would have been rejected on the ground that the marriage had already been dissolved. If in any proceedings in the courts of Israel the defendant's status had been called in question, it would undoubtedly have been held that her status was that of a single person; if the defendant had married while in Israel, the marriage being valid according to the law of Israel should be recognised as valid in Ontario. It seems to me that the legal result should not be different because the marriage took place in Ontario. . . .

In the present case the Waktors were divorced in a country in which they were temporarily resident but not domiciled and by whose laws the divorce was not recognised as a valid divorce, nor was it recognised as such in the country of their domicile of origin. In this respect this case differs from any reported case I have found. It was, however, recognised as valid by the laws of the country in which they later became domiciled and I think must be regarded as an exception to the general rule that a divorce is not valid under the law of Ontario when it is not recognised as valid by the laws of the country of the domicile of the parties at the time it was obtained. This is so because the defendant subsequently, before coming to Ontario, and before she acquired a domicile in Ontario by her marriage to the plaintiff, acquired

1 [1895] AC 517, 64 LJPC 97.
2 [1906] P 135, 75 LJP 42.
3 [1959] P 43, [1959] 1 All ER 99.
4 [1953] P 220, [1953] 2 All ER 373.
5 7th edn (1958) pp 223–225, 249, 256, 307.

a domicile in a country by whose laws the divorce was recognised as a valid divorce. . . .[6]

Appeal allowed.

R v Brentwood Superintendent Marriage Registrar (p 251 above)

Recognition of Divorces and Legal Separations Act 1971

7. Where the validity of a divorce obtained in any country is entitled to recognition by virtue of sections 1 to 5 or section 6 (2) of this Act or by virtue of any rule or enactment preserved by section 6 (5) of this Act, neither spouse shall be precluded from remarrying in the United Kingdom on the ground that the validity of the divorce would not be recognised in any other country.

QUESTION

H, domiciled in England, obtains a divorce from his wife W1 in the English court. This divorce is not recognised in Spain. After the divorce H, still domiciled in England, marries W2. He dies intestate domiciled in Spain leaving movables in England. Will W1 or W2 or both or neither succeed to these movables?

---

6 This judgment was upheld on appeal to the Supreme Court of Canada [1965] SCR 148, 48 DLR (2d) 644.

CHAPTER 28

The Time Factor

English courts sometimes refuse to give effect to retrospective changes in foreign law made after the relevant date.

Lynch v Provisional Government of Paraguay (1871) LR 2 P & D 268, 40 LJP & M 81 (Court of Probate)

Francisco Solano Lopez died on 1 March 1870, domiciled in Paraguay. He left a will appointing the plaintiff his executrix and making her his universal legatee. He left movable property in England. By a decree of the government of Paraguay dated 4 May 1870, all the property of the deceased, wherever situated, was declared to be the property of the state; and the decree declared that no will of his was entitled to probate in England or elsewhere.

The plaintiff claimed probate of the will. The government of Paraguay entered a caveat. The plaintiff demurred.

Lord Penzance: The general proposition that the succession to personal property in England of a person dying domiciled abroad is governed exclusively by the law of the actual domicile of the deceased was not denied; but it was affirmed by the plaintiff that this proposition had relation only to the law of the domicile as it existed at the time of the death of the individual in question, and that no changes made in that law after the date of the death can by the law of this country be recognised as affecting the distribution of personal property in England. This contention appears to me well founded. A general statement of the rule of law on this head is to be found in s 481 of Story's *Conflict of Laws*. He says: 'The universal doctrine now recognised by the common law, although formerly much contested, is, that the succession to personal property is governed exclusively by the law of the actual domicile of the intestate at the time of his death.' The words 'at the time of his death' are here carefully inserted as part of the principal proposition, and a long list of authorities is cited in support of that proposition, in none of which is any passage to be found indicating that those words are not a necessary part of it. But it was ingeniously argued that the decree in question has by the law of Paraguay a retrospective operation, and that, though the decree was, in fact, made since the death, it has by the law of Paraguay become part of that law at the time of the death. In illustration of this view it was suggested, that if the question were to arise in a court of Paraguay such court would be bound by the decree, and therefore bound to declare the provisions of the decree to be effective at and from the time of the death. This may be so; but the question is, whether the English courts are bound in like manner; or, more properly speaking, the question is, in what sense does the English law adopt the law of the domicile? Does it adopt the law of the domicile as it stands at the time of the death, or does it undertake to adopt and give effect to all retrospective changes that the legislative authority of the foreign country may make in that law? No authority has been cited for this latter proposition, and in principle it appears both inconvenient and unjust. Inconvenient, for letters of administration or probate might be granted in this country which this court might afterwards be called upon, in conformity with the change of law in the foreign country, to revoke. Unjust, for those entitled to the succession might, before any change, have acted directly or indirectly upon the existing state of things, and find their interests seriously compromised by the altered law. As, therefore, I can find no warrant in authority or principle for a more extended proposition, I must hold myself limited to the adoption and application of this proposition, that the law of the place of domicile as it existed at the time of the death ought to regulate the succession to the deceased in this case. Under that law the present defendants have no locus standi to oppose any will the testator may have made, and no concern with his estate. The demurrer must therefore prevail.

But usually they will give effect to such changes.

Phillips v Eyre (p 467 above)

Starkowski v A-G (p 221 above)

R v International Trustee (p 506 above)

Re Helbert Wagg & Co Ltd's Claim (p 559 above)

Wills Act 1963, s 6 (3) (p 580 above)

CHAPTER 29

Statutes and the Conflict of Laws

Section A. Types of Statutes

NOTE

It has been suggested[1] that from the point of view of the conflict of laws, statutory provisions may conveniently be divided into six classes: (1) those which lay down a rule of domestic law without any indication of its application in space; (2) those which lay down a particular or unilateral rule of the conflict of laws indicating when a rule of domestic law is applicable; (3) those which lay down a general or multilateral rule of the conflict of laws indicating what law governs a given question; (4) those containing a limitation in space or otherwise which restricts the scope of a rule of domestic law (self-limiting statutes); (5) those which apply in the circumstances mentioned in the statute, even though they would not be applicable under the normal rules of the conflict of laws (overriding statutes); and (6) those which do not apply in the circumstances mentioned in the statute, even though they would be applicable under the normal rules of the conflict of laws (self-denying statutes).

Not unnaturally, courts sometimes differ as to the category into which a particular statute should fall. Thus in *Sayers v International Drilling Co*[2] the majority of the Court of Appeal treated section 1(3) of the Law Reform (Personal Injuries) Act 1948 (below) as inapplicable unless English law was the proper law of the contract. In other words they treated it as belonging to class (1). But in *Brodin v A/R Seljan* (below) the Court of Session treated the same statute as applicable irrespective of the proper law of the contract or, it would seem, of the place where the tort was committed. In other words, the court treated it as belonging to class (5).

(1) *Statutes with no choice of law clause.* Statutes of this kind are of course by far the most common. A typical example is section 2 of the Marriage Act 1949 (below). Obviously, this enactment cannot be read literally so as to apply to all marriages in the world. Obviously, it must be limited in some way, either personally, or territorially, or both. Does it apply to all marriages celebrated in England, or to all marriages between parties domiciled in England, or only to marriages celebrated in England between parties domiciled in England?

A court, when confronted by a statute expressed in general terms like this, could use one of two methods to determine its scope. The first is to interpret the statute in the light of its background and purpose so as to read into it the limitations which the legislature would have expressed if it had given thought to the matter. The second is to apply general principles derived from the conflict of laws, eg first characterise the question as relating to capacity to marry, and then apply the relevant conflict rule to the question so characterised. In *Pugh v Pugh,*[3] the court adopted both of these methods, and reached the surprising conclusion that the section applies to all

---

1 Dicey and Morris *Conflict of Laws* (10th edn, 1980) pp 14–23.
2 [1971] 3 All ER 163, [1971] 1 WLR 1176; p 497 above.
3 [1951] P 482, [1951] 2 All ER 680; p 246 above.

marriages between parties one at least of whom is domiciled in England, even if the party domiciled in England was over 16 and the party under 16 had capacity to marry under the law of her domicile.

2) *Statutes with a particular choice of law clause.* A statute of this type answers the question, When does the system of law of which the statute forms part apply? A good example is section 1 of the Marriage (Scotland) Act 1977 (below), which neatly avoids the strange result which the English court reached in *Pugh v Pugh*. Further examples are provided by section 1 (3) of the Marriage (Enabling) Act 1960[4] and by section 1(2) of the Legitimacy Act 1976.[5]

(3) *Statutes with a general choice of law clause.* A statute of this type answers the question, What law applies? Examples are rare in English law, but they can be found in section 72 of the Bills of Exchange Act 1882 (formal and essential validity of bills of exchange) and the Wills Act 1963 (above). Another example can be constructed from sections 2 and 3 of the Legitimacy Act 1976.[6] Section 2 provides that where the parents of an illegitimate person marry one another, the marriage shall, if the father is at the date of the marriage domiciled in England, render that person, if living, legitimate from the date of the marriage. Taken by itself, this would be a rule of English domestic law coupled with a particular or unilateral conflict rule answering the question, When does English law apply? But section 3 provides that where the parents of an illegitimate person marry one another, and the father is not at the time of the marriage domiciled in England but is domiciled in a country by the law of which the illegitimate person became legitimated by virtue of such subsequent marriage, that person, if living, shall in England be recognised as having been so legitimated from the date of the marriage. These two sections, added together, yield a general or multilateral conflict rule to the effect that the law of the father's domicile at the date of the marriage determines whether an illegitimate person is legitimated by the subsequent marriage of his parents.

(4) *Self-limiting statutes.* A statute may provide that some of its provisions apply only to British subjects, or to British ships, or to the capital city, or on Sundays, or during the close season for various classes of game birds, or to certain kinds of employees. Such 'self-limiting provisions' are clearly not rules of the conflict of laws, whether multilateral or unilateral. They limit the application of the statute to certain persons, things, events, times or places connected in a specified way with the country whose legislature enacted the statute. A good example for our purposes is section 141 of the Employment Protection (Consolidation) Act 1978 (below).

(5) *Overriding statutes.* These must be applied regardless of the normal rules of the conflict of laws, because the statute says so. A statute does not normally apply to a contract unless it forms part of the proper law of the contract or unless (being a statute of the forum) it is procedural. To this general proposition, overriding statutes are an exception. An example is furnished by section 153 (5) of the Employment Protection (Consolidation) Act 1978 (below). The subsection makes the proper law of the contract of employment irrelevant to the application of the Act. Other examples are furnished by section 1 (3) of the Law Reform (Personal Injuries) Act 1948, as interpreted by the Court of Session in *Brodin v A/R Seljan* (below), by section 1 of the Carriage of Goods by Sea Act 1971 (and the Hague-Visby Rules incorporated thereunder) as interpreted by *The Hollandia*, (below) and by section 27 (2) of the Unfair Contract Terms Act 1977 (below). That Act lays down certain mandatory rules in the interests of consumers. The parties to certain contracts cannot contract out of these rules;[7] and to prevent them from doing so indirectly by choosing some

---

4 Above, p 240.
5 Above, p 410.
6 Above, p 420.
7 Unless the contract is an 'international supply contract' as defined in s 26.

foreign law as the proper law of the contract, section 27 (2) provides that the Act has effect notwithstanding any such choice, if either of two conditions is satisfied.

(6) *Self-denying statutes*. These are the opposite of overriding statutes: they do not apply in the circumstances where the statute says they shall not apply, even though they would apply under the normal rules of the conflict of laws. The only example of such a statute in English law which we have been able to find is section 27 (1) of the Unfair Contract Terms Act 1977 (below), which is the converse of section 27 (2).

The two Law Commissions have explained why it was necessary to include section 27 (1) in the Act.[8] They point out that the parties to contracts of which the proper law would otherwise be the law of some country other than England or Scotland often choose English law or Scots law as the proper law of their contracts, sometimes by an express term to that effect, more often through the medium of an arbitration clause. The Commissions then point out that the effect of imposing the controls contained in the Act in relation to these contracts might well be to discourage foreign business men from agreeing to arbitrate their disputes in England or Scotland. The suggestion is that this would strike a heavy blow at the City of London as a centre for international arbitration.

The truth is that English law is now having to pay the price for its decision[9] to allow contracting parties almost unlimited freedom to choose the proper law. Section 27 (1) and (2) of the Unfair Contract Terms Act 1977 are part of that price.

(1) *Statutes without a choice of law clause.*

Marriage Act 1949

2. A marriage solemnized between persons either of whom is under the age of sixteen shall be void.

Pugh v Pugh (p 246 above)

(2) *Statutes with a particular choice of law clause.*

Marriage (Scotland) Act 1977

1.—(1) No person domiciled in Scotland may marry before he attains the age of 16.

(2) A marriage solemnised in Scotland between persons either of whom is under the age of 16 shall be void.

(3) *Statutes with a general choice of law clause.*

Wills Act 1963 (p 579 above)

---

8 Second Report on Exemption Clauses, Law Com No 69, Scots Law Com No 39 (1975) para 232.
9 *Vita Food Products Inc v Unus Shipping Co Ltd* [1939] Ac 277, [1939] 1 All ER 513; p 443 above.

(4) *Self-limiting statutes.*

Employment Protection (Consolidation) Act 1978

141.—(1) Sections 1 to 4 and 49 to 51 do not apply in relation to employment during any period when the employee is engaged in work wholly or mainly outside Great Britain unless the employee ordinarily works in Great Britain and the work outside Great Britain is for the same employer.

(2) Sections 8 and 53 and Parts II, III, V and VII do not apply to employment where under his contract of employment the employee ordinarily works outside Great Britain.

(5) *Overriding statutes.*

Employment Protection (Consolidation) Act 1978

153.—(5) For the purposes of this Act it is immaterial whether the law which (apart from this Act) governs any person's employment is the law of the United Kingdom, or of a part of the United Kingdom, or not.

Law Reform (Personal Injuries) Act 1948

1.—(3) Any provision contained in a contract of service or apprenticeship, or in an agreement collateral thereto, (including a contract or agreement entered into before the commencement of this Act) shall be void in so far as it would have the effect of excluding or limiting any liability of the employer in respect of personal injuries caused to the person employed or apprenticed by the negligence of persons in common employment with him.

Brodin v A/R Seljan 1973 SC 213, 1973 SLT 198 (Court of Session)

The pursuer was a Norwegian national who had lived in the United Kingdom since the age of four and could neither speak nor read Norwegian. He was employed as an able seaman on board a Norwegian oil tanker owned by the defenders, whose registered office was in Norway. He was injured in an accident at Bowling in Dunbartonshire owing, as he alleged, to the fault of certain officers employed by the defenders who were on the bridge of the vessel at the time. His contract of employment was written in Norwegian and signed by him and by the master of the ship on behalf of the owners. It was governed by Norwegian law. It provided that service on board the ship should be governed by Norwegian legislation, under which he was entitled to payment of wages for 12 weeks after the accident and of medical expenses, but nothing more.

The pursuer brought an action in Scotland to recover reparation. The defenders submitted to the jurisdiction of the court.

Lord Kissen: The essence of the argument for the pursuer was that the delict, which is the basis of the pursuer's action, occurred in Scotland, that

therefore the law which governs the rights of the parties in this action is Scots
law, that said section 1 (3) of the said Act of 1948 accordingly applies and
that the defence, based on Norwegian law, is irrelevant. The submission was,
in other words, that the lex loci delicti, which in this case is also the lex fori,
was paramount. The essence of the argument for the defenders was that the
law which governed the rights of the parties in this reparation action was the
proper law of the said contract of service, under which the pursuer was
employed at the material time, that this was Norwegian law, and that said
section 1 (3) could not apply in these circumstances. The fact that the said
accident occurred in Scotland had, it was said, no bearing on the rights of
the parties.

There was no reported case in which the legal question which I have to
decide in this case was considered. There was, however, a recent decision by
the Court of Appeal in England in which said section 1 (3) of the said Act of
1948 was considered and on which defenders' counsel strongly relied. I
commence by a consideration of that case.

That case is Sayers v International Drilling Co.[10] The facts of that case have
some resemblance to the facts of this case but there is at least one vital
difference. (His Lordship stated the facts in that case and continued): The
vital difference from the present case is that the accident occurred when the
plaintiff was employed on the defendants' oil rig off the Nigerian coast and
in the territorial waters of Nigeria. The Court of Appeal decided that said
section 1 (3) did not apply and could not be invoked by the plaintiff. The
ground of the decision by Lord Denning MR was that the proper law of the
tort was Dutch, and that, as the claim was founded on tort, the issue of
liability should be decided by Dutch law, despite the fact that, according to
him, the proper law of the contract of employment was English.[11] On the
other hand, the ground of the decision by both Salmon LJ and Stamp LJ
was that the proper law of the contract of employment was Dutch and that
accordingly the rights of the plaintiff were governed by Dutch law.

I do not think that this case can assist the defenders. The facts were
different in that, in the present case, the accident occurred in Scotland where
section 1 (3) of the said Act of 1948 is part of the law relating to delicts.
Another difference is that the terms of employment were such that the
pursuer in the present case would be employed, at times, in ports in England
where said section 1 (3) is also part of the law relating to torts. Apart
altogether from this, I have some difficulty in finding any consistent principle
from the differing grounds for that decision. The defenders' counsel founded
strongly on the majority grounds but they cannot, in my opinion, apply to
the completely different circumstances here. It might be possible to argue,
from Lord Denning's opinion, that the 'law of the tort' in this case was Scots
law in that the acts done have most connection with Scotland where the
accident occurred and where the deceased was domiciled. I think, however,
as I have said, that this case is of no assistance. I add that I was referred by
pursuer's counsel to strong criticisms of this decision in two articles in
Volume 21 of the International and Comparative Law Quarterly at pp 164 and
335.

The principle governing the decision in Sayers was, it was maintained by

10 [1971] 3 All ER 163, [1971] 1 WLR 1176; p 497 above.
11 Sed quaere: is this an accurate summary of Lord Denning's ratio decidendi? (Ed).

the defenders' counsel, in line with a general principle which supported their argument. This general principle of statutory construction was that there was a presumption against the application of a statute 'extra-territorially', that 'extra-territorially' included the operation of a contract which was governed by foreign law and that said section 1 (3) could not therefore apply to the contract of employment which was governed by Norwegian law. They referred to *Dicey and Morris*,[12] and to some reported cases as authority for this general principle. The exact words used in *Dicey and Morris* are:— 'If the statute is silent, the general rule of interpretation comes into play, according to which an English statute is not to be deemed to have any extra-territorial operation unless such operation is required by the terms of the Act or by its "object, subject-matter or history".' They add that:— ' "Extra-territorial" operation in connection with the law of contract will sometimes mean operation with regard to a contract governed by foreign law.' The passage which I have quoted from *Dicey and Morris* occurs in the discussion on Rule 128 which is thus stated: 'The validity or invalidity of a contract must be determined in accordance with English law, independently of the law of any foreign country whatever, if and in so far as the application of foreign law would be opposed to the public policy of English law, or to the provisions of an Act of Parliament which, by the terms of the Act or by virtue of established principles of statutory interpretation, applies to the contract.' It will be observed that there is a difference between the general principle as stated by the defenders' counsel and the passages quoted from *Dicey and Morris*. I stress the use of the word 'sometimes' in the second passage quoted. I refer also to Cheshire's *Private International Law*.[13]

Applying this general principle of construction which I have mentioned, it was then maintained for the defenders that it was plain from the terms of said section 1 of the said Act of 1948 that it was not intended to apply to foreign contracts of employment. The terms of subsection (1) were particularly founded upon as was the legal basis for the pre-1948 law relating to common employment as explained by Lord Watson in *Johnson v Lindsay*.[14] It was said that subsection (1) could only affect contracts of employment which were governed by Scots and English law, that they could not affect contracts governed by a foreign system of law and that, therefore, section 1 (3) must be similarly restricted. This line of argument seems to me to beg the question. Said subsection (1) altered the law of Scotland relating to liability of employers for accidents occurring in Scotland. A foreigner who meets with an accident in the course of his employment in Scotland can found on the law of Scotland to make a claim in the courts of Scotland against his foreign employer for negligence, if he can establish jurisdiction. See Anton, *Private International Law* at p 238. That employer would be liable, if negligence was established, unless he could show that his liability was excluded. Prior to 1948, that employer could, inter alia, have founded on common employment. I cannot see why subsection (1) should or could have the limited effect suggested. It seems to me that the locus delicti is of importance and there is nothing to suggest, in my opinion, that subsection (1) was only intended to apply to delicts in Scotland which were based on

12 *Conflict of Laws* (8th edn, 1967) p 732.
13 8th edn, pp 209, 212, 223 et seq.
14 [1891] AC 371 at 382.

contracts whose proper law was Scots or English. The intention was simply to alter the law of Scotland to rid it of a rule which had been much criticised. These observations also apply to said subsection (3). The suggestion that said section 1 (3), if applicable, would mean an application 'extraterritorially' of an Act of Parliament is, in my view, incorrect. The validity of the contract or of the provision to which said section 1 (3) is applied is not affected generally. The court, in applying it, is simply saying that for the purpose of Scots law, applied by a court in Scotland, that provision is unenforceable. I prefer the use of the word 'unenforceable' to 'void', as used in the pursuer's averments. It follows that I cannot accept the submissions made for the defenders.

The opinion which I have reached, that the defenders' contention is incorrect, is reinforced by the case of *English v Donnelly*[15] to which I was referred by pursuer's counsel. As is pointed out in *Anton*, above at p 209 that case illustrates the general principle that 'a contract is unenforceable in Scotland, whatever may be the proper law, if it requires doing what is expressly forbidden by a statute which is binding on the Scottish courts'. It is also referred to in *Dicey and Morris* above as an illustration of Rule 128. That case related to hire purchase legislation but, in my opinion, the principle does not depend on that. The relevant contract had a provision that the law of England was to apply. The Inner House held that, despite this provision, section 2 of the Hire Purchase and Small Debt (Scotland) Act 1932, which applied only to Scotland, applied to the transaction, and that the contract was void and could not be enforced because of non-compliance with the said section 2. The terms of said section 1 (3) of the said Act of 1948 are as mandatory and as peremptory as said section 2 of the said Act of 1932. An object of the contract on which the first defenders found in this case is the 'contracting out' of a peremptory statutory provison of the lex fori and the lex loci delicti. There is, furthermore, no limitation stated and the application must be to persons and conduct in, among other places, Scotland. Whatever the law chosen by the parties to govern a contract or whatever the law of a contract may be, that law must, I think, yield to an Act of Parliament which has provided otherwise. The provision is, in other words, unenforceable in Scotland, whatever its effect elsewhere.

Carriage of Goods by Sea Act 1971

1.—(1) In this Act, 'the Rules' means the International Convention for the unification of certain rules of law relating to bills of lading signed at Brussels on 25 August 1924, as amended by the Protocol signed at Brussels on 23 February 1968.

(2) The provisions of the Rules, as set out in the Schedule to this Act, shall have the force of law.

The Hollandia [1983] 1 AC 565, [1982] 3 All ER 1141 (House of Lords)

The plaintiffs shipped a large machine on board the Dutch vessel, *The Haico Holwerda*, at Leith in Scotland for carriage to Bunaire in the Dutch West

15 1958 SC 494.

Indies. Condition 2 of the bill of lading issued by the carriers, the Royal Netherlands Steamship Co, provided in paragraph 1 that the law of the Netherlands should apply and that the maximum liability per package was D fl 1250; and in paragraph 3 that the court of Amsterdam should have exclusive jurisdiction. While the machine was being unloaded at Bunaire it was dropped and severely damaged. The plaintiffs estimated the damage at about £22,000 and brought an action in rem against *The Hollandia*, a sister ship in the same ownership as *The Haico Holwerda*, claiming damages for breach of contract and negligence.

Dutch law at the date of issue of the bill of lading still applied the unamended Hague Rules under which the limit of the carrier's liability was about £250. Under the amended Hague/Visby Rules scheduled to the United Kingdom Carriage of Goods by Sea Act 1971, the limit of liability was about £11,000.

Article X of the Hague/Visby Rules provides that the Rules shall apply to every bill of lading relating to the carriage of goods between ports in different states if (a) the bill of lading is issued in a contracting state, or (b) the carriage is from a port in a contracting state, or (c) the contract provides that the Rules or legislation of any state giving effect to them are to govern the contract. Article III, paragraph 8, provides that any agreement in a contract of carriage relieving the carrier or the ship from liability for loss or damage to goods arising from negligence, fault or failure in the duties and obligations provided in that article or lessening such liability otherwise than as provided in the Rules shall be null and void and of no effect.

The carrier applied for a stay of the action on the ground that it could only be brought in Amsterdam. Sheen J granted a stay because he regarded the third paragraph of condition 2 as severable from the first. The Court of Appeal (Lord Denning MR, Ackner LJ and Sir Sebag Shaw) reversed his decision. The carrier appealed.

Lord Diplock (after stating the facts, and reading section 1 of the 1971 Act and articles III paragraph 8 and X of the Rules, continued):

My Lords, the provisions in section 1 of the Act that I have quoted appear to me to be free from any ambiguity perceptible to even the most ingenious of legal minds. The Hague/Visby Rules, or rather all those of them that are included in the Schedule, are to have the force of law in the United Kingdom: they are to be treated as if they were part of directly enacted statute law. But since they form part of an international convention which must come under the consideration of foreign as well as English courts, it is, as Lord Macmillan said of the Hague Rules themselves in *Stag Line Ltd v Foscolo, Mango & Co Ltd*.[16]

> 'desirable in the interests of uniformity that their interpretation should not be rigidly controlled by domestic precedents of antecedent date, but rather that the language of the rules should be construed on broad principles of general acceptance.'

They should be given a purposive rather than a narrow literalistic construction, particularly wherever the adoption of a literalistic construction would enable the stated purpose of the international convention, viz, the

16 [1932] AC 328 at 350.

unification of domestic laws of the contracting states relating to bills of lading, to be evaded by the use of colourable devices that, not being expressly referred to in the Rules, are not specifically prohibited.

The bill of lading issued to the shippers by the carriers upon the shipment of the goods at the Scottish port of Leith was one to which the Hague-Visby Rules were expressly made applicable by article X; it fell within both paragraph (a) and paragraph (b); it was issued in a contracting state, the United Kingdom, and it covered a contract for carriage from a port in a contracting state. (His Lordship held that the first paragraph of condition 2 was rendered null and void by article III, paragraph 8. He referred to the decision of Sheen J and continued):

Counsel for the carriers sought to justify the judge's decision on this point by putting a narrow literalistic interpretation on article III, paragraph 8 of the Hague-Visby Rules. A choice of forum clause, he contended, is to be classified as a clause which only prescribes the procedure by which disputes arising under the contract of carriage are to be resolved. It does not ex facie deal with liability at all and so does not fall within the description 'Any clause, covenant, or agreement in a contract of carriage . . . lessening . . . liability', so as to bring it within article III, paragraph 8; even though the consequence of giving effect to the clause will be to lessen, otherwise than is provided in the Hague-Visby Rules, the liability of the carrier for loss or damage to or in connection with the goods arising from negligence, fault or failure in the duties and obligations provided in the Rules.

My Lords, like all three members of the Court of Appeal, I have no hesitation in rejecting this narrow construction of article III, paragraph 8, which looks solely to the form of the clause in the contract of carriage and wholly ignores its substance. The only sensible meaning to be given to the description of provisions in contracts of carriage which are rendered 'null and void and of no effect' by this rule is one which would embrace every provision in a contract of carriage which, if it were applied, would have the effect of lessening the carrier's liability otherwise than as provided in the Rules. To ascribe to it the narrow meaning for which counsel contended would leave it open to any shipowner to evade the provisions of article III, paragraph 8 by the simple device of inserting in his bills of lading issued in, or for carriage from a port in, any contracting state a clause in standard form providing as the exclusive forum for resolution of disputes what might aptly be described as a court of convenience, viz, one situated in a country which did not apply the Hague-Visby Rules or, for that matter, a country whose law recognised an unfettered right in a shipowner by the terms of the bill of lading to relieve himself from all liability for loss or damage to the goods caused by his own negligence, fault or breach of contract.

My Lords, unlike the first paragraph of condition 2 a choice of forum clause, such as that appearing in the third paragraph, does not ex facie offend against article III, paragraph 8. It is a provision of the contract of carriage that is subject to a condition subsequent; it comes into operation only upon the occurrence of a future event that may or may not occur, viz: the coming into existence of a dispute between the parties as to their respective legal rights and duties under the contract which they are unable to settle by agreement. There may be some disputes that would bring the choice of forum clause into operation but which would not be concerned at all with negligence fault or failure by the carrier or the ship in the duties and obligations provided by article III; a claim for unpaid freight is an obvious example. So a choice of forum clause which selects as the exclusive forum for the resolution of disputes a court which will not apply the Hague-Visby Rules, even after such clause has come into operation, does not necessarily always have the effect of lessening the liability of the carrier in a way that attracts the application of article III, paragraph 8.

My Lords, it is, in my view, most consistent with the achievement of the purpose of the Act of 1971 that the time at which to ascertain whether a choice of forum clause will have an effect that is proscribed by article III, paragraph 8 should be when the condition subsequent is fulfilled and the carrier seeks to bring the clause into operation and to rely upon it. If the dispute is about duties and obligations of the carrier or ship that are referred to in that rule and it is established as a fact (either by evidence or as in the instant case by the common agreement of the parties) that the foreign court chosen as the exclusive forum would apply a domestic substantive law which would result in limiting the carrier's liability to a sum lower than that to which he would be entitled if article IV, paragraph 5 of the Hague-Visby Rules applied, then an English court is in my view commanded by the Act of 1971 to treat the choice of forum clause as of no effect. . . .

Having regard to the nature of the dispute which the carriers asserted brought into operation the choice of forum clause that forms the third paragraph of condition 2 of the bill of lading, Sheen J was, for the reasons that I have given, bound to treat the bill of lading as if it contained neither the first nor the third paragraph of condition 2 and consequently was without any choice of forum clause. That did not deprive the learned judge of all discretion to grant a stay if the carriers were able to satisfy him that, independently of condition 2, the Court of Amsterdam was a forum conveniens and the Admiralty Court in London was not. But in exercising his discretion to grant the stay the learned judge gave decisive weight to the fact that by accepting the bill of lading, even though it was a contract of adhesion so far as the 'Company's Standard Conditions' were concerned, the shippers had agreed not to bring any action under the contract against the carriers in any court other than the Court of Amsterdam. Since by English law he was required to treat the choice of forum clause as null and void and of no effect, it follows that by giving any weight to it in deciding how to exercise his discretion he was taking into consideration a matter which he was not entitled to take into consideration.

The choice of forum clause being eliminated from the contract of carriage, the shippers as plaintiffs, were prima facie at liberty to avail themselves of the right of access to the Admiralty Court. In determining whether to grant a stay that would deny them that prima facie right the principle to be followed became that which I stated in *MacShannon v Rockware Glass Ltd*[17]—a formulation that was subsequently accepted by this House in *Castanho v Brown & Root (UK) Ltd*:[18]

> 'In order to justify a stay two conditions must be satisfied, one positive and the other negative: (a) the defendant must satisfy the court that there is another forum to whose jurisdiction he is amenable in which

17 [1978] AC 795 at 812, [1978] 1 All ER 625 at 630; pp 130–131 above.
18 [1981] AC 557, [1981] 1 All ER 143; p 138 above.

justice can be done between the parties at substantially less inconvenience or expense, and (b) the stay must not deprive the plaintiff of a legitimate personal or juridical advantage which would be available to him if he invoked the jurisdiction of the English court.'

It has not been seriously contended that either of these conditions are fulfilled in the instant case if the third paragraph of condition 2 is, like the first paragraph, struck down by the Act of 1971.

As foreshadowed at an earlier point in this speech I must return in a brief postscript to an argument based on certain passages in an article by a distinguished commentator, Dr F. A. Mann 'Statutes and the Conflict of Laws' which appeared in (1972–73) 46 BYIL 117, and which, it is suggested, supports the view that even a choice of substantive law, which excludes the application of the Hague-Visby Rules, is not prohibited by the Act of 1971 notwithstanding that the bill of lading is issued in and is for carriage from a port in, the United Kingdom. The passages to which our attention was directed by counsel for the carriers I find myself (apparently in respectable academic company[19]) unable to accept. They draw no distinction between the Act of 1924 and the Act of 1971 despite the contrast between the legislative techniques adopted in the two Acts, and the express inclusion in the Hague-Visby Rules of article X (absent from the Hague rules), expressly applying the Hague-Visby Rules to every bill of lading falling within the description contained in the article, which article is given the force of law in the United Kingdom by section 1 (2) of the Act of 1971. The Act of 1971 deliberately abandoned what may conveniently be termed the 'clause paramount' technique employed in section 3 of the Act of 1924, the Newfoundland counterpart of which provided the occasion for wide-ranging dicta in the opinion of the Privy Council delivered by Lord Wright in *Vita Food Products Inc v Unus Shipping Co Ltd*.[20] Although the actual decision in that case would have been the same if the relevant Newfoundland statute had been in the terms of the Act of 1971, those dicta have no application to the construction of the latter Act and this has rendered it no longer necessary to embark upon what I have always found to be an unrewarding task of ascertaining precisely what those dicta meant.

I would dismiss this appeal.

Lords Keith of Kinkel, Roskill, Brandon of Oakbrook and Brightman concurred.

Appeal dismissed.

Unfair Contract Terms Act 1977

27.—(2) This Act has effect notwithstanding any contract term which applies or purports to apply the law of some country outside the United Kingdom where (either or both)

(a) the term appears to the court or arbitrator to have been imposed wholly

---

19 The reference is apparently to an article by Morris on 'The Scope of the Carriage of Goods by Sea Act 1971' (1979) 95 LQR 59, an article much relied on by Lord Denning MR in the court below. Notice that Dr Mann is 'distinguished' but Dr Morris is merely 'respectable' (*Ed*).

20 [1939] AC 277, [1939] 1 All ER 513; p 443 above.

or mainly for the purpose of enabling the party imposing it to evade the operation of this Act; or

(b) in the making of the contract one of the parties dealt as consumer,[1] and he was then habitually resident in the United Kingdom, and the essential steps necessary for the making of the contract were taken there, whether by him or by others on his behalf.

(6) *Self-denying statutes.*

Unfair Contract Terms Act 1977

27.—(1) Where the proper law of a contract is the law of any part of the United Kingdom only by choice of the parties (and apart from that choice would be the law of some country outside the United Kingdom) sections 2 to 7 and 16 to 21 of this Act do not operate as part of the proper law.

Section B. Interpretation of statutes implementing international conventions

When interpreting a statute implementing an international convention English courts are willing to relax some of their traditional rules of interpretation in order to promote uniformity between all contracting states.

James Buchanan & Co Ltd v Babco Forwarding and Shipping (UK) Ltd [1978] AC 141, [1977] 3 All ER 1048 (House of Lords)

The defendants agreed to carry a quantity of whisky from the plaintiffs' bonded warehouse in Glasgow to Teheran via Felixstowe. The contract was expressed to be subject to the Convention on the Carriage of Goods by Road scheduled to the Carriage of Goods by Road Act 1965. Owing to the negligence of the defendants' lorry driver in leaving the lorry containing the whisky unattended in a lorry park in North Woolwich for three days,[2] the whisky was stolen. The value of the whisky when it left the bonded warehouse was £7000. But the plaintiffs, being unable to prove that the whisky was exported, were obliged by law to pay and did pay £30,000 to the Customs and Excise by way of duty. They sought to recover £37,000 from the defendants, who admitted liability for £7000 but denied that they were liable to pay more. Article 23 (1) and (2) of the Convention provided that the compensation payable by the carrier should be calculated by reference to the value of the goods at the place and time at which they were accepted for carriage. Article 23 (4) provided that, in addition, the carriage charges, customs duties and other charges in respect of the carriage of the goods should be refunded.

1 'Deals as consumer' is widely defined in s 12 (*Ed*).
2 Since North Woolwich is 80 miles off the direct route from Glasgow to Felixstowe, what was the lorry driver doing spending a long week-end there? Your guess, gentle reader, is as good as ours (*Ed*).

Master Jacob held that the plaintiffs could recover £37,000. The Court of Appeal affirmed his judgment. The defendants appealed.

Lord Wilberforce (having stated the facts, and held that the value of the whisky within the meaning of article 23 (1) and (2) was £7000, continued): I therefore reject the respondent's first argument.

The second is one which I find to be of difficulty. Is the excise duty a 'charge incurred in respect of the carriage'? I can see that there are powerful arguments to the contrary. The charge upon the owners arises under section 85 of the Customs and Excise Act 1952—effectively because the owners, having held the goods in a bonded warehouse, and having removed the goods therefrom without payment of duty, are unable to produce to the customs documents of export clearance, or to avail themselves of the other escape provisions in section 85. The section is stated (subsection (3)) to apply in relation to the goods 'in the course of that removal' which I take to mean during the period of the carriage. There is, it may be said, a difference between 'during the period of the carriage' and 'in respect of the carriage': a loss may occur during the carriage but have nothing to do with the carriage itself. In the present case, the charge arises from the presumed release of the whisky on to the home market. This is a narrow distinction, but not an impossible one: I think that Lord Denning MR took this view of the meaning, at least the literal meaning, of the expression used in article 23, paragraph 4.

There are three different routes by which it has been found possible to reach the opposite conclusion, viz, that excise duties arising in the circumstances of this case come within the words 'charges incurred in respect of the carriage'. These are: 1. That there is a gap in the Convention which can be filled by judicial decision following a 'continental method' of interpretation (Lord Denning MR). 2. That the relevant words can be expanded in scope by looking at the French text of the Convention (Roskill LJ and Lawton LJ). 3. That the relevant words—in English—are, in the context of an international convention, wide enough to include the duty (Master Jacob). These arguments call for some consideration of the correct principles of interpretation.

Conventions, when made part of English law, may be expressed in language texts in various ways. There may be only an English statutory text which is based upon the convention, the convention itself not being incorporated in the statute. There may be an English convention text which is incorporated in the statute. There may be a French (or other language) convention text with an English translation adopted by the English statute; there may be convention texts in two languages with or without a provision that one shall prevail in case of doubt (contrast this case with the Hague Convention of 1961 on Wills). Different principles of interpretation may apply to each of these cases.

The Convention of 1956 is in two languages, English and French, each text being equally authentic. The English text alone appears in the Schedule to the Act of 1965 and is by that Act (section 1) given the force of law. Moreover the contract of carriage seems to have incorporated contractually this English text. It might therefore be arguable (though this was not in fact argued)—by distinction from a case where the authentic text is (for example) French and the enacted text an English translation—that only the English text ought to be looked at. In my opinion this would be too narrow a view to take, given the expressed objective of the Convention to produce uniformity in all contracting states. I think that the correct approach is to interpret the English text, which after all is likely to be used by many others than British businessmen, in a normal manner, appropriate for the interpretation of an international convention, unconstrained by technical rules of English law, or by English legal precedent, but on broad principles of general acceptation: *Stag Line Ltd v Foscolo, Mango & Co Ltd,*[3] per Lord Macmillan. Moreover, it is perfectly legitimate in my opinion to look for assistance, if assistance is needed, to the French text. This is often put in the form that resort may be had to the foreign text if (and only if) the English text is ambiguous, but I think this states the rule too technically. As Lord Diplock recently said in this House the inherent flexibility of the English (and, one may add, any) language may make it necessary for the interpreter to have recourse to a variety of aids: *Carter v Bradbeer.*[4] There is no need to impose a preliminary test of ambiguity.

My Lords, I would not lay down rules as to the manner in which reference to the French text is to be made. It was complained—by reference to the use of the French text made by Roskill LJ and Lawton LJ—that there was no evidence as to the meaning of the French text and that the Lords Justices were not entitled to use their own knowledge of the language. There may certainly be cases when evidence is required to find the exact meaning of a word or a phrase; there may be other cases when even an untutored eye can see the crucial point (cf *Corocraft Ltd v Pan American Airways Inc*[5] (insertion of 'and' in the English text)). There may be cases again where a simple reference to a good dictionary will supply the key (see per Kerr J in *Fothergill v Monarch Airlines Ltd,*[6] on 'avarie'). In a case such as I think the present is, when one is dealing with a nuanced expression, a dictionary will not assist and reference to an expert might also be unhelpful, for the expert would have to direct his evidence to a two-text situation rather than simply to the meaning of words in his own language, so that he would be in the same difficulty as the court. But I can see nothing illegitimate in the court looking at the two texts and reaching the conclusion that both are expressed in general or perhaps imprecise terms, so as to justify rejection of a narrow meaning.

I find myself unable to follow the first of the above-mentioned routes— that which attracted Lord Denning MR. I cannot detect that this is a case of a gap in the legislation. The question simply is whether this loss is to fall on the owner or on the carrier. The words used must cover the case in one way or the other—we have to decide which: if they are not such as to impose liability on the carrier, the owner is left to bear his loss. Furthermore, the assumed and often repeated generalisation that English methods are narrow, technical and literal, whereas continental methods are broad, generous and sensible, seems to me insecure at least as regards interpretation of international conventions. (In the present context I do not get assistance from methods said to be used in interpreting the Treaty of Rome by the

3 [1932] AC 328 at 350.
4 [1975] 3 All ER 158 at 161, [1975] 1 WLR 1204 at 1206.
5 [1969] 1 QB 616, [1969] 1 All ER 82.
6 [1978] QB 108, [1977] 3 All ER 616; p 691 below.

Court of Justice of the European Communities.) We have our share of technical decisions but I do not know that this is greater than other jurisdictions can claim: the often quoted case of *Ellerman Lines Ltd v Murray*[7] is untypical and in my opinion should no longer be followed. English judges have been interpreting such international instruments as the Hague Rules and commercial documents for many years with some success and international approbation. This (CMR) Convention has been accepted by more than 20 states some of them close to English ways of thought. I cannot credit them all, or some average of them, with recognisably superior, or even different, methods of interpretation. We should of course try to harmonise interpretation but, as Megaw LJ pungently shows (*Ulster-Swift Ltd v Taunton Meat Haulage Ltd*[8]) on this very Convention, courts in 6 member countries have produced 12 different interpretations of particular provisions—so uniformity is not to be reached by that road. To base our interpretation of this Convention on some assumed, and unproved, interpretation which other courts are to be supposed likely to adopt is speculative as well as masochistic.

My Lords, some further material, available in this House and not before the Court of Appeal, illustrates the danger of this speculative method. A decision of the Court of Appeal of Paris (5th Chamber) of 30 March 1973,[9] appears to have adopted in relation to a charge of VAT (TVA) the interpretation contended for by the respondents (see the 'Observations' appended which relate the decision to article 23 of the CMR). But a decision of the Amsterdam Arrondissementsrechtbank (3rd Chamber) of 30 March 1977,[10] in a matter concerning excise duty, on facts very similar to the present, decided against the carriers' liability, holding that, to come within article 23, paragraph 4, the charges must have been incurred in direct connection with the carriage such as it should have been performed. The levy in question (of excise duty) was held to be more of a 'subsequent levy or administrative fine than an item of charges in respect of carriage' ('dan van vervoerskosten', an expression which seems to overlook the distinction between 'carriage charges' and 'other charges' in article 23, paragraph 4). The court took the French text 'encourus à l'occasion du transport' into consideration but thought that the case was basically different from one where customs duties—on passing a frontier—were concerned, which case could be covered by the phrase. These cases show that there is no universal wisdom available across the Channel upon which our insular minds can draw. We must use our own methods following Lord Macmillan's prescription and taking such help as existing decisions give us.

The crucial words occur in an international convention a reading of which at once shows that it is not drafted in language of precision or consistency— see, for example, the varied expressions used in article 6 paragraph 1 (i), as compared with article 23, paragraph 4. In it we have the phrase 'other charges incurred in respect of the carriage' which is on the face of it uncertain. We can see, with the minimum of linguistic skill, that the French version 'frais encourus à l'occasion du transport' is equally a phrase drawn with a broad brush. Are we to give the words a narrow meaning so that they

7 [1931] AC 126, 100 LJP 25.
8 [1977] 3 All ER 641 at 646, [1977] 1 WLR 625 at 631.
9 *Cie L'Helvetia v Cie Seine et Rhone*, Bulletin des Transports, 1973, p 195.
10 *British American Tobacco Co (Nederland) BV v van Swieten BV* (unreported).

cover and only cover such charges as arise from the carriage 'such as it should have been performed'[11] or a broad meaning so as to cover charges arising in the course of the removal from the failure to carry in accordance with the carriage. We must decide this without any presumption in favour of a 'liberal' interpretation, for, even if such a presumption exists, it cannot help us to decide, as we must, whether the carrier, or the owner, is to bear the loss. Whichever decision prevails will be claimed as liberal by one side and illiberal by the other.

My Lords, I take from the judgments of Roskill LJ and Lawton LJ the approach that these words, appearing in this international Convention, as both texts show, are loosely drafted and cannot be expected to be applied with taut logical precision. With this approach, I find that the judgment of Master Jacob carries conviction. The duty, he says, became chargeable having regard to the way in which the goods were carried by the defendants. 'In respect of' is wide enough to include the way in which the goods were carried, miscarried or lost. I think this is right—and I do not consider that it is answered by saying that the charge would not have arisen if the thieves had exported the goods or if the whisky had flowed away. No doubt this is true but the fact that an exemption might have arisen does not prevent the charge which did arise from being 'in respect of the carriage.' The carriers' duty was to carry the whisky to the port of embarkation—their failure to do so might, or might not, bring a charge into existence. But if it did, I think it right to say that the charge was in respect of the carriage.

I would dismiss the appeal.

Lords Dilhorne and Salmon delivered judgments to the same effect. Lords Edmund Davies and Fraser of Tullybelton dissented.
Appeal dismissed.

Fothergill v Monarch Airlines Ltd [1981] AC 251, [1980] 2 All ER 696 (House of Lords)

The plaintiff returned by air to Luton airport from a holiday in Italy, the carrier being the defendants. The carriage was 'international carriage' and was therefore subject to the Warsaw Convention as amended by the Hague Protocol scheduled to the Carriage by Air Act 1961. The Schedule is in two parts, containing an English and a French text. Section 1 (1) of the Act provides that the Convention as set out in the Schedule shall have the force of law in the United Kingdom, and section 1 (2) provides that if there is any inconsistency between the English and French texts, the French text shall prevail.

Some time after he got home the plaintiff noticed that some of the contents of his suitcase were missing. The defendants rejected his claim for £16.50 for compensation for the loss on the ground that he had not notified them within seven days as, they alleged, he should have done under article 26 (2) of the Convention. This provides that 'in the case of damage, the person entitled to delivery must complain to the carrier forthwith after the discovery of the damage, and at the latest within seven days of the date of receipt'.

Kerr J gave judgment for the plaintiff. His judgment was affirmed by the

11 *British-American Tobacco Co (Nederland) BV v van Swieten BV.*

Court of Appeal (Browne and Geoffrey Lane LJJ; Lord Denning MR dissenting on the main point, but agreeing in the result on a subsidiary point). The defendant appealed.

Lord Scarman: My Lords, I agree with the speech delivered by my noble and learned friend, Lord Wilberforce. If there be any difference between us, it relates only to our respective views as to the ordinary, or more common, meaning of the word 'damage' in the English usage. But for the reasons appearing in his speech, and mine, the difference, if any there be, is of no moment.

I venture, however, to add some comments of my own as to the correct approach by our courts to the interpretation of international conventions. I do so because of the growing importance of the task. I confidently expect that the municipal courts of the United Kingdom will have increasingly to tackle this job: and, if they are to do it successfully, they will have to achieve an approach which is broadly in line with the practice of public international law. Faced with an international treaty which has been incorporated into our law, British courts should now follow broadly the guidelines declared by the Vienna Convention on the Law of Treaties, to which my noble and learned friend refers. Lord Denning MR reconnoitred the ground—or, rather, the waters—of this new judicial operation in the area of the common market when he spoke of an incoming tide of law flowing into our rivers and estuaries: see his dicta in *H. P. Bulmer Ltd v J. Bollinger SA*.[12] But the waters are not confined to the legal outpourings of the Rhine and the Scheldt: they comprise the oceans of the world. The Warsaw Convention is itself world-wide.

The case concerns the Warsaw Convention for the Unification of Certain Rules relating to International Carriage by Air. Upon a literal construction of article 26 (2) of the Convention I would agree with the interpretation placed upon the word 'damage' in the article by Kerr J at first instance and by Browne and Geoffrey Lane LJJ in the Court of Appeal. I would construe it as meaning physical injury to the baggage (or cargo) and as excluding a partial loss of the contents. Linguistically I agree with the American judge (Shapiro J) in *Schwimmer v Air France*[13] that in ordinary usage 'damage is damage and loss is loss'. Moreover I am satisfied that the ordinary meaning of 'avarie', the word used in the French text, is physical harm, or injury to an object. Notwithstanding the specialist meaning of 'avarie' in French maritime law where it does also include a maritime loss (compare the use of our word 'average' in marine insurance), there would be no inconsistency between the English and French texts unless the context of article 26 (2) be such that one must give to 'avarie' this highly specialised meaning: but, in my opinion, the context does not so require.

If, therefore, the literal construction be legitimate, I would dismiss the appeal. But, in my judgment, it is not. It makes commercial sense to apply, if it be possible, the same time limits for giving notice of a complaint of partial loss of contents as for one of physical damage: and I am equally in no doubt that it is the duty of the English courts to apply, if possible, an interpretation which meets the commercial purpose of the Convention. In my judgment,

12 [1974] Ch 401 at 418, 425, [1974] 2 All ER 1226 at 1231, 1236–1237.
13 (1976) 14 Avi 17, 466.

such an interpretation is possible; and I have derived a measure of assistance in reaching my conclusion from certain aids to interpretation which, if we were not concerned with an international convention, it would not be legitimate to use.

The trial judge's error was, I think, to construe the article as though it were merely a term of a ticket contract. It is much more than that. It is part of a convention intended to unify the rules relating to the carriage of persons and goods by air. The majority of the Court of Appeal (Browne and Geoffrey Lane LJJ) was, I think, also misled by the ordinary meaning of 'damage' into interpreting the Convention in a way inconsistent with its purpose. It is because I consider it our duty to interpret, if it be possible, article 26 (2) in a way which is consistent with the purpose of the Convention that I think it necessary to discuss the intricate questions raised as to the correct approach of a British court to a convention of this character.

The issue between the parties is as to the construction to be put upon an Act of Parliament. But the Act requires the courts to interpret an international convention. The Convention is in French. The French text, as well as an English text, is scheduled to the Act. In the event of any inconsistency between the two texts, the French is to prevail. The French text is, therefore, English law. The English text is secondary—a statutory translation. Three problems of importance arise:

(1) What is the approach to be adopted by British courts to the interpretation of an international convention incorporated by statute into our law?

(2) To what aids may our courts have recourse in interpreting such a convention?

(3) If our courts may have recourse to 'travaux préparatoires', to foreign judicial decisions, and to the writings of distinguished jurists expert in the field of law covered by the Convention, by what criteria are they to select such material and what weight are they to give it?

The broad approach of our courts to the interpretation of an international convention incorporated into our law is well settled. The international currency of the convention must be respected, as also its international purpose. The convention should be construed 'on broad principles of general acceptation'. The approach was formulated by Lord Macmillan in *Stag Line Ltd v Foscolo, Mango & Co Ltd*;[14] it was adopted by this House in the recent case of *James Buchanan & Co Ltd v Babco Forwarding and Shipping (UK) Ltd*.[15]

The implications of this approach remain, however, to be worked out by our courts. Some can be explored in this appeal: but it would be idle to pretend that all can be foreseen. Our courts will have to develop their jurisprudence in company with the courts of other countries from case to case—a course of action by no means unfamiliar to common law judges. I propose, therefore, to consider only the implications and difficulties which arise in the instant case, and to direct myself broadly along the lines indicated by article 32 of the Vienna Convention on the Law of Treaties.

First, the problem of the French text. Being scheduled to the statute, it is part of our law. Further, in the event of inconsistency, it shall, as a matter of law, prevail over the English text. It is, therefore, the duty of the court to

14 [1932] AC 328 at 350.
15 [1978] AC 141, [1977] 3 All ER 1048; p 687 above.

have regard to it. We may not take refuge in our adversarial process, paying regard only to the English text, unless and until one or other of the parties leads evidence to establish an inconsistency with the French. We are to take judicial notice of the French. We have to form a view as to its meaning. Given our insular isolation from foreign languages, even French, and being unable to assume that all English judges are familiar with the language, how is the court to do its duty? First, the court must have recourse to the English text. It is, after all, the meaning which Parliament believes the French to have. It is an enacted translation, though not binding in law because Parliament has recognised the possibility of inconsistency and has laid down how that difficulty is to be resolved. Secondly, as with the English language, so also with the French, the court may have recourse to dictionaries in its search for a meaning. Thirdly, the court may receive expert evidence directed not to the questions of law which arise in interpreting the convention, but to the meaning, or possible meanings (for there will often be more than one), of the French. It will be for the court, not the expert, to choose the meaning which it considers should be given to the words in issue. The same problem arises frequently with the English language, though here the court relies on its own knowledge of the language supplemented by dictionaries or other written evidence of usage. At the end of the day, the court, applying legal principles of interpretation, selects the meaning which it believes the law requires.

I come now to consider to what aids our courts may have recourse in interpreting an international convention. It matters not how the convention has entered into our law. Once it is part of our law, its international character must be respected. The point made by Lord Macmillan in *Stag Line Ltd v Foscolo, Mango & Co Ltd* is to be borne in mind. Rules contained in an international convention are the outcome of an international conference; if, as in the present case, they operate within the field of private law, they will come under the consideration of foreign courts; and uniformity is the purpose to be served by most international conventions, and we know that unification of the rules relating to international air carriage is the object of the Warsaw Convention. It follows that our judges should be able to have recourse to the same aids to interpretation as their brother judges in the other contracting states. The mischief of any other view is illustrated by the instant case. To deny them this assistance would be a damaging blow to the unification of the rules which was the object of signing and then enacting the Convention. Moreover, the ability of our judges to fulfil the purpose of the enactment would be restricted, and the persuasive authority of their judgments in the jurisdictions of the other contracting states would be diminished.

We know that in the great majority of the contracting states the legislative history, the 'travaux préparatoires', the international case law ('la jurisprudence') and the writings of jurists ('la doctrine') would be admissible as aids to the interpretation of the Convention. We know also that such sources would be used in the practice of public international law. They should, therefore, also be admissible in our courts: but they are to be used as *aids* only.

Aids are not a substitute for the terms of a convention: nor is their use mandatory. The court has a discretion. The exercise of this discretion is the true difficulty raised by the present case. Kerr J at first instance and Geoffrey

Lane LJ in the Court of Appeal plainly thought it was unnecessary to have recourse to any aids to interpretation other than the words of the Convention. Although I disagree with their conclusion, I think their initial approach was correct. They looked to the terms of the Convention as enacted, and concluded that it was clear. I agree with them in thinking that the court must first look at the terms of the convention as enacted by Parliament. But, if there be ambiguity or doubt, or if a literal construction appears to conflict with the purpose of the convention, the court must then, in my judgment, have recourse to such aids as are admissible and appear to it to be not only relevant but helpful on the point (or points) under consideration. Mere marginal relevance will not suffice: the aid (or aids) must have weight as well. A great deal of relevant material will fail to meet these criteria. Working papers of delegates to the conference, or memoranda submitted by delegates for consideration by the conference, though relevant, will seldom be helpful: but an agreed conference minute of the understanding upon the basis of which the draft of an article of the convention was accepted may well be of great value. And I agree with Kerr J that it would be useful if such conferences could identify—perhaps even in the convention—documents to which reference may be made in interpreting the convention.

The same considerations apply to the international case law and the writings of jurists. The decision of a supreme court, or the opinion of a court of cassation, will carry great weight: the decision of an inferior court will not ordinarily do so. The eminence, the experience and the reputation of a jurist will be of importance in determining whether, and, if so, to what extent, the court should rely on his opinion.

Nevertheless the decision whether to resort to these aids, and the weight to be attached to them, is for the court. However, the court's discretion has an unusual feature. It is applied not to a factual situation but to a choice of sources for help in interpreting an enactment. It operates in a purely legal field. An appellate court is not, therefore, bound by the lower court's selection of aids, but must make its own choice, if it thinks recourse to aids is necessary. This legal process is not unlike the use made by our courts of antecedent case law, though it lacks the inhibitions of any doctrine of precedent. To those who would say that there is a risk of our courts becoming burdened with an intolerable load if this material is to be available, I would reply that the remedy lies with the court. It need look at no more than it thinks necessary.

I now apply these criteria to the present case. First, I look at the terms of the Convention. The two texts of article 26 (2) are not inconsistent. Their literal construction suggests, in the absence of indications to the contrary, that 'damage' or 'avarie' is limited to physical harm or injury. But this appears, for the reasons which my noble and learned friend has developed and which I accept, to be inconsistent with the purpose of article 26. Moreover, it is possible, linguistically, to construe 'damage', or 'avarie', as covering not only damage to, but partial loss of contents of, baggage or cargo; for—a common feature of language in a complex society—each word can, and does, take a different shade of meaning from its context. Which construction is to be accepted? At this stage, it is helpful to have regard to the aids which the courts of other contracting states would use in ascertaining the meaning of 'damage' or 'avarie' in the context of the article.

The minutes of the conference of 1955, the outcome of which was the Convention enacted by the Act of 1961, suggest that 'damage' in the context of the article was intended to cover partial loss of contents. These minutes, it should be noted, were published in 1956, not only in Montreal (the headquarters of the International Civil Aviation Organisation) but also by Her Majesty's Stationery Office in London: and, probably, elsewhere as well. They are in no way secret. But they are not conclusive. Further, the weight of the international case law and of the writings of jurists supports the same conclusion. For all these reasons, therefore, ie the commercial sense of such an interpretation, the context (including in particular article 22 (2) (b) of the Convention), the minutes of the conference, the case law and the writings of jurists, I conclude that in article 26 (2) of the Convention damage to baggage includes partial loss of its contents. Unless, therefore, complaint of the loss be made within the time limited by the article, no action lies against the carrier.

Lords Wilberforce, Diplock and Roskill delivered judgments to the same effect. Lord Fraser of Tullybelton dissented in part: he would not look at the travaux préparatoires.

Appeal allowed.

The Hollandia (p 682 above)

CHAPTER 30

American Methods for Choice of Law

NOTE

Over the past few decades there has been in the USA what has been described as a 'revolution' in the approach of both courts and writers to the question of determining the applicable law. The focal point for these developments has been the choice of law rules in tort. Whilst there has been very widespread rejection of the rule of the first Restatement on the Conflict of Laws, namely the uniform application of the lex loci delicti, there has been no unanimity as to the new approach which should be adopted. Whilst there is little doubt that the 'revolution' owes much to the writing of Brainerd Currie,[1] David Cavers[2] and Willis Reese[3] and to the judgments of Chief Justice Traynor[4] of California and Chief Judge Fuld[5] of New York, no one view has come to prevail throughout the USA.

Although this chapter tries to give some idea of the breadth of the differing approaches in the USA and allocates both academic views and judicial decisions into particular categories, a preliminary word of caution is called for. Complete isolation of individual approaches is not possible. For example, later academic writings build on earlier views. Cavers adopts the same approach as Currie to the issue of true and false conflicts but they propose different solutions to true conflicts. Leflar,[6] Reese and the Restatement Second on the Conflict of Laws isolate similar choice-influencing considerations but only Leflar (and the courts which have adopted his approach as in *Clark v Clark*[7]) places emphasis on the 'better rule of law'.

A similar combination of approaches is seen in the cases. The use of an 'interest analysis' approach may be as likely to cause a court to conclude that the conflict is false, because the law of only one state has an 'interest' in being applied (as in *Williams v Rawlings Truck Line*[8]) as to conclude that the interest of the law of one state prevails (as in *Reich v Purcell*).[9] Again, in a situation where the law is in a state of fluid development, in over 50 different jurisdictions, it is not surprising to find reliance in

1 *Selected Essays on the Conflict of Laws* (1963).
2 *The Choice-of-Law Process* (1965).
3 Eg 'General Course on Private International Law' (1976) 150 Hague Recueil des Cours 1–193. Professor Reese was also the Reporter for (and thus architect of) the Restatement on Conflict of Laws, Second.
4 See *Bernkrant v Fowler* 360 P 2d 906 (1961), p 631 above; *Reich v Purcell* 432 P 2d 727 (1967), p 713 below.
5 See *Babcock v Jackson* 191 NE 2d 279 (1963), p 501 above; *Neumeier v Kuehner* 286 NE 2d 454 (1972), p 721 below.
6 *American Conflicts Law* (3rd edn, 1977).
7 222 A 2d 205 (1966); p 737 below.
8 357 F 2d 581 (1965); p 700 below.
9 432 P 2d 727 (1967); p 713 below; and see also *Pfau v Trent Aluminium* 263 A 2d 129 (1970); p 704 below.

any one case on several, not wholly mutually consistent theories for the basis of the decision,[10] nor indeed that within one jurisdiction the courts have developed variants on the new approaches.[11] One of the most striking illustrations of the diversity of approach in the USA is provided by federal court cases where claims by a large number of plaintiffs, all claiming against the same defendant, are consolidated, as happens in the case of litigation arising out of a major air disaster. For example, in *Re Air Crash Disaster Near Chicago Illinois on May 25, 1979*,[12] the court had to examine the present choice of law rules relating to tort in several different states. The result was that the same federal court applied 'the most significant relationship'[13] test to those claims which originated in Illinois and the Restatement Second test[14] to those from New York, but the 'comparative impairment' test[15] to the California claims, and the old lex loci delicti rule to the Puerto Rican claims.[16]

Section A: Preliminary matters

(1) *Rule selection or jurisidiction selection?*

Leflar, American Conflicts Law (3rd edn, 1977) pp 198–200*

§ 100. *Choice of Jurisdictions or Choice of Law.*—Traditionally, the choice-of-law process has been assumed to involve first a choice of jurisdictions to be followed later by an inquiry as to what is the relevant law of the selected state. The theory was that the first choice, as between states, is not affected by the content of the laws of the respective states, but somehow proceeds independently of the laws' content, which is newly discovered at a later stage of the inquiry.

Every participant in the process knows that it does not happen that way. The lawyer representing one side or the other in a case starts, at least approximately, with the result he wants to reach. Having characterised his problem sufficiently to know what areas of law he is concerned with, he checks the laws of the connected states and ascertains which are favorable to him and which unfavorable. Then he looks at the conflicts rules which choose a state rather than a law, and selects a characterisation or a conflicts theory that will under the rules lead him to the previously chosen law with its desired result.

When he comes before the court, he reverses the reasoning process and argues first for his ultimate characterisation and conflicts theory, then leads on to the concluding result which was in fact his starting point. Since both sides normally present their choice-of-law reasoning in this final form, it is understandable that courts accept the form and in their decisions adopt it as presented by one side or the other. But it is also likely that a court will

---

10 *Mitchell v Craft* 211 So 2d 509 (1968).
11 See, for example, the differing approaches of the Supreme Court of California in *Reich v Purcell*, above, and *Offshore Rental Co v Continental Oil Co* 583 P 2d 721 (1970); p 715 below.
12 644 F 2d 594 (1981).
13 Below, pp 728–731.
14 Ibid.
15 Below, pp 715–719.
16 As for the two other states involved, one was Hawaii whose choice of law rule could not be identified and the other Michigan whose courts had abandoned the lex loci delicti rule but put nothing clear in its place.
* Extract reproduced by kind permission of The Michie Company, Charlottesville, Virginia.

understand what the lawyers have done and follow the order of their unstated as well as of their stated argument. The court's desire to achieve justice is just as real as that of the opposing lawyers, the difference being that the court's definition of justice is not controlled by the identity of the lawyers' clients. The court can concern itself with the quality of the opposing laws between which it has to choose, and any serious study of the cases clearly indicates that courts do concern themselves with the content of the laws even though they do not often frame their opinions in those terms. The lawyer who omits argument on the inherent superiority of the opposing laws, apart from their territorial origins, is crediting the average court with less sophisticated wisdom than it possesses.

Professor David F. Cavers of Harvard many years ago[17] suggested that the selection of governing law ought to be a process of choice between rules of law rather than a choice between jurisdictions. He criticised systems under which

> [t]he forum's choice is made simply by locating that place (ie, jurisdiction), the law's content being irrelevant to the choice. In contrast, a true choice of law would confront the forum with the competing rules of law on which the respective parties rely.[18]

His point is that a court choosing between the laws of two states must look at the rules of law themselves and evaluate them with reference to the facts in the case and with reference to the social policies inherent in them as they relate to the facts. He concedes, however, that:

> My position does not stigmatise jurisdiction-selecting rules as bad per se; a good jurisdiction-selecting rule may emerge from a process of evaluating the claims of the competing rules in contrasting law-fact patterns.[19]

It is not suggested that policy values or judicial preferences for one rule of law over another should become the whole basis for choice of law, but only that they may be (are) a part of the bases, and that it is just as inaccurate to omit them from analysis of the process as it would be to regard them as the only considerations that affect choice-of-law decision. Most courts today would pay some attention to the 'governmental interests' of the states, or at least of their own state. There is no chance of doing this without taking into account the content of the rules of law between which a choice is to be made, and of the policies and purposes behind them.

The technique of choice between laws, as distinguished from choice of jurisdictions, is accepted in the courts more by deed than by word. It is easiest to accept when the laws of two involved states are substantially identical, or give the same result in the pending dispute, so that the court can apply the rule or reach the result, perhaps as against the contrary rule of

---

17 Cavers 'A Critique of the Choice-of-Law Problem' 47 Harv L Rev 173, 194, 201 (1933).
18 Cavers 'Re-Restating the Conflict of Laws: The Chapter on Contracts' in *XXth Century Comparative and Conflicts Law; Essays in Honour of Hessel E. Yntema*, 349, 350 (K. Nadelmann, A. von Mehren & J. Hazard, eds 1961).
19 Cavers *The Choice-of-Law Process* (1965) p 238, n 26. See also Cavers 'Comments on *Babcock v Jackson*' 63 Col L Rev 1219, 1222 (1963).

a third state, without having to choose between the first two.[20] There are but few cases of that sort, however. Most choice-of-law cases require a deliberate choice between the opposing rules of two states. At one time judges would have self-consciously denied that they gave any weight to the quality of the rules of law between which choice was made. A vested rights approach called for a choice between states, not between laws, and there was thought to be some tinge of the unethical in the conduct of a judge who, unlike blind Justice, admittedly opened his eyes to see the consequences of his choice. Even today some jurists assert the blind ideal, though none would deny the reality, sometimes partially concealed but readily discoverable, of weight given to the content of rules and the policies they represent.

(2) *True or false conflicts*

Westen, 'False Conflicts' (1967) 55 California L Rev 74, 75–78, 122

The concept of 'false conflicts' came into the choice-of-law world through a series of articles written by Professor Brainerd Currie between 1958 and 1965.[1] Other commentators have since asserted that the idea of false conflicts is an old concept which Currie simply clothed in new terminology. Professor Cavers did, in fact, propose an approach to choice-of-law problems in 1933 which was very similar in principle and wording to the one advanced by Currie.[2] Currie, however, was the first to analyse systematically the disposition of what he called 'false problems'. The phrase 'false conflicts' which Currie himself never used, has nonetheless been consistently attributed to him by others. While most commentators agree on the disposition of 'false conflicts' cases, they have not yet agreed when such cases—not to mention 'classic' false conflicts cases—may occur. Nor have they agreed on terminology. Hereinafter, the phrase 'false conflicts' will be used to group together what have been variously called 'false problems', 'spurious conflicts', 'illusory' conflicts, 'apparent' conflicts, 'avoidable' conflicts, 'pseudo conflicts' and 'superficial' conflicts.

In his book, *The Choice-of-Law Process*, Professor Cavers enumerates four kinds of 'false conflicts':[3]

1. Cases in which the laws of both states are the same.
2. Cases in which the laws of two states, though different, yield identical results with respect to the specific issue before the court.
3. Cases in which two states have different laws, but only one state has an *interest* in having its law applied. This is the case Currie referred to as a 'false problem', and one which the court in *Williams v Rawlings Truck Line, Inc*[4] identified as a 'classic "false conflicts" situation'.
4. Cases in which states with different laws both have an interest in applying

20 The importance of doing this as a means of avoiding 'false conflicts' when the laws of all involved states would produce the same result in litigation is evident.
1 Currie *Selected Essays on the Conflict of Laws* (1963).
2 Cavers 'A Critique of the Choice-of-Law Problem' 47 Harv L Rev 173, 176–177 (1933).
3 Cavers *The Choice-of-Law Process* pp 63–64, 89–90 (1965).
4 357 F 2d 581 (DC Cir 1965); p 700 below.

their own law, but in which 'the forum [is] prepared, when the circumstances warrant, to give a moderate and restrained interpretation to the policy or interest of one state or the other and thus avoid the conflict'.

Three more situations, not discussed by Cavers, have been referred to by other commentators as 'false conflicts' and should be added to the list:

5. Cases in which the laws of two states are involved, but neither has an interest in having its law applied. Related to this is the case of a *disinterested forum* confronting a true conflict between two other states but having itself no rational preference for one rather than the other law.
6. Cases in which foreign law (or forum law, as the case may be) is referred to not for the *rule of decision,* but as a *datum* for the state applying its law.
7. Cases in which the law of only one of several contact-states has been pleaded.

The concept of false conflicts has wide appeal and diverse meaning. In some cases, it is used to describe situations in which choice of law is moot. In other cases, it is used to describe the choice-of-law process itself. And in still other cases, it is used to describe situations in which choice of law has already been made. In each case, however, by characterising a choice-of-law problem as a false conflict, the courts are asserting that only one law can be rationally applied to the facts at issue. The concept of false conflicts has value for courts which are sufficiently sophisticated to engage in the kind of reasoning it presupposes. The concept is also useful in eliminating as forceful precedent those choice-of-law cases which are found to have involved no real conflict. But it is no shibboleth for solving the problems of private international law. Rather it is a challenge to counsel and courts alike to abandon the talismans of the past by confronting the task of accommodating legitimate state interests.

Williams v Rawlings Truck Line Inc 357 F 2d 581 (1965) (United States Court of Appeals, District of Columbia Circuit)

The appellant, Williams, was injured in a car accident in the District of Columbia. He was a passenger in the car which collided with a truck. The driver of the car (Rivera) disappeared and Williams sued the owners of the truck (Rawlings Truck Line) and the man (Goldberger) whose New York car registration tags were on the car. One month before the accident Goldberger, who lived in New York, had sold the car to Rivera but had allowed Rivera to take the car whilst still bearing licence plates issued in Goldberger's name. The trial judge directed a verdict in favour of Goldberger and Williams appealed to the United States Court of Appeals, the District of Columbia Circuit.

Per curiam: Appellant asserts that Goldberger's liability for the alleged negligence of Rivera is to be determined solely by New York law. A New York statute requires that upon transfer of a vehicle registered in New York

the licence plates must be removed from the car.[5] Another section provides
that:

> 'Every owner of a vehicle . . . shall be liable and responsible for death or
> injuries to person or property resulting from negligence in the use or
> operation of such vehicle . . . by any person using or operating the same
> with permission, express or implied, of such owner.'[6]

Were New York statutory law to be applied, an important issue would be
whether Goldberger 'owned' the car within the meaning of section 388. The
New York courts have developed the common law doctrine that the former
owner of a car who fails to comply with the statutes governing transfer of
title, is estopped from denying his ownership in order to avoid liability.
Thus, as Goldberger himself recognises, if New York law in its entirety were
applied, he would experience difficulty in avoiding liability for any negligent
act committed by Rivera while driving the car.

Appellee Goldberger counters that the law of the District of Columbia
should be applied. Our Motor Vehicle Safety Responsibility Act declares in
language similar to that of New York that, 'Whenever any motor vehicle . . .
shall be operated [within the District] . . . by any person other than the
owner, with the consent of the owner, express or implied, the operator
thereof shall in case of accident, be deemed to be the agent of the
owner . . .'.[7] We have read the statute as creating a new rule of liability in
which agency is based upon consent. However, the District's decisional law
recognises that the registered owner is free to prove passage of equitable title
and that such proof will relieve the former owner of liability under section
40–424.

We are thus confronted with what appears to be a classic conflict of laws
problem. As we stated in the recent case of *Tramontana v S. A. Empresa de
Viacao Aerea Rio Grandense*:[8] 'The Supreme Court . . . has recognised the
inadequacies of the theoretical underpinnings of *Slater v Mexican National
R. R.*[9] and its progeny. The latter cases have a highly attenuated
precedential weight, both in authority and reason. Thus we are free to
explore the question presented by this appeal in the light of the newer
concepts of conflict of laws.'

Two separate but closely related issues are at once apparent, each
requiring an independent evaluation of the respective interests of New York
and of the District in the outcome of this case. The first is whether
Goldberger is the 'owner' of the car—eg, whether the New York rule of
estoppel or the District of Columbia rule allowing proof of sale applies. The
second is, assuming that Goldberger is found to be the 'owner' of the car,
whether his liability is to be measured under New York's or the District's
statute rendering an automobile owner vicariously liable for the torts of
another committed while driving his car. We turn first to the issue which was
raised in the District Court and presented to us in brief and argument—that
of Goldberger's 'ownership' of the vehicle.

Resolution of this issue turns upon whether the District of Columbia has

5 NY Vehicle and Traffic Law, § 420.
6 Ibid, § 388.
7 DC Code § 40–424 (1961).
8 350 F 2d 468, 471 (1965), cert denied 86 S Ct 1195 (1966).
9 194 US 120 (1904).

any significant interest in applying its rule of 'ownership' to this case. The basic policy which motivated passage of section 40–424 'was to control the giving of consent to irresponsible drivers by the one having that power rather than to impose liability upon one having a naked legal title with no immediate right of control'.[10] An additional goal presumably was 'To furnish a financially responsible defendant . . .'. In short, section 40–424 and the doctrine of allowing a registered owner to disprove ownership were designed to protect the persons and property of District residents by encouraging safe driving and by providing injured parties with potential defendants. Yet, none of the parties to this suit is a resident of the District, nor was the car registered here. The place of the accident was, in this sense, wholly fortuitous. Hence, the District is not in a position to assert an interest in the application of its law to this case; such an application would not further the policies underlying the District's law. Conversely, no policy of the District would be impinged upon by application of the New York estoppel doctrine under which Goldberger might be held liable for the alleged negligence of Rivera.

New York, on the other hand, has a substantial interest in the application of its rule of estoppel to this case. This New York doctrine is designed to enforce by its in terrorem effect the vehicle registration laws of the state, and thereby to maintain the integrity and accuracy of that state's vehicle registration system. Fulfillment of this basic goal would require extra-territorial application of the estoppel doctrine. Otherwise, New York residents could improperly transfer their cars any time the car was to be permanently, or even temporarily, removed from the state without fear of liability; ultimately such a circumstance might lead to a significant impairment of New York's record-keeping system.

In sum, this case presents a classic 'false conflicts' situation. Adoption of the New York doctrine of estoppel will further the interests of New York, but will not interfere with any of the articulated policies of the District of Columbia. On the other hand, application of the District's rule allowing proof of sale would impinge upon New York's interests, without furthering any of the recognisable policies of the District. As a false conflicts case, our decision becomes simple: we apply the estoppel rule of New York, the only jurisdiction with an interest in having its law applied to the issue of defining *ownership* of the vehicle. We conclude that the District Court erred in directing a verdict in favour of Goldberger.

With the 'ownership' aspect determined as we have seen, the parties and the court at a new trial may be confronted with a consequential problem, not previously reached because of the directed verdict. Is Goldberger's potential *liability* as 'owner' of the car to be measured under the law of New York or under our statute, previously cited? We note that the New York statute, section 388, is similar both in purpose and in wording to our own which gives rise to the likelihood that defenses under both statutes may be identical. If so, the problem of selecting the applicable statute will become moot. If not, however, a 'true conflicts' question will then be presented. It may be that the courts of New York have not insisted that the interests of that state require that its section 388 be applied to accidents outside the state. If that be so, there is no reason why the District's rules of liability

---

10 *Mason v Automobile Finance Co* 121 F 2d 32, 35 (1941); *Forrester v Jerman* 90 F 2d 412 (1937).

under section 40–424 might not apply. Granting that the District of Columbia has no interest in the issue of defining 'ownership' of a vehicle, the District may nevertheless have an interest in the application of other facets of section 40–424 to an accident which has occurred here.

We simply point, without further comment, to a possible liability question, the answer to which will depend upon an analysis of the interests and policies of the respective jurisdictions and of the relationships of the parties to New York and to this District.

Affirmed as to Rawlings Truck Line and Willis.

Reversed as to Goldberger.

Gaither v Myers (p 710 below).

Pfau v Trent Aluminum Co 263 A 2d 129 (1970) (Supreme Court of New Jersey)

The plaintiff was domiciled in Connecticut but he was a student at a college in Iowa. The second defendant, Trent, was a fellow student of the same college and he was domiciled in New Jersey. He had the use, whilst in college, of a car which belonged to the first defendants, a New Jersey company which his father owned. The car was registered and insured in New Jersey. Trent and Pfau agreed to spend a weekend away from college on a trip, in the car, to Missouri. Whilst still in Iowa, the car hit another car and the plaintiff was injured and claimed damages. In Iowa, but not in New Jersey, there was a guest statute which provided that a host-driver was not liable to his passenger-guest for ordinary negligence. The trial judge in New Jersey held that this defence was not available, as New Jersey law was to be applied. The Appellate Division reversed this decision and the plaintiff petitioned the Supreme Court of New Jersey for certification of this decision.

Proctor J (who gave the judgment of the court): The sole question presented by this appeal is whether the Iowa guest statute is applicable to this action.

In *Mellk v Sarahson*[11] this court abandoned the old lex loci delicti rule for determining choice of law in tort cases, and adopted the governmental interest analysis approach. We did so because we believed that the lex loci delicti doctrine worked unjust results in many cases and ignored the interests which jurisdictions other than that where the tort occurred may have in the resolution of the particular issues involved. In *Mellk*, the plaintiff was injured while riding as a passenger in the defendant-driver's car when it struck a parked vehicle in Ohio. Plaintiff and defendant were both New Jersey domiciliaries and their guest-host relationship began in this state. When the accident happened, they were returning from a brief visit to the home of a mutual friend in Wisconsin. Defendant's automobile was insured and registered in New Jersey. In those circumstances we declined to apply the Ohio guest statute. The purposes discerned in the Ohio statute by that state's own courts were the prevention of collusive suits and the preclusion of suits by 'ungrateful guests'. Since both plaintiff and defendant were New Jersey domiciliaries and since the car was insured in New Jersey, we did not believe that Ohio had any interest in the application of its guest statute to the case.

11 229 A 2d 625 (1967).

Instead, we applied New Jersey's strong declared policy of requiring a host to exercise at least ordinary care for the safety of his guest.

Our decision in *Mellk* followed *Babcock v Jackson*,[12] in which the New York Court of Appeals rejected the traditional choice of law rule which looked invariably to the place of the tort, and reached the same result as *Mellk* on similar facts. There, two New York residents began an automobile trip from that state to Ontario. The plaintiff, a guest in defendant's car, was injured when the defendant-driver struck a stone wall in Ontario. Although the Ontario statute barred any recovery by a guest-passenger against a host-driver, the court applied New York law which permitted the guest to sue his host. *Babcock* achieved widespread acclaim from legal scholars, eg, Cavers, Cheatham, Currie, Ehrenzweig, Leflar and Reese,[13] and New York has continued to apply the *Babcock* approach in subsequent decisions. These post-*Babcock* decisions have indicated some of the difficulties which are inevitable when a court applies a new approach to various factual patterns. We are faced with the same problem in the present case, for defendants do not argue that New Jersey should return to lex loci delicti; they disagree, however, with the plaintiff over what state's law modern conflicts principles dictate should be applied.

In order to determine whether the Iowa guest statute should apply to this case, we must first examine its purposes as articulated by the Iowa courts. See *Mellk v Sarahson*, above. These purposes are: 'to cut down litigation arising from the commendable unselfish practice of sharing with others transportation in one's vehicle and protect the Good Samaritan from claims based on negligence by those invited to ride as a courtesy', to prevent ingratitude by guests, to prevent suits by hitchhikers, 'to prevent collusive suits by friends and relatives resulting in excessively high insurance rates'.

The above policies expressed by the Iowa courts would not appear to be relevant to the present matter. This action will not increase litigation in the Iowa courts; no hitchhiker is involved; no Iowa insurer will be subjected to a 'collusive suit' since the insurer is a New Jersey corporation; there is no 'Good Samaritan' Iowa host-driver to be protected; and finally, there is no Iowa guest displaying his 'ingratitude' by suing for ordinary negligence. The desire of Iowa to prevent collusive suits and suits by ungrateful guests and to cut down litigation would ordinarily apply to Iowa domiciliaries, defendants insuring motor vehicles there, and persons suing in its courts. *Mellk v Sarahson*, above.

Defendants contend, however, that application of the Iowa guest statute is required because the plaintiff and the individual defendant were residing in Iowa at the time of the accident, because the host-guest relationship began and ended in Iowa, and because non-guest Iowa domiciliaries were injured in the accident. These factors were treated as significant in the post-*Babcock* decision of *Dym v Gordon*.[14]

(The court then examined a number of recent New York and New Jersey tort cases and continued:) While Iowa was the 'seat of the relationship' in the instant case, this 'contact' does not relate to any interest or policy behind Iowa's guest statute. Nor do we attach any importance to the temporary

12 191 NE 2d 279 (1963), p 501 above.
13 'Comments on *Babcock v Jackson*' 63 Col LR 1212 (1963).
14 209 NE 2d 792 (1965).

Iowa residence of plaintiff and defendant. Both parties were still permanently domiciled in other states which retained interests. Moreover, the insurer is a New Jersey corporation which issued its policy at rates applicable to New Jersey. Iowa's interest in these temporary residents is limited to enforcement of its rules of the road at least where the litigation is not in that state. Finally, we are not persuaded by the third-party-fund theory. Iowa has never expressed such a purpose behind its guest statute, and it is not appropriate for us to impute inarticulated purposes to the legislature of another state. The danger of injured Iowa domiciliaries being deprived of available funds because of recovery by the negligent driver's guest is merely speculative. If Iowa had identified the protection of these third parties as a policy underlying its guest statute, we could still give effect to that policy by giving priority to the third party's judgment lien against defendant's assets. We need not decide whether such a procedure is the proper solution to this problem because the claims of the Iowa domiciliaries have been settled.

It is clear to us that Iowa has no interest in this suit. Recovery for negligence in this action will not transgress any of the purposes behind Iowa's guest statute as enunciated by that state's courts or legislature, and will not in the slightest impair traffic safety in Iowa. Nor do we believe that the reasons urged by defendants for applying Iowa law are valid. We are convinced that if the plaintiff were a New Jersey domiciliary Iowa's guest statute would be inapplicable.

In this case, however, we are faced with a more complex situation since plaintiff is a domiciliary of Connecticut. Thus, we must consider the law of both New Jersey and Connecticut. Connecticut long ago repealed its guest statute and now permits guest-passengers to recover from their host-drivers for ordinary negligence. There is no doubt that if this plaintiff-guest had been injured in a Connecticut accident by a Connecticut host-driver, there would be no bar to recovery for ordinary negligence if suit were brought in that state.

Turning to New Jersey's law, we are led to *Cohen v Kaminetsky*,[15] where we held that the strong policy of this state is to allow a guest-passenger to be compensated by his host-driver in cases of ordinary negligence. Thus, the substantive laws of Connecticut and New Jersey are in accord.

In *Reich v Purcell*,[16] the California Supreme Court was faced with a situation similar in principle to the present case. There the court dealt with a Missouri statute which limited damages for wrongful death. Lee and Jeffry Reich, father and son, brought a wrongful death action for damages arising out of a head-on collision between two automobiles in Missouri. One of the automobiles was owned and operated by the defendant, a domiciliary of California, who was on his way to a vacation in Illinois. The other automobile was owned and operated by plaintiffs' decedent, Mrs Reich. The Reichs were domiciled in Ohio and Mrs Reich and her two children were on their way to California where the family was contemplating settling. Mrs Reich and one child were killed in the collision. Plaintiffs later became California domiciliaries. The estates of Mrs Reich and the deceased child were being administered in Ohio. Neither Ohio nor California limits

15 176 A 2d 483 (1961).
16 432 P 2d 727 (1967); p 713 below.

recovery in wrongful death actions. Missouri's statute limits damages in such cases to a maximum of $25,000. It was stipulated that the damages for Mrs Reich's death were substantially in excess of that amount.

Writing for a unanimous court Chief Justice Traynor rejected defendant's contention that the Missouri ceiling applied. The court held that Missouri had no substantial interest in extending the benefits of its statute to travelers from states having no similar limitation. Having resolved that Missouri law did not apply, Justice Traynor next examined the interests of California and Ohio. He refused to give any weight to the plaintiffs' California domicile since they had moved to California after the accident. Nor did he believe that defendant's California domicile was significant since that state did not have any limitation on damages to protect its defendants. Accordingly, he concluded that Ohio, the state of decedents' domicile at the time of the accident, was the only interested state and that its law should apply to the case.

It may well be that in this case, however, New Jersey has an interest. We are not certain that a defendant's domicile lacks an interest in seeing that its domiciliaries are held to the full measure of damages or the standard of care which that state's law provides for. A state should not only be concerned with the protection and self-interest of its citizens. In *Cohen v Kaminetsky*, above, we emphasised a host's *duty* to his guests. There we said: 'We see no reason why the host should be less vigilant for his own guest than he must be for the guest in another car. The duty to exercise reasonable care is as appropriate in the one situation as in the other.' It would not seem just to limit the imposition of this duty to instances where a New Jersey host negligently injures a New Jersey guest in a state which has a guest statute. See *Mellk v Sarahson*, above. Therefore, if Connecticut had a guest statute in this case, we would be forced to choose between our state's policy of holding our hosts to a duty of ordinary care and Connecticut's policy of denying a guest recovery for the ordinary negligence of his host and we might have a true conflict. But since Connecticut has the same policy of applying principles of ordinary negligence to the host-guest relationship as does New Jersey, this case presents a false conflict and it is unnecessary for us to decide whether this state has an interest sufficient to warrant application of its law.

It would appear that Connecticut's substantive law allowing a guest to recover for his host's ordinary negligence would give it a significant interest in having that law applied to this case. Defendants argue, however, that if we apply Connecticut's substantive law, we should apply its choice-of-law rule as well. In other words, they contend Connecticut's interest in its domiciliaries is identified not only by its substantive law, but by its choice-of-law rule. Connecticut adheres to lex loci delicti and according to its decisions would most likely apply the substantive law of Iowa in this case. Defendants contend that plaintiff should not be allowed to recover when he could not do so in either Iowa where the accident occurred or in Connecticut where he is domiciled. We cannot agree for two reasons. First, it is not definite that plaintiff would be unable to recover in either of those states. More importantly, however, we see no reason for applying Connecticut's choice-of-law rule. To do so would frustrate the very goals of governmental-interest analysis. Connecticut's choice-of-law rule does not identify that state's interest in the matter. Lex loci delicti was born in an effort to achieve simplicity and uniformity, and does not relate to a state's interest in having its law applied to given issues in a tort case. It is significant that in *Reich v Purcell*, above, the California Supreme Court applied the substantive law of Ohio to the Missouri accident. The court did not apply Ohio's choice-of-law rule which was lex loci delicti, and would have called for application of the Missouri limitation on damages. Professor Kay[17] in her comment on *Reich v Purcell* was in agreement with the above authorities that only the foreign substantive law should be applied, and she agreed with the court in *Reich* that Ohio's choice-of-law rule should be ignored.

We conclude that since Iowa has no interest in this litigation, and since the substantive laws of Connecticut and New Jersey are the same, this case presents a false conflict and the Connecticut plaintiff should have the right to maintain an action for ordinary negligence in our courts. In this situation principles of comity, and perhaps the equal protection and privileges and immunities clauses of the Constitution, dictate that we should afford the Connecticut plaintiff the same protection a New Jersey plaintiff would be given.

For the reasons expressed the order of the Appellate Division is reversed and the order of the trial court striking the separate defense of the Iowa guest statute is reinstated.

Reich v Purcell (p 713 below)

Section B: Governmental interest analysis

Currie 'Comments on Babcock v Jackson: A recent development in Conflict of Laws' (1963) 63 Columbia L Rev 1233, 1242–1243.

In short, the problems of choice of law consist of false problems that, once identified, need not trouble anyone further, and real problems that cannot be judicially solved except by means of arbitrary and unreasonable demands that one state or the other sacrifice its legitimate interest.

Understandably, this is an unpalatable concept to those who aspire to compile a reasonable set of choice-of-law rules for the solution of such problems. We have long harbored the delusion that in dealing with cases involving more than one state we can escape, by easy generalisation, the hard problems of construction and interpretation that we cannot avoid in other contexts. The passion for such generalisation dies hard. The question will inevitably be asked: If the governmental-interest analysis of *Babcock v Jackson*[18] is to prevail, must all choice-of-law problems be solved on an ad hoc basis, or will new generalisations be possible? My response is that, for the time being at least, new efforts to find short cuts and syntheses should be sternly discouraged. We are beginning to recover from a long siege of intoxication resulting from overindulgence in generalities; for a while, at least, total abstinence should be enforced.

When we have regained our health, or our senses, it is conceivable that we may be able to attempt a limited synthesis without excessive danger of

17 'Comment on *Reich v Purcell*' (1968) 15 UCLA L Rev 551, 589 n 31.
18 191 NE 2d 279 (1969); p 501 above.

relapse. I venture on such speculations with the utmost fear of jeopardising the process of recovery; but my position regarding the feasibility and utility of choice-of-law rules is a drastic one, and I suppose whatever concessions can be made should be stated.

1. Offhand, there is only one class of laws with respect to which I am prepared to generalise. Traffic regulations, I assume, are intended to apply to all vehicles and drivers, domestic and foreign, in operation within the enacting state, and to no others. I am not at all sure of this, but it is a starting point for those who insist on generalisation.

2. Especially in fields that I have not studied closely in terms of governmental-interest analysis—perhaps in the field of real property—there may be classes of laws with respect to which a particular connecting factor readily identifies the one state having such an obvious interest that no other state could conceivably claim a conflicting interest; but at this writing I am not prepared to specify those laws.

3. When the forum state is disinterested, and there is a genuine conflict of interests between two (or more) other states, there is a difficult problem that cannot be satisfyingly dealt with by applying the law of the forum, which is the reasonable solution when the forum is interested. For these cases it is perhaps feasible to construct general principles for choice of law on a reasonable basis; thus far, however, I have been unable to visualise a satisfactory system.

These generalisations will not get us very far. In the main they will help us to identify the false problems. For the real problems, in which the forum's interests are at stake, there can be no judicial solution except application of the law of the forum.

If I were asked to restate the law of conflict of laws I would decline the honor. A descriptive restatement with any sort of internal consistency is impossible. Much of the existing law, or pseudo law, of the subject is irrational; profound changes destructive of the fundamental tenets of the traditional system are gathering momentum. On the assumption that the project admits of a statement of what is reasonable in existing law and what may reasonably be desired for the future, however, I volunteer the following as a substitute for all that part of the Restatement dealing with choice of law (for the purpose of finding the rule of decision).

§ 1. When a court is asked to apply the law of a foreign state different from the law of the forum, it should inquire into the policies expressed in the respective laws, and into the circumstances in which it is reasonable for the respective states to assert an interest in the application of those policies. In making these determinations the court should employ the ordinary processes of construction and interpretation.

§ 2. If the court finds that one state has an interest in the application of its policy in the circumstances of the case and the other has none, it should apply the law of the only interested state.[19]

§ 3. If the court finds an apparent conflict between the interests of the two states it should reconsider. A more moderate and restrained interpretation of the policy or interest of one state or the other may avoid conflict.[20]

19 This is what the court did in *Babcock v Jackson*.
20 This is what the California Supreme Court did in *Bernkrant v Fowler* 360 P 2d 906 (1961); p 631 above.

§ 4. If, upon reconsideration, the court finds that a conflict between the legitimate interests of the two states is unavoidable, it should apply the law of the forum.

§ 5. If the forum is disinterested, but an unavoidable conflict exists between the laws of the two other states, and the court cannot with justice decline to adjudicate the case, it should apply the law of the forum—until someone comes along with a better idea.

§ 6. The conflict of interest between states will result in different dispositions of the same problem, depending on where the action is brought. If with respect to a particular problem this appears seriously to infringe a strong national interest in uniformity of decision, the court should not attempt to improvise a solution sacrificing the legitimate interest of its own state, but should leave to Congress, exercising its powers under the full faith and credit clause, the determination of which interest shall be required to yield.

The explanatory note might run a little longer.

Bernkrant v Fowler (p 631 above)

Gaither v Myers 404 F 2d 216 (1968) (United States Court of Appeals, District of Columbia Circuit)

The plaintiff, Myers, was resident in Maryland where he was injured in a collision between his car and a car owned by the defendant, who lived in the District of Columbia. The defendant had left his car unattended, with the keys still in it. The car was stolen and was driven by the thief from the District of Columbia to Maryland where the plaintiff was injured. The stolen car was then abandoned and the thief disappeared. The plaintiff alleged that the defendant, as owner of the car, was liable for the injuries he suffered. Under the law of the District of Columbia, the owner of a car can be held liable in negligence in leaving the keys in a parked and unattended car even though the plaintiff's injuries are directly caused by a thief. There is no such liability under the law of Maryland, where it is held that the intervening conduct of the thief breaks the chain of causation from the defendant. The trial judge had directed a verdict for the defendant. The District of Columbia Court of Appeals upheld the plaintiff's appeal and ordered a new trial. The defendant appealed to the United States Court of Appeals, District of Columbia Circuit.

Leventhal, Circuit Judge (giving the judgment of the court): The question for decision is whether the District's tort rule concerning liability for violation of the traffic regulation[1] applies where: the conduct prohibited by the regulation takes place in the District; and the immediate consequence of that violation (stealing of the car) occurs here; but the final sequence resulting in damage takes place in Maryland. To answer this question it is first necessary to ascertain the underlying policies and interests sought to be regulated and protected by the rules of the relevant jurisdictions and to

---

1 Article XIV, § 98 of the District of Columbia Traffic and Motor Vehicle Regulations.

determine whether on the facts of the case these differing state interests are in conflict.

We begin with the rule of the District, turning to the 1943 landmark case of *Ross v Hartman*.[2] There the court said:

> The evident purpose of requiring motor vehicles to be locked is not to prevent theft for the sake of the owners or the police, but to promote the safety of the public in the streets. An unlocked motor vehicle . . . creates much more risk that meddling by children, thieves, or others will result in injuries to the public. . . . The rule we are adopting tends to make the streets safer by discouraging the hazardous conduct which the ordinance forbids. It puts the burden of the risk, as far as may be, upon those who create it.

The doctrine of *Ross v Hartman* has been reaffirmed in intervening decisions of this court. The strength of the District's policy of 'discouraging the hazardous conduct which the ordinance forbids' has not diminished during the intervening 25 years. On the contrary we have never had greater need for doctrines helping to deter injuries and crimes traceable in significant measure to keys left in unattended cars.

On 1 March 1968, the Attorney General of the United States and 19 responsible organisations, including national associations of mayors, police chiefs, district attorneys, municipal law officers, launched the National Auto Theft Prevention Campaign in a nationwide effort to reduce automobile theft. The data distributed by the Campaign include the estimate that in 1966 more than a million cars were stolen nationally and that about 24% of the stolen vehicles were involved in accidents. The theft problem is acute in the District of Columbia where, during 1967, there were over 13,000 auto thefts, an increase over 1966 of 30% as opposed to a national rise of 17%. The accident rate for stolen cars is estimated to be approximately 200 times the normal accident rate. And in the District of Columbia, 85% of the thieves do not possess operator's permits. A study has disclosed that of the total cars stolen, the key had been left in either the ignition or in the car in 42.3% of the cases.

Moreover, the authorities point out that auto theft is to a large extent a crime of opportunity, unusually inviting to young people, and is often the first major episode in a criminal career. The data reveal that 70% of the District of Columbia auto thefts are by offenders under the age of 21.

The District has a strong policy of deterrence of auto theft. That policy must be viewed in the light of the probabilities of consequential hazards. This perspective fosters our conclusion that there is a significant District of Columbia interest in the application of the District rule of liability to an actor who leaves his car keys accessible to a thief in the District, and sets in motion the sequence of events that enlarges the probability of, and in a significant number of instances contributes to, results of death, disability and destruction.

Aside from the purpose served by the tort rule of *Ross v Hartman* in deterring highly hazardous motorist conduct, tort liability also has the purpose of shifting the loss from the injured victim and his creditors to the vehicle operator who, in turn, if he chooses, may procure insurance. It is true

---

2 139 F 2d 14 (1943), cert denied 321 US 790 (1944).

that this compensatory policy has the greatest relevance to cases when the mishap occurs in the District and when District residents are plaintiffs. However, to confine the benefits of the *Ross* rule to the territory ceded by the states of Maryland and Virginia to form the Nation's Capital would be to shun the present reality of the economically and socially integrated greater metropolitan area. It is a commonplace that residents of Maryland are part of the Washington metropolitan trading area, and that District residents and businesses have an interest in the well-being of these citizens of the Free State. We cannot fairly impute to Congress, or its delegate, the parochial intention to restrict recovery based on violation of the District regulation to District residents, especially taking into account the national constituency of Congress, in the absence of an express disclaimer.

It is plain, in short, that a legitimate and indeed powerful policy and interest of the District of Columbia is involved in this case and is furthered by application of the rule of *Ross v Hartman*.

Looking to the interests of Maryland, where the accident occurred and the plaintiff resides, its highest court has interpreted a nearly identical statute as being aimed at preventing theft, tampering with a car, or the starting of a car under its own momentum if the brakes should slip.[3] While that court agrees that the statute creates a duty of safety to the public, this apparently is limited to the immediate vicinity of the parking place for the court says it does not extend 'to all the world, but must be a foreseeable duty to a class of which the plaintiff was a member'. The court feels that the thief, an 'independent intervening cause', and not the car owner, is the proximate cause of the accident.

Thus Maryland's interests are aimed at prevention of theft, tampering, accidental starting of a car, and possibly some very immediate injury. Maryland, however, also expresses an interest in protecting car owners from tort liability for injury caused by car thieves. Yet, that interest of Maryland in curtailing liability of a car owner, would not seem to extend to an owner like our defendant, who is not a citizen of Maryland but rather a resident of the District of Columbia. This seems especially true where it is a Maryland citizen who is being compensated for his injuries. It is obvious that the finding of such liability would in no way violate the other interest in Maryland in preventing theft or tampering with cars by requiring removal of keys from parked cars; if anything, it fosters that interest.

Thus, we are not concerned with any real 'conflict' between the interests of Maryland and the District in this case. The fact that two states have different rules where all the factors are oriented to one state does not necessarily mean that there is a 'conflict' in which one state demands and the other rejects the application of its rule to a situation where the pertinent factors arise in two or more states. Where there is no such conflict of interest in a multi-state situation, as this court and others have noted, there is a 'false conflicts' situation. In such a case application of the appropriate rule is simplified. We think the DC Court of Appeals was correct in its conclusion that appellant's liability turns on the District of Columbia's rule in *Ross v Hartman*.

The cause is remanded for further proceedings consistent with this opinion. So ordered.

3 *Liberto v Holfeldt* 155 A 2d 698 (1959).

Reich v Purcell 432 P 2d 727 (1967) (Supreme Court of California)

Traynor, Chief Justice: This wrongful death action arose out of a head-on collision of two automobiles in Missouri. One of the automobiles was owned and operated by defendant Joseph Purcell, a resident and domiciliary of California who was on his way to a vacation in Illinois. The other automobile was owned and operated by Mrs Reich, the wife of plaintiff Lee Reich. The Reichs then resided in Ohio and Mrs Reich and the Reichs' two children, Jay and Jeffry, were on their way to California, where the Reichs were contemplating settling. Mrs Reich and Jay were killed in the collision, and Jeffry was injured.

Plaintiffs, Lee Reich and Jeffry Reich, are the heirs of Mrs Reich and Lee Reich is the heir of Jay Reich. Plaintiffs moved to California and became permanent residents here after the accident. The estates of Mrs Reich and Jay Reich are being administered in Ohio.

The parties stipulated that judgment be entered in specified amounts for the wrongful death of Jay, for the personal injuries suffered by Jeffry, and for the damages to Mrs Reich's automobile. For the death of Mrs Reich they stipulated that judgment be entered for $55,000 or $25,000 depending on the court's ruling on the applicability of the Missouri limitation of damages to a maximum of $25,000. (Vernon's Ann.Mo.Stats. § 537.090.) Neither Ohio nor California limit recovery in wrongful death actions. The trial court held that the Missouri limitation applied because the accident occurred there and entered judgment accordingly. Plaintiffs appeal.

For many years courts applied the law of the place of the wrong in tort actions regardless of the issues before the court, eg, whether they involved conduct, survival of actions, applicability of a wrongful death statute, immunity from liability, or other rules determining whether a legal injury has been sustained. It was assumed that the law of the place of the wrong created the cause of action and necessarily determined the extent of the liability.[4] This theory worked well enough when all the relevant events took place in one jurisdiction, but the action was brought in another. In a complex situation involving multistate contacts, however, no single state alone can be deemed to create exclusively governing rights. The forum must search to find the proper law to apply based upon the interests of the litigants and the involved states. Such complex cases elucidate what the simpler cases obscured, namely, that the forum can only apply its own law. When it purports to do otherwise, it is not enforcing foreign rights but choosing a foreign rule of decision as the appropriate one to apply to the case before it. Moreover, it has now been demonstrated that a choice of law resulting from a hopeless search for a governing foreign law to create a foreign vested right may defeat the legitimate interests of the litigants and the states involved.

Accordingly, when application of the law of the place of the wrong would defeat the interests of the litigant and of the states concerned, we have not applied that law. (*Grant v McAuliffe;*[5] *Emery v Emery.*[6]) *Grant* was an action for personal injuries arising out of an automobile accident in Arizona between

---

4 *Slater v Mexican National RR Co* 194 US 120 (1904).
5 264 P 2d 944 (1953).
6 289 P 2d 218 (1955).

California residents. The driver whose negligence caused the accident died, and the court had to choose between the California rule that allowed an action against the personal representative and the Arizona rule that did not. We held that since 'all of the parties were residents of this state, and the estate of the deceased tortfeasor is being administered in this state, plaintiffs' right to prosecute their causes of action is governed by the laws of this state relating to administration of estates'. Under these circumstances application of the law of the place of the wrong would not only have defeated California's interest and that of its residents but would have advanced no interest of Arizona or its residents. In *Emery* members of a California family were injured in Idaho when another member of the family who was driving lost control of the car and it went off the road. The question was whether Idaho or California law determined when one member of a family was immune from tort liability to another. We applied the law of the family domicile rather than the law of the place of the wrong. 'That state has the primary responsibility for establishing and regulating the incidents of the family relationship and it is the only state in which the parties can, by participation in the legislative processes, effect a change in those incidents. Moreover, it is undesirable that the rights, duties, disabilities, and immunities conferred or imposed by the family relationship should constantly change as members of the family cross state boundaries during temporary absences from their home.'

Defendant contends, however, that there were compelling reasons in the *Grant* and *Emery* cases for departing from the law of the place of the wrong and that such reasons are not present in this case. He urges that application of that law promotes uniformity of decisions, prevents forum shopping, and avoids the uncertainties that may result from ad hoc searches for a more appropriate law in this and similar cases.

Ease of determining applicable law and uniformity of rules of decision, however, must be subordinated to the objective of proper choice of law in conflict cases, ie, to determine the law that most appropriately applies to the issue involved. Moreover, as jurisdiction after jurisdiction has departed from the law of the place of the wrong as the controlling law in tort cases, regardless of the issue involved, that law no longer affords even a semblance of the general application that was once thought to be its great virtue. We conclude that the law of the place of the wrong is not necessarily the applicable law for all tort actions brought in the courts of this state.

As the forum we must consider all of the foreign and domestic elements and interests involved in this case to determine the rule applicable. Three states are involved. Ohio is where plaintiffs and their decedents resided before the accident and where the decedents' estates are being administered. Missouri is the place of the wrong. California is the place where defendant resides and is the forum. Although plaintiffs now reside in California, their residence and domicile at the time of the accident are the relevant residence and domicile. At the time of the accident the plans to change the family domicile were not definite and fixed, and if the choice of law were made to turn on events happening after the accident, forum shopping would be encouraged. Accordingly, plaintiffs' present domicile in California does not give this state any interest in applying its law, and since California has no limitation of damages, it also has no interest in applying its law on behalf of defendant. As a forum that is therefore disinterested in the only issue in dispute, we must decide whether to adopt the Ohio or the Missouri rule as the rule of decision for this case.

Missouri is concerned with conduct within her borders and as to such conduct she has the predominant interest of the states involved. Limitations of damages for wrongful death, however, have little or nothing to do with conduct. They are concerned not with how people should behave but with how survivors should be compensated. The state of the place of the wrong has little or no interest in such compensation when none of the parties resides there. Wrongful death statutes create causes of action in specified beneficiaries and distribute the proceeds to those beneficiaries. The proceeds in the hands of the beneficiaries are not distributed through the decedent's estate and, therefore, are not subject to the claims of the decedent's creditors and consequently do not provide a fund for local creditors. Accordingly, the interest of a state in a wrongful death action in so far as plaintiffs are concerned is in determining the distribution of proceeds to the beneficiaries and that interest extends only to local decedents and beneficiaries. Missouri's limitation on damages expresses an additional concern for defendants, however, in that it operates to avoid the imposition of excessive financial burdens on them. That concern is also primarily local and we fail to perceive any substantial interest Missouri might have in extending the benefits of its limitation of damages to travelers from states having no similar limitation. Defendant's liability should not be limited when no party to the action is from a state limiting liability and when defendant, therefore, would have secured insurance, if any, without any such limit in mind. A defendant cannot reasonably complain when compensatory damages are assessed in accordance with the law of his domicile and plaintiffs receive no more than they would have had they been injured at home. Under these circumstances giving effect to Ohio's interests in affording full recovery to injured parties does not conflict with any substantial interest of Missouri. Accordingly, the Missouri limitation does not apply.

The part of the judgment appealed from is reversed with directions to the trial court to enter judgment for the plaintiffs in the amount of $55,000 in accordance with the stipulations of the parties.

McComb, Peters, Tobriner, Mosk, Burke and Sullivan JJ concur.

Pfau v Trent Aluminum Co (p 704 above)

Section C: Comparative impairment

Offshore Rental Co Inc v Continental Oil Co (1978) 583 P 2d 721
(Supreme Court of California)

The plaintiff was a California corporation with its main place of business in California. One of its main activities was to lease oil drilling equipment in Louisiana and one of its employees was injured in Louisiana as the result of the alleged negligence of the defendant company. This employee was a vice-president of the plaintiff company, a 'key' employee for whose loss of services the plaintiffs claimed $5 million damages. Such an action could be maintained under the law of California but not of Lousiana. The trial court applied Lousiana law and dismissed the complaint. The plaintiff appealed to the Supreme Court of California, alleging that Californian law should be applied.

Tobriner J (giving the judgment of the court):   Questions of choice of law are determined in California, as plaintiff correctly contends, by the 'governmental interest analysis' rather than by the trial court's 'most significant contacts theory'. As we announced in *Reich v Purcell*,[7] under the governmental interest analysis approach, the forum in a conflicts situation 'must search to find the proper law to apply based upon the interests of the litigants and the involved states'. As we shall explain, however, we have concluded that despite its analytic error, the trial court correctly dismissed plaintiff's cause of action.

The matter presently before us involves two states: California, the forum, a place of business for defendant, as well as plaintiff's state of incorporation and principal place of business; and Louisiana, the locus of the business of both plaintiff and defendant out of which the injury arose, and the place of the injury. As we pointed out in our decision in *Hurtado v Superior Court*,[8] however, the fact that two states are involved does not in itself indicate that there is a 'conflict of laws' or 'choice of law' problem. As we stated in *Hurtado*, '[t]here is obviously no problem where the laws of the two states are identical.'

Here, however, the laws of Louisiana and California are not identical. In the leading case interpreting Louisiana law, *Bonfanti Industries Inc v Teke Inc*[9] a Louisiana corporation, relying on Louisiana Civil Code article 174, brought suit for the loss of services of one of its key officers occasioned by the Louisiana defendant's negligence. Although article 174 provides that 'The master may bring an action against any man for beating or maiming his *servant*' (emphasis added), the Louisiana court held that the *corporate plaintiff* could state no cause of action in modern law for the loss of services of its officer.

On the other hand, expressions in the California cases, although chiefly dicta, support the present plaintiff's assertion that California Civil Code section 49 grants a cause of action against a third party for loss caused by an injury to a key employee due to the negligence of the third party. Section 49 provides that 'The rights of personal relations forbid: . . . any injury to a servant which affects his ability to serve his master. . . .' Plaintiff contends that the master-servant relation protected by section 49 encompasses plaintiff's employment relationship with its injured vice-president, and thus that section 49 grants a cause of action against defendant for damages to plaintiff caused by defendant's negligence.

If we assume, for purposes of analysis, that section 49 does provide an employer with a cause of action for negligent injury to a key employee, the laws of California and Louisiana are directly in conflict. Nonetheless, '[a]lthough the two potentially concerned states have different laws, there is still no problem in choosing the applicable rule of law where only one of the states has an interest in having its law applied. . . . When one of the two states related to a case has a legitimate interest in the application of its law

7 432 P 2d 727 at 729 (1967); p 713 above.
8 522 P 2d 666 (1974).
9 224 So 2d 15; affd 226 So 2d 770 (1969).

and policy and the other has none, there is no real problem; clearly the law of the interested state should be applied.' (Currie, *Selected Essays on The Conflict of Laws* (1963) p 189) (*Hurtado v Superior Court*).

We must therefore examine the governmental policies underlying the Louisiana and California laws, 'preparatory to assessing whether either or both states have an interest in applying their policy to the case.'[10] Only if each of the states involved has a 'legitimate but conflicting interest in applying its own law' will we be confronted with a 'true' conflicts case. (*Bernhard v Harrah's Club.*[11])

Turning first to Louisiana, we note that Louisiana'a refusal to permit recovery for loss of a key employee's services is predicated on the view that allowing recovery would lead to 'undesirable social and legal consequences'. (*Bonfanti Industries Inc v Teke Inc.*) We interpret this conclusion as indicating Louisiana's policy to protect negligent resident tortfeasors acting within Louisiana's borders from the financial hardships caused by the assessment of excessive legal liability or exaggerated claims resulting from the loss of services of a key employee. Clearly the present defendant is a member of the class which Louisiana law seeks to protect, since defendant is a Louisiana 'resident' whose negligence on its own premises has caused the injury in question. Thus Louisiana's interest in the application of its law to the present case is evident: negation of plaintiff's cause of action serves Louisiana's policy of avoidance of extended financial hardship to the negligent defendant.

Nevertheless, we recognise as equally clear the fact that application of California law to the present case will further California's interest. California, through section 49, expresses an interest in protecting California employers from economic harm because of negligent injury to a key employee inflicted by a third party. Moreover, California's policy of protection extends beyond such an injury inflicted within California, since California's economy and tax revenues are affected regardless of the situs of physical injury. Thus, California is interested in applying its law in the present case to plaintiff Offshore, a California corporate employer that suffered injury in Louisiana by the loss of the services of its key employee.

Hence this case involves a true conflict between the law of Louisiana and the law of California. In *Bernhard v Harrah's Club* we described the proper resolution of such a case. We rejected the notion that in a situation of true conflict the law of the forum should always be applied. Instead, as we stated, 'Once [a] preliminary analysis has identified a true conflict of the governmental interests involved as applied to the parties under the particular circumstances of the case, the "comparative impairment" approach to the resolution of such conflict seeks to determine which state's interest would be more impaired if its policy were subordinated to the policy of the other state. This analysis proceeds on the principle that true conflicts should be resolved by applying the law of the state whose interest would be the more impaired if its law were not applied.'

As Professor Horowitz has explained, this analysis does not involve the court in 'weighing' the conflicting governmental interests 'in the sense of determining which conflicting law manifest[s] the "better" or the "worthier" social policy on the specific issue. An attempted balancing of conflicting state

10 Kay 'Comments on *Reich v Purcell*' (1968) 15 UCLA L Rev 584, 585.
11 546 P 2d 719, 722 (1976).

policies in that sense . . . is difficult to justify in the context of a federal system in which, within constitutional limits, states are empowered to mold their policies as they wish'.[12]

Rather, the resolution of true conflict cases may be described as 'essentially a process of allocating respective spheres of lawmaking influence.'[13] The process of allocation demands several inquiries. First, while '[i]t is not always possible to say fairly whether [the] policy [underlying a state's law] is one that was much more *strongly held* in the past than it is now, . . . this ground of analysis should not be ignored'.[14]

The current status of a statute is an important factor to be considered in a determination of comparative impairment: the policy underlying a jurisdiction's law may be deemed 'attenuated and anachronistic and properly . . . be limited to domestic occurrences in the event of [a multistate] clash of interests'.[15] Moreover, a particular statute may be an antique not only in comparison to the laws of the federal union, but also as compared with other laws of the state of its enactment. Such a statute may be infrequently enforced or interpreted even within its own jurisdiction, and, as an anachronism in that sense, should have a limited application in a conflicts case.

Another chief criterion in the comparative impairment analysis is the 'maximum attainment of underlying purpose by all governmental entities. This necessitates identifying the focal point of concern of the contending lawmaking groups and ascertaining the *comparative pertinence* of that concern to the immediate case'.[16] The policy underlying a statute may be less 'comparatively pertinent' if the original object of the statute is no longer of pressing importance: a statute which was once intended to remedy a matter of grave public concern may since have fallen in significance to the periphery of the state's laws. As Professor Currie observed in another context, 'If the truth were known, it would probably be that [those few states which have retained the archaic law of abatement have done so] simply because of the proverbial inertia of legal institutions, and that no real policy is involved.'[17]

Moreover, the policy underlying a statute may also be less 'comparatively pertinent' if the same policy may easily be satisfied by some means other than enforcement of the statute itself. Insurance, for example, may satisfy the underlying purpose of a statute originally intended to provide compensation to tort victims. The fact that parties may reasonably be expected to plan their transactions with insurance in mind may therefore constitute a relevant element in the resolution of a true conflict.

In sum, the comparative impairment approach to the resolution of true conflicts attempts to determine the relative commitment of the respective states to the laws involved. The approach incorporates several factors for consideration: the history and current status of the states' laws; the function and purpose of those laws.

12 Horowitz 'The Law of Choice of Law in California: A Restatement' (1974) 21 UCLA L Rev 719, 753.
13 Baxter 'Choice of Law and the Federal System' (1963) 16 Stan L Rev 1, 11–12.
14 Von Mehren and Trautman *The Law of Multistate Problems* (1965) p 377 (emphasis added).
15 Freund 'Chief Justice Stone and the Conflict of Laws' (1946) 59 Harv L Rev 1210, 1224.
16 Baxter 'Choice of Law and the Federal System' (1963) 16 Stan L Rev 1, 12 (emphasis added).
17 Currie *Selected Essays on the Conflict of Laws* p 143.

Applying the comparative impairment analysis to the present case, we first probe the history and current status of the laws before us. The majority of common law states that have considered the matter do not sanction actions for harm to business employees, recognising that even if injury to the master-servant relationship were at one time the basis for an action at common law, the radical change in the nature of that relationship since medieval times nullifies any right by a modern corporate employer to recover for negligent injury to his employees. With the decision in *Bonfanti Industries Inc v Teke Inc* discarding the obsolete concept of recovery for loss of a servant's services, the Louisiana courts have thus joined the 'main stream' of American jurisdictions: Louisiana law accords with the common law's consistent refusal generally to recognise a cause of action based on negligent, as opposed to intentional, conduct which interferes with the performance of a contract between third parties or renders its performance more expensive or burdensome.

Indeed California has itself exhibited little concern in applying section 49 to the employer-employee relationship: despite the provisions of the antique statute, no California court has heretofore squarely held that California law provides an action for harm to business employees, and no California court has recently considered the issue at all. If, as we have assumed, section 49 does provide an action for harm to key corporate employees, in Professor Freund's words the section constitutes a law 'archaic and isolated in the context of the laws of the federal union'. We therefore conclude that the trial judge in the present case correctly applied Louisiana, rather than California, law, since California's interest in the application of its unusual and outmoded statute is comparatively less strong than Louisiana's corollary interest, so lately expressed, in its 'prevalent and progressive' law.

We have explained that Louisiana law precludes a corporate employer from stating a cause of action for losses caused by negligent injuries to a key employee. We have assumed for the purposes of the present case that California law grants a cause of action for such injuries, and thus directly conflicts with the law of Louisiana. Upon examination of the nature and purpose of the states' respective laws, however, we have determined that the California statute has historically been of minimal importance in the fabric of California law, and that the Louisiana courts have recently interpreted their analogous Louisiana statute narrowly in light of that statute's obsolescence. We do not believe that California's interests in the application of its law to the present case are so compelling as to prevent an accommodation to the stronger, more current interest of Louisiana. We conclude therefore that Louisiana's interests would be the more impaired if its law were not applied, and consequently that Louisiana law governs the present case. Since the law of Louisiana provides no cause of action for the present plaintiff, we hold that the trial court correctly dismissed plaintiff's cause of action.

Section D: Principles of preference

Cavers, The Choice of Law Process (1965), pp 139, 146, 159, 166, 177, 181, 194

1. Where the liability laws of the state of injury set a *higher* standard of conduct or of financial protection against injury than do the laws of the state where the person causing the injury has acted or had his home, the laws of the state of injury should determine the standard and the protection applicable to the case, at least where the person injured was not so related to the person causing the injury that the question should be relegated to the law governing their relationship.

2. Where the liability laws of the state in which the defendant acted and caused an injury set a *lower* standard of conduct or of financial protection than do the laws of the home state of the person suffering the injury, the laws of the state of conduct and injury should determine the standard of conduct or protection applicable to the case, at least where the person injured was not so related to the person causing the injury that the question should be relegated to the law governing the relationship.

3. Where the state in which a defendant acted has established special controls, including the sanction of civil liability, over conduct of the kind in which the defendant was engaged when he caused a foreseeable injury to the plaintiff in another state, the plaintiff, though having no relationship to defendant, should be accorded the benefit of the special standards of conduct and of financial protection in the state of the defendant's conduct, even though the state of injury had imposed no such controls or sanctions.

4. Where the law of a state in which a relationship has its seat has imposed a standard of conduct or of financial protection on one party to that relationship for the benefit of the other party which is *higher* than the like standard imposed by the state of injury, the law of the former state should determine the standard of conduct or of financial protection applicable to the case for the benefit of the party protected by that state's law.

5. Where the law of a state in which a relationship has its seat has imposed a standard of conduct or of financial protection on one party to that relationship for the benefit of the other party which was *lower* than the standards imposed by the state of injury, the law of the former state should determine the standard of conduct or financial protection applicable to the case for the benefit of the party whose liability that state's law would deny or limit.

6. Where, for the purpose of providing protection from the adverse consequences of incompetence, heedlessness, ignorance, or unequal bargaining power, the law of a state has imposed restrictions on the power to contract or to convey or encumber property, its protective provisions should be applied against a party to the restricted transaction where (a) the person protected has a home in the state (if the law's purpose were to protect the person) and (b) the affected transaction or protected property interest were centered there or, (c) if it were not, this was due to facts that were fortuitous or had been manipulated to evade the protective law.

7. If the express (or reasonably inferable) intention of the parties to a transaction involving two or more states is that the law of a particular state which is reasonably related to the transaction should be applied to it, the law of that state should be applied if it allows the transaction to be carried out, even though neither party has a home in the state and the transaction is not centered there. However, this principle does not apply if the transaction runs counter to any protective law that the preceding principle would render applicable or if the transaction includes a conveyance of land and the mode

of conveyance or the interests created run counter to applicable mandatory rules of the situs of the land. This principle does not govern the legal effect of the transaction on third parties with independent interests.

Neumeier v Kuehner 286 NE 2d 454 (1972) (New York Court of Appeals)

Fuld, Chief Judge: A domiciliary of Ontario, Canada, was killed when the automobile in which he was riding, owned and driven by a New York resident, collided with a train in Ontario. That jurisdiction has a guest statute, and the primary question posed by this appeal is whether in this action brought by the Ontario passenger's estate, Ontario law should be applied and the New York defendant permitted to rely on its guest statute as a defense.

The facts are quickly told. On 7 May 1969, Arthur Kuehner, the defendant's intestate, a resident of Buffalo, drove his automobile from that city to Fort Erie in the Province of Ontario, Canada, where he picked up Amie Neumeier, who lived in that town with his wife and their children. Their trip was to take them to Long Beach, also in Ontario, and back again to Neumeier's home in Fort Erie. However, at a railroad crossing in the Town of Sherkston—on the way to Long Beach—the auto was struck by a train of the defendant Canadian National Railway Company. Both Kuehner and his guest-passenger were instantly killed.

Neumeier's wife and administratrix, a citizen of Canada and a domiciliary of Ontario, thereupon commenced this wrongful death action in New York against both Kuehner's estate and the Canadian National Railway Company. The defendant estate pleaded, as an affirmative defense, the Ontario guest statute and the defendant railway also interposed defenses in reliance upon it. In substance, the statute provides that the owner or driver of a motor vehicle is not liable for damages resulting from injury to, or the death of, a guest-passenger unless he was guilty of gross negligence (Highway Traffic Act of Province of Ontario).[18] It is worth noting, at this point, that, although our court originally considered that the sole purpose of the Ontario statute was to protect Ontario defendants and their insurers against collusive claims (see *Babcock v Jackson*).[19] 'Further research . . . has revealed the distinct possibility that one purpose, and perhaps the only purpose, of the statute was to protect owners and drivers against ungrateful guests.'[20]

The plaintiff, asserting that the Ontario statute 'is not available . . . in the present action', moved to dismiss the affirmative defenses pleaded. The court at Special Term, holding the guest statute applicable, denied the motions but, on appeal, a closely divided Appellate Division reversed and directed dismissal of the defenses. It was the court's belief that this result was dictated by *Tooker v Lopez*.[1]

In reaching that conclusion, the Appellate Division misread our decision

---

18 RSO 1960, c 172, s 105 (2) (as amended by statute of 1966, c 64, s 20 (2)). This s was repealed by the Highway Traffic Amendment Act 1977, s 16 (1) *(Ed)*.

19 191 NE 2d 279, 283–284 (1963), p 501 above.

20 Reese 'Chief Judge Fuld and Choice of Law' 71 Col L Rev 548, 558; see Trautman 'Two Views on *Kell v Henderson:* A Comment' 67 Col L Rev 465, 469.

1 249 NE 2d 394 (1969).

in the *Tooker* case—a not unnatural result in light of the variant views expressed in the three separate opinions written on behalf of the majority. It is important to bear in mind that in *Tooker*, the guest-passenger and the host-driver were both domiciled in New York, and our decision—that New York law was controlling—was based upon, and limited to, that fact situation. Indeed, two of the three judges who wrote for reversal—Judge Keating and Judge Burke—expressly noted that the determination then being made left open the question whether New York law would be applicable if the plaintiff passenger happened to be a domiciliary of the very jurisdiction which had a guest statute. Thus, *Tooker v Lopez* did no more than hold that, when the passenger and driver are residents of the same jurisdiction and the car is there registered and insured, its law, and not the law of the place of accident, controls and determines the standard of care which the host owes to his guest.

What significantly and effectively differentiates the present case is the fact that, although the host was a domiciliary of New York, the guest, for whose death recovery is sought, was domiciled in Ontario, the place of accident and the very jurisdiction which had enacted the statute designed to protect the host from liability for ordinary negligence. It is clear that although New York has a deep interest in protecting its own residents, injured in a foreign state, against unfair or anachronistic statutes of that state, it has no legitimate interest in ignoring the public policy of a foreign jurisdiction—such as Ontario—and in protecting the plaintiff guest domiciled and injured there from legislation obviously addressed, at the very least, to a resident riding in a vehicle traveling within its borders.

To distinguish *Tooker* on such a basis is not improperly discriminatory. It is quite true that, in applying the Ontario guest statute to the Ontario-domiciled passenger, we, in a sense, extend a right less generous than New York extends to a New York passenger in a New York vehicle with New York insurance. That, though, is not a consequence of invidious discrimination; it is, rather, the result of the existence of disparate rules of law in jurisdictions that have diverse and important connections with the litigants and the litigated issue.

The fact that insurance policies issued in this state on New York-based vehicles cover liability, regardless of the place of the accident, certainly does not call for the application of internal New York law in this case. The compulsory insurance requirement is designed to *cover* a car-owner's liability, not *create* it; in other words, the applicable statute was not intended to impose liability where none would otherwise exist. This being so, we may not properly look to the New York insurance requirement to dictate a choice-of-law rule which would invariably impose liability. We must observe that Judge Keating's statement in *Tooker*, that the legislature 'has evinced commendable concern not only for the residents of this state, but residents of other states who may be injured as a result of the activities of New York residents' was in the context, not of proving that New York had a governmental interest in overriding foreign rules of liability, but of demonstrating that it was immaterial in that case that the driver and passenger, while domiciliaries of New York, were attending college in Michigan. While New York may be a proper forum for actions involving its own domiciliaries, regardless of where the accident happened, it does not follow that we should apply New York law simply because some may think it is a better rule, where doing so does not advance any New York State interest, nor the interest of any New York State domiciliary.

When, in *Babcock v Jackson*, we rejected the mechanical place of injury rule in personal injury cases because it failed to take account of underlying policy considerations, we were willing to sacrifice the certainty provided by the old rule for the more just, fair and practical result that may best be achieved by giving controlling effect to the law of the jurisdiction which has the greatest concern with, or interest in, the specific issue raised in the litigation. (See, also, *Tooker v Lopez*.) In consequence of the change effected—and this was to be anticipated—our decisions in multistate highway accident cases, particularly in those involving guest-host controversies, have, it must be acknowledged, lacked consistency. This stemmed, in part, from the circumstance that it is frequently difficult to discover the purposes or policies underlying the relevant local law rules of the respective jurisdictions involved. It is even more difficult, assuming that these purposes or policies are found to conflict, to determine on some principled basis which should be given effect at the expense of the others.

The single all-encompassing rule which called, inexorably, for selection of the law of the place of injury was discarded, and wisely, because it was too broad to prove satisfactory in application. There is, however, no reason why choice-of-law rules, more narrow than those previously devised, should not be successfully developed, in order to assure a greater degree of predictability and uniformity, on the basis of our present knowledge and experience. 'The time has come', I wrote in *Tooker*, 'to endeavor to minimise what some have characterised as an ad hoc case-by-case approach by laying down guidelines, as well as we can, for the solution of guest-host conflicts problems.' *Babcock* and its progeny enable us to formulate a set of basic principles that may be profitably utilised, for they have helped us uncover the underlying values and policies which are operative in this area of the law. To quote again from the concurring opinion in *Tooker*, 'Now that these values and policies have been revealed, we may proceed to the next stage in the evolution of the law—the formulation of a few rules of general applicability, promising a fair level of predictability'. Although it was recognised that no rule may be formulated to guarantee a satisfactory result in every case, the following principles were proposed as sound for situations involving guest statutes in conflicts settings:

'1. When the guest-passenger and the host-driver are domiciled in the same state, and the car is there registered, the law of that state should control and determine the standard of care which the host owes to his guest.

2. When the driver's conduct occurred in the state of his domicile and that state does not cast him in liability for that conduct, he should not be held liable by reason of the fact that liability would be imposed upon him under the tort law of the state of the victim's domicile. Conversely, when the guest was injured in the state of his own domicile and its law permits recovery, the driver who has come into that state should not—in the absence of special circumstances—be permitted to interpose the law of his state as a defense.

3. In other situations, when the passenger and the driver are domiciled in different states, the rule is necessarily less categorical.

Normally, the applicable rule of decision will be that of the state where the accident occurred but not if it can be shown that displacing that normally applicable rule will advance the relevant substantive law's purposes without impairing the smooth working of the multistate system or producing great uncertainty for litigants.'

The variant views expressed not only in *Tooker* but by Special Term and the divided Appellate Division in this litigation underscore and confirm the need for these rules. Since the passenger was domiciled in Ontario and the driver in New York, the present case is covered by the third stated principle. The law to be applied is that of the jurisdiction where the accident happened unless it appears that 'displacing [the] normally applicable rule will advance the relevant substantive law purposes' of the jurisdictions involved. Certainly, ignoring Ontario's policy requiring proof of gross negligence in a case which involves an Ontario-domiciled guest at the expense of a New Yorker does not further the substantive law purposes of New York. In point of fact, application of New York law would result in the exposure of this state's domiciliaries to a greater liability than that imposed upon resident users of Ontario's highways. Conversely, the failure to apply Ontario's law would 'impair'—to cull from the rule set out above—'the smooth working of the multistate system [and] produce great uncertainty for litigants' by sanctioning forum shopping and thereby allowing a party to select a forum which could give him a larger recovery than the court of his own domicile. In short, the plaintiff has failed to show that this state's connection with the controversy was sufficient to justify displacing the rule of lex loci delicti.

(Breitel J gave a concurring opinion with which Jasen J agreed. Burke, Scileppi and Gibson JJ concurred with Fuld CJ. Bagen J dissented.)

First National Bank in Fort Collins v Rostek 514 P 2d 314 (1973)
(Supreme Court of Colorado)

Mr and Mrs Rostek were killed in a plane accident. Mr Rostek was the pilot and his wife the guest-passenger in the plane. The plaintiff bank acted as the guardian of Mrs Rostek's children. The defendant was the administratrix of Mr Rostek's estate. Both Mr and Mrs Rostek were citizens and residents of Colorado, as were the children. The couple had flown on a business trip from Colorado to South Dakota where the accident occurred. The trial judge applied the law of South Dakota to the claim on the ground that, under Colorado choice of law rules, the issue was governed by the lex loci delicti. A South Dakota guest statute required proof of wilful or wanton misconduct on the part of an operator of an aircraft. Leave to appeal to the Supreme Court of Colorado was given on the issue of whether the Colorado courts were compelled to apply the lex loci delicti in the circumstances of this case.

Pringle CJ (who gave the judgment of the court): A brief review of Colorado case law convinces us that the issue presented in this case has in reality never been previously decided by this court, and that the doctrine of lex loci delicti appears in Colorado law more by default than by design.

This court in effect has not previously been confronted with the issue of the propriety and the justice of the doctrine of lex loci delicti, nor has this court previously held that such a broad rule unfailingly applies in all multistate controversies. We conclude, therefore, that stare decisis does not compel this court to apply the rule of lex loci delicti without regard to the facts and circumstances in the particular case. Instead, this court must decide, as a matter of first impression, whether the broad rule of lex loci delicti should be adopted and applied to this case, or whether a more flexible choice of law rule should control.

When the doctrine of lex loci delicti was first established in the mid-nineteenth century, conditions were such that people only occasionally crossed state boundaries. Under those circumstances, there was legitimacy in a rule which presumed that persons changing jurisdictions would be aware of the different duties and obligations they were incurring when they made the interstate journey. Further, even if persons making these occasional journeys into neighboring states were not actually aware of the changing duties and responsibilities, enforcing the laws of the jurisdiction in which they were wronged was justified because of the 'vested rights' doctrine that was prevalent and widely accepted at that time. Thus, the rule of lex loci delicti was originally viewed as a practical formula by which individuals could govern their actions in accordance with prevailing attitudes and customs, providing both uniformity of application and predictability of results.

However, with the industrial revolution and the passage of time, the interstate mobility of the citizenry increased in speed and availability to such an extent that persons no longer regarded an interstate journey as a rare occurrence entailing a significant change of surroundings. As these attitudes and conditions changed, it became clear that the mechanical application of lex loci delicti to every multistate tort controversy often yielded harsh, unjust results, unrelated to the contemporary interests of the states involved or the realistic expectations of the parties.

To avoid the growing number of undesirable results which strict adherence to lex loci delicti produced, courts devised various methods of characterising the issues in the controversy to allow them to deviate from the application of lex loci delicti without offending stare decisis. By labeling a matter as 'procedural' rather than 'substantive', or 'contractual' rather than 'tortious', courts were able to apply a law other than the law of the place of the wrong. In the process the courts were, in effect, making a choice of law decision without exposing the real choice influencing factors for objective classification and criticism. This constant search for a result which would comport with reason and justice made it evident by the mid-twentieth century that the doctrine of lex loci delicti no longer provided the high degree of predictability and uniformity which were considered its primary virtues.

The questionable viability of the lex loci delicti rule in today's society has been recognised by courts and commentators alike. In the last ten years, while several states have retained adherence to the broad lex loci delicti rule, a greater number of jurisdictions have abandoned or rejected lex loci delicti in favor of a more flexible and rational choice of law approach in multistate tort cases. The majority of those cases rejecting the lex loci delicti rule have involved the application of host-guest statutes or the question of interspousal liability for injuries received in automobile or airplane accidents. Additionally, the overwhelming majority of commentators are opposed to the mechanical application of the place of wrong rule, largely for the reasons previously discussed.

The rationale of the cases rejecting lex loci delicti, the views of eminent authorities in the field of tort law, and our own observations and experience convince us a more flexible and rational approach than lex loci delicti affords is necessary. We fully appreciate the arguments made by the defendant that lex loci delicti retains some predictability of result and ease of application by courts. Yet, the facts in the case at bar classically demonstrate the injustice and irrationality of the automatic application of the lex loci delicti rule. Both Carol and John Rostek were citizens of Colorado. The airplane in question was registered in Colorado and was returning to Colorado when the accident occurred. The lawsuit was brought in a Colorado forum with a Colorado resident as defendant. It becomes evident, therefore, that South Dakota's only interest in this controversy is the fortuitous occurrence of the accident within its borders. Thus the trial court's decision to apply South Dakota law to this case can be affirmed only if we are to adhere to a mechanical and unfailing application of the place of wrong rule, regardless of the interests of the states involved or the expectations of the parties. This we refuse to do.

Although most courts and commentators are united in their opposition to the use of the general lex loci delicti rule, there is disagreement as to which approach should be adopted. Some would emphasise the law of the place of the forum, while others would place more emphasis on the expectations of the parties. Still others stress the need to consider the interests of the various governmental entities involved. All of the generally accepted approaches, however, suffer from a similar defect; namely, they are all 'approaches', to be applied in a more or less ad hoc fashion, and containing indeterminate language with no concrete guidelines. Thus, quite naturally, these approaches have exhibited a certain lack of both predictability of result and uniformity of application. This situation cannot be completely disregarded. While we recognise that a rational and equitable approach to choice of law is desirable, we now harmonise that approach with the genius of the common law which always sought to provide to its consumers some degree of predictability and consistency in application. As we have said, accidents occurring in states not the domicile of all of the parties are commonplace in today's society. The law should not deal with them as if they were rare and exotic hypotheticals, to be solved by exercises in intellectual gamesmanship. The events in this case, and their probable reoccurrence, are real world concerns, and the law in this area should provide a concrete and viable system for the equal application of just laws.

Because of the lack of consistency and predictability exhibited by various proposed choice of law 'approaches', the principal question in choice of law today is whether or not to adopt rational choice of law 'rules', or to deal with each case as it comes to us on an ad hoc basis. Rules are employed in most areas of the law because they provide the benefits of certainty and predictability. To some extent the existence of a rule in any area of the law serves the ends of justice since it furnishes the juridical machinery by which like situations are equally adjudged. In short, rules are one of the laws' attributes, and fulfill an essential function of concrete justice.

Thus, in order to provide some predictability of result and uniformity of application, this court turns to the adoption of some rules dealing with choice of law. In so doing, we begin with the particular issue presented in this case, namely, the application of a guest statute to a host-guest controversy. We consider this issue a narrow one, occurring with enough frequency and repetitiveness to enable us to extract specific guidelines that will satisfactorily regulate this issue.

Our search for a workable choice of law rule in the guest-host area leads to the majority opinion in *Neumeier v Kuehner*[2] written by Chief Judge Fuld. In *Neumeier* the court was faced with a guest-host accident situation involving a citizen of Canada and a resident of New York. Judge Fuld admitted that the recent choice of law 'approach' in guest-host controversies, initiated in *Babcock v Jackson*[3], had, until *Neumeier*, lacked consistency. The New York court then proceeded to formulate a specific rule governing the application of guest statutes in multistate tort controversies. This rule generally embodies the rational underpinnings of the newer approaches to choice of law problems, emphasising the expectations of the parties and the interests of the different jurisdictions involved. We are persuaded that it is just and equitable and ought to be accepted in Colorado with respect to the first two sections thereof and we now do so. As stated by the New York court, those sections provide:

'1. When the guest-passenger and the host-driver are domiciled in the same state, and the [vehicle] is there registered, the law of that state should control and determine the standard of care which the host owes to his guest.

2. When the driver's conduct occurred in the state of his domicile and that state does not cast him in liability for that conduct, he should not be held liable by reason of the fact that liability would be imposed upon him under the tort law of the state of the victim's domicile. Conversely, when the guest was injured in the state of his own domicile and its law permits recovery, the driver who has come into that state should not—in the absence of special circumstances—be permitted to interpose the law of his state as a defense.'

We must now apply the aforementioned choice of law rule to determine if the South Dakota guest statute should be applied to the case at bar. Both the guest-passenger and the host-pilot were domiciled and residing in Colorado, and the airplane was registered in Colorado. Thus, the facts in this case are governed by the first statement of the rule. Under this statement, the rights and liabilities of the parties are governed by the law of the place of domicile which in this case is Colorado. Accordingly, South Dakota law, including its Airplane Guest Statute, is not the appropriate law to apply under this new rule. We recognise that this case is a comparatively easy one and in cases like it the result will hereafter be reasonably easy for lawyers and judges to reach. Admittedly, there will be harder cases, more difficult to decide even under the narrow host-guest *rule*. However, we believe that the application of this rule promises a fair level of predictability and uniformity in the application of a rational and modern set of choice of law considerations.

Since the scope of our decision to reject the mechanical application of the rule of lex loci delicti extends to all multistate tort controversies, we must now address ourselves to the question of what rules govern choice of law in Colorado outside the rules laid down with respect to host-guest controversies which fit those rules. We announce that Colorado will adopt the general rule

2 286 NE 2d 454 (1972), p 721 above.
3 191 NE 2d 279 (1963), p 501 above.

of applying the law of the state with the most 'significant relationship' with
the occurrence and the parties, as presented and defined in the Restatement,
(Second) Conflict of Laws, Vol 1, Sec 145 (1969). Generally, the
Restatement requires the application of separate rules to various kinds of
torts, and defines 'significant contacts' in terms of the issues, the nature of the
tort, and the purposes of the tort rules involved. While this Restatement rule
is somewhat broad, it is no less precise than the concepts of 'reasonableness'
or 'due process' which courts have applied for many years. Hopefully, at
some time in the future, as the body of case law develops, we can lay down
more specific choice of law rules governing other areas, as we have done
today in the area of guest statutes. However, at present, in all areas of
multistate tort controversies other than those involving the situations we
have dealt with in the specific rules laid down today, we will use and apply
the rule articulated in Sec 145 of the Second Restatement on Conflict of
Laws.

Since Colorado law was the appropriate law to be applied to the issues in
this case, it was error for the trial court to grant respondent's summary
judgment motion on the grounds that South Dakota law barred the suit.

The judgment is reversed and the cause remanded to the trial court for
further proceeding not inconsistent with the views herein expressed.

Section E: Most Significant Relationship

Restatement, Conflict of Laws, Second, §145

§145.   *The General Principle*

(1) The rights and liabilities of the parties with respect to an issue in tort
are determined by the local law of the state which, with respect to that issue,
has the most significant relationship to the occurrence and the parties under
the principles stated in §6.

(2) Contacts to be taken into account in applying the principles of §6 to
determine the law applicable to an issue include:
(a) the place where the injury occurred,
(b) the place where the conduct causing the injury occurred,
(c) the domicil, residence, nationality, place of incorporation and place of
business of the parties, and
(d) the place where the relationship, if any, between the parties is centered.
These contacts are to be evaluated according to their relative importance
with respect to the particular issue.

Babcock v Jackson (p 501 above)

First National Bank in Fort Collins v Rostek (p 724 above)

Pancotto v Sociedade de Safaris de Mocambique SARL 422 F
Supp 405 (1976) (United States District Court, Northern District of Illinois)

The Pancotto family, who were domiciled in Illinois, visited Mozambique in
1973 on a safari holiday directed by the defendants. Mrs Pancotto, the

plaintiff, was injured whilst taking photographs when a swamp buggy driven by one of the defendants' employees ran into her. She claimed damages for her injuries. The defendants argued that the issues of liability and of assessment of damages should be governed by the law of Mozambique.

Marshall, District Judge: The plaintiff, Rosemary Pancotto, has brought this diversity action to recover damages for a personal injury she sustained in 1973 while on a hunting safari in Mozambique. Pending for decision is the motion of defendant Sociedade de Safaris de Mocambique (Safrique), to apply the law of Mozambique to the substantive issues in the action, and for a determination of the relevant Mozambique law. Under the rule of *Klaxon v Stentor Electric Mfg Co*,[4] a federal court sitting in diversity applies the conflicts law of the state in which it sits. Thus our task regarding the first part of defendant's motion is to determine and apply the Illinois choice of law rule.

Illinois modified its choice of law rules for tort cases in *Ingersoll v Klein*.[5] 'In our opinion, the local law of the state where the injury occurred should determine the rights and liabilities of the parties, unless Illinois has a more significant relationship with the occurrence and the parties, in which case, the law of Illinois should apply.'

The first step in the choice of law analysis is to isolate the substantive legal issues and determine whether the various states' tort rules conflict. If a potential conflict is discovered, the next step is to examine the contacts with the states, evaluating the importance of each contact in relation to the legal issues of the case. Finally, under the Illinois choice of law rule, the law of the state or country of the place of injury is followed, unless Illinois is more significantly interested in the resolution of a particular legal issue.

I. The Defendant's Liability

Defendant's motion identifies the two substantive legal issues to be addressed by this choice of law analysis, each of which will be considered in turn: (1) the defendant's liability; and (2) the appropriate measure of damages. A cursory look at the defendant's materials outlining Mozambique law indicates that the standard of care there was different from Illinois'. Briefly, the Mozambique standard of care upon which defendant relies was the 'diligence with which a law abiding male head of a family would act'. Portuguese Civil Code, art 487 (2). Although this standard of care bears an analytical similarity to Illinois' reasonable man standard, it may be more or less demanding of an alleged wrongdoer. This putative difference could lead to a different result if Mozambique rather than Illinois law is applied. Consequently, we are faced with a true conflict of laws and must evaluate the parties' contacts with the two states to determine which law should control.

Ingersoll refers us to what is now Restatement (Second) of Conflict of Laws §145 (1971), for a listing of the contacts to be evaluated in determining which jurisdiction is most significantly concerned with the liability of the alleged tortfeasor. The first of these is the place where the injury occurred. The parties do not dispute that plaintiff sustained her injuries in Mozambique.

4 313 US 487 (1941).
5 262 NE 2d 593 (1970).

The place of injury has an interest in applying its own tort principles to discourage harmful behavior within its borders. This interest in controlling the tortfeasor's conduct is strongest when the alleged tort is intentional. If the harmful contact is unintentional, however, the interest of the place of injury is attenuated. Realistically, the negligent tortfeasor is not affected by a state's civil liability laws because he does not premeditate before he acts. Nonetheless, to the extent that such conduct is shaped by legal standards, Mozambique was, at the time of the alleged wrong, interested in the choice of the standard of care to be imposed upon the defendant.

The second contact listed in the Restatement is the place of the conduct which caused injury, which is again clearly Mozambique. The interest of the jurisdiction where the conduct occurred is similar if not identical to that of the place of injury. Again, however, Mozambique's valid interest in controlling harmful conduct assumes less importance when the alleged tortfeasor was not governed by conscious reference to a behavioral standard.

The Restatement's third contact is the domicile or place of business of the parties. This consideration refers us to both Illinois law and that of Mozambique. The plaintiff's domicile, Illinois, is interested in compensating both the victim and her creditors. Mozambique, on the other hand, as the defendant's domicile and principal place of business, is concerned that defendant's conduct conforms to its standards, and may also have an interest in insulating a domiciliary from liability.

The Restatement's final contact point is the place where the parties' relationship is centered. The relationship here has an international flavor. The safari was arranged in large part by intercontinental telephone calls and cables. In addition, certain employees of the defendant visited the plaintiff's husband in Illinois approximately three times prior to the safari, although the parties dispute the business as opposed to personal significance of the visits. Regardless of the nature of the Illinois contacts, they obviously were preparatory to an extended, well-planned interaction in Mozambique. Plaintiff's ultimate presence in that country was hardly fortuitous. In short, although the relationship had international aspects, it can fairly be characterised as centering in Mozambique.

These contacts and the state interests evoked by them indicate that both Illinois and Mozambique are interested in the resolution of the liability issue. Both jurisdictions' interests are significant. The numerous Mozambique contacts highlight that government's interest in controlling the conduct of those who take action within its borders, and the interest in affording the protection of its laws to its domiciliaries. Illinois, on the other hand, has a strong interest in seeing that its residents are adequately compensated for tortious injuries. The Illinois interest, although based upon a single contact, cannot for that reason be automatically dismissed as less significant. A contact assumes significance only in view of the legal issue to which it relates. Our evaluation of the contacts indicates that both Illinois and Mozambique are validly interested in the resolution of the issue of defendant's liability, and we hesitate to characterise either jurisdiction's interest as more significant.

In general, the Illinois courts have chosen their own law rather than the law of the place of injury only if the majority of the significant contacts were in Illinois, and the tort's occurrence in the foreign state was fortuitous. Given that both states here may assert significant although distinct interests in the outcome of the liability issue, the Illinois choice of law rule directs the application of the law of the place of injury, Mozambique.

(The judge concluded that further evidence was required on the standard of liability under Mozambique law.)

II. The Measure of Damages

A brief look at Mozambique's and Illinois' laws on recoverable damages reveals an acute conflict. Illinois permits recovery for medical expenses due to the injury, and, inter alia, compensation for the injury itself, for disfigurement, and for pain and suffering. In contrast, art 508 of the Portuguese Civil Code limits liability for travel accidents to 600 contos, or approximately $6,600 in United States dollars. This limit is not inflexible, however. A Mozambique court may apparently, in its discretion, award damages to the full extent of the plaintiff's out-of-pocket loss, although the typical recovery is less generous. And, under Mozambique law, the plaintiff recovers nothing for pain and suffering, disfigurement, or loss of enjoyment of life as she might under Illinois law.

The defendant argues that the Illinois choice of law rule dictates the application of Mozambique law to this issue also. And, in fact, the analysis of the two jurisdictions' interests in the measure of damages leads to such a result. As the place of conduct, injury, defendant's domicile, and the place where the parties' relationship centered, Mozambique has a strong interest in the resolution of this issue. As plaintiff's domicile and the place where the consequences of the injury are felt, Illinois is concerned that plaintiff receives compensation. Plaintiff, however, contends that the application of Mozambique's damage limitation would be so grossly repugnant to Illinois' public and constitutional policy of providing a remedy for all injuries that an Illinois court would refuse to follow Mozambique law, even if the *Ingersoll* rule would normally dictate its application. . . .

In conclusion, although the Illinois choice of law rule indicates the application of Mozambique's law to the substantive issues in this action, we feel the Illinois courts would refuse to enforce the Mozambique policy of not providing a remedy for personal injuries. Foreign substantive law is not unenforceable simply because it differs from our own law, but because the differences are against public policy. The refusal to enforce a foreign law should not be lightly made. But when no justification is offered for a policy which contravenes a sound public policy of the forum, and the defendant is not unfairly surprised, we believe that the Illinois courts would decline to apply the foreign limitation.

Section F. Choice Influencing Considerations

Leflar, American Conflicts Law (3rd edn, 1977) pp 193–195*

§96. Choice-Influencing Considerations. The list of five choice-influencing considerations,[6] proposed some years ago by the present author as a

---

6 Leflar 'Choice-Influencing Considerations in Conflicts Law' 41 NYU L Rev 267 (1966); Leflar 'Conflicts Law: More on Choice-Influencing Considerations' 54 Cal L Rev 1584 (1966).

* Extract reproduced by kind permission of The Michie Company, Charlottesville, Virginia.

practical working basis for choice-of-law decisions, has been employed in a number of states. It must be taken into account as a major element in the modern law of choice of law.

The considerations that influence choice of law have always been present and operative in the cases. They have not always been recognised, let alone clearly identified, nor has the weight given to one or another among them always been logical or sensible. That is a criticism that can be, and is, directed at today's choice-of-law decisions as well as at those handed down a half-century ago. Identification of the relevant choice-influencing considerations and attachment of appropriate significance to each of them is a task that will have to be worked at indefinitely, with little prospect of complete agreement among either judges or commentators.

An article by Cheatham and Reese[7] in 1952 was the first thorough effort to list and analyse all the choice-influencing considerations. The American Law Institute's *Restatement (Second)* makes frequent reference to the Cheatham-Reese list of nine 'policies'[8] as explanations of black-letter rules. . . . Professor Ehrenzweig throughout his writings pointed out and relied upon choice-influencing factors as he identified and weighed them. He saw considerations that had not been noted by others, and he was willing to apply them in more detail to a wider variety of fact situations than have others. Professor Brainerd Currie, on the other hand, deliberately narrowed and thinned out the list of choice-influencing considerations. Simplicity of rule and ease of judicial administration were the prime considerations underlying Currie's system[9] just as with Beale's system, though for different reasons. Beale would have recognised the validity of almost every choice-influencing consideration that can be reasonably urged today, but he concluded that the virtues supporting his conceptually logical rules were the most worthy ones. Contrariwise, Currie said that many of the considerations that are asserted today ought not to be taken into account at all by the courts. He regarded these considerations as matters of 'policy' or 'politics' that are outside the proper ken of courts, that should be left for legislatures to pass upon. Under his system the overt weighing of choice-influencing considerations would be kept to a minimum, though it was inevitable that the considerations would have a part in any process by means of which 'governmental interests' were territorially assigned.

The relevant choice-influencing considerations had to be reduced to manageable number and identity if they were to be used as a practical basis for actual decision in choice-of-law cases. The availability of a long catalog of policy factors is not of much help to lawyers and judges working on specific cases. The considerations had to be restated and defined with particularity, and brevity, before they could be used as a realistic test of the rightness of choice-of-law rules and decisions.

Some of the policy factors named by Cheatham and Reese and by others appear in or affect more than one of the ultimately listed considerations. There is some contradiction within them, because all the opposing values must be included in the restated list of considerations. Testing of rules or decisions under such a set of standards is a qualitative process of evaluation,

7 Cheatham and Reese 'Choice of the Applicable Law' 52 Col L Rev 959 (1952).
8 See *Restatement (Second) of Conflict of Laws* §6 (1971); p 733 below.
9 See Currie *Selected Essays on the Conflict of Laws* (1963) pp 285, 476–77, 580 n, 213, 614, 700.

and there is room for difference of opinion in it. That is inherent in the nature of conflicts problems; solutions to them should usually not be mechanical, though the relevant considerations should include an indication of when mechanical rules are appropriate.

Standards expressed in these terms usually justify choice-of-law rules that apply to categories of cases, so that reexamination of the considerations will not be required for every case that comes along, though oftentimes uniqueness or divergencies of fact or law will make such standardised generalisations improper. Such inexactness is not new in conflicts law, and an effort to eliminate it would be a step backward toward mechanical jurisprudence. The societal function of each area of law within which a conflicts case arises, as well as the locally conceived functions of the specific rules between which conflict exists, ought to be tied into the choice-of-law process. Identification and express employment of choice-influencing considerations can aid in achieving predictability for some types of transactions, but different values will be promoted for other types of transactions.

The effort to systematise and correlate the choice-influencing considerations produced a list of five, which seem to incorporate all that are in the longer lists:

(A) Predictability of results;
(B) Maintenance of interstate and international order;
(C) Simplification of the judicial task;
(D) Advancement of the forum's governmental interests;
(E) Application of the better rule of law.

No priority among the considerations is intended from the order of listing. Their relative importance varies according to the area of law involved. Some will be more important in one area of law, others in another. But all should be considered regardless of the area. This list of considerations, it has turned out, itself affords a manageable basis for judicial decision of specific choice-of-law cases.

Restatement, Conflict of Laws, Second, §6.

§6. *Choice-of-Law Principles*

(1) A court, subject to constitutional restrictions, will follow a statutory directive of its own state on choice of law.

(2) When there is no such directive, the factors relevant to the choice of the applicable rule of law include
(a) the needs of the interstate and international systems,
(b) the relevant policies of the forum,
(c) the relevant policies of other interested states and the relative interests of those states in the determination of the particular issue,
(d) the protection of justified expectations,
(e) the basic policies underlying the particular field of law,
(f)   certainty, predictability and uniformity of result, and
(g) ease in the determination and application of the law to be applied.

Turcotte v Ford Motor Co 494 F 2d 173 (1974) (United States Court of Appeals, First Circuit)

The plaintiff's son was killed in a road accident in Massachusetts. The car in which he was a passenger caught fire when hit by another car. The owner of the car, his son (the driver) and the deceased all came from Rhode Island. The car had been bought in Massachusetts and the driver of the other vehicle involved came from Massachusetts. It was claimed, in an action for damages against Ford, that the Ford Maverick car in which the deceased burnt to death would not have caught fire in the accident had it not been of a faulty design. The plaintiff succeeded at first instance and Ford appealed to the United States Court of Appeals, the only issue of concern here being the question whether Rhode Island law or Massachusetts law should be applied to this claim.[10]

McEntee, Circuit Judge (with whom Coffin CJ concurred and Moore J concurred in part and dissented in part):   The threshold issue is whether the trial court correctly decided that Rhode Island's wrongful death statute and its law on strict liability govern the instant case. Ford, a Delaware corporation, contends that Massachusetts law should have controlled. Applying the conflict of laws rules of Rhode Island, the forum state, see *Klaxon Co v Stentor Elec Mfg Co*,[11] we hold that Rhode Island law was properly invoked on both questions.

Rhode Island has abandoned the old lex loci delicti theory of conflict of laws, in which the law of the place of the tort governed, in favor of a modern 'interest-weighing' approach. The Supreme Court of Rhode Island has summarised the interests it will consider under this new approach in a five-point guideline:

(1)   Predictability of results.
(2)   Maintenance of interstate order.
(3)   Simplification of the judicial task.
(4)   Advancement of the forum's governmental interests.
(5)   Application of the better rule of law.

Woodward v Stewart.[12] We will consider these interests separately with respect to, first, the appropriate wrongful death statute and, second, the appropriate tort law.

Plaintiff brought this suit under the Rhode Island wrongful death statute,[13] which measures damages by a quasi-compensatory standard with no ceiling on recovery. In contrast, the Massachusetts wrongful death statute[14] measures damages by a purely punitive standard, ie, solely by the degree of defendant's culpability rather than plaintiff's actual loss. Also, at the time of this collision recovery was limited to $50,000. Application of the Massachusetts statute would thus preclude the $500,000 judgment entered for the plaintiff.

---

10 On the other issues in the case, the court upheld the finding of liability but ordered a new trial on the issue of damages.
11 313 US 487 (1941).
12 243 A 2d 917, 923 (1968).
13 Gen Laws of RI §10-7-1 (1956) as amended.
14 Mass Gen Laws Ann ch 229 §2 (Supp 1973).

Applying the Rhode Island interest-weighing approach to this conflict of laws, we find that the fourth factor listed above, advancement of the forum's governmental interests, strongly points towards the Rhode Island wrongful death statute as more appropriate in the instant case. Rhode Island's interest here is in seeing that plaintiff, its citizen, is adequately compensated for a wrongful death. While of course the forum has some interest in protecting its citizens in any situation, such interest is particularly compelling in a tort case involving substantial personal injury or death because failure there to provide adequate compensation could mean that the plaintiffs will later become burdens on the state. In the instant case, this Rhode Island interest would plainly be defeated if recovery were limited to $50,000 under the Massachusetts statute. The jury found actual loss of $500,000.

Moreover, consideration of Rhode Island's interest in maintaining interstate order does not indicate contrary application of the Massachusetts statute. Under this heading, Rhode Island courts inquire whether another state's law and policy would be 'offended' by application of Rhode Island law. See *Brown v Church of the Holy Name of Jesus*.[15] Ford is not a Massachusetts corporation. Therefore, Massachusetts does not have as immediate an interest in making available the $50,000 recovery limitation in its statute as it would if defendant were a Massachusetts citizen. Similarly, in view of the fact that the conduct allegedly causing the injury, the design of the Maverick, occurred outside of Massachusetts, the punitive aspect of the Massachusetts wrongful death statute is of marginal relevance here. On the other hand, Massachusetts may have an interest in protecting non-citizen businesses, such as Ford, from unlimited wrongful death liability as a means of encouraging these businesses to continue operating in the state, providing local jobs and tax revenues. We first note in response to this interest that the existence of unlimited wrongful death liability in Rhode Island has not deterred Ford from continuing to supply automobile dealerships in that state. But in any event, we find that the Massachusetts interest in encouraging non-citizen business enterprises is weak in the instant case when compared to the Rhode Island interest in protecting its citizens from uncompensated harm.

The remaining three interests considered under the Rhode Island conflicts approach are either inconclusive or point to Rhode Island's statute.[16]

---

15 252 A 2d 176, 180 (1969).

16 The first listed interest, predictability of results, refers to the commendable policy of enabling parties to know at the time they enter a transaction that it will produce the same set of socio-economic consequences regardless of where disputes occur. As applied to the instant case, this interest compels us to inquire whether Ford had a reasonable expectation when it transferred the Maverick to a Massachusetts dealership that a wrongful death action arising from alleged defects in the car would be brought under the Massachusetts statute and whether Ford planned the transaction accordingly. We cannot find that such reasonable expectation or planning existed. Under either the old lex loci delicti approach to conflicts law or the modern interest-weighing approach, it was at least as likely that actions arising from the design of a car sold to a Rhode Island resident would be brought under Rhode Island's statute as under Massachusetts' statute, even though such car was purchased in Massachusetts. Moreover, although Ford has not provided us with its insurance rate figures, we note that most interstate businesses calculate insurance rates on the assumption that there will be no state imposed ceilings on wrongful death recoveries, contrary to Massachusetts law.

The interests of simplification of the judicial task and application of the better rule of

Therefore, we hold that Rhode Island's wrongful death statute properly governed the measure of damages in the instant case.

With regard to choice of appropriate strict liability law, we note first that it is somewhat unclear whether a conflict of laws in fact exists between Massachusetts and Rhode Island. Massachusetts courts apparently have never expressly adopted, or rejected, the doctrine of strict products liability. In the absence of relevant case law, the trial court and the parties proceeded on the arguendo assumption that strict liability would not be a permissible basis for recovery in Massachusetts. In contrast, Rhode Island has expressly adopted this doctrine. *Ritter v Narragansett Elec Co.*[17] Moreover, the trial court in the instant case held that, if presented with the issue, the Supreme Court of Rhode Island would interpret that doctrine as authorising liability where defects in the design of an automobile do not cause a collision but rather exacerbate the injuries resulting therefrom. The court thus found a true conflict of laws between Massachusetts and Rhode Island on strict liability which the court resolved in favor of Rhode Island law. Reviewing this second conflicts decision, we, too, will assume arguendo that Massachusetts would not recognise strict products liability in any form. To resolve the conflict, we again apply Rhode Island's interest-weighing approach.

Clearly Rhode Island has a significant governmental interest to advance by applying its own law on strict liability rather than the law of Massachusetts which denies recovery on that theory. Rhode Island's interest is the protection of its citizens from defective products. Such citizens include plaintiff, his son, and Sullivan, the purchaser of the Maverick. Application of Massachusetts law would plainly defeat this Rhode Island interest.

At the same time, application of Rhode Island law would not appear to offend Massachusetts law and policy. We again note that Ford is not a Massachusetts corporation. Thus, even if we assume that Massachusetts' failure to adopt strict products liability represents an intention to protect that state's manufacturers from excessive liability, Ford is outside of the protected class. Even if we assume a Massachusetts interest in encouraging non-citizen manufacturers to sell their products in the state, such interest is insubstantial when the product here was sold to a Rhode Island citizen and another Rhode Island citizen allegedly died as a result of a defect in it. Massachusetts' undeniable interest in controlling driving behavior on its highways—a factor which caused the Supreme Court of Rhode Island to apply Massachusetts negligence law to a Massachusetts collision in the *Woodward* case—is also not a significant consideration here. Where plaintiff complains of defective design which occurred in Michigan on a car sold to a Rhode Island resident, the fact that the alleged defect had tragic results on a Massachusetts highway is something of a fortuity. The causes of the collision in Massachusetts are not at issue. Instead plaintiff alleges that once the collision occurred, from whatever cause, the defect which existed in

___

law also point to Rhode Island's statute. Rhode Island courts are probably more adept at computing damages under their own compensatory standard than under Massachusetts' punitive standard and it is clear the Supreme Court of Rhode Island would find the compensatory measure with no ceiling to be the better rule of law.

17 283 A 2d 255, 261 (1971).

Sullivan's car caused the death of his son. Massachusetts has no significant interest in adjudicating a claim of that nature.

The remaining three interests considered under the Rhode Island conflicts approach also indicate application of this state's strict liability law.[18] We therefore hold that the trial court correctly chose to apply Rhode Island laws on strict liability.

Clark v Clark 222 A 2d 205 (1966) (Supreme Court of New Hampshire)

Kenison CJ (giving the judgment of the court, other than Duncan J who dissented): The plaintiff is the wife of the defendant and in this action she seeks damages for personal injuries caused by her husband's alleged negligence in operating a motor vehicle in which she was riding with him. The parties now and for some time previous to the accident were domiciled in Lancaster, New Hampshire. On the evening of 26 June 1964 the parties left Lancaster for Littleton, New Hampshire, intending to return to their home later that evening. This trip took them into Lunenberg, Vermont where the accident occurred.

The plaintiff moved for a pre-trial order that the substantive law of New Hampshire governs the rights of the parties. All questions of law raised by the motion were reserved and transferred without ruling by Leahy CJ.

Vermont has a guest statute under which a host is liable to his automobile guest only if the injuries are caused by the 'gross and willful negligence' of the operator. This state has no guest statute and a guest may recover if the injuries are caused by the host's lack of ordinary care under the circumstances. The question is whether the law of Vermont or the law of New Hampshire governs.

In years gone by the choice of law rule of such cases was thought to be settled and the governing law was invariably that of the place where the injury occurred. That old rule is today almost completely discredited as an unvarying guide to choice of law decision in all tort cases due in no small part to the trenchant criticism of Cheatham, Cook, Currie, Lorenzen, Stumberg and Yntema. No conflict of laws authority in America today agrees that the old rule should be retained. See eg texts and articles by Cavers, Ehrenzweig, Hancock, Leflar, Morris, Reese, Rheinstein, Trautman, Traynor, von Mehren and Weintraub, to mention only a few. No American

---

18 Predictability of results does not appear to be an important interest here. Ford could not reasonably foresee or plan that its liability for defects in a car delivered to a Massachusetts dealership and sold to a Rhode Island resident would be governed by Massachusetts law rather than Rhode Island law. Under either the lex loci delicti or the interest-weighing approach, Rhode Island law was at least as likely to govern. Ford has not provided the court with its specific insurance rates, which might have indicated that it planned otherwise. We note that generally products liability insurance is computed on a national basis, not state-by-state. Simplification of the judicial task might seem to point to application of Massachusetts law because obviously it is simpler to apply a rule denying any recovery on strict liability grounds than to grapple with the intricacies of that doctrine. But Rhode Island's courts, having adopted strict liability, have committed themselves to dealing with its interpretation in difficult cases. Cf *Brown v Church of the Holy Name of Jesus* 252 A 2d at 180–181 (rejecting proposition that simplification of task resulting from application of Massachusetts charitable immunity doctrine warrants that outcome). With regard to the better rule of law, the *Ritter* case above makes clear Rhode Island's approval of the doctrine of strict liability. And we hold today, below, that the Rhode Island courts would extend that doctrine to encompass strict liability for design defects.

court which has felt free to re-examine the matter thoroughly in the last decade has chosen to retain the old rule. It is true that some courts, even in recent decisions, have retained it. But their failure to reject it has resulted from an unwillingness to abandon established precedent before they were sure that a better rule was available, not to any belief that the old rule was a good one. The only virtue of the old rule, apart from the fact of its pre-existence, was that it was easy for a court to apply. It was easy to apply because it was a mechanical rule. It bore no relationship to any relevant consideration for choosing one law as against another in a torts-conflicts case.

This state has recognised the inadequacy of the old rule but has up to now broken away from it only to a limited extent. We have recognised that this mechanical rule ought to be discarded, but unlike some of the other states have been unwilling to abandon it completely until reasonably sure that a more satisfactory rule was available to take its place. Accordingly, we have used the place of wrong rule for want of a better one even though our dissatisfaction with it and with its application was evident.

Some jurisdictions, experiencing the same dissatisfaction with the mechanical place of wrong rule, have substituted a straight characterisation approach. This approach would reach different results according to whether a torts case could be technically re-characterised as a contracts case, as a family law case, as one presenting a procedural question, or under some other key-number section heading which would enable a court to vary its choice of law subjectively. This court prefers not to rely on such a technique because it overlooks policy considerations that should underlie choice of law adjudication.

The relevant considerations in choice of law decision are fairly well known. Courts and writers have identified and cited them, or most of them, down through the years, though they have not often been separately analysed and summarised. One of the first thorough analyses of them was in Cheatham and Reese 'Choice of the Applicable Law,' 52 Col L Rev 959 (1952). They have been expressly taken into account in the drafting of the Restatement (Second), Conflict of Laws (Tent Draft No 9) and specifically in s. 379, the basic tort section. There is a difference of opinion as to the exact content of these considerations and the relative weight to be accorded different ones among them, but they are identified and knowable. We have concluded that choice of law decisions ought to be based directly upon these relevant considerations, rather than upon any mechanical rule or technique of ad hoc characterisation derived indirectly from such considerations.

The relevant choice-influencing considerations can be summarised without great difficulty. Obviously, some of them will be more relevant to some types of cases, less to other types. The process of applying them to particular cases will not be a subjective one. It will be typical of the judicial process in nonconflicts cases.

One of the considerations is predictability of results. It basically relates to consensual transactions, in which it is important that parties be able to know in advance what law will govern a transaction so that they can plan it accordingly. Reliance upon a predictable choice of law protects the justifiable expectations of the parties. Also, it assures uniformity of decision regardless of forum, thus discouraging 'forum shopping'. Except for the evils of forum shopping, the predictability consideration does not have much to do with automobile accident cases. They are not planned.

A second consideration is the maintenance of reasonable orderliness and good relationship among the states in our federal system. State chauvinism and interstate retaliation are dangers to be avoided. Any choice of law that would unduly favor one state, the forum perhaps, or interfere with easy movement from state to state, would be questionable. Open disregard of another state's clear interests might have bad effects. In terms of interstate automobile trips and accident litigation growing out of them, no more is called for under this head than that a court apply the law of no state which does not have substantial connection with the total facts and with the particular issue being litigated.

Simplification of the judicial task is another important consideration. It underlies that practice by which a court applies its own procedural rules in suits on foreign facts. It may be easier also for a court to apply its own substantive law than another state's law, because it understands its own law better and therefore can do a better job of administering justice under it. Mechanical choice of law methods, such as that the law of the place of injury always governs, also make the judicial task easier. But simplification of the judicial task is not the whole end of law, and opposing considerations may outweigh it.

A fourth consideration is inherent in the obvious fact that every court is more concerned with the advancement of its own state's governmental interests than with those of other states. Governmental interest, however, is not necessarily synonymous with domestic law. A state often has no particularly strong policy in reference to local rules of law which happen through the vagaries of legislative or judicial law making to differ from a neighbor's view. Strong policy concerns can underlie local rules, and they sometimes do, but often they do not. In most private litigation the only real governmental interest that the forum has is in the fair and efficient administration of justice, which is usually true of automobile accident cases.

Finally, a fifth consideration, too often disguised, is the court's preference for what it regards as the sounder rule of law, as between the two competing ones. Professor Cavers has for years been pointing out that in choice of law cases courts have the opportunity to make, and do make, a choice between rules of law, as distinguished from the choice between jurisdictions that they have traditionally purported to make in conflicts cases. We prefer to apply the better rule of law in conflicts cases just as is done in nonconflicts cases, when the choice is open to us. If the law of some other state is outmoded, an unrepealed remnant of a bygone age, 'a drag on the coattails of civilisation,' we will try to see our way clear to apply our own law instead. If it is our own law that is obsolete or senseless (and it could be) we will try to apply the other state's law. Courts have always done this in conflicts cases, but have usually covered up what they have done by employing manipulative techniques such as characterisation and renvoi.

After this review of the relevant choice-influencing considerations, application of them in the present case becomes not unduly difficult, and a lawyer advising these parties—either the plaintiff or the defendant, or insurance company—after the accident could anticipate with reasonable certainty that the law suit would be brought in a New Hampshire court under New Hampshire law. Predictability of legal results in advance of the event is largely irrelevant, since automobile accidents are not planned. The expectations of the present parties, if they had any, as to legal liabilities and insurance coverage for accidents, would be with reference to their own state, and they would think in terms of lawsuits brought in New Hampshire courts under New Hampshire law, if they thought about the matter at all.

Maintenance of interstate orderliness presents no problems, one way or the other. Interstate travel by residents of the two states will not be affected, nor will the sensibilities of either state, whichever law is applied.

Simplification of the court's task is almost irrelevant here too. We are accustomed to applying our own ordinary negligence rule, and our judges could administer a trial under it a bit more confidently than under Vermont's gross negligence rule, but they could with relative ease use either rule.

As to New Hampshire's governmental interests, it is our duty to further them. We in this instance believe in our own law. Our negligence rule is common law, made by this court, and our legislature more than once has refused to change it. We have an interest in applying it to New Hampshire residents, especially when such advance expectations as they may have had, based upon their domicile in New Hampshire, their maintenance of a car under our laws, and going on a short trip that was both to begin and end here, would have led them to anticipate application of our law to them. Unlike 'rules of the road', as to which every consideration requires obedience to the rules that prevail at the place where the car is being driven, the factors that bear on this host-guest relationship all center in New Hampshire.

The only reasons that have ever been given, or that Vermont could possibly have, for enactment of its guest statute are (1) to protect kindly hosts from ungrateful guests ('don't bite the hand that feeds you'), and (2) to protect liability insurance companies from suits brought by guests colluding with their hosts. Vermont's interests under its statute are in suits brought in its own courts affecting hosts, guests and insurance companies subject to its jurisdiction. Our primary interest arising out of our ordinary negligence law correspondingly applies to suits in our courts affecting people and relationships with which we have a legitimate concern. That interest in this case is a real one.

Finally, we conclude that our rule is preferable to that of Vermont. The automobile guest statutes were enacted in about half the states, in the 1920s and early 1930s, as a result of vigorous pressures by skillful proponents. Legislative persuasion was largely in terms of guest relationships (hitchhikers) and uninsured personal liabilities that are no longer characteristic of our automotive society. The problems of automobile accident law then were not what they are today. New Hampshire never succumbed to this persuasion. No American state has newly adopted a guest statute for many years. Courts of states which did adopt them are today construing them much more narrowly, evidencing their dissatisfaction with them. Though still on the books, they contradict the spirit of the times. Unless other considerations demand it, we should not go out of our way to enforce such a law of another state as against the better law of our own state.

Taken altogether, this analysis of the relevant choice of law considerations leads clearly to the application of New Hampshire's law in the present case. The '. . . circumstances under which a guest passenger has a right of action against the driver of an automobile for injuries suffered as a result of the latter's negligence will be determined by the local law of their common domicil, if at least this is the state from which they departed on their trip and that to which they intended to return, rather than by the local law of the state where the accident occurred.' Restatement (Second), Conflict of Laws, s 379, comment d, p 9 (Tent Draft No 9). See also *Babcock v Jackson*.[19] This case is a comparatively easy one, and in cases like it the result will hereafter be reasonably easy for lawyers and trial judges to calculate. Admittedly there will be harder cases, more difficult to decide, cases that will not yield sure answers in terms of proper choice-influencing considerations as readily as this case does. That will not be a new phenomenon in conflict of laws. Nor will it be as bad as choice based on mechanical rules which do not take the relevant considerations into account. In course of time perhaps we will develop 'principles of preference' based upon the relevant considerations, to guide us more exactly.[20] Most of the choice of law rules and results that have been reached in the past were supported by good sense and sound practical analysis, and will not be affected by re-examination in terms of the relevant choice-influencing considerations. Some, like the place of injury rule for torts, clearly will be affected. That is as far as this decision need go.

The Superior Court is advised that it should enter a pre-trial order that the New Hampshire law pertaining to husband and wife and host and guest governs the rights of the parties in this action.

NOTE

Many commentators frown on the application of the better rule of law, and with good reason. It is not the function of the courts to reform the law of other countries (still less of their own country) by giving it the narrowest possible scope or refusing to apply it in a conflict of laws case. That is a task better left to legislatures or law reform bodies. As Cavers says, to ask the judge simply to express a preference between two rules of law on the ground of justice and convenience 'is to abolish our centuries-old subject'.[1]

QUESTIONS

1. Do you think that any of the approaches in this chapter can properly be applied in England where our concern is with international, rather than interstate, cases?
2. In an action in England against an English defendant for damage caused in France by the escape of water from a dam, how would the court establish the English interest in the application of the rule in *Rylands v Fletcher* (1868) LR 3 HL 330, 37 LJEx 161 as against the French interest in applying the equivalent rule of the Code Civil, article 641? In considering the interest behind these rules, should you consider the purpose they were originally designed to fulfil or their purpose now, and how would one discover these?
3. By what criteria can a court determine whether its rule of law is a 'better rule of law' than that of another interested state?
4. How justified is the criticism of s 6 of the Restatement Second that it is both jurisdiction-selecting and rule-selecting at the same time?

19 191 NE 2d 279 (1963); p 501 above.
20 Cavers *The Choice of Law Process* (1965) p 114.
1 Cavers *The Choice of Law Process* (1965) p 86.

Index

743